AMERICA'S
GARDEN BOOK

AMERICA'S GARDEN BOOK

by

James and Louise Bush-Brown

Revised Edition by

THE NEW YORK BOTANICAL GARDEN
BRONX, NEW YORK

CHARLES SCRIBNER'S SONS
NEW YORK

Library of Congress Cataloging in Publication Data

Bush-Brown, James.
  America's garden book.

  Previous editions entered under Louise Carter
Bush-Brown.
  Includes index.
  1. Gardening. 2. Gardening—United States.
I. Bush-Brown, Louise Carter, 1897–1974 joint author.
II. New York (City). Botanical Garden.
SB453.B9 1979   635.9′0973   79-17303
ISBN 0-684-16270-9

A Note from the Garden

When a work has for so long been so eminently successful as the Bush-Browns' *America's Garden Book*, it behooves one to be cautious about meddling with what is obviously the right formula. However, in the two decades and more since publication of the last edition much has happened in and out of horticulture that unavoidably affects the gardening avocation.

Our nation's population is even more urbanized, with gardening in some cases focused on the small privately owned lot, in others on the rented, leased or owned apartment, often with rooftop access, and always with special challenges. Law has intruded somewhat, as with the many regulations governing the availability and use of chemical substances employed to control plants and animals unwanted in the garden. There have been many changes in the lexicon of plant names, both because of newly introduced strains that have in some cases replaced old ones and because taxonomic interpretations of some old favorites have led to nomenclatural adjustments.

Throughout the country, people in swelling numbers have turned to plants and gardening as they look for communion with nature as a way to find new meaning in their lives. Heightened awareness of environmental responsibility has given thoughtful people a new perspective on the colors, forms and rhythms in plant life and has offered urban denizens a facet of experience refreshingly outside the works and workings of man. Although these and other aspects of change are reflected in this new edition, the book remains essentially the work of Louise and James Bush-Brown. In this revision changes have been introduced in substance and emphasis only where the staff specialist committee, chaired by Carlton B. Lees, has felt them necessary.

The approach remains topical rather than encyclopedic. Species and strains are recommended not merely according to popularity but rather according to their likelihood of success. Cultural procedures are advocated by virtue of proven worth, not in response to fad or to archaic if venerable tradition. Every attempt has been made to acquaint the reader with the best in the current horticultural catalog and the most effective and environmentally responsible in horticultural practice.

We at The New York Botanical Garden are honored to have been asked to collaborate in this revision and are pleased to have had a role in preparing the text in its present form. Our experience with James and Albert Bush-Brown and with the publisher has been intellectually stimulating and personally satisfying, for we have dwelt upon ideas that combine the science and art of horticulture, as leavened by the experience of knowledgeable practitioners.

Whether you grow vegetables, flowers, bulbs or herbs, or content yourself with trees and shrubs; whether your gardening site is indoors, outdoors, skyward, in shade or somewhere in the house or highrise; whether you are interested in the literature of gardening for reasons other than practical guidance, we believe this edition of *America's Garden Book* will contribute much to your enjoyment and your understanding of plants and their culture.

—HOWARD S. IRWIN

Advisory Committee
Dr. Howard S. Irwin, Chairman
Dr. Albert Bush-Brown
James Bush-Brown
Ingrid Eisenstadter
Carlton B. Lees

Contributors

Carlton B. Lees, Committee Chairman. Senior Vice-President, The New York Botanical Garden. Author of *Budget Landscaping; Gardens, Plants and Man* and *New Budget Landscaping.* Former Executive Director, Massachusetts Horticultural Society, Pennsylvania Horticultural Society; past president, Garden Writers of America.

    Chapters: *The Heritage of Gardening; Design; Terraces and Patios; Pools and Fountains; The Home Swimming Pool; Hardy Bulbs and Lilies; Annuals and Biennials; Flower Boxes.*

Dr. Arthur Bing, Professor of Ornamental Horticulture, Cornell University.

    Chapter: *The Control of Weeds and Undesirable Plants.*

Karl Grieshalber, Rock Garden Horticulturist, The New York Botanical Garden. Former Senior Gardener, Longwood Gardens.

    Chapters: *Terraces and Patios; Garden Walls, Banks, Paths and Steps; Fences; Hardy Bulbs and Lilies; Rock and Wall Gardens; Coldframes and Hotbeds; Greenhouse Gardening.*

Robert S. Hebb, Horticulturist, Cary Arboretum of The New York Botanical Garden. Former Assistant Horticulturist, Arnold Arboretum. Author of *Low Maintenance Perennials.*

    Chapters: *Hedges; Trees; Shrubs; Vines; Ground Covers; Herbaceous Perennials; Annuals and Biennials; The Woodland Garden.*

Dr. Bruce McAlpin, Fern Horticulturist, The New York Botanical Garden.

    Chapters: *Gardening Indoors; Gardening under Artificial Light; Plant Societies.*

Arthur H. Ode, Director of Horticulture, The New York Botanical Garden. Former Assistant Director of Parks, Milwaukee.

    Chapters: *Grading; Mulches; Tools and Garden Equipment; Prairie and Meadow; Water and Bog Gardens; Inviting the Birds; Soils and Soil Improvement; Garden Practices.*

Marvin Olinsky, Assistant Director of Horticulture, The New York Botanical Garden.

    Chapters: *The Home Vegetable Garden; The Fruit Garden; Greenhouse Gardening.*

Dr. Pascal P. Pirone, Senior Plant Pathologist, The New York Botanical Garden. Author of *Tree Maintenance.*

    Chapter: *Plant Diseases and Insect Pests.*

Dr. John E. Voight, Director, retired, Alfred L. Boerner Botanical Gardens.

    Chapter: *Roses.*

Helen Whitman, Proprietor, Tool Shed Herb Farm, New York.

    Chapter: *The Herb Garden.*

Carol Young, Assistant Horticulturist, Cary Arboretum of The New York Botanical Garden.

    Chapter: *Propagation.*

Valery Saint-Rossy, Managing Editor

Illustrations by Dorothy Irwin

Contents

Preface

Well before its second edition appeared in 1958, *America's Garden Book* had become a national classic, offering accessible and authoritative information about all the important aspects of gardening.

First published in 1939, *America's Garden Book* was the work of Louise Bush-Brown, then Director of the Pennsylvania School of Horticulture at Ambler, Pennsylvania, and her husband, James Bush-Brown, Landscape Architect. Writing in longhand, drawing with pen and ink, and sorting thousands of index cards, they worked nights and weekends to produce a practical reference manual, a compendium for the craft of gardening, with essays that emphasize artistic design and lasting construction. The display of information, which was supported by an excellent index, and the illustrations of techniques, plant materials and gardens soon won a national following among professional horticulturists and amateur gardeners alike. Its essential emphasis on conservation and organic gardening assured continuing respect, even today.

The revised edition of 1958 gave readers currency with many recent developments in horticulture, but, remarkable though its prescience was, *America's Garden Book* could not then anticipate six major movements affecting gardening in the last two decades. One was the enormous extension of sites, soils and climates as urban, suburban, northern, western and southwestern regions opened new opportunities for gardening. A second was the change in artistic taste that introduced new shapes, structures and palettes, enriching the repertory of landscaped forms that were no longer only the Renaissance vista or the English Romantic park. A third was the change to outdoor living and dining, which imposed new requirements upon the terrace and garden. A fourth was the growing popularity of indoor gardening, helped by artificial light and easily maintained greenhouses. A fifth was the increased knowledge of plant pathology, with concomitant improvement of sophisticated fertilizers and pesticides. And, sixth, the years since 1958 saw vast developments in plant topology, including the perfection of new species and national, indeed international, exchanges of plant materials, not described in the 1939 or 1958 editions.

Recognizing the need for revising *America's Garden Book,* the publishers, Charles Scribner's Sons, wrote to the Bush-Browns in 1977, requesting that they discuss a new edition. But Louise had died in 1974, and James was eighty-five years old, retired and, though still an avid student of horticulture, unable to undertake so formidable a task.

The Scribner letter was brought to the attention of the authors' son, Albert, who, being an architectural historian and chancellor of a university, could do little more than suggest a way to renew *America's Garden Book.* He proposed to Charles Scribner that Dr. Howard Irwin and the staff of The New York Botanical Garden be invited to review and revise the book and share in the income.

By happy confluence, then—an enlightened and generous publisher, a respected botanical garden, its staff of scholars led by a fine scientist, its writers and editors, all working to improve a book written four decades earlier by the Bush-Browns — the new edition of *America's Garden Book* was begun in the spring of 1978 and is now ready again to provide, as the Bush-Browns wrote in an earlier foreword, "accurate information and sound counsel on the process of garden making."

On behalf of the authors, thanks are given to The New York Botanical Garden and to Charles Scribner's Sons, with the hope that *America's Garden Book* will serve generations of gardeners for decades to come.

For James and Louise Bush-Brown
by Albert Bush-Brown

1980

1

GARDEN DESIGN

1.1 Court of the Pool, the Generalife, Granada, Spain. Photo Carlton Lees

1

The Heritage of Gardening

The word "garden" in today's America is not always thoroughly understood. More often than not, it is used to refer to a piece of tilled or otherwise intensively cultivated land such as vegetable garden, rose garden or flower garden—the last, perhaps, no more than a small bed of petunias. As a verb, "to garden" implies the growing of plants, while "gardening" becomes a synonym for horticulture (from the Latin: *hortus,* garden). Yet the origins of the word derive from a larger and broader concept: that of landscapes which have been altered or rearranged by man to render them more useful, more pleasing and more comfortable. Within this context, a garden is fine art.

In the history of gardens, we study not the culture of plants but the design of outdoor spaces for human habitat. The concept is clouded and complicated, however, by the fact that it deals with living materials as well as with abstract design. By their very nature, gardens are changing continually. They change moment by moment, with the hours, the days and the seasons. A few years can bring awesome maturity or disappointing ruin to a garden. The success of the art, therefore, cannot be separated from the pure sciences of botany or biology, or from the applied science of horticulture.

GARDENING CONCEPTS

The words "garden," "yard," "orchard" and "paradise" all stem from a single concept: a more or less enclosed outdoor space, sheltered, leafy, refreshing, often bright with color and alive with fragrances, bird song, the sounds of splashing water and cooling breezes. Indeed,

Pliny the Younger wrote of one of his villas (Tuscum): "I can enjoy a profounder peace there, more comfort, and fewer cares; I need never wear a formal toga. . . . Everywhere there is peace and quiet. . . ." Pliny had created his own paradise, that most beautiful and wonderful of gardens of Eastern philosophy to which the departed go in afterlife. In the medieval garden, the orchard was not a place for growing apples, but rather a grove of trees planted to provide cooling shade on hot summer days. So much was pleasure emphasized in these gardens that Sir Francis Bacon, the sixteenth-century philosopher and statesman, referred to them as gardens of "pleasant delytes." And our own word "yard" stems directly from that medieval orchard.

That the American backyard might be a cool and shady retreat on hot summer days is an appealing idea. Many homeowners already know that home can be a paradise; others, not so fortunate, continue to dash from place to place seeking it. With today's increasing concern over dwindling and costly energy supplies, it would make great sense if more of us turned to our own backyards to create oases at home. In order to do so, however, we must consider the backyard as living space rather than as vegetable plots and petunia patches. Within this larger concept, then, a garden becomes, by definition, outdoor space organized for our use, comfort and pleasure. It is a place where family and friends can meet in relaxation and pleasure, where we need not always wear our best "togas."

While gardens have been a continuing source of inspiration for philosophers, poets, painters and musicians, they take on added significance

3

today as outposts of reality in this increasingly crowded and artificial world. A near renaissance in urban tree planting, in the creation of mini-parks, green spaces, plazas, garden shopping malls and "vacant lot" gardening has taken place in the recent past. The current boom of interest in houseplants, for example, is something no one would have predicted a few years ago. It all adds up to expression of a basic human need: to have direct contact with reality as represented by the natural world. This is especially so in our modern, hard, artificial urban environments. We are, after all, natural creatures, more related to trees than to machines. And while individual plants may help to reassure us, the broader experience of unlimited landscape reveals a great deal more. As the world grows increasingly crowded, however, for many the opportunity to experience unlimited landscape becomes infrequent, if not impossible. Gardens, therefore—whether elaborate, or minuscule, or in between—have come to symbolize the natural landscape that twentieth-century people are searching for. In other words, gardens have become more and more important to our survival as rational creatures.

While gardens have to do with the manipulation of landscape as art, they also have to do with conservation, a concept that is growing in importance daily. Landscape can be organized for many purposes, to reach many goals—from the architectural sophistication of a city plaza to the biological sophistication of a country bog. Amos Bronson Alcott, the famous nineteenth-century educator, mystic and author, wrote in one of his essays: "Who loves a garden, still his Eden keeps; Perennial pleasures, plants, and wholesome harvests reaps." And, it should be added here, he helps also to preserve a part of the total landscape. "Gardeners make extraordinarily good citizens," said Barbara Ward (Lady Jackson), the eminent British economist and writer. We couldn't agree with her more.

How it all began is a subject for conjecture. It is generally accepted that sometime after early men came down from the trees to live on the ground, they began to feel the need for a "home place" from which they could go out and to which they could return, a place where they could gather and store their possessions and food, a place they would find familiar and comfortable. Perhaps this first home was no more than a small area cleared within a thicket or in the shelter of an overhanging bluff. When the first man organized that first bit of landscape, however, he created the first garden. Architecture, as we understand it, came much later.

Sir Francis Bacon is also credited with saying: "Man comes to build stately sooner than to garden finely, as if the latter were the greater perfection." A civilization requires maturity before it can achieve great architecture or great gardens; these are not portable arts like music, dance, poetry and various other creative forms. Fortunate are we, indeed, that this stability has provided us with a rich heritage of gardens, from ancient Persia and China, from Rome and Renaissance Italy, from the France of Louis XIV, and from the England of Capability Brown.

HISTORICAL BACKGROUND

Our heritage is anything but meager; though civilizations rise and fall, gardens continue to persist through the ages. The ancient Egyptians, the Assyrians and the Persians all developed gardens of majestic grandeur and opulence. The Chinese, with their deep sensitivity to beauty, laid the foundations for a form of garden art that was to have, in years to come, great influence upon other lands.

The Greeks also gave to the world a new concept of gardening. Their homes were adorned with flowers, but it was in their civic design and public buildings that they most skillfully applied their garden art. Their temples were surrounded by groves of trees, and trees lined the important streets and marketplaces in their principal cities.

Much of the knowledge and skill in garden craft possessed by the Romans was acquired from the Greeks. In the second century A.D. the Romans began to build gardens on a tremendous scale, inspired by the precedent of the vast palace gardens of Mesopotamia, which they had conquered. They studied hydraulics and brought water from great distances by conduit to supply the ornamental fountains that adorned their villa gardens. These great villas were later to inspire the Italian garden architects to follow the Roman precedent.

During the Dark Ages, those centuries of almost complete barbarism and ignorance, the art and practices of gardening were kept alive by monks in the monasteries. They made their work the interpretation of goodness and their study the means of gaining a deeper knowledge of life.

The gradual emergence of Europe into an era of revived culture and intellectual enlightenment; the spread of the study of the classics, brought about by the founding of the universities; the rise of an independent class of citizen craftsmen, unattached to the feudal system; the growing importance of the great free cities of Europe—all combined to usher in an age of increased prosperity and greater accomplishment in the arts. It was a remarkable era, destined to become known as "the Renaissance," the time of rebirth of Western civilization.

It is only natural that while this great surge of rebuilding and rediscovery of learning was taking possession of the ambitions and imaginations of free men, experiments should be undertaken in many fields, each with the hope of capturing something of the unknown and mastering it. Painting, sculpture, architecture, garden design, music and literature, all supported by the skilled crafts, were the outgrowths of this resurgent spirit of the times. And all the while, the gains in the arts were upheld by the firmer economy, based on a lively production of goods and an ever-expanding commerce.

It was during this period that some of our most notable examples of garden art were produced: the great villas of Italy, the palace gardens of Spain, the vast estates of the French châteaux, the careful parterres of the Dutch and the beautiful manor-house gardens of England.

In the sixteenth century the Italians began to build palatial country villas after the manner of the Romans, and they designed and planted these gardens with all the artistic and poetic refinement of their sensitive natures. The results were marvelous essays of merged architecture, verdure, trees, sculpture, flowers and watercourses, all woven into designs of subtle harmony and perfect proportions. So beautiful were these visual compositions that they won

the admiration and attention of the many visitors from all parts of Europe who flocked to Italy, with the result that the Italian style, with some variations, soon spread to other realms and other climates. Italian artists and architects were invited to France and Spain to practice their professions and to teach. Thus the Italian Renaissance garden became the European Renaissance garden.

For 200 years this formal, architectural style of garden art was practiced throughout Europe. The artist-architects of each nation designed in this grand manner and modified the work of their predecessors to suit their times and their own countries. In all these gardens, formal shapes, symmetrically placed, predominated. The details expressed the basic character of the design, with emphasis on straight pathways, clipped hedges, balustrades, fountains, pools and sculpture.

The Spaniards copied the geometric patterns of the Moors and, later, the excessively ornamented details of the baroque Italian gardens. The French enlarged the scale of garden building to include many acres in their far-spreading bosques and greenswards. The Dutch reduced the scale in order to fit their gardens compactly into the inevitably small areas available to them in their comparatively little country. And the English gleaned from Italian, French and Dutch styles in developing their formal gardens, adding notable touches of their own, such as the mount, the "ha-ha" and the long perennial border.

In the early days of our own country, the colonists naturally drew their inspiration from the familiar scenes of their homes in England. The villages of New England resembled the villages of old England, except that most of the houses here were built of wood instead of stone or brick or half-timber and plaster. The plantations of Virginia, Maryland and the Carolinas were set out in much the same arrangement as the manors of England. Their concept of garden art was that of seventeenth- and eighteenth-century England.

Thus, precedent for garden design in the colonies was drawn from the English interpretation of the Renaissance spirit, just as the architecture we now describe as colonial was copied from the Georgian period in England, itself a translation from Italian Renaissance into English methods and materials. The gardens were geometric in major lines. Even in the small dooryard gardens of New England, Elizabethan patterns persisted. Prim, patterned flower beds, straight paths edged with boxwood or with flowers, fruit trees in rows, turf squares bordered with flowers—these were typical features of the colonial garden. As architectural features and purely decorative ornaments were rarely included, the design was expressed almost entirely in plant materials, a medium that greatly softens the regularity of the formal style. The faithfully restored gardens at Williamsburg and at Mount Vernon are fine examples of gardens of this period.

In the latter years of the eighteenth century, the Spanish tradition of the secluded patio was brought into New Orleans and to southern California by the Spanish missionaries and early settlers, and, with modifications, these have remained a feature of most gardens in these areas to this day.

The Renaissance tradition in America lost its vitality during the early years of the Republic. In order to infuse new life into the thread of design, Greek forms were resorted to in architecture, as if design could go no further and must, therefore, return to the ultimate source of classic precedent. The Greek revival had its brief day during the early part of the nineteenth century. But so utterly unadapted was it to domestic needs of the times in this country that it was soon abandoned, and for the next seventy years no serious attempt was made to derive inspiration from the classic monuments of architecture.

This trend of architecture was also the trend of garden design of that period and was only a phase of what was happening in the composite mind of the growing nation. The attention and efforts of the people were absorbed in the great tasks of winning the West, extending the railroads and developing industries. To build a civilization in the wilderness was, in itself, a work demanding the energies of several generations. It is small wonder, then, that until Americans finally achieved the leisure to travel in Europe and to see for themselves their art heritage, no great awareness of art developed in this country. The nineteenth century produced new and unfamiliar forms and expressions, and with the restoration of Colonial Williamsburg in the 1930s came a period of eighteenth-century revival. It was almost as if "good taste" ended in 1800. Much of our architectural heritage of the nineteenth century was destroyed, ersatz eighteenth-century flourished, and not until the 1960s did the nineteenth century come to be appreciated for what it was: a lively expression of a period in which the pioneering spirit excelled—in western expansion, in politics, in letters, and although belatedly recognized, in architecture and the other arts as well.

Through much of this period the concept of a garden was that of a collection of plants, purely horticultural in purpose. There was great interest in botany, in the introduction of new plants and in the growing of fine horticultural specimens, and these interests completely occupied the minds of the gardeners of the period. But this phenomenon did not take place in America alone. In England, control of the garden passed from the landscape gardener to the collector-horticulturist. Save for the efforts of Andrew Jackson Downing in America to introduce the romantic, naturalistic expression of landscape design, as expressed in England by the works of Sir Humphrey Repton, no attempt was made to produce examples of garden art of any significance.

During the last decades of the nineteenth century and the early decades of the twentieth many educated Americans traveled widely in Europe, and in doing so, they renewed a close contact with that rich culture after a lapse of several generations. In the same period, the country home in America was assuming a more important aspect, and gardening was again looked upon as a valid field of artistic expression. The garden styles of Italy, France and England were diligently studied and copied here. English, Scots, Dutch and Italian gardeners came to this country in great numbers to carry on their craft in a land of widening opportunities. Nurseries expanded to meet the steadily increasing demands for choice plant materials. Yet, although during this era of prosperity the art flourished as never before, no really new statements were made. Most gardens, however well planned, were mere reproductions of a past age. The estate, with its expansive lawns, its woodland and its well-de-signed and superbly maintained garden, was the part-time residence of only the person of wealth. These were gardens for the privileged few, cared for by professional gardeners.

After World War I, the building of large and magnificent estates continued, but a change gradually became perceptible. In the many small homes that were being built in rapidly spreading suburbs during that time, people began to take an interest in the development of their home grounds. Gardening was no longer for the few, but for the many. Each decade since then has witnessed an ever-increasing number of enthusiastic home gardeners, with new forms and variations coming steadily into favor—rooftop gardening, indoor "container" gardening, and so on.

These new gardens are of necessity different from the old. They frequently are more utilitarian; they are not limited by the tradition of formality and style. They demand less in the way of maintenance, are more "lived in" and are, more often than not, considered an integral part of one's home. And this is as it should be. A garden should reflect the time in which it is built. It should not imitate styles of other lands. The very life of all arts is the power to rise, phoenixlike, from the past. People of the twentieth century are amply endowed with both tradition and precedent. Knowledge of what has been accomplished in past centuries is helpful and often inspiring, but it is not the goal. Today, the purpose of garden design is to provide an environment for happy living, according to one's needs. This is a do-it-yourself age; it is an ecologically aware age that is short on supplies of energy. Gardens are bound to reflect these times, just as the gardens of the past reflected theirs. All art forms demand honesty, and in that honesty lies the germ of distinction, whatever the age.

It is interesting to reflect on the gardens of history that were, by and large, the property of royalty, princes of the church and the privileged landed gentry. In mid-twentieth-century America, new statements for small gardens began to emanate from California—a straightforward, almost sculptural approach that emphasized above all the need for family use, comfort and pleasure. This concept for gardens proved so popular and successful that it soon set a new direction throughout the country for gardens as organized spaces. These gardens, in turn, not only revived ancient traditions but also came to influence the design of larger gardens, industrial parks, shopping malls, mini-parks. And while most of these new large gardens are privately owned in democratic America, they are open to all.

2.1 The first goal of landscape design should be to fit ourselves into the existing environment with as little disruption as possible. This house seems always to have been here. Photo Grant Heilman

2

Design

The visual appearance of the natural landscape is the result of many gradual changes in its geologic formation, climate and vegetation through the ages. The intensive use of land by man has brought about further changes that have altered and sometimes even destroyed natural features. Farms, towns, cities and highways replaced the forest and prairie; as a result, the natural landscape has been damaged and sometimes even irrevocably changed.

The design of the landscape for human use begins with a careful study of the natural conditions of a site. These conditions guide the modifications in the use and appearance of the land so that the resultant forms will be appropriate, pleasing and convenient. The preservation of natural beauty and the development that best conserves and adapts a landscape to new uses is the function of landscape architecture or design.

Landscape design is a subtle art. It requires an understanding and an appreciation of natural conditions, imagination in foreseeing a site's possibilities, skill in creating pleasing compositions, taste in selecting materials and ingenuity in adjusting to diverse requirements. Unless it is well designed, a landscape that is being modified is likely to become an inconvenient arrangement of parts that will lack comfort and beauty. But in terms of good living, a well-organized landscape will bring deeply rewarding satisfactions.

HISTORIC STATEMENT AND STYLE

In architecture itself, as well as in landscape architecture, style is intimately connected with the social customs and economic and political structure of its time. But it only becomes live style when it is repeated with or without variation (and often foolishly) after the time of the original statement.

Every important place and time in history has developed a recognizable statement and has done so out of its environment, distinctive culture, and sense of beauty and order. Habit and tradition tend to fix these statements into styles, while changing social customs tend to bring about new statements.

Landscape architecture and design, because of the very nature of their material, are more limited by local conditions than is architecture itself because they are more intimately involved with natural elements: contours, trees, sky, sunlight, rainfall, and so on. In general, plant materials can be used only in climatic zones that are similar to those of their place of origin. While an Italian villa can be built in New England and its design may be architecturally correct, it cannot be embellished by the cypresses, the stone pines and the olive trees traditional in the Italian landscape.

Style is as recognizable in garden art as it is in architecture. Our American heritage includes the simple dignity of the New England colonial village, the restricted, prim yards of the formal town houses in Philadelphia, the spacious formality of the southern plantation home and the secluded patios of New Orleans and the early Spanish missions in California.

The precedents for these early gardens in America were the abundant gardens of England, both great and small; the stately, architectural gardens of Italy; the measured formality of gardens in France; and the secluded patios of Spain. All of these older styles were faithfully

9

2.2 This house seems to occupy its own landscape space, which is distinct from the public street space. The result suggests shelter and comfort. Photo Grant Heilman

based on the formal plan: trees in balanced symmetry, straight paths paved and precisely edged, a flat terrace with a clipped hedge at the outer rim to provide transition between the formality of the garden and the naturalness of the outer landscape.

But also strongly rooted in our American tradition is the naturalistic style of England. In this graceful, flowing style, symmetry is discarded in favor of sweeping curves and a balanced asymmetry of masses, of open lawns and meadows, flanked by groves of trees.

Contemporary design sometimes seems to have no relationship to the past while at the same time often echoing it: "California gardens," they were often called through the 1950s. Yet the freedom provided by this approach to design has made it possible to break away from the limitations of past concepts and styles that were too often imposed, inappropriately, on landscape.

This new approach afforded the freedom to shape landscape directly in order to meet practical needs, and to provide comfort while at the same time being interesting. Not everyone thought these gardens were beautiful, just as some may not think abstract expressionism, in painting, is beautiful. The designers of these gardens were more concerned with organizing space as a sculptural concept than as a pictorial composition. These gardens are what can only be described as "hollow sculpture"—people containers—compositions to be experienced from within. They are not pictorial compositions just to be looked at. Herein, then, lies the strength of this newer approach: to adapt landscape to meet our needs while at the same time recognizing and taking advantage of the demands, limitations and opportunities of the site. At its best, nothing is forced upon the landscape or superimposed; rather, the forms and shapes grow out of or are determined by that landscape.

The speed with which this new approach to garden design was accepted is tribute to its validity. We see it everywhere: in shopping malls, new parks and urban plazas; in corporate and industrial parks; and in private gardens, both vast and small. And as this approach has matured, it seems less self-conscious and more relaxed; more and more, it echoes the past. Zen-like landscapes of the Orient, Italian and French Renaissance parterres and allées, Roman atria and Spanish patios; instead of copying from the past, we use our rich heritage to provide inspiration for refreshing new statements.

GARDEN PLANNING

Except possibly for someone very skilled and talented, it is virtually impossible to create a new garden—or even refurbish an old one—without a plan. Planning on paper allows for an orderly process of thought and decision making to achieve a result that will meet your particular needs within the limitations of your site, budget and interest. It is much less costly to make mistakes on paper, in the planning stage, than to try to correct them in the landscape itself. The planning process allows decisions to be made on interrelating factors. If a tree is needed to shade the west windows of a living room, for example, how does the same tree relate to shading an outdoor sitting area, to bedroom windows above, neighbor's view, spring flowers, autumn color, septic tank leaching field where certain tree roots cause problems? Working on paper stimulates the kind of analysis that answers such practical, as well as aesthetic, questions. This is the function of a good landscape architect or designer; it is not the function of a nurseryman or landscape contractor. It is important to realize the distinction between organization of landscape in a spacial sense and the installation of plants, paving materials, fences, etc. While some contractors and nurserymen are also qualified landscape designers, this does not necessarily follow. So, when selecting a landscape architect, designer, nurseryman or contractor, ask to see other work he or she has done. You may want to design your own property with or without assistance from an architect or designer. There are several good books on do-it-yourself

2.3 Trite foundation plantings should be avoided at all costs. Here the forthright geometry of the house and the simplicity of the ground cover and tree trunks provide a quiet and satisfying entrance garden. Reich-Versen Landscape Architects. Photo Carlton Lees

design on the market. Be sure to study them carefully to find the best approach for you.

Every site has its assets and its liabilities, some apparent, some latent. The creative designer must be able to see through the actual conditions to arrive at possible solutions of the practical problems. One of the first steps in planning is the evaluation of these possibilities and the summing up of the practical facilities that must be provided. One must endeavor to plan for these necessary facilities in such a way as to preserve, as far as possible, the best qualities of the site. Major decisions come first; details later.

In developing a new piece of property, an early decision is the exact position of the house: its situation in respect to sunshine, prevailing winds and views; its relationship to the land forms and to other features of the landscape — these are all important considerations. Many suburban houses are placed on their lots with utter disregard for such factors. All too frequently a house is placed nearly in the center of a lot and the garage at the rear in the hope that the latter will be less conspicuous. This means that the garage often appropriates for the driveway 20 percent of all the land not occupied by the house and, if repeated by the neighbors, results in a panorama of unattractive garages as well. The most functional arrangement, and the most economical of space, is one in which the service door, the kitchen and the purely utilitarian part of the grounds and house are grouped together facing toward the street. The other rooms thus occupy the more remote part of the house and look out on a comparatively secluded area that can be developed for satisfactory outdoor living.

While the architectural period or style of the house should be taken into consideration when determining scale, proportion and materials (i.e., brick paving for a colonial house, terrazzo or precast blocks for a contemporary one), the garden design should grow out of the needs of the occupants. If the fundamentals cited above are adhered to and the existing character of the landscape respected, the garden need not repeat patterns of the past. Just because you live in a Cape Cod cottage, it is not necessary to have a dooryard garden or herb knot any more than it is necessary to create boxwood parterres if you live in a reproduction of an Elizabethan manor. A sensitive approach to both will relate house and garden while not necessarily restricting the solution to a reproduction of the past.

The three major functional units of the home property are the approach, the service area and the area devoted to family living and recreational pursuits. In general, the approach should be reasonably direct, the service area convenient and accessible, and the living area ample, secluded and attractive. Each of these units should be contiguous with the corresponding portion of the house, each should be as complete and as segregated from the others as is practical. Local topographic conditions may dictate compromises, but wherever it is possible to adhere to this program, the plan should result in a convenient, economical and functional arrangement.

After assigning different areas of the ground to certain uses, these areas must next be separated from one another and connected logically. This is best done by masses of foliage, trees, shrubs, hedges, fences or walls. The designer should indicate on the plan the position of open lawn and of trees; the position of screen plantings to hide unsatisfactory views; the positions of viewpoints; and the directions of distant views. There is an element of the practical and an element of the aesthetic in each of these decisions.

On a small property, space must be very carefully planned and economically used. No amount of embellishment can overcome the inconvenience of an ill-adapted plan or make up for the loss of available space caused by an illogical arrangement of parts. The needs and desires of the family must be carefully considered and one alternative weighed against another—whether a certain space would be of more value if used as a play area than a vegetable garden, for example. And here let it be said that even in progressive and enlightened communities where public playgrounds exist, nothing quite takes the place of a sandpile or a favorite tree to climb in a child's own homeyard.

On a very small lot, bounded as it is by straight property lines and the straight lines of the house, a rectilinear design is sometimes the most logical and most effective plan for a garden. This does not imply that the design must be symmetrical. The placing of a few well-cho-

sen trees and the developing of one or two focal points or axes will be enough to make the plan harmonize with its restricted, geometric site. The planting of the shrubs and flowers may be incidental. Unity of design may be obtained by emphasizing the boundaries, by separating the property from adjoining neighbors and by concentrating interest within the area. The boundary may take the form of a hedge, or a fence or wall, which sets off and enhances the composition within.

One sees so many examples of efforts wasted because of the lack of a definite plan. Trees, shrubs and flowers are so often planted in haphazard fashion without regard for the beauty of the composition as a whole, or the eventual size of the plants. The same amount of diligent effort and money applied to carrying out a well-conceived plan would result in a much more satisfying, useful and beautiful picture. It is not the amount expended, but rather the exercise of forethought that is necessary to create beautiful surroundings, and the small property deserves as much consideration as any, perhaps even more.

2.4 (left), 2.5 Two views of this entrance garden emphasize how this space serves as an outdoor entry hall and excludes auto-mobile parking and nearby highway noises. Alice Milton, Landscape Architect. Photos Carlton Lees

Trees and Shrubs
in the Landscape Composition

Plantings of trees and shrubs form the masses in the landscape plan. Not only are they important objects in themselves, interesting in outline, texture and color, but they are one of the best means of marking the boundaries of a site and separating the various functional areas from each other. A mass of flowering shrubs, a hedge or a vine-covered fence each makes an excellent screen about the service yard. Where a view is to be kept open, the most effective means of relating it to the foreground is to frame it within the branches of trees in the middle distance. This separates it from every other scene, fixes the attention upon the distance, and contrasts the shadowy foreground with the light-filled countryside. At the same time, the trees afford shade that makes the house and its adjoining lawn or terrace more livable in summer. Trees and shrubs determine, by their position, the shapes of open areas in the design, contrasting the solid masses with the open spaces, the shade with the sunlight. The designers of the Italian villas were masters of the use of this kind of dramatic contrast.

The owner should see that care is taken to protect the existing healthy trees on a piece of property that is to be developed. It is well to remember that the building of a house is apt adversely to affect nearby trees. Foundations frequently cut through the root system, excavations lower the water level of the subsoil, thus reducing the tree's available water supply, and paved areas of driveway or terrace deprive the soil of its normal supply of water and air. In many instances, trees become so adversely threatened as a result of building operations that they die after several years of struggle. Prompt and adequate feeding of the trees may occasionally save them, but careful preliminary planning is a much more judicious and sensible procedure. It is an obvious absurdity to compromise a house plan in order to save an existing tree and then have it die from lack of consideration of its needs. A new structure should be kept at a distance from any tree you wish to save, so that only a fractional portion of the root system is disturbed in the course of construction.

2.6 This dooryard is not only a colorful entrance garden but a pleasant reminder of gardens of the past. Garden design and photo by Carlton Lees

Each new tree should be selected for a variety of purposes—shade, flowers, fruit or picturesque outline. To fulfill most completely the exacting requirements of the home property, trees should have the following characteristics: they should be in scale with their surroundings; they should have good habits, that is, they should never drop sections of bark (sycamore) or unpleasant fruit (female ginkgo) on the terrace; they should not be the habitual home of insects (wild cherry), or require much spraying and attention to protect them from insect and disease infestations. They should not produce flowers with a disagreeable odor, like the hawthorns and privets; they should not be brittle and lose great branches in the storms; and they should not disperse a quantity of seedlings. If, besides these negative qualities, they possess well-shaped, symmetrical heads or picturesque outlines, if they produce beautiful flowers or fruits, or if they turn to gorgeous hues in autumn, then they are especially desirable.

For the small suburban property the choice is necessarily limited, as the matter of scale must be given consideration. In most designs, a sense of proper scale is one of the most difficult qualities to preserve. For example, if a small house is given a big chimney, the house is made to appear even smaller than it really is, and so the chimney is considered to be "out of scale." The same thing applies to the design of a residential property. A small yard may seem even smaller because of the presence of very large trees. This changing of the apparent scale may be just what we wish to accomplish. Certainly there is no more homelike picture than a little New England farmhouse standing in the shelter of a great elm tree. But some houses do not belong to this type of setting. In the suburbs there is no open countryside to make the elm tree seem at home and appropriate. And, alas, the Dutch elm disease has so reduced the number of elms in our landscape that the sight is now a rare one. Everywhere is evident that saving of space that is forced on us by the high price of land. Today, the typical lots are narrow, usually too narrow for the houses on them; the street may be narrow in proportion to the amount of traffic it carries. The elm tree in such a situation may very well be too large—much as we love the elm. Smaller trees are better adapted to the small suburban home.

And adequate expenditure on trees and shrubs is an excellent investment. As they grow and mature over the years, the plants will continue to increase in value and to contribute, as nothing else can, to the value of the property.

Architectural Features in the Garden

A garden composed entirely of plant material is apt to lack precision and definiteness of design. An architectual feature placed at the end of an axis, or used as a central motif, will serve to emphasize the major lines of the design and to impart to it that note of regularity so important in the more highly wrought surroundings of the house.

Pavements of flagstone and brick have an architectural function, as their regular pattern

2.7 Good design implies respect for existing conditions. Here the natural rock outcropping has been used to great advantage. Photo Grant Heilman

and outline give form to the overall plan. Walls, fences and even hedges are essentially architectural, and as such, they can be very decorative with their rhythmic repetition of parts. But the principal architectural embellishments of a garden are those structures that are functional as well as beautiful. The well-designed toolhouse or dovecote at the corner of the garden wall, the summerhouse, the potting shed, even the rear or side wall of a garage—all offer infinite possibilities for pleasant architectural treatment. Lattices, arbors, trellises and pergolas not only provide practical support for vines but also contribute to the architectural enrichment of the garden. Fountains, sundials, sculptured seats and benches—all these may be treated as incidental ornaments or as dominant features, but in either case they are architectural in character and give a sense of permanence to scenes made up largely of changing plant forms. How and when these forms should relate to the architecture of the house is difficult to determine. The most important relationship is that of scale—size, rather than period or style. Huge pieces of contemporary welded sculpture seem perfectly at home in some English landscapes of the eighteenth century, while ancient Japanese stone figures can fit equally well into contemporary gardens.

Planting Design

By grouping and placing plants in a way that emphasizes their similarities and differences, it is possible to change an ordinary site that has no distinction and no natural advantages into one of rare beauty and much interest. The many forms, colors and textures found in plants offer infinite possibilities.

One of the most important considerations in arranging plants in a landscape composition is the viewpoint from which the plants will be seen. So important is this that unless the viewpoint is carefully chosen, the beauty of the plants may be greatly diminished or even lost entirely. For example, many small, delicate rock plants are best seen at close range and should be planted on a bank or at the top of a ledge or wall where they are near eye level, whereas the effect produced by other rock plants is that of a broad carpet of color that should be looked down upon or viewed from a distance. The blossoms of the red maple in early spring are far more beautiful when viewed from a distance with the gray winter forest behind them than they are when seen at close range. Sugar maples in their autumn brilliance are finer when seen in masses at a distance than they are in the foreground. One could recall

2.8 *From our colonial past came many garden patterns that are more suited to the growing of roses, perennials and annuals in rigid beds than to meeting the more casual outdoor living needs of today. Photo Grant Heilman*

or a winter's snowstorm will bring into silhouette trees that at other times merge with those about them. Different species of native trees have typically characteristic outlines that make them recognizable by their silhouette alone. Hickory, sugar maple, black walnut, tulip tree, white ash and the Kentucky coffee tree are among the native trees most easily distinguished from a distance.

The three outstanding aspects of a plant are form, texture and color. The outline of a tree seen as a silhouette is a print of its form, but the more subtle modeling is better appreciated by the play of light on the surface of the masses of foliage. The importance of form in design can hardly be overemphasized, as it is this that gives balance and substance to the composition. And form is much more than outline. Whereas the outline of *Juniperus chinensis* 'Pfitzerana' and the outline of *Taxus cuspidata* are very similar, their forms are quite different, because the branches of the yew are in somewhat flat planes, while the many fine branches of the juniper are grouped in thick masses.

example after example of the effect of viewpoint upon the appearance and beauty of plants. But we must also remember that people move about in a landscape, so that while we may enjoy the sugar maple as an object to be seen from a distance, we may also walk under its sheltering canopy and experience sunlight shimmering through its golden autumn leaves.

The simplest aspect of a plant is its silhouette. In some situations, the shadowy trunks of trees contrasted with a sunny meadow or against an open sea beyond, or even against the wall of a building, produce a picturesque composition in lines, as in the case, for instance, of the twisted trunks of sassafras along a shoreline. In other instances, trees make a silhouette by spreading dark masses of foliage against the sky, the pines being distinguished by their bold outlines. Another dramatic silhouette is made by white birch seen against a background of hemlocks. Any tree of distinctive outline, such as the American elm, the white oak or the Lombardy poplar, is excellent in silhouette. Often a mist

2.9 *This city garden provides shelter, shade and a place where spring's arrival is obvious. Photo Grant Heilman*

Texture is a matter of leaf size and distribution. The contribution that some trees and shrubs make to a landscape composition is largely in the texture of their foliage. Notable for this rather subtle beauty are the Katsura tree *(Cercidiphyllum japonicum)*, the birches, the locusts, the English maple and the English oak. Many of the azaleas have leaves grouped at the end of the branches that make beautiful patterns. The same effect on a larger scale is produced by the compound leaves of the horse chestnut. Trees and shrubs with compound leaves are apt to have finer textures than those with simple leaves. This is not true in all cases, however, because the ash and cherry are about the same in texture. The leaves of some plants are so large that it is difficult to adjust them to the textures of other plants. In this group we find such plants as the castor bean, elephant ears and *Magnolia macrophylla*.

Plants provide the color scheme, and every plant contributes its facet of color to the whole mosaic. Some of the colors—in fact, many of them—change with the seasons, the gray of winter merging into the green of spring, with a short period of brilliance at blossom time or at the time of fruiting. Outline, form, mass and texture are all important elements in the design, but in many compositions, particularly in the flower garden, color has the strongest appeal. It is dangerous to give flower color first consideration when designing a garden; better get the more subtle basic greens, grays and autumn colors of the woody plants first, then concentrate on the relatively short duration color of annuals, perennials and roses.

Garden Lighting

In the eighteenth century, the magnificent gardens at Versailles were illuminated with

2.10 Even a very small city lot offers the opportunity to experience the comfort of a garden. Note sitting and dining areas near house, large window that brings the garden indoors, sheltering tree, enclosing fence and shrubs. Photo Grant Heilman

thousands of torches for the delight of Louis XVI and his courtiers as they strolled through the great plaisances. Today, the illumination of gardens is no longer the luxury of kings, as even the most modest garden may achieve the special enchantment that skilled lighting effects can provide.

Lighting makes possible more hours of outdoor living, and for many people, the evening hours are their only time for leisure and relaxation. Well-planned lighting extends the usefulness of the terrace, patio and the recreation areas. Such lighting dramatizes the beauty of the garden as viewed from the house or terrace; it highlights special points of interest; and it makes safe and pleasurable the use of garden paths and steps.

Light emphasizes the texture and pattern of foliage silhouetted against the darkness, and it brings out interesting details. A greater feeling of depth and form will be obtained if trees and flowers are lighted from the side rather than from the front; when dramatic effect is desired, it is usually best to concentrate on one or two points of interest, rather than on too broad an area.

2.11 A substantial surface for garden furniture is essential. Dinner by candlelight, surrounded by roses, after the hot summer sun has gone down, would be pleasant here. But we ask ourselves, would not service be more convenient if this dining space were closer to the house? Photo Grant Heilman

With the development of waterproof extension cords, moisture-proof outlets and connections and attractively designed lamps, garden lighting has become a simple and comparatively inexpensive undertaking. There are fixtures of many types—lamps suitable for lighting outdoor dining areas and reading chairs; low, mushroom-type fixtures that direct the light downward, being specifically designed for lighting paths or steps; and spotlights of various types designed for general overall illumination or for highlighting some special group of plants or some garden feature.

For lighting paths and steps, ordinary bulbs are usually satisfactory. A 60-watt bulb in a mushroom-type fixture will light an area about 20 ft. in diameter. For larger areas, or for creating dramatic effects at a distance, 150-watt bulbs, or PAR spot or floodlamps may be used. A 150-watt PAR bulb with a bullet-type reflector will illuminate a group of trees or a garden feature at a distance of 40 ft. Some fixtures are portable, others are stationary. Most spotlights are arranged so that they can be turned at any angle. All outdoor lighting fixtures should be of rugged construction and weatherproof.

It is important that the wiring and the laying of the cables meet the specifications of the local electical code, and it is advisable to have a well-qualified electrician do the work.

Foundation Planting

Foundation planting is a uniquely American phenomenon. It has been practiced with the often expressed purpose of fitting the house to the surrounding area, harmonizing its vertical surface with the horizontal lines of the ground about it, compromising the artificiality of the architecture with the naturalness of the landscape. These purposes are worthy, but how much harmony is there in the monotony of stiffly spotted little evergreens? Does a building fit into its site better if it is surrounded by a smothering mantle of greenery? And will evergreen trees in a variety of form and color and texture, trimmed to resemble croquettes, really serve to harmonize a dignified piece of architecture with its surroundings? A finely designed house that has a charm arising from its own design has more in common with a simple, dignified landscape of trees and graceful lawn than it has with what we have come to mean by "foundation planting."

It is time we stopped thinking about foundation planting altogether, and allowed ourselves to think about the whole setting of the house, its background and foreground, the ground forms, and the play of lights and shadows upon its walls. Then we would let the planting at the base of the walls be as unobtrusive as possible, and so moderate would we be in both the quantity and variety of plants used that attention would remain on the structure, where it should rightly be. The planting in the foreground of the house should contain only such plants as harmonize with each other. A few varieties in greater number are more easily harmonized than are many varieties. Yet variety enriches and makes possible a succession of interests as the season advances. With care in the selection, it is possible to use variety and yet keep to a fixed general character. This may be accomplished to a considerable extent by avoiding the use of plants that are conspicuous because they are unique in form or color. A beautiful house needs a beautifully designed setting, one that embraces the whole house as a dominant element in the composition and subordinates the details to their proper places. A planting that is simple and dignified will always remain satisfying.

Built-in Planting Beds

A modification of the usual foundation planting area is the built-in, raised planting bed found in an increasing number of homes of contemporary design. This consists of a low retaining wall built about 3 ft. out from the base of the house, and usually of the same material as the house. Such beds are suitable only for houses built of stone, brick or some other form of masonry.

Planting beds vary in height according to the design of the house. They should be deep enough to provide a good bed of soil for the plants. The bed should have no bottom, the soil in the bed being contiguous with the soil below. Thus the capillary movement of water in the soil will prevent an excessive evaporation of moisture from the bed, and will also aid in the drainage of surplus water.

An exposure of partial sun and partial shade is ideal for most plants grown in raised planting beds. Beds exposed to full sun throughout the day tend to dry out rapidly and many plants are unable to withstand the combination of full sun and reflected heat from the wall of the building, which can be very intense during the mid-summer months. In such an exposure, the choice of plant materials is definitely restricted.

The selection of plants for built-in beds needs careful consideration; it should include such points as hardiness, ultimate size and good year-round appearance. Some of the dwarf evergreens and shrubs meet these exacting requirements well, and certain perennials and bulbs may be used to bring animation and color into the planting composition during the spring and summer months.

For partial shade in cool climates, the following plants are recommended: azaleas of the smaller types, such as *kaempferi* and *kurume; Ilex*

2.12 Safe and comfortable walking surfaces are essential to those parts of the garden that bear heaviest traffic. In this instance, where rains are frequent and the lawn often wet, a raised boardwalk provides a useful and attractive solution at the garden entryway. Reich-Versen Landscape Architects. Photo Carlton Lees

2.13 Because trees, shrubs and other plants are irregular in shape, the ground pattern should provide the structure upon which garden spaces are organized. Even with the flower beds empty, the design holds together.

2.14. Lawn panels are used like carpets; even without the flowers, the panels, paving and balustrade define the garden. Photos Carlton Lees

2.15 The influence of Japan on American gardens has been substantial. This garden has been designed more as a restful vista in a city neighborhood where eighteenth- and twentieth-century architecture come together than as a space to be occupied. Photo Grant Heilman

crenata 'Convexa'; *Lonicera nitida;* and the spreading junipers. Among the shrubby perennials *Iberis sempervirens* and *Daphne cneorum* are particularly good, and tuberous begonias and achimenes may be used along the front of the bed to give a brilliant note of color during the summer months. Patches here and there of early spring bulbs, such as the species crocus, the scillas, the narcissus and the lovely species tulips like *T. kaufmanniana,* will give added interest in the spring, as will the colchicums and autumn-flowering crocus in the fall.

For more dense shade, *Leucothoë catesbaei, Pieris japonica, Ilex glabra* and *Sarcococca hookerana* may be used, with *Vinca minor* and *Ajuga reptans* as a ground cover in the foreground, enlivened with occasional clumps of violas and primroses in the spring.

In mild climates not subject to frosts, there is a wide choice of material: *Fatsia japonica,* with its striking, large leaves, may be used to achieve very dramatic effects, as may *Fatshedera lizei* and the lovely fern pine, *Podocarpus elongata; Aucuba japonica variegata; Phormium tenax,* the New Zealand flax; *Agapanthus africanus,* the blue lily-of-the-Nile; and *Plumbago capensis* may also be used very effectively.

CITY GARDENS

No garden is more artificially situated or beset with greater disadvantages than the garden in the city. It is cramped for space. Neighboring buildings often deprive it of adequate sunshine and circulation of air. And getting quite ordinary materials in and out of a city backyard garden (soil, mulch, new plants, pruning refuse) is often a tiresome, cumbersome, disruptive task.

If, by ingenious design, the space has been well utilized, and, by technical skill, the cultural requirements for healthy plant growth have been provided, such a garden can bring real satisfaction to the owner.

The surroundings of the city garden make an architectural approach to its design the most logical one. The garden site should be enclosed by a wall or fence, thus securing privacy. Axes should be employed as a framework of the design, giving it strength of form and harmonizing it with the adjoining architecture. However, exact symmetry may not necessarily be important in so small a space. Such architectural features as sculpture, a wall fountain, balustrades, wrought-iron grills, colored tiles and pavement all express the formal style and add color and interest of detail to a garden in which flowering plants do not play a dominant part. The design should be simple, straightforward, small in scale and economical of space, and not crowded.

As with so many gardens, the background is an important part of the composition. Walls 8 ft. or 9 ft. high are an effective means of blocking unsatisfactory views, but in some positions they shut out too much sunshine and air circulation, and they should be used with a careful regard for the points of the compass. Brick, hollow tile with stucco surface, hollow tile with colored-tile surface, or combinations of these, are all satisfactory. The coping on the top of the wall—tile, flagstone or brick—can be made a decorative color note. To mitigate the severity of wall surfaces and the heat radiating from them, vines should be grown on the walls. Such vines as English ivy and Boston ivy cling to brick by rootlets, but clematis, *Polygonum,* silver lace vine and many other vines require lattices on which to climb. Lattices of painted wood can be of simple decorative patterns. Wood frames

2.16 *The old-fashioned porch provided comfortable and useful living space—close to indoors and yet a part of outdoors—and served as a logical link between house and garden. Photo Carlton Lees*

are good, but wrought iron is preferred for wisteria, which is so strong that it can wreck wooden trellises in a few years.

A combination low brick wall and high brick piers with fencing between the piers is satisfactory when designed in good proportions. It is more permanent than a fence with wooden posts, and the combination of materials makes it an interesting architectural feature.

There are numerous types of wooden fences that may be used very satisfactorily. The close-woven type of fence made of cedar pickets is obtainable in various heights and affords excellent protection. The basket-weave type with a lattice top to provide support for vines is attractive, reasonable in price and easily erected. Modern louver fences are excellent, as they provide for a good circulation of air and at the same time ensure privacy and protection. Well-

designed board fences are also very satisfactory. (See Chapters 5 and 6 for the design and construction of walls and fences.)

Paths

Concrete is permanent and the most practical and economic material for walks, but it is harsh and glaring and its use should be avoided if possible. Its combination with colored pebbles of a fairly uniform size may give pattern to an otherwise monotonous surface. In this type of pavement, the pebbles are pressed into the surface of the concrete while it is still mobile, and protrude above the surface, forming a knobby, rough floor. Such a pavement may be combined with flagstone. In districts where frost action in the soil is not the usual winter condition, "popple" stones may be used. These are small cobblestones set on edge into the ground

2.17 *Essential to garden design is the manipulation of space to create rooms. Here the fence and gate provide separation between inner and outer spaces, yet are open enough to invite us to enter. Photo Carlton Lees*

and firmed by tamping. The art of laying such a pavement is practiced in southern England; and in Spain, where the passion for decoration is so strong, these stones are placed in patterns of varied colors and sizes, especially in the enclosed courts or patios of town houses.

Brick and flagstone are the most satisfactory materials for paths in the city garden. They are in harmony with the architectural surroundings, and are attractive and permanent. Paths of loose pebbles or crushed gravel are also appropriate with small formal schemes but require a certain degree of maintenance and are less comfortable to walk on.

(See Chapter 5 for the design and construction of garden paths.)

Many a city-yard garden is also the means of access from delivery truck to kitchen. As a yard it must provide receptacles for waste containers. A cupboard for containing rubbish cans may sometimes be concealed behind a low wall, the top of which is a broad shelf for potted plants. If the path to the alley is at a slightly lower level than the rest of the garden, this concealment is all the more easily accomplished.

Practical Considerations

As drainage of surface water and air circulation are apt to be poor in city gardens, it is advisable to plan for raised planting beds when possible in order to help mitigate these handicaps. Such beds may be held in place by narrow walls of brick, by flagstones set on end, by planks or old railway ties.

Soil is always a problem in a city garden. Usually it must be purchased and brought in by truck from the country. It is wise to obtain a sample of the soil before the purchase is made, as there is a great difference in the quality of topsoil. The ideal soil is a good loam well supplied with humus, such as is found in old pastures or in well-managed fields. When highways are put through, or when areas are sold for development and roads are put in, such soil may become available, and one is fortunate indeed to be able to obtain it. When purchasing soil, one should stipulate that it is not to be loaded and delivered when too wet. This is particularly important in the case of clay soils, as they can become lumpy and extremely difficult

2.18 Success in garden design also depends upon appropriate elements that add extra interest, comfort or pleasure. Plastic flamingos and ceramic gnomes are out of place. Here the gardener's imagination and direct approach provide a pleasant and unexpected resting place along a woodland path. Photo Carlton Lees

PLANTS THAT MAY BE GROWN UNDER CITY CONDITIONS

DECIDUOUS TREES

Betula alba	white birch	*Magnolia soulangiana*	saucer magnolia
Carpinus betulus	European hornbeam	*Magnolia stellata*	star magnolia
Cornus florida	flowering dogwood	*Malus*—spp. and cultivars	flowering crabs
Crataegus oxycantha	Washington thorn tree	*Prunum subhirtella*	Japanese flowering cherry
Crataegus phaenopyrum	English hawthorn	*Sophora japonica*	Chinese scholar tree
Ginkgo biloba	maidenhair tree	*Styrax japonica*	Japanese snowbell
Ilex opaca	American holly	*Syringa pekinensis*	Pekin lilac
Magnolia glauca	swamp magnolia	*Ulmus pumila*	Siberian elm

EVERGREEN TREES

Pinus mughus	Mugho pine	*Taxus cuspidata*	Japanese yew
Pinus sylvestris	Scots pine	*Thuja occidentalis*	arborvitae

DECIDUOUS SHRUBS

Acanthopanax pentaphyllum	five-leaf aralia	*Philadelphus* (most spp.)	mock-orange
Berberis thunbergii	Japanese barberry	*Physocarpus opulifolius*	ninebark
Deutzia scabra	rough deutzia	*Rhododendron* spp.	azalea
Exochorda grandiflora	pearlbush	*Rhodotypus kerrioides*	jetbead
Forsythia spp.	all species	*Rhus cotinus*	smokebush
Hibiscus syriacus	rose-of-Sharon	*Spiraea vanhouttei*	bridal-wreath
Lagerstroemia indica	crape myrtle	*Symphoricarpos vulgaris*	snowberry
Ligustrum ibota	Ibota privet	*Syringa vulgaris*	lilac
Ligustrum ovalifolium	California privet	*Tamarix varius*	tamarisk
Myrica caroliniensis	bayberry	*Vitex agnus-castus*	chaste tree
Nandina domestica	heavenly bamboo	*Weigela*, hybrids	weigela

EVERGREEN SHRUBS

Buxus microphylla var. *koreana*	Korean box	*Pyracantha coccinea*	firethorn
Ilex crenata (and varieties)	Japanese holly	*Rhododendron*	rhododendron
Kalmia latifolia	mountain laurel	R. *carolinianum*	
Osmanthus aquifolium	holly olive	R. *mucronulatum*	
Pieris japonica	Japanese andromeda	R. hybrids	

VINES

Calonyction aculeatum	moonflower	*Parthenocissus quinquefolia*	Virginia creeper
Cobea scandens	cup and saucer vine	*Phaseolus coccineus*	scarlet runner bean
Hedera helix	English ivy	*Polygonum aubertii*	China fleece vine
Humulus japonicus	Japanese hop vine	*Wisteria floribunda*	wisteria
Parthenocissus tricuspidata	Boston ivy		

GROUND COVERS

Hedera helix	English ivy	*Pachysandra terminalis*	Japanese spurge	*Vinca minor*	periwinkle or creeping myrtle

ROSES

climbing roses	floribundas	grandifloras	rugosas	shrub roses	species roses

FLOWERS

PERENNIALS				ANNUALS		
bleeding-heart	delphinium	iris	phlox	alyssum, var. 'Snowdrift'	lobelia	*Salvia farinacea*
columbine	eupatorium	peony	primrose	dahlia (seedling type)	marigold	snapdragon
daylily	hosta			larkspur	petunia	torenia
						zinnia

FLOWERS (Continued)

BIENNIALS			POTTED PLANTS		LILIES
Canterbury-bells	foxglove	wallflower	achimene	geranium	candidum lily
English daisy	pansy		caladium	tuberous begonia	regal lily
Forget-me-not	viola		coleus	wax begonia	

BULBS

Crocus	*Chionodoxa*	*Muscari*	*Narcissus*	*Scilla*	Tulip
crocus	glory-of-the-snow	grape hyacinth	daffodil	squill	

PLANTS FOR SHADY AREAS

(partial shade)

achimene	caladium	fern	lily-of-the-valley
bleeding-heart	coleus	hosta	tuberous begonia

to handle if they are loaded and dumped when saturated with water.

The care of the plants in a city garden poses very special problems. All plants suffer from smoke and soot in city areas. This is particularly true in the case of the broad-leaved evergreens. The best way to overcome the harmful effects of soot and other similar residues is to syringe the foliage at frequent intervals with a strong force of water from a hose nozzle.

Since plants are in a more or less restricted soil area in a city garden, special care must be taken to see that their nutrient requirements are met and that a pH is maintained that will meet their specific needs.

Although the city gardener labors under definite handicaps, much may be accomplished if plants are selected with care and a good maintenance program is followed.

Plant Materials

Vines on walls and arbors, potted plants, shrubs and small trees as background and accents, bulbs heralding the arrival of spring in the city, roses in flower from June until late autumn, the colorful bloom of petunias, dahlias and lantana, the dramatic coloring of fancy-leaved caladiums, hanging baskets of the lovely achimenes with their cascades of richly colored flowers — much of the beauty of the surrounding countryside may be enjoyed in the small city garden if the kinds of plants are selected with care.

There are many plants that cannot survive city conditions. There are others, however, that will make themselves quite happily at home in a city garden. Surprisingly, we find in this group some plants that are inhabitants of the wild and yet will thrive under city conditions if given the proper soil.

Since a city garden is usually small, special thought and study should be given to the planting design, as each individual plant assumes an importance it would not have in a large-scale planting. Instead of long beds filled with tulip or iris, there may be room for only one or two groupings and the varieties to be used should be chosen with great care; instead of a wealth of spring bloom from a variety of flowering trees, there may be room for but one tree, and the selection of that particular tree, whether a star magnolia, a Japanese flowering cherry, a dogwood or a lilac, is a matter of great importance.

Since comparatively little space can be devoted to flower beds and borders in a city garden, plants in pots and tubs can be used effectively, and with careful planning a succession of bloom may be achieved from early spring until late autumn. Pots of early spring bulbs may be followed by tulips and bleeding-heart, foxgloves and Canterbury-bells. And an array of

2.19 In a small garden, turf, brick edging and evergreen groundcover establish the basic floor shapes. Garden design by Carlton Lees, photo by Gretchen Harshbarger

terials, its charm is dependent to a considerable extent upon its design and architectural embellishment. Because of the restrictions of the surroundings, the design should be formal, simple, yet interesting. If space permits, a pleasant sitting area and an attractive place for outdoor dining should be provided. Instead of a spacious, overall design, it is sometimes possible to design a series of outdoor rooms separated by low hedges or walls with wrought-iron grills, reminiscent of Spanish patios. Such an arrangement will afford a feeling of intimacy and will provide welcome protection from high winds.

Well-placed architectural features, such as a wall fountain with a pool below, antique oil jars or a piece of sculpture, will contribute greatly to the charm of the penthouse garden.

The areas devoted to outdoor living may be paved with tile, brick or flagstone, or they may be carpeted with turf. If turf is used, there should be at least 4 in. of good topsoil, and a

tuberous begonias, fancy-leaved caladiums, geraniums and annuals will carry on until the chrysanthemums come into flower in early autumn. (For more on plants in pots, see Chapter 4.)

The plants included in the following lists will thrive under average city conditions and are well suited to the small city garden. The list is not all-inclusive. There are many trees that will grow well in the city and are excellent as street trees, but if planted in a garden would soon become too large and would rob the shrubs and flowers of light and food. And there are other plants that would thrive but are of inferior character, so they have not been included.

PENTHOUSE AND ROOF GARDENS

The trend toward city apartment living has led to the development of penthouse gardens and terraces high above the ground. The problems and hazards of developing a penthouse garden are many.

Since a penthouse garden must necessarily have distinct limitations in the use of plant ma-

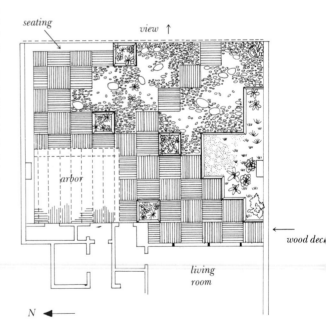

Fig. 2.1
Plan for a roof garden using prefabricated wood decking units, planting boxes, rocks and arbor for shade.

good maintenance program is essential. (See Chapter 12 on lawns.)

Structural and Gardening Considerations

In developing a penthouse garden, one must make sure that the supporting structure can carry the weight to be added to it. Most of the materials used in constructing a roof garden, such as tile, brick, soil, planting tubs and boxes, are heavy, and the sum total of the weight may reach a considerable figure. Expert advice on this matter may be advisable in order to prevent the possibility of future trouble. A structural engineer can answer questions about weight limitations and distribution.

Raised planting beds may be constructed or, if desired, all the planting may be done in tubs or planting boxes. Such boxes should be built of good materials. If wood is used, the outside of the boxes should be painted or treated with a wood preservative penetrating stain, and the inside treated with cuprinol, which is a good wood preservative nontoxic to plants. For trees, shrubs, roses and vines, the planting boxes should be at least 18 in. in depth and any length and width required. For bulbs and annuals, boxes 10 in. to 12 in. in depth will be satisfactory. Brass screws should be used in the construction of the boxes and angle irons at the inside corners. Holes should be bored in the bottom of the boxes to facilitate drainage, and at least 1 in. of drainage material, such as gravel or rubble from broken bricks or crocks, should be spread over the bottom. The boxes should be raised slightly above the floor in order to facilitate drainage.

Excellent tubs are available in a wide variety of sizes, and casks and hogsheads can be cut down to any desired height and used for growing trees.

Obtaining good soil for the tubs and planting boxes is a matter of importance. Soil transported to the city and then delivered to a penthouse garden is expensive, largely because of the high costs of transportation and handling. It costs just as much to transport poor soil as it does to transport good soil, and purchasers should make sure they are getting good, fertile topsoil.

The greatest hazards of roof gardening are wind and intense summer sunshine. It is difficult for anyone who has not experienced it to realize what the full force of a strong wind can be on a rooftop high above city streets, and for many plants some protection must be provided. Above the walls, which are usually part of the structure of the building, it may be advisable to construct a barrier that will provide additional protection from wind. A close-woven cedar picket fence, obtainable in sections of varied heights, is excellent for this purpose; a latticed Chinese fence with translucent panels is both decorative and practical; and various types of panel-wood fences may be used.

Selection of Plants

The kinds of plants for the roof garden must be selected with great care as there are many plants that are unable to survive the hazards of strong wind and intense summer sun.

The planting compositions should be carefully studied. There should be trees to give height and scale to the planting; shrubs with good evergreen foliage to provide year-round beauty; vines to adorn and soften the walls that provide enclosure for the garden; bulbs for the special joy they bring to any garden in spring; and freely flowering plants throughout the season.

Trees

A number of trees have proved well adapted to the trying conditions on a roof garden and can be grown very satisfactorily in large tubs, casks and planting boxes. When the root growth is thus restricted, the trees will seldom attain their normal size, but in many cases this is an advantage when they are used in a penthouse garden. The ubiquitous ailanthus will thrive anywhere, under any conditions, but there are so many other superior trees that it is hardly deserving of a place in a penthouse garden. The lovely mimosa tree *(Albizzia julibrissin)* does well in an eastern exposure and with its feathery, interesting foliage has unique charm, its one disadvantage being that in the latitude of New York it may not survive an extremely severe winter. Both the river birch and the white birch will thrive and are decorative and full of grace. The beautiful Burford holly will do well if given a location in partial shade; and with its deep green, glossy foliage and red berries, it will be a thing of joy throughout the year. The Lombardy poplar is best used as an accent where a tree of slender, tapering height is desired, and although not long-lived even under the most favorable conditions, it will usually remain vigorous and attractive for a good many years on a rooftop terrace. Willows are among the easiest trees to grow, and they withstand the wind well. Graceful in form, they will often reach a height of 20 ft. or more on a rooftop terrace. Also graceful in form, and lovely when in flower, are the Japanese cherries.

Some of the fruit trees, such as apples and pears, may be grown in planting boxes and trained to the espalier form against the walls. When trained in this way, they become a decorative feature of the penthouse garden and in time may bear a small quantity of delicious fruit.

2.20 This garden on a roof incorporates the essential elements of any successful garden: comfortable walking surface, shelter overhead, enclosure and the green of plants. Photo William Curtis

Shrubs

There are a number of very choice shrubs as well as many of the commoner types that may be grown successfully in tubs and planting boxes in the penthouse garden. Many of the azaleas thrive, and with their abundant and colorful bloom they add greatly to the charm of the garden in spring. Some of the hardiest species of the camellia, such as *Camellia sasanqua,* will thrive if grown in a protected corner where they can have partial shade during the summer and some light protection during the winter. They will come into flower in October and remain in bloom for a month of more. Forsythia may be allowed to assume its naturally graceful form, or it may be trained as an espalier against a wall where its branches will form a cascade of golden bloom in the spring. Among the evergreen shrubs particularly valued because of their beauty at all seasons are *Pieris japonica* and *Pyracantha* or firethorn, which, with its brilliant orange berries, is one of the glories of autumn. *Pyracantha* may be easily trained to any desired form against a wall and is a most decorative feature in a planting composition. Both Regel's privet and the more common California privet also thrive under rooftop conditions, as does *Taxus cuspidata,* the Japanese yew.

Vines

Because of the great expanse of wall that often encloses a penthouse garden, vines play an important part in the planting design. English ivy will usually thrive against a north or east wall but will be unable to endure the intensity of the sun on a wall with a southern or southwestern exposure. Japanese honeysuckle is beloved for its fragrance and will give intermittent bloom from June to November, and the decorative China fleece vine *(Polygonum aubertii)* will thrive under almost any conditions. Fortunate is the penthouse gardener whose wisteria, one of nature's masterpieces, will also do well on rooftop terraces, for it makes the weeks when it is in flower a memorable occasion. For rapid growth and quick shade the Puerto Rican yam is very satisfactory, and many of the annual vines, such as the moon flower, the morning glories, the scarlet runner bean and the cypress vine, are also excellent and may be used very happily while the more permanent vines are becoming established.

Roses

Some roses, such as the lovely floribundas and the more stately grandifloras, grow extraordinarily well in the environs of a penthouse garden. In the latitude of New York they are often in full leaf by the middle of March and are in almost continuous bloom from June until late autumn. They may be grown in tubs, in planting boxes or in specially prepared raised beds. Among the most dependable varieties for the penthouse garden are 'Betty Prior,' which will reach a height of 4 ft. to 5 ft. and is never out of bloom, 'Carrousel,' 'Floradora,' 'Spartan' and 'Vogue.'

Flowers

With careful planning, a succession of bloom may be achieved in the penthouse garden from early spring until late autumn. The spring bulbs, pansies, violas and forget-me-nots, all of which may be purchased in pots or baskets, usher in the season of spring and are followed by greenhouse-grown annuals brought into early bloom. Perennials play a minor role in the penthouse garden. Their period of bloom is usually comparatively short and planting space is at such a premium that it cannot be spared. Some of the perennials, such as the lovely old-fashioned bleeding-heart, and some of the biennials, such as the Canterbury-bells and sweet William, can be purchased in large tar-paper pots when just coming into bloom and will continue to flower for many weeks. Among the sun-loving annuals there is a wide choice: the ever dependable petunias, which are available in enchanting colors and will give abundant bloom throughout the season, ageratum, alyssum, including the new tetraploid giant variety, 'Snowdrift,' which will continue to flower until heavy frost; seedling dahlias in lovely colors, lantana, which thrives in intense heat, zinnias in the new pastel shades, and the mari-golds, which never fail to be prolific with their blooms.

For fragrance there are nicotiana, night-blooming stock, heliotrope and lavender, and for accents here and there, geraniums.

For shady areas there are the foliage plants such as coleus and named varieties of fancy-leaved caladiums. For north and west exposures, where they will receive good light but little direct sunshine, there are begonias and fuchsias.

In autumn, potted chrysanthemums may be used to replace some of the annuals that have begun to look a bit shabby, and a patch here and there of autumn crocus and colchicums, which should be planted in August, will bring added interest into the penthouse garden.

Herbs

Even a few herbs can be grown on a rooftop terrace, and a strawberry jar, the pockets filled with some of the delectable varieties suited only to the home garden, will yield an occasional picking.

Maintenance

It is important to follow a good maintenance program. The routine care of the plants in a penthouse garden differs somewhat from the care of such plants in the usual type of garden. Since the plants on a rooftop terrace tend to dry out rapidly as a result of the effects of wind and brilliant sunshine, more attention must be given to watering. In order to conserve as much moisture as possible in the soil, a good system of mulching should be adopted. (See Chapter 8 on mulches.) Because of the shallow depth of soil and the restricted root area in which the plants are grown, special care must be taken to see that the plants are adequately supplied with the nutrients necessary for good growth. A monthly application of a high-analysis, quickly soluble fertilizer is advisable (for methods of application, see index).

Careful watch should be kept for evidence of disease or insect pests; if trouble occurs, prompt control measures should be undertaken.

3

Grading

The process of covering land to more intensified use is apt to involve changes in the grades of ground surfaces. Such constructions as roadways and the immediate surroundings of house and play areas need to conform to certain standards of practicality and use. Local zoning ordinances also may dictate grade changes. Sloping surfaces, too steep for convenient travel, must be brought down to more gentle grades in order to accommodate new roads. The formality appropriate for the terraces of a house usually demands flat surfaces of ground, although contemporary architecture often weds the structure to the building site with a minimum of disturbance. The games of tennis, bowls, baseball, and so on require carefully leveled areas. These operations of changing the levels of ground are classed as grading.

GRADING FOR A NEW HOUSE

The subject of grading a new house usually receives scant attention on the part of the owner. There are so many questions of furnishings and fixtures to be decided that problems of landscape design tend to be postponed until these are disposed of. Meanwhile, the earth from the cellar excavation often has been dumped and spread over a considerable area, thus covering up much valuable topsoil, and the floor levels are fixed, regardless of the design of the surrounding ground areas.

Adjusting a house to its site is not an easy problem at best. When it has been complicated by postponing the task until the house has imposed a new set of conditions, it is even more difficult to reach a satisfactory solution. However, when a house and the surrounding areas

have been designed simultaneously, it is possible to compromise one to accommodate the other. The raising of the floor grades by a few inches above the level originally planned may be enough to save several hundred dollars in the grading item alone, or will make possible an easier transition between architecture and landscape. The shifting of the house several feet from the site originally selected may make possible a better grade and an easier curve in the driveway. These results are worth attaining and can be achieved by carefully designing a general landscape plan of the property, with a grading plan of the house site, *before* the house is built. All these things may be considered a part of design and, of course, they are. But because there are certain factors such as maximum grade and minimum curve that limit road forms, the problems of grading in many cases determine what the design may be.

Planning changes in ground form requires careful measurement and the recording of existing grades as a basis for studies. Such a record of the site is called a topographic plan because it represents the ground slopes. By a series of lines called contour lines, each connecting all points on the earth's surface that are at an equal elevation, the plan readily expresses the configuration of the ground. Where the lines are close together, the ground is steep; where they are far apart, the ground is nearly level.

The finished plan representing the original ground form and the ground levels after they have been adjusted to new requirements is called a grading plan. It is the working drawing controlling the excavating and filling operations. From this plan, earthwork quantities are computed and the new levels staked out.

It is perfectly possible to grade land without using a plan. Simply cut where necessary and fill the excavated earth wherever it is most needed, or wherever it will do least damage. The only difficulty with this procedure is that there is no way of knowing in advance how much earth must be handled, whether there will be enough or too much to make the fills required, or even how far the fills will extend. It also results in an uneven layer of topsoil that will make for uneven growth of whatever planting is done later. If the design is for the environs of a new house not yet built, the grading plan should be made in order to determine not merely the cuts and fills but the position and floor levels of the house. By adjustment of the floor grade, the quantities of earth excavated and filled may be made to balance, thus reducing to a minimum the cost of grading. If too much earth is cut, the surplus must be hauled away. If not enough earth comes from the cuts, then additional earth must be hauled in to make the fills. In either case, more earth is handled than is necessary to do the job.

The suburban home site often abounds in valuable plant life that is unwittingly destroyed during the grading process. Large, valuable trees can frequently be saved by building walls or wells around them, and by providing proper drainage and aeration. Not so obviously salvageable are smaller trees, which many times can be transplanted to a safe location or even temporarily heeled in and replanted once grading is finished. Even less often considered are shrubs, wildflowers and grasses, which similarly be saved and utilized. These adventitious plants may be particularly useful to the homeowner who is interested in creating a natural landscape.

The importance of topsoil or loam cannot be too strongly emphasized. Every finished surface of the open ground should have a top layer of loam for the support of plant life. The under earth or subsoil is not productive and will support only the toughest weeds. Even if much of the finished area of the property is to be converted to driveways, pavements and house site, the topsoil originally on these areas should be scooped off and saved, and later added to the topsoil in areas devoted to garden, terrace and lawn. In this way a natural topsoil only 6 in. in

depth may be increased to 12 in. or 24 in. in special places where extra depth will be an advantage. Garden flowers grow better, bloom better and resist drought better in deep loam than in shallow soil. Fertilizer may be used to make up for the lack of proper depth in soil, but its effect is temporary at best, whereas a rich topsoil 15 in. deep is a permanent asset.

GRADING PROCEDURE

When grading begins, all the topsoil should be removed with a scoop from the whole area and dumped conveniently near but outside the field of operations. It is wise to save all available topsoil. If some is left over, the surplus will help make compost and topdressing and will renew the soil in the greenhouse and coldframes for several years to come.

The next step is to excavate for the foundations and for the areas to be lowered. The earth thus removed should be placed, whenever possible, in its final position, handling the earth only once. The spreading of earth in areas of fill should be done in layers not deeper than 6 in., and each layer should be rolled before the next is spread. This method compacts the earth so firmly that there will be practically no settling of subsoil during subsequent years. Care should of course be exercised so that soil is not unnecessarily compacted near existing trees.

Failure to compact the earth while it is being filled will cause a gradual settling of the earth during the next three or four years. In some places this settling is no detriment, but in other areas, such as those adjacent to terrace steps, the settling will cause the steps to appear above their normal position, sometimes by as much as several inches—a very awkward condition in a finished landscape.

The grades of the subsoil should be brought to levels below the proposed final grade equal to the thickness of topsoil or paving required in these various areas. Thus, if it is intended that a terrace should be furnished with 15 in. of topsoil, the subsoil should be smoothed off at a level 15 in. below final grades.

No area of turf or pavement should be absolutely level, or so shaped that a concave surface will collect water. Though they should look level, terraces actually should slope away from the building with a fall of at least 1 ft. (preferably more) to 100 ft.

Lawns for tennis should be graded to an even, smooth surface but should not be absolutely level. One method is to slope the ground away from the net to the backstop fence at the minimum degree of slope. This has the effect of making the top of the net actually higher than it should be in relation to players on the baseline. Other methods are to slope the whole court evenly from end to end or to slope it from the center foul lines toward the sides and from the baselines out to the end fences.

DRAINAGE

Catch basins and drain inlets are important adjuncts to the driveway, court, terrace and flower garden. Properly placed and connected with a drain, they will remove surface water before it has a chance to flood flower beds or wash out banks. The drains should extend in straight lines from one basin to the next and should be at least 1 ft. below the surface. The smallest size practicable for drains is 6 in. in diameter. Drains that take the outflow of three or more basins should be 8 in. or more in diameter. Unless the town has separate storm-water sewers, the outlet of drains usually must be taken care of on the property, either by being brought to the surface, distributed through a tile field or emptied into a dry well or stream.

A tile or drainage field is a series of tile pipes, flexible plastic tubing with slits in it or asphalt piping with holes, branching off from the main drain in parallel lines 10 ft. or 15 ft. apart and about 15 in. below the surface. The pipes are laid in trenches and are filled with crushed stone. The upper few inches of the trench are filled with topsoil. The water flowing through the pipes seeps out into the crushed stone, saturates the soil, and the grass roots absorb the water. It is important to locate the field in open ground away from trees. Sunshine keeps the soil in condition to absorb the water. Tree roots are likely to find their way into the drain and clog it. Also important is the grade of the pipe. It should fall at the rate of 1 percent ($^{1}/_{16}$ in. to the foot). A steep pitch in the pipes will cause the water to run to the end.

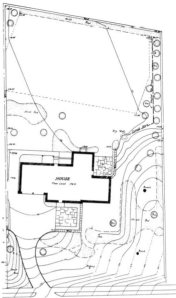

Fig. 3.1
Grading plan of a suburban property. Contour lines indicate slopes.

A dry well is an excavation into the subsoil, usually 6 ft. or 8 ft. deep and 4 ft. or 6 ft. in diameter, the sides of which are walled with stone. It is covered by a stone or concrete slab. It fills up in a storm, and the water seeps away slowly into the subsoil.

The back-filling of trenches must be done with great care. The earth should be filled in layers of 6 in. and each layer sprinkled with water and tamped into place. This method will prevent future settling of shallow trenches. Deep trenches of sewer and water lines should be thoroughly soaked, using a 4-ft. length of pipe attached to a garden hose and inserted at intervals the length of the excavation. Do not mound soil over the excavation in anticipation of eventual settling, since it may take years to do so. Thorough compaction with water, tamping and rolling is the better method.

After the subsoil has been brought to the proper grades by excavating and filling, and the trenches have been refilled, the topsoil may be brought back and spread. If the grading has been in process for several months and the topsoil has been piled up during the house-building operation, many of the old grass roots should be pretty well decomposed, but the pile may be covered with weeds, and the soil will be full of weed seeds. Spreading it out in its final position will give the weeds a chance to germinate. Then if the ground is cultivated before grass seed is sown, many of the weeds may be eliminated. If time permits, it is an advantage to let three or four weeks elapse between finished grading and sowing. Whether such a program can be followed will depend on the time of year the grading is completed. The most favorable time for starting a lawn is August or early September, and the next best is early spring. If topsoil has been spread in the autumn too late for starting a lawn, then the ground should go through the winter with a cover crop of rye that can be sown in October and turned under in the spring. Rye should be sown at the rate of 1.5 bushels per acre. Rye sown during summer can also be cut very short in mid-August or September, the ground then scarified and overseeded with permanent lawn grasses.

WATER-SUPPLY SYSTEMS, UNDERGROUND PIPELINES AND UNDERDRAINAGE

After subgrades are finished, and if possible, before the topsoil has been spread, the utility lines may be laid. House water-supply pipes must be in trenches at a depth greater than the maximum frost penetration for the region. House sewers and drains from catch basins and from the roofs need not be as deep, although 15 in. or 18 in. of soil over the pipes is advisable to keep them out of the way of planting operations.

Water-supply pipes leading to garden-hose connections need not be below frost line, if they are constructed in such a way as to permit the emptying of the pipe when the water is shut off for the winter. For this reason the pipes should slope to an outlet at the cut-off valve or at the spigot. An all-season outdoor water-supply system must have pipes below the frost line and self-draining hydrants rather than faucets.

Gas pipes may be shallow, but they must be so graded that there is a moisture outlet at each low point in the line.

Catch basins are so constructed that the outlet is well above the bottom. The sediment that collects should be removed periodically before it reaches the level of the outlet drain. Neglected catch basins are the principal cause of stoppages in the drainage system.

The size of the drain from the catch basin is dependent on the area of land it is to drain. The table opposite gives the pipe sizes and grades for draining areas of turf under conditions of rainfall prevailing in eastern North America.

The minimum grade for 6-in. tile drains is 1 percent, but 2 percent or more is better because the faster flowing water keeps the pipe clear. Increase in the grade of the pipe increases the flow and capacity.

Land that contains too much moisture, or that is so slow to dry out in early spring that spring operations are retarded, may be greatly improved by drainage lines. The pipes for draining land should be laid about 18 in. to 24 in. below the surface, and the ditch should be filled with crushed stone or gravel to within 8 in. of the surface. Strips of roofing paper or polyethylene should be spread over the stone ballast and then covered with topsoil to bring the trench to an even grade. The pipes should be laid at a grade of about 2 percent in parallel lines 15 ft. or 20 ft. apart, and the outlet should be carried to a stream. The pipes most often used for this purpose are 3-in. agricultural drain pipes, but the main carrying off the outlet from several laterals should be a 4-in. or 6-in. vitrified tile or cast concrete drain pipe. Flexible plastic tubing is a suitable alternative to concrete or vitrified pipe, and its ease of installation renders it most practicable in many cases.

SIZE OF PIPE (TILE)	GRADE OF PIPE (%)	AREA TO BE DRAINED	
		IN TURF (SQ. FT.)	IN PAVEMENT (SQ. FT.)
6″	2	7,000	3,500
8″	2	12,000	6,000
10″	2	19,000	9,500
6″	4	10,000	5,000
8″	4	18,000	9,000
10″	4	28,000	14,000

4.1 In the cool of a canopy suggestive of a lath house, fuchsias flower in abundance and provide a delightful ceiling for an evening meal. Photo Grant Heilman

4

Terraces and Patios

TERRACES

The terrace is an important feature of the modern home. It can be defined as a raised level space with one or more vertical or sloping sides, and usually marks the transition between house and garden.

In the great Italian villas, the terraces commanded views over the surrounding countryside. They often extended across the whole garden scheme, and by the architectural treatment of their outlines with balustrades, they pleasantly combined architecture with plant forms. Often they were embellished with sculpture, fountains, potted plants and patterned pavements, and usually they were shaded by large trees. Wherever garden art has felt the Italian influence, terraces have formed an important element in the landscape design.

Because of its architectural form, almost every house requires some degree of structure in its immediate surroundings; terraces, clipped hedges, parapets, balustrades, paving and fences provide transition between the architectural and the natural landscape. The terrace makes a platform for the house and thereby adjusts it to its site in a graceful and easy transition. Furthermore, the terrace is another room to the house, useful when it is pleasant enough to sit out of doors. In this respect the terrace should be arranged for various weathers, part of it being open to the breezes of summer and part hemmed in by the house so that it is exposed to the warm sunlight of early spring mornings.

The size and proportions of a terrace are a matter of scale. The bulk of the house, the size of the property and the extent of the lawn are factors, and function is also to be considered. It is safe to say that one is more apt to make a terrace too narrow than too broad. The broad terrace has an air of spaciousness and makes a good foreground to a distant view. A narrow terrace is appropriate only on a restricted site where other elements, such as the lawn, are also compact, or where a broader terrace would cut off a pleasant view down into a valley. Unless conditions of the site dictate otherwise, the terrace should be at least as broad as the height of the house façade flanking it. It is probably better to build the terrace slightly oversize in order to provide ample space for outdoor activities.

The house terrace may be raised above surrounding land by a wall or bank; it may be level with the lawn, the separation being made merely by the edge of the pavement; or it may be sunk below the adjacent ground. The grading will be suggested by the conditions of the site. The terrace floor should slope slightly away from the house and the surface water should be collected in drain inlets at the outer rim. The terrace floor may be treated in a number of ways: pavement to accommodate the furniture, smooth turf, small pebble surface, or, what is usually better, a combination of these materials. A broad expanse of stone paving just outside the house can be uncomfortably hot. If only a small part of the terrace is paved and if it is shaded by large trees, summer heat will be greatly mitigated.

Built upon the side of a hill, the terrace floor is maintained by a masonry wall or by a smoothly graded bank. If the hill ascends above the terrace, it, too, must be retained, and the treatment of this wall may be made an interesting feature of the design. A long, unbroken masonry wall may be monotonous; but divided into bays by buttresses or pilasters, or surmounted by a balustrade, it becomes architectural, something in harmony with the artificiality of the place. Vines clinging to the wall or hanging down over it from above, or fruit trees pleached against it, impart a softness of texture in pleasing contrast to the rugged masonry.

Because of the importance of ridding the terrace of rainwater promptly, drain inlets should be placed at frequent intervals. On a terrace 80 ft. or 100 ft. long, four drain inlets at the outer margin are sufficient to carry off the surplus water of a storm. The ground surface should slope toward the drain inlets. The inlet gratings may be small and inconspicuous, 8 in. by 12 in. being ample. (For the construction of drains and inlets, see index.)

A very pleasant effect of stone paving is produced by planting little flowering plants or herbs between the flagstones. Such a paving is not laid on a concrete base but on a cushion of sand and pockets of soil, for the plants are prepared beneath the crevices.

PATIOS

Twentieth-century gardeners owe a debt of gratitude to the ancient Greek civilization, because it was that distant culture which contributed both the patio and the concept of pot-gardening so familiar to us today.

The Greeks worshipped Adonis as the spirit of the green-growing world, and it was in the open inner courts of their dwellings dedicated to the god Adonis that baskets and pots, carefully filled with quickly sprouting seeds, were religiously nurtured. Thousands of years later, the patio or courtyard became one of the main architectural features in Spain, where it was introduced by the Moors during their conquest in the seventh century. These courts were enclosed within walls but were open to the sky and were enlivened with fountains and adorned with plants.

PLANTS APPROPRIATE FOR PLANTING IN SOIL BETWEEN PAVING STONES

Arabis blepharophylla	Rock cress
Arabis ferdinand-coburgi	Rock cress
Arabis hirsuta	Rock cress
Arabis muralis	Rock cress
Arabis muralis var. rosea	Rock cress
Arabis procurrens	Rock cress
Arenaria montana	Sandwort
Gypsophila cerastioides	Baby's-breath
Gypsophila repens	Baby's-breath
Gypsophila silenoides	Baby's-breath
Herniaria glabra	Herniary
Herniaria glabra var. aurea	Herniary
Mazus reptans	Mazus
Minuartia verna	Minuartia
Sagina glabra	Pearlwort
Sagina subulata	Pearlwort
Sagina subulata var. aurea	Pearlwort
Sedum acre	Sedum
Thymus doerfleri	Thyme
Thymus hirsutus	Thyme
Thymus serpyllum	Thyme
Thymus serpyllum var. coccineus	Thyme
Thymus serpyllum var. pseudolanuginosus	Thyme
Thymus vulgaris var. aureus	Thyme

In the elegant homes built by members of the Spanish nobility and the wealthy aristocracy in Seville, Granada and other cities of southern Spain in the sixteenth century, the protected patios were the center of family life, as they are even today. The central feature was usually a fountain around which potted plants were grouped; some special planting was usually featured in each patio and gave it its name—the patio of the orange trees, or the patio of the box, or of the laurel or the myrtle. The white stucco walls that divided one patio from another were adorned with gracefully arched openings that had delicate, wrought-iron grills, or *rejas*, through which pleasant vistas were glimpsed. The walks were made of glazed tiles or river pebbles, or of colored earth, such as bright ocher clay, firmly tamped. Vines or trees were intertwined against the walls, and there were low, clipped beds of ivy and myrtle, and pomegranate and pepper trees for accents, while in the spring the patios were fragrant with the scent of orange blossoms. The rooms of the house opened upon the various patios,

4.2 The true patio is a roofless room surrounded by house on four sides. Photo Carlton Lees

and picturesque balconies looked down upon the patterned walks and beds, with here and there a descending staircase, its graceful wrought-iron railing entwined with vines.

The early Spanish explorers and missionaries brought with them the memories of these lovely, secluded patios; when they built their homes and their missions in the New World, the enclosed patio was its central feature. This tradition has persisted for many years in some sections of Florida and in southern California—but mostly in New Orleans—and in these sunny regions it has come to seem indigenous.

In contemporary garden design, which allows great freedom and originality of expression, the patio has assumed a variety of forms. It may be a paved area open to the sky and either partly or wholly enclosed by the walls of the house. It may be partly covered by a roof or by vines on a latticed support. It is usually adja-

4.3 In New Orleans many patios exist and are wonderful retreats away from city clamor. Some are large, with overhanging balconies; and some are small, restful nooks. Photo Carlton Lees

cent to the house, being the transition between the house and the out of doors, although it may be a paved area separated from the house with a supporting wall of its own and perhaps a roof.

A patio can be designed to fulfill a variety of functions. It may be an entrance patio, separated from the street by a wall or fence. Small as such a patio must often be, it can possess great charm and provide a most attractive entrance to a home. A patterned pavement, a choice vine espaliered against the wall, a few well-chosen plants in pots and tubs can bring distinction to such an area.

An area may be designed as an intimate patio, entirely enclosed, and to be entered from but one room—a guest room or the master bedroom. Here again, the treatment should be restrained and the planting composition handled with great sensitivity and skill, since such a secluded patio is for repose and quiet meditation. For a small child's patio opening off of a nursery, the treatment would be imaginative and playful.

The most usual type of patio is that designed for the enjoyment of the family and for entertaining. Such a patio is generally of ample proportions and is made bright with plants in pots and tubs and hanging baskets. It has the pleasing aspect of partial enclosure, and if it is partly protected by a roof, it affords a pleasant place for the enjoyment of social pleasures in sunshine or in shadow. It is usually adjacent to the recreational area—the pool, the outdoor grill, the sandpile—and is the center of family life.

Because of the enclosure and the regulation of sunshine and shade, conditions for plant growth may be made almost ideal on the patio. Shelter from the wind and the concentration of sunshine tend to prolong the season and make this a warm spot in winter where one may grow tender plants without protection. On the other hand, protection from too much sun in summer by vines on a lattice or by a louver roof, and the play of water in a fountain, make possible cooler conditions than would be attained on an open, sunny terrace. The patio has become, in the hands of a skillful designer, a versatile and charming adjunct to the modern home, one that contributes greatly to the comfort and enjoyment of outdoor living.

PAVEMENTS FOR TERRACES AND PATIOS

For pavements that are to be in constant use several months each year, the qualities most desired are firmness, smoothness and watertightness. In cold climates it is also important that the pavement have foundations that will be undisturbed by frost heaving.

The paving materials generally used are brick, flagstone, wood-block and concrete. The construction of brick and flagstone pavings is described in Chapter 5, on garden paths.

Wood-block paving is laid in the same manner as brick, on a foundation of sand. The blocks, which are about the size of bricks, are set close together with the end grain on the surface. Such a pavement will dry rapidly after a summer rain, the moisture draining down between the blocks to the sand beneath.

As it is usually used for pavements, concrete makes a wonderful, firm, smooth, quick-drying surface, durable and therefore practical. Fur-

4.4 A cool, comfortable and quiet place for summer afternoons and evenings, this terrace is shaded partly by house and partly by large dogwood trees. Tuberous and fibrous-rooted begonia and other plants provide color. Garden design and photo by Carlton Lees

thermore, it is economical and rapid to cast, and it is enduring. But it is not in the least interesting: it lacks texture and color, and it imparts a mechanical artificiality that is quite foreign to the hand-wrought refinement of a garden or patio.

Concrete used with imagination and skill may be quite different. Indeed, it can give variety, interesting texture and color to a pavement. One of the most satisfactory methods of using concrete is to substitute small natural pebbles for the crushed stone in the mixture, and then to brush off with a wire brush the upper surface of the cement before it has finished setting, and thus expose the pebble aggregate. The surface will be made up of the many irregular, rounded forms of the pebbles, which will impart their color and roughness to the floor.

Broad expanses of this pavement may be divided into squares of 3- or 4-ft. by 2-in. strips of redwood set on edge in the cement so that the wood and pebble surfaces are flush. Further variety may be made by using two or three sizes or colors of pebbles, each in a separate square. The result will be a pattern of several hues and an interesting sequence of textures, each catching the light in a different way.

POT PLANTS
FOR TERRACES AND PATIOS

Few outdoor areas offer such dramatic opportunities for the use of different plants as do the terrace and patio.

Because the area is small and intimate, each plant assumes an importance it would not have in a more expansive setting, and the plants should therefore be chosen with special care.

There can be great variety and distinction in the planting. Plants may be grown in pots and tubs, in portable planting boxes and in hanging baskets, and there is a wealth of material available from which selections can be made.

In the .gardens of southern France and in Spain and Italy, potted plants are used in profusion. Many a low wall or parapet and many a balcony is thus pleasantly adorned, and they bring vivid animation to otherwise placid scenes. But nowhere can potted plants be used better than on the terrace or patio.

With careful planning, a succession of bloom may be enjoyed from very early spring, when the first diminutive blooms of *Iris reticulata* unfold, to be followed by the starry flowers of the water-lily tulip, to late autumn when the last of the chrysanthemums are over.

In order to be of value for pot culture, a plant must measure up to certain requirements. It should thrive under the particular conditions that pot culture necessitates, it should be reasonably easy to grow, and it should flower over a long period. A surprising number of plants adapt well to pot culture. Among them we find not only the usual pot plants, such as the geraniums, fuchsias and begonias, but also many annuals, a number of very decorative biennials such as foxgloves and Canterbury-bells, and a few of the herbaceous perennials, among them the lovely, old-fashioned bleeding-heart, sea lavender and chrysanthemums.

A large number of bulbs and tubers, including the colorful tuberous begonias, the exotic lily-of-the-Nile and many of the early spring bulbs may also be grown as potted plants.

In growing potted plants successfully, there are a number of points to be taken into consideration: the selection of the right type and size of pot, the soil mixture, watering, feeding and general care.

Selection of Pots

For centuries, plants have been grown, and grown very successfully, in clay pots. However, as with so many other facets of modern living, the high cost of production and labor has made the old-fashioned and efficient clay pot almost obsolete, with the result that today many nurseries are using the less expensive plastic pot.

There are both advantages and disadvantages to the plastic pot. Essentially, it is cheaper to produce, easier to clean and to handle in large quantities and less subject to breakage; also, it needs less frequent watering. However, even if as many as five drainage holes are provided, there is a danger, especially during periods of heavy rain, that the soil in such pots will become waterlogged. Some plants will be harmed. This problem can be partially over-

4.5 This terrace is a level place higher than the adjacent landscape. Both patios and terraces offer special opportunities for gardening in pots, boxes, tubs and other containers. Photo Anita Sabarese

come by providing additional internal drainage with ½ in.-size gravel filled from the bottom up to one-fourth of the height of the pot.

The quality and color of the plastic pot also are important. The pot should be strong and thick enough so that the plant can readily be lifted with the thumb and index finger only, without breaking or cracking the pot. The very thin and soft plastic pots should be used only for shipping plants, not for growing them. A plastic pot should also be dark enough so that light will not penetrate. In light-colored and white pots, algae will form that can be harmful to some plants. However, many growers of epiphytic orchids prefer the white plastic pots so that light *will* penetrate to the roots.

The plastic pot is practical for fast-growing, one-year crops and for seedlings, though for slow-growing plants that remain in the same pot for a longer period, the old-fashioned clay pot is still the best.

If one's garden budget is ample enough, beautiful handmade clay pots with fluted or rolled rims may be used. Pots of this type, skillfully molded by hand, lend great distinction and charm to the serried patios of southern Spain and the terraced gardens of Italy. They were the only type of flowerpot available in colonial days and have been reproduced in this country for use in the garden at Mt. Vernon

and in the gardens at Williamsburg, which have been so faithfully restored.

Sizes of Pots

Pots are obtainable in various styles and sizes. The standard type, the kind most generally used, is always as wide across the top as it is high. A pot 4 in. across the top is also 4 in. high. Standard pots come in sizes beginning at 1 in. and increasing up to 14 in. The increase in the smaller sizes occurs at intervals of ½ in., in the medium sizes at intervals of 1 in. and in the larger sizes at intervals of 2 in.

Pots commonly referred to as "pans" are one-half as high as they are wide, the smallest of this type being 5 in. in diameter. Pots known as "azalea" or "three-quarter" pots are three-quarters as high as they are wide. These pots are very popular for shallow-rooted plants, such as tuberous begonias, as they are broad at the base and cannot be easily tipped over.

Care of Pots

New clay pots should always be soaked overnight before they are used. Unless this is done, the pot will draw from the soil water that is needed by the plant. Old pots should be washed thoroughly before they are reused. Hot soapy water and a small, stiff scrubbing brush will do a good job. If, because of the possible presence of disease, it seems desirable to disinfect pots, they may be put in a large kettle and boiled for thirty minutes.

Providing Drainage

In preparing the pots for planting, one must provide adequate drainage. An inverted piece of broken crock placed over the hole in the bottom of the pot will usually be sufficient. In the case of tuberous begonias, achimenes and other plants that demand exceptionally good drainage, 1 in. of broken crocks or gravel should be placed in the bottom of the pot and a thin layer of damp sphagnum moss spread over it.

Potting Mixtures

It is well to have a good basic potting mixture that can be altered, when necessary, to meet the specific needs of certain plants. In general, such a mixture should be well supplied with humus and should be light, porous and well drained, being made up of good garden loam, well-decayed compost, a moderate amount of sand and a small quantity of damp peat moss. For plants that prefer a somewhat heavy soil, less sand and more garden loam would be used. For plants requiring a soil exceptionally high in organic matter, an additional amount of compost or well-decomposed leaf mold would be added. For plants requiring soil of very high fertility, well-rotted manure or, if such manure is not available, a small amount of dried cow manure mixed with damp peat moss could be included. If the only garden soil available for use in the mixture is a very heavy clay loam, a soil conditioner should be applied before it is used.

Potting

At the time of potting, the soil mixture should be damp but not in the least soggy. The usual test may be applied. Take a handful and

4.6 An antique urn, draped with ivy, strikes a romantic note in a city patio and offers the opportunity to experiment with plant combinations. Photo Amy Duevell

squeeze it. Then let it drop to the ground. If it crumbles when dropped, it is in good condition to handle. If it retains its shape in the ball, it is too wet and sticky to use. The soil in the flats, trays or pots, in which the plants to be potted are growing, should also be moderately moist but not saturated with water. If the soil is too wet at the time of potting, it is apt to form a solid mass through which the delicate feeding roots cannot penetrate, and the supply of oxygen will also be diminished. Consequently, the plants will fail to become well established and will not grow well. Overwatering of slow-growing seedlings can be avoided by transplanting them into clay pans or wooden flats. Fast-growing seedlings can be potted directly into small clay or plastic pots.

4.7 Calendulas in pots—dozens of them—at the Alhambra (Granada, Spain), with the Generalife across the ravine. Photo Carlton Lees

After plants have been potted, they should be watered and kept in semishade for a few days until they have become reestablished.

Repotting

Young, actively growing plants should be repotted as soon as their roots have filled the pot. This stage may be determined by knocking the plant out of the pot, which is a simple process. Turn the pot upside down, placing the left hand over the top of the pot, with the stem or crown of the plant held between the index and middle fingers. Tap the rim of the plant against a hard, wooden surface. The rootball will dislodge more easily if it is watered first. After one or two taps the plant will be dislodged from the pot. If no roots, or only a very few roots, are visible, the plant is not ready for repotting.

When plants are being shifted to larger pots, the pot next in size should be selected. For example, a plant in a 3-in. pot should be shifted into a 4-in. pot. It is a great mistake to shift a plant into too large a pot, as it will not be able to make use of the moisture or nutrients. Consequently, the soil in the pot is apt to become soggy and sour and the plant will fail to thrive. If the pots are dry, it is wise to soak them before they are used.

When old plants that have become badly potbound are being repotted, it is wise to rub off some of the soil on the surface so that the young feeding roots can come into contact with the fresh soil.

As plants reach maturity, they can be maintained for long periods without repotting, provided a good program of feeding is put into effect.

Watering

In general, plants in pots dry out more quickly than plants in garden beds, and plants in clay pots dry out faster than plants in plastic pots. The rapidity with which they dry out depends upon whether the plants are in active growth, whether the pots are in an exposed position in full sun or are protected by other plants, or whether they are in a shady location. It is important to know the requirements of the various plant groups and to try to meet their specific needs. Some plants, such as impatiens and the tuberous begonias, require large amounts of water and suffer seriously if neglected, while other plants thrive on a moderate amount of moisture, and some, such as lantana, prefer to be kept on the dry side.

If it is necessary to keep potted plants in a sunny location during very hot weather, it is possible to reduce the loss of moisture appreciably by burying the pots in soil, peat or sand, or by using the "pot-within-a-pot" method. The pot containing the plant may be set into a larger pot, the space between the two pots being filled with wet sphagnum moss or with damp peat moss. Potted plants thrive extraordinarily well when this practice is followed and practically never suffer from lack of sufficient moisture. A planting box or tub may be used to serve the same purpose.

Syringing the foliage occasionally with a fog nozzle will help to keep the foliage clean and in good condition and will also help to increase the humidity. This should be done when the sun is not on the plants.

Feeding

As plants in pots have a very restricted soil area from which to draw their nutrients, adequate fertilization plays an important part in a good maintenance program. Here again, it is necessary to understand the needs of the various plant groups, and no general rule can be applied to all types of plants. Geraniums and impatiens will give their best bloom on a rather meager diet, and many a tuberous begonia has suffered and died from the effects of overfeeding. On the other hand, there are plants that require liberal feeding if good growth is to be obtained. The majority of potted plants will benefit from biweekly feedings of a well-balanced, high-analysis, soluble fertilizer.

General Maintenance

Potted plants require faithful attention and respond well to the thought and care bestowed upon them. Dead blooms and dead leaves should be removed promptly; pinching back to induce bushy growth, and judicious pruning to maintain a shapely form, should be practiced, and an ever vigilant eye should be on the alert for the first signs of insect infestation or disease. Shabby, neglected plants are no credit to the gardener.

PLANTS IN TUBS AND VERY LARGE POTS

There are many shrubs and a few small trees that will grow satisfactorily in wooden tubs, boxes or very large pots. Such material lends height and substance to the planting on a patio or terrace.

Some shrubs and trees are particularly well adapted to growing in tubs, while others do not thrive under such conditions. Some plants may be grown in tubs almost indefinitely; others

ANNUALS FOR POT CULTURE

Alonsoa warscewiczii	*Lobelia erinus*
Browallia americana	*Lobelia tenuior*
Browallia viscosa	*Lobularia maritima*
Calendula officinalis	*Nicotiana* (all var.)
Catharanthus (Vinca) roseus	*Petunia* (all var.)
Catharanthus (Vinca) roseus	*Phlox drummondii*
var. *albus*	*Salpiglossis sinuata*
Celosia plumosa	*Schizanthus hybridus*
Clarkia elegans	*grandiflorus*
Heliophila longifolia	*Tagetes* (all var.)
Impatiens holstii	*Torenia* (all var.)

BIENNIALS FOR POT CULTURE

Campanula	*Myosotis*
Cheiranthus	*Viola*
Digitalis	

PERENNIALS FOR POT CULTURE
(*tender perennial)

Chrysanthemum	*Hosta*
Coleus	*Lantana*
Dicentra spectabilis	*Limonium perezii*
Fuchsia	*Pelargonium*

SPRING-FLOWERING BULBS FOR POT CULTURE

Crocus	*Muscari*
Hyacinth	*Narcissus*
Iris	*Scilla*
Leucojum	*Tulip*

SUMMER-FLOWERING BULBS AND TUBERS FOR POT CULTURE

Achimenes	*Caladium*
Amaryllis	*Lilium*
Begonia (tuberous)	*Polianthes*

AUTUMN-FLOWERING BULBS FOR POT CULTURE

Colchicum	*Sternbergia*
Crocus (autumn-flowering)	

may be grown in this way for a few years and then begin to deteriorate. In Italy, one occasionally sees orange trees or laurel trees that have been growing in tubs or huge pots for more than 100 years.

It is wise to choose plants known to grow well under the restricting conditions of pot and tub culture. Fortunately, a wealth of material is available from which selections may be made.

Unless shrubs are purchased as large specimen plants, they usually begin their sojourn on the terrace or patio in medium-sized pots; they are then shifted into larger pots and eventually, as they become more mature, into tubs. Some trees and shrubs that normally grow to a considerable size will never attain their full development when grown in a tub, and, with judicious pruning and wise handling, may be kept at almost any desired size.

When growing plants in tubs, many practical points must be taken into consideration, such as the size and type of tub best suited to the needs of the plant, methods of shifting from one tub to another, soil mixtures, general maintenance requirements and the wintering of plants in tubs.

Size and Type of Tub

Plant tubs may be purchased in a variety of types and sizes, or they may be constructed at home. Whether purchased or homemade, tubs should be made of durable wood that is resistant to decay. Such a tub will give years of service, whereas a tub constructed of cheap lumber that lacks the ability to resist decay will deteriorate rapidly and will be worthless after a few years. The best and most durable woods are redwood, cypress and cedar.

Tubs may be round, square or hexagonal. The bottom of a tub should always be supplied with holes, approximately five ½ in. holes per square foot, for drainage, and it should be raised slightly above the base of the tub to permit good air circulation, which will prevent it from rotting and will facilitate drainage. If the bottom is flush, the tub may be placed on small blocks of wood, or cleats may be used.

Commercially available tubs range in size from small tubs 8 in. to 12 in. in diameter, suit-

able for fuchsias and other small shrubs, to large tubs 20 in. to 30 in. in diameter, suitable for growing large shrubs or small trees. The depth of a tub will vary according to the needs of the plant for which it is to be used. Plants that are shallow-rooted or that never attain great size, such as the azaleas, bouvardia, fuchsias and lantanas, require tubs from 12 in. to 15 in. in depth, while such plants as camellias, laurel, crape myrtle, pittosporum and other plants that grow to considerable size require tubs with a depth of 18 in. to 24 in.

A very satisfactory type of tub that can be made by a good home carpenter is one square in shape, fastened together with removable bolts. This makes it possible to remove only one side, if desired, or all four sides, and greatly facilitates the shifting of a plant from one tub to another of larger size. It also makes easier such routine practices as root pruning and the addition of fresh soil or compost.

If ball-bearing casters are placed on the bottom of plant tubs, it will greatly facilitate moving them from one location to another.

4.8 Gardening in containers is not limited to the ordinary. Here a small tropical aquatic garden — with fish, no doubt — has been created in a tub. Photo Amy Duevell

Methods of Shifting

When a plant is to be shifted from a pot into a tub, it is important to select a tub only slightly larger in size than the pot in which the plant has been growing. The same premise holds true in shifting a plant from a small tub into a larger tub. The increase in diameter should not exceed 1 in. to 2 in. A plant in a 10-in. pot may be shifted into a 12-in. pot or tub; a plant in a 12-in. tub may be shifted into a 13-in. or 14-in. tub when its roots have begun to fill the smaller tub.

The size to which a plant develops can be controlled by regulating the size of the tub. If a plant normally reaches considerable size and one wishes to maintain it at a size below the maximum, this may be achieved by keeping it in a small container. The procedure, therefore, it to continue shifting the plant from one tub to a slightly larger tub until it attains its normal size *or* until it attains the smaller than normal size desired. There are instances in Italy where plants have been kept in the same sized tubs or huge pots for seventy years or more and have still retained their vigor and flowered regularly, although no increase in overall size has occurred.

Soil

The soil mixture should be one that will best meet the needs of the specific shrub. The great majority of shrubs will thrive in a good basic soil mixture, such as 2 parts good garden loam, 1 part compost or leaf mold and 1 part sharp sand. Some shrubs, such as the rhododendrons and many of the azaleas, require a definitely acid soil (see rhododendron). Some need exceptionally light, well-drained soils, and others prefer slightly heavy soils.

Maintenance

General maintenance requirements include watering, feeding, mulching and pruning.

Plants in wooden tubs do not dry out as rapidly as plants in pots, and in hot weather the soil remains at a cooler temperature, as wood is a poor conductor of heat. Most shrubs require a moderate amount of water, although some need a more abundant supply and others need to be kept on the dry side. Frequent, light waterings should be avoided, as this tends to induce shallow rooting. It is best to give a thorough watering once or twice a week, depending on the weather and if the tub is in full sun or in shade, and then to wait until the soil appears dry on the surface. A mulch of peat moss will help to conserve moisture in hot, dry weather.

If a good soil mixture is used, three feedings per year of a high-analysis soluble plant food are usually sufficient. The first should be given early in the spring to encourage good growth. If the condition of the plant indicates by the

4.9 The wide overhang of a ranch house provides hanging space for plants that winter indoors. Photo Grant Heilman

color of its leaves or its general appearance that it would benefit from further feedings, additional applications may be given. If plants are to be given a winter rest period, no feedings should be given from midsummer on.

Judicious pruning should be done occasionally to maintain an attractive shape and to remove dead wood or growth that is too twiggy.

Wintering Plants in Tubs

In mild climates it is possible for the plants to remain on the patio or terrace throughout the year; but where winters are severe, it is necessary to move the tubs into some suitable area where they will be adequately protected from cold. Success with many shrubs depends on being able to winter them well. A cool sun porch or a conservatory that can be maintained

at a very low temperature provides ideal conditions, but when such a place is not available a cool cellar proves a good substitute. The matter of temperature is the chief consideration. It is more important than the question of light, as little light is required during this period of semidormancy. The temperature should range between 45° and 55° F. Warm temperatures in cellars are apt to prove disastrous, as the combination of high temperature and lack of light will cause serious damage to the plants.

Certain plants, such as the fuchsia, require special pruning or other care at the time of winter storage; careful attention must be given to such details.

Some plants do not adapt well to a period of winter storage, and in selecting plants to be grown in tubs in northern areas, one must keep this fact in mind. Those starred on the following list are recommended as adaptable.

PLANTS ADAPTED TO GROWING IN TUBS

(*Will adapt to winter storage in northern areas)

	HEIGHT IN FEET		HEIGHT IN FEET
*Abelia grandiflora	2 to 5	*Ligustrum japonicum	3 to 6
*Agapanthus africanus (lily-of-the-Nile)	3	*Mahonia lomarifolia	3 to 6
*Aucuba japonica	4 to 5	*Myrtus communis	3 to 5
Azalea (in great variety)	2 to 5	*Nandina domestica	3 to 6
*Bougainvillea glabra (trained as shrub)	4 to 5	*Nerium oleander (oleander)	4 to 6
Bouvardia	3 to 6	Osmanthus fragrans (sweet olive)	6 to 8
*Buddleia davidii	4 to 5	Pittosporum tobira	6 to 8
*Buxus japonica and B. sempervirens	3 to 5	*Plumbago capensis	3 to 5
Camellia japonica and C. sasanqua	5 to 10	Podocarpus elongata	8 & up
*Ceanothus delilianus	3 to 5	Podocarpus macrophylla	6 to 10 & up
Citrus aurantium (Seville orange)	4 to 10	*Prunus laurocerasus	3 to 6
*Datura arborea and D. suaveolens	4 to 6	*Punica granatum nanum	3 to 8
Fatsia japonica	4 to 8	Pyracantha (firethorn)	5 to 6
*Ficus carica	4 to 6	*Raphiolepis umbellata (Yedda hawthorn)	3 to 5
*Fuchsia	4 to 5	Rhododendron (in variety)	5 to 6
Gardenia florida	3 to 6	*Roses (in great variety)	4 to 6
*Hibiscus rosa-sinensis	5 to 8	*Strelitzia regiuae (bird-of-paradise)	3
Ilex aquifolium (English holly)	10 & up	*Streptosolen jamesonii	3 to 5
*Laburnum watereri	5 to 8	*Viburnum tinus	4 to 6
*Lagerstroemia indica	5 to 8	*Vitex agnus-castus (chaste tree)	4 to 6
*Lantana camara	3 to 5	*Wisteria floribunda macrobotrys (standard)	5 to 6
*Laurus nobilis	4 to 8		

HANGING POTS AND BASKETS

Hanging pots and baskets filled with cascades of bloom have a unique charm and may be used most delightfully to adorn a terrace or patio.

Flower baskets are used with great distinction on the West Coast and in New England seaside communities, not only in private gardens but also along the streets, at the doorways of shops and in other public places. They are used on balconies and porches and hang from the beams of pergolas and arbors. For shady places, there are hanging types of tuberous begonia and fuchsia, both of which may be seen to the best advantage when growing in hanging pots or baskets. A superbly grown basket of begonia is breathtaking and memorable. For hot, sunny situations, there is trailing lantana, portulaca and *Anagallis*, with its dainty sky-blue flowers. On porches that get only a few hours of morning sun and then shade for the rest of the day, achimenes thrive.

Types of Containers

Various types of containers may be used. Pots, wooden baskets, small wooden tubs and wire baskets are all satisfactory. Pots especially designed for hanging, complete with saucer to reduce dripping after watering, have become extremely popular and, indeed, have helped to create a boom in the use of hanging plants. The light weight of these plastic hanging pots is a great advantage. A disadvantage is their color: the bright white pots are often more conspicuous than the plants they contain. A small can of a gray-green latex paint and a brush is the answer: simply paint the pot (even with the plant in it), and in a matter of minutes the paint dries and focus is back on the plant itself.

Especially constructed wire hangers are available that can be attached to the rim of any ordinary clay pot. These have a hook at the top, sometimes on a swivel type that greatly facilitates turning the pot. Clay pots are much heavier than plastic ones, however, so more attention must be given to securing them to sufficiently strong hooks or hangers.

Baskets made of small redwood or cedar slats are very popular on the West Coast. They are available in a number of sizes, and are attractive and durable. Small redwood tubs or boxes are widely used in California and are the best type in which to grow tuberous begonias and fuchsias, as they retain moisture better than any other type of hanging receptacle. They come in various shapes: square with a tapered base, octagonal and round. They may be obtained in various sizes.

Open-mesh wire baskets are also obtainable in a great variety of shapes and sizes. They are considerably less expensive than the other types and are very satisfactory for many plants if careful attention is given to the method of planting and to watering. Copper wire is superior to galvanized wire, as it will not rust and will give more years of service. Similar baskets may be fashioned at home, if desired.

Pots, redwood containers and wire baskets are also available with one flat side for use on walls, fences and posts.

Planting

Slatted and wire baskets should be lined either with sheets of wood moss or with wet sphagnum moss. Osmunda fiber may also be used but is less satisfactory, as it is difficult to pack the soil in firmly and there is more danger of rapid drying out. All of these materials are usually available from florist supply houses. If it is not too conspicuous, burlap or even Saran Wrap (plastic) screening can be used in some instances. The lining will serve two purposes: it will retain the soil within the basket and will provide for good drainage of surplus water. Slatted and wire baskets tend to dry out rapidly, and if they are to be used in a sunny location it is advisable to place a flower pot saucer in the bottom of the basket, covering it lightly with a layer of sphagnum moss. This will act as a reservoir for surplus water.

After the baskets have been lined, the soil may be added. If one desires to have plants growing out of the sides of wire baskets as well as dropping down from the top, the planting should be done when the basket is about half filled with soil. The plants should be placed on their sides, the ball of earth around the roots being kept intact. The moss lining should be temporarily pulled aside, and the leaves and stems should be worked carefully through the

PLANTS FOR HANGING POTS AND BASKETS

(*For complete cultural details, see under individual plant entries in the index)

Abronia umbellata	sand-verbena	rosy-lavender flowers; full sun
*Achimenes		
Anagalis	pimpernel	annual; blue flowers; full sun
*Begonia	(pendula type)	
Beloperone guttata	shrimp plant	showy, pinkish bracts; partial shade
Browallia speciosa		tubular, clear blue flowers; light shade
Campanula		
C. fragilis		pale blue, star-shaped flowers, gray foliage;
*C. isophylla		partial shade
Coleus	trailing types	brilliant foliage; sun or light shade
Convolvulus mauritanicus		lavender-blue flowers; sun or light shade
Dianthus		
D. latifolius 'Beatrix'		double pink flowers; full sun
D. plumarius		spicy fragrance, many colors; full sun
*Dimorphotheca aurantica	cape marigold	
*Fuchsia	hanging varieties	
Hedera helix	English ivy	many types and varieties; full shade
Hoya carnosa	wax plant	partial shade
Lantana montevidensis	trailing type	lavender-purple flowers; full sun
Lobelia (many varieties)		blue flowers; sun or light shade
*Lobularia maritima	sweet alyssum	
Lotus berthelotii		gray foliage, scarlet flowers; sun or light shade
Mimulus tigrinus	monkey flower	yellow, trumpet flowers; shade
Pelargonium		
P. peltatum	ivy-leaved geranium	pink and lavender flowers; sun or light shade
P. tomentosum	peppermint geranium	scented foliage; light shade
*Petunia	(balcony type)	
Portulaca	rose-moss	flowers in many colors; full sun
Saxifraga sarmentosa	strawberry geranium	white flowers; sun or shade
*Schizanthus	poor man's orchid	
Sedum sieboldii		blue-green foliage, pink flowers; partial shade
Thunbergia alata	clock vine	orange, buff, apricot flowers; sun or light shade
*Torenia fournieri		
Tropaeolum majus	nasturtium	yellow, orange, gold flowers; full sun
Zebrina pendula, 'Quadricolor'	wandering Jew	blue flowers; sun or shade

wires. The remaining soil should then be added.

Adequate drainage material must be put into the bottom of the container—whether it is a pot, basket or a solid wooden box. The soil may then be added, and the flowers planted. The number of plants used will be determined by the size of the container and the ultimate size the plants will attain.

Watering

Hanging pots and baskets, particularly when in full sun, dry out rapidly and require faithful care. Daily watering is usually essential, and on days when there are hot, drying winds it may be necessary to water twice. Pots and wire baskets dry out much more rapidly than solid wooden boxes. Glazed pots dry out less rapidly than clay pots. If, however, a coat of shellac is applied to clay pots, it will reduce evaporation.

One of the most effective ways to overcome the loss of moisture is to follow the "pot-within-a-pot" method, or a variation of it—a "pot-within-a-basket" method. A plant such as fuchsia or tuberous begonia, in a pot of adequate size, may be placed in a larger pot or in a wire basket, the space between being filled with either damp peat moss or damp sphagnum moss. Excellent growth is usually obtained with this method, other conditions being favorable.

If a number of baskets are to be watered, a hose attachment may be purchased that will greatly facilitate the task. This consists of a long, metal tube with a spray at the end, which is put on at a convenient angle for overhead watering.

PLANTS IN PORTABLE BOXES

Portable planting boxes are a recent innovation and have increased the opportunities for an ever-changing succession of bloom on the patio and terrace. Indeed, if they are skillfully planted and maintained, one may experience within a small paved area all the pleasures of a veritable garden.

Planting boxes of the portable type have great versatility. They may be moved easily from one location to another on the patio, and interesting effects may often be obtained by combining boxes of different sizes and shapes. They offer almost unlimited opportunities for dramatic and beautiful combinations of color, texture and form, as plants may be removed as soon as they have completed their period of bloom and be replaced with other plants just coming into flower. Thus, in the North a succession of bloom may be maintained from early spring, when the first bulbs come into flower, until late autumn; in mild climates a full year's cycle of bloom may be enjoyed. And special gems, such as some of the dainty and exquisite cyclamens and the lovely Christmas rose, which require special culture, may be grown in small boxes and used where their beauty will be most fully appreciated and enjoyed.

To the gardener, planting boxes offer solutions to many practical problems, as they make it possible, in many instances, to provide conditions that approximate the ideal. Soil mixtures may be prepared that best meet the needs of special plants. One box may contain a rich, woodsy soil for tuberous begonia, while another box may contain a lean, sandy mixture to restrain the often too rampant growth of lantana and thus produce more abundant flowering. And in areas where nematodes are troublesome, sterilized, nematode-free soil may be used. Conditions involving exposure, humidity,

watering and feeding may also be controlled more readily than is possible when plants are grown in the open ground.

Types of Boxes

The two most satisfactory materials for portable plant boxes are wood and fiberglass and plastics of various sorts.

Boxes made of wood have special advantages. In many areas they may be purchased ready-made, or they may be easily constructed at home by anyone who is handy with tools, as the making involves very simple carpentry. If durable lumber is used and the boxes are carefully made, they should last for ten years or more. Wooden boxes may be purchased in a wide variety of shapes and sizes, and if well designed they may be attractive in appearance. Boxes made of wood also provide good growing conditions for plants.

Some nurseries and garden supply centers offer planting boxes in modular sizes. These are often made up in units of 8 in., available in the following sizes: 8 in. by 8 in.; 8 in. by 16 in.; 8 in. by 32 in.; 16 in. by 16 in. and 16 in. by 32 in.

Wooden plant boxes should always be made with cleats on the bottom to facilitate lifting and moving and to provide for the circulation of air and good drainage. Ball-bearing casters may be attached to the cleats if desired and will greatly facilitate the ease of shifting boxes from one location to another.

(For full details concerning selection of wood and construction, see index.)

Fiberglass Boxes

This material offers certain advantages. Boxes made of fiberglass or plastic are light in weight, are easily handled and are extremely durable. As it is not easy to attach cleats to the bottom, the cleats should be placed directly on the paving and the box rested upon them.

Drainage

It is essential to provide good drainage in planting boxes. A narrow space may be left between the bottom boards, or if a solid board is used, drainage holes should be provided. In addition, it is advisable to place a 1-in. layer of broken crocks, bricks or gravel on the bottom of the box over which a thin layer of moist sphagnum moss should be spread.

Soil

A soil mixture should be used that will meet the needs of the plants to be grown in the box. Unless plants have specific requirements, a general purpose mixture that is light in texture and contains abundant humus will be the most satisfactory, as it will tend to drain well.

Maintenance

The usual good maintenance practices should be followed. The boxes should never be allowed to dry out completely but should be watered with care and good judgment, as over-watering can be as harmful as underwatering. Most plants will benefit from feedings of a high-analysis, soluble fertilizer at intervals of two to four weeks.

For tuberous begonias and caladiums it may prove most satisfactory to grow the plants in pots and sink the pots in peat moss rather than to fill the box with soil. The peat moss should be kept thoroughly damp.

5.1 *A dry stone wall, whether free-standing (as above) or retaining, is a special work of art. Photo Carlton Lees*

5

Garden Walls, Banks, Paths and Steps

GARDEN WALLS

In ages past, high walls were built around gardens to protect them. Often a moat also surrounded the garden. In some cases the walls were built as much for shelter against winds as for protection, and they provided supports for fruit trees that were trained against them. A southern wall surface stimulated spring growth in the espalier trees and induced earlier flowering and fruiting. Besides these practical functions, garden walls also served as a background for flowers and foliage, in addition to providing both privacy and seclusion.

A broad, unbroken surface of masonry is not always interesting, but a wall divided into panels or interrupted by projecting buttresses, or one built with a pleasing combination of materials, has architectural significance. It is the link that unites the garden and the house as parts of one composition.

Freestanding Walls

It is essential that the top of the wall be protected from the weather. One of the most practical means of preventing the moisture from entering the masonry from above is to cover the wall with a coping of flagstones set in cement mortar joints. In addition to its practical function, this definite edge also gives a finished "look" to the structure. A sharp-pitched roof of slate, brick, shingles or painted boards is sometimes used, the last being common in Pennsylvania. A brick coping is also frequently used for this purpose, and a wedge-shaped top built of brick courses in diminishing thicknesses is picturesque. Molded brick set on edge is a favorite wall finish in Virginia.

In the South, walls are sometimes built with some of the bricks omitted, leaving holes to allow for the passage of air currents. For obvious reasons, it is important not to exclude all the breezes in the warmer parts of our country, and the perforated wall serves as a practical screen but not an absolute barrier to circulating air. During the last fifteen years the ornamental cement block has found its way into the garden. These comparatively inexpensive blocks, which come in different designs, are usually 12 in. by 12 in. square and 4 in. to 5 in. thick. They are cemented between piers of 6-in. or 8-in. cement blocks and are plastered with white stucco. Like the perforated brick wall, these blocks prevent a complete view of the area behind, while at the same time allowing for the passage of air currents.

A wall typical of South Carolina is brick with panels of stucco. The piers are thick, while the panels are only one brick in thickness. Thomas Jefferson's famous serpentine wall is only one brick thick. Structural strength comes from the serpentine construction.

Retaining Walls

A retaining wall must hold its position against the pressure of the earth behind it. At seasons of alternate freezing and thawing, ground pressure is considerable. We see its effect when paved roads heave in early spring. If the wall is not adequate to hold, the pressure thus exerted may be translated into one of four kinds of movement: (1) The wall may be forced to bulge out of shape, opening cracks in the masonry. This is apt to happen in dry walls in which there is no mortar to hold the stones together. The pressure and strain is there in all walls. (2) The whole wall may slide away from the hill. This can happen if the footings of the wall are not deep enought to have a firm hold in the soil. (3) The wall can be forced to revolve about its baseline, and thus it is forced to lean forward out of position. (4) The wall may be lifted up vertically by the action of frost beneath the footings. This can happen when the foundations do not extend below the frost line of the region.

It has been found by long practice that the proportions shown in the sectional sketch are adequate to withstand the pressures in the soil. The footings are below frost line and slope down toward the rear. The thickness of the wall at the base equals one-third of the height measured from the lower ground level. The top of the wall is 18 in. thick. Special conditions, such as heavy moving traffic along the top of the wall, will make necessary a greater bulk of masonry than for normal conditions.

By building projections or buttresses into the face of the wall at intervals of 10 ft. or 12 ft., the effective base of the wall is widened, thus making the structure more resistant to the tendency to revolve about its base, and hence more secure. Any revolving of the wall would have to become a lifting of the center of gravity. The buttresses must be built with the wall as an integral part of the structure. The wider the projection of the base of the buttresses, the greater is the resistance to pressure. A buttressed wall may be built thinner than, and still be as strong as, a plain wall of the same height. Buttresses may be made a decorative element, dividing a long wall into bays.

Pressure from wet soil is greater than pressure from dry soil. To prevent the soil behind a retaining wall from becoming saturated, or simply to permit the normal flow of water through the subsoil to continue uninterrupted by the wall, small holes should be left in the masonry near the base of the wall at intervals of 10 ft. or 12 ft.

Stones should be laid into the wall in such a

5.2 A stone wall laid up with mortar requires more complex drainage beneath and a coping (cap) to prevent water penetration.
Photo Grant Heilman

way as to form a strong bond. That is, the long dimension of the stone should be horizontal, and each stone should bridge over the joint between the two stones in the course below. In this way no long, vertical joint will appear. In any retaining wall some stones should run from the front to the back face across the wall in order to tie the masonry more firmly together.

The mortar should be a mixture of 1 part Portland cement and 2 parts sand.

The well-built masonry wall is a structure of great strength and should serve as a permanent installation. The retaining walls of the great Italian villas, for example, have remained intact for 400 or 500 years.

Reinforced Concrete Wall

Another type, known as the "cantilever" wall, holds partly by the weight of earth upon a broad projecting footing. This is built of reinforced concrete, and is therefore a monolith.

Such walls are much lighter and thinner in construction than the gravity wall and are used in regions where sand is common and stone is scarce.

Concrete is made by mixing cement, gravel and water; after it cures, the mixture turns into the equivalent of artificial stone. Because of its strength, permanence and relatively low cost, concrete is one of the most important building materials used in modern construction. Though concrete is strong in compression, it is relatively weak in tension, and structures in which the concrete is likely to be subject to tension must be reinforced with steel rods that can sustain such tension.

The concrete used for reinforced walls is poured between temporary forms built of lumber. Steel reinforcing rods form a mesh of 12-in. or 15-in. squares, which gives the concrete great rigidity and prevents it from cracking under unequal pressure. The inner surface of a concrete wall should be sealed with an application of a waterproofing compound. Unless this

5.3 *This brick wall not only defines the edge of the terrace but with its wood planking becomes a comfortable seat-wall. Reich-Versen Landscape Architects. Photo Carlton Lees*

5.4 The seat-wall in this example frames the deck and also prevents one from stepping off by accident. Such a wall provides extra seating as well as eliminating the confusion of other furniture. Reich-Versen Landscape Architects. Photo Carlton Lees

is done, the concrete is likely to become porous and will crack. With this protection from groundwater, a concrete retaining wall may be faced either with a coat of stucco or with brick. But unless the wall has been waterproofed as described above, the stucco will peel off and the brick will blossom out with rosettes of lime deposited by moisture coming through the bricks and then evaporating.

GARDEN BANKS

In many cases, a simply treated, evenly sloping bank will be appropriate and will function as well as a retaining wall. The advantages of the wall are its architectural character, its economy of space and its permanence. The advantages of the bank are its more natural character and economy of construction. The bank that either slopes down or up from a terrace may be planted with interesting ground cover plants to prevent erosion and to reduce maintenance costs. The bank may also rise from the top of a low retaining wall, an arrangement of form and material that imparts a note of precision in harmony with the formality of the terrace.

Turf Bank

Turf-clad banks have been used for many centuries, and with good reason. Nothing else presents such a finished effect as an accurately graded and well-maintained turf terrace bank, but such banks should not be graded to a steeper slope than 1 ft. of rise to 2 ft. of horizontal dimension. Starting turf on a slope is more difficult than on level land. A heavy rain coming just before the turf has formed will erode the soil and will necessitate patching, regrading and reseeding. Laying turf over the whole bank is the most certain method of starting grass on a bank. If the surface water from the hillside above the bank is diverted by turf gutters, the bank grass may be started with seed sowing. In this case, strips of turf placed in horizontal lines along the banks at intervals of 4 ft. or 6 ft. will arrest the washing away of soil. This precaution is worth the additional cost and effort.

Planted Bank

A bank well furnished with topsoil and covered with densely spreading plants is perhaps the most satisfactory and economical treatment of the change in levels. The slope should be 1 ft. of rise to 2½ ft. of horizontal dimension, or it may be even less steep. By a careful selection of plants, the bank may be made very beautiful. Conditions of soil and exposure may affect or even dictate a choice of plants, but such a great variety of plants are suitable for covering a bank that a wide range of choice is possible.

Ground Cover Plants for Banks

For a sunny bank that slopes down from the terrace, a good ground cover is *Plinus mugo*, *Cotoneaster horizontalis* or *Juniperus* (horizontal forms). A strong color effect in late spring can be achieved by using groups of different *Rhododendron* ssp. (azaleas). For a shady or partially shaded bank, *Vinca minor* (periwinkle) and *Hedera helix* (English ivy) can be planted, with various spring and fall bulbs naturalized throughout the area. These will provide welcome color in spring and fall in an otherwise green ground cover throughout the season.

WOODY PLANTS

Arctostaphylos uva-ursi	bearberry
Calluna vulgaris	heather
Comptonia asplenifolia	sweetfern
Cotoneaster horizontalis	rock cotoneaster
Erica carnea	spring heath
Euonymus fortunei 'Colorata'	spindle tice
E. fortunei var. *radicans*	
Euonymus nana	
Jasminum nudiflorum	winter jasmine
Juniperus chiueusin 'Pfitzerana'	spreading juniper
Juniperus communis depressa	ground juniper
Juniperus conferta	shore juniper
Juniperus horizontalis 'Bar Harbor'	creeping juniper
J. horizontalis 'Plumosa'	
Juniperus procumbens	
Pachysandra terminalis	Japanese spurge
Rosa rugosa	Japanese rose
Spiraea tomentosa	hardhack

HARDY PERENNIAL PLANTS

Ajuga reptans	carpet bugle
Arabis alpina	mountain rock cress
Arenaria montana	mountain sandwort
Cerastium tomentosum	snow-in-summer
Ceratostigma plumbaginoides	bunge
Convallaria majalis	lily-of-the-valley
Hemerocallis fulva	tawny daylily
Lysimachia nummularia	moneywort
Nepeta mussini	catmint
Phlox subulata	moss phlox
Sedum acre	gold moss
Thymus serpyllum	thyme

GARDEN PATHS

A garden path—the very words bring to mind old brick walls bordered with boxwood; strips of turf between long flower borders; flagstones interspersed with tiny herbs and overarched with spreading branches of magnolias. The path is one of the components of the garden plan that gives expression to the design: in some cases by making a pattern among the flower beds, or by accenting the lines of symmetry, and in others by the use of a subtle turn or graceful curve.

In considering the construction of paths, there are a number of matters that should be given careful thought—the selection of the materials to be used, the suitability, the original cost and the expense of upkeep.

Often the suitability of one material over another will be the deciding factor. On an area where there is much activity, turf would not be desirable, as it would lack the essential quality of durability. Within the confines of a garden, however, where there is comparatively little traffic, grass paths are entirely satisfactory. On the other hand, if one has a wooded tract developed along informal or naturalistic lines, a path of tanbark, fir bark or wood chips would be suitable. In this kind of setting, wooded paths of brick or gravel would be out of harmony with the surroundings. For a pathway leading from the sidewalk to the door, where there is much activity, some durable material such as gravel, brick or flagstones should be used.

Costs will vary considerably in different parts of the country. In areas where there are natural outcroppings of rock, and where stone is plentiful, flagstone paths might be the most economical, while in other areas where such stone is scarce, they might be almost prohibitive in price because of the expense of shipping the materials. For turf and tanbark paths, much of the work may be done by the average amateur gardener and the costs may consequently be kept low. On the other hand, a turf path requires more upkeep than do most of the other types. It must be kept mowed and edged, for nothing detracts more from the trim and pleasing appearance of a garden than straggly grass and unkempt edges. This question of upkeep should be taken into careful consideration before the final decision is made on what type of garden path to use.

Lines and Grades

In a formal garden, the lines and dimensions of paths must be laid out with great care. The best way to establish a straight line is to stretch a cord between two stakes. A steel tape or a heavy cloth tape is essential, and a surveyor's transit is a great help. Without a transit, right angles may be marked off on the ground by the 3–4–5 method. This is most easily done by three persons, using a tape and three stakes.

If one takes three sections of tape, the lengths of which are proportioned to one another as 3 is to 4 and as 4 is to 5, and places them end to end in a triangle, the angle between the "3" section and the "4" section will be a square angle, or 90°. The reason for this is the old geometric theorem, "The square of the hypotenuse of a right-angled triangle is equal to the sum of the squares of the other two sides." Thus, $3^2 + 4^2 = 5^2$ or $9 + 16 = 25$. If the lengths of the two lines are to extend some distance, it is best to use longer pieces of tape than 3 ft., 4 ft. and 5 ft., because a slight error in holding the tapes together would increase proportionally with the distance to the end of the line. Sections 9 ft., 12 ft., and 15 ft. are convenient.

The most direct and satisfactory way of

5.5 *Whether a part of the entrance garden or the private outdoor living space, paved surfaces that are used for walking and for furniture should be comfortable underfoot. A great many materials can be used in a variety of ways. Concrete paving, when will designed and installed, can be interesting and smooth. Reich-Versen Landscape Architects. Photo Carlton Lees*

marking a "freehand" curve is to fling a section of garden hose or heavy rope on the ground. The hose may be adjusted until the desired alignment is reached, and it may then be marked by frequent stakes. However, never make a curve or series of curves in a walk just for the sake of having them. A natural obstacle, such as a tree, shrub or boulder, is the reason for a curve, both in nature and in garden design.

Grades are important in path building. Surface water must be induced to run off promptly, and this can best be done by making the center of the paths slightly higher than the sides. (On a 6-ft. brick path, $3/4$ of an in.; on a 6-ft. flagstone, $1/2$ in.; on a 6-ft. gravel, 1 in.) Also, the path must slope slightly lengthwise (at least 1 ft. in 100 ft.) and there should be catch basins or drain inlets at points where water may be collected and carried off by underground pipes. These subjects have been more fully treated in the chapter on grading.

Path materials

Brick

Brick walks are usually very pleasant, and they age with an appealing mellowness and charm. The initial cost is comparatively high, but if a good quality of brick is used and the walk is carefully laid, it should give service for many years. In some of our old colonial gardens, we find paths laid two centuries or more ago that are still in good condition and attest to the worth of the fine craftsmanship of our forefathers.

In those parts of the country where there is a minimum of frost action each winter and where there is a natural layer of sandy or gravelly soil, no additional foundation is needed for a brick path. If frost seldom penetrates more than 1 in. or 3 in. into the ground, it is possible to lay the bricks directly upon a cushion of sand after the subgrades have been determined. In the North, however, it is much more expensive and laborious to install a brick wall, and a foundation course must be carefully prepared before the bricks are laid. Unless this is done properly, the

action of the frost will gradually heave the bricks out of place, causing some to crack and break, and before many years have elapsed, one will have an unsightly and unsatisfactory garden path.

Bricks may be laid either upon a concrete base with a crushed stone or gravel foundation or upon a cushion of sand above a gravel foundation. Gravel known as "pit gravel" is greatly to be preferred to washed gravel for the surfacing of walks and should be obtained whenever possible. If it is necessary to use washed gravel, limestone dust to the amount of approximately 15 percent should be mixed with it to help bind the surface. Gravel or stone dust used for the wearing surface of paths should be of a size that will pass a $1/4$-in. mesh.

Where the bricks are to be laid with mortar joints, the concrete base should be used. After the grades have been established and the earth has been excavated to a depth of 12 in. below the finished grade, a 6-in. layer of gravel should be put in place. A 3-in. layer should first be spread, watered thoroughly and then rolled or tamped. The second layer should be handled in the same manner. The base course of concrete should then be prepared and spread over the gravel to a depth of 3 in. A mixture of 1 part cement, 3 parts sand and 5 parts gravel is recommended for this purpose. After this concrete foundation has set for twenty-four hours, the bricks should be laid according to the desired pattern on a thin coat of mortar, which should consist of 1 part cement to 3 parts sand. When the mortar has set and the bricks are firmly in place, the joints should be filled. This may be done in one of two different ways. If the joints are $1/4$-in. or less in width, a dry mixture of cement and sand in the proportion of 1 of cement to 2 of sand may be swept into the joints. After the bricks have been swept entirely free of cement, the walk should be watered with a fine, gentle spray until all the cement in the joints has become thoroughly wet. Where the joints are large, it is advisable to prepare a wet mixture of the same proportions and carefully pour it between the bricks until the joints are filled.

When a brick walk is to be laid upon a sand cushion, a similar foundation course of gravel is used. Upon the surface of the gravel a 2-in.

Fig. 5.1   Brick walks

Section:

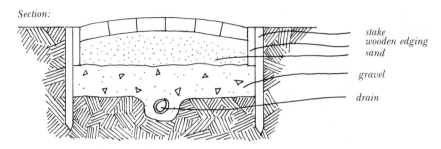

stake
wooden edging
sand

gravel

drain

Running Bond

Soldier courses

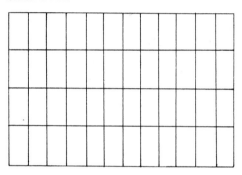

Herringbone

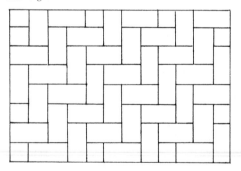

Basket-weave

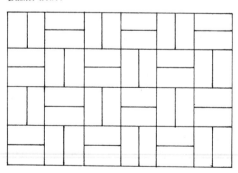

layer of fine sand should be spread, and it should be thoroughly rolled or tamped before the bricks are set in place. After the bricks are laid, the joints should be filled with sand. As the bricks are being laid, the surface of the walk should be kept at an even and uniform level. This may easily be done by placing a wide board crosswise with the path and tamping it until the surface is even. A curb should always be used when brick walks are laid in sand, because such walks have a tendency to creep, with the joints gradually becoming wider and wider as a result.

Bricks may be laid in various patterns, the Running Bond, Herringbone and Basket being the most usual.

Brick and Cement in Combination

In France one often sees paths constructed of brick combined with cement. If the workmanship is quite good, a path of this type is very pleasant and certainly possesses much more character and charm than a plain concrete walk. The construction is comparatively simple and the cost is not unduly high. After the grades have been established, the soil should be excavated to a depth of 10 in. A 6-in. foundation course of gravel should then be laid in the same manner as that prescribed for brick walks. A very thin coat of cement mortar, hardly more than 1 in. in thickness, should then be spread over the gravel, and upon this foundation the bricks should be placed in any desired pattern. The spaces between the bricks should then be filled with cement and the surface brought to an absolutely true level. A small quantity of terracotta dye mixed with the cement will give it a slightly reddish tone that harmonizes more pleasantly with the color of the bricks.

The bricks may be placed according to various patterns. In constituting a narrow path, the area of cement between the patterned bricks should be relatively small, while in a path of more ample proportions, the scale could be increased accordingly.

Flagstone

Flagstone paths have decided character and charm and are widely used. In sections of the country with an abundant supply of local stone, such paths are not expensive and are easily laid. There are various types: those made from

5.6 Terracotta tiles at the entryway are embedded in a concrete base. Photo Carlton Lees

Fig. 5.2
Stone pavements

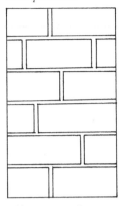

1½-in. to 2-in. flagstones

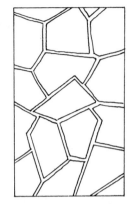

1½-in. irregular flagstones

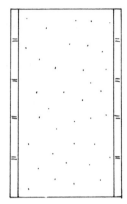

3-in. macadam pavement
with stone or brick edging

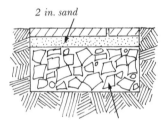

2 in. sand

6 in. crushed stone

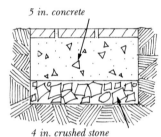

5 in. concrete

4 in. crushed stone

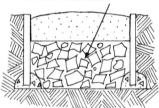

6 in. crushed stone

Edging can be of 2-in. precast
cement edgings or 3-in. flagstones,
15 in. to 18 in. deep and set in concrete.

stones of square or rectangular shape with cut edges are laid in a perfectly formal or symmetrical manner, while those made from stones of more or less irregular shape are laid in a random pattern.

The stones may be laid either upon a sand cushion with soil joints or upon a cement foundation with mortar joints. Laying them with earth joints makes possible the growing of turf or low-creeping plants between the stones, an attractive feature greatly to be desired. The laying of a flagstone path on a sand cushion is a simple matter and does not require a great amount of skill. The ground should be excavated only to a depth that will bring the stones to the desired level. A layer of fine sand about ½ in. in depth should then be spread over the surface of the soil. A 3-in. to 4-in. layer of crushed stones between soil and sand will prevent the accumulation of water, which, if frozen

during the winter, will heave the flagstones. The flagstones may then be put in place; care should be taken to see that they are firm, with no tendency to wobble or teeter. If the lower surface of the stone is uneven, it will be necessary to remove a portion of the soil directly under the protruding point in order that it may settle firmly into its bed. The surface of the path should be true to the desired grade, and as the stones are set in place a carpenter's level should be used to check the surface. After the stones are properly positioned, sand should be spread over the surface of the path and swept into the joints or, if desired, the joints may be filled with small strips of turf. There are a number of low-creeping rock plants that are particularly suitable for planting between flagstones. Creeping thyme is dainty and pleasing, as it emits a sweet, pungent fragrance when crushed underfoot. *Gypsophila repens* and *Veron-*

5.7 The same kind of tiles as in the previous photo here are laid on a well-drained sand base. Photo Carlton Lees

ica repens are also excellent for this purpose.

When flagstones are to be laid with mortar joints, they must be set in cement. The soil should be excavated to a depth of 10 in., and a 6-in. layer of crushed stone or gravel should be spread in two layers 3 in. thick, each layer being watered, rolled or tamped. A 3-in. layer of cement should be spread upon this foundation course of gravel, being mixed in the proportions of 1 part cement, 3 parts sand and 5 parts gravel. After the cement has set for 24 hours, a thin coat of cement mortar should be spread over it and the flagstones set in the mortar. When the stones have become form, mortar should be poured into the joints.

Gravel

Gravel walks were often used during colonial times, and they have maintained their popularity throughout the years. There are numerous methods of construction. If the walk will not have too much traffic, and if the ground is naturally well drained, the gravel may be laid directly upon the soil after the subgrade has been established. However, a walk constructed in this manner will not withstand hard wear, and during wet weather it will have a tendency to become very soft and springy. A much better walk

will result if a foundation course of slag or crushed stone is used. In the construction of a walk of this type, the soil should be excavated to a depth of 7 in. below the finished grade. A 5½-in. layer of slag or crushed stone of a size that will pass a 2½ in. screen should then be spread and thoroughly tamped or rolled. The gravel should be spread upon this surface and then should be well watered and rolled.

Stepping Stones

Stepping stones laid in turf also make a very pleasant path. Because of their rather informal character, however, they are perhaps more suitable for a casual or incidental path than for a walk that is rather heavily used.

The stones selected for a path of this type should be of comfortable size, at least 12 in. to 15 in. square, and the upper surface should be reasonably smooth. It is not necessary for the stones to be absolutely regular in shape, as very pleasant effects may be obtained with stones of slightly irregular outline. They should be placed at even intervals and spaced far enough apart to permit a pleasant, easy stride from one stone to the next, 18 in. being the usual comfortable distance.

The setting of the stones is very simple. If a

5.8 Cut bluestone in irregular rectangles, laid on a sand bed in this example, is much more pleasant to live with than the irregular and sharply cut slate all too commonly seen. Note that the same stone has been used to edge the planting bed. Photo Carlton Lees

new walk is being made, they may be set at the same time that the surrounding area of grass is sown, or they may be easily set in a piece of established turf. Initially, the stones should be placed upon the surface of the ground and their final position determined. The outline of each stone should then be marked with the edge of a trowel; after the stone has been lifted to one side, the soil within the prescribed area should be removed to the proper depth. A light layer of fine sand should be placed at the bottom of the excavation, as this makes a better bed upon which to rest the stone and settle it into its final position. When placing the stones, one should make certain that they are perfectly firm and that they do not teeter from side to side. If the bottom of the stone is uneven, it may be necessary to remove it several times and cut one portion of the excavation or build up another until the stone is absolutely firm. The surface of the stone should be level with the area of turf around it. Not only does this make a difference in the general appearance of the path but it greatly facilitates the use of the lawn mower. If the stepping stones are set too low, each will form a puddle of water after rain. In order to prevent this, the soil should be rammed in close around the edges after the stones have been set in place.

Tanbark

Tanbark, the bark used in the tanning of leather, is particularly suitable for woodland walks and is also frequently used in gardens of formal design. Licorice root is similarly used and available in 80-lb. bags. Tanbark has much to recommend it as a material for the surfacing of paths. It is comparatively inexpensive; its mellow, reddish-brown color forms a pleasing contrast with the areas of turf and foliage about it; it is easy to handle, and under ordinary conditions no elaborate system of underdrainage is necessary; it offers an unusually pleasant and springy surface; and it dries almost immediately after a rain. Even during the heaviest rains tanbark never becomes muddy, and it is so porous that it seldom retains standing pools of water.

For constructing paths, a good quality of tanbark should be procured. A poor grade is not cheap at any price, as it is apt to contain large, lumpy pieces and various foreign substances. The best grades usually are obtained from oak and hemlock barks. Unless the path is to be constructed in a very low, swampy area, no underdrainage is necessary. In a cast of this sort, either a foundation course of gravel or a tile drain may be used. Ordinarily, however, all that is necessary is to see that the ground is leveled to the desired grade before the tanbark is spread. A layer 3 in. in depth makes an excellent and very durable path. Immediately after it is spread, the tanbark should be soaked and rolled. One ton of tanbark will provide a 3-in. layer for a path 3 ft. wide and 60 ft. long.

Turf

A turf path has a number of advantages. The initial cost of materials is comparatively low, and the construction requires no great degree of skill. And undoubtedly, green, luxuriant turf possesses a beauty and a charm that are difficult to equal in other materials.

Turf paths may be readily established from seeding, or, if immediate effect is desired, sod may be laid. In either case the preliminary preparation of the ground is very much the same. If the soil is a medium or light loam, no underdrainage will be necessary. If, however, the soil is of heavy clay texture or if the path is to be constructed in a low area that has poor natural drainage, some means of artificial drainage should be provided. A 6-in. vitrified tile drain laid 2 ft. below the surface of the soil directly under the middle line of the path will usually prove entirely adequate. It will add greatly to the enjoyment of a turf walk that might otherwise be soggy and practically unusable after heavy rains or in the early spring when the frost is coming out of the ground. Instead of using tile drains, this channel can be filled with crushed stones, or the soil may be excavated to a depth of 12 in. and a 6-in. layer of 2-in.-sized crushed stones placed over the subsoil. A 6-in. layer of good top soil should be placed above the crushed stones. This should be leveled off to the proper grade and then raked until it is finely pulverized. The first rolling will reveal any slight unevenness, which may then be corrected by subsequent rakings. Where the path is to be seeded, approximately 1 lb. of seed will be required per 30 sq. yd. Only seed of the highest quality should be used, and it is wise to obtain a mixture that does not contain any clover if one wants to achieve a turf of fine texture. Clover also has an unfortunate tendency to become rather slippery when it is

5.9 Roman bricks, in this example, are larger than ordinary bricks. Here, as an extension of the paved seating area, they invite exploration of the garden beyond. Garden design by Carlton Lees, photo Gretchen Harshbarger

wet, which is a decided disadvantage to a turf walk. The various bent grasses are excellent for this purpose, however, and mixtures containing Kentucky bluegrass, Chewings New Zealand Fescue and Redtop are very desirable. The seed should be sown both lengthwise and crosswise with the path in order to get an even distribution. The ground should be rolled immediately after the seed is sown, as a firm seedbed is one of the secrets of success for this type of walk.

If the walk is sodded, great care should be taken to obtain sod of the best quality. Nothing is more disappointing than to go to the trouble and expense of sodding only to find, later on, that one has purchased poor, coarse grass that will never make a really good turf. The sod, which usually comes in long rolls, should be laid lengthwise with the path, and care should be taken to see that the joints are broken. After it is laid, the sod should be rolled and thoroughly soaked. It should not be allowed to dry out until it has become well established.

Interlocking Paving Stones

This type of paving stone for garden walks and driveways was first devised and produced in Europe in 1962. It proved so successful that many private and public garden administrators adopted it for use as a permanent outdoor floor covering. It is functional, not slippery, and blends very well into the landscape.

The interlocking paving stones, which come in different colors, are made of compressed concrete and are manufactured in ordinary brick sizes. The evenly mixed aggregates produce a matte finish that prevents the stones from becoming slippery when wet. As a result, these paving stones are ideal for use on swimming pool decks.

In the northeastern United States, the Z-shaped block paver has been increasingly used for malls, plazas and sidewalks. The price range varies with the thickness, color and number of edge units required; the 3¼-in. thickness is especially good for vehicular traffic, while for pedestrian traffic the 2½-in. thickness is adequate. A paved area of this kind is frostproof if the underlying bed of sand and gravel is properly prepared to provide good drainage.

The ease with which Z-shaped blocks can be installed makes it feasible for the average homeowner to do this without professional help. In order to assure a long-lasting paving job, however, the soil should be checked and the substructure designed in accordance with the ground conditions prevailing in the immediate area.

Install 2 in. of sand over the subbase and screed level. The sand should be accurately

5.10 This roughly cobbled surface is not intended for foot traffic; rather, it is practical and attractive for a Virginia driveway. Photo Carlton Lees

sloped for desired pitches, and then it should be compacted. The screeded sand should be ¾ in. higher than required. The brick-sized pavers should then be laid directly into the sand, starting with the edging pieces. All interlocking pavers should be set at 45° angles to the road axis. They must be laid close-jointed, and their alignment should be checked periodically.

After the pavers are set—they will be ¾ in. higher than required, if the work has been

Fig. 5.3
Interlocking concrete pavers

Surface view:

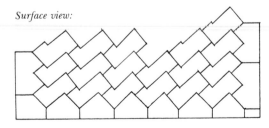

Cross section:

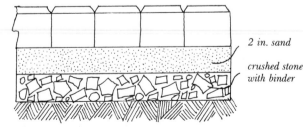

2 in. sand

crushed stone with binder

5.11 Concrete paving: Here a 2 in. by 6 in. wooden framework, after being treated with preservative, serves as a form for concrete but stays in place as part of the paving pattern. Note nails protruding from the inside edge of each square to ensure locking of timbers to the concrete. For a textured surface, pebbles are pounded into the surface of unset mortar, and just before the concrete is thoroughly set, the surface is washed and scrubbed. Photo Carlton Lees

done properly—they should be vibrated with a vibrator-compactor to the desired elevation. The joints of the pavers should be filled, but not completely, with a substantial quantity of sand, which is spread over the completed area. The sand should then be vibrated or hosed into the joints, until all the joints are properly and completely filled.

Concrete

On the whole, the increasing use of concrete is rapidly changing the appearance of cities throughout the world. Ordinarily, the familiar, plain gray troweled concrete of city sidewalks does not make for attractive garden paving; but with just a little additional effort and expense, concrete *can* become both useful and attractive. This can easily be accomplished if color, texture and pattern are added to the basic mix. Earth colors are the safest, because greens and blues tend to fade and compete with foliage colors. New and different techniques can readily be combined with many styles of surface treatment today. For example, casting may be made with such patterns as burlap, reed mats or the grain of weathered lumber. The knots

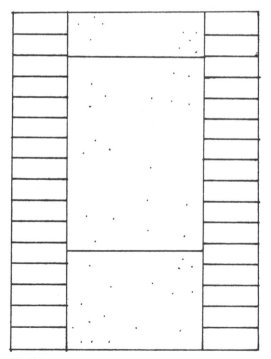

Fig. 5.4
Concrete sidewalk widened with bricks

5.12 Screed: when laying bricks on sand or fine gravel, this simple device helps smooth the bed. Photo Carlton Lees

and even nailheads in such lumber stand out most attractively in such impregnation. Sandblasting, washed concrete with exposed aggregate surface, and plastering with pattern are other methods that can mellow the hard, dull look of concrete.

These new approaches to the use of concrete are rapidly gaining acceptance among gardeners and landscape designers. For example, Burle Marx, the famous Brazilian architect who is equally eminent as a gardener and a painter, pioneered the use of solid decorative walls in unfaced concrete for the first time in 1956 in a garden he designed in São Paulo.

Several general requirements affect concrete surface finishes. The most important of these is the quality of the mix. For example, if the mix is too wet, the materials will tend to segregate and lead to sand streaking, dusting, cracking and discoloration. Conversely, too stiff a mix will create workability problems at corners and around patterns, and it may also lead to honeycombing and finishing problems. The method of placing the concrete, the shape and thickness of the section, and the complexity of the surface pattern will all contribute to determining how workable the individual mix should be.

CONCRETE MIXES IN DIFFERENT PROPORTIONS FOR DIFFERENT PURPOSES

	CEMENT	SAND (in parts)	GRAVEL
Foundations and footings	1	3	5
Walks	1	2½	4
Floors	1	2	4
Rough and smooth finishes	1	2	—

Edgings

The best method of keeping the margins of garden paths permanently neat is to build edgings or small curbs on each side of the path. Many materials may be used for marking the path and separating it from the garden beds. Bricks on edge, or on end, are appropriate for brick or gravel paths. The use of planks dipped in creosote and held at intervals by stakes is an old and effective colonial method, particularly appropriate in an old-fashioned garden with gravel paths. It is also good with tanbark. Flagstones set on edge are appropriate with flagstone paving or gravel, while tile is interesting in an architectural garden. Metal strips are also sometimes used, and though not very attractive, they also serve the purpose of keeping path edges neat and trim. After experiments with iron for these strips, it has been found that zinc is more durable and unobtrusive. It is excellent for use between driveway and lawn and also in geometric patterns of garden beds and paths.

GARDEN STEPS

As a change in levels in a garden necessitates a pleasant and easy transition from one level to another, garden steps may become an important landscape feature. Unless the steps are rus-

5.13 When brick and other paving materials are laid in a sand bed, it is generally better to choose another material for steps, as in this example. (If the steps were of brick, mortar would be necessary and the combination of mortared and unmortared brick would be incongruous.) The granite blocks, though slightly uneven, are an excellent choice. Photo Carlton Lees

tic in character, such as split logs, hewn railroad ties or long heavy stones, they should rest on a foundation with footings below the frost line. The steps should be in harmony with the surrounding area and should be as broad as the path that leads to them.

The angle of ascent of outdoor steps should be less steep than that of interior stairways. In general, the broader the tread, the lower should be the riser. A good formula for determining proportions in the size of individual steps is as follows: one tread plus two risers should equal 27 in. Thus, steps 6 in. high will require 15 in. treads, while steps 5 in. high should have 17 in. treads. The treads should be constructed so that they pitch about ¼ in. toward the front in order that the water may drain off readily after a rain.

Foundations

Foundations for stone or brick steps may be built of rubble masonry. Any irregular pieces that are not easily used in finished masonry

5.14 A hedge of fragrant lavender tops this wall of native stones, which has been laid up with mortar. Note that steps and wall are of the same material; the walkway is cut bluestone on sand. Photo Carlton Lees

5.15 Gravel can be used in many gardens for walkways, paths, or as flooring for larger areas that are subject to little foot traffic yet need definition (visualize the sand gardens of Japanese temples). In this example, timbers have been used to edge the walkway, and mortared stone for the steps, which results in three different elements. Successful garden design depends on limiting the number of materials; a better solution would have been to use timbers for the steps as well. Photo Anita Sabarese

walls will be good enough for foundations. The stones are thrown in with enough mortar to hold them together. The footings must be below frost line. The foundation for concrete steps, or a concrete foundation for stone or brick steps, need not be so solid. The concrete may be formed like a bridge and reinforced with steel rods. The top and bottom treads rest on footings below frost line, but the others are supported on the concrete slab cast between the supports. It is not necessary to excavate the earth between the supporting footings. On such a foundation, the stone or brick or tile treads and risers are set upon the concrete base with cement mortar.

The proper mixture for a concrete foundation is 1 part cement, 2 parts sand and 3 parts aggregate—crushed stone in sizes from ¾-in. to 1 in. The steel rods should be ⅝-in. square section placed at intervals of 12 in. or 15 in.

Step Arrangements

Long, unbroken flights of steps should be avoided. If the difference in grade between the upper landing and the bottom is greater than 6 ft., a landing should be interposed. Do not use more than six steps between landings in a series of steps. Steps sunken into a bank blend better into the landscaping and can be used safely without handrails, compared to steps exposed above the bank. Steps ascending a terrace held by a retaining wall may either project out from the wall or be recessed into the wall, or they may combine both of these arrangements, often with a landing at the wall itself. If it is a high wall, the most harmonious arrangement is a flight of steps parallel to the wall, with landings near the top and bottom. Such a flight should have a hand railing of wrought iron, a balustrade or a parapet.

5.16 This flight of brick-and-timber stairs is an excellent example of how well ordinary materials can be used. Reich-Versen Landscape Architects. Photo Carlton Lees

Ramped Steps

Ramped steps are a series of sloping surfaces alternated with single steps. They are useful where the sloping hillside of the ascent is too steep for a path (10 percent or more), and not steep enough for a flight of steps. Twenty percent is about minimum for such steps. The risers are formed of narrow stones set on edge and sunk deeply into the ground. The treads or ramps are built of the same material as the pathways, flagstone or brick being the materials most frequently used in this country. The narrow streets of hillside towns in Europe are often made into ramped steps, with stone risers and cobblestone ramps. A rustic path in a woodland is frequently stepped by placing logs across the

path for the risers. Railroad ties are also good for this purpose.

The proper dimensions for ramped steps may be determined by establishing the distance between the risers at three normal paces, between 6 ft. 3 in. and 8 ft., and the height of the riser as from 3 in. to 5 in. The slope of the ramp should not be greater than 12 percent. Obviously, the steeper the ramp and the higher the tread, the shorter should be the length of the ramp.

Construction of Garden Steps

Rule: All steps should be based on the length of the pace. Twice the riser plus tread is the length of a stride. For example, stride is 24 in.:

$$riser = 5 \text{ in.} + 5 \text{ in.}$$
$$tread = \underline{14 \text{ in.}}$$
$$stride = 24 \text{ in.}$$

1. Outdoor risers are usually lower than indoor ones and therefore have a wider tread than the steps within a building.
2. If the tread overhangs the riser by ½ in. to 1 in., the steps create a better appearance and also use less space.
3. The riser of a step should rest on the tread of the preceding step. This is most important on steps built without the use of cement.
4. Steps, like walks, should be below ground level and should not protrude from the bank.
5. Tread and landing should have a slight fall to the front to assure proper drainage of any surface water.
6. Never change your riser or tread in a series of steps.
7. Don't place too many steps in succession. Four to six steps is a good average. The landings between the steps should also be based on the length of the pace. At least one to two strides should be allowed between steps.
8. Wide Steps: The best way to change direction in such steps is by staggering them so that they won't narrow on one side and widen on the other.
9. Smaller Steps: The best way to change direction in such steps is to build them sideways in the bank and protect them on the bank side by a retaining wall.

6.1 In gardens, fences provide more than enclosure. They also serve as backgrounds for choice plants, frames for dooryards and other small spaces. Photo Gretchen Harshbarger

6

Fences

A fence is an element of the landscape capable of great variety of form and with limitless possibilities for distinctive design. Today, it has become a background for much of our outdoor living.

Both as barriers and as ornaments, fences are conspicuous. As elements of design and as aids in the use of land, they are important and often indispensable. For the homeowner who desires privacy, the fence provides a screen against too much publicity and is a barrier against intrusion. Beyond these practical uses, a fence should be an expression of pure design, a frame for the grounds and an architectural element in harmony with the house.

Materials and methods have brought about the designs of several distinctive types of fences. In certain regions the abundance of some good material has made a special type of fence structure typical of that locality. Thus the stone wall and the picket fence express New England; the zigzag rail fence, Virginia and Kentucky; the post and rail fence, Virginia; and the post and board fence, Pennsylvania and Maryland.

Today, transportation makes available materials other than those from local sources and has opened markets for the best materials, which in earlier times were used only in the regions of their origin. As a result, in New England one can have for posts not merely the red cedar of the neighboring pastures but cypress as well, which will outlast it. Also available are fence materials assembled in manageable units made in Virginia, Michigan, New Jersey and California, and shipped all over the country.

As with so many other products of modern manufacture and distribution, local tradition in fence design is no longer dominant. The decision as to the type of fence for a certain place should be based on considerations of strength, durability, appearance and cost.

The practical attributes of a good fence are strength sufficient to hold its place against wind; durability—that is, soundness after many years of exposure to weather—good appearance, meaning the ability to remain neat and trim without much attention to maintenance; and economy of construction cost in relation to the life of the fence.

A fence should be so firmly fixed in the ground that it will withstand many years of wind pressure and the effects of summer sun and winter freezing.

Posts should be set into the ground to a depth of 2½ ft. to 3 ft. for firm anchorage. In cold climates, the base of the post should be below the frost line in order to prevent heaving caused by frost pressures. Fences that are to serve as snow barriers should have an extra anchorage, such as a second post slanting into the ground on the leeward side.

The back-filling of the earth around the posts, after they have been set in the hole, must be accompanied by firm tamping; any tendency to wiggle will be increased by the force of wind and weather.

All fence corners should be cross-braced to provide additional strength.

Wood is the most generally available material for fences and is widely used for the enclosure of home properties. Metal is also used in the form of galvanized iron, wrought iron and woven wire. For posts, wood, concrete and steel are commonly used.

WOOD FENCES

There are many types of wood fences, some very simple in design and construction, others more elaborate. Regardless of the type, there are certain points that should be taken into consideration: the durability of the wood selected, the setting of the posts, details of construction and the upkeep of the fence.

When board fences or picket fences, except those of rustic type, are being constructed, the surfaces of the pickets and rails where they join one another, and the surfaces of the rails and posts where they, in turn, join, should be painted before the fence is put together. It is in these crevices that moisture is most apt to lodge, and the paint will provide protection against decay. At no later time can the painting of these particular spots be done so easily or so

6.3 The Los Angeles State and County Arboretum contains many examples of fences as a demonstration for homeowners. Photo Carlton Lees

6.2 From the simplicity of the two-rail example in the preceding photo, fence design varies to include sophisticated screens like the one shown here. Photo courtesy Los Angeles State and County Arboretum

effectively. The extra labor required to do this will be more than repaid in the increased life of the fence.

Woods vary greatly in their durability. Some woods will give many years of service, while in certain climates other wood will last for only a few years under outdoor conditions. The durable woods are usually more expensive but will prove to be the best investment in the end. It is poor economy to select a cheaper, less durable wood that will have to be replaced within a few years.

The decay of wood is caused by certain wood-destroying fungi. In order to function, these fungi must have favorable conditions, the important factors being moisture, air, a warm temperature and food, which is supplied by the wood. If the temperature is too cold, if the supply of air is completely shut off, or if insufficient moisture is present, as in desert areas, the decay of wood is greatly retarded or does not occur. But in humid areas with mild climates, conditions are particularly favorable, and under certain circumstances, such as at the ground line, decay takes place rapidly. It is at this point that posts always decay, and only woods that are extremely resistant to decay or that have been chemically treated should be used for fence posts.

Among the most durable woods are cypress, redwood, red cedar, arborvitae, white cedar, black locust and sourgum. These woods possess remarkable ability to resist decay and are therefore recommended for posts.

In order to increase its durability, wood may be treated with a chemical preservative. To be fully effective, the chemical should be applied under pressure so that sufficient penetration is obtained. In some cases, the entire post is treated; in other cases, the treatment extends only to well above the ground line, which is entirely satisfactory. In many areas, treated posts

are available. Such treatment will greatly prolong the life of the less durable woods and will sometimes prove the best choice if the more durable woods are very costly or unobtainable.

For rails, pickets, palings, spindles and panels, less durable woods may be used. Although redwood, cedar and cypress will outlast them, such woods as pine, hemlock, spruce and fir will give many years of good service for these purposes, particularly if they are kept painted. For rustic fences, redwood, cedar and imported chestnut are most frequently used.

Split Rail Fence

The "snake fence," or split rail fence, is one of the most picturesque for open farmlands. It originated in Virginia in colonial times and is often called Virginia rail fence, though more properly Kentucky rail fence, because of its frequent use in that state. It is made of rails split from poles cut in the woods close at hand.

6.4 The horizontal laths of this fence create a complementary background for the vertical delphinium. Photo Carlton Lees

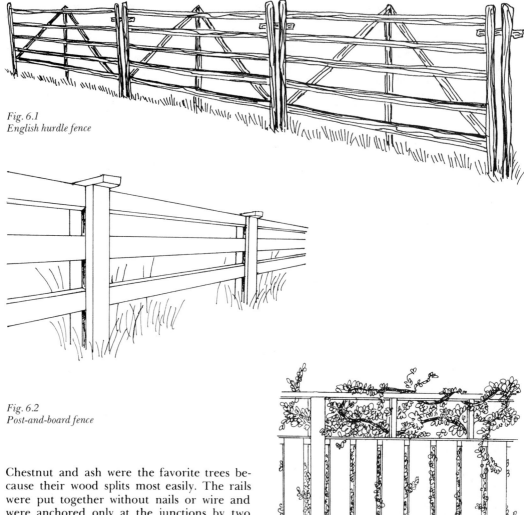

Fig. 6.1
English hurdle fence

Fig. 6.2
Post-and-board fence

Fig. 6.3
Board fence

Chestnut and ash were the favorite trees because their wood splits most easily. The rails were put together without nails or wire and were anchored only at the junctions by two slanting rails leaned against the junction of horizontal rails. A great deal of wood is required for the construction of this fence, but no other tool except the axe and no other materials are required. It is, therefore, the fence of the pioneer. As forests became depleted, a modification of this fence, which requires less wood, was developed: the Virginia rail fence, strictly speaking. With this, the rails are laid end overlapping end in a straight line, their points of junction being kept upright by two posts set in the ground, one on each side, and wired together at the top. A more modern version of this is the post and rail fence, with three slots cut in the single post to receive the ends of the rails.

Post and Rail Fence

A very handsome pasture enclosure, this fence is suitable for the property lines of country residences. White cedar and black locust posts with large slots cut in them are erected at intervals of about 10 ft. The rails—half-round arborvitae poles of the same wood as the posts, or a softer wood, and 11 ft. long—are tapered to flat ends thrust through the slots in the posts. There are two sizes of posts, making two-or three-rail fences. It is an easy type of fence to erect and most satisfactory for its rugged appearance and durability. The weathering gives it a warm gray color, harmonizing well with the tones of the countryside.

Reinforced concrete posts may be used instead of wooden posts and will outlast them by many years. When concrete posts are used, heavy planks may be substituted for split rails and will be more enduring.

Hurdle Fence

Originally developed in England as a pasture fence, hurdle is light, strong and attractive, and is excellent for use as a boundary fence on suburban properties of moderate size. It is picturesque, easily erected and as easily moved, and it provides an excellent background for climbing roses and other vines. The panels come in 8-ft. lengths in both 3-ft. and 4-ft. heights. They may be purchased already assembled or, at more moderate cost, in a knocked-down state ready for the homeowner to put together. It is one of the quickest and easiest fences to erect. The sharpened posts are driven into the ground with a sledgehammer, and each panel is then pegged to the next.

Post and Board Fence

This type of fence is framed on red cedar or cypress posts erected at 10-ft. or 12-ft. intervals. Three or four horizontal rough boards 1 in. by 8 in., or 1 in. by 6 in., are nailed to the posts with wide spaces between them. A vertical 6-in. board covers the board ends against each post, and a 6-in. square board caps the post like a shed roof. Rough sawed pine boards are usually used. Whitewashed or, even better, painted white, this makes a very neat fence for a suburban property, especially one with a house of colonial architecture.

Board Fence

With lattice top, this is a very attractive type of fence and is appropriate for town yards, especially where the house is of colonial tradition; it may also be used as a garden enclosure. Many variations in design and proportion are possible. The posts are usually spaced about 10 ft. apart, and several horizontal rails provide a framework to which the upright boards can be nailed. The lattice top, if strongly built, will provide a support for light, graceful vines, such as clematis and akebia. Wisteria should never be used for this purpose, as it is too rampant.

Louver Fence

This is a modification of the board fence, in which the boards are set at an angle to let the breezes through. It is used to achieve privacy and at the same time to provide for a good circulation of air. Fences of this type are very popular in hot climates, and they are also excellent for city gardens, where conditions are often not favorable for good air circulation. Sections of louver fences can be made so that they are adjustable and a slight push will control the breeze. Lightly constructed louver sections are often used as movable wind baffles and can be made into quite a decorative feature on a terrace or patio.

Woven Split Sapling Fence

This fence is rustic in character and makes an opaque screen. The construction is simple and strong. Posts are set at 10-ft. intervals and are connected with two or three cedar rails. Panels of split saplings about 1½ in. wide, woven together with wire, are nailed to the rails, so that the finished fence is a continuous wall of rustic vertical lines. With the bark still on, the fence immediately has an old appearance, but with the bark stripped off, a year of mellowing will be required. Fences of this type are usually made of cedar, arborvitae or imported French chestnut and are very durable. They may be obtained in various heights and provide an excellent barrier where complete privacy or protection is desired. They are manufactured at the mill and are shipped as panels with the requisite number of posts and rails.

Picket Fence

This has long been popular and has been used for the enclosure of town yards and gardens since colonial times. In the early New England villages, the white clapboard houses were grouped about the central green, and their dignified, spacious yards were always enclosed with picket fences. Within these enclosures flourished pleasant little flower gardens. Like the details of the houses, the fences were often designed with great distinction and gave an architectural expression to the house settings.

The picket fence requires careful construction and the proper spacing of parts, as it expresses the qualities of rightness and precision. Great variance in design and proportion may be achieved.

The simplest type of picket fence has natural, round posts. The upper rail, a 2 in. by 4 in. set flat, rests on the top of the posts and is nailed to them. The lower rail, a 2 in. by 4 in. set on edge, is mortised into the face of the post and nailed. The pickets, ¾ in. by 3 in. or ¾ in. by 4 in., are nailed to the outer side of the rails, and a picket covers each post.

Fences of more carefully studied design may have posts topped by beautiful turned finials. The shafts of such posts are of planed lumber,

6.3 This fence not only provides background and a degree of privacy but allows for air movement as well. Photo Amy Duevell

and the bases and caps have appropriate moldings. The pickets, also, may have specially designed tops. A fence of such finished carpentry should be supported on concrete footings under the posts so that the base of the wood is several inches above the ground. This feature will greatly prolong the life of the fence, as there will be no ground rot.

Rustic Picket Fence

The rustic picket fence has the same structural lines and general character as the picket fence but is less formal. Rustic pickets are made of split wood, usually arborvitae, cedar or redwood, and the pickets should not be painted.

Spindle Fence

This is a refinement of the picket fence and is suitable for the formal dooryard or garden of a colonial mansion. The spindles are round, about 1¼ in. in diameter, and pass through holes in the rails at intervals of 5 in. to 7 in. Variations from this are made by giving the fence a solid board base, or even a third rail 16 in. above the lower rail, and filling the space with a lattice of square bars in diamond pattern—the round spindles extending from the intermediate rail through the upper rail. Such a fence with graceful fenceposts is in keeping with the careful carpentry of modillioned cornices and a carved broken pediment above the door.

"Snow Fence"

This consists of pickets woven by horizontal wires and fastened to metal posts driven into the ground. Used as a winter precaution, such fences are erected at a distance of 50 ft. or 75 ft. from the road, toward the prevailing wind; they create enough obstacles to cause snow to form drifts in the lee close to the fence and not in the road. They may be used for any other temporary purpose, to surround play yards or

dog runs. The life of the fence is usually about ten years.

Lattice Fence

The lattice fence is most closely associated with the French style of garden art, for the French developed the intricate lattice patterns. But very simple lattices were used in colonial gardens as supports for vines, particularly climbing roses. Painted white to harmonize with the frame house or the white trim of brick or stone structure, the lattice is an adjunct of formal design.

Chinese Lattice Fence

Used in California with such distinction, this fence has large patterns of irregularly spaced rectangular openings. Only a few of the horizontal bars extend to both sides of the panel. The resulting design is balanced but informally asymmetrical. When used in combination with translucent plastic, it makes a pleasing background for flowering plants and also provides protection from the wind.

Fig. 6.4
Picket fence with gate

Grape Stake Fence

A rustic structure used around many small homes in certain sections of California, this fence is reminiscent of early pioneer days. The stakes are driven into the ground close together, forming a sort of miniature stockade. The tops are cleated together with stakes placed horizontally, or a little on the slant. The tops of the stakes are not cut back to an even saw-line, and the effect is most casual. Its great advantages are that the materials are inexpensive, its erection requires a minimum of skill and it will last for many years. Redwood or cedar are the woods most commonly used. The height may be varied to suit the desires of the owner.

Basket-weave Fence

This is becoming increasingly popular and has much to recommend it. It consists of thin strips of wood woven horizontally between upright supports set about 3 ft. apart. The fencing is made up in panels of several heights, ranging from 4 ft. to 8 ft. It is light in weight, easily erected and comparatively inexpensive. It forms an excellent screen, providing complete privacy and protection, yet permitting some circulation of air. The modern basket-weave fence is made of redwood and is available in preassembled sections of 8-ft. lengths in both 6-ft. and 8-ft. heights. It is simple to install and very durable.

FENCES OF OTHER MATERIALS

Plastic Fence

Post fences with top and bottom rails can be finished with sheets of translucent plastic. This is one of the least attractive types of fence but is inexpensive and requires little skill in its erection.

Canvas Fence

The canvas fence is best adapted to dry climates, or for use where temporary protection from wind or from the public gaze is desired. The construction requires posts with top and bottom rails between. The sheets of canvas are laced to the posts and rails. The ropes should be loosened in wet weather and tightened on sunny days. Such a fence has a certain novelty and charm when used in appropriate surroundings, as in the environs of an informal summer home.

Chain-link Fence

Often used for swimming pool enclosures, this fence is not good-looking in itself but can be used to support vines and eventually will disappear from view.

Woven-wire Fence

Used for pasture, this is probably the least expensive type of fence as far as initial cost is concerned, but its period of usefulness is short compared with that of most other fences, and the style is completely lacking in charm.

If it is necessary to use such a fence, its appearance can be greatly enhanced by training

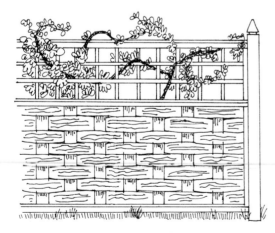

Fig. 6.5
Basket-weave fence with lattice top

English ivy through the wire mesh. If this is faithfully done, the fence will eventually become a wall of solid dark green foliage.

Live Basket-weave Fence

This is a "living" fence, made of 4-ft. to 5-ft.-long saplings of hornbeam, crataegus, willows and the like. They are planted in a row 6 in. apart and woven into each other at a 45° angle. Eventually, the overlapping stems and branches will grow together to form a strong, impassable barrier. An annual pruning and shaping of the side branches will be necessary.

MAINTENANCE OF FENCES

Almost all fences, except those of rustic character, require periodic painting.

New wooden fences should have two priming coats of paint and one finishing coat. Repainting should be done *before* the paint has worn off and the wood has become exposed to the weather. The intervals between paintings will depend somewhat on the climate and also on the quality of the paint and of the workmanship that goes into the job.

All iron work should receive a coat of special rust-resisting paint before it is erected and should be repainted at intervals of about every three years.

A periodic inspection of fences is a good practice. One broken picket will spoil the appearance of a fence; a few minutes of work with a hammer, saw and paintbrush will restore the rhythm and avoid the suggestion of shabbiness.

Posts occasionally become weak and should be tamped firmly into place, or, if decay has set in, they should be replaced before the fence is allowed to sag out of place.

6.6 A board fence interrupted by an old tree meet in complementary fashion. Photo Carlton Lees

7.1 Garden hedges have been providing enclosure and creating privacy for hundreds of years. Here a hedge is put to twofold use — creating private space and furnishing an entrance into it. Photo Carlton Lees

7

Hedges

The hedgerow has been a familiar feature of the landscape in Europe since medieval times. But the hedge itself antedates the medieval garden. The ancient Romans used hedges of myrtle, laurel and box in their gardens. Indeed, so important a feature was the hedge in gardens of this period that the gardener who cared for it and kept it faithfully trimmed to the desired form and height was given the dignity of a special title, being known as "topiarius."

The designers of the Italian villas used hedges of *Ilex* and cypress as great walls of green and made them architecturally important components of the design. The French gave the hedge even greater scale to conform to their vast estates by using large trees, such as elm, linden, hornbeam and beech, trimming them to vertical form. In England, hedges played an important part in the design of the "knott" gardens, laid out in geometric patterns. Sometimes the spaces within the hedges were flower beds, but more often they were bits of turf. Herb gardens were frequently designed in this style, each plot being planted to a single herb, and the whole forming a pleasing pattern. In the gardens that surround the Elizabethan manor houses of England, there are magnificent yew hedges which were planted more than 400 years ago and which have been carefully tended throughout the years.

The primary purpose of a hedge is enclosure. The second purpose is shelter from the wind; and the third is protection and privacy. In designing a landscape, the hedge is one of the best means of enclosing a formal area and separating it from the outer world. But not only does a hedge enclose and frame the garden; it may also frame the scenes within the garden and provide a background for flowering plants.

It would be difficult indeed to find a more satisfactory background for masses of bright flowers than the deep green of an evergreen hedge. The colors of the blossoms are contrasted effectively with the dark green of the background. The hedge is interesting enough in texture but is not conspicuous or obtrusive.

Furthermore, a hedge has the great attribute of permanence. It fixes the major lines of the design. It establishes the background for the garden, against which the succession of color and mass moves in ever-changing sequence. The hedge is not changeless in itself but grows in a slower cycle and thereby imparts an air of stability to the scene. It even invites confidence. By its continued existence it links the past with the present. There is the hedge. Season after season the flowers come and go. Generation after generation those who care for the garden come and go—but the hedge remains.

TYPES OF HEDGES

Hedges vary in size from small edging plants hardly 1 ft. in height to towering trees. They may be extremely formal in outline, being trimmed to even surfaces and regular lines, or they may be natural in growth, with billowing masses of foliage and a profusion of flowers. Every kind of hedge has its own particular adaptation.

The width of a hedge is not always easy to predict. Theoretically, most hedges can be kept at any desired dimension of height or width. In actual practice, however, it is not always possible to do this, for the plants must be allowed to make some growth each year or they will suffer both in vigor and appearance. It is essential that adequate space be allowed for the eventual spread of a hedge. One occasionally sees box hedges, originally planted beside the garden paths as edgings of the flower beds, which have grown so wide that they entirely overshadow the path.

Hedge materials may be derived from many sources: from deciduous trees of naturally thick growth, branching close to the ground; from evergreen trees that have a fine texture and closely massed foliage; from deciduous shrubs that have dense foliage and that make vigorous growth; from evergreen shrubs; from herbs; and from vines that may be trained to grow on a frame of any desired shape. But in order to be satisfactory as a hedge plant, a tree or shrub must meet certain very definite requirements. It must possess thick foliage of fine texture; it must be capable of even growth; it must produce branches and foliage close to the ground; and in the case of trimmed, formal hedges, it must have the ability to withstand repeated cutting.

PLANTING

As the roots of hedge plants are bound to be restricted, it is important to have the soil well prepared before planting is done. For soil of average fertility, the addition of manure at the rate of 1 ton to 200 linear ft. is recommended. If manure is not available, comparable amounts of compost, peat moss or other well-decomposed organic matter should be worked into the soil. Since hedge plants are to form a dense wall of green, the individual plants should grow so closely that they are not distinguishable in the general mass. The plants are therefore set much closer than in the usual shrub border. There should be good light and air on each side of the hedge in order to make up for this deficiency in the interior. A hedge placed too close to a wall not only looks out of place but seldom does well. Hedges under trees are rarely satisfactory. The root system of a hedge is necessarily crowded. When to this handicap is added the competition of tree roots, it is impossible for the hedge to obtain vigorous growth and development. We have frequent examples of this in the case of privet hedges that thrive in the open

but become weak and spindly at the point where they pass under trees. A few hedge plants such as *Taxus cuspidata* and *Ilex glabra* are exceptions; these grow reasonably well under the shade of trees.

In order to increase the density of the growth, hedges are sometimes planted in double rows, with the plants either staggered or paired. The advantages to be gained from this procedure are somewhat doubtful, and a single row is usually adequate.

During the planting, a trench should be opened to a depth approximately equal to the depth of the balls of earth, or, in the case of plants that are not balled, to the depth of the root system. After the plants have been spaced in the trench, each individual plant should be adjusted for depth and the earth should be filled in around it, as in any planting operation. A tape stretching along the side of the trench will aid in the correct spacing of the plants. Care should be taken to see that the plants are in an absolutely vertical position and in line with each other. The usual watering and trimming should follow planting.

PROTECTION AGAINST ENCROACHING ROOTS

Some of the more vigorous hedge plants have root systems that reach out long distances in search of the nourishment they require to maintain their rapid growth and abundant foliage. Privet is one of the most greedy in this respect, and for this reason it is a bad neighbor for the flower border. The bush honeysuckles, the viburnums and the lilacs are also greedy feeders. If close proximity of such hedges to flower beds is unavoidable, then it is wise to interpose a barrier between them. One device is to dig a trench along the garden side of the hedge 18 in. deep and as wide as the spade. Fill the trench with rocks and a lean mixture of cement, about 1 part cement, 3 parts sand and 5 parts coarse aggregate (gravel or crushed stone). This will keep the roots from intruding into the garden, but it will be necessary to watch for surface roots hurdling over this barrier. A possible modification of this scheme on sloping land is to have the garden on ground higher than that outside, and in this case the barrier becomes a retaining wall, with its foundation below the frost line. The same results could be obtained from burying sheets of transite—a concrete/asbestos board available in flat or corregated panels—in a vertical plane parallel to the hedge.

No precaution need be taken against the roots of box, arborvitae or junipers because these roots are confined closely under the plant in a dense mat. Hemlock roots are a little more rangy but are not very damaging to other plants; a separation of 3 ft. of space (path or turf) will be enough protection against these roots.

CARE

Untrimmed hedges require no more care than any ordinary planting of the same material. A hedge that is to be trained to a certain form, however, requires periodic care. In establishing a new hedge, it is frequently advisable to cut back annual growth by about one half until the ultimate desired height and width has been obtained. Such treatment encourages dense branching and the strongest possible structure for the new hedge. Formal hedges should have one clipping or more each year, depending upon the type of material used. Yew, arborvitae and hemlock may be kept in excellent condition with one trimming a year, although two clippings are sometimes given. Privet should have three or four clippings a season, being trimmed whenever it has outgrown its prescribed size. Box and lilacs require but one clipping; beech, one clipping—never more.

The purpose of trimming is to keep the hedge thick and neat and within bounds. Sometimes an informal hedge may be trimmed lightly to help thicken the mass of foliage. For most evergreen hedges, the best season of the year for clipping is spring, before new growth starts. But because this is a very busy time for gardeners, summer trimming is common, and the results are entirely satisfactory. In this case, trimming should be done after growth has practically ceased. Lilac hedges should be trimmed in June; box hedges in August. The

7.2 In Spanish gardens, elaborate patterns of hedges often enclose roses. Photo Carlton Lees

only tool necessary for clipping a small hedge is a pair of shears with long blades and handles. The type with the handles placed at an angle with the blades is the most desirable, as it enables the worker to reach the lower parts of the plant without undue bending. A number of excellent electric hedge trimmers are available; these are of great value if extensive hedges are to be kept trimmed. The blades are set in a series, cutting much as do the blades of a hay mower, and the work can be done rapidly and efficiently. Ladders on wheels are a great aid to clipping high hedges; sometimes a scaffolding becomes necessary.

A taut line of string set at the desired height of the hedge and attached to stakes on either end will serve as a precise guide while clipping and will ensure a neat and straight planting. It is well to use a line level—a simple device available in hardware stores—to ensure that the string guide is level. Always avoid clipping a hedge to a shape that is narrow at the base and

Fig. 7.1
Good hedge forms

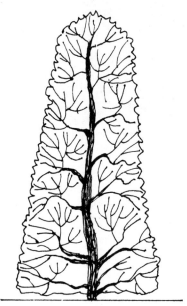

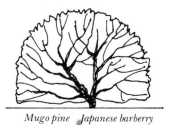

Hemlock   Japanese yew

Mugo pine   Japanese barberry

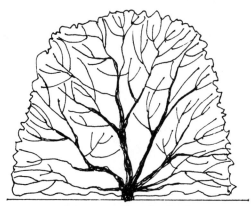

Japanese yew (spreading form)
Regel's privet

Beech   Hornbeam

wider at the top; this will result in undue shading and eventual weakening (or even drying) of
the lower branches. Vertical lines are satisfactory for the sides of a hedge, but the ideal
shape is with a base several inches wider than
the top, with the sides sloping gradually in from
ground up.

Hedges of regular and geometric outline
require more frequent clipping than do the
simpler forms. Few things give a garden an

appearance of neglect more quickly than a
formal hedge in the stages of reverting to the
wild. The trimming of hedges into definite
forms and shapes is time-consuming and requires endless patience and much practice.

The general care of hedge plants does not
differ appreciably from the usual gardening
routine. An occasional cultivation is beneficial
and prevents the intrusion of large weeds or
encroaching trees. Nothing spoils the beauty of

Fig. 7.2
Privet form

 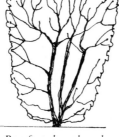

Good form: lower	*Poor form: lower branches*
branches get sunlight	*shaded by upper ones.*

a hedge more surely than seedling trees that have been allowed to grow up beside it, or within it. At first such seedlings are unnoticed, but by the time they are well above the top of the hedge, they are difficult to remove, and their removal creates an unslightly gap in the hedge.

The yearly application of a complete fertilizer is one of the best means of promoting vigor and growth. A mulch of manure appplied in the autumn will not only increase the fertility of the soil but will give protection to the roots during the winter. Box hedges respond remarkably well to an application of humus. This should be worked into the soil along the two sides of the hedge just outside the root ends. In order to rejuvenate an old box hedge that has suffered from neglect, the soil should be trenched along each side at the outer edge of the roots. The soil should be removed to a depth of about 15 in. and the trench refilled with a mixture of humus and top soil. The amount of humus will depend on the quantity available; any proportion up to 1 part humus to 1 part topsoil will be satisfactory—the more humus the better.

If a box hedge has been killed to the ground by an unusually severe winter, do not make the mistake of digging it up. Cut it back to stubs about 3 in. high and wait. Box has wonderful vitality and often has the power to recuperate, if given a chance. This salvaging job should be done early in the spring before the rush of spring work begins. If it is not done then, it will probably be postponed until summer; in the meantime the box, in trying to regain life, will send its sap feebly into all the twigs instead of concentrating its efforts on a few adventitious buds at the end of the stubs. The same treatment will often save a privet hedge that has been injured by severe cold.

HEDGE PLANTS OF SPECIAL MERIT

Abelia x *grandiflora* (glossy abelia)

This makes an excellent, graceful hedge, which is evergreen in mild climates but deciduous in the North. The leaves are glossy and the small, pale pink, tubular flowers are borne almost continuously throughout the summer and fall. It should not be trimmed, but should be allowed to maintain its natural grace. Height 5 ft. to 6 ft. Spacing of plants, 4 ft.
Zone of hardiness: 6.

Berberis x *mentorensis* (barberry)

This is a semievergreen, hybrid barberry that has dark green leaves and a dense habit of growth. It is very adaptable, being tolerant of heat and dry conditions, and from Baltimore southward it is evergreen. Height 6 ft. Spacing of plants. 2½ ft.
Zone of hardiness: 5.

Berberis thunbergii (Japanese barberry)

One of the old reliable hedge plants, it is hardy, stands exposure well, and because of its thorns it affords good protection against intruding animals. As a hedge it forms a dense foliage mass close to the ground. In autumn the foliage has beautiful tones of orange, red and yellow, and the bright red berries hang among the gray twigs well into the winter. It can be maintained at any desired height but reaches a natural height of about 5 ft. Spacing of plants, 3 ft.
Zone of hardiness: 4.

Berberis thunbergii 'Crimson Pygmy'

This is a dwarf form, 2 ft. high, with handsome red leaves if grown in full sun, but similar to the species in all other respects. Spacing of plants, 1½ ft.
Zone of hardiness: 4

Buxus sempervirens Suffruticosa (dwarf box)

A boxwood of antiquity and of English and colonial gardens, this makes one of the most satisfactory hedges. Dense but gracefully irregular, and with foliage close to the ground, boxwood makes an excellent hedge for bordering paths and terraces or as a background in the flower garden. Boxwood hedges may be trimmed to exact lines, or left to develop their picturesque, undulating surfaces. The rate of growth is hardly more than 1 in. a year in the North, but more than twice this in the South, where it is so generally used that it has become almost a symbol of stability and charm. Many a box hedge in the South was planted before the Revolution and has been kept to low proportions by careful trimming or by being cut down to short stumps about every thirty years and allowed to grow up again. The "sempervirens" in the name means that it lives always. Height 6 ft. Spacing of plants, 2 ft. In Zone 5, *Buxus microphylla* var. *Koreana* is a good substitute.
Zone of hardiness: 6

Cotoneaster divaricatus (spreading cotoneaster)

A wide-spreading, dense shrub that will form a compact hedge when trimmed, this plant can be kept at any desired height. The leaves are small, oval and a lustrous dark green, and in the autumn it is bright with small red berries. Height 6 ft. Spacing of plants, 2 ½ ft.
Zone of hardiness: 5

Euonymus alata 'Compacta' (winged spindle tree)

'Compacta' is a dwarf form of the winged euonymus. Its great glory is its brilliant crimson autumn color and its scarlet fruits. It is deciduous but forms a dense hedge and even in winter the thick twigs give it a special solidity. Height 5 ft. Spacing of plants, 3 ft.
Zone of hardiness: 3.

Ilex crenata 'Convexa' (Japanese holly)

'Convexa' makes a fine evergreen hedge. A low shrub, with leaves convex on the upper surface, it is compact and dense in habit of growth. It will need an annual trimming back of the more vigorous branches, but will maintain itself without further attention for years. Height 5 ft. Spacing of plants, 3 ft.
Zone of hardiness: 6.

Ilex crenata 'Microphylla'

'Microphylla' is one of the best cultivars of the Japanese holly for use as a hedge. With careful pruning it forms a dense evergreen hedge, with foliage close to the ground. It is slow-growing but lives for many years and improves with age. It reaches an ultimate height of about 15 ft. but can easily be maintained at any desired height. Spacing of plants, 3½ ft.
Zone of hardiness: 6.

Laurus nobilis (Grecian laurel)

This tree of classic poetry is an evergreen shrub or small tree. It is slow in growth. Its leaves make a dense wall, and its tapering form and upright growth provide an ascending screen. It may be sheared into formal outlines and reaches an eventual height of about 30 ft. but may be maintained at any desired height by judicious pruning. It is widely used in the Pacific Northwest. Spacing of plants, 4 ft.
Zone of hardiness: 7–8.

Ligustrum sinense (privet)

One of the best of the privets; it remains evergreen in most winters in Zone 7 and is defi-

nitely evergreen further south. Less rapid in growth than other privets, it forms a dense hedge, and can be trimmed to formal lines, with leaves right down to the ground. It may be maintained at any desired height. Ultimate height 12 ft. Spacing of plants, 3 ft.
Zone of hardiness: 7.

Pittosporum tobira (**Japanese pittosporum**)

Japanese pittosporum is an evergreen shrub that makes an interesting hedge. Although it is not agreeable to shearing, it will form untrimmed hedges up to 15 ft., and by selective cutting of branches, it can be kept to a lower height. Suited to California and the South. Height 15 ft. Spacing of plants, 4 ft.
Zone of hardiness: 8.

Pyracantha coccinea (**firethorn**)

Firethorn is a useful and versatile evergreen shrub closely related to the hawthorns. It is notable for its generous clusters of orange-vermilion fruits that hang on all autumn. Because it is not discouraged by severe pruning and because of its evergreen foliage, it will form a dense hedge. It is wide-spreading in habit of growth and requires plenty of space. It should not be used where a narrow hedge is desired, but where it can develop its natural form, it makes a magnificent hedge. It will require a little annual pruning and possibly some spraying against scale. Height 10 ft. Spacing of plants, 3 ft.
Zone of hardiness: 6.

Rosa rugosa (**Japanese rose**)

Rosa rugosa is highly satisfactory as an informal, unclipped hedge where summer bloom is desirable. Flowers are pink or white, single or double, depending on the variety of cultivar chosen. They are followed in autumn by large, handsome red fruits. Height 5 ft. Spacing of plants, 2 ft.
Zone of hardiness: 2.

Sarcococca hookerana 'Humilis' (**sweet box**)

'Humilis' is a very choice, dwarf evergreen shrub related to the boxwood, which can be trained into an attractive hedge. The dark green, narrow, tapering leaves make solid masses of foliage close to the ground. It is equally at home in either continuous shade or partial shade but will be scorched on a sunny bank. Height: often only 1½ ft high, it can grow to 4 ft. Spacing of plants, 15 in.
Zone of hardiness: 6.

Spiraca vanhouttei (**bridal-wreath**)

This is an excellent shrub for an informal flowering hedge. It is best not to prune it at all, because any cutting back will spoil the effect of

7.3 On a steep San Francisco street, the zigzagging hedge not only adds green to the hillside but also reduces the sense of exposure and danger. Photo William Curtis

the graceful arching branches. Covered with small clusters of white flowers in May, it provides a gay background for flowers, or it may be used as a border for the lawn. Height 6 ft. Spacing of plants, 4 ft.
Zone of hardiness: 4.

Taxus canadensis 'Stricta' (ground hemlock)

'Stricta' is a cultivar of the Canadian yew. Its upright branches and rich green needlelike foliage make it appropriate for low hedges. It is very hardy, being at home in Zone 2. It may be clipped but is more interesting in its natural form. Height usually 3 ft., occasionally 5 ft. Spacing of plants, 12 in. to 15 in.
Zone of hardiness: 2.

Taxus media 'Hatfieldii'

'Hatfieldii' is a hybrid yew with upright branches and radially spreading needles. Its dark green foliage is an excellent background for bright flowers, and its columnar form makes it adaptable for a hedge in a narrow space. Height 6 ft. Spacing of plants, 2½ ft.
Zone of hardiness: 4.

7.4 Old boxwood hedges with their irregular billowy growth habit are of longstanding tradition in gardens. At the top of this planted retaining wall, the dark green provides excellent background. Photo Grant Heilman

Thuja occidentalis (**American arborvitae**)

This is the old and trusted hedge plant used ever since the early settlers first domesticated it. Hardy, persistent, slow-growing, it has an air of serenity. Old hedges of 100 years or more and 30 ft. in height still persist in New England and elsewhere. Good cultivars for hedges include 'Nigra', which maintains a good green leaf color during the winter, and 'Spiralis', which has a narrower form. Height 60 ft. at maturity. Spacing of plants, 4 ft.
Zone of hardiness: 1.

Tsuga canadensis (**Canada hemlock**)

This makes an excellent dense hedge. It should be sheared only lightly in order to thicken the foliage, but not deeply enough to discourage growth. Old hedges 20 ft. high have remained in excellent condition for many years. Once established, it can be kept at any desired height above 8 ft. to 10 ft., but for low hedges some other plant should be chosen. Height 10 ft.+ Spacing of plants, 4 ft.
Zone of hardiness: 4.

HEDGE MATERIAL—EVERGREEN TREES

SCIENTIFIC NAME	COMMON NAME	SUITABLE FOR CLIPPED (C) OR UNCLIPPED (U) HEDGE	MAXIMUM EFFECTIVE HEDGE HEIGHT	MINIMUM HEIGHT BY TRIMMING	SPACING	ZONE OF HARDINESS
Chamaecyparis lawsoniana cultivars	Lawson cypress	C and U	30'	5'	2–3'	5, 6
Chamaecyparis obtusa	Hinoki cypress	C and U	20'	8'	2–3'	4
C. obtusa 'Crippsii'	Cripps golden cypress	C and U	20'	8'	2–3'	4
C. obtusa 'Gracilis'	slender Hinoki cypress	C and U	12'	6'	2–2½'	4
Chamaecyparis pisifera	Sawara cypress	C and U	30'	6'	2–3'	3
C. pisifera 'Plumosa'	plume cypress	C and U	30'	5'	2–3'	4
C. pisifera 'Squarrosa'	moss cypress	C and U	20'	5'	2–3'	4
Ilex aquifolium	English holly	C and U	20'	5'	2½'	6
Ilex opaca	American holly	C and U	20'	5'	2½'	5
Juniperus chinensis 'Pfitzerana'	Spreading juniper	C and U	8'	4'	3–4'	4
Juniperus virginiana	eastern red cedar	C and U	25'	6'	2½–3'	2
J. virginiana 'Canaertii'	Cannart red cedar	C and U	25'	6'	2½–3'	2
J. virginiana 'Glauca'	silver red cedar	C and U	20'	6'	2½–3'	2
Laurus nobilis	bay	C only	40'	6'	4'	7
Picea abies	Norway spruce	C and U	30'	6'	3'	2
Picea glauca	white spruce	U only	30'		3'	2
Pinus strobus	white pine	C and U	40'	10'	3–6'	3
Pinus sylvestris	Scots pine	U only	20'		3–5'	2
Pinus thunbergiana	Japanese black pine	U only	40'		3–6'	5
Platycladus orientalis and cultivars	oriental arborvitae	C and U	25'	8'	2–3'	6
Pseudotsuga menziesii	Douglas fir	U only	30'		3–5'	4, 5, 6
Taxus baccata	English yew	C and U	20'	4'	3–5'	6
Taxus cuspidata cultivars	Japanese yew	C and U	12'	4'	2½–4'	4
Taxus x *media* 'Hicks'	Hicks yew	C and U	8'		2–2½'	4
Thuja occidentalis	American arborvitae	C and U	30'	8'	2–3'	2
T. occidentalis 'Douglasii Pyramidalis'		C and U	20'	8'	2–3'	2
T. occidentalis 'Wareana'	Ware arborvitae	C and U	30'	8'	2–3'	2
Tsuga canadensis	Canada hemlock	C and U	30'	8–10'	3–4'	3
Tsuga caroliniana	Carolina hemlock	C and U	30'	8–10'	3–4'	4

HEDGE MATERIAL—EVERGREEN SHRUBS AND DWARF EVERGREEN TREES

SCIENTIFIC NAME	COMMON NAME	SUITABLE FOR CLIPPED (C) OR UNCLIPPED (U) HEDGE	MAXIMUM EFFECTIVE HEDGE HEIGHT	MINIMUM HEIGHT BY TRIMMING	SPACING	ZONE OF HARDINESS
Berberis julianae	barberry	C and U	6'	3'	2'	5
Berberis verruculosa	warty barbery	C and U	3'	2'	1½'	5
Buxus sempervirens 'Suffruticosa'	dwarf box	C and U	6'	1½'	½ – 1½'	6
Chamaecyparis obtusa 'Compacta'	dwarf cypress	C and U	7'	3'	1½ – 2'	4
C. obtusa 'Nana'		C and U	4'	2½'	1½ – 2'	4
Euonymus fortunei var. *radicans*	spindle tree	C and U	4'	2'	2 – 2½'	5
E. fortunei 'Minimus' (kewensis)		C and U	3'	1'	1½'	5
E. fortunei 'Vegetus'		C and U	5'	2'	2 – 2½'	5
Ilex crenata	Japanese holly	C and U	8'	3'	2'	6
I. crenata 'Convexa'		C and U	4'	2'	1 – 2½'	6
I. crenata 'Latifolia'		U only	8'		2 – 2½'	6
I. crenata 'Microphylla'		C and U	6'	2½'	1 – 2'	6
Lonicera nitida	box honeysuckle	C and U	5'	1½'	15 – 21''	7
Picea abies 'Maxwellii'	dwarf Norway spruce	U only	2½'		1' or less	2
Pinus mugo var. *mugo*	Mugo pine	C and U	8'	4'	2 – 4'	2
Pittosporum tobira	Japanese pittosporum	C only	12'	6'	4'	8
Pyracantha coccinea	firethorn	C only	12'	4'	3'	6
Taxus baccata 'Repandens'	spreading English yew	U only	3'		2'	5
Taxus canadensis 'Stricta'	ground hemlock	C and U	3'	1'	1½'	2
Taxus cuspidata 'Brevifolia'	dwarf Japanese yew	C and U	6'	2'	1¼ – 2'	4
T. cuspidata 'Densa'		C and U	4'	2'	1¼ – 2'	4
T. cuspidata 'Nana'		C and U	4'	2'	2 – 3'	4
Teucrium chamaedrys	germander	C and U	1'		1½'	5
Thuja occidentalis 'Hoveyi'	American arborvitae	C and U	6'	4'	2 – 3'	3
T. occidentalis 'Reidii'		C and U	6'	3'	1½ – 2½'	3

HEDGE MATERIAL—DECIDUOUS TREES

Acer campestre	hedge maple	U only	25'		3–6'	4
Acer ginnala	Amur maple	U only	25'		3–4'	2
Carpinus betulus	European hornbeam	C only	20'	6'	2–3'	5
Carpinus caroliniana	American hornbeam	C only	20'	6'	2–3'	2
Crataegus crus-galli	cockspur thorn	C and U	20'	10'	3'	4
Crataegus oxyacantha	English hawthorn	C and U	20'	10'	3'	4
Crataegus phaenopyrum	Washington thorn tree	U only	20'		3'	4
Elaeagnus angustifolia	Russian olive	U only	25'		4–6'	2
Fagus sylvatica	European beech	C only	30'	8'	4–5'	4
Maclura pomifera	osage orange	U only	25'	may be cut to 1' and will resprout	3–4'	5
Ostrya virginiana	American hop hornbeam	C and U	25'	6'	4–6	4
Quercus inbricaria	shingle oak	C only	20'	6'	3–5'	5
Salix pentandra	laurel willow	U only	25'		3–6'	4
Tilia cordata	little-leaf linden	C only	30'	10'	4–6'	3
Ulmus pumila	Siberian elm	C only	25'	8'	4'	4

HEDGE MATERIAL—DECIDUOUS SHRUBS

SCIENTIFIC NAME	COMMON NAME	SUITABLE FOR CLIPPED (C) OR UNCLIPPED (U) HEDGE	MAXIMUM EFFECTIVE HEDGE HEIGHT	MINIMUM HEIGHT BY TRIMMING	SPACING	ZONE OF HARDINESS
Abelia x *grandiflora*	glossy abelia	U only	6'		3'	6
Acanthopanax sieboldianus	five-leaf aralia	C and U	5–6'	3'	2–3'	4
Berberis thunbergii	Japanese barberry	C and U	4–6'	3'	1½–2	4
B. thunbergii 'Atropurpurea'	red-leaved barberry	C and U	4–5'	3'	1½–2'	4
B. thunbergii 'Crimson Pygmy'	crimson pgymy barberry	C and U	2'	1'	9–12''	4
Caragana arborescens	pea-tree	U only	10'		2½–3'	2
Chaenomeles japonica	Japanese quince	C and U	3'	3'	2–4'	4
Cotoneaster adpressus	creeping cotoneaster	U only	5'		1–2'	4
Cotoneaster divaricatus	spreading cotoneaster	C and U	5'	3'	2–2½'	5
Cotoneaster microphyllus	small-leaved cotoneaster	C and U	3'	2'	1–1½'	5
Deutzia gracilis	slender deutzia	U only	3'		1½–2'	4
Deutzia x *lemoinei*	Lemoine's deutzia	U only	3'	1½–2'	1½–2'	4
Euonymus alata 'Compacta'	winged spindle tree	C and U	6'	4'	3–4'	3

(Continued)

HEDGE MATERIAL—DECIDUOUS SHRUBS (Continued)

SCIENTIFIC NAME	COMMON NAME	SUITABLE FOR CLIPPED (C) OR UNCLIPPED (U) HEDGE	MAXIMUM EFFECTIVE HEDGE HEIGHT	MINIMUM HEIGHT BY TRIMMING	SPACING	ZONE OF HARDINESS
Hydrangea arborescens	hills-of-snow	U only	4′		2′	4
Hydrangea paniculata 'Grandiflora'	Peegee hydrangea	U only	15′		2½–3′	4
Ligustrum amurense	Amur privet	C and U	15′	4′	1–2′	3
Ligustrum obtusifolium 'Regelianum'	Regel's privet	C and U	6′	3′	1½–2′	3
Ligustrum ovalifolium	California privet	C and U	15′	3′	1–1¼	5
Ligustrum sinense	Chinese privet	C and U	6′		3′	7
Ligustrum vulgare	European privet	C and U	15′	3′	1–1½′	4
Lonicera fragrantissima	winter honeysuckle	U only	6′		3–6′	5
Lonicera maackii	Amur honeysuckle	U only	15′		4–6′	2
Lonicera morrowii	Morrow honeysuckle	U only	6′		3–5′	4
Lonicera tatarica	Tatarian honeysuckle	U only	10′		3–6′	5
Myrica pensylvanica	bayberry	C and U	9′	4′	2–3′	2
Philadelphus coronarius	mock-orange	U only	9′		3–5′	4
Philadelphus x *lemoinei* cultivars	Lemoine's mock-orange	U only	6′		2′	5
Physocarpus opulifolius	ninebark	U only	9′		3′	2
P. opulifolius 'Nanus'	dwarf ninebark	C and U	3′	2′	1½–2	2
Rhamnus frangula 'Tallhedge'	tallhedge buckthorn	C and U	15′	5′	2½–3′	2
Rhodotypos scandens	jetbead	U only	6′		2–3′	5
Ribes alpinum	Alpine currant	U only	7′		1½–2′	2
Rosa rugosa	Japanese rose	U only	6′		2–3′	2
Spiraea x *arguta*	garland spirea	U only	5′		2½–3′	4
Spiraea prunifolia	bridal-wreath spirea	U only	10′		3–4′	4
Spiraea thunbergii	Thunberg spirea	U only	4–5′		2–3′	4
Spiraea x *vanhouttei*	bridal-wreath spirea	U only	6′		3′	4
Syringa x *persica*	Persian lilac	U only	6′		2½′	5
Syringa vulgaris	common lilac	U only	15–20′		3′	3
Viburnum dilatatum	linden viburnum	U only	9′		3′	5
Viburnum lantana	wayfaring tree	U only	15′		3′	3
Viburnum opulus 'Nanum'	dwarf highbush cranberry	C and U	3′	1½′	1–1½′	3
Viburnum plicatum tomentosum	doublefile viburnum	U only	9′		3–4′	4
Viburnum prunifolium	black-haw	C and U	15′	8′	3–4′	3
Viburnum sieboldii	Siebold viburnum	U only	25′		3–5′	4

8

Mulches

Mulches not only have a very beneficial effect upon plant growth but also reduce to a minimum the time and labor required for garden maintenance. On the well-managed home property, mulching becomes a year-round operation.

A good mulch, consisting of suitable materials properly applied at the correct time, serves many functions. The most important of these functions is the conservation of moisture. A good mulch readily permits the penetration of water into the soil. During periods of heavy precipitation it checks the full force of the rain, lessening the danger of surface runoff, and permits the water to sink gently into the soil. It also protects the soil from the drying effects of sun and wind, thus preventing the evaporation of moisture from the soil surface. On soils protected by a mulch, one never finds a hard, baked crust such as is found all too frequently on soils exposed to the sun's rays. Even during periods of intense summer heat and drought, the soil under a heavy mulch will remain cool and moist. It is usually dark and crumbly, characteristics of a soil that will provide favorable conditions for good root development.

The application of a mulch is one of the most effective measures of weed control. There are few weeds that can push up through a heavy mulch, and if they occasionally succeed, they are so straggly that they can easily be pulled out.

A mulch also serves as an insulating material and helps to maintain more even soil temperatures. In summer the soil under a mulch is sometimes as much as 20° F. cooler than surrounding soils, and in winter the soil under a blanket of mulch retains some of its heat and is warmer than surrounding soil areas. More uniform soil temperatures usually result in better plant growth and, in the case of vegetables, in superior quality. Newly transplanted trees and shrubs especially should receive a thorough mulching during the first winter, to prevent frost heaving and root desiccation.

The end result of an organic mulch is that it eventually decomposes and adds humus to the soil. During this process of decomposition valuable plant nutrients are released that increase the fertility of the soil. In the course of time, soil under a heavy mulch will resemble woodland soil that is always richly supplied with natural humus resulting from the slow decay of fallen leaves and branches. It will become crumbly to the touch, dark in color and have a clean, woodsy smell. The upper few inches of soil will be full of healthy feeding roots and will be well supplied with earthworms and beneficial soil microorganisms. If plants are kept mulched with organic materials year after year, there will be a constantly replenished supply of humus for their needs.

SELECTING MATERIALS FOR MULCHES

The points in favor of mulching are so convincing that the gardener is usually not faced with the problem of whether to mulch or not to mulch, but rather with the question of which kind of mulch to use.

In selecting materials for mulches, there are a number of factors to be considered: the availability of the material; the cost, compared with that of other materials; the appearance of the mulch; the effect it will have on the soil; the acidity of its reaction on the soil; its durability; whether it presents a fire hazard; whether it decomposes rapidly or slowly; whether it is comparatively weed-free; and whether there is danger of introducing disease through its use. In general, organic mulches are to be preferred to inorganic mulches because of their benefit to the soil.

Aluminum Foil

In experimental tests aluminum foil has proved to be an effective mulch. It conserves moisture well, the moisture content of the soil under an aluminum mulch usually being at least 8 percent higher than that of the surrounding soil. This is due in part to the fact that water vapor coming to the surface of the soil condenses on the underside of the foil and drips back into the ground. While often unsightly, aluminum foil also serves as an insulating material against both heat and cold. As it reflects the sun's rays, it has an extraordinarily cooling effect on the soil in summer. Tests show that on a hot, sunny day the soil under an aluminum mulch will often be 20° F. cooler than that of the surrounding soil, and on cold nights the soil under the mulch will retain its heat and remain 8° to 10° F. warmer than the surrounding area. This even soil temperature results in more uniform growth and, in the case of vegetables, in improved quality. Aluminum foil is also one of the most fire-resistant of all mulches.

In spite of its many good qualities, however, aluminum foil has certain limitations as a mulch. It is comparatively expensive, it adds no humus or nutrients to the soil, it must be anchored down along the edges to prevent blowing and tearing, and it is suitable only for plants grown in rows. It has proved of special value as a mulch in vegetable gardens, in areas where flowers are grown in rows for commercial production or for cutting, in nurseries where small plants are set out in rows and for strawberries. It has resulted in increased yields of both vegetables and flowers, in an improvement in quality, and in better disease and insect control.

When an aluminum foil mulch is applied, the soil should be completely covered with the foil except for a 2-in. strip where the plants come through. The most suitable grade for garden use is a .001- or a .0015-in. gauge.

The foil is obtainable in widths varying from 1 ft. to 3 ft.

Buckwheat Hulls

Buckwheat hulls are an excellent mulch for rose beds and flower borders. They are clean, light in weight and easy to apply. They are weed-free and make a mulch that is inconspicuous and that can be raked up and reused a second year if desired. Its greatest disadvantage is that in exposed areas it has a tendency to blow around. It should be applied in a layer from 1 in. to 3 in. in depth.

Corncobs

Corncobs ground into small pieces make a very satisfactory mulch, and in some sections they are readily obtainable at moderate cost. They are weed-free, clean, light in weight and easy to handle. They rot down into excellent humus, but in order to avoid a deficiency of nitrogen in the soil during decomposition extra nitrogen should be applied in some form. When used on roses or on shrubs, a 3- to 4-in. layer should be applied, while on perennial beds a 2-in. layer is sufficient. If canker on roses is prevalent, it will be advisable to spray the canes and the mulch with Fermate (see index).

In some sections of the country, very finely ground corncobs are being used as a mulch on greenhouse crops and have given excellent results on roses, carnations, chrysanthemums, snapdragons and stocks. A 3-in. to 4-in. mulch is recommended for greenhouse roses, a 1-in. mulch for other crops.

Glass Wool

This material has been used experimentally and provides an effective mulch, one of its chief advantages being that it is fireproof. It is too expensive for extensive home or commercial use and lacks the many good qualities of an organic mulch.

Grass Clippings

Raked-up grass clippings provide a good home-grown mulching material. Because they tend to form a rather dense mat, it is advisable to mix them with some coarse material such as partially rotted leaves, sawdust or corncobs. If lawn grasses are treated with weedkillers, particularly products containing the herbicide 2,4-D, the clippings must not be used for mulching or in composts since the residual chemical may harm valuable ornamentals or fruits and vegetables.

Hay

Rain-damaged hay unfit for livestock feed may sometimes be procured in rural areas at a very low cost, and it makes an excellent mulch for the vegetable garden and for shrubbery borders. It may be used either as long hay or as chopped hay. It rots down into good humus and is very beneficial to the soil. If the hay is from a legume crop such as alfalfa, clover, soybeans or cowpeas, it will supply a considerable amount of additional nitrogen to the soil as it decomposes.

Hops

In some areas, spent hops from breweries are readily available. These have much to recommend them as a mulch for shrub plantings and for use around specimen trees. They decay very slowly and need to be renewed only once in every three or four years. And they are one of the most resistant of all mulches to fire; they do not catch fire as do most dried materials, they do not even smolder, they merely blacken. When first applied, the mulch exudes an objectionable odor, but this is soon dissipated. Spent hops are used extensively at Harvard University's Arnold Arboretum as a deep mulch on some of the prized shrubbery plantings and around valuable specimen trees.

Leaves

Leaves are nature's favorite mulching material and are ideal for mulching trees and shrubs. A mulch of leaves 4 in. to 8 in. deep applied to a shrub border or to trees in the autumn will afford excellent protection and will add large quantities of humus to the soil. Oak leaves are acid in their reaction on the soil and are the

standard mulch for broad-leaved evergreens. Some leaves, such as those of silver maple, elm and birch trees, have an unfortunate tendency to mat and soon become a soggy mass. In the flower garden there is danger of having leaves of this kind mat down and destroy the crowns of valuable plants. Shredded leaves do not mat as readily as whole leaves and have the added advantage of decomposing more quickly. If shredding is impracticable, the leaves may be composted for a season before they are used, or they may be mixed with straw, ground corncobs or some other light material. Leaves of oak, beech and sycamore do not have a tendency to mat down.

Manure

Most animal manures available for mulches are mixed with straw, sawdust or some other form of absorptive organic material that has been used as bedding. They are, therefore, mulches with "built-in" fertility and are of great value. Such materials could be easily obtained half a century ago, but they are at a premium today and usually available only to people living in rural areas. When used for mulching purposes, manures are most satisfactory if they have been composted.

Paper

Paper first came into use as a mulch on the pineapple plantations in Hawaii. A heavy grade of tough, black paper has been developed for mulching purposes; it is very effective in controlling weeds and in conserving moisture. However, it is higher in cost than many other mulching materials, it must be weighted down to prevent blowing and tearing, it is suited only to row crops and it lacks the values of an organic mulch. As it will exclude all light, it is particularly useful for killing such weeds as quack grass, Canada thistle and bindweed on very small areas where it can be heavily weighted down with boards or stones.

Peat Moss

Peat moss is one of the most widely used of all mulching materials. It is obtainable in medium-sized bags or in large burlap-covered bales. It makes a mulch that is attractive, clean, easy to handle and weed-free; it is slow to decompose and therefore has to be renewed less frequently than many other organic materials, and its reaction is so mildly acid that it may be used on a wide variety of plants. It is suitable for use in the flower garden, on rose beds, on shrubbery borders and around specimen plants. Peat moss should be thoroughly moistened before it is applied as a mulch, and the mulch should be kept moist and loose. If it is permitted to dry out, it has a tendency to form a crust that is almost impervious to water, creating a condition that is extremely detrimental to plant growth. Peat moss is very absorptive, and if it is partially dry it sometimes does not permit light rains to percolate down into the soil. Under conditions of normal rainfall, this is not apt to occur.

Pine Needles

Pine needles make an airy, attractive mulch and in many areas are available for the raking. In the South they are widely used as a mulch for camellias. They are slightly acid in reaction, light in weight, clean, weed-free and pleasant to handle.

Plastic

Black polyethylene plastic is widely used as a mulch in many commercial vegetable areas and to some extent in home gardens. It is usually spread between the rows, being weighted down with soil or with stones. Plants may also be set out through slits in the mulch. Its advantages are that it eliminates the need for cultivation as it prevents the growth of weeds completely, it conserves the moisture in the soil and, since it is dark, it absorbs the rays of the sun and therefore maintains a high soil temperature. On cold nights the soil temperature is from 10° to 15° F. warmer under a black plastic mulch. This is of great advantage in starting crops in the vegetable garden early in the spring. A plastic mulch is also valuable for strawberries, as it results in early maturity, clean berries free from grit and reduced decay in ripening berries. The disadvantages for the home garden are that it is not

an organic mulch, it is not attractive, and in midsummer, soil temperatures under it may become too high for some plants. It is obtainable in rolls of various widths and may be used for a number of seasons.

Salt Hay

Salt or marsh hay is extensively used as a mulch in many sections. It is light, clean, pest-free and weed-free, and is long lasting. After a season of use, it may be raked up, stored and used again. It never mats, and it makes an excellent winter mulch for perennial beds and borders, being of particular value for mulching plants with leafy crowns. A bale of salt hay will provide a light covering for an area of approximately 1,200 sq. ft.

Sawdust

Sawdust makes a very effective mulch, and in areas where it is readily available, it is widely used. As a year-round mulch on blueberries and other small fruits, and in vegetable gardens, a mulch 4 in. to 6 in. deep is usually applied. Sawdust is less desirable as a mulch in flower gardens, as it is apt to encourage the development of crown rot in plants that are particularly susceptible, probably because the moisture is held so closely around the crown. The acid reaction of sawdust will depend on the source. Sawdust from some trees is very acid in its reaction; from other trees it is nearly neutral (see table on page 99). For some plants it is desirable to use an acid type of sawdust; for other plants a neutral type will best meet their requirements. To lessen the effect of an acid type of sawdust, 10 lb. of ground limestone may be used per 200 lb. of dry sawdust, which will help to maintain a more nearly neutral pH. When using sawdust as a mulch, it is essential that additional nitrogen be applied to the soil (see page 100).

Stones

Flat stones can be used as a mulch in areas where they are readily available and in a location where a permanent mulch is desired. They will conserve the moisture in the soil, will prevent the growth of weeds, and will provide a cool root-run for the plants; however, on the whole, organic materials are to be preferred. Stone chips are excellent for use in rock gardens, as they prevent erosion in the soil pockets and help to lower soil temperatures. Heavy polyethylene plastic sheeting weighted by decorative stones provides a weed-free and moisture-retentive mulch of great aesthetic value; it has gained much favor in recent years.

Straw

All the cereal straws, such as wheat, oat, barley and rye straw, provide excellent mulching material. Long straw may be used satisfactorily in the vegetable garden and for the mulching of trees and shrubbery, but straw is not suitable for use in the flower garden unless it is shredded. After one season, straw is usually pretty well decomposed and becomes valuable humus. Nitrogen should be applied when straw is used as a mulch.

Tobacco Stems

Where they are available, tobacco stems make an effective and economical mulch. Because of the danger of introducing mosaic disease, they should never be used on bulb plantings, or even near lilies or tomato plants.

Walnut Shells

In some areas, ground black walnut shells are available as a mulching material, and they have much to recommend them. They provide a fairly permanent mulch, as they do not rot readily and therefore do not have to be replaced as frequently as many other mulches. They are pleasing in appearance, with a cinnamon brown color; they do not wash away during heavy rains, and since the shells do not actually absorb any moisture themselves, even light rains percolate down into the soil. A mulch of this type is also very resistant to fire,

---

ACID MULCHES

Acid mulches are recommended for use on azaleas, rhododendrons, pieris, camellias and other broad-leaved evergreens, and on blueberries.

Apple pomace from cider mills
Oak leaves: very acid
Peat moss: slightly acid
Pine needles: moderately acid
Sawdust
    Black oak: moderately acid
    Cypress: very acid (pH 3.5 to 3.9)
    Maple: mildly acid
    Red oak: mildly acid
    White oak: moderately acid

NONACID MULCHES

Nonacid mulches are recommended for use on perennial flower beds, on rose beds, in the vegetable garden and on deciduous shrub borders. Peat moss is so mild in its acid reaction that it may also be used safely on most plants in this group.

Buckwheat hulls	Sawdust
Corncobs	Elm
Grass clippings	Hemlock
Leaves (except oak)	Locust
Salt hay	Straw

---

and since the material is extremely rot-resistant, it has little tendency to reduce the supply of nitrogen in the soil.

Wood Chips

In forested regions, wood chips are often available from utility companies, city parks departments and arborists. They are very effective as a mulch and will, in time, become completely decomposed and add humus to the soil. Extra nitrogen should be supplied when wood chips are used.

ADDITIONAL NITROGEN

Certain raw organic materials, such as sawdust, wood chips, corncobs and, to some extent, cereal straws, will cause a depletion of nitrogen in the soil during decomposition. This is due to the fact that the soil bacteria that cause the breakdown of raw organic materials into humus require large amounts of nitrogen during the process, and they make use of the available nitrogen in the soil, sometimes causing the plants to suffer from nitrogen starvation. This may be prevented by increasing the supply of nitrogen in the soil when such mulches are applied, so there will be a sufficient amount to meet the needs of both the soil bacteria and the plants. Ammonium sulphate, nitrate of soda, ammonium nitrate or a complete fertilizer high in nitrogen may be used. The following amounts are recommended for use on soils of average fertility, per 100 sq. ft.: $\frac{1}{2}$ lb. of ammonium sulphate or nitrate of soda, or $\frac{1}{3}$ lb. of ammonium nitrate or 1 lb. of a complete fertilizer 10–6–4.

On large areas, the fertilizer is usually applied directly to the soil. If it is necessary to apply it after a mulch has been put on, it may be applied on the surface of the mulch and watered in, or it may be dissolved in water and applied to the mulch in the form of a solution.

When small quantities of sawdust are used for mulching individual plants, the fertilizer may be mixed with the sawdust as it is applied.

SUMMER MULCHES

Summer mulches are of great value in conserving moisture and controlling weeds and are widely used in flower gardens, vegetable gardens, on small fruits and trees and shrubs.

In the Flower Garden

The summer mulch in the flower garden should be applied in the late spring or early summer, after the ground has become thoroughly warm. Buckwheat hulls and peat moss are recommended as the most satisfactory materials for use on flower beds, as they are weed-free, clean, easy to handle and make an inconspicuous mulch. A mulch 2 in. deep will usually be sufficient. When plants have low, leafy crowns, the mulch should be worked in carefully about the plant in order to avoid covering the crown. If peat moss is used, it should be thoroughly wet before it is applied and should be

maintained in a moist, fluffy condition, never being allowed to dry out and form a crust.

If slugs are troublesome, precautions must be taken in mulching herbaceous plants and annual flowers. A slug killer should be applied to the soil before the mulch is put on, and careful watch should be kept. If the slug killer was not applied to the soil, an application on the surface of the mulch may prove helpful.

In the Vegetable Garden

A summer mulch in the vegetable garden will reduce to a minimum the labor required and will also appreciably increase yields and improve the table quality of the crops. And if an organic mulch is used, the benefit to the soil will be great. Sawdust, straw, aluminum foil and paper may be used.

On Small Fruits

When summer mulches are used on small fruits, such as raspberries, blackberries and blueberries, it will not only result in the control of weeds and a consequent saving in labor but also in more vigorous growth and increased production. Sawdust, straw and hay are excellent mulching materials. A year-round sawdust mulch on blueberries is recommended.

On Trees and Shrubs

Broad-leaved evergreens, being shallow-rooted, thrive best under a permanent mulch that should remain undisturbed. As the older layers decompose, new material should be added. This may be done whenever materials such as leaves, especially from oaks, are available. Permanent mulches may also be maintained on deciduous trees and shrubs. Permanent organic mulches of leaves, straw or sawdust should be maintained at a depth of 4 in. to 6 in.

WINTER MULCHES

In the Flower Garden

In the North a winter mulch serves several important functions in the flower garden. It protects the plants from severe cold; it protects the foliage of certain plants from the effects of drying winds and brilliant winter sunshine that are apt to sear and scorch tender growth; it prevents plants from starting into growth too early in the spring; and, perhaps most important, it prevents the alternate freezing and thawing of the soil that, during the late winter and spring months, is so harmful to many herbaceous plants, heaving the crowns out of the soil and leaving the roots exposed. Young plants whose roots are very near the surface, and shallow-rooted plants, such as columbines, are the most likely to be injured. In many parts of the country, winter-killing is more often due to this cause than to the effect of extremely low temperatures.

Materials

A number of materials, such as salt hay and straw, may be used very satisfactorily as winter mulches in the flower garden.

If small evergreen boughs are available, they offer excellent material for winter covering, as they are light in weight and permit a good circulation of air. They may also be used to hold leaves, straw or other light materials in place. Fallen leaves are one of nature's own coverings, but if they are to be used as a winter protection on garden beds, only those kinds should be selected that will not mat and will not become a soggy mass before spring. Leaves from oak, beech and sycamore trees are excellent, while leaves from maples, elms and other hardwood trees should not be used.

When to Apply the Mulch

The winter mulch should not be applied until the plants are completely dormant and the ground is frozen. The purpose of the mulch is not only for the protection against cold but also to protect the plants from the temporary warmth of late winter and early spring days, which can be so deceptive and so damaging to herbaceous plants when it is followed by a return to severe weather.

Depth of the Mulch

The depth of the winter mulch will depend on the type of material used and the severity of the winter climate. It is as disastrous to apply too heavy a mulch and smother the plants as it is to apply too light a covering. Care should be taken not to cover the crowns of such plants as foxgloves, Canterbury-bells, hollyhocks, heuchera, garden pinks or anchusa, all of which retain their succulent foliage throughout the winter. The mulch should be worked in about the roots, with only a few light wisps of salt hay over the foliage.

Removal of the Winter Mulch

The removal of the winter mulch is always a matter of concern to the gardener. If a fairly heavy mulch was used, it should be removed gradually and the final covering should, if possible, be lifted off on a cloudy day in order that any young shoots that have started into growth may not be too suddenly exposed to brilliant sunshine.

It is unwise to leave the winter mulch on too late in the spring, as it will seriously retard the growth of the plants, and shoots that have tried to push through will be spindly and weak. It is usually safe to begin to remove the mulch as soon as the cold weather seems to be over and the early, small bulbs, such as the squills and crocus, are in bloom.

On Evergreens

The evergreen, particularly the broad-leaved evergreens, are greatly benefited by a winter mulch. Under an adequate winter mulch the soil does not freeze as quickly or as deeply as soil that is exposed. This is a matter of considerable importance with evergreens, as they are never completely dormant. They continue to need water during the winter, and are able to obtain it much more readily from heavily mulched soils than from bare, frozen ground. Under a system of permanent mulching, this advantage is gained.

9.1 *This mosaic fountain from Damascus, surrounded by pots of clipped myrtle* (Myrtus communis), *is typical of the gardens of ancient Persia. Photo Carlton Lees*

9

Pools and Fountains

Water traditionally has been the symbol of life, and with good reason. It makes all life possible. In Central Asia and in northern Africa, where a garden is a highly developed oasis in an arid land, water is indispensable. The sound of a trickling fountain is pleasant indeed to those whose senses are accustomed to the barren dryness of the outer world.

While garden pools had their origin in warm countries and their primary purpose was to cool the atmosphere, the almost universal appeal of sparkling water has made them equally appreciated in northern climes. The idea of a fountain or pool as a garden feature was first brought to Europe by the Crusaders after their contacts with the older and more highly developed culture of the Near East. Even in the comparatively damp climate of England and Scotland, the fountain idea has persisted, although with somewhat less elaboration and emphasis than it has received in Italy and Spain.

POOLS

Besides its original function of providing refreshment in hot weather by cooling the surrounding air, the garden pool serves a distinctly decorative purpose. Set in a frame of stone, the gleaming mirror of its surface becomes an object of admiration and attention. It may be used as the central feature of the garden, or it may be used as a terminal motive for a major or minor axis. It often provides a fitting foreground for a piece of sculpture, and its usefulness and charm can be heightened by making it the habitation of fish and water-loving plants.

In the design of a garden pool, the major

decisions are the size, the shape, the material to be used for the coping, the depth of the water and the color of the bottom.

It is important that the pool should be in harmony with its surroundings, and that it should be in scale as a detail of the garden design. Its setting, in patterned paving or in turf, should be carefully studied. The shape will largely depend on the general plan of the garden and, to a limited extent perhaps, on the personal preference of the owner. In some gardens a round pool would be the most logical and pleasing from a standpoint of design; while in other gardens a square or oblong pool would be more in keeping with the general scheme.

The material to be used in the construction of the coping is largely a matter of personal choice. A simple flagstone coping is always pleasant and is particularly suitable if the garden is small and informal. For gardens of more formal and elaborate design, a coping of cut stone might be preferred. Colored tiles are very decorative and lovely, and they can be used both as a coping and as a complete lining for the pool. While concrete may be used as a coping, it is decidedly less attractive and less interesting than most other materials.

Special paints are available for use in the interior of concrete pools. If the bottom is painted black, it gives an appearance of much greater depth. Blue is the most popular color, as it gives a reflection of the sky, but care must be taken not to choose too harsh a tone, which would be artificial in the landscape.

When considering the construction of a pool, it must be borne in mind that the initial cost is usually the last. A pool is a permanent feature of the garden, requiring little or no upkeep. When once its construction has been com-

103

pleted, it will be a source of satisfaction for years to come. Fortunately for the homeowner, a garden pool need not be elaborate or expensive. A small, simple pool may be constructed for a very modest sum, and most of the work can be done by the owner.

In constructing a garden pool, the major considerations are: absolute watertightness; drainage; and water supply, including the control of inlet, outlet and overflow. The walls of the pool are, essentially, retaining walls, and as such they must be strong enough to withstand the soil pressure against them and also to resist the pressure of frost. There must be no heaving caused by the action of frost, as this will crack the walls and throw the coping out of level. A poorly constructed pool, which consequently is cracked by frost year after year, can become a source of constant annoyance. It is difficult to repair a pool that has developed a leak, and it is therefore a matter of sound economy to see that the pool is well constructed in the beginning.

The ground surrounding the pool should be absolutely level. This is a matter of vital importance, which is sometimes overlooked by the amateur builder. If a pool is constructed on ground that is only slightly uneven, the result will be unsatisfactory. If there is no other alternative, and if a pool must be constructed on ground that is slightly sloping, it will be necessary to raise the coping on one side. If this is not done, the surface will be unattractive and have the appearance of a tilted dish.

Construction Materials

Concrete

Concrete is one of the best materials to use for the construction of garden pools. For a pool of 100 sq. ft. or less, the bottom should be 5 in. thick and the walls 8 in. thick. For very large pools these figures should be slightly increased, while for very small pools they may be somewhat reduced, although not to any appreciable extent. In constructing a small pool, it is not necessary to reinforce the sides. In a pool that is more than 15 ft. in length, however, the sides

should be reinforced with steel rods in order to maintain the concrete in a monolith against varying pressures.

The soil should be excavated to a depth of from 12 in. to 18 in. below the proposed floor level of the pool. The sides of the excavation should be vertical and in line with the outside wall of the pool. A layer of gravel should be spread over the bottom of the excavation and tamped firmly into place. If the gravel is sprinkled with water, it will help the mass to settle into place. This layer will act as a drain and will keep the groundwater away from the undersurface of the concrete, thus reducing the danger of heaving caused by the action of the frost. The actual depth of the layer of gravel will depend somewhat upon the character of the soil. In light, sandy soils a layer only a few inches in depth will be satisfactory; while in soils of a heavy clay texture, a layer 12 in. deep is advisable.

Sheet Lead

Sheet lead, since ancient times, has been the ideal material for constructing small and irregularly shaped pools and ornamental basins for gardens because it is pliable and practically indestructible; it is also much better looking and less bulky than concrete. In spite of its advantages, however, it is heavy to handle, has become almost impossible to obtain and is outrageously expensive. Fortunately, polyvinylchloride (PVC) — the kind of plastic used as swimming pool liners — is an adequate replacement.

Polyvinylchloride

Polyvinylchloride can be used to make pools of almost any size and shape, provided this durable and flexible material is bedded in a firm base.

The first step is to establish the outline of the pool, then to determine the size of the liner needed. To do so, measure a rectangle that will cover the ground area occupied by the pool as outlined. Then add twice the depth of the pool, plus another 1½ ft. for the edge, to each side of the rectangle. In other words, if the outline of the pool on the ground is contained within a 3-

ft. by 5-ft. rectangle and you are planning to have a pool 1 ft. deep, you add twice the depth plus 1½ ft. to each of the dimensions—the 3-ft. dimension of the original rectangle becomes 6½ ft. and the 5-ft. dimension becomes 8½ ft.

After determining the outline of the pool and obtaining the liner, excavate to a depth of 1 ft. or more, sloping the sides toward the center. Be sure to remove stones, sticks, roots and other materials that might cause damage to the liner. After the rough excavation has been completed, tamp all surfaces firmly. Then add 2 in. or 3 in. of damp builder's sand and tamp firmly into place. To avoid the typical swimming pool aqua color in a garden pool, simply use the PVC to expose the reverse side, which is a dull gray-black. This dark bottom will add to the reflecting quality of the water. Be sure, also, to excavate a rim or step at the pool edge so that you can completely conceal the plastic where it emerges above the water level.

After placing the liner in the excavation, fill with water to hold it in place and cut off any excess material on the edges, leaving a flap of about 1 ft. This then can be hidden under rocks and soil in the case of a natural-looking pool or bog, or you can have a more formal coping of stone slabs and concrete blocks set in the sand or soil.

Since no plumbing is involved, a hose will have to be used to add water as needed; and if the pool has to be drained, a bucket and siphon or pump will be necessary.

Be sure not to place sharp stones and other sharp objects in the pool as these could puncture the lining. If a bucket or pot holding a water lily or other plants or objects is desired, place a scrap of the plastic, or some similar material that will keep the hard edges from coming into direct contact with the liner, between the container and the pool bottom.

Clay-lined

A modification of the concrete pool is the pool with a clay bottom. The clay pool is similar to a natural pond in its formation because the bottom is a layer of clay. Spread evenly 2 in. or 3 in. thick and worked into the consistency of a mud pie, it will hold water remarkably well. In regions where clay is obtainable, it has many

9.2 The ancient concept of the oasis—water bubbling from the earth—in a twentieth-century statement. Reich-Versen Landscape Architects. Photo Carlton Lees

advantages as a material for a large pool. No serious injury can come to the clay floor. No forms are required for building, and the actual labor of handling the material in construction is less than for concrete.

Fiberglass

Fiberglass is a light, durable material that is cast to size and shape at the factory and brought to the job in one piece. The floor and walls form a deep bowl with a smooth, curved surface. It is comparatively inexpensive. The excavation of the pit and the setting of the bowl in sand are the only items of construction. It may be fitted with inlet, outlet and overflow, as with any pool, and the joints may be sealed with liquid fiberglass, which hardens.

There are many prefabricated fiberglass pools available in shapes varying from the standard rounds, squares and rectangles to irregular and sometimes ugly "natural" and free-form shapes.

Maintenance

With adequate facilities for maintaining a flow of water through the pool, and for emptying it, care and general upkeep are made easy. An occasional cleaning out of sediment and fallen leaves is practically all that is necessary. In northern regions the concrete pool should be protected from the action of the frost during the winter months. The water should be drained off before the onset of freezing weather, and a few sticks or boards placed in the bottom to absorb the thrust of any small amount of ice that may form after snow has melted.

A concrete pool may be arranged for winter with a water level just a little below normal by placing a few large floating logs in the water. The logs will absorb the thrust from the ice, thus relieving the pressure on the concrete walls. Another device is to build the pool with such sharply sloping sides that when the ice forms, it merely slides up the sides as it expands, and no pressure is transmitted to the structure.

Ways of Reducing Costs

Those who desire a garden pool but are deterred by the apparently high cost of installation may be interested in methods of reducing the costs. Plumbing is a major item. Its need may be eliminated by using the garden hose to fill and empty the pool. Reinforcing rods comprise a big item. They may be omitted if the pool is small and of simple shape.

Emptying a pool with a garden hose is a simple trick, requiring only a place lower than the pool floor within reach of the hose, whence the water may flow off. To start the working of a siphon, place one end of the hose down the slope at this low point. Hold the other end near the edge of the pool and pour water into it out of a watering can. When the water begins to flow out of the lower end of the hose and while still pouring water into the upper end, plunge

9.3 In this patio, the fountain and pool are good to look at and listen to, and also provide a cooling effect as the water evaporates. Photo Carlton Lees

the end of the hose, together with the watering can, into the pool. The flow thus started will continue until the pool is practically empty. The watering can may be removed as soon as the flow from the pool has been established. The flow will continue until the water level reaches the end of the hose.

FOUNTAINS

In centuries past, a fountain was the most finely wrought and most decorative feature of a garden. In dry climates where the presence of water was always highly prized, the fountain symbolized the life-giving power of water. Water was piped to the fountains at great expense and from the fountains it flowed in little canals throughout the garden to irrigate the soil and make possible the growing of the plants.

During the Italian Renaissance the fountain became an elaborate work of art, combining spouting jets of water with architectural and sculptural forms. The Italian noblemen vied with each other in the display of animated water features in their villas. The water was often piped from streams several miles away to supply a series of fountains, which were so arranged that the overflow of one fountain supplied the next fountain on a lower terrace.

The fountain in most American gardens today is a much less complicated feature but is nonetheless important, and it is often the one note of architectural embellishment. The simplest type is the pool fountain with a single stream rising in a vertical jet from the center. The structure of such a fountain consists merely of a brass nozzle on the supply pipe at the water level. An elaboration of this arrangement is a central pedestal supporting a shallow basin, from the rim of which the water drips into the pool. In such a fountain the central jet is sometimes replaced by a sculptured figure. Greater elaboration occasionally takes the form of minor jets of water near the rim. But as in so many other garden elements, simplicity is the keynote of a successful fountain.

The wall fountain as a terminal feature at the end of a garden walkway possesses infinite possibilities for artistic expression. Water coming from a spout or through a trough-shaped stone and falling in a narrow stream to the pool below is one of the most satisfactory arrangements for the inlet.

Since fountains are architectural in character, they may be used either as the dominating motif in a garden or as a mere incidental feature.

10

Tools and Garden Equipment

Gardening is a craft. Good craftsmen have good tools. For the greatest efficiency in all gardening operations, good tools are essential. Not only should gardeners know how to select strong and durable tools that will give good service over a period of many years, but they should also know how to care for tools properly in order to keep them in good condition.

It is a matter of sound economy to buy well-made tools. A good tool differs from a poor one in the materials used in its manufacture and in its type of construction. Good tools are more durable than cheap tools and are usually more efficient. This is particularly true in the case of tools used for cutting purposes, such as lawn mowers, pruning shears, grass shears and hedge trimmers, as they may be sharpened more readily and will retain a better edge.

The most satisfactory spade is that with a metal shank which extends part way up the handle, as this makes for additional strength. The same type of construction is desirable for spading forks and for long-handled shovels. Trowels made from a single sheet of metal stamped into shape are not so strong or so durable as trowels with wooden handles driven into a forged metal shank.

The most satisfactory small hand cultivator for use in flower borders is the weeder with three clawlike prongs that are not rigid. It is capable of doing rapid and efficient work and leaves the soil in excellent tilth. It is also possible to work with it among very small seedling plants. There are a number of other types on the market that are reasonably satisfactory.

The garden hoe has been designed in a great variety of sizes and shapes. A hoe that is too large and heavy is cumbersome and is better fitted for the mixing of cement than for garden work. The 6-in. draw hoe, the 6-in. scuffle hoe and the lightweight pointed hoe are all satisfactory for general garden cultivation. The pointed type is of particular value for opening seed drills in the vegetable garden. If the broad-bladed type of hoe is used, its efficiency will be greatly increased by keeping it well sharpened.

Modern wheelbarrows of metal, or metal and wood, are made in a variety of sizes and designs. They should be carefully chosen for the purpose in mind and the storage space available. With proper care, quality wheelbarrows will last a gardening lifetime.

The garden hose is one of the most indispensable pieces of equipment in any suburban or country place. If a hose of good quality receives good care, it should last for many years, whereas a cheap hose of inferior quality will need to be replaced within a comparatively short time. A one-ply rubber hose has the advantage of being light and is therefore easily handled, and if it is of superior quality, it will give excellent service. A two-ply rubber hose will give longer wear, as it is made for heavy service and has the added advantage that it will not kink, but it is heavy to move from place to place. The light, plastic hose has been a great boon to the gardener and has largely replaced the rubber hose. It is supple and easy to handle, and may be moved from one part of the garden to another with little effort. A good quality plastic hose has a long life of service. Soil soakers are available both in plastic and in canvas and are exceedingly useful where a gentle flow of water that will soak into the ground is desired.

Various new hose attachments have made watering less of a problem for gardeners. The fog nozzle gives a very fine, mistlike spray and is excellent for watering newly sown seedbeds and young seedlings. It is also valuable for syringing the foliage of broad-leaved evergreens and for increasing the humidity for tuberous begonias, achimenes and other plants that thrive best in a moist atmosphere. A hose attachment for applying liquid fertilizers is used by many commercial growers and is another useful piece of equipment for the home gardener. Similar attachments are available for the application of pesticides.

CARE OF TOOLS

Tools should be cleaned immediately after use and before they are returned to their place. It is far easier to remove soil from a spade or hoe when it is still moist than when it is hard and dry and has become encrusted onto the metal. A blunt wooden blade of the type used to mix paint is the most convenient thing to use in removing soil from spades and hoes. If the soil has been allowed to become badly encrusted, it may be removed by rubbing the surface vigorously with a wet cloth or with a rag soaked in kerosene.

When tools are to be put away for the winter, they should first be thoroughly cleaned. Rust can easily be removed with steel wool. A protective coating of wax or grease should then be applied. Ordinary floor wax may be used or almost any type of grease or a light grade of rust-inhibiting oil—a cheap grade of vaseline is excellent, cup grease is entirely satisfactory or lard may be used. It is wise to ensure that such tools as pruning shears, lawn mowers, knives and hoes are sharpened before they are put away so that they are ready for use when the rush of spring work begins.

Sprayers should always be rinsed out after use. In order to keep the leather from drying out, the plunger rod and leather plunger should be oiled at frequent intervals during the spraying season and especially when the sprayer is to be stored for the winter. Before storing, worn washers should be replaced and the hose cleaned with a mild vinegar solution, then rinsed with clear water. During the winter the sprayer should be stored in a dry place. This is particularly important in the case of ungalva-

RECOMMENDED TOOLS AND EQUIPMENT

CUTTING TOOLS	CULTIVATING TOOLS
grass clippers	hand cultivator
hedge trimmers	hand weeder
lawn mower	hoe
lopping shears	rake
pruning saw (hand, pole)	shovel (long, short handle)
pruning shears	spade and spading fork
	trowel

WATERING EQUIPMENT	MISCELLANEOUS
hose	duster
nozzles	lawn fertilizer spreader
oscillating sprinkler	mason's twine
soil soaker	sprayer
watering can	stakes
	wheelbarrow

nized steel sprayers in order to prevent them from rusting.

The lawn fertilizer spreader should be thoroughly cleaned after use, and the wheels should be oiled at the axle to prevent rusting. It should be kept in a dry place. Most fertilizers are very corrosive to metal, and the distributor's period of usefulness will be greatly extended if these simple precautions are followed.

When not in use, a garden hose should be kept on a reel or a mounted fixture in a shaded place. Nothing shortens the life of a hose more rapidly than to allow it to lie out in the sun day after day. When a hose is put away for the winter, care should be taken to see that it is carefully drained.

The lawn mower should be given a thorough cleaning at the end of the season. All grass clippings, dirt and grease should be removed. A steel brush is excellent for this purpose. Any parts that show evidence of rust should be cleaned with steel wool. All exposed metal parts should receive a coating of oil. All bearings should be oiled. In power mowers the oil filter should be cleaned and rinsed in gasoline, and clean oil should be added. All gasoline should be removed from the tank, as it is liable to leave a gummy residue as it evaporates. Run the engine until all the gasoline in the tank, fuel line and carburetor is used up. In order to remove all sediment, drain the crankcase oil while the engine is still warm, and then add fresh oil.

Remove the spark plug and pour 1 oz. of No. 20 grade oil into the cylinder. Cover the cooled mower with a plastic, waterproof cover to protect it from dampness and dust. Similar maintenance should be performed on Rototillers, chain saws and other motorized equipment.

STORAGE FACILITIES

A well-organized toolroom where the tools may be kept in good order and where supplies — spray materials, stakes, labels and other garden accessories — may be kept readily at hand, will be a source of constant satisfaction.

The ideal arrangement is to have a small building specially designed for such a purpose, with racks and hanging space for the tools, shelves and cupboards for supplies, a small potting bench, bins for soil and compost, and floor space for the wheelbarrow and lawn mower. Such a building need not be large: a floor area of 60 sq. ft. to 100 sq. ft. is ample; but it should be conveniently arranged and, although simple in design, should have architectural merit and be in harmony with the style of the house.

As it is not always possible to plan for a separate toolhouse, various compromises may be acceptable. A portion of the garage may be used, the mower being stored in one corner and the tools hung along one of the side walls. The simplest arrangement for hanging the tools is to nail a 2 in. by 4 in. strip on the wall about 4 ft. above the floor and screw into it a half dozen inexpensive spring steel broom holders procurable at any hardware store. All the tools with long handles, such as rakes, hoes, spading fork, etc., can be easily kept in place in this way, the handle of each being slipped into its holder when it is not in use. A piece of pegboard nailed against the wall will provide more flexible facilities, as the small tools as well as the larger ones may be hung on it, and it presents a neat appearance.

When a garage with a gable roof is being constructed, it may be possible, at very little additional expense, to extend the roofline on one side to include a separate area for tools. Such an arrangement can be functional and also quite attractive. In some cases a small projection can be built at the rear of the garage to serve as a storage space for tools.

In providing storage space for supplies, it must be borne in mind that all spray materials should be stored in locked cupboards where children and pets will have no access to them. The importance of this can hardly be overemphasized.

Seeds should be stored in tight metal containers where they will be protected from dampness and from mice. They should be in a cool place where the temperature does not fall below freezing.

Fertilizers that are not to be used within a short time should be stored in large glass jars or plastic containers with tight lids, and should be labeled. If paper or cloth bags are used, the containers will soon disintegrate entirely.

11

The Home Swimming Pool

A home swimming pool that is well designed, carefully built and conscientiously maintained can be a source of endless pleasure for many people. It can also be an investment in healthful, wholesome recreation for the entire family and a contribution to happy living.

The swimming pool first became a feature at country clubs and hotel resorts, and in some cities public pools were built as part of municipal recreational systems. In recent years, however, improvements in the methods of construction—particularly the vinyl-lined, steel-walled method for in-ground pools and the vinyl-lined wood and steel frame technique used for above-ground pools—and the perfection of filter systems have combined to make the swimming pool increasingly popular and affordable. In fact, to a great extent, the swimming pool has refocused attention on the home as a center of social activity and stimulated development of the backyard as a private, enclosed living space.

Besides their comparatively low cost, the great advantage of the vinyl-lined, steel-walled swimming pools over yesterday's cast concrete ones is that both the vinyl and the steel walls are flexible and can withstand the expansion and contraction caused by the freezing and thawing of the water in winter. It is necessary to put one or two logs into a concrete pool before freezing so that the wood may absorb the pressure of the ice; nonetheless, because of the rigidity of concrete, such pools are subject to cracking under severe stress, and leaks frequently occur. The vinyl liner in the newer types of pools can be punctured and may also develop leaks, but most of these can readily be repaired because patches can be applied underwater, thus obviating the necessity of draining the pool.

The decision to build a home swimming pool is one that must be made with full recognition of a number of attendant conditions, especially that of an adequate water supply. In addition, the type of filtration system, the size and location of the pool, the choice of materials and methods, the overall construction costs, maintenance expenses, and finally, the duties and obligations of the owner, all must be carefully considered before a final decision is made.

WATER SUPPLY AND FILTER SYSTEMS

A swimming pool must have clear, pure water. However, even pure water that remains standing will become clouded with algae in a few summer days. In order to overcome this condition, the water must be circulated through a filter. The advantages of the filter system are that the same water can be purified and used constantly while simultaneously maintaining a fairly even temperature.

There are two types of filters: the sand filter and the diatomite filter. The sand filter has been in use for many years and requires that the water be "backwashed," or periodically pumped back through the filter in the opposite direction. Such "backwashing" serves to wash out the impurities by discharging the flow into the drain. The diatomite filter makes use of a fine-grained or diatomaceous earth, which does not require rewashing, but rather holds the impurities in the filter. In this method, the water passes through a series of bags of filter cloth, and the collected material is removed with the filter bags periodically. Because the filter bags expand as the sediment accumulates, long periods of operation are possible before

111

11.1 This deck seems to cantilever outward into space, taking advantage of the hillside placement of the pool. Reich-Versen Landscape Architects. Photo Carlton Lees

changing or cleaning the filter elements becomes necessary. It is therefore an economical system to operate. But the schedule must be faithfully followed.

A regular schedule of vacuuming the pool and of testing and adding chlorine and other chemical purifiers when necessary is a very important part of pool maintenance. The process is simple, however, even when preparing the pool for the winter. If proper procedures have been followed, the water will be clear when the pool cover is removed in the spring, and only the sediment in the bottom need be vacuumed away. Fine mesh covers are now available for winter protection; these are light and easy to use, and seem to work better than the solid vinyl plastic covers.

SIZE AND LOCATION

In general, the size of a pool should be in proportion to the number of people expected to use it. But there is a minimum size, fixed by the natural requirements of safety. For diving there should be a depth of at least 8½ ft. at one end. Standard pools start at 12 ft. by 32 ft. A larger one, 18 ft. by 32 ft., of course, is better and is well worth the extra cost of construction. But a pool 20 ft. or 25 ft. wide and 40 ft. or 50 ft. long is a far more desirable size. For children and beginners there should be a shallow area at one end with the floor sloping from 3 ft. to 4 ft., at which point it should slope steeply down to the deep diving area.

The placement of the pool in the landscape should be very carefully studied. Because the swimming pool is likely to be the most conspicuous element in the home landscape, it should be integrated with other landscape factors. It should be convenient to use, private and enclosed. While in most neighborhoods fencing is required as a safety precaution for both children and adults, the fencing need not be immediately adjacent to the pool, thereby restricting the adjoining spaces. As long as the area containing the pool is adequately fenced and gated according to local codes, it can be either nearby or relatively far away from the pool itself. Since the pool invites active recreation, it is foolish to restrict space around it. Nor need the fence be conspicuous in order to serve its purpose. Even a utilitarian chain-link fence can be made more attractive by the use of climbing vines, or it can be obscured by a hedge.

The best location for a pool is in open sunshine, sheltered from the wind and unencumbered by nearby trees. Falling leaves and twigs can make the task of keeping the water clear all the more difficult; in addition, uninterrupted sunshine is preferred by most swimmers.

It is also wise to place the deep end of the pool away from the major sitting area for three reasons: (1) when small children are present, it is less worrisome to have them close at hand while they are in the pool, and at the nearby shallow end, right by the sitting area; (2) if someone falls into the pool at the shallow end, there is less need for alarm; and (3) the splash made by divers should be away from people who may be sitting and relaxing beside the pool.

Obviously, a swimming pool is a great addition to the garden and to the quality of life for those who enjoy it. However, the obligations of maintenance — not only for appearance but also for health and safety — must be recognized and assiduously adhered to. Once these responsibilities are accepted, however, the pleasure of a pool is immeasurable.

2

PLANT SELECTION
AND
CULTURE

12.1 A shadow-splashed lawn is cooling balm on a hot day. A good lawn is also the basic floor of the garden and is the best of all carpets. Photo Grant Heilman

12

Lawns

When one plants a tree, it is done with the full realization that one may be planting for posterity—that it will increase in dignity as the years pass, and that a century or more hence it may still provide welcome shade for those who linger beneath its branches.

It is difficult to realize, however, that a lawn may be as permanent a planting as the trees that cast their shade upon it. Many of the lawns that surround the beautiful manor houses of England were planted more than 500 years ago, and today the fine quality of this English turf is an inspiration to gardeners throughout the world. There are few achievements that bring more lasting satisfaction to the homeowner than a fine, well-maintained lawn. Such a piece of turf, luxuriant in growth, healthy and weed-free, is the result of intelligent study of the requirements of lawn grasses, careful planning, adequate preparation and the faithful adherence to a program of good management.

In the establishment of a new lawn, there are many factors to be considered: the selection of the grass or mixture of grasses, the preparation of the soil and improvement of its fertility, the time and method of seeding, and the program of subsequent feeding, mowing and general management.

Some grasses thrive best under cool, moist growing conditions, while others will withstand extreme heat and drought. Some grasses require a very high level of soil fertility, other types will grow on relatively poor soils; some will grow well in partial shade, other types prefer full sun; some are suited to withstand heavy traffic and endure hard wear, while others need careful management.

It is therefore important to select a grass or a mixture of grasses that will be well adapted to the climate and will meet one's specific need, whether it be exceptionally fine turf for a terrace or rugged turf upon which strenuous games will be played or a good general purpose lawn for family use and enjoyment.

Before reaching a final decision, it is wise to become familiar with the advantages and disadvantages of the various grasses that are adapted to one's locality.

The quality of the seed is also important. In purchasing grass seed, it is poor economy to buy cheap or "bargain" seed. A lawn should be viewed as a long-term investment, and only the best quality of seed from a reliable source should be considered. Cheap seed will usually be low in germination and is apt to contain a high percentage of chaff and weed seeds or seeds of inferior grasses. State laws require that all grass seeds be labeled and that the following information be available on the tag: percentage of germination, name of each grass and its percentage by weight.

In purchasing grass seed, it is important to note the percentage of germination as stated on the tag. In high-quality seed, the germination percentage should run not lower than 80 percent and preferably 90 percent or higher.

When grass seed mixtures are purchased, it is also important to make certain what type of grasses are included in the mixture and the proportions in which they are used. A mixture that includes a high percentage of grasses, such as Redtop, timothy, Canada bluegrass, sheep fescue and meadow grass, should not be considered, since those species are inferior as lawn grasses. Perennial ryegrass and Redtop are used in mixtures as cover crops while permanent grasses are establishing; they are acceptable in small percentages.

117

IMPORTANT LAWN GRASSES FOR COOL CLIMATES

Bent Grasses

If one does not have to take into consideration the costs of establishment and maintenance, it is possible to achieve a lawn with turf of such supremely fine quality that it will resemble a putting green. It is sometimes possible to develop such a lawn on a small area—a house terrace or a grass panel in the flower garden—where it would not be practical to attempt it on a larger scale. For such a turf, the bent grasses are the most desirable.

Most of the bent grasses are of low-growing, semicreeping habit, and if given proper care, they produce a turf of superior quality and beauty. All of the bents can tolerate considerable soil acidity and thrive best on soils with a pH between 5.5 and 6.5. They do well on moist soils, and since they also are extremely well adapted to close mowing, it is best to keep a bent lawn at a height of ¼ in. to ½ in. The seeds of the bent grasses are very fine, and they should be sown at the rate of not more than 2 lbs. per 1,000 sq. ft.

In general, the bent grasses are much more exacting in their demands than are most of the other lawn grasses. In addition to an adequate program of fertilization, watering and mowing, it is necessary to apply frequent topdressings of rich compost in order to provide ideal conditions for vigorous growth. The bent grasses are also more subject to attacks from various fungus diseases than are most other grasses. It is wise, therefore, not to attempt to develop a bent grass lawn unless one is fully prepared to meet the additional requirements of labor and expense involved.

The three most desirable types of bent grass are Colonial Bent, Creeping Bent and Velvet Bent.

Colonial Bent

This produces an excellent quality of turf. It is not tolerant of shade but will grow on soils that vary widely in type, and it is moderately drought-resistant. It is frequently used as a component of grass seed mixtures and may also be sown alone. A number of strains of Colonial Bent have been developed in various parts of the country to meet specific conditions, the most widely used being Astoria, Highland, New Zealand, Oregon, Penncross and Rhode Island. The Highland strain is often used as a companion grass with Bermuda grass in the coastal areas of California, where it retains its green color throughout much of the winter. It is also recommended as a companion for Merion bluegrass in the north central and eastern states.

Velvet Bent

The true aristocrat among lawn grasses, this is considered one of the most desirable of all the bent grasses. Once well established, it is persistent, vigorous and hardy, and it produces a remarkably fine-textured turf with a velvetlike quality. It is more tolerant of heat than the Creeping Bent, is also more drought-resistant and grows fairly well in light shade. In addition, it has the decided advantage of being more resistant to fungus diseases. Velvet Bent may be grown either from seed or from stolons. It may be grown alone or in mixture with other grasses. As the seed germinates quickly, it does not require a nurse grass when sown alone.

Bluegrass

Kentucky Bluegrass

The majority of homeowners wish to have a lawn of luxuriant green turf that will withstand a reasonable amount of wear and can be easily maintained. If climate and soil conditions are favorable, Kentucky bluegrass will meet these requirements more completely than any other type of grass. There is no other lawn grass that can equal Kentucky bluegrass in its ability to produce a fine dense turf under average conditions of care and maintenance.

However, Kentucky bluegrass has a few very definite requirements for satisfactory growth. It perfers a cool climate, it requires abundant moisture, it thrives best on a mellow, loam soil of good fertility, and it requires a neutral or very slightly acid soil with a pH between 6.0 and

7.0. Kentucky bluegrass is not satisfactory in shady areas, it does not thrive well on sandy, droughty soils or on soils of low fertility, and it is not tolerant of intense midsummer heat. Under such conditions, it soon develops into a thin, unsatisfactory turf and is eventually crowded out by inferior grasses and weeds. Kentucky bluegrass makes luxuriant growth during the cool, moist weather of early spring. It tends to go dormant when temperatures remain above 80° F. for any length of time, and during prolonged periods of summer heat and drought it makes little or no growth, often becoming parched and brown in appearance. However, with the onset of cooler weather it revives and continues growth until late in the autumn.

Kentucky bluegrass germinates more slowly than many other lawn grasses and also requires a longer time to become established. It does not begin to form a dense, springy sod until the second year after sowing.

The results will usually be most satisfactory if Kentucky bluegrass is sown in combination with other good lawn grasses, but it should form 50 percent or more of the seed mixture. It is an extremely long-lived and persistent grass and if conditions are favorable, it eventually will crowd out the other grasses and become completely dominant.

Merion Kentucky Bluegrass

Merion Kentucky bluegrass is the first improved strain of Kentucky bluegrass. This deep-rooting, somewhat creeping strain of bluegrass was observed at the Merion Golf Club in Ardmore, Pennsylvania, by Mr. Joseph Valentine, who noted a small patch of it there in 1936. After watching it closely for a few years, Mr. Valentine sent samples of it to the Green Section of the U.S. Golf Association at Beltsville, Maryland, where it was subsequently developed and tested under the direction of Dr. Fred Grau. Merion Kentucky bluegrass has a wider climatic range than Kentucky bluegrass. It thrives in the more southern sections of the bluegrass region where Kentucky bluegrass is sometimes difficult to maintain, and it also thrives on the West Coast. It does not do well on very light, sandy soils.

Merion Kentucky bluegrass is a deeper green than Kentucky bluegrass, is more spreading in habit of growth and slightly coarser in texture. It has a deep root system and requires a good soil and liberal feeding. It is more drought resistant than Kentucky bluegrass, red fescue or the bent grasses, and will remain green during periods of heat and dry weather when most other grasses are brown and dormant. Merion Kentucky bluegrass does not go dormant in the summer until the temperature reaches the upper 90's. Merion Kentucky bluegrass also retains its green color during the winter better than almost any other grass. It is in active growth every day of the year when the temperature is above freezing. When planted alone, Merion Kentucky bluegrass forms a beautiful, dense turf that is reasonably resistant to wear. When grown under favorable conditions, it will produce a better turf than any other species of grass commonly used for home lawns. In a well-managed Merion Kentucky bluegrass turf, there should be few, if any, weeds.

The seed of Merion Kentucky bluegrass is usually of high quality, but is slow in germination, and even under very favorable conditions it sometimes requires from eight to ten weeks to become established. The usual rate of seeding is considerably lower than for most other grasses, which helps to compensate for the higher cost of the seed. A rate of 1 lb. to 2 lb. per 1,000 sq. ft. is recommended.

Since the advent of Merion Kentucky bluegrass, additional highbred bluegrass strains, such as K 31, Delta, Pennstar and others, have been introduced on the market. Although each has its particular attributes, its color or leaf texture, Merion Kentucky bluegrass is the oldest and most tested variety and probably remains the best Kentucky bluegrass hybrid choice for the homeowner.

When a lawn area is to be seeded with Merion Kentucky bluegrass, the soil must be carefully prepared. A pH of 6.5 to 7 is considered optimum. (For preparation for seeding, see index.) Merion Kentucky bluegrass should be seeded as soon after August 15 as possible. This is earlier than most autumn seedings but is advisable as it will give the young grasses a chance to become established before winter. Seeding may also be done in very early spring, but the results are usually far less satisfactory, and autumn seeding is strongly recommended.

For best results, Merion Kentucky bluegrass should be seeded alone or in combination with some other grass known to be a good companion. It has very slow starting habits, and when it is seeded with an ordinary lawn grass mixture it sometimes fails to get started at all, or is crowded out before the young seedlings become established. The fact that its cultural requirements differ from those of the more common lawn grasses also make such a seeding inadvisable.

On the West Coast an excellent turf that will remain green throughout all or most of the year can be obtained by seeding Merion Kentucky bluegrass and U3 Bermuda grass in combination. It is advisable, however, to use regular applications of fertilizer throughout the autumn months in order to encourage the growth of the Merion Kentucky bluegrass, which is the dominant grass during the winter months while the U 3 Bermuda is dormant.

When attempts are made to seed Merion Kentucky bluegrass in already established turf, the results are apt to be disappointing, although under ideal conditions one may meet with success. The most favorable time for seeding Merion Kentucky bluegrass on established turf is during late winter, from the middle of February to the middle of March, when the soil is undergoing alternate freezing and thawing and is in a honeycomb condition. At this time no coverage is necessary. If an attempt is made to seed Merion Kentucky bluegrass on established turf in the autumn, the existing grass should be cut very close, 1/2 in. or less, and the soil should be thoroughly aerated. Lime and fertilizer should be added before the seed is sown. The seed should be worked into the soil with the back of an iron rake, or with a rough fiber doormat, which may be used as a drag. The soil should be kept moist until germination has taken place and the young seedlings have become established. During this period the existing grass should be kept cut very short. When Merion Kentucky bluegrass is seeded on established turf, it may take two or three years before it begins to take hold and becomes at all evident.

Merion Kentucky bluegrass may also be established by the vegetative method, either sprigs or plugs being planted.

In the management of a Merion Kentucky bluegrass turf, mowing, fertilization and aeration all play important parts. As Merion Kentucky bluegrass thrives on close cutting, the mower should be set to cut at a height of 1/2 to 3/4 in. When a cut higher than 1 in. is maintained, Merion Kentucky bluegrass fails to form a dense, closely knit, weed-free turf. Mowing should begin as soon as it has reached a height where there is anything to cut; the grass should not be mown when wet, however. It must be borne in mind that close mowing is possible only in pure stands of Merion Kentucky bluegrass or when it is in mixture with bent grasses, U3 Bermuda grass or Meyer Zoysia. If a Merion Kentucky bluegrass turf is well fertilized and is mown closely, a dense turf will be formed that will resist the invasion of weeds and weedy grasses.

Merion Kentucky bluegrass requires heavier applications of fertilizer than many other grasses and is particularly dependent on an adequate supply of nitrogen.

It has been found that if too much water is applied to Merion Kentucky bluegrass, it tends to become shallow-rooted and fails to do well. It requires a well-drained soil, rather infrequent watering and a thorough soaking every ten days or so during periods of prolonged dry weather.

It is recommended that Merion Kentucky bluegrass turf be aerated thoroughly in the spring and again in the early autumn. It is not advisable, however, to aerate the turf the first spring following fall planting.

While Merion Kentucky bluegrass is not immune to disease, it is highly resistant to leaf spot, a disease common to Kentucky bluegrass. Rust occasionally appears on Merion Kentucky bluegrass in the autumn but under a system of good management is seldom serious. Merion Kentucky bluegrass possesses high sensitivity to phenylmercury compounds, and their use should be avoided in a program of disease control. As grubs make no distinction between the roots of Merion Kentucky bluegrass and other grasses, the usual precautions should be taken.

Rough-stalk Bluegrass *(Poa trivialis)*

This grass is of value chiefly because it is one of the few lawn grasses that will grow in moist, shady locations. It is light green and forms a reasonably good turf under rather unfavorable conditions. It is often included in shady mixtures.

Fescue

The fescues are among the most adaptable of lawn grasses, and while they do not form a turf of superior quality, they are valuable in specific lawn grass mixtures and for use under certain adverse conditions where better grasses would fail to thrive. The fescues will thrive almost equally well in sun or shade, and when used in a general purpose mixture, they will usually become dominant in the shady areas beneath the trees on the lawn. Fescues are tolerant of both moist and dry conditions, and although appreciative of good fertility, they will grow surprisingly well on soils low in nutrients. A pH between 5.5 and 6.5 best meets their needs, but they will do reasonably well on more acid soils. The fescues are cool climate grasses and will not endure extreme heat well.

The turf formed by the fescues is deep green, dense and fine in texture but somewhat stiff and wiry. However, the very qualities that make it less desirable as a lawn impart to it a ruggedness that makes it of special value on areas subjected to rough usage, such as playing fields and parks, where there is heavy foot traffic. It is also one of the best grasses for dry slopes. The fescues should not be mown closer than 2 in.

Creeping Red Fescue

The improved strains of Creeping Red Fescue are best suited for general use and are included in many all-purpose lawn mixtures. The Illahee and Pennlawn strains are considered two of the most superior in the East; Rainier is popular on the West Coast. Other excellent strains include Penn State Chewings and Trinity.

MIXTURES FOR SPECIFIC PURPOSES IN COOL CLIMATES

GENERAL PURPOSE MIXTURE	PERCENTAGE
Kentucky bluegrass	65
Creeping Red Fescue, Illahee	
or Pennlawn strain	25
Redtop	10
MIXTURE FOR MOIST SHADE	
Chewings Fescue	50
Poa trivialis	40
Kentucky bluegrass	10
MIXTURE FOR DRY SHADE	
Chewings Fescue	70
Colonial Bent	15
Redtop	15
MIXTURES FOR A SUPERIOR TURF	
1. Merion Kentucky bluegrass	100
2. Merion Kentucky bluegrass	65
Pennlawn Fescue	30
Redtop	5

Redtop

Redtop is a comparatively short-lived grass and its chief value is as a nurse grass. It germinates very quickly, within a few days after sowing if conditions are favorable, and gives a newly seeded lawn the appearance of green while the other more slowly germinating grasses are becoming established. It is fine-textured when young but somewhat coarse when mature. When used in a mixture, it disappears as soon as the superior grasses have formed a good sod. The proportion of Redtop in a general purpose lawn mixture should not exceed 10 percent.

Zoysia

The improved strain of Zoysia, known as Meyer Zoysia, is one of the most valuable lawn grasses in the South. Zoysia has been grown successfully in Massachusetts, New York, Pennsylvania, Michigan, Iowa, Nebraska and Colorado, but it should be stressed that it turns brown with the first heavy frost and does not become green again until the warm days of spring. During the winter, in the North, the mat-brown is conspicuous and emphasizes the fact that the bluegrasses remain green all winter. For full cultural requirements of Zoysia, see the index.

IMPORTANT LAWN GRASSES FOR MILD AND DRY CLIMATES

Bermuda Grass

Bermuda grass is one of the most widely used lawn grasses throughout the southern states and in the Southwest. It possesses many admirable qualities but also has very definite limitations. It is tolerant of intense summer heat and of drought conditions, it is comparatively free from pests and diseases, it is resistant to wear, and, if well managed, makes an excellent and attractive turf with good summer color. Its chief disadvantages are that it is an extremely invasive grass and can become a serious pest in flower beds and the vegetable garden unless restrained; it does not thrive in shady areas; and in most areas where it is grown, it turns a dead-looking brown during the winter months.

Bermuda grass may be propagated either by seed sown at the rate of 1 lb. per 1,000 sq. ft. or by planting sprigs or plugs of sod. It makes the best turf when mowed very closely, being kept at almost putting-green height, not over 3/8 of an inch. At this height, it has less tendency to mat badly. If permitted to grow too tall before it is cut, the turf loses its green color and remains brown until new growth occurs.

Liberal feeding is required for best results. Two feedings of a good complete fertilizer, at the rate of 20 lbs. per 1,000 sq. ft., should be given, one in the early spring and another in the early autumn; and additional nitrogen should be applied during the early summer. The urea-form type will give a slow release of nitrogen over a long period.

During periods of prolonged dry weather Bermuda grass should be watered thoroughly every week or ten days. Several improved strains of Bermuda grass have been developed. Ormond and Tifton 57 are two that are popular in the Gulf states and will make a very satisfactory lawn under average conditions.

U3 Bermuda grass is a very superior strain developed in Savannah, Georgia. It is a fine-textured grass and produces an excellent, tight, velvety turf. The seed germinates quickly and makes rapid growth, forming a fairly good turf six weeks or more after sowing. U3 Bermuda grass is very hardy and will survive zero temperatures; it can therefore be grown further north than any of the other strains. Like common Bermuda grass, it turns brown during the winter months but retains its green color for a longer period. On the West Coast it produces a year-round green turf when grown in combination with Merion Kentucky bluegrass.

U3 Bermuda grass requires very close mowing and liberal feeding for best results.

Buffalograss

Buffalograss (*Bouteloua curtipendula*) is one of the best grasses for the dry-land regions of the West. Few grasses can endure the difficult conditions found in these areas, but this native of the Great Plains will make a very satisfactory lawn if given good care. It is very adaptable, able to withstand extremes of heat and cold, and it has the ability to endure long periods of drought, growing vigorously under very adverse conditions. It is low-growing and produces a dense turf, a soft gray-green in color.

Buffalograss may be seeded in the spring at the rate of 1 lb. per 1,000 sq. ft., or it may be established vegetatively through the use of sod. The plugs should be set out during late spring 1 ft. to 1 1/2 ft. apart. The soil should be well prepared and moist at the time of planting and should be kept well watered until the plugs have become established. Once established, the lawn will require no watering and little or no mowing. Its chief drawback is that it does not green until warm weather, a fact that limits its applications.

St. Augustine Grass

St. Augustine grass is adapted only to frost-free areas and therefore is used extensively for lawns in Florida and the Gulf states. It thrives in either sun or shade, requiring abundant moisture and moderate fertility. The turf is coarse and, under good management, retains its deep green color throughout the year. It requires little mowing. St. Augustine sod does not withstand heavy wear. Since seed is not available, it must be planted vegetatively with plugs or sprigs.

Zoysia

The Zoysia grasses, natives of Japan and Korea, are among the most valuable of all lawn grasses throughout the South.

An improved strain of the common *Zoysia japonica* has been developed through the cooperative efforts of the U.S. Golf Association Green Section and the U.S. Department of Agriculture. This superior, fine-textured strain is known as Meyer (Z-52) Zoysia, and is gaining rapid popularity as a desirable lawn grass. Another excellent strain, introduced under the name 'Emerald,' has been developed by the Georgia Improvement Association.

Meyer Zoysia produces a firm, resilient turf with a pleasing texture and color, closely resembling a Kentucky bluegrass sod. A Zoysia lawn is durable and very resistant to wear when it is in active growth. Grown under favorable conditions, Meyer Zoysia forms a very dense turf and has the ability to crowd out summer weeds and undesirable grasses.

Meyer Zoysia will grow on soils of almost any type, thriving equally well on very sandy soils and rather heavy clay soils. Exceptionally well adapted to sandy soils, it is widely used in coastal areas. It is also more tolerant of low soil fertility than most grasses. However, if a turf of superior quality is desired, regular and liberal applications of a high nitrogen fertilizer must be made.

Meyer Zoysia is deep-rooted and extremely drought-resistant. It is primarily a warm climate grass, being tolerant of extreme heat, and it thrives best during the heat of midsummer. In Florida, Meyer Zoysia remains green during the entire year, and throughout the lower South it retains its green color during much of the year.

Meyer Zoysia must be grown vegetatively. Either plugs of sod or sprigs, consisting of roots and stolons with no soil, may be used. Plug-planting is preferred. Meyer Zoysia is some-times rather slow to establish itself and may take several years to cover an area. If 2-in. plugs are used, planted 12 in. apart each way, a good solid turf may usually be obtained within two years. Plugs are removed from a pure stand of Meyer Zoysia sod with a simple tool designed for this purpose and with the same tool are plugged into a freshly prepared lawn area or into an existing lawn. Plugs may be purchased from a nursery, and, for reasonably small areas, the cost is not excessive. A homeowner may obtain a few packages of them and establish his own turf nursery, upon which he can later draw. Most nursery plugs measure about 2 in. in diameter. The plugs should be pressed firmly into the soil and should be kept watered until established, one or two soakings usually being sufficient except in very hot, dry weather. Plugs should be set from 6 in. to 12 in. apart, usually being planted on 12-in. centers. Plug-planting may be done at any time when the ground is not frozen or is not baked hard by drought.

Sprig-planting is a simple process but is suited only to newly prepared lawn areas. If sprigs are planted on established turf, the competition of the other grasses will be too great, and such a procedure is seldom successful. Plugs can be divided into sprigs having two to three joints each. The sprigs should be spaced from 2 in. to 3 in. apart and pressed firmly into the soil. They should be only partially covered, with as much leaf growth left exposed as possible. The soil should be kept moist until the young sprigs have taken root. Sprigs may be planted at any time from spring to midsummer.

Meyer Zoysia grows rather slowly and therefore requires mowing at less frequent intervals than most grasses. It forms the best quality of turf when a 1/2-in. to 3/4-in. cut is maintained. When it is cut too high, it develops more slowly and produces an inferior turf that will permit the encroachment of weeds and undesirable grasses.

Since Meyer Zoysia makes its most active growth in midsummer, it requires its fertilization at this time. If luxuriant growth is desired, three applications during late spring and early summer are recommended.

Meyer Zoysia seems to be unaffected by turf insects and the various diseases that affect other lawn grasses.

Zoysia matrella, **var.** *Emerald*

This is an excellent type of Zoysia grass that is particularly well adapted to the deep South. It is fast-growing, fine in texture, deep green and makes an attractive turf. It is also tolerant of shade. Under favorable conditions it becomes established rapidly and is one of the best varieties for use in the Gulf states. It may also be grown successfully further north.

LAWN GRASS SUBSTITUTES

There are numerous low-growing plants that are sometimes classed as lawn grass substitutes, but many of these plants actually belong in the category of ground covers. In order to justify its use as a lawn grass substitute, a plant should be of extremely low growth, should have the general appearance of a green lawn and should have some of the same attributes that the lawn grasses possess. In order to function as a lawn, it should be able to withstand at least a moderate amount of tramping and use, it should maintain a pleasing green color throughout the major portion of the year, it should not be unduly expensive to establish, and its maintenance requirements should be moderate.

If one prefers to grow a ground cover *instead* of having a lawn, there is a wide choice of material available. (See Chapter 16 on ground covers.)

The following plants meet the requirements of a lawn grass substitute reasonably well, although each has its special limitations.

Anthemis nobilis (chamomile)

A low-growing herb of dense, compact growth, with finely cut foliage, it thrives in full sun, prefers a light, well-drained soil and is particularly well adapted to planting on sunny slopes where it is difficult to maintain a satisfactory stand of grass. It retains its beautiful green color throughout the year. It will withstand moderate use but is not well suited to areas that are subjected to constant wear, as under such conditions it has a tendency to become shabby and die out, leaving bare, brown patches that

require renovation. Its appearance will be improved if it is cut and rolled once or twice a year.

Arenaria verna **var.** *caespitosa* (Irish moss)

Irish moss is a mosslike plant of dense, compact growth. Its color is a pleasing shade of bright green, and it bears tiny white flowers during the summer. It is very hardy, prefers partial shade but will also grow in full sun, and requires a moist, friable soil well supplied with organic matter. It withstands some trampling and does not usually require any clipping. It has a tendency to become humpy, but this may be controlled by occasional thinning out. Plants may be obtained from nurseries and should be spaced 6 in. apart. It is best suited for small areas in partial shade where a bright green carpet is desired.

Dichondra carolinensis (*D. repens,* **lawn leaf**)

This is one of the most widely grown and most satisfactory of the lawn grass substitutes, its chief limitation being its lack of hardiness. It suffers serious damage at temperatures below 20° F. and is killed by a hard freeze. However, young self-sown seedlings sometimes replace the plants that have been killed. *Dichondra* is a very low, spreading, matlike plant with small rounded or heart-shaped leaves. It thrives in sun or partial shade, is as tolerant of traffic and wear as most lawn grasses and has a pleasing appearance. It prefers a moist but well-drained fertile soil and can tolerate both acid and alkaline conditions. It withstands intense summer heat well, provided it has plenty of moisture. Weeds are often a problem until it has become established. It may be readily grown from seed, or plants may be obtained from nurseries. In areas where root-knot nematodes are prevalent, seeding is preferable, as there is danger of introducing the nematodes with purchased plants. Mowing is not necessary, but an occasional clipping will improve the appearance of the turf and will prevent bunching up.

Dichondra is well suited to the milder areas in

California and to the Gulf Coast and the middle South.

Lippia canescens (L. repens)

This low-growing, matlike plant will withstand extreme heat and thrives under desert conditions. The foliage is grayish in tone, and tiny, pinkish-lilac flowers are borne during the summer. The plants appear shabby and dead-looking for about two months in the winter. It is tolerant of any type of soil, is highly drought-resistant and grows well in either sun or shade. No mowing is necessary unless growth becomes too vigorous. It withstands hard wear well. New areas are established by setting out young plants in the spring 4 in. to 6 in. apart. There is some danger of the plants spreading to other areas and becoming difficult to eradicate.

PREPARATION OF THE SOIL

It is a far easier task to improve the condition of the soil before planting a lawn than it is to improve either its texture or fertility afterward. So the importance of adequate soil preparation before the seed is sown can hardly be overemphasized. The establishment of proper grades, the need for more adequate drainage, the physical texture and fertility of the soil and the degree of soil acidity must all be taken into consideration.

If grading is to be done, the topsoil should be carefully removed; and after the grading has been completed, it should be replaced. This procedure will increase the cost of the grading but will prove to be a matter of sound economy in the end. (See the instructions on grading in Chapter 3.)

Unless the area to be seeded possesses low spots that are apt to be soggy at some seasons of the year, underdrainage will not be necessary. Frequently, such low spots can be improved with proper grading, but if this is not possible, they may be effectively drained with agricultural tile. The trenches being from 15 in. to 24 in. deep and approximately 20 ft. apart, there

should be a fall of at least 3 in. in every 50 ft. The tile should be laid end to end and the joints covered with strips of tar paper in order to keep the soil out of the tile.

Organic Matter

The physical texture of the soil plays a major role in establishing a fine turf. It may be improved to a very marked degree by the addition of organic matter. Most soils, with the exception of woodland and prairie soils, are deficient in humus. Soils with a marked deficiency of organic matter present very serious problems as they are low in water-holding capacity, are poorly aerated, become too readily compacted, tend to be less fertile and, in general, provide a very poor medium for the healthy, vigorous growth of lawn grasses. It is an accepted fact that practically all of our better lawn grasses thrive best on a soil that is well supplied with organic matter.

Organic matter may be supplied in the form of well-rotted manure, spent mushroom soil, compost, cover crops, raw native peat and the commercial peat moss. Manure has the disadvantage of introducing weed seeds into the lawn area, and in many communities it is not readily available at a reasonable price. The great point in its favor is that it increases the fertility of the soil as well as adding organic matter. If it is applied several months before planting, the weed seeds will germinate and can be controlled by cultivation before the grass seed is sown. Spent mushroom soil is a mixture of rotted manure and soil that is particularly valuable in improving the texture of sandy and shaly soils. In areas of the country where mushrooms. are grown commercially, such soil is readily available at a reasonable price and is one of the most satisfactory forms in which organic matter can be supplied. Good garden compost is similar to mushroom soil and is also an excellent source of organic matter. If it is possible to plan the program of work well in advance and to devote several months to the preparation of the soil, one or more cover crops may be grown and the organic content of the soil increased in this way with comparatively little expense. When a new home is being built, it is frequently possible to do this in the course of construction. The following cover crops are recommended.

Fall sowing: Per acre, 1 bushel rye and 1 peck winter vetch; per 1,000 sq. ft., $1\frac{1}{2}$ qt. rye and $\frac{1}{2}$ pt. vetch. Sow in September or early October. Plow or spade the crop under in the spring when it has attained a height of 12 in.

Early spring sowing: Per acre, 2 bushels oats and 1 peck Canada field peas; per 1,000 sq. ft., $1\frac{1}{2}$ qt. oats and $\frac{1}{2}$ pt. Canada field peas. Sow as early in the spring as possible and plow or spade under about the middle of June.

Late spring sowing: Per acre, 1 bushel soybeans, 1 peck of millet; per 1,000 sq. ft., 1 qt. soybeans, 1 cup of millet. Sow between the middle of May and the middle of June. Inoculate the soybeans before planting in order to gain the full benefit of their nitrogen-fixing abilities. Plow or spade under at least one month before the time of lawn seeding.

Peat moss should always be thoroughly moistened before it is applied to the soil. If applied dry, it may actually do more harm than good, as it will take up the moisture from the soil. On areas where grass is to be sown, it should never be allowed to remain as a layer on the surface of the soil. It should always be thoroughly worked into the upper few inches of topsoil.

The rate of application of organic matter will depend on the character of the soil. Light, sandy soils will require liberal applications so that they may become more retentive of moisture. Soils of a dense, heavy texture will also be greatly improved and the drainage of the surface water facilitated if liberal quantities are applied. Manure should be applied at the rate of 1,000 lb. to 1,500 lb. per 1,000 sq. ft. of lawn area, or 20 tons to 30 tons per acre. Peat moss should be applied at the rate of 4 bales per 1,000 sq. ft. of lawn area, or approximately 170 bales per acre. Native moist peat should be applied at the rate of 2 cu. yd. per 1,000 sq. ft. of area, 86 yd. per acre.

In whatever form it is applied, it is essential that the organic matter be thoroughly incorporated with the upper 5 in. or 6 in. of topsoil. The organic matter, particularly when applied in the form of peat moss, should never be allowed to form a definite layer, either upon the surface of the soil or below, as such a layer has a very undesirable effect on plant growth. The organic matter should be thoroughly plowed, forked or spaded into the upper 5 in. or 6 in. of topsoil. A Rototiller is excellent for this purpose and leaves the soil in fine tilth.

Fertilizers

The fertility of the soil is one of the most important factors in establishing a new lawn. It is a widely accepted premise that all of our most desirable lawn grasses require a soil of fairly high fertility if they are to produce a fine quality of turf. It is well, therefore, to see that adequate nutrients are supplied before planting. The application of a well-balanced complete fertilizer will usually give the most satisfactory results, the amount required depending upon the natural fertility of the soil. On soils of medium fertility an application of 15 lb. to 20 lb. per 1,000 sq. ft. will usually be sufficient, or approximately 650 lb. to 700 lb. per acre. On soils of low fertility the application should be increased to 25 lb. to 30 lb. per 1,000 sq. ft. or 1,000 lb. to 1,200 lb. per acre. (For soil tests and fertilizers, see index.)

Soil Acidity

The majority of our better lawn grasses prefer an almost neutral or very slightly acid soil. A few types, such as the bent grasses and the fescues, while tolerant of rather strong soil acidity, will also make healthy growth on soils that are more nearly neutral. For practically all types of desirable lawn grasses, it is therefore advisable to have an acidity that does not fall below a pH value of 5.5 and that preferably ranges between pH 6 and pH 7. Soil tests should be made to determine the existing degree of acidity. If the tests show that the soil is too acid, the condition may be readily corrected by an adequate application of lime.

Lime may be applied in the form of hydrated

lime or ground limestone, but hydrated lime is more rapid in its action. One pound of a good-quality hydrated lime is equal in value to 1½ lb. of ground limestone. When the application is made, it is important that the lime be distributed uniformly over the surface of the soil and worked lightly into the upper few inches of topsoil. The lime will move downward in the soil but not laterally and, therefore, any soil areas not directly covered by the lime will receive no benefit from the application. There are various mechanisms on the market for the distribution of lime, but on very small areas where the use of machinery is not justified, one of the most satisfactory methods is to place the hydrated lime in a coarse, loosely woven burlap bag and to drag it back and forth over the area. If one prefers, the bag may be held a few inches above the soil and the lime shaken out onto the surface.

The importance of applying lime at the time the seedbed is prepared can hardly be overstressed. If applications are delayed until after the sod has become established, it will require several years to correct any marked degree of acidity entirely, whereas this condition may be rapidly and thoroughly overcome if an adequate application is made at the time of planting.

The rate of application will depend entirely on the degree of soil acidity. On soils of extremely high acidity it is advisable to make several applications, as the heavy liming of strongly acid soils is detrimental to normal plant growth. This extreme condition would be met only very occasionally. Soils testing over pH 6 will require no application of lime. Soils testing between pH 5 and pH 6 should receive an application of 50 lb. of hydrated lime or 75 lb. of finely ground limestone per 1,000 sq. ft., or 1 ton of hydrated lime per acre or 1½ tons of ground limestone. Soils testing between pH 4 and pH 5 or below should receive two or more applications, the total amount varying from 60 lb. to 145 lb. per 1,000 sq. ft. of hydrated lime, or 2¼ tons to 3 tons per acre. Only in very extreme cases would as much as 145 lb. per 1,000 sq. ft. be necessary. In general, sandy soils of a given degree of acidity require lighter applications of lime than do heavy clay soils of the same pH value. Applications should therefore be slightly adjusted to meet the various soil types. Not more than 50 lb. or 60 lb. of hydrated lime or its equivalent in ground limestone should be applied at one time to 1,000 sq. ft. If heavier applications are necessary, the amount should be divided. It must be borne in mind that lime not only corrects conditions of soil acidity but serves other functions as well. It helps to improve the physical structure of the soil, and consequently increases its water-absorbing capacity, and it also provides both calcium and magnesium, which are essential elements for normal plant growth.

Preparation of the Seedbed

After the organic matter, fertilizer and lime have been thoroughly incorporated with the soil, the seedbed may be prepared for planting. On large areas this is done with the use of spike tooth and drag harrows and a smoothing board. On small areas it may be easily accomplished with an iron hand rake. The surface should be reasonably firm and absolutely even, with no hollows or small depressions.

Lawns for Poor Soils

In establishing a lawn on soil that is definitely low in fertility and cannot be immediately improved to a point where it will be able to support the better types of lawn grasses, it is wise to use some of the varieties that are less exacting in their demands. The fescues are the most satisfactory grasses for this purpose, as they thrive on poor, sandy soils, are tolerant of acidity, will endure considerable shade and will withstand long periods of drought. The leaves of the fescues are tough and wirelike, and in habit of growth the plants are low and inclined to be bunchy. It is advisable, therefore, to sow the fescues in mixture with other grasses in order to obtain a better quality of turf. Of the many varieties, Chewings Fescue and True Creeping Red Fescue are the most desirable for lawn purposes. The seeds of the fescues lose their vitality rapidly, and as a poor percentage of germination is frequently achieved, it is necessary to make rather heavy seedings. For a lawn on poor, sandy soil or on extremely acid soil, the following mixture is recommended:

	PERCENTAGE
Chewings Red Fescue	40
Fine-textured Kentucky bluegrass	40
Ryegrass	20

Lawns for Shady Areas

For shady areas it is necessary to choose grasses that are tolerant of such conditions. It must be borne in mind that all grasses require some sunlight for satisfactory growth, and if the shade is too dense, it is well to resort to some evergreen ground cover rather than to attempt to produce a lawn. A careful program of pruning will frequently mitigate the density of the shade sufficiently to make it possible to grow lawn grasses under large trees. If the pruning program is carried out over several years, it may be done without injuring the form or beauty of the trees. The program consists of gradually removing the lower branches of the trees so that the morning and afternoon sun may reach the grass. The tree will put on additional growth at the top to compensate for what has been cut away and will continue to maintain its natural form. Two ft. or 3 ft. of the lower branches may be cut away entirely each year, and at the end of five years, the foliage level will have been raised as much as 10 ft.

Temporary Lawns

It occasionally happens that one desires to plant a purely temporary lawn. If one moves into a new home late in the spring, it would be folly to attempt to plant a permanent lawn at a season of the year when it is most difficult for the better types of lawn grasses to establish themselves, and under such conditions it is wise to resort to temporary measures. Within a few brief weeks it is possible to obtain a rich and almost luxuriant growth of turf if the correct type of seed is used. Either the perennial ryegrass or the domestic ryegrass should be selected for this purpose. The growth is somewhat coarse and rank, but at least the grass will form a welcome covering of green on ground that might otherwise be bare. Before planting, a complete fertilizer (6−8−4 analysis) should be worked into the soil at the rate of 10 lb. per 1,000 sq. ft. in order to stimulate growth. The seed should be sown at the rate of 6 lb. per 1,000 sq. ft. The soil should be kept moist until the seed has germinated, and the grass should be mown when it has reached a height of 2 in. This temporary grass may be plowed or spaded under when the time approaches to prepare the seedbed for the permanent lawn, and it will benefit the soil by adding a small amount of organic matter.

SEEDING

Time of Sowing Grass Seed

The one point on which all authorities seem to agree is that the most desirable time for sowing lawn grasses is in late August or early September. If it is not possible to do the work at this season, seed may be sown in *early* spring. Late spring and summer sowings are not recommended except in the case of purely temporary lawns. Early autumn sowing has several advantages over spring sowing. Practically all of the lawn grasses make their best growth during cool, moist weather and the autumn months usually provide very favorable conditions for good germination of the seed and for the sturdy, vigorous growth of the young grass. There is comparatively little competition from weeds at this season of the year and by the following summer the autumn-sown turf should be so well established that it will not suffer seriously from drought or other adversities.

Method of Sowing

In sowing grass seed, the chief aim is to provide for an even distribution of seed over the lawn area. The seed may be sown by hand or with a hand-operated seeder, or with a mechanical seeder mounted on wheels.

For small areas, sowing may be done very sat-

RATE OF SEEDING

The quantity of seed required will depend upon the type of grass seed or the mixture used.

TYPE OF GRASS	SEED REQUIRED PER 1,000 SQ. FT.
bent grasses	2 lb.
Bermuda grass	1 lb.
Kentucky bluegrass	4 lb.
Merion Kentucky bluegrass	1 – 2 lb.
fescues	3 – 6 lb. (the heavier seeding on dry, sandy soil)
Poa trivialis	3 lb.
General Purpose Mixture (for cool climates)	4 lb.

isfactorily by hand if care is taken to get an even distribution. Hand sowing should be done on a calm day when there is little or no wind, as it is otherwise impossible to make an even sowing. It is wise to divide the quantity of seed in half and to sow in two directions, walking first north and south and the second time east and west, thus covering the area twice.

Seeding with a hand-operated seeder is much more rapid than sowing by hand and a fairly accurate distribution can usually be obtained. The most approved method, however, is to sow the seed with a mechanical distributor. Such a machine represents a small investment, but as it can also be used for the annual applications of fertilizer, its purchase is often justified even for lawns of moderate size. Such a machine can be adjusted to sow the seed at the desired rate.

After it has been sown, the seed should be raked into the soil *very* lightly with an iron rake, being covered by not more than 1/8 in. It is very important not to cover it too deeply, as poor germination will result. After the raking, the area should be lightly rolled to establish good contact between seed and soil.

From the time of sowing until the grass seed is well up, the area should be kept moist. Water should be applied in the form of a fine, mistlike spray. A fog nozzle is ideal for this purpose. A heavy spray will tend to cause a crust to form on the surface of the soil that may seriously interfere with germination.

Mowing New Grass

Young, newly sown grass (with the exception of the bent grasses, Bermuda grass and Merion Kentucky bluegrass) should not be cut until the grass has reached a height of 2 in. The mower blades should be carefully set so that the final cut will not be closer than 1 1/2 in. If young grass is mown too closely, it will prevent the formation of a vigorous root system and will seriously injure the quality of the turf.

Sodding New Areas

Undoubtedly, the most rapid method of establishing turf is sodding. It consists of cutting strips of sod from an existing lawn, laying them carefully together on the new area and encouraging the grass roots to reestablish themselves in the soil. Under certain conditions this method may be preferable to starting grass from seed or stolons, because it has the advantage of being so quickly accomplished that there will be no opportunity for a hard rain to wash away the soil and ruin the surface of newly prepared ground. On banks or steep slopes this is an advantage.

Turf selected for cutting and transplanting should be well-established grass growing in open ground and free from crabgrass and weeds. The best source is a lawn grown from seed and composed of a mixture, bluegrass predominating over Redtop and fescue, with little or no clover.

Pastures that have been well cared for also provide an excellent source of good sod.

Sodding should be done when there will be at least four or five weeks of good growing weather before the onset of either winter or summer. Unless the roots become established well enough to supply moisture and nourishment, warm growing weather before the beginning of winter frosts will kill the grass altogether.

When purchasing sod, it is very important to make sure it is of good quality.

Before cutting sod, the area should be mown closely. The edges of the sod strips are then cut by a rotary blade or a spade held in a vertical position. The sod is thus divided by these vertical cuts into strips 12 in. or 15 in. wide and 10 ft. or more long. If the job is a small one, cutting sod into squares may be more convenient. A specially built sod spade with its handle at an angle with the blade is forced under the sod, cutting off the lower roots and lifting up a mat of upper roots about 1½ in. thick. The strips are then rolled up and loaded onto a truck or wheelbarrow. It is important to keep the edges of the strips straight, parallel and at a uniform distance apart. To facilitate this, a wide plank is laid on the sod with its edge at the last cut, and the new cut is made along the opposite side. This regularity will simplify the task of laying the sod.

The ground on which the sod is to be laid must be graded to an even surface, cultivated, raked and rolled, and any irregularities smoothed out. The turf is then laid, the strip being unrolled into place, firmed with blows of the back of the spade. Any irregularities caused by an uneven thickness of the sod should be adjusted at this time by rolling back the strip, and filling or cutting the soil below as required. This is the part of the work in which skill and patience are important and which will make the difference between an uneven turf and a smooth one. After rolling with a hand roller, the whole area should be watered until it is thoroughly soaked; it should not be allowed to dry out until it has become well established.

Commercial sod farms have been established in virtually all large metropolitan areas, and the process is now highly mechanized and competitive. Sodding has become an increasingly attractive alternative for both the homeowner and the commercial and industrial developer.

MAINTENANCE OF EXISTING LAWNS

It is advisable for every homeowner to work out a careful program of lawn maintenance and to adhere faithfully to the schedule. The majority of the lawns in this country suffer sadly from neglect. After a lawn is once established, the owner is all too apt to assume that the only subsequent care required is that of periodic mowing. Under such conditions of neglect, how-

ever, it does not take many years for a good lawn to deteriorate into a poor lawn. The fertility of the soil becomes gradually depleted to the point where it can no longer support the better types of lawn grasses, and the inferior grasses consequently become more and more dominant; the soil becomes increasingly more acid in its reaction and therefore more impervious to water; the lawn becomes less resistant to injury from drought and from insect attacks; and weeds gradually creep in and will, in time, almost entirely crowd out the grasses. It is therefore a matter of sound economy to follow a carefully planned program of lawn maintenance.

Rolling

The question of lawn rolling is a much-debated one, on which authorities fail to agree. It is undoubtedly true that rolling has been much overdone in the past, and the present consensus seems to be in favor of one or two light rollings in the spring. Rolling should not be done until all possibility of alternate thawing and freezing is past. It should be done when the soil is moderately moist—never when it is soggy. Too frequent rolling is apt to cause an undesirable compaction of the soil, which tends to interfere with the normal, thrifty growth of the turf. This danger is much greater on heavy soils than on soils or a more sandy character. A water-ballast roller is the most desirable type for lawn use, as the weight may be adjusted to meet varying conditions. The roller should be just heavy enough to press the crowns back into the soil without making the soil unduly compact.

Fertilization

The maintenance of soil fertility is one of the major considerations in any program of lawn management. All of our most desirable lawn grasses require a soil of reasonably good fertility for satisfactory development. It is wiser, and better economy, to maintain this fertility from year to year by periodic applications of commercial fertilizers and composts than it is to allow the soil to become depleted.

The three most important elements of fertility needed by lawn grasses for satisfactory growth are nitrogen, phosphorus and potash. Nitrogen produces a vigorous growth of leaves and stems; phosphorus is needed for good root development; and potash is valuable in promoting general vigor and resistance to disease. A complete commercial fertilizer contains these three essential elements. The true value of a commercial fertilizer, however, depends not only on the actual content of plant food but also on the form in which the nutrients are supplied. This point is of particular importance when fertilizing lawn grasses.

Nitrogen may be supplied in the form of ammonia compounds, nitrate compounds, urea-formaldehyde compounds and organic compounds. Ammonia compounds, such as sulphate of ammonia, are quickly available after application. When used year after year, sulphate of ammonia will tend to increase the acidity of the soil appreciably, but this may be overcome by sufficient application of lime. Nitrate compounds, such as nitrate of soda, are also quickly available and do not tend to increase the soil acidity. They are, therefore, preferred for use on soils that are strongly acid or for grasses that require a nearly neutral soil. The urea-formaldehyde compounds, known as urea-form fertilizers, release nitrogen very slowly over a period of many months. This is one of the best forms in which to supply nitrogen to lawn grasses, as there is no danger of burning and the nitrogen needs of the plants for the entire season can be supplied with one application—a matter of considerable importance in managing large areas of turf. The various organic forms of nitrogen, such as cottonseed meal, soybean meal, dried blood, tankage, fish meal and sludge, decompose slowly and are not active in releasing plant nutrients except under conditions of warmth and moisture. Although they may be applied in early spring, they supply very little nitrogen until the beginning of summer. If organic nitrogen is derived from but one source, it may cause delayed nitrogen burn when it is released during a period of hot, dry weather. Therefore, organic fertilizers applied to lawns should supply nitrogen from a number of sources so that it will be released over a period of time, thus avoiding the danger of delayed nitrogen burn. In general, the organic compounds are more

valuable for use on sandy soils than on heavy, clay soils, since they are not lost through leaching as are some of the more readily available inorganic forms.

Phosphorus is usually supplied in the form of superphosphate; it is an important ingredient of a complete lawn fertilizer.

Potash is commonly supplied in the form of muriate of potash, and is included in all complete fertilizer mixtures for turf areas.

Even distribution of the fertilizer is essential, as areas not covered will receive little or no direct benefit from the application.

If fertilizers are used in the dry form, they should be applied with a fertilizer distributor that can be adjusted to apply the material at the desired rate and that will make possible an even coverage. This is an essential piece of equipment for the establishment and maintenance of a good lawn and if well cared for, it should last for many years.

Fertilizer in the dry form should always be applied when the grass is dry in order to avoid the danger of burning the leaves.

Planning a Fertilization Program

Soil tests: The kind of fertilizer that should be applied and the amount required can be most accurately determined by soil tests. The advisability of having such tests made can hardly be overemphasized. Unless this is done, one is working in the dark. A reliable soil test will indicate whether or not an application of lime is needed, and the amount required to obtain the desired pH can be readily figured (see page 564). Whether or not a deficiency of nitrogen, phosphorus, potash or any of the minor elements exists can also be accurately determined, and a fertilizer program can be worked out that will best meet specific needs.

Most state colleges and state universities offer a Soil Testing Service. In some states this service is free to residents of the state, while in other states there is a nominal charge.

Requirements of a good lawn fertilizer: A good lawn fertilizer should contain the essential elements of fertility—nitrogen, phosphorus and potash in the correct proportions. In general, a ratio of 2:1:1 (2 parts nitrogen to 1 part phosphorus and 1 part potash) will best meet the needs of the average lawn. A fertilizer with an analysis of 10−5−5 (10 parts nitrogen, 5 parts phosphorus and 5 parts potash) is an example of a 2:1:1 ratio. If a heavier application of phosphorus than of potash is needed, a ratio in which the sum of the phosphorus and potash equals the amount of the nitrogen may be used, such as a 10−6−4 analysis. Adjustments of these ratios may be made very readily if indicated as advisable by soil tests. However, they form a good basis on which to develop a program.

In addition to the above requirements, a good lawn fertilizer should contain nitrogen in several forms, derived from both quickly available and slowly available sources. The most favorable ration is 1 to 3, 1 part from quickly soluble sources and 3 parts from slowly available sources. This makes it possible to avoid having more nitrogen available than is needed shortly after an application of fertilizer followed by a deficiency of nitrogen later in the season. And it also makes it possible to reduce the number of applications required per season.

Rate of application: The rate of application will depend upon the analysis of the fertilizer used, the fertility requirements of the soil as indicated by soil tests, the kind of grasses that compose the turf and, to some extent, upon the structure of the soil.

Without the benefit of soil tests, only very general recommendations can be made. The amount of fertilizer to apply can best be figured on the basis of the actual nitrogen required, the level of fertility and the type of grass being taken into consideration.

The amount of fertilizer that must be applied per 1,000 sq. ft. in order to supply 1 lb. of nitrogen may be obtained by dividing 100 by the percentage of nitrogen contained in the fertilizer.

Analysis of fertilizer 5−10−5; $100 \div 5 = 20$

Therefore, it would require 20 lb. of a 5−10−5 fertilizer to supply 1 lb. of nitrogen per 1,000 sq. ft.

Analysis of fertilizer 10−5−5; $100 \div 10 = 10$

Therefore, it would require 10 lb. of a 10−5−5 fertilizer to supply 1 lb. of nitrogen per 1,000 sq. ft.

A fertilization program may be worked out for any type of grass, on soils of varying fertility, and with fertilizers of varied analyses if this procedure is followed and the proper ratio maintained.

RATE OF APPLICATION CHART

GENERAL RECOMMENDATIONS

KIND OF GRASS	SOIL FERTILITY	LB. OF NITROGEN REQUIRED PER 1,000 SQ. FT. PER YEAR	LB. OF FERTILIZER TO APPLY PER YEAR PER 1,000 SQ. FT. ANALYSIS 10−5−5 OR 10−6−4
Kentucky Bluegrass	high	2 to 3 lb.	20 to 30 lb.
predominating in	medium	3 to 5 lb.	30 to 50 lb.
the mixture	low	5 to 6 lb.	50 to 60 lb.
Merion Kentucky	high	3 to 4 lb.	30 to 40 lb.
Bluegrass	medium	4 to 5 lb.	40 to 50 lb.
sown alone	low	6 to 6½ lb.	60 to 65 lb.
Fescues	high	1 to 1½ lb.	10 to 15 lb.
predominating in	medium	1½ to 2 lb.	15 to 20 lb.
the mixture	low	2½ to 3 lb.	25 to 30 lb.
Bermuda Grass	high	1½ to 2 lb.	15 to 20 lb.
	medium	3 to 4 lb.	30 to 40 lb.
	low	4½ to 5 lb.	45 to 50 lb.
Zoysia Grass	high	1½ to 2 lb.	15 to 20 lb.
	medium	2 to 3 lb.	20 to 30 lb.
	low	3 to 4½ lb.	30 to 45 lb.

Time of application: The time of application will depend on the type of grass, the fertility of the soil and the kind of fertilizer used.

Bluegrass mixtures: On soils of high fertility, one application in the autumn (late August to mid-October) will be sufficient, provided the fertilizer contains ⅔ of its nitrogen in a slowly available form, such as ureaform. On soils of low fertility, it is advisable to make two applications of fertilizer of this type—two-thirds of the total amount in the autumn and one-third in late spring. If the fertilizer used does not contain slowly available forms of nitrogen, three applications should be made, the first very early in the spring, the second in early May and the third in early autumn.

Bermuda grass: First application should be made in early spring, second application in early autumn. Additional application of nitrogen should be made in early summer if the need is indicated.

Zoysia grass: First application should be made in early spring, second in late spring or early summer.

Fescue mixtures: Same program as for bluegrass.

Topdressing

One method of supplying additional fertility to lawn areas and of improving the texture of the soil is through the use of topdressings. Topdressings in the form of rich topsoil, compost or spent mushroom soil are widely used on many golf courses to keep the putting greens, which are composed largely of bent grasses, in the best possible condition.

In using topsoil and compost for this purpose, it is extremely important that it be free of weed seeds. It is a disheartening experience to go to the labor and expense of applying a topdressing only to find that one has introduced new weeds into the lawn area. It is, however, possible to destroy the weed seeds in the soil before it is spread so that there will be no danger of having this occur. The chemicals most satisfactory for this purpose are calcium cyanamide and Vapam.

The topdressing, which may be applied at any time during the growing season, should be spread as a thin layer over the surface of the lawn and worked into the turf with the back of an iron rake.

Liming

In order to promote a vigorous, healthy growth of the lawn grasses, the soil reaction should be kept as nearly neutral as possible. While it is true that the bent grasses and the fescues are decidedly tolerant of acid soil, they will grow better on more nearly neutral soils.

Normally, grasses produce a new crop of roots each year. The old roots die, adding humus to the soil. On extremely acid soil, however, these old roots fail to decay, and the soil tends to become seriously sod-bound.

Another point in favor of maintaining a neutral soil reaction is the fact that on highly acid soils the grasses are unable to use nitrogen in the form of ammonium compounds. Under such conditions the grass apparently absorbs the nitrogen but cannot assimilate it, and a toxic reaction occurs. It is also a well-known fact that when soils become highly acid, something happens to the structure of the soil itself, and it gradually becomes less and less permeable to water. An adequate application of lime, therefore, not only overcomes the acidity of the soil but also improves the soil structure and increases its water-absorbing capacity, as well as supplying small quantities of plant food in the form of calcium and magnesium.

If soil tests indicate a degree of acidity below a pH of 6, an application of lime should be made, either in the form of hydrated lime or of finely ground limestone. The most favorable seasons for applying lime are autumn, winter and very early spring, when the alternate freezing and thawing of the ground will enable the lime to penetrate more deeply into the soil. It may, however, be applied at any season of the year. Lime is slow in its reaction and no appreciable benefits will be noticed until five or six months after the application has been made. However, the eventual beneficial effects of lime are of long duration and will be apparent for several years. Unless the soil is intensely acid, which occurs infrequently, an application of lime once every two or three years will be sufficient to maintain the correct soil reaction. (For the rate of application, refer to the table on page 565.)

Mowing

The height at which a lawn should be maintained depends on the type of grass or grasses that compose the turf. Some grasses thrive best, and present the most attractive appearance, when they are cut very close, while other grasses must be maintained at a greater height in order to produce a healthy, vigorous turf.

	HEIGHT AFTER MOWING
bent grasses	1/4 to 1/2 in.
Bermuda grass	3/16 to 3/8 in.
fescues	1 1/4 to 2 in.
Kentucky bluegrass	1 1/4 to 2 in.
Merion Kentucky bluegrass	1 1/4 to 2 in.
Zoysia	1/2 to 3/4 in.

The lawn mower should be checked periodically and adjusted whenever necessary. In order to adjust a mower to cut at a given height, set the roller on the back of the mower so that the bedknife (the long flat blade against which the blades on the revolving reel cut) is at the desired height.

Frequent, wisely regulated mowing tends to produce a fine-textured turf, as new leaf growth is stimulated. If a lawn is neglected and the grass is allowed to become too tall before it is cut, the results are unfortunate, as growth becomes coarse and tough and the leaves lose their healthy deep green color. This is particularly true in the case of Bermuda grass.

Extremely early mowing should be avoided on lawns that are predominantly Kentucky bluegrass, as the root system is entirely renewed each spring, and if the grass is closely mown early in the season there will be a decided reduction in root development. The quality of the turf will suffer considerably, and the grass will be less able to withstand the vicissitudes of summer droughts. To ensure vigorous root growth, the first spring mowing should not be done until the grass has reached a height of 2 in.

Under normal conditions the grass clippings should be allowed to remain on the lawn, thus helping to maintain the humus supply in the soil. If, because of a long period of wet weather or for some other unavoidable cause, the grass has become unusually long and rank in growth, the clippings will have a tendency to form a mat on the surface of the newly mown lawn and will have a detrimental effect on the growth of the turf. If the clippings are heavy, they should be raked up with a light bamboo rake and removed. Of course, if the lawn mower is equipped with a grass catcher, the necessity of raking will be eliminated.

In selecting lawn mowers of the motor type, it is advisable to avoid those that are equipped with heavy rollers, as they have a tendency to make the soil too compact. The danger of soil compaction is far greater on heavy soils than on light, sandy soils.

Reel-type or rotary mowers are equally acceptable for use on most home lawns. A small lawn can often be mowed easily with a nonmotorized reel mower. Power mowers may have either reel or rotary blades, the reel-type providing a somewhat finer cut. The advantage of the rotary mower is that it can handle taller grass; but it is also the cause of frequent and serious injuries. Rotary mowers should *not* be used by anyone inexperienced, particularly children. These mowers are also very much more noisy and are more likely to throw stones and other objects. Although all rotary models have power-driven blades, they are available either as the push-type or self-propelled, the choice depending upon the size and terrain of the lawn. Estate lawns may require riding mowers, and the choice then widens to include flail-type and sickle-bar mowers. The flail cuts tall grass fairly well, and is safer than a rotary mower; the sickle-bar is suitable only for rough areas, such as roadsides, meadow edges, fence rows or infrequently maintained lawns.

Aeration

Many soils tend to become very compact and therefore detrimental to the growth of turf. Clay and clay-loam soils are more subject to compaction than are soils of other types, but even sandy soils may become somewhat compact and crusted on the surface.

On lawns that are too compact, water fails to penetrate into the soil and there is apt to be considerable surface runoff. Grasses on such soils tend to become shallow-rooted, and the turf suffers seriously in time of drought. When fertilizers are applied, they often fail to penetrate to the lower root levels where they are most needed, and the grasses also suffer from a lack of oxygen since sufficient air cannot enter the soil.

Adequate aeration of lawn areas therefore serves many functions. It reduces surface runoff and, by permitting water to percolate down into the soil, encourages deeper and more vigorous roots. It makes it possible for fertilizers to penetrate to a depth where the roots can readily make use of the nutrients, and provides for a better circulation of air in the soil, thus lessening the danger of oxygen starvation.

Aeration is usually done at the time when fertilizer is applied in the spring, and again in the early autumn.

Many tools are suitable for the aeration of lawn areas. The simplest is an ordinary garden fork, practical only on very small lawns as it is laborious to use. The fork should be inserted into the turf at a 45° angle to a depth of 4 in. to 6 in., and a slight downward pressure should be exerted on the handle before it is withdrawn. This procedure should be repeated at distances of 1 ft. A fork especially designed for this purpose, known as an Aeri-fork, is also available. Another simple method is to drive spikes, several inches apart, through a board. The board is then placed on the turf, and by walking along it the spikes will be driven into the ground. This procedure is repeated over the area and is effective but it is practicable only on very small lawns. Flat wooden sandals with spikes on the bottom strapped onto the feet can perform much the same function. For larger lawn areas there are numerous excellent spike-disc tools on the market that can be pushed along like a hand lawn mower. For extensive park and golf areas, power-driven machines are available.

Watering

Watering a lawn must be done with intelligence and discretion, otherwise more harm than good may result, A thorough watering once a week during dry weather is of far greater value than daily sprinklings. Frequent light waterings tend to make the plants shallow-rooted and consequently less vigorous, and by keeping the surface constantly moist ideal conditions are provided for the growth and spread of fungus diseases, the germination of weed seeds and the spread of crabgrass.

The water should be applied in the form of a fine, mistlike spray that will fall gently and evenly on the surface. If an ordinary garden hose is used, a fog nozzle should be attached rather than the usual type. Perforated hoses are excellent for supplying water to small areas as they deliver small, mistlike jets of water and can be easily shifted from one section to another. The oscillating type of sprinkler is also very satisfactory, as it applies water evenly and slowly.

It is important not to apply water faster than the soil can absorb it, nor in the form of a coarse, heavy spray, as the surface then becomes so thoroughly saturated that normal percolation is hindered. For the grass roots to derive the fullest benefit, the water should penetrate to a depth of at least 4 in. to 6 in.

Subirrigation Systems

Before the introduction of plastic piping, an irrigation system for the lawn was seldom within the range of the small homeowner, due to the high cost not only of materials but also of installation. Today, however, there are a number of excellent products on the market that are moderate in price and may be installed by the "do-it-yourself" method.

Polyethylene plastic pipe has many advantages over the various types of metal pipe. It is light, pliable and easy to handle; it will not rust, rot or corrode; it does not need to be buried in a deep trench, as it will not freeze and crack; and it contains no substances that are toxic to plants.

Most of these products are equipped with noncorrosive brass fittings, and the sprinkler heads are set flush with the turf so that they will not interfere with the mowing of the lawn. These are suited to both low- and high-pressure water systems, and they are obtainable in various sizes, covering from 1,000 sq. ft. upward. The sprinkler heads deliver a fine spray similar to a gentle rainfall.

Since most lawn grasses are very dependent on an adequate supply of moisture to maintain an active, vigorous growth, it is a tremendous advantage to be able to supply water *when* it is needed; although an irrigation system involves an initial outlay, it may be considered as a permanent investment, and the cost is relatively small when spread over a period of years.

Renovation of Old Lawns

The renovation of old lawns presents special problems. If, through neglect, a lawn has become shabby, and if the better grasses have been crowded out by grasses of inferior quality and encroaching weeds, it is important to determine how far this deterioration has progressed. If it is evident that the existing sod still contains a fair proportion of good grasses, much may be accomplished by initiating a good program of fertilization, careful mowing, watering and weed control. In all probability the lack of adherence to such a program was the cause of deterioration in the first place.

If, however, the weeds and inferior grasses have become so dominant that they have almost entirely crowded out the good lawn grasses, more drastic measures will have to be taken and the entire area should be prepared for reseeding. This may be done in a number of ways. If the area is small, it may be spaded or forked over by hand and a good seedbed prepared. If it is a comparatively large area, a Rototiller or some similar implement may be used, which will leave the soil in excellent tilth. In most communities such work may be done on the custom basis.

CONTROL OF LAWN PESTS

Precaution: As is true of insecticides, the chemicals used for the control of lawn pests are poisonous and must be handled with care. Special care should be taken not to inhale the dusts or the wettable powders, and not to let the materials come into contact with the skin as, in some cases, there is danger of absorption.

Chlordane, DDT and other chlorinated hydrocarbons are no longer available for home use. The salts of heavy metals, such as arsenic and lead, are environmentally damaging and are becoming less prevalent for general use. As active research is conducted on alternative controls, more substitutes will become available.

Chinch Bug (Hairy Chinch Bug)

Identification

The adults are about 1/8 in. in length. The body is black, with short, white wings. The young nymphs are very small, bright red with a white crossband. As they mature, they become brownish, then black. Upon close examination both the adults and the young nymphs may be seen, in infested areas, at the base of the stems near the crown.

Injury

The young nymphs feed at the base of the grass blades, sucking the juices from the plants. The turf becomes brown and irregular, somewhat circular, and dead patches are formed. The margin is usually a sickly yellow and it is in this area that the young nymphs may be found feeding. The injury from chinch bugs is differentiated from injury caused by beetle grubs in that the infested grass cannot be rolled back like a piece of carpet.

Life History

The adults usually winter in tall grasses and weeds. In the spring they migrate to the lawn and the females lay their eggs at the grass roots. The eggs hatch during June and the young nymphs begin feeding on the turf. They pass through several molts before becoming adults. A second brood, which is often more damaging than the first, appears in August, and the nymphs and adults continue to feed until well into October.

Control

There are several chemicals that will give excellent control. When dusts are applied, they should be worked well into the turf with the back of an iron rake.

The first application of the chemical should be made in June. If there is still evidence of infestation, a second application should be made in August. Close cutting and a topdressing of fertilizer following treatment will aid the recovery of the injured turf.

Grubs

There are numerous grubs that cause severe damage to lawns. Among them are the grubs of the Asiatic beetle, the European lawn chafer, the Japanese beetle, the May beetle or June bug, the Oriental beetle, and the southern masked chafer.

Identification

The grubs are whitish, with dark, yellowish-brown heads and three pairs of legs. They vary in size from $\frac{1}{4}$ in. to $1\frac{1}{2}$ in. in length.

Injury

The grubs feed upon the roots of the grasses. If they are present in great numbers, they seriously injure the growth of the turf; and if measures of control are not taken, they may kill the grass entirely. Badly infested turf appears brown and dead and can be rolled back like a carpet.

By cutting out a square foot of sod to a depth of 3 in. to 4 in. and examining it, one may readily determine whether it is seriously infested with grubs. The presence of five to ten grubs would indicate light infestation, but enough to warrant treatment. A count of thirty to fifty would indicate very heavy infestation.

Life History

The adult beetles lay their eggs in the green turf or under the grass roots during the summer months. The grubs hatch and begin feeding on the roots immediately. During the winter they move downward in the soil to a depth that will protect them from freezing, moving upward again in the spring, where they feed once more prior to passing into the pupa stage. Some types, such as the May beetle, require two years to complete their life cycle.

Control

Grubs can be completely controlled through the use of chemical insecticides. These may be applied at any time of the year except when the ground is frozen. Application during April and early May is recommended. One application of some chemicals will provide effective control for a period of three to five years. All grub-proofing insecticides should be watered in with a heavy spray as soon as possible after application in order to become immediately effective and to lessen the danger of harm to birds and pets.

Moles

Moles often cause severe damage to lawns. As beetle grubs are one of their chief sources of food, the best measure of control is to deprive moles of their food supply in the lawn area by eradicating the grubs.

Sod Webworm (Lawn Moth)

The sod webworms are most prevalent on bent grass and bluegrass lawns, and are more damaging in warm climates than in the North. There are a number of species that cause damage to lawns.

Identification

Although the adult moths and the caterpillars differ somewhat in appearance, according to the species, they all have certain common characteristics. The small moths are usually seen at dusk, flying low over the grass where the eggs are dropped. The small, thick-bodied caterpillars, from $\frac{1}{4}$ to $\frac{3}{4}$ in. in length, make silk-lined tunnels between the grass blades near the ground.

Injury

When young, the caterpillars skeletonize the grass blades while feeding; but as they mature, they chew off the blades, causing the lawn to become ragged in appearance. If the infestation is heavy and measures of control are not taken, large areas of turf may be killed out.

LAWN DISEASES

Brownpatch

Brownpatch is a fungus disease caused by *Rhizoctonia solani*. Many species of lawn grasses are affected, the bent grasses being particularly susceptible to injury. Some soils seem to be comparatively free from the fungus causing brownpatch, while other soils are badly infected. The disease is particularly prevalent during long periods of hot, humid weather. An excessive supply of nitrogen, overwatering, poor drainage conditions and high soil acidity are contributing factors in the spread of the disease.

When the turf first becomes affected, it turns a very dark green in color, then gradually becomes a light brown, having the appearance of dead, dried grass. The patches are somewhat circular in outline although very irregular, and they vary in size from a diameter of a few inches to a diameter of several feet.

There are a number of preventive measures that should be followed to lessen the occurrence of brownpatch.

1. Excessive applications of quickly available fertilizers high in nitrogen should be avoided.

2. Watering should be done in the morning to avoid having the grass wet during the night.

3. Good air circulation should be provided for the lawn area, even if it means sacrificing some trees and shrubs.

4. Adequate drainage should be provided for low areas.

Under ordinary conditions it is the practice to treat a lawn for brownpatch only upon the appearance of the disease. However, in sections where it is very prevalent, periodic treatments are advised.

Leaf Spots

The various leaf spots, which cause the diseases commonly known as melting-out and going-out, seriously damage lawns in some areas of the country. Kentucky, Canada and annual bluegrasses are particularly susceptible; Merion Kentucky bluegrass, on the other hand, is highly resistant.

Going-out disease, sometimes called Foot rot, occurs in the spring from March through May and occasionally reoccurs in the autumn. The leaves attacked by the fungus shrivel, the crowns turn brown and the rhizomes and roots rot away. Large areas of turf may become affected unless control measures are undertaken.

Copper Spot

This fungus disease sometimes appears on bent grass lawns after a prolonged rainy spell during the late spring or summer months. Upon close observation salmon-pink spores may be seen on the grass blades.

Dollarspot

This is a form of brownpatch, causing small, circular patches hardly more than 2 in. in diameter. The patches are of a somewhat lighter color than those typical of brownpatch.

Fading-out or Black Mold *(Curvularia)*

A fungus disease that usually occurs on bent grasses, the fescues and annual bluegrass. Velvet Bent is particularly susceptible.

The injury is most severe during the heat of midsummer, but the disease may also appear in late spring or early autumn. Lawns affected with the fungus develop a yellowish-green dappled appearance, similar in some respects to iron chlorosis, and the grass eventually dies out. Upon examination under a lens, a black mold may be observed on affected blades.

Snow Mold (Winter Scald)

When the last of a heavy snow has melted, patches of turf may be found that are covered with a grayish-white or pinkish mold. This is caused by a fungus that thrives at low temperatures, and serious damage to the turf may occur. Low areas are particularly susceptible to attack.

Overfertilizing and overwatering are prime causes of disease, and a healthy, well-cared-for turf is the best insurance against such hazards. If fungicides must be used, a number of products are currently available, among them Acitidione, DuPont 1991, Daconil, etc. As with pesticides, fungicides must be applied specifically and carefully. The mercury compounds formerly used so widely are no longer available because of environmental restrictions.

CONTROL OF LAWN WEEDS

On areas where a sound program of turf management is faithfully carried out, there will be comparatively little trouble with weeds. Vigorous, rapidly growing grass is capable of crowding out many of the existing weeds and also of preventing new weeds from gaining a foothold. Many excellent lawns that are virtually free from weeds have been established and are maintained solely through the application of the fundamental practices of good lawn management.

If, however, these practices have been neglected, and if a lawn area has become badly infested with weeds, very definite measures of weed eradication should be adopted, along with a general improvement in the management program for the lawn.

On very small areas weeding by hand produces excellent results. It is of vital importance, however, that the weeds be removed before seed has formed. After the weeding has been completed all bare areas should be prepared for reseeding in accordance with the general principles involved in the seeding of new lawns.

While weeding by hand may be practical on small areas or where the infestation is very light, it is not feasible for large areas, as it is far too tedious and costly a method. On large areas effective weed control may best be obtained through the use of various chemicals. Within recent years a great deal of research has been completed by the various experimental stations on the chemical control of weeds, and it has been proved conclusively that practically all of our common lawn weeds can be entirely eradicated by the proper and timely use of various chemicals. The factors contributing to the success of this method are: the selection of the chemical most effective for the control of each particular weed or group of weeds; the method and time of application; the rate of application; and the subsequent method of revitalizing the turf.

Most lawn weeds may be divided into three classes according to their general habit of growth. It has been found that for each of these groups, some one method of chemical control will give the best results. It is, therefore, important to select the chemical most effective for the particular type of weed to be eradicated.

Weedy Grasses

Crabgrass

Of the weedlike grasses that infest lawn areas, crabgrass is by far the most troublesome. In order to eradicate it or to keep it under control, it is well to know something of its habit of growth. Crabgrass is a tender annual, thriving in full sun and unable to endure shade. The seed germinates late in the spring, and the plants grow slowly during early summer. They then develop rapidly in late July and August, reseed prolifically, and are killed by the first light frost. In controlling crabgrass, we have three points of attack: to hand-weed the young plants if the area is small; to provide for such a luxuriant growth of the better lawn grasses and to maintain the lawn at a sufficient height (1½ in.) so that the young crabgrass seedlings cannot gain a foothold; or to use some chemical measure of control, which will either kill the crabgrass or prevent it from reseeding.

Preemergence weedkillers (available under various trade names) have been used with varying success on lawns. The purpose is to prevent germination of crabgrass seed and to kill small seedling plants before they have had time to make any growth. As crabgrass seeds continue to germinate over a period of six weeks or more, from mid-spring to early summer, two to four applications are necessary. In some instances the preemergence materials have given excellent control, while in others they have been less satisfactory. The manufacturer's instructions should be followed carefully.

Mat-forming Weeds

In this group we find several weeds that are sometimes very troublesome on lawns.

Chickweed

Both the common chickweed (*Stellaria media*) and the mouse-ear chickweed (*Cerastium* spp.) may be controlled by spraying with potassium cyanate. Control is most effective when the application is made during moderately warm weather. If spraying is undertaken during the cooler months, it should be done on a warm, sunny day and hot water should be used when mixing the spray.

Potassium cyanate is also recommended as a control for crabgrass and it is effective against chickweed, veronica, knotweed and goosegrass as well. It possesses the additional advantages of having very low toxicity to human beings and to animals, and of having some fertilizing value. When potassium cyanate comes into contact with the soil, it is rapidly broken down into potash and nitrogen. Two or three applications are recommended, the first early in July, the last by mid-August. On large areas applications may be made with a power sprayer, while on small areas a hand sprayer may be used very satisfactorily. Applications of potassium cyanate should be made only when lawn grasses are making active, vigorous growth, Under such conditions there will be little injury to most lawn grasses other than a slight and very temporary discoloration of the tips. However, if application is made during periods of extreme heat, or when growth is stunted because of drought, severe injury may result. Bent grasses are susceptible to injury and potassium cyanate is not recommended for use on bent grass lawns. Potassium cyanate may be combined with 2,4–D, but when this is done there is greater danger of injury to the turf.

Rosette-forming Weeds

Dandelion

Control may be obtained by spraying with 2,4–D, one of the hormone weedkillers (available under various trade names). Applications are most effective when made in the spring shortly before the plants come into full bloom, or in the autumn from mid-October to early November. Results are not as satisfactory from applications made in late spring or during the summer. If the infestation is light, spot treatment may be done; but if the infestation is heavy, it will be advisable to treat the entire lawn area.

2,4–D may be used either as a spray or in the dry form, being applied with a fertilizer distributor.

See precautions under Plantain (below) on use of 2,4–D on lawn areas.

Plantain

Both the broad-leaved plantain and the narrow-leaved plantain, or buckhorn, may be effectively controlled by treatment with 2,4–D. Applications are most effective when made during the spring or early summer. When the infestation is light, spot treatment may be done; but if the lawn is heavily infested, the entire area should be treated.

2,4–D may be used either as a spray or in dry form, applied with a fertilizer distributor.

Precautions: Most lawn grasses are extremely resistant to the effects of 2,4–D and will show practically no injury if it is applied at the prescribed rate. It will, however, definitely depress the growth of bent grasses and clover, and in some cases they will be seriously injured or killed.

Young seedling grasses of all species will be seriously injured or killed out entirely by an application of 2,4–D. A new lawn should not be sprayed until it has been mown at least twice and the plants have begun to form a crown. The same precautions should be observed in cases where an established lawn has been seeded with a superior grass, such as Merion Kentucky bluegrass.

When applying 2,4–D on lawns, precautions must be taken to prevent the material from drifting onto other areas, as many flowering plants, vegetables, trees and shrubs are very susceptible to 2,4–D and serious injury may occur. Applications should be made on a day when there is little or no wind.

A sprayer used for 2,4–D should be used for no other purpose with the exception of the hormone sprays.

Garlic

In many sections of the country garlic has become a serious weed pest on lawns. It is particularly unsightly in the early spring and gives a lawn a very unkempt and shabby appearance. Mowing is not effective, as it is only a temporary measure and the garlic will reappear the following spring more vigorously than before. The most effective means of eradication is to spray with the ester form of 2,4–D. Complete eradication requires a three-year spraying program. This is necessary because of the nature of the growth of the garlic plant, which consists of the mother bulb, the young bulbs clustered about the mother bulb and the tiny bulblets. If one year in the three-year spraying schedule is missed, it will start the cycle again. Best results will be obtained when spraying is done during January, February or March. Later sprayings are much less effective, since it becomes more difficult to kill the plants as they reach maturity.

13

Trees

Ever since the dawn of civilization, the forest and its products have affected the economics as well as the aesthetics of human life. A love and respect of trees has been characteristic of mankind since the beginning of human evolution. Instinctively, we understood the importance of trees to our lives long before we were able to ascribe reasons for our dependence on them. Today, the importance of trees in our welfare and happiness is a commonplace fact of daily life and one that is almost universally understood. And in today's urban and suburban world, we remind ourselves of our primeval link with trees—as well as their physical and aesthetic value—by sheltering our homes whenever possible with the benevolent shade and symbolic strength of trees.

Trees are grown for many purposes. They may be grown for the sheer beauty of their form, foliage or flowers. They may be grown to provide shelter from the wind or to provide shade. They may be grown for the production of fruits, nuts, timber, wood pulp, sugar or turpentine. And in addition to these many uses, trees fulfill other important functions. Though some trees must be considered weeds or pests, the beneficial trees far outnumber the less worthy ones.

In a landscape composition the trees native to a region are usually to be preferred to exotic trees that would be alien to the immediate surroundings. In New England and the northern states, for example, the American elm, sugar maple, white oak and white pine are typical trees dominant in the landscape, and their use in plantings in these areas is appropriate and satisfying. On the other hand, on the coastal plains where spruce trees are not native, Norway spruces and blue spruces will always look artificial and out of place.

This does not mean that foreign trees should not be used, but rather that they should be used with discretion. As a matter of fact, in formal designs there is no such restriction. But if a naturalistic scene is desired, then the trees selected should either be native or have an appearance similar to native trees. For instance, the Chinese scholar tree (*Sophora japonica*), though it comes from the Orient, blends agreeably with the foliage of native deciduous trees and will be pleasing as a specimen flowering tree or as a member of a grove. But *Sciadopitys verticillata*, the umbrella pine, another Oriental, being unlike anything we have in this country, would seem an intrusion if placed in a naturalistic setting.

Trees are a very important element in landscape composition and are used for various purposes in design. Groups of them may form the masses in the design as contrast to an open area. Many trees together make a background for the structure and for the more intimate details of the design. Individual trees may serve as accents in the overall design or as incidental notes of the picturesque. By their shapes, trees express line as well as mass in the composition. Thus the famous group of cypresses at Villa Falconieri in Italy gives dominant vertical line to the composition. The windswept Monterey cypresses of California make dramatic horizontal lines against the sky and sea.

Many trees produce showy or conspicuous flowers in profusion, thus giving the garden picture greater scale and variety and more richness of color. Still others are adorned with ornamental fruit, or with a foliage that turns a glorious color in autumn, while some trees have picturesque branching forms that are particularly interesting in winter.

Trees, especially ornamental trees, should be

considered as a long-time though continuous crop. The mature trees immediately surrounding a house will eventually become aged and subject to decay, and homeowners with forethought will plant young trees to take their place, long before the old trees start to deteriorate. In this way the general form of the original landscape design will be maintained, although individual members of the group may change. Seedling trees frequently come up in places where they are not wanted. If these are not removed while young, they may spoil the appearance of the hedge or shrub border or rob the soil in the flower bed.

In planting new trees, their eventual dimensions should be considered. Otherwise, within a few years, the inevitable crowding will occur, to the detriment alike of the overall design and each of the individual trees. It is sometimes hard to cut down trees we enjoy. It is an advantage to plant woodland trees closely because young trees benefit by mutual protection. But although a young forest thus started may be thinned out later, there is no justification for crowding specimen lawn trees.

Sometimes it is a great advantage to transplant semimature trees and to place them where they are most needed. This shortens the waiting period. But in most cases, especially when the cost of investment must be considered, smaller trees are better. On the other hand, it is a great mistake for an owner to postpone planting trees for several years. The money invested in small trees during the first year on a new property will greatly enhance the property's value. In addition, the trees themselves will increase in value, and a $25 tree may be worth $100 after only six years of growing.

SELECTION OF TREES

When selecting trees for one's property, there are many points to be considered in addition to the basic question of the size of the tree at maturity. Other factors of equal importance are the tree's hardiness in the climate; its resistance to wind; its adaptability to soil conditions; its habits and rapidity of growth; its production of flowers or fruit; and its undesirable habits—such as shedding bark or poisonous fruit. All these points should be taken into account.

If selection is being made for ornamental reasons, those trees that have outstanding beauty during several seasons of the year should be given preference, especially if the property is a small one. Trees form the backbone of any garden and we must live with them for fifty-two weeks of the year, not just the brief period they are in flower. A tree that produces a good display of blossoms in spring, displays ornamental fruits in autumn, shows good autumnal leaf color and presents a pleasing growth habit in winter is thus far more desirable than one that merely blossoms well in the spring and has no outstanding features throughout the rest of the year.

From a list of fairly dependable trees, a great variety may be selected for a large property, so that together they will produce bloom over a period from April to August, followed by a succession of ornamental fruit and rich autumn coloration. There are trees that are suitable for all purposes and for unusual growing conditions. There are trees for wet soil, dry gravelly soil, city atmosphere, wind, heat, and drought, while there are others that for one reason or another are not dependable or satisfactory at all.

Trees for the small property should be chosen particularly carefully. Few features enhance the surroundings of a home more than the flowering trees. And, fortunately, many of our most beautiful flowering trees are not large and are therefore well adapted to planting on the small property, as they will not outgrow the restrictions of the site. There are many to choose from: the lovely star magnolia, which greets the spring with its display of delicate white flowers; the dogwoods, with their wealth of ivory-tinted bloom and their picturesque, horizontal branches extending outward in rhythmic waves; the lovely silverbell tree, hung with a myriad white bells in May; the flowering crabs and cherries, with their deep pink buds and their profusion of bloom; the snowbell tree from Japan, with its dainty, pendent bells that open early in the summer after the flowering period of most of the other trees has passed; and the sourwood, which in autumn brings to the small suburban home a touch of woodland glory, for there are few trees that have a more beautiful fall coloring or retain their leaves over so long a period. In addition to these, there are many other flowering trees from which selections may be made.

There are also a number of small trees that do not bear conspicuous flowers but, because of their picturesque form or other desirable characteristics, deserve to be considered. In this group are the English maple and the white birches. The English maple is a sturdy, compact tree and offers to children welcome opportunities for climbing and for building tree houses among its branches. A clump of white birches on the edge of the lawn area is always aesthetically pleasing, and when a planting of primroses and early spring bulbs is grouped beneath their branches, it makes a lovely composition.

If space permits, it is desirable to have one or two larger trees for shade. Considerable thought should be given to the choice of such trees, however. A tree should be selected that will cast high shade and under which grass will grow well. The frequently planted Norway maple is objectionable from this point of view because the dense shade it casts, combined with its thick, shallow roots, conspire to keep virtually any other plant from succeeding underneath. It should be a tree that is graceful in form and that remains modest in size. Trees with side-spreading branches that sweep the ground are not suited to the small place, as year by year they diminish the area needed for lawn and recreation, and gradually the property becomes too heavily shaded. It should be a tidy tree, which does not shed its bark or drop objectionable fruits upon the lawn. Among the trees that are excellent as shade trees on the small home property are thornless honey locust, sweet gum, male ginkgo, the Katsura tree and little-leaf linden.

TREES FOR THE SMALL PROPERTY

SCIENTIFIC NAME	COMMON NAME	HEIGHT IN FEET	SPREAD IN FEET
Acer campestre	English or hedge maple	25	15–20
Acer palmatum	Japanese maple	15–20	20–25
Betula pendula	European white birch	40–60	20–30
Cercidiphyllum japonicum	Katsura tree	50–60	40–50
Cercis canadensis	eastern redbud	20–30	20–25
Cornus florida	flowering dogwood tree	15–25	12–18
Cornus kousa	Japanese dogwood	15–20	15–18
Crataegus laevigata 'Paulii'	Paul's scarlet hawthorn	12–15	12–15
Franklinia alatamaha	franklinia tree	15–20	12–15
Ginkgo biloba (male)	maidenhair tree	100–125	40–50
Gleditsia triacanthos var. inermis cultivars	thornless honey locust	100–125	30–40
Halesia carolina	Carolina silverbell	20–30	25–30
Koelreuteria paniculata	golden-rain tree	20–30	20–30
Liquidambar styraciflua	sweet gum	70–90	35–40
Magnolia x soulangiana	saucer magnolia	20–30	15–25
*Magnolia stellata	star magnolia	12–15	12–15
Malus spp. and cultivars	flowering crab apple	20–25	20–25
Oxydendrum arboreum	sourwood, sorrel tree	20–30	12–18
Pinus nigra	Austrian pine	80–90	30–35
Prunus subhirtella	Japanese flowering cherry	25–30	15–20
Sorbus aucuparia	European mountain ash	30–35	20–25
Styrax japonica	Japanese snowbell	20–25	15–20
Syringa reticulata	Japanese tree lilac	20–25	12–20
Tilia cordata	little-leaf linden	70–90	35–40

*Best treated as a shrub

PREPARATION OF SOIL FOR PLANTING

Trees growing in the woods often have a soil that is unusually rich in humus and porous but moist; in other words, they have natural built-in conditions most favorable to growth. On the other hand, trees growing in lawn or field have a soil usually less rich in humus, less porous and commonly matted with grass roots. Therefore, carefully preparing the soil before trees are transplanted is one of the essentials to success. Rich soil stimulates the vigor of trees and equips them with abundant vitality that will make them less subject to disease and less vulnerable to attack by insects. Undernourished trees start with a handicap in the battle for survival. The proper preparation of soil for tree planting should include the following: plowing and harrowing to eliminate turf roots, or deep hand-digging if the area to be planted is comparatively small; the addition of humus or peat moss to lighten the soil and make it porous but moisture-conserving; sand added to lighten a soil that is too heavy with clay; and breaking up the clay subsoil with deep plowing as necessary. Well-rotted manure may be added to improve the soil texture and will, in addition, increase the available nourishment.

In preparing soil for the planting of large deciduous trees, the topsoil should be removed, subsoil excavated to a depth of 18 in. or 2 ft. below the final grade, and the hole filled with additional topsoil. The shock of transplanting is more severe to a mature tree than a young tree, and the added depth of rich soil will contribute greatly in reestablishing the root system. The planting bed should be round and 3 ft. wider than the diameter of the ball of earth that will come with the roots. If possible, this preparation should be done six months or a year in advance of planting to allow the soil to settle.

In preparing the soil for tree planting, if rock is encountered at a depth too shallow to permit the proper soil preparation, one of three alternative procedures must be chosen. In some situations, the grade of the ground may be raised by filling in topsoil over a wide area to a depth that will cover the rock by 18 in. of earth. In other cases, the position of the tree may be changed, without seriously affecting the pictori-

al composition, to a place where the underlying rock is deeper. But if a tree must be planted at a certain position where rock is near the surface, the rock will have to be removed. Blasting a hole in the rock, removing the pieces and filling the place with soil is the best method. But if blasting is impracticable, the rock may be broken by the following traditional method that our forefathers used very effectively. On a cold day, build a wood fire on the rock, so heating it. Rake away the ashes and pour cold water on the rock. The rapid and uneven change of temperature will crack the rock and the pieces can then be pried up with a crowbar and wedge.

TRANSPLANTING TREES

Digging and Transplanting Seasons

In most parts of the country, trees purchased from nurseries in containers or with adequate balls of soil around their roots may be planted any time during the growing season, but extra attention should be paid to watering if they are planted during hot periods in summer. Because of the severe winters in Canada, northern New England, Michigan, Wisconsin and west of Omaha, spring planting is preferable there, though this period cannot be fixed by calendar. The spring planting season begins as soon as the ground is dry enough to work, and continues until the buds of deciduous trees have sent forth their young leaves to ½ in. or 1 in. in length. Thus oaks, which leaf out late, may be transplanted later than horse chestnut trees.

The evergreen planting season continues longer. The autumn season begins in late August for evergreens, and with the turning color of the leaves for deciduous plants, and continues until freezing weather, except for evergreen trees and the broad-leaved evergreens, which should not be moved after the middle of October. Many evergreen trees and most deciduous trees may be transplanted with a frozen ball of earth during the winter as described for transplanting large trees.

Some trees can be transplanted safely only at one season. Magnolias, for example, should be moved only in very early spring. Their roots are easily broken, and since loss of root activity is to be expected after transplanting, it is wise to move these trees when root growth is most active, before flowering in the spring.

Other trees that are best moved only in early spring include the following:

Betula spp.	birch
Carpinus spp.	hornbeam
Carya spp.	hickory
Cornus spp.	dogwood
Cladrastis spp.	yellowwood
Gymnocladus spp.	Kentucky coffee tree
Juglans spp.	walnut
Liquidambar styraciflua	sweet gum
Liriodendron tulipifera	tulip tree
Nyssa spp.	tupelo
Ostrya spp.	hop hornbeam
Quercus alba	white oak
Taxodium distichum	bald cypress
Xanthoceras	shinyleaf yellowhorn

Plastic Sprays and Defoliation

The use of plastic antitranspirant sprays appreciably reduces losses after transplanting. Diluted in water, the plastic may be sprayed over the entire tree so that not only the trunk but all surfaces are covered with a thin film that is flexible, colorless and long-lasting. While it retards evaporation, it does not arrest transpiration. These sprays can be applied to large trees with a power sprayer or to small trees and bushes by a hand spray. This method is so effective that when it is used on deciduous stock in a dormant state, the need for pruning after planting is considerably reduced; it also makes for better bark protection than wrapping the trunk with paper. One spraying is ususally enough. Spraying should be done when the temperature is 50° F. or warmer. In transplanting evergreen trees, the spraying of plastic before digging is an enormous help in retarding evaporation.

While the transplanting of deciduous trees in full leaf is not recommended, it may be done with some success if the whole plant is sprayed with plastic to cover both sides of the leaves. The use of these sprays not only reduces the need for severe pruning but also enables one to

prolong the planting season into the late spring and to start it earlier in the autumn.

Another method of preparing trees for transplanting is called defoliation. It consists of cutting with shears (not pulling off from the twigs) all the leaves from the tree, or all but one-fourth of the leaves. This method is used particularly on both American and English holly when they are being transplanted in northern regions. New leaves will reappear in due time and meanwhile the tree will not be losing moisture. Nursery staff report that they never lose a holly from transplanting if it has been defoliated.

Methods of Transplanting

Bare Root Transplanting

This popular method of moving many deciduous shrubs and young deciduous trees from the nursery to their permanent locations depends for its success on taking up a large proportion of the root system, placing it in the ground again as soon as possible, and removing enough of the top (branches and foliage) to compensate for the temporary reduction of activity in the roots. This operation is best accomplished either in early spring, when the twigs are bare, or in the autumn when the plant is losing its leaves.

To transplant a tree, the gardener begins by digging into the ground in a circle at the outer ends of the roots, and works in toward the trunk, carefully forking the earth from the roots. Thus, practically all the important main roots and a large portion of the fibrous roots remain intact. Any soil left clinging to the roots is carried with them, and is a great benefit to the plant while it is reestablishing itself in the new place. These little particles of soil held by the fine roots keep the contact and hence capillary action uninterrupted during transportation, and they continue to function unless they become very dry while out of the ground.

The time that elapses between digging in the nursery and planting in the new position should be reduced to a minimum. The roots should never be exposed to the sun or wind during this interval. If a group of plants must be kept out of the ground for several hours, as is usual on a large planting job, they should at least be in the shade of a tree or building and their roots should be covered with burlap. A better precaution against drying of the roots is to heel the trees in at once in a convenient place. Then if planting work is interrupted or delayed, the trees can wait until all is ready. This also is the best procedure to follow when bare-rooted trees are obtained from mail order sources and time must elapse before they are properly planted. To heel in trees or shrubs, dig a trench large enough to accommodate the roots, throwing the soil to one side. Place the roots of the plants in the trench in such a way that the stems are inclined at an angle of 45° or lower, and cover the roots with the loose soil. If the roots are very dry when the plants are received, they should be soaked in a container of water for a half hour before being heeled in. The soil covering the roots should be kept wet. In such a situation, trees and shrubs may be kept safely for a few weeks.

When trees are dug in the nursery, they are bundled, labeled and gathered for shipment. The risk of injury from chafing of the bark on the side of the truck may be minimized by placing a wad of burlap bagging where the trunk rests on the brim. An injury to the bark at this time is apt to cause a lowering of vitality in the plant and consequent failure.

Transplanting trees from the woods or from your own grounds entails more risk than transplanting from the nursery. In the nursery, each tree has been transplanted or root-pruned once or twice to induce the growth of fibrous roots in a concentrated mass. On the other hand, the roots of forest-grown seedlings are rangy, and it is difficult to dig them up and make them stay together. If a tree is to be transplanted from the woods, it should be prepared for the change of location by pruning its roots a year in advance. This is best accomplished by digging a trench around the tree at a distance from the trunk equal in feet to the diameter of the trunk in inches. The trench should be deep enough to cut through all the lateral roots, 18 in. or 24 in., according to the size of the tree. The soil is then returned to the trench and new roots will develop within the circle and in the trench. When the tree is taken up, it should be done according to one of the methods of transplanting described in this chapter.

In placing the tree in its new location, make sure that the hole is large enough to accommodate the roots without bending them. The roots

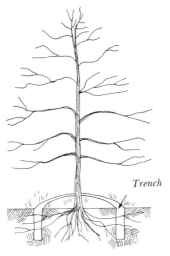

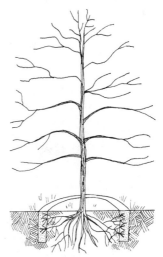

Trench

Topsoil fills trench.

Fig. 13.1 Root pruning
The effect of root pruning is to concentrate the roots in a ball.

should be spread out evenly and the topsoil thrown in among the roots and allowed to settle. When the roots are covered with loose soil but the hole not yet filled, the earth should be packed in among the roots by treading on it. More earth must be added and firmed by treading, and the hole thus filled. When adding soil, approximately one-third by volume of peat moss should be thoroughly mixed in and thus incorporated into the planting. Deciduous trees should be planted 1 in. or 2 in. deeper than they were in the nursery. This permits the roots to be better protected from drying, pending the establishment of the plant. Evergreens should be planted at the same level, never deeper than their former position. Deep planting of evergreens may result in depriving the roots of adequate air in the soil.

The top of the tree should be cut back quite severely, to equalize the rate of evaporation with the ability of the reduced root system to supply water. It also should be pruned the same day that the tree is planted. This is particularly true of oaks and other slow-growing trees. Postponement of this part of the work results in loss of moisture and vitality for the plant; when the tree is pruned later, the pruning will need to be even more severe and the results will not be so satisfactory. The amount of pruning required will depend on the kind of tree, and on the season, *early* spring planting needing less pruning than later plantings. As a general rule, about one-third of the growth should be removed. This should be done in such a way that the main shoot or leader will not be interfered with, thus spoiling the ultimate shape of the tree. Rather, the pattern of the lateral branches should be carefully studied before pruning is started. The aim is to remove one-third of the growth by eliminating some of the lateral branches entirely and cutting others back by about one-half to one-third until the desired result is obtained (see diagram, page 150). If the tree has developed two leaders, one should be completely removed. This procedure will ensure that the tree develops a single straight trunk, so eliminating the possibility of a weak crotch union later in the life of the tree.

The ground surrounding the newly planted tree should be shaped like a saucer to receive a generous supply of water from the first day onward. The function of the water at first is not so much to give the plant the extra moisture it needs but rather to firm the soil about its feeding roots and to drive out the air pockets that inevitably remain in newly turned soil. The roots can take up only so much water, no matter how much is put on the soil, but the air in the soil can dry out the little roots before they become established. Water should be frequently given after planting and for the remainder of the growing season. But this watering should be intermittent, so that several days are allowed for drying and aeration of the soil.

Trees that are at least 12 ft. high should be held in place by three or five guy wires fastened to stakes radiating from the trunk. The upper end of the wire should be looped through a piece of old garden hose and passed around a lower crotch of the tree. The wires are tightened by twisting two strands about a stick. Loose guy wires are of no use at all, because they will not prevent the tree trunk from shaking in a heavy wind or storm, thus loosening the roots in the soil.

Transplanting with a Ball of Earth

Most evergreen trees, deciduous trees 8 ft. to 10 ft. in height and some large shrubs require a more painstaking method of transplanting. The slow rate of growth of the evergreens prevents them from becoming established after transplanting with bare roots. For this class of trees and for a few species of shrubs, transplanting is done with a ball of earth, wrapped tightly about with burlap and tied securely with rope. The roots of such plants as box and hemlock form a dense mass in the soil and it is easy to keep the earth together with burlap and hemp cord; but in moving plants with more loosely arranged roots, such as many of the junipers, it is harder to prevent the ball from cracking. A broken ball or crumbling earth is apt to lead to a dead tree. The ground must be in good condition before the trees are dug. If it is too dry, the earth will crack away from the roots in balling or while moving. This condition may be remedied by a thorough watering several days before transplanting. If it is too wet, the earth will cling to tools and cannot be worked.

The method used by nursery staff in transplanting evergreens that are to be handled in this way is to dig a trench around the specimen at a distance outside the ends of the fibrous roots and as deep as the roots may penetrate. When carefully dug, the side of the trench is beyond the root ends and the earth is then gradually cut away until the roots are encountered. In digging deciduous trees, the outer roots are cut off and the ball made smaller. The trench is usually wide enough for a man to work in, and this space enables him to get his pick and spade well under the rim of the ball. By digging a gallery under and all around the rim, he carves out the undersurface of the ball, leaving it perched on a pedestal in the center. If the tree is a particularly large one and cannot be maneuvered out of its hole, then an incline is dug at one side to the floor of the hole up which the ball can be dragged. Burlap bagging is wrapped about the sides and bottom of the ball and laced very tightly with hemp twine. When all is in readiness to take the tree out of the ground, a chain is passed around the ball, and the end of the chain is hooked on to one of its links at a point about one-third or one-fourth of the circumference from the direction of pull. In other words, the pulling chains start to work tangentially to the edge of the ball. The pull twists the ball off its perch and thus frees it from the ground. A steel or wooden platform is then placed under the ball while the ball is tipped up on edge. The ball is firmly fastened to the platform by ropes passing over the ball from rings at each of the four corners of the platform. A block and tackle fastened to the platform and anchored in the direction of pull helps drag the plant out of the hole. The power used may be three or four men or a truck with a power winch.

The tree is loaded onto the truck by skidding or rolling the platform up heavy planks. The planks are used again to unload it, to roll it across lawns and to ease it into the new hole. Metal rollers on the planks make moving easier. The planks hold the ball while the platform is yanked out from beneath the ball, and by carefully sliding out the planks, the ball is allowed to settle to the floor of the hole. If the hole has been properly prepared, it will have a flat floor covered by a 2-in. layer of topsoil (in the case of box bushes and hemlocks, a mixture of topsoil

and humus is better) and at such a depth that the top of the ball will be flush with the grade of the ground around it. Deciduous trees may be placed 2 in. lower. The hole will be about 2 ft. wider in diameter than the ball of earth, and the soil thrown out of the hole will be in two separate piles, one all topsoil and the other subsoil. Topsoil, or topsoil mixed with humus, should be used for filling in around the ball. The subsoil should then be carted away.

When the tree is in the hole, if the ball does not come to the proper level – which sometimes happens in spite of careful measuring – the ball should be tipped up on one side and more soil added or removed from beneath it. The tree can then be revolved so that it faces in the desired direction. Not until this point should the twine and burlap be removed, at which time the space surrounding the ball may be filled with humus and topsoil. The filling should be tamped with a tamper or, if the plants are small, with a pick handle or any other tool that will firmly pack the soil against the roots. Watering and puddling is not satisfactory because it is apt to make the soil around the tree too loose and consequently more vulnerable to accidental movement from wind or other unexpected sources. Water may be applied later, after the hole is almost filled with firm soil, but not during the filling process. If the outer surface of the ball has become dry and caked during transportation, this should be remedied by watering the ball before the earth is filled in. Here the gardener must choose between two risks: that of having unstable soil about the ball saturated with water, or of permitting the tree roots to suffer from being encased in a hard crust of dry clay soil.

After placing the ball in the hole, the burlap should be carefully removed. If the earth has not held well and the ball is about to crack, one is tempted to leave on the bagging, cutting away the burlap at the base, but leaving a circle of material beneath the ball to rot during the two or three succeeding years. If this expedient is adopted, the lateral roots will not be affected and the down-growing roots will eventually find their way through the bagging. But plastic "burlap," or the burlap treated with chemical preservatives used by some nurseries, will rot away so slowly that new root growth may be se-

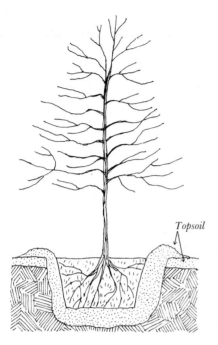
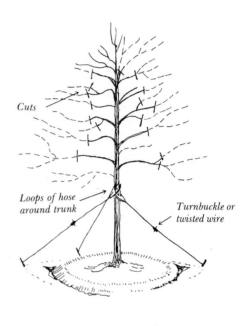

Cuts

Loops of hose around trunk

Turnbuckle or twisted wire

Topsoil

Fig. 13.2 Transplanting a tree with a ball
After removal of burlap, tree is planted in topsoil (left). Tree is guyed with wire and pruned (right). The soil is graded in the form of a dish to conserve water.

riously retarded. This type of burlap, therefore, should always be carefully removed.

The topsoil must be placed around the ball in such a way as to assure firmness of the plant in the ground and exclusion of air pockets in the soil. A layer of soil should be thrown in and trodden and tamped until it is firm. Another layer should then be added and made compact, and the process repeated until the hole is filled. If all the soil is tossed into the hole at one time and then tamped, the lower soil cannot be firmly packed and too much air will remain in the soil.

After planting is finished, the precautions and technique described for planting with bare roots should be followed. Evergreen trees and broad-leaved evergreen shrubs will benefit by a permanent mulch of peat moss, wood chips or a carpet of rotting leaves to retain moisture and retard its evaporation from the soil.

Any tree with a trunk larger than 6 in. in diameter should be transplanted with ball and burlap. Smaller sizes of the following trees also should be transplanted by this method:

Japanese maple	birch
hickory	magnolia
persimmon	sourwood
beech	sassafras
sour gum	sugar maple
walnut	dogwood
tulip tree	oak (nearly all)
sweet gum	evergreen (nearly all)

Transplanting Trees Grown in Containers

It is now a very common practice for nurseries to offer young trees that have been grown entirely in metal or plastic containers, or field-grown trees that have been transplanted into such containers one or two seasons before sale. Such practices frequently reduce production and transportation costs for the nursery, are an efficient and attractive way to display and maintain the plants in retail garden centers and, in addition, they offer greater convenience to the customer.

If a tree has been kept in its container too long, however, or if it has dried out several times or has not been fertilized on a regular basis in the garden center, serious problems can result when the tree is finally transplanted to its permanent location in the home garden. If the tree has been kept too long in its container, the root system may have been too crowded and major roots will have become entwined and entangled. In this case, the danger is that when the tree starts to mature and the roots that were once crowded in the container expand in diameter, they begin to choke out each other. Also, surface roots may have followed the periphery of the container, wrapping themselves around the trunk and eventually girdling the tree completely. These conditions usually do not start to appear until the tree is several years old, or sometimes not until the tree is nearly mature. Symptoms may range from delayed growth after planting to a general decline in vigor later on or even the outright death of the tree caused by the reduced ability of the "choked" roots to transport water and nutrients. Sometimes a major root may completely encircle the base of the trunk and cause the tree to die for no readily visible reason.

In general, do not purchase container-grown trees from a nursery unless the plant shows signs of active, uninterrupted, healthy growth during the current season. If the leaves are few or appear undersized, pale green, or otherwise discolored or drooping, the plant has probably dried out several times or nutrients have been leached out of the soil. If the tree appears quite large for its container, it probably has been in there far too long. Such trees will likely suffer root girdling and thus are no bargain at any price, even though the end-of-the-season sale is very tempting.

When removing a tree from its container just prior to planting, examine the root system thoroughly. If roots appear crowded or matted at the outer edges, they should be gently but thoroughly pried apart. If they are too densely entwined for this to be effective, several longitudinal cuts should be made with a sharp knife around the entire ball right through the outer-

most roots. Sometimes a spaghettilike mass of thick roots will be seen at the base of the container. These too should either be pried apart or cut. In each case the aim is to break up the twining mass of roots and attempt to have as many roots as possible face outward into the new soil in which the plant is placed.

If root disturbance or cutting must be severe, then a corresponding amount of top growth should be pruned away.

Transplanting Very Large Trees

Transplanting large semimature trees is a job to be undertaken only by experienced nursery staff with adequate equipment. The same precautions must be taken with large trees as with shrubs. The roots must be kept moist while they are out of the ground, and they must be carefully placed and firmly packed about with soil. The amount of leafage (evaporation surface) must be reduced in proportion to the loss of feeding roots. The task is made more difficult by the great weight of soil that must be moved with the roots, and by the longer period of time that the tree is out of the ground, but the principles remain the same. The size of the ball of earth required for proper transplanting is proportionate to the size of the tree. It is almost impossible to take all the roots of a large deciduous tree, but for most species the diameter of the ball in feet should at least equal the diameter of the trunk in inches.

Transplanting is a shock to a tree under the best of circumstances, but a shock that may be reduced by preparing the tree for its removal. A year in advance of the transplanting, the circle of the ball is marked out and a trench is dug to a depth of 2 ft., cutting through existing roots. The trench is then filled entirely with topsoil. During the year the tree will form a dense mat of fibrous roots in the topsoil, which will be ready to grow out into a new layer of topsoil in the new location. When the tree is lifted, the new fibrous roots will hold the soil firmly together. The transplanting may be done in early autumn or in spring, and sometimes even in the winter when the ground is frozen solid. Winter transplanting also is best done in a series of operations, beginning the previous year by preparing the ball as described before. In the late autumn the trench is dug and the tree ball twisted off its ground base. There it is left, with the open trench around it, until the ground is frozen. During the winter the tree can be bound up with burlap and cord, tilted up and placed on a platform and removed to the new position, put into the hole and left there still unplanted until spring weather thaws the ground. Then the space about the tree is filled with good topsoil.

In handling large trees, all the sliding, lifting, rolling on rollers and skidding of the ball down into the hole should be done without sudden jostling or bumping. A block and tackle anchored to a "dead-man" will transmit the power of the winch and motor or the pull of a gang of men at a slow, steady motion. The descent into the hole by an inclined plane is the part most apt to bring disaster. Unless the power is strong enough to hold it back, the tree ball may roll with great force down the sloping planks and strike the earth side of the excavation, where it will crack. If the platform is on rollers, the tree ball can be gently eased down into the hole by slacking up slowly on the rope of the block and tackle.

CARE OF TREES AFTER TRANSPLANTING

Transplanting necessarily interrupts or somewhat retards the life processes of any tree. The diminished vitality of the tree renders it more vulnerable to attack by insects and diseases, and less able to withstand the effects of unusual weather conditions.

Moisture Requirements

The greatest danger to the tree both during and after transplanting is from desiccation, or excessive loss of moisture through natural transpiration of foliage while the disturbed roots are unable to replace water and thus maintain a normal moisture content in the tissues. The function of pruning is to diminish the area of foliage and hence reduce the amount of water lost by the tree in a given period.

Watering the tree at intervals is a very impor-

tant part of aftercare. The soil should be thoroughly soaked once a week if rain is insufficient, because the soil should never be allowed to become really dry. On the other hand, in a soil kept constantly saturated, the water will exclude the air from the roots. Proper watering will enable the roots to take up the soil moisture rapidly and will encourage root growth. Evaporation through the bark and the danger of sun scald and splitting of the trunk during warm spells in winter is sometimes a problem, especially with larger trees. A method long in use by planters to retard this evaporation during the first year after transplanting is to wrap the trunk and larger branches with burlap. It is effective, especially against winter drying, but has the disadvantage of harboring insects, and in some positions the objection of unsightliness. Commercially manufactured crepe paper wrapping is sometimes used as a substitute for burlap.

Mulches

To keep the soil about newly planted trees in condition, mulching is advisable. For method of application and materials to be used, etc., see Chapter 8 on mulches.

Ground Covers as Root Protection

A treatment beneficial to trees, and one that may be used in certain situations where lawn is not essential, is a base planting of pachysandra, periwinkle or English ivy. These plants have the ability to thrive even in dense shade, in many places doing better than grass, and what is most important for the tree, they will collect fallen leaves, thus adding annually to the leaf mold in the soil. This subject is more fully discussed in Chapter 16 on ground covers.

Fertilizing Trees

In their natural habitat in the forest, trees are nourished by a soil rich in organic material that is annually replenished by the decaying of fallen leaves. Under conditions where leaves are raked up, this renewing does not take place.

To compensate for the lack of soil fertility, solutions of nitrates, phosphates and potash

13.1 Trees, large and small, help to define landscape space, provide canopy overhead and create shelter. Without such effects, provided here by the large oak on the left and the flowering dogwood on the right, this garden would not invite us to enter. Photo Grant Heilman

should be applied to the soil every three or four years.

No commercial fertilizer should be placed in the hole in which a tree is to be planted, as the risk of burning the roots is too great.

Time of Application

Applications of fertilizer may be made at any time from early spring until midsummer and from the middle of September until late November. No applications should be made between July 15 and September 15 as there is danger of stimulating a late, succulent growth that will be subject to winter-killing. Tree roots take in nutrients most readily during the period of early spring growth, and they continue to absorb nutrients in the autumn long after the leaves have been shed.

Method of Application

The feeding roots of most trees occur in a zone that begins approximately one-third the distance from the trunk to the outer branches and extends to just beyond the limit of the outermost branches. Fertilizer should be applied over this entire area. Holes, varying in depth from 12 in. to 15 in. should be drilled and spaced from 15 in. to 18 in. apart. A mature tree will need about 100 holes. Into each of these holes is put from $1/10$ lb. to $1/4$ lb. of complete fertilizer, and the holes are then filled with water to dissolve the fertilizer.

Kind and Amount of Fertilizer

A 10–6–4 complete fertilizer is recommended for trees, and it should be applied at the rate of 2 lb. to 5 lb. per inch of trunk diameter. Trees with a trunk diameter less than 6 in. should receive about half this amount of fertilizer. For a soil markedly deficient in phosphorus and potash, a 4–8–7 mixture is recommended. A soil test will help in determining what mixture to use.

Spraying to Diminish the Effects of City Soot and Gas

Sulphur dioxide and other gases so prevalent today in the air in cities are detrimental to many trees. The accumulation of soot on the surface of leaves clogs the pores and retards respiration. These conditions are particularly hard on evergreen trees, the leaves of which remain active for several years. To minimize the damage to trees from such atmospheric impurities, the foliage may be washed with a hose spray about once a week during the growing season. This treatment will help deciduous trees and such evergreens as arborvitae and *Chamaecyparis.*

Pruning

Shade trees require comparatively little pruning. The removal of dead or diseased wood and the cutting out of crowded or interfering branches is usually all that is necessary. Pruning of small dead branches will often prevent the large branches or the trunk from rotting. The cut should be made through live wood and close to the junction with the larger stem. In removing small branches, cut from below, part way through, then from above. This lower cut will prevent the weight of the branch, in falling, from ripping off a section of bark below the branch just before the saw cuts through. Larger and heavier branches need even more precaution to prevent this splitting of the bark. (See sketch, Chapter 35.)

First cut part way through from below in the position of the final cut. Then cut through from above at a distance out from the crotch.

After the limb is cut off leaving this stump, cut the stump to a flat surface. Recent research has shown that pruning paint does little to retard decay by preventing the entrance of fungi or other damaging organisms, so the purpose of painting is mostly cosmetic.

Trees that have been injured by storm or that have begun to decay will require more attention than mere pruning. The rotted wood in the cavity should be removed down to the live wood. A hammer and chisel may be used to cut away the decayed wood. It is important that damp or saturated rotten wood be removed, leaving only hard, healthy tissue.

For control of insect pests and diseases, see Chapter 32.

Grading Around a Tree

If the grades around a tree are to be altered by filling soil over the original ground level, then special precautions should be taken to prevent the smothering of the roots. A fill of 4 in. of good topsoil over the roots of deciduous trees will usually do no damage, although it might affect evergreens unfavorably. A fill of 12 in. or more would be very harmful. The quantity of air and water in the soil diminishes with the depth. Thus, when roots growing at a depth of 18 in. are covered so that they are 36 in. from the surface, they are deprived of their normal oxygen and water rations. To overcome this handicap, it is advisable to construct some device for maintaining a contact between the air and the root-containing soil. It is important to do this before the fill is made. First, the original soil is loosened by forking. Then a dry stone wall is built up around the tree, if possible at a distance of several feet from the base of the trunk and to the level of the new grade. Several 4-in. agricultural tile drains are laid in lines radiating from the inner surface of this wall. The entire area is then spread with a course of crushed stone or large gravel. This material is put on to a depth of 6 in. or to within 12 in. or 15 in. of the final grades. Above this is spread a layer of straw or, preferably, manure to prevent the soil above from sifting down through the stones or slag. Finally, a layer of topsoil is spread to a depth of 6 in. or 8 in. This construction should cover the whole area of tree roots. The tile pipes may be used to conduct water to the roots and may be filled by a hose.

If soil has been washed away from the roots of large trees, as sometimes happens on steep slopes, or if the ground is worn down by pedestrian traffic, the damage to the trees may eventually be fatal. Restoration of the natural grade by applying a layer of topsoil to cover the roots and establishing a turf or a gound cover crop to retain the soil is the only permanent remedy for this situation.

DECIDUOUS TREES OF MERIT

Acer campestre (English maple or hedge maple)

This pleasant shade tree, with its dense dark green foliage, forms a broad dome with branches near the ground. The leaves are small, with five rounded lobes. It is a handsome lawn tree and is excellent for children to climb in because of its broad, spreading, sturdy branches. Very slow growth.

Height 25 ft. Zone 5 – 6.

Acer saccharum (sugar maple)

One of the noblest American trees, its dense habit of growth and its gorgeous autumn color make it a tree to remember. This is one of the trees that has made New England famous for its fall foliage. It is much used as a street tree and shades many a New England village green. It cannot be surpassed as a shade tree on a broad home lawn or as a forest tree. The sugar maple is not a rapid grower but it is long-lived. Plant this tree for your children, and they will be able to pass it on to their grandchildren.

Height 125 ft. Zone 3 (northern limit).

Betula pendula (*B. alba.* European white birch, and *B. papyrifera* (canoe birch)

These are among the most picturesque trees. They have bright, smooth white stems and in autumn clear yellow foliage. They are fre-

quently planted as accents and are at home among evergreen trees and with mountain laurel.

Height 60 ft. Zone 2.

Other birches, especially the river birch and the yellow birch, are picturesque but not as striking as the white birches.

Cercidiphyllum japonicum (Katsura tree)

A native of Japan, planted for its beautiful foliage. It usually grows with several stems to form a broad, spreading dome with leaves and branches reaching to the ground, a most graceful structure. The delicate heart-shaped leaves turn to bright yellow and scarlet in autumn.

Height 50 ft. to 60 ft., spread 50 ft. Zone 4.

Cercis canadensis (eastern redbud)

An undergrowth tree common in the woods of Maryland and southward, where it blooms with the dogwood. Its deep pink buds cling to the branches for several weeks before opening into rose-pink, pealike blossoms.

It does best in the shade of larger trees, in rich, humus soil.

Height 30 ft. Zone 4.

Cladrastis lutea (yellowwood)

Native to a small region in the mountains of North Carolina and eastern Tennessee, the yellowwood has a smooth, gray bark resembling that of a beech. The leaves are compound and turn a brilliant yellow in late September. Its glory is its large hanging panicles of creamy-white fragrant flowers in June.

Height 50 ft. Zone 3.

Cornus florida (flowering dogwood tree)

A native of the understory of our eastern forests, and one of the most beloved and most beautiful of our flowering trees, flowering dogwood is a sturdy, small tree with spreading, drooping branches. Its quantities of white flowers, consisting of four spreading bracts, greet the spring before the leaves appear. In October the leaves turn crimson and the twigs are adorned with tight bunches of scarlet fruits.

Height 25 ft. Zone 4.

Cornus kousa (Japanese dogwood)

A native of Japan and Korea, its broad, spreading habit and dense foliage make this an excellent tree for background and screen. Its chief beauty is its white blossoms, which cover the branches in June. Unlike our native eastern dogwood, the bracts end in short, sharp points. The large reddish fruits ripen in August and hang on through the autumn, and the foliage turns scarlet in October.

Height 20 ft. Zone 5.

Crataegus phaenopyrum (Washington thorn tree)

This is one of the best native hawthorns. It is excellent when used as an untrimmed hedge, as a windbreak and as a specimen. Its horizontal branches and drooping twigs bear quantities of small, bright scarlet applelike fruits in September, which hang on well into the winter. The leaves also turn scarlet and orange in the autumn. The thorns are 2 in. or 3 in. long and are sharp.

Height 30 ft. Zone 4.

Fagus sylvatica (European beech)

This beech has a dignity and refinement deriving from its rugged form and smooth bark. The leaves are finely toothed, the buds long and sharp and tapering, the twigs small and widespreading. The tree reaches up to 100 ft., yet the lower branches touch the ground. The autumn color is at first clear yellow turning to rich brown, and the lower leaves hang on all winter. Numerous forms have appeared, the most notable of which is the copper beech.

Height 90 ft. Zone 4.

Franklinia alatamaha (franklinia tree)

A small tree of very slow growth, native to Georgia, where it was discovered by John Bartram in 1770. It has not been found wild since 1790, and all the trees we have today are descended from the seedlings Bartram raised. It prefers sheltered valleys and the partial shade of large trees. Its lovely flower is a pure white cup of five petals with golden stamens, measuring about 3 in. across. The flowers appear in late summer and open in succession over a period of many weeks. The leaves turn crimson in the autumn. This is a rare and lovely small tree that deserves to be more widely grown.

Height 20 ft. Zone 5–6.

Ginkgo biloba (maidenhair tree)

Brought from China two centuries ago, this tree has since been distributed widely in Europe and America. The growth is sparse, usually with upward-directed branches, giving it a rather angular outline. The leaves are its chief beauty. Each is a little fan with conspicuous, radiating veins and an undulate outer rim. In autumn the maidenhair is a glorious clear yellow. It is used quite often as a street tree, but its value as a lawn tree is well recognized. It is dioecious, and the odor of the fruit is so unpleasant that one should be careful to obtain the male form.

Height 100 ft. Zone 4.

Gleditsia triacanthos var. inermis 'Moraine' (Moraine locust)

Valued for its rapid growth, lacy foliage, vaselike form and freedom from disease, this tree has no thorns and is well adapted for use as a street tree and on the home lawn. It thrives well in many types of soil.

Height 100 ft. Zone 4.

Halesia carolina (Carolina silverbell)

This lovely small tree is a native of the South. In late spring it bears thousands of small, white, bell-shaped flowers, followed by interesting four-winged fruits that are greatly relished by squirrels. Rapid in growth, and not subject to diseases, this shrublike spreading tree is excellent for the small property. The leaves turn clear yellow in October.

Height 30 ft. Zone 5.

Koelreuteria paniculata (golden-rain tree or varnish tree)

A most picturesque Oriental tree. Its rather wide-ranging twisted branches and its feathery, compound, light green foliage give it a characteristic contrast to our familiar forms. But its great beauty bursts forth in late June or early July, when the large panicles of bright yellow blossoms open. Later, when the blooms fall, they cover the ground with a carpet of yellow. The flowers are followed by conspicuous bladderlike pods that remain on the tree into early winter, thus greatly extending the season of ornamental interest. The autumn foliage is yellow.

Height 30 ft. Zone 5.

Liquidambar styraciflua (sweet gum)

A native forest tree that forms extensive stands in the lowlands of New Jersey and Maryland. It is a tree with a conspicuous central trunk and a tapering apex. Its star-shaped leaves turn a brilliant crimson in September. The crooked, corky-barked branches are picturesque in winter, as are the hanging fruit balls that persist until spring.

Height 90 ft. Zone 5.

Liriodendron tulipifera (tulip tree)

A majestic tree, with a straight trunk often rising 30 ft. to the first branch. It is a very fast grower, achieving 50 ft. in fifteen years. The large four-lobed leaves turn clear yellow in September. The blossoms, which are greenish-yellow marked with orange and tulip-shaped, stand erect at the twig ends at the top of the

13.2 The white oak's magnificent proportions in maturity give it a dignity beyond that of all other native trees. Photo Grant Heilman

tree where they are not easily seen. An excellent tree for planting on the home grounds as it casts high shade and permits grass to flourish beneath. It is used to line the avenues of southern plantations and to shade the mansions.

Height 120 ft. Zone 4.

Magnolia x *soulangiana* (saucer magnolia)

One of the most spectacular of flowering trees. The whole tree is covered in April or May with lavender, cup-shaped blossoms. The bark is light gray and smooth, and the rich foliage is a medium green. The magnolias are remarkably free from disease, and usually live for many years. They grow extremely well under city conditions if the soil is fairly rich and moisture-retentive.

Height 30 ft. Zone 5.

Magnolia stellata (star magnolia)

This much-loved shrub or small tree is of very slow growth, but begins to bloom when it is only 3 ft. high. The white flowers, with many ribbonlike white petals, open in early spring before the forsythias and, unless they are frost-touched, remain open for many days. It is one of the loveliest of the small trees and deserves to be widely planted.

Height 15 ft. Zone 5.

Malus floribunda (Japanese flowering crab apple)

This is one of the finest of the many flowering crabs, and a most beautiful sight when in full bloom in mid-spring. Thousands of carmine-pink buds open into pure white flowers, which resemble small apple blossoms and remain in bloom for several weeks. In September the tree is covered with small, pale yellow apples about 1/3 in. in diameter. It will thrive for at least fifty years.

Height 30 ft. Zone 4.

Oxydendrum arboreum (sourwood)

A small, deciduous tree, native to the forests in the Alleghenies from Pennsylvania southward. It is a member of that large family the Ericaceae, and is thus related to rhododendrons. Its blossoms, hanging in branched tassels, resemble the white bells of *Pieris,* but its great glory is its autumn coloring. By late August the leaves are beginning to turn, and they remain a bright crimson until mid-October. It is very slow in growth, occasionally reaching an eventual height of 40 ft, but usually remaining much smaller.

Zone 5.

Platanus x *acerifolia* (London plane tree)

A hybrid of the American and the European sycamores, this is a much-used street tree. Its picturesque cream or white trunk and branches give it great distinction, but the shedding bark and the fruit heads clutter the ground beneath. However, it is one of our best shade trees, branching very broadly, casting a deep shade and living for 100 years. Regrettably, it has become subject to disease as a result of overplanting.

Height 100 ft. Zone 5.

Prunus subhirtella (Higan cherry)

One of the most disease-resistant and long-lived of the many Japanese flowering cherries, and a tree of graceful habit and great beauty. Pink buds and pale pink blossoms cover it in April. A pathway beneath a double row of these trees is very impressive. A weeping form, *P. subhirtella* 'Pendula,' is also very popular.

Height 30 ft. Zone 5.

Quercus alba (white oak)

Almost in a class by itself, the white oak's light gray bark and rugged branches make it easily distinguishable from the other oaks, and its magnificent proportions in maturity give it a dignity beyond that of all other native trees. This is also a tree to plant for one's grandchildren; it will live hundreds of years and will grow very slowly. The leaves are deeply indented with rounded lobes. In autumn the colors range through pink-scarlet to deep bronze-brown. It will grow on almost any soil except wet bottomland. A fine tree for the home property of ample size.

Height 125 ft. Zone 4.

Several other oaks are worthy of special mention. Among the best for shade and autumn color are:

Quercus coccinea	scarlet oak (Zone 4)
Quercus laurifolia	laurel oak (Zone 7)
Quercus palustris	pin oak (Zone 4)
Quercus rubra	red oak (Zone 3)
Quercus virginiana	live oak (Zone 7)

Except for the pin oak, oaks are rather difficult to transplant. It is therefore prudent to purchase small young trees, not more than 2 in. in diameter.

Salix babylonica (Babylon weeping willow)

This has long been a popular tree with romantic association, the subject of Chinese and occidental art. In this country it rarely reaches a height of more than 40 ft. Its long, hanging twigs moving in the wind are most graceful and as winter begins to give way to spring, the twigs suddenly turn a light yellow, bringing life to the somber landscape. The leaves are long and narrow and remain green until late autumn. The true *S. babylonica* is not reliably hardy north of New York City, and in colder climates *S.* x *elegantissima* (Thurlow weeping willow) is frequently planted as a substitute of very similar appearance.

Height 35 ft. Zone 6.

Sophora japonica (Chinese scholar tree)

Brought from China two centuries ago, the scholar tree is still not well enough known. It is a graceful and wide-spreading tree when growing alone. The leaves are compound and resemble those of the locust. In August and September great panicles of pale yellow, pealike blossoms are produced in profusion, and these are followed by picturesque green pods. It is a very handsome shade tree suitable for the home lawn of spacious proportions.

Height 75 ft. Zone 4.

13.3 Sugar maple trunks turn to silver in the warming sunlight of spring. Photo Carlton Lees

Sorbus aucuparia (European mountain ash)

A small tree, with compound leaves, white blossoms in flat clusters followed by gorgeous, orange-vermilion fruit in August and September. This is excellent for the small property, graceful and distinctive, but it is slow to mature. Trunk borers are occasionally a problem, so it is not wise to plant more than one or two on a small property.

Height 40 ft. Zone 3.

Styrax japonica (Japanese snowbell)

A compact tree, with wide-spreading, horizontal branches and deep green leaves. In June and July the branches are hung with little, white, fragrant, bell-like flowers, and in August the oval green fruits appear, which turn brown as they ripen. This neat and attractive tree is excellent for small home grounds, and has few, if any, disease problems.

Height 25 ft. Zone 5.

Syringa reticulata (Japanese tree lilac)

This attractive small tree is well suited to the suburban home property, is compact in habit of growth and in June bears large trusses of white flowers. It is remarkably free from pests and diseases and requires little maintenance.

Height 25 ft. Zone 5.

13.4 While magnolia flowers are spectacular, in winter sunlight the branches are sculpturelike. Photo Carlton Lees

Taxodium distichum (bald cypress)

Although this deciduous conifer grows in the swamps of the South from Maryland to Louisiana, it is nevertheless hardy in upland soil as far north as central New York State. One of the most beautiful sights of the southern spring is cypress trees with their new feathery leaves of pale green covering them like a mist. Contrary to popular belief, bald cypress will thrive in any reasonably moisture-retentive soil, and swampy conditions are not necessary for successful cultivation within its range of hardiness.

Height 100 ft. Zone 4.

Tilia cordata (littleleaf linden)

This has been planted as a shade tree since ancient times. It has a broad, spreading base, with branches close to the ground, and a rounded head. The leaves are small, broad and irregularly heart-shaped.

Height 100 ft. Zone 3.

Tilia x *euchlora* (Crimean linden)

One of the most handsome of all trees for planting as a specimen on a lawn because the picturesque growth habit is pleasing in all seasons. The lower branches are pendulous, the middle branches nearly horizontal and the uppermost branches ascending in form.

Height 60 ft. Zone 4.

Zelkova serrata (Japanese zelkova)

Zelkova has received much publicity as an excellent substitute for the American elm. It is true that zelkova is fairly resistant to the ravages of Dutch elm disease, and it does possess an upright habit, many wide-spreading ascending branches and leaves quite similar to the American elm. However, it is a short-trunked tree and does not grow to the majestic proportions of our native elm. It makes an excellent shade tree and is fairly rapid in growth. Although it is being widely planted as a substitute, one should not expect the stately proportions and massive trunk of the American elm, once the most popular and handsome shade tree.

Height 60 ft. Zone 5.

EVERGREEN TREES OF MERIT

Abies concolor (white fir)

One of those adaptable trees that seem to make themselves at home in almost any situation. Native to the Rocky Mountains, it tolerates dry soil and windy exposures. Its great beauty is its majestic, columnar form and soft, blue-green needles, which are long and waxy smooth. In the West attains a height of 125 ft.

Zone 4.

Cedrus atlantica (Atlas cedar)

This is the hardiest of the three true cedars, and comes from the mountains of Spain. Because the needles are arranged in starlike clusters covering the twigs and branches with a fine pattern, this cedar is a beautiful symphony of line. In maturity the tree is 125 ft. tall and very broad at the base, with branches to the ground. The cultivar 'Glauca' is frequently planted for its attractive bluish needles.

Zone 6.

Cedrus libani, the cedar of Lebanon from Syria, and *Cedrus deodara*, the deodar cedar from the foot of the Himalayas, are even more beautiful, with longer needles, but they are less hardy and are suited only to mild climates. *C. libani* var. *stenocoma* (hardy cedar of Lebanon) is a much hardier form, only occasionally available from nurseries. It survives winter cold at least as far north as Boston.

Zone 5.

Chamaecyparis pisifera (Sawara cypress)

Brought from Japan, along with its cultivars 'Plumosa' and 'Squarrosa,' this cypress is used frequently in suburban plantings. It keeps a neat shape and density without shearing, though shearing will thicken the foliage. It should not be planted where it will outgrow a restricted space. It has a good, erect, tapering column of feathery evergreen foliage. 'Plumosa' is very fine in texture, and 'Squarrosa' has bluish scales that stand out as needles in fluffy masses. In Japan it grows to 150 ft., but in this country it is rarely higher than 50 ft.

Zone 3.

Ilex opaca (American holly)

This tree, beloved by every generation of Americans, has unfortunately been exterminated in many regions by the vendors who fill the markets with its branches for Christmas greens. In maturity the magnificent slow-growing evergreen reaches a height of 60 ft., although usually much less in the North, and it will live for 200 years. The dark green and flat leaves are stiff, with several spines on the rim. The bright red berries ripen in October and remain all winter.

Zone 5.

Juniperus virginiana (eastern red cedar)

This is not in fact a cedar at all, but a juniper. It is familiar to all in the Northeast as a shaft of

deep green, fine in texture. In the North it normally matures at about 35 ft. and widens at the base. In Maryland, Virginia and southward, where it grows more rapidly, it is often 80 ft. or 90 ft. tall and very broad at the base. The wood is very hard and is one of the best for farm fence posts as it resists decay for 50 years or more.

The best cultivar is 'Canaertii,' which has a richer green and a denser mass of foliage.

Zone 2.

Laurus nobilis (Grecian laurel)

A small evergreen tree of slow growth used for hedges and as specimens on the coasts of the Mediterranean and in the Pacific Northwest. Its picturesque branching and compact form (it reaches a height of about 30 ft.) produce a rather tapering outline. It may be pruned into any formal shape. This is the laurel of history and poetry.

Zone 7.

Magnolia grandiflora (southern magnolia, bull bay)

This is the famous magnolia of the southern plantations. Its height, and its large, lustrous dark green leaves, give it great distinction. But the great waxy-white, cup-shaped blooms that adorn the upper branches from May to August are perhaps its finest asset. A native throughout the lower South, it is hardy only as far north as Virginia except in very sheltered locations.

Height 70 ft. Zone 7.

Pinus nigra (Austrian pine)

The old reliable among the pines, hardy in nearly any exposure, almost free from insects and diseases, a pine of rugged character that is also a thing of simple beauty. Masses of stiff long needles cover the twigs and outer branches. Small, broad, dark brown cones cling close to the stems, decorating the top. This tree is used as specimen, as a shade tree and often as a windbreak.

Height 100 ft. Zone 4.

Pinus strobus (eastern white pine)

One of the glories of New England, sought since earliest colonial years for its timber and famous as the mast tree of the sailing ships of Britain and America. As a tree for suburban home grounds, the white pine is unsurpassed. One towering by the house can be a joy for every nature lover through winter and summer; it is the gathering place of warblers and finches, the shelter for juncos and the home of nuthatches. In the carpet of its fallen needles in the forests grow the elusive pink lady's slipper, the Indian pipe and *Clintonia borealis*. Its soft needles clothe the twigs in a rich green verdure.

Height 100 ft. to 150 ft. Zone 3.

Several other pines are of landscape value. Among them are *Pinus sylvestris* (Scots pine), a tree of picturesque outline, and *Pinus thunbergii* (Japanese black pine), which will stand terrific wind.

Pseudotsuga menziesii (Douglas fir)

This is one of the valuable timber trees of the Pacific Northwest, where it grows to 300 ft. In domestic use it is a graceful spire of rich green, far more beautiful than the spruces and more dependable than the true firs.

It is best as a specimen or as one of several ascending evergreens in a group.

Height 80 ft. to 100 ft. Zone 4.

Quercus virginiana (live oak)

The live oak was often planted along the avenues of southern homes, where it has attained great age. The tree has wide, horizontally spreading limbs, but it does not reach great height. It is of rapid growth and will adjust itself to almost any soil. Although it is a forest tree, live oak makes a magnificent specimen for the lawn. Native from Virginia to Mexico.

Height 60 ft. to 70 ft. Zone 7.

13.5 Flowering dogwood in a grove of oak, pine and other native trees provides shelter and shade as well as an abundance of long-lasting flowers. Photo Grant Heilman

Thuja occidentalis (American arborvitae)

A tree for many climates and for a wide range of soil conditions. Normally the arborvitae is a solid column of rich dark green with scalelike leaves arranged in broad fans that hang irregularly on the twigs.

It is best when used as an ornamental, in groups or as a single accent, but it is often also used in hedges or windbreaks. Arborvitae is a hardy, persistent and healthy tree, which gives satisfaction in heavy soil, damp or dry. Be watchful for bagworm infestations (see index). Height usually 35 ft. but occasionally 60 ft.

Zone 2.

Tsuga canadensis (Canada hemlock)

In the forests and glens hemlock grows to 100 ft. or more, with a trunk 6 ft. in diameter. In suburban settings it reaches half these proportions. The slender nodding top and the drooping branches give it a gracefulness not seen in any other evergreen tree. The lower branches spread widely and sweep the ground; it is important, therefore, to give it plenty of room. This tree is excellent when used as a background, as a clump or among pines in a grove. It may be clipped into a very dense hedge. It is sometimes wrongly used next to a house where in ten years it will have outgrown the location: do not compromise its beauty by crowding it. Hemlock is not subject to insects and diseases but deserves good care and consideration. Water it during a dry season.

Height 100 ft. Zone 3.

TREES FOR DRY, SANDY SOIL

DECIDUOUS

Acer negundo	box elder
Ailanthus altissima	tree of heaven
Betula davurica	Dahurian birch
Betula populifolia	gray birch
Broussonetia papyrifera	paper mulberry
Gleditsia triacanthos	honey locust
Koelreuteria paniculata	golden-rain tree
Maclura pomifera	osage orange
Populus alba	white poplar
Populus grandidentata	largetooth aspen
Populus tremuloides	quaking aspen
Quercus prinus	chestnut oak
Robinia pseudoacacia	black locust
Sassafras albidum	sassafras
Sophora japonica	Chinese scholar tree
Ulmus pumila	Siberian elm

EVERGREEN

Juniperus spp.	juniper
Pinus banksiana	jack pine
Pinus rigida	pitch pine
Pinus virginiana	Virginia pine

TREES RELATIVELY FREE FROM INSECT PESTS AND DISEASES

DECIDUOUS

Ailanthus altissima	tree of heaven
Cercidiphyllum japonicum	Katsura tree
Elaeagnus angustifolia	Russian olive
Ginkgo biloba	maidenhair tree
Gleditsia triacanthos	honey locust
Gymnocladus dioica	Kentucky coffee tree
Halesia carolina	Carolina silverbell
Koelreuteria paniculata	golden-rain tree
Liquidambar styraciflua	sweet gum
Magnolia (all species)	magnolia
Nyssa sylvatica	sour gum
Oxydendrum arboreum	sourwood
Phellodendron (all species)	cork tree
Sophora japonica	Chinese scholar tree

EVERGREEN

Sciadopitys verticillata	umbrella pine
Tsuga (all species)	hemlock

TREES OF RAPID GROWTH

DECIDUOUS

Acer negundo	box elder
Acer rubrum	red maple
Acer saccharinum	silver maple
Ailanthus altissima	tree of heaven
Betula maximowicziana	monarch birch
Betula populifolia	gray birch
Catalpa speciosa	western catalpa
Fraxinus americana	white ash
Ginkgo biloba	maidenhair tree
Gleditsia triacanthos	honey locust
Gymnocladus dioica	Kentucky coffee tree
Larix decidua	European larch
Liriodendron tulipifera	tulip tree
Magnolia acuminata	cucumber tree
Magnolia tripetala	umbrella magnolia
Paulownia tomentosa	empress tree
Platanus x *acerifolia*	London plane tree
Populus alba	white poplar
Populus nigra 'Italica'	Lombardy poplar
Prunus serotina	black cherry
Quercus palustris	pin oak
Robinia pseudoacacia	black locust
Salix alba	white willow
Sorbus aucuparia	European mountain ash
Syringa reticulata	Japanese tree lilac
Tilia americana	American linden
Ulmus pumila	Siberian elm

EVERGREEN

Picea abies	Norway spruce
Pinus rigida	pitch pine
Pinus resinosa	red pine
Pinus strobus	white pine

TREES THAT WILL FORM GOOD WINDBREAKS

DECIDUOUS

Acer ginnala	Amur maple
Acer negundo	box elder
Acer platanoides	Norway maple
Acer pseudoplatanus	sycamore maple
Crataegus mollis	downy hawthorn
Crataegus phaenopyrum	Washington thorn tree
Maclura pomifera	osage orange
Morus alba	white mulberry
Populus alba	white poplar
Populus balsamifera	balsam poplar
Quercus imbricaria	shingle oak
Quercus palustris	pin oak
Quercus phellos	willow oak
Rhamnus davurica	Dahurian buckthorn

DECIDUOUS *(Continued)*

Tilia spp.	linden
Ulmus pumila	Siberian elm

EVERGREEN

Juniperus virginiana	eastern red cedar
Picea abies	Norway spruce
Picea glauca	white spruce
Pinus nigra	Austrian pine
Pinus rigida	pitch pine
Pinus strobus	eastern white pine
Pinus sylvestris	Scots pine
Pinus thunbergii	Japanese black pine
Thuja occidentalis	American arborvitae
Tsuga canadensis	Canada hemlock

TREES FOR THE SEASHORE

(WILL WITHSTAND STRONG WIND)

DECIDUOUS

Acer pseudoplatanus	sycamore maple
Acer rubrum	red maple
Aesculus hippocastanum	horse chestnut
Ailanthus altissima	tree of heaven
Amelanchier canadensis	shadblow
Carpinus betulus	European hornbeam
Crataegus oxyacantha	English hawthorn
Gleditsia triacanthos	honey locust
Platanus occidentalis	American plane tree
Populus alba	white poplar
Populus balsamifera	Carolina cottonwood
Populus tremuloides	quaking aspen
Prunus maritima	beach plum
Prunus serotina	black cherry
Quercus laurifolia	laurel oak
Quercus rubra	red oak
Quercus virginiana	live oak
Salix alba	white willow
Sassafras albidum	sassafras

EVERGREEN

Juniperus horizontalis	creeping juniper
Juniperus virginiana	red cedar
Pinus mugo	Swiss mountain pine
Pinus nigra	Austrian pine
Pinus pinaster	cluster pine
Pinus rigida	pitch pine
Pinus sylvestris	Scots pine
Pinus thunbergii	Japanese black pine

SHADE TREES FOR STREETS

(Those marked with an asterisk* are particularly suitable for confined or narrow areas or where the lawn strip is 3 ft. or less in width. Many require special pruning while young to encourage an upright growth habit. Many maples do not appear on this list because they heave sidewalks.)

*Acer campestre**	English or hedge maple
*Acer ginnala**	Amur maple
Acer saccharum f. *monumentale**	Newton Sentry sugar maple
Aesculus hippocastanum 'Baumannii'	double-flowering horse chestnut
*Carpinus betulus**	European hornbeam
Carpinus betulus 'Fastigiata'*	upright European hornbeam
*Carpinus caroliniana**	American hornbeam or ironwood
Celtis occidentalis	hackberry
Cornus florida and cultivars*	flowering dogwood tree
Crataegus x *lavallei**	Lavalle hawthorn
Crataegus oxycantha 'Crimson Cloud'*	Crimson Cloud hawthorn
*Crataegus phaenopyrum**	Washington thorn tree
Cladrastis lutea	yellowwood
Fraxinus pennsylvanica 'Marshall's Seedless'	seedless green ash
Ginkgo biloba	maidenhair tree
Ginkgo biloba 'Fastigiata'*	upright maidenhair tree
Gingko biloba 'Princeton Sentry'*	Princeton Sentry maidenhair tree
Gleditsia triacanthos var. *inermis* cultivars	thornless honey locust
*Koelreuteria paniculata**	golden-rain tree
Liquidambar styraciflua	sweetgum
Liriodendron tulipifera	tulip tree
Malus baccata 'Columnaris' and other flowering crab apples*	upright Siberian crab apple
Metasequoia glyptostroboides	dawn redwood
Morus alba 'Kingan'	Kingan mulberry
Nyssa sylvatica	sourgum
Ostrya virginiana	American hop hornbeam
Platanus x *acerifolia*	London plane tree
Prunus sargentii	Sargent cherry
Prunus yedoensis	Yoshino cherry
Pyrus calleryana 'Bradford'	Bradford pear
Quercus coccinea	scarlet oak
Quercus macrocarpa	bus oak
Quercus palustris 'Crownright'	Crownright pin oak
Quercus palustris 'Sovereign'	Sovereign pin oak
Quercus phellos	willow oak
Quercus rubra (*Q. borealis*)	red oak
Sophora japonica	Chinese scholar tree
Sorbus alnifolia	Korean mountain ash
*Syringa reticulata**	Japanese tree lilac
Tilia americana 'Redmond'	Redmond basswood
Tilia cordata	littleleaf linden
Tilia tomentosa	silver linden
Zelkova serrata	Japanese zelkova
Zelkova serrata 'Village Green'	Village Green zelkova

TREES THAT TOLERATE MOIST TO WET SOIL

DECIDUOUS

Acer negundo	box elder
Acer rubrum	red maple
Acer saccharinum	silver maple
Alnus glutinosa	European alder
Betula lutea	yellow birch
Betula nigra	river birch
Betula populifolia	gray birch
Carpinus caroliniana	American hornbeam
Carya ovata	shagbark hickory
Fraxinus caroliniana	water ash
Fraxinus pennsylvanica var. *lanceolata*	green ash
Gleditsia aquatica	water locust
Larix laricina	American larch
Liquidambar styraciflua	sweet gum
Magnolia virginiana	sweet bay
Nyssa sylvatica	sour gum
Platanus occidentalis	buttonwood
Populus balsamifera	Carolina cottonwood
Populus grandidentata	largetooth aspen
Quercus bicolor	swamp white oak
Quercus palustris	pin oak
Quercus phellos	willow oak
Salix alba	white willow
Salix alba 'Vitellina'	golden willow
Salix babylonica	weeping willow
Salix fragilis	brittle willow
Salix nigra	black willow
Salix pentandra	laurel willow
Taxodium distichum	bald cypress
Tilia americana	American linden

EVERGREEN

Abies balsamea	balsam fir
Chamaecyparis thyoides	white cedar
Picea mariana	black spruce
Picea rubra	red spruce
Thuja occidentalis	American arborvitae
Tsuga canadensis	Canada hemlock

DECIDUOUS TREES

SCIENTIFIC NAME	COMMON NAME	ZONE OF HARDINESS; HEIGHT IN FEET; PREFERRED SOIL	BLOOM; SEASON OF BLOOM; FRUIT	REMARKS
Acer buergerianum	trident maple	6; 20 (rounded); rich, moist	greenish, May; 2-winged samara	good small shade tree, delicate foliage
Acer campestre	English or hedge maple	5–6; 25 (round, low); good	greenish; May; 2-winged samara	delicate foliage, excellent for screen or clipped hedge
Acer ginnala	Amur maple	2; 20 (upright to rounded); good	yellowish-white; May; 2-winged bright red samaras in summer	brilliant scarlet autumn foliage; requires little care
Acer griseum	paperbark maple	5; 25 (rounded); good, moisture-retentive	greenish; May; 2-winged samara	Handsome reddish-brown peeling bark
Acer japonicum	fullmoon maple	5; 20 (rounded); rich, moisture-retentive	purple; May; 2-winged samara	red autumn leaves; several cultivars with interesting foliage variations
Acer negundo	box elder	2; 60 (wide-spreading); not particular	yellowish-green; March; 2-winged samara	rapid growth, weak-wooded; makes quick screen
Acer palmatum	Japanese maple	5; 20 (rounded); rich, moisture-retentive	purple; June; 2-winged samara	many cultivars selected for foliage color and texture
Acer pensylvanicum	moosewood	3; 30 (open); moisture-retentive	yellow; May; 2-winged samara	greenish bark with white stripes
Acer platanoides	Norway maple	3; 90 (rounded); moisture-retentive	yellow, showy; April–May; 2-winged samara	very dense shade; roots heave widewalks
Acer pseudoplatanus	sycamore maple	4; 90 (spreading; moisture-retentive	yellowish-green; May; 2-winged samara	excellent near the sea
Acer rubrum	red maple	3; 120 (round-headed, pyramidal); wet to ordinary	red to yellow; March–April; 2-winged samara	autumn leaves scarlet and yellow
Acer saccharinum	silver maple	4; 125 (spreading); moisture-retentive	greenish; Feb.–March; 2-winged samara	rapid growth, very weak branches
Acer saccharum	sugar maple	3; 125 (round head); good, moisture-retentive	red; April; 2-winged samara	excellent shade tree, red or yellow autumn foliage
Acer tataricum	Tatarian maple	4; 30 (round-topped); ordinary soil	greenish-white; May; 2-winged samara	red fruit in August
Aesculus x *carnea*	red horse chestnut	3; 70 (round head, pyramidal when young); rich, moist	pink to red; May; smooth shell containing glossy brown nut	'Briotii' has larger scarlet flowers than the sp.
Aeschulus glabra	Ohio buckeye	3; 30 (round); rich, moist	greenish-yellow; May; smooth shell containing glossy brown nut	brilliant orange autumn foliage—only horse chestnut with this feature
Aesculus hippocastanum 'Baumannii'	double flowering horse chestnut	3; 75 (rounded, massive); deep, rich	double white, tinged red; May–June; sterile—no fruit	dense shade; good flowers; no mess from fruit
Ailanthus altissima	tree of heaven	4; 60 (open to rounded); any soil	small yellow; late June; female plants have greenish to red samaras	rapid-growing; withstands smoke and city conditions; self-sows easily and may become a pest
Albizia julibrissin 'Rosea'	hardy silk tree	6 (5); 30 (flat-topped); well drained	rounded heads of pink stamens; July–August; tan-colored pod	tropical appearance; finely divided leaves; hardy to Boston

DECIDUOUS TREES (Continued)

SCIENTIFIC NAME	COMMON NAME	ZONE OF HARDINESS; HEIGHT IN FEET; PREFERRED SOIL	BLOOM; SEASON OF BLOOM; FRUIT	REMARKS
Alnus glutinosa	European alder	3; 60 (oval-headed); moist	catkins; March; small conelike fruit	excellent for wet places
Alnus incana	white alder	2; 60 (round head); moist	yellow catkins; March; small conelike fruit	excellent for wet places
Amelanchier canadensis	shadblow serviceberry	4; 50–60 (upright); moist to well drained	white, nodding; late April; edible, maroon-purple, berrylike	handsome light gray bark; yellow to red autumn foliage
Amelanchier x *grandiflora*	apple serviceberry	4; 20–25 (spreading); moist to well drained	white; early May; edible, red to black, berrylike	handsome light gray bark; yellow to orange autumn foliage
Aralia elata	Japanese angelica tree	3; 15–30 (wide-spreading, with several stems); indifferent	12–18″ pyramidal spikes of small white flowers; August; large clusters of small black berries	thorny, stems; large bicompound leaves
Asimina triloba	pawpaw	5; 25–35 (upright); rich, moisture-retentive	maroon; late May; yellow to brown fruit, edible and delicious	interesting large drooping leaves
Betula davurica	Dahurian birch	4; 40–60 (spreading); well drained	catkins; late April; inconspicuous	exfoliating reddish-brown bark
Betula lenta	sweet birch	3; 50–70 (dense, white when young, rounded at maturity); well drained	catkins; late April; inconspicuous	cherrylike reddish-brown to black bark
Betula maximowicziana	monarch birch	4; 60–80 (open at maturity); well drained	catkins; late April; inconspicuous	gray to orange-gray exfoliating bark
Betula nigra	river birch	4; 60–90 (pyramidal); moist to well drained	catkins; late April; inconspicuous	rugged appearance; reddish-brown to silver-gray exfoliating bark
Betula papyrifera	canoe birch	2; 60–90 (pyramidal); well drained	catkins; late April; inconspicuous	handsome white exfoliating bark
Betula pendula	European white birch	2; 40–60 (pyramidal); well drained	catkins; late April; inconspicuous	handsome white exfoliating bark
Broussonetia papyrifera	paper mulberry	6; 40 (wide-spreading); well drained	globular female catkins; May; ¾ in. diam.; orange to red	interesting, irregularly lobed leaves; good in difficult situations
Carpinus betulus	European hornbeam	5; 60 (rounded); moisture-retentive	catkins; late April; pendulous clusters of leaflike bracts bearing small nutlets	good foliage plant; can be sheared as a screen, hedge or for pleached allée
Carpinus caroliniana	American hornbeam or ironwood	2; 30 (rounded); moisture-retentive	catkins; late April; pendulous clusters of leaflike bracts bearing small nutlets	often with several trunks; interesting "muscled" gray bark
Carya illinoinensis	pecan	5; 100–150 (rounded, massive branches); rich, moisture-retentive	unisexual, in drooping catkins; May; edible nut	fast-growing; season often too short in North for nuts to ripen
Carya ovata	shagbark hickory	4; 90 (upright with round head); rich, moisture-retentive	unisexual, in drooping catkins; May; edible nut	bark exfoliates in long plates; excellent nuts
Castanea mollissima	Chinese chestnut	4; 50–60 (dense, rounded); well drained	unisexual, male flowers in catkins, female at base of male; June; large brown nuts in green burs	highly desirable edible nuts

DECIDUOUS TREES (Continued)

SCIENTIFIC NAME	COMMON NAME	ZONE OF HARDINESS; HEIGHT IN FEET; PREFERRED SOIL	BLOOM; SEASON OF BLOOM; FRUIT	REMARKS
Catalpa bignonioides	southern catalpa	4; 40 (broadly rounded); well drained to dry	upright clusters, white with yellow and brown markings; late June; long beanlike pods	leaves not as coarse as the following species
Catalpa speciosa	northern catalpa	4; 60–90 (pyramidal); well drained to dry	upright clusters, white with yellow and brown markings; late June; long beanlike pods	coarse-texture foliage
Celtis occidentalis	hackberry	2; 60–100 (rounded); moist to dry	inconspicuous; May; orange-red to dark purple drupe	smooth, gray bark
Cercis canadensis	eastern redbud	4; 20–35 (irregular); well drained, acid or neutral	pealike, purplish or pink in clusters; May; pods	attractive heart-shaped leaves; free-flowering, shade-tolerant
Cercidiphyllum japonicum	Katsura tree	4; 40–80 (rounded); rich, moisture-retentive	inconspicuous; April; inconspicuous "dried" follicles on female trees	delicate leaf texture; insect- and disease-free
Cladrastis lutea	yellowwood	3; 50 (rounded); rich, moisture-retentive	fragrant pendulous clusters of white wisterialike flowers; June; dried pods in clusters	valuable flowering specimen tree; smooth, light gray bark; may not blossom every year
Cornus florida	flowering dogwood tree	4; 20–40 (rounded, with horizontal branches); rich, moisture-retentive	showy white bracts surrounding inconspicuous flowers; May; clusters of red berries	scarlet autumn foliage; one of the best small trees for spring blossoms; many cultivars
Cornus florida 'Rubra'	pink flowering dogwood	4; 20–40 (rounded, with horizontal branches); rich, moisture-retentive	showy pink to reddish bracts surrounding inconspicuous flowers; May; clusters of red berries	scarlet autumn foliage
Cornus kousa	Japanese dogwood	5; 20 (horizontal branches); rich, moisture-retentive	showy pointed cream bracts surrounding inconspicuous flowers; mid-June (after leaves); 1/4–1/2 in., red	the best small tree for late spring or early summer blossoms
Corylus colurna	Turkish filbert	4; 50–75 (pyramidal); moisture-retentive or dry	long catkins; late winter, early spring; brown nuts	withstands drought; good form and foliage
Crataegus crus-galli	cockspur thorn	4; 30 (round- to flat-headed, dense); good to poor	white in clusters; late May; bright red berries	horizontal branches; makes good hedge; orange to scarlet autumn foliage
Crataegus laevigata (oxyacantha) 'Paulii'	Paul's scarlet hawthorn	4; 15 (dense, rounded); good to poor	scarlet, double in clusters; late May; dark red	one of the showiest of the hawthorns for flowers
Crataegus x lavallei	Lavalle hawthorn	4; 20 (dense); good to poor	white in clusters; late May; red to orange berries	2-in. thorns; fruit persisting all winter
Crataegus monogyna	single-seeded hawthorn	4; 30 (dense, rounded); good to poor	white in clusters; late May; dull red	lustrous leaves; fruit persisting all winter
Crataegus nitida	glossy hawthorn	4; 30 (dense, rounded); good to poor	white in clusters; late May; dull red	lustrous leaves; fruit persisting all winter
Crataegus phaenopyrum	Washington thorn tree	4; 30 (dense, round head at maturity); good to poor	white in clusters; June; bright red	fruit persisting all winter; brilliant orange to scarlet autumn foliage

DECIDUOUS TREES (Continued)

SCIENTIFIC NAME	COMMON NAME	ZONE OF HARDINESS; HEIGHT IN FEET; PREFERRED SOIL	BLOOM; SEASON OF BLOOM; FRUIT	REMARKS
Davidia involucrata var. *vilmoriniana*	Vilmorin dove tree	5; 30–60 (pyramidal); rich, moisture-retentive	two showy white pendulous bracts surrounding flower "ball"; May; green drupe	unusual and interesting in flower
Diospyros virginiana	common persimmon	4; 60–75 (round-headed); good, moisture-retentive	greenish-yellow, inconspicuous; June; orange to yellow, edible after frost	interesting specimen tree; fruit useful for many culinary purposes
Elaeagnus angustifolia	Russian olive	2; 20 (open, spreading); good to poor; well drained	fragrant, silvery and yellow; June; yellow with silvery scales	valuable for silvery gray foliage
Eucommia ulmoides	hardy rubber tree	5; 40–60 (rounded); well drained	inconspicuous; May; oblong, winged	small specimen tree; produces rubber
Euonymus bungeana var. *semipersistens*	mid-winter euonymus	4; 15 (open); good to poor	inconspicuous; June; yellowish to pinkish white	fruit persisting into winter; subject to attack by euonymus scale
Fagus grandifolia	American beech	3; 90 (pyramidal); good, good, well drained	inconspicuous; three-angled nut	forms copses or groves; smooth gray bark; golden-bronze autumn foliage
Fagus sylvatica	European beech	4; 90 (pyramidal); good, well drained	inconspicuous; three-angled nut	massive specimen tree, smooth gray bark; many cultivars
Franklinia alatamaha	franklinia	5; 15–20 (upright); rich, moisture-retentive	single white; Sept.–Oct.; woody capsule	excellent for autumn flowers; bright scarlet autumn foliage
Fraxinus americana	white ash	3; 100 (erect, with rounded top); not particular	inconspicuous; clusters of winged samaras	fast-growing; deep purple or yellow autumn foliage
Fraxinus ornus	flowering ash	5; 40–60 (rounded); not particular	small, white, fragrant, in dense clusters; May; clusters of winged samaras	dense foliage; flowers and fruit very ornamental
Fraxinus pennsylvanica var. *lanceolata*	green ash	2; 60 (rounded, dense); not particular	inconspicuous; winged samaras	vigorous, dense, seedless forms preferable
Ginkgo biloba	maidenhair tree	4; 80–100+ (open, spreading); good, well drained	inconspicuous; fruit ovoid, with obnoxious odor (plant male trees only)	fine-textured, fan-shaped leaves; golden autumn foliage; excellent in cities
Gleditsia triacanthos var. *inermis* cultivars	thornless honey locust	4; 80–100+ (open, wide); not particular	sterile	fine-textured foliage; withstands city conditions well; numerous cultivars
Gymnocladus dioica	Kentucky coffee tree	4; 60–80 (open, wide); good to poor, well drained	inconspicuous; thick brown pod	picturesque growth habit; large bicompound leaves
Halesia carolina	Carolina silverbell	5; 25 (rounded); good, moisture-retentive	white, bell-shaped; May; dry winged pods	valuable small spring-flowering tree
Halesia monticola	mountain silverbell	5; 40–60 (pyramidal); good, moisture-retentive	white, bell-shaped; May; dry winged pods	valuable spring-flowering tree
Hippophae rhamnoides	sea buckthorn	3; 20 (open, rounded) good to poor, well drained	inconspicuous, sexes separate; large clusters of bright orange berries	grayish-green to silvery leaves, especially good for seashore

DECIDUOUS TREES (Continued)

SCIENTIFIC NAME	COMMON NAME	ZONE OF HARDINESS; HEIGHT IN FEET; PREFERRED SOIL	BLOOM; SEASON OF BLOOM; FRUIT	REMARKS
Juglans nigra	black walnut	4; 80–120 (upright, with rounded head); good, moisture-retentive	inconspicuous; large edible nuts	valuable timber tree; coarse leaves
Juglans regia	English or Persian walnut	5–6; 60 (rounded, with broad head); good, moisture-retentive	inconspicuous; large edible nuts	the cultivar 'Carpathian' fruits best under northern conditions
Kalopanax pictus	castor-aralia	4; 40–60 (open and rounded, massive branches); good to poor, well drained	small white, in large clusters; late July; black seeds	large-lobed leaves, tropical in appearance; seeds relished by birds
Koelreuteria paniculata	golden-rain tree	5; 20–30 (rounded); good to poor, well drained	small yellow, in large pyramidal upright clusters; early summer; bladderlike pods	long season of interest from flowers and fruit
Laburnum alpinum	Scots laburnum	4; 20–30 (upright); good, well drained	yellow, pealike, in pendulous clusters; May; small pods	superior small spring-flowering tree
Laburnum x *watereri*	Waterer laburnum	5; 20–30 (upright); good, well drained	yellow, pealike, in pendulous clusters, May; small pods	superior, spring-flowering
Larix decidua	European larch	2; 60–90 (irregular at maturity); good to poor to moist	inconspicuous; 2-in. cones	rapid growth, handsome at all seasons
Larix laricina	tamarack	1; 60 (irregular at maturity); good to poor to moist	inconspicuous; 2-in. cones	rapid growth, handsome at all seasons
Larix leptolepis	Japanese larch	4; 60–90 (irregular at maturity); good to poor to moist	inconspicuous; 2-in. cones	rapid growth, handsome at all seasons
Liquidambar styraciflua	sweet gum	5; 60–100 (pyramidal); moist to ordinary	inconspicuous; round, horned balls 1 in. in diam.	attractive star-shaped leaves turning brilliant scarlet in autumn
Liriodendron tulipifera	tulip tree	4; 100+ (pyramidal, massive branches); moist to ordinary	greenish-yellow with orange markings, shaped like tulips; June; dry pods	stately tree with interesting but not conspicuous flowers
Maackia amurensis	Amur maackia	4; 30–40 (upright); poor to ordinary	small white in erect panicles; summer; pods	good small tree for summer flowers
Maclura pomifera	osage orange	5; 30–50 (irregular, open); poor to ordinary	inconspicuous; green, like a large wrinkled orange	drought-resistant, good as screen or impenetrable barrier in difficult growing situations
Magnolia acuminata	cucumber tree	4; 60–90 (massive and wide-spreading); good, moisture-retentive	greenish-yellow; not conspicuous; June; reddish, in cucumber-shaped shells	bold foliage and rugged habit at maturity
Magnolia heptapeta (*M. denudata*)	yulan magnolia	5; 20–30 (rounded); rich, moisture-retentive	white, fragrant; early May; bright red seeds in pods	handsome in flower, especially with flowering cherries
Magnolia x *loebneri* 'Merrill'	Merrill magnolia	4; 40–50 (pyramidal to rounded); rich, moisture-retentive	white, fragrant, 8–15 petals; late April; red seeds in pods	vigorous and free-flowering, blossoms when quite young
Magnolia macrophylla	big-leaf magnolia	6–5; 40–50 (round-headed); rich, moisture-retentive	creamy-white, 10–12 in. in diam., fragrant; July; red seeds in pods	leaves 20–30 in. long, striking effect

DECIDUOUS TREES (Continued)

SCIENTIFIC NAME	COMMON NAME	ZONE OF HARDINESS; HEIGHT IN FEET; PREFERRED SOIL	BLOOM; SEASON OF BLOOM; FRUIT	REMARKS
Magnolia x *soulangiana*	saucer magnolia	5; 20–30 (upright to rounded); rich, moisture-retentive	white to purple, 5–10 in. in diam.; April–May; red seeds in pods	many cultivars; the most popular magnolia in North
Magnolia stellata	star magnolia	5; 8–20 (bushy, moundlike); rich, moisture-retentive	white, 12–15 petals, fragrant; March–April; red seeds in a pod	early blossoms sometimes injured by late frosts
Magnolia virginiana	sweet bay	5; 20–60 (treelike in South, shrubby in North); wet to ordinary	white, fragrant; early summer; handsome pods with red seeds	leaves green above, nearly white below, persist into winter; evergreen in South
Malus x *arnoldiana*	Arnold crab apple	4; 20 (mounded, dense); ordinary, well drained	buds rose, flower pink outside fading to white inside; May; yellow and red	beautiful contrasting flowers; bears annually
Malus x *atrosanguinea*	carmine crab apple	4; 20 (mounded, dense); ordinary, well drained	buds crimson, flowers deep rose; May; dark red	bears annually; resistant to apple scab; fruits not particularly ornamental
Malus baccata	Siberian crab apple	2; 30–50 (upright, dense); ordinary, well drained	white, fragrant; May; red or yellow	bears annually; resistant to apple scab; best small flowering tree for tubs or containers
Malus 'Blanche Ames'	Blanche Ames crab apple	4; 20 (rounded, dense); ordinary, well drained	pink and white, delicate; May; yellow	bears annually; resistant to apple scab; graceful in flower
Malus 'Bob White'	Bob White crab apple	5; 20 (rounded, dense); ordinary; well drained	buds pink, fading to white flowers; May; yellow	fruit remains well into winter and provides food for birds; alternate bearer
Malus 'Dolgo'	Dolgo crab apple	3; 30–40 (vigorous, open); ordinary, well drained	white, fragrant; May; bright red	useful in very cold areas; alternate bearer
Malus 'Dorothea'	Dorothea crab apple	4; 25 (rounded, dense); ordinary, well drained	buds, rose, semidouble deep pink flowers; May; bright yellow	graceful in blossom; resistant to apple scab; bears annually
Malus floribunda	Japanese flowering crab apple	4; 30 (rounded, dense); ordinary, well drained	buds deep pink, flowers fading to white; May; yellow and red	handsome color contrast when flowers partly open; bears annually
Malus huepehensis	tea crab apple	4; 20 (vase-shaped, handsome); ordinary, well drained	buds deep pink, flowers fade to white; May; greenish-yellow to red	flowers in alternate years, but one of the most handsome of all crabapples in blossom
Malus 'Prince Georges'	Prince Georges crab apple	4; 20–25 (upright, dense); ordinary, well drained	delicate pink, double; May; no fruits	excellent where fruiting is not desired; flowers annually
Malus x *purpurea* 'Lemoinei'	Lemoine crab apple	4; 25 (rounded, dense); ordinary, well drained	deep magenta; May; purplish-red	resistant to apple scab; strong color not appreciated by all; bears annually
Malus 'Red Jade'	red jade crab apple	4; 20 (pendulous); ordinary, well drained	small, white; May; bright red	interesting growth habit, fruit persists into winter; alternate bearer

DECIDUOUS TREES (Continued)

SCIENTIFIC NAME	COMMON NAME	ZONE OF HARDINESS; HEIGHT IN FEET; PREFERRED SOIL	BLOOM; SEASON OF BLOOM; FRUIT	REMARKS
Malus sargentii	Sargent crab apple	4; 8 (mounded, broad and low); ordinary, well drained	white; May; dark red	the only shrubby crabapple; many landscape uses
Metasequoia glyptostroboides	dawn redwood	5; 100 (upright, pyramidal); moist to ordinary	inconspicuous flowers and fruit	rapid-growing and problem-free, fine-textured foliage
Morus alba	white mulberry	4; 40 (rounded, dense); ordinary or poor	inconspicuous, white, pinkish or purplish like blackberries	good for poor soil; fruit messy and foliage coarse
Nyssa sylvatica	sour gum or black gum	4; 60–90 (dense to open, pyramidal and picturesque); wet to ordinary	inconspicuous; small blue berries	slow-growing, glossy leaves; brilliant scarlet autumn foliage
Ostrya virginiana	American hop hornbeam	4; 50–60 (pyramidal); ordinary	inconspicuous; hoplike fruit clusters	slow-growing, trouble-free small tree
Oxydendrum arboreum	sourwood or sorrel tree	5; 20–40 (pyramidal); rich, moisture-retentive	racemes of small white flowers; July; dried capsules	handsome in flower; brilliant scarlet autumn foliage; fruit effective into winter
Paulownia tomentosa	empress tree	5; 40 (rounded, open); ordinary to poor	violet, fragrant, in large pyramidal clusters before leaves; May; large brown dry capsules	rapid-growing; large leaves; self-sows
Platanus x *acerifolia*	London plane tree	5; 80–100 (open, spreading); ordinary to poor	inconspicuous; pendulous ball-like clusters	exfoliating bark, underbark light-colored; grows well in cities but often overplanted
Populus alba	white poplar	3; 60–80 (open, irregular); poor to ordinary, well drained	flowers and fruits inconspicuous, but fluffy white seeds noticeable when dispersed by breeze	handsome silvery pubescence under leaves, very wide-spreading at maturity; good in littoral areas
Populus maximowiczii	Japanese poplar	4; 60 (open, wide-spreading); poor to ordinary	flowers and fruits inconspicuous, but fluffy white seeds noticeable when dispersed by breeze	vigorous in growth; interesting specimen tree; somewhat coarse foliage
Populus nigra 'Italica'	Lombardy poplar	3; 90 (dense, columnar); poor to ordinary	flowers inconspicuous	very rapid growth, short-lived; use only as temporary screen
Populus simonii 'Fastigiata'	pyramidal Simon poplar	2; 50 (loosely columnar); poor to ordinary	flowers and fruits inconspicuous, but fluffy white seeds noticeable when dispersed by breeze	a substitute for Lombardy poplar, but not as columnar
Prunus 'Hally Jolivette'	Hally Jolivette cherry	5; 10–15 (dense, rounded); good, moisture-retentive	double white, pink in bud; May; sterile	buds do not open all at once, long period of bloom
Prunus maackii	Amur chokecherry	2; 30 (rounded, dense); ordinary	white in racemes, not showy; May; black berries	striking brownish-yellow flaking bark, excellent for winter interest

DECIDUOUS TREES (Continued)

SCIENTIFIC NAME	COMMON NAME	ZONE OF HARDINESS; HEIGHT IN FEET; PREFERRED SOIL	BLOOM; SEASON OF BLOOM; FRUIT	REMARKS
Prunus sargentii	Sargent cherry	4; 40–50 (upright, with rounded top); good, moisture-retentive	single, deep pink; late April; dark purple, not freely produced	one of the best flowering cherries, few disease problems, large in stature; red autumn foliage
Prunus serrula		5; 20 (spreading); good, moisture-retentive	white; May; fruit not freely produced	superlative glossy, brilliant reddish-brown bark; good winter interest; often not long-lived
Prunus serrulata cultivars	Oriental cherries	5–6; 20–25 (upright to spreading); good, moisture-retentive	white to pink, May, single and double; May; mostly sterile	handsome flowers but demand good growing conditions, frequently short-lived in eastern U.S.A.
Prunus subhirtella	Higan cherry	5; 30 (rounded, dense); good, moisture-retentive	pale pink; late April; not freely produced	very floriferous, long-lived, with few disease problems
Prunus subhirtella 'Pendula'	weeping Higan cherry	5; 30 (gracefully pendulous); good, moisture-retentive	pale pink; late April; not freely produced	very floriferous, long-lived and relatively disease-free; purchase plant on own roots rather than grafted
Prunus yedoensis	Yoshino cherry	5; 40 (flat-topped); good, moisture-retentive	single, white; late April; not freely produced	very floriferous, long-lived and relatively disease-free
Pseudolarix amabilis	golden or false larch	5; 60–80 (open, broad and pyramidal); good, moisture-retentive	inconspicuous; beautiful pale green cones	refined texture, golden autumn foliage; needs much space to develop
Pterostyrax hispida	epaulette tree	5; 30 (open-headed, slender); good, moisture-retentive	creamy-white, fragrant, 4–9-in. pendulous panicles in June; bristly in panicles	unusual small specimen tree, easily grown
Pyrus calleryana 'Bradford'	Bradford pear	4; 30 (pyramidal); good	white; May; small, russet-colored	good small tree for streets, easily grown
Quercus acutissima	sawtooth oak	6–5; 45 (wide-spreading, with rounded head); ordinary	inconspicuous; acorn	lustrous chestnutlike leaves, bold appearance
Quercus alba	white oak	4; 90+ (massive, wide-spreading); ordinary	inconspicuous; acorn	very long-lived, of slow growth, one of the most majestic trees
Quercus coccinea	scarlet oak	4; 75 (open, rounded head); ordinary	inconspicuous; acorn	difficult to transplant; scarlet autumn foliage
Quercus imbricaria	shingle oak	5; 75 (round-topped at maturity); ordinary	inconspicuous; acorn	lustrous laurel-like leaves persisting into winter; handsome specimen tree
Quercus laurifolia	laurel oak	7; 60 (dense, rounded); ordinary	inconspicuous; acorn	good street tree in South; semievergreen; lustrous leaves
Quercus nigra	water oak	6; 60 (round-topped); moist to wet	inconspicuous; acorn	good for wet situations, also as a street tree

DECIDUOUS TREES (Continued)

SCIENTIFIC NAME	COMMON NAME	ZONE OF HARDINESS; HEIGHT IN FEET; PREFERRED SOIL	BLOOM; SEASON OF BLOOM; FRUIT	REMARKS
Quercus palustris	pin oak	4; 75 (pyramidal, dense, drooping lower branches); ordinary	inconspicuous; acorn	excellent specimen tree; transplants easily
Quercus phellos	willow oak	5; 50 (round-topped); ordinary	inconspicuous; acorn	beautiful fine-textured foliage; withstands city conditions
Quercus prinus (*Q. montana*)	chestnut oak	4; 70 (dense, rounded head); ordinary to poor	inconspicuous; acorn	one of the best oaks for dry soils
Quercus robur	English oak	5; 75–100 (open, broad); ordinary	inconspicuous; acorn	not long-lived in all situations in U.S.A.
Quercus rubra (*Q. borealis*)	red oak	3; 75 (round-headed at maturity); ordinary	inconspicuous; acorn	rapid-growing, withstands city conditions, easily transplanted
Quercus virginiana	live oak	7; 60 (open, wide-spreading); ordinary	inconspicuous; acorn	evergreen in deep South, massive in habit
Robinia pseudoacacia	black locust	3; 75 (upright and open at maturity); ordinary to very poor	white, pealike, in fragrant clusters; June; dried pods	use only for poor soils; often troubled by borers and leaf miners in some areas
Salix alba	white willow	2; 75 (open, wide); wet to moist to ordinary	inconspicuous flowers and fruit	best of the upright willows
Salix alba 'Tristis'	golden weeping willow	2; 30 (pendulous branches); wet to moist to ordinary	inconspicuous flowers and fruit	attractive golden pendulous branches
Salix babylonica	Babylon weeping willow	6; 30 (pendulous branches); wet to moist to ordinary	inconspicuous flowers and fruit	best of the weeping willows south of New England
Salix x *elegantissima*	Thurlow weeping willow	4; 40 (pendulous branches); wet to moist to ordinary	inconspicuous flowers and fruit	best weeping willow for colder areas
Salix matsudana 'Tortuosa'	corkscrew willow	4; 30 (broadly upright); wet to moist to ordinary	inconspicuous flowers and fruit	twisted, contorted branches provide unusual winter interest
Salix pentandra	laurel willow	4; 60 (rounded); wet to moist to ordinary	inconspicuous flowers and fruit	large lustrous dark green leaves
Sophora japonica	Chinese scholar tree	4; 75 (rounded, spreading); ordinary	creamy, pealike, in large upright clusters; August; greenish in clusters	valuable flowering time; fine texture of foliage; messy flowers and fruits
Sorbus alnifolia	Korean mountain ash	4; 30–60 (rounded at maturity); ordinary	white in clusters; May; clusters of orange berries	smooth gray bark, larger than other mountain ashes; easily grown
Sorbus aucuparia	European mountain ash	3; 30–40 (open at maturity); ordinary	white, in flat clusters; May; red to orange berries	good, small tree in fruit; borers attack trunk
Stewartia koreana	Korean stewartia	5; 30 (dense, pyramidal); rich, moisture-retentive	white, 3 in., conspicuous yellow stamens; July; dry capsule	beautiful flowers, interesting bark; orange-red autumn color
Stewartia pseudocamellia	Japanese stewartia	5; 30 (dense, pyramidal); rich, moisture-retentive	white, 3 in., conspicuous yellow stamens; July; dry capsule	beautiful flowers, interesting bark; purplish autumn color

DECIDUOUS TREES (Continued)

SCIENTIFIC NAME	COMMON NAME	ZONE OF HARDINESS; HEIGHT IN FEET; PREFERRED SOIL	BLOOM; SEASON OF BLOOM; FRUIT	REMARKS
Styrax japonica	Japanese snowbell	5; 30 (wide-spreading, flat top); rich, moisture-retentive	white, pendulous, bell-shaped; June; drupe	beautiful flowers, good foliage; easily grown
Syringa reticulata	Japanese tree lilac	5; 25–30 (pyramidal); ordinary	creamy-white, large pyramidal clusters; June; leathery capsules	train to single trunk or several stems; interesting cherry-like bark
Taxodium distichum	bald cypress	4; 100+ (pyramidal); wet to ordinary	inconspicuous flowers and fruit	fine-textured foliage; does not need wet conditions for good growth
Tilia cordata	littleleaf linden	3; 90 (pyramidal, dense); ordinary	small, yellowish, fragrant; July; nutlike	excellent shade tree, withstands city conditions
Tilia x *euchlora*	Crimean linden	4; 50 (lower branches pendulous); ordinary	small, yellowish, fragrant; July; nutlike	beautiful growth habit
Tilia petiolaris	pendent silver linden	5; 70 (narrow head, with drooping branches); ordinary	small, yellowish, fragrant; July; nutlike	beautiful growth habit
Tilia tomentosa	silver linden	4; 90 (erect branches, broad, pyramidal, dense); ordinary	small, yellowish, fragrant; July; nutlike	striking growth habit in winter
Ulmus parvifolia	Chinese elm	5; 40–50 (rounded); ordinary	flowers and fruit fairly inconspicuous	handsome mottled exfoliating bark; resistant to Dutch elm disease
Ulmus pumila	Siberian elm	4; 70 (rounded, open); ordinary	flowers and fruit relatively inconspicuous	very rapid growth, weak wood; resistant to Dutch elm disease
Zelkova serrata	Japanese zelkova	5; 60–70 (ascending branches, round-headed); good	flowers and fruit relatively inconspicuous	leaves and habit of growth like American elm, but smaller stature

EVERGREEN TREES

SCIENTIFIC NAME	COMMON NAME	HEIGHT IN FEET	ZONE OF HARDINESS	REMARKS
Abies balsamea	balsam fir	70	3	prefers moist places; for cold areas only
Abies concolor	white fir	60–100+	4	handsome bluish-green foliage
Abies homolepis	Nikko fir	60–90	4	wide-spreading, vigorous, deep green foliage
Abies koreana	Korean fir	50	5	slow-growing; formal in appearance
Abies nordmanniana	Nordmann fir	80–120	4	glossy dark green foliage
Abies veitchii	Veitch fir	60–75	3	stiffly pyramidal, leaves with beautiful white undersurface
Calocedrus decurrens (Libocedrus)	California incense cedar	40–80	5	very ornamental narrow columnar shape; requires good soil
Cedrus atlantica 'Glauca'	blue Atlas cedar	60–80+	6	graceful widely pyramidal habit; blue-green foliage
Cedrus deodara	deodar cedar	60–80	7(6)	graceful in habit of growth and texture

(Continued)

EVERGREEN TREES (Continued)

SCIENTIFIC NAME	COMMON NAME	HEIGHT IN FEET	ZONE OF HARDINESS	REMARKS
Cedrus libani	cedar of Lebanon	60–80	6	deep green foliage
Cedrus libani var. *stenocoma*	hardy cedar of Lebanon	60–80	5	hardy at least to Boston; upright growth habit
Chamaecyparis lawsoniana	Lawson cypress	80–120	5	slender to broadly pyramidal growth habit; many cultivars for specimen use, screens, hedges, etc.
Chamaecyparis obtusa	Hinoki cypress	60	4	pyramidal growth habit; many cultivars for specimen use, screens, hedges, etc.
Chamaecyparis pisifera	Sawara cypress	60–80	3	narrowly pyramidal growth habit; many cultivars for specimen use, screens, hedges, etc.
Cryptomeria japonica	Japanese cedar	80	6(5)	symmetrical while young; rapid-growing; scalelike needles
Cunninghamia lanceolata	China fir	60	7(6)	spreading branches, with soft-textured needles
Ilex aquifolium	English holly	30–60	6	deep green leaves; red berries; many cultivars
Ilex cassine	dahoon	30	7	dense habit of growth; profuse clusters of red berries
Ilex latifolia	lusterleaf holly	40–60	7	dark green lustrous leaves; dense clusters of pale red berries
Ilex opaca	American holly	20–40	5	spiny leaves are not lustrous; hardier than English holly; many cultivars
Ilex pedunculosa	longstalk holly	15–30	5	lustrous spineless leaves; profuse red berries borne on long stalks
Ilex pernyi	Perny holly	20–30	6	attractive glossy leaves; conspicuous clusters of red berries
Juniperus chinensis	Chinese juniper	40–50	4	upright growth habit; scalelike leaves; many cultivars
Juniperus excelsa 'Stricta'	Greek juniper	20–30	7	dense, compact, pyramidal
Juniperus rigida	needle juniper	20–30	5	graceful pendulous branchlets; open habit, long scalelike leaves
Juniperus scopulorum	Rocky Mountain juniper	30	5	drought-resistant; upright growth habit; many cultivars
Juniperus virginiana	eastern red cedar	60	2	hardiest of the upright cedars; numerous cultivars
Libocedrus, **see** *Calocedrus decurrens*				
Magnolia grandiflora	southern magnolia or bull bay	50–80	7	large lustrous leaves; large fragrant white flowers
Photinia serrulata	Chinese photinia	30	7	lustrous dark green leaves, new leaves reddish; clusters of bright red berries
Picea abies	Norway spruce	100–120	2	stiff appearance, especially when young; massive at maturity
Picea engelmannii	Engelmann spruce	80	2	dense habit of growth; bluish needles
Picea glauca	white spruce	80	2	pyramidal growth habit; withstands heat and drought
Picea omorika	Serbian spruce	60	4	narrow growth habit with graceful pendent branches
Picea orientalis	oriental spruce	80	4	glossy green needles; dense pyramidal growth habit
Picea pungens	Colorado spruce	80	2	stiff, formal appearance; many forms with bluish foliage

EVERGREEN TREES (Continued)

SCIENTIFIC NAME	COMMON NAME	HEIGHT IN FEET	ZONE OF HARDINESS	REMARKS
Pinus aristata	bristlecone pine	8–40	5	extremely slow-growing; open picturesque growth habit
Pinus bungeana	lace-bark pine	40	4	beautiful exfoliating bark, light creamy-colored patches; unusual specimen tree
Pinus cembra	Swiss stone pine	30–60	2	slow-growing; handsome dense habit of growth
Pinus densiflora	Japanese red pine	60–90	4	handsome irregular growth habit; flat-topped; orange-red bark
Pinus flexilis	limber pine	40	2	slow growth; broad habit at maturity; fine texture
Pinus koraiensis	Korean pine	60–90	3	slow-growing; dense; fine texture
Pinus monticola	western white pine	60	5	growth habit narrow and symmetrical; handsome specimen tree
Pinus nigra	Austrian pine	60–80+	4	fast-growing, stiff appearance; adapts to difficult growing situations
Pinus parviflora	Japanese white pine	60	5	wide-spreading; short needles; dark green
Pinus ponderosa	ponderosa pine	80	5	fast-growing; massive and open growth habit
Pinus resinosa	red pine	60	2	broadly pyramidal growth habit; soft texture; reddish-brown bark; disease problems in some areas
Pinus strobus	eastern white pine	100–120	3	soft green, refined foliage; rapid growth; the best native pine
Pinus sylvestris	Scots pine	60–70	2	bluish-green needles; attractive open habit at maturity; older trunks and branches have orange-red bark
Pinus thunbergii	Japanese black pine	60	5	picturesque open growth habit; excellent for seashore plantings
Pseudotsuga menziesii	Douglas fir	100+	4	rapid growth; weak wood; pyramidal growth habit
Sciadopitys verticillata	umbrella pine	30–60	5	whorls of long needles; densely pyramidal; excellent specimen tree
Sequoia sempervirens	redwood	100+	7	straight massive trunk; fine-textured foliage
Sequoiadendron giganteum	giant sequoia	100+	6	straight massive trunk; dense appearance while young
Taxus baccata	English yew	30–50	6	develops slowly into a small tree if not pruned; many cultivars
Taxus cuspidata	Japanese yew	30–50	5	develops slowly into a small tree if not pruned; many cultivars
Thuja occidentalis	American arborvitae	30–60	2	columnar growth habit; many cultivars for specimen planting, screens or hedges
Thuja orientalis	oriental arborvitae	30–50	6	columnar growth habit; many cultivars for specimen planting, screens or hedges
Thuja plicata	giant arborvitae	50–100	5	foliage does not turn brown in winter; excellent for screens or hedges
Tsuga canadensis	Canada hemlock	90	3	rapid growth; fine texture; many cultivars for specimen planting, screens or hedges;
Tsuga caroliniana	Carolina hemlock	70	4	delicate, dense growth habit; specimen, screens or hedges

14.1 Old rhododendrons and azaleas—and many other shrubs—create garden walls that provide enclosure, privacy and protection from unwanted intrusion. Photo Grant Heilman

14

Shrubs

In the planting design for a home property shrubs should be given an important place, not merely because they function so well as a natural screen but for the sake of their own beauty. In wealth and color of bloom, in range of flowering season, in richness and variety of foliage, in diversity of shape and form, in vivacity of fruit effect and individual interest of twig color in winter, no other plant group can surpass this type of display.

Shrubs form the intermediate plantings on the home property. They may be used with restraint and distinction in the planting about the house; they may be used as low ornamental hedges to form the boundary of the property or as a high hedge to screen unsightly objects; they may be used as specimen plants where the beauty of their bloom or foliage can be enjoyed to advantage; they may be planted in groups or as borders to bring a variety of form, bloom and autumn coloring into the landscape picture, and to provide a nesting place and perhaps even some berries or other food for birds. They may be used as a background for tall perennials and lilies, and some of the smaller species may be used in rock gardens to give character and form to the planting. Some types may be grown in tubs or planting boxes to be used for decorative effect on terrace or patio, and a few, such as the evergreen firethorn (*Pyracantha coccinea*) and the wintercreeper (*Euonymus for-*

tunei var. *radicans*) can be trained as vines against the house wall.

Most shrubs are long-lived and, like the trees, are considered a permanent or long-time investment. However, unlike the trees, they mature in a very few years and thus begin early to pay dividends. Four or five years after planting, a shrub border or a boundary screen should usually be high and dense enough to start to obliterate whatever lies behind it, and mature enough to bear blossoms and fruit in profusion.

Before winter is really over, some shrubs are already in bloom, followed by others that carry on through the season until the onset of autumn frosts or even later. The great majority of shrubs bloom in spring or early summer. From mid-July on there is only an occasional shrub in flower, but by careful selection a homeowner may have some bloom in almost every season except the colder parts of winter. Shrubs with interesting fruit begin to produce it in late June or July, and the succession continues without intermission until midwinter or early spring. Some of the fruits are pure colors of red, purple, orange, yellow or blue. Some are only dry capsules but interesting nonetheless because of their form. Fruits of many shrubs are frequently used for indoor flower arrangements. Color, form, texture, line — all the essentials of composition — are to be found in twigs and fruit as well as in leaves and blossoms of shrubs. The leaves of some shrubs turn to brilliant colors in the autumn, some of the viburnums, enkianthus and euonymus being as beautiful as any tree.

Like any other types of plants, shrubs should be adapted to the soil and other conditions of the site. Some shrubs thrive in dry soil, others in wet soil, while the majority prefer a soil that is midway between the two. Some respond to cultivation and enrichment of the soil; others prefer a meager diet. Some are hardy on exposed summits; others require protection from the wind. Some grow well in shade, while most prefer plenty of sunshine. And then there is an easily satisfied group of shrubs that seem at home in any environment. All of these factors, while they may somewhat limit the use of some shrubs, also enlarge the possibilities of others.

SELECTION OF SHRUBS

The selection of shrubs for a garden site may be approached in two different ways. In the first, the existing conditions of the site are (and very often must be) accepted, and only the shrubs that thrive in those conditions are used. In the second, existing conditions are modified to make possible a wider range in the use of shrubs. Sometimes conditions cannot be changed except at great expense. Sometimes it requires time to effect the change. But usually growing conditions may be improved by the application of organic matter and fertilizer, by cultivation and the removal of grass and weeds, by drainage or by irrigation. If the second method is used, shrubs may be selected solely for their quality and for their special contributions to the general composition. For methods of modifying acidity or alkalinity of the soil, altering drainage, and increasing fertility and organic matter content, see index.

If on a bare, open ground with alkaline or neutral soil we insist upon having rhododendrons and azaleas, then we will have to make changes in the site, underdrain the soil, plant oak trees for shade and for acidity of soil, add humus and leaf mold to the soil and mulch every year with a carpet of oak leaves. Only when these changed conditions are established can we plant rhododendrons and laurel with any possibility of success.

But if we accept existing conditions without making any changes, we must be content with the shrubs that grow under such conditions. So long as conditions are favorable, with an ordinary garden soil, some sun, not too much shade, and protection from wind, then the range of selection is very wide and our choice can be made entirely on climatic and aesthetic considerations.

The cultural requirements of all shrubs to be used in a planting scheme must be thoroughly understood before final selections can be determined or decisions made about the extent to which the site should be modified. The most critical factor is each shrub's ability to adapt to the existing or modified soil conditions. This includes tolerance of varying degrees of soil acidity or alkalinity (pH), availability or lack of moisture during various periods of the year (including whether the plant can withstand the extremes of these conditions), and the ability to grow well in various types of soil—sandy, gravelly, clayey, loamy, or any mixtures of these. The manner in which a plant can adapt to varying degrees of sunlight and shade is equally important and will affect such characteristics as general vigor, height, habit or growth, heaviness of flowering and fruiting, and, to some extent, hardiness. Other environmental and special site conditions to be considered include the resistance of the shrub to strong winds, glaring or reflected sunlight, snow or ice damage and atmospheric pollution.

Matching a shrub's cultural requirements to existing or modified site conditions is only half the problem, however. No planting scheme will be ultimately successful if the shrubs fail to perform the function intended for them in the landscape. Prior knowledge of the habit of growth, height and spread at maturity, and of flowering or fruiting characteristics, is essential and can save the homeowner considerable disappointment or expense later on.

All too frequently shrubs are selected that will grow too large for the space allotted to them. Frequent pruning to keep them within bounds then becomes necessary, which often leads to distorted, unnatural shapes and the ultimate need to replace them. Careful initial selection of less vigorous or more compact types can prevent this problem. Some shrubs, such as *Philadelphus, Deutzia* or *Weigela,* have very attractive flowers for a few weeks in the spring, but undistinguished foliage during the growing season and no ornamental fruits, autumn leaf color, handsome stems or outstanding interest during the winter. On smaller properties we must live in intimate contact with shrubs the whole year round and those that possess ornamental features during two or more seasons are consequently much more rewarding. Interesting fruit, foliage, twig and bark characteristics, autumn color and habit of growth are equally as important as heavy flowering. Few shrubs possess all these combinations; but the more combinations they do have, the greater will be their value in the landscape.

Knowledge of the various shrubs' ornamental characteristics will lead to further rewards when one is trying to select and combine shrubs that will provide pleasing seasonal or year-round contrasts. Interesting shapes may be juxtaposed one against another, attractive combinations of flower and fruit colors may be arranged, leaf shapes and textures may be used to create special effects, combinations of evergreen and deciduous shrubs may help liven the winter landscape and shrubs with interesting or unique habits of growth may be used to create accents and focal points.

Selecting shrubs may be likened to selecting furnishings for a room. They should be seen and studied from all points of view, and finally chosen with great care. Glowing descriptions in textbooks or nursery catalogues serve only as an introduction. There is no substitute for actually seeing the plant beforehand, especially when it is at full maturity, and preferably in as many seasons of the year as possible. Numerous opportunities for such studies exist. Examples of ornamental plantings in one's own neighborhood make a good starting point. Conspicuous instances of successes and failures are easy to find. Local public parks, tours of private gardens and estates open to the public, and the display plantings of local nurseries and garden centers are good places to study various shrubs. Visits to botanical gardens, arboreta and display gardens can be most rewarding. In such gardens, shrubs may be planted among their close relatives, and opportunities exist to make comparisons between the ornamental value of the different varieties. Often, too, shrubs may be seen in such gardens at full maturity in uncrowded settings. The specimens displayed have withstood the test of time and climate, and frequently represent the best species and cultivated varieties adapted to the local area.

PLANTING AND TRANSPLANTING SHRUBS

Shrubs Balled and Burlapped

Shrubs that have been field grown in the nursery and purchased with balls of soil about the roots should be transplanted either in early spring, which is the more favorable time, or in the autumn. Each planting season has its advantages. Except for the very early spring-flowering shrubs, the spring transplanting is preferred by many gardeners because it gives the plants increasingly good growing weather in which to reestablish themselves. However, spring is a busy time for all gardeners, and in apportioning the year's work it often is advisable to plan the transplanting of new shrubs and trees in the autumn when such work may be spread over a longer period of good transplanting weather. In sections of the country from the shores of Chesapeake Bay southward through the coastal plains to Texas, in the central valley of California and on the coast of Oregon, transplanting operations are safely carried on throughout the winter months because many parts of these regions have six months of continuous good transplanting weather. In colder portions of the Northeast, Midwest and the Plains states, the seasons for transplanting are very short, September and May for evergreens and September through October and May for deciduous plants.

Container-grown Shrubs

It is becoming standard practice for nurseries and garden centers to sell shrubs (and to some extent, trees too) that have been raised in containers of various sorts. In many instances such plants have spent their entire life in the container; but sometimes they have been field grown and transplanted into the container a season or two before sale. Shrubs obtained in this manner may be planted almost any time during the growing season, and the shock of transplanting can be reduced to a minimum. When selecting container-grown plants, be sure that plenty of healthy new vigorous growth is in evidence. This will indicate that the plant has not been kept in the container too long, and that it has been well fed and continuously well watered in the nursery. Shrubs that have been kept in their containers too long, or those that have had their growth seriously checked by inadequate watering and fertilizing, may take several seasons to recover and grow vigorously when planted in their final site in the garden.

Water the plant thoroughly a few hours before it is removed from the container for planting. Upon removal, examine the root system carefully. If dense masses of roots are found at the perimeter of the soil mass, they should be pried gently apart before the plant is set into its hole. If the roots are especially dense and tangled, they should be cut with a knife. Make several slits no larger than 1/4 in. into the root mass around the ball; each slit should run vertically from top to bottom, and should be parallel to the next. Whether to separate the outermost roots by hand or to cut them with a knife will depend upon the severity of the crowding. This is a very important operation, however, as it will ensure that new roots will grow out into the surrounding soil. Planting methods for container-grown shrubs are otherwise similar to those for balled and burlapped shrubs and trees. Pruning need not be as severe, but if a considerable amount of root disturbance has been necessary, then the tops should be cut back correspondingly by at least one-fourth or one-third.

Bare Root Shrubs

Shrubs that have been purchased with bare roots from nurseries or mail-order sources should be planted immediately upon receipt. Delivery should be arranged so that the plants arrive in early spring, while they are still dormant and just before new growth commences. If the ground is still frozen when the plant ar-

rives, or if the weather does not permit immediate planting, then the plants should be stored indoors in a cool (35°–45°F.), shady place and the roots kept well covered and damp. Thoroughly moistened (but not soggy) burlap, peat or sphagnum moss makes an ideal covering for this purpose. Soaking the roots for an hour or so in a bucket of water soon after receipt will help the plants to recover the moisture lost in shipping. If for any reason bare-rooted shrubs must be left longer than a week before planting, they should be placed in trenches out of doors and the roots covered with soil. This procedure, called heeling in, should be done in a sheltered, shady place. A coldframe, if available, is ideal for this purpose.

Many shrubs may be moved from one location in the garden to another with bare roots, especially while young. Older, well-established plants with an extensive root system (especially broad-leaved evergreens and conifers) should be carefully dug and balled and burlapped. This method requires more time and effort but involves less risk than moving shrubs with bare roots. Early spring, just prior to the onset of new growth, is the best time for either of these procedures, with early autumn being a second preference.

The following shrubs are usually difficult to transplant and should be handled by the method recommended for each:

Abelia x *grandiflora*	ball and burlap
Ceanothus	''
Corylus	''
Cotoneaster adpressus	potted plants
Cotoneaster horizontalis	''
Cotoneaster microphyllus	''
Exochorda	ball and burlap
Hibiscus syriacus	''
Ilex serrata	''
Magnolia (all)	''
	(early spring only)
Myrica	''
Pyracantha	potted plants
Rhamnus	ball and burlap
Tamarix	''
Viburnum plicatum	''
Viburnum plicatum f. tomentosum	''
Broad-leaved evergreens (all)	'' except stock grown in containers

Shrubs that should be moved only in spring include *Buddleia, Abelia* and *Magnolia* (very early). Shrubs that should be moved only in the autumn include *Chaenomeles japonica, Cornus mas* and *Hamamelis vernalis*.

The procedures for digging, moving, planting and transplanting bare-rooted shrubs and for balling and burlapping are the same as those for trees, and are fully discussed in Chapter 13. The same general precautions as for trees are taken to get the plants into the ground as soon as possible, to water soon after planting and frequently thereafter, to prune back to compensate for root loss, to provide shade at first and to mulch the ground about the more tender ones. Shrubs will stand even more pruning than seems necessary for trees. It is the roots that count most at first, and healthy roots will send up enough new shoots to balance the intake and evaporation of moisture. If the shrubs are not pruned enough when first transplanted, the tops will wilt and gradually die back. Much more severe pruning will then be required to save the plants, and in the meantime much vitality has been lost. As a rule of thumb, approximately one-fourth to one-third of the branches and twigs should be removed, the exact amount depending upon the severity of the root loss. Entire branches should be removed to ground level, rather than giving the plant a "haircut." Large shrubs that tend to form only a few main leaders, such as magnolias and hollies, should be pruned by thinning the side branches. Cutting back the leaders will ruin the habit of growth of these shrubs.

Some shrubs are much more subject to wilting after transplanting than others. The honeysuckles are particularly fast wilters and should never be transplanted while in leaf. Forsythia, on the other hand, may be moved while in full flower.

The best days for transplanting are cloudy, cool days, with a high degree of humidity and no wind. Seldom are we able to pick ideal weather, however, and reasonable precautions against the rapid drying of stems and roots must be taken if satisfactory results are to be obtained.

Transplanting is a shock to the plant, even if the person doing the job solemnly swears that "the thing will never know it has been moved."

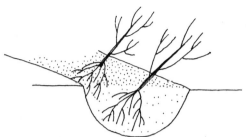

Fig. 14.1 Heeling in

Unless the humidity of the air is 90 percent or more, the plant is losing moisture all the time that it is out of the ground, not only through its stems and leaves but, what is more harmful, through its roots. Some of the roots are cut and a proportionate part of the top should be cut off to equalize the loss. Dry roots cause more failures after transplanting than any other factor. Whatever precaution we can take to prevent or retard this loss of moisture will reduce the effect of the shock on the vitality of the plant. With boxwood, no trimming of stems and branches is necessary because of the dense mat of roots that have remained intact in the ball. The plant should be watered thoroughly at first and frequently throughout the remainder of the season, the foliage being watered as well as the soil, ending with a generous application of water in mid-autumn. This autumn watering is especially important for rhododendron, mountain laurel and broad-leaved evergreens in general. These plants all lose moisture through their leaves during the winter and chances for survival are increased if they can store up a supply of water before winter freezing of the ground about their roots sets in. After freezing, the roots cannot replenish the plant's water supply.

Preparation of Beds for Planting

Areas to be planted with shrubs should be plowed or dug to a depth of 12 in., and the soil thoroughly broken up and loosened. Well-rotted manure should be worked into the soil by forking. Heavy soils should be improved by the addition of sandy loam, and sandy soil should have an application of humus or decomposed vegetable matter. The whole planting bed should thus be prepared, not merely little pockets where each shrub is to go. After all, this preparation and improvement of the soil is the last this area is likely to receive for many years and a good soil is essential to the robust growth of any plant.

The real test of success in transplanting shrubs that have been moved comes the second year after planting. In the first year the new growth comes from the vitality in the plant, stored up from previous years. In the second year its growth is dependent on the nourishment taken in from the new roots made during the first year. If the root growth is satisfactory the first year, top growth and general vigor should be good the second year. The importance of good rich soil about the roots of the newly planted shrub cannot be too strongly emphasized.

Pruning

The best time to prune shrubs depends upon their individual flowering habits. Those shrubs that bear blossoms on *new* growth in late spring or summer should be pruned in early spring or during the last weeks of winter. In this group are:

Abelia	Hydrangea	Rosa
Acanthopanax	Hypericum	Salix
Berberis	Indigofera	Spiraea
Buddleia	Kerria	Staphylea
Callicarpa	Lagerstroemia	Stephanandra
Caryopteris	Lespedeza	Tamarix (late-
Ceanothus	Ligustrum	flowering kinds)
Clethra	Lonicera	Vitex
Colutea	Neillia	
Franklinia	Rhus	
Hibiscus		

Shrubs that bear blossoms on *last year's* wood should be pruned soon after blooming. In this group, flower buds have been formed late in the previous growing season, and heavy winter or early spring pruning will remove many potential flowers that could otherwise be enjoyed during the spring. Pruning after flowering will also prevent the formation of seed pods and

thus conserve the vitality of the plant, and in the case of some plants such pruning even improves their appearance. In this group are:

Azalea	Deutzia	rose (climbers)
Caragana	Exochorda	Spiraea
Cercis	Forsythia	Syringa
Chaenomeles	Magnolia	Tamarix (early-flowering
Chionanthus	Philadelphus	kinds)
Cytisus	Ribes	Viburnum

A few shrubs should be pruned lightly after blooming and again lightly in early spring:

Cornus alba 'Sibirica'	Sambucus	Viburnum opulus
Cornus racemosa	Spiraea bumalda	Viburnum
Cornus stolonifera	Symphoricarpos	tomentosum
Lonicera		Weigela

The primary purpose of pruning most shrubs is to keep them vigorous and to maintain their blooming ability. This is done by removing old wood, and with it the parts of the stems that no longer bloom freely. The healthy, active root system will then stimulate new top growth the following year and thus increase the quantity of stems that bear blossoms. This is particularly effective with spirea, lilac, hydrangea, mock-orange, shrub honeysuckle and many other deciduous shrubs.

Many gardeners seem to think that the way to prune shrubs is to cut off all the branches to an even length. This "haircut" treatment ruins the grace of the shrub and frequently diminishes its vitality or flower production. Proper pruning technique calls for cutting branches to their bases and each year removing only about one-fifth or one-fourth of the entire mass. The purpose of this kind of pruning is to give new stems a better opportunity to develop from the bottom, thus improving the entire plant. This method requires less time than cutting a multitude of stems near the tops, and it also helps to maintain the natural shape of the shrub.

If shrubs have to be pruned to keep them from growing too large for their specific location, then the wrong shrubs were selected for the planting scheme. If this is the case, such shrubs should then be transplanted to more ample surroundings and their place taken by smaller ones.

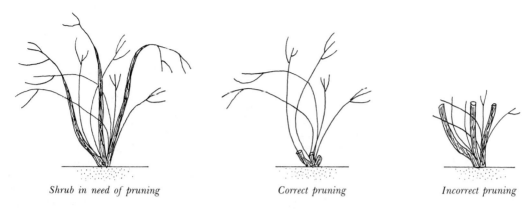

Shrub in need of pruning   Correct pruning   Incorrect pruning

Fig. 14.2 Pruning an established shrub

Some kinds of shrubs, however, do need annual pruning to keep them in good condition. Those shrubs that habitually have dead branches or often are winter-killed should have old, mature wood thinned out. Some deutzia, hydrangea, privet, mock-orange, buddleia, spirea, snowberry, tamarix, chaste tree, *Kerria, Stephanandra, Cornus sericea* and *C. alba* 'Sibirica' are all in this class. Those that winter-kill in the North will need a spring clearing of dead stems. They include some of the preceding list plus *Abelia, Callicarpa, Chimonanthus, Corylopsis, Genista*, some *Hypericum* species, *Ilex aquifolium, Kolwitzia, Jasminum nudiflorum, Osmanthus aquifo-lium, Mahonia aquifolium, Pieris japonica*, some azaleas and a few less well-known shrubs.

Some shrubs benefit from removing the flower heads after blooming and before seeds are set. This practice, traditionally known as "dead-heading," diverts nutrients and energy ordinarily used for seed production into increased growth and flowering for the next season. Lilac, azalea, rhododendron, magnolia, buddleia and mountain laurel all benefit from this treatment, but it is by no means essential to the health of the shrub.

Some shrubs, especially lilacs, sucker badly and are improved by the periodic removal of

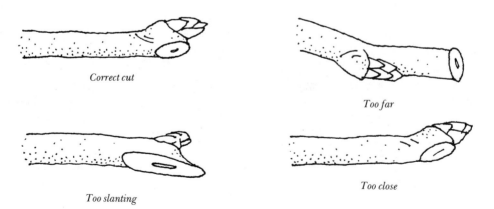

Correct cut

Too slanting

Too far

Too close

Fig. 14.3 Twig pruning

the suckers. Regular annual removal of most suckers on old lilac bushes, coordinated with annual removal of one or two of the oldest branches to ground level, will encourage maximum flowering and keep the plants from becoming overgrown. One or two suckers, however, should be retained each year to replace the older branches that have been removed.

Some shrubs may be cut to within a few inches of the ground and will grow again from the roots. This should only be done when plants have become hopelessly overgrown or leggy and other less drastic pruning methods cannot be employed. Such shrubs as lilac, sumac, lycium, honeysuckle, privet, forsythia, bayberry and box are in this group. On the whole, shrubs have great vitality. Many will withstand utter neglect and even much abuse, living for years without attention. Those that are particularly self-reliant are forsythia, barberry, shrub honeysuckle, hypericum, the broad-leaved evergreens in general, sumac, wild rose, viburnum, *Elaeagnus,* aronia and *Potentilla.*

WINTER PROTECTION

There are so many hardy shrubs that there seems little justification in trying to maintain species which are not really hardy in the region. Those that may be induced to survive the winters by protecting them and that reward the gardener for this extra care are rare indeed, for an occasional exceptionally severe winter may make the protection of no avail.

The need for special winter protection is greatly reduced whenever broad-leaved evergreens can be planted in sites that do not receive excessive amounts of sunlight and wind in winter. Damage may be especially severe on such exposed sites during late February and March while the ground is still frozen and the sunlight is becoming more intense.

One of the most satisfactory methods of providing winter protection for broad-leaved evergreens or newly planted conifers is by the use of plastic sprays known as antidesiccants. The thin film of spray should be applied to the leaves and twigs between mid-November and early December. It is important to cover the undersurfaces of the leaves as thoroughly as possible because much moisture is lost by transpiration through the stomata or pores located in these areas. Roots cannot absorb moisture to replace this loss while the soil is frozen.

For the protection of half-hardy shrubs, of broad-leaved evergreens in a very windy site or of newly planted shrubs, some shelter from wind is advisable, and a windscreen should be constructed. This may be made of any material that will remain in place and will not rot. Commercially manufactured mats of straw are often used. These are usually available at garden centers, and can be rolled up and put away at the end of the season and used year after year. Burlap tacked securely onto lath frames set about 1 ft. out from the plant and surrounding it completely (but not covering it) is also very satisfactory. Whatever method is chosen, it is important not to wrap protective material—particularly plastic—too tightly around the shrub. In such cases, winter sun will heat the shrub under the wrapping, creating a "greenhouse" effect. A sudden lowering of the temperature when the sun goes down can produce heavy damage to plant tissues, and plants "protected" by this method frequently are killed outright.

The winter screen should not be removed in the spring until all danger of a return to winter conditions has passed. March is one of the most difficult months, with much wind and brilliant sunshine while the ground is still frozen, and since the screen is to serve as a protection against these factors, not against cold, it should remain in place until the weather is springlike and settled.

Winter protection is often of great value for newly planted evergreen shrubs, such as the Rhododendrons, *Ilex, Leucothoë* and *Mahonia,* and as a general practice it is wise to provide some protection for two years following transplanting.

Some shrubs suffer seriously from the weight of heavy snow upon their branches. Boxwood is particularly subject to such injury, and suffers also from the action of sunshine on melted snow that has refrozen to form ice. In many parts of the country it is therefore wise to construct wooden frames around the bushes and cover them with heavy canvas, burlap, chicken wire or even cornstalks in order to prevent the snow from falling on the foliage and branches. If no covering is provided, careful vigilance should be practiced, and snow should be swept from branches as soon as it has fallen.

Breakage from heavy wet snow, ice or a combination of these conditions accompanied by high winds can cause severe damage to the branches of large shrubs, or they are frequently broken or bent out of shape. To prevent this from happening, the snow should be shaken from the branches as soon as possible after the storm has passed. A coating of ice on the branches, however, should be left alone. Attempts to remove it may only increase the chances of breaking the branches.

SHRUBS OF SPECIAL MERIT

Abelia x *grandiflora* (glossy abelia)

Evergreen in the South, leaves semipersistent in the North. Refined habit of growth. The foliage is glossy and somewhat coppery in tone. The small, pink tubular flowers are borne in terminal racemes, and continue from midsummer through autumn. Dense in habit of growth, abelia at maturity will reach a height of 6 ft. to 8 ft. It is useful in a shrub border, in foundation planting or as a specimen. Makes a good unclipped hedge.
Zone of hardiness: 6 (5 in sheltered sites).

Soil requirements: A good garden loam.

Exposure: Sun or partial shade.

Culture: Requires light pruning to maintain its natural, graceful shape. Prune in late winter or very early spring.

Acanthopanax sieboldianus (five-leaf aralia)

Attractive compound leaves plus the ability to survive under difficult conditions, including city life, are the chief merits of this infrequently used shrub. The flowers and fruit are rather inconspicuous. It can be clipped into an interesting hedge, used as a specimen plant or as a tall cover on steep banks. It can also be used to make a dense barrier plant if unclipped, eventually reaching a height of 7 ft. to 9 ft. with an equal spread.
Zone of hardiness: 4.

Soil requirements: Good to poor; will withstand dry soil.

Exposure: Sun or partial shade.

Acer ginnala (Amur maple)

An extremely hardy and dense shrub or small tree, especially useful for screening purposes or for specimen planting. Eventual height 15 ft. to 20 ft. Leaves small, only 3 in. long, with excellent scarlet autumn coloration. The fruits turn bright red in summer while the leaves are still green.
Zone of hardiness: 2.

Soil requirements: Good to poor.

Exposure: Full sun; good for exposed windy situations.

Culture: Cutting back to encourage several leaders while young will produce a more dense, shrublike habit of growth.

Aucuba japonica (Japanese aucuba)

A rugged and reliable broad-leaved evergreen shrub for milder climates, with thick, glossy leaves 5 in. to 7 in. long. The brilliant red berries are very effective in winter, but both male and female plants must be present for their production. The species has green leaves, while the leaves of *A. japonica* 'Variegata' are mottled and yellow and extremely attractive.

There are several cultivars available, which differ in sex, size and degree of variegation.
Zone of hardiness: 7 (6 in very sheltered sites).

Soil requirements: Good garden loam that retains moisture well.

Exposure: Light to medium shade. Leaves may burn badly in full sun.

Berberis julianae (wintergreen barberry)

One of the best of the hardy, evergreen barberries. Its rather dense foliage and its height, 6 ft. or more, make it a dependable background shrub. The yellow flowers are borne in conspicuous clusters in spring and have a most decorative value.
Zone of hardiness: 5, northern limit.

Soil requirements: A good garden loam.

Exposure: Full sun is best, but will withstand partial shade.

Berberis thunbergii (Japanese barberry)

This is one of the most rugged and versatile shrubs for the garden. It has a very dense habit of growth, thorny branches and bright red berries that are retained throughout the winter. Nearly oblivious to soil conditions except the extremes, it can be grown as a specimen plant, a clipped formal or unclipped unformal hedge, in the shrub border or as dense cover on banks that are difficult to maintain. The species attains heights of 4 ft. to 7 ft., depending upon location. There are many selected forms, including 'Atropurpurea', with reddish leaves (reddish-green in shaded locations); 'Erecta,' with an upright habit of growth; 'Aurea,' with bright yellow leaves; and 'Crimson Pygmy,' which grows to only 2 ft. to 2½ ft. It has red leaves, and is most useful as a woody ground cover or low hedge.

Zone of hardiness: 4.

Soil requirements: Good to poor; will withstand dry soil.

Exposure: Sun or shade (the cultivars with red or yellow leaves retain their color best in full sun).

Buddleia davidi (orange-eye butterfly bush)

A welcome addition to any planting, as it blooms during the summer months when few other shrubs are in flower. The foliage is a soft gray-green and the tall, slender wandlike branches are gracefully arched. The beautiful fragrant flowers are borne in terminal clusters and are violet-purple with a small orange eye. The flowering period extends from early July well into the autumn. It often reaches 6 ft. to 7 ft. in height and from 5 ft. to 6 ft. in spread. The butterfly bush is excellent as a source of cut flowers. Good cultivars include 'Charming,' with pink flowers; 'Dubonnet,' with dark purple flowers; 'Empire Blue,' with deep blue flowers; and 'Peace,' with white flowers.
Zone of hardiness: 6 (5). In northern extremes of their hardiness range, including most of Zone 5, butterfly bushes may be expected to die to the ground during severe winters and are thus treated in a similar manner to the herbaceous perennials. Resprouting and subsequent summer flowering is heavy, so the dying back need not exclude their cultivation in these areas.

Soil requirements: Good; well drained.

Exposure: Full sun.

Buxus (box, boxwood)

Beloved and cherished in the gardens of our ancestors, *Buxus sempervirens*, the common or true box, is as highly appreciated now as it ever has been. Indeed, its popularity has so increased that collectors search the countryside for fine old specimens, and nurseries raise it from cuttings by the thousands.

The various species of box are native to Europe and parts of Asia and Japan. *B. sempervirens* has been in cultivation since the times of the Roman Empire. In ancient gardens it was cut into geometric or complex shapes (topiary) and occupied conspicuous positions in the formal gardens. Through the Middle Ages it was cultivated in cloister garths, in castle gardens, and in town yards. Because of its very general use in English gardens during the seventeenth and eighteenth centuries, it was brought to America by the colonists, who established gardens here similar to those they had known and loved in the old country.

The climate of Virginia, Maryland and the Carolinas is particularly favorable for growing box, and while its growth is slower, it is also hardy in southeastern Pennsylvania, Delaware, New Jersey and Long Island. Further north (Zone 5), common box should be grown only in locations that are protected from strong winds and glaring winter sun. Breakage from heavy snow or ice may be more severe in these areas. (Varieties and selections of *B. microphylla,* the littleleaf box, are much more hardy and deserve wider planting in Zone 5.)

Beyond question, box is one of the most valuable plants for landscape purposes and it possesses many excellent qualities. Not only is it evergreen but it retains its deep green color and freshness throughout the year. When well established, it will thrive for many years and can endure considerable neglect. It withstands severe pruning and clipping better than almost any other cultivated plant, and some varieties can be kept at any desired height. Box hedges 10 in. high and seventy-five years old are a matter of record. Broken off 1 in. above the ground, box will send up new shoots and recover with surprising vigor.

It is not a voracious feeder and for this reason is particularly well suited for edging garden beds, as it will not rob the flowers of food and moisture or send its roots out to encroach upon the roots of neighboring plants. The wood is strong, heavy and very enduring, with a close, almost indistinguishable grain of rich yellow hue. It is highly prized for fine cabinet work

and is used for the most delicate sculpture tools, and for architects' scales.

The foliage of box has a very distinctive odor, considered delightful by some people but repugnant by others. As an individual specimen plant it possesses great dignity and beauty, as well as individual character, the billowy foliage masses in some cases taking irregular forms always expressive of great vitality. Indeed, it is this tremendous vitality, this ability to overcome adversity, this marvelous longevity linking past to present, that is one source of its enduring charm.

Zone of hardiness: 6 (5 in sheltered locations).

Soil requirements: Deep rich loam with plenty of humus and a porous subsoil is ideal for box. A constant supply of moisture is indispensable to good growth. For the transplanting of large specimens, a clay loam is preferable to a sandy soil.

Exposure: Partial shade is better than full sunlight in the North, but in the South either sunshine or shade is satisfactory. While these conditions are ideal, box will grow and thrive in a great variety of soils and in many kinds of exposure.

Culture: Box has a fibrous and extremely compact root system. It may therefore be transplanted with ease, using the ball and burlap method.

Where a box hedge is to be trimmed, the pruning should be done in August. Box bushes that have been recently transplanted, especially in regions north of Philadelphia, should be given winter protection. A barrier of cornstalks, or straw matting as shelter from the wind, and even a roof to keep off the weight of snow, are reasonable precautions during the first few winters. The barriers should not be removed until late March. If box bushes are not protected, snow should be carefully brushed off the foliage as soon as it has fallen. Snow damage by breaking and by freezing into ice is the most serious winter hazard for box.

Buxus microphylla (littleleaf box)

Hardier than common box, it is quite slow-growing, and has a compact, low habit of growth. The cultivar 'Compacta' never grows over 1 ft. in height, but with age may attain a spread of 2 ft. to 4 ft.

Buxus microphylla var. *koreana* (Korean box)

Although it is the hardiest box of all (Zone 4), this develops a somewhat untidy habit of growth if not pruned, and the foliage turns an unattractive brown in the winter. The cultivars 'Tide Hill' and 'Wintergreen' are somewhat more compact, and retain green foliage throughout the winter. These are the preferred cultivars to choose in areas where hardiness is a problem with box.

Buxus sempervirens (common box)

Numerous cultivars are available, which differ in habit of growth, height, leaf color, leaf size and hardiness. The following are some of the more popular ones: 'Handsworthiensis' — makes an excellent hedge plant, has dark green foliage and a wide upright habit of growth; slow-growing. 'Newport Blue' — has very attractive bluish-green foliage and a dense, rounded habit of growth. 'Suffruticosa' — this is the box used for edging flower beds; very slow-growing, compact, and has fragrant leaves. 'Vardar Valley' — undoubtedly the hardiest cultivar of common box (suited to Zone 5), it is very slow-growing, not exceeding 2 ft. to 2½ ft. in height, and much broader than tall. 'Pendula' — a tall-growing cultivar, to 15 ft., with pendulous branches. 'Argenteo-variegata' — leaves variegated with white; and 'Aureo-variegata' — leaves variegated with yellow.

Calycanthus floridus (strawberry shrub, sweet shrub)

C. floridus is particularly beloved because of its association with old-time gardens and the delightful and pungent fragrance of its flowers. It is rather coarse and open in its habit of growth and is therefore better adapted to mass planting than for specimen purposes. It attains a height of about 8 ft. The flowers, which come in June, are a dull reddish-brown and when crushed give off a very spicy fragrance. The branches also exude a strange, almost camphorlike odor.

Zone of hardiness: 4.

Soil requirements: Rather rich, moist loam.

Exposure: Shade or open sun.

Camellia

Few flowers have enjoyed such an upsurge of popularity as the camellias within recent years. And the popularity is well deserved, for the blooms of the camellia have a chaste and sculptured beauty that few other flowers possess.

With the introduction of hardier varieties, the camellia belt is gradually being extended northward. Whereas several decades ago an occasional southern or West Coast nursery listed perhaps a dozen varieties, there are now numerous large nurseries devoted entirely to the propagation of camellias and many hundreds of cultivars are listed. Some of these new cultivars are of breathtaking beauty and are the sensation of many camellia shows held throughout the country. *Camellia japonica* is the species most widely grown, but two other species, *Camellia reticulata* and *Camellia sasanqua*, have been gaining rapidly in popularity.

Camellia japonica

An evergreen shrub with dark, glossy foliage, *C. japonica* has several distinct types of flowers: single; loose semidoubles; large peoniforms; and imbricated sorts. Some varieties are stiffly formal, others charming and dainty, and some gracefully asymmetrical in form. The flowers range in color from white to cream, through shades of pink to brilliant scarlets and deep reds.

Climatic requirements: C. *japonica* thrives best with moderate temperatures and high humidity. It is grown in the southeastern sections of the United States from Florida to Texas and northward along the coast to Virginia. It does not bloom well in the southern portion of Florida. Some of the hardier cultivars may be grown in the northern part of Georgia and Alabama and in Tennessee, and, if planted in sheltered locations, certain cultivars of exceptional hardiness may be grown as far north as Pennsylvania, Long Island and Westchester County, New York. C. *japonica* is also well adapted to the Pacific Coast area from California to Washington.

Exposure: C. *japonica* prefers a semishaded location, and there are only a few varieties that will thrive in full sun. Dense shade is not desirable, as it results in a heavy growth of foliage and sparse bloom. Camellias should not be planted under trees that are heavy surface feeders, as they will be robbed of nourishment and moisture, two of their chief requirements. They thrive well in the shelter of live oaks, pines and other needle-leaved evergreens. When planted adjacent to a building or a wall, a northern or eastern exposure is considered best. But this does not hold true in more northerly areas, where plantings on the north and west sides usually show less winter injury than those with southern or eastern exposures. This is due to the fact that they are protected from the morning sun which, if the temperature has fallen below freezing during the night, hastens thawing and seriously injures the foliage, particularly if it is wet. When plants are protected from the sun, they will thaw gradually and little damage will result. C. *japonica* should never be planted where it will be exposed to strong winds.

Soil requirements; C. *japonica* requires a light, acid soil that is abundantly supplied with organic matter. Soils with a pH ranging from 4.5 to 6.5 are suitable, a pH of 5.5 being considered the optimum.

Good drainage is absolutely essential, as C. *japonica* will not grow well in waterlogged soil.

Camellias will endure many adverse conditions provided this requirement is adequately met.

Culture: In the camellia belt of the South camellias are usually planted in the autumn. In more northern latitudes spring is often preferred.

Fertilization: After the blooming period is over, two or three feedings are recommended, to be given about six weeks apart. This will stimulate new growth and a good production of flower buds for the following year. An acid type of fertilizer should be used. The following mixtures are recommended:
1. 5 parts cottonseed meal
   3 parts superphosphate
   2 parts sulphate of potash
2. 35 lb. superphosphate
   28 lb. cottonseed meal
   17 lb. sulphate of potash (high-grade)
   10 lb. ammonium sulphate
   10 lb. aluminum sulphate (used as an acidifier)

Commercial preparations specifically formulated for camellias are available from garden supply stores in the camellia belt, and may be purchased in small quantities for homeowners with only a few plants.

No applications of a nitrogen fertilizer should be given after late spring or early summer. This period of less active growth is important, as it allows the new spring shoots to harden, thus reducing the danger of winter injury. An application of 1 part sulphate of potash to 5 parts superphosphate in August will be of benefit in hardening new growth and improving the quality of the flowers.

When applied in the dry form, the fertilizer may be spread as a topdressing on top of the mulch and watered in. The application should reach the outer spread of the branches.

Overfertilization of camellias should be guarded against, as its effects can be disastrous.

Watering: The soil should be kept moist at all times but should never be allowed to become soggy. Thorough waterings should be given as needed, rather than frequent light waterings, which encourage surface root growth and lessen the vigor of the plant. An adequate supply of moisture is of particular importance during the period when the plants are making new growth and when they are in flower.

Mulching: Camellias should be mulched in order to conserve the moisture in the soil, and to afford protection for the roots, which tend to be near the surface. The following materials are recommended: peat moss, partially rotted oak leaf mold, pine needles, sawdust and acid compost.

Disbudding: On one- or two-year-old plants all but one or two buds should be removed in order to conserve the vigor of the plant.

On older plants, disbudding should be practiced if blooms of maximum size are desired. One bud should be left to every 2 in. to 4 in. of stem.

Pruning: Camellias require little or no pruning, merely the removal of dead wood and the cutting back of an occasional shoot to improve the shapeliness of the bush. Where particularly compact dense growth is desired, it may be encouraged by judicious pruning.

Protection from cold: It is important to know how to protect camellias from unexpected cold spells. This is particularly important if they are grown along the northern limit of the camellia belt.

A sudden drop in temperature is far more damaging than a gradual decline, and cold weather during or following a long, dry spell is especially harmful. Under such conditions the danger of injury can be lessened by watering the soil and spraying the foliage with a mistlike spray of water. Plants that are in active growth have less resistance to cold than those that have been gradually hardened to it. An early freeze after a long spell of warm weather can be particularly disastrous. If a freeze occurs, the following precautions should be taken: as soon as the temperature rises above freezing, the foliage should be watered with a fine, mistlike spray, and should be protected from direct sun. This will greatly reduce the danger of severe injury.

Control of insect pests and diseases: See Chapter 32.

Camellia reticulata

In its wild form, *C. reticulata* bears single medium pink flowers that are 3 in. to 4 in. in diameter. The foliage is a dull green, entirely lacking the glossy sheen of the other species.

The flowers of the modern cultivars, the result of hybridization, are of spectacular beauty, being semidouble in form, 5 in. to 8 in. in diameter, with superb texture, grace and richness of color.

The reticulatas bring the camellia season to a close, as they are the last to bloom, coming into flower in March and continuing until May. The flowers open quite slowly, some varieties requiring a week or ten days, but they remain in bloom over a long period.

Exposure: *C. reticulata* tolerates more sun than does *C. japonica* and will thrive in a half-sunny exposure.

Fertilization: The reticulatas do not thrive on heavy feeding and will sometimes show signs of leaf burn even under conditions of moderate feeding.

For planting and further cultural requirements, see *C. japonica.*

Camellia sasanqua

Like the other camellias, *C. sasanqua* is an evergreen shrub. The flowers are smaller and more fragile in appearance than are the blooms of *C. japonica* and *C. reticulata,* but they are borne in profusion, are obtainable in a wide range of beautiful colors and are delicately fragrant. The typical form of the flower is single, with wide-open petals and prominent stamens. There are also semidouble and fully double varieties. The flowers of *C. sasanqua* do not have the substance or the long-lasting qualities when cut that the bloom of *C. japonica* possess, but for landscape effects their value is unequaled. The flowers of *C. sasanqua* range from white through various shades of pink to deep red, with some blendings in between. Cultivars of *C. sasanqua* vary considerably in habit of growth, some varieties being much more compact than others. The Sasanqua camellias are predominately autumn flowering, coming into bloom in September and continuing into December.

Uses: Sasanqua camellias have great decorative value in the landscape scheme. They may be used as specimen plants, in shrubbery borders and in foundation plantings. They make exceedingly handsome hedges and are often used in this way in California. *C. sasanqua* can also be trained very readily to an espalier form and can be used as a decorative feature against a wall or garden fence.

Climatic requirements: *C. sasanqua* can be grown successfully throughout the same range as *C. japonica*. However, it can withstand greater extremes of heat and cold and may therefore be grown farther south as well as farther north. In southern Florida it is far more satisfactory than *C. japonica*, and it has played an important part in extending the camellia belt northward. Within recent years the hardier cultivars of *C. sasanqua* have been found more and more frequently in gardens in southeastern Pennsylvania, in New Jersey, on Long Island, New York State, and in very sheltered sites even farther north. For northern areas the earlier blooming varieties should be selected.

Exposure: Sasanqua camellias require more sun than the cultivars of *C. japonica* for their best development and they will thrive in full sun as well as in light shade. When grown in the North they should, however, be planted in a location where they will be protected from full winter sun, and from winter winds. Sasan-

qua camellias can also be grown successfully along the Gulf Coast and the seacoast, as they possess considerable tolerance to salt spray and can be planted within a few feet of open water, provided other conditions are favorable.

Soil requirements: *C. sasanqua* will tolerate a rather poor soil better than any of the other species. It will often thrive reasonably well on soils where *C. japonica* would not make satisfactory growth. It does, however, respond to good soil preparation and its general soil requirements are similar to those of *C. japonica*.

Culture: While the Sasanqua camellias are less exacting in their cultural requirements than the other species, their general requirements for fertilization, watering, mulching and protection from cold are very similar to those of *C. japonica* (see above).

Planting: In the North spring planting is recommended for *C. sasanqua*.

Pruning: If *C. sasanqua* is to be used as a hedge and compactness is desired, some pruning back of the shoots may be necessary. When Sasanqua camellias are trained to an espalier form, they will require only a minimum of pruning to keep them within desired limits. On slow-growing cultivars all that is usually necessary is a mere tip pinch during the blooming season.

Cercis chinensis (Chinese redbud)

This interesting Asian relative of our native redbud is a large shrub reaching 10 ft. or 15 ft. (or a bit more or less than this, depending upon climate). In May (earlier in the South) its numerous branches are heavily covered with rosy-purple pealike flowers. It is seen to best advantage when used as a specimen plant on a smaller property, or when planted in groups where its spread of 8 ft. to 10 ft. can be accommodated. It is also most effective when planted against an evergreen backdrop, or when com-

bined with flowering dogwoods, silverbells or many of the azaleas that blossom at the same time.
Zone of hardiness: 6 (5 in a sheltered location).

Soil requirements: Good loamy soil.

Exposure: Full sun for best flowering; tolerates partial shade.

Chaenomeles japonica (**Japanese quince**)

This is a close cousin of the lovely flowering quince but is less widely known. It is a low-growing shrub, seldom over 3 ft. high, and of very picturesque outline. The flowers borne in great profusion during the month of May are an orange-scarlet in color, a most striking shade. It is a shrub of great beauty and individuality, and gives a note of brilliant color when used in a foundation planting. *C. japonica* var. *alpina* is a wonderful dwarf, dense shrub, seldom over 1 ft. high, with handsome orange flowers.
Zone of hardiness: 4.

Soil requirements: Good loamy soil.

Exposure: Sun.

Fruit: The fruit, resembling quinces, is hard and green and not edible raw, but is occasionally used in preserving.

Chaenomeles speciosa (**flowering quince**)

Blooming in late April or early May, the myriad, brilliant blossoms of the flowering quince are very striking. The shrub is of irregular and rather picturesque growth, varying in height from 4 ft. to 6 ft. As a specimen plant, it is a thing of unique and brilliant beauty. It also lends itself well to mass planting and makes a

most attractive flowering hedge. Branches may be cut in late winter and readily brought into bloom indoors.

Of the many available cultivars, some of the better ones are: 'Apple Blossom,' with single white to pink flowers; 'Knap Hill Scarlet,' with single, deep pink flowers; 'Nivalis,' with single white flowers; 'Simonii,' with vivid double red flowers; and 'Coral 'Beauty,' with single reddish-orange flowers.

Zone of hardiness:

Soil requirements:

Exposure: See *C. japonica*

Fruit:

Chionanthus virginicus (**fringe tree**)

This is one of the finest of out native shrubs. It develops into a multi-branched large shrub or small tree and is particularly well suited for specimen purposes or for planting along an edge of woodland. It usually attains a height of from 10 ft. to 12 ft. but occasionally grows considerably taller if conditions are very favorable. In late spring it is a glorious mass of bloom, the cream-white flowers being borne in large, drooping panicles. Fruits (produced only on female plants) are small, blue in color, produced in clusters. There are few shrubs more beautiful or more showy than the fringe tree when it is in flower, and in habit of growth it is also decorative and graceful. A literal interpretation of the name "Chionanthus"—coming from the Greek *chion*, meaning "snow," and *anthos* "flower"—would give this plant the name "snowflower." Endures smoky and bad atmosphere well.
Zone of hardiness: 5. Native from Pennsylvania to Texas.

Soil requirements: Sandy, fertile loam. Likes subacid, pH 5.0–6.0 soil conditions.

Exposure: Open, sunny location; does reasonably well in partial shade.

Culture: This shrub should never suffer from lack of moisture.

Clethra alnifolia (sweet pepperbush)

C. alnifolia is valued for its fragrant white flowers in midsummer when few other shrubs are in bloom. A shrub of slender, erect habit, it reaches a height of 4 ft. to 5 ft. It should be kept well mulched with leaves or peat moss as it suffers under dry conditions.

The cultivar 'Rosea' bears flowers of a charming shade of pink.

Zone of hardiness: 3.

Soil requirements: Thrives best in moist, acid soil.

Exposure: Prefers partial shade, but also thrives in full sun.

Cornus alba 'Sibirica' (Siberian dogwood)

Although not at all distinctive in flower, this exceptionally hardy member of the dogwood family bears conspicuous white fruits, and is also a choice shrub for its effect in the winter landscape. The stems and twigs are a bright coral-red, and when seen either as a single specimen or massed, they add a distinctly warm touch to even the coldest winter day. The effect is particularly charming against snow and can be enhanced if interplanted with *C. sericea* 'Flaviramea,' which has bright yellow stems.

Zone of hardiness: 2.

Soil requirements: Does well on almost any soil; excellent for moist soils and planting near water.

Exposure: Full sun.

Culture: Every few years the oldest branches should be cut to ground level to encourage new sprouts that will have more vivid color. If the plants become overgrown, they may be cut entirely back to 1 in. or so of ground level. Recovery from such treatment is very rapid.

Cornus sericea 'Flaviramea' (yellow-twig dogwood)

The branches and twigs of this shrub are brilliant yellow in winter. All the comments on *C. alba* 'Sibirica' pertain here.

Cotinus coggygria (smokebush)

The large pinkish to grayish plumelike fruiting panicles that cover the bush in summer give a definitely "smoky" appearance. These may persist into early winter, thus creating a very long period of effectiveness. The shrubs grow large, up to 15 ft., and may be planted as single specimens or massed for spectacular effect on a larger property. Several cultivars, such as 'Purpureus,' 'Flame,' 'Royal Red' and others, have purplish to pinkish fruiting panicles and purple leaves.

Zone of hardiness: 5.

Soil requirements: Good soils, but will survive in acceptable condition upon poor soil.

Exposure: Full sun will produce maximum fruiting and best foliage color on the purple-leaved varieties; will withstand some shade.

Cotoneaster horizontalis (rock cotoneaster)

Here is one of the finest of this large and aristocratic group. The branches are horizontal in habit of growth, being almost prostrate, and it seldom grows taller than 2 ft. The foliage is small, dark green and very glossy. In the North the leaves turn a brilliant red in the autumn and drop, while in the South they are practically evergreen. The flowers, which are white with a pinkish tinge, are small and are not in the least showy but are followed by myriad bright red fruits that are very decorative.

Plants may be trained informally up a masonry wall for an interesting effect and make a delightful informal espalier in such a situation if pruned. It may also be used as a woody ground cover, especially on steep banks.

Zone of hardiness: 5. Evergreen in the South.

Soil requirements: Likes a well-drained soil.

Exposure: Sunny.

Other species

C. apiculatus: similar to *C. horizontalis*, but bears much larger, bright red fruits; red autumn color.

C. divaricatus: spreading growth to a height of 6 ft.; quantities of small red fruits in the autumn.

C. franchetii: reaches a height of 6 ft.; orange fruits.

C. microphyllus: evergreen to semi-evergreen; low-growing, reaching a height of 3 ft.; scarlet fruits.

C. salicifolius: open habit of growth with arching stems; evergreen foliage; height 10 ft. to 15 ft.; red fruits.

Deutzia gracilis (slender deutzia)

This deutzia is a dainty shrub that seldom grows more than 3 ft. tall and is particularly desirable for foundation planting. It is of dense, upright growth, with gracefully arching branches which, in late May, are festooned with flowers. The pendulous, white, bell-shaped blossoms are borne in clusters.

Zone of hardiness: 5 (needs protected location farther north).

Soil requirements: Well drained, with plenty of humus.

Exposure: Partial shade as well as in full sun.

Culture: The wood of the deutzia is not long-lived; therefore, it must be renewed. This is done by cutting out the old shoots from the base of the plant and allowing new branches to take their places. Shearing should not be practiced on this shrub as it promotes too bushy and top-heavy an appearance. If the new tender growth has been killed by cold in the spring in northern climes, it should be pruned back early in order to allow new growth to take its place.

Deutzia lemoinei 'Compacta' (Lemoine deutzia)

'Compacta' is one of the beautiful hybrid deutzias and particularly desirable as a specimen shrub because of its graceful habit and its profusion of bloom. It seldom attains a height of more than 3 ft. or 4 ft. It blooms about the middle of May, and the masses of white flowers that are borne in thickly clustered panicles are very showy and attractive.

Zone of hardiness, soil, etc.: See *Deutzia gracilis.*

Elaeagnus angustifolia (Russian olive)

Here is a fast-growing, hardy shrub that will endure extremely difficult conditions. It is often used as a windbreak in the Great Plains section and in the West. The foliage is a soft, gray-green, the flowers, which are not showy, are a yellowish-orange, the fruits red. It attains a height of about 20 ft.

Zone of hardiness: 2

Soil requirements: Tolerant of almost any soil.

Exposure: Will withstand sun, wind and drought.

Elaeagnus multiflorus (cherry elaeagnus)

E. multiflorus is noted particularly for the silvery sheen of its leaves and for its brilliant fruit. It is a shrub of upright, spreading growth, often reaching a height of from 9 ft. to 10 ft. The small, greenish-white flowers, which are very fragrant, are borne in the axils of the leaves and are not showy. The fruits, which ripen through the summer, are orange-red and somewhat cherrylike in appearance. They are edible but very tart, and are sometimes used for making jelly.
Soil requirements: Well drained; sandy or clayey; a good drought-resistant shrub.

Exposure: Sunny.

Enkianthus campanulatus (redvein enkianthus)

This is a very striking shrub because of its beautiful glossy foliage, which is bronze through the early part of the season, turning a brilliant red in the autumn. In habit of growth it is refined and upright, reaching a height of about 9 ft. The drooping clusters of white to pale orange, bell-shaped flowers are borne at the ends of the branches in May and June.
Zone of hardiness: 5.

Soil requirements: Acid, moist, sandy soil.

Exposure: Sunny.

Euonymus alata (winged spindle tree)

For either individual or group planting the winged euonymus is a lovely thing. It is of regular, rather horizontal growth, 6 ft. to 8 ft. in height. The small, delicate flowers are borne in late spring and are followed by red fruits. The curious corky bark on the branches gives it a winged effect, hence the common name. The leaves are small and finely toothed, and in the autumn they turn a bright scarlet.

E. alata 'Compacta' (dwarf winged spindle tree)

More refined in growth habit, this tight-leafed shrub seldom reaches over 5 ft. to 6 ft., with a dense branching pattern. It makes an excellent hedge that frequently can go for two years without clipping.
Zone of hardiness: 4.

Soil requirements: Not particular.

Exposure: Sunny.

Euonymus japonicus (Japanese spindle tree)

Here is a very handsome evergreen shrub. Unfortunately, it is not hardy north of the latitude of Philadelphia except in very protected places and commonly fails to set fruit except in warm latitudes. It is of upright growth, reaching a height of 8 ft. to 10 ft., and is well adapted for specimen purposes or for hedges. The broad, oval leaves are thick and glossy. A shrub of unique character and great dignity. There are several cultivars that have leaves variegated in differing patterns.
Zone of hardiness: 7 or 8.

Soil requirements, etc.: See *E. alatus.*

Forsythia x intermedia 'Spectabilis' (showy border forsythia)

One of the best of this large group, *F. intermedia* reaches a height of from 8 ft. to 10 ft., and in early April, before the leaves unfold, it is a mass of glorious golden bloom. The flowers are larger and more perfect in form than in some of the other types; it also has the advantage of coming into bloom just late enough to escape danger from severe frosts.
Zone of hardiness: 5.

Soil requirements: Any soil except overly wet or dry.

Exposure: Full sun.

Culture: Forsythias require pruning immediately after blooming, cutting several of the oldest stalks a few inches above ground level in order to allow new growth to take their place. This method allows the shrub to bear its blossoms on gracefully arching branches, making a compact appearance of bloom, rather than far out on old, heavy branches. The practice of shearing forsythias back to a predetermined height and width should be avoided whenever possible. It should be remembered that a full-grown forsythia will be 8 ft. to 10 ft. in width, and sufficient space should be allotted for natural development. Forsythias really are not suitable in foundation plantings as seems to be their common fate.

Forsythia ovata (early forsythia)

This Korean species has ascending branches that arch gracefully. The flowers are pale primrose-yellow, borne singly, and are produced ten days before any other type of forsythia. Its advantages are the time of bloom and its hardiness.
Zone of hardiness: 4. It is said to be much hardier than the others, the buds withstanding temperatures well below zero degrees F.

Soil requirements, etc.: See *F.* x *intermedia* 'Spectabilis'.

Forsythia suspensa (drooping or weeping forsythia)

Growing to 10 ft. or more *F. suspensa's* slender branches often bend to the ground and root at the tips. In bloom it forms a golden-yellow mound. Var. *sieboldii* has more slender branches and can be used effectively to clothe a wall or arbor. It is also very effective when trailing over a rock or wall.
Zone of hardiness: 5.

Soil requirements, etc.: See *F.* x *intermedia* 'Spectabilis'.

Ilex crenata (Japanese holly)

I. crenata and its several varieties and cultivars are among our most useful evergreen shrubs. The leaves are small, dark green and dense; the flowers inconspicuous. It combines well with other evergreens in the shrub border, and may be used in foundation planting and for hedges. Attains a height of 10 ft. to 20 ft.
Zone of hardiness: 6.

Soil requirements: Rich loam, acid or nearly neutral.

Exposure: Sun or partial shade.

Culture: Should be watered during periods of drought. Prune only to thicken growth and to remove dead wood.

Cultivars:
I. crenata 'Convexa: low-growing to 4 ft. to 6 ft.; broader, convex leaf.
I. crenata 'Latifolia': tall-growing to 12 ft. to 20 ft.; wider, larger leaf.
I. crenata 'Microphylla': upright growth to 10 ft.; smaller leaf.

Ilex verticillata (winterberry)

One of the best of the native shrubs in the East. This is a deciduous member of the holly family, producing quantities of red berries that remain throughout the early winter. A few twigs tucked into a Christmas wreath will brighten it with its sparkle. As a cultivated

shrub it is dense and handsome, often reaching a height of 12 ft.
Zone of hardiness: 4.

Soil requirements: Moist, rich, woodsy, somewhat acid or neutral is best, but will thrive in most normal soil conditions.

Exposure: Sun or light shade.

Jasminum nudiflorum (winter jasmine)

This is a shrub of trailing, almost vinelike habit. The long, slender stems are green throughout the winter months and in February or very early March, almost before the snows have gone, the small clear yellow flowers begin to open. They are borne very close to the stem and appear well before the leaves. Winter jasmine may be readily trained upon a trellis as a vine and is often happily used in this way. Its habit of early flowering endears it to every homeowner, for in its golden cup of bloom it seems to hold the very promise of spring.
Zone of hardiness: 6. (As far north as New York. Winter protection in Zone 5.)

Soil requirements: Good loam.

Exposure: Sunny position.

Juniperus chinensis 'Pfitzerana' (spreading juniper)

One of the larger of the spreading forms, this Pfitzer reaches a height of 5 ft. to 10 ft. It is very graceful in its habit of growth, rather open and vase-shaped. The dense foliage is a soft, cool green and retains its fresh coloring throughout the year. It is adaptable to any position where low bulk is required and is considered one of the best of the spreading junipers.
Zone of hardiness: 4. Withstands extremely hard winter conditions.

Soil requirements: Thrives in poor soil; preferably sandy and dry.

Exposure: Nearly any exposure; prefers sun.

Culture: Cultivation improves the condition of the plant. If there are wounds on lower branches that have died, investigate for gnawing mice.

Juniperus horizontalis 'plumosa' (*Juniperus depressa plumosa*, Andorra juniper)

Of all the spreading junipers this is the most satisfactory and the most generally used. Hardy, compact but graceful, long-lived, low, it has a feathery texture and a pleasing appearance. It requires almost no care and year after year it is dependable. It may be used for covering banks, for foundation planting and as foreground to larger evergreens. Height 1½ ft.
Zone of hardiness: 3, northern limit.

Soil requirements: Light, sandy soil.

Exposure: Full sun.

Kalmia latifolia (mountain laurel)

Here is one of the most beautiful of our native evergreens. It is a very valuable shrub for mass planting and is also well adapted for foundation planting under certain conditions, and for underplanting in woodland areas. It has a decided preference for an acid and rather sandy soil; under favorable conditions the plants often attain a height of 8 ft. The handsome foliage is a dark, glossy green and the lovely flower clusters that open in late May and June vary from rose to pure white. There are few shrubs more beautiful than our native mountain laurel.
Zone of hardiness: 4, sometimes 3.

Soil requirements: Sandy, acid soil.

Exposure: Dense or semishade; or in sun with a mulch.

Culture: Transplanting should preferably be done with ball and burlap. If this is not possible, the plants should be cut down to the ground and allowed to resprout before transplanting.

Kerria japonica (kerria)

K. japonica is a dainty and very useful shrub. The slender, wandlike branches retain their soft green color throughout the year and are particularly lovely during the winter months after the leaves have fallen. The flowers are a deep golden-yellow and there are both single and double forms. It is especially good for foundation planting because it is not too dense and heavy in texture and rarely grows more than 4 ft. or 5 ft. high.
Zone of hardiness: 5. Tops will be killed back if exposed to temperatures much below zero.

Soil requirements: Well drained.

Exposure: Sheltered, partial shade, to preserve color from bleaching.

Culture: Pruning is done for two reasons: (1) to prolong the length of bloom by cutting the branches back to various lengths and thus delaying the bloom on some; (2) to cut off any wood that was winter-killed. This last should be done very early in the spring.

Kolkwitzia amabilis (beautybush)

This is a very showy and decorative shrub. Of upright habit, with arching branches, it reaches a height of about 10 ft. The flower buds are deep pink while the open blooms borne in such profusion in May and June are somewhat paler, with delicate orange veins in the tubular throat. The weigela-like, flowers are borne in pairs, from twenty-five to fifty in a single cluster. The light-colored bark exfoliates or peels from stems and twigs, and thus gives added interest in winter.
Zone of hardiness: 5.

Soil requirements: Soil of poor fertility and good drainage.

Exposure: Full sun and open position for free air circulation. Without free circulation, beauty bush is apt to winter-kill.

Leucothoë fontanesiana (drooping leucothoë)

A low, evergreen shrub with gracefully arching branches, the foliage is a dark, deep green and in winter turns a rich bronze with purple tints. It seldom grows more than 3 ft. to 4 ft. tall and is often broader than it is high. The flowers, which are borne in late May, resemble those of the lily-of-the-valley, and are very lovely. The little clusters of drooping, bell-shaped waxy flowers appear at the tips of the branches and are quite fragrant. Leucothoë is a very choice shrub, particularly useful as a filler between large evergreen shrubs or for foundation planting.
Zone of hardiness: 4.

Soil requirements: Rich loam soil of considerable acidity; subacid, pH 5.0–6.0.

Exposure: Partial shade.

Culture: Set balled plants in spring 2 ft. to 4 ft. apart.

Ligustrum lucidum (glossy privet)

A native of the Orient, this is a handsome evergreen with lustrous leaves. Like most of the

privets, it grows rapidly and attains a height of over 30 ft. Useful as an untrimmed hedge and windbreak in the South, and also often used as a specimen shrub.
Zone of hardiness: 7, northern limit.

Lonicera morrowi (Morrow honeysuckle)

One of the loveliest of our bush honeysuckles, this is of wide, spreading growth with crooked, angular branches, and reaches an ultimate height of about 8 ft. The foliage is a soft gray-green and the myriad cream-white flowers, which appear in May, are followed by brilliant red berries. As the fruits are greatly relished by the birds, it is a particularly desirable shrub for planting in a bird sanctuary.
Zone of hardiness: 5.

Soil requirements: Not particular provided soil is good. In poor soil, flowers are deficient in size. Circumneutral, pH 6.0–8.0.

Exposure: Open, sunny.

Culture: New plantings should be made preferably in late fall or early spring. If medium or late spring deliveries are made and leaf growth has started, the transplanting is somewhat of a shock. In this case, hard pruning should be done to avoid a scraggly appearance the first year. After the shrub is established, pruning should consist only of removing dead branches and sometimes the oldest, thick branches in the spring. This will invigorate the bush and start new growth.

Mahonia aquifolium (Oregon hollygrape)

M. aquifolium is an evergreen shrub, of rather low habit, seldom attaining a height of more than 3 ft. or 4 ft. The handsome foliage is glossy, rather leathery in texture and prickly. To the casual observer it resembles the foliage of our

Christmas holly although it is much more shiny. The young growth has a very characteristic bronze tint and the leaves turn a reddish-bronze during the winter months. The flowers are yellow, borne in dense clusters at the ends of the branches in late April and early May. The small blue-black fruits ripen in September.
Zone of hardiness: 5.

Soil requirements: Any soil (Circumneutral, pH 6.0–8.0), even dry and sandy. Likes moisture. Manure or bone meal will keep plants from becoming straggly.

Exposure: In dense or partial shade; foliage burns in sun.

Culture: Better if moved with ball of earth, but not absolutely necessary.

Myrica pensylvanica (northern bayberry)

Bayberry is very useful for general planting and its merits are, perhaps, not fully appreciated. It grows from 5 ft. to 9 ft. tall. The foliage is a medium green, smooth, glossy and very attractive in appearance. It has a delicious and pungent fragrance. The flowers are inconspicuous and the handsome gray fruits are borne in dense clusters close to the stem. These remain on the plant throughout the winter months. As fruits are produced only on female shrubs, one or two male plants are necessary in any planting.
Zone of hardiness: 2.

Soil requirements: Prefers a moist, peaty soil; subacid pH 5.0–6.0.

Exposure: Open, sunny.

Culture: Of easy culture, but best to start with plants that have been balled and burlapped.

Paeonia (tree peonies):

See Chapter 17 on perennials.

Philadelphus x *virginalis* (virginal mock-orange)

This lovely hybrid mock-orange was produced by the famous French hybridizer, Victor Lemoine, and it is without doubt one of the most beautiful of the group. The white flowers, which are large and semidouble in form, are borne in profusion and are very fragrant. It blooms during the month of May and occasional flowers are produced later in the season. The ultimate height varies from 6 ft. to 8 ft. Like many of the other hybrids of this family, it has the advantage of flowering while still quite small.
Zone of hardiness: 5.

Soil requirements: Not particular, as long as it is not soggy.

Exposure: Full sun is best, but withstands shade better than most flowering shrubs.

Culture: Prune after flowering.

Photinia villosa (Oriental photinia)

This is a very desirable shrub wherever it can be grown. It is large and upright, reaching a height of 12 ft. to 15 ft. The oval leaves are sharply toothed, and are lustrous and glossy in appearance, turning a scarlet or deep red in the autumn. The white flowers, which are borne in May in rounded panicles, resemble those of the hawthorn, and are followed by bright red berries that last well into the winter.
Zone of hardiness: 4.

Soil requirements: Light, sandy, loamy soil; requires perfect drainage and likes plenty of leaf mold.

Exposure: Prefers sun.

Pieris japonica (Japanese andromeda)

One of the most beautiful, as well as one of the most dependable, of evergreen shrubs, *P. japonica* is almost always adorned with gracefully hanging tassels that in winter are the flower buds; for six weeks in April and May waxy, white, bell-shaped blossoms; and for the rest of the season picturesque seed capsules. The foliage is gracefully spreading in clusters of somewhat glossy leaves. Height: 6 ft. to 9 ft.
Zone of hardiness: 5.

Soil requirements: Neutral or acid.

Exposure: Sun or partial shade.

Culture: Very easily transplanted and requires no particular attention.

Pittosporum

The Pittosporums are widely used in the South and on the Pacific Coast. They are large, evergreen shrubs and may be used either as background plants or as accents.

P. phillyraeoides is of slow growth, graceful and willowlike in form, reaching a height of about 20 ft. It will withstand long-continued heat spells.

P. tobira is of spreading form, reaching a height of about 15 ft. The foliage is thick, leathery and dark green. The creamy-white flowers, which are borne in clusters, are fragrant.
Zone of hardiness: 7 and 8.

Soil requirements: Rich garden loam.

Exposure: Sun or partial shade.

Pyracantha coccinea 'Lalandei' (scarlet firethorn)

A shrub of striking beauty, *P. coccinea* reaches a height of 8 ft. to 10 ft. The evergreen foliage is dark and glossy and the branches are thorny. The white flowers are borne in clusters and are followed by brilliant orange-scarlet fruits that last well into the winter. For its beautiful evergreen foliage, its flowers and its highly ornamental fruits, this is a most desirable and prized shrub. It may be used as an individual specimen and in group plantings, or trained against a building or over a doorway, where it creates a unique and handsome effect.

Zone of hardiness: 6.

Soil requirements: Well drained; likes lime, circumneutral, pH 6.0–8.0.

Exposure: Full sun.

RHODODENDRONS: EVERGREEN SPECIES AND CULTIVARS OF MERIT

There are few shrubs that can compare with the dramatic beauty of the rhododendrons when they are in full flower. Thousands of hybrids have been developed in this country and in England and Europe, where rhododendrons have long been highly prized. The hybrids offer a wide range of beautiful colors and have great landscape value as specimen plants and for mass effects. Some sections of the country, such as the Pacific Northwest and the central mountainous region of the East, are particularly well suited to their culture. But so highly valued are the rhododendrons that gardeners in the South and Midwest, where conditions are less favorable, make every effort to meet their exacting requirements in order to enjoy their spectacular beauty.

Exposure

Some rhododendrons, such as *R. maximum*, are tolerant of rather dense shade, but the majority prefer light shade. In their native habitats, rhododendrons are denizens of the forest. On the home property the most favorable exposure is a location where they will be protected from hot afternoon sun in the summer and where early morning sun will not strike them in the winter. A northeastern exposure meets these requirements well. Such a location may be in the shelter of buildings, or in an area protected by trees.

Where climatic conditions are not naturally favorable to the growth of rhododendrons, such as in the South and the Midwest, a northern exposure is always desirable in order that the plants may have full protection from intense sunshine and searing winds. They will thrive well in areas where they receive good light, but no direct sun. In the Midwest honey locusts afford an excellent overhead canopy for rhododendron plantings and in the North and South pines and oaks provide favorable conditions, if the lowest branches are about 12 ft. above the ground.

Never plant rhododendrons under trees that develop dense surface soil root systems and thereby deplete the soil of moisture and nutrients. Rhododendrons have shallow, very fibrous root systems, and generally will not grow well under most maples or beeches.

Soil Requirements

In growing rhododendrons, a congenial soil is one of the most important factors for success. They require a soil rich in humus and high in acidity (pH 4.5–5.5).

Planting

Rhododendrons should be planted in very early spring before growth starts, or in August and September.

Plants that are at least 15 in. to 18 in. in height and well branched, with foliage low to the ground, are the most desirable for planting. If special soil preparation is required, an area of at least twice the depth and width of the ball of earth surrounding the plant should be prepared for each plant used as an individual specimen. If a mass planting is to be done, the entire area may be prepared at one time. In areas where the soil is definitely alkaline, or where it is poorly drained and there is danger of its becoming waterlogged, it is advisable to plant rhododendrons in raised beds. This will not only provide for good drainage but will prevent surface water from seeping into the bed. This is the method followed so successfully in England when rhododendrons are grown in areas where the soil is highly alkaline.

Rhododendrons must always be planted at the same depth as they were growing in the nursery. And after planting they should be thoroughly watered, then mulched with peat moss or acid leaf mold.

Culture

The soil beneath rhododendrons should not be cultivated. It should be kept mulched at all times. During dry periods a thorough soaking every ten days or two weeks is recommended. Heavy watering in August and September should be avoided, because the current season's growth is "hardening off" during this period and will be in better condition to survive low winter temperatures if not encouraged by too much water.

In severe climates winter protection is advisable. A heavy 8-in. mulch of oak leaves may be applied in the fall or early winter, a portion of the mulch being removed in the spring and the rest left to decay. A snow fence or burlap protection should be provided in areas where winter winds are severe. Young plants, or even older ones in very windy sites, will benefit by winter application of an antidesiccant plastic spray.

If the faded blooms are removed and seed capsules not allowed to form, bloom will likely improve the following season. Such "deadheading" is, of course, possible only in small plantings.

Fertilization

Rhododendrons planted in soil that is rich in organic matter and quite acid do not, in general, require great quantities of fertilizer to maintain healthy growth. Most of their nutritional requirements are obtained from decomposition of the mulching material and humus in the soil. A 5-10-10 fertilizer spread at the rate of 3 lb. per 100 sq. ft. yearly, or even every other year, is usually quite sufficient. This should be done as early in the growing season as possible (before mid-May). Later applications may stimulate new tender growth at the end of the season and result in considerable burning or winter-kill. Cottonseed or soya bean meal applied at the rate of 4 lb. per 100 sq. ft. is also an excellent fertilizer to use with rhododendrons.

Control of Insect Pests and Diseases
See Chapter 32.

Rhododendron carolinianum (Carolina rhododendron)

This lovely, low-growing species seldom attains a height of more than 5 ft. or 6 ft. The flowers, which are borne in great profusion in mid-spring, are a pale, rose-pink and possess an unusually dainty and decorative quality. Although native to the mountains of North Carolina, this is a hardy species, and because of its habit of growth it is one of the best rhododendrons for the small property. It may be used, provided the exposure is favorable, in foundation plantings and in the foreground of large mass plantings, as underplanting in a grove of trees or as a specimen shrub. The evergreen foliage is attractive throughout the year. Protection from wind and strong sunshine is advisable. *R. carolinianum* var. *album* has glistening white flowers, and usually blooms about a week later than the species.
Zone of hardiness: 5.

Rhododendron catawbiense (Catawba rhododendron)

This is one of the finest of the native rhododendrons, its natural habitat being the mountains of Virginia, the Carolinas and Georgia.

Many beautiful hybrids have been developed from this species, and among them there are a number of named varieties of exceptional merit and hardiness, the colors ranging from white through light lavender to crimson, purple and red. The plants usually reach a height of about 6 ft. (see lists below).

Zone of hardiness: Zone 4 is the northern limit without some protection.

Rhododendron fortunei (fortune rhododendron)

A beautiful species from China, with very large fragrant flowers varying from white to deep rose. It becomes a very large shrub, 10 ft. to 15 ft. in height, with attractive foliage and a very free-flowering habit. It has been used extensively in breeding programs, and has produced some of the most beautiful of all the hybrids now available for planting in areas as cold as Zone 5 (see lists below).

Rhododendron maximum (rosebay rhododendron)

This is one of the best known of our native rhododendrons and a shrub of great beauty. It is extremely hardy, is of dense growth, and although it is generally seen at a height of about 10 ft., under very favorable conditions it will grow considerably taller. The leaves are larger than in any of the other hardy species, and the flowers, which vary from white to rose-pink, are produced in large clusters during June and July. *R. maximum* is particularly well adapted for mass plantings, for underplanting in woodlands and along wooded walks and drives, as it thrives best in shaded areas. It is not suitable for foundation planting, or for the small property, as its growth is too bold and vigorous.

Zone of hardiness: 3.

Rhododendron mucronulatum (Korean rhododendron)

This beautiful rhododendron from Korea is of particular value because of its early flowering. It is one of the first shrubs to come into bloom in the spring. The soft, rosy-lavender blooms, which are borne in great profusion, open before the leaves unfold, and in full flower it is a dramatically lovely thing. In the au-tumn the handsome foliage is scarlet-tinted. It attains an ultimate height of about 6 ft. Unlike most other members of the rhododendron family, *R. mucronulatum* will thrive well in rather dry soils that are not strongly acid. It is one of the few rhododendrons that can be grown in slightly alkaline soils.

Although classified as a true rhododendron, it loses its leaves during winter as the azaleas do. *R. mucronulatum* 'Cornell Pink' is a handsome selection with rose-pink flowers.

Zone of hardiness: 4.

Rhododendron smirnowii (Smirnow rhododendron)

One of the hardiest rhododendrons, *R. smirnowii* when planted in colder areas will provide a much more spectacular display of blossoms than *R. maximum*. It also is more compact in habit (6 ft. to 8 ft.), and grows more slowly. The flowers are a bright purplish-rose, and the petals are frilled at their margins. The deep green leaves are thickly coated underneath with a soft white or fawn-colored matting known as an indumentum.

Zone of hardiness: 4.

Rhododendron yakusimanum (Yakushima rhododendron)

A marvelous species from northern Japan, this has skyrocketed to fame among rhododendron fanciers in recent years, and deservedly so. It grows very slowly and, after many years, forms a dense mound eventually 3 ft. to 4 ft. high, with extremely handsome foliage. The leaves, which are about $3\frac{1}{2}$ in. long, are deep green, very glossy and down-curved at the edges. The undersurfaces are coated with a dense wooly brown matting—the indumentum. The flowers are exquisite, a deep rose color in bud, delicate pink when partially open and near white at maturity. The effect of a flower truss exhibiting all these stages simultaneously has been likened to apple blossoms. This rhododendron will withstand sunny conditions better than most of the others.

Zone of hardiness: 5.

HARDY CULTIVARS (ZONES 4, 5 AND 6)

NAME AND PARENTAGE	FLOWER COLOR, TIME. ETC.	HARDINESS
R. 'Album Elegans' (*catawbiense* hybrid)	white with lilac tinge; June	−20°F.
R. 'America' ('Parsons Grandiflorum' x dark red hybrid)	dark red; late May	−20°F.
R. 'Anna Baldsiefen' ('Pioneer' x 'Pioneer')	light pink; April	−10°F.
R. 'Atrosanguineum' (*catawbiense* hybrid)	red; late May	−20°F.
R. 'Belle Heller' ('Catawbiense Album' x white *catawbiense* hybrid)	glowing white; early May	−10°F.
R. 'Blue Peter' (*ponticum* hybrid)	lavender blue; early May	−10°F.
R. 'Boule de Neige' (*caucasicum* x *catawbiense* hybrid)	white; late April; very compact	−25°F.
R. 'Caractacus' (*catawbiense* hybrid)	red; June	−25°F.
R. 'Caroline' (*decorum* hybrid)	lavender; fragrant, late May; good in hot climates	−15°F.
R. 'Catawbiense Album' (*catawbiense* selection)	white; late May	−25°F.
R. 'Charles Dickens' (*catawbiense* hybrid)	red; late May; slow-growing	−25°F.
R. 'Conewago' (*carolinianum* x *mucronulatum*)	pink; early April; low-growing	−25°F.
R. 'Dora Amateis' (*carolinianum* x *ciliatum*)	white; late April; low-growing	−15°F.
R. 'Dr. V. H. Rutgers' ('Charles Dickens x Lord Roberts')	aniline red; late May	−15°F.
R. 'Everestianum' (*catawbiense* hybrid)	rosy-lilac; late May; shade or sun	−15°F.
R. 'Goldsworth Yellow' ('Jacksonii' x *campylocarpum*)	apricot buds, yellow flowers; late May	−10°F.
R. 'Great Lakes' (*catawbiense* var. *album* 'Glass' x *yakusimanum*)	white; semidwarf	−25°F.
R. 'Henrietta Sargent' (*catawbiense* hybrid)	rose-pink; late May	−25°F.
R. 'Holden' (red *catawbiense* sdlg. x 'Cunningham's White')	red; late April; compact	−15°F.
R. 'Ice Cube' ('Catalgla' x 'Belle Heller')	white; early May	−20°F.
R. 'Janet Blair' (Dexter hybrid x unknown parent)	pink; early May; tall	−15°F.
R. 'King Tut' (*smirnowii* x 'America')	pink; early May	−20°F.
R. 'Lady Armstrong' (*catawbiense* hybrid)	rose-pink, white throat; late May	−20°F.
R. 'Lee's Dark Purple' (*catawbiense* hybrid)	dark purple; late May	−15°F.
R. 'Meadowbrook' ('Mrs. C. S. Sargent' x 'Everestianum')	frilly pink; late May	−15°F.

HARDY CULTIVARS (Continued)

NAME AND PARENTAGE	FLOWER COLOR, TIME, ETC.	HARDINESS
R. 'Mrs. Charles S. Sargent' (*catawbiense* hybrid)	rose, yellow throat; late May	−25°F.
R. 'Mrs. Wm. R. Coe' (*fortunei* hybrid)	deep pink with crimson throat; late May	−5°F.
R. 'Nova Zembla' ('Parsons Grandiflorum' x hardy red hybrid)	red; early May; heat-tolerant	−20°F.
R. 'Parsons Gloriosum' (*catawbiense* hybrid)	lavender-pink; late May	−25°F.
R. 'Pioneer' ('Conemaugh' x *mucronulatum*)	light mauve-pink; early April; low-growing	−20°F.
R. 'P.J.M.' (*carolinianum* x *dauricum*)	lavender-pink; early April; low-growing; mahogany-colored leaves in winter	−25°F.
R. 'Purpureum Elegans' (*catawbiense* hybrid)	bluish-purple; late May	−25°F.
R. 'Ramapo' (*fastigiatum* x *carolinianum*)	violet-blue; early April; dwarf	−25°F.
R. 'Trilby' (*griffithianum* hybrid)	deep red, almost black; late May	−10°F.
R. 'Windbeam' (*carolinianum* x *racemosum*)	white to soft pink, fragrant; early April; semidwarf	−25°F.
R. 'Wyanokie' (*carolinianum* x *racemosum*)	white; early May	−25°F.

CULTIVARS FOR MILD CLIMATES (ZONES 7 AND 8)

NAME AND PARENTAGE	FLOWER COLOR, TIME, ETC.	HARDINESS
R. 'Anna Rose Whiteney' (*griersonianum* x 'Countess of Derby')	pink; handsome foliage; late May	0°F.
R. 'Blue Diamond' ('Intrifast' x *augustinii*)	blue; early April; low-growing	0°F.
R. 'Cilpinense' (*ciliatum* x *moupinense*)	pink; March; low-growing	+5°F.
R. 'Cornubia' (*arboreum* x 'Shilsonii')	rich red; March	+15°F.
R. 'Cream Crest' (*chryseum* x 'Cilpenense')	light yellow; early April; low-growing	0°F.
R. 'David' ('Hugh Koster' x *neriiflorum*)	blood-red; early May	+5°F.
R. 'Earl of Athlone' ('QueenWilhelmina' x 'Stanley Davies')	blood-red; late April; compact growth	0°F.
R. 'Fabia' (*dichroanthum* x *griersonianum*)	orange, bell-shaped; late May; low-growing	+10°F.
R. 'Fragrantissimum' (*edgeworthii* x *formosum*)	white; early April; very fragrant	+20°F.

(Continued)

CULTIVARS FOR MILD CLIMATES (Continued)

NAME AND PARENTAGE	FLOWER COLOR, TIME, ETC.	HARDINESS
R. 'Golden Belle' (discolor x 'Fabia')	apricot, yellow centers; saucer-shaped; late May; compact	0°F.
R. 'Grierosplendour' (griersonianum x 'Purple Splendour')	plum; late May; low-growing	0°F.
R. 'Harvest Moon' ('Mrs. Lindsay Smith' x campylocarpum hybrid)	pale yellow with red spots; early May	0°F.
R. 'Jean Marie de Montague' (griffithianum hybrid)	bright red; early May; compact	0°F.
R. 'Jingle Bells' ('Lem's Goal' x 'Fabia')	yellow, tubular; early May; low-growing	0°F.
R. 'King of Shrubs' (discolor x 'Fabia')	apricot-yellow; late May	+5°F.
R. 'Lady Chamberlain' (cinnabarinum var. roylei x 'Royal Flush')	orange to salmon-pink, tubular; late April	+10°F.
R. 'Lady Roseberry' (cinnabarinum var. roylei x 'Royal Flush')	Pink, tubular; late April	+5°F.
R. 'Little Gem' ('Carmen' x elliottii)	blood-red; early May; dwarf	+5°F.
R. 'Loderi King George' (griffithianum x fortunei)	large, white, fragrant; early May	0°F.
R. 'May Day' (haematodes x griersonianum)	orange-scarlet; early May; low-growing	+5°F.
R. 'Mrs. Horace Fogg' (griersonianum x 'Loderi Venus')	pink with dark throat; early May	0°F.
R. 'Polar Bear' (diaprepes x auriculatum)	white, green throat; June	0°F.
R. 'Romany Chal' ('Moser's Maroon' x eriogynum)	dark scarlet; June; shade	0°F.
R. 'Sapphire' ('Blue Tit' x impeditum)	blue, fragrant; early April; dwarf	0°F.
R. 'Spitfire' (griffithianum hybrid)	deep red; early May	0°F.
R. 'Tidbit' (dichroanthum x wardii)	yellow; early May; low-growing	+5°F.
R. 'Unique' (campylocarpum hybrid)	yellow-tinged peach; late April	0°F.
R. 'Vanessa Pastel' ('Soulbut' x griersonianum)	red turning to apricot, then yellow; late May	+5°F.

Azaleas: Rhododendron Species of Merit

The azaleas, botanically rhododendrons, are among the most beautiful of the flowering shrubs. Native to eastern Asia, North America and Europe, they have been developed in the skillful hands of the plant hybridizers until today we have many varied and brilliantly flowered forms. There are both evergreen and deciduous types. Most azaleas possess considerable hardiness, while a few are suited only to mild climates.

Azaleas and other rhododendrons are more exacting in their cultural requirements than are most of the other commonly grown flowering shrubs. However, their profusion and beauty of bloom, combined with their wide range of glorious colors and their dependable flowering year after year, more than repay the extra effort expended upon them.

Exposure

Most azaleas prefer a sunny exposure, or a location where they will receive direct sunlight for at least a portion of the day. Some types may be grown successfully under trees that cast high shade and provide filtered sunlight. Many will make satisfactory growth in areas where they are in partial shade, but no azalea will grow well in dense shade. Most azaleas withstand exposure to wind extremely well, but the evergreen types may burn severely under such conditions, especially when grown near their northern limit of hardiness.

Soil Requirements

Most azaleas require an acid soil. A pH range of 4.5 to 5.5 is considered optimum for most types.

The texture of the soil is also important. Azaleas require a soil that is abundantly supplied with humus, mellow and fibrous in texture, retentive of moisture yet well drained. They will not thrive in heavy, poorly drained, waterlogged soil.

If the soil in the area where azaleas are to be planted does not meet these requirements, measures should be taken to correct its deficiencies. (For methods that may be used to increase soil acidity, see index.) If the soil is a good garden loam, its texture may be improved by incorporating into it liberal quantities of compost, acid peat and other suitable organic materials. If, however, it is a heavy clay, or a very light, sandy soil, it would be wise to remove it and fill the bed or the planting hole with a good mixture—peat, oak leaf mold and humus as recommended for the plant. The area should be excavated to a depth of 12 in. to 15 in. and refilled with the planting mixture. It requires considerable labor to accomplish this but it must be borne in mind that an azalea planting is a very permanent one and will be a source of satisfaction over a period of many years. The cost of the plants is also compara-

tively high, and it is a matter of poor economy and unsound judgment to fail to provide congenial soil that will be conducive to their best growth. If this is not done in the beginning, the results will be disappointing. The plants will fail to flower well and will tend to die out after a few years.

Planting

Except in the case of extremely small plants, azaleas should always be planted with a ball of earth and not with bare roots. They may be purchased in pots or tubs, or with the ball of earth wrapped in burlap. In the North spring planting is advisable. In the South azaleas should preferably be transplanted during the period between the time they have set their flower buds in the autumn and spring. If possible, the deciduous azaleas should be planted after they have dropped their leaves and while they are completely dormant. It is very important that azaleas be planted at the same depth at which they were growing in the nursery. Planting them too deeply is the cause of many failures. The ball of earth should not be allowed to dry out between the time of digging and planting, and after the bushes are in place the area should be well watered, and a good mulch of acid leaf mold, wood chips or peat should be applied.

Fertilization

In order to maintain an azalea planting in vigorous, healthy condition and to ensure abundant bloom, two annual applications of fertilizer are desirable, one early in the spring and the other between the middle of June and the middle of July. Fertilizers that are acid in their reaction upon the soil should be used. A commercially prepared complete fertilizer for acid-loving plants may be used.

Cottonseed meal applied alone is an excellent fertilizer on soils that are not low in potash. The same rate of application as for broad-leaved evergreen rhododendrons is recommended. The fertilizer should be spread evenly over the surface of the ground about the plants, extending out slightly beyond the spread of the branches, and should be watered in.

14.2 *Azalea flowers are a special experience. Colors range from clean white to shockingly bright pinks, coral and purple. And some are wonderfully fragrant. Photo Grant Heilman*

Culture

The soil about azaleas should never be cultivated, as the feeding roots are very near the surface and might be severely injured. A good mulch of acid peat, wood chips or oak leaf mold should be maintained. This will help to keep the soil cool and moist and provide conditions favorable to good growth.

For control of insect pests and diseases, see Chapter 32.

Rhododendron calendulaceum (flame azalea)

This lovely azalea, known as the flame azalea, is one of the most beautiful of our native shrubs. It grows wild in the Appalachian Mountains from northern Georgia to Pennsylvania and in the spring the woods are aglow with its beauty. The flowers vary in color from pale yellow to brilliant orange and a well-grown specimen is a glorious sight when in full bloom. It requires an acid soil, rich in humus and well drained, and under favorable conditions it will attain a height of 8 ft. to 9 ft. It thrives best in light woodland shade but will withstand consid-

erable exposure to sun and wind. The foliage is deciduous.

Zone of hardiness: 5, northern limit.

Exbury and Knap Hill Hybrids

This large group is the result of intercrossing numerous Ghent hybrids and also using a few species such as *R. occidentale* and *R. molle*. The cultivars exhibit an astounding array of flower colors, ranging from white through pink and rose, to yellow, orange, red and scarlet—often in stunning combinations. Many of the cultivars tend to be somewhat less robust than the older Ghent Hybrids, but wherever they are hardy, members of this outstanding race of relatively new azaleas are a decided asset to the spring garden.

Zone of hardiness: 5–6.

Rhododendron x gandavense (Ghent Hybrids)

The Ghent Hybrids are noted for their wide range of beautiful colors. The flowers are smaller than those of some of the other types but are borne in great profusion, the colors ranging from white to lilac-pink, deep pink,

golden-yellow, orange-red and brilliant scarlet. The Ghent Hybrids are hardy, dependable and of easy culture, reaching a height at maturity of about 6 ft.
Zone of hardiness: 4.

Rhododendron (Glendale Hybrids)

These lovely, large-flowered evergreen azaleas were developed by Mr. B. Y. Morrison. Most varieties that have been introduced are hardy from New York southward. Plants range in height from 4 ft. to 8 ft., according to variety. Many varieties produce flowers that are flecked, striped or blotched with a contrasting color, making them distinctive in appearance. Others are clear self-colors. Most varieties are single, but some are of the semidouble type.
Zone of hardiness: 6 – 7.

Rhododendron (Indian group)

This group of azaleas includes many of the beautiful large-flowered, evergreen varieties that are grown so widely in the South and have made many gardens in that section of the country famous. The colors range through white, lavender, rose-pink, salmon and orange-red to the variegated types. Although most of the members of this diverse group are suited only to mild climates, a few are very hardy, among them *R. mucronatum (R. ledifolia alba)*, one of our best white azaleas.
Zone of hardiness: 7 (*R. mucronatum:* Zone 6)

Rhododendron (Mollis Hybrids)

The Mollis Hybrids are vigorous and hardy and prefer full sun, but they will grow fairly well in light shade, are less exacting in their soil requirements than many other types and may be transplanted when small without a ball of earth. In this group there is a wide range of unusually beautiful colors, some being soft, pastel shades, others of a more brilliant hue – delicate yellow, deep Indian yellow, apricot-yellow, and brilliant, coppery-flame. The Mollis

Hybrids are excellent for a mass planting in beds or for the foreground of shrubbery borders, and they may also be used in foundation planting and as specimens. The plants vary in height from 3 ft. to 6 ft., depending upon the variety.
Zone of hardiness: 5.

Rhododendron obtusum (Kurume azaleas)

The Kurume azaleas were introduced into this country from Japan by the great plant explorer, Dr. E. H. Wilson. Fifty varieties were shipped to Harvard University's Arnold Arboretum in 1919, and since that time they have gained tremendous popularity in many areas of the country. The plants are evergreen, the leaves small, and the characteristic growth is dense and twiggy. The height ranges from 4 ft. to 8 ft. according to variety. The flowers, which are smaller than those of many other types, are produced in great profusion. Most are single, others of the type known as semidouble. Among the many varieties there is a wide range of color, from white, pale pink, lavender and salmon to brilliant scarlet. Some of the more brilliant colors are difficult to combine harmoniously with other plants, and should be used with great restraint. Many named varieties are available.

The Kurume azaleas are widely grown from Pennsylvania southward and on the Pacific Coast. In colder sections they require a sheltered location or some winter protection.
Zone of hardiness: 6 – 8.

Rhododendron obtusum var. *kaempferi* (torch azalea)

In its native habitat in Japan the torch azalea grows in thickets and along the edge of woodlands, and it is therefore well adapted to growing in light shade. The *R. obtusum* var. *kaempferi* Hybrids offer a wide range of color – from soft lilac and pink to lilac-rose, deep mauve, orange-pink, and pale orange, light rose to rose-red and bright brick-red. The flowers are produced in large clusters. The plants are vigorous, hardy and free-flowering, and attain a height of 8 ft.

to 10 ft. at maturity. The deciduous foliage turns a brilliant orange-scarlet in the autumn.
Zone of hardiness: 5.

Rhododendron periclymenoides (R. nudiflorum, pinxter flower)

This lovely azalea is a native of the woodlands in the East from North Carolina to Massachusetts. It is one of the most satisfactory azaleas for undergrowth planting in moist wooded areas. In early spring, before the leaves appear, it brings a touch of color to the gray woods with its masses of small pink flowers, which are delicately fragrant. It is upright in growth habit, reaching a height of 6 ft. to 10 ft.
Zone of hardiness: 3.

Rhododendron schlippenbachii (royal azalea)

This beautiful azalea from eastern Asia blooms in early spring before the leaves unfurl. The wide-open flowers are very large, a lovely shade of soft pink, and they are borne in clusters at the tips of the twigs. Its growth is slow and widely branched, but after many years it sometimes attains a height of 15 ft. It is hardy and well adapted to cool climates. It thrives in very light shade and can tolerate a greater range of soil acidity than some other types.

Rhododendron vaseyi (pinkshell azalea)

This is one of our most beautiful native azaleas, its natural habitat being the ravines and swampy areas in the mountains of North Carolina. The clear pink flowers are borne in clusters in early spring before the leaves unfold. In habit of growth it is upright and somewhat irregularly spreading, usually attaining a height of about 15 ft. It begins to flower when quite small. In autumn the foliage turns a bright crimson. It is hardy, and is best adapted to cool climates and high altitudes. It requires a soil that is abundantly supplied with moisture.
Zone of hardiness: 3.

Rosa rugosa (Japanese rose)

Perhaps the most dependable of all the shrub roses for general planting. The flowers are pink or white, depending on variety, and appear in early June. The handsome brick-red to orange fruits (1 in. diameter) are very effective in autumn. *Rosa rugosa* is widely naturalized along the coast in the Northeast, and is one of the best of all shrubs for seaside gardens. Normal height ranges from 5 ft. to 6 ft., and this species

*14.3 The rugosa rose (*Rosa rugosa*) is a familiar seaside plant in New England but grows equally well in many other situations. Flowers are white and magenta-pink, are very fragrant and appear throughout the summer. Photo Grant Heilman*

adapts itself well to treatment as a hedge, either clipped or unclipped. There are many cultivars with single or double flowers, and colors range from white through pink and rose-purple.
Zone of hardiness: 2.

Soil requirements: Not particular.

Exposure: Full sun.

Culture: Thrives without attention for many years; occasional cutting out of older branches for rejuvenation purposes may be desirable.

Sarcococca hookerana 'Humilis' (sweet box)

This is a small, evergreen shrub that has proven itself of value in planting compositions. Its dark, glossy leaves and compact form make it an excellent ground cover in semishaded areas and it may also be used very effectively as a foreground planting in an evergreen shrub bed or border. The flowers are white and inconspicuous. The leaves are 3 in. to 4 in. long and taper to a slender point. It is a shrub that grows slowly but, eventually, after many years, attains a height of 3 ft. to 4 ft.
Zone of hardiness: 6.

Soil requirements: A good loam.

Exposure: Prefers partial shade. Does well on the north side of a building.

Culture: Mulch with leaves and do not disturb the roots by cultivation.

Spiraea prunifolia (bridal-wreath)

A comparatively small shrub, seldom growing more than 4 ft. or 5 ft. tall. It is of upright, spreading growth, with graceful branches that are wreathed with bloom in early spring. The small white flowers are quite double in form and are borne in great abundance. It has a tendency to become a bit leggy near the ground and is best used in mass or foundation plantings. In spite of this fault it is desirable because of its daintiness, and when it is in flower it seems to have about it the very breath of spring.
Zone of hardiness: 4.

Soil requirements: Any good soil, but thrives best in a rich, moist loam.

Exposure: Sunny position.

Culture: Pruning is necessary to keep the shrub from becoming too leggy below. Cut out all dead wood from the center that does not bear bloom, allowing new growth to come up. Pruning for this early spring-blooming type should take place after flowering, inasmuch as bloom is borne on the previous year's growth.

Spiraea thunbergii (Thunberg spirea)

S. thunbergii is well adapted for the foreground of mass plantings as it rarely grows more than 3 ft. tall. It is of bushy habit, with very slender, twiglike branches. The leaves are small, narrow and quite pointed. They are a slightly yellowish-green, turning orange and red in the autumn. It blooms very early in the season, in March or early April, the myriad small white flowers appearing before the leaves unfold.
Zone of hardiness: 4.

Soil requirements:
Exposure: } See *S. prunifolia.*

Culture: Prune immediately after blooming.

Spiraea x Vanhouttei (bridal-wreath)

A veritable fountain of bloom when it is in flower, this is a shrub of graceful form, 5 ft. to 6 ft. in height, and the finely cut, delicate foliage is attractive throughout the season. The large white flower clusters are borne in lavish profusion during the month of May. It may be used as a specimen shrub, for both foundation and mass planting, and as a flowering hedge.
Zone of hardiness: 4.

Soil requirements:

Exposure:

} See *S. prunifolia.*

Culture: Pruning for this early spring-blooming type should take place after flowering, inasmuch as bloom is borne on the previous year's growth.

Symplocos paniculata (sapphire berry)

Valued for its brilliant blue fruit, borne in hanging clusters in the early autumn. These are highly attractive to the birds, large bushes often being stripped of the fruit very soon after the berries change color. The small white flowers, which appear in late spring, are borne in panicles. The height varies from 15 ft. to 25 ft. The foliage, although small, is dense, and the shrub can be used either as a background or as an accent in a formal setting.

Zone of hardiness: 5 — northern limit.

Soil requirements: A rich garden loam.

Exposure: Full sun or partial shade.

Syringa vulgaris (common lilac)

A native of the mountainous regions of Rumania, Yugoslavia, Bulgaria and Greece, lilac was highly prized by the Turks, and from Constantinople was introduced into Europe about 1550. It is a vigorous shrub, growing to a height of 15 ft. or more, bearing large trusses of blossoms. Its ability to naturalize and thrive caused it to run wild throughout western Europe, so that by 1780 it was a common hedgerow shrub in parts of Italy and France. When or how it was brought to America is not known, but in all likelihood it reached the colonies before 1750. It was greatly appreciated by colonists because of its ability to survive severe winters and long periods of neglect. In 1823 its name appeared in American nursery catalogues. It is hardy in Zone 3.

By the early years of the nineteenth century horticulturists were experimenting with lilacs, producing new varieties and discovering those with distinctive characteristics. Hundreds of varieties have been produced, in France, Belgium, Holland, Germany, Canada, and the United States, and many of these are now offered by American nurseries.

Soil requirements and exposure: Lilacs are not exacting about soil, but they thrive in rich garden loam with a pH value of 6.0 to 8.0 (slightly acid or slightly alkaline). Though lilacs endure shade, they should have plenty of sunshine and moisture to bloom well. When well established they withstand wind, deep snows, hard winters and years of neglect.

Culture: Young lilac bushes should be trained to several main stems so that damage from borers is reduced to a minimum. If borers are detected in one stem, it may be removed and burned and the borers with it, while the other stems carry on. Many lilacs have a habit of suckering. This should be checked by annual pruning. Likewise the central or interior stems tend to become crowded and should be thinned out occasionally. Dead flower clusters should be removed to prevent the formation of seed. With abundantly blooming shrubs, the flowering stems may be cut long to include much foliage and may be used in decorating the house. This is one of the easy methods of pruning. Failure to bloom regularly may be due to too severe pruning or to no pruning the preceding season, or to the accumulation of suckers or to heavily shaded conditions.

Lilacs are subject to borers and scales. The borer is most active in June and July, and its presence is made evident by piles of sawdust and dying branches.

Oyster shell scale and San José scale are both damaging to lilacs. Their presence in clusters on the twigs and branches results in the shriveling of leaves and general lack of vitality. Measures of control for borers and scales are described in Chapter 32.

LILAC CULTIVARS OF MERIT

'Adelaide Dunbar': double; purple
'Ami Schott': double; bluish
'Capitaine Baletet': single; magenta
'Charles X': single; magenta
'Christophe Colomb': single; lilac
'Congo': single; magenta
'De Miribel': single; violet
'Ellen Willmott': double; white
'Jan Van Tol': single; white
'Katherine Havemeyer': double; pink
'Lucie Baltet': single; pink
'Ludwig Spaeth': single; purple
'Marechal Lannes': double; violet
'Mme. F. Morel': single; magenta
'Monge': single; purple
'Paul Hariot': double; purple
'Paul Thirion': double; magenta
'President Lincoln': single; bluish
'Primrose': single; yellowish
'Victor Lemoine': double; lilac

Besides *Syringa vulgaris*, there are a number of species native to different parts of Asia and Europe, but none native to America.

Syringa x chinensis (Chinese lilac)

This is not a Chinese species at all but a hybrid between *S. persica* and *S. vulgaris*. It appeared in the nurseries of a French grower at Rouen about 1777 and was first supposed to be an imported species when it was named. Its blossoms are larger and more compact than those of *S. persica*, reddish purple, dark red, or white. The leaves are larger and broader than those of *S. persica*. Height 15 feet.
Zone of hardiness: 5.

Syringa microphylla 'Superba' (Daphne lilac)

A small, compact shrub. The mahogany-red buds open to soft, pink flowers in large panicles in May in such quantities that the whole shrub becomes a large bouquet. The leaves are very small. It sometimes blooms again in the autumn. Height 5 feet.
Zone of hardiness: 5 — northern limit.

S. x persica (Persian lilac)

Although for centuries supposed to have originated in Persia, this really comes from China. Many hundreds of years ago it was brought over the great caravan route to Persia, where it has been cultivated ever since. The plant and leaves are smaller and narrower than *S. vulgaris* and are rarely over 10 ft. tall. Another difference is in the arrangement of flowers, which are borne on lateral leafy branches, in small clusters of pinkish bloom. Its existence in Europe is recorded as early as 1660.
Zone of hardiness: 5.

S. villosa (late lilac)

A very hardy shrub, 11 ft. high, with broad leaves often 7 in. long and pale rose or flesh-colored flowers in late May. To some people the odor of the bloom is disagreeable. It is one of the hardiest of all the lilacs (Zone 2), and one of the last to blossom, in early June. Crossing this species with *S. reflexa* has yielded a series of cultivars, collectively known as the *S. x prestionae* Hybrids. These blossom well into June and thus considerably prolong the lilac season. Two tree-like forms are *S. reticulata* and *S. pekinensis*.

S. reticulata (Japanese tree lilac)

A rapidly growing plant 25 ft. or 30 ft. tall, with a central stem, low forked branches and cherry like bark. The cream-white blossoms are borne in enormous, loose panicles in June and July. The odor resembles that of privet, to which lilacs are related.
Zone of hardiness: 4.

S. pekinensis

Although this is 20 ft. tall, it has a shrubby form. Its bark is yellowish-brown and peels off like birch bark. The flowers are yellowish-white in large panicles in June. It was introduced from China about 1880.
Zone of hardiness: 5.

Viburnum

Viburnum carlesii (Korean spice viburnum)

Native to Korea and noted particularly for the sweet fragrance of its blossoms. It is a shrub of somewhat rounded form, reaching a height of about 5 ft. The flowers, which form a close,

compact head, are a delicate pink in color when they first open in early April, gradually fading to white, and their fragrance is suggestive of the trailing arbutus.
Zone of hardiness: 4.

Soil requirements: Not particular, but does best in a cool, moist, fertile soil.

Exposure: Full sun.

Culture: Shrubs of large size do not withstand transplanting too well, so when purchasing them it is wise to choose small specimens.

Viburnum x *carlcephalum* (fragrant snowball)

A hybrid of *V. carlesii* and *V. macrocephalum* that possesses many of the best characteristics of both parents. It is hardy and vigorous in growth, reaching a height of 6 ft. to 9 ft. It combines the fragrance and early season of bloom of *V. carlesii* with the large, rounded white flower clusters of *V. macrocephalum*. The blooms are borne in great profusion and in the autumn the foliage turns a brilliant color.
Zone of hardiness: 5.

Soil requirements: Thrives equally well in acid or neutral soils.

Exposure: Full sun or light shade.

Viburnum *dilatatum* (linden viburnum)

Like the other viburnums, this is a vigorous shrub of dense habit. It is covered with panicles of white flowers in May and June, and in September and October it bears masses of showy scarlet berries, which hang on well into the winter. Excellent in the mixed shrub border. Height 6 ft. to 9 ft.

V. *dilatatum* 'Xanthocarpum'

Has yellow berries and is somewhat less vigorous in growth.
Zone of hardiness: 5, northern limit.

Viburnum *plicatum* f. *tomentosum* (doublefile viburnum)

This is a strikingly handsome shrub in flower. In the autumn the dark green leaves take on a somber bronzy purple. It is of upright habit, with wide-spreading, horizontal branches. The white flowers, which come in May, are borne in flat clusters and line the upper side of the branches, producing an unusually interesting effect. The small fruits are red at first, then turn gradually to a bluish-black. A very desirable shrub both for specimen use and for mass planting.
Zone of hardiness: 4.

Soil requirements:

Exposure: } See *V. carlesii.*

Culture: Care should be used when transplanting, as it is moved with difficulty.

Viburnum *rhytidophyllum* (leatherleaf viburnum)

One of the few hardy members of this large group that is evergreen. It is a shrub of vigorous growth, with strong, stout branches, and it reaches a height of about 10 ft. The yellow-white flowers open in May and June and are borne in broad heads well above the foliage. The fruits are characteristically red, changing to black. The handsome foliage is a deep, dark green, very shiny and somewhat wrinkled in texture.
Zone of hardiness: 6 and sometimes in 5. Hardy in the North, but kills back in below-zero weather. Needs protected position for foliage to remain evergreen.

Soil requirements:

} See *V. carlesii.*

Exposure:

Viburnum setigerum 'Aurantiacum' (V. theiferum, tea viburnum)

A shrub for special consideration, that is not dense but has beautiful slender leaves and a profusion of white flowers in midsummer. In autumn the clusters of brilliant red berries give

it distinction and beauty. It is slow to mature but reaches an eventual height of about 10 ft. to 12 ft.

Zone of hardiness: 5.

Soil requirements: Thrives equally well in acid or neutral soils.

Exposure: Sun or partial shade.

RELIABLE SHRUBS

(Those that thrive without care, and even in spite of abuse. Rarely attacked by insects or diseases.)

Acanthopanax sieboldianus	*Elaeagnus umbellata*	*Myrica pensylvanica*
Acer ginnala	*Euonymus alata*	*Physocarpus opulifolius*
Actinidia arguta	*Forsythia* x *intermedia* cultivars	*Pieris floribunda*
Aronia arbutifolia	*Forsythia ovata*	*Potentilla fruticosa*
Aronia prunifolia	*Forsythia suspensa* var. *sieboldii*	*Prunus triloba*
Berberis julianae	*Hamamelis* (all)	*Rhododendron maximum*
Berberis koreana	*Hydrangea paniculata* 'Grandiflora'	*Rosa multiflora*
Berberis thunbergii	*Ilex verticillata*	*Rosa rugosa*
Calycanthus floridus	*Kolkwitzia amabilis*	*Spiraea* x *vanhouttei*
Caragana arborescens	*Leucothoë fontanesiana*	*Symphoricarpos albus* var. *laevigatus*
Caragana maximowicziana	*Lindera benzoin*	*Taxus cuspidata* and *T.* x *media* cultivars
Cephalanthus occidentalis	*Lonicera* x *amoena*	(most, if left unpruned)
Clethra alnifolia	*Lonicera maackii*	*Vaccinium* spp.
Cornus mas	(most of the bush honeysuckles)	*Viburnum* spp. (most)

RECOMMENDED SHRUBS FOR AUTUMN COLOR

Acer ginnala	red	*Nandina domestica*	red
Amelanchier x *grandiflora*	yellow to orange	*Photinia villosa*	red-bronze
Aronia arbutifolia	red	*Rhododendron schlippenbachii*	orange to crimson
Aronia melanocarpa	red	*Rhododendron vaseyi*	light red
Aronia prunifolia	red	*Rhus aromatica*	yellow and scarlet
Berberis koreana	deep red	*Rhus copallina*	red
Berberis thunbergii	scarlet	*Rhus typhina*	red
Calycanthus floridus	yellow	*Rosa rugosa*	orange
Chionanthus virginicus	yellow	*Rosa virginiana*	scarlet
Cotinus coggygria	yellow to orange	*Spiraea prunifolia*	red to orange
Enkianthus campanulatus	red	*Vaccinium corymbosum*	scarlet
Euonymus alata	scarlet	*Viburnum dilatatum*	red
Fothergilla major	yellow to scarlet	*V. latana*	red
Franklinia alatamaha	red	*V. lentago*	purplish red
Hamamelis x *intermedia* cultivars	reddish	*V. opulus*	red
Hamamelis mollis	yellow	*V. prunifolium*	red
Hamamelis virginiana	yellow	*V. rufidulum*	red
Itea virginica	red	*V. trilobum*	red

SHRUBS WITH CONSPICUOUS FRUIT

Aronia arbutifolia	red	Sept. – winter
Aronia arbutifolia 'Brilliantissima'	red	Sept. – winter
Berberis thunbergii	bright red	winter
Berberis vulgaris, etc.	red or purple	winter
Callicarpa dichotoma	purple	Oct. – Nov.
Callicarpa japonica	purple	Oct. – Nov.
Chionanthus virginicus	blue	Sept.
Cornus mas	scarlet	August
Cornus racemosa	blue	Sept. – Oct.
Cotoneaster divaricatus	red	Sept. – Nov.
Cotoneaster horizontalis	bright red	Sept. – winter
Cotoneaster hupehensis	bright red	Aug. – Sept.
Cotoneaster simonsii (and others)	scarlet	Oct.
Elaeagnus umbellata	orange	July
Euonymus alata	red and orange	Sept. – Oct.
Euonymus americanus	light scarlet	Aug. – Oct.
Euonymus europaeus	pink or red	Sept. – Oct.
Ilex laevigata	orange-red	Sept.
Ilex opaca	red	winter
Ilex serrata	red	Oct. – winter
Ilex verticillata	bright red	Oct. – winter
Ligustrum x *ibolium*	black	Sept. – Dec.
Ligustrum vulgare	black	Sept. – Dec.
Lonicera maackii	crimson	Sept. – Nov.
Lonicera tatarica	crimson	July
Mahonia aquifolium	blue	Sept.
Myrica pensylvanica	gray	Sept. – April
Nandina domestica	bright red or purple-red	Sept.
Photinia serrulata	red	Oct.
Photinia villosa	bright red	Oct. – Nov.
Pyracantha coccinea 'Lalandei'	orange-scarlet	winter
Rhodotypos scandens	black	Oct. – Nov.
Rosa multiflora	red	winter
Rosa rugosa (and other spp.)	orange-red	winter
Sambucus canadensis	black	Sept.
Sambucus racemosa	red	Sept. – Oct.
Symphoricarpos albus var. *laevigatus*	white	Sept. – Nov.
Symphoricarpos orbiculatus	purplish-red	Oct. – Dec.
Symplocos paniculata	blue	Sept.
Vaccinium corymbosum	blue	July – Aug.
Viburnum dilatatum	red	Oct. – Nov.
V. lantana	purple	July – Sept.
V. opulus	red	Aug. – winter
V. prunifolium	blue-black	Sept. – Oct.
V. sargentii	red	Sept. – Oct.
V. setigerum 'Aurantiacum'	orange	Oct. – Nov.

SHRUBS FOR WET PLACES

(Moist to wet soils)

Alnus spp.	*Magnolia virginiana*
Amelanchier spp.	*Myrica gale*
Aronia arbutifolia	*Myrica pensylvanica*
Calycanthus floridus	*Rhododendron canadense*
Cassandra (Chamaedaphne) calyculata	*R. nudiflorum*
Clethra alnifolia	*R. vaseyi*
Cornus alba	*R. viscosum*
Cornus amomum	*Rosa palustris*
Cornus sanguinea	*Salix caprea*
Cornus sericea	*Salix discolor*
Dirca palustris	*Salix purpurea* (and many others)
Hypericum densiflorum	*Sambucus canadensis*
Ilex glabra	*Spiraea tomentosa*
Ilex laevigata	*Taxus canadensis*
Ilex verticillata	*Vaccinium macrocarpum*
Ilex vomitoria	*Viburnum alnifolium*
Itea virginica	*V. cassinoides*
Kalmia angustifolia	*V. dentatum*
Ledum groenlandicum	*V. lentago*
Lindera benzoin	*V. opulus*
	V. trilobum

SHRUBS FOR DRY PLACES

(Survive in poor, sandy soil)

Acanthopanax spp.	*Lonicera* spp.
Acer ginnala	*Lycium* spp.
Amorpha spp.	*Myrica pensylvanica*
Arctostaphylos uva-ursi	*Physocarpus* spp.
Artemisia spp.	*Potentilla* spp.
Baccharis halimifolia	*Prunus besseyi*
Berberis thunbergii	*P. maritima*
Caragana spp.	*Rhamnus* spp.
Ceanothus americanus	*Rhus* spp.
Ceanothus fendleri	*Ribes alpinum*
Colutea spp.	*Robinia hispida*
Comptonia peregrina	*Rosa caroliniana*
Cornus racemosa	*R. gallica*
Cotinus coggygria	*R. nitida*
Cytisus species	*R. rugosa*
Elaeagnus angustifolia	*R. setigera*
Elaeagnus umbellata	*R. spinosissima*
Epigaea repens	*R. virginiana*
Gaylussacia baccata	*Rosmarinus officinalis*
Hypericum prolificum	*Salix tristis*
Indigofera species	*Santolina chamaecyparissus*
Juniperus communis	*Shepherdia argentea*
Juniperus conferta	*Shepherdia canadensis*
Juniperus horizontalis cultivars	*Sophora davidii*
Juniperus virginiana cultivars	*Spartium junceum*
Lavandula species	*Tamarix* spp.
Lespedeza bicolor	*Viburnum lentago*
Ligustrum spp.	*Yucca* spp.

SHRUBS FOR CUT FLOWERS

Buddleia	Forsythia	Sorbaria
Caryopteris	Hamamelis	Spiraea
Chaenomeles	Philadelphus	Syringa
Cornus mas	Prunus	Tamarix
Corylus	Salix	Weigela
Deutzia		

SHRUBS OF NEAT GROWTH HABIT

(Will never grow too tall for a position under windows)

HEIGHT IN FEET

Abilia x grandiflora	5
Berberis x chenaultii	4
Cotoneaster adpressus	3
Cotoneaster apiculatus	3
Cotoneaster horizontalis	2½
Deutzia gracilis	3
Enkianthus perulatus	5
Ilex crenata 'Helleri'	4
Ilex glabra	6
Juniperus horizontalis	1½
Juniperus sabina var. tamariscifolia	3 – 4
Leucothoë fontanesiana	3 – 5
Lonicera alpigena 'Nana'	3
Lonicera nitida	5 – 6
Mahonia aquifolium	3 – 4
Myrica gale	3
Myrica pensylvanica	6
Pieris floribunda	5
Polentilla fruticosa cultivars	2 – 4
Rhododendron 'Boule de Neige'	3
R. carolinianum	3 – 6
R. laetevirens	3 – 4
R. obtusum var. kaempferi	5
R. 'P.J.M.'	6
R. yedoense var. poukhanense	3
Sarcococca hookerana 'Humilis'	2
Spiraea x arguta 'Compacta'	4
Spiraea japonica var. alpina	1
Spiraea x vanhouttei	5 – 6
Stephanandra incisa	5
Taxus baccata 'Repandens'	3
Taxus canadensis	3 – 5
Taxus cuspidata 'Densa'	4

SHRUBS OF RAPID GROWTH HABIT

(For quick screen or windbreak)

HEIGHT IN FEET

Acanthopanax sieboldianus	9
Elaeagnus angustifolia	20
Elaeagnus umbellata	10 – 12

SHRUBS OF RAPID GROWTH HABIT (Continued)

Euonymus europaeus	25
Forsythia x intermedia cultivars	10
Forsythia suspensa var. sieboldii	3 – 10
Ligustrum species	15
Lonicera fragrantissima	10
Lonicera maackii	15
Philadelphus coronarius	10
Rosa multiflora	8 – 10
Salix pentandra	30
Salix purpurea	9
Viburnum dentatum	15
V. lentago	20 – 25
V. prunifolium	15

SPREADING SHRUBS FOR COVERING A BANK

(See also vines and ground covers)

SIZE OF AREA COVERED

Arctostaphylos uva-ursi	small
Berberis thunbergii	medium to large
Cornus alba	''
Cornus amomum	''
Cornus sericea	''
Cotoneaster horizontalis	small to large
Cytisus scoparius	medium to large
Forsythia 'Arnold Dwarf'	medium to large
Forsythia x intermedia cultivars	large
Forsythia suspensa var. sieboldii	''
Hypericum buckleyi	small to medium
Hypericum calycinum	small to large
Indigofera incarnata var. alba	small to medium
Indigofera korolkowii	''
Jasminum nudiflorum	medium to large
Juniperus chinensis var. sargentii	''
Juniperus conferta	''
Juniperus horizontalis	''
Leucothoë fontanesiana	small to large (shade)
Lycium halimifolium	medium to large
Myrica species	''
Physocarpus opulifolius	large
Pieris floribunda	medium to large
Rhus aromatica	''
Robinia hispida	medium to large
Rosa 'Max Graf'	''
R. multiflora	''
R. virginiana	''
R. wichuraiana	''
Spiraea salicifolia	medium
Stephanandra incisa 'Crispa'	medium to large
Symphoricarpos species	''
Vaccinium angustifolium	small to medium
Viburnum dentatum	medium to large
V. lentago	''
V. trilobum	''
Vinca minor	small to large
Xanthorhiza simplicissima	medium to large

OLD-FASHIONED SHRUBS

(Appropriate for colonial gardens)

SHRUBS FOR SHADY PLACES

(Those marked with an asterisk will withstand fairly deep shade)

EVERGREEN

Aucuba japonica
Berberis julianae
Buxus spp. and cultivars
Camellia spp. and cultivars
Euonymus fortunei and varieties
Euonymus kiautschovicus
Fatsia japonica
Gaultheria shallon
Ilex crenata cultivars
**Ilex glabra*
**Kalmia latifolia*
Laurus nobilis
**Leucothoë fontanesiana*
**Mahonia* species
**Pieris* spp. and cultivars

**Rhododendron* spp. and cultivars
Sarcococca spp.
Skimmia japonica
**Taxus* spp. and cultivars
**Taxus canadensis* cultivars
Thuja spp. and cultivars

DECIDUOUS

Abelia x *grandiflora*
**Acanthopanax sieboldianus*
Amelanchier species
**Aronia* species
Berberis thunbergii and cultivars
Cercis chinensis
Chionanthus virginicus
**Clethra alnifolia*

**Corylopsis* species
**Cornus alba* and cultivars
**Cornus amomum*
**Cornus mas*
**Cornus racemosa*
**Cornus sericea* and cultivars
Daphne spp.
Fothergilla spp.
**Hamamelis* spp.
Hydrangea anomala var. *petiolaris*
Hydrangea quercifolia
Hypericum calycinum
Hypericum frondosum
Hypericum prolificum
**Ilex verticillata*
Ligustrum spp. and cultivars
**Lindera benzoin*

Lonicera spp.
Magnolia virginiana
Myrica spp.
Nandina domestica
Photinia spp.
Pyracantha spp.
Raphiolepis umbellata
Rhamnus spp.
Rhododendron spp. and cultivars
Rhodotypos scandens
Ruscus aculeatus
Stephanandra incisa
Symphoricarpos spp.
**Vaccinium* spp.
**Xanthorhiza simplicissima*

SHRUBS

KEY: s – sun
      sh – shade
      p sh – partial shade

( )   indicates possible hardiness only;
See Zone of Hardiness map on pages 796 – 97

SCIENTIFIC & COMMON NAME	ZONE OF HARDINESS; HEIGHT IN FEET	EXPOSURE; PREFERRED SOIL	COLOR; SEASON OF BLOOM	COLOR OF FRUIT; REMARKS
Abelia x *grandiflora* glossy abelia	6; 6 – 8	s or sh, protected; light, peaty	white, flush pink; June – November	inconspicuous
Abelia x Edward Goucher abelia	6; 5	s or sh, protected; light, peaty	pink; August	inconspicuous
Abeliophyllum distichum Korean abelialeaf	5; 5	s, protected; ordinary	white; April	inconspicuous
Acanthopanax sieboldianus five-leaf aralia	5; 4 – 6	s; rich, heavy	inconspicuous	inconspicuous
Acer ginnala Amur maple	2; 20	s; ordinary to poor	red; summer	inconspicuous

SHRUBS (Continued)

SCIENTIFIC & COMMON NAME	ZONE OF HARDINESS; HEIGHT IN FEET	EXPOSURE; PREFERRED SOIL	COLOR; SEASON OF BLOOM	COLOR OF FRUIT; REMARKS
Aesculus parviflora bottlebrush buckeye	4; 8–12	s or sh; moist	white; July	horse chestnutlike
Amelanchier canadensis shadbush	4; 30	s or sh; limestone, loamy	white; May	maroon-purple
Amorpha canescens leadplant	2; 4	s; poor, dry	blue; June	inconspicuous
Aralia spinosa Hercules club	5; 30	s or sh; ordinary	white; August	black
Arbutus unedo strawberry tree	8; 8–20	s; porous	white; September	red, yellow; evergreen
Aronia arbutifolia 'Brilliantissima'	5; 10	s or sh; moist to ordinary	white; April	red, persistent
Aronia arbutifolia red chokeberry	5; 9	s or sh; moist to ordinary	white, pinkish; May	red
Aronia prunifolia purple-fruited chokeberry	4; 12	s or sh; moist to ordinary	white; May	purplish-black
Aucuba japonica Japanese aucuba	7; 6–10	sh; heavy	maroon; March	red; evergreen
Baccharis halimifolia groundsel bush	4; 6–12	s; ordinary to dry	white; September	white; withstands salt spray
Berberis buxifolia var. *nana* dwarf Magellan barberry	6; 3	s	orange-yellow	dark purple; evergreen, compact
Berberis julianae wintergreen barberry	(5); 5	neutral	yellow; April	bluish-black; evergreen
Berberis koreana Korean barberry	5; 6	s	yellow	red, persistent; deciduous
Berberis x *mentorensis*	5; 6	s; rich	yellow; April	red; evergreen in Zone 6
Berberis sargentiana	6; 6	neutral	yellow; April	bluish-black; evergreen
Berberis thunbergii Japanese barberry	5; 3–6	s or sh; neutral	yellow; April	red
Berberis thunbergii 'Erecta' columnberry	5; 6	half sh; neutral	yellow; April	red
Berberis thunbergii 'Minor' dwarf Japanese barberry	5; 1½	s; neutral	yellow	red; very dense growth
Berberis verruculosa warty barberry	6 (5); 2	s, protected; neutral	yellow; April	violet-black; evergreen
Berberis wilsonae Wilson's barberry	6 (5); 1½	s; neutral	yellow; April	salmon-red
Buddleia alternifolia fountain buddleia	5; 10–12	s; well drained	pale purple; May	inconspicuous
Buddleia davidii orange-eye butterfly bush	6 (5); 8–10	s; well drained	lilac; July–autumn	inconspicuous
Buxus microphylla var. *japonica* littleleaf box	5; 6	half sh; rich	cream; inconspicuous, axillary	inconspicuous; evergreen
Buxus microphylla var. *koreana* Korean box	5; 2	half sh; rich	cream; inconspicuous, axillary	inconspicuous; evergreen, very hardy
Buxus sempervirens 'Arborescens' tree box	6; 30	half sh; rich	inconspicuous	inconspicuous; evergreen, grows rapidly
Buxus sempervirens 'Suffruticosa' dwarf box	6; 10	half sh; rich in humus		evergreen
Buxus sempervirens 'Vardar Valley' Balkan box	4; 2	half sh; rich	inconspicuous	inconspicuous; exceptionally hardy
Callicarpa dichotoma Chinese beautyberry	(5); 4	s; well drained for hardiness	pinkish; August	lilac-violet
Callicarpa japonica Japanese beautyberry	(5); 4	s; well drained for hardiness	pink; August	violet
Calluna vulgaris heather	6; 3	s or p sh; semiacid	rosy pink; July–Sept.	evergreen
Calycanthus floridus Strawberry shrub, sweet shrub	4; 8	s; moist loam	purplish red-brown; June–July	inconspicuous
Caragana arborescens Siberian peatree	2; 15–18	s; dry or poor	yellow; May	brown

(Continued)

SHRUBS (Continued)

SCIENTIFIC & COMMON NAME	ZONE OF HARDINESS; HEIGHT IN FEET	EXPOSURE; PREFERRED SOIL	COLOR; SEASON OF BLOOM	COLOR OF FRUIT; REMARKS
Caragana maximowicziana Maximowicz pea-tree	2; 4–5	s; dry or poor	yellow; May	brown
Caryopteris x *clandonensis* bluebeard	5; 3½–4	s; well drained for greater hardiness	blue; August	inconspicuous; cut back in spring
Ceanothus americanus New Jersey tea	5; 3	s; well drained	white; June	inconspicuous; difficult to move
Cephalanthus occidentalis buttonbush	4; 8–15	s or sh; wet to moist	white; July	inconspicuous
Cephalotaxus harringtonia Japanese plum-yew	5; 6–25	s or sh; good, well drained	inconspicuous	green
Cercis chinensis Chinese redbud	6 (5); 10–30	s or sh; good, well drained	rose-purple; May	brown
Chaenomeles japonica Japanese quince	4; 3	s; good, well drained	red; May	yellow, applelike
Chaenomeles speciosa cultivars flowering quince	4; 4–6	s; good, well drained	white, pink, red, orange; May	greenish-yellow applelike
Chamaecyparis lawsoniana dwarf cultivars, vars. of Lawson cypress	5; 2–8	s; good, well drained	inconspicuous	inconspicuous; evergreen, varying foliage, color and texture
Chamaecyparis obtusa cultivars vars. of Hinoki cypress	3–4; 2–8	s; good, well drained	inconspicuous	inconspicuous; evergreen, varying foliage, color and texture
Chimonanthus praecox wintersweet	7; 6–8	s or light sh; good, well drained	yellowish, fragrant; March–April	inconspicuous
Chionanthus virginicus fringe tree	4; 10–25	s or sh; moist to well drained	white; June	blue on female plants
Clerodendrom trichotomum harlequin glory-bower	6 (5); 6–15	s; good, well drained	white, fragrant; August	blue with reddish-maroon calyx
Clethra alnifolia sweet pepperbush	4; 4–8	sh; wet, peaty or acid, sandy	white, pink tinge; July–Sept.	inconspicuous; fragrant flowers
Colutea arborescens bladder senna	5; 12	s or sh; dry	yellow; June–Sept.	bronze-red
Comptonia peregrina sweetfern	2; 2–4	s or sh; peaty, sandy or sterile	inconspicuous	inconspicuous
Cornus alba Tatarian dogwood	2; 5–10	s or sh; wet	creamy-white; May or June	bluish-white
Cornus alba 'Sibirica' Siberian dogwood	4; 10	s or sh; wet	creamy-white; May–June	bluish-white; bright coral-red branches
Cornus amomum silky dogwood	5; 3–10	s; wet	white; June	blue
Cornus mas cornelian cherry	5; 10+	s or sh	golden-yellow; March	scarlet; often treelike
Cornus racemosa gray dogwood	4; 3–15	s	creamy-white; June	white or pale blue
Cornus sericea red osier dogwood	2; 8	s; wet	dull white; May	white; bright red twigs
Corylopsis glabrescens winter hazel	5; 6	s or sh; peaty, sandy	yellow, fragrant	inconspicuous
Corylus americana American hazelnut	4; 10	s or sh; moisture-retentive	drooping catkins	brownish
Cotinus coggygria (Rhus cotinus) smokebush	5; 15	s; well drained	inconspicuous	pinkish to grayish; plumelike fruiting panicles
Cotoneaster adpressus creeping cotoneaster	4; prostrate	s; well-drained soils preferred	pink; June	red; evergreen in the South
Cotoneaster apiculatus cranberry cotoneaster	4; 3	"	pink; June	red; evergreen in the South

SHRUBS (Continued)

SCIENTIFIC & COMMON NAME	ZONE OF HARDINESS; HEIGHT IN FEET	EXPOSURE; PREFERRED SOIL	COLOR; SEASON OF BLOOM	COLOR OF FRUIT; REMARKS
Cotoneaster dielsianus Diel's cotoneaster	6 (5); 6	''	pinkish; June	scarlet
Cotoneaster divaricatus spreading cotoneaster	5; 6	''	pink; June	red
Cotoneaster franchetii Franchet's cotoneaster	7; 6–10	''	pink; June	orange-red
Cotoneaster horizontalis rock cotoneaster	5; 3, semiprostrate	''	pink; June	red
Cotoneaster microphyllus	6; 3	''	white; May	scarlet
Cotoneaster rotundifolius roundleaf cotoneaster	5; 6–10	''	white; June	scarlet
Cotoneaster salicifolius willowleaf cotoneaster	6; 15	s; well-drained soils preferred	white; June	red; evergreen to semievergreen
Cydonia japonica See *Chaenomeles japonica*				
Cyrilla racemiflora cyrilla	6 (5); 6–25	s; moist to well drained	white; June–July	inconspicuous; beautiful dense foliage
Cytisus hirsutus broom	5; 2	s; neutral	yellow; May–June	inconspicuous
Cytisus x *praecox* Warminster broom	5; 6	s; well drained	pale yellow; May	inconspicuous
Cytisus scoparius Scotch broom	6; 6–8	s; well drained	yellow to red; May or June	inconspicuous
Daphne cneorum rose daphne	5; ½–1	s; peaty or sandy alkaline	rose; April and Sept.	inconspicuous, poisonous
Daphne genkwa lilac daphne	6 (5); 3	s; peaty or sandy alkaline	violet; April	inconspicuous, poisonous
Daphne mezereum February daphne	4; 3	s; alkaline	pink, rose, purple; April	scarlet, poisonous
Deutzia gracilis slender deutzia	5; 3–5	s; well drained for greater hardiness	pink, white; May	inconspicuous
Deutzia x *lemoinei* Lemoine deutzia	5; 3–6	s; well drained for greater hardiness	white; May	inconspicuous
Elaeagnus angustifolia Russian olive	2; 20	s; sandy or clay	yellow, fragrant; June	yellowish
Elaeagnus multiflora cherry elaeagnus	4; 9	s; sandy or ordinary	yellowish-white, fragrant; May	red
Elaeagnus pungens thorny elaeagnus	7; 10–12	s; sandy or ordinary	white, fragrant; May	brown turning red; evergreen
Elaeagnus umbellata autumn elaeagnus	3; 10	s; sandy or ordinary	yellowish-white, fragrant; May	silvery turning red
Elsholtzia stauntonii mintshrub	4; 3–5	s; well drained	lilac-purple; August–Sept.	inconspicuous
Enkianthus campanulatus red vein enkianthus	4; 8–20	s or sh; acid	pink; May	inconspicuous; excellent scarlet foliage in autumn
Enkianthus perulatus white enkianthus	5; 4–6	s or sh; acid	white; May	inconspicuous; excellent scarlet foliage in autumn
Euonymus alata winged spindle tree	3; 9–12	s or sh; indifferent	inconspicuous	scarlet; excellent scarlet foliage in autumn
Euonymus alata 'Compacta' dwarf winged spindle tree	3; 5–7	s or p sh; indifferent	inconspicuous	scarlet; excellent scarlet foliage in autumn
Euonymus europaeus 'Aldenhamensis' Aldenham spindle tree	3; 12–20	s or p sh; indifferent	inconspicuous	bright pink; red autumn color
Euonymus fortunei 'Vegetus' bigleaf wintercreeper	5; 4	s or sh; indifferent	inconspicuous	pinkish and orange; evergreen to semievergreen

(Continued)

SHRUBS (Continued)

SCIENTIFIC & COMMON NAME	ZONE OF HARDINESS; HEIGHT IN FEET	EXPOSURE; PREFERRED SOIL	COLOR; SEASON OF BLOOM	COLOR OF FRUIT; REMARKS
Euonymus japonicus Japanese spindle tree	8; 10–15	s or sh; moisture-retentive	inconspicuous	pinkish to orange; evergreen
Exochorda giraldii var. *wilsonii* Wilson pearlbush	5; 12–15	s; moisture-retentive	white; May	brown, dry capsules
Fatsia japonica Japanese fatsia	7; 8–15	sh; moisture-retentive	white; Sept. – Oct.	blue, effective in winter; evergreen
Forsythia 'Arnold Dwarf'	5; 4	s or sh; indifferent	yellow, not abundant; April	inconspicuous; excellent for steep slopes
Forsythia x *intermedia* 'Spectabilis' showy border forsythia	5 (4); 9	s or sh; indifferent	yellow; April	inconspicuous
Forsythia ovata early forsythia	4; 8	s or sh; indifferent	yellow; April	inconspicuous
Forsythia suspensa var. *sieboldii* Siebold forsythia	5; 3–9	s or sh; indifferent	yellow; April	inconspicuous
Forsythia viridissima 'Bronxensis'	5; 2	s or sh; indifferent	yellow; April	inconspicuous; free-flowering dwarf
Fothergilla major fothergilla	5 or 6; 4	sh; light	white; April	inconspicuous
Fothergilla monticola Alabama fothergilla	5; 6	s; damp	white; May	larger flower
Gaultheria shallon salal	6 (5); 3–5	s or sh; acid, moisture-retentive	white; June	purple; edible
Gaylussacia brachycera box huckleberry	5; 1–1½	s or sh; dry, sandy	white; May	blue
Hamamelis japonica Japanese witchhazel	5; 15–30	s or sh; indifferent	lemon-yellow; Feb. or March	inconspicuous
Hamamelis mollis Chinese witchhazel	5; 15–30	s or sh; indifferent	golden-yellow; Feb. or March	inconspicuous
Hamamelis vernalis spring witchhazel	5; 6–10	s or sh; indifferent	light yellow; Feb. or March	inconspicuous
Hamamelis virginiana common witchhazel	4 (3); 10–20	s or sh; indifferent	yellow; Oct. or Nov.	inconspicuous
Hibiscus syriacus rose of Sharon	5; 15	s; not too sandy	white, red, purple; August	inconspicuous
Hydrangea arborescens 'Grandiflora' hills of snow	4; 3	s or sh; neutral, moisture-retentive	white; June–July	dry flower heads
Hydrangea paniculata 'Grandiflora' peegee hydrangea	4; 25	s or sh; neutral, moisture-retentive	white, pink, greenish-bronze; July	dry flower heads
Hydrangea quercifolia oak-leaf hydrangea	6 (5); 4–6	s or sh; moisture-retentive	pinkish-white purplish; July	dry flower heads
Hypericum x *moserianum* goldflower	(7); 1½	sh; sandy	yellow; nearly all summer	inconspicuous
Hypericum prolificum	4; 5	s; sandy, rocky	yellow; July–Sept.	inconspicuous
Ilex cornuta Chinese holly	6 or 7; 9–15	s; well drained	inconspicuous	red; evergreen
Ilex cornuta 'Burfordii' Burford holly	6; 9	s; well drained	inconspicuous	red; evergreen
Ilex crenata Japanese holly	6; 10–15	p sh; acid, moisture-retentive	inconspicuous	black; evergreen
Ilex crenata 'Convexa' convex Japanese holly	5; 4	s or sh; rich	inconspicuous	black; evergreen
Ilex crenata 'Microphylla'	4; 4	sh; rich, well drained	inconspicuous	evergreen
Ilex glabra inkberry	5; 8	sh; acid, moisture-retentive	inconspicuous	black; evergreen
Ilex verticillata winterberry	3; 8	s; wet to ordinary	inconspicuous	red; deciduous

SHRUBS (Continued)

SCIENTIFIC & COMMON NAME	ZONE OF HARDINESS; HEIGHT IN FEET	EXPOSURE; PREFERRED SOIL	COLOR; SEASON OF BLOOM	COLOR OF FRUIT; REMARKS
Jasminum nudiflorum winter jasmine	6; 4–6	s or p sh; rich, moisture-retentive	yellow; Feb.–March	inconspicuous; green stems, 3-part leaves
Juniperus chinensis 'Pfitzerana' spreading juniper	4; 10	s; dry, sandy	inconspicuous	blue-gray; evergreen
Juniperus communis common juniper	2; 30	s; well drained	inconspicuous	dark blue; evergreen
Juniperus horizontalis creeping juniper	2; 1½	s; well drained	inconspicuous	blue; evergreen
Juniperus horizontalis 'Douglasii' Waukegan juniper	4; 1½	s; well drained	inconspicuous	blue; evergreen
Juniperus horizontalis 'Plumosa' Andorra juniper	3; 3–4	s; well drained	inconspicuous	blue; evergreen
Juniperus sabina var. 'Tamariscifolia' savin juniper	4; 3	s; well drained	inconspicuous	evergreen
Kalmia latifolia mountain laurel	4; 8	s or sh; sandy, acid	white, pink; June	inconspicuous
Kerria japonica kerria	5; 4–6	s or sh; moisture-retentive	golden-yellow; June–Sept.	inconspicuous
Kolkwitzia amabilis beautybush	4; 10	s; good drainage	pink; June	inconspicuous
Lagerstroemia indica crape myrtle	7; 15–20	s; well drained	purple to white; August–Oct.	inconspicuous
Laurus nobilis Grecian laurel	7; 12–30	s; rich, well drained	inconspicuous	black; evergreen
Leucothoë fontanesiana drooping leucothoë	4; 3–5	sh; acid, moisture-retentive	white; April–May	inconspicuous
Ligustrum amurense Amur privet	3; 15	s or sh; indifferent	white; June	black
Ligustrum x *ibolium* ibolium privet	4; 12	s or sh; indifferent	white; June	black
Ligustrum japonicum Japanese privet	7 or 8; 10–15	s or sh; indifferent	white; July	black; evergreen
Ligustrum lucidum glossy privet	7; 25	s or sh; indifferent	white; August–Sept.	black; evergreen
Ligustrum obtusifolium var. *regelianum* Regel's privet	5; 15	s or sh; indifferent	white; June–July	black
Ligustrum ovalifolium California privet	5; 15	s or sh; indifferent	white; June	black
Lonicera fragrantissima fragrant honeysuckle	5; 5–6	s; indifferent	white; March–April	red
Lonicera korolkowii blueleaf honeysuckle	2; 12	s; indifferent	rose; May	red
Lonicera maackii Amur honeysuckle	2; 12–15	s; indifferent	white; May	red
Lonicera morrowii Morrow honeysuckle	5; 8	s; indifferent	white; May–June	blood-red
Lonicera nitida shiny honeysuckle	7 or 8; 6	s; indifferent	white; June	blue, purple; evergreen
Lonicera pileata privet honeysuckle	6; 12	s or sh; indifferent	whitish; May–June	purple
Lonicera tatarica Tatarian honeysuckle	3; 9	s; indifferent	rose, white; May	red
Mahonia aquifolium Oregon hollygrape	5; 3–5	sh; well drained	yellow; April–May	black; evergreen
Mahonia bealei leather-leaf hollygrape	6; 6–12	sh; well drained	yellow; April–May	black
Myrica gale sweet gale	1; 4	s; moist	inconspicuous	gray

SHRUBS (Continued)

SCIENTIFIC & COMMON NAME	ZONE OF HARDINESS; HEIGHT IN FEET	EXPOSURE; PREFERRED SOIL	COLOR; SEASON OF BLOOM	COLOR OF FRUIT; REMARKS
Myrica pensylvanica northern bayberry	2; 9	s; well drained	inconspicuous	gray; semievergreen
Nandina domestica nandina	7; 3–6	s or sh; peaty loam	white; June–July	red; evergreen
Osmanthus heterophyllus holly olive	6; 7–20	s or sh; protected peaty spots	white; June–July	bluish; evergreen
Philadelphus coronarius sweet mock-orange	4; 10	s; alkaline to neutral	white; June	inconspicuous
Philadelphus grandiflorus big-flowered mock-orange	4; 9	s; well drained, neutral	white; June	inconspicuous; scentless flowers
Philadelphus x *lemoinei* 'Avalanche'	5; 6	s; alkaline to neutral	white, fragrant; June	inconspicuous; large flowers
Philadelphus x *virginalis* virginal mock-orange	5; 6	s; alkaline to neutral	white; May	racemes of white, semidouble flowers
Photinia serrulata Chinese photinia	7; 30	s; well drained	white; May	red; evergreen
Photinia villosa oriental photinia	4; 15	s; well drained	white; May	red
Pieris floribunda mountain andromeda	5; 8	sh; acid, well drained	white; April–May	inconspicuous
Pieris japonica Japanese andromeda	5; 8	sh; acid, well drained	white; April	inconspicuous
Potentilla fruticosa shrubby cinquefoil	2; 3–4	s; dry or wet	yellow and white; June–Sept.	inconspicuous
Prunus laurocerasus cherry laurel	6; 18	s or sh; rich, moisture-retentive	white; May	purple, black; evergreen
Prunus maritima beach plum	3; 6	s; sandy, dry	white; May	purple or yellow; seashore
Prunus tomentosa Nankin cherry	2; 8	s; good, well drained loam	white; April	scarlet
Pyracantha coccinea 'Lalandei' scarlet firethorn	6; 6–20	s; alkaline, well drained	white; May–June	scarlet; evergreen, bunches of fruit
Rhododendron arborescens sweet azalea	4; 6–9	s or sh; acid, moisture-retentive	white, very fragrant; June	inconspicuous
Rhododendron calendulaceum flame azalea	5; 8–12	s or sh; acid, moisture-retentive	yellow, orange, scarlet; June	inconspicuous
Rhododendron carolinianum Carolina rhododendron	5; 4–6	ʼʼ	pink, white; May	inconspicuous; evergreen
Rhododendron catawbiense Catawba rhododendron	4; 6–12	ʼʼ	white-rose, purple, to reddish; June	inconspicuous; evergreen
Rhododendron x *gandavense* Ghent azalea	4; 6–10	ʼʼ	white, pink, red, orange, yellow; May	inconspicuous
Rhododendron indicum Indian azalea	6; 3–6	ʼʼ	red, pink, white; June	inconspicuous
Rhododendron maximum rosebay rhododendron	3; 12–25	ʼʼ	rose to pink; late June	inconspicuous; evergreen
Rhododendron mucronulatum Korean rhododendron	4; 6–7	ʼʼ	rosy purple; April	inconspicuous
Rhododendron obtusum var. *kaempferi* torch azalea	5; 6–10	sh; acid, moisture-retentive	salmon red; May	inconspicuous
Rhododendron schlippenbachii royal azalea	4; 8–12	ʼʼ	pink; May	ʼʼ
Rhododendron vaseyi pinkshell azalea	4; 6–8	ʼʼ	pink; May	ʼʼ
Rhododendron viscosum swamp azalea	3; 7–12	ʼʼ	white, very fragrant; July	ʼʼ

SHRUBS (Continued)

SCIENTIFIC & COMMON NAME	ZONE OF HARDINESS; HEIGHT IN FEET	EXPOSURE; PREFERRED SOIL	COLOR; SEASON OF BLOOM	COLOR OF FRUIT, REMARKS
Rhododendron yedoense Yodogawa azalea	5; 3–5	′′	mauve-purple, double; May	′′
Rhodotypos scandens jetbead	5; 5	s or sh; indifferent	white; May to fall	black
Rhus cotinus See *Cotinus coggygria*				
Rhus glabra smooth sumac	2; 9–15	s; well drained	greenish; June–July	scarlet
Rhus typhina staghorn sumac	3; 15–25	s; indifferent	greenish; June–July	crimson and hairy
Ribes odoratum clove currant	4; 6	s or sh; moderately fertile	yellow, fragrant; April	red
Robinia hispida rose acacia	5; 6	s; dry	rose-pink; June	pods
Robinia viscosa clammy locust	6; 40	s; indifferent	pink; May–June	pods
Rosa alba 'Incarnata' cottage rose	5; 6	s; moisture-retentive	white or pinkish; June	orange to red
Rosa blanda meadow rose	2; 6	′′	pink, single; May–June	red
Rosa carolina Carolina rose	4; 3	s; moisture-retentive	pink; June–July	red
Rosa centifolia cabbage rose	5; 6	′′	pink, very double; June	
Rosa cinnamomea cinnamon rose	4; 6	′′	red, fragrant; June	red
Rosa damascena damask rose	4; 6	′′	pale pink to red, double, fragrant; June	red
Rosa eglanteria sweetbrier rose	4; 6	′′	pink; June	red
Rosa gallica French rose	5; 4	′′	pink to crimson, solitary; June	red; flower 3 in. wide
Rosa x *harisonii* Harison's yellow rose	4; 6	′′	yellow, double; June	orange
Rosa hugonis Father Hugo's rose	5; 8	s; moisture-retentive	sulphur yellow; May	dark red
Rosa moschata var. *nastarana* Persian musk rose	6; 6	′′	pink; June	red
Rosa multiflora Japanese rose	5; 10	′′	white; June	red
Rosa nitida bristly rose	3; 1½–2	′′	deep pink; June	red
Rosa palustris swamp rose	4; 6	s; swampy to moist	pink; June–August	red
Rosa rugosa Japanese rose	2; 6	s; moisture-retentive	pink, white; June	red, large
Rosa setigera prairie rose	4; 15	′′	pink; July	red
Rosa spinosissima Scotch rose	4; 3	s; moisture-retentive	yellow, pink, white; June	black
Rosa virginiana Virginia rose	3; 6	′′	pink; June–July	red
Rosa wichuraiana memorial rose	5; prostrate	′′	white, fragrant; June	red
Salix caprea goat willow	4; 25	s; wet to moist	catkins; March	inconspicuous

(Continued)

SHRUBS (Continued)

SCIENTIFIC & COMMON NAME	ZONE OF HARDINESS; HEIGHT IN FEET	EXPOSURE; PREFERRED SOIL	COLOR; SEASON OF BLOOM	COLOR OF FRUIT; REMARKS
Salix discolor pussy willow	2; 20	s; wet to moist	catkins; March	inconspicuous; hardy to Nova Scotia
Sambucus canadensis American elder	3; 5–8	s or sh; indifferent	white; June–July	black
Sambucus racemosa European red elder	4; 6–8	s or sh; indifferent	white; April–May	red
Sarcococca hookerana var. 'Humilis' sweet box	6; 1½	sh; rich	white; Oct.–March	black; evergreen
Skimmia japonica Japanese skimmia	7 (6); 3–4	sh; moisture-retentive	white; May	bright red on female plants; evergreen
Sorbaria aitchisonii Kashmir false spirea	6; 6–8	s; indifferent	white; July	inconspicuous
Spiraea x *arguta* garland spirea	4; 6	s; neutral, well drained	white; May	''
Spiraea x *billardii* Billard spirea	4; 6	''	rose; June	''
Spiraea bumalda Bumalda spirea	5; 2–3	''	red; June and July	''
Spiraea x *bumalda* 'Froebelii'	5; 4	''	deep rose; June	''
Spiraea prunifolia bridal-wreath	4; 4–6	s; neutral, well drained	white; May	inconspicuous
Spiraea thunbergii Thunberg spirea	4; 5	''	white; May	''
Spiraea x *vanhouttei* bridal-wreath	4; 3–6	''	white; May	''
Staphylea colchica bladdernut	5; 10	sh; moist, rich	yellow-white; May–June	green, bladderlike pod
Stephanandra incisa 'Crispa' cutleaf stephanandra	5; 3–4	s or sh; peaty	white; June	inconspicuous
Stewartia ovata var. *grandiflora* showy stewartia	5; 15	s or sh; moisture-retentive	white, purple stamens; July	inconspicuous
Stranvaesia davidiana Chinese stranvaesia	6; 6–20	s or sh; good, moisture-retentive	white; June	red; evergreen
Symphoricarpos albus var. *laevigatus* snowberry	3; 6	s or half sh; lime and clay	pinkish; June	white
Symphoricarpos orbiculatus coralberry	3; 4–5	s or sh; moisture-retentive	inconspicuous	purplish-red
Symplocos paniculata sapphire berry	5; 15–25	s or sh; moisture-retentive	white; May–June	blue; very fine fruit cluster
Syringa x *chinensis* Chinese lilac	5; 10–15	s; neutral, well drained	purple-lilac; May	inconspicuous
Syringa x *persica* Persian lilac	5; 5–6	''	pale lilac; May	''
Syringa reticulata Japanese tree lilac	4; 20–30	''	creamy-white; June	''
Syringa villosa late lilac	2; 9	''	lilac to white; June	''
Syringa vulgaris common lilac	3; 10–20	s; neutral, well drained	lilac; May	inconspicuous
Tamarix parviflora tamarisk	4; 15	s, salt air and wind; not too much lime	pink; May	inconspicuous
Tamarix pentandra five-stamen tamarix	2; 15	s; indifferent	pink; July	inconspicuous; frequent pruning
Taxus baccata 'Repandens' English yew	6; 3–4	s or sh; indifferent		evergreen
Taxus canadensis ground hemlock	3; 6	s or sh; acid, moisture-retentive	evergreen	

SHRUBS (Continued)

SCIENTIFIC & COMMON NAME	ZONE OF HARDINESS; HEIGHT IN FEET	EXPOSURE; PREFERRED SOIL	COLOR; SEASON OF BLOOM	COLOR OF FRUIT; REMARKS
Taxus cuspidata 'Densa' Japanese yew	4; 3–4	s or sh; indifferent		red; evergreen
Taxus x *media* 'Hicksii'	4; 20	s or sh; indifferent		red; evergreen
Vaccinium corymbosum highbush blueberry	3; 12	moist; acid	white; April	blue; edible fruit; crimson autumn leaves
Vaccinium angustifolium lowbush blueberry	3; 1½	dry; acid	white; April	blue; edible fruit, crimson autumn leaves
Viburnum acerifolium mapleleaf viburnum	3; 5	sh; dry	white; June	black
Viburnum americanum See *Viburnum tribolum*				
Viburnum x *burkwoodii* Burkwood viburnum	5; 6	sh; moist	white; April	black
Viburnum x *carlcephalum* fragrant snowball	5; 7	s; rich	white; April	black
Viburnum carlesii Korean spice viburnum	5; 4–6	s	pink; April	black
Viburnum cassinoides withe-rod	2; 6	s; wet	white; May	black; crimson autumn leaves
Viburnum dentatum arrowwood	2; 10	s or sh	white; June	black
Viburnum dilatatum linden viburnum	5; 7–9	s	white; June	red; one of the best red-fruited shrubs
Viburnum lantana wayfaring tree	3; 15	s	white; June–July	black
Viburnum molle Kentucky viburnum	5; 12		white; May	black
Viburnum opulus European cranberrybush	6; 10	s or sh	white; May–June	red
Viburnum opulus 'Nanum' dwarf cranberrybush	6; 3	s or sh	no flowers	good accent plant
Viburnum plicatum Japanese snowball	4; 10	s	white; May or June	blue-black; one of the best white-flowering shrubs
Viburnum plicatum f. *tomentosum* doublefile viburnum	5; 10	s	white; June	
Viburnum prunifolium blackhaw	3; 30	s or sh	white; April	black
Viburnum rhytidophyllum leatherleaf viburnum	6 (5); 9	shaded in winter; well drained	white; May	red to black; evergreen
Viburnum setigerum 'Aurantiacum' tea viburnum	5; 12	s or sh	creamy-white; May–June	red
Viburnum sieboldii Siebold viburnum	4; 10–25	s; damp	white; May–June	black; lustrous leaves
Viburnum trilobum (americanum) American cranberrybush	2; 12	s or sh	white; May	red
Viburnum wrightii Wright viburnum	5; 6–8	s or sh	white; May	red
Vitex agnus-castus chaste tree	7 (6); 10	s; slightly acid	lilac; July–Sept.	inconspicuous; stems winter-kill in Penna.
Weigela cultivars weigela	5; 3–8	s; well drained	white through pink, to reddish; May	inconspicuous
Xanthorhiza simplicissima yellowroot	4; 2	s or sh	brownish-purple, inconspicuous; May	inconspicuous

15.1 Even in restricted space, vines can produce opulence—as in the case of this wisteria welcome to an old New England house. Photo Carlton Lees

15

Vines

By its proper botanical definition, the word "vine" refers to grapes or members of the genus *Vitis*. It is used here in its broad popular sense to refer to slender-stemmed, woody plants that climb, scramble up, cling to or in other ways attach themselves or become attached to supporting structures.

Vines in a garden have an important role because they are both decorative and functional. Probably the earliest use of vines was for fruit and wine production, but the decorative value of the grapevine was so apparent that the garden builders of Italy occasionally used grape arbors as part of the scheme in their formal gardens.

Each vine possesses distinctive characteristics that suit it to certain locations in the landscape. Some vines are valued for the welcome shade they provide when trained upon arbors or pergolas; other vines lend distinction to a planting when skillfully trained against the wall of a house or patio, or when used to gracefully frame a doorway. Some vines can be used to relieve the monotony of a large expanse of wall, being trained to a definite pattern, or allows to clothe it completely with leafy green. With their blossoms and delicate tracery of leaf form, certain vines can make an otherwise commonplace fence seem a thing of exciting and even exotic beauty, and there are others that will form a cascade of bloom on rough, steep banks, while holding the soil in place.

Different vines are admired and valued for many reasons: for their decorative habit of growth; for the fragrance or spectacular beauty of their flowers; for the graceful tracery of their supple stems; or for the beauty of their leaf patterns and overall foliage texture. In the hands of the skillful designer and gardener, vines offer a rich source of material with which to create compositions of striking beauty.

SUPPORT FOR VINES

Most vines must have support. And since the various vines differ according to their habits of growth and climbing strategies, the support must be suitable to the type of vine selected. Those that climb by stems twining around the support, such as wisteria, and those that have tendrils which reach out and grasp small objects in the manner of the grapevine, need a lattice, arbor or fence type of support. Those that cling to things by means of rootlets, rootlike "holdfasts" or tendrils with adhesive disks need brick, stone or masonry walls, or even great boulders as support. Boston ivy, climbing hydrangea and creeping fig are examples that need this type of support.

Some vines will grow without supports, but the amazing fact about many of them is that when grown in this manner they lose their vine characteristics and become shrublike in form. *Euonymus fortunei* var. *radicans* is an outstanding example of this modification. In some cases

231

such vines will send out quantities of long, straight stems along the surface in an effort to find a support. Such are the tactics of the wisterias. Many others, like Virginia creeper, memorial rose and English ivy, are quite content to scramble on the ground and often make good ground covers. However, when they reach a support, up they go, for vines are essentially outlaws. They are opportunists in the plant kingdom; if they did not grow rapidly up and over their neighbors, they would not reach the light. The vine's self-preservation comes from its capacity to grow up rapidly without taking time to produce wood strong enough to support itself. It depends on its neighbors for support, and eventually it may even kill the very tree that offers it support by smothering its foliage. Furthermore, the roots of some vines range as widely and freely as their stems. This makes them bad neighbors for many plants. A gardener should understand these tendencies in vines and make provision for them.

The best type of support for vines is the one that gives the required structural strength and stability, and at the same time makes a neat appearance.

15.2 The word "vine," strictly speaking, should be applied only to the grape, but it is now used to include all climbing plants. Photo Anita Sabarese

In a sophisticated garden, the more architectural arbor has its place, but in many cases the growth of the vines will so completely cover all but the posts that such embellishment seems unwarranted.

Vines that clamber up a trellis on a frame house are a serious obstacle to the periodic painting the house requires. If rambler roses are trained on the trellis, the job of painting will be both difficult and uncomfortable. To overcome this trouble, the trellis should be built so that, together with the vines, it may be detached from the building. One of the best ways to accomplish this is to hinge the trellis at the bottom and fasten the top to a cleat on the house wall by means of a bolt. When the painting begins, the bolt may be removed, the trellis swung out and held in a slanting position by a strut. There will be sufficient pliancy in the stems of the vine to bend along with the hinge.

For the support of rather small twining vines or shrubs against a stone or brick wall, a special nail is manufactured and can readily be purchased from most garden centers. From the head projects a strip of soft metal, which is bent around the vine stem to hold it in place. The nails are driven into the cement mortar joint and, because of the rough surface of the metal, hold firmly in the mortar. This is a most satisfactory device for training jasmine, forsythia or firethorn against a masonry wall.

For the support of large, stem-twining vines against a masonry wall, metal frame lattices are good. Less expensive but equally effective is a large mesh network of wire cables fastened to expansion bolts, which project out about 8 in. from the face of the wall. The wires are made tight by turn buckles. This is suitable for such strong vines as wisteria and actinidia, and if the wires are placed 3 ft. apart, forming squares, a very pleasing pattern of greenery and masonry is produced. This is a satisfactory means of covering a large bare wall surface flanking a city garden.

MAINTENANCE

Pruning vines to produce better bloom or to keep the plants within bounds is an annual task requiring patience and skill. The removal of the old wood may involve several cuts to each stem so that they can be untangled. The same principles of pruing apply to flowering vines as to fruit trees. Prune to guide future growth.

Vines like wisteria produce quantities of large stems that tangle in grotesque knots. As the stems grow and expand, the knots become tighter, and in this way the vine is apt to strangle itself. This may be avoided in part by reducing the number of major stems when the vine is still young, and by training the early growth in such a way as not to form heavy twisted ropes made up of several stems. If the central part of the plant is well branched, the formation of tangles in the outer parts is not so serious. They can be removed without spoiling the vine.

Spraying against insects should be done as part of the general spraying program for the whole area.

VINES OF MERIT

Actinidia polygama (silver vine)

A vigorous and tall-growing vine, with a handsome foliage that is remarkably free from insect pests and diseases. It produces small, fragrant white flowers in cymes of three blossoms at the axils of the leaf in June, and the fruit, which ripens in September or October, is a greenish-yellow berry about 1 in. long. As the plant is sometimes dioecious, a vine that does not bear fruit occasionally appears. This is of little consequence, however, as staminate plants tend to have more handsome silvery leaves. This species, like catnip, is extremely attractive to cats, and young plants may be completely destroyed by them if not protected.
Zone of hardiness: 4.

Height: To 30 ft.

Exposure: Sun or shade.

Culture: Occasional thinning out of the mass of stems to improve appearance.

Uses: Makes an attractive pattern on trellis, fence or wall.

Akebia quinata (five-leaf akebia)

A charming, slender vine, with beautiful foliage made up of five-parted leaves. The flowers are a deep rosy-purple, waxy in texture, opening valvelike into three parts. They are not conspicuous or fragrant but as cut flowers they are delightful. The vine is rather low-growing and is excellent on a trellis or for covering a low wall. It needs the support of a wall or wires.
Exposure: Sun or shade.

Culture: Occasional thinning out of the mass of stems to improve appearance. If plants become overgrown, they may be cut back to near ground level and will resprout rapidly.

Uses: Forms a pleasant, delicate tracery against a wall or fence.

Caution: May become a pest if allowed freedom to romp. It could easily choke out and kill shrubbery if allowed to get out of control.

Ampelopsis brevipedunculata (porcelain berry)

A hardy, deciduous vine of rampant growth. The three-lobed leaves are large and handsome, though the flowers are inconspicuous. The fruit appears in autumn in clusters of berries that change from pale lilac to yellow to bright blue, an unusual and highly attractive combination of colors.
Zone of hardiness: 4.

Height: 20 ft.

Exposure: Full sun or shade.

Culture: Thrives in any good garden soil.

Uses: On trellis or arbor. Useful for quickly covering unattractive chain-link fences.

Aristolochia macrophylla (Dutchman's-pipe)

An old-fashioned favorite, not often seen nowadays. It is a foliage vine, with large heart-shaped leaves thickly overlapping one another. If grown on a series of horizontal slats or wires, it will form an opaque wall of green. The flowers, although not conspicuous, are very entertaining; they resemble a Dutchman's pipe, and from this comes its common name. *A. macrophylla* is native to the woodlands of the eastern United States from Pennsylvania and Minnesota southward to Georgia, and has long been in cultivation.
Zone of hardiness: 4.

Height: 20 ft.

Exposure: Sun or partial shade.

Culture: A good, garden loam with a pH between 6.0 and 7.0. Should be watered well in dry weather.

Uses: On arbor, trellis or wires. Makes a dense shade; excellent for screen or barrier.

Bignonia capreolata (crossvine)

A near relative of the trumpet vine, *B. capreolata* is prized for its profusion of orange-red flowers in late spring and its evergreen foliage. It is quite vigorous and needs plenty of space to develop properly. As with *Akebia*, care should be taken to see that it does not run out of control.
Zone of hardiness: 7 (6 in protected spots).

Height: 50 ft. to 60 ft.

Exposure: Sun or partial shade.

Culture: Fair to good soil.

Uses: Tendrils attach by adhesive disks, so this is an excellent vine for covering walls. Also good on large trellises, and will climb trees.

Campsis grandiflora C. chinensis, (Chinese trumpet creeper)

This creeper has very few aerial rootlets, and therefore requires the support of a trellis. It may be distinguished from its relatives by the fact that it generally has fewer leaflets, seven or nine. The bright scarlet flowers are larger and open in August and September. Many gardeners consider it superior to the native trumpet creeper, partly because of its less vigorous habit of growth.
Zone of hardiness: 7.

Height: 20 ft. to 25 ft.

Exposure: Full sun.

Culture: Adaptable to ordinary culture.

Uses: On a trellis against a wall or fence; on arbors.

Campsis radicans (native trumpet creeper)

A wonderful vine, with orange and scarlet tubular blossoms in terminal clusters in summer, each blossom 3 in. or 4 in. long. The coarse-textured foliage is very dense and consists of compound leaves of nine or eleven leaflets. It is native to forests from Pennsylvania to Texas and has been in cultivation since colonial times. *C. radicans* 'Flava' has pure yellow flow-

ers, and the hybrid *C.* x *tagliabuana* 'Madame Galen' has showy scarlet flowers.
Zone of hardiness: 4

Height: 20 ft. to 40 ft.

Exposure: Sunshine.

Culture: Requires no attention; good garden soil.

Uses: Against brick, stucco and stone walls, to which it clings by means of aerial rootlets. Can be trained along the edge of a roof, over arbors, along sturdy fences. It can also be used as a flowering hedge, as the branches become self-supporting after the first year if they are pruned and guided correctly. It is very rampant in growth and can easily choke out shrubs and other vegetation if allowed to get out of control.

Celastrus (bittersweet)

C. orbiculatus (Oriental bittersweet)
Much more vigorous than the native bittersweet, this produces an abundance of billiant orange and scarlet fruit. The flowers, being in axillary clusters, are somewhat hidden in the leaves, and the fruit is not really conspicuous until the leaves fall. Conditions and requirements are similar to those of *C. scandens* (below).
Zone of hardiness: 4.

C. scandens (American bittersweet)
Another native of our forests that is an old but still very popular favorite. It is related to *Euonymus*, which it somewhat resembles in its fruit formation. This vigorous, high-climbing vine, with rich foliage in a great variety of shapes, has strong, twining stems. The orange and red fruit, which ripens in October, lasts all winter, even when brought into the house to decorate the mantle or table. The fruit is borne on terminal panicles, which makes it conspicuous. Although *C. scandens* will ascend to the top

of any deciduous tree and is at home in the shadiest forest glade, it may strangle some trees and should be watched. This vine is dioecious, the pistillate and staminate flowers being borne on separate plants.
Zone of hardiness: 2.

Height: 20 ft. to 40 ft.

Exposure: Shade or sunshine.

Culture: Requires no attention.

Uses: On fences and arbors and clambering over rocks and stone walls.

Clematis

The various species of *Clematis* are among the most decorative and beautiful vines. Some species are of vigorous growth and will do well under widely varying conditions, while others are somewhat temperamental and will thrive only when their specific cultural requirements are met.

Some species of *Clematis* have solitary or small clusters of bell-shaped or urn-shaped flowers; others bear numerous small blooms in panicles or loose-spreading clusters; and others again bear large, open, starlike blooms. The flowering season is long, beginning when *Clematis montana* unfolds its lovely blossoms in May, and drawing to a close when the last white blooms of the large-flowered hybrid, 'Duchess of Edinburgh,' have shed their petals in late autumn.

Of the numerous species of *Clematis* comparatively few are widely grown, but those that are add grace and charm to a garden composition wherever they are used.

C. armandii
A lovely evergreen *Clematis* that is hardy in mild climates and is much valued for both its foliage and flowers wherever it can be grown. The leaves are a dark, glossy green, and the

15.3. Hybrid Clematis (in this case, pale mauve 'Nelly Mosier') bring exclamations of pleasure because of their very special qualities. Photo Grant Heilman

glistening white, starlike flowers are borne in clusters in early spring.
Zone of hardiness: 7.

Height: To 20 ft., eventually with a very wide spread.

Exposure: Sun or light shade.

Culture: Slow in becoming established, but makes rapid growth later on. Should be trained at frequent intervals to prevent the branches from becoming tangled. It is wise to remove all branches except those desired to form a pleasant pattern. Flowers are formed on the previous year's wood, so it should be pruned immediately after flowering only.

Uses: To train over doorways, along a cornice or to outline a gable. May also be used along fence tops if carefully trained, or on walls if supported.

C. crispa (marsh or curly clematis)
A lovely species native in southern swamps, but hardly also in northern New York. The dainty steel-blue flowers are bell- or urn-shaped, and are borne from July to September.
Zone of hardiness: 5.

Height: To 8 ft.

Exposure: Full sun or light shade.

Culture: Thrives well in ordinary soil. Prune in early spring only.

Uses: On trellis, fence or stone wall.

C. paniculata (sweet autumn clematis)
One of the most vigorous and fast-growing of all the *Clematis.* In September and October it bears an abundance of small, white, fragrant flowers, which are followed by a profusion of feathery, twisted seed pods (achenes).
Zone of hardiness: 5.

Height: 10 ft. to 20 ft.

Exposure: Sun or light shade.

Culture: The flowers are produced on new growth; therefore, severe pruning may be practiced in early spring.

Uses: On arbors or trellis; clambering over old stone walls.

C. x jackmanii cultivars (Jackman clematis)
The large-flowered hybrid cultivars of this group result mainly from the crossing of *C. lanuginosa* and *C. viticella. C. x jackmanii* has very large, violet-purple four-petaled, star-shaped flowers, 5 in. to 7 in. in diameter. The cultivars, in both single and double forms, range from

pure white through pink and wine-red to purple, and there are also bicolor forms.
See Clematis Cultivars of Merit
Zone of hardiness: 5.

C. lanuginosa 'Alba' (wooly-leaved clematis)
   Has very large, pure white flowers that are borne in profusion throughout the summer. Vigorous in growth and flowering over a long season, from June to September, this species bears flowers of rosy-mauve flushed with bluish-purple.
Zone of hardiness: 6.

Height: 6 ft. to 15 ft.

Exposure: Full sun.

Culture: Flowers borne on new wood; can be pruned severely.

Uses: On arbor, pergola or trellis.

C. macropetala (big-petal clematis)
   One of the most beautiful of all the species, hardy in the North for spring flowering. The large (2½ in. to 4 in. in diameter) azure blue, semidouble flowers present a handsome nodding appearance.
Zone of hardiness: 5.

Height: 10 ft.

Exposure: Full sun.

Culture: Flowers borne on previous year's wood; prune lightly only after flowering, if at all.

Uses: Arbor, pergola, trellis; on a wall if supported.

C. montana
   A lovely, vigorous vine, that is completely covered with anemonelike flowers in June. The flowers are small, about 2 in. across, and are white when first open, turning to a pale pink.

C. montana var. rubens
   Called the pink-anemone clematis, the flowers being a deep, rich pink.
Zone of hardiness: 5.

Height: 10 ft. to 15 ft.

Exposure: Full sun or light shade.

Culture: As the flowers are borne on old wood produced the previous season, very light pruning is recommended.

Uses: On arbor, trellis or fence; on walls, if supported.

C. virginiana (virgin's bower)
   A vigorous native vine, delicate in appearance, and useful for its numerous small white flowers, which appear in late August. These are followed by attractive plumelike seed heads.
Zone of hardiness: 4.

Height: 18 ft.

Exposure: Full sun or light shade.

Culture: Adaptable to many soil conditions, will tolerate wetter soil than most other species.

Uses: Best in a naturalistic setting or woodland garden; on stone walls, fences or trellises.

C. vitalba (traveler's joy)
   One of the easiest of all *Clematis* to grow. It is a vigorous vine of Europe, with very dense,

somewhat coarse foliage. The rather small (1 in. in diameter) white flowers are quite fragrant and appear in clusters in late August.

Zone of hardiness: 4.

Height: 30 ft.

Exposure: Full sun.

Culture: Adaptable to many soil conditions.

Uses: Covering a fence, trellis or pergola, especially where dense growth is wanted.

General Cultural Requirements of *Clematis*

Exposure: Full sun should be provided wherever possible. Most clematis require maximum sunlight in order to produce the fullest amount of bloom. However, when planted in very lightly shaded locations, many of them will grow reasonably satisfactorily and flower well. They will not thrive in full shade or on the north side of the house where they receive little direct sunlight. The location selected should be protected from strong winds.

Soil: *Clematis* prefers a soil that is neutral or slightly alkaline in its reaction. A test for acidity should be made, preferably before planting, and lime should be applied if it is needed. A sandy loam well supplied with organic matter is considered ideal; heavy loam or clay soils do not provide favorable growing conditions. Good drainage is essential. However, the roots of clematis require cool, evenly moist soil conditions. Soils that tend to bake or dry out for long periods definitely are not suitable.

The soil should be carefully prepared before planting. It is well to dig a hole of generous size, from 18 in. to 24 in. deep. If draining is likely to be a problem, a layer of gravel or rubble should be placed in the bottom. The soil that has been removed may be mixed with well-decomposed leaf mold, compost and dampened peat moss, with a little superphosphate added

CLEMATIS CULTIVARS OF MERIT

The most beautiful and the most widely grown of the *Clematis* are the large-flowered hybrids that have been developed from the various species. These lovely hybrids are both the joy and despair of many a gardener. They are so decorative that one longs to be able to grow them to perfection, yet they are fastidious in the extreme and perfection is hard to obtain.

'Belle of Woking' (*C. florida* hybrid) – Flowers double, silvery-gray, May to June, on previous season's growth.

'Comtesse de Bouchard' (*C.* x *jackmanii* hybrid) – Flowers satiny rose, July to October, on previous season's growth.

'Crimson King' (*C. lanuginosa* hybrid) – Flowers crimson, with chocolate-colored anthers, July and August.

'Duchess of Albany' (*C. texensis* hybrid) – Flowers bell-shaped, pink, July to September, on current year's growth.

'Duchess of Edinburgh' (*C. florida* hybrid) – Flowers double, pure white, fragrant, May and June, on previous season's growth.

'Ernest Markham' (*C. vitifolia* hybrid) – Flowers vivid red, July to September, on current year's growth.

'Henryi' (*C. lanuginosa* hybrid) – Enormous white flowers with dark stamens, June and July, on current season's growth.

C. x *jackmanii* 'Alba' – White single and double flowers produced both on previous and current season's growth.

C. x *jackmanii* 'Rubra' – Dark red flowers produced both on previous and current season's growth.

C. x *jackmanii* 'Superba' – Dark purple flowers produced both on previous and current season's growth.

'Lord Neville' (*C. lanuginosa* hybrid) – Dark purple flowers, June to August, on current season's growth.

'Nelly Moser' (*C. patens* hybrid) – Mauve-pink flowers with deeper pink markings, May and June, on previous season's growth.

to the mixture. The advisability of using manure is debatable. If it is used it should be very well rotted and should not come into direct contact with the roots at time of planting.

Planting: Autumn is considered the most favorable time for planting. It is wise to purchase plants that have been grown on their own roots, as they are considered superior to grafted plants. Most nurseries supply young, vigorous own-root plants in pots. The crown of the plant should be set from 2 in. to 3 in. below the level of the soil, and all plants should be watered thoroughly at the time of planting. Some type of support, such as a bamboo stake or a bit of wire mesh, must be provided immediately. It is important that this is done at the time of planting as the stems twist and break very easily. The young plant should also be protected at the base from possible injury. A circle of small stakes may be used. A large clay flowerpot broken in half vertically provides an excellent protective collar.

Mulching: Regardless of its location, whether it be planted in full sun in an exposed situation or in light shade, it is essential that a clematis vine be protected at the base in order that the roots may be kept cool and moist. A mulch 2 in. deep and extending out at least 2 ft. from the plant is recommended. Dampened peat moss or rotting leaf mold may be used. In some cases a shallow-rooted shrub or other low-growing plants near the base of the vine will give sufficient protection.

Fertilization: In early spring a good complete fertilizer, such as a 5-10-5, may be applied at the rate of 1 tablespoonful per square foot of area, and watered in well; or an application of a high-analysis, soluble fertilizer may be made. Repeat every six weeks during the growing season.

Pruning: It is wise to allow young clematis plants to become well established before any pruning is done. The amount of pruning advisable for established plants will depend upon the type. Vines that flower early on old wood produced during the previous year require only the removal of dead, weak or crowding stems. Vines that flower later on the new growth of the current season should be pruned more severely. Pruning should be done in late winter or early spring. Maintaining six to eight vigorous stems will result in an attractive vine. Unless height is desired for some special purpose, the stems should be cut back to from 12 in. to 18 in. in order to encourage vigorous growth and more abundant bloom.

Even when killed to the ground during a particularly severe winter *Clematis* will usually renew itself.

COMMON CAUSES OF FAILURE

Too shallow planting.
Too much shade.
Soil that is too high in acidity.
Soil that is too heavy and poorly drained.

Support: Clematis vines require some type of support in order to prevent them from becoming a tangle of stems. The stems should be encouraged to spread out on the trellis or wire so that all parts will receive maximum sunlight and also so that a pleasant pattern may be maintained. A light trellis, a fence, a post or wire mesh will all make very satisfactory supports. Sometimes adjacent shrubs are used for this purpose. A brick or high stone wall furnished with adequate wire supports will form a handsome backdrop for most clematis.

Winter protection: In cold climates where winter protection is needed, soil, sand, peat moss or coal ashes may be mounded about the base of the plant and covered with a layer of leaves or straw.

Uses: The clematis are among the most versatile of vines. They are lovely when trained on a trellis against the wall of a house or a patio, or when used to frame an entrance. Intermingled with not-too-rampant varieties of climbing roses on a fence they prolong the season of bloom, and when carefully trained on their own support they lend added interest to a perennial border. Planted in large pots or tubs, they add distinction and charm to the planting on a patio or terrace. Such plants should be trained on bamboo stakes and the tips should be pinched out when the shoots are 2 ft. high to encourage lateral branching. The soft, exquisite coloring and texture of the flowers, the delicate tracery of the stems and tendrils and the long-lasting quality of the blooms make clematis a favorite among those who delight in arranging flowers.

Euonymus fortunei

E. fortunei var. radicans

This is an evergreen vine of exceptional merit. Hardy, vigorous and handsome at all seasons of the year, the foliage is a fine, glossy green, and in autumn and winter the bright red berries add a note of welcome cheer to a planting composition.
Zone of hardiness: 4.

Height: To 30 ft.

Exposure: Sun or partial shade.

Culture: Extremely hardy and of easy culture. *Euonymus* is often slow at starting but after the first year or so it makes vigorous growth. It is semishrubby in form, so that in order to train it as a vine it must be given support when first planted and induced to grow upward. Otherwise, it has a tendency to remain bushy. It is subject to attack by oyster shell scale.

E. fortunei 'Vegetus'

Similar to *E. fortunei* var. *radicans,* with the exception that the leaves are larger and the berries an orange-red. Considered by some to be superior to *E. fortunei* var. *radicans.* It also requires support until it starts to climb.

Hedera

H. canariensis (Algerian ivy)

Comes from the Canary Islands, and is adapted only to mild climates. It is more tolerant of hot sun than the English ivy and is therefore more satisfactory in southern areas. The leaves are more widely spaced on the stems than are those of the English ivy, and are three- to five-lobed, measuring from 5 in. to 8 in. in width. The cultivar 'Canary Cream' bears leaves edged with greenish-white.
Zone of hardiness: 7.

Uses: Valued for its ability to cling to brick, stone and stucco walls, and as one of the best evergreen vines for planting against the wall of house, patio or garden.

H. helix (English ivy)

A sturdy, evergreen vine that has many uses and is widely grown. It clings by means of aerial rootlets, and the handsome, dark green, somewhat glossy foliage is attractive throughout the year when grown under favorable conditions.
Zone of hardiness: 5–6.

Height: Will eventually reach the top of a building or tree trunk.

Exposure: Does best on a north or east wall where it is protected from too much sun. Susceptible to sunburn in winter if given a southern exposure.

Culture: An annual trimming and pruning back is advisable in order to prevent the vines from becoming too bunchy at the top.

Uses: Clothes brick, cement and stucco walls, where it clings tenaciously when once established. May also be used as a ground cover (see Chapter 16) or as a fence or screen by weaving the shoots through a woven wire livestock-type fence. In a season or two the wire will be completely covered.

There are many varieties and cultivars of English ivy, each having distinctive characteristics of leaf form and habit of growth that make it suitable for specific uses. Those specially noted below as being extra hardy may be used in Zones 4 and 5 wherever shelter from wind and winter sun can be provided:

Var. *baltica*—noted for its hardiness; the leaves are somewhat smaller than those of the type; perfectly hardy as far north as Boston.
'Bulgaria'—another hardy selection; has proven satisfactory around St. Louis, where winters may be particularly difficult on evergreens.
'Conglomerata'—has stiff upright stems and small leaves arranged in ranks of two along the stems.
'Minima'—has very small leaves, but shows a

15.4. As wall covering, particularly in city gardens, some vines are almost necessary. Photo Anita Sabarese

tendency to revert to type if not watched carefully; reverting shoots should be pruned away quickly.
'Rumania'—similar to 'Bulgaria,' and quite hardy.
'238th Street'—a selection of the New York Botanical Garden that is quite hardy and resistant to burn by winter sun.

Hydrangea anomala var. *petiolaris* (climbing hydrangea)

This climbing form of the hydrangea clings by means of small rootlike "holdfasts," and is a hardy, vigorous vine. The leaves are heart-shaped and the creamy flowers, which are borne in June in wide, flat clusters, are very decorative. The peeling, reddish-brown bark is another interesting feature that makes this vine particularly attractive in winter.
Height: To 75 ft. depending upon use.

Exposure: Full sun or partial shade.

Culture: No special care, nearly problem-free.

Uses: Handsome when used against the wall of a building. Clings to stone, masonry and wood.

Dramatically effective if allowed to climb up the trunk of a tree, but it must be grown slowly enough so that it will not overpower the tree; the effect of the flowers covering the trunk and major limbs is very beautiful. Also very effective if allowed to cover a stone wall, and can be used as a ground cover on a steep bank. Climbing hydrangea is one of the most interesting, versatile and trouble-free vines, and should be used more frequently in gardens.

Jasminum

J. mesnyi (primrose jasmine)
A strong-growing evergreen vine, with long, arching branches. The bright, lemon-yellow flowers are borne from February to April. One of the most handsome of all the jasmines for mild climates.
Zone of hardiness: 8.

Height: To 20 ft.

Exposure: Sun or semishade.

Uses: Because of its arching habit of growth, best used when a cascade of foliage and flowers is desired.

J. nudiflorum (winter jasmine)
A graceful vine, with slender, green, willowy branches. It is among the first vines to bloom, often flowering in January or February when in a protected position. The flowers are borne before the foliage unfolds.
Zone of hardiness: 6 (or 5 if sheltered).

Height: 10 ft. to 15 ft.

Exposure: Sun or partial shade.

Culture: Occasional pruning is necessary to remove untidy growth and pruning out dead branches after severe winters.

15.5 Climbing hydrangea (Hydrangea anomala var. petiolaris) and Virginia creeper (Parthenocissus quinquefolia), while not evergreen, are vigorous and sturdy wall-hugging plants. Photo Anita Sabarese

Uses: Best when carefully trained against a wall or on a trellis, where it will be enjoyed for its early bloom; also lovely when allowed to cascade over a wall or bank.

J. officinale (poet's jasmine)

One of the most beloved of the jasmines, this has small, fragrant white flowers. Blooms throughout the summer. Not hardy where the climate is severe. Semievergreen.
Zone of hardiness: 7.

Height: To 30 ft.

Exposure: Sun or partial shade.

Uses: On trellis, arbor or pergola.

Lonicera (honeysuckle)

L. heckrottii (everblooming honeysuckle)

A deciduous honeysuckle of vigorous growth. The fragrant flowers are borne in profusion from spring until autumn. The blooms are tubular in form, creamy-white within and pink to rose on the outside.

Height: To 15 ft.

Exposure: Sun or partial shade.

Culture: Adaptable.

Uses: On trellis and arbor; one of the best of the honeysuckle vines to grow for flowers.

L. henryi

See Chapter 16 on ground covers, page 247.

L. japonica 'Halliana' (Hall's climbing honeysuckle)

An evergreen to semievergreen honeysuckle of rampant growth, with deep green leaves. The axillary flowers are borne in pairs and are white at first, changing to yellow as they mature. The flowers are fragrant and are in almost continuous bloom throughout the summer.
Zone of hardiness: 4.

Height: To 30 ft. or more.

Exposure: Full sun or partial to dense shade.

Culture: A rampant grower that *must* be kept within bounds.

Uses: On trellis or arbor; as a cover on rough banks.

Caution: When left undisturbed, this honeysuckle is capable of making a wild tangle and of smothering or strangling anything with which it comes into contact (see index for measures of control and eradication). In very cold areas where choices are limited, Hall's climbing honeysuckle is of definite value, but it should be used with extreme caution elsewhere.

*15.6 While the common Japanese honeysuckle (*Lonicera japonica*) is a rampant weed in many parts of the mid-Atlantic and other states,* Lonicera sempervirens *and its cultivars, such as 'Dropmore Scarlet,' 'Sulphurea' and 'Superba,' provide bright flowers on plants that can be confined with ease. Photo Carlton Lees*

L. sempervirens (scarlet trumpet honeysuckle)

This is one of the most showy and most desirable of the honeysuckles. The leaves are semi-evergreen. The scarlet flowers have very long tubes and are borne in long clusters of six; they are not fragrant. The period of bloom lasts from May to August. Cultivars include:

'Dropmore Scarlet'—a vigorous hybrid with scarlet flowers.
'Sulphurea'—with yellow flowers.
'Superba'—with bright scarlet flowers.

Parthenocissus

P. quinquefolia (Virginia creeper)

A well-known native vine that clambers over stone walls and fences, clinging by tendrils with disklike ends. This special equipment for climbing enables it to ascend masonry walls as readily as does English ivy, and it has been much used since colonial times. Its compound leaves make a beautiful pattern and turn a brilliant crimson in the autumn. The bluish-black fruit ripens in September. A very useful foliage plant, it grows well in shade or sun, is hardy as far north as Ottawa and is a common native from Maine to Florida.

Zone of hardiness: 3.

Height: To 30 ft.

Exposure: Full sun, partial or deep shade.

Culture: Prune in early spring if necessary to keep it within restricted bounds.

Uses: On masonry walls, on arbors and fences, as a ground cover or clambering over old stone walls in a natural setting.

P. quinquefolia var. *engelmannii*

Has leaves much smaller and foliage more dense than *P. quinquefolia*.

P. tricuspidata (**Boston ivy or Japanese creeper**)

One of the strongest and most rapidly growing of vines, being able completely to cover the entire façade of a large building within a few years. The leaves are large, with long petioles. It clings tenaciously to almost any surface and makes a very dense pattern on a wall. The foliage turns a brilliant color in the autumn.

P. tricuspidata 'Lowii'

Has foliage that is small and deeply lobed.

P. tricuspidata 'Veitchii' (**small leaved Boston ivy**)

A very desirable form of *P. tricuspidata*. Makes a more attractive pattern and has the ability to cling to even the smoothest surface. Leaves small, purple when young.
Zone of hardiness: 4.

Height: 30 ft. and up.

Exposure: Full sun and partial shade.

Culture: Vigorous, and needs little care.

Uses: Where the complete coverage of a stone, stucco or brick wall is desired, few vines can compare with Boston ivy.

Polygonum aubertii (**China fleece vine**)

This rapidly growing vine blooms abundantly for a long period. In general disposition it resembles sweet autumn clematis. The flowers are creamy-white and are borne in long, threadlike panicles that completely cover the top of the vine. It is prolific in the production of seedlings, which spring up everywhere, and should be planted only where its vigorous growth will not become a threat to other plants.
Zone of hardiness: 4.

Height: Will reach the top of almost any structure.

Culture: Water thoroughly during the blooming season. Its growth may be controlled by severe pruning.

Uses: On a trellis against a wall, on fences and on arbors. It does extremely well under adverse city conditions, and is particularly useful in quickly covering the ugliness of tall chain-link fences.

Vitis coignetiae (**crimson glory vine**)

Probably the best of the numerous species of *Vitis* (or grape) to grow for ornamental purposes, *V. coignetiae* grows very rapidly, and can be counted upon to produce a screen quicker than almost any other hardy vine. The leaves (10 in. in diameter) impart a bold, coarse appearance. They turn a brilliant red in autumn. Like all grapes, this species is subject to attack by Japanese beetles. The fruits are not edible, so its main value is as a rapid-growing ornamental screen.
Zone of hardiness: 5.

Height: 60 ft.

Exposure: Full sun. Not demanding as to soil.

Culture: Frequent pruning to keep in bounds if space is restricted.

Wisteria

The wisterias are superbly beautiful vines, with great hanging panicles of lavender-purple, pink or white flowers that are borne in profusion during the spring. The vine is hardy, vigorous and high-climbing, and is remarkably long-lived.

W. *floribunda* (Japanese wisteria)

A species that blooms somewhat later than *W. sinensis* (below), and thus extends the season of bloom for *Wisteria*. The following are some of the better cultivars available from nurseries:

'Alba' – white, flower clusters 11 in. long.
'Longissima Alba' – white, flower clusters 15 in. long.
'Macrobotrys' – violet, flower clusters an incredible 18 in. to 36 in. long (even longer under ideal conditions).
'Rosea' – pink, flower clusters 15 in. long.
Zone of hardiness: 4.

Culture: See *W. sinensis.*

W. *sinensis* (Chinese wisteria)

This species from China is the one that is most widely planted. The flowers are of exquisite beauty and are slightly fragrant. There is a white cultivar, *W. sinensis* 'Alba.'
Zone of hardiness: 5.

Height: Wisteria will climb to almost any height, to the top of any support or to the top of the tallest tree.

Exposure: Full sun or partial shade.

Culture: It is essential that wisteria have a strong support and that it be kept within bounds. When planted on the wall of a building, it should preferably have a metal support. Because wisteria has such great vitality and so easily outgrows its situation, it should be pruned back severely every year. This pruning will induce it to bloom more abundantly and will also restrain the venturesome stems before they do any damage to shutters, cornice or roof. It is imperative that such pruning is done every year. If it is omitted, up the vine goes, over the roof, working its way under shingles and gutters, and the contest is on. But because of the beauty of its bloom, wisteria deserves more than this annual care. Pruning

VINES FOR MILD CLIMATES

Allamanda cathartica	common allamanda
Antigonon leptopus	queen's wreath, coral vine, rosa de montana
Beaumontia grandiflora	Easter lily vine, herald trumpet
Bougainvillea	bougainvillea
Clytostoma callistegioides	violet trumpet vine
Distictis lactiflora	vanilla-scented trumpet vine
Ficus pumila	creeping fig
Hibbertia scandens	snake vine
Jasminum mesnyi	primrose jasmine
Jasminum nudiflorum	winter jasmine
Jasminum officinale	poet's jasmine
Jasminum x *stephanense*	
Mandevilla suaveolens	Chilean jasmine
Passiflora manicata	red passionflower
Passiflora mollissima	soft-leaf passion vine
Stephanotis floribunda	Madagascar jasmine
Thunbergia grandiflora	sky flower
Trachelospermum jasminoides	star jasmine

should preferably be done after the blooming season and before the growth of new wood. And one should also be watchful to see that no side runners are sent out by the parent trunk at the base.

Vines that have failed to bloom should be pruned during the summer, reducing new growth to about six buds.

As the tendency to produce abundant bloom seems to be an inherited characteristic, it is wise, when purchasing plants that have been produced from cuttings, to make sure that they have come from freely blooming vines. Grafted plants, produced from scions taken from heavy-blooming plants, are apt to bloom at an earlier age than plants grown from cuttings.

Uses: On walls of buildings, adequate support being necessary; on stoutly constructed arbors and pergolas.

Caution: Wisteria may become a very serious problem if allowed to get out of bounds. (See index for measures of control.)

16.1 Myrtle (Vinca minor), *with its periwinkle-blue flowers and evergreen foliage, carpets this woodland hillside while at the same time complementing the yellow daffodils. Photo Grant Heilman*

16

Ground Covers

When certain plants are grown closely together under just the right conditions, they form dense carpets that tend to discourage competition from weeds or other plants in the garden. Such plants are known as ground covers, and included in this group are herbaceous perennials, many evergreen and deciduous shrubs of various heights, and even certain vines that creep over the ground. The uses and usefulness of these plants vary considerably according to situation, and many are adapted to grow in problem areas where it is difficult to maintain lawns or other less vigorous plants. A popular misconception, however, is that ground covers are the answer to most garden maintenance problems, and that they may also be used extensively to create trouble-free plantings. This impression is erroneous because all ground covers require some periodic maintenance, and most ground covers are truly effective under a very limited range of conditions only. Three of the most important uses for ground covers are: (1) to create textural and color contrasts in the landscape; (2) to define special spaces or areas; and (3) to cover the ground in areas where grass is difficult to maintain. If the plants chosen as ground covers are adapted to grow well in the situations provided for them, maintenance may be kept to a minimum, and landscape use therefore becomes as important a consideration as ease of care.

In addition to their landscape value, ground covers fulfill other important functions. Wherever planted, they help protect the soil by conserving moisture and, during periods of extreme heat, by maintaining lower temperatures in the soil, a matter of considerable importance in hot climates. When planted on steep banks, they protect the soil from heavy rains and thus reduce erosion. And by spreading their green carpet of foliage over areas of bare ground, they prevent or limit the encroachment of weeds.

In developing a home property, ground covers can be used in many ways. They can be planted as a pleasant foreground for the shrub border, and are of particular value for use among plantings of broad-leaved evergreens. Cultivation of the soil disturbs the roots of rhododendrons and mountain laurels, and ground cover plants afford welcome protection, serving much the same purpose as a mulch in that they keep the soil cool and moist. Ground covers may also be used very successfully on narrow or odd-shaped areas that are often difficult to maintain. Some are well suited for use as a green carpet on areas where it is difficult to establish good turf, as under trees that cast dense shade, or on banks where mowing would become difficult. Though most ground covers are not a substitute for lawn grasses, since they do not possess the same appearance or qualities, some may be used as a substitute for a lawn and will provide pleasant verdure on such areas.

The extent to which ground covers are used to replace lawns should be considered carefully. Lawn itself is, of course, a ground cover. In fact, it is not only the most extensively used ground cover but probably the least expensive to install and maintain when used to cover most large areas. Grass is the *only* ground cover that can be closely clipped and walked upon extensively. Areas around the home used for recreation, relaxation and various other utilitarian purposes requiring random access should not be planted with any other types of ground covers. (For alternative low-maintenance lawn management techniques, see Chapter 12.) Very pleasing foliage as well as textural and color contrasts can be achieved when lawn and ground cover areas are considered as complementary design elements, and are used to create special contrasting effects.

SELECTION OF GROUND COVER PLANTS

The selection of an attractive and suitable ground cover will depend upon the area where it is to be used. There are ground covers that will grow well only in partial shade, others that require full sun, while others again are tolerant of both sun and shade. Some prefer moist soils rich in humus, others are particularly well adapted to dry, shady soils. Some are low and matlike, hugging the soil closely, while others are somewhat tall and spreading, and of a shrubby character. Some are evergreen and are lovely at every season of the year, whereas others are deciduous and present a pleasing appearance only during the growing season.

It is therefore important that the ground cover best adapted to the particular location is chosen. Where a low evergreen ground cover is desired for a lightly shaded area, there are a number that meet the requirements and from which a selection could be made. Among these are *Ajuga reptans*, English ivy, *Pachysandra* and *Vinca minor*. For clothing a sunny bank, some of the prostrate junipers or cotoneasters, with their spreading branches and interestingly textured foliage, would be a worthy choice; or, in very mild climates, *Gazania* or one of the *Mesembryanthemums* could be used. For use on the

16.2 Ajuga reptans—*for some reason sometimes called bugle—is a nonevergreen ground cover that is useful in shady places, but may escape into lawns and other undesirable areas. Photo Anita Sabarese*

north side of buildings where there is continual shade, the choice is more limited, the most dependable ground covers for such a location being English ivy, lily-of-the-valley, *Ajuga reptans* or *Euonymus fortunei*.

Occasionally two ground covers can be grown as companions. One of the pleasantest of such associations is that of periwinkle (*Vinca minor*) and leadwort (*Ceratostigma plumbaginoides*). The soft, lavender-blue flowers of the periwinkle come in early or mid-spring and the brilliant blue flowers of the leadwort carry the period of bloom well into the autumn. During the spring months one is hardly aware that the leadwort forms a part of the planting, but in late summer it begins to assume a more important role and by September it has become almost completely dominant.

Spring-flowering bulbs, such as snowdrops, scilla and narcissus, and the autumn-flowering crocus (*Colchicum*) may be planted among some of the low-growing ground covers, such as periwinkle or ivy, and are very effective.

There are a few plants which are so invasive that they should never be used as ground cover plants. Some are occasionally used to clothe steep banks along highways, but they should never be used on the home property as they are extremely difficult to restrain and to eradicate.

It sometimes requires a year or more for a ground cover planting to become established. Some ground cover plants grow fairly rapidly and look good at the end of the first season, while others may require several seasons before a good cover is obtained. The spacing of the plants has some bearing on this, and in every case the advantages of immediate results should be weighed against those of economy.

Plantings that are slow to become established should be mulched well to retain moisture and prevent encroachment by weeds. Hand weeding at frequent intervals is also important. If certain persistent weeds successfully invade a ground cover planting, they may be difficult or impossible to eradicate once the cover becomes established.

Large or steeply sloping banks present special problems while ground covers are becoming established. In such situations, erosion and encroaching weeds must be assiduously dealt with, and heavy mulching is essential. Sometimes covering the bank with black plastic and planting through it is an effective solution. Be sure to make numerous holes through the plastic with a spading fork so that ample moisture can penetrate through to the roots below. Covering the plastic with a light mulch of wood chips or other suitable mulching material will prevent excessive heat from building up under the plastic, and will also hide it from view.

GROUND COVER PLANTS OF SPECIAL MERIT

Aegopodium podograria (bishop's goutweed)

Herbaceous perennial; 6 in. (12 in. to 14 in. in flower); good to poor soil.

Useful in areas where it can be restrained, otherwise can get out of bounds and become invasive. Tolerates shade, dry soil; does well in sun. Can be cut to ground occasionally with a mower and will recover. The species has green

GROUND COVER PLANTS THAT ARE INEXPENSIVE BUT TROUBLESOME

(The following frequently become weeds and, once established, are difficult to restrain or eradicate)

Glechoma hederacea	ground ivy, gill-over-the ground
Lonicera japonica	Japanese honeysuckle
Lonicera japonica 'Halliana'	Hall's climbing honeysuckle
Lycium chinense	Chinese matrimony vine
Lycium halimifolium	matrimony vine
Lysimachia nummularia	moneywort, creeping charlie
Polygonum cuspidatum	Japanese knotweed, false bamboo
Pueraria lobata	kudzu vine

leaves. In 'Variegatum,' the leaves are margined with white.

Zone of hardiness: 4. *Spacing:* 12–15 plants per sq. yd. Suitable for covering large areas.

Ajuga reptans (carpet bugle)

Semievergreen perennial; 4 in. (6 in. to 12 in. in flower); dark green foliage; flowers blue, white, purple; full sun or semishade; any garden soil, even poor.

Very rapid growth that quickly forms a dense mat. Handsome flowers May to June. Can invade the lawn and become a serious pest, so do not plant next to lawn areas. 'Alba,' white flowers; 'Atropurpurea,' leaves bronze-purple, flowers dark purple; 'Multicoloris,' leaves mottled red, white and yellow on green; 'Variegata,' leaves mottled creamy-white.

Zone of hardiness: 4. *Spacing:* 18–20 plants per sq. yd. Suitable for covering fairly large areas.

Akebia quinata (five-leaf akebia)

Woody deciduous vine; flowers purple, fairly inconspicuous, May; full sun; any garden soil, even poor.

Fast-growing and rampant. Use only to cover large banks where there are no objects for it to climb.

Zone of hardiness: 4. *Spacing:* 1 plant per sq. yd. Suitable for covering large areas.

Arctostaphylos uva-ursi (bearberry)

Evergreen creeping shrub; small white flowers in May; red berries summer to early winter; full sun to partial shade; acid, well-drained sandy soil; fairly slow-growing.

One of the best evergreen ground covers for sandy soil, especially near the sea. Because it is very difficult to transplant, better to purchase plants already established in pots.
Zone of hardiness: 2. *Spacing:* 4 plants per sq. yd. Suitable for covering small to medium-sized areas.

Asarum europaeum (European ginger), Asarum shuttleworthii (Shuttleworth ginger)

Handsome evergreen perennials, with lustrous dark green leaves (some forms of *A. shuttleworthii* mottled white); 4 in. to 6 in.; flowers inconspicuous; semishade to deep shade; rich moist garden soil well supplied with humus.

One of the most handsome evergreen ground covers for shady places. Slow-growing and never invasive.
Zone of hardiness: 5. *Spacing:* 12–16 plants per sq. yd. Suitable for covering small to medium-sized areas. Expensive and slow for large areas.

Ceratostigma plumbaginoides (frequently listed in catalogues as Plumbago larpentiae; blue leadwort)

Herbaceous perennial; 6 in. to 1 ft.; deep blue flowers late August to September; handsome reddish-bronze autumn color; full sun or partial shade; good moisture-retentive soil.

Very effective for bloom late in the season; forms dense, neat tufts of growth. Starts to grow quite late in the spring, and thus is effective when combined with other ground covers such as *Vinca*. May become invasive unless confined.
Zone of hardiness: 6. *Spacing:* 9 plants per sq. yd. Suitable for covering small to medium-sized areas.

Convallaria majalis (lily-of-the-valley)

Herbaceous perennial; 8 in.; fragrant white flowers in May; poisonous orange berries in autumn; does best in partial or dense shade, in rich soil with good organic matter content, but also successful on poorer soils.

Plants increase rapidly and require almost no care. Foliage yellows and tends to become unattractive toward end of growing season. Dies to ground and leaves soil bare throughout winter.
Zone of hardiness: 2. *Spacing:* 9–12 plants per sq. yd. Suitable for covering medium- to large-sized areas.

Coronilla varia (crown vetch)

Herbaceous perennial; 1 ft. to 2 ft.; pink pea-like flowers in dense clusters freely produced June to September; full sun; dry or well-drained soils.

Very rapid-growing, especially useful in covering steep dry banks and is now seen planted frequently along highways. 'Penngift' is especially suited for this purpose. Dies to ground in winter.
Zone of hardiness: 3. *Spacing:* 1 plant per sq. yd. Suitable for covering medium-sized to very extensive areas, especially slopes.

Cotoneaster horizontalis (rock cotoneaster)

Creeping, deciduous shrub; 1½ ft. to 3 ft.; full sun or partial shade; persistent red berries; flat, nearly horizontal branches; semievergreen in mild areas; thrives in good, moisture-retentive soils.

Excellent for covering a bank, but good on flat areas too. Profits from occasional pruning to maintain neat habit of growth.
Zone of hardiness: 4. *Spacing:* 2 plants per sq. yd. Suitable for covering medium- to large-sized areas.

Other excellent cotoneasters for ground cover purposes include *C. adpressus* var. *praecox; C. apiculatus; C. congestus; C. dammeri;* and *C. microphyllus.*

Epimedium grandiflorum (bishop's hat)

Deciduous perennial; 9 in.; red, violet and white flowers May to June; partial or deep shade; good soil.

Forms very dense carpets and survives well under heavy shade of trees. One of the few ground covers that will usually survive at the base of a tree. Foliage should be left on the plant throughout winter and cut to ground in early spring before the flowers appear. Slow to become established. Other good species of *Epimedium* for ground cover purposes include *E. alpinum*; *E. pinnatum*; *E.* x *versicolor* 'Sulphureum'; and *E.* x *youngianum* 'Niveum.'
Zone of hardiness: 3. *Spacing:* 12–15 plants per sq. yd. Suitable to cover small to medium-sized areas, but expensive and slow to establish on larger areas.

Euonymus fortunei (spindle tree)

Evergreen creeping (or clinging) vine; 4 in.; light shade; rich soil.

Branchlets root where they come in contact with moist soil. Will quickly climb up or over any object with which it comes in to contact. One of the hardiest evergreen vines for ground cover purposes, but can be seriously affected by euonymus scale (for control, see index). Other *Euonymus* excellent for use as ground covers include *E. fortunei* 'Colorata,' purplish to bronze color in winter, vigorous and can be grown in full sun; *E. fortunei* 'Minima,' very small leaves, 5/8 in. long or less.
Zone of hardiness: 5. *Spacing:* 1 plant per sq. yd. Suitable for covering medium- to large-sized areas.

Forsythia 'Arnold Dwarf' (Arnold dwarf forsythia)

Shrub to 3 ft.; branches root at tips where they touch the ground; full sun; ordinary, well-drained soils; flowering quite sparse.

Low stature and tendency to tip-root makes this an excellent selection for covering steep slopes. Plants will withstand periodic heavy pruning.
Zone of hardiness: 5. *Spacing:* 1 plant per sq. yd. Suitable for covering medium-sized to large areas.

Hedera helix (English ivy)

Evergreen vine; light shade; good soil.

One of the best of the broad-leaved evergreen ground covers, withstands the shade of trees particularly well. Many kinds of bulbs can be naturalized in it. Hardy selections for colder areas in the north include 'Baltica', 'Bulgaria,' 'Rumania' and '238th Street.'
Zone of hardiness: 5. *Spacing:* 3 plants per sq. yd. Suitable for covering medium- to large-sized areas.

Hemerocallis fulva (orange daylily)

Herbaceous perennial; 2 ft. to 3 ft.; full sun or partial shade; good or poor soil; orange flowers, July to early August.

Naturalized throughout the eastern United States, will thrive indefinitely without any attention whatsoever. Forms very dense colonies. Flowering stalks should be removed after blooming to give a neater appearance. Does well on a steep bank, but good on flat areas too. 'Kwanso' has double flowers.
Zone of hardiness: 3. *Spacing:* 2–3 plants per sq yd. Suitable for covering medium-sized to large areas; very hardy.

Hosta (plantain lily)

Herbaceous perennial; 1½ ft. to 3 ft., depending upon species; flowers July to late summer, depending upon species; partial shade; good, moisture-retentive soil with ample humus.

Excellent for foliage at varying heights, and to provide bold textural contrast to other plants. Flower stalks should be removed after blossoms fade. Dies to ground in winter. Survives well under the shade of trees, but should not have considerable root competition from trees. Valuable species and cultivars include *H. decorata*, 1 ft. to 2 ft., with pointed, oval 6 in. leaves; *H. fortunei*, 2 ft., 5 in. leaves; *H. fortunei* 'Marginato-alba,' 11 in. leaves with a broad white margin; *H. lancifolia*, 1½ ft. to 2 ft., tapering 5 in. leaves; *H. sieboldiana*, robust to 2½ ft. to 3 ft., with very glaucous thick leaves and prominent veins; *H. undulata*, 2 ft. to 3 ft., 6 in.

leaves striped with cream or white; withstands more sun than the others.
Zone of hardiness: 3–4. *Spacing:* 1–3 plants per sq. yd. Suitable for covering small to medium-sized areas.

Hydrangea anomala subsp. petiolaris (climbing hydrangea)

Deciduous woody climber; 2 ft. to 3 ft. as ground cover; full sun or partial shade; good moisture; retentive soils; large flat clusters of white flowers in June; lustrous foliage.

Unusual flowering ground cover for flat places or steep slopes. Interesting reddish-brown peeling bark in winter. Slow to become established, but will climb any tree it comes into contact with. Tends to form a moundlike cover of irregular height. Withstands periodic pruning. Excellent for binding the soil on steep banks.
Zone of hardiness: 4. *Spacing:* 1 plant per sq. yd. Suitable for covering medium-sized to large areas.

Hypericum calycinum (Aaronsbeard, St. Johnswort)

Semievergreen to evergreen sub-shrub; spreads freely by stoloniferous roots; full sun or partial shade; good well-drained soils; bright yellow flowers in profusion in late July and August.

Excellent for sandy soil conditions. This is one of the best ground covers for midsummer bloom.
Zone of hardiness: 6. *Spacing:* 4 plants per sq. yd. Suitable for covering small to large-sized areas.

Juniperus horizontalis (creeping juniper)

Creeping coniferous evergreen shrub; 12 ft. to 18 ft.; full sun; poor to dry soils.

One of the best plants for covering steep slopes, but satisfactory on flat areas too. Requires almost no attention once established. Foliage has bronze tints in winter. Excellent cultivars include 'Douglasii,' foliage steel-blue dur-

ing growing season, tinged purple in winter; 'Plumosa,' more feathery, lighter green foliage that turns purple in autumn; and 'Wiltonii,' a beautiful slower-growing form of 'Douglasii.'

Other very satisfactory junipers for ground cover include the following: *J. chinensis* var. *sargentii,* a dense, moundlike shrub to 1 ft.; *J. conferta,* a very low-growing species 1 ft. and under, especially suited to conditions by the sea; *J. chinensis* var. *procumbens,* a dense, somewhat stiff shrub to 2 ft., with attractive blue-green color throughout the winter; *J. sabina* 'Tamariscifolia,' 2 ft., and more upright than those previously mentioned. Withstands city conditions, and will grow on limestone soils.
Zone of hardiness: 2–5. *Spacing:* 1–2 plants per sq. yd. Suitable for covering medium-sized to large areas.

Leucothoë fontanesiana (drooping leucothoë)

Broad-leaved evergreen shrub; 2 ft. to 5 ft.; light to deep shade; good moisture-retentive soil with ample humus.

Has long, arching, graceful stems. Does best with the same conditions as for rhododendrons. Periodic pruning out of the older stems will keep the plants more vigorous. If planted in full sun, foliage will burn in late winter. Handsome, and nearly trouble-free.
Zone of hardiness: 4. *Spacing:* 1 plant per sq. yd. Suitable for covering small to large areas.

Lonicera henryi (Henry honeysuckle)

Semievergreen twining vine; as a ground cover, 6 in.; yellowish-red to purplish flowers in June; black berries, September to December; full sun or partial shade; ordinary to poor soil.

Less vigorous and not quite so invasive as *L. japonica* and *L. japonica* 'Halliana,' and in most situations will not get out of hand so rapidly. However, will climb any tree or shrub it contacts. Suited to steep slopes or flat areas.
Zone of hardiness: 4. *Spacing:* 3 plants per sq. yd. Suitable for covering medium-sized to large areas.

Pachysandra terminalis (Japanese pachysandra)

Broad-leaved evergreen perennial; 6 in.; full sun to deep shade; flowers inconspicuous; good to somewhat poor soil.

The most popular and versatile ground cover of all. Spreads rapidly by underground stolons. One of the few ground covers that can withstand competition from surface-rooted trees such as maple.
Zone of hardiness: 4. *Spacing:* 1 ft. apart. Suitable for covering small to very large areas.

Potentilla tridentata (wineleaf cinquefoil)

Evergreen, semiwoody perennial with lustrous leaves; 2 in. to 1 ft.; acid soil; full sun or partial shade.

A plant of very refined foliage and texture. Rather slow to become established, but very long-lasting and trouble-free. Does not grow well on alkaline soils.
Zone of hardiness: 2. *Spacing:* 1 ft. apart. Suitable for covering small to medium-sized areas.

Rhus aromatica (fragrant sumac)

Deciduous shrub; 3 ft.; full sun or partial shade; flowers inconspicuous; fruit red berries in summer; autumn color yellow and scarlet; good to poor soil conditions.

Leaves somewhat resemble those of poison ivy, but are harmless. Excellent, vigorous shrub as a tall ground cover, spreading by underground stems. Can be cut back severely to within 6 in. of ground if it becomes overgrown. Equally good for flat areas or slopes.
Zone of hardiness: 3. *Spacing:* 1 plant per sq. yd. Suitable for covering medium-sized to large areas.

Rosa wichuraiana (memorial rose)

Trailing semievergreen rose with lustrous foliage; 1 ft.; flowers single, white, 2 in., mid-July; fruits reddish, less than 1/2 in. in diameter; full sun; any soil.

The best rose for ground cover. Very vigorous and especially suited for planting on banks. Tree seedlings occasionally becoming established in this ground cover will require periodic removal.
Zone of hardiness: 5. *Spacing:* 1 plant per sq. yd. Suitable for covering medium-sized to very large areas.

Sedum acre (gold moss)

Perennial evergreen succulent; 2 in.; flowers bright yellow in May and June; full sun or partial shade; any soil, particularly if dry.

Forms dense mats and is very vigorous even under trying, dry soil conditions.
Zone of hardiness: 3. *Spacing:* 9 plants per sq. yd. Suitable for covering small to medium-sized areas.

Vinca minor (periwinkle, creeping myrtle)

Evergreen, semi-woody trailing plant; 6 in.; full sun or partial to deep shade; flowers lavender-blue in late April or May.

Vies with pachysandra as the best evergreen ground cover. Especially good on banks or in shady places. Cultivars include 'Alba,' white flowers; 'Bowlesii,' flowers darker blue, freely produced; 'Flore Pleno,' double, purplish-blue flowers.
Zone of hardiness: 4. *Spacing:* 9 plants per sq. yd. Suitable for covering small to medium- to large-sized areas.

Xanthorhiza simplicissima (yellowroot)

Deciduous shrub; 1 1/2 ft. to 2 ft.; inconspicuous flowers and fruits; full sun to partial shade; soil moist and rich in humus.

Increases very rapidly by underground stolons, and forms very dense clumps that thrive for years with no attention. Interesting yellowish to orange autumn color, no particular winter interest. One of the most trouble-free ground covers if soil conditions are suitable.
Zone of hardiness: 4. *Spacing:* 9 plants per sq. yd. suitable for covering areas of any size.

17.1 A country border of black-eyed Susan (Rudbeckia hirta), *sunflower* (Helianthus), *larkspur* (Delphinium) *and daylily* (Hemerocallis) — *some perennial, some annual — makes a welcome summertime sight. Photo Grant Heilman*

17

Herbaceous Perennials

The large group known as herbaceous perennials includes many of our most beloved garden flowers. Although very diverse in form and habit of growth, there is one characteristic that members of this group share in common: they die down to the ground in winter and renew their growth again in the spring. Some herbaceous perennials live on almost indefinitely, while others have a tendency to die out after a few years.

All of these common and familiar garden flowers originally came from wildflowers. They were brought into cultivation because of their beauty, and by selection and hybridization many of them have been developed and improved to such an extent that their relationship to their ancestors is difficult to recognize today. Indeed, with some flowers it is impossible to determine their place of origin or their line of descent, so dissimilar are they to wild species. Most of these domesticated plants are more vigorous in growth, the flowers larger and more varied, than in wild counterparts, and in some instances the blossoms have become so specialized that they no longer set seed.

Some perennials have been in cultivation for many centuries, even since ancient times, while others were introduced more recently, following the era of extensive exploration. Those plants that have been cultivated in gardens since ancient times were first grown in the countries of their origin. Later they were introduced into Europe by the returning Crusaders or by travelers or explorers. Thus, the flowers that were originally gathered together in the monastery gardens, and then displayed in public botanic gardens, gradually became the familiar flowers of the European flower garden.

The early colonists who established homes in the New World brought with them many of the perennial flowers they had known and loved in their native lands. Their qualities of hardiness, long life, and their thriftiness under adverse and widely varying conditions made these perennials particularly welcome to the early settlers of this country, and these same sturdy qualities in the perennials make them just as valuable today.

SITE CONSIDERATIONS

The ideal site for a perennial garden is one that (1) will receive direct sunlight for as many hours during the day as possible (a minimum of four or five, preferably at least six to eight); (2) is sheltered from strong winds; (3) possesses deep, fertile, well-drained, loamy and neutral soil, rich in organic matter; (4) is on flat or only slightly sloping land; and (5) occupies a conspicuous location on the property. Few gardeners are blessed with such a site! Fortunately, poor soil can be enriched and improved. By proper selection, plants that tolerate a fairly

PERENNIALS FOR WET SOIL CONDITIONS

(Asterisk indicates suitability for quite wet conditions; all others are suitable for moderately wet soils only)

Aruncus sylvester	*Hibiscus* hardy cultivars
Arundo donax	*Hosta* spp.
Astilbe spp. and cultivars	*Iris kaempferi*
Astrantia major	*Iris sibirica*
Boltonia asteroides	*Iris versicolor*
Caltha palustris	*Ligularia* spp.
Chelone spp.	*Lobelia cardinalis*
Cimicifuga spp.	*Lobelia syphilitica*
Epilobium angustifolium	*Lysimachia clethroides*
Eupatorium purpureum	*Lythum salicaria*
Filipendula palmata	*Myosotis palustris*
Gentiana andrewsii	*Trollius* spp.
Helenium autumnale	*Vernonia noveboracensis*
Hemerocallis cvs.	

PERENNIALS FOR SHADY CONDITIONS

(Asterisk indicates suitability for either light or deep shade; others are suitable for light shade only and will also withstand full sun)

Aconitum	*Geranium* spp.
Actaea	*Hemerocallis*
Ajuga	*Heuchera*
Anchusa azurea	*Hosta*
Anemone x *hybrida*	*Iberis sempervirens*
Aquilegia	*Lobelia cardinalis*
Aruncus	*Mertensia*
Asperula odorata	*Phlox*
Astilbe	*Platycodon*
Brunnera	*Polemonium*
Campanula	*Polygonatum*
Chelone	*Primula*
Cimicifuga	*Pulmonaria*
Convallaria	*Silene caroliniana*
Corydalis	*Smilacina*
Dicentra	*Thalictrum*
Digitalis	*Tradescantia virginiana* cultivars
Doronicum	*Trillium* spp.
Epimedium	*Trollius* spp.
Eupatorium coelestinum	*Uvularia*
Eupatorium rugosum	*Viola* spp.
Filipendula spp.	

wide range of soil or light conditions may be chosen, and some species adapt to special situations with very poor soil or heavy shade. The further one departs from the ideal conditions outlined above, however, the more limited the choices will be.

The worst site for a perennial garden is one where the soil is poorly drained, especially during the winter. In such conditions, the hardiness of many perennials is considerably reduced; plants tend to be heaved out of the ground during periods of alternate freezing and thawing, and the choice of suitable plants for such a situation is thus very restricted. Unless considerable time and expense can be spent to drain the site extensively, a major herbaceous perennial garden should not be attempted in such a location.

Another limiting location for a perennial garden is one that receives less than four hours of direct sunlight a day. The choice of plants for such a situation is again restricted, though admittedly not so limited as in wet locations. Although many sun-loving perennials tolerate partial shade, the greater the degree of shade, the greater will be the need for staking. Moreover, such gardens will be subject to increased attack from fungus and other diseases, in addition to the likelihood that some plants will produce rampant growth.

Traditional perennial plantings are most effective against a backdrop, such as a hedge or wall. Good hedge plants for this purpose include yew, privet or hemlock. Wooden or metal fences are also appropriate, and a well-planned perennial border can mask the ugliness of a chain-link fence as effectively as it complements the beauty of a wooden fence or screen. Many other backdrops are possible, including the walls of the house itself, a mixed shrub border or outbuildings on the property.

In contemporary gardens, the perennial border is frequently liberated from the prescribed, often stereotyped backdrop. It may be placed in the lawn, independent of any single feature or structure, yet be in complete harmony with the overall landscaping plan. The shape may be linear in general outline or free-form. It may be defined by gently curving lines, or sometimes raised or contoured in elevation. In such situations, use of shrubs with contrasting shapes, leaf colors and textures will complement the perennials and add interest during both the growing season and the bleak months of winter when perennial gardens usually are least attractive.

Many other sites on the average home property present possibilities as good locations for a perennial garden. These include areas along driveways, parallel to walks within or partially surrounding vegetable gardens, around existing specimen shrubs or small trees, mixed into annual borders, adjacent to terraces or patios, at the base of a rock outcrop, near a fence or hedge, or among the shrubs of the foundation planting or shrub border. The possibilities are almost equal to the myriad of sites to be found or created on any property.

PLANNING THE PERENNIAL BORDER

No planting problem is more diverse and intricate than that of the perennial flower border. No planting plan requires more careful thought, more detailed study or more creative skill. It is the aim of the designer to produce a succession of color harmonies that will merge imperceptibly, one into the other, as the season advances. No other type of plant material offers such infinite possibilities for color compositions as do the perennials, and the gardener finds in this ever-changing medium wide scope for his artistic skill and creativity.

It must be borne in mind, however, that perennials alone will not produce as full an effect of bloom and color throughout the season as will perennials supplemented with spring- and summer-flowering bulbs, and with annuals and biennials. Therefore, in planning the border for continuous bloom, it is an advantage to include a few plants of these other valuable groups as well.

When designing the perennial garden, the entire life cycle of each plant must be taken into consideration to determine its position — its period of growth, blossoming and retrogression. In selecting and arranging plant material, the most important factors are the ultimate height of the plants, the color range and the season of

bloom. But there are other factors also to be taken into consideration, such as the texture and color of the foliage, the longevity of the plant and its cultural requirements. All of these considerations may at first seem confusing, especially to the novice, but they need not be so if the decisions are made in logical sequence.

The usual procedure in preparing a planting plan for a perennial garden is first to draw to scale a diagram showing the outline of the various beds or borders. A scale of $\frac{1}{2}$ in. to 1 ft. will usually provide for a plan of workable size, unless the garden is unusually large, in which case the scale may be reduced to $\frac{1}{4}$ in. to 1 ft. The next step is to compile a list of the plants and bulbs one wishes to include in the planting plan. On this list they may either be jotted down quite at random as they come to mind, or listed alphabetically, or in some other logical order such as blooming sequence. Such a list, set down at random, might appear as follows:

Anemone x *hybrida*	Japanese anemone
Aquilegia	columbine
Artemisia lactiflora	white mugwort
aster	
chrysanthemum	
Delphinium	
Dicentra spectabilis	bleeding-heart
Hemerocallis	daylily
Heuchera	coralbells
Iris	
Linum perenne	blue flax
Lupinus	lupine
peony	
Phlox divaricata	wild sweet William
Phlox paniculata	perennial phlox
Salvia farinacea	mealycup sage
Thalictrum aquilegifolium	meadow rue
viola	violet

When this tentative list has been completed, it should be broken up into a number of subgroupings, according to (1) season of bloom, (2) color and (3) height.

Biennials, bulbs or annuals may be added to the list to provide more abundant bloom at certain seasons, or because they are particularly good companions.

Thus the above list would be arranged into the following groupings:

PERENNIALS ACCORDING TO SEASON OF BLOOM

SPRING PERENNIALS	EARLY SUMMER PERENNIALS	MIDSUMMER PERENNIALS	AUTUMN PERENNIALS
Aquilegia	*Delphinium*	*Artemisia lactiflora*	*Anemone japonica*
Dicentra spectabilis	*Hemerocallis*	*Hemerocallis*	aster
Iris	*Heuchera*	*Lupinus*	chrysanthemum
peony	*Linum perenne*	*Phlox paniculata*	
Phlox divaricata	peony	*Salvia farinacea*	
Thalictrum aquilegifolium	*Phlox paniculata*		

SPRING PERENNIALS

Aquilegia
Dicentra spectabilis
Iris
peony
Phlox divaricata
Thalictrum aquilegifolium

BIENNIALS

English daisy
pansy

BULBS

Narcissus
scilla
tulip

EARLY SUMMER PERENNIALS

Delphinium
Hemerocallis
Heuchera
Linum perenne
peony
Phlox paniculata

BIENNIALS

Canterbury-bells
foxglove
sweet William

BULBS

lily

MIDSUMMER PERENNIALS

Artemisia lactiflora
Hemerocallis
Lupinus
Phlox paniculata
Salvia farinacea

BULBS AND CORMS

lily
gladiolus

ANNUALS

Ageratum   *Nicotiana*
Antirrhinum *Torenia*
Cleome   zinnia
marigold

TUBERS

dahlia

AUTUMN PERENNIALS

Anemone japonica
aster
chrysanthemum

ANNUALS

Ageratum
Antirrhinum
Cleome
marigold
Nicotiana
petunia
Torenia
Verbena
zinnia

PERENNIALS ACCORDING TO HEIGHT

LOW PERENNIALS

aster (dwarf var.)
Linum perenne
Phlox divaricata

BIENNIALS

English daisy
pansy
viola

BULBS

Narcissus
scilla

ANNUALS

Ageratum
marigold (dwarf var.)
petunia
Verbena

MEDIUM PERENNIALS

Anemone japonica
Aquilegia
chrysanthemum
Dicentra spectabilis
Hemerocallis
Heuchera
Iris
Lupinus
peony
Phlox paniculata
Salvia farinacea

BIENNIALS

Canterbury-bells
sweet William

BULBS AND CORMS

Gladiolus tulip
lily

ANNUALS

Antirrhinum marigold
Cleome   zinnia
Nicotiana

TALL PERENNIALS

Artemisia lactiflora
aster
Delphinium
Hemerocallis
Thalictrum aquilegifolium

BIENNIALS

foxglove

BULBS

lily

ANNUALS

marigold (giant var.)
zinnia (giant var.)

PERENNIALS ACCORDING TO COLOR

WHITE PERENNIALS	BLUE, LAVENDER, PURPLE, MAUVE PERENNIALS	PINK, SALMON, ROSE, RED PERENNIALS	YELLOW, ORANGE, BRONZE PERENNIALS
Anemone japonica	*Anemone japonica*	*Anemone japonica*	*Aquilegia*
Aquilegia	*Aquilegia*	*Aquilegia*	chrysanthemum
Artemisia	aster	aster	*Hemerocallis*
aster	chrysanthemum	chrysanthemum	*Iris*
chrysanthemum	*Delphinium*	*Dicentra spectabilis*	
Delphinium	*Iris*	*Heuchera*	
Iris	*Linum perenne*	*Iris*	
peony	*Phlox divaricata*	*Lupinus*	
Phlox paniculata	*Phlox paniculata*	peony	
	Salvia farinacea		
	Thalictrum aquilegifolium		

ANNUALS	ANNUALS	ANNUALS	ANNUALS
Antirrhinum	*Ageratum*	*Antirrhinum*	*Antirrhinum*
Cleome	*Antirrhinum*	*Cleome*	marigold
Nicotiana	*Nicotiana*	*Nicotiana*	zinnia
Torenia	petunia	petunia	
Verbena	*Torenia*	*Verbena*	
zinnia	*Verbena*	zinnia	
	zinnia		

BIENNIALS	BIENNIALS	BIENNIALS	BIENNIALS
Canterbury-bells	Canterbury-bells	Canterbury-bells	foxglove
English daisy	foxglove	English daisy	pansy
foxglove	pansy	pansy	
pansy		sweet William	
sweet William			

BULBS	BULBS AND CORMS	BULBS AND CORMS	BULBS AND CORMS
gladiolus	gladiolus	gladiolus	gladiolus
lily	lily	lily	lily
Narcissus	scilla	tulip	*Narcissus*
tulip	tulip		

TUBERS		TUBERS	TUBERS
dahlia		dahlia	dahlia

With these lists at hand, one is ready to select the plant material for the overall plan. A piece of tracing paper may be laid over the outline plan, which has been carefully drawn to scale, and the notation of the plant names made on this rough sketch sheet. The most orderly and logical sequence is to begin with spring bloom and to place the names of the plants on the plan in the approximate positions they are to occupy. In this early stage of the design, the exact outline of the clumps need not be indicated, nor should the quantity of each group be consid-

ered. At this point, the designer is concerned only with color harmonies, the sequence of bloom and height.

The selection of plants for early summer, late summer and autumn bloom is then made, and the names indicated upon the plan. If it is not possible to indicate the interplanting of annuals because of lack of space on the plan as sketched out, the name may be written outside the area of the border with an arrow pointing to the spot each plant will occupy.

After the color harmonies and the sequence

of bloom have been determined, and the sketch plans and all final decisions have been made, the plant names should be placed on the final plan, the outline of each clump should be indicated and notation should be made of the number of plants to be used in each group. The groups should be large enough to give an effective display and prevent an appearance of spottiness. Low-growing plants, such as violas and *Phlox divaricata,* may be used in long drifts along the front of the border; the taller plants may be used in groups of five, eight or ten, depending upon the size of the garden; and an occasional plant, such as bleeding-heart, may be used as an accent and planted alone, rather than in a group.

In general, the overall plan of the border should be to place lower-growing species toward the front and taller ones at the rear. The designer can create even greater interest, while at the same time giving the border a feeling of greater depth, if occasionally a group of taller perennials is brought out into the middle, and groups of plants of medium height are brought toward the front of the border. The reverse, however, should not be attempted, as low perennials would definitely appear out of place in the middle of the border or those of medium height at the rear.

Herbaceous perennials may be propagated in various ways: by seed, cuttings, division of old clumps, layering, division of tubers and rhizomes, and in a few very exceptional cases, by grafting. Some perennials may be readily propagated by several methods, some by only one method, but division is the most common practice. For detailed directions concerning seed sowing, division and the various other methods of propagation, see Chapter 34 on propagation. Purchasing enough plants to establish a large perennial garden can be quite expensive. The gardener who is familiar with the above-listed, relatively simple methods of increasing his or her perennials has a big advantage over the novice. Only one or two plants of each species need be purchased when the border is first established. During the year or two required for these to increase in size for propagation purposes, the gaps in the garden may be filled in with less expensive annuals.

PREPARATION OF THE SOIL

Since perennial beds and borders constitute a more or less permanent type of planting, the soil should be adequately prepared. Most herbaceous perennials attain their maximum perfection in a fertile, well-drained loam, which is high in organic content, neutral or very nearly neutral in reaction, and which has been deeply and thoroughly prepared previous to planting.

Since many perennials are deep-rooted, and as it is well to induce the more shallow-rooted types to send their feeding roots downward, the soil should be prepared to a depth of at least 15 in., preferably to a depth of 24 in. Trenching and double digging are the most approved methods for the preparation of the soil in perennial beds and borders. For detailed information concerning these practices, consult Chapter 35. If the soil is poorly drained, this condition should be remedied at the time that the beds are initially prepared.

Soil Reactions

A few perennials definitely prefer a soil that is slightly alkaline in reaction, while others are either acid-tolerant or even entirely indifferent. The vast majority, however, prefer a soil that is neutral or very nearly neutral in reaction, with a pH ranging from 6.5 to 7.5. In preparing the soil for perennial beds, samples should be taken and the soil reaction should be definitely determined. If the soil tests show that the reaction is below a pH of 6.5, an application of lime should be made. See the chart in Chapter 30 that indicates the exact amount that should be applied. The application should be made after the beds have been prepared for planting. The lime should be sprinkled over the surface of the bed and then cultivated lightly into the soil. In order to meet the needs of those perennials that definitely prefer a slightly alkaline soil, a sufficient quantity of lime should be applied over the area where they are to be planted in order to bring the reaction to a pH of approximately 7.5.

Almost all other perennials may be grouped among those that prefer a neutral or nearly

---

PERENNIALS THAT PREFER SLIGHTLY ALKALINE SOIL

Anemone x *hybrida* (*A. japonica*)   *Dictamnus*
Clematis — herbaceous species   *Gypsophila*
Delphinium

PERENNIALS THAT PREFER ACID SOIL

Actaea   *Mertensia*
Cimicifuga   *Trillium*
Digitalis

---

neutral soil, or those that are entirely indifferent to soil conditions.

GENERAL MAINTENANCE

A perennial garden requires faithful care and maintenance throughout the season. In the spring a general inspection of the garden should be made. Any plants that have been partially heaved out of the soil during the winter should be gently pressed back into place, and notations should be made of any plants that have failed to survive the winter. During this first spring survey the needs of each individual group of plants should be carefully studied, and the plans for spring work should be outlined. Some plants will need to be divided, others will need to be replaced with younger, more vigorous stock, and plans must be made for the spring feeding (see index for details on maintenance of fertility). It is also wise to make a few soil tests at this time to determine whether an application of lime is advisable. During the early spring, also, any remaining dead leaves and stalks should be removed and the beds and borders should be edged, so that the garden looks neat and trim from the very beginning of the season.

The first cultivation should be given as soon as the soil is warm and mellow and sufficiently dry to be workable. Soil should never be cultivated when it is too wet, as that would seriously injure its physical condition by causing the formation of many hard lumps. An excellent way to test the workability of the soil is to take a small amount and squeeze it tightly in your hand. If it crumbles when it falls to the ground, it is in good condition to be cultivated. If, however, it remains in a firm, compact lump, it contains too much moisture and should not be worked until it has become drier. Subsequent cultivations should be given throughout the season at intervals of every week or ten days unless a summer mulch is applied. A small weeder with three flexible prongs is one of the most convenient and efficient tools for cultivating perennial beds. It is possible to cultivate very close to the plants without causing damage to the roots or crown; the soil is left in excellent tilth, and the work may be done very rapidly, provided that the soil is in good condition for cultivation, being neither too wet nor too dry.

In order that perennials may be kept vigorous and healthy, it is necessary to be constantly alert to detect the first signs of disease or insect infestation, and as soon as trouble is noticed control measures should be put into effect immediately. (For the control of insect pests and diseases, see Chapter 32.)

Throughout the season, all flower stalks should be cut down as soon as the blooms have faded. Not only will this improve the overall appearance of the garden but it will also help to conserve the vigor of the plants, as the production of seed is a heavier drain upon the vitality of a plant than any other function it is required to perform. There are other advantages to be gained as well: in the case of some plants (such as *Achillea* and *Dicentra eximea* cultivars), it is possible to prolong their blooming season to a considerable extent if seed pods are not allowed to form, and, with other plants such as the delphiniums and some *Campanula* (such as *C. lactiflora*), it is possible to induce a second period of bloom. In some cases, with *Hemerocallis*, for example, the removal of old flowers each day adds immeasurably to the overall appearance of the garden.

Included also under the term of general maintenance are such tasks as watering, staking, feeding and the occasional division and replanting of established plants.

Watering

For their best development, most perennials require an adequate but not overabundant supply of moisture throughout the season. A few perennials thrive on very dry soils, and there are others that have the ability to thrive under extremely moist conditions, but the vast majority prefer a moderate and fairly constant supply of moisture. In most areas of the country these requirements are met by normal rainfall. If, however, the rainfall is insufficient at any time during the season to meet the needs of the plants, it is advisable to resort to artificial watering. Frequent, light waterings are of little value and usually do far more harm than good as they tend to draw the roots toward the surface. A very thorough watering should be given once every five to ten days, depending on weather conditions, making sure that the moisture penetrates to a depth of at least 1 ft. Late afternoon and early evening are the most favorable times for watering as there is less evaporation and the soil retains the moisture more readily then. There are a number of excellent sprinkling attachments for an ordinary garden hose that make it possible to cover a considerable area simultaneously. If the garden is large, it is possible to water a section of it each evening and thus an entire area can be watered with comparatively little effort.

Staking

Staking appears to be such a very simple operation, yet it is seldom done in an entirely satisfactory manner. Staking is necessary for two purposes: either to provide support for weak and floppy stems, or to protect tall flower spikes from being bent and broken by winds and heavy storms. Whatever the purpose, the staking should be done in such a way that the natural form and beauty of the plant are preserved and the stakes themselves are as inconspicuous as possible.

Some perennials produce a quantity of small stems that have a tendency to be floppy and consequently need some support. In this group we find *Achillea ptarmica, Coreopsis grandiflora, Gypsophila, Platycodon* and *Veronica.* For such plants, twiggy tree or shrub branches may be used very successfully. Birch and alder are particularly good for this purpose. While the plants are still young, the twigs may be stuck into the ground close beside them and as the foliage develops the twigs will be entirely concealed. Such twigs offer a very satisfactory framework for the support of weak, floppy stems.

Plants such as delphiniums, asters, dahlias and many others require fairly tall, strong stakes. Bamboo stakes can be obtained in a variety of sizes and are very satisfactory. Those stained a soft green become almost invisible after they are in place. Strong wire stakes are also satisfactory and can be purchased in various styles and sizes. The type with spiral turns is particularly valuable for supporting individual flower stalks. Wooden stakes are often used, and if painted a dull green, they are reasonably unobtrusive in appearance. However, they lack the suppleness of bamboo and wire and frequently have a tendency to snap off. It is wise to keep a variety of stakes on hand in order to be prepared for every need. Some plants require stout stakes for adequate support, while others will require more slender ones. When staking large clumps, it is advisable to use more than one stake. When tall flower stalks are to be staked, they should be tied to the stake at several points. The tape should first be wound firmly about the stake and then wound about the stalk, being brought back and tied to the stake rather loosely. A flower stalk should never be tied tightly to a stake lest the beauty and grace of the plant are impaired. When a large clump is to be staked, the tape may first be attached to one of the stakes and then woven through the clump, being wound about each individual stalk until it reaches the far side of the clump, where it is attached to the opposite stake. Clumps of peonies may be supported by special wire hoops that may be placed about the entire plant, the legs resting upon the soil.

The material to be used in tying must be chosen carefully. Stems that are hollow and brittle must be tied with some very soft material that will not cut or bruise the stalk. Various types of plastic tape are available that are excellent for this purpose. These tapes are an inconspicuous green, are soft in texture, strong and durable, and have much to recommend them.

Feeding

In order to maintain the perennial border at its best from year to year, the fertility of the soil must be kept at a constantly high level. Two applications of a good complete fertilizer should be given during each season, one in spring after the plants have started into active growth and one early in the summer. Late summer and fall applications are not advisable as they tend to stimulate a rather succulent growth that would cause the plants to enter the winter in an unhardened condition.

The fertilizer may be applied in the form of a standard analysis complete fertilizer, such as a 4–12–4 or a 4–8–6, or it may be applied in the form of a high analysis, water-soluble fertilizer. The standard complete fertilizer should be applied at the rate of 3 oz. per 1 sq. yd. or 2 lb. per 100 sq. ft. It should be sprinkled over the surface of the bed, cultivated lightly into the soil and watered in thoroughly. Fertilizers such as bone meal and cottonseed meal are traditional, but as they release nutrients very slowly and do not become active until warm weather, they are less efficient than a well-balanced complete fertilizer.

The water-soluble fertilizer should be one that contains both trace elements and major elements. See index for details concerning the use of high-analysis, water-soluble fertilizers.

During periods of prolonged rain it may be necessary to supply additional amounts of nitrogen, as all the available supply of nitrogen in the soil is rapidly leached out under such conditions. This may be applied in the form of a top-dressing of nitrate of soda or sulphate of ammonia.

Division and Replanting

At the end of every five or six years, it is usually advisable to remake the perennial garden entirely. Groups of plants will have become too crowded, many of the original clumps will be in need of division and the soil will be depleted of nutrients. If the garden is large, a small section may be renovated each year. The work may be done either in the autumn or in the early spring, although autumn is preferable not only because there is usually more leisure to undertake such work but also because new bulbs may be planted and old bulbs may be divided at this season. The plants should be lifted from the beds, the soil should be rotoretrenched or double-dug and liberal quantities of well-rotted manure should be incorporated. Where necessary, the plants should be divided before they are reset. Such permanent plants as peonies and bleeding-heart, *Dictamnus* and *Platycodon*, which resent being moved, may be left undisturbed during this process of rejuvenation without any serious interference to the work.

RENEWING PERENNIAL PLANTS

When applied to plants, the term "perennial" denotes permanence. It cannot be assumed, however, that when perennial plants have once become established they will bloom on year after year without further thought or care on the part of the gardener. A few of the exceedingly robust types, such as gas plant, might measure up to such an expectation; but the vast majority of our more desirable perennials do require a reasonable amount of care if they are to grow satisfactorily and provide an abundance of bloom.

Some perennials are comparatively short-lived, and new plants should be grown to replace those that have served their period of usefulness in the garden. In this group we have the beautiful hybrid columbines, which have a tendency to die out after several years of luxuriant bloom; the lupines; the glorious hybrid delphiniums, which often fail to carry on over a period of many years unless conditions are extremely favorable for their growth; *Linum perenne*, *Anchusa*, primroses and many others. As some of our most choice perennials are to be found in this group, it is well to recognize the fact that these plants are more or less transient in the garden and that new specimens should be propagated at intervals of every few years.

Other perennials will thrive well for a year or two after they are planted but will then begin to deteriorate rapidly unless the clumps are divided. In this group we have the chrysanthemums, *Physostegia*, the hardy asters, *Iris* and *Phlox*. Chrysanthemums should be lifted and divided each year, or new plants should be started from cuttings, as the old clumps usually produce inferior blooms. *Physostegia* should also be lifted and divided annually, not only for the sake of better bloom but also in order to prevent it from encroaching upon its neighbors and becoming a pest. Hardy asters should be lifted and divided every two or three years. *Iris* should be divided every three or four years; *Phlox* every five or six years.

There are a few perennials that will thrive for many years without being divided and replanted; in fact, in some cases such plants seriously resent being disturbed. In this group we find *Dicentra spectabilis* (bleeding-heart), the peonies, the Oriental poppies, *Dictamnus* and *Platycodon*.

In maintaining a perennial garden, it is well to know the requirements of each individual group and to meet these needs as adequately as possible.

SUMMER AND WINTER MULCHES

A summer mulch fulfills several functions and may be used very advantageously in the perennial garden. Such a mulch reduces to a minimum the labor required for general care and cultivation, conserves the moisture in the soil and helps to maintain a more even soil temperature.

Winter mulch plays an important part in the successful maintenance of the perennial garden. Which plants should be mulched and which plants should be left unprotected; what materials should be used and how heavily should they be applied; when should the mulch be put on and when should it be removed—all these points must be taken into consideration.

For details concerning the use of summer and winter mulches, see Chapter 8.

PERENNIALS OF SPECIAL MERIT

Aconitum (monkshood)

The aconites derive their common name of monkshood from the characteristically hooded

or helmet-shaped flowers, and there are a number of varieties that are valued for their rich autumn effect in the garden. The aconites are also well adapted to a seminaturalistic setting, being suitable for use in the foreground of a shrubbery border or along a fringe of woodland.

A. carmichaelii (listed in most catalogues as A. fischeri) (azure monkshood)

Grows to only 2½ ft. in sun and to 3½ ft. in shade. It blooms in early autumn and is one of the hardiest of all the monkshoods.

A. carmichaelii var. wilsonii (listed in most catalogues as A. wilsonii, or A. fischeri var. wilsonii)

It blooms in late autumn and is distinct both in form and coloring. The flowers are a delicate violet-mauve, and the tall spikes tower to a height of 6 ft. or more and require staking.

A. henryi (listed in many catalogues as A. autumnale)

Plants reach a height of from 3 ft. to 4 ft. and bear racemes of large, dark blue flowers in late September and October.

A. napellus (aconite monkshood)

Blooms earlier than most—in August and early September, and has very attractive, finely divided foliage. Flower color varies from blue to violet. Plants reach a height of 3½ ft. to 4 ft.

A. napellus var. bicolor

Has flowers with a two-toned appearance. The outer edges are bright blue, fading to white in the center.

A. 'Sparks Variety'

Flowers are deep violet-blue and appear in August. Plants reach a height of 3 ft. to 4 ft.

Exposure: Semishade is preferred although the plants will also grow well in full sun if the soil is moisture-retentive in summer.

Soil requirements: Monkshood will thrive in any good garden loam but prefers a moist soil well supplied with organic matter.

Propagation: Monkshood may be propagated either by the division of old clumps or by seed. The seed is very slow to germinate, often requiring a month or more, and its viability is apt to be poor unless fresh seed is secured.

Culture: During dry seasons the aconites should be watered liberally. As the plants are difficult to move, they should be left undisturbed for many years after they have once become established. Planting distances vary from 8 in. to 10 in.

Caution: All parts of monkshood are poisonous, including flowers, stems and roots. It would probably be prudent not to plant them in areas frequented by small children.

Anchusa azurea (listed in many catalogues by the old name *A. italica*) (Italian alkanet)

This tall-growing *Anchusa* is useful for the perennial border, but because it is robust and has a somewhat branching habit of growth, it requires ample space and is not suitable for small garden beds. The small, intensely blue flowers are borne in rather loose clusters on ascending, heavy stems, being produced abundantly in June and intermittently throughout the summer.

'Dropmore'

The flowers are a deep, gentian blue. The plants are very vigorous in growth habit and reach a height of nearly 5 ft.

'Opal'

The flowers are a clear, pale blue in color and the plants range in height from 3ft. to 4 ft.

'Little John'

Only 1 ft. to 1½ ft. tall; deep blue flowers.

'London Royalist'

Another good, blue, low-growing variety, not over 3 ft. tall.

'Pride of Dover'

One of the most desirable of the recent introductions, with true heavenly blue color.

Exposure: Full sun.

Soil requirements: A fertile garden loam that is moist and well drained is considered ideal. Although the plants will grow reasonably on soils of moderate fertility, they respond remarkably well to liberal feeding.

Propagation: *Anchusa azurea* may be propagated by the division of old clumps, by root cuttings or by seed.

Culture: Transplanting should be done with care as the roots are very brittle. The plants attain considerable size and should be spaced from 15 in. to 18 in. apart. During the growing season, the anchusas require large quantities of water. After the second growing season, clumps start to degenerate and must be divided. They also have a tendency to self-seed.

Anemone x hybrida (listed in most catalogues as *A. japonica*, Japanese anemone)

The Japanese anemones are among the loveliest of our autumn flowers. The cup-shaped blooms with their brilliant golden stamens are borne on tall, slender stems that rise far above the dense clumps of foliage, often attaining a height of 3 ft. or more. The plants are in flower almost continuously from early September until late autumn, when they are cut down by heavy frosts. The flowers are exceedingly decorative in the garden and also are very lovely for cutting.

JAPANESE ANEMONE CULTIVARS OF MERIT

'Alba'; single; white
'Queen Charlotte': semidouble; rose-pink
'September Charm': single; silvery-pink
'Whirlwind': semidouble; white

Exposure: Full sun or partial shade. The Japaese anemones do exceedingly well at the edge of a shrubbery border where they are protected from strong winds and have the benefit of light shade for a portion of the day.

Soil requirements: The Japanese anemones thrive best in a cool, moist, yet well-drained soil, rich in humus and of a slightly alkaline reaction. The soil should be deeply prepared and liberal quantities of well-rotted cow manure, leaf mold or commercial humus should be incorporated previous to planting. Wet soil in the winter is one of the worst enemies of *A.* x *hybrida,* and considerably lessens its ability to withstand cold temperatures.

Propagation: Japanese anemones may be propagated by the division of old clumps in the spring, by root cuttings taken at any time during the growing season or by seed. In purchasing plants from a nursery, young pot-grown plants will usually give the best results.

Culture: The plants should be spaced from 15 in. to 18 in. apart. They require liberal quantities of moisture throughout the growing season, and will benefit tremendously from a summer mulch of half-rotted leaves. When once well established, the plants should be left undisturbed, as they do not transplant readily and resent interference. When the winters are of considerable severity a mulch of leaves or salt hay should be provided. This is particularly advisable for areas north of New York City.

Aquilegia (columbine)

The columbines are among the most beautiful of our garden flowers. They possess an exquisite daintiness and charm equaled by few other perennials, and no spring garden is quite complete without them. Many new and very beautiful strains have been introduced.

There are many species of *Aquilegia* and they vary considerably in form, in coloring and in adaptability. Some are definitely perennial in habit and will continue to bloom year after year, while others are comparatively short-lived. Some are particularly well suited to the rock garden, others thrive best in a woodland setting and others again are happily at home in the herbaceous border. Of the many species there are less than a dozen in common cultivation today.

A. alpina

Comes to us from the Alps and is one of the most cherished plants in many rock gardens. It seldom reaches a height of more than 9 in.; the flowers, which are borne in May and June, vary in color from clear blue to white. The spurs are short and stout and distinctly incurved. The plants prefer a light, well-drained, rather stony soil, which is not too rich, and they thrive in either full sun or partial shade. They may be spaced from 6 in. to 8 in. apart.

A. caerulea

Known as the Rocky Mountain columbine, this is one of the most beautiful of all species. It is a native of our mountain regions from Colorado south to Mexico. The lovely, long-spurred flowers are a clear blue with a white cup and golden anthers, and they are borne in great profusion. The plants are considered short-lived in eastern gardens as they frequently die out after two or three years, but recent experiments tend to show that they will persist considerably longer if given a soil of moderate acidity. Many of our beautiful hybrid strains have been developed from this species.

A. canadensis (wild columbine)

A native of this country east of the Rocky Mountains, usually found growing on dry, stony ledges. It prefers partial shade and a neutral soil, as it will not tolerate either extreme acidity or extreme alkalinity. It is a modest little plant, seldom growing more than 10 in. or 12 in. high. The blooms are of a scarlet and yellow hue. It is most happily at home in a woodland setting or in some partially shaded corner of the rock garden. There is also a very dwarf form known as *A. canadensis* 'Nana.'

A. chrysantha (golden columbine)

Bears flowers of clear yellow, tinted with claret, and the spurs are long, slender and graceful. It comes into flower a little later than some of the other species but has the pleasant habit of blooming intermittently throughout the season. In fact, it is sometimes in flower when cut down by frost in the autumn. The deep, glossy green foliage is particularly good, and usually retains its healthy, vigorous appearance throughout the summer months. The plants reach a height of from 18 in. to 24 in. and are well adapted either for the woodland or for use in the garden.

A. glandulosa (Altai columbine)

A rare and beautiful species that comes from the mountain regions of Siberia. The large, pendent, wide-spreading flowers are a bright, lilac-blue tipped with white, and the spurs, like those of *A. alpina*, are short and distinctly incurved. *A. glandulosa* is one of the first of the columbines to come into flower, blooming from early May until well into June. The foliage is very lovely, having a soft, velvety quality with rich, coppery shadings. The plants vary in height from 12 in. to 15 in. and are lovely both in the herbaceous border and in the rock garden, thriving either in full sun or in light shade.

A. vulgaris (European columbine)

The common columbine of Europe and the one so frequently found in old-time gardens. It reaches a height of from 18 in. to 24 in., and the blooms are heavy, short-spurred and lacking in grace and beauty. There are, however, a number of improved varieties, and some of our lovely hybrid strains have been developed by crossing *A. vulgaris* with other species.

Hybrid strains: Many of our most beautiful columbines today are hybrids, and among the choicest of these recent introductions are several distinct strains. The Mrs. Scott Elliott strain bears flowers of large size with long, graceful spurs, the colors varying from deep purple through violet and pink to a deep wine-red. The outer petals are often of one color and the corolla of another color, and many of the flowers offer the most subtle and exquisite harmonies and contrasts.

Sutton's selected long-spurred hybrids are an excellent strain. The plants are hardy and vigorous, and the lovely, long-spurred flowers, which vary in color from light to deep colors, are borne in great profusion.

The Rainbow Blend is a strain that was introduced many years ago by one of our western growers. The flowers are very large, with long, slender spurs, and for brilliancy of color they are quite unsurpassed. Pink, rose, scarlet, deep reds and purples and many other unusual and very beautiful shades are found among them. The McKana's Giant Hybrids strain has an extensive color range. The plants are of very sturdy growth, 2½ ft. to 3 ft. in height, and produce large flowers with spurs at least 4 in. long.

Propagation: Columbines may be propagated by seed and by the division of old clumps. It is advisable to grow new plants from seed, as the division of old clumps is not very satisfactory and the results are often disappointing.

It is better to purchase seed of the hybrid strains from commercial sources. The plants do not reproduce true from seed, and if seed is saved from garden plants, the resultant seedlings will be of "mongrel" type. In order to produce plants that will give good bloom the following season, it is essential that the seeds be sown early. If greenhouse space is not available, they may be sown in frames or in a seedbed in the open later in the season. In any case, it is well to have the seed sown before the middle of May so that the seedlings may have as long a growing season as possible. The seedbed should be carefully prepared. A mixture of equal parts of good garden loam, peat moss and sand provides excellent conditions for germination. The bed should be partially shaded after sowing and the soil should never be allowed to dry out. Growth is rather slow for the first month or so, but after the seedlings have been transplanted they will begin to develop more rapidly. If the young seedlings are protected by a lath shade during the summer months, they will grow much more rapidly and vigorously than they will if exposed to full sunlight. The young plants need a light, mellow soil with excellent drainage. They should be given good cultivation and abundant water throughout the season and should never be allowed to become stunted as a result of overcrowding. Given good care they will develop into thrifty, vigorous plants by autumn; they may then be moved to their permanent position in the garden or may be wintered over in the nursery beds.

Soil requirements: Although one or two species among the columbines have decided soil requirements, the long-spurred hybrids, which are those most commonly grown in our gardens, will thrive in any good garden loam. They respond to a moderate quantity of well-rotted manure, but fresh manure should never be allowed to come into direct contact with the plants. On the whole they are most at home in a loose, friable soil. In poorly drained locations they are apt to die out during the winter and are also more subject to root rot.

Culture: Most of the hybrid columbines will thrive either in full sun or in light shade. As the mature clumps attain considerable size, they should be allowed ample room for development and the plants should be spaced from 15 in. to 18 in. apart in the flower border. During the first year when the plants are small, interplantings of *Phlox divaricata* may be made. Even under the most favorable conditions many of the new hybrid strains of columbines are comparatively short-lived and will die out after a few years of bloom. It is well, therefore, always to have a few young plants coming on to take the place of those that do not survive.

Columbines may be transplanted with the greatest ease and large clumps may be moved when in full flower, provided they are watered well and are taken up with a generous quantity of soil. In fact, there are very few other perennials that may be moved with such certainty of success.

Season of bloom: If each individual bloom is nipped off as it fades, new buds will develop along the stems and columbines may be kept in flower for a month or six weeks. By prolonging their blooming season in this way, one

greatly increases their value in the spring garden. The bloom of some perennials is so fleeting that it hardly seems worthwhile to grow them, but when plants may be kept continuously in flower for nearly a month and a half, they soon become indispensable to the avid gardener. Columbines are particularly lovely when grown in combination with lupines, blue flax, *Nepeta* x *faassenii* (*N. mussini*) and *Thalictrum*, and the most exquisite color harmonies may be obtained by such combinations.

Not only are columbines lovely in the garden but they are among the choicest of all our flowers for cutting. They last unusually well and their daintiness and lovely soft colorings make possible the most beautiful indoor flower arrangements. The pink varieties are lovely when arranged with *Nepeta* x *faassenii* (*N. mussini*) and those with deep purple tints make a lovely contrast when arranged with sprays of bleeding-heart.

Winter protection: Columbines are very hardy and need no winter protection except in severe climates. Dry oak leaves, which will not mat down over the crowns, afford an excellent covering and may be held in place by small evergreen boughs. Salt hay is also good as a winter mulch.

Insect pests and diseases: See Chapter 32.

Artemisia lactiflora (white mugwort)

With its creamy-white blossoms, which are borne on tall, graceful stems *Artemisia lactiflora* is one of the most useful background plants for the perennial border. When grown under favorable conditions, the plants reach a height of 5 ft. or more. The soft tone of the flowers is a pleasant foil for blossoms of a more brilliant hue, and they may be used very effectively in combination with *gladiolus*, *Salvia farinacea* and *S. azurea*. The foliage is somewhat coarse and heavy and forms a dense background mass.

Exposure: *Artemisia lactiflora* thrives best in full sun.

Soil requirements: If the plants are to reach maximum development they should be grown in a fertile, deeply prepared, fairly moist soil. On poor soil, and with an inadequate supply of moisture, *Artemisia* will make spindly growth and produce but little bloom.

Propagation: Usually by the division of old clumps in early spring or in the autumn. The plants may also be propagated by seed or by cuttings.

Culture: *Artemisia lactiflora* is one of the few tall border plants that usually do not require staking. The plants must, however, be given ample room to spread and should be spaced at least 15 in. apart.

Asclepias tuberosa (butterfly weed)

There is hardly a flower of greater decorative value in the garden than the brilliant and beautiful butterfly weed, which blooms during the midsummer months. The myriad orange flowers are borne in broad, flat umbels of irregular outline. They are lovely both in the garden and for cutting, and are particularly striking when planted in combination with some of the tawny daylilies and the dwarf *Kniphofia*. The plants reach a height of 12 in. to 18 in. and remain in flower for many weeks.

Exposure: Full sun is essential.

Soil requirements: A light, sandy, exceedingly well-drained soil of medium fertility. If soil conditions are favorable, the plants will continue to thrive year after year, but in a heavy, poorly drained soil they are short-lived.

Propagation: The plants may be grown very easily from seed that is sown in the coldframe in early spring or in the open ground later in the season. The young seedlings must be transplanted carefully, as they suffer seriously if the fleshy tap root is broken or unduly disturbed. The seedling plants should be placed in their permanent location when still quite small, as the transplanting of old, established plants is very difficult and seldom successful. If plants are purchased from a nursery, they should be well established in pots to lessen the shock of transplanting.

Culture: The plants should be spaced from 10 in. to 12 in. apart. When they have once become well established, they will give generous bloom year after year provided that conditions of soil and exposure are favorable. They will withstand long periods of drought better than almost any other perennial.

Hardy Asters

Few perennials will give such a lavish display of autumn bloom as the hardy asters. In England one sees them used in profusion, and it is there that many of our most beautiful hybrid varieties have been developed, mostly from hybridization using our native American species. In the herbaceous garden, as a foreground for a shrub border or along the edge of a woodland, the hardy asters are happily at home. In the rock garden, the dwarf varieties are a welcome addition because they bloom at the end of the season and thus bring autumn color to a garden that has too often been considered only for its springtime effect.

Exposure: Most of the hardy asters prefer full sun but will thrive reasonably well in very light shade.

Soil requirements: Asters will thrive under almost any soil conditions, provided that the soil is not too saturated with moisture during the winter months. A medium to heavy loam is considered ideal — there are few perennials that are less exacting than the hardy asters. A soil that is exceedingly high in fertility is less desirable than one of moderate fertility, as the plants have a tendency to make too rank a growth and become somewhat leggy.

Propagation: Although hardy asters may be propagated very easily from seed, this method is seldom used. The usual method of propagation is by the division of the clumps in early spring, the young vigorous shoots being used.

ASTER CULTIVARS OF SPECIAL MERIT

LOW-GROWING	INTERMEDIATE TO TALL
'Audrey': pale blue	'Arctic': white
'Constance': shell pink	'Crimson Brocade': bright red
'Jean': lilac-blue	'Harrington's Pink': soft pink
'Jenny': cerise	'Marie Ballard': pale blue
'Lilac Time': lilac	'Ryecroft Purple': purple
'Niobe': white	'Winston Churchill': ruby red
'Snowsprite': white	

Cuttings may also be made from young shoots in the spring. New plants are usually purchased as rooted cuttings, but sometimes are field-grown divisions.

Culture: About every three years the clumps should be dug up, divided and replanted. If frequently renewed this way, the plants will not deteriorate. The dwarf varieties may be placed 1 ft. apart in the beds, and the larger growing ones 2 ft. The cushion types sometimes attain a spread of 2 ft. and should therefore be given ample room.

Campanula

The bellflowers are a large and varied group, and its members range in size from the tiny *C. caespitosa* of the rock garden to *C. pyramidalis*, which grows to a height of 6 ft. or more in the border. The flowers of all the species are bell-shaped; in some species they are produced singly, while in others they are borne in clusters. A few campanulas bloom in May, most bloom in June and July, and several last until August. Blue is the dominant color among the campanulas, with some white forms and pink in a few species. Many are perennial, while others are either annual or biennial. So varied and adaptable is the genus that few modern gardens should be without some form of *Campanula*.

C. carpatica (tussock bellflower)

The Carpathian harebell, which grows 12 in. tall, is delightful as an edging in the flower border, or along the top of a rock wall. It is graceful yet compact, with quantities of upturned bluebells. Plant from 8 in. to 10 in. apart.

C. elantines var. *garganica*

A trailing plant spreading to broad tufts. The flowers are wide bluebells that are divided into five petal-like points. Plant from 8 in. to 10 in. apart.

C. glomerata (clustered bellflower)

Has rather stiff stems bearing closely clustered, blue funnel-form flowers. Best in full sun or it may become invasive. *C. glomerata* 'Crown of Snow' has white flowers, and *C. glomerata* 'Joan Elliott' deep violet-blue flowers.

C. persicifolia (peach-bells)

Attains a height of 2 ft. to 3 ft. and produces violet-blue, wide, bell-like flowers in June and July. An improved variety with large purple-blue flowers known as 'Telham Beauty' is even more beautiful. 'Moerheimi' is semidouble, creamy-white. The plants should be spaced from 12 in. to 15 in. apart, and they should be lifted and divided every second or third year.

C. pyramidalis (chimney bellflower)

A narrow, columnar form that reaches a height of 5 ft. or 6 ft. The flowers, which open in August, are a clear, deep blue and continue in bloom for five or six weeks. Plant from 15 in. to 18 in. apart.

C. rotundifolia (common harebell)

The famous and well-loved bluebells of Scotland. It is a compact plant, 6 in. or more high, which sends up thin stems bearing hanging blue, bell-shaped flowers from June to September. Plant from 4 in. to 6 in. apart.

Exposure: Most of the bellflowers are best grown in a sunny location, although several of the dwarf species will thrive in partial shade.

Soil requirements: The bellflowers require a rich garden loam with a neutral or slightly alkaline reaction. The soil should be well prepared before planting.

Propagation: Almost all bellflowers may be raised from seed, by cuttings made from young growth in spring or by the division of old clumps. Seedlings raised to partial growth by autumn are carried over the winter in cold-frames and transplanted to the garden in the spring.

Chrysanthemum

The brilliant autumn tones of ash, oak and maple in the woodlands, and the deep bronze and golden russets of the chrysanthemums in the garden, bring to a close the season's pageantry of color and bloom. No other flowers can take the place of the chrysanthemums in the autumn garden, and from mid-September on until frost cuts them down, they hold the center of the stage. With the introduction of hybrids that are noted both for their early bloom and for their winter hardiness, the season of bloom has been greatly extended, and it is possible to grow chrysanthemums in northern gardens with every assurance of success.

Chrysanthemums may be handled very satisfactorily in several ways. They may be grown throughout the season in beds or borders of mixed perennials, or they may be grown in nursery plots until they are almost ready to come into bloom, at which time they should be lifted and moved into the garden. If facilities permit, it is wise to follow the latter procedure, as the plants may be grown under more carefully controlled conditions and will consequently make better growth. If grown this way, they will give a greater abundance of bloom, which will usually more than compensate for the additional labor involved.

The essentials for the successful culture of hardy chrysanthemums are: vigorous, healthy plants for spring planting; a sunny location; a well-drained, fertile soil; an adequate supply of moisture throughout the growing season; careful attention to the pinching back of the plants; and protection against insect pests and diseases.

Exposure: Chrysanthemums thrive best in a sunny location. If grown in partial shade, the plants have a tendency to become spindly and the lower leaves are apt to shrivel and turn brown.

Soil requirements: A light, rich, well-drained soil is considered ideal for chrysanthemums. The plants are notoriously rank feeders and require abundant quantities of plant food to attain their maximum development. Liberal quantities of manure or compost should be incorporated in the bed before planting, and the condition of the soil may be further improved by an application of a 5−8−6 complete fertilizer, applied at the rate of 1 lb. to every 30 sq. ft. The application of fertilizer should be made in early spring, at least a week or more before planting. Chrysanthemums grow best in a soil with a pH that is just below the neutral point, and lime should be applied if the soil has a tendency to be acid. During the summer months, from the time of the last pinching back until the time when the buds begin to show color, it is wise to make weekly applications of liquid manure. This practice will greatly stimulate growth and will prove to be of decided benefit to the plants. If liquid manure is not readily available, a biweekly application of a high-analysis, quickly soluble fertilizer may be made.

Propagation: Well-rooted cuttings, sold as small pot-grown plants, may be purchased in the spring from any reliable nursery. After a selection of desirable varieties has been obtained, it is possible to maintain or increase the stock by propagating new plants each spring. This may be done either by the division of old clumps or by cuttings taken from the young shoots as they start into growth in the spring. (See Chapter 34 on propagation.)

Culture: Chrysanthemums make their maximum growth during hot weather, and throughout this period they require a liberal supply of moisture. If the plants suffer a serious check at any time during this period, it will often result in a loss of the lower leaves, which seriously injures the general appearance of the plant.

The pinching back of the plants, which is sometimes spoken of as summer pruning, is a factor of great importance in the culture of garden chrysanthemums. After three or four pairs of leaves have formed, the growing tip of the shoot should be pinched back. From three to five side shoots will then develop and these, in turn, should be pinched back to induce further branching. For the early-flowering varieties, no pinching should be done after the middle of July; the late-flowering types should not be pinched back after the early part of August. The importance of this summer pruning can hardly be overemphasized. If it is neglected, the plants will assume a spindly habit of growth, sprawling out over the garden in an ungainly fashion, and will produce but little bloom. If the pinching is done systematically, however, the plants will develop into broad, spreading bushes, bearing many strong, flowering stems.

Hardy varieties may be left in the garden during the winter, while the more tender types will need the protection of a coldframe. Many gardeners prefer to dig such clumps as may be needed for propagation as soon as the flowering season is over, and to heel them in, in a coldframe. In the spring, as soon as the plants start into growth, they may be lifted and divided, or cuttings may be taken.

For the control of insect pests and disease on chrysanthemums, see Chapter 32.

Types of Hardy Chrysanthemums

Thousands of chrysanthemum cultivars have been developed and any selection of the better ones available today would not only be arbitrary but soon superseded by newer versions.

Classification of the numerous types available is based mainly on flower form and, to a lesser extent, on their habit of growth.

Cushion type—the dwarf hardy spreading types.

Decorative type—the most common garden type. Petals are regularly or irregularly reflexed. The flowers are 1½ in. to several inches across, with the petals varying in length.

Pompon type—the flowers are usually spherical, not over 4 in. broad. Some have incurved petals in the center of the flower head.

Spoon type—the disk florets (those that form the central "eye") are rather flat, while the ray florets (those that form the "petals") are regularly arranged and spoon-shaped.

Single and Daisy-flowered types—the disk florets form a daisylike "eye" in the center, while the ray or petallike florets are arranged in not more than five rows.

Delphinium

Delphiniums contribute great distinction to a garden composition by the sheer beauty of their form and the richness of their coloring. The low-growing types with their starry, single flowers of clear sky-blue are delightful when used in great drifts along the front of the border, and the towering, majestic blooms of the larger types are a veritable glory during the days of early summer.

Many fine hybrid strains of delphinium have been developed both in this country and in England (D. elatum hybrids). The flower spikes of these hybrids are broad at the base and taper toward the tip, the blooms being clustered closely along the stem. The plants are of extraordinarily vigorous growth and often attain a height of 6 ft. to 8 ft. There is considerable variance in the seedlings, both single and double forms being common, and the flowers range in color from deep purple and maroon through the lighter shades, many very beautiful contrasts being found.

Although the spectacularly beautiful new hybrid types have largely superseded the older types, there are still many gardeners who love the lighter form and the clear, sky-blue coloring of the old-fashioned Delphinium x belladonna. It most surely deserves a place in the cutting garden, as it is generous with its bloom, and is lovely when used in combination with roses and other June flowers. It is also less exacting in its cultural requirements and less susceptible to disease than some of the newer types, and it will often thrive in areas where the giant hybrids have proved difficult of culture. 'Connecticut Yankees,' an all-American selection, is a distinctly new type and blooms the first year, base branching, often with up to twenty-five spikes on mature plants; lilac, purple, light, medium and dark blue. Excellent for cutting; 2½ ft. to 3 ft.

There are also several intermediate and low border types *(D. grandiflorum)*, which are of great merit and deserve to be more widely grown. The very dwarf forms are hardly more than 8 in. to 10 in. in height, the intermediate forms about 15 in. The colors range from a deep gentian blue to the lovely, soft, clear blue known as Cambridge blue; there is also a pure white form. The plants are branching in habit and the single flowers are borne in great profusion. The plants remain in flower for many weeks and are particularly lovely when grown in combination with some of the annuals along the front of the border. If the seeds of these dwarf and intermediate types are sown early in the spring, they will usually bloom well the first season.

Climatic range: Delphiniums thrive in a moderately cool climate, and they do exceedingly well in high altitudes or near the seashore. They are unable to withstand intense summer heat and are therefore not well adapted to the South. If grown in southern climates, they are usually treated as annuals.

Propagation: Delphiniums may be propagated by seed, by cuttings or by the division of old clumps. As the plants seldom come true from seed, unless careful hand pollination is practiced, it is necessary to resort to cuttings or to the division of old clumps if one desires to perpetuate new plants of a given cultivar such as those named above. It is possible, however, to obtain many very beautiful plants from carefully selected seed. There are several large firms both in this country and in England that have made a specialty of delphiniums. For years they have maintained extensive trial grounds, and by crossing desirable varieties they have produced some fine hybrid strains. If seed is obtained from any of these reliable sources, one will usually find that a large percentage of the plants are of excellent type and possess great beauty. A few may be disappointing, but these can readily be discarded. It is an excellent practice to allow the young seedling plants to

DELPHINIUMS OF SPECIAL MERIT

D. x *belladonna* (garland larkspur): low-growing, 3 ft. to 4 ft. Open-branching habit, with numerous short spikes and looser flower arrangement than hybrids of the *D. elatum* group; also blooms for a longer period. Light blue flowers.

D. x *belladonna* ('Bellamosa'): dark blue flowers, 3 ft. to 4 ft.

D. x *belladonna* 'Casa Blanca': pure white flowers, vigorous growth, to 5 ft.

D. x *belladonna* 'Lamartine': deep purplish-blue flowers, 3 ft. to 4 ft.

D. 'Connecticut Yankees': densely branched, to 2½ ft.; very free-flowering. Blossoms loosely arranged on the spikes in shades of blue, purple, lavender and white.

D. elatum hybrids: the large-flowered, stately hybrids growing to 6 ft. to 8 ft. in height. English strains include the Blackmore and Langdon Hybrids and the Wrexham Hybrids. The Pacific Hybrids, developed on our own West Coast, are among the most beautiful of all garden flowers ever developed scientifically. They include the following named cultivars:

D. 'Astolat': shades of lavender and pink with a black or gold "bee" or central "eye."

D. 'Black Night': deep purple with a black "bee."

D. 'Blue Bird': medium blue with a white "bee."

D. 'Blue Jay': dark blue, no contrasting "bee."

D. 'Elaine': pink to rosy-lilac with a white "bee."

D. 'Galahad': pure white, no contrasting "bee."

D. 'Guinevere': inner petals lavender, outer petals light blue, with a white "bee."

D. 'King Arthur': deep violet with a white "bee."

D. 'Percival': pure white, with a black "bee."

D. 'Summer Skies': soft blue, with a white "bee."

D. grandiflorum (often listed in catalogues as *D. chinense,* Siberian or bouquet larkspur): Frequently treated as a biennial. Grows to 1½ ft. to 2 ft., flowers in late summer and has a slender branching habit. Flowers violet-blue.

D. grandiflorum 'Album': white.

D. grandiflorum 'Blue Mirror': gentian blue.

D. grandiflorum 'Cambridge Blue': rich, light blue.

produce one or two blooms during the first season while they are in the nursery rows, as it is then possible to select those of merit and to discard those that are less desirable.

By seed Delphinium seed loses its vitality very rapidly if kept under average storage conditions, but if stored at a cold temperature, the seed will retain its viability for many months. If delphinium seed, whether home-produced or purchased, is to be kept for any length of time before it is sown, it should be stored in the refrigerator in a moisture-proof container.

There are a number of flower seeds that require low temperatures for best germination and delphinium seeds are in this group, the optimum temperature range being 42° to 55° F. Reasonably good germination can usually be obtained by sowing under ordinary conditions, provided the seed is viable, but the nearer one approaches the optimum temperature the better the germination will be. An excellent way for the home gardener to obtain maximum germination is to mix the seed with sterile damp sand and moist peat moss and to place it in a sealed polyethylene bag in the refrigerator. It must be watched carefully. As soon as the seed sprouts, it should be removed and the sand, peat moss and sprouted seeds may be sown immediately in flats or seedbed, where the medium is sterile, being handled from this point on in the usual way. When delphinium seeds are sown under ordinary conditions, every effort should be made to keep the temperature as cool as possible. If sown in late summer in a frame or out of doors, the seedbed should be shaded. If sown indoors early in the spring, the seed pan or flat should be placed in the coolest place possible until after germination has occurred.

As delphinium seedlings are very susceptible to damping-off, every precaution should be taken to ensure protection. The seeds should be treated before they are sown, in order to control preemergent damping-off, and the medium in which the seeds are sown should be sterile. (For complete details of seed sowing, see Chapter 34 on propagation.)

By cuttings Some delphinium plants may be propagated very readily from cuttings, while an attempt to secure rooted cuttings from others results only in failure. Best results will be obtained from plants that are brought into the greenhouse and forced slowly, rather than from those that are left in the open ground, as more cuttings will be produced and they will root more readily. Those plants that are to be used for propagation should be lifted in the autumn after the first killing frost and placed in a coldframe, where they should be allowed to remain until late in January. When brought into the greenhouse, they should be placed in a moderately cool temperature.

Cuttings may be taken when the shoots have reached a height of from 2 in. to 3 in., each cutting being taken with a very small heel and treated with a weak-strength root-inducing hormone. (See Chapter 34 on propagation.) The cuttings should be soaked in water for an hour before they are placed in the propagating bench. Either pure sand or a mixture of sand and peat moss may be used as the rooting medium, and every precaution should be taken during the first few days to see that the cuttings do not wilt. After the first week watering should preferably be done by subirrigation, as it is wise to keep the foliage and stems free from moisture. The shading should be gradually diminished, and as soon as new leaf growth appears, the shade may be entirely removed. When the cuttings have become well rooted, they may be lifted with care and planted in pots.

By division Old clumps of delphiniums may be lifted and divided in early spring. (See Chapter 34 on propagation.) The work must be done carefully if success is to be assured. The soil should be shaken away from the roots and the plants should be gently pulled apart with the fingers. If the clump is cut or roughly torn apart, the crown is apt to be badly bruised and various forms of fungus and bacterial rot will gain easy entrance.

Exposure: Delphiniums thrive best in a sunny location where there is sufficient protection from severe wind. Good air circulation is essential. If delphiniums are planted in a shady position, or where the circulation of air is poor, the growth tends to be weak and spindly and the blooms are inferior.

Soil requirements: Delphiniums require a mellow, well-drained, deeply prepared soil of a neutral or slightly alkaline reaction. They are not acid-tolerant and if the soil has a pH lower than 6.0, an application of lime should be made to bring the soil reaction up to neutral or slightly above neutral. The application should preferably be made several months previous to planting.

The texture of the soil does not seem to be a matter of great importance, as delphiniums grow almost equally well in a fairly heavy clay or in a light, sandy loam, provided that the soil is well drained and that other conditions are favorable.

The small-flowered, small-spiked types give the most satisfactory results when grown on a soil of moderate fertility. If such plants are grown on an exceedingly rich soil or if they are fed heavily, they have a tendency to become floppy and leggy and the size and quality of the blooms show little or no improvement. The large-flowered types, which normally produce tall, massive spikes of bloom, present quite a different problem. If maximum development of the plant, and flower spikes of superior quality are desired, the soil must be of high fertility and heavy annual feeding is necessary. For many years it was the common practice to use manure in liberal quantities in the preparation of delphinium beds, but the present consensus is in favor of commercial fertilizers, as it has been found that manure is conducive to the spread of crown rot and other fungus diseases and therefore its use is not advisable. Some of the most successful growers of delphiniums of exhibition quality follow the practice of mixing a 12–16–12 complete fertilizer with the soil at the time of planting. A topdressing of the same fertilizer is applied to established clumps early in the spring, and after the first blooming period an application is made of a fertilizer with a lower nitrogen content, a 4–16–20 complete fertilizer being recommended.

Culture: Delphiniums are very dependent upon an adequate supply of moisture during their active period of growth and the soil should receive a thorough soaking at least once a week. In many seasons the natural rainfall will supply the needed moisture, but if this is not adequate, it is wise to resort to artificial watering.

It is possible to transplant delphiniums either in the autumn or in the spring, and since the plants have a fine and fibrous root system they may be moved with comparative ease. As delphiniums are among the first herbaceous plants to start growth in the spring, autumn planting is generally preferred as the plants undoubtedly suffer less shock. If the work is done with extreme care, it is possible to move quite large plants when they are just coming into bloom. The plants must be lifted with a generous quantity of earth in order that the root system may remain practically intact. This work should preferably be done on a cloudy day, otherwise it will be advisable to provide light shade for a few days. The plants should be kept thoroughly watered until they are well established.

When planting delphiniums, it is advisable to use a mixture of sand and charcoal about the crown of each plant as this facilitates drainage and consequently lessens the danger of crown rot.

If blooms of superior exhibition quality are desired, not more than three flower stalks should be allowed to develop on a single plant. The remaining stalks should be cut away before they have had an opportunity to make any growth. When grown for mass effect in the garden, however, healthy, vigorous plants should be capable of producing from six to eight good spikes of bloom.

The large-flowering types should be given adequate room for development and the plants should be spaced from 18 in. to 2 ft. apart. The more dwarf types such as *D. chinense* should be spaced from 12 in. to 15 in. apart.

As soon as the flowering period is over, the plants should be given a topdressing, as recommended under Soil Requirements, and the flower stalks should be partially cut down. A small portion of the stalk and the lower leaves should be left until new growth has appeared at the base of the plant. The old stalks should then be cut down level with the surface of the ground, in order that water may not collect in the hollow stems projecting above the soil. If new growth has already started at the base of the plant before the flowering period is over, as occasionally happens, the stalks may be cut down to the ground as soon as the blooms have faded. The second bloom will never quite equal the first in size or quality, but through the late summer months the blue of the delphiniums is a very welcome note in the garden and the plants will provide good material for cutting.

It is good common practice to lift and divide

17.2 Who has not childhood memories of bleeding-heart (Dicentra spectabilis)? *Photo Grant Heilman*

delphinium clumps every second year. If this procedure is followed, a stock of young and vigorous plants of the most desirable types and varieties is constantly maintained.

Staking: The proper staking of delphiniums is of utmost importance. Unless one is fortunate enough to have an unusually sheltered location, staking is absolutely essential, and even in positions that may seem very protected the wind will occasionally work havoc with these plants. The stems of delphiniums are rather hollow and brittle, and as the flower spikes of some of the improved types are exceedingly heavy when wet, the stems are not strong enough to resist the combination of rain and wind. An excellent method of staking is to place three light bamboo stakes close to each plant and, at a distance of about 18 in. above the soil, tie a loop of plastic tape or twine, winding it securely about each stake. During heavy storms when there is driving wind and rain, it may be necessary temporarily to protect some of the individual flower spikes by tying them as far up as the very tip to a stout stake.

Winter protection: Delphiniums are far more sensitive to heat than they are to cold, and they are capable of withstanding severe winter weather with very little protection. It is the alternate freezing and thawing of the ground and excessive amounts of surface water that are usually responsible for losses during the winter months. It is, therefore, advisable to provide good drainage about the crown of each plant. A little mound of sand placed over the crown late in the autumn will facilitate drainage and will afford excellent protection.

For control of insect pests and diseases, see Chapter 32.

Dicentra spectabilis (bleeding-heart)

Bleeding-heart is an old favorite, associated with gardens of long ago, but its popularity has remained undiminished through the years. It is one of the most beautiful of our spring-flowering perennials and deserves a place in every garden. Its graceful form, the beauty of its bloom and the quality of its foliage make it one of the most valuable plants for the spring border. Even in a small garden bleeding-heart does not seem out of place in spite of the wide spread of its arching branches. The foliage is a delicate green in color with a glaucous sheen, and the graceful stems bear hanging, deep pink, heart-shaped flowers that diminish in size toward the tip of the branches. It flowers in spring, with the tulips and the late narcissus, and remains in bloom for almost six weeks. By midsummer the foliage begins to die down and gradually disappears entirely. The plants reach a height of from 2 ft. to 4 ft. with an almost equal spread.

Exposure: Full sun or partial shade.

Soil requirements: A deep, rich loam, well supplied with organic matter, is desirable, and an adequate supply of moisture is essential.

Propagation: Bleeding-heart may be propagated by seed, by division, by root cuttings or by stem cuttings. Cuttings may be taken from the young shoots as they start into growth in the spring or soon after flowering.

Culture: When in flower, the plants need ample room and should be spaced at least 2 ft. apart. They are seldom planted in clumps, but rather are used as accent plants in the overall planting scheme. After the leaves have begun to die down, shallow-rooted annuals or chrysanthemums may be planted to fill the vacancy left by the disappearing foliage of the bleeding-heart. The plants resent frequent moving and when once well established they may be left undisturbed for many years. The roots should be planted in an upright position and placed at a depth of 2 in. to 3 in.

Gypsophila (baby's breath)

The wiry, twisted stems of *Gypsophila* bear their narrow, gray-green leaves so sparsely that the plants seem almost transparent. The myriad small flowers are borne in great profusion, and the effect is that of a veil thrown over a portion of the garden, a fairylike foil for the more colorful flowers of the border.

G. paniculata

The old-fashioned type, forming a symmetrical mass almost 3 ft. in height and with an almost equal spread. There are both single- and double-flowered forms, blooming in late summer.

G. paniculata 'Bristol Fairy'

One of the finest cultivars, flowering almost continuously throughout the summer. The flowers are much larger than those of the type, being fully double and pure white in color.

G. paniculata 'Compacta'

Has single flowers and only grows 2 ft. to 2½ ft. high, with a similar width.

G. paniculata 'Compacta Plena'

A double-flowered form of the above type.

G. paniculata 'Perfecta'

Similar to *G. paniculata* 'Bristol Fairy,' but the flowers are nearly two times larger, double and exceedingly handsome.

G. repens

A dwarf, trailing type suitable for the front of the perennial garden, bearing myriads of tiny white flowers in July and August.

G. repens var. 'Rosy Veil'

A dwarf form bearing double flowers of a clear, soft pink. It blooms fully two weeks earlier than the larger types and flowers almost continuously throughout the summer. It reaches a height of about 2 ft. and is excellent for use in the front of the border.

Exposure: Full sun is essential as the plants will not thrive in even light shade.

Soil requirements: A light, well-drained soil of medium fertility and high in lime content is necessary. The very name *Gypsophila,* meaning gypsum-loving, denotes the preference these plants show for limestone soils. Gypsophilas are noted for their ability to grow well on dry, rather poor soils. Wet soil, particularly in winter, is not suitable.

Propagation: By seed, by cuttings and by the division of old plants. The double-flowered varieties are usually grafted on the roots of the single-flowering types.

Culture: The gypsophilas require very little in the way of care and attention. The dwarf types should be spaced from 15 in. to 2 ft. apart, the larger types from 2½ ft. to 4 ft. as they form large masses.

Hemerocallis (daylily)

The modest lemon lily, long a favorite in old-time gardens, is now available in lovely new forms and in enchanting colors. The botanical name, derived from two Greek words—*hemera,* meaning "day," and *kallos,* meaning "beautiful"—was bestowed upon it because of the fleeting beauty of the flowers, which last only for a day. The daylilies are native to Asia. The lemon lily was introduced into England in 1596 from Siberia and was brought to this country by the early colonists. Other species were brought in by the captains of the early clipper ships and thus found their way into the gardens of New England.

During the latter years of the nineteenth century interest in the daylily waned, and it was not until the development of the new hybrids that it again became appreciated. The pioneer work in breeding, which resulted in the introduction of the first hybrid daylilies to be developed in this country, was done by Dr. A. B. Stout at the New York Botanical Garden. Work in hybridization is now being carried on in every section of the country by professionals and amateurs alike, and there is a steadily increasing demand for varieties of proven merit. Literally thousands of cultivars have been produced, and the existence of the thriving American Hemerocallis Society attests to the present popularity of the daylily.

SPECIES HEMEROCALLIS

Hemerocallis aurantiaca (orange daylily): Has rich orange flowers shaded to brown in June and July.
Hemerocallis citrina (citron daylily): Has fragrant pale yellow blossoms in June and July.
Hemerocallis dumortieri: Has flowers of rich yellow inside and bronzy-yellow outside, blooming in May.
Hemerocallis fulva (tawny daylily): Deep coppery-orange, darkening to crimson, with flowers in great numbers in July and August. This is the species that has naturalized itself so profusely throughout the eastern states.
Hemerocallis lilioasphodelus (syn. *H. flava,* lemon daylily): Has fragrant lemon or canary flowers in May and June; grows about 3 ft. high.
Hemerocallis middendorffii: Has deep orange flowers in June and July.

Among these beautiful new hybrids there is considerable variation in form and a wide range of colors. Some varieties have wide, overlapping petals, others have slightly recurved petals, and others frilled, crinkled and ruffled petals. Some of the blooms resemble wide, flaring trumpets, others are graceful, chaliced cups and some are almost bell-like. The colors range from palest lemon-white through tones of ivory-buff to a soft yellow, golden-yellow, apricot and orange; and from rose-pink, delicate shrimp-pink and violet-pink to wine-red, Indian red, claret, deep maroon and dark ebony-purple. And there are many lovely intermediate pastel shades and polychromes.

Considerable attention is now being given to a relatively new group known as the tetraploid daylilies. These are cultivars whose chromosomes have been doubled; they are generally more robust and have larger flowers than the standard or diploid cultivars. There are tall, intermediate, dwarf and midget types. The dwarf varieties have large blooms but low-growing foliage, and attain a height of 18 in. to 24 in. The midget varieties have small flowers, slender grasslike foliage and seldom reach a height of more than 12 in. to 18 in.

The blooms of most daylilies last only a single day. Toward evening the flowers close and wither. But as long as flower buds continue to form, the bloom of today is replaced with a fresh bloom on the morrow, and many varieties continue to bloom for six weeks or more. The flowers of some of the new hybrids remain

17.3 Daylilies (Hemerocallis), *in hundreds of cultivars ranging from creamy-yellow through butter, apricot and orange to tawny garnet and smoky brown-purple, are dependable, prolific and long-seasoned. Photo Carlton Lees*

open until very late in the evening, while a few varieties even remain open a full twenty-four hours. Some of these are evening bloomers, which open at dusk and remain open until the following evening. These varieties are very popular in some sections of the South.

By selecting early, mid-season and late varieties, it is possible to obtain a succession of bloom throughout the season. The very early cultivars will come into bloom with the iris, and some of the late cultivars will continue to flower until severe frosts bring the season to a close.

Daylilies can be used with dramatic effect in many planting compositions: in the perennial border, in the foreground of shrubbery plantings, as an accent in a foundation planting or beside a pool. They are particularly effective when planted in sweeping drifts or masses against a wall or fence, or when used as a ground cover to clothe an unsightly bank. A clump planted at the base of a small tree has an informal charm, and they will adapt themselves very happily to odd corners that might otherwise be bare and uninteresting.

The daylily, beautiful when in bloom, can also be enjoyed for its foliage. The foliage is at-

tractive, appealing when the young growth is pushing upward in the spring and valued, too, for its lush, all-season effect. Some cultivars have foliage that is evergreen, but with most the foliage dies down in the autumn.

Each year sees the advent of many new cultivars. Demand is so great among fanciers that some of these may command initial prices of $100 or more. Numerous nurseries exist in this country that specialize in *Hemerocallis* exclusively and there are an almost bewildering number of cultivars available, most of which are excellent. Any listing of the better cultivars would be highly arbitrary and very soon out of date. Each year a popularity poll is published in the *Hemerocallis Journal* (American Hemerocallis Society). This includes all the current favorites on a regional basis, and those who wish to keep their daylily collection up to date with the most popular cultivars would do well to consult this publication.

Climate and exposure: The daylily is one of the few perennials, if not the only perennial, that will flourish and give a good account of itself in all parts of our country. It is immune to heat, is completely winter hardy, and possesses an extraordinary capacity to survive floods and drought.

Most daylilies will thrive well in either full sun or partial shade. There are a few cultivars that will even do reasonably well in heavy shade. The flowers of some of the new hybrids have a tendency to fade or wilt in very intense sun and are at their best when grown in a location where they will receive light shade, or shade for at least a portion of the day. In general, most daylilies prefer morning sun and some afternoon shade.

Soil requirements: A good, sandy loam is considered ideal, but most daylilies will thrive on soils of widely varied types and are not exacting in their demands. Good drainage is, however, an important consideration.

Propagation: Daylilies are very easily propagated by the division of old clumps. The plant should be lifted with a spading fork and the clump gently pulled apart. The most favorable time for dividing old clumps and resetting the plants is from late summer to late autumn. Planting may also be done in very early spring but is less advisable.

When planting divisions or newly purchased plants, a hole should be made that is large enough to accommodate the entire root system when it is spread out in a natural position. A little cone of soil should be made in the center of the hole to support the crown, as this will permit the roots to fan outward and downward. The soil should be worked in carefully among the roots. The crown should be set so that it is not more than an inch below the surface of the soil.

Tall varieties should be spaced about 30 in. apart, small varieties from 18 in. to 24 in. apart.

Culture: Daylilies are among the most adaptable of plants and there are few perennials less exacting in their demands. Indeed, they rate near the top among perennials requiring little care. They have practically no pests and diseases, and therefore require no spraying. The stems are strong and supple and require no staking. Daylilies thrive and bloom well on a meager diet, and the foliage shades the ground so completely that they require almost no cultivation. When the clumps become crowded, they benefit from being lifted, divided and replanted, and this should be done every few years if possible. But if it is not done the plants carry cheerfully on with somewhat less abundant bloom.

Heuchera (coralbells or alumroot)

The coralbells are charming, graceful plants with geraniumlike, evergreen to semievergreen foliage that forms a broad mat close to the ground. The wiry stems, rising above the leaves, bear panicles of tiny, nodding bells. The brilliant hue of the flowers, dispersed as it is into many small particles, makes a delightful sparkle of color and gives life and vivacity to the garden. The coralbells make excellent border plants, and they are also frequently used in rock gardens with pleasing effect. The flower stems vary in height from 12 in. to 18 in.

DAYLILY SPECIES AND CULTIVARS OF MERIT

H. x *brizoides*

The flowers are pale pink to white and are produced freely in May. The plant is robust in habit of growth, with excellent foliage.

H. sanguinea

The best known of all the coralbells. The brilliant crimson flowers are lovely for cutting and are produced in abundance over a period of several months, beginning in June. It is one of the principal parents of the following cultivars:

H. 'Chartreuse': flowers an unusual soft chartreuse color
H. 'Chatterbox': flowers deep rose-pink
H. 'Fire Sprite': large rose-red flowers
H. 'June Bride': large pure white flowers
H. 'Peachblow': flowers pink, tipped with white
H. 'Perry's White': pure white flowers from June to September
H. 'Rosamundi': one of the finest of the hybrids; the brilliant coral-pink flowers are borne in profusion over a period of several months; it is strong and robust in habit of growth
H. 'Scarlet Sentinel': large scarlet-red flowers
H. 'White Cloud': creamy-white flowers

Exposure: Full sun, or partial shade.

Soil requirements: A rich, well-drained loam is considered ideal, as the plants will not thrive in a heavy clay soil and tend to be easily heaved out of the ground in winter if the soil is overly wet.

Propagation: The most satisfactory method of propagation is the division of established plants. The plants may be lifted and divided either in the spring or in the autumn. If the divisions are made in the autumn, the young plants should be wintered over in a coldframe, and they should be kept well watered until they have become established. *Heuchera* may also be propagated by seed but since the seeds are usually of poor viability and do not germinate well, they should not be used to perpetuate named cultivars. Leaf cuttings may also be made. The leaf should be cut at the base of the leaf stalk with a sliver of the main stem attached.

Culture: Coralbells may be planted in the autumn or in early spring and the plants should be spaced from 6 in. to 8 in. apart. Spring planting is preferred in sections where the winters are severe.

As coralbells have a tendency to be heaved out of the soil during the winter, due to the alternate freezing and thawing of the gound, it is well to give plants extra attention in the early spring. If the plants have suffered from heaving they should be gently pressed back into the soil and a light mulch of compost should be placed around the crowns.

If plantings of coralbells are to be maintained in good condition, the plants should be lifted and divided every third or fourth year, the soil being well enriched before the plants are reset.

Hosta (plantain lily)

The plantain lily is valued for both its foliage and its flowers. The flower spikes rise above the dense masses of broad, green leaves, reaching a height of 1½ ft. to 2 ft., and bear small tubular flowers in shades of lavender and white. *Hosta* will flourish at the foot of a wall or on the north side of a building where little else will grow, and it is therefore of particular value for positions in semishade.

Hosta may be used to introduce interesting textural contrasts into the garden. The bold leaves of some species, and the contrasting heights, leaf shapes, colors and flowers of others, are ideal for this purpose. Massing plants together will produce valuable ground cover effects, but the larger-leaved species and cultivars are also effective as single specimens where their beautiful radial symmetry is best appreciated.

Hosta is very valuable where low maintenance is a concern. The plants practically never require division, and they survive for years with almost complete neglect. The only seasonal chore is the removal of the stems after the flowers have faded. These stems can be quite unat-

tractive if left on the plants, and if seed production is prevented by their removal, unwanted seedlings will not appear in the garden.

Exposure: Partial shade.

Soil requirements: Hosta does well in any ordinary garden soil but is better in a soil with a high moisture content. It makes luxuriant growth in rich, moist loam.

Propagation: The plants may be lifted and divided in early spring.

Culture: Since the plantain lily requires ample space for its best development, the plants should be spaced from 2 ft. to 3 ft. apart. They are of exceedingly simple culture, and demand little in the way of care and cultivation.

17.4 Hosta, *in many species and cultivars, is an extremely useful perennial, particularly in shaded places. Photo Carlton Lees*

HOSTA SPECIES AND CULTIVARS OF SPECIAL MERIT

H. decorata (blunt-leaved plantain lily)
Leaves oval with blunt tips, about 6 in. long, with prominent silvery margin. Clumps spread to about 2 ft. Flowers deep lilac on 2-ft. stems in August.

H. fortunei var. gigantea
Very large form of the above. Clumps may be up to 5 ft. in diameter at full maturity with good growing conditions; leaves up to 12 in. in length.

H. fortunei 'Marginato-alba'
Edges of the leaves have irregular shiny white bands.

H. fortunei 'Marginato-aurea'
Leaves have yellow borders.

H. lancifolia (narrow-leaved or Japanese plantain lily)
Lance-shaped leaves, 6 in. in length. Forms dense clumps about 2 ft. wide. Flowers pale lilac on 2-ft. stems in August.

H. plantaginea (syn. H. subcordata, fragrant plantain lily)
Has large white trumpetlike flowers up to 4 in. long, which are very fragrant. These appear on 2-ft. stems in late August and September. Mature clumps about 3 ft. wide.

H. sieboldiana (syn. H. glauca, blue-leaved or Siebold plantain lily)
One of the most beautiful of all foliage plants for the shaded perennial garden. The large, 12-in. long leaves are quite heavy in texture and gray-green with a bluish cast. Clumps at maturity are up to 3 ft. in width. The white flowers appear in July and frequently are hidden among the leaves.

H. sieboldiana 'Frances Williams'
A very desirable cultivar, with rounded glaucous leaves bordered cream and yellow.

H. tardiflora (autumn plantain lily)
Very small species, clumps seldom over 12 in. in width or height. The deep lavender-purple flowers appear in October.

H. undulata (wavyleaf plantain lily)
One of the most commonly grown of the plantain lilies, it withstands sunny conditions better than most other types. Leaves have wavy margins and are variegated white on green; flowers are pale lavender and appear in July. The plant forms clumps about 20 in. in diameter.

H. 'Betsy King'
Grown for its flowers, which are a rich purple and appear in August on 20-in. stems.

H. 'Honeybells'
The very fragrant striped lilac-lavender flowers appear in August on 3-ft. stems.

H. 'Royal Standard'
The white flowers are very sweetly scented, and appear in August and September on 2-ft. stems.

Iris

Irises contribute to the garden a quality distinctively their own. They have been important garden flowers for many centuries, and with their grace, delicacy of form and luminous colors they impart a radiance to the garden that is not equaled by any other flower.

In medieval times, the iris was so beloved by the people of France that it was given a special distinction and became the symbol of the royal house of France, and hence of the entire realm. It appears in many illuminated manuscripts, and in the heraldry, architecture and jewelry of the early Renaissance in France it was affectionately called *"Fleur-de-Lis."*

Not only are irises valued today for the rare quality they contribute to a planting composition but they are also greatly prized for their decorative qualities as cut flowers.

During the past quarter of a century remarkable progress has been made in breeding new and superbly beautiful varieties of iris. The color range has been extended to include dramatically lovely shades of pink and also many subtle and muted tones of rose, tawny sunset reds and violets, as well as exquisite blends.

Each year new varieties of iris are introduced. Medals and certificates of merit are awarded by the American Iris Society to varieties considered worthy of these coveted honors. Thus, over the years, a great number of varieties of exceptional merit, vigorous in growth and indescribably beautiful in form and color, have gradually replaced the older types. When new varieties are first introduced they are often very high in price, but within a few years, when stock has become more plentiful, they become available at more modest figures that are well within the budget of the average gardener.

There are many species, groups and subgroups of iris, each endowed with a special charm. Some are stately and majestic, others are diminutive in size; some prefer dry situations, others are at their best when grown by the waterside; some grace the spring garden with their bloom, others bring dramatic beauty to the garden in midsummer, and the fall-blooming irises are often in flower until late in the autumn.

With careful planning, many months of iris bloom may be obtained in the garden. A succession of bloom can be achieved, however, only through the planting of many species, groups and varieties. The diminutive and enchantingly lovely *I. reticulata*, blooming in very early spring, is the herald among the irises. This is followed in due succession by the Dutch iris, the dwarf bearded, intermediate bearded and tall bearded groups. During the summer months the Siberian, Spuria, Louisiana and Japanese groups carry on the gay pageantry of bloom, and the fall-blooming irises often continue to flower until cut down by heavy frosts.

Irises are classified into several groups, according to their root characteristics and their flower forms. Most of the more commonly cultivated types have fleshy roots known as rhizomes, while some types are cormous and a few have fibrous root systems.

Many of our garden irises, which originally came from central Europe, have a bearded tongue on the lower petals of the flowers.

These are known as the Pogoniris Group, *pogon* being the Greek word for beard. The beardless iris group, which includes many species from the Orient, is known as the Apogoniris Group, meaning "without a beard." Iris belonging to the Crested Group have a ridged growth on the lower petals in place of the beard.

Pogoniris Group (Bearded Iris)

Dwarf Bearded

This group includes several species, such as *I. pumila*, as well as many hybrid forms. Some types are miniature in size, hardly more than 3 in. or 4 in. high, while others reach a height of 10 in. There is also considerable variance in the form of the flowers, and a wide color range. The blooms of some varieties are of exquisite daintiness, while others are more voluptuous, resembling in form the blooms of the tall bearded group.

Dwarf irises are at home in well-drained pockets in the rock garden. They also are very effective when planted in drifts along a path or when used as an edging in a flower border, particularly combined with primroses and *Narcissus* and the early tulips. They are lovely, too, when planted in masses on a sunny slope, either alone or in combination with *Arabis alpina*, *Phlox subulata*, *Arenaria* and some of the other rock plants. Most dwarf irises bloom early in the spring, several weeks before the tall, bearded type, and there are also several autumn-blooming varieties.

The culture of dwarf bearded irises is similar to that of the tall bearded groups. Good drainage and a position in full sun are essential to their happiness. If conditions are favorable, they increase very rapidly and a single plant will develop into a large clump within a few years. In order to prevent crowding, they should be divided and replanted about every three years.

Intermediate

Many of the varieties in this group have been developed by hybridizing some of the dwarf types with the tall bearded types. The flowers are lovely in form, possessing many of the characteristics of the tall, bearded group, but are smaller and more delicate. Some varieties have ruffled or frilled petals, giving them distinction and charm. In height and season of bloom they are intermediate between the two groups, ranging in height from 12 in. to 18 in. and blooming with the mid-spring tulips. There are also several autumn-blooming varieties within the Intermediate Group.

Tall Bearded

The decorative landscape value of the tall bearded irises remains unchallenged through the years.

It is in this group that we find many of our most magnificent garden irises, superb in form and indescribably beautiful in color. No garden is complete without them, and in spring they bring dramatic beauty to many a planting composition.

Autumn-Flowering Group

After years of patient effort on the part of plant hybridizers, a new race of iris has been introduced that extends the flowering period through the autumn months. These irises have two or more distinct flowering periods, blooming in the spring and again in autumn, beginning in September and continuing until growth is checked by heavy frosts. Some varieties also flower intermittently throughout the summer months. Although hardy in northern gardens, these autumn-flowering irises are specially recommended for the South where the fall-blooming season may extend over many months. The plants vary in height from 15 in. to 30 in.

Culture of Bearded Iris

Climatic range: Bearded irises have an extraordinarily wide climatic range and are able to endure the intense heat of southern summers as well as the extreme cold of winters in the far North.

Exposure: Bearded irises should be planted in a sunny location if they are to be grown at their best. If planted on the north side of a building or in an otherwise shady location, they seldom thrive, the plants being weak and spindly in growth and the flowers decidedly inferior in size and in quantity of bloom.

Soil requirements: Bearded irises may be grown successfully on soils of widely varying types; it has been found that they do almost as well on

Fig. 17.1
Iris division
Below: *Cluster of iris to be divided.*

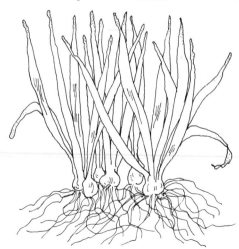

Division trimmed and ready for planting.

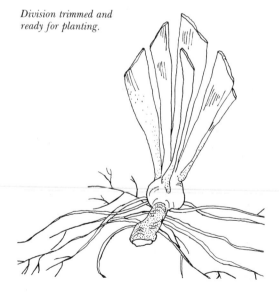

heavy clay soils as on sandy loam, provided that the soil is well drained. Good drainage is absolutely essential, as they do not thrive on soils that are saturated with moisture. Unless the soil is naturally well drained, some provision must be made for artificial drainage. While it is true that many irises will do reasonably well on rather poor soils, the fact must not be overlooked that the most thrifty plants capable of producing an abundance of bloom are to be found on soils of good fertility. If special beds or borders are to be devoted to irises, the soil should preferably be prepared several months in advance of planting. Well-rotted manure, compost or some commercial form of humus should be thoroughly incorporated into the soil and the soil should be deeply prepared. Although the bearded irises are generally classed among the more shallow-rooted plants, many of the feeding roots penetrate to a considerable depth. At the time of planting, an application of commercial fertilizer should be made at the rate of ½ lb. per square yard. The bearded irises prefer a soil that is very nearly neutral in reaction, although they will tolerate a very mildly acid soil as well as one with a considerable degree of alkalinity. As a general rule, they are classed among lime-loving plants.

Propagation: Bearded irises are propagated by the division of the rhizomes. The clump should be lifted from the soil with a spading fork and the rhizomes either cut or broken apart. Each fan of leaves should have a short, sound piece of rhizome with a number of strong, vigorous feeding roots attached to it. Any dead or shriveled leaves should be removed, and in the case of the tall bearded group, the foliage should be cut back to within 6 in. to 8 in. of the rhizome. The dwarf and intermediate types should be cut back proportionately. The ideal time for the division of bearded irises is the period immediately after flowering. As new root growth is made at this time, new plants will have an opportunity to become well established before winter and will usually produce a few blooms the following year. Late autumn planting is not advisable because the plants have had no opportunity to become anchored and are likely to be heaved

out of the soil during the winter. Clumps may be divided in the early spring, but the bloom is then sacrificed for that season as the plants will not flower until the following year.

Planting: The dwarf types of bearded iris may be planted from 5 in. to 6 in. apart if the effect of a large clump is desired. The intermediate and tall-growing types should be planted from 15 in. to 18 in. apart. If immediate mass effect is desired, the rhizomes may be placed as closely as 8 in. to 10 in. apart, but this practice is not recommended except as an occasional expedient, as the clumps soon become crowded and growth and vigor are sacrificed. When planting irises, the rhizome should not be covered deeply. The feeding roots should be spread out in a natural position, a hole of sufficient size having been prepared, and the upper portion of the rhizome should be barely covered with soil. Deep planting, particularly in heavy soils, makes the rhizomes more susceptible to rot. The nearly planted rhizomes should always be well firmed into the soil.

Culture: The cultural requirements of the bearded iris are not exacting. The plants require an abundance of moisture during the blooming season but are able to endure long periods of drought at other periods. The best bloom is usually produced the second, third and fourth years after planting. As soon as the rhizomes show evidence of becoming crowded, the clumps should be lifted and divided. Most iris plantings will continue to bloom well and will remain in good condition for a period of about five years. After this period, the rhizomes in the center of the clump usually become so crowded that the plants begin to deteriorate.

Each spring the soil about the clumps should be lightly cultivated, and if it seems advisable to improve the fertility of the soil an application of commercial fertilizer may be applied at the rate of ½ lb. per square yard. This should be sprinkled on the surface of the soil about the plants and cultivated lightly. The soil should then be thoroughly watered.

In the autumn the foliage should be cut back to within 4 in. or 5 in. of the rhizome and all dead or shriveled leaves should be removed.

Winter protection is not necessary except in areas where the winters are of extreme severity.

Throughout the season one should be constantly alert to detect the first signs of insect infestation or disease. Iris borers are a particular problem and should be controlled as soon as they are noticed. (See Chapter 32.)

Cultivars of Merit

So many cultivars of dwarf, intermediate or tall bearded iris are available from nurseries that any list of superior cultivars would be highly arbitrary and soon out of date. Each year the American Iris Society publishes a popularity poll in the *Bulletin of the American Iris Society,* which should be consulted by those who wish to maintain collections of the most popular cultivars.

Apogoniris Group (Beardless Iris)

Japanese iris *(I. kaempferi)*

The Japanese irises have become increasingly popular because of their great beauty and dignity. The flowers are characteristically flat and broad, the standards and falls being horizontal rather than ascending and descending. The flowers possess colors dominantly in the red-purple, purple, lavender, blue and white sector of the color scale. Some are a mahogany red and a few have a gray background tone with deep purple, violet or wine-red markings. The leaves are narrow and reedlike and the blooms, with their broad, crepelike petals, are borne on tall, erect stems that attain a height of 2½ ft. to 5 ft. With the exception of the fall-blooming bearded varieties, they are among the last of the irises to flower, blooming in late June and throughout July.

Exposure: Full sun is necessary for at least the major portion of the day.

Soil requirements: The Japanese irises require an abundance of moisture until after their flowering season is over. They are then able to withstand considerable drought, although they should never be allowed to dry out com-

JAPANESE IRIS CULTIVARS OF MERIT

'Eleanor Parry': hyacinth-violet
'Great White Heron': tall, white
'Iso-no-Kamone': medium, white
'Mountain Grotto': orchid-blue
'Nishike Yama': pansy-violet
'Repsime': azure blue
'Suehiro': deep lavender
'Summer Storm': deep purple

pletely. During the winter months they prefer a soil that is free from excessive moisture. It is almost the universal custom in Japan to flood the iris plantings during the period when the plants are in bud and in bloom, but during the balance of the year the soil is kept comparatively dry. Japanese irises should never be planted in a location where the water table rises to the surface of the ground during the winter months as such a condition will usually prove fatal.

Japanese irises grow best in a rich, highly fertile soil well supplied with organic matter and definitely acid in reaction. In preparing the soil, liberal quantities of leaf mold (preferably oak), peat moss and well-rotted cow manure (if obtainable) should be used. Lime should never be spread where Japanese irises are growing; liberal doses of this often prove fatal.

Propagation: Japanese irises may be readily propagated by the division of old clumps, the ideal time being late August or early September. If the divisions are made at this season, the young plants will reestablish themselves quickly and may give some bloom the following summer. Clumps may also be divided early in the spring, but the results are not as satisfactory because many of the divisions may fail to grow and only a small percentage will flower the following year. An entire clump may be lifted and divided, being pried apart with two strong spading forks until it is sufficiently loosened to fall into many natural divisions, or large pieces may be removed from established clumps without lifting them. It requires a stout spading fork with considerable pressure behind it to accomplish this feat. The rhizomes should not be allowed to dry out before planting. If immediate effect is desired in the garden, the divisions should consist of three fans of leaves. If, however, rapid increase of stock is desired, single fans may be planted. The foliage should be cut back to within 5 in. to 6 in.

Japanese irises may also be propagated by seeds. If the seeds are sown out of doors in the autumn as soon as they are ripe, they will germinate in the spring and will bloom in two to three years. They do not, however, come true from seed.

Planting: The rhizome of the Japanese iris is very slender, with many fibrous roots. At the time divisions are planted, these roots should be shortened to 5 in. or 6 in. The new roots develop from the backs of the leaf fans and the crowns should be planted 2 in. below the surface of the soil in order to enable these new roots to gain anchorage. For mass plantings that will remain undisturbed for many years, the plants should be spaced from 18 in. to 2 ft. apart. If clumps of Japanese irises are to be used in herbaceous borders or in other similar

17.5 Siberian iris (Iris sibirica) *by a rail fence at the edge of a meadow. Photo Grant Heilman*

locations, more immediate effect may be obtained if three, four or five divisions are planted about 10 in. apart.

Winter protection: With the exception of newly planted divisions, Japanese irises require no winter protection. Young plants that have not had an opportunity to become established are liable to suffer severely from the effects of heaving and it is, therefore, wise to protect them during the first winter. Oak leaves are excellent as a mulch if they are held in place by evergreen boughs. Stable manure may also be used. The Japanese iris is one of the very few members of the iris family for which a mulch of rotted manure can be used with impunity.

Siberian iris (*I. sibirica*)

The Siberian irises are of great decorative value in the garden and are enchantingly lovely as cut flowers. They are lavish with their bloom, a well-established clump sometimes producing more than fifty flowers. The blooms are borne well above the narrow, swordlike leaves, each slender stalk bearing from five to ten graceful flowers on branching pedicels. Varieties range from 2 ft. to 4 ft. in height and there is a wide range of colors, from pure white through delicate blue, lavender and violet to rich, velvety purple, with a few deep reds and reddish-purples.

Exposure: The Siberian irises are at their best when grown in full sun but will produce some bloom in partial shade if they receive several hours of sunlight during the day. In dense shade the plants exist but will not flower.

Soil requirements: For best development the plants prefer a fairly moist, highly fertile soil. Good drainage is essential, however, and Siberian irises should never be planted in a location where the crowns might be covered with water during the winter as they cannot survive the effects of a saturated soil during freezing weather. Before planting, the soil should be well enriched with rotted cow manure, rich compost or leaf mold. The plants are acid-tolerant but prefer a soil within the near neutral range.

Although Siberian irises are appreciative of soils that are high in fertility, they will make a remarkably good showing on rather poor soils. This is particularly true of some of the old cultivars such as 'Snow Queen,' which will thrive under the most adverse conditions.

Propagation: The clumps should be lifted and divided in late August and early September. Divisions may also be made in spring or immediately after flowering, but the percentage of plants that survive is far less than when divisions are made in late summer. The methods of making the divisions and of planting are the same as those for the Japanese iris, described in detail on page 286. The rhizomes should be planted 2 in. deep and the plants should be spaced from 15 in. to 18 in. apart.

In order to achieve a clump effect as quickly as possible in the garden, a small section containing from five to seven slender rhizomes should be selected for planting. If, however, rapid increase in stock is desired, smaller sections should be used. The Siberian irises have long, fibrous roots and when planting the divisions, it is important to see that the hole is of ample size so that the roots will not be cramped. Long-established clumps are sometimes very difficult to divide, as their roots have often formed a very dense mass.

Siberian irises may be propagated by seed but wide variation is found among the seedlings and it is a method seldom employed except by hybridizers.

Culture: Siberian irises are of extremely easy culture and are almost certain to do well under average conditions. They require abundant moisture before and during the flowering period if maximum bloom is to be obtained, but beyond this they need little care. They are rarely attacked by pests or diseases and the clumps may be left undisturbed for many years. No winter protection is necessary except in very cold climates, or in the case of young plants that have not become established. Under such conditions a light mulch of salt hay or some similar material will prove helpful.

SIBERIAN IRIS CULTIVARS OF MERIT

'Caesar's Brother': pansy-purple
'Congo Drums': deep purple
'Eric the Red': deep red
'Gatineau': clear, light violet
'Mountain Lake': clear blue
'Periwinkle': porcelain blue
'Seven Seas': violet-blue
'Snow Crest': pure white
'Snow Egret': ruffled petals, white
'Tycoon': rich, velvety purple
'Summer Sky': wisteria blue
'White Dove': tall, pure white

Spuria Iris Group (*I. spuria*)

The lovely spuria irises, often called the butterfly iris, are prized not only for their landscape value but also for their distinction as cut flowers. They have a unique and sprightly charm and are considered by many to be the best of all the irises for use in flower arrangements.

In height the spurias range from 2½ ft. to 5 ft. Each flower stalk usually produces four pairs of buds, the flowers being similar in form and size to the larger types of Dutch iris. The colors range from white through shades of yellow and bronze to deep brown, and from pale blue and lavender to deep blue. Some of the new hybrids are very beautiful in coloring.

The spurias bloom in midsummer, following the Siberian irises and overlapping the Japanese irises. In the South the period of bloom often lasts two months or more.

These irises may be grown in all sections of the country and have proved to be of particular value in the lower Rio Grande Valley.

Exposure: The spuria irises do best in full sun but will thrive in semishade. They are tolerant of large amounts of water but also have the ability to withstand long periods of drought.

Soil requirements: Members of this group reach their best development in a fertile soil that is retentive of moisture, but they are much less exacting regarding soil conditions than are many other iris. They can tolerate some acidity as well as mild alkalinity.

Propagation: The spuria irises may be easily increased by division, the clumps being lifted and divided in late summer or early autumn.

Culture: These hardy irises are of easy culture. To be brought to perfection they require abundant moisture throughout the growing season. They will form large clumps and may be left undisturbed for years.

Louisiana Iris (hybrid complex involving several *Iris* species native in the Southeast)

The beautiful Louisiana irises, although native to the swamps and bayous of the lower Mississippi, have proved extraordinarily hardy and adaptable and are now widely grown in many sections of the country. Unique in color and form, many of these species and their hybrids are startling in their beauty. They range in height from 2 ft. to 4 ft. Many of the flowers are flat in form, while others have flaring or hanging segments. In color the blooms range through velvety tones of deep garnet, rosy apricot, rose-petal pink, deep pansy-violet, pale lavender and ivory white.

Exposure: The Louisiana irises thrive either in sun or semishade.

Soil requirements: Members of this group prefer an acid soil with a very high moisture content.

Culture: Before planting, the soil should be well and deeply prepared. Liberal quantities of peat moss of the coarsest grade, coarse leaf mold, unscreened compost and rotted cow manure, if available should be thoroughly worked into the soil to a depth of 12 in. to 18 in. Although Louisiana irises can hardly be supplied with too much water during the growing season, care must be taken when they are being planted in a northern garden not to select a location where water would freeze about their roots during the winter, as this can prove fatal to the plants.

Vesper Iris (*I. dichotoma*)

The lovely vesper iris is unique among the irises, both in its habit of bloom and in the character of its root system. The flowers open in mid-afternoon and remain open until late in the evening. During the night the petals droop and curl into a small spiral, the faded flowers falling to the ground, to be followed the next afternoon by crisp, fresh blooms. There are sometimes as many as 50 to 100 blooms on a single plant. The flowers, which are borne on candelabrumlike branches, are dainty and graceful in form, hardly more than 2 in. across, and the flaring petals, in shades of blue, lavender or wine-red, are marked with touches of orange and grayish-blue tones. In height the plants range from 2 ft. to 3 ft., some being slightly taller. The vesper iris comes into flower in late July or early August and continues to produce its bountiful bloom until frost. The flowers are very attractive to hummingbirds, and to honeybees.

Exposure: The vesper iris will thrive either in full sun or in partial shade. It is extremely hardy and after it is well established can withstand temperatures as low as 15° F. below zero.

Soil requirements: A rich, heavy loam will provide soil conditions most favorable to good growth, but the vesper iris will also grow reasonably well in almost any type of soil.

Propagation: Unlike most members of the iris family, the vesper iris has a fibrous root system and does not produce a definite rhizome. It may be propagated both by seed and by the division of old clumps. Each division should have two or three strong eyes. The clumps should always be divided and the division replanted in the spring. If done in the autumn the young plants will not have time to become established before winter, and their chances of survival are slight.

After the divisions have been planted growth is slow at first, but when they are well started growth is more rapid and there is often some bloom the first year.

Culture: The vesper iris is of very easy cul-

IRIS PSEUDACORUS
CULTIVARS OF MERIT

I. pseudacorus 'Alba': a beautiful pure white form
I. pseudacorus 'Gigantea': a giant-flowered form
I. pseudacorus 'Immaculata': pure yellow without throat
 markings
I. pseudacorus 'Sulphurea': sulphur-yellow form

ture. It is subject to few pests and diseases and will do well under ordinary garden conditions. It prefers abundant moisture but will tolerate long periods of dry weather. If, during the blooming period, it suffers from lack of sufficient moisture it will cease flowering, but will bloom again when it receives the moisture it requires.

Iris pseudacorus (yellow flag)

The rich yellow blooms of *I. pseudacorus* are of striking beauty, being borne on tall, erect stems from 3 ft. to 4 ft. in height. There is no finer iris for the water garden or for naturalization along the banks of a stream.

Exposure: Full sun.

Soil requirements: *I. pseudacorus* will thrive in almost any location but prefers a very damp soil.

Propagation: Readily propagated by division of the rhizomes.

Culture: As *I. pseudacorus* is very hardy, it demands little in the way of care and cultivation after it has once become established.

American Beardless Species

Iris versicolor

This is the beardless marsh iris of our northern states. It is of particular value for the water garden or for naturalization along the banks of streams. The flowers are of a lavender-purple hue.

Exposure: Sun or semishade.

Soil requirements: Rich, very moist soil.

Propagation: The division of the rhizomes.

Culture: As *I. versicolor* is perhaps the most rugged of the irises, it requires no special culture. It thrives in almost any location and is most amazing in its adaptability.

Crested Iris

Iris cristata (dwarf crested iris)

This lovely native of the southern highlands is found growing on thinly wooded hillsides and along stream banks from Virginia southward to Georgia and westward to Missouri. It is exquisite, though hardly more than 4 in. in height. The diminutive flowers, their lavender petals touched with crested gold, spread their bloom above the carpet of soft green leaves in late spring, and sun-splashed patches of it along a woodland path hold joy for all who pass. *I. cristata* 'Alba' is a beautiful white-flowering cultivar.

Exposure: Partial shade is best and *I. cristata* thrives in open woodlands. It also does reasonably well in full sun, but definitely prefers afternoon shade.

Soil requirements: A gravelly, well-drained soil, rich in humus, is ideal, although *I. cristata* will succeed well in almost any good garden soil.

Propagation: This species is readily propagated by division of the small rhizomes. This may be accomplished with a fair degree of success at almost any time during the growing season, but very early spring is preferred. The roots should be spread out in a natural position and the rhizomes should be barely covered with soil.

Culture: The rhizomes should be planted from 5 in. to 6 in. apart. When the clumps become too crowded, the plants should be lifted and divided. Careful weeding must be done throughout the season in order to prevent more vigorous plants from crowding out the small, delicate rhizomes of *I. cristata.*

In its native habitat *I. cristata* is accustomed to an annual leaf cover, and if grown in cultivated ground where leaves do not provide such a covering it has a tendency to grow itself out of the ground. In such locations it should be given an annual topdressing of screened compost or leaf mold.

As slugs have a special fondness for members of the iris family and are capable of destroying large clumps of *I. cristata* in an incredibly short time, one should be on the alert to detect the first signs of infestation. Fortunately, with simple precautions, damage from slugs can be easily prevented (see Chapter 32 for measures of control).

Iris gracilipes (Japanese crested iris)

In Japan, this dainty little crested iris is found growing in the woodlands and although it is a bit temperamental when transplanted from its native habitat, it may, with a little coaxing, adapt readily to either the woodland or a partially shaded spot in the rock garden. The foliage is slender and grasslike, and the miniature flowers, of a pinkish-lavender hue, are borne on branching stems hardly more than 8 in. in height.

Exposure: Light shade is essential, as it will not thrive in a hot, dry position. Good air circulation is also necessary.

Soil requirements: A fairly moist but well-drained soil, loose in texture and well supplied with humus, is considered ideal. This species is not tolerant of any degree of alkalinity and does best in a slightly acid soil.

Propagation: The division of the rhizomes should preferably be done in July when new root growth is active. If attempted at other seasons of the year, it is less apt to be successful.

Culture: As the plants are somewhat frail, careful weeding is necessary throughout the season in order to prevent more vigorous plants from encroaching upon the clumps of *I. gracilipes.* In early spring and again in late June, the plants should be given a top dressing of compost or well-decayed leaf mold.

Iris tectorum (roof iris)

This is the roof iris of China and Japan, so famed in song and story. The flowers are a clear blue in color. The foliage is broad and heavily ribbed, and the flower stalks reach a height of 12 in. to 15 in.

The white form, *I. tectorum* 'Alba,' is considered one of the most exquisite of flowers. Anyone who has once seen it will never forget the chaste perfection of its bloom, which resembles a magnified snowflake. The flowers are fragile and suffer from wind and rain, but during periods of unfavorable weather they may be cut in bud and allowed to open in the house. The white form is the less hardy type.

Exposure: Full sun or light shade.

Soil requirements: *I. tectorum* will grow in soils of widely varying types. It does extremely well in the strong limestone clay soil of the Shenandoah Valley in Virgina, equally well in the well-drained, sandy-loam soils of Connecticut hillsides, but is best in a garden loam, well supplied with humus.

Propagation: Plants should be divided shortly after the flowering period is over. They may also be readily propagated by seed.

Culture: This species is considered rather temperamental, sometimes thriving in one location and not in another. It is one of the most shallow-rooting of all the members of the iris group and requires frequent division and enrichment of the soil. It may be planted in clumps or in drifts, the rhizomes being spaced from 6 in. to 8 in. apart. It should preferably be lifted and divided every second year. Where the winters are severe, it should be given the protection of leaves and brush.

For the bulbous (cormous) iris, see Chapter 18 on Hardy Bulbs and Lilies.

Linum perenne (blue flax)

This lovely flower, which reflects the blue of soft spring skies, is of particular value in the perennial border because of its airy grace and its long season of bloom. The fine, delicate foliage is a pale-bluish-green, and the lovely, single flowers of soft azure blue are borne in great profusion on slender, graceful stems. On days of brilliant sunshine the petals fall before evening, but in cloudy weather they remain open throughout the day. The plants vary in height from 18 in. to 24 in. *Linum perenne* is particularly charming when grown in combination with the dainty little Iceland poppy, 'Coonara Pink,' and with the columbines. 'Album' is a good, white-flowered cultivar and 'Tetra Red' has satin-red flowers.

17.6 For connoisseurs, hybrid lupine (Lupinus polyphyllus) is a challenge. Photo Grant Heilman

Exposure: Full sun.

Soil requirements: A light, sandy, well-drained garden loam of moderate fertility is considered ideal. *Linum perenne* will not thrive in a heavy soil that becomes saturated with moisture.

Propagation: Blue flax is readily propagated by seed. The seeds are of excellent vitality, germinate well, and the young seedlings make rapid growth. The seeds may be sown in the coldframes early in the spring or in the open ground later in the season and will produce vigorous flowering plants the following year.

Culture: The plants should be spaced from 8 in. to 10 in. apart. Being fibrous-rooted, *Linum perenne* may be transplanted with the greatest ease and large, established plants may be moved with a fair degree of success if they are lifted with a sufficient quantity of earth and if the root system remains intact. If half of the flower stalks are cut back early in the season, and allowed to grow up later to replace those that are ready to go to seed, the flowering period will be greatly prolonged and the energy of the plant will not be exhausted. Under such treatment the plants will sometimes flower almost continually from May to September.

Winter protection::   No winter protection is required if the plants are grown in light, well-drained soil. Serious losses sometimes occur where the soil is heavy and poorly drained.

Lupinus (lupine)

In English gardens, lupines frequently are grown to perfection, and anyone who has seen and admired the beauty of their stately blooms and glorious colors comes away with a longing to produce comparable specimens here in America. Unfortunately, we do not have a combination of English soil and English climate, which contribute so much to these beauties, and in many parts of our country these lovely hybrid lupines will not thrive. In gardens along the New England seacoast, in some sections along the Great Lakes, and on the Pacific coast, where the atmosphere is moist, they do exceedingly well; but where the summers are hot and dry, and where soil conditions are not to their liking, it is almost useless to attempt to grow them, for in spite of all one's efforts to provide favorable conditions, they will only sicken and die. After the introduction of the magnificent Russell lupines, with their tall flower spikes and veritable rainbow of color forms, there is an increased desire on the part of many gardeners to attain success with these rather temperamental perennials.

Exposure: Full sun and a somewhat sheltered location suit lupines best.

Soil requirements: A light, moist, yet well-drained soil of good fertility and with a slightly acid reaction is considered ideal.

Propagation: Lupines may be propagated very readily from seed.

Culture: As lupines are of a somewhat spreading growth habit, the plants should be allowed ample room for development and should be spaced from 12 in. to 15 in. apart. They require an abundance of moisture throughout the growing season, and respond well to an annual topdressing of well-rotted cow manure.

Lythrum salicaria (purple loosestrife)

Because of their long season of bloom and their showy flower spikes, lythrums are an asset in the perennial garden during the summer months. A dozen or more flower spikes will often be produced on a single plant and they make a brilliant note of color in the midsummer garden, blooming from late June to well into September. There are several varieties that reach a height of 3 ft. to 4 ft., while some are more dwarf in form, not exceeding 1½ ft.

LYTHRUM CULTIVARS OF MERIT

'Columbia': soft pink, 3½ ft. high
'Dropmore Purple': rich violet-purple, 3 ft. to 4 ft. high
'Firecandle': intense rosy-red, 3 ft. high
'Happy': dark pink, 15 in. to 18 in. high
'Morden's Pink': clear pink, 3 ft. to 4 ft. high
'Morden's Rose': bright rosy-red, 3 ft. high
'Purple Spires': rose-purple, 3½ ft. to 4 ft. high
'Robert': bright rose-red, 2 ft. high

Exposure: Lythrum salicaria will thrive well in full sun or in partial shade. However, it is usually at its best in a moist, sunny location.

Soil requirements: Any ordinary garden soil will give good results. Although reasonably tolerant of drought, lythrums reach perfection in a moist soil that is well supplied with organic matter.

Propagation: Lythrum is usually propagated by the division of old clumps. These may be lifted and divided either in early spring or in the autumn, as soon as the flowering period is over.

Culture: As *Lythrum* soon forms large clumps, it should be given plenty of room to develop without encroaching upon its neighbors. The tall varieties should be spaced from 2 ft. to 3 ft. apart, small varieties somewhat closer. The best bloom will be obtained if the clumps are lifted and divided every third year.

Lythrum is hardy and vigorous and will repay with generous bloom the care that is bestowed upon it.

Macleaya cordata (syn. *Bocconia cordata*, plumepoppy)

Plumepoppy is a magnificent perennial with large, deeply lobed, glaucous leaves, and tall, handsome flower spikes that often reach a height of 6 ft. to 8 ft. The individual flowers, which are creamy-white in color, are small but are borne in large showy terminal panicles. In late summer these panicles bear quantities of small, almost transparent, pale green pods that become suffused with reddish-purple, and these fruits are almost as beautiful as the flowers. Plumepoppy should be used only where it can have ample space. At the rear of a deep, long border its huge spires of bloom and its gray-green foliage are magnificent. In a small garden it would be entirely out of scale, but when planted in bold masses with a background of evergreens or against a high wall it produces a striking effect. Both the flowers and the seed pods are excellent for bold, decorative arrangements in the house.

Exposure: Full sun or partial shade.

Soil requirements: A rich, moist, deeply prepared soil is considered ideal, although the plants will grow reasonably well in any garden soil of moderate fertility.

Propagation: By seed, by the division of old clumps and by suckers. The plants will attain a height of 3 ft. or 4 ft. the first year from seed.

Culture: Plumepoppy may be planted either in the autumn or in early spring and the plants should be given ample room to develop, being spaced from 2 ft. to 3 ft. apart. As these plants produce suckers very freely, they are capable of becoming a pest unless kept within reasonable bounds.

Paeonia (peony)

The peony has long been a favorite among gardeners, and it is one of the hardiest and most easily grown of any of the perennials. When once established, peonies will continue to flower year after year. Indeed, some of the old-fashioned types are still blooming in gardens where they were planted more than a hundred years ago.

In a small garden peonies are often out of scale. The blooms are so large and the plants themselves require so much room that they should be used sparingly, if at all. However, in a large garden where quantity of bloom and mass

effect are desired, peonies may play an important part in the planting composition. They are lovely when planted in groups along the front of a shrubbery border, or when used as specimen or accent plants. They may also be used very effectively as a low, herbaceous hedge.

With the selection of early, mid-season and late-blooming varieties, six weeks of bloom may be enjoyed.

Exposure: While peonies do best in full sun, they will grow reasonably well in light shade. The more shade, however, the fewer number of blossoms. Deep shade should be absolutely avoided.

Soil requirements: Peonies thrive fairly well in almost any soil, but do best in a rather heavy clay loam that is well drained. The soil reaction should be as nearly neutral as possible because peonies do not grow well in acid soil. The soil should be deeply prepared and well enriched at the time of planting. At no future time will it be possible to supply fertility so effectively, and the plant will derive benefit from it for years to come. A hole of generous proportions should be dug. Well-rotted manure or rich compost should be mixed with the topsoil and placed in the bottom of the hole and firmed well to prevent too much settling later on. Over this a few inches of good topsoil should be spread to prevent the roots of the plants from coming into direct contact with the manure before they have become established.

Planting: Peonies should be planted in the autumn, September and October being the most favorable months. Spring planting is sometimes done but is much more of a shock to the plant and is not recommended as a desirable practice. Depth of planting is a matter of great importance with peonies, as more failures are probably due to planting them too deeply than to any other cause. The division — containing at least three buds — should be placed in the hole so that the tip of the buds will be from 1 in. to 2 in. below the surface of the soil. If planted too deeply, it may never bloom. Good topsoil should be filled in about the roots and firmed well, and the plant should be watered thoroughly immediately after planting. It is wise to allow the plants ample room for full development, and they should be spaced approximately 3 ft. apart.

Fertilization: Although peonies grow reasonably well in rather poor soil, they respond remarkably to good care and to high soil fertility. If blooms of the finest quality are to be produced, it is necessary to see that conditions most favorable to the full development of the plant are provided.

Two applications of a complete fertilizer, such as a 5–10–5, are recommended. The first application should be made in the spring when the new shoots are about 12 in. high. The second application should be made after the period of bloom is over.

The fertilizer should be applied at the rate of approximately ¼ cupful per plant. It should be sprinkled on the surface of the soil about the plant, and worked into the soil lightly with a small hand weeder. The ground should then be watered thoroughly so that the fertilizer will be made immediately available to the plant. In applying the fertilizer, care must be taken to see that it does not come into contact with the stems or leaves as this might result in severe burning, particularly if the foliage is wet.

Culture: Peonies resent being moved; when once well established, they may be left undisturbed for many years.

Some varieties do not produce stems strong enough to hold the full-blown flowers erect, and for such plants some form of support should be provided. Stakes may be put in at intervals about the plant and a loop of tape used to encircle it, or a ready-made support may be used.

For general garden effect peonies are not usually disbudded. However, if exhibition blooms are desired, all of the side buds on the flower stems should be removed, leaving only the large central bud.

When cutting blooms, it is wise to leave two or three leaves on each stem in order that the foliage of the plant may not become too depleted, as the leaves are needed for the manufacture of food.

Old blooms should be removed as soon as they have faded in order to conserve the vigor of the plant.

After the foliage has died down in the autumn the stems should be cut off *just* below ground level, raked up and burned, as a precautionary measure against the spread of blight.

Ants on peony buds are a perfectly natural phenomenon, and should not be a cause for alarm. They are merely seeking nectar produced on the buds and will not damage the plant in any way.

For control of insect pests and diseases, see Chapter 32.

Peony Classification

There is considerable variability in the flower forms of peonies. The following classification has been drawn up by the American Peony Society.

Single: These consist of a ring of a few broad petals, the center being filled with pollen-bearing stamens and seed-bearing carpels.

Japanese: These show the beginnings of doubling. The outer ring or guard petals are like those in the singles but some of the filaments of the stamens have become petaloid. As long as anthers are present, class as Japanese.

Anemone: The next step in doubling—the anthers have disappeared from the petal-like filaments. The central petaloids still are narrow and short.

Semidouble: Similar to the anemone, except that instead of the petaloids being uniformly wide, they occur in all stages of transformation, the formation being loose.

Crown: The carpels are partly or fully transformed into petaloids, which differ from the guard petals and from the petaloids derived from stamens.

Bomb: The next step in doubling finds the petaloids much wider but still differentiated in form from the guard or outer petals, and no anthers are found scattered through the center of the bloom. No collar or crown is in evidence.

Semirose: The carpels are fully transformed. The only thing that differentiates this class from the rose is the fact that an occasional pollen-bearing stamen is found.

Rose: This is the fully doubled type, in which the stamens and carpels are completely transformed to more or less evenly arranged petaloids, which are not distinguishable from the guard petals. If the guard petals are distinct, the flower is classed as a bomb, the line of division being arbitrary.

Tree Peonies

History: Tree peonies are native to the Orient, where they have been cherished and greatly honored since the sixth century. They have figured in the art and literature of the Far East since ancient times, and in the garden they were always accorded a special place of honor. In the imperial gardens, where they were regarded as great treasures, they were usually grown on stepped terraces, and in other gardens they were often planted in high, raised beds, enclosed with stone or marble. Today, tree peonies grace many a temple and monastery garden in the Orient, where they continue to be regarded as sacred plants, and in these gardens specimens are sometimes found that are 300 years old.

The tree peony was not imported into this country until the early 1800s, and for more than a century it remained a plant cherished by connoisseurs and collectors, and was seldom seen except in botanic gardens and in a few gardens on large private estates. Within recent years, however, tree peonies have become increasingly popular and are now more widely grown.

Description: Tree peonies have an ornamental value throughout the year, and lend distinction to any garden. The deciduous foliage is deeply

PEONY CULTIVARS OF MERIT

DARK RED

'Matilda Lewis'   'Nippon Beauty'
                   'Philippe Rivoire'

SINGLE WHITE	DOUBLE WHITE
'Krinkled White'	'Festiva Maxima'
'LeJour'	'Kelway's Glorious'
'Mildred May'	'Le Cygne'

SINGLE PINK	DOUBLE PINK
'Harriet Olney'	'Alice Harding'
'Helen'	'Moonstone'
'Wild Rose'	'Mrs. Franklin D. Roosevelt'

SINGLE RED	DOUBLE RED
'Gopher Beauty'	'Burma'
'Kickapoo'	'Longfellow'
'President Lincoln'	'Mary Brand'

JAPANESE PEONIES

WHITE	LIGHT PINK
'Lotus Queen'	'Akashigata'
'Shaylor's Sunburst'	'Apple Blossom'
'Toro-no-maki'	'Kathalo'

RED	DARK PINK
'Mikado'	'Filagree'
'Nippon Beauty'	'Nippon Gold'
'Red Star'	'Tamate Boku'

cut, soft in tone and texture and very decorative; the shrublike, woody stems have a striking quality in the winter landscape picture, and the flowers are of superb beauty. The blooms possess both delicacy and elegance. The texture and sheen of the petals has been described as "like Oriental silk, ruffled taffetas or crimped and glistening satins." The flowers vary in size from 6 in. to 10 in. across; they also vary considerably in form. There are the beautiful single-saucered types, the semidouble and the fully double types. And there is a wide color range, extending all the way from white through pink to rose, scarlet and red, deep mahogany and maroon; lilac and purple, and even occasional yellows in the hybrid species. Plants vary in height from 3 ft. to 6 ft., with a spread often equal to the height. Some cultivars are compact in form, others spreading, while some have an upright habit of growth. Well-established plants sometimes bear as many as forty or fifty blooms.

Climatic requirements: Tree peonies have a wide range of adaptation. Their native home in the Orient is in mountainside forests, in areas where the climate is rigorous and subject to extremes of heat and cold. They have, however, readily adapted themselves to the windswept hills of northern New York, to the more mellow humid climate of Philadelphia and to the burning summer heat of St. Louis and the Midwest. They are not hardy in the subzero areas of northern Minnesota and Canada.

Exposure: Although tree peonies grow well in light shade, they are not suited to heavily shaded areas. They also do well in full sun. In general, plants grown in full sun are larger, more vigorous and tend to hold their leaves longer in the autumn than those grown in partial shade.

Uses: One of our early horticultural writers, Charles Mason Hovey, referred to the tree peonies as "those truly magnificent undershrubs." And, indeed, in the general landscape scheme this is one of their greatest values. They are particularly well adapted for planting toward the front of shrub borders, and they may also be used in foundation plantings when choice plant materials are desired. Tree peonies are often grown as specimen plants or as accent plants in the garden. For a dramatic display of bloom in late spring, they may be planted in a specially prepared bed.

Soil requirements: Tree peonies grow best in a deep, sandy loam soil that contains an abundance of organic matter. Good drainage is es-

sential. A pH of between 6.5 and 7.0 is considered the most satisfactory, although plants will do reasonably well within a somewhat wider range. Since tree peonies are noted for their longevity, it is wise to see that the soil is well prepared prior to planting. If ideal conditions are to be provided, the soil for each plant should be prepared to a depth of 2 ft.

Planting: Tree peonies may be planted either in the autumn or in the spring, provided the plants are dormant. Plants of small size are usually available as pot-grown plants. Field-grown plants are usually shipped with bare roots, and large specimen plants are best transplanted with a ball of soil wrapped in burlap. Occasionally, fine specimen plants may be obtained in tubs or large pots. Small potted plants may be transplanted with little difficulty, the only precaution recommended being the removal of flower buds in order to encourage good root and leaf growth while the plant is becoming established. If flower buds are removed during the first season after planting, it will increase the vigor of the plant and will ensure more abundant bloom the following season. The depth of planting is a matter of great importance. For years shallow planting (2 in. to 3 in.) had been advocated, but research has now proven conclusively that deep planting is preferable. For best results, the crown of the plant should be set at least 6 in. below the surface of the ground. Deep planting results in a much more vigorous root system than shallow planting and it is one of the keys to success in growing tree peonies.

Fertilization: Well-rotted cow manure and bone meal are regarded as the best fertilizer for tree peonies.

Pruning: Mature tree peonies require little pruning. Dead wood should be cut out, and an occasional shoot should be removed to improve the shape of the plant. A good specimen plant should have from three to seven vigorous stems. When large, bare root plants are transplanted in the spring, some growers prune them severely, cutting the stems back almost to the ground. Some authorities also recommend that where fine specimen plants are desired, it is sometimes advisable to cut the plant back to the ground three or four years after it was set out. This should be done in the early autumn and will result in a new growth of vigorous, healthy stems the following spring.

Mulches: In areas where there is excessive summer heat frequently accompanied by drought, as in the Midwest, the mulching of tree peonies is definitely advisable. Under a heavy mulch it is possible to maintain the soil in a reasonably cool and moist condition. Sawdust has proved one of the most satisfactory materials for mulching, although other materials such as straw, wood chips, leaves, buckwheat hulls, peat moss and corncobs may be

17.7 The explosion of an Oriental poppy (Papaver orientale). *Photo Grant Heilman*

used. In more humid areas of the country mulching is not necessary as it may tend to encourage fungus diseases.

Staking: When the production of blooms is unusually heavy, it may be necessary to stake some of the lateral branches in order to relieve them of excessive weight.

Control of pests and diseases: See Chapter 32.

Papaver orientale (Oriental poppy)

The Oriental poppy is native to southwest Asia and has long been a popular garden flower. In June, the large, flamboyant blooms are borne in profusion above the rough, hairy leaves and there are few perennials that can equal the Oriental poppy in intensity of hue. The old-fashioned varieties vary from pure scarlet to deep red in color, but many of the newer hybrids offer flowers of more delicate and subtle tones.

Soil requirements: Oriental poppies prosper in any well-drained garden loam. If they possess any definite preference, it is for a sandy, gritty loam rather than for a soil of a heavier type.

Exposure: Full sun.

Culture: There are no special cultural requirements for Oriental poppies, for they do well under average garden conditions. As they have a large, fleshy tap root, they are very difficult to transplant except when dormant. This period of dormancy follows the blooming season, and if transplanting is necessary, it should preferably be done at this time. If spring transplanting is necessary, it may be accomplished successfully if great care is taken not to bruise the roots. The plants should not be kept out of the ground for any length of time and they should be shaded for at least a week after being transplanted. It is also essential that they be kept thoroughly watered until they have become well established.

ORIENTAL POPPY CULTIVARS
OF MERIT

'Barr's White': pure white, with purplish-black markings at the base of the petals

'Beauty of Livermore': deep red, black spots at the base of the petals

'Bonfire': bright orange-red, crinkly-edged petals

'Burgundy': maroon-red

'Carnival': vivid orange-red, lower half of each petal white

'Crimson Pompon': deep red, double

'Dubloon': clear orange, double

'Glowing Rose': watermelon-pink, luminous

'Harvest Moon': golden-orange

'Helen Elizabeth': light pink, darker markings at base of petals

'May Curtis': watermelon-red

'Raspberry Queen': raspberry

'Warlord': very fine, deep crimson-red

Oriental poppies require ample room for development during the period when they are in bloom, and they should be spaced from 15 in. to 18 in. apart. Annuals and summer-flowering bulbs may be planted between the poppies in order to carry on a succession of bloom after the poppies have become dormant.

As the Oriental poppies reseed readily, it is important to see that the flower stalks are cut down before the seed pods form. If this is not done, colonies of sturdy young plants will develop the following year that will bear flowers of every hue, most of them reverting to the brilliant flame of the old-fashioned type.

Propagation: As Oriental poppies seldom come true from seed, they should be propagated either by the division of old clumps or by root cuttings. After the blooming period is over, the plants die down entirely and remain practically dormant for a month or more. About the middle of August new growth begins and a little tuft of green leaves appears. The plants should be lifted and divided while they are dormant or just after the new growth begins. Root cuttings may also be made at this time and are very easily handled. The roots should be cut into small pieces 1 in. to 2 in. long, each piece containing at least one joint. These should be placed on a bed of soil, either in a flat or in a coldframe, and laid in a horizontal position. A light covering of sand or sandy loam should be spread over them to a depth of about 1/2 in., and the bed should be kept well watered and partially shaded until active growth has started. If conditions are favorable, roots will develop from each joint and in a short time the leaves will begin to appear. This is undoubtedly the most satisfactory method of propagation. A single plant will yield a large number of cuttings.

Phlox

The tall, hardy types of phlox are the pièce de resistance of most midsummer gardens and with the careful selection of varieties the period of bloom may be extended from June until early September. They are among our most useful plants for the perennial garden and give lavish bloom when color and mass effect are most needed.

The two types of hardy phlox most valuable for summer bloom are *Phlox carolina (P. suffruticosa)* and *Phlox paniculata*. The plants in the *P. suffruticosa* group bloom early, have glossy, deep green foliage and are very resistant to disease. The members of the *P. paniculata* group prolong the season of bloom through the summer. (*Phlox paniculata* is sometimes listed by nurseries as *P. decussata*.)

Phlox carolina (P. suffruticosa)
'Miss Lingard: white; 'Reine du Jour': white with crimson eye.

Climatic requirements: The garden types of phlox are best adapted to areas where the summers are warm and the winters are cold. They do not thrive in hot, dry climates or where the winters are extremely mild.

Exposure: Phlox plants grow well either in full sun or in light shade. In sections of the country where the summer sun is intense, partial shade, or shade for a portion of the day, is preferable, as the colors of some varieties tend to bleach in brilliant sunlight.

PANICULATA PHLOX CULTIVARS OF MERIT

'Blue Ice': flowers pinkish-blue at center when first open, turning white as they age
'Dodo Hanbury Forbes': huge heads of clear pink flowers
'Dresden China': soft, shell-pink flowers, deeper "eye" at center
'Juliet': pale pink flowers
'Lilac Time': lilac-blue flowers
'Mount Fujiyama': pure white flowers
'Orange Perfection': near-orange flowers
'Pinafore Pink': very low, only growing to 4 in.; bright pink flowers with a deeper pink "eye" at center
'Rembrandt': flowers pure white
'Russian Violet': flowers bright violet-purple
'Sir John Falstaff': large, luminous salmon-pink flowers, with a darker "eye" at center
'Starfire': flowers brilliant red
'World Peace': late-flowering, September; flowers pure white

Soil requirements: Phlox has long been recognized as a voracious feeder. For maximum growth and for a fine quality of bloom, phlox requires a rich, well-drained garden loam, high in organic content and very slightly acid. It is important that nutrients be readily available to the plant in the upper 8 in. of topsoil, as phlox are very shallow-rooted. They respond well to heavy applications of potash, so a fertilizer should be used that has a high potash content. An application of wood ashes worked into the soil about the plants is very beneficial. A summer mulch of rotted manure or rich compost will supply additional nutrients and keep the roots cool and moist.

During the growing season phlox plants require an abundance of moisture and suffer seriously from the effects of drought. However, an extremely wet soil and poor air circulation are very injurious and are conducive to poor growth and the spread of various diseases.

Propagation: Phlox may be propagated by the division of old clumps, by root cuttings and by cuttings made from young, growing shoots. Old clumps may be lifted and divided either in the spring or in the early autumn. New root growth is made in the autumn, shortly after the flowering season is over. September is considered the most favorable time for dividing old clumps and replanting, as it is then possible to take full advantage of this new root formation. The earth should be shaken away from the roots and the clumps should be gently pulled apart into small divisions containing from one to three stems. Only the young shoots on the outside of the clump should be used for replanting, and the hard, woody center of the old clump should be discarded. In replanting the divisions, a hole of sufficient size should be dug and the roots should be carefully spread out, the crown of the plant being covered with not more than 1 in. of soil. The soil should be firmed well about the roots, and the plants should be watered thoroughly until they have had an opportunity to become well established. If planting is done in the autumn, a light mulch of strawy manure may be placed over the crowns, and worked into the soil about the plant in the spring. The plants should be spaced from 15 in. to 18 in. apart. The largest flower trusses are usually obtained from newly made divisions. Clumps of phlox are at their best from the second to fourth years after planting. After this period the plants usually begin to lose their vigor. The clumps should therefore be lifted, divided and reset every fourth or fifth year.

Culture: If blooms of exhibition quality are desired, not more than three stalks should be allowed to develop from one crown. Under ordinary garden conditions, however, where a mass of bloom is desired, the stems should be allowed to develop naturally. As soon as the plants have completed their flowering period, the fading blooms should be cut off in order to prevent the plants from reseeding. Phlox plants reseed prolifically and these young, self-sown seedlings are a great liability in a planting composition, as they seldom come true to color, usually reverting to an ugly magenta shade. If the fading flower stalks are removed promptly, a second period of bloom will sometimes be induced. Another method of extending the blooming season is to pinch back from one-fourth to one-half of the stems before the flower buds have begun to form. The remaining stems will produce bloom at the normal time while those which have been cut back will bloom several weeks later.

For insect pests and diseases, see Chapter 32.

Salvia azurea (blue salvia)

This hardy perennial is a very satisfying addition to a garden. The flowers, which are borne on long spikes, are a clear, azure blue and are very decorative and lovely both in the garden and for cutting. *Salvia azurea* is particularly charming when grown in combination with pink gladioli, *Artemisia lactiflora*, white phlox, and pale pink snapdragons, and it may be used in generous quantities for late summer and early autumn bloom.

Exposure: *Salvia azurea* is very hardy and will withstand long periods of drought with no ill effects. A position in full sun is preferred.

Soil requirements: *Salvia azurea* does well on poor soil. Indeed, it seems to reach its best development on soils of medium or low fertility. When it is given an excessively rich diet, it attains too great a height and has a tendency to become floppy and untidy.

Propagation: The plants may be propagated either by seed or by cuttings. The seeds are usually of excellent vitality and germinate readily. They may be sown in the greenhouse in February or March, or they may be sown later in the season either in a coldframe or in the open ground. If sown before the middle of April, the young plants will give some bloom the first year. The seedlings should be transplanted before they become crowded, and when they reach a height of 6 in. or 8 in. they should be pinched back so that they will become bushy and well branched.

Culture: After the plants are well established, they will thrive for many years. Each year they should be cut back severely when they have reached a height of about 8 in. Staking is occasionally necessary in order that the plants may be pleasing and symmetrical in form. The plants vary in height from 2 ft. to 4 ft., and they should be spaced from 12 in. to 15 in. apart.

Salvia farinacea (mealycup sage)

Few flowers bloom over as long a period as *Salvia farinacea*, and it is one of the loveliest members of this group. The flowers are a soft lavender-blue in color and are borne on slender, graceful spikes. The plants are upright in habit of growth, branching freely, and attaining a height of 3 ft. to 4 ft. The flower stems are held erect and have no tendency to become floppy. The foliage is a cool, rather light green. From midsummer until frost the plants will give generous bloom and they are lovely both as part of the garden composition and for cutting.

Although a true perennial, *Salvia farinacea* is often treated as an annual in the North, as it is not hardy where the winters are of extreme severity.

Exposure: The plants thrive best in full sun but will make reasonably good growth in partial shade.

Soil requirements: *Salvia farinacea* will grow well on almost any type of soil.

Propagation: The plants may be raised very easily from seed. For early bloom the seeds may be sown in the greenhouse or hotbed in March. For later bloom they may be sown either in the coldframe or in the open ground. The seeds germinate readily and the young plants make rapid growth. They should be transplanted or thinned out before they become in the least crowded, and when they have reached a height of about 6 in. they should be pinched back, unless very early bloom is desired.

Culture: *Salvia farimacea* may be transplanted with ease, and the plants should be spaced from 8 in. to 10 in. apart.

For insect pests and diseases, see Chapter 32.

Thalictrum (meadow rue)

Light and graceful in form, the thalictrums contribute to the garden a unique quality. Of the many species and varieties there are five that are of particular value in the garden of herbaceous perennials.

T. adiantifolium

The foliage resembles that of the maidenhair fern and the myriad small, creamy-white flowers are produced in abundance in June and early July. The plants attain a height of from 3 ft. to 4 ft. and as they develop into large clumps, they should be spaced from 15 in. to 18 in. apart.

T. aquilegifolium

The flowers are borne on tall, graceful stems, which rise above the foliage to a height of 3 ft. or more. They may be obtained in shades of pink, lavender and creamy-white, and bloom throughout the month of June. The foliage bears a striking resemblance to that of the columbines. The plants should be spaced from 12 in. to 18 in. apart.

T. rochebrunianum

By far the most beautiful of all the meadow rues. The flowers are lavender and bear many soft yellow stamens. These appear from mid-July through August on stems 5 ft. to 6 ft. in height. Plants are somewhat slow to establish, but they are well worth waiting for until they come into their own in a few years. A much more satisfactory and undemanding plant than *T. dipterocarpum*, which also has lavender or mauve flowers.

T. speciosissimum (often listed in catalogues as *T. glaucum*)

The glaucous leaves are a soft blue-gray, and the fragrant yellow flowers are borne on tall, erect stems, varying from 3 ft. to 4 ft. in height. The plants are more compact and erect in habit of growth than most of the other *Thalictrum* and they should be spaced from 12 in. to 15 in. apart.

Exposure: Full sun or partial shade.

Soil requirements: A well-drained, moderately fertile graden loam.

Propagation: By seed or by the division of clumps.

Culture: Thalictrum may be planted either in the autumn or in the early spring. No winter protection is required.

PERENNIALS THAT WILL GROW IN POOR SOIL

Achillea spp.	millfoil or yarrow
Ajuga genevensis	bugleweed
Arabis caucasica	wallcress
Artemisia spp.	
Aurinia (Alyssum) saxatilis	basket-of-gold
Baptisia australis	blue or false indigo
Cerastium tomentosum	snow-in-summer
Dianthus deltoides	maiden pink
Dianthus plumarius	cottage pink
Eryngium spp.	sea holly
Euphorbia myrsinites	myrtle spurge
Geranium maculatum	spotted cranesbill
Geranium sanguineum	blood-red cranesbill
Gypsophila paniculata	baby's breath
Helianthemum nummularium	rock or sun rose
Iberis sempervirens	evergreen candytuft
Linaria vulgaris	toadflax
Phlox subulata	moss phlox
Potentilla tridentata	wineleaf cinquefoil
Salvia azurea	azure sage
Saxifraga pensylvanica	Pennsylvania or swamp saxifrage
Sedum acre	gold moss
Sedum stoloniferum	running sedum
Sempervivum spp.	roof houseleek
Verbascum thapsus	common mullein
Viola cucullata	blue marsh violet

PERENNIALS FOR DRY, SANDY SOIL

(Drought-resistant)

Achillea millefolium	millfoil
Achillea ptarmica	sneezewort
Ajuga reptans	carpet bugle
Anthemis tinctoria	yellow camomile
Artemisia spp.	
Asclepias tuberosa	butterfly weed
Aster novae-angliae	New England aster
Callirhoe involucrata	poppymallow
Cassia marilandica	wild senna
Coreopsis grandiflora	tickseed
Dianthus plumarius	cottage pink
Echinops ritro	steel globe thistle
Eryngium spp.	sea holly
Gaillardia aristata	blanket flower
Helianthus spp.	sunflower
Iris	bearded iris
Liatris pycnostachya	cattail gay-feather
Papaver nudicaule	Iceland poppy

PERENNIALS FOR BORDERS OF PONDS AND STREAMS

(Well-drained soil)

SUNNY LOCATIONS

Astilbe cultivars	astilbe
Brunnera macrophylla (Anchusa myosotidiflora)	Siberian bugloss
Cimicifuga racemosa	black cohosh
Grasses	ornamental grasses
Hemerocallis cultivars	daylily
Iris cultivars	iris
Lythrum salicaria	purple loosestrife
Myosotis scoipioides var. *semperflorens*	dwarf perpetual forget-me-not
Tradescantia virginiana	spiderwort
Trollius europaeus	globeflower

SEMISHADY LOCATIONS

Anemone x *hybrida*	Japanese anemone
Cimicifuga racemosa	black cohosh
Epimedium grandiflorum	barrenwort, bishop's hat
Eupatorium purpureum	Joe-Pye weed
Iris cristata	crested iris
Lythrum salicaria	purple loosestrife
Tradescantia virginiana	spiderwort

FRAGRANT PERENNIALS

Arabis	arabis
Artemisia abortanum	southernwood, old-man
Asperula odorata	sweet woodruff
Centranthus ruber	Jupiter's-beard
Convallaria majalis	lily-of-the-valley
Dianthus plumarius	cottage pink
Dictamnus albus	gas plant
Hemerocallis flava	tawny daylily
Hesperis matronalis	dame's rocket
Hosta plantaginea 'Grandiflora'	big plantain lily
Iris — Pallida section	
Lathyrus grandiflorus	everlasting pea
Lychnis viscaria	German catchfly
Monarda didyma	bee balm
Oenothera spp.	evening primrose
Paeonia	peony
Phlox paniculata	phlox
Valeriana officinalis	common valerian
Viola cornuta	horned violet
Viola odorata	sweet violet

HERBS:

Lavandula angustifolia	lavender
Origanum majorana	sweet marjoram
rosmarinus officinalis	rosemary
Thymus spp.	thyme

LOW-GROWING PERENNIALS FOR EDGING

Achillea tomentosa	wooly yarrow
Ajuga reptans	carpet bugle
Alchemilla vulgaris	lady's-mantle
Aquilegia flabellata 'Nana Alba'	dwarf fan columbine
Arabis alpina	Alpine rockcress
Arabis caucasica	wallcress
Armeria maritima	thrift
Aubrieta deltoidea	purple rockcress
Aurinia saxatilis 'Compacta'	dwarf goldentuft
Bellis perennis	English daisy
Campanula carpatica	Carpathian harebell
Cerastium tomentosum	snow-in-summer
Ceratostigma plumbaginoides	leadwort
Dianthus deltoides	maiden pink
Dianthus plumarius	cottage pink
Festuca ovina var. *glauca*	sheep fescue
Heuchera sanguinea	coralbells
Iberis sempervirens	evergreen candytuft
Oenothera missouriensis	evening primrose
Papaver nudicaule	Iceland poppy
Phlox x *procumbens*	hairy phlox
Phlox subulata	moss phlox
Primula veris	cowslip primrose
Sedum reflexum	Jenny stonecrop
Sedum stoloniferum	running stonecrop
Stellaria holostea	chickweed or starwort
Stokesia laevis	Stokes' aster
Veronica incana	wooly speedwell
Veronica latifolia	rock speedwell
Viola spp.	violet

PERENNIALS THAT HAVE ESPECIALLY LONG BLOOMING SEASONS

Achillea filipendulina cultivars	fernleaf yarrow
Anchusa azurea	bugloss
Aquilegia chrysantha	golden columbine
Campanula carpatica	Carpathian harebell
Coreopsis auriculata 'Nana'	dwarf-eared coreopsis
Coreopsis verticillata	thread-leaf coreopsis
Delphinium (requires cutting back)	delphinium
Dicentra eximia (recurrent blooming cultivars)	plume bleeding-heart
Heuchera sanguinea	coralbells
Hibiscus moscheutos cultivars	hardy hibiscus
Iris fall-blooming varieties	
Lathyrus latifolius	perennial pea
Lychnis coronaria	dusty-miller
Phlox (requires cutting back)	summer phlox
Scabiosa graminifolia	pincushion flower or mourning-bride
Tradescantia virginiana cultivars (requires cutting back)	spiderwort
Verbascum (requires cutting back)	mullein
Viola cornuta	horned violet
Viola tricolor	heart's-ease, Johnny-jump-up, pansy

PERENNIALS THAT DO NOT REQUIRE FREQUENT DIVISION

(Those marked by an asterisk resent disturbance)

Acanthus spp.	bear's-breech
Aconitum spp.	monkshood
Adenophora spp.	ladybells
Amsonia	bluestar
*Anemone x hybrida	Japanese anemone
Armeria	thrift
*Asclepias tuberosa	butterfly weed
Baptisia australis	blue or false indigo
Bergenia	
Brunnera	Siberian bugloss
*Callirhoe	poppy mallow
Cassia	wild senna
Cimicifuga	bugbane, cohosh
*Clematis (herbaceous)	
Convallaria	lily-of-the-valley
*Dictammus	gas plant
Echinops	globe thistle
Epimedium	bishop's hat
*Eryngium	sea holly
Euphorbia	spurge
Gentiana	gentian
*Gypsophila	baby's breath
*Helleborus	Christmas or lenten rose
Hemerocallis	daylily
Hosta	plantain lily
*Incarvillea	hardy gloxinia
Kniphofia	torch flower
*Lathyrus	perennial pea
*Limonium	sea lavender
Lythrum	purple loosestrife
Mertensia	bluebells
Oenothera	evening primrose
Paeonia	peony
*Papaver	poppy
*Platycodon	balloon flower
Polygonatum	Solomon's-seal
Scabiosa	pincushion flower
Sedum	stonecrop
Smilacina	false Solomon's-seal
Thalictrum	meadow rue
Thermopsis	false lupine
Trollius	globeflower

PERENNIALS THAT REQUIRE THE MOST FREQUENT DIVISION

Achillea ptarmica cultivars	yarrow
Anthemis	golden marguerite
Aster	
Boltonia	
Cerastium tomentosum	snow-in-summer
Chrysanthemum maximum cultivars	shasta daisy
Chrysanthemum x morifolium cultivars	chrysanthemum

Erigeron	fleabane
Eupatorium coelestinum	hardy ageratum
Eupatorium rugosum	white snakeroot
Gaillardia	blanket flower
Helenium	sneezeweed
Monarda	bee balm
Physostegia	false dragonhead

PERENNIALS FOR OLD-FASHIONED GARDENS

Aconitum spp.	monkshood
Aclea rosea	hollyhock
Arisaema triphyllum	Jack-in-the-pulpit
Aster old cultivars	hardy aster
Campanula spp.	bellflower
Convallaria majalis	lily-of-the-valley
Delphinium x belladonna	garland larkspur
Delphinium formosum	Formosa delphinium
Dianthus arenarius	sand pink
Dianthus barbatus	sweet William
Dianthus plumarius	cottage pink
Dianthus superbus	lilac pink
Dicentra spectabilis	bleeding-heart
Dictamnus	gas plant
Digitalis	foxglove
Hemerocallis	lemon lily
Hepatica triloba	hepatica
Hesperis matronalis	sweet rocket
Lilium candidum	madonna lily
Lilium tigrinum	tiger lily
Lunaria	honesty (biennial)
Lupinus polyphyllus	lupine
Lychnis chalcedonica	Maltese cross or scarlet lychnis
Mertensia	bluebells
Myosotis spp.	forget-me-not
Paeonia lactiflora	peony
Primula veris	primrose
Trillium spp.	trillium, wake-robin
Viola odorata	sweet violet
Viola tricolor	heart's ease, Johnny-jump-up, pansy

PERENNIALS THAT CAN BECOME INVASIVE

Achillea ptarmica cultivars	yarrow
Achillea tomentosa	wooly yarrow
Artemisia stelleriana	old-woman, dusty-miller
Boltonia	
Cerastium tomentosum	snow-in-summer
Convallaria	lily-of-the-valley
Coronilla varia	crown vetch
Eupatorium coelestinum	hardy ageratun
Eupatorium rugosum	white snakeroot
Helianthus	sunflower
Hemerocallis fulva	tawny daylily
Lysimachia clethroides	gooseneck loosestrife
Macleaya cordata	plumepoppy
Monarda didyma	bee balm
Phlox subulata	moss phlox
Physostegia	false dragonhead

HARDY PERENNIALS FOR BOLD OR SUBTROPICAL EFFECTS

Acanthus latifolius	acanthus
Aruncus sylvester	goatsbeard
Cimicifuga racemosa	black cohosh
Dipsacus sylvestris	common teasel
Echinops ritro and *Echinops exaltatus*	globe thistle
Elymus arenarius	wild-rye grass
Eulalia japonica	eulalia grass
Helianthus salicifolius	sunflower
Heracleum laciniatum	cow parsnip
Kniphofia uvaria	torch flower
Macleaya cordata	plumepoppy
Onopordum acanthium	Scotch thistle
Polygonum sachalinense	giant knotweed
Silphium perfoliatum	rosinweed
Telekia speciosa	telekia
Verbascum olympicum	mullein
Yucca filamentosa	yucca, Adam's needle

TALL-GROWING PERENNIALS FOR BACKGROUND PLANTING

Aconitum carmichaelii	azure monkshood
Aruncus sylvester	goatsbeard
Aster novae-angliae	New England aster
Aster tataricus	Tatarian aster
Boltonia asteroides	white boltonia
Campanula latifolia 'Macrantha'	great bellflower
Cassia marilandica	wild senna
Cimicifuga racemosa	black cohosh
Delphinium hybrids	delphinium
Echinops sphaerocephalus	great globe thistle
Helenium autumnale	sneezeweed
Helianthus maximiliani	Maximilian sunflower
Hibiscus moscheutos hybrids	hardy hibiscus
Macleaya cordata	plumepoppy
Rudbeckia laciniata	golden-glow
Valeriana officinalis	common valerian

HERBACEOUS PERENNIALS

SCIENTIFIC NAME	COMMON NAME	HEIGHT IN INCHES	DISTANCE APART IN INCHES	SEASON	COLOR	REMARKS
Acanthus mollis	bear's-breech	36		July – August	lilac, rose	deeply toothed leaves; sun; good drainage
Achillea filipendulina	fernleaf yarrow	36	10–12	June – July	yellow	fernlike foliage; full sun; good drainage; cut flowers
Achillea filipendulina 'Coronation Gold'		24–30	10–12	June – July	yellow; large	"
Achillea filipendulina 'Gold Plate'		48–50	12–15	June – July	yellow; large	"
Achillea 'Taggeta'		18	10–12	June – July	yellow	"
Achillea millefolium cultivars	millfoil	18–24	12	June – August	pink to red	
Achillea ptarmica cultivars	sneezewort	24	12	July – August	white	any soil; cut flowers; frequent division
Achillea tomentosa cultivars	wooly yarrow	10	8	July – August	canary yellow	spreads rapidly
Aconitum carmichaelii	azure monkshood	30–42	10–12	August – Sept.	pale blue	shade or sun; infrequent division; good soil; poisonous
Aconitum napellus	aconite monkshood	24–40	12	August	blue and white	"
Aconitum napellus 'Spark's Variety'		36–48	15	August – Sept.	violet, blue	"
Adenophora confusa (*A. farreri*)	Farrers ladybell	30	12	July – August	deep blue	sun; resents disturbance
Adenophora liliyfolia		24–36	12	July – August	blue	sun; resents disturbance

(Continued)

HERBACEOUS PERENNIALS (Continued)

SCIENTIFIC NAME	COMMON NAME	HEIGHT IN INCHES	DISTANCE APART IN INCHES	SEASON	COLOR	REMARKS
Adonis amurensis	Amur adonis	10	12	April	yellow	
Adonis vernalis	spring adonis	12	10	April	yellow	
Aethionema grandiflorum	stonecress	12	6	May	pink	
Ajuga genevensis	bugleweed	6–9	6	May–June	bright blue	invasive in the lawn
Ajuga reptans and cultivars	carpet bugle	3–6	6	May–June	blue	''
Alchemilla vulgaris	lady's-mantle	12	10	May–June	greenish	shade; handsome foliage
Alyssum saxatile (see *Aurinia saxatilis*)						
Amsonia tabernaemontana	bluestar	24–30	12	May–June	steel-blue	sun or shade; infrequent division
Anchusa azurea and cultivars	bugloss	36–60	36	June–July	deep blue	frequent division; self-sows
Anemone hupehensis var. *japonica*	Japanese anemone	12	12	August–Sept.	rose-pink	partial shade
Anemone x *hybrida* cultivars	Japanese anemone	36	15	Sept.–Oct.	white through pink and rose	''
Anemone vitifolia 'Robustissima'	grape-leaved anemone	30–36	12	Sept.–Oct.	light pink	''; hardiest of the fall anemones
Anthemis tinctoria and cultivars	golden marguerite	18	12	June	yellow	sun; tolerates poor soil
Aquilegia caerulea	Colorado columbine	18	12	April	blue and white	graceful; good color; long spurs
Aquilegia canadensis	wild columbine	18	9	April	red and yellow	self-sows
Aquilegia chrysantha	golden columbine	24	12	May–August	yellow	long spur; very long flowering season
Aquilegia flabellata	fan columbine	12–18	10	May–June	lilac, white	
Aquilegia flabellata 'Nana Alba'	dwarf fan columbine	8–12	8	May–June	white	
Aquilegia x *hybrida*	long-spurred columbine hybrids	18–36	10–12	May–June	various	long spurs; frequent replanting necessary
Aquilegia glandulosa	Altai columbine	12	9	May–June	blue and white	
Aquilegia skinneri	Mexican columbine	12	9	April	yellow and red	
Aquilegia vulgaris	European columbine	18	12	May–July	violet	short spurs
Aquilegia vulgaris hybrids	short-spurred columbine	18	12	May–July	various	
Arabis alpina	Alpine rockcress	12	9	April	white	spreading, carpetlike
Arabis caucasica (*A. albida*)	wallcress	12	9	April	white	spreading, carpetlike
Armeria maritima and cultivars	thrift	3–5	9	June–July	pink to white	good for edgings and seashore paintings
Artemisia abortanum	southernwood, old-man	24	18	August	yellow	common in old gardens
Artemisia absinthium	absinthe	24	18	August	white, yellow	
Artemisia lactiflora	white mugwort	48–72	24	August–Sept.	white	fragrant cut flower
Artemisia ludoviciana var. *albula*	silver-king	24–36	18	summer	white	an everlasting; grown for its gray foliage
Artemisia schmidtiana 'Nana'	silver mound	18–24	30	all season		moundlike; silver leaves
Artemisia stelleriana	old-woman, dusty-miller	18	10–12	June–July	white	can become invasive; silver leaves
Aruncus sylvester	goatsbeard	60	24	June–July	white	excellent for rear of border
Asclepias tuberosa	butterfly weed	18–24	12	July–August	orange	dry, sunny places; resents disturbance
Asperula odorata	sweet woodruff	6–12	9	May–June	white	partial shade; fragrant spreading
Aster alpinus	Alpine aster	8–10	9	May–June	violet	sun
Aster amellus	Italian aster	18	12	July–August	purple	sun
Aster x *frikartii*	wonder of Staffa	18–24	12	July–Nov.	blue	sun
Aster novae-angliae	New England aster	48–72	24	Sept.–Oct.	purple	sun; spreading
Aster novae-angliae cultivars	Michaelmas daisies	36–72	24	Sept.–Oct.	pink and purple	sun; spreading

HERBACEOUS PERENNIALS (Continued)

SCIENTIFIC NAME	COMMON NAME	HEIGHT IN INCHES	DISTANCE APART IN INCHES	SEASON	COLOR	REMARKS
Aster novae-belgi	New York aster	36–72	24	Sept.–Oct.	violet to blue	sun; spreading
Aster novae-belgi cultivars	Michaelmas daisies	36–72	24	Sept.–Oct.	various	sun; spreading
Astilbe x arendsii cultivars	astilbe	24–30	12	June–July	white, rose, red, etc.	likes moist soil
Astilbe japonica	spirea	24	12	June–July	pink or white	likes moist soil
Astrantia major	masterwort	24–36	12	May	silvery-pink	good foliage plant
Aubreta deltoidea	purple rockcress	3–6	6–8	April–May	purple, white	spreading, matlike
Aurinia (Alyssum) saxatilis	basket-of-gold	12–18	12	May	yellow	sheets of yellow
Aurinia saxatilis 'Citrinum'		12–18	12	May	citron	pale gold
Aurinia saxatilis 'Compactum'		8–10	12	May	yellow	more compact than the species
Baptisia australis	blue or false indigo	24–30	24–30	June	indigo	flowers resemble lupines; handsome foliage
Belamcanda chinensis	blackberry lily	36–42	24	July–August	orange	sun; good drainage, handsome black seeds
Bergenia cordifolia	bergenia	12	12	April–May	rosy-purple	any soil; excellent bold foliage
Bergenia crassifolia	bergenia	12	12	April–May	rosy-purple	'' ''
Boltonia asteroides	white boltonia	60–72	36	September	creamy-white	spreading; rear of border; like wild aster; grayish leaves
Brunnera macrophylla (Anchusa myosotidiflora)	Siberian bugloss	12	12	May–June	blue	sun or shade; flowers like forget-me-not
Caltha palustris	marsh marigold	12–18	12	April–May	yellow	moist or wet soil
Campanula carpatica	Carpathian harebell	8	12	July–Sept.	blue, white	edging
Campanula glomerata	clustered bellflower	12–18	9	July–August	violet	spreads
Campanula lactiflora	milky bellflower	36–60	12–36	June–Sept.	blue, white	excellent for rear of border
Campanula latifolia 'Macrantha'	great bellflower	36–48	24–30	May–June	royal blue	striking plant for rear of border
Campanula persicifolia and cultivars	peach-bells	24–30	9	June–July	blue, white, pink	good cut flower
Cassia marilandica	wild senna	36–60	36	July	yellow	good background plant; infrequent division
Catanache caerulea	cupid's dart	18–24	12	Sept.	blue	dry places; everlasting; frequent division
Centaurea dealbata 'Sternbergii'	Persian centaurea	24	18	July–August	bright, purple, white center	sun; endures dry soil
Centaurea macrocephala	globe centaurea	36–48	18–24	June–July		bold effects; sun; endures dry soil
Centaurea montana	mountain bluet	18–24	12	June–July	violet	sun; endures dry soil; frequent division
Cerastium tomentosum	snow-in-summer	6	10	June	white	spreading; edging or ground cover; can become invasive
Ceratostigma plumbaginoides (Plumbago larpentiae)	blue leadwort	8–12	10	August–Oct.	blue	growth starts very late in spring
Chelone glabra	turtlehead	30–36	12	July–Sept.	pinkish to white	good for moist soil
Chelone lyonii	pink turtlehead	36–40	12–15	August–Sept.	deep rose	good for moist soil
Chrysanthemum arcticum	Arctic daisy	6–12	8–10	Sept.–Oct.	white	good, dark foliage
Chrysanthemum coccineum cultivars	painted daisy, pyrethrum	24	12	June	various	good for cut flowers
Chrysanthemum maximum cultivars	Shasta daisy	24	12	June–Sept.	white (single and double)	good for cut flowers; sun; good drainage
Chrysanthemum x morifolium cultivars	garden chrysanthemum	12–48	12–18	autumn	various	see under index for details

(Continued)

HERBACEOUS PERENNIALS (Continued)

SCIENTIFIC NAME	COMMON NAME	HEIGHT IN INCHES	DISTANCE APART IN INCHES	SEASON	COLOR	REMARKS
Chrysanthemum nipponicum	Nippon daisy	12		Sept.	white	shrubby; cut back to maintain good shape
Cimicifuga foetida	Kamchatka bugbane	36–60	24–36	Sept.	white	excellent for background
Cimicifuga racemosa	black cohosh	48–60	24–36	July	white	"
Cimicifuga simplex		24–48	24–36	Sept.–Oct.	white	shorter than others
Clematis heracleifolia var. *davidiana*	blue tube clematis	36–48	36–38	August	deep blue, fragrant	resents disturbance
Clematis integrifolia 'Coerulea'	blue solitary clematis	18–24	12	June–Oct.	porcelain blue, fragrant	"
Clematis recta 'Grandiflora'	ground clematis	36	20	June–July	white	"
Convallaria majalis	lily-of-the-valley	6–8	8–10	May	white, fragrant	survives neglect; spreads; fruits poisonous
Convallaria majalis 'Rosea'	pink lily-of-the-valley	6–8	8–10	May	pale pink, fragrant	"
Coreopsis auriculata 'Nana'	dwarf-eared coreopsis	6	10	June–August	orange-yellow	sun; long period of bloom; front of the border; tolerates dry soil
Coreopsis grandiflora	tickseed	36	18	May	yellow	sun; good cut flower; tolerates dry soil
Coreopsis lanceolata 'Sunburst'		24	10–12	July–Sept.	yellow, semidouble	good cut flower; long period of bloom; tolerates dry soil
Coreopsis rosea	pink tickseed	12	12	August–Sept.	pink	good cut flower; long period of bloom; tolerates dry soil
Coreopsis verticillata	thread-leaf coreopsis	18–24	10–12	July–Sept.	bright yellow	sun; long period of bloom; tolerates dry soil; moundlike
Delphinium x *belladonna* and cultivars	garland larkspur	24–40	12	June–July	blue, white, purplish	good cut flower (see under index for all delphiniums)
Delphinium 'Connecticut Yankees'	Connecticut Yankee delphinium	30	12	July	blue, purple, lavender, white	good cut flower
Delphinium elatum hybrids	common delphinium	48–60	18	June–July	various	
Delphinium grandiflorum and cultivars	Siberian or bouquet larkspur	18	9	July–Sept.	blue, white	fine foliage
Delphinium nudicaule	orange larkspur	18	9	July	orange	rather tender; not easy in all gardens
Delphinium semibarbatum (*D. zalil*)	yellow larkspur	12–24	9	June–July	yellow	tuberous
Dianthus x *allwoodii* hybrids	Allwood's pink	12–18	9	June–July	various	tender in North
Dianthus barbatus hybrids	sweet William	(See biennials, page 378)				
Dianthus caesius (See *D. gratianopolitanus*)						
Dianthus deltoides and cultivars	maiden pink	6–9	9	June	various	
Dianthus gratianopolitanus	Cheddar pink	8–10	9	June–July	pink to rose	forms mats or cushions; edging
Dianthus x *latifolius* and cultivars	button pink	12–18	9	July–Sept.	various	edging
Dianthus plumarius and cultivars	cottage pink	12–18	12	June	various	edging
Dicentra eximia and cultivars	plume bleeding-heart	12–18	12	May and some recurrent blooms till frost	pink to rose	edging; sun or partial shade
Dicentra spectabilis	bleeding-heart	24–36	36	May	pink	best in partial shade
Dictamnus albus	gas plant	30–36	24	May	white	resents disturbance
Dictamnus albus 'Rubra'	gas plant	30–36	24	May	rose	"
Digitalis (See biennials, page 378)						
Doronicum austriacum	leopard's-bane	24	12	May–June	yellow	earliest yellow daisies

HERBACEOUS PERENNIALS (Continued)

SCIENTIFIC NAME	COMMON NAME	HEIGHT IN INCHES	DISTANCE APART IN INCHES	SEASON	COLOR	REMARKS
Doronicum cordatum and cultivars (*D. caucasicum*)	leopard's-bane	18–24	9	May–June	yellow	earliest yellow daisies
Doronicum plantagineum	leopard's-bane	36	12	June	yellow	
Echinacea purpurea	purple coneflower	36	24	Sept.	rosy-purple	well-drained soil
Echinops ritro	small globe thistle	36	24	July	blue	full sun; good drainage; foliage coarse, thistlelike
Echinops sphaerocephalus	great globe thistle	60	24	July–August	pale blue to whitish	''
Echinops 'Taplow Blue'		48–60	24	August	rich steel-blue	''
Epimedium alpinum	barrenwort, bishop's hat	10–12	12	April–May	red and yellow	semishade; good for edging or ground cover
Epimedium grandiflorum	barrenwort, bishop's hat	10–12	12	April–May	red, violet and white	''
Epimedium pinnatum	barrenwort, bishop's hat	10–12	12	April–May	yellow and red	''
Epimedium x *rubrum*	barrenwort, bishop's hat	10–12	12	April–May	crimson and yellow	''
Epimedium x *versicolor* 'Sulphureum'	barrenwort, bishop's hat	10–12	12	April–May	pale yellow	''
Epimedium youngianum 'Niveum'	barrenwort, bishop's hat	10–12	12	April–May	pure white	''
Eremurus himalaicus	foxtail lily, desert-candle	48–70	12	May	white	full sun; well-drained soil
Eremurus robustus	giant foxtail-lily	48–70	24	May–June	pink	full sun; well-drained soil
Erigeron aurantiacus	double orange daisy	9	12	July–August	bright orange, semidouble	full sun
Erigeron hybridus cultivars	fleabane	15–24	12	July–August	various	full sun
Erigeron speciosus	Oregon fleabane	18–24	12	June–July	violet blue, yellow center	full sun
Eryngium alpinum	bluetop eryngo	18–24	12	August–Sept.	silvery-blue	sun; handsome thistlelike plant; resents disturbance; good drainage
Eryngium amethystinum	amethyst sea holly	24	12	July–August	steel-gray to amethyst	''
Eryngium bourgatii	Mediterranean sea holly	18	10	June–August	steel-blue	''
Eryngium planum	flat-leaved sea holly	36	12	July–August	steel-blue	''
Eupatorium coelestinum	hardy ageratum	24–30	12	Sept.–Oct.	blue	flowers resemble ageratum
Euphorbia corollata	flowering spurge	36	12	July	white	cut flowers; sun, tolerates dry soil
Euphorbia epithymoides (*E. polychroma*)	cushion spurge	18	12	May	yellow	symmetrical moundlike plant
Euphorbia myrsinites	myrtle spurge	6	8	April and May	yellow	sun; poor soil; blue-green evergreen leaves; creeps
Filipendula hexapetala (See *E. vulgaris*)						
Filipendula rubra	queen-of-the-prairie	48–72	36	June–July	pink	handsome for rear of border; infrequent division
Filipendula ulmaria	queen-of-the-meadow	48	36	June–July	white, fragrant	''

(Continued)

HERBACEOUS PERENNIALS (Continued)

SCIENTIFIC NAME	COMMON NAME	HEIGHT IN INCHES	DISTANCE APART IN INCHES	SEASON	COLOR	REMARKS
Filipendula vulgaris	dropwort	18–24	12	June	creamy-white	round foliage; sun; tolerates dry soil
Filipendula vulgaris 'Flore Pleno'	double dropwort	15–18	10–12	June	double white	''
Gaillardia x *grandiflora* cultivars	blanket flower	6–36	10–12	May–Sept.	various	sun; good drainage
Geranium cinereum cultivars		4–6	10	June–August	lilac to bright magenta	long period of bloom
Geranium dalmaticum		4–6	10	May–June	pale pink to white	
Geranium endressii and cultivars		15–18	10–12	May–August	blue, pink, white	long period of bloom
Geranium grandiflorum (See *G. himalayense*)						
Geranium himalayense	lilac cranesbill	18–24	12	May–June	magenta	long period of bloom; spreads rapidly
Geranium ibericum	Iberian cranesbill	18–24	12	June–July	violet-blue	
Geranium sanguineum	blood-red cranesbill	12	12	May–August	purple-red	long period of bloom
Geranium sanguineum var. *prostratum* (*G. lancastrense*)		6	10	May–August	bright pink	compact, not as rampant as the species
Geum coccineum and *G. quellyon* (*G. chiloense*) hybrids and cultivars	geum	30	12–18	May–August	various	sun; good drainage
Gypsophila paniculata	baby's breath	30–36 similar spread	single specimens	July	white, single	alkaline soil; good drainage
Gypsophila paniculata 'Bristol Fairy'		36 similar spread	single specimens	July	white, double	alkaline soil; good drainage; very floriferous
Gypsophila repens 'Bodgeri'		18	12	May–June	white to pinkish, semidouble	''
Helenium autumnale cultivars	sneezeweed	30–60	12–18	Sept.–Oct.	yellow through red-bronze	sun; frequent division
Helenium hoopesii		24–30	12	June	orange	''
Helianthus angustifolius	swamp sunflower	36	24	Sept.	yellow	background plant; cut flowers
Helianthus decapetalus	thin-leaf sunflower	72	36	August	sulphur-yellow	background plant; cut flowers
Helianthus maximiliani	Maximilian sunflower	84	36	Oct.	gold	''
Heliopsis helianthoides ssp. *scabra* 'Gold Greenheart'		36–40	12	July–Sept.	bright yellow, double	full sun; moisture-retentive soil
Heliopsis helianthoides ssp. *scabra* 'Incomparabilis'		36–40	12	July–Sept.	yellow, semidouble	''
Helleborus niger	Christmas rose	10–12	12	late winter	white	neutral to slightly alkaline soil; partial shade
Helleborus orientalis	Lenten rose	10–12	12	late winter	white through brown to purple	''
Hemerocallis aurantiaca	orange daylily	36	20–24	June	orange	naturalizing; ground cover or flower border; semishade to full sun
Hemerocallis dumortieri	Dumortier's daylily	18	20–24	June	bright orange	''
Hemerocallis fulva	tawny daylily	36	20–24	July	bronze	''
Hemerocallis hybrids	daylily	24–36	20–24	May–Oct.	various	flower border; long season of bloom by selecting early mid-season or late cultivars

HERBACEOUS PERENNIALS (Continued)

SCIENTIFIC NAME	COMMON NAME	HEIGHT IN INCHES	DISTANCE APART IN INCHES	SEASON	COLOR	REMARKS
Hemerocallis lilioasphodelus (*H. flava*)	lemon daylily	24	24	June	canary yellow	naturalizing; ground cover or flower border; semishade to full sun
Hemerocallis middendorffi	Amur daylily	24	20–24	June	gold	''
Hemerocallis minor	dwarf yellow daylily	18–24	20	June–July	yellow	''
Hemerocallis thunbergii	Thunberg daylily	40–48	24	July	canary yellow	''
Hesperis matronalis	dame's rocket	36	12	June–July	purple	fragrant; sun or light shade
Heuchera sanguinea cultivars	coralbells, alumroot	12–24	9	July	red, pink, white	well-drained soil
Hibiscus moscheutos hybrids and cultivars	hardy hibiscus	48–60	36	August–Sept.	red, pink, white	sun; moist to wet soils
Hosta (See descriptive list, page 281)						
Iberis sempervirens and cultivars	evergreen candytuft	9–12	12	March–April	white	cut back after flowering; well-drained soil
Iris species and cultivars (See descriptive list, page 282)						
Kniphofia cultivars	torch lily	18–48	18	June–Sept.	orange, red, yellow, white	full sun; excellent drainage
Lathyrus latifolius	perennial pea	60–100	24	July–Sept.	deep rose	sun
Lathyrus latifolius 'Albus'	white perennial pea	60–100	24	July–Sept.	white	''
Liatris pycnostachya	cat tail gay-feather	48–60	12	August–Sept.	pinkish-lavender	blooms from top of spike down; moisture-retentive soil
Liatris scariosa and cultivars	tall gay-feather	24–36	12	August–Sept.	purple	''
Liatris spicata and cultivars	spike gay-feather	24–60	12	August	pink to purple	''
Ligularia dentata 'Desdemona'		30–42	30	August	yellow	bold, handsome dark foliage; moisture-retentive soil
Limonium latifolium and cultivars	sea lavender	20	18–24	August	lavender-blue to pink	everlasting flowers; sun; good drainage; resents disturbance
Linum flavum	golden flax	12–15	9	June–August	gold	full sun; well-drained soil
Linum narbonense	Narbonne flax	18–24	12	May–June	azure blue	full sun; well-drained soil
Linum perenne and cultivars	blue flax	18–24	12	June–August	blue, white	''
Lobelia cardinalis	cardinal flower	24–36	9–12	August–Oct.	scarlet	light shade; moist to ordinary soil; short-lived but self-sows
Lupinus polyphyllus cultivars	perennial lupine	36–48	12–24	June	various	sun; well-drained soil
Lupinus Russell hybrids	Russell lupines	36–48	12–24	June	various	sun; well-drained soil; dislikes summer heat
Lychnis chalcedonica	Maltese cross	24–30	12	July–August	scarlet	well-drained soil
Lychnis viscaria	German catchfly	12–18	9	June	magenta	''
Lysimachia clethroides	gooseneck loosestrife	24	12	July–August	white	sun to semishade; forms large clumps
Lysimachia punctata	yellow loosestrife	30–36	12	June	yellow	light shade
Lythrum salicaria cultivars	(See descriptive list, page 293)					
Macleaya cordata	plumepoppy	60–96	36	July	cream-white	sun; large clumps; bold foliage; may become invasive
Mertensia virginica	Virginia bluebell	18	9	May	blue	partial shade; dies to ground in summer

(Continued)

HERBACEOUS PERENNIALS (Continued)

SCIENTIFIC NAME	COMMON NAME	HEIGHT IN INCHES	DISTANCE APART IN INCHES	SEASON	COLOR	REMARKS
Monarda didyma cultivars	bee balm	24–36	12	July–August	scarlet through pink and white	full sun; moisture-retentive soil; spreads rapidly
Myosotis scorpioides var. *semperflorens*	forget-me-not	9	8–10	May–Sept.	lavender-blue	moisture-retentive soil; very free flowering
Nepeta x *faassenii* (*N. mussini*)	Fassen catmint	15–18	12	May–July	blue-violet	moundlike; good for edging
Oenothera fruticosa 'Major' (*youngii*)		24–30	12	June–July	lemon-yellow	sun; well-drained soil
Oenothera missourensis	evening primrose	10–12	12	July–August	yellow	sun; well-drained soil; blooms at night; appears late in spring
Oenothera tetragona and cultivars	common sundrop	24	12	July–August	pale to deep yellow	sun; well-drained soil
Paeonia	peony (See descriptive list, page 294)					
Papaver nudicaule	Iceland poppy	12	10	June–Oct.	yellow, orange	sun; well-drained soils; dislikes hot summers
Papaver orientale	Oriental poppy	(See descriptive list, page 298)				
Penstemon barbatus	beard-tongue	30–36	12	June–July	red	sun; well-drained soil
Phlox divaricata	blue phlox	12	9	May	lavender	excellent with daffodils, primroses or tulips
Phlox paniculata	garden phlox	(See descriptive list, page 380)				
Physostegia virginiana and cultivars	false dragonhead	18–36	12–18	July–Sept.	pink to bright pink	sun; can become invasive
Platycodon grandiflorus	balloon flower	24	12	May–Sept.	blue, white	well-drained soil; resents disturbance
Platycodon grandiflorus var. *mariesii*	Maries balloon flower	12	9	May–Sept.	blue, white	''
Polemonium caeruleum	Jacob's ladder	18	9	May–June	blue, white	light shade; moisture-retentive soil
Polemonium reptans	Greek valerian	9	9	May	blue	''
Potentilla nepalensis	Nepal cinquefoil	18	9	June–August	rose	well-drained soil
Primula denticulata	Himalayan primrose	10	9	May	pink, white	light shade; moisture-retentive soil; cool places
Primula japonica	Japanese primrose	24	9	June	crimson to white	''
Primula x *polyantha*	polyanthus	6–10	9	April–May	various in combination	''
Primula sieboldii	siebold primrose	10	9	May	white, rose, purple	''
Primula veris	cowslip primrose	9	9	April–May	yellow	''
Primula vulgaris and cultivars (*P. acaulis*)	English primrose	6	9	April–May	various in combination	light shade; moisture-retentive soil; cool places
Pulmonaria officinalis	Jerusalem sage, lungwort	6–12	9	April	purple	light shade; moisture-retentive soil
Pulmonaria saccharata	Bethlehem sage	6–12	9	April–May	reddish-violet	light shade; moisture-retentive soil; handsome spotted foliage

HERBACEOUS PERENNIALS (Continued)

SCIENTIFIC NAME	COMMON NAME	HEIGHT IN INCHES	DISTANCE APART IN INCHES	SEASON	COLOR	REMARKS
Rudbeckia fulgida var. *sullivantii* 'Goldsturm'	coneflower	30	10–12	July–August	yellow with black "eye"	sun; well-drained soil; the epitome of the "black-eyed Susan"
Rudbeckia laciniata 'Goldquelle'	golden-glow	30	12	July–Sept.	yellow, double	sun; well-drained soil; profuse bloomer
Salvia azurea var. *grandiflora* (*S. pitcheri*)	azure sage	48	24	August–Sept.	light blue	sun; well-drained soil
Salvia farinacea	mealycup sage	36	12	August–Sept.	light blue	use as annual north of Washington, D.C.; sun; well-drained soil
Salvia glutinosa	Jupiter's distaff	36	12	July	pale yellow	coarse texture
Salvia pratensis	meadow clary	36	12	July	pale yellow	sun; well-drained soil
Scabiosa caucasica and cultivars	Caucasian scabiosa	24	12	June–Sept.	white blue, lilac	best in regions with cool summers
Sedum spectabile and cultivars	showy stonecrop	18	12	August–Oct.	red through pink to white	sun; well-drained soil
Sidalcea malviflora cultivars	checkerbloom	36	12–15	June–July	pink, white or purplish	sun; well-drained soil; like small hollyhocks
Solidago cultivars	goldenrod	18–40	12	August–Sept.	yellow	sun; almost any soil
Stachys grandiflora	big betony	18–24	12	May–June	purple	good cut flowers; takes partial shade
Stachys byzantina (*S. lanata*)	lamb's ears	12	10	July	purple	sun; handsome wooly leaves; forms a mat; spreads rapidly
Stokesia laevis and cultivars	Stokes' aster	12–24	12	July–August	blue, lilac, white	well-drained soil
Thalictrum	meadow rue	(See descriptive list, page 301)				
Thermopsis caroliniana	false lupine	36–48	15	June	yellow	survives considerable neglect
Tradescantia virginiana cultivars	spiderwort	18–24	15	May–Sept.	various	tolerates most poor growing conditions
Trollius europaeus cultivars	globeflower	24	12	April–June	yellow	moisture-retentive or wet soil
Trollius lederbourii	globeflower	24–30	12–18	June	golden	''
Trollius pumilus	globeflower	6–8	10	May–June	yellow	''
Valeriana officinalis	common valerian	36–60	12	July	lavender to white	for informal border only
Veronica grandis var. *holophylla*	Japanese speedwell	12	8–10	August–Oct.	vivid blue	sun; well-drained soil
Veronica incana	wooly speedwell	12	6	June–July	blue	sun; well-drained soil; white wooly leaves
Veronica latifolia	rock speedwell	12–24	12	June–August	blue	sun; well-drained soil; forms mats
Veronica longifolia (*V. maritima*)	beach speedwell	24	10	August	lilac-blue	sun; well-drained soil
Veronica spicata and cultivars	spike speedwell	14–18	10	July–August	blue or white	sun; well-drained soil
Veronica spicata 'Blue Peter'		18	10	July–August	deep blue	''
Veronica spicata 'Icicle'		24	10	June–Sept.	white	sun; well-drained soil
Veronica spicata 'Minuet'		12	10	June–August	pink	''
Veronica spicata 'Saraband'		20	10	June–August	violet-blue	''
Viola cornuta and cultivars	horned violet	6–10	6	April–Oct.	various	very hardy; long flowering season if seed formation is prevented
Yucca filamentosa	yucca, Adam's needle	60–72	36	June–July	white	sun; well-drained soil; coarse foliage

18.1 Crocus, *here popping through a ground cover of* Pachysandra, *are among the first of the so-called small bulbs to bloom in spring. Photo Grant Heilman*

18

Hardy Bulbs and Lilies

In the pageantry of the seasons bulbs play an important part. From the first flowers of the diminutive snowdrops in late winter to the last lingering blooms of the autumn crocus there is an ever-changing succession. The fleeting beauty of the crocus, the scillas and the grape hyacinths gives way to the far-flung loveliness of the narcissus, and as the season advances the tulips, with their sculptured beauty, hold the center of the stage.

There are few flowers that give so generously of their bloom and beauty as do the bulbs. Many of the spring-flowering bulbs, when once established, will increase rapidly and will form large colonies. This is particularly true of the early bulbs, such as the snowdrops and scillas, the grape hyacinths and the narcissus. Wide-spreading clumps of snowdrops along a woodland path in very early spring, the intense blue of a carpet of squills beneath the spreading branches of a great beech tree, a meadow with a myriad grape hyacinths in bloom, a bank where hundreds of narcissus sway in the spring breeze — these are among the joys of spring.

SPRING-FLOWERING BULBS

Narcissus

The narcissus, with its wealth of sunny and lovely flowers, is among the most adaptable of bulbs and deserves a place in every garden. It is hardy and dependable, demands little in the way of care and will continue to bloom blithely for many years, whether planted in long drifts in the garden, in masses along the edge of the woodland or on grassy slopes.

Narcissus are classified according to flower types and how they are borne on the scape of stem. The flower parts are essentially two for classification purposes: trumpet or corona, and perianth (the saucerlike disc of petals).

Division I – Trumpet Narcissus
Distinguishing characters: One flower to a stem; trumpet or corona as long as or longer than the perianth segments.
- (a) Perianth colored; corona colored, not paler than the perianth.
- (b) Perianth white; corona colored.
- (c) Perianth white; corona white, not paler than the perianth.
- (d) Any color combination not falling into the other groups.

Division II – Large-cupped Narcissus
Distinguishing characters: One flower to a stem; cup or corona more than one-third but less than equal to the length of the perianth segment.
- (a) Perianth colored; corona colored, not paler than the perianth.
- (b) Perianth white; corona colored.

315

18.2 Daffodils (Narcissus) — the most dependable and durable of the hardy bulbs — are wonderful when planted in great sweeps in a meadow, at the edge of a woodland or in an outcropping as above. Photo Carlton Lees

    (c) Perianth white; corona white, not paler than the perianth.
    (d) Any color combination not falling into the other groups.

Division III — Small-cupped Narcissus of Garden Origin
Distinguishing characters: One flower to a stem; cup or corona not more than one-third the length of the perianth segments.
    (a) Perianth colored; corona colored, not paler than the perianth.
    (b) Perianth white; corona colored.
    (c) Perianth white; corona white, not paler than the perianth.
    (d) Any color combination not falling into the other groups.

Division IV — Double Narcissus of Garden Origin
Distinguishing character: Double flowers.

Division V — Triandrus Narcissus
Distinguishing characters: Characteristics of *Narcissus triandrus* clearly evident.
    (a) Cup or corona not less than two-thirds the length of the perianth segments.
    (b) Cup or corona less than two-thirds the length of the perianth segments.

Division VI — Cyclamineus Narcissus of Garden Origin
Distinguishing characters: Characteristics of *Narcissus cyclamineus* must be clearly evident.
    (a) Cup or corona not less than two-thirds the length of the perianth segments.
    (b) Cup or corona less than two-thirds the length of the perianth segments.

Division VII — Jonquilla Narcissus of Garden Origin
Distinguishing characters: Characteristics of any of the *Narcissus jonquilla* group clearly evident.
    (a) Cup or corona not less than two-thirds the length of the perianth segments.
    (b) Cup or corona less than two-thirds the length of the perianth segments.

Division VIII — Tazetta Narcissus of Garden Origin

Distinguishing characters: Characteristics of any of the *Narcissus tazetta* group clearly evident.

Division IX — Poeticus Narcissus of Garden Origin

Distinguishing characters: Characteristics of any of the *Narcissus poeticus* group without a mixture of any other.

Division X — Species and Wild Forms and Hybrids

All species and wild, or reputedly wild, forms and hybrids.

Division XI — Split Corona Narcissus

Distinguishing character: Corona split for at least one-third of its length.

Division XII — Miscellaneous Narcissus

All narcissus not falling into any of the foregoing divisions.

Time of planting: When grown under natural conditions, narcissus produce their new root growth in the late summer and early autumn, and by the time the ground becomes frozen a strong root system has been developed. The ideal time for planting is during the dormant or rest period that occurs after the foliage has died down and before active root growth commences. If old clumps of narcissus are to be lifted and divided, it should preferably be done at this season. Bulbs that have been purchased from commercial growers are usually shipped early in the autumn and should be planted as soon as possible after their arrival, in order that full advantage may be taken of the good growing weather. If, for some unavoidable reason, planting must be delayed until late in the season, the ground should be kept mulched with straw or fresh manure to prevent it from freezing, and the mulch should be replaced again after the bulbs have been planted, in order to give them an opportunity to make as much root growth as possible. Late planting is never very successful. Both the quantity and quality of the spring bloom are dependent to a considerable extent upon the root development that the bulb has made the previous autumn. Good root development means good flowers, other conditions being favorable.

Method of planting: The depth of planting will vary according to the size of the bulb. A generally accepted rule is to cover each bulb with twice its own depth of soil. The small bulbs of the jonquil type should, therefore, be planted from 1 in. to 3 in. deep, while the very large bulbs of some of the trumpet varieties should be planted at a depth of 6 in. or more. The smaller varieties should be spaced from 3 in. to 4 in. apart, the larger varieties from 10 in. to 12 in. apart. If the bulbs are to be planted in well-prepared soil in a garden bed, a trowel or a bulb planter may be used to open the holes. Care should be taken to see that the base of the bulb is resting upon firm soil in order to avoid an air pocket beneath it. If bulbs are to be planted in an area of sod, or in a woodland, the digging of the holes is often very tedious and difficult. The work can be done more rapidly and efficiently with a mattock than with any other tool. A sharp stroke with the mattock should be used to pry up a piece of sod; it should not be torn entirely loose. The bulb should then be placed in the hole and the sod pressed back into position. Another method for planting a mass of bulbs into sod or woodland is to use a large electric drill or steel bar.

Soil requirements: Narcissus may be grown successfully in almost any type of soil. A well-drained, sandy loam is considered ideal. An application of well-rotted manure is beneficial in increasing the fertility of the soil and in improving its structure, but fresh manure should never be used as it is apt to cause serious injury. Some varieties of narcissus are more sensitive than others, but it is wise never to use manure in any form until it has become throughly rotted. Bone meal is the most satisfactory fertilizer for narcissus and may be applied at the rate of ½ lb. to every 25 sq. ft., being worked into the upper 2 in. or 3 in. of soil in the autumn.

After the period of bloom is over, the withered flowers should be cut off in order to prevent the formation of seed pods. No leaves should be removed until the foliage has turned a yellowish-brown and has died down. The vigor of the bulbs will be seriously affected if the foliage is removed while still green. If the bulbs

NARCISSUS VARIETIES OF MERIT

DIVISION I—TRUMPET NARCISSUS

YELLOW	BICOLOR	WHITE	PINK
'Arctic Gold'	'Lunar Sea'	'Beersheba'	'Mrs. R. O. Backhouse'
'Golden Harvest'	'Queen of Bicolors'	'Broughshane'	'Pink Glory'
'Golden Rapture'	'Spellbinder'	'Cantatrice'	'Rima'
'Hunters Moon'	'Spring Glory'	'Empress of Ireland'	
'King Alfred'	'Trousseau'	'Mount Hood'	
'Kingscourt'		'Vigil'	
'Slieveboy'			

DIVISION II—LARGE-CUPPED NARCISSUS

YELLOW PERIANTH, COLORED CORONA	WHITE PERIANTH, COLORED CORONA	WHITE PERIANTH, WHITE CORONA	PINK CORONA OR PINK-EDGED
'Armada'	'Duke of Windsor'	'Easter Moon'	'Accent'
'Binkie'	'Festivity'	'Ice Follies'	'Louise de Coligny'
'Butterscotch'	'Green Island'	'Pigeon'	'Passionale'
'Carlton'	'Kilworth'	'Sleveen'	'Pink Rim'
'Galway'	'Singal Light'	'Stainless'	'Roseyards'
'Gigantic Star'	'Tudor Minstrel'		'Rosy Sunrise'
'St. Keverne'			'Salmon Trout'
			'Toscanini'

DIVISION III—SMALL-CUPPED NARCISSUS

YELLOW PERIANTH, COLORED CORONA	WHITE PERIANTH, COLORED CORONA	WHITE PERIANTH, WHITE CORONA
'Apricot Distinction'	'Aircastle'	'Chinese White'
'Barrett Browning'	'Blarney'	'Cushendall'
'Chungking'	'Firetail'	'Dreen Castle'
'Edward Buxton'	'La Riante'	'Frigid'
'Irish Coffee'	'Verger'	'Polar Ice'
		'Portrush'

DIVISION IV—DOUBLE NARCISSUS

YELLOW	BICOLOR	WHITE
'Golden Ducat'	'Irene Copeland'	'Cheerfulness'
'Inglescomb'	'Mary Copeland'	'White Lion'
'Yellow Cheerfulness'	'Texas'	

DIVISION V—TRIANDRUS NARCISSUS

YELLOW	WHITE
'Hawera'	'Shot Silk'
'Liberty Bells'	'Silver Chimes'
	'Thalia'
	'Tresamble'

DIVISION VI—CYCLAMINEUS NARCISSUS (YELLOW)

'Charity May'	'March Sunshine'
'February Gold'	'Peeping Tom'
'Jack Snipe'	'Tete-a-tete'

NARCISSUS VARIETIES OF MERIT (Continued)

DIVISION VII — JONQUILLA NARCISSUS (YELLOW, LARGE AND SMALL)

'Cheri'	'Pipit'
'Lintie'	'Suzy'
Narcissus jonquilla	'Trevithian'

DIVISION VIII — TAZETTA NARCISSUS

YELLOW	BICOLOR	WHITE
'Early Perfection'	'Cragford'	'Bridal Crown'
'Scarlet Gem'	'Geranium'	'Cheerfulness'
'Yellow Cheerfulness'	'Laurens Koster'	
	'Minnow'	

DIVISION IX — POETICUS NARCISSUS (WHITE WITH RED-RIMMED CUPS)

'Actaea'	*Narcissus poeticus recurvus*
'Cantabile'	'Red Rim'

DIVISION X — SPECIES AND WILD FORMS AND HYBRIDS

Narcissus bulbocodium conspicuus	*Narcissus jonquilla* 'Rip Van Winkle'
Narcissus gracilis	*Narcissus watieri* 'W. P. Milner'

have been planted in an area of sod, the grass should not be cut until the foliage of the bulbs has matured. If the yellowing foliage becomes unsightly in the garden, the leaves may be braided or rolled into a small mass and tucked under the foliage of neighboring plants.

Narcissus bulbs increase very rapidly, and when the bulbs have become too crowded, they should be lifted, divided and replanted as soon as the foliage has ripened. In naturalistic plantings, where the size and perfection of the flowers are not matters of great importance, the bulbs may be left undisturbed for a period of many years. In the garden, it is advisable to lift them every six or eight years, as the blooms have a tendency to become smaller, and the bulbs are less thrifty when they have become overcrowded.

Tulip

There are few flowers that offer the gardener so great an opportunity for color harmonies as the tulips. In the skillful hands of the artist they may be used to create the most subtle and beautiful compositions in the spring garden. If some of the lovely species tulips are grown, a succession of bloom may be had extending from very early spring, when *Tulipa kaufmanniana*, the exquisite waterlily tulip, opens its graceful flowers to late May when the last of the stately Breeder tulips bring the season to a close.

Exposure: Tulips prefer a sunny location where they will be protected against strong winds. Partial or heavy shade is not desirable, as the stems have a tendency to bend toward the light and to become weak and floppy. Tulips will, however, do well where they receive shade for a few hours each day, and in some cases the colors seem to fade less and the flowers last longer when protected from full sun, particularly afternoon sun.

Soil: The ideal soil for tulips is a light, fertile, well-drained loam. Fresh manures should never be used in the preparation of tulip beds. Very well-rotted manure or compost may be used in fairly liberal quantities. Bone meal is one of the best fertilizers and may be applied to the tulip beds at the rate of ½ lb. per 25 sq. ft.

Planting: Where soil conditions permit, deep planting is recommended, the bulb being placed so that the top is from 10 in. to 12 in. below the surface. Deep planting has a number of advantages over shallow planting. The bulbs will continue to flower well for a greater number of years; there is less danger of injury from botrytis blight; it is possible to plant annuals and gladioli in the same space after the tulips have finished blooming without running the risk of injuring the bulbs; and there is less danger of loss from mice. However, in planting tulips at this depth it is essential that the soil be well drained, and there must be no danger of having standing water near the surface at any season of the year. There must also be a sufficiently deep layer of topsoil to provide a fertile soil of good texture beneath the bulb. In soils that are not well drained, or where there is only a shallow layer of topsoil, it is wiser to plant tulips at a depth of 4 in. to 6 in.

The early-flowering varieties may be spaced 4 in. apart, the later varieties, such as the Darwins and the Breeders, 6 in. apart. If tulips are to be planted in drifts in the herbaceous border, a trowel or a bulb planter may be used to open the holes, care being taken to see that the base of the bulb is resting on firm soil in order to avoid an air pocket beneath it. When a large bed or border is to be planted entirely with tulips, it is sometimes a wise plan to remove the upper 4 in. to 6 in. of topsoil. The floor of the bed may then be slightly loosened and raked until the surface is level. The bulbs may be placed in position, being pressed firmly into the soil, and the topsoil carefully replaced. This method will assure absolute uniformity of planting, which is necessary if precise regularity is desired.

Tulips should preferably be planted between the middle of October and the middle of November. If the bulbs are planted too early in the autumn, they are apt to start into active growth, and will suffer a severe setback during the win-

ter. Tulips should, therefore, not be planted as early as narcissus. It is important, however, that the bulbs are planted far enough in advance of freezing weather to enable them to make sufficient root growth. A strong, vigorous root system produced during the autumn has a very direct effect upon the quality of the bloom the following spring. If planting must be delayed until very late in the season, the same procedure may be followed as that recommended for narcissus.

Mice are extremely fond of tulips, and if they are prevalent they can completely destroy an entire planting in a single season. In gardens where mice are known to be troublesome it is wise to use every possible measure to eradicate them. And where it is not possible, because of soil conditions, to plant the bulbs at a depth of 10 in. to 12 in., it is recommended that the bulbs be planted in wire baskets that will afford excellent protection. Such baskets can be pur-

18.3 Tulips, while not as durable over the years as daffodils, are essential to spring. Photo Carlton Lees

chased from garden supply stores or can be fabricated from hardware cloth or similar close-meshed wire.

Care after blooming: Tulips will produce their best bloom the spring following planting. Some varieties will bloom well over a period of years, while other varieties deteriorate rapidly and show a decided decline after the first season. Some of the older varieties such as 'Clara Butt,' 'William Copeland' and 'Rev. Ewbank' will continue to flower for twenty years, while some of the newer varieties are comparatively short-lived. If tulips are planted in a bed with herbaceous perennials or as a foreground to a shrubbery border, the foliage may be allowed to die down naturally. If young plants of quick-growing annuals such as snapdragon, petunia and verbena are set among the tulips the yellowing of the foliage will hardly be noticed. If tulips are planted in solid beds or borders, and if the space they occupy is desired for other plantings, the bulbs may be lifted very carefully after blooming, the roots and leaves remaining intact, and they may then be removed to a partially shaded spot where they can be heeled in and then left to ripen. When the leaves have turned brown and the bulbs are thoroughly mature, they may be placed in storage until planting time in the autumn. The bulbs should be stored in a cool, dark, dry place.

Tulips for Southern Gardens

It was long a matter of regret to southern gardeners that tulips were among the flowers that would not thrive in southern climates, and for generations those who have gardened in the South have had to be content with miserably weak and floppy specimens, or have had to forgo their beauty entirely.

Today, of course, tulips may be grown quite as successfully in the South as in the North, provided that the bulbs are placed in cold storage for several months before they are planted. Excellent results may be obtained if the bulbs are held in storage at a temperature of 45° F. for about six months prior to actual planting. Obviously, this time span means that the southern gardener who wants to look forward to an impressive tulip display must have the foresight to order bulbs well in advance of planting time. Bulbs usually may be planted any time from December through early February, though in the case of later plantings, active growth will probably begin almost immediately. If this method is followed, an abundance of tall, strong-stemmed blooms may be had.

As soon as the foliage has died down and the bulbs have ripened, they should be lifted and placed in storage. Some bulbs will flower well for several seasons if accorded this treatment, while others deteriorate rapidly and must be replaced by new stock, which has been specially prepared for southern planting.

Species Tulips and Hybrids

The species tulips and their hybrids possess a sprightliness and charm that is quite distinctive. Most of them flower early and when once well established they will usually continue to bloom on year after year. As a group they prefer dry, sunny locations and are most happily at home when planted in some sheltered nook where they add a welcome touch of bright color in the early spring.

Among the most appealing and beloved in this group are *T. biflora; T. clusiana; T. dasystemon; T. fosteriana* and its hybrids, which include *T. fosteriana* 'Red Emperor'; *T. kaufmanniana* and its many lovely hybrids; and *T. sylvestris.*

Hyacinth

Hyacinths lack the grace and charm of tulips and narcissus and it is sometimes difficult to find a place in the garden where they seem at home. If planted as a foreground for a shrubbery border, they present a striking display of color and are effective in such a location.

The bulbs should be planted in the autumn between the middle of September and the middle of October. The depth of planting will vary according to the size of the bulb. The top of the bulb should be approximately 3 in. below the surface if the soil is of a heavy texture; 5 in. in a light, sandy soil. They may be set from 6 in. to 8 in. apart.

TULIP VARIETIES OF MERIT

SINGLE EARLY TULIPS

PINK	RED	WHITE	YELLOW	ORANGE
'Princess Irene'	'Brilliant Star'	'Diana'	'Bellona'	'De Wet'
'Christmas Marvel'	'Couluer Cardinal'		'Joffre'	'Dr. Plesman'
'Ibs'	'Keizerskroon'			'Princess of Austria'
'Le Reve'				

PURPLE

'Van der Neer'

DOUBLE EARLY TULIPS

PINK	YELLOW-ORANGE	RED	WHITE
'Murillo Max'	'Goya'	'Dante'	'Schoonoord'
'Peach Blossom'	'Marechal Niel'	'Electra'	
	'Mr. Van der Hoef'	'Jewel Dance'	
	'Orange Nassua'	'Vuurbaak'	

TRIUMPH TULIPS

RED	YELLOW-ORANGE	WHITE	PURPLE
'Elmns'	'Cup Final'	'Hibernia'	'First Lady'
'Garden Party'	'Kees Nelis'	'Kansas'	'Purple Star'
'La Suisse'	'Orange Wonder'		
'Lucky Strike'	'Ornament'		
'Paul Richter'			
'Prominence'			

MENDEL TULIPS

PINK-RED	WHITE	YELLOW-ORANGE
'Apricot Beauty'	'Athlete'	'Golden Triumph'
'Golden Olga'	'White Sail'	'Sulphur Triumph'
'Olga'		
'Pink Trophy'		
'Ruby Red'		

COTTAGE TULIPS

PINK	RED	WHITE	YELLOW	ORANGE
'Artist'	'Burgundy Lace'	'Maureen'	'Georgette'	'Bond Street'
'Greenland'	'Halcro'	'Sorbet'	'Golden Harvest'	'Dillenburg'
'Rosy Wings'	'Henry Ford'		'Mrs. John D. Scheepers'	'Orange Bouquet'
'Smiling Queen'	'Renown'		'Princess Margaret Rose'	

VIOLET-PURPLE

Blue Heron

TULIP VARIETIES OF MERIT (Continued)

DARWIN AND DARWIN HYBRID TULIPS

YELLOW	RED	ORANGE	WHITE	PINK-ROSE
'Beauty of Apeldoorn'	'Apeldoorn'	'Orange Sun'	'Duke of Wellington'	'Aristocrat'
'Golden Age'	'Apeldoorn Elite'	'Elizabeth Arden'	'Magier'	'Clara Butt'
'Gudoshnik'	'Flying Dutchman'			'Dreamland Gander'
'Jewel of Spring'	'Hollands Glory'			'Queen of Bartigons'
'Niphetos'	'Landseadel's Supreme'			
'President Kennedy'	'Oxford'			
'Sunkist'	'Parade'			
'Sweet Harmony'	'Spring Song'			
'Yellow Dover'				

PURPLE-BLACK	MAUVE-LILAC
'Queen of Night'	'Bleu Aimable'
'Scotch Lassie'	'Insurpassable'
'The Bishop'	'William Copeland'

LILY-FLOWERING TULIPS

RED	YELLOW	WHITE	ROSE-PINK	VIOLET
'Aladdin'	'Alaska'	'White Triumphator'	'China Pink'	'Maytime'
'Queen of Sheba'	'West Point'		'Mairette'	
'Red Shine'				

DOUBLE LATE TULIPS

PINK	RED	WHITE	YELLOW	ORANGE
'Angelique'	'Bonanza'	'Mount Tacoma'	'Gold Medal'	'Orange Triumph'
'Eros'	'Uncle Tom'			
'May Wonder'				

PARROT TULIPS

PINK	ORANGE	RED	YELLOW	PURPLE
'Fantasy'	'Orange Favorite'	'Estelle Rignveld'	'Karel Doorman'	'Black Parrot'
		'Firebird'	'Texas Gold'	'Blue Parrot'

WHITE
'White Parrot'

SPECIES HYBRIDS

'Cape Cod'	'Salmon Trout'
'Daylight'	'Shakespeare'
'Purissima'	'Stresa'
'Red Emperor'	'Yellow Emperor'
'Red Riding Hood'	

Hyacinths will produce good bloom in any type of moderately fertile soil provided that it is well drained.

After the bulbs have flowered, the foliage should be allowed to ripen. If desired, the same treatment may be accorded hyacinths as that recommended for tulips.

SMALL SPRING-FLOWERING BULBS

These early harbingers of spring hold a very special place in our affections, and they may be planted in drifts along the edge of the flower borders or they may be naturalized in great masses.

All of these small bulbs should be planted during the early autumn. They may be spaced from 3 in. to 4 in. apart and the depth of planting will vary from 2 in. to 3 in., depending upon the size of the bulb. After they have once become established, they will increase rapidly and may be left undisturbed for many years. They thrive well in any type of well-drained soil and will require no further care or attention.

Anemone apennina

This is a good species to grow in meadows leading to the rock garden, or to naturalize in woodlands where, if left undisturbed, it will develop extensive colonies over the years. The plants reach 6 in. when in flower. The blue, white or pink flowers have ten to twenty petals, and are about 1¼ in. in diameter. This spe-

*18.4 This lovely anemone (**Anemone** blanda), when in a woodsy, humusy soil and where other conditions are suitable, covers the ground with sparkling blue stars in early spring. Photo Grant Heilman*

cies differs from *A. blanda* (below) mainly by being taller and having a rather elongated rhizomatous root, while *A. blanda* has a rather rounded tuber. It occurs wild in southern Europe and flowers in March and April.

Anemone blanda

Dainty and charming, this little anemone comes into flower in very early spring, soon after the snowdrops and winter aconites are over. It is a winsome thing, hardly more than 3 in. in height, and the star-shaped flowers are nestled in a spreading growth of fernlike leaves. It prefers light shade and is lovely in the rock garden, and when naturalized under trees or in the foreground of shrub plantings. A little patch near the house will become a joy for a few brief weeks each succeeding spring. *Anemone blanda atrocaerulea* is a rich violet-blue in color. There is also a pink shade.

Since new tubers are very dry and shriveled, and winter moisture still a long way off, it might be a good idea to soak the tubers for one hour in water before planting. The little bulbs (actually tubers) should be planted 3 in. deep, and spaced about 2 in. apart. It is most effective when the bulbs are planted in clumps of six or more.

Anemone pavonina

In this species the roots are misshapened knobby tubers. The flowers are 1½ in. to 2 in. in diameter and scarlet, pink or purple, often with a yellowish or white eye. There are many cultivars that are good garden plants with a long flowering period. Native to the northern Mediterranean area, *A. pavonina* flowers from February to April. Where the ground freezes, it needs winter protection. It is not reliably hardy north of Philadelphia.

Convallaria majalis (lily-of-the-valley)

This lovely little member of the lily family is an old-time favorite. The nodding creamy-white bells are very fragrant and a few stalks tucked into a flower arrangement will bring a pervading perfume into a room. The pips should be planted in the autumn; when once established, they spread very rapidly if conditions are favorable. They prefer a fertile soil well supplied with humus, abundant moisture and a position in partial shade. They are one of the few flowering plants that will thrive in really dense shade, although they do not flower as abundantly as when grown in partial shade. In time the clumps tend to become crowded and the blooms sparse. In order to prevent this, the clumps should be lifted, divided and replanted occasionally.

Crocus

Among the most beloved and most widely grown of the small, spring-flowering bulbs are the crocuses. The "Dutch" crocus is the garden type most commonly grown and, when planted in masses, it gives a lavish display of color. The jaunty, erect, cuplike flowers come in a variety of colors—white, deep violet, porcelain blue, dark lilac and golden-yellow.

Lovely as are the Dutch crocuses, any gardener who has never grown some of the smaller, more dainty species crocuses has missed one of the greatest joys of very early spring. They come into flower soon after the snowdrops are over, and they possess a sprightliness and a piquant charm that is very endearing. A little patch of species crocuses near the house, in some sheltered corner where they will catch the first warm rays of spring sunshine, will be a source of joy year after year. They may be tucked into all sorts of places: along a path, on a bank, in front of shrub plantings, anywhere, provided they can be left undisturbed after they have flowered, and each spring one will find oneself eagerly watching for the first blooms. Colors vary according to the species. *Crocus aureus* is a deep golden-yellow; *C. korolkowii*, the very earliest to bloom, is a brilliant yellow, shading to orange, the reverse of the petals touched with bronze; *C. chrysanthus* is pale yellow with brilliant orange stamens; the flowers of *C. sieberi* are a delicate blue with a golden throat; and *C. tomasinianus,* one of the most

CROCUS VARIETIES OF MERIT

SPRING-BLOOMING DUTCH

BLUE	WHITE	YELLOW
'Enchantress'	'Jeanne d'Arc'	'Golden Yellow'
'Paulus Potter'	'Kathleen Parlow'	'Yellow Mammoth'
'Pickwick'	'Peter Pan'	
'Queen of the Blues'	'Snowstorm'	
'Remembrance'		
'Striped Beauty'		
'The Sultan'		

SPECIES AND THEIR CULTIVARS

BLUE	YELLOW	WHITE
Crocus biflorus	*Crocus aureus*	*Crocus fleischeri*
C. imperati	*C. chrysanthus* and cultivars	
C. sieberi and cultivars	*C. korolkowii*	
C. tomasinianus and cultivars	*C. sulphureus concolor*	
C. veriscolor	*C. susianus*	

charming of all the species, is more than generous with its bloom, the flowers being a soft, pale lavender.

Culture: All types of crocus are of easy culture. They prefer a light, somewhat sandy soil, not too rich a diet, and an exposure in full sun or very light shade. The corms of the Dutch crocuses should be planted about 4 in. deep, the species from 2 in. to 3 in., and all should be spaced from 2 in. to 4 in. apart.

Where crocuses are planted in a lawn, the grass should not be cut until after the foliage has matured and begins to die down.

Crocuses increase very rapidly, both by the production of new corms and by reseeding. Most of the species crocuses reseed readily and sometimes appear in the most surprising places as a result. From a modest initial planting large colonies will often develop over a number of years.

In areas where mice and other rodents are common, crocus plantings should be protected with ½-in. wire mesh or netting, laid flat over the bed and turned down several inches into the soil at the edges. Squirrels and chipmunks are particularly assiduous at finding, digging up and eating newly planted crocus.

Eranthis hyemalis (winter aconite)

Blooming with the snowdrops, this endearing little flower seems to hold within its golden cup the very promise of spring. Borne on a stem hardly more than 2 in. or 3 in. tall, each little flower is surrounded by an Elizabethan ruff of green leaves. Eranthis reseed readily and large colonies soon develop from a small planting. Patches of them are lovely in an open woodland, on a bank, or in the foreground of a shrub planting. They will thrive in full sun or partial shade but prefer light shade during the summer. The little tubers should be soaked in water immediately upon arrival for one or two hours, and planted at a depth of about 2 in., spaced about 3 in. apart. If they appear shriveled and dry, it is advisable to bury them in moist sand or in wet peat moss for a few days before planting them.

Galanthus nivalis (snowdrop)

Because the snowdrop is the true harbinger of spring, often coming into flower while there is still snow on the ground, it is especially cherished and beloved. Diminutive in size, hardly

18.5 The autumn-flowering crocus (Crocus longiflorus) *and the closely related* Colchicum *are always a pleasant surprise. Photo Grant Heilman*

more than 3 in. or 4 in. tall, it possesses the ability to survive a heavy snowfall quite unharmed and will bloom blithely on after the snows have melted. Preferring partial shade and a rather cool, moist, heavy soil, snowdrops will increase slowly over the years until large clumps are formed from an original planting of a few bulbs. The small, dropping white blooms are of great daintiness, and clumps of snowdrops are lovely when naturalized in open woodland areas, or at the base of trees on the lawn, or in the foreground of a planting of evergreen shrubs. A patch by the door or below a window will bring to those within a message that spring is soon to come.

Leucojum (snowflakes)

The leucojums resemble the snowdrops, having pendent, bell-shaped flowers, tipped with green. They bloom later than the snowdrops, however, and are much taller and more robust.

They may be naturalized in a woodland planting, or used in the foreground of a shrub planting or may even be planted in the perennial border, being pleasant companions for tulips, *Phlox divaricata* and bleeding-heart. They are very long-lived and when once established will continue to bloom on year after year, requiring only an occasional digging. The bulbs should be planted in the autumn about 3 in. deep, and spaced 4 in. to 5 in. apart. There are several types and varieties, some blooming earlier than others.

Muscari (grape hyacinth)

Always dependable and bountiful with their bloom are the lovely little grape hyacinths. Some species flower in very early spring, others come later with the narcissus and tulips. Amazingly adaptable, they will do well in full sun or partial shade and will increase rapidly, soon forming large colonies that will continue to bloom year after year with no care or attention whatsoever. For many years there was a meadow in the countryside near Philadelphia where grape hyacinths had naturalized themselves and in spring thousands of them flowered, spreading their expanse of blue over an acre or more.

M. armeniacum
One of the largest species, bearing flowers of a deep, cobalt blue on sturdy stems 5 in. to 6 in. in height. It is one of the best for mass plantings and comes into flower with the daffodils.

M. azureum
The earliest to flower, blooming with the early species crocuses. It is a dainty, lovely little thing with flowers of a bright, azure blue.

M. botryoides caeruleum
Bears flowers of bright blue, coming into bloom with the late crocuses. It is more compact in growth than most of the other species and is expecially well adapted to the rock garden. There is a white variety.

M. plumosum **(feather hyacinth or plume hyacinth)**

This is quite different in character from the other species. The little feathery plumes are a clear violet color and are borne on stems about 7 in. in height. It flowers in May with the tulips and remains in bloom over a long period.

Scilla

The various species of *Scilla* are among the loveliest of the small spring-flowering bulbs. When once established, the *Scilla* will increase rapidly and will bloom on almost indefinitely. They are particularly fine for naturalizing in a woodland area or on shady banks. They prefer partial shade but will also do well in full sun.

S. hispanica **(*S. campanulata* in many catalogues, wood hyacinth or Scotch Bluebell)**

Comes into bloom with the Darwin and cottage tulips and is lovely in flower beds and borders or for naturalizing. Patches of them here and there in a woodland or along a wooded path are superb in springtime. The dainty flowers are borne on stalks about 10 in. to 12 in. tall and are excellent for cutting. They come in several colors, deep blue, pale blue, porcelain blue, white, pale pink and deep pink.

S. nonscripta **(*S. nutans*)**

The true English bluebell. Taller and more robust than *S. hispanica*, it comes into flower a week or ten days later, with the last of the late tulips. It is particularly valuable for naturalizing and will, in time, completely cover a bank or a wooded area. The banks along Hobby Drive in the lovely little Devonshire village of Clovelly in England are carpeted with bluebells and are an enchanting sight during the month of May.

S. siberica **(squill)**

The smallest of the *Scilla* species and the first to come into flower. The color is a very intense, bright blue, and the bell-like, drooping flowers are borne on slender stems hardly more than 3 in. or 4 in. in height. There is also a white form, *S. siberica* 'Alba.' Squills are most effective when planted in masses. A sheet of blue squills beneath the newly unfolding leaves of a copper beech is a thing of breathtaking beauty. They are also effective when used to border prim garden paths in a colonial garden, or in the foreground of a planting of evergreens.

SUMMER-FLOWERING BULBS AND TUBERS

Achimene (pronounced a-kim′e-ne)

This lovely member of the Gesneriad family, to which the *Saintpaulia* and *Gloxinia* belong is a dainty, charming thing, prodigal with its bloom, and adapted to many uses. It offers delightful material of distinction and charm for porch and window boxes, and for hanging pots and baskets. It is colorful and gay when used in flat containers against the wall of a patio, or in small strawberry jars or decorative pots on the terrace. It is lovely on low walls along the edge of terraced beds, or at the edge of raised planting beds by the house. It may be grown under deeply rooting trees that cast high shade, and will thrive in the foreground of shrub plantings, provided the exposure is favorable. And it may be used to grace many a window sill during the summer months.

There are numerous types and varieties of achimenes, and there is considerable variation in the size and shape of the blooms, as well as in their coloring and general habit of growth. Some types are dwarf and compact, others taller and more robust, reaching a height of 10 in. to 12 in.; most types are definitely trailing in habit. Some, however, may be easily trained on small stakes to upright form if desired for use on window sills. The flowers are most attractive. A few varieties bear slipper-shaped flowers resembling those of the *Gloxinia*, but most varieties have a curved tube, the petals opening into dainty pansy-faced or petunialike flowers. The colors range from white through delicate mauve, violet, and pale lavender-blue to deep purple, with a few pink and scarlet types.

After the plants come into bloom, they will bear continually until the end of the season, often flowering over a period of four or five months.

Exposure: The achimenes are native to tropical America, from Mexico southward to Brazil, and they are unable to withstand cold. The very name indicates this, being derived from the Greek word *achaimems* meaning "suffers from cold." In very mild climates they may be grown out of doors, remaining in the ground throughout the year. In cooler regions they should not be planted outside until all danger of sudden drops in temperature below 45° F. They thrive within a temperature range of 55° to 80° F. Locations where the plants would be exposed to high winds or to heavy rains should be avoided.

One of the most important requirements of achimenes is shade. It is essential that semi-shade be provided. They require plenty of light, and will not thrive in dense shade, but must be protected from midday sun. Sun in the early morning and in late afternoon, but no direct sun between 9 o'clock and 5, is a safe rule to follow. Plants will usually thrive in the foreground of shrub plantings on the north and east sides of the house.

Soil requirements: A coarse, loose soil mixture is ideal, and good drainage is essential. The pH is not a matter of importance, as achimenes thrive equally well in neutral or strongly acid soils. The following soil mixtures are recommended:
  (1) 1 part sandy loam, 1 part sifted peat moss, 1 part leaf mold
  (2) 1 part coarse sand, or fine gravel or vermiculite
  1 part fibrous loam, rich in humus
  1 part milled sphagnum moss, or sifted peat moss or coarse leaf mold
  (3) A loose, fibrous, sandy loam, rich in humus

Propagation: Achimenes may be propagated by the division of the tuberlike rhizomes, by stem cuttings and by little axillary cones. The tubercles, which form on the roots in late summer and fall, range according to variety from ½ in. to 1 in. or more in length. Some are oval, some roundish, others long and slender. Stem cuttings should be taken just below a node and

will root very readily in moist vermiculite or some similar rooting medium. During the latter part of the growing season little axillary cones, which are dark in color and covered with a waxy substance, develop in the axils of the upper leaves. These should be gathered just before they are ready to drop off the plants, and stored in vermiculite during the winter, until time for planting in the spring. They are slow to sprout but will develop into good plants.

Planting: The tubercles and the axillary cones may be planted at any time from February to late May. In mild climates they may be planted out of doors or in suitable containers in lath houses. In the North they must be started indoors.

In outdoor beds the tubercles should be spaced 3 in. to 4 in. apart. In pots or hanging baskets they should be spaced as follows: 1 in a 2-in. pot; 2 to 5 in a 4-in. pot; 3 to 7 in a 5-in. pot; 5 to 6 in a 6-in. hanging basket; 10 to 12 in a 12-in. basket; 20 to 25 in a 16-in. basket. When planting the more vigorous types or varieties, use the smaller number; for the more dwarf and more delicate types, use the larger number per pot or basket.

Several planting methods may be followed.

Method 1. Plant directly in the pot or basket in which they are to be grown. If a pot is used, provide at least 1 in. of good drainage material, such as broken crocks or gravel in the bottom. Add the soil to within 1½ in. to 2 in. of the rim. Place the tubercles in a horizontal position on the surface of the soil. Cover with ¾ in. to 1 in. of soil. Water *sparingly* until growth starts and maintain a temperature of 70° to 75° F. if possible. After shoots appear, shift to a slightly cooler temperature and keep pots always moist but never soggy.

Method 2. If the tubercles have not started to sprout when received, growth may be hastened by placing them on milled sphagnum moss or vermiculite or screened peat moss that has been thoroughly moistened. The container should be kept in a warm place with a temperature between 75° and 90° F. until the shoots appear. They should then be planted in pots or baskets according to the procedure followed in Method 1.

If the plants are to be used in beds out of doors, the tubercles may be started in flats and later transplanted.

Culture: The young plants need warmth and care in watering. The pots should be turned regularly in order that growth may be symmetrical, and when a few inches high the plants may be pinched back to make them more bushy. High humidity is desirable throughout the growing season, and abundant moisture is essential. If the plants are allowed to become completely dry when in active growth, they may become prematurely dormant. Cold water will cause a spotting of the leaves. Tepid water should therefore be used and it is advisable to avoid wetting the leaves. A very fine, mistlike spray is not harmful.

The size and quantity of the bloom will depend to a considerable extent upon the nutrients available to the plant. An application of a high-analysis, quickly soluble fertilizer (1 heaping teaspoonful to 1 gallon of water) every few weeks will encourage good bloom.

In the autumn when the lower leaves begin to shrivel it is a sign that the period of dormancy is approaching and water should be withheld. As soon as the stems are completely dry, they should be cut off and the pots or baskets stored in a cool, dry place. A temperature of 60° F. is ideal, and the temperature should never drop below 50° F. In the spring (from February to May) the containers may be placed in a warm temperature, given good light and watered sparingly until the shoots appear. Plants may usually be grown for two seasons in the same pot, or for three years in the same hanging basket, before being divided and replanted.

Hanging baskets: Achimenes are well adapted to pot culture but are at their best when grown in hanging baskets. Baskets of various shapes and sizes can be made out of hardware cloth (1/4-in. mesh wire), or wire baskets may be pur-

ACHIMENES OF MERIT

'Adelaide': pale blue
'Galatea': medium size, showy, blue flowers; early
Jaureguia maxima: white
'Margaritae' ('Purity'): white
'Mauve Queen': large flowers of delicate mauve
'Pink Beauty': clear pink flowers
'Pulchella': small, scarlet flowers, fernlike foliage
'Purple King' ('Royal Purple'): sturdy, free blooming, of easy culture
'Violetta': a lovely, trailing variety from Holland
'Vivid': purple with bright orange tube

chased. The baskets should be lined with a good layer of coarse sphagnum moss and then filled with the soil mixture. A row of tubercles, with tips pointing outward, should be placed close to the edge of the basket, spaced about 3 in. apart, and a few should be planted in the center. The tubercles should be covered with 3/4 in. to 1 in. of soil. If very large wire baskets are used, a row of tubercles may be planted near the edge when the basket is half filled with soil and others planted at the top in the manner outlined above. This method will give a charming effect.

Anemone coronaria (anemone)

Anemones are delightful for cutting and may be had in a wide variety of colorings — white, deep purple, lavender, and brilliant scarlet. The cup-shaped flowers are borne on slender, graceful stems that attain a height of from 12 in. to 15 in. The St. Brigid strain is considered one of the finest.

Exposure: An eastern exposure is ideal, where they may be protected from afternoon sun.

Soil requirements: A soil mixture of 1 part loam, 1 part leaf mold and 1 part sand is considered ideal.

Propagation: By tubers. Care must be taken to see that the tubers are not planted upside down. The top of the tuber may be recognized by its fuzzy appearance; the bottom of the tuber is usually pointed.

Culture: In warm climates the tubers may be planted in the open ground from August to November. In areas where the climate is severe, anemones may be planted either in coldframes or in the greenhouse.

Begonia, tuberous

Tuberous begonias are among the most beautiful and most decorative of flowering plants. The blooms, which vary widely in form, have a sculptured quality, and the glowing colors will highlight a planting composition with great distinction.

Tuberous begonias may be grown in garden beds, in pots and in hanging baskets. When planted in beds, it is wise not to attempt to combine them with other flowers because of their specific cultural requirements. When grown in pots, tuberous begonias offer exciting material for the decoration of terrace or patio, and in such a location the rare beauty of the blooms can be enjoyed to the fullest extent. On the West Coast the pendula type is used extensively in pots and baskets, which are hung on balconies and porches, suspended from the beams of patio roofs and arbors, or hung from the picturesque branches of live oak trees arching over patio walls. A large pot or basket with its cascade of drooping branches and its myriad blooms is a thing of breathtaking beauty, and when used in great numbers, as on a long balcony or beneath the beams of a pergola, the effect is dramatic.

Types: The tuberous begonia is often spoken of as the "mockingbird flower" because in its widely varied forms the flowers of the camellia, the rose, the carnation, the hollyhock and even the daffodil have found their counterparts.

From the various wild species discovered in the western hemisphere many beautiful forms of the tuberous begonia have been developed through hybridization and careful selection. In most types there is a wide color range—unusually beautiful shades of pink, salmon, apricot and orange; brilliant scarlets, crimsons and deep reds; pure, glistening white and pale yellow.

The types most popular with commercial growers and with home gardeners include: the double camellia and the ruffled camellia types, the rose form, the picotee, and the carnation or *fimbriata* types, the pendula or hanging type, and the small, multiflowered type.

Culture: Start tubers in February or March by placing them in leaf mold or peat moss in shallow boxes at a temperature of 65° to 70° F. When rooted, plant in small pots, and afterwards transfer to larger ones. Water moderately at first, then more fully later on. Feed with diluted liquid manure when active growth takes place.

Exposure: Except in the coolest of summer climates tuberous begonias require *partial* shade. The ideal type of shade is that provided by the high, arching branches of trees through which the plants receive filtered sunlight. This type of sunlight and shade is provided when begonias are grown in lath houses. In dense shade tuberous begonias do not grow satisfactorily or flower well. A northern or northeastern exposure that receives early morning and late afternoon sun usually provides conditions for good growth. When grown in pots or in porch or window boxes, tuberous begonias will do well if they receive strong light but little or no direct sunlight.

Tuberous begonias grow best in moderately cool climates where there is an abundance of moisture in the atmosphere. They reach their maximum perfection in the fog-belt on the Pacific Coast, and the northern New England coast, and sometimes at high altitudes. They do not do well under conditions of intense or prolonged summer heat.

Soil requirements: Tuberous begonias require a mellow, fibrous soil, rich in organic matter

POTTING MIXTURES

(1) 2 parts well rotted leaf mold   (2) 2 parts leaf mold
     1 part coarse sand   1 part loam
     1 part well rotted cow manure   1 part compost
     1 part good loam

Ample drainage should be provided for in the bottom of the pot.

and slightly on the acid side, a pH of 6.5 being satisfactory. Good drainage is essential. When preparing garden beds, liberal quantities of coarse leaf mold should be worked into the soil and a rich compost or very well-rotted cow manure may be added, if available.

For soil mixtures for plants grown in pots and baskets, see Chapter 30.

As tuberous begonias are shallow-rooted, many people prefer to use the azalea-type pot, which has less depth than the standard pot. For tubers from 1½ in. to 2 in. in diameter, an 8-in. pot is usually sufficiently large; for larger tubers, 10- to 12-in. pots are best.

The potting mixture is of great importance in growing fine quality tuberous begonias. It should be rich in humus, friable and slightly on the acid side with a pH of about 6.5.

Growing the pendula type: This is the type that is suitable for hanging pots and baskets. The flowers are considerably smaller than those of the large-flowered types but they are beautifully formed and are borne in great profusion, some plants producing more than 100 blooms.

It requires a longer time to produce a flowering-size tuber of the pendula type than it does to produce a tuber of the large-flowered types, and most commercial growers offer two-year-old tubers. Some offer three-year-old tubers.

The tubers may be started in flats or planted directly in the container in which they are to be grown. If started in flats, they should be transplanted into the permanent pot or basket when 3 in. to 4 in. high.

Adequate drainage should be provided and the same potting mixture may be used as that recommended for the large-flowered types. If wire or slatted redwood baskets are used, they should be lined with coarse sphagnum moss or with fresh green sphagnum, if available. About 2 in. of coarse sand should be placed in the bottom of the pot or basket before the soil is added.

Several types of containers may be used. Hanging pots and baskets are not attractive unless they are well filled with graceful, drooping branches and abundant blooms. It is therefore necessary for a tuber to produce several shoots. Very large tubers are preferable to small ones, as they will produce a greater number of shoots, the stems will be longer and the branching better. The best practice is to plant one large tuber in each container. However, several small tubers may be used if large tubers are not available. If only one or two shoots develop they should be pinched back to induce branching.

The shoots will be upright at first and will then gradually droop down over the sides of the container. They should not be staked or trained in any way, but should be allowed to arrange themselves naturally.

Fertilization: As the nourishment for the plant during its early stages of growth is contained within the tuber, it is wise not to apply fertilizers until growth is well started. Overfertilization when the plants are young will often result in spindly, leggy plants with weak stems. When the plants are being grown in a good soil mixture, many people prefer to delay supplementary feedings until the flower buds begin to form. In the case of potted plants many people begin feeding when the pot is well filled with roots.

The appearance of the plant will give some indication whether fertilization is desirable. If the leaves are dark green in color and tend to crimp downward, and if the stems are strong and vigorous, it will be an indication that satisfactory growth is being maintained, whereas if the leaves are light green or yellowish and tend to cup upward it is evident that the plant is suffering from lack of food and an application of fertilizer should be made.

One of the safest fertilizers to use is a solution of liquid cow manure, made by soaking 1 lb. of dried cow or sheep manure in 5 gallons of water. The solution should be diluted until it is the color of weak tea before it is applied. Application may be made every three weeks. Fish meal is an excellent fertilizer, and commercial fertilizers are also used.

Certain precautions should be observed in fertilizing tuberous begonias. The soil should always be thoroughly moist before an application of fertilizer is made, and care should be taken to see that the fertilizer does not come into contact with the foliage.

Overfertilization should be avoided, as it may cause the flower buds to fall, and if fertilizers are used in great excess the plant will die.

Watering: Tuberous begonias require an ample supply of water; the plants suffer seriously if they are allowed to become too dry. Good drainage is essential, whether the plants are grown in beds or in pots, for although abundant water is needed the soil should never become soggy. Overwatering may cause the flower buds to drop.

Disbudding: When begonias are grown in garden beds, disbudding is seldom practiced. However, when they are grown in pots, and when exhibition blooms are desired, disbudding will result in larger, better developed plants and more spectacular flowers. The first flower buds should be nipped off when they are small and very immature. If early flowering is desired, this practice should not be followed.

Tuberous begonias normally bear three blossoms on each flower stem. The large flower is the male blossom, which produces the pollen, and the two small flowers on either side, which are often single, are the female flowers, which produce the seed. If blooms of maximum size are desired, the female flowers should be removed in the early bud stage. When the effect of a mass of flowers is desired, this is not done. In some of the newer types the female flowers are double and almost as large as the male flowers. After flowering, gradually withhold water and keep the plants dry until February.

Wintering dormant tubers: Given proper care, tubers may be carried over from one year to another. Although they tend to become less vigorous with age and to loose their vitality after a number of years, there are instances where tubers have flowered satisfactorily over a period of ten to fifteen years. However, in the hands of the amateur their longevity is usually considerably less.

In the autumn when the foliage begins to turn yellow, it is evident that the plants are preparing for their period of dormancy. At this time water should be gradually withheld but should not be omitted entirely. If plants have been grown in a greenhouse or indoors they should, at this time, be moved to an open shed or on to a porch. The foliage will gradually die down and drop off and it is wise to remove it from the plants before it begins to decay. At this stage water should be withheld entirely. The main stem will eventually drop off or may be carefully severed by hand. It should never be cut off at the point of junction with the tuber or forcibly broken off. If a portion remains, it is wise to leave it on until it will disjoint easily during the curing process.

If the tubers have been growing in garden beds, they should be dug with care and prepared for storage. If the tubers have been grown in pots, some people merely turn the pots on the sides and store them in this manner in a dry, cool place. However, the majority of gardeners prefer to remove the tubers from the pots after the plants have lost their foliage and become completely dormant. After the tubers have been dug from outdoor beds, or turned out of pots, the soil should be removed with care. Some growers recommend that the tubers be washed so that all soil is removed before it dries, as there is then less danger of injuring the skin of the tuber and the larger attached roots.

It is essential that the tubers be completely dry before storage. The best method is to spread them out in flats and place them in the sun. If this is not possible, they may be cured in any dry, well-ventilated place. The purpose of the drying process is to permit all excess moisture to evaporate from the tubers and to obtain a completely dry, clean crown before storage. After about two weeks of drying, the tubers are usually ready for storage.

During the winter months the tubers should

be stored one row deep in shallow trays or flats in a cool, dry place where the temperature can be maintained between 45° to 50° F. There should be as little fluctuation in temperature as possible. The tubers may be left uncovered or may be very lightly covered with dry peat moss, vermiculite or dry sand, just enough being used to sift down between the tubers and to give the barest covering.

In late winter or very early spring the tubers should be uncovered and moved to a warm, light place so that the buds will begin to sprout and show color, preparatory to planting.

Control of diseases and pests: See Chapter 32.

Caladium

The fancy-leaved caladiums are among the most decorative of foliage plants, and some of the varieties and cultivars with their distinctive colorings, ranging from silvery whites through translucent rose to brilliantly variegated reds and greens, are of exotic and exciting beauty.

In mild climates the fancy-leaved caladiums may be grown outdoors, and in Florida and Texas and along the Gulf Coast extensive plantings are often made in gardens and parks, and private drives are sometimes bordered with them. The foliage remains beautiful from spring until frost, and in semitropical climates they often retain their beauty until late December or early January.

In less favorable climates caladiums may be started indoors and grown in pots until the weather is warm enough to transfer them to the garden. They may then be shifted from the pots to the garden bed, or the pots may even be sunk directly in the ground. Pots of fancy-leaved caladiums are very decorative when grouped in a shady corner of a terrace or placed on a low, shady ledge by a fountain. They may also be used effectively as a foreground planting in shrubbery borders, provided they are not exposed to too much sun.

As house plants caladiums may be used effectively in many ways and add a touch of dramatic beauty to the decor. They thrive best in low light intensity and may therefore be grown in windows where they receive little or no sun.

They are also of great decorative value in room dividers and niches when they can be grown under artificial light (see Chapter 37).

Exposure: The natural habitat of the caladium is the tropical forest region of South America. They therefore thrive under conditions of great heat and prefer a temperature that ranges well into the 90's. In areas where the summer temperature ranges around 70° F. or lower, caladiums do not grow satisfactorily.

The caladiums require a semishaded location. If the shade is too dense it will prevent a full coloration of the leaves, and in full sun the leaves of some of the more delicate and most beautiful varieties tend to burn.

Planting: When grown out of doors, the dormant tubers should be planted when all danger of frost is over. They should be planted about 2 in. deep and spaced from 8 in. to 10 in. apart. Good drainage is essential, as the tubers will rot in water-logged soil or in soil that is cold and soggy.

In regions where the climate is not mild enough to plant caladiums in the garden, they may be started indoors in pots or in flats. If started in flats, plants should be shifted to pots after the leaves begin to develop. One tuber can be started in a 4-in. pot or several tubers in a larger pot. A deep greenhouse flat with an inch or so of sand on the bottom, covered with a deep layer of milled sphagnum moss, makes an excellent medium for starting the tubers. The tubers should be started in a temperature ranging between 80° and 85° F. In the house such conditions can best be obtained by placing the pots or flats on a piece of tin or on a board directly over a hot-water radiator. The tubers should be watered sparingly but should never be allowed to dry out. When good root growth has been made and the first leaves reach a height of 4 in to 8 in., the tubers, if they are being grown in flats, should be carefully shifted into 6- or 8-in. pots.

Soil: The soil for fancy-leaved caladiums should be rich in humus and well drained,

18.6 Caladiums (Caladium hortulanum) *in lovely variations of pale and deep pink and in cool, green-veined white, are remarkably useful summertime plants both in pots and in the ground. Photo Grant Heilman*

slightly on the acid side, the optimum pH being from 6.2 to 6.5. High fertility is essential, as caladiums do not do well in poor soil. When the tubers are to be planted in garden beds, the soil should be well prepared. If obtainable, well-rotted cow manure should be forked into the bed. As a substitute, compost or leaf mold may be used.

When the tubers are grown in pots, the following mixtures are recommended:

(1) 25% rotted cow manure
    20% peat moss
    20% sand
    35% good garden loam

(2) 1 part leaf mold
    1 part rotted cow manure
    1 part good garden loam

The pots should be kept in the greenhouse or indoors on a window sill until all danger of frost is over and the weather is warm and settled. They should never be allowed to dry out, and liberal feeding with a good soluble fertilizer is desirable.

In the autumn, when the foliage begins to droop, water sparingly until the leaves are dry and slough off. During the winter the pots should be stored in a dry, warm place where the temperature ranges around 70° F.

If the tubers are either removed from the pots or lifted from garden beds after the foliage has ripened, they should be spread out on shallow trays or flats and kept in a dry warm place.

Canna

In Victorian days cannas were so overused for mass plantings and the colors were so garish that they gradually lost favor and for years were relegated to formal beds around railway stations or to dreary city parks. However, new strains and hybrids have now been developed, which may be obtained in glowing shades of apricot, coral, watermelon-pink and other dramatic ranges. There are both dwarf forms and tall-growing varieties, such as the Grand Opera Series. The giant forms make excellent accents for the rear of wide perennial borders, and the dwarf forms may be used effectively in the foreground of shrubbery borders and in large tubs as part of the decor on terrace or patio.

Climatic range: As cannas are native to the tropical and subtropical regions, they should not be planted in the North until all danger of frost is over.

Soil requirements: A fertile, moist, well-prepared soil will provide ideal conditions for good growth.

Culture: Old roots should be divided in the spring with a sharp knife, allowing a bud to each piece. Set 12 in. to 24 in. apart and from 3 in. to 5 in. deep. Lift in the fall when the tops have been killed by frost and store like dahlias. For control of pests and diseases, see Chapter 32.

CANNA VARIETIES OF MERIT

DWARF (2½–3 ft.)	GIANT (3–5 ft.)
'Pfitzer's Cherry Red'	'Black Knight'
' '' Chinese Coral'	'City of Portland'
' '' Primrose Yellow'	'Orange Beauty'
' '' Salmon Pink'	'Pink President'
' '' Lippo Tangerine'	'Red King Humbert'
' '' Stadt Fellbach'	'Richard Wallace'
	'The President'
	'Wyoming'
	'Yellow King Humbert'

GRAND OPERA SERIES (4 ft.)

'Aida'
'La Boheme'
'La Traviata'
'Mme Butterfly'
'Rigoletto'

Dahlia

Few flowers offer us such variety in form and coloring as the dahlias. All the glorious, translucent tones of a sunset sky, all the warm rosy hues of a summer's dawn are to be found among them, and they bring a richness and a glory to the late summer garden that nothing else can equal. The tall-growing varieties may be used delightfully at the rear of the herbaceous border, the dwarf sorts are more suitable for bedding purposes, and all types and varieties are invaluable for the cutting garden.

Dahlias are grouped into several distinct classes according to the form and size of the flower. The classification adopted by the American Dahlia Society is as follows:

Class 1. Incurved Cactus

Fully double flower with the margins of the majority of the floral rays revolute (rolled or quilled) for one-half or more of their length; the floral rays tending to curve toward the center of the flower.

Class 2. Recurved and Straight Cactus

Fully double flowers with the margins of the majority of the floral rays revolute for one-half of their length or more; the floral rays being recurved or straight.

Class 3. Peony

Open-centered flowers with not more than three rows of ray florets regardless of form or number of florets, with the addition of smaller curled or twisted floral rays around the disk.

Class 4. Semicactus

Fully double flowers with the margins of the majority of the floral rays revolute for less than one-half their length.

Class 5. Formal Decorative

Fully double flowers, rays generally broad, either pointed or rounded at tips, with outer floral rays tending to be cupped, all floral rays in somewhat regular arrangement.

Class 6. Informal Decorative

Fully double flowers, floral rays generally long, twisted or pointed and usually irregular in arrangement.

Class 7. Ball

Fully double flowers, ball-shaped or slightly flattened, floral rays in spiral arrangement, blunt or rounded at tips and quilled or with markedly involute margins; 2 in. or more in diameter.

Class 8. Anemone

Open-centered flowers with only one row of ray florets regardless of form or number of florets, with the tubular disk florets elongated, forming a pincushion effect.

Class 9. Single

Open-centered flowers, with only one row of ray florets regardless of form or number of florets.

DAHLIA VARIETIES OF MERIT

A — anemone
B — bedding
C — cactus
D — dwarf
FD — formal decorative

IC — incurved cactus
ID — informal decorative
M — miniature
SC — semicactus
STC — straight cactus

LARGE DAHLIAS

RED

'Arthur Godfrey' (FD)
'Autumn Blaze' (ID)
'Dark Desire' (ID)
'Mary Elizabeth' (ID)
'The Cardinal' (SC)

PINK AND ROSE

'Canby Charm' (ID)
'D-Day' (FD)
'Enchantment' (ID)
'Jersey Beauty' (FD)
'Morning Kiss' (SC)

YELLOW AND ORANGE

'Croydon Ace' (ID)
'Croydon Masterpiece' (FD)
'First Lady' (FD)
'House of Orange' (FD)
'Moonglow' (SC)

PURPLE AND LAVENDER

'Blue River' (FD)
'City of Wellston' (FD)
'Lavender Perfection' (FD)
'Night Editor' (ID)
'The Commando' (FD)

WHITE

'Alabaster' (FD)
'Lula Pattie' (ID)
'My Love' (SC)
'Robens White Dove' (ID)
'Snow Country' (ID)

BICOLORS

'Flying Saucer' (STC)
'Grand Prix' (ID)
'Holland's Festival' (FD)
'Lois Walcher' (FD)
'Tartan' (ID)

SMALL DAHLIAS

RED

'Bishop of Llandaff' (M,A)
'Fabel' (A)
'Fred Springer' (B)
'Nelly Geerlings' (DB)
'Wing' (DB)

PINK AND ROSE

'Honey' (B)
'Murillo' (B)
'Park Princess' (M,SC)
'Preference' (M,C)
'Siemon Doorents' (B)

YELLOW AND ORANGE

'Brio' (A)
'Flashlight' (M,C)
'Irene Van der Zwet' (B)
'Venturas Yellow' (M,FD)
'Yellow Cheer' (M,FD)

LAVENDER

'Alice B. Clayson' (M,FD)
'Cheerio' (M,C)
'Julie R.' (M,SC)
'Mrs. C. J. Robertson' (M,IC)
'Regina' (B)

WHITE

'All Triumph' (M,SC)
'Bride' (M,C)
'Sneezy' (B)
'Toto' (A)

POMPONS

RED

'Alize'
'Fuji'
'Kochelsee'

PINK AND ROSE

'André Menou'
'Betty Ann'
'Tiki'

YELLOW

'Drumstick'
'Margaret John'
'Mimosa'

LAVENDER

'Andrew Lockwood'
'Morning Mist'
'Royal Willow'

WHITE

'Albino'
'Celestia'
'Little Willow'

Class 10. Duplex

Open-centered flowers, with only two rows of ray florets regardless of form or number of florets.

Class 11. Pompon

Fully double flowers, ball-shaped or slightly flattened, floral rays in spiral arrangement, blunt or rounded and quilled or with markedly involute margins; less than 2 in. in diameter.

Class 12. Collarette

Open-centered flowers with only one row of ray florets, with the addition of one or more rows of petal lids, usually of a different color, forming a collar around the disk.

Class 13. Miniature Decorative

All dahlias that normally produce flowers that do not exceed 3 in. in diameter, pompons excluded, to be classified according to the foregoing definitions.

Climatic range and exposure: Although dahlias are natives of the mountainous sections of Mexico and thrive luxuriantly in the hot, high, dry climate of these regions, they are remarkably adaptable and may be grown in almost every section of the United States. They require an exposure of full sun. If grown in a shady location, the plants have a tendency to become spindly and the blooms are poor in quality.

Propagation: By division of the tubers, by cuttings, by seed.

(1) By Tubers: Dahlia tubers are produced in clumps, which are attached very firmly to the parent stems. If the entire clump is planted, the results are unsatisfactory, as a mass of thin, weak stems will be produced and the flowers will be poor in quality. The tubers should therefore be divided before planting. Dahlias seldom produce buds on the tuber itself, the buds being found only at the neck of the tuber. When

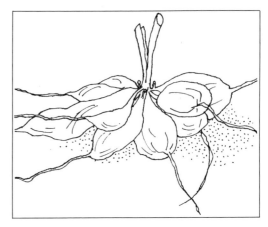

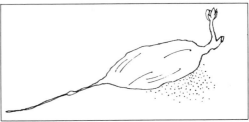

Fig. 18.1
Dahlia division
Top: *Dahlia clump to be divided.* Bottom: *Division including bud, ready for planting.*

dividing the tubers, it is essential to include the neck, which will usually produce from one to three buds. Many gardeners find it an advantage to cover the clumps with damp earth, moist peat moss, or sand, and to place them in a warm temperature for a week or ten days before planting. Under these favorable conditions the buds or eyes will start into growth and when the tubers are divided those may be selected for planting that have strong, well-developed buds. The clumps should not be kept under these conditions for too long a period as the actual sprouts will begin to develop, which will necessitate very careful handling at planting time.

(2) By Cuttings: If a rapid increase of stock is desired, cuttings may be taken from the sprouted shoots produced by the tubers. Where this method is to be followed, the tubers should be

started into growth during February or March. They may be planted in flats in the greenhouse, being given ample light, heat and moisture in order to induce quick growth. When the shoots have formed two sets of leaves, cuttings may be taken. A clean, sharp cut should be made just below the first set of leaves. These lower leaves should then be carefully cut from the stem and the cutting should be inserted in the propagating case. If conditions are favorable, dahlia cuttings root very readily, and as soon as roots have developed, the cuttings may be potted up in small 2½ or 3-in. pots, a mixture of 2 parts loam, 1 part sand and 1 part leaf mold being used. If the cuttings make rapid growth and transplanting seems advisable, they may be shifted to larger pots before they are planted in the open. When planted in the garden, they should be set from 1 in. to 2 in. deeper than they were when growing in the pot.

(3) By Seed: Dahlias do not come true from seed. New varieties are always produced by seed, and some of the small bedding types are frequently grown from seed. A few seed firms offer these bedding types in separate colors, but most of such seed comes in mixed packets and the flowers vary greatly. The seed may be sown under glass early in the season or in the cold-frame later in the spring. The young seedlings may be transplanted into small pots when the second pair of leaves has developed, and they may be set in the open ground after all danger of frost is over.

Soil requirements: Dahlias have very definite soil preferences. They thrive best on a sandy loam with a gravelly subsoil and they require a soil that is abundantly supplied with organic matter. It is unwise to attempt to grow dahlias on a heavy, clay soil that is poorly drained, as they will make but little growth and will produce blooms of an inferior quality. The texture of a heavy soil may be greatly improved by the addition of liberal quantities of well-rotted manure, rich compost, and sand, or through the use of a good soil conditioner. If the natural drainage is exceedingly poor, the entire area upon which the dahlias are to be grown may be underdrained by a tile drain, or the soil where each individual tuber is to be planted may be

18.7 Dahlias, when properly pruned and disbudded, are magnificent for late-summer cut flowers. Photo Grant Heilman

excavated to a depth of 15 in. and a width of 3 in. Coarse cinders, gravel or some form of rubble may then be placed in the bottom to improve the drainage.

Dahlias are notoriously heavy feeders and if blooms of superior quality are desired, the plants must have an abundant and well-balanced supply of nutrients throughout the season. An excess of nitrogen should be avoided as it encourages too rank a growth of leaves, which are produced at the expense of flower buds. Phosphorus and potash may be supplied in more liberal quantities as they are the nutrients most needed. Unless the soil is naturally fertile and well supplied with humus and with the necessary nutrients, it is wise to prepare it thoroughly before planting the tubers. The exact location where each tuber is to be planted may be marked off by a stake and the soil excavated to a depth of 8 in. The soil below this depth should be loosened with a spading fork and a shovelful of humus, rich compost of well-rotted manure may be worked into it. The topsoil that was removed should be enriched with a similar amount of humus, and the hole should then be refilled until the soil is within 6 in. of the surface.

Planting tubers: As dahlias are very sensitive to frost, the tubers should not be planted until the ground is warm and mellow and there is no danger of a sudden drop in temperature. In the vicinity of New York, dahlias are usually planted between the middle of May and the middle of June. Little is to be gained from very early planting as the tubers make but slow, unhealthy growth if the soil remains cold and wet. The stakes that are to provide future support for the plants should be driven into the ground at the time the tubers are planted. If this operation is delayed until the plants have grown far enough actually to require staking, the tubers may be seriously injured. Dahlias of the large type require ample space for their best development, and they should be planted at least 3 ft. apart in rows that also are 3½ ft. to 4 ft. apart. The dwarf types require less space, but as they are inclined to be somewhat bushy in growth habit, they should be allowed a minimum of 15 in. to 18 in. each way. After the ground has been prepared (see *Soil Requirements*) and the stakes driven into the ground, the tubers may be planted. The excavation should be approximately 6 in. in depth. The tuber should be placed on the prepared bed, the buds or shoots pointing upward, and it should be covered with 2 in. of earth. It is well to have the neck of the tuber from which the shoots rise near the point where the stake was driven. As the shoots develop, the soil may be filled in about the plant, until the surface of the ground is level. The tuber should be approximately 6 in. below the surface.

Culture: If the finest quality of bloom is desired, only one stalk should be allowed to develop from each tuber. If several shoots have developed, the strongest should be selected and the remaining shoots discarded. When the main stalk has reached a height of about 1 ft. and has formed two or three pairs of leaves, the tiny growing tip may be nipped out. Care must be taken not to cut the stalk back too severely, as the hollow stem will have difficulty in healing—just the growing tip should be removed. From four to six strong, vigorous stalks will then develop.

If exhibition blooms are to be produced, disbudding is advisable. The lateral or side buds on each terminal branch should be pinched out in order that the middle bud may have every chance to produce a flower of perfect size and substance. The two series of buds below the terminal buds should also be pinched out in order to increase the length of the stem. If the flowers are desired for cutting, severe disbudding is not usually practiced.

Frequent, shallow cultivations are advisable until the middle of July. At this time cultivations should cease, an application of fertilizer should be made and a good mulch should be applied. A fertilizer mixture consisting of 1 part bone meal, 1 part pulverized manure and 1 part commercial fertilizer (a 2–10–6 or a 4–8–6) may be applied at the rate of 3 handfuls per plant, being broadcast over the surface of the soil about 6 in. away from the base of the plant. The fertilizer should be watered in thoroughly and a good mulch 2 in. to 3 in. deep applied. (See Chapter 8 on Mulches.)

At no time during the growing season should dahlias be allowed to suffer from lack of moisture. A thorough soaking once a week should be sufficient. A soil soaker is excellent for this purpose.

One of the most important factors in the culture of dahlias is to keep the plants in vigorous, continuous growth. If growth is seriously checked at any time due to lack of sufficient moisture or lack of nutrients, the stems tend to become hard and woody, the plants remain stunted, and produce poor bloom.

As the plants grow, the stems should be securely fastened to the stakes. Dahlia stems are hollow and pithy and they are easily broken by heavy winds.

Autumn care: Being extremely sensitive to cold, the plants will be killed with the first heavy frost. The stalks should then be cut off to within

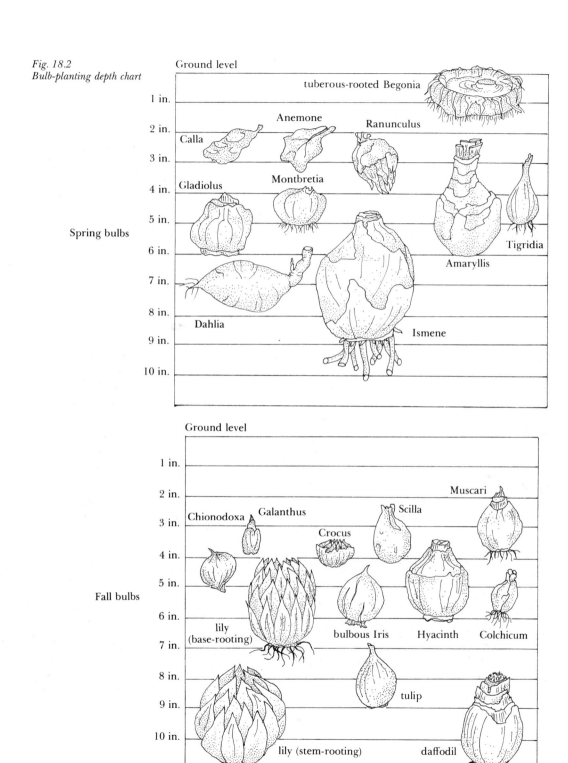

Fig. 18.2
Bulb-planting depth chart

Ground level

Spring bulbs

1 in.
2 in.
3 in.
4 in.
5 in.
6 in.
7 in.
8 in.
9 in.
10 in.

tuberous-rooted Begonia

Anemone

Ranunculus

Calla

Montbretia

Gladiolus

Tigridia

Amaryllis

Dahlia

Ismene

Ground level

Fall bulbs

1 in.
2 in.
3 in.
4 in.
5 in.
6 in.
7 in.
8 in.
9 in.
10 in.

Muscari

Scilla

Chionodoxa

Galanthus

Crocus

lily
(base-rooting)

bulbous Iris

Hyacinth

Colchicum

tulip

lily (stem-rooting)

daffodil

6 in. of the surface of the ground and the tubers should be left in the ground for a week or ten days to become thoroughly ripened. They should then be dug and prepared for storage. A spading fork should be thrust into the ground beside the tubers, and they should be pried loose from the soil with the greatest of care so that no injury occurs. The clump of tubers should be turned upside down in order that any sap or moisture may drain from the stalk, and should be exposed to full sunlight for several hours until thoroughly dry.

During the winter dahlia tubers should be stored in a dry, frost-proof place where the temperature ranges between 45° and 55° F. One of the best methods of storing dahlias is to dip the tubers in Wilt-Pruf, using 1 part of Wilt-Pruf to 4 parts of water. Allow the tubers to dry and then store them in dry peat moss. This method prevents the loss of moisture and the tubers come through the storage period in excellent condition.

Insect pests and diseases: See Chapter 32.

Eremurus (foxtail lily, desert-candle)

Coming to us from the deserts of Persia, the Himalayas and Turkestan, the giant blooms of the *Eremurus* are dramatic when planted against a background of deep green, where they can be viewed from a distance. The flower spikes often attain a height of 8 ft. or more, the individual, bell-shaped flowers being closely set upon the stalk. The plants flower during June and July, and vary in color from creamy-white through yellow, rose and pink.

Exposure: A sunny and somewhat sheltered position is desirable. The roots are not particularly hard, and in the latitude of New York and northward the crowns should be protected with a heavy mulch of straw. An inverted box filled with straw affords an excellent means of protection.

Soil requirements: Eremurus prefers a rich, moist, but well-drained soil.

EREMURUS SPECIES AND HYBRIDS

SPECIES

Eremurus altaicus: yellow, very hardy, 3 ft. to 4 ft., Siberia
Eremurus bungei: citron yellow, June and July, 1 ft. to 3 ft., Persia
Eremurus elwesii: white, 6 ft. to 9 ft., Himalayas
Eremurus himalaicus: white, May to June, 6 ft. to 8 ft., Himalayas
Eremurus robustus: rosy pink, May to June, 6 ft. to 10 ft., Turkestan

HYBRIDS

A number of hybrids are offered in trade lists, and most of these bloom in early summer. These include:
'Himrob': pink, 7 ft. to 9 ft.
'Shelford Hybrids': pastel shades, 4 ft. to 5 ft.

Planting: The fleshy roots of *Eremurus* should be planted in the autumn. A hole of ample size should be dug in order that these roots may be spread out in a natural position. The plants should be entirely surrounded with sand and the crown of the plant should be only just beneath the surface of the soil. As the roots are very brittle, they must be handled with great care. The plants should be spaced from 18 in. to 2 ft. apart.

Culture: As growth begins very early in the spring, the winter mulch should be removed as soon as weather conditions permit. The young growth is very subject to injury from frost and during any cold spells that occur after the mulch has been removed the plants should be protected by a burlap covering or an inverted receptacle of some kind. During the growing season the plants require an abundance of moisture. After flowering the leaves disappear entirely and during this period of dormancy practically no water is required. After the plants are once established, they will thrive for many years if conditions are favorable. Large plants do not transplant easily and should be left undisturbed. If *Eremurus* is grown in the flower border, great care must be taken not to injure the roots when cultivating after the leaf growth has died down.

Propagation: Eremurus may be propagated either by the division of the root clumps or by seed, the latter process being exceedingly slow and seldom practiced.

Galtonia candicans (summer hyacinth)

The creamy-white, bell-shaped flowers of the *Galtonia,* which is a native of South Africa, are decorative and lovely either in the perennial border or against a background of deep green shrubbery. The flowers come into bloom in late August and frequently continue until cut down by frost. The flower stalks usually attain a height of 18 in., sometimes growing as tall as 3 ft., and the flowers hang suspended from the tall, leafless stems.

Exposure: Full sun.

Soil requirements: A deep, rich garden loam.

Culture: The bulbs may be planted in the spring at a depth of approximately 6 in., and should be spaced from 8 in. to 12 in. apart. The bulbs are not hardy in the latitude of New York and should be lifted in the autumn and stored in a frost-proof place. As the old bulbs frequently fail to bloom a second season, it is wise to replenish the stock each year.

Propagation: Galtonia may be grown very easily from seed as well as from bulbs. It requires two years to produce flowering bulbs from seed; during the winters the small bulblets must be lifted and stored.

Gladiolus

Gladioli are amazing in their adaptability, and because they demand so little in the way of care and cultivation and give so generously of their bloom and beauty they are looked upon as one of our most useful flowers. They are invaluable for cutting and may be had in bloom during every month of the year; and they are

GLADIOLUS VARIETIES OF MERIT

LARGE-FLOWERED TYPE

RED	PINK AND SALMON
'Albert Schweitzer'	'Mexicali Rose'
'Fire Chief'	'Miss America'
'Oscar'	'Spic and Span'
'Peter Pears'	'Spring Song'
'Sans Souci'	'True Love'

VIOLET	BLUES
'Sandstorm'	'China Blue'
'Stormy Weather'	'Green Lilac'
	'Purple Splendor'
	'Salman's Blue'
	'Sugar Plum'

YELLOW AND ORANGE	WHITE AND CREAM
'Brightside'	'America'
'Canary Bird'	'Day Dream'
'Orange Gold'	'Glacier'
'Pay Dirt'	'Morning Kiss'
'Sundown'	'White Friendship'
'Sunshine'	

GREEN AND OTHERS

'Brown Glow'
'Chocolate Sundae'
'Copper Lustre'
'Green Woodpecker'
'Lemon Lime'

MINIATURES

RED	WHITE
'Atom'	'Daintiness'
'Bravo'	'Mighty Mite'
'Red Bantam'	

equally prized for their decorative value in the garden. They may be planted in great drifts through the garden beds and borders, becoming the dominant note in the planting composition from midsummer on; or they may be used in an incidental way to fill in an occasional gap here and there.

Climatic range: Few flowers have a wider climatic range than the gladiolus, for they may be grown in every section of the United States. During the winter months, one sees them blooming in profusion throughout the South, ranging all the way from southern Florida to California. During the summer one finds them in all parts of the country, even in dooryard gardens of remote northern villages.

Soil requirements: Gladiolus will thrive well on almost any soil of medium fertility. On soils of a slightly heavy texture the flowers are of a superior quality but only a comparatively small number of cormlets are formed. On a light, sandy-loam soil, the flowers are not quite as fine but a large number of cormlets are produced.

Gladiolus are moderately acid-tolerant and prefer a soil with a pH of approximately 6.0. If the soil is extremely acid, the condition should be remedied with an application of lime the autumn before planting. Gladiolus will not thrive well in a soil with a reaction of more than pH 7.0, and if the alkalinity runs as high as pH 7.5, the growth will be decidedly inferior.

Superphosphate has proved to be the most effective fertilizer for gladiolus as it will increase production and will produce earlier and better bloom. It should be applied in the furrow at the rate of 5 lb. to every 100 ft. of row. The fertilizer, which is best applied in the form of 16 percent superphosphate, should be covered lightly with soil before the corms are planted in the furrow. A complete fertilizer such as a 4–12–4 may be used instead of the superphosphate, but nitrogenous and potassic fertilizers should never be used unless they are liberally supplemented by phosphorus, as the results are definitely detrimental and growth will be seriously checked.

Planting: Gladiolus may be planted at any time after danger of frost is over and the soil has become warm and mellow. In order to provide for a succession of bloom, they may be planted at intervals every two weeks until midsummer. The corms come into flower from eight to ten weeks after planting. Gladiolus corms are graded according to size. The blooming sizes are Nos. 1, 2, and 3. No. 4 will sometimes bloom. The smaller sizes are considerably less expensive than the No. 1 grade, and will give equally good results. If grown in rows in the cutting garden, the corms may be planted 4 in. apart in rows 18 in. apart. In garden beds and borders the corms should be spaced about 6 in. apart. The depth of planting will vary somewhat according to the texture of the soil. In light, sandy soil, the corms may be planted 6 in. deep; in heavy, clay soil, a depth of 4 in. is preferable. If the corms are planted as deeply as possible, the stalks will be held more firmly in position and less staking will be required.

Culture: Gladiolus require no special care. They thrive best in a sunny location, require a moderate amount of moisture and respond to a reasonable amount of cultivation. They will reward one generously for the small amount of time that must be spent upon them.

When gladiolus are to be used for decorative purposes in the house, they should be cut as soon as one or two of the blossoms have opened, as the remaining buds will open after the spikes have been placed in water. When cutting gladiolus, it is very important to leave two or three of the broadest leaves at the base of the stalk. If all of the foliage is cut away, the development of the new corm and the cormlets will be seriously impaired. All flower stalks should be cut as soon as the flowers have faded, as the development of the seed pods also affects the vitality of the corm.

Winter care: As soon as the foliage has turned yellow, which usually occurs about six weeks after the period of bloom is over, the corms are ready to be dug. The leaf stalks should be cut off within about 2 in. of the ground. The corms should then be lifted gently with a spading fork or spade, care being taken to scatter as few of the small cormlets as possible. The corms should be placed in flats and stored in an airy, frostproof shed for several weeks in order that they become thoroughly mature. If, as sometimes happens in the case of late-planted corms, the foliage has failed to ripen before midautumn, the leaf stalks may be allowed to remain on the plant when the corms are dug.

After the period of ripening is over, the leaf stalks should be cut off and the corms prepared for winter storage. The old mother corm, which was planted in the spring, and the roots should be removed from the new corm and the little cormlets should be separated. The corms may be placed on shallow trays and should be stored in a cool, well-ventilated cellar. The temperature should range between 40° and 45° F. and the air should have a humidity of approximately 80 percent. If the trays are piled one upon another, a free circulation of air must be provided.

Propagation: Gladiolus are propagated by means of the small cormlets produced at the base of the corm. These may be separated from the corm at the time of harvest, and they may be stored in paper bags during the winter. In the spring they may be planted in shallow furrows, being lifted in the autumn and stored during the winter. The cormlets will produce flowering-size corms the second or third year.

Insect pests and diseases: See Chapter 32.

Iris, bulbous

Exquisite in form, varied and lovely in coloring, the bulbous (actually cormous) irises are unexcelled as cut flowers, and their decorative value in the garden is coming to be more and more appreciated. The erroneous and widespread impression that these lovely bulbous irises are not hardy has meant that they have been used to only a very limited extent for outdoor planting, and it is indeed unfortunate that many of them are known to us only as cut flowers that have been grown in the greenhouse during the winter months. In fact, the bulbous irises are quite as hardy as tulips, are able to withstand subzero temperatures with no ill effects, and are practically never injured by the most extreme cold.

There are several species and types of bulbous iris belonging to the same botanical subgenus, *xiphium.* Those that are considered the

IRIS VARIETIES OF MERIT

'Blue Ribbon': deep blue standards, bronze falls
'Bronze Queen': blue and bronze
'Gold and Silver': white standards, gold falls
'Golden Emperor': golden yellow
'Golden Harvest': yellow
'H. C. Van Vliet': dark violet-blue
'Wedgewood': porcelain blue
'White Superior': white

most desirable for garden plantings and for cut flowers are the Spanish iris, the English iris and the Dutch iris.

Iris xiphium (Spanish iris)

A species that includes many named varieties. This is also true for *Iris xiphiodes*, or English iris. The so-called Dutch irises, named because they were originally bred and are grown in the Netherlands, are hybrids of *Iris xiphium* and other species. Their heavier stems bear larger blooms than the Spanish parent. These are the irises commonly sold as cut flowers in florists' shops. The flowers of all three types are showy and suggest orchids in their beauty. There is a broad color range, with many fine porcelain blues among them.

Dutch iris

Produces heavy single-flowered stems 1½ ft. to 2 ft. in height. They are sold as cut flowers and are also good as garden flowers. The bulbs are usually sold in the United States in mixtures. The Dutch hybrids bloom outdoors in late May, followed by the Spanish irises in early June and the English irises in late June.

Exposure: A position in full sun is essential for iris in order that the foliage may become fully ripe after the flowering season is over.

Soil requirements: A moderately fertile, well-drained soil is desirable, a light, sandy loam being considered ideal. The bulbs are decidedly indifferent to the reaction of the soil and will thrive equally well in slightly acid, neutral or mildly alkaline soils.

Planting: Shipment of bulbs is usually made in late September or early October. The bulbs should be planted immediately, being spaced from 6 in. to 8 in. apart and at a depth of 4 in. to 5 in. As the bulbous irises are apparently considered a great delicacy by field mice, some protection should be given if they are planted in an area where rodents are troublesome. (See Chapter 32.)

Culture: Active growth begins soon after the bulbs are planted, and most varieties will send up several green, spearlike shoots during the autumn. After the flowering period is over in late June, the foliage should be allowed to ripen and it is essential that it be exposed to full sun during this period. When the leaves have become brown, the bulbs may be lifted. They should be placed on shallow trays, covered with dry sand, and stored in the hottest attic available, where conditions will approximate as nearly as possible the conditions found in their native habitat. If the bulbs are not lifted, but instead are left undisturbed after the foliage has died down, some few varieties will persist for several years while others will fail to reappear after the first season of bloom. If the flowers are used for cutting, the foliage will be reduced to such an extent that the vigor and vitality of the bulb will be impaired, and new bulbs should therefore be planted the following year.

Winter protection: For the Dutch iris this is absolutely necessary for areas north of Washington, D.C. An effective and simple mulch is a layer of pine needles and/or evergreen boughs, applied *after* the first hard freeze.

Iris danfordiae
Yellow with an orange crest on the falls. Native to south and central Turkey.

Iris histrioides
Extremely hardy and early flowering, with leaves not yet visible at flowering time. The flowers are very large, with falls spreading nearly horizontally. The color is a very dark, intense blue, with a paler spotted area around the orange crest. The cultivar 'Lady Beatrix Stanley' is a paler blue with a larger area of spotting of the falls.

Iris reticulata
This lovely species of iris, native to the Near East, is available in a wide range of cultivars. The ordinary commercial form has very deep violet-blue flowers. These include:
'Cantab': light blue
'Clariette': sky-blue with white markings
'J. S. Dijt': deep red-purple
'Royal Blue': a very deep Oxford blue

Iris vartanii
Native to Israel, where it grows on stony hillsides, *I. vartanii* thrives best in an alpine house or bulb frame, though even under these conditions it is somewhat difficult to produce blooms because the bulbs tend to split into tiny bulblets.

Iris winogradowii
Native to the Caucasus, this iris provides large, lemon-yellow flowers and is very hardy.

Exposure: A somewhat protected position with a sunny exposure is desirable.

Soil requirements: A moderately fertile and very well-drained neutral or slightly alkaline soil is considered ideal.

Planting: The bulbs should be planted in the autumn, in late September or October, being spaced from 4 in. to 6 in. apart. When once established, the bulbs will continue to bloom year after year and under favorable conditions will increase rapidly. In exposed situations light winter protection should be given.

Ismene (Hymenocallis calathina, basket flower)

This showy, tender, summer-flowering bulb has long been popular, sold commercially as Peruvian daffodil or spider lily. The large, fra-

ISMENE VARIETIES OF MERIT

'Daphne': very large white flower
'Festalis': hybrid with extravagantly curved perianth petals
'Sulphur Queen': yellow hybrid

grant white flowers have tubular crowns 4 in. long, surrounded by fringed perianth segments 2 in. long. The very handsome, glossy green straplike foliage is decorative in the garden long after bloom is over and often until the bulbs are lifted.

The funnel-shaped white flowers of the ismene, with their fringed crown and long, threadlike stamens, are unique in form, and add a note of interest to a planting composition. The flowers are borne at the top of a stout, leafless scape that often attains a height of 15 in. or more.

Exposure: Full sun.

Soil requirements: Any ordinary garden soil.

Propagation: By offsets.

Culture: The bulbs should be planted in spring at a depth of approximately 3 in., being spaced from 8 in. to 10 in. apart. In the early autumn the bulbs should be lifted. They should then be dried off in an inverted position (foliage down), being careful not to cut off the fleshy roots. They should be stored during the winter at a temperature of 60° F. in a cool, dry, frost-proof place.

Kniphofia (*Tritoma,* **torch lily**)

The decorative value of the *Kniphofia* is appreciated by the florist and the gardener alike. The brilliant flowers of red and yellow hue are borne on stout, fleshy stems above sword-shaped leaves and are unique in form and striking in appearance. The dwarf types, reaching a height of 18 in. to 24 in., are of more value as cut flowers in the home than are the larger

types, and they combine well with *Asclepias tuberosa* (butterfly weed) and the tawny daylily. *Hemerocallis fulva.*

Exposure: A sheltered, sunny location.

Soil: A loose, well-drained soil of moderate fertility is considered ideal. A soil that is too rich causes an over-rampant growth.

Propagation: By seed, by the division of the rhizomes and by offsets. If the seed is sown under glass in January or February, flowering plants may be produced the same season.

Culture: The rhizomes may be planted in the spring after all danger of frost is over, being set from 9 in. to 12 in. apart. In the North the rhizomes should be dug up in the autumn and stored in dry earth in a cool but frost-proof place.

Tigridia (**tiger flower, Mexican shell flower**)

The brilliant blooms of the *Tigridia*—a native of Mexico, Central and South America—are unique in form, and its colors range from flame-red through orange and yellow to buff, with spotted centers. The corms are generally available in assorted colors only. Although the individual flowers last only a day each, the blooms are produced in succession over a period of nearly two months. Very few species are in cultivation, and only *Tigridia pavonia,* the showiest species, is commonly grown. Flowers July through October.

Exposure: Full sun.

Soil requirements: A light, rich garden loam.

Culture: Tigridia requires a warm temperature and abundant moisture during the growing season. The corms should be planted in early spring about 2 in. deep, being spaced from 6 in. to 8 in. apart. In warm regions where there are no heavy frosts the corms may be left undisturbed for many years, and they will give generous bloom each season. Where the climate is severe, the corms should be dug before the ground freezes. It is essential that the corms be stored in a cool, airy, dry, frost-proof place. One of the · most satisfactory methods of handling them is to tie the dried leaves and stems into small bundles and hang them up in a cool, dry room. Care must be taken to see that mice cannot reach them. If the top growth is cut off, the corms may be stored in wire trays. The corms are very sensitive to dampness; if they are not kept properly dry, they will decay.

Propagation: *Tigridia* may be grown very readily from seed, as well as from corms. If the seed is sown early in the season, about 20 percent of the plants will bloom the first year.

Tritonia (montbretia)

Tritonia crocata
Belongs to the iris family. It is a half-hardy cormous plant similar to gladiolus. The common montbretia of gardens is *Crocosmia* x *crocosmiiflora*, also often known as *Tritonia*.

The brilliant, colorful flowers of the various *montbretia* native of South Africa, are among the most beautiful and most decorative of all the summer-flowering bulbs. The flowers are borne on tall graceful spikes varying in height from 2 ft. to 4 ft. ; they are lovely for cutting as they last extremely well, often remaining fresh for two weeks or more. Some of the recently introduced varieties of the Earlham strain are of striking beauty, with their wide, flaring flowers in lovely tones of orange and apricot.
Exposure: Full sun.

Soil requirements: *Montbretia* prefers a rather sandy soil well supplied with rotted manure or some other form of humus.

Planting: In sections of the country where the climate is mild, *Montbretia* may be planted in the autumn. In sections where the temperature is apt to drop much below 20 degrees above zero, it is wise to plant the corms in the spring. The depth of planting is approximately 4 in. and the corms may be spaced from 5 in. to 6 in. apart.

Culture: *Montbretia* requires an abundance of moisture during the growing and flowering season. When the flowering season is over, the foliage will ripen more quickly if moisture is reduced to a minimum. After the first frost, the corms may be lifted and stored for the winter in the same manner as are gladiolus corms.

AUTUMN-FLOWERING BULBS

Colchicum (meadow saffron, autumn crocus)

The crocuslike blooms of the *Colchicum* are dainty and appealing, and bring a shy, bright touch to the autumn landscape. They come into flower in September and October, and as they bloom on naked stems with no foliage at this season they are at their best when planted among *Vinca minor* (periwinkle or creeping myrtle) or some other low ground cover. They are charming in the foreground of a shrubbery border or along the outer fringe of a woodland or in the rock garden. A small patch near the terrace or the entrance will lend added interest to the planting.

COLCHICUM OF MERIT

C. *autumnale:* lilac-rose
C. *autumnale album:* white
C. *giganteum:* soft violet
C. *speciosum*
'Autumn Queen': rose-purple
'The Giant': lilac

CROCUS SPECIES OF MERIT

WHITE	BLUE
Crocus laevigatus	Crocus asturicus
C. speciosus 'Albus'	C. longiflorus
	C. medius
	C. sativus (saffron crocus)

Culture: The corms are usually shipped in August and should be planted immediately upon arrival. If they are held even for a few days, the flowers may begin to appear. They should be planted at a depth of 3 in. to 4 in. *Colchicum* blooms a few weeks after planting but the foliage does not appear until the following spring. It is very important that the foliage be allowed to mature and die down naturally.

Crocus

Crocus bulbocodium vernum

An early-flowering plant that is widely distributed in the mountains from the Pyrenees to the Caucasus. It bears flowers resembling those of a small colchicum that are a bright reddish-purple with a white center. The leaves remain short until after flowering.

Autumn-flowering species

There are a number of delightful species crocus that flower during the autumn months, the early ones blooming in September and others carrying the period of bloom through October and November. The flowers are piquant and dainty, and when once established they will bloom year after year. They are lovely when planted along the edge of a shrub border or in little patches at the base of trees or near the terrace.

Culture: The corms should be planted as soon as they have been received, at a depth of 2 in. to 4 in. Although they thrive best in full sun, they will also adapt themselves quite happily to light shade, and they prefer a rather light, sandy soil.

MISCELLANEOUS BULBS

Lycoris squamigera (Amaryllis Hallii, **magic lily)**

The lilylike pink flowers, with a tint of lavender, are borne on 3-ft. stalks in clusters of six to nine, and are delicately fragrant. They flower during August and September, and are lovely when planted among ferns or in the foreground of a shrubbery border.

Culture: Lycoris prefers a position in partial shade and a fertile soil, well supplied with humus. The bulbs should be planted in August as soon as they arrive, at a depth of 5 in. The following spring large, straplike leaves will appear. They make remarkably rapid growth and after reaching their full height of about 2½ ft. they begin to mature, turn brown and disappear entirely. In August the naked flower stalks emerge and within a week or two will reach full height and come into bloom. The bulbs will live on almost indefinitely and should not be disturbed.

Sternbergia lutea (**winter daffodil, lily-of-the-field**)

This brings a touch of lovely autumn color to the garden. The crocuslike flowers, surrounded by glossy foliage, are a clear golden-yellow. They come into bloom in October and remain in flower for several weeks. They are lovely when planted in patches under trees or along the edge of a walk and will bloom bountifully year after year.

Culture: The bulbs should be planted just as soon as they arrive at a depth of about 4 in.

They prefer a light, well-drained soil and a warm, sunny exposure, although they will also thrive in light shade.

LILIES

The stateliness of lilies, their beauty of form and their subtle color harmonies make them one of the most highly prized flowers in a landscape composition. In the hands of a skillful designer lilies may be used to achieve dramatic and superbly beautiful effects.

When planning for their use in a planting design, a few points should be borne in mind. Lilies are far lovelier planted in groups of three or more than when they are used as individual specimens. Tall lilies are seen to best advantage against a pleasing background, such as a garden wall, a shrub border or a planting of low-branching evergreens.

18.9 Lilium 'Golden Clarion' is a modern trumpet lily carrying the fragrance of one of its regal lily ancestors. Photo Carlton Lees

Lilies that are to be used in the perennial border should be selected with care. The colors should be in harmony with the surrounding plants, and the height and character of the flowers should also be considered.

There are lilies to suit nearly every location and every purse. The novice in the art of gardening should select some of the more easily grown varieties, many of which are very beautiful, while the more experienced gardener will find keen interest and joy in growing some of the more temperamental types.

Remarkable progress has been made in the hybridization of lilies during the past few decades, resulting in the production of many hybrid strains and clones that offer to the gardener new types possessing vigor, hardiness and resistance to disease, as well as perfection of form and color.

18.8 Turk's cap lily (Lilium superbum) is soft orange and has reflexed flower form. Other species and cultivars are so acutely reflexed that the face is almost flat and the petals are curled back on themselves. Photo Grant Heilman

Culture: The essential requirements of success with lilies are: a well-drained soil, abundantly supplied with organic matter; good air

18.10 The upright-facing lily 'Enchantment' (Lilium tigrinum × Lilium hollandicum *var. 'Enchantment') reflects the sunshine in brown-spotted brilliant orange. Photo Grant Heilman*

circulation; shelter from high winds; disease-free bulbs; the correct time, method and depth of planting; an adequate mulch during the winter and a protective covering for the surface of the bed during the growing season; full sun or partial shade, to meet the requirements of the individual groups; and protection against rodents and disease.

Soil requirements: Good drainage is an absolutely essential factor; nothing is so destructive to the life of a lily bulb as standing water or a soggy, saturated soil. Even those native lilies that prefer a moist situation are unable to endure standing water; they must have their

moisture in motion, rapidly trickling through the soil. Therefore, unless the soil is naturally well drained, artificial drainage must be provided. The bed may be drained by the use of 4-in. agricultural tile laid 2 ft. below the surface of the soil, or the soil in the bed may be excavated to a depth of 2½ ft. and a 6-in. foundation of crushed stone or coarse hard-coal cinders placed in the bottom. If the bed is raised slightly above the surrounding area, drainage will also be facilitated.

Lilies thrive best in a good loam soil supplied with an abundance of organic matter. If a new bed is being made, the humus should be incorporated into the soil well in advance of planting, and may be supplied in the form of leaf

18.11 The trumpet lily (Lilium regale) *most resembles the madonna lily of Renaissance tapestries and paintings and the modern-day Easter lily. The royal lily above is overwhelmingly fragrant. Photo Grant Heilman*

mold, good compost, cultivated peat or well-rotted cow manure. If the soil is naturally heavy, its physical texture will be greatly improved by the addition of liberal quantities of humus, and it will thus be made a more suitable medium for growing lilies. Most lilies thrive best in a soil that is nearly neutral, with a pH ranging between 6.5 and 7.5.

Exposure: Good air circulation is closely related to the problem of disease control, and most lilies, except those that are definitely shade-loving, will thrive in a sunny, airy situation. Disease is much more apt to be prevalent in a low, badly drained spot where there is poor air circulation than on gently sloping, well-drained ground.

Planting: The time of planting as well as the method and depth of planting will depend to a considerable extent upon the type of lily being grown, although there are a few general rules that apply to practically all members of the lily group. Lily bulbs mature, or ripen, after the flowering period is over, and should be dug as soon as possible after the bulbs have ripened. Most lily bulbs resent being out of the ground, and some varieties deteriorate rapidly during the process of shipment. It is essential, therefore, that the bulbs be planted without delay as soon as the shipment has been received. The ground should be prepared well in advance, and everything should be ready for immediate planting as soon as the bulbs arrive. The more promptly the shipment can be made after the bulbs have ripened, and the more promptly the bulbs are planted, the greater are the chances of success. Because of the distances involved in some shipments, it occasionally is impossible to plant the bulbs at the most favorable time. Another problem facing the gardener is that of shipments that arrive late in the autumn when the ground is no longer in suitable condition for planting, being either frozen or soggy. This situation may be met in either one of two ways.

The bed may be prepared well in advance, and the area where these late arrivals are to be planted may be mulched with fresh manure, leaves, or straw, to prevent the ground from freezing and to maintain it in a favorable condition for planting. Even when this is done, however, the bulbs frequently arrive too late to make sufficient autumn growth to carry them through the winter and they suffer seriously in consequence. In handling bulbs that arrive after the middle of November (in the latitude of Philadelphia) a more favorable procedure seems to be to pot the bulbs in fairly dry soil and to store them during the winter in a root cellar where the temperature will range between 38° and 50° F. The pots may be buried in dry sand, and kept without moisture during the winter. In early spring the pots should be set outdoors and covered with straw or half-rotted leaves until growth has started. Later in the season, when the ground is in good condition, the bulbs may be gently removed from the pots and placed in their permanent position in the garden, care being taken not to disturb the roots. This method of winter storage is preferable to the use of coldframes for the wintering of bulbs that arrive too late to be planted in the open.

Some growers supply lilies for spring planting that have been dug in the autumn, placed in a plastic bag filled with slightly damp peat moss, and then stored in an air-conditioned warehouse at a temperature of 34° F. Such bulbs give excellent results when planted in the garden in the spring or when used as potted plants. They offer an alternative to late autumn planting under unfavorable conditions. They also make it possible for anyone establishing a new garden to have lilies in flower the first season. And they are of special value as potted plants on terrace or patio.

The method and depth of planting are discussed in detail under cultural requirements of each species.

Winter mulch: In the North, most lilies, with the exception of a few exceedingly hardy varieties, require the protection of a winter mulch. Well-rotted leaf mold makes an excellent mulch for lilies as it can be left on the ground throughout the year and will aid in increasing the organic content of the soil. Salt hay is also excellent. (See Chapter 8 on Mulches.)

Summer mulch: Lilies prefer a cool, moist root-run; only a few will thrive in a soil that becomes hard and parched during the growing season. A soil well supplied with organic matter will naturally be more retentive of moisture than a soil deficient in humus and will, therefore, provide more favorable growing conditions. The surface of the soil, however, should have some form of protective covering. When lilies are grown in the herbaceous border, this covering is provided by the natural growth of other plants which, in many cases, will afford sufficient ground cover for the bulbs. If lilies are grown in beds or borders by themselves, the surface of the soil should be kept mulched throughout the growing season. Peat moss, well-rotted leaf mold, lawn clippings and buckwheat hulls may be used successfully for this purpose.

Protection against rodents: Mice are, unfortunately, passionately fond of most varieties of lily bulbs and in gardens where mice are apt to be troublesome it is useless to attempt to grow lilies unless some adequate protection is provided. The most effective protection is to use ¼ in. mesh galvanized wire. If the lilies are to be grown in a bed or border by themselves, it is best to line the bottom, sides and ends of the entire bed with wire. When the wire is purchased by the roll it is not prohibitively expensive, and it will afford absolute protection from rodents over a period of many years. It may be put in place at the same time that the bed is prepared for planting, and therefore does not require much extra labor. If the lilies are to be planted in groups in the border, wire baskets of any size can be made or purchased and the bulbs planted within the basket. Although many other means of protection have been tried, such as planting the bulbs in camphor or in medicated peat moss, no method has been found as entirely dependable as the use of wire. For the control of field mice by the use of poison baits, see Chapter 32.

Propagation

Lilies may be propagated by seed, by scales, by bulbils and by bulblets. Some lilies may be propagated more readily by one method than by another.

Propagation by seed

Many lilies may be grown very readily from seed, if one does not mind the years of waiting that intervene between the sowing of the seed and the flowering of the plant. Propagation by other methods is more rapid, however.

Propagation by bulbils

In some species of lilies small bulbils are produced in the axils of the leaves. When the bulbils are ready to be gathered, they will drop from the stem almost at the touch of the fingers. They should be sown in shallow drills in light, well-prepared soil, and handled in very much the same manner as are lily seedlings.

Propagation by bulblets

Most of the stem-rooting lilies produce bulblets on the underground stem. When these bulblets are left undisturbed, they produce a

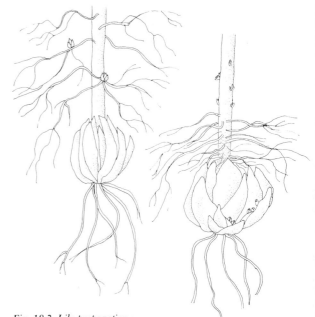

Fig. 18.3. Lily propagation
Lilium regale *with bulblets forming along underground stem.* Lilium auratum *with bulblets forming on stem and scales.*

cluster of small leaves about the base of the main stem and soon become overcrowded. It is well, therefore, to remove them, even though one does not wish to use them for propagation. In the autumn the earth should be carefully dug away from the main stem with a trowel and the small bulblets removed. In some cases the stem may be ripe enough so that it may be gently pulled out without harming the bulbs, in which case the bulblets may be picked off. These bulblets may be planted in shallow drills, being handled in the same manner as are the bulbils.

Lilies of Special Merit

Division 1

Asiatic Lilies and Their Hybrids. The familiar tiger lily *(L. tigrinum)* of old-fashioned gardens belongs here—not to be confused with the tawny daylily *(Hemerocallis fulva)*, which is common along roadsides and on old farm properties but is not a true lily. The new hybrids in this group are, by and large, variations of yellow and orange, but they range from cream to deep brown-reds, then generally are spotted though sometimes without spots. They are divided into three groups: with upright-facing, outward-facing and downward-facing flowers.

Some outstanding lilies in the upright-facing group include 'Black Bear,' 'Cinnabar,' 'Connecticut King,' 'Delicious,' 'Enchantment,' 'Golden Chalice,' 'Golden Coronet,' 'Golden Star,' 'Harmony,' 'Polar Bear,' 'Ruby,' 'Sundrop' and 'Tabasco.'

Those outstanding in the outward-facing group are 'Apricot Glow,' 'Bittersweet,' 'Burgundy,' 'Corsage,' 'Firebright,' 'Paprika,' 'Paul Bunyan' and 'Red Velvet.'

Those outstanding in the downward-facing group are 'Aureola,' 'Connecticut Yankee,' 'Fiesta,' 'Golden Wedding,' 'Harlequin Hybrid,' 'Hornback's Gold,' 'Marlin,' 'Nutmegger,' 'Scarlett' and 'Sonata.'

Division 2

Lilium martagon and Its Hybrids. The species bears small, dull purple, recurving, waxy flowers, but it has given rise to some very pleasing offspring in a group called Paisley Hybrids. These range from white to pale yellow, gold and orange, lilac, purple and mahogany. All are spotted. The 6-ft.-tall stems bring the flowers to impressive height.

Division 3

The lovely and familiar madonna lily *(L. candidum)* is in this division—a favorite in European gardens for hundreds of years and common in engravings of medieval, Italian Renaissance and Elizabethan gardens. The flowers are white, beautifully shaped and borne on stalks 4 ft. to 6 ft. tall. The Cascade strain is an improvement over the species. Madonna lily is unique in that it should be planted in August and covered with only about 1 in. of soil. (All others can be planted in the spring or, prefera-

bly, fall, and covered with 4 in. to 6 in. of soil.) Also in this group is *L. chalcedonicum.*

Division 4

Hybrids derived from native American lilies such as *Lilium canadense, L. humboldtii, L. pardalinum, L. parryi, L. philadelphicum* and *L. superbum.* These are much varied, ranging in color from clear yellow and orange to scarlet, creamy lavender, blue and deep vermilion. Included are Bellingham Hybrids, 'Banting,' 'Nightingale' and 'Robert Simonet.'

Division 5

The Easter lily *(L. longiflorum)* and its many hybrids are in this group, which also includes the interesting species *L. formosanum,* with its very long, white, trumpet-shaped flowers. Most Easter lilies are unreliable in northern gardens.

Division 6

The hardy trumpet lilies, mostly derived from *L. henryi,* are in this group, listed in catalogues as Hybrid Trumpet Lilies or Aurelian Hybrids. Some are distinctly trumpet-shaped, such as 'Black Dragon,' 'Golden Splendor Strain,' 'Pink Perfection' and 'Sentinel Strain.' Others are bowl-shaped: 'Heart's Desire Strain' and 'Thunderbolt.' The 'Sunburst' types— 'Golden Sunburst'—are lilies of clear golden yellow. All of the above are large-flowered, spectacular, large-growing lilies. Many are very fragrant.

Division 7

This group features some of the most spectacular and largest flowers in garden lilies. The species, often referred to as 'Orientals,' includes *L. auratum, L. japonicum, L. rubellum, L. speciosum,* and their crosses with *L. henryi.* Some are bowl-shaped, some recurve until the flowers are flat-faced. Many are variations of pink, red and white, for example: 'Black Beauty,' 'Cover Girl,' 'Empress of India,' 'Imperial Crimson Strain,' 'Imperial Gold Strain,' 'Jamboree' and 'Pink Glory.'

19.1 Portulaca *requires a hot, sunny site in the garden to produce carpets of electric color. Photo Grant Heilman*

19

Annuals and Biennials

ANNUALS

Annuals are plants that complete their life cycles within one growing season. In this group are such useful flowering plants as petunia, zinnia and marigold. Other plants such as snapdragon and geranium, for example, are not true annuals, but are handled as such because they come to flower quickly and are not hardy in most areas of the country.

Annuals have many uses. They are indispensable for cutting, and they give a wealth of bloom throughout the summer and early autumn months. They are useful in flower beds and herbaceous borders to extend color into summer and fall, and if a garden is new or only temporary, such as a rental property, annuals may very satisfactorily be used as the only material in the planting scheme. For window and porch boxes, for potted plants on the terrace or on the low coping of a wall, for the indoor window garden and for winter bloom in the small greenhouse, annuals can hardly be equalled.

In both form and color these flowers offer an extraordinarily wide range, which makes them useful in many ways. For edging beds and other plantings or for solid low carpets of color, there are lobelia, fibrous-rooted (wax) begonia, verbena, sweet alyssum, *Phlox drummondii* and low-growing petunia. For border plants of medium height, there is a wealth of material from which to choose: aster, marigold, poppy, salpiglossis, larkspur, zinnia and countless others, while

tithonia and the exotic castor bean are excellent for use as tall background plants.

The terms "hardy annual," "tender annual" and "winter annual" are used to indicate various things. Tender annuals generally will not withstand even the slightest frost; petunia is a tender annual. Hardy annuals often will withstand frost. Indeed, in some, such as larkspur, seed that falls to the ground in autumn may germinate and the small plants survive through the winter to the next spring, whereupon they will grow to maturity. A winter annual refers to those plants that, in warmer sections of the world (southern California, Florida, the Mediterranean), are planted in the fall and provide flowers all through the winter. Calendula is an excellent example. In fact, calendula responds so well to cool temperatures that in northern gardens it might start out with a burst of bloom in June and early July, only to go dormant in the very hot weather of August, then respond again to the cooler temperatures of September and October and produce what may be the best flowers of the year.

Tremendous advances have been made in the production of new and superior types among many of the more widely grown annuals. Plant breeders have succeeded in doubling the chromosomes of some annuals, with the result that these plants have greater vigor, larger flowers, longer stems and foliage of a more luxuriant green. Among these improved annuals are such flowers as the giant ruffed tetra-

357

ploid snapdragon and the lovely tetraploid alyssum 'Snowdrift.'

Through controlled pollination and planned breeding, new strains of petunia, begonia, snapdragon, impatiens and other annuals are now abundantly available. The plant breeder inbreeds to get two lines which, when crossed, give predictable and superb results. This is known as the F_1 generation, the seeds of which produce superior petunias, snapdragons, and so forth.

Exposure: Annuals generally require full sun; there are comparatively few members of this group that will thrive in even partial shade. In selecting a site for the annual garden or flower border, therefore, it is well to choose an open, sunny location where there is good air circulation.

Soil requirements: The majority of annuals will thrive in a soil of reasonably good fertility that is amply supplied with organic matter, a good, mellow garden loam with a reaction varying from pH 6.5 to pH 7.5 being considered ideal. A few annuals will grow well on extremely poor soils, some will tolerate a considerable degree of acidity and some seem to be entirely indifferent to soil conditions. For the annual garden, the soil may be prepared either in the autumn or in the early spring as soon as the ground is workable. Adequate preparation will bring increased rewards in the form of more vigorous growth and more abundant bloom. If well-rotted manure or good compost is available, it may be spread over the surface of the beds and then forked or spaded in, or if time and labor do not have to be taken into consideration the beds may be prepared by "double-digging" (see index). If the beds are prepared in the autumn, the surface of the soil should be left rough during the winter. However, if the surface of the bed is prepared in the spring, it should be carefully leveled and raked with an iron rake until the soil is of fine tilth.

If it seems advisable to increase the fertility of the soil, a topdressing of commercial fertilizer may be applied early in July and again in early August. A 4-12-4 or a 5-10-5 complete fertilizer will give excellent results; it should be applied at the rate of 2 lb. to every 100 sq. ft. When the application is made, care should be taken not to get any of the fertilizer on the foliage of the plants as it might cause burning. It should be sprinkled lightly on the surface of the soil and watered in.

The high-analysis, quickly soluble fertilizers are also of great value. They may be applied as a booster application at the time of transplanting and again in midsummer when the plants are flowering heavily. If the soil tests below a pH of 6.5, lime should be applied. (See Chapter 30 on Soils and Soil Improvement.)

Propagation: Most annuals are propagated by seed. Sowing seed of annuals in the open ground is generally poor practice, especially after investing in good-quality seed, because soil contains too many insect and disease organisms that may destroy or damage the small seedling. It is wiser to sow seed in sterilized media (commercial potting soil, perlite, vermiculite, etc.) in flats or pots to ensure success. For detailed directions on seed sowing, both in the open ground and under glass, see Chapter 34 on propagation.

Some annuals "self-sow," that is, their seeds survive the winter to germinate in the spring, and though some of these flowers are desirable, others are rather inferior. When self-sowing occurs, the young seedling plants frequently require thinning, as it is essential that each individual plant be allowed ample space for its full development if good bloom is to be obtained. The ultimate space required by the plants should be determined (see tabular list on pages 387 to 393), and the thinning should be done before the plants start becoming overcrowded. In some cases, such as with zinnia and marigold, the plants that are thinned out may be transplanted to another section of the garden. In the case of seedlings that do not transplant readily (poppy, mignonette, etc.), it is best to discard those that have been thinned out. Thinning of young seedlings should be done on a cloudy day when the ground is moist, as those that remain in the ground will suffer less shock if their root systems are only slightly disturbed. They also will suffer less

19.2 Petunia and sweet alyssum (Lobularia maritima) *worked into a foundation planting add summer color. Photo Grant Heilman*

from sudden exposure to full sunlight if they have been somewhat shaded by the close proximity of other seedlings.

Transplanting: When annuals are transplanted from seed flats to the garden, they should be protected from shock as much as possible. Transplanting also should preferably be done on a cloudy day or late in the afternoon. Plants should be handled gently to minimize root damage and should be watered immediately. An extra boost can be given the plants at this time by watering them with a weak starter solution of a water-soluble fertilizer, after which they should be covered with newspaper, baskets or some similar covering to protect them from too much sunlight for a day or two after planting if the heat is excessive.

Some annuals should be allowed to develop their natural habits of growth and will either produce a spire of bloom or will branch quite freely if they are given ample space for their full development. There are a number of annuals, however, that definitely benefit from judicious pinching back. Left entirely to their own devices these seedlings will make rather tall, spindly growth and will produce only scanty bloom. It is, therefore, wise to nip out the terminal bud or the tip of the plant when two or three sets of leaves have developed along the main stem, so that the plant has an opportunity to become bushy and well branched. In some cases further pinching may be desirable after the side shoots have developed.

Culture: The cultivation of the soil plays an important part in the success of the annual garden. Frequent, shallow cultivation should be given, the most satisfactory tool for this purpose being the small weeder with three flexible prongs. The soil should be kept in excellent tilth throughout the season and a hard crust should never be allowed to form upon the surface of the bed.

Some annuals, such as poppy, portulaca and *Phlox drummondii*, do not mind a high soil temperature and a minimum supply of moisture in the soil. However, many other annuals such as zinnia, marigold and snapdragons may be greatly benefited by a summer mulch of peat moss or some similar material that will help to conserve the moisture in the soil and will maintain a lower soil temperature.

The period of bloom of most annuals may be greatly prolonged if the fading flowers are regularly removed. This detail of good garden maintenance, called "dead-heading," is more important when one is dealing with annuals than it is in the case of any other group of flowers. The chief function of an annual plant is to blossom and produce seed; having fulfilled this function, it has no further reason for existence. The prevention of seed formation, therefore, stimulates additional flowering. In the case of low border plants such as sweet alyssum, it is sometimes wise to shear the plants back if they become somewhat shabby, and vigorous new growth will thus be induced. Some cool weather annuals such as calendula can be cut back severely in the heat of August to stimulate new growth and a good autumn crop of flowers.

Specific recommendations for the treatment of diseases and pests of annuals are given in Chapter 32 on plant diseases and insect pests.

Selection of Cultivars

From the long lists of annuals in the seed catalogues, it is difficult to make wise selections for one's own gardening needs unless one has had an opportunity to become familiar with them. They are all listed in these voluminous catalogues—the dependable ones and the fickle ones; the sturdy ones and the temperamental ones; those with flowers of exquisite daintiness and those that have a bold form or hue; those that are planted for their fragrance and those that may have an objectionable odor, but nevertheless would serve to fill in a particularly

troublesome spot. Several good seed catalogues from leading seedhouses should be studied carefully for a range of flowers from which to choose for one's own specific purposes.

It is impossible to discuss them all, obviously. Here those annuals have been selected for inclusion that, because of some particular merit, seem well worth considering in the general garden scheme. One nice aspect about growing annuals is that we can experiment with new ones each year, while we also continue to include "tried-and-true" old favorites.

ANNUALS OF MERIT

(alphabetical by common name)

African daisy (*Arctotis grandis*)

Arctotis is classed among the worthy annuals because of the simple beauty of its flowers, which resemble a white daisy with long pointed petals, lavender on the under side, with a steel-blue center. The flowers are borne on long, graceful, almost leafless stems and are excellent for cutting as they last extremely well. The plants reach a height of 15 in. to 18 in., and will continue to bloom throughout the summer if the fading blooms are removed.

Culture: The plants are very tolerant of poor soil and of drought, which makes them particularly valuable for the gardener who must struggle against such handicaps. *Arctotis* is classed as a half-hardy annual. The seeds may be sown early in the spring indoors, or later in the season either in coldframes or directly in the garden where they are to flower. The plants should be spaced from 10 in. to 12 in. apart. They are remarkably free from pests and diseases, and since they are so modest in their demands regarding soil and moisture, they may be classed among the most easily grown annuals.

Ageratum, floss flower (*Ageratum*)

Ageratum varies in size from the very dwarf, compact type, hardly more than 3 in. high, to the tall, branching varieties, which often reach a height of from 15 in. to 18 in. The pale lavender-blue flowers of the larger types are lovely in the flower border and are also excellent for cutting. White and dark blue varieties are also obtainable but are less satisfactory.

The tetraploid cultivar 'Blue Mink' is an excellent dwarf variety and was a major improvement over older sorts. Since then, however, many newer and even smaller ageratums have appeared in a constant effort on the part of plant breeders to improve compactness, flower color, durability and showiness. Vigorous and uniform in growth, the plants are crowned with a myriad of small, lavender-blue flowers.

Culture: *Ageratum* is classed as a tender annual. For early bloom the seed should be sown indoors in March and the young seedlings transplanted to the garden when all danger of frost is over. Sowings made in the open ground after it has become warm and mellow will give later bloom. The plants reseed so abundantly that they will often establish themselves in a garden, new plants appearing year after year. If the faded blooms are removed and the plants are not allowed to reseed, *Ageratum* will remain in bloom over a period of many months until the plants are killed by the first frost. The dwarf varieties may be used as edging plants and should be spaced from 4 in. to 6 in. apart. The taller varieties are excellent for the front of the flower border and should be spaced from 10 in. to 12 in. apart.

Alyssum, sweet alyssum (*Lobularia maritima*)

Sweet alyssum is one of the most popular of the annual edging plants. Several of the exceedingly dwarf forms attain a height of hardly more than 3 in., while some of the larger types are fully 9 in. tall. The plants begin to flower when still very small, and they are covered with a profusion of bloom throughout the summer months. The varieties most commonly used are white, although there are several strains that bear flowers of a deep lavender hue. The plants are very uniform both in height and in habit of growth.

The dwarf cultivar 'Royal Carpet' is a lovely shade of royal purple and makes an excellent edging. The tetraploid giant alyssum 'Snowdrift' reaches a height of almost 10 in. and bears a profusion of snowy flowers, continuing in bloom until late autumn.

Culture: Sweet alyssum is a hardy annual and may be sown outdoors as soon as the frost is out of the ground, the plants being thinned to stand 6 in. apart. The young seedlings make rapid growth and will begin to bloom in less than six weeks from the date of planting. Seeds may also be sown indoors or in coldframes, being later transplanted to the garden, so that a very early bloom can be obtained.

Browallia, bush violet (*Browallia* spp.)

Blue is a color that is found none too frequently among the annuals and for this reason *Browallia* is especially prized for its abundant bloom throughout the summer. The small, tubular flowers are a clear violet-blue or white, and they are excellent for their decorative value in the garden, for cutting and as potted plants. *Browallia elata* is ideal for bedding purposes, attaining a height of about 1½ ft. *B. speciosa (major)* produces larger flowers, and it is of especial value as a potted plant, for window boxes and for hanging baskets.

Culture: The seeds may be planted early in the season under glass or later in the open ground. The young seedlings should be pinched back when about 6 in. tall to induce a bushy, well-branched plant. The plants prefer a position in full sun and will thrive in any good garden soil. They should be spaced from 6 in. to 8 in. apart, and will give a profusion of bloom throughout the season.

Butterfly flower (*Schizanthus* spp.)

Schizanthus is sometimes called the poor man's orchid because of the form and color of its dainty flowers and because it may be so easily grown. The foliage is a soft light green, finely cut, and the myriad delicate flowers form a pyramid of bloom, in tints of lavender, rose and brown.

Culture: The seed may be sown either out of doors or under glass, and the plants come into bloom in less than six weeks from sowing. They are so profligate with their flowers, however, that the period of bloom is somewhat short. *Schizanthus* is exceedingly well adapted to pot culture in the greenhouse, and beautiful plants may be produced that are charming for decorative purposes in the house. The taller types, which grow from 2 ft. to 3 ft., should be planted from 1 ft. to 1½ ft. apart. The more dwarf varieties reach a height of about 1 ft. and should be spaced about 9 in. apart.

Calendula *(Calendula officinalis)*

There is a quality about the great golden and orange blooms of the calendulas that is very appealing. The plants are extremely hardy, and in the South they may be grown outdoors during the winter months. In the North, calendulas are popular both as a greenhouse plant to supply flowers for cutting during the winter and as a summer-flowering annual.

Types and varieties: Since calendulas are considered winter annuals in frost-free (or nearly so) climates, they do not do well in very hot weather. In recent years breeders have attempted to develop heat-resistant sorts, such as the 'Pacific Beauty' hybrids. Dwarf cultivars also are now available.

Culture: The plants are of easy culture and are not exacting in their demands. The seeds may be sown indoors for early bloom or directly in the garden as soon as the ground can be worked in the spring. The plants reach a height of from 12 in. to 18 in., and they should be spaced about 1 ft. apart. They are excellent for the front of the border and for the cutting garden.

California poppy *(Eschscholzia* spp.)

The California poppy is among the gayest of our summer-flowering annuals and beloved by many a gardener. It was named in honor of a Dr. Eschscholtz, a Russian ship's surgeon, who found it growing wild on our western coast more than a century ago. While some members of the genus are true perennials in their native habitat, they are not able to survive the extreme cold of northern winters and are therefore usually treated as annuals.

Types and varieties: The plants vary considerably in height, some of the miniature varieties being hardly more than 6 in., while the larger, more vigorous types often reach a height of from 12 in. to 15 in. The foliage is finely cut, a soft gray-green in color, and the lovely flowers are borne on slender, upright stems. During the night and on dull, cloudy days the petals remain closed, but when the sun shines on them they open wide. The flowers are lovely both in the garden and for cutting as they last exceedingly well when cut and require no special attention. The true California poppy (*E. californica*) varies in color from a soft cream to a deep golden-orange. Many of the varieties we have today, however, are hybrid forms and offer a much wider range of color, being obtainable in shades of ivory, shell pink, salmon, rose, scarlet, crimson and a deep tawny orange. Special cultivars are available, such as 'Mission Bells' and 'Ballerina,' which are double and semidouble respectively.

Culture: *Eschscholzia* are of very easy culture. Although they prefer a light, sandy soil, they will thrive in soil of almost any type and will give an abundance of bloom provided that they are planted in full sun. The seeds may be sown in late autumn, shortly before freezing weather sets in, or they may be sown in the open ground in very early spring. The plants make their most rapid growth during the cool, moist days of early spring. The seeds should always be sown where they are to flower, as *Eschscholzia* do not take kindly to transplanting. To make the spreading of seed for such plants easier, mix the tiny seeds with about a cupful of dry vermiculite. By doing so, the plants will be more evenly distributed, and fewer will be wasted in the thinning process. If the blooms are cut off as soon as the petals have fallen and no seed pods are allowed to form, the plants may be kept in flower for many months. The plants should be thinned out so that they are spaced from 8 in. to 10 in. apart.

Cape marigold *(Dimorpotheca sinuata)*

This bright little orange daisy deserves a place both in the cutting garden and in the flower border. It may also be grown very successfully in the greenhouse, and although the flowers are modest in form and size, they are lovely when used in mixed bouquets. In the garden the plants seldom reach a height of more than 12 in. The flowers are daisylike in form, with long, slender, somewhat pointed petals that seem to shimmer in the sunlight. They range in color from pale lemon-yellow to deep orange and salmon-pink.

19.4 Popular for dried winter bouquets is the old-fashioned cockscomb (Celosia cristata). *Photo Grant Heilman*

Culture: The seed may be sown in the open ground or the young seedlings may be started under glass. Cape marigolds prefer an open, sunny location in the garden and will thrive even in very poor soil. They are also more tolerant of drought than some of the other annuals. The plants should be spaced 8 in. to 10 in. apart.

Celosia, cockscomb *(Celosia argentea, C. cristata)*

Garden plants, like many other aspects of modern life, are frequently subject to fashion vagaries. Celosia suffered a sort of Victorian hangover when it was fashionable to be anti-Victorian. Now we are more generous in our attitudes and this, along with some good hybridizing, gives us a very useful group of annuals.

Most valuable are the tall plume celosias for great masses of color in the garden. They grow to about 2½ ft. and produce plumes of red, tangerine and gold. The golden varieties ('Golden Torch,' 'Golden Triumph,' 'Tango') have yellow-green leaves, and such reds as 'Forest Fire' have purple-bronze leaves that are quite striking and vivid. These plume types also are available in dwarf plants ('Feathery,' 'Fiery,' 'Lilliput'), which are good for edging beds.

The cockscomb celosias—those having the flowers in a roosterlike comb arrangement, rather than in soft plumes—are less successful as bedding plants because each plant tends to be an individual, whereas the plume types mass together in such a way that you can hardly tell where one plant ends and another begins. But in spite of this they can be rewarding plants to grow. Cockscombs can be had either in tall sorts, bearing huge combs 8 in. to 10 in. across ('Fireglow,' 'Toreador'), or in delightful small plants less than 12 in. tall yet bearing large combs, ('Empress,' 'Jewel Box'). Celosias are superb also for cutting and using either fresh or dried in winter bouquets.

Culture: Celosias are easy to grow from seed, and seem to have practically no insect or disease pests. Sow seed indoors in the greenhouse or under lights. They grow particularly well in a good garden soil and require plenty of moisture, but they will also tolerate poor soil provided the moisture is adequate.

China asters *(Callistephus chinensis)*

Long one of the most popular of annual flowers, these are obtainable in a wide variety of form and colorings and will give abundant bloom throughout the season. They are lovely in the flower garden and are quite indispensable in the cutting garden. If early, mid-season and late varieties are selected, the period of bloom may be extended from late June until frost.

Types and varieties: Although annual or China asters are frequently used in garden beds and as border plants, they are most successful and rewarding when used for cut flowers, and few annuals can surpass them for this purpose. The flower forms vary from formal powder-puff shapes to curled, fluffy forms and wide-eyed singles. And the color range, from deep rich purple through many variations of lavender and pink to white, is appealingly distinctive.

Culture: China asters thrive best in a fairly fertile soil, and while they prefer full sun they will also do reasonably well in light shade. In the North the seed should be sown indoors or in a coldframe. As asters are shallow-rooted, close cultivation should be avoided, and they require ample moisture during periods of drought. Wilt-resistant varieties should be selected.

Clarkia, farewell-to-spring *(Clarkia unguiculata, C. pulchella)*

Clarkia is a native of our own Northwest and was first discovered at the time of the Lewis and Clark expedition, being named in honor of the explorer. There are two types, *Clarkia elegans,* which bears its flowers in long, loose sprays, and *Clarkia pulchella,* which bears its flowers in clusters. The stems are of a coppery tone and the dainty flowers are beautiful both in form and in coloring, ranging from white through salmon-pink to purple and crimson. The blooms are excellent for cutting, and as the plants do extremely well under greenhouse conditions, they are often grown for cut flowers during the winter months.

Culture: The seeds may be sown in the autumn in the open ground, in the greenhouse or in cold frames for very early bloom, and directly in the garden as soon as the soil is mellow and workable. The plants reach a height of 15 in. to 18 in. and should be spaced from 10 in. to 12 in. apart.

Coleus *(Coleus blumei)*

This is another plant which, along with geraniums and impatiens, used to be limited to baskets, boxes and Grandma's window sill. Plant breeders, however, have brought it out of these limitations so that today many cultivars are available that can be grown from seed with predictably good results. The 'Carefree' series is available either in mixture or in individual variations, such as 'Carefree Jade,' 'Carefree Golden,' and so on. Other cultivars range from 'Candidum' (creamy-white leaf with green edge) to 'Red Velvet,' which has solid, deep crimson leaves. There are large-leaved and small-leaved cultivars, large plants and dwarf. Shade or partly shaded growing sites intensify the color and variations in each leaf.

Culture: Sow indoors, in greenhouse or under lights in March, and grow in good soil with a plentiful water supply. These plants will not do well in a hot, dry, poor soil location. At the end of summer, take cuttings of special plants to root and hold through winter for next year, or for indoor plants, if desired. Coleus also is excellent for window boxes, pots and outdoor containers.

Cornflower, bachelor's-button *(Centaurea cyanus)*

The cornflower may be classed in the group of absolutely dependable annuals. They are of vigorous habit, will thrive on poor, sandy soil and ask almost nothing in the way of care and cultivation.

Culture: If the seed is sown outdoors late in autumn, it will lie dormant during the winter and will germinate with the first warm days of spring. The lusty, vigorous seedlings make rapid growth and will soon come into bloom. Seed may also be sown in the open ground at any time during the spring months. As the period of bloom is rather short, successive sowings should be made. The plants reseed readily and young seedlings will often appear as volunteers year after year. Cornflowers are especially recommended for cutting and for children's gardens. They seem to hold a special delight for children and are so dependable and of such easy culture that they make failure almost impossible. The tall cornflowers reach a height of about 18 in. to 3 ft. Dwarf cultivars such as 'Jubilee Gem' are compact and only about 12 in. high.

Cosmos *(Cosmos bipinnatus, C. diversifolius, C. sulphureus)*

Cosmos is of particular value because of its height, the giant varieties often reaching 6 ft. or more. If both early and late varieties are planted, bloom may be had from July until frost. In habit of growth cosmos is somewhat spreading and spindly, and lacks the grace and charm of many other flowers. It is best adapted to the rear of border planting and to the cutting garden. The so-called 'Sensation' cosmos are variations of pink, mauve, white and crimson, and are marvelously refreshing as cut flowers. Quite different in flower form, color and even plant are the 'Klondike' cosmos, which range in color from lemon-yellow through gold and orange to deep burnished red. 'Diablo' is a compact, exceptionally free-flowering, fiery red, which makes a brilliant mass of color in the garden.

Culture: Cosmos is classed as a tender annual and the seeds should not be sown until all danger of frost is over. If early bloom is desired, the seedlings may be started under glass. As the plants have a decidedly branching habit of growth, they should be allowed ample room to develop. The dwarf varieties should be spaced 2 ft. apart, the tall varieties from 2½ ft. to 3 ft. apart. The tall varieties frequently require staking.

Flowering tobacco *(Nicotiana)*

The flowering tobacco is one of the most valuable of the tall growing annuals, and it is so well adapted to a variety of planting compositions that it should be widely grown. In the evening when the lovely white, tubular flowers recede into the twilight, its delicate fragrance pervades the garden and the night moths hover above it in the dusk. Unfortunately, many of the more compact modern hybrids do not exude the lovely evening fragrance of the species *N. affinis.*

Some varieties remain closed during the day but many of the newer varieties, such as 'Sensation Daylight,' remain open. A wide range of color is now available among the *Nicotiana* species, including such lovely shades as lavender, coral, soft pink, rose-mahogany, crimson and even green.

Culture: The plants are easily grown, and when once well established in a garden they reseed very readily and the seedlings will come up year after year. The seed is exceedingly fine and may be sown under glass for early bloom or in the open where the plants are to flower. The plants may be transplanted with ease, and they may be moved into the garden when they are in full flower if they are lifted with ample soil, and if the transplanting is done on a cloudy, moist day. The plants bloom over a long period and may be used very satisfactorily in the herbaceous border after some of the early flowering biennials have been removed. The flowering tobacco is also lovely when used as a house plant during the winter months. Seedlings that have been potted up in the autumn before frost will give generous bloom throughout the winter.

Geranium *(Pelargonium x hortorum)*

While geraniums have traditionally been purchased at the local greenhouse each spring, a major breakthrough occurred in the gardening world when it became possible not only to grow geranium by seed in great numbers but also to produce seedlings true to form. The first of these was the 'Carefree' series, and it made possible the large-scale use of geranium in gardens. A newer but similar series of seed-grown geranium is 'Sprinter.' The plants are self-branching, stocky and prolifically flowering.

Geranium must be started indoors, either in a greenhouse or under lights, in order to have plants of sufficient size for planting outdoors. Seedlings should be pricked off into pots to give maximum opportunity for each plant to grow to good size before planting in the garden.

Impatiens *(Impatiens wallerana, I. platypetala)*

Impatiens is a relatively new addition to the list of popular annuals, due to the hybridization efforts of plant breeders and the introduction of many large-flowered and variegated leaf varieties from the islands of the South Pacific. They are valued for their persistent flower production, bright and clear colors and, equally important, for their ability to grow and flower well in the shade. There are tiny dwarf cultivars ('Elfin'), starred-flower cultivars ('Twinkles') and a wide assortment of colors, ranging all the way from white through pink to red, scarlet to orange.

Impatiens can be grown from seed if started early indoors either in a greenhouse or under lights. If, in a mixture, a particular plant is considered choice, it can readily be wintered as a pot plant and propagated by cuttings for use in next year's garden.

Larkspur *(Consolida ambigua, C. regalis)*

The annual larkspur is among the loveliest and most decorative of our garden flowers. The stately spires of bloom add their full measure of beauty to any garden composition, and they are highly valued for cutting as well. Several new and greatly improved varieties of annual larkspur have been introduced within recent years. The plants reach a height of from 3 ft. to 4 ft., and the massive spires of bloom are very beautiful, being obtainable in a wide range of colorings—white, shell-pink, rose, lavender and

purple. The plants should be given ample room to develop and should be spaced about 9 in. apart.

Culture: The seed and seedlings are quite hardy, and the seed may be sown in the open ground late in the autumn, germinating with the first warm days of spring; or it may be sown as soon as the ground is workable in March. Autumn sowing and early spring sowing are desirable, as seedlings started later in the season do not thrive as well and the plants do not grow as vigorously. It is possible to start the seedlings under glass for early transplanting to the open ground.

Annual larkspur is extremely popular for greenhouse culture during the winter months. The lovely spikes of bloom are very decorative as cut flowers and require no special care or attention in the greenhouse benches.

Lobelia *(Lobelia erinus)*

The intensity of the blue found in the lobelia is equalled in almost no other flower. The several newer cultivars such as 'Crystal Palace' and 'Bright Eyes' have greatly increased the popularity of these highly valued edging plants. There are several types: an exceedingly dwarf form suitable only for edgings; a trailing form, which is of particular value for porch and window boxes; and an upright form, which reaches a height of almost 15 in.

Culture: The plants are tender and the seeds should be started under glass early in the season, the young seedlings being transplanted into the garden when all danger of frost is over. The plants are of simple culture and will thrive well in any good garden soil. They should be set 4 in. to 6 in. apart.

Lupine *(Lupinus)*

Although the annual forms are not as large or as decorative as the perennial types, they possess a certain distinction and charm that make them well worth growing. The plants do well either in full sun or in partial shade, and if the seed pods are not allowed to form, they will bloom over a very long period. The tall spikes of bloom are graceful and lovely, and come in such colors as a clear soft blue, pink, mauve and white. Because of the decorative value of the blooms as cut flowers, the annual lupines are frequently grown in greenhouses during the winter months.

Culture: The seeds may be planted in the open ground where they are to flower or they may be started under glass. As they do not tolerate transplanting as readily as some other annuals, an ideal method of growing the plants, if they are to be started indoors for early bloom in the garden, is to sow the seeds in peat moss pots. The plants may then be moved into the garden when they are about to flower. By using such peat moss pots, the roots will be undisturbed and the plants will suffer no setback. The plants grow from 2 ft. to 2½ ft. tall and should be spaced from 12 in. to 15 in. apart.

Marigold (*Tagetes* spp.)

Although the terms "French," "African" and, most recently, "American" have been applied to marigold, the species is originally from tropical America. In recent years, hybridizers have performed near miracles with these wonderful flowers. There are now "carnation"-flowered, "chrysanthemum"-flowered, singles, bicolored, cream, yellow, red, orange and gold, huge plants with large flowers and dwarf plants with lovely small flowers. Marigolds are both useful and aesthetic. They are supposed to deter rabbits and nematodes, yet they provide more color for effort expended than almost any other annual.

From midsummer until frost the marigolds may be counted upon for generous bloom. They may either be used as the dominant note in the late summer garden or they may play a minor role by filling in an occasional gap here and there. In the cutting garden they are in-

19.5 Marigolds (Tagetes), *along with* Zinnia *and* Petunia, *are among the most popular of garden annuals and are available in many flower types and growth habits. Photo Grant Heilman*

dispensable. They are so profligate with their bloom that they may be cut with lavish abandon and great bowls of them will carry the rich yellow and orange tones of late summer into the house, until the onset of the first frost.

Culture: The marigolds are of the most simple culture. The seeds are large and germinate readily, and the young plants may be transplanted with the greatest ease, it being possible to move them into the garden when they are in full flower. They are tolerant of poor soil, and will thrive under almost any conditions, in full sun or in partial shade, and in wet or dry soil. The seeds may be sown in the open where they are to flower or they may be sown early under glass.

Painted tongue (*Salpiglossis sinuata*)

The trumpetlike flowers of this plant come in shades of dusky purple, deep wine-red and ivory, with stencilings of gold. They are very decorative both in the garden and for cutting, as they last unusually well in water.

Culture: The plants reach an ultimate height of from 2 ft. to 2½ ft., and should be given ample space in which to develop, being spaced from 8 in. to 10 in. apart. *Salpiglossis* is not of as easy culture as are many of the annuals, and the young seedlings require considerable pampering. The seeds should be sown indoors early in the spring, and the young plants should not be set out until all danger of frost is over. The seedlings should be kept growing rapidly and should not be allowed to suffer from overcrowding in the seedbed or from lack of moisture. The plants prefer full sun and a deep, rich, loam soil.

Petunias

In the skillful hands of the hybridizers, the petunia has been developed into one of our most useful flowers. Always dependable, demanding almost nothing in the way of care and cultivation, thriving under most adverse conditions of soil and climate, it offers us an abundance of bloom and beauty throughout the long summer season. For porch and window boxes, for masses of bloom about a summer cottage, as border plant in the flower garden, the petunia is quite indispensable. Single or double, ruffled or fluted, it offers a wider range of color than almost any other flowering annual. Some of the new shades of velvety purple, pale rose and deep wine-red are especially lovely when used in combination with other annuals. The lovely F_1 hybrids attest to the skill of our modern plant breeders. The 'Hybrid Multiflora' petunia is extremely prolific and now includes yellow in its color range. The 'Hybrid Grandifloras' have larger flowers, are often ruffled and striped or veined with contrasting colors. All are extraordinarily reliable in growth habit and possess a perfection of bloom that places them quite in a class by themselves.

Culture: For early bloom the seeds should be sown indoors and the young plants may be transplanted into the garden when they are ready to come into flower. Seed may also be sown in the open ground, being covered very lightly with well-sifted soil, since it is so fine. Petunia has a longer season of bloom than most flowers, and if the plants become spindly at any period in their growth they may be cut back and will soon branch out again. The tall, spreading varieties that reach from 1 ft. to 2 ft. should be spaced about 1 ft. apart. The dwarf varieties reaching a height of 6 in. to 8 in. should be spaced about 6 in. apart.

Phlox, annual *(Phlox drummondii)*

Annual phlox was originally found growing wild in Texas. Since its introduction into cultivation it has become one of our most useful edging and low border plants. It is especially well adapted to cool, seaside location. There are many variations in flower color, which together provide a carpet of bright, jewel-like tones.

Culture: In the South annual phlox is often grown as a winter annual, and since it is extremely hardy it can survive many sudden cold snaps and bloom blithely on. In the North the seeds may be planted in the autumn or in very early spring in the open. Sowings under glass are also frequently made. The plants can readily be transplanted and, if they are not allowed to reseed, will remain in bloom for many months. There are low-growing, dwarf types reaching a height of about 6 in., which should be spaced about 6 in. apart. The larger, more spreading types, which attain a height of from 10 in. to 12 in., should be planted about 9 in. apart. *Phlox drummondii* thrives best in an open, sunny position and does exceedingly well on poor, sandy soil.

Pincushion flower, mourning-bride *(Scabiosa atropurpurea)*

The flowers of the annual *Scabiosa* are borne in profusion from midsummer until frost. The plants are of rather thin growth and scant foliage, but the flowers are excellent for cutting and are attractive in the garden as well. The plants reach a height of about 2½ ft., and the flowers are borne on long, wiry stems.

Culture: The seeds may be sown in the open where the plants are to flower, or under glass for early bloom. The flowers come in a wide range of colors—white, lavender-blue, flesh-pink, rose, crimson, purple and deep maroon. They should be planted about 1 ft. apart.

Pink, annual *(Dianthus chinensis)*

The annual pinks have long been popular. They will produce generous bloom throughout the summer months. Both single and double varieties are obtainable in a wide range of color-ings—white, salmon-pink, crimson and deep red. The plants are branching in habit of growth and reach a height of about 1 ft. They are especially useful in the front of the border.

Culture: The seeds may be sown in a cold-frame or in the open ground after the soil has become warm and mellow. The plants prefer a sunny location, and they thrive in a rich, rather moist garden soil. They should be spaced from 8 in. to 10 in. apart.

Poppy *(Papaver* spp.)

Of all the annual poppies, the Shirley poppy *(P. rhoeas)* is among the most appealing. Its flowers are of exquisite daintiness and are love-ly both in the garden and for cutting. The Shir-ley poppy is a distinct strain developed from the little corn poppy, which is found growing wild throughout Europe, and it owes its origin to that wonderful student of plant life, the Rev-erend W. Wilks, who in the year 1880 found a modest little corn poppy with a fine line of white along the edge of the petals growing in his garden at the Shirley Vicarage in England. He saved the seed, and the following year from the resultant 200 seedling plants he obtained 4 or 5 others with the same fine white line. For many years he worked patiently with these poppies, gradually developing a new and very beautiful strain known as the Shirley poppy. In habit of growth the plants are somewhat branching, reaching a height of almost 2 ft., and they bear a profusion of flowers of beauti-ful form. The single varieties are far more ex-

quisite than the heavy-headed double types, and there is a wide color range—white, salmon-pink, apricot, rose and deeper shades of red and crimson. 'Wild-rose Pink' is one of the love-liest varieties.

Culture: The Shirley poppy, with its long, slender, hairy stems, thrives best in full sun in a light, sandy loam soil. It requires a free cir-culation of air, and if planted in a damp, poorly drained situation, the young plants have a ten-dency to rot off. They also are apt to suffer during a rainy season, as the flower buds fre-quently rot before they open under such con-ditions.

The opium poppy *(P. somniferum)* differs from the Shirley poppy in that its stems are smooth and glaucous and somewhat thicker. This poppy attains a greater height and the flowers are larger. There are single and double types, carnation- and peony-flowered forms, and they all are decorative and lovely.

All members of the poppy family are hardy. The seeds may be sown either in the autumn or early in the spring. Since it is almost impossible to transplant the young seedlings with much success, they should be sown where the plants are to flower. The seed is very fine and should be covered lightly with sifted soil. The young seedling plants should be thinned out to a dis-tance of 6 in. or 8 in. apart before they become in the least crowded.

Poppies thrive best during the cool, moist, growing weather of spring, and they should, therefore, be sown as early in the season as pos-sible. This is very important in sections of the country where the summer heat is intense.

Snapdragon *(Antirrhinum majus)*

There are few annuals that are more useful than the snapdragon. It is indispensable in the flower beds and borders, and is equally valuable in the cutting garden. It is lovely in form, and the colors are infinitely varied. ranging from delicate apple-blossom pink through shades of salmon and apricot, to tawny yellow and deep wine-red. The intermediate type, reaching a height of about 18 in., is the most popular, but for the rear of the flower border the giant types are preferable, since they often reach a height of 3 ft. or more. Snapdragon also is available in dwarf form, but somehow the tall spikes are still most appealing. The flower forms range from the familiar "snapping dragon" to double and bell-flower forms in which the flowers are open and resemble *Gloxinia*.

Culture: For early spring bloom the seeds may be sown in August and the young plants wintered over in coldframes, or the seeds may be sown in the greenhouse in January or February or in hotbeds in March. The young seedlings should be pricked out as soon as they have reached sufficient size, and, as they develop, they should be pinched back to make them well branched. The young seedlings may be transplanted to the garden as soon as the soil has become warm and mellow, being spaced about 1 ft. apart.

If the faded flowers are removed regularly, and if the plants are given good care and cultivation, they will give generous bloom over a period of many months. Snapdragon thrives best in a rich, mellow soil rather high in lime content, but is tolerant of widely varying conditions. In mild climates, snapdragon will live through the winter, and it may be regarded as a perennial.

Since the introduction of the rust-proof varieties, the gardener need have little cause for concern over this disease, which formerly took such a heavy toll of these flowers.

Stock *(Matthiola incana, M. longipetala)*

Stock is beloved for its spicy fragrance and for its association with old-fashioned gardens. When grown in the greenhouse during the winter months, the flowers are lovely for mixed bouquets and they are lovely, too, when grown outdoors if the plants are given proper care.

Culture: Stock is a bit more temperamental than many of the annuals and sometimes fails to flower well. For most satisfactory results, the seeds should be sown indoors or in coldframes and the young plants set out in the garden when all danger of frost is over. There are both tall-growing and dwarf-growing types, and both single and double forms, and there is a wide range of color: white, cream, lavender, purple, pink, rose, red, crimson and a dusky shade of antique copper. The tall-growing types, reaching a height of from 2 ft. to 2½ ft., should be planted from 1 ft. to 1½ ft. apart, while the dwarf varieties of 1 ft. to 1½ ft. in height should be planted from 6 in. to 9 in. apart.

Sunflower *(Helianthus annuus)*

Although many of the members of this family are of such coarse and ungainly growth that they are ill-suited to the flower border, there are several that are outstanding as cut flowers or as large background plants in a country garden. A whole group of burnished red-brown, some with rays of yellow, can be had under such names as 'Color Fashion,' 'Excelsior Mixed,' 'Piccolo,' 'Sutton's Red'—these all have small flowers 4 in. across, and when used as cut flowers are pure sunshine. 'Italian White' and the large-flowered double 'Dwarf Sungold' are also interesting to use.

Culture: The seeds may be sown in the greenhouse or in coldframes for early bloom, or they may be sown in the open ground after all danger of frost is over. The plants should be spaced from 15 in. to 18 in. apart. The sunflower is among the least exacting of plants and requires little in the way of cultivation. It prefers full sun, but will tolerate poor soil and drought to an extraordinary degree.

Sweet pea *(Lathyrus odoratus)*

Early sowing is one of the secrets of success with sweet pea. If greenhouse space is available the seeds should be sown in January, in small flower pots. If seed is to be sown in the open ground, it should be planted as early as possible in the season. In the South autumn sowing is preferred. In order to facilitate early spring sowing, it is wise to prepare the trench in autumn. Sweet pea requires a deep, rich soil, and a trench at least 18 in. deep should be prepared with liberal quantities of well-rotted manure and rich compost. A comparatively short trench that has been carefully prepared will produce vigorous plants and abundant bloom. It is, therefore, wise to prepare a small area thoroughly, rather than to attempt too much. In the spring the trench should be opened to a depth of 6 in. and the seeds placed in the bottom of the furrow, 4 in. apart, being covered with about 1 in. of soil. If the seeds are either nicked or soaked in water for twenty-four hours before planting, germination will be hastened. As the young plants develop, the trench should be gradually filled until it is almost level, a slight depression being left to conserve moisture. Sweet pea grows best during the cool, moist days of early spring and is seriously affected by heat and drought. Wire or brush may be used as a support for the vines.

Verbena *(Verbena hybrida)*

Like the petunia, the verbena is classed among the ever-dependable annuals. There are dwarf types suited to the front of the flower border and taller types that are remarkably free-flowering. Verbena comes in a wide range of lovely colors and is generous with its bloom, continuing until frost.

Culture: Verbenas are of easy culture and will give generous bloom throughout the long summer season. The seeds may either be started under glass or sown in the open where they are to flower. The seedlings are sturdy and bear transplanting well. Of low, somewhat spreading growth, verbena is of particular value as a border plant. The parti-colored types with white eyes are far less lovely than the self-colors, which come in shades of pink, rose, lavender and deep purple. The dwarf varieties, reaching a height of about 6 in., should be planted 9 in. apart, while the taller varieties should be planted 1 ft. apart.

19.3 Modern cultivars of fibrous-rooted (wax) Begonia *are very reliable bedding plants even in full sun. Photo Grant Heilman*

Wax begonia *(Begonia semperflorens)*

Though these wax-leaved begonias were once limited to the houseplant or the Memorial Day "cemetery basket" kind of gardening, plant breeders today have created one of the most useful of garden plants with an impressive array of new hybrids. These neat, mound-shaped plants seem to be forever in bloom. They are very adaptable, and will even take full sun in cooler locations (where temperatures seldom exceed 90°F.), though they are perhaps best in light shade. The leaves are clean and shiny, and come either in green- or bronze-leaved varieties. The dwarf begonias grow to a height of only 6 in. to 8 in. and make tight carpets of color. 'Rose Perfection' is one of the outstanding green-leaved cultivars in the dwarf group; several other varieties are available in both green- and bronze-leaved sorts. The Intermediate group, which grows to about 12 in., are just as compact and rich in bloom and are available both in specific varieties ('Pink Charm') and in mixed colors.

Plant breeders have also succeeded in enlarging the size of the flowers themselves, and a group named Glamour Hybrids has been introduced. The prolific flowers are single and 2 in. across; they are especially good for pots, window boxes and baskets.

Culture: These begonias are particularly well adapted to culture under artificial light, and should be started early in the year to ensure garden-sized plants. The seedlings are tiny, and more horizontal than vertical in growth habit as the flat, broad leaves develop. They should be sown thinly and pricked off into individual pots or bands as early as possible. In the garden they seem to thrive in any good soil, provided that ample moisture is present. If these begonias are to be planted in areas that are shaded by trees or large shrubs, it is especially important to check the water supply regularly because of competition from the neighboring tree and shrub roots.

Wishbone flower *(Torenia fournierii)*

The quaint little blossoms of the *Torenia* are borne in profusion throughout the summer, and the plants are barely affected by either heat or drought. Attaining hardly more than 1 ft. in height, *Torenia* is excellent as an edging plant or when planted in drifts along the front of the border. The small flowers are semitrumpetlike in form, and come in shades of lavender and deep violet with a yellow blotch on the lower petal. There is also a white form. The plants are admirably adapted to pot culture.

Culture: *Torenia* is a tender annual. The seed may be sown in the greenhouse or in a cold-frame early in the spring or in the open ground after all danger of frost is over. The seed is very fine and should be covered but lightly. The young seedling plants may be transplanted readily. If they have been started indoors they

may be moved to the garden when danger of frost is over, being spaced from 6 in. to 8 in. apart. *Torenia* thrives either in full sun or in partial shade, and the plants will continue to bloom throughout the season until killed by autumn frosts.

Zinnia *(Zinnia elegans)*

Zinnias are among the most popular of the annuals, and they have much to recommend them. They offer wide variations in form and coloring; they bloom over a long period; they will endure drought and neglect, and will succeed when all else fails; and the brilliantly colored flowers add immeasurably to the beauty of midsummer and early autumn gardens. In size, zinnias range from the tiny Lilliput varieties, suitable for edgings and borders, to the giant, branching types, which reach a height of over 3 ft. There also are single and double forms, crested, curled and quilled forms.

As a midsummer-cut flower, zinnia is difficult to surpass. It is even superior to the marigold, because it has the added advantage of a much wider color range. Zinnia is so varied that any good seed catalogue carries three to five pages of zinnia cultivars in several flower types and plant habit. Flowers can be large and formal ('Mammoth Dahlia Type'), or shaggy ('Giant Cactus-flowered'), or quilled and twisted ('Ruffles Hybrid') or formal buttons ('Cherry Buttons'). Plants range from large (the Dahlia types grow to 3 ft.) to such small ones that some—'Thumbelina,' for example—carry an abundance of 1-in. flowers on mounded plants only 4 in. high. And zinnia colors also have been so vastly improved in recent years that subtle variations are now available in pinks, reds, yellows and oranges, along with a marvelous rich cream cultivar named 'Carved Ivory.' Some flowers are even multicolored ('Whirligig' and 'Chippendale'), while 'Envy' is an interesting pale yellow—green cultivar.

Culture: Zinnia is of the easiest possible culture and will thrive under widely varying conditions. It is a tender annual, and the seed may be started under glass for early bloom, or sown in the garden after all danger of frost is over. Zinnia may be transplanted with ease, and it is possible to move the plants when they are in full flower. Although it thrives in full sun, zinnia will also endure partial shade. The dwarf varieties, reaching a height of 1 ft. to 1½ ft., should be planted about 9 in. apart, while the taller 3-ft. varieties should be spaced about 1 ft. apart.

BIENNIALS

A biennial is a plant that completes its life cycle within the space of two years. During the first year leafy vegetative growth is produced at ground level, and during the second year the plant blooms, produces seed and dies.

In this group we find some of our most beautiful garden flowers, and yet, because the individual plants are not permanent residents of the garden, we are inclined to underestimate their potentialities. It is true that they are but transients in the flower border—that few, if any of them, may be counted upon for even one full season of bloom; yet during the space of the few or several weeks when they are in flower, biennials contribute a full measure of beauty to any planting.

Indeed, this transient quality of biennials may be considered one of their greatest assets, for it makes it easier to plan for a long succession of bloom. Whereas perennials, such as the columbines, iris, phlox and peonies, must be left undisturbed in the border throughout the season, much of it outside their period of bloom, biennials may be moved into the garden a few weeks before they are to flower and then, without a qualm, they may be ruthlessly uprooted as soon as their blooming period is over, leaving welcome space for the planting of annuals and summer-flowering bulbs and perennials. Foxgloves may be followed by hardy chrysanthemums, gladiolus may be planted as soon as the Canterbury-bells have been removed, and pansies and English daisies, which make such a colorful spring border, may be followed, later in the season, by some of the low-growing annuals such as *Phlox drummondii*, lobelia and *Torenia*.

So, while we may continue to consider the perennials as the mainstays of our flower gardens, and while some of the annuals—particularly those that can be counted upon for a long season of bloom—may be considered almost equally invaluable, we must not overlook the possibilities of the biennials, for they have much to offer.

Almost all biennials are propagated by seeds. For general techniques of sowing seeds and caring for seedlings, see Chapter 34 on propagation.

Most biennials are very easy to transplant. Whenever possible the transplanting should be done on a cloudy day and the plants should be moved with as much soil about the roots as possible. An application of high-analysis, liquid or water-soluble fertilizer, watered in at the time of transplanting, at the rate of ¼ cupful for small plants, ½ to 1 cupful for medium-sized and large plants, will help to prevent a setback at time of transplanting (see index under soluble fertilizers).

When weather conditions are not favorable for transplanting (during periods of intense sunshine and hot, drying winds) or when transplanting hollyhocks and other biennials that are difficult to move, and when large plants already in flower are to be transplanted, temporary shading with evergreen boughs, shade cloth, baskets or even newspaper "tents" for a day or two after transplanting will help to reduce wilting.

For control of insect pests and diseases, see Chapter 32.

BIENNIALS OF MERIT

Canterbury-bells (*Campanula medium*)

Canterbury-bells are among the most beautiful and most showy of the biennials. In the South they come into bloom in March and April, while in the latitude of Philadelphia and New York they reach their height of bloom during June. Coming as they do just after the columbines and iris and foxgloves are over, they may be used as the dominant planting in the garden or they may assume a minor role by filling in an occasional gap here and there.

Culture: Canterbury-bells are easily grown from seed. Sow the seeds in June, either in cold-frames or in a carefully prepared seedbed. The seed has excellent vitality, and a high percentage of germination is usually secured. Transplant the seedlings before they become in the least crowded. Do not expose young Canterbury-bells to full summer sunshine. After the first transplanting they will make much more rapid growth if they are protected by a lath frame, through which dappled sunlight may filter. A coldframe sloping to the north, which does not receive sunlight throughout the entire day, offers a very satisfactory location for the growth of the young plants.

Canterbury-bells have a very fibrous root system and may consequently be transplanted with the greatest ease. If the plants are lifted with ample soil about the roots and if the transplanting is done on a damp, cloudy day, Canterbury-bells may be moved into the garden when they are in full flower. As one cannot always be sure of good transplanting weather, however, it is advisable to move them after growth has started in the spring and before the plants come into bud. They will then have an opportunity to become well established before flowering. If the fading blooms are pinched off at the base, smaller auxiliary flower buds will develop and the flowering period may be considerably prolonged. In the border, the plants should be set 1 ft. apart.

Canterbury-bells may be obtained in both single (*Campanula medium* mixtures) and double (*Campanula medium* 'Calycanthuma') forms and in a wide range of color: delicate pink, deep rose, white, pale lavender-blue and a deep bluish-purple. Some mail-order nurseries sell year-old plants ready to bloom. Those who want only a few Canterbury-bells in the garden may prefer to obtain plants in this manner rather than raising their own.

Soil requirements: The plants thrive in almost any soil, provided that it is well drained, but they will attain a greater size and give more abundant bloom if given a soil of high fertility.

In mild climates, Canterbury-bells may be wintered in the open ground, if the soil is well drained; but where the winters are severe they require the protection of a coldframe. If only a few plants are being grown and if a frame is not available, large inverted flower pots placed over the plants will afford excellent protection. No covering should be used that will mat down over the crowns, as the plants are rather sensitive to crown rot.

English daisies *(Bellis perennis)*

In England these winsome spring daisies re-seed so prolifically that they are apt to infest the lawns and consequently are frequently regarded as a pest. The wild form is seldom cultivated in gardens, however. The selected large, double-flowered garden strains come in shades of pink, deep rose and white, and they may be used in pleasant combination with pansies, violas and forget-me-nots.

The English daisy is actually a perennial, and in the garden may be treated as such. Often, however, it is treated as a biennial and discarded as soon as flowering has finished. If this is not done, it will often self-sow and revert to the common single form.

Culture: English daisies are of very easy culture. Sow the seeds in July or early August in flats or in frames, and transplant the young seedlings when small, 4 in. to 6 in. apart. In the North they will require some winter protection; in the South they may be wintered in the open ground. In spring the plants may be transplanted very successfully when in bud or in full flower. They have no decided soil preferences and no pests or diseases, and yet, modest and humble though they may be, they add their share of bloom and beauty to the spring border.

Forget-me-not *(Myosotis)*

Some species of forget-me-not, such as *Myosotis scorpioides,* are true perennials, while others, such as *M. sylvatica*, are biennials. The perennial species are better suited for naturalizing or for the rock garden, while selections of *M. sylvatica*, a true biennial, are excellent additions to the perennial border. The species self-sows itself abundantly and can actually become a pest. For this reason the named cultivars with deeper blue or white flowers are to be preferred and raised on an annual basis. To prevent self-sowing and reversion to the wild type, plants are best removed from the garden and destroyed as soon as the flowering period is over.

For spring bloom, sow seed in late July or early August, transplant the seedlings to winter over in frames or in the open. As the young seedling plants are rather susceptible to damping-off, every precaution should be taken to see that the soil in the seedbed is free from contamination. For the control of damping-off, see Chapter 32. The plants may be transplanted to the flower border in spring, and may be moved with great ease. While forget-me-not prefers a damp, woodsy soil, it will settle down quite happily in any location in the garden. The plants should be set from 6 in. to 8 in. apart.

The pale blue of forget-me-nots is lovely in combination with other flowers in the spring border. They may also be used very delightfully as an under planting in tulip beds. Varieties: Selected forms of *M. sylvatica* include 'Alba' — with white flowers; 'Compacta' — dense growth; 'Oblongata Perfecta' — large blue flowers; 'Rosea' — rose-colored flowers; and 'Robusta Grandiflora' — vigorous growth and large flowers.

Foxglove *(Digitalis)*

Although there are several species of *Digitalis* that are true perennials, those most commonly grown in the flower garden are biennials. There is no other flower that can quite take the place of the foxgloves in the spring border. They are among the first flowers of the season to give height and substance to the garden composition, and the stately spires of bloom against a background of hedge or wall add beauty and distinction to any planting. Coming into flower just as the first flush of spring bloom

19.6 Foxglove (Digitalis), *particularly the biennial Shirley Hybrid, comes in rich variations of cream, pink and lavender. Photo Carlton Lees*

has passed, they may be used as the dominant note in the garden until the delphiniums and roses are ready to claim the stage.

Types and varieties: Digitalis purpurea is the wild foxglove of Europe, and it is from this species that most of our improved strains have been developed. *Digitalis purpurea* 'Gloxiniiflora' is an old-fashioned cultivar that is still popular. It closely resembles the wild type, being more vigorous in habit and bearing longer spikes of bloom. The flowers are always spotted and are available in a variety of colorings — white, rose, purple and mixed. While it is lovely in itself, it cannot compare in size or in beauty of coloring with some of the more recent introductions. The Shirley Hybrids developed by the Reverend W. Wilks at his home in Shirley, England, bear witness to his skill as a plant breeder. The plants are of large size and vigorous, often reaching a height of 6 ft., and the large, drooping flowers clustered closely along the flower spikes range in color from white to dark rose and purple, many of them being spotted with crimson and maroon. The strain known as the 'Excelsior Hybrids' is the most spectacular and beautiful of all the foxgloves. Plants are as tall in stature as the 'Shirley Hybrids,' with the same beautiful range of flower colors, but the flowers completely encircle the stem and are flaringly horizontal. This unique flower habit, combined with the immense, 4-ft. to 6-ft. flowering spikes, produces such an effect that many gardeners have completely abandoned other types of foxgloves in its favor. *D.* x *mertonensis* is a tetraploid hybrid. The 2-in. long strawberry-red flowers appear on 3-ft. to 3½-ft. stems in June and July.

Culture: As the seeds of foxgloves are exceedingly fine, the seedbed should be well prepared. If the seeds are sown in June and if the young seedlings are given good care, they will develop into large, vigorous plants by autumn and will give generous bloom the following spring. It is unwise to delay the sowing of the seed until August as the plants will be so small that they will not be capable of giving good bloom the following season. Sow the seed either in flats or in a coldframe. The seeds are usually of excellent vitality and germinate within a week or ten days after sowing. Care should be taken to see that the young seedlings are transplanted before they become in the least crowded. The young plants need an abundance of water during the growing season and should never be allowed to become stunted. If growth is at any time seriously checked, due to overcrowding, insufficient moisture or lack of nourishment, the young plants have difficulty in making a full recovery. If conditions are favorable, however, the seedlings make rapid growth. They should be pricked out soon after the first true leaves have formed, and about a month or six weeks later they will again require transplanting, as it is essential that they be given ample room to develop.

Where the climate is mild, foxgloves may be wintered over in the open ground; but where the winters are severe it is advisable to give them the protection of a frame, which not only protects them from extreme cold but also from excessive moisture. The thick fleshy leaves and the crown buds rot very easily if the soil remains soggy for any length of time. When the plants are wintered in frames they should be spaced 8 in. to 10 in. apart, in order that the air may circulate freely between them. In spring the plants may be moved from the frames to their permanent location in the garden. If the plants are lifted with an ample quantity of earth, and if the transplanting is done on a cloudy day, they will suffer practically no check and will continue perfectly normal growth. If, however, the soil falls away from the roots or if the plants are exposed to wind and brilliant sunshine at the time of transplanting, they will suffer seriously and will never reach full perfection of bloom. Plant, outdoors, from 10 in. to 12 in. apart.

Foxgloves grow reasonably well in almost any type of good garden soil provided that is well drained, but they prefer a rich friable loam, and will make good use of a hearty diet of well-rotted manure or rich compost.

Hollyhock (*Althaea rosea* syn. *Althea rosea*)

Picturesque and lovely, the hollyhocks are reminiscent of old-time gardens, and they seem equally at home beside a modest cottage doorway or in the long herbaceous borders of a formal garden. There are both single and double forms, and a wide range of colors—white, rose, salmon, pale primrose-yellow, scarlet, crimson, purple and maroon. Hollyhocks are among our most useful background plants, attaining a height of from 6 ft. to 8 ft. They are particularly lovely when planted against an old wall or picket fence. The period of bloom extends through the month of July into early August.

While hollyhocks are mostly biennial, some plants survive for more than one blooming period, and because they self-sow so liberally, they often create patches or colonies in a garden that are perennial in effect. Some of the newer dwarf cultivars bloom the first year, which is also atypical of true biennials.

Culture: Although hollyhocks grow best in full sun, they will also do reasonably well in partial shade, and they may be grown very successfully in a flower border with a northern exposure.

Preferring a light, well-drained soil of a neutral or slightly alkaline reaction, hollyhocks will thrive in almost any garden, provided that the soil does not remain too saturated with moisture throughout the winter months. The plants respond well to good fertility but they will make fair growth on very poor soil.

Hollyhocks may be grown very easily from seed. The seeds may be planted either in a coldframe or in the open ground in late July or early August. The plants will bloom the following season. As hollyhocks produce a strong tap root, it is very difficult to move the plants after they have attained any size. It is, therefore, wise to transplant the young seedlings to their permanent position in the garden while they are still quite small. Seedling plants grown from seeds sown in July may be transplanted to the garden in early autumn or early the following spring. Hollyhocks reseed so readily that after they are once established it is seldom necessary to make additional sowings. If a few flower stalks are allowed to produce seeds, these self-sown seedlings may be transplanted to any desired position in the garden. The chief disadvantage of this method is the fact that these self-sown seedlings will produce a variety of colorings and it is not possible to carry out a definite color scheme. However, if only soft, pastel shades are used in the original planting, the colors usually blend harmoniously and mixed seedlings are often very lovely.

Because of their robust habit of growth, hollyhocks should be given ample space for their development, and should be planted from 2 ft. to 2½ ft. apart. As soon as the blooms have faded, the flower stalks should be cut down unless seed is to be produced.

Hollyhocks may be obtained as started plants from many nurseries. In addition to the species, which is available mostly in double-flowered forms, the following strains are also available: *A. rosea* 'Chaters Double'—full double, plants somewhat smaller in stature than the species; *A. rosea* 'Newport Pink'—fully double pink flowers; *A. rosea* 'Pompadour'—double flowers in the full range of colors, petals crinkled with a single row of outer petals surrounding the usual double, "half-ball" of petals; *A. rosea* 'Powderpuff Hybrids'—double flowers, flower spikes often taller than the 'Chaters Double' forms.

Japanese beetles and hollyhock rust disease are serious problems in some parts of the country. For control, see Chapter 32.

Iceland poppy *(Papaver nudicaule)*

Although the Iceland poppy is a true perennial in its native habitat, it has assumed all the characteristics of a biennial when grown in our gardens and is best treated as such. It blooms luxuriantly the year following sowing, and then usually dies out, an occasional plant surviving through another year.

The soft, gray-green leaves form a rosettelike growth just above the ground, and the delicate, lovely flowers are borne on long, slender, leafless stems. The plants vary in height from 12 in. to 20 in., and as many as fifty blooms may be produced upon a single plant. The cup-shaped flowers are very lovely, with delicately crinkled petals.

Iceland poppies may be obtained in a wide variety of colorings ranging from pure white to salmon-pink and from pale yellow to deep orange. Both single and double forms are available.

They come into flower in spring, about the time that the late narcissus are in bloom, and if the seed pods are not allowed to develop, the plants will give scattered bloom throughout the rest of the season.

Culture: Sow the seeds in August, or under glass in January or February. If the seed is sown during the summer, the young plants may be wintered over either in the frames or in the open. As the Iceland poppy is a native of the Arctic regions, it is extremely hardy and will withstand the most severe winter cold. Since all poppies are difficult to transplant (they develop long, threadlike tap roots), it is well to sow seeds in small pots, if sowing indoors. Thin out to two or three seedlings per pot and grow on until ready to be planted in the garden. The plants should be set 1 ft. apart.

Pansy (*Viola* x *wittrockiana*)

No spring garden is quite complete without the piquant blossoms of the pansy, upturned to the sun. Many types and strains are now available and although the giant types have lately come into vogue, the smaller, quainter kinds will probably always be preferred by many gardeners. In planning special schemes, it is a decided advantage to be able to obtain pansies in separate colors: blue, deep purple, wine-red, maroon and yellow.

Culture: Pansy seeds germinate most satisfactorily when there are wide fluctuations in temperature. Best results will therefore be obtained if sowing is delayed until cool nights follow warm days, as in late August and early September. Sowings may also be made in January in the greenhouse. These plants will come into bloom later than the fall-sown plants but will continue in flower throughout most of the summer.

Seedlings from fall-sown seed may be wintered over in the coldframe or, in mild climates, in the open ground. If wintered in the open, some protection against rabbits should be provided. They may be transplanted with the utmost ease, being moved when in full flower with no apparent setback to the plant. If the seed pods are not allowed to form, pansies may be kept in flower over a period of several months. When they begin to appear spindly and leggy, the plants may be cut back almost to the ground and a handful of fertilizer may be cultivated into the soil about them; in reward for one's labor there will be a second blooming.

Pansies may be readily propagated by cuttings as well as by seed, the cuttings being taken in late spring or early summer.

Set the plants 6 in. to 8 in. apart.

Purple Mullein (*Verbascum phoeniceum*)

This member of the Mullein genus is not as well known as many of the other biennials, yet it is a worthy addition to any garden. The leaves form a small rosette of green upon the surface of the soil, and the flowers, which come in soft shades of mauve and lavender, are borne on erect flower stalks, varying from 15 in. to 24 in. in height. This species is one of the parents of several named cultivars, which include: 'Cotswold Beauty'—with bronze flowers; 'Cotswold Gem'—with soft terra cotta shades; 'Cotswold Queen'—with salmon-bronze flowers; 'Gainsborough'—with soft yellow flowers; and 'Pink Domino'—with rose-colored flowers.

Culture: Grow the plants from seed sown in July. Because of the long, fleshy tap root the plants move with difficulty and must be handled with extreme care at the time of transplanting. The plant must be lifted from the soil in such a manner that the tap root is not broken, and the soil about the roots must be disturbed as little as possible. The verbascums are reasonably hardy and may be wintered in the open except in locations where the climate is of extreme severity. They may be used as individual accents or massed 18 in. apart.

Sweet William (*Dianthus barbatus*)

Sweet William, although actually a perennial, is best treated as a biennial for garden purposes. Its pleasing form and wide range of color (pastel shades of pink, salmon and rose, as well as deeper tones of red and scarlet) makes it an important part of the spring garden. Among the most beautiful cultivars are 'Fairy,' 'Newport Pink' and 'Sutton's Pink Beauty.'

Culture: Sow the seeds in June so the young plants may reach a good stage of development before winter. If the seeds are not sown until August the plants will be too small to give good bloom the following spring. In the South the plants may be wintered in the open. In the North they should be carried over in frames, moved into the garden in early spring and set 9 in. apart.

Wallflower, English (*Cheiranthus cheiri*)

Throughout England wallflowers grow in cracks and crannies in the walls, and in Ireland

19.7 Sweet William (Dianthus barbatus) *is another old-fashioned garden plant that deserves to be seen in more gardens. Photo Grant Heilman*

one even sees their tawny yellow blossoms on cottage rooftops. They are, indeed, a poignant part of an English spring, and it is to be regretted that they are not more widely grown in our gardens in America.

Culture: Sow seed in July or very early August, and transplant the young seedlings twice so they develop good, fibrous root systems. The young plants should also be pinched back occasionally in order that they may become stocky and well branched, as they have a tendency to make a rather spindly growth if they are left entirely to their own devices. If the plants are wintered over in frames they will be among the first of the spring flowers to come into bloom, and they may be moved into the garden, 10 in. to 12 in. apart as soon as the ground is workable.

When mixed seed is sown many of the flowers are apt to be streaked and blotched, and it is more satisfactory to obtain the seeds in self colors such as pale lemon, buttercup-yellow, deep wine-red and mahogany. Both single and double forms are obtainable.

Wallflower, Siberian *(Erysimum hieraciifolium syn. Cheiranthus allionii)*

The Siberian wallflowers are among the most effective of our spring plants for the low border, and their bright orange blooms may be used in pleasant contrast with flowers of a more subtle hue. They may be used very effectively in combination with the late-blooming narcissus and the lovely, early-blooming tulip, 'General De Wet,' with an occasional clump of *Phlox divaricata* and *Mertensia* as a foil for the brilliant tones of the tulips and wallflowers.

Culture: Sow the seeds in July and transplant the young seedlings when of sufficient size. In mild regions the plants may be wintered in the open very successfully, but in the north the protection of a coldframe is advisable. Being fibrous-rooted, the plants may be moved easily in the spring to the desired location in the garden, 1 ft. apart, and as soon as their period of bloom is over the plants may be discarded, making room for other flowers.

ANNUALS FOR COOL OR SHADY PLACES

Anchusa spp.	alkanet
Campanula spp.	annual Canterbury-bells
Impatiens spp.	impatiens
Nemophilia spp.	love-grove
Nicotiana spp.	flowering tobacco
Oenothera	evening primrose
Omphalodes spp.	navelwort

ANNUALS AS EVERLASTINGS

Acroclinium (Helipterum roseum)	everlasting
Catanache caerulea	Cupid's dart
Gomphrena globosa	globe amaranth
Helichrysum bracteatum	strawflower
Limonium bonduellii	statice or sea lavender
Rhodanthe (Helipterum manglesii)	Swan River everlasting
Xeranthemum annuum	immortelle

ANNUALS THAT WILL GROW IN VERY POOR SOIL

bartonia	*Mentzelia lindleyi*
California poppy	*Eschscholtzia californica*
calliopsis	*Coreopsis tinctoria*
corn poppy	*Papaver rhoeas*
feather cockscomb	*Celosia argentea*
four-o'clock	*Mirabilis jalapa*
gaillardia	*Gaillardia pulchella*
garden balsam	*Impatiens balsamina*
godetia, Whitney	*Clarkia amoena*
love-lies-bleeding	*Amaranthus caudatus*
nasturtium	*Tropaeolum majus*
petunia	*Petunia hybrida*
rose moss	*Portulaca grandiflora*
spiderflower	*Cleome hasslerana*
sweet alyssum	*Lobularia maritima*
sweet-sultan	*Centaurea moschata*

ANNUALS THAT WILL ENDURE HEAT AND DROUGHT

calliopsis	*Coreopsis tinctoria*
cape marigold (winter)	*Dimorpotheca sinuata*
cornflower	*Centaurea cyanus*
four-o'clock	*Mirabilis jalapa*
ice plant	*Mesembryanthemum crystallinum*
larkspur, rocket	*Consolida ambigua*
morning-glory	*Ipomoea purpurea*
morning-glory (dwarf)	*Convolvulus tricolor*
perilla, green	*Perilla frutescens*
pricklypoppy, showy	*Argemone grandiflora*
rose moss	*Portulaca grandiflora*
scarlet sage	*Salvia splendens*
sanvitalia	*Sanvitalia procumbens*
snow-on-the-mountain	*Euphorbia marginata*
summer-cypress	*Kochia scoparia*
sunflower	*Helianthus annuus*
zinnia	*Zinnia elegans*

ANNUALS WITH A SHORT SEASON OF BLOOM

(Several sowings should be made for succession of bloom)

annual phlox	*Phlox drummondii*
baby's breath	*Gypsophila elegans*
calliopsis	*Coreopsis tinctoria*
candytuft, purple	*Iberis umbellata*
cape marigold (winter)	*Dimorphotheca sinuata*
cornflower	*Centaurea cyanus*
forget-me-not	*Myosotis sylvatica*
love-in-a-mist	*Nigella damascena*
mignonette	*Reseda odorata*
poppy	*Papaver* spp.
sweet alyssum	*Lobularia maritima*

ANNUALS THAT MAY BE SOWN IN THE FALL

baby's breath	*Gypsophila elegans*
calendula	*Calendula officinalis*
California poppy	*Eschscholtzia californica*
calliopsis	*Coreopsis tinctoria*
candytuft	*Iberis* spp.
clarkia	*Clarkia unguiculata*
cornflower	*Centaurea cyanus*
cosmos	*Cosmos bipinnatus*
cow soapwort	*Vaccaria pyramidata*
herb treemallow	*Lavatera trimestris*
larkspur, rocket	*Consolida ambigua*
love-in-a-mist	*Nigella damascena*
pansy	*Viola tricolor*
pink, Chinese	*Dianthus chinensis*
poppy	*Papaver* spp.
snapdragon	*Antirrhinum majus*
sweet alyssum	*Lobularia maritima*
sweet pea	*Lathyrus odoratus*

ANNUALS THAT FREQUENTLY SELF-SOW

baby's breath	*Gypsophila elegans*
bush violet	*Browallia* spp.
calendula	*Calendula officinalis*
California poppy	*Eschscholtzia californica*
calliopsis	*Coreopsis tinctoria*
cornflower	*Centaurea cyanus*
cosmos	*Cosmos bipinnatus*
flowering tobacco	*Nicotiana sylvestris*
four-o'clock	*Mirabilis jalapa*
larkspur, rocket	*Consolida ambigua*
mealycup sage	*Salvia farinacea*
morning-glory	*Ipomoea purpurea*
petunia	*Petunia hybrida*
rose moss	*Portulaca grandiflora*
snow-on-the-mountain	*Euphorbia marginata*
spiderflower	*Cleome hasslerana*
summer-cypress	*Kochia scoparia*
sweet alyssum	*Lobularia maritima*

ANNUALS THAT BENEFIT FROM PINCHING BACK

ageratum	*Ageratum houstonianum*
bush violet	*Browallia* spp.
calendula	*Calendula officinalis*
chrysanthemum, annual	*Chrysanthemum* spp.
petunia	*Petunia hybrida*
phacelia	*Phacelia* spp.
phlox	*Phlox drummondii*
pink, China	*Dianthus chinensis*
salpiglossis, painted tongue	*Salpiglossis sinuata*
schizanthus	*Schizanthus pinnatus*
snapdragon	*Antirrhinum majus*
verbena	*Verbena hybrida*
zinnia	*Zinnia elegans*

ANNUALS DIFFICULT TO TRANSPLANT

(Should be sown where they are to flower)

baby's breath	*Gypsophila elegans*
California poppy	*Eschscholtzia californica*
evening primrose	*Oenothera drummondii*
herb treemallow	*Lavatera trimestris*
laceflower, blue	*Trachymene coerulea*
love-in-a-mist	*Nigella damascena*
lupine	*Lupinus* spp.
nasturtium	*Tropaeolum majus*
poppy	*Papaver* spp.
pricklypoppy, showy	*Argemone grandiflora*
rose moss	*Portulaca grandiflora*
scarlet runner	*Phaseolus coccineus*
sunflower	*Helianthus annuus*
sweet pea	*Lathyrus odoratus*

ANNUALS THAT ARE SLOW-GROWING

(Requiring a long season to bloom)

China aster	*Callistephus chinensis*
everlasting, winged	*Ammobium* spp.
flax	*Linum grandiflorum*
golden-cup	*Hunnemannia fumariifolia*
immortelle, everlasting	*Xeranthemum annuum*
lobelia	*Lobelia erinus*
petunia	*Petunia hybrida*
pincushion flower	*Scabiosa atropurpurea*
rhodanthe	*Helipterum humboldtianum*
salpiglossis, painted tongue	*Salpiglossis sinuata*
snapdragon	*Antirrhinum majus*
strawflower	*Helichrysum bracteatum*
sweet-sultan, basket flower	*Centaurea* spp.
verbena	*Verbena hybrida*

ANNUALS THAT TOLERATE ACIDITY

calliopsis	*Coreopsis tinctoria*
flowering tobacco	*Nicotiana* spp.
marigold	*Tagetes* spp.
verbena	*Verbena hybrida*

ANNUALS THAT SUCCEED IN A NEUTRAL OR ALKALINE SOIL

balsam	*Impatiens* spp.
candytuft	*Iberis* spp.
corn poppy	*Papaver rhoeas*
annual phlox	*Phlox drummondii*
mignonette	*Reseda odorata*
nasturtium	*Tropaeolum majus*
zinnia	*Zinnia elegans*

ANNUALS FOR TEMPORARY HEDGES

cucumber sunflower	*Helianthus debilis*
strawflower	*Helichrysum* spp.
balsam	*Impatiens balsamina*
summer cypress	*Kochia trichophylla*
four-o'clock	*Mirabilis jalapa*
fountain grass	*Pennisetum ruppelii*

ANNUALS THAT WILL ENDURE LIGHT SHADE

basket flower	*Centaurea americana*
begonia (fibrous-rooted)	*Begonia semperflorens*
Chinese forget-me-not	*Cynoglossum amabile*
clarkia	*Clarkia unguiculata*
annual phlox	*Phlox drummondii*
impatiens	*Impatiens wallerana*
lupine	*Lupinus hartwegii*
pansy	*Viola tricolor*
snapdragon	*Antirrhinum majus*
sweet alyssum	*Lobularia maritima*
sweet-sultan	*Centaurea moschata*
sweet-sultan, royal	*Centaurea moschata* var. imperialis

ANNUALS THAT WILL ENDURE CONSIDERABLE SHADE

calliopsis	*Coreopsis tinctoria*
cockscomb	*Celosia argentea*
flowering tobacco	*Nicotiana* spp.
godetia	*Clarkia amoena*
impatiens	*Impatiens* spp.
lobelia	*Lobelia erinus*
monkeyflower	*Mimulus* spp.
periwinkle	*Catharanthus rosea*
Virginia stock	*Malcomia maritima*

ANNUALS FOR POTS IN GREENHOUSE OR CONSERVATORY

begonia (fibrous-rooted)	*Begonia semperflorens*
bush violet	*Browallia speciosa*
Canterbury-bells	*Campanula* spp.
cockscomb	*Celosia* spp.
cup-and-saucer vine	*Cobaea scandens*
twinspur	*Diascia barberae*
everlasting	*Helipterum* spp.
impatiens	*Impatiens* spp.
morning-glory	*Ipomoea purpurea*
flowering tobacco	*Nicotiana* spp.
beard-tongue	*Penstemon gloxinioides*
mignonette	*Reseda odorata*
butterfly flower	*Schizanthus pinnatus*
wishbone flower	*Torenia* spp.
nasturtium	*Tropaeolum majus*

ANNUALS FOR CUT FLOWERS

(*salable cut flowers; †everlasting flowers)

†*Acroclinium (Helipterum roseum*	everlasting
Amaranthus caudatus	love-lies-bleeding
**Antirrhinum majus*	snapdragon
Arctotis grandis	bushy arctotis
Argemone spp.	pricklypoppy
Browallia demissa	bush violet
Browallia speciosa	bush violet
Calendula officinale	calendula
**Callistephus chinensis*	China aster
**Centaurea moschata*	sweet-sultan
Chrystanthemum spp.	annual chrysanthemum
Clarkia elegans	clarkia, farewell-to-spring
**Consolida ambigua*	rocket larkspur
Coreopsis stillmanii	Stillman coreopsis
Coreopsis tinctoria	calliopsis
**Cosmos* spp.	cosmos
**Dianthus chinesis*	China pink
Dimorphotheca sinuata	cape marigold
Emilia javanica	tasselflower
Eschscholtzia californica	California poppy
Gaillardia spp.	gaillardia
†*Gomphrena globosa*	globe amaranth
**Gypsophila* spp.	baby's breath
Helianthus annuus	sunflower
†*Helichrysum bracteatum*	strawflower
Lathyrus odoratus	sweet pea
Lavatera trimestris	treemallow
†*Limonium sinuatum*	notchleaf statice
**Lupinus* spp.	lupine
Matthiola bicornis	stock
Matthiola incana	stock
Nicotiana spp.	flowering tobacco
Nigella damascena	love-in-a-mist
Papaver glaucum	tulip poppy
Papaver rhoeas	Shirley or field poppy
Papaver umbrosum	field poppy
Phacelia campanularia	California bluebell
Phacelia tanacetifolia	fiddleneck
Phlox drummondii	annual phlox
Polygonum orientale	prince's feather
Psylliostachys suworowii	Suworow sea lavender
Reseda odorata	mignonette
Salpiglossis sinuata	salpiglossis, painted tongue
Scabiosa atropurpurea	pincushion flower
Senecio elegans	purple groundsel
Tagetes spp.	marigold
Tripleurospermum maritimum	double daisy
Verbena erinoides	moss vervain
Verbena x *hybrida*	garden verbena
Zinnia elegans	zinnia
Zinnia haageana	orange zinnia

ANNUALS FOR MOIST PLACES

Ionopsidium acaule	diamondflower
Nemophilia spp.	love-grove
Mimulus spp.	monkeyflower

ANNUALS THAT SHOULD NOT BE PINCHED BACK

balsam	*Impatiens balsamina*
cockscomb	*Celosia argentea*
everlasting	*Helichrysum*, etc.
poppy	*Papaver* spp.

ANNUALS FOR WINDOW AND PORCH BOXES

Ageratum houstonianum	Mexican ageratum
Begonia semperflorens	begonia (fibrous-rooted)
Browallia speciosa	bush violet
Catharanthus rosea	periwinkle
Centaurea candidissima	dusty-miller
Impatiens spp.	impatiens
Lobelia erinus	lobelia
Lobularia maritima	sweet alyssum
Maurandia barclaiana	climbing snapdragon
Petunia hybrida	petunia
Phlox drummondii	annual phlox
Portulaca grandiflora	rose moss
Tagetes signata var. *pumila*	dwarf marigold
Thunbergia alata	clockvine
Tropaeolum majus	nasturtium
Verbena hortensis	verbena
Zinnia elegans (dwarf)	zinnia, dwarf

EDGING ANNUALS

Ageratum houstonianum	Mexican ageratum
Anagallis monelli	pimpernel
Anagallis phillipsii	pimpernel
Antirrhinum majus	dwarf snapdragon
Asperula azurea setosa	woodruff
Calendula officinalis	dwarf calendula
Centaurea candidissima	dusty-miller
Celosia, spp.	dwarf celosia
Charieis heterophylla	South African daisy
Collinsia bicolor	collinsia
Coreopsis tinctoria	calliopsis
Dianthus sinensis	annual pink
Eschscholtzia californica	California poppy
Iberis umbellata	candytuft
Linum grandiflorum	scarlet flax
Lobelia erinus	dwarf lobelia
Lobularia maritima	sweet alyssum
Matricaria inodora	double daisy
Mesembryanthemum crystallinum	iceplant
Nemophila insignis	baby-blue-eyes
Phacelia campanularia	phacelia
Phlox drummondii	annual phlox
Sanvitalia	sanvitalia
Saponaria calabrica	Calabrian soapwort
Silene pendula	catchfly
Tagetes spp.	marigold
Torenia spp.	wishbone flower
Tropaeolum majus	nasturtium
Verbena hortensis	vervain

SCENTED ANNUALS

(*night-scented)

Ageratum houstonianum	Mexican ageratum (delicate)
Antirrhinum majus	snapdragon (delicate)
Calendula	calendula (pungent)
Centaurea moschata	sweet-sultan (delicate)
Heliotropium arborescens	heliotrope (one of the loveliest)
Iberis coronaria	candytuft
Iberis umbellata	purple candytuft
Lobularia maritima	sweet alyssum (delicate)
Lupinus luteus	yellow lupine
*Matthiola bicornis	night-scented stock
Matthiola incana	ten-week stock
Mimulus moschata	muskplant
*Nicotiana affinis	flowering tobacco
*Oenothera lamarckiana	evening primrose
Petunia hybrida	petunia (heavy)
Reseda odorata	mignonette (delightful)
Scabiosa atropurpurea	pincushion flower (dainty)
Tagetes	marigold (pungent)
*Verbascum phlomoides	tall mullein
Verbena erinoides	moss vervain
Verbena x *hybrida*	garden verbena

ANNUAL GROUPS OR GENERA FOR SEASHORE AND MOUNTAIN

(For cooler and more moist regions)

Alonsa	maskflower
Chrysanthemum	annual chrysanthemum
Clarkia	clarkia
Collinsia	collinsia
Cosmos	cosmos
Eschscholtzia	California poppy
Gilia	gilia
Godetia	godetia
Hymenoxys (*Actinolepis*)	
Layia	tidytips
Leptosiphon (*Gilia*, in part)	
Lupinus	lupine
Mentzelia	mentzelia
Mimulus	monkeyflower
Nemesia	nemesia
Nemophila	love-grove
Nigella	love-in-a-mist
Papaver	poppy
Phacelia	phacelia
Reseda	mignonette
Saponaria	Calabrian soapwort
Scabiosa	pincushion flower

ANNUALS

(Listed by scientific name first)

WHITE

Ageratum houstonianum	Mexican ageratum
Ammobium alatum	winged everlasting
Antirrhinum majus	snapdragon
Arctotis stoechadifolia	African Daisy, bushy arctotis
Argemone grandiflora	pricklypoppy
Browallia demissa elata	bush violet
Campanula spp.	annual Canterbury-bells
Catharanthus rosea	periwinkle
Centaurea spp.	royal sweet-sultan, cornflower, etc.
Centranthus macrosiphon	spur valerian
Chrysanthemum spp.	annual chrysanthemum
Clarkia amoena	farewell-to-spring, godetia
Clarkia pulchella	clarkia
Cleome hasslerana	spiderflower
Collinsia bicolor	Chinese-houses
Datura metel	yellow floripondio
Dimorphotheca sinuata	cape marigold
Echium plantagineum hybrids	viper's bugloss
Gilia tricolor	bird's-eye gilia
Gypsophila elegans	baby's breath
Helichrysum bracteatum	strawflower
Iberis amara	candytuft
Impatiens balsamina	garden balsam
Lathyrus odoratus	sweet pea
Lavatera trimestris	treemallow
Limonium sinuatum	statice or sea lavender
Lobelia erinus and *tenuior*	lobelia
Lobularia maritima	sweet alyssum

(Continued)

ANNUALS (Continued)

WHITE

Lupinus mutabilis	lupine
Malcomia maritima	Virginia stock
Matthiola incana	stock
Nemesia strumosa	nemesia
Nemophila maculata	five-spot
Nicotiana spp.	flowering tobacco
Oenothera americana	evening primrose
Papaver somniferum	opium poppy
Petunia hybrida	petunia
Phlox drummondii	annual phlox
Portulaca grandiflora	rose moss
Scabiosa atropurpurea	pincushion flower
Schizanthus pinnatus	butterfly flower
Senecio elegans	purple groundsel
Tolpis barbata rubra	hawkweed
Vaccaria pyramidata	soapwort
Verbena erinoides	moss vervain
Viola tricolor	pansy
Xeranthemum annuum	immortelle
Zinnia elegans	zinnia

RED, ROSE AND PINK

Abronia umbellata	pink sand verbena	rose
Adonis spp.	pheasant's eye	red
Alonsoa acutifolia	mask flower	scarlet
Alonsoa warscewiczii		orange to scarlet
Amaranthus caudatus	love-lies-bleeding	crimson
Antirrhinum majus	snapdragon	shades red to pink
Calandrinia ciliata	red maids	ruby-red
Calandrinia grandiflora	calandrinia	rose
Callistephus chinensis	China aster	shades red to pink
Campanula spp.	annual Canterbury-bells	pink
Celosia spp.	cockscomb	crimson
Centaurea cyanus	bachelor's-button	pink
Centaurea moschata var. *imperialis*	royal sweet-sultan	pink
Centaurea moschata	sweet-sultan	rose
Centranthus macrosiphon	spur valerian	rose
Clarkia pulchella	clarkia	rose, pink
Collinsia bicolor	Chinese-houses	pink
Collomia cavanillesii	collomia	scarlet
Cosmos bipinnatus	cosmos	crimson to white
Cuphea ignea	firecracker plant	scarlet
Diascia barberae	twinspur	pink
Echium creticum	viper's bugloss	red
Echium plantagineum hybrids	viper's bugloss	pink
Emilia flammea and *sagittata*	tasselflower	scarlet
Eschscholtzia californica	California poppy	red, pink
Gilia spp.	gilia	scarlet
Gilia micrantha (Leptosiphon hybrida)		rose to carmine
Godetia grandiflora	godetia	rose to white
Gypsophilia muralis	baby's breath	rose
Helichrysum bracteatum	strawflower	red, pink
Helipterum manglesii and *H. roseum*	Swan River everlasting	rose
Iberis umbellata	candytuft	carmine, pink
Impatiens balsamina	balsam	rose, pink
Lathyrus odoratus	sweet pea	rose, pink
Lavatera trimestris and *L. rosea*	treemallow	rose
Linaria bipatita	cloven-tip toadflax	crimson, pink
Linum grandiflorum	flowering flax	crimson

ANNUALS (Continued)

RED, ROSE AND PINK

Lupinus hartwegii	Hartweg lupine	pink
Lychnis coeli rosa	rose-of-heaven	flesh
Malcomia maritima	Virginia stock	pink
Malope trifida 'Grandiflora'	mallowwort	rose-red
Matthiola incana	stock	rose, pink
Mimulus spp.	monkeyflower	scarlet
Myosotis sylvatica	forget-me-not	pink
Nemesia strumosa	nemesia	rose, pink
Nicotiana sanderae and *N. sylvestris*	flowering tobacco	crimson to white
Papaver rhoeas	Shirley or field poppy	crimson to pink
Papaver somniferum	opium poppy	red to white
Petunia hybrida	petunia	bright rose to pink
Phlox drummondii	annual phlox	rose to white
Psylliostachys suworowii (Limonium suworowii)	statice or sea lavender	rose
Portulaca grandiflora	eleven o'clock	purplish-crimson to white
Salvia splendens	scarlet sage	scarlet
Saponaria calabrica	Calabrian soapwort	rose
Scabiosa atropurpurea	pincushion flower	rose to white
Schizanthus pinnatus	butterfly flower	rose to white
Senecio elegans	purple groundsel	rose to white
Silene armeria	catchfly, campion	rose
Tolpus barbata	hawksbeard	rose
Tropaeolum majus	nasturtium	scarlet, rose
Vinca rosea	Madagascar periwinkle	rose to white
Zinnia elegans	zinnia	scarlet to white

BLUE, LAVENDER, PURPLE AND MAUVE

Ageratum houstonianum	ageratum	blue
Anchusa capensis	alkanet	blue
Angallis indica	blue pimpernel	blue
Asperula azurea setosa	blue woodruff	blue
Browallia demissa elata	browallia	lavender
Callistephus chinensis	China aster	blue and lavender
Campanula macrostyla	blue bellflower or annual Canterbury-bells	blue
Centaurea spp.	batchelor's-button, sweet-sultan	blue and lavender
Clarkia elegans and *C. pulchella*	clarkia	lavender
Collinsia bicolor	Chinese-houses	blue
Cosmos diversifolius	black cosmos	lilac
Cynoglossum amabile	hound's tongue	blue
Datura fastuosa	downy thorn apple	purple
Delphinium ajacis	larkspur	blue
Echium plantagineum	echium	purple to blue
Felicia bergeriana	kingfisher daisy	blue
Gilia spp.	gilia	purple and blue
Godetia grandiflora	godetia	purple
Heliophila spp.	heliophilia	blue
Iberis spp.	candytuft	lilac shades
Impatiens balsamina	balsam	lilac shades
Lathyrus odoratus	sweet pea	lilac and purple
Limonium sinuatum	statice or sea lavender	lilac
Linaria spp.	toadflax	purple
Lobelia spp.	lobelia	violet and blue
Lupinus spp.	lupine	purples and lilacs
Malcomia maritima	Virginia stock	purple
Martynia fragrans	unicorn plant	mauve
Matthiola incana	stock	lilac and purple
Myosotis	forget-me-not	blue
Nemophila insignis	baby-blue-eyes	blue

(Continued)

ANNUALS (Continued)

BLUE, LAVENDER, PURPLE AND MAUVE

Nigella damascena	love-in-a-mist	blue
Papaver rhoeas	Shirley or field poppy	blue
Petunia hybrida	petunia	purple and lilac
Phacelia whitlavia	California bluebell	lavender and blue
Phlox drummondii	annual phlox	purple and lilac
Salpiglossis sinuata	salpiglossis, painted tongue	purple
Salvia spp.	sage	blue
Scabiosa atropurpurea	pincushion flower	purple and blue
Schizanthus pinnatus	butterfly flower	purples and mauves
Senecio elegans	purple groundsel	purple
Torenia fournieri	wishbone flower	blue and purple
Trachymene caerulea	laceflower	blue
Viola tricolor	pansy	varied purple and blue
Xeranthemum annuum	immortelle	purple

YELLOW AND ORANGE

Alonsoa warscewiczii	mask flower	orange to scarlet
Antirrhinum majus	snapdragon	orange, yellow
Argemone mexicanum	Mexican pricklypoppy	yellow or orange
Calendula officinalis	calendula	gold, sulphur
Callistephus chinensis	China aster	yellow, orange
Celosia spp.	cockscomb	yellow, orange
Chrysanthemum spp.	annual chrysanthemum	yellow, orange, bronze
Coreopsis spp.	goldenwave and calliopsis	yellow, brown to red
Coreopsis stillmanii	Stillman coreopsis	yellow
Cosmos sulphureus	yellow cosmos	yellow
Datura metel	downy thorn apple	yellow
Diascia barberae	twinspur	orange
Dimorphotheca sinuata	cape marigold	orange, lemon
Emilia javanica	tasselflower	orange
Eschscholtzia californica	California poppy	yellow, orange
Gaillardia pulchella	rose-ring gaillardia	yellow
Gamolepsis tagetes	yellow chrysanthemum	orange to yellow
Helianthus annuus	sunflower	golden, red to brown
Helichrysum spp.	strawflower	yellow
Hunnemannia fumariifolia	tulip poppy	yellow
Lathyrus odoratus	sweet pea	yellow, orange
Layia elegans	tidytips	yellow
Limonium bonduellii	statice or sea lavender	yellow
Linaria bipartita	cloven-tip toadflax	yellow
lupinus luteus	European yellow lupine	yellow
Mimulus luteus	monkeyflower	yellow
Nemesia strumosa	nemesia	orange
Oenothera drummondii	evening primrose	yellow
Papaver rhoeas	Shirley or field poppy	orange
Portulaca grandiflora	rose moss	yellow
Reseda odorata	mignonette	greenish yellow
Rudbeckia hirta var. *pulcherrima*	pinewoods coneflower	yellow
Salpiglossis sinuata	salpiglossis, painted tongue	variegated yellow
Sanvitalia procumbens	sanvitalia	golden yellow
Sphenogyne speciosa (Ursinia pulchra)	ursinia	yellow
Tagetes spp.	marigold	yellow, tawny
Thunbergia alata	clockvine	yellow
Tithonia rotundifolia	Mexican sunflower	rich orange
Tropaelum majus	nasturtium	yellow, orange
Ursinia anethoides	jewel-of-the-veldt	orange
Venidium fastuosum	monarch-of-the-veldt	orange
Viola tricolor	pansy	yellow
Zinnia elegans	zinnia	yellow

ANNUALS

SCIENTIFIC NAME	COMMON NAME	HEIGHT IN INCHES	DISTANCE APART IN INCHES	COLOR	MONTHS OF SOWING INDOORS (I) OUTDOORS (O)	REMARKS
Abronia umbellata	sand verbena	6	6	rose	I. March	really a perennial but usually treated as an annual
Acroclinium (see *Helipterum roseum*)						
Adonis aestivalis	summer adonis	12	6	crimson	I. March	
Adonis aleppica	pheasant's eye	18	6	red	O. April	not easy
Ageratum houstonianum	Mexican ageratum	18–24	12	blue, white	I. March	reseeds prolifically and when once established, comes up year after year from self-sown seed
intermediate		9–12	9	blue, white	I. March	
dwarf		4–8	6	blue, white	I. March	
Alonsoa acutifolia	mask flower	24	9	scarlet	I. April	
Alonsoa warscewiczu	mask flower	18	6	orange-scarlet	I. April	also good as potted plant; does not endure a hot, humid climate.
Amaranthus caudatus	love-lies-bleeding	48–72	18	crimson	O. May	
Ammobium alatum	winged everlasting	24	12	white	I. April	
Anagallis arvensis forma *caerulea*	blue pimpernel	6	6	blue	O. April, May	
Anchusa capensis var. 'Blue Bird'	blue bird anchusa, alkanet	18	9	bright blue	O. May	one of the best of the blue annuals
Antirrhinum majus dwarf varieties	snapdragon	6	6	orange,		select rust-proof varieties
intermediate varieties		18	10	yellow, pink, red,	I. March	
tall varieties		36	12–18	white, purple	O. April	
Arctotis grandis	bushy Arctotis	24	10	white, bluish eye	I. March	excellent for cutting
Arctotis stoechadifolia	African daisy, bushy arctotis	24	10	white, bluish eye	I. March O. April	excellent for cutting
Argemone grandiflora	pricklypoppy	36	12	white	O. May	likes warm soil and hottest exposure
Argemone mexicana	Mexican poppy	24–36	12	yellow, orange	O. May	
Asperula setosa	blue woodruff	9		gray-blue		does well in poor soil or light shade
Aster (see *Callistephus chinensis*)						
Begonia spp.	fibrous-rooted begonia	6–10	6–12	red, pink, white	I. Feb., long season bloom	long season of bloom
Brachycome iberidifolia	Swan River daisy	12	6	blue, pink, white	I. April O. May	good edger; short period of bloom. Sow for succession
Browallia americana	bush violet	12–18	9	purple-blue, white	I. April O. May	
Browallia speciosa major	sapphire flower	12–24	9	purple-blue	I. Feb.	good pot plant
Cacalia (see *Emilia javanica*)						
Calandrinia grandiflora	calandrinia	18	10	rose		
Calandrinia ciliata	red maids	9	6	ruby-red		
Calendula officinalis	calendula	12–24	12–15	gold, sulphur	O. April	very hardy; may be grown in South for winter bloom
Callistephus chinensis	China aster	18	10	various (blue, lavender, white, pink, red, yellow)	I. March	

(Continued)

ANNUALS (Continued)

SCIENTIFIC NAME	COMMON NAME	HEIGHT IN INCHES	DISTANCE APART IN INCHES	COLOR	MONTHS OF SOWING INDOORS (I) OUTDOORS (O)	REMARKS
Campanula ramosissima (*attica*)	bluestar bellflower	12	6	blue	I. March	
Campanula macrostyla	annual Canterbury-bells	24	12	pink, white, blue	I. March O. April	blooms in late summer and early fall
Catharanthus rosea	Madagascar periwinkle	18	9	rose, white	I. Jan., Feb.	
Celosia argentea (*plumosa*) and all varieties	feather cockscomb	36–48	12–18	yellow to crimson	O. April	yellow and orange varieties are very effective for autumn bloom in border
Celosia argentea dwarf		12	9	yellow to crimson	O. April	
Celosia cristata	cockscomb	24		yellow to crimson	O. April	
Centaurea americana	basket flower	36–48	18	lavender	O. April	
Centaurea cineraria	dusty-miller	24	15	purple-rose	I. March	
Centaurea cyanus	cornflower	36	12	blue, pink, white	O. Sept. or April	short period of bloom
Centaurea moschata	sweet-sultan	36	12	blue, pink, white	I. April O. May	
Centaurea moschata var. *imperalis*	royal sweet-sultan	36	12	blue, pink, white	I. April O. May	
Centranthus macrosiphon	spur valerian	12	10	rose, white	O. April	
Cheiranthus cheiri	English wallflower	30	10–12	yellow	July	
Chrysanthemum carinatum	annual chrysanthemum	24	9	white, marked variously	O. April	
Chrysanthemum coronarium	crown daisy	24	12	sulphur yellow	O. April	
Chrysanthemum parthenium	feverfew	12–30	9			
Chrysanthemum segetum	corn marigold	24	12	golden		
Clarkia amoena (*Godetia*)	farewell-to-spring, godetia	24	12	rose to white	O. April	
Clarkia grandiflora	Whitney godetia	18	9	purple, rose to white	O. April	
Clarkia unguiculata	clarkia, farewell-to-spring	12–24	9	rose to white and purple	I. April	excellent for cutting; prefers cool growing weather
Clarkia pulchella	clarkia	12–24	9	rose to white and purple	I. April	
Cleome spinosa	spiderflower	48–60	24	magenta, white	O. April	excellent in border because of its height
Coleus blumei	coleus	36		white, crimson	I. March	
Collinsia heterophylla	Chinese-houses	18	6	blue, pink and white	I. April	
Collomia cavanillesii		24	6	scarlet	I. March O. April	
Consolida ambigua (*Delphinium ajacis*)	rocket larkspur	24–36	9	various blues	O. Sept., March	
Consolida regalis (*Delphinium condolida*)	field larkspur	18–24	9	various blues	O. Sept., March	
Coreopsis basalis	goldenwave	24	12	yellow	O. April	
Coreopsis maritima (*Leptosyne maritima*)	sea dahlia	24–36	12	yellow	O. April	
Coreopsis stillmanii (*Leptosyne stillmanii*)	Stillman coreopsis	18	15	large yellow,	O. April	

ANNUALS (Continued)

SCIENTIFIC NAME	COMMON NAME	HEIGHT IN INCHES	DISTANCE APART IN INCHES	COLOR	MONTHS OF SOWING INDOORS (I) OUTDOORS (O)	REMARKS
Coreopsis tinctoria	calliopsis	36	15	yellow; brown-red	O. April – June, Sept.	
Coreopsis tinctoria var. 'Crimson King'		8	6	yellow; brown-red	O. April – June, Sept.	
Cosmos bipinnatus	cosmos	48 – 62	18 – 24	crimson to white	O. April	valuable for cutting
Cosmos diversifolius	black cosmos	36	18	lilac	O. April	
Cosmos sulphureus	yellow cosmos	48 – 72	18 – 24	yellow	I. March	
Cuphea ignea	firecracker plant	18	12	scarlet	I. June	
Cynoglossum amabile	hound's tongue	24	9	blue	I. April O. May	
Datura fastuosa D. metel, D. cornucopia)	downy thorn apple	24	18	yellow, white, purple reverse	I. April	
Dianthus chinensis	rainbow pink	12 – 18	6	various	O. Sept., April I. March	
Diascia barberae	twinspur	18	6	pink, orange	I. March	
Didiscus (see *Trachymene caerulea*)						
Dimorpotheca sinuata	cape marigold	12 – 18	8 – 10	orange, lemon to white	I. March	excellent for hot, dry position
Echium creticum	viper's bugloss	12 – 18	12	red	I. Jan.	
Echium lycopsis		18 – 24	15	purple-blue	I. Jan.	very effective in border
Echium lycopsis hybrids		18 – 24	15	pale blue, pink, mauve, white	I. Jan.	
Emilia javanica (*E. sagittata*)	tasselflower	18+	9	scarlet, orange	O. April	
Eschscholzia californica	California poppy	12	9	yellow, pink, red	O. March, Sept.	do not transplant; good cut flower
Euphorbia heterophylla	painted spurge	36	12	red leaves at tips	O. April	
Euphorbia marginata (*E. variegata*)	snow-on-the-mountain	36 – 48	12	leaves margined white	O. March	milky juice is poisonous
Felicia bergeriana	kingfisher daisy	6	6	blue with yellow disks		daisylike flower
Gaillardia amblyodon	maroon gaillardia	18 – 24	9	brown-red or maroon	O. April	
Gaillardia pulchella	rose-ring gaillardia	18 – 24	9	yellow and rose-purple	O. April	
Gamolepis tagetes	gamolepis	12	10	orange-yellow	I. March O. May	
Gilia capitata	globe gilia	24	9	blue	I. March O. April	
Gilia micrantha (*Leptosiphon hybrida*)		12	10	rosy-carmine	I. April	
Gilia tricolor	bird's-eye gilia	24	9	white, purple	O. April	
Gomphrena globosa	globe amaranth	24	12	magenta, amaranth, salmon-white	I. March O. May	
Gypsophila elegans	baby's breath	12 – 18	6	white	O. April	
Gypsophila muralis	cushion gypsophila	12	6	rose	O. April	
Helianthus annuus	sunflower	96 – 108	3	golden	O. April	
Helianthus debilis	cucumber sunflower	48	2	golden, sulphur	O. April	
dwarf varieties		12 – 36	12	yellow or red-brown		
Helichrysum bracteatum	strawflower	36	9 – 12	red, pink, yellow, white	I. March O. May	excellent for winter bouquet
Heliophila leptophylla		18	10	blue, white-eyed	I. March O. May	
Heliophila longifolia		18	10	blue, white-eyed	I. March O. May	

(Continued)

ANNUALS (Continued)

SCIENTIFIC NAME	COMMON NAME	HEIGHT IN INCHES	DISTANCE APART IN INCHES	COLOR	MONTHS OF SOWING INDOORS (I) OUTDOORS (O)	REMARKS
Heliotropium arborescens	heliotrope	10	12	lavender, purple	I. March	sweet-scented
Helipterum manglesii	Swan River everlasting	18	6	rose	I. March O. May	
Helipterum roseum	rose everlasting, acroclinium	12 – 18	6	rose	I. March O. May	
Hunnemannia fumariifolia	golden-cup, tulip poppy	18 – 24	9 – 12	soft yellow	I. April, pots	
Iberis amara	candytuft	16	12 – 16	white, often with lilac tinge	O. April	sometimes fragrant
Iberis umbellata	globe candytuft	16	16	purple, carmine, pink	O. April	
Impatiens balsamina	garden balsam	12 – 18	9	various – pink, rose, purple, violet, white	O. April	
Impatiens platypetala	orange patience	15	9	orange	O. April	
Impatiens wallerana	impatiens	12 – 15	12	red, pink, white	I. March	exceptionally prolific
Incarvillia sirenis		18	8 – 10	yellow, pink, white	I. March O. May	
Ipomopsis rubra (Gilia coronopifolia)	texasplume	36	9	scarlet	I. March O. May	
Kochia scoparia (trichophila)	belvedere or summer cypress	18 – 24	12 –.18		O. May	makes an excellent low hedge
Lathyrus odoratus	sweet pea	48+ (climbing)	6	white, pink, rose, purple, yellow, peach, orange	O. Oct., April	prefers cool growing weather
Lathyrus odoratus dwarf varieties	dwarf sweet pea	8	6	''	O. Oct., April	
Lavatera trimestris	treemallow	24 – 60	12 – 18	rose, white	O. May	
Lavatera trimestris 'Splendens'		36	18	white, rose	O. May	
Layia platyglossa	tidytips	12	10	yellow, tipped white	O. May	
Limonium bonduellii	sea lavender or statice	18 – 24	15	yellow	I. March	
Limonium sinuatum	notchleaf sea lavender	18 – 24	15	violet to white	I. March	
Linaria bipartita	cloven-tip toadflax	18 – 24	15	yellow to crimson, pink and purple	O. April, May	
Linaria maroccana	Moroccan toad flax	12	4	bright purple with yellow spot	O. April, May	
Linum grandiflorum	flowering flax	8 – 12	9	crimson	O. April	
Lobelia erinus, dwarf varieties	edging lobelia	4 – 6	6	violet, blue, white	I. Feb., March	excellent as an edging plant
Lobelia tenuior		12 – 18	6	bright blue or white	I. March O. May	
Lobularia maritima compact varieties	sweet alyssum	3 – 4	6	white	I. March O. April	fine edging plant
spreading varieties		6 – 10	9	white	I. March O. April	fine edging plant
Lunaria annua	honesty	18	12	magenta	I. March O. April	
Lupinus hartwegii	Hartweg lupine	36	12 – 18	purple, pink	I. March pots O. May	very effective in the border and good for cutting
Lupinus hirsutus	blue lupine	24	12	blue	I. March pots O. May	

ANNUALS (Continued)

SCIENTIFIC NAME	COMMON NAME	HEIGHT IN INCHES	DISTANCE APART IN INCHES	COLOR	MONTHS OF SOWING INDOORS (I) OUTDOORS (O)	REMARKS
Lupinus luteus	European yellow lupine	24	12	yellow	I. March pots O. May	
Lupinus mutabilis	Andes lupine	24	18	violet, yellow pink and white	I. March pots O. May	
Lupinus, dwarf varieties	dwarf annual lupine	12	9	violet, yellow and white	I. March pots O. May	
Lychnis coeli-rosa	rose-of-heaven	12	6	flesh	O. April	
Malcomia maritima	Virtinia stock	4–8	3	purple, pink, white	O. April	
Malope trifida 'Grandiflora'	mallowwort	30	12	rose-red	O. April	
Matthiola incana, dwarf	stock	12–18	9	tones of rose and purple, also white	I. March O. April	
Matthiola incana, tall	stock	24–30	12–18	tones of rose and purple, also white	I. March O. April	
Matthiola longipetala	evening stock	12	6	lilac		night-blooming, grown for fragrance
Mentzelia lidleyi (*Bartonia*)	bartonia	36–48	24	white, yellow	O. May	opens in the evening, fragrant
Mimulus luteus	monkeyflower	18	9	scarlet, crimson, yellow, mottled	I. March to April	
Mimulus hybridus	monkeyflower	12–18	9	red and yellow	I. March O. May	
Mirabilis jalapa	four-o'clock	24	12	pink, white, yellow	O. May	flowers open at four o'clock
Myosotis sylvatica	forget-me-not	12	6	blue, pink	I. April	lovely as an edging plant
Nemesia strumosa	nemesia	18	9	orange, rose to white	I. March	prefers cool growing weather
Nemophila maculata	five-spot	10	8	white, black, spotted	I. April	
Nemophila menziesii	baby-blue-eyes	9	12	clear blue	O. April	
Nicotiana alata	winged tobacco	36–48	12	white	I. March O. April	delightfully fragrant
Nicotiana sanderae	flowering tobacco	24–36	12	red	I. March O. April	
Nicotiana sylvestris	flowering tobacco	36–48	12	white to crimson	I. March O. April	
Nigella damascena	love-in-a-mist	18–24	9	blue	O. April	short season of bloom
Oenothera americana	evening primrose	12	6	white	O. May	
Oenothera drummondii	Drummond evening primrose	12	6	yellow	O. May	
Papaver rhoeas	Shirley or field poppy	18–36	12	tones of scarlet	O. Nov., March	hairy stems and buds
Papaver somniferum	opium poppy	24–36	9	various (white to red)	O. Sept., March	smooth stems and buds
Pelargonium spp.	geranium	12–18	18–24	white, pink, salmon-red	I. Feb.	very compact, heavy growers
Penstemon gloxinioides	beard-tongue	24–36	9	many		for use in pots for the greenhouse
Petunia hybrida, dwarf	petunia	6–8	6	white to bright rose	I. March O. April	long season of bloom
Petunia hybrida, tall and trailing		12–24	12	white to bright rose and purple	I. March O. April	

(Continued)

ANNUALS (Continued)

SCIENTIFIC NAME	COMMON NAME	HEIGHT IN INCHES	DISTANCE APART IN INCHES	COLOR	MONTHS OF SOWING INDOORS (I) OUTDOORS (O)	REMARKS
Phacelia campanularia	California bluebell	12	9	blue	I. March O. April	
Phacelia ciliata		12	9	blue	O. April	
Phacelia tanacetifolia	fiddleneck	24	12	light purple	O. April	
Phacelia viscida		12	9	blue	O. April	
Phaseolus coccineus	scarlet runner		8	red	O. May	rapid climber
Phlox drummondii	annual phlox	6	6	white, magenta, rose, tawny and purple	I. March O. May	plan for successive plantings
dwarf varieties		6–12		white, magenta, rose, tawny and purple		
tall varieties		12–18	9	white, magenta, rose, tawny and purple	I. March O. May	
Portulaca grandiflora	portulaca, rose moss	8	6	purplish-crimson, yellow, white	O. April	excellent for hot, dry situations
Proboscidea fragrans (*Martynia fragrans*)	unicorn plant	24	12	mauvé	O. April	Wooly foliage, sweet-scented
Psylliostachys suworowii (*Limonium suworowii*)	Suworow sea lavender	18	15	rose	I. March	
Rehmannia elata		48	18	rose	I. March	lovely perennial treated as annual
Reseda odorata, dwarf varieties	mignonette	6	12	greenish-yellow	I. April pots	lovely fragrance; does not like transplanting
tall varieties		12–18	12	greenish-yellow	I. April pots	lovely fragrance; does not like transplanting
Rudbeckia hirta var. *pulcherrima*	black-eyed Susan	24	18	yellow, black center	O. April	
Salpiglossis sinuata	salpiglossis, painted tongue	18–24	9	purples and yellows variegated	I. March O. May	rather tempermental
Salvia patens	gentian sage	18	12	deep blue	I. March	intense and lovely blue
Salvia farinacea	mealycup sage	24	9	blue	I. March O. May	half-hardy perennial treated as annual; very useful for the border
Salvia splendens	scarlet sage	36	18	scarlet	I. Feb., March O. May	should be used in moderation
Salvia splendens var. 'Welwyn'	Welwyn sage	36	18	pink	I. March O. May	
Sanvitalia procumbens	sanvitalia	6, tr.	9	golden	I. March O. May	
Sanvitalia procumbens 'Flore Pleno'		6	9	golden	I. March O. May	double-flowering
Saponaria calabrica	Calabrian soapwort	12+	10	rose	I. March O. April	
Saponaria vaccaria pyramidata	dairy pink	18	9	pink, white	I. March O. April	
Scabiosa atropurpurea	pincushion flower	36	12	purple, blue, mahogany, rose, white	I. March O. April	attracts humming-birds
Schizanthus pinnatus dwarf varieties	butterfly flower	12	9	white, rose, purple spotted	I. June, April O. May	
tall varieties		24–36	12–18	white, rose, purple spotted	I. June, April O. May	

ANNUALS (Continued)

SCIENTIFIC NAME	COMMON NAME	HEIGHT IN INCHES	DISTANCE APART IN INCHES	COLOR	MONTHS OF SOWING INDOORS (I) OUTDOORS (O)	REMARKS
Seneccio elegans	purple groundsel	18	6	purple, rose to white	I. March	
Silene armeria	sweet William campion	12	6	rose	O. April	
Solanum integrifolium	tomato eggplant	36	24	inconspicuous, white	I. March	grown for orange-red fruit for indoor decoration
Ursinia anthemoides speciosa	sphenogyne	10	6	yellow, daisylike		
Statice (**see** *Limonium bondvellii*)						
Tagetes erecta	Aztec or African marigold	48	12–18	gold, lemon	I. March O. May	excellent for cutting
Tagetes patula	French marigold	18	9	gold, spotted maroon	I. March O. May	very effective in fall garden
Tagetes tenuifolia	Mexican marigold	12	6	gold	I. March O. May	
Thunbergia alata	clockvine	9	12	yellow with dark center	I. March O. May	trailer
Tithonia rotundifolia (T. speciosa)	Mexican sunflower	72–100	36	rich orange	I. March O. May	coarse; spectacular flowers
Tolpis barbata	hawkweed	12	6	rose, white (daisylike)		
Torenia fournierii	wishbone flower	9–12	6	blue and velvety purple	I. March O. May	sun or partial shade; endures intense heat well
Trachymene caerulea	laceflower	24	9	soft blue	I. March	
Tropaeolum majus	nasturtium	48, cl.	12–15	scarlet to yellow	O. April	pungent odor
Tropaeolum minus	dwarf nasturtium	12	6	scarlet to yellow	O. April	pungent odor
Ursinia anethoides		12	6	orange, daisylike	I. March O. April	good for very sunny border
Ursinia anethoides hybrids		12–24	10	orange, daisylike	I. March O. April	good for very sunny border
Venidium fastuosum	cape daisy	24–36	12	orange, with dark centers	I. March O. April	spectacular, spiny-looking foliage
Verbena erinoides	moss vervain	8, tr.	9	magenta to white	I. March	long season of bloom
Verbena erinoides hybrida	verbena	8, tr.	9	magenta to white	I. March	long season of bloom
Verbena erinoides, tall varieties		12	12	magenta to white	I. March	long season of bloom
Viola tricolor	pansy	8–12	9	varied purple, blue, yellow or white	I. Feb. O. April, or Aug.	usually bienniel, but may be treated as an annual
Viscaria (**see** *Lychnis coeli-rosa*)						
Xeranthemum annuum	immortelle	24–36	9	purple, white	I. March	everlasting
Zinnia elegans	giant zinnia	36	12	scarlet, rose, white, orange and yellow	I. March O. April	long season of bloom
Zinnia elegans dwarf	dwarf zinnia	15	9	scarlet, rose, white, orange and yellow	I. March O. April	
Zinnia haageana	orange zinnia	18	9	yellow, blotched maroon	I. March O. April	

20.1 Modern roses, such as Hybrid Perpetual 'Tiffany,' were developed from a myriad of ancestors. Photo Grant Heilman

20

Roses

Since ancient times the rose has held a very special place in the hearts of people throughout the world. Because of its significance as a symbol of purity and faith, because of the many associations, legends and traditions surrounding it, because of its sheer beauty, it has been loved and revered by countless generations.

The romance of the rose has come down to us in song and story and it is interwoven into the very fabric of our history. The Greek poetess, Sappho, sang of its beauty as far back as the sixth century B.C. The Roman matron of the first century A.D. took pride and pleasure in arranging her roses for the flower shows of her day. The symbols of the two factions contending for supremacy in strife-torn England during the fifteenth century were the white rose of York and the red rose of Lancaster. "The War of the Roses" was so called because of these symbols.

One of the first flowers to become domesticated, the rose has been faithfully protected, treasured and planted wherever civilization has spread. Universal in its appeal to the spirit of man, it is equally at home over the cottage doorway and within the proud gates of royal palaces.

Since the dawn of science, and its application to the study of plants, no other flower has received so much attention as the rose. Plant explorers and botanists have discovered and named more than 200 species in the northern hemisphere alone and, after more than a century of plant breeding, we now have many hundreds of varied forms. When we compare the wealth of material available to us today with the very limited number of varieties and types that were available only a few generations ago, we realize what a debt of gratitude we owe to our modern plant hybridizers.

Today there is a rose for every place and purpose: for formal beds and borders, for arbors, trellises and fences, for hedges, for ground covers on steep banks, for edgings, for accent plants in perennial borders, for use as specimen shrubs and decorative features in portable containers on terrace and patio, and even for planting in little rose bays along crowded streets in the heart of great cities. Roses are one of the most versatile and exciting plant groups with which to work today in creating landscape compositions.

ROSE GARDEN DESIGN

Partly because of the special esteem in which the rose is held, partly because the cultural requirements of the rose differ from those of other flowers, and partly because the rose lacks the fullness of growth of many other cultivated plants and therefore needs special compositional arrangement, a separate garden or planting area or bed for roses is the most satisfactory method of planting. Such a specialized garden may seem to be too great an undertaking for

395

the average gardener, but it is not impossible to attain even on a small property and where resources are limited. A rose garden need not be large in scale or lavish in details of construction.

In planning a traditional rose garden, a few essential considerations should be borne in mind: an enclosure that is not too close and airless yet gives adequate shelter from the wind and provides a background against which the blooms may be seen to the best advantage; a geometric pattern to give the design definite form, so that the garden will have a beauty of its own quite independent of the flowers; and paths of some material such as brick, flagstone or turf that will be in harmony with the surroundings.

In a rose garden of contemporary design the composition will be more casual and varied, and will permit greater freedom. Such rose beds may be designed to create an interesting and dramatic pattern within the surfaced area of the patio, or roses may be planted in raised beds against the free-sweeping curve of the patio wall. Planted in tubs, roses may also be used as specimen or accent plants to highlight a planting composition.

If the grounds of a suburban home or apartment dwelling are too limited to permit the development of even a very small garden, roses may still be grown and enjoyed—perhaps as a single lovely bush beside the door, or a few floribundas or miniature roses planted in a group near the corner of the house, or some of the graceful, climbing hybrid tea roses on a low fence. Few flowers bring such touches of warmth and graciousness, of color and beauty to any home—be it large or small—as does the rose in any form.

CULTURAL REQUIREMENTS

The factors that contribute to success in growing roses of fine quality include: a suitable location; a fertile, friable soil; good drainage; the selection of vigorous, disease-free plants; correct planting procedures; and good cultural practices—pruning, fertilization, mulching winter protection and the control of insect pests and diseases.

20.2 Arches and arbors of old-fashioned rambler roses, although they only bloom once, are a special experience. Photo Anita Sabarese

Location: In order to produce good bloom, roses require a minimum of six hours of sun during the day. Shade during the afternoon is preferable to morning shade. In fact, some afternoon shade is desirable, as the blooms tend to retain their color for a longer period. Roses will not thrive in situations where the shade is too dense, and they should not be planted in close proximity to trees, shrubs or hedges that are heavy surface feeders. Under such conditions, the roses will be deprived of both food and moisture.

Air circulation is also important. Roses do not make satisfactory growth in closely confined areas where there is insufficient circulation of air currents.

SOIL REQUIREMENTS

The actual structure of the soil is not as important as its drainage capacity and its fertility. Roses will thrive in both fairly heavy clay and in sandy-loam soils, provided the requirements of drainage and fertility are met. The ideal soil is a good garden loam, well supplied with organic matter.

Drainage: Good drainage is absolutely essential. While roses require large quantities of water for their best growth, they are seriously injured by an excess of standing water in the soil. They will not thrive in soils that do not drain readily or where the water table rises to within a few feet of the surface at any time of the year.

If the natural drainage is not adequate to take care of surplus water, the beds may be underdrained with either tile or with crushed stone or cinders.

Four in. agricultural tile should be used, being laid end to end at the bottom of a 2-ft. trench. The tile joints should be covered with strips of tar paper to keep the soil out of the tile while the trench is being refilled. Whatever material is used, there should be a fall of at least 3 in. in every 50 linear ft. While agricultural tile is traditional, cement-asbestos perforated pipe, which is available in 8-ft. lengths, is easier to handle. Even easier and much less expensive is corrugated PVC drain, which is flexible.

If crushed stone or cinders are used, a 6-in. layer placed at the bottom of the trench will usually be sufficient to provide adequate drainage.

Acidity of the soil: Roses prefer a slightly acid soil with a pH ranging between 5.5 and 6.5. If the soil is too strongly alkaline, or if it becomes too acid, roses have a tendency to become chlorotic—a condition indicated by a characteristic mottling of the leaves, the veins remaining dark green and the leaf areas between the veins turning yellow, or in extreme cases, almost white. When such a condition becomes evident, the soil should be tested to determine whether the trouble is due to either too much acidity or alkalinity, or to a lack of available iron. (See index for the use of iron chelate.) If the chlorosis is caused by too high a degree of acidity, the condition may be remedied by an application of lime. (See chart on page 565 for rate of application.) In preparing new beds the soil should be tested and a pH between 5.5 and 7.0 should be definitely established.

PREPARATION OF THE SOIL

It is important that the soil for roses be well prepared. The roots of a vigorous rosebush will extend to a depth varying from 15 in. to 20 in.; the best time to improve the fertility and texture of the soil in the area where the roots can derive the greatest benefit from it is *before* planting.

If the soil is decidedly sandy, its texture may be improved and its water-holding capacity greatly increased by adding clay loam, compost, peat moss and other organic materials to it. Similarly, the texture of extremely heavy clay soils may be improved by the addition of sand, compost, strawy manure, or some comparable material.

The methods of preparing soil for rose beds will depend to a considerable extent upon the desires of the owner. If one's means are limited, the old English practice of "double-digging" will give satisfactory results. If, however, time, labor and expense do not have to be taken into consideration, and if one wishes to provide conditions as nearly ideal as possible, the beds should be trenched.

"Double-digging" is a simple, comparatively rapid and very efficient method of soil preparation. It consists of removing the top spadeful of soil from one end of the bed and placing it at the other end of the bed, ready for later use. A generous layer of well-rotted cow manure or rich compost, to which a few handfuls of superphosphate have been added, should then be worked well into the lower stratum of soil that was left exposed after the top spadeful was removed. The next layer of topsoil is then spaded forward upon this lower stratum, and the process is continued until the end of the bed has been reached. The pile of topsoil removed from the first trench is used to fill the last trench. The organic matter should, if possible, be applied at the rate of 5 to 6 bushels per 100 sq. ft. of area.

Essentially the same procedure may be followed when individual holes are being prepared for specimen roses.

If the roses are to be planted in the spring, the beds should, if possible, be prepared the previous autumn. The preparation of the bed should be completed at least three weeks before planting so that the soil may have time to settle.

The final level of the rose bed should be about 2 in. or 3 in. above the surface of the surrounding area.

MAINTENANCE OF SOIL FERTILITY

If the rose beds have been well prepared, no further fertilization will be necessary during the first season of growth. During the second year a definite program of fertilization should be adopted, which may then be followed annually so that the soil does not become deficient in nutrients. Roses are vigorous feeders and require a soil well supplied with the essential elements of fertility. An adequate supply of nitrogen is necessary to promote rapid, vigorous growth and good foliage. Phosphorus induces good root development, stimulates flower bud formation and also increases the size and color of the blooms. Potash is essential in that it gives strength to the cell walls, increases the resistance of the plant to disease, and aids in the ripening and hardening of the wood in the autumn.

In planning a program for the maintenance of soil fertility the following points should be taken into consideration: the time of application, the formulation or analysis of the fertilizer to be used, as well as the method and rate of application.

In order to obtain vigorous growth and abundant bloom, roses should be given at least two feedings a year, and, if weather permits, a third may even be made. The first application should be made in the spring, soon after the pruning has been done. The second should be made in June about the time that the roses are coming into bloom, and the third may be given in the summer, provided the weather is neither too hot nor too dry. No application of fertilizer should be made after the middle of August, as it will tend to encourage succulent fall growth that will be subject to winter injury.

Most rose growers use a complete, commercial fertilizer such as a 5-10-5. Some prefer to use a fertilizer with an organic base containing the trace elements.

The soil should be fairly moist when the application is made. The fertilizer should be sprinkled on the soil about the plant and worked in lightly with a hand cultivator. Unless a rainfall occurs shortly afterward, the soil should be watered in order that the fertilizer may go into solution and be readily available for absorption by the roots. The foliage of the plants should be dry at the time that the application is made and no fertilizer should be allowed to come into contact with the leaves or the canes as it may cause severe burning, particularly if the foliage is wet.

The rate of application will vary somewhat according to the fertility of the soil. For soils of high fertility, 2 tbs. of 5-10-5 fertilizer per plant at each application is recommended. For soils of average fertility, the amount should be increased to 3 tbs., and for poor soils 4 tbs. are recommended.

High-analysis, soluble fertilizers may also be used if desired, but they are considerably more expensive than the commercial fertilizers. The instructions on the container should be carefully followed.

SELECTION OF STOCK

The importance of purchasing good stock from a reliable source can hardly be overemphasized. It is poor ecomony to purchase cheap rose bushes or "bargain" stock. Such plants are almost invariably of inferior quality and rarely make vigorous growth or bloom satisfactorily.

For the protection of the buyer, roses are graded into several standard classes. The top grade is listed as No. 1. In order to be graded No. 1, a bush must have three or more vigorous canes and, if carefully planted, it is almost certain to develop into a satisfactory plant.

TIME OF PLANTING

Roses may be planted in the autumn after the bushes have stopped active growth and are dormant but before the ground freezes; they may be planted in early spring while the plants are still dormant; or they may be planted as potted roses after growth is well started. Some growers are enthusiastic about autumn planting, while others prefer very early spring planting. A method which, in some ways, is a combination of both fall and spring planting has been employed very successfully in some parts of the country and is highly recommended by some rose authorities. The plants are dug and shipped in the autumn, and upon arrival they are placed in a trench, the bushes being completely covered with soil. In the spring, when the soil is in ideal condition, the plants are lifted and placed in their permanent position in the bed. When this method is followed, the wood and buds remain plump and firm throughout the winter, and the bushes are in perfect condition for planting in the spring. Planting does not have to be delayed until a spring shipment arrives, but may be done when both soil and weather conditions are most favorable; and one also has the advantage of being able to obtain superior stock. Most of the large commercial rose growers and seed firms dig their plants in the autumn, and store them during the winter in specially constructed storage houses. Consequently orders shipped out in the autumn are filled before the stock has become depleted, and plants of the finest quality may be obtained.

Spring planting should be done as soon as the ground can be worked. Since spring-shipped roses have usually been held in storage over the winter, they should be completely dormant upon arrival and should be planted immediately.

If a delay in planting new roses is necessary because of unfavorable weather conditions, they should be unpacked and buried in a trench. If the stems are dry and shriveled or the plants are light in weight, this will help to "plump" up the buds. Soaking the bushes for several hours will serve the same purpose.

Many retail growers now lift their roses in the autumn, or have wholesale orders shipped to them at this time. They pot them up during the winter in deep, heavy, tar-paper pots, ready to sell in the spring after the bushes have leafed out, or later when they are in bud or in bloom. If good, top-grade plants are used, and if they are potted skillfully and are well cared for, roses may be handled very successfully in this way. When planting potted roses, care must be taken to make sure that the ball of earth is not broken.

METHOD OF PLANTING

Planting distances will depend almost entirely upon the type of rose. Because of their very vigorous habit of growth, the hybrid perpetuals should be planted from 2 ft. to 3 ft. apart. For the hybrid teas and the tea roses a distance of 2 ft. is preferred, except in the case of some of the very vigorous varieties. Floribundas and grandifloras should also be spaced 2 ft. apart. There is great variance in spread among the varieties of floribundas.

Never let the roots be exposed to sun or wind before planting. They should be kept in shade, and wrapped in wet sphagnum moss or wet paper until ready to be placed in the hole.

Before planting, all injured or broken roots should be carefully pruned away, a clean, slanting cut being made. Any long, straggly roots should be cut back sufficiently so that they will not have to be twisted or bent when the plant is set. A hole of ample size should be dug for each plant. If the loose soil is mounded slightly in the bottom of the hole, the roots can be placed in a natural position, extending both out and down.

The depth of planting also is a very important factor. The plant should be placed so that the bud, or crown, which is the point of union between the stock and scion, is 1 in. below the surface of the soil. If the bush is planted too deeply, with the point of union more than 2 ins. below the surface, the roots will receive an inadequate supply of oxygen from the air, and the growth of the plant will be seriously affected as a result. This factor is of particular importance in heavy clay soils. If roses are planted too shallowly, the root stock will send up shoots and produce flowers of the species on which the rose that one desired was grafted. This understock is usually *Rosa multiflora,* which is very vigorous and is undesirable in a rose garden.

After the plant is in place, the soil should be packed firmly about the roots. Many failures are caused by loose, careless planting, and if success is to be assured it is necessary that a few simple rules be observed. Packing the soil about the roots with the blunt end of a trowel handle is very effective, though care must be taken not to bruise the roots. When the hole has been filled almost to the top, the soil may be tramped firmly about the bush. The plants should then be watered thoroughly, and the beds should not be allowed to dry out until the plants have become well established. Such watering is quite as necessary for roses planted in the autumn as it is for those planted in the spring, as the soil about the roots should always be moist when the ground freezes. Immediately after the first watering has been given at the time of planting, the soil should be mounded up about the plants. In the case of roses planted in the autumn this will serve as a winter protection for the plants, and the beds may then be mulched in the usual way. When roses are planted in the spring this hilling up of the soil is equally advisable, as it protects the canes from the drying effects of sun, late frosts and wind while the new feeding roots are being developed that will, later in the season, supply the moisture the plant needs. In the spring these temporary mounds of earth should be left about the plants for three or four weeks, at which time the soil may then be gradually worked back into the beds.

PRUNING

The method and the time of pruning depend, to a large extent, upon the type of rose and the locality. However, there are a few fundamentals that apply to all types and to all parts of the country.

The objectives in pruning roses are twofold: to remove dead, weak and diseased wood; and to maintain the desired height and form of the bush. All dead canes should be removed at the base. Canes should be examined for wounds, split bark and signs of canker or other disease, and such canes should be cut back below the point of injury or attack. Where the tips of canes have died back during the winter, they should be cut back to sound wood. Canes that interfere with the desired height or shape of the bush should be cut back or removed, and where canes rub against each other one cane should be removed to at least below the point of contact.

Sharp pruning shears are essential. Dull shears will make a jagged cut and tend to crush or bruise the stems, thus making conditions more favorable for the entrance of fungi and bacteria. A clean, slanting cut should be made just above a vigorous bud, the slant being in the same direction as the bud. The cut should be as close as possible to the bud without causing injury to it; it should never be more than $1/4$ in. above the bud. Long stubs die and tend to permit the entrance of fungi. As a precaution against fungi the end of the stems may be treated with tree-wound paint. This is a tedious process, however, and is not practical on a large scale.

Climbing Roses

The large-flowered climbers, such as 'Silver Moon' and 'Dr. Van Fleet,' require rather drastic pruning in order to restrain their usual rampant growth. Pruning should be done in late winter or early spring. Each year several of the oldest canes should be removed at the base to make room for new, vigorous growth, and long, unwieldy canes should be cut back. Most of the large-flowered climbers bear their blooms on the new shoots produced by the

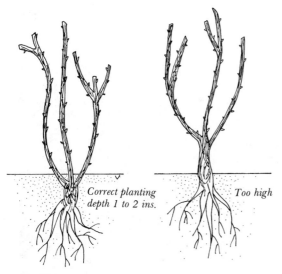

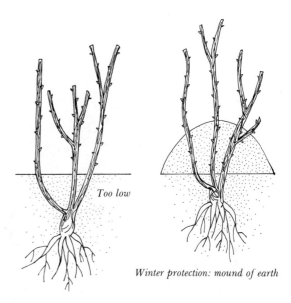

Fig. 20.1
Rose bushes—planting and protection

strong branches that form the framework of the bush, and after bloom these laterals should be cut back to 6 in. to 12 in. It is unwise to permit a large-flowered climber to become too rampant. With careful training and judicious pruning the full beauty of the bush may be maintained, but if it is allowed to grow unrestrained it will, in the course of a few years, become a tangled, unsightly mass. Where growth must be very much restricted it is wiser to plant a climber of more delicate habit.

The Climbing Hybrid Teas

These are much less vigorous in growth than other types of large-flowered climbers and require little pruning beyond the cutting back of canes that may have been winter-killed at the tip.

Floribundas

Pruning should be done in the spring just as the buds begin to swell. As a class the floribundas require very little pruning. They should be allowed to grow to their natural height unchecked. Dead and diseased wood and crowding canes should be removed. Occasionally an old cane will die back and a new cane grow up.

Grandifloras

The same methods apply as to the floribunda class.

Hybrid Perpetuals

Prune in early spring when the buds begin to swell. Cut out dead and diseased wood. Prune back canes to the desired height and prune canes where necessary to maintain the symmetry of the bush.

Hybrid Teas

Prune in the spring as the buds begin to swell. If hybrid tea roses are pruned severely, leaving only two to four buds on a cane, it will result in a few, somewhat late but very large blooms suitable for exhibition purposes. If this practice is continued over a period of years, however, it may shorten the life of the bush.

Unless exhibition blooms are specifically desired, moderate pruning is recommended. When canes are pruned back to a height of 12

20.3 *After their first burst of flowers in June, modern climbers, unlike their earlier counterparts, continue to bloom intermittently throughout the season. Photo Grant Heilman*

in. to 18 in., an abundance of bloom will be assured and the bush will produce sufficient foliage to manufacture the food so necessary for its continued vigor. The beauty and symmetry of the bush should be maintained by the removal of crowding or angular canes. Whenever possible the cut should be made just above an *outside* bud as this tends to keep the center of the bush open.

Polyanthas

Roses in this class require very little pruning. Dead or unhealthy wood should be removed and each spring, before the buds swell, a few of the old canes should be cut out in order to induce the growth of young, vigorous shoots.

Ramblers

The members of this class should be pruned immediately *after* their period of bloom is passed. Much of the old, recently flowered wood may be cut away, as the true ramblers will produce their flowers the following season on the new canes arising from the base of the plant. In this respect they differ markedly from the large-flowered climbing roses. Unless pruned vigorously, ramblers will become an unsightly mass of briers.

Shrub Roses

Remove any dead, unhealthy or crowding branches to maintain a bush of pleasing scale.

CUTTING ROSES

When roses are cut for decorative purposes, many of the same principles may be applied that are used in the pruning of the plants. A clean, sharp, slightly slanting cut should be made, approximately ¼ in. above a leaf bud. The symmetry of the bush may be maintained by cutting either at an outside or inside bud, though it is advisable to direct the growth outward whenever it is possible to do so. The quality and abundance of future bloom will depend upon the number of leaf buds left on the stem after the flower has been cut. If the shoot is strong and vigorous, three buds may be left — two if the shoot is weak. The length of the stem of the cut flower will, therefore, be determined by the number of buds to be left on the cane. Roses should preferably be cut early in the morning before they have been touched for many hours by the sun.

WATERING

Roses make their best growth during moderately cool weather when the soil is well supplied with moisture. Although roses resent a soil that is too saturated, or a water table that has risen above the level of the roots, they require an adequate and fairly abundant supply of moisture throughout the growing season. During periods of drought roses should be watered thoroughly once a week. The bed should be soaked until the water has penetrated into the soil to a depth of at least 1 ft. Frequent light waterings are of little value and do more harm than good.

Overhead watering is not recommended as it is conducive to the spread of black spot, mildew and other diseases. It is preferable to use a soil soaker or underground irrigation.

For control of diseases and insect pests, see Chapter 32.

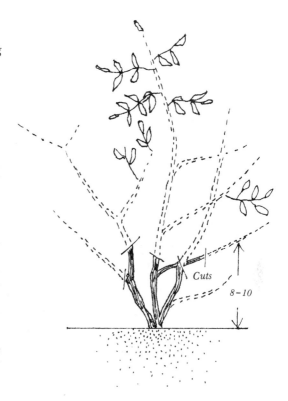

Fig. 20.2
Hybrid tea rose pruned for bloom

SUMMER MULCHES

Roses benefit greatly from a summer mulch. This is particularly true of bush-type roses. A number of materials may be used — buckwheat hulls, ground corncobs, peat moss, shredded sugar cane fiber, rice hulls, wood chips, coconut hulls, sawdust and tobacco stems. Of these, buckwheat hulls have proved one of the most satisfactory. They are light in weight and easy to handle, they may be applied dry, they are permeable to water, do not cake and have a dark, pleasing color. If peat moss or sawdust is used, it is essential that it be thoroughly wet before being applied. The long-continued use of peat moss year after year may cause the soil to become too loose in texture and may tend to increase its acidity slightly. If corncobs or sawdust are used, extra nitrogen must be supplied to compensate for the loss of nitrogen from the soil during the period of decomposition.

The soil should always be moist at the time the mulch is applied, and the mulch should be at least 1 in. deep.

(See Chapter 8 on Mulches.)

WINTER PROTECTION

The amount of winter protection necessary depends upon three factors: the severity of the climate; the exposure of the rose garden; and the natural hardiness of the varieties selected.

Winter injury is usually attributable either to the actual freezing of the twigs and roots, which breaks down the cell tissues, or to the loss of moisture from the twigs caused by excessive evaporation. Winter injury is quite as likely to be caused by strong, drying winds and by brilliant sunshine as by extreme cold. Throughout the winter the roots continue to absorb water from the soil and a slow evaporation of moisture continues from the canes. If an undue amount of wind and sunshine increases evaporation beyond the point where the roots can supply sufficient moisture to the twigs, the canes will begin to shrivel, and if the process is prolonged the plant will die, even though no actual freezing of the plant tissues has taken place. One of the first preparations for winter, therefore, should be to see that the soil is well supplied with moisture. The normal autumn rains will often provide for an adequate storage of moisture, but if the autumn season is deficient in rainfall, artificial watering should be done before the ground freezes.

In the South roses require practically no winter protection. In areas of the North, however, where the cold is so severe that the thermometer will range much below 10° F. it is wise to provide adequate protection for the majority of the hybrid teas, for the grandifloras, for all the tea roses and for some of the floribundas, hybrid perpetuals and polyanthas, as well as for a few of the more tender climbers.

In a normal season the early frosts of autumn will harden and ripen the wood, and the plants will gradually become dormant. It is a wise precaution to rake and destroy all fallen leaves and bits of twig in order to prevent them from harboring bacterial and fungus diseases. Soil brought into the beds may be mounded up about the bushes to a height of from 10 in. to 12 in. This mound of earth will afford considerable protection about the crown of the plant and will also prevent the wood and buds of the lower portion of the stem from drying out. If a summer mulch was used, this must be removed before application of the soil mound. After the ground has frozen, a mulch of salt or marsh hay or some similar material may be spread over the beds. It is important that the mulch is not applied until after the ground has frozen. In the case of the less hardy varieties each individual bush may be protected with a covering of salt or marsh hay or dry leaves, and in sections where the winters are of extreme severity a generous covering of salt or marsh hay or dry leaves may be heaped over the entire bed until only the tips of the bushes are left exposed. The covering may be held in place by evergreen boughs, a snow fence or by a wire framework. If leaves are used for this purpose, choose only those that do not rot readily, such as oak leaves. Leaves from maples and elms soon form a soggy mat when used for winter covering and usually do more harm than good.

There are various climatic conditions that frequently contribute to the winter-killing of roses, conditions over which one has very little control. If there is a long spell of warm, growing weather in the autumn, the plants will not become sufficiently hardened to withstand the rigors of a severe winter. Under such conditions the bushes will have a tendency to continue growth until late in the autumn and the new shoots will be so soft and succulent that considerable injury may result. In such cases it is wise to provide careful protection for the bushes, even though it may not normally be necessary.

Protection for Climbers and Standard Roses

Some of our most beautiful climbers, such as 'Jacotte' and 'Emily Gray,' are not able to survive the extreme severity of a northern winter unless given sufficient protection.

Some very interesting experiments have been carried out at Cornell University to determine the most satisfactory method of affording protection for climbing roses. It has been found that cornstalks and evergreen boughs, while affording satisfactory protection, often harbor field mice and rabbits to such an extent that considerable damage may be done to the bush. Burlap is not satisfactory as it holds too much moisture. The most approved method, and one that has given absolute satisfaction, consists of removing the canes from the trellis or support early in October while they are still supple, and allowing them to remain procumbent upon the ground, where the grass will grow up among them and where the falling leaves that are blown in upon them will afford natural protection. Soil is then mounded up about the base of the plant, and after the ground has become frozen a mulch of salt marsh hay or straw is placed over the mound of soil. In order to hold the canes in a procumbent position two strong pieces of wood may be driven into the earth at right angles to each other, forming a wedge to hold the canes in place. This method of protection has proved so satisfactory that even during several winters of extreme severity, when the temperature reached 20° below zero, no injury resulted. Early in the spring, after danger from frost is over, the mounds of soil may be gradually removed from the base of the plant, and the canes may then be easily refastened to their supports.

Standard or tree roses require careful winter protection. The soil should first be removed from the side of the roots, and the rose tree then bent down into an improvised trench and covered with a heavy layer of soil.

CLASSIFICATION OF ROSES

Roses may be grouped into several classifications, one of the most logical being their adaptability to certain uses.

For the formal pattern of beds and borders in the rose garden, the six types that are of the greatest value are the floribundas, the grandifloras, the hybrid perpetuals, the tea roses, the hybrid teas and the polyanthas.

For use on arbors, lattices, pergolas and walls, the large-flowered climbing roses, the climbing hybrid teas, the pillar types, and the semiclimbing, ever-blooming types are the most desirable.

As a ground cover on steep banks some of the species roses are of value, and in this group we also find a number of recent introductions that are of outstanding merit.

For massed shrubbery plantings, for hedges and for beautiful specimens, the brier roses, the rugosas and rugosa hybrids and some of the delightful species roses may be used.

And, quite in a class by themselves, we have the old-fashioned roses — the Provence rose and moss rose; the Damask rose and the bourbon rose; the noisette rose and the China rose; and many others.

ROSES FOR GARDEN BEDS AND BORDERS

Floribunda Roses

Seldom has a new type of rose gained so rapidly in popularity as has the floribunda class, which is a comparatively recent introduction. The result of a cross between the low-growing polyanthas and the chaste and lovely hybrid tea rose, the floribundas have inherited many of the best characteristics of each parent. Hardy, adaptable and vigorous, almost prodigal in their bloom and lovely in form and coloring, the floribundas have won the hearts of rose lovers throughout the country.

Varieties vary greatly in size, some being semidwarf in habit and others, such as 'Betty Prior,' reaching a height of 5 ft. to 6 ft. There is also considerable variation in the flower form, from single to semidouble to fully double. And there is a wide range of color: white, pink, salmon, coral, scarlet, deep red, yellow and two-tone. The floribundas are generous with their bloom, flower over a long season and demand less care and attention than the more fastidious hybrid teas.

The versatility of the floribunda is one of the qualities that has made it so popular with gardeners everywhere. Its charm and piquant beauty make it a welcome addition to the formal rose garden. It is happily at home in the foreground of a shrubbery planting; it can be

FLORIBUNDA CULTIVARS OF MERIT

Bon Bon: Attractive mass effect, pink reverse on white, large flat blooms; fruitlike fragrance; 24 in. to 36 in. tall; 1974 All-America winner

Eutin: Huge clusters of red double flowers; 36 in. and sometimes even taller; excellent hedging variety

Fabergé: Profuse, beautifully formed, lovely pink with white and yellow blooms; low habit of 24 in. or less; bushy, dark leathery foliage

Fire King: Orange-red bloom with long stems; excellent for cutting, above average hardiness; 24 in. to 36 in. tall

Iceberg: Medium size, white decorative blooms; medium height of 24 in. to 36 in.; fruitlike fragrance

Jolly Roger: The brightest, most lasting in the orange-red color range; low habit of 24 in. or less

Lilli Marlene: Most reliable, low-growing, vigorous red; 24 in. to 36 in. tall

Merci: Attractive deep red rose with maximum bloom; holds its color well, excellent plants, lush green foliage

Saratoga: Good vigor and attractive foliage; white bloom with fruitlike fragrance; 1964 All-America winner

Tamango: Deep cherry-red with decorative lasting blooms; slight fragrance; 24 in. to 36 in. tall

Woburn Abbey: Well-formed yellow and orange bicolor blooms, dark leathery foliage; moderate growth; free bloomer

used as a hedge or as a solid border along the base of a wall; it gives added interest to the planting in a perennial border; and if there is space for only a bush or two on a tiny suburban plot, the floribundas are the ideal choice.

Grandiflora Roses

The lovely, recently developed grandiflora class attests the skill of the modern rose hybridizer and it has been, with justification, enthusiastically received by rosarians throughout the country.

Roses in this class are extremely vigorous, free-blooming, and among the easiest roses to grow. The buds and flowers have the exquisite perfection of the hybrid tea but are borne in clusters. The flowers are long and tapering, the blooms large and delicately formed, often measuring more than 4 in. across. The grandiflora roses are noted particularly for their almost incredible profusion of bloom, their robust growth and healthy foliage, and for the long-lasting qualities of the flowers. Some varieties are fragrant and others almost thornless.

GRANDIFLORA CULTIVARS OF MERIT

Camelot: Salmon-pink flower that is fragrant and semidouble; vigorous uniform growth habit: 36 in. or more in height; All-America winner for 1965

Garden State: Two-tone fragrant pink blooms; above average hardiness; 36 in. or more in height

Montezuma: Coral to pink blooms, long-lasting, attractive pointed buds; 36 in. or more in height; handsome foliage

Pink Parfait: Attractive pink blend with unusual buds; 36 in. or more high; above average hardiness; 1961 All-America winner

Queen Elizabeth: A superbly formed, fragrant flower of lovely clear pink and unusually long-lasting; excellent cut flower; tall, erect plant with handsome foliage; 1955 All-America winner

Hybrid Perpetuals

The hybrid perpetuals were introduced in 1830 by Laffray, who had succeeded in crossing the lovely old damask rose with the China rose. The name "hybrid perpetual" is, unfortunately, very misleading, as the members of this group bloom freely during the month of June and only yield but occasional, scattered bloom throughout the rest of the season. The term-"perpetual" was originally intended to refer to the hardiness of the plant instead of to its blooming period. The hybrid perpetuals are the "June Roses," which were so cherished by gardeners early in this century. Even today, when they are no longer classed among our favorites, we recognize the fact that they pos-

HYBRID PERPETUAL CULTIVARS OF MERIT

Arrillaga: Large, glowing pink buds developing into immense flowers of a vivid pink with a golden glow at the base of the petals; blooms fragrant and long-lasting

Frau Karl Druschki: Considered the best white rose in cultivation and often called "the white American Beauty." The large, pure white blooms are borne on long, strong stems and are unexcelled for cutting. The flower is of beautiful form; its one failing seems to be that it has no fragrance

George Arends: The pink form of Frau Karl Druschki; very fragrant

Paul Neyron: Very large blooms of a deep pink shade

Ulrich Brunner: Brilliant scarlet-crimson; a rose of vigorous habit and very hardy

sess many virtues and that they will never be entirely replaced by the newer hybrid teas. The hybrid perpetuals are very hardy, and are able to withstand winters of extreme severity. In habit of growth they are strong and vigorous. The flowers are large and well formed and are produced on long, strong stems.

Tea Roses

Tea roses were introduced from China in the year 1810 and they have long been classed among the favorites.

Wherever tea roses can be grown they are greatly prized. The foliage has a coppery tint and the sweetly scented flowers are exquisite in form. Unfortunately, tea roses are not hardy in the North unless very elaborate winter protection is provided. They are, therefore, seldom grown except in the lovely gardens of the South. They prefer a rich, well-drained soil and require severe prunning.

TEA ROSE CULTIVARS OF MERIT

Lady Hillingdon: Beautifully pointed buds, flowers a clear saffron yellow
Maman Cochet: Large, fragrant flower of carmine pink
William R. Smith: Creamy-white flowers tinged with pink

Hybrid Tea Roses

The first hybrid tea rose was produced by Guillot in 1867 as the result of crossing the hybrid perpetual rose 'Mme Victor Verdier' with the tea rose 'Mme Bravy.' This cross resulted in the lovely hybrid tea rose known as 'La France,' which has maintained its popularity for many decades. Many later crosses were made between hybrid perpetuals and tea roses, and again between hybrid tea roses and other hybrid teas, and as a result of these crosses many strains have been developed.

Our finest and most desirable garden roses are to be found in this group. Most varieties within the group are of a sturdy, vigorous growth habit and are hardy in the North if given moderate winter protection. Under favorable cultural conditions the hybrid tea roses will give generous bloom from June well into October. During the heat of midsummer the bloom is more scattered and the different varieties vary somewhat in their blooming habits, some giving better autumn bloom than others. There is also considerable variation in habit of growth, some varieties attaining a height of 3 ft. or more, while other varieties are somewhat low and spreading in form and produce but scanty foliage. Some hybrid tea roses are exceptionally vigorous and very long-lived, while other varieties have a tendency to die out after a few years, even when grown under the most favorable cultural conditions. The hybrid teas possess a wide range of color and form, and they are the most desirable type for the average garden.

HYBRID TEA ROSE CULTIVARS OF MERIT

American Heritage: A good, hardy grower of medium height; long, urn-shaped buds produce an abundance of yellow blend flowers; 1964 All-America winner
Bewitched: Attractive form, clear, bright, typical pink fragrant flowers; 24 in. to 36 in. tall
Charlotte Armstrong: Delightful long, slender red buds opening to a striking rose-pink; vigorous grower, excellent cut rose, slight fragrance
Chicago Peace: Has all the characteristics of the famous Peace rose, with the addition of color and fragrance; a bicolor multicolor blend
Chrysler Imperial: Dark red, outstanding fragrance, good form; 24 in. to 36 in. tall; 1953 All-America winner
Double Delight: Unique combination of red and white bloom; medium height of 24 in. to 36 in.; above average hardiness, delightful fragrance
Electron: Bright pink with a glow, attractive dark green foliage; medium height, compact bushy plants; 1973 All-America winner
Fragrant Cloud: Well-formed large flowers of a coral-red shade, old rose fragrance; glossy dark foliage; vigorous habit
Heirloom: A clear, decorative, lilac-colored flower, intensely scented, produces an abundance of bloom on single stems; medium to tall; attractive pointed oval buds.
Helen Traubel: All-weather pink blend rose, large blooms borne singly on vigorous, medium-size plants; mild fragrance; 1952 All-America winner
Irish Gold: Attractive lemon-colored blooms, vigorous upright habit, excellent foliage, sweet fragrance; low-growing to 24 in. or less
King's Ransom: Pure yellow flowers, long attractive bud form, sweet fragrance; upright, sturdy plants with strong stems
Kordes Perfecta: Creamy-white petals edged with carmine; very fragrant, vigorous plants, attaining 3 ft. or more

HYBRID TEA ROSE CULTIVARS (Continued)

Mr. Lincoln: Strong, upright, vigorous grower; striking dark red flower, delightful fragrance; 1964 All-America winner

Mojave: A deep coppery flower combining the tones of a desert sunset; medium height, upright habit, mild fragrance; 1955 All-America winner

Old Smoothie: Almost thornless, extreme deep red decorative bloom; vigorous grower, 36 in. or more in height

Reichprasident von Hindenburg: An unusual large pink flower that resembles a peony; vigorous, well-scaled plants; grows from 3 ft. to 5 ft.

Sutter's Gold: Long slim buds of reddish-orange opening to deep yellow; strong, vigorous plants with a rich tea fragrance

Swarthmore: Classic hybrid tea buds, deep pink bloom on long stems; vigorous habit, 36 in. or more in height; sweet fragrance

Tiffany: A striking pink rose with a yellow glow at the base; outstanding tapering buds, highly fragrant blooms; vigorous plants of good habit

Tropicana: Brilliant orange, free-blooming and long-lasting; holds its color exceptionally well; strong sturdy stems

White Masterpiece: Breathtaking large white blooms, low-growing—24 in. or less—with attractive, large glossy leaves

Yankee Doodle: Showy, large pinkish-yellow blooms, long-lasting quality; vigorous tall grower; delightful fragrance; 1976 All-America winner

Single Hybrid Tea Roses

In this group are some of our most beautiful hybrid tea roses, exquisite both in form and in coloring. They are decorative and lovely in the garden and offer most delightful possibilities for cut flower arrangements.

Polyantha Roses

The polyantha or cluster roses are used extensively for mass plantings, for the foreground of shrubbery borders and for edging purposes. They are very hardy and require comparatively little care and attention. Gay and colorful, they give generous bloom throughout the season and are rapidly becoming more popular.

SINGLE HYBRID TEA ROSE CULTIVARS OF MERIT

Dainty Bess: An attractive, five-petaled pink flower; sweet fragrance; constantly recurring bloom

Dainty Maid: A cerise single rose opening to a silvery-pink; dark leathery foliage, vigorous compact bushy habit

Elsie Poulsen: A single, bright rose-pink; blooms in clusters on long stems; vigorous and floriferous

Golden Wings: A single, five-petaled sulphur yellow flower; extremely vigorous, bushy and profuse; recurrent bloom; exceptionally hardy

Irish Fireflame: Large, single, crimson flowers, very fragrant; dark glossy foliage; compact bushy habit

White Wings: A single, white fragrant flower with a long pointed bud; dark leathery foliage; vigorous bushy upright habit

POLYANTHA CULTIVARS OF MERIT

Cameo: The tiny flowers are borne in great profusion and are of a most lovely tone of shell-pink shading to orange-salmon

Improved Cecile Brunner: Known also as the sweetheart rose. The flowers are small and exquisitely formed, being particularly charming when in bud. The color is a delicate shade of pink, tinted with yellow at the base

Gloria Mundi: Flowers are borne in clusters and are of a most unusual scarlet-orange hue

Golden Salmon: Small flowers, produced in great abundance, of a bright scarlet-salmon hue

The Fairy: A polyantha with unique and endearing qualities. Hardy and vigorous, it reaches a height of 1½ ft. to 2 ft. and often attains a spread of 3 ft. The rosette-type flowers are a charming shade of pink and are borne in great abundance in small clusters. The Fairy is seldom out of bloom.

ROSES FOR ARBORS, PERGOLAS AND WALLS

Climbing Roses

In this class we find roses that are of particular value for use on arbors, fences, pergolas, pillars, trellises and walls.

Some varieties are very robust, inclined to be rampant in habit of growth, and require ample room for development and adequate support. Others are more restrained in growth and less apt to outgrow their location. Some give a profusion of bloom during the height of the rose

CLIMBING CULTIVARS OF MERIT

Blaze: Great clusters of brilliant red flowers, dark leathery foliage; vigorous grower with moderate recurrent bloom

Chesterfield: Medium-size white flowers; a strong and hardy grower

Dr. J. H. Nicholas: Large, double pink fragrant flowers; vigorous grower; rich, dark leathery foliage

Golden Showers: Medium vigorous habit; daffodil-yellow fragrant flowers, recurrent bloom; dark and glossy foliage

High Noon: Upright vigorous habit; lemon-yellow flowers, glossy leathery foliage; moderately hardy

RAMBLER CULTIVARS OF MERIT

Aviateur Blériot: Saffron buds and flowers in small clusters, light yellow fading to white; magnolia fragrance

Evangeline: One of the strongest-growing climbers, with excellent glossy foliage, and bearing its soft pink, single flowers in enormous clusters; lovely fragrance

Phyllis Bide: A graceful rambler with exquisitely formed little buds of pale gold and pink, opening to small buff-yellow flowers

Sanders' White Rambler: Flowers pure white, double and sweetly fragrant, in huge clusters; a strong grower with good, disease-resistant foliage

White Dorothy: A pure white counterpart of the common pink Dorothy Perkins.

season and do not bloom again, while others continue to produce either abundant or intermittent bloom after the peak of bloom is passed. Some varieties are extremely hardy, while others are suited only to a mild climate. Some are particularly well adapted to growing on pillars and low fences, while others are best when allowed to climb on arbors or pergolas, or when trained on a trellis against a wall.

Ramblers

The rambler roses are particularly well suited for the covering of rough banks, or can be used on fences, walls, posts, arches and other latticelike structures. Unfortunately, some of the more common varieties, such as the Crimson Rambler and Dorothy Perkins, have been very much overplanted and it is usually possible to find roses that can be grown under similar conditions and that are far superior both in habit of growth and in quality of bloom. As a group the ramblers are prone to attacks of mildew and the foliage is apt to become unsightly.

SHRUB ROSES

Roses of numerous types, many of them species roses or hybrids, fit into this class. They have considerable decorative value when used as specimens or accent plants, and some are at home in the shrub border. Most are hardy and vigorous and require comparatively little care and attention.

Austrian Brier Rose (*R. foetida*)

A shrub rose reaching a height of 8 ft. to 10 ft. Flowers bright yellow, single.

Austrian Copper (*R. foetida bicolor*)

A lovely brier rose with single flowers of an intense coppery-red hue, the reverse side of the petals being a bright, golden-yellow.

Harison's Yellow (*R. foetida hybrid*)

Originated in 1830 by the Reverend Harison, this lovely brier rose has maintained its popularity for more than a century. It is hardy and vigorous in habit of growth and the semidouble yellow flowers are produced in great profusion. When it is in flower, every branch and twig seems to have blossomed forth, so full is it of starry blooms.

Persian Yellow (*R. foetida 'Persiana'*)

A fine, old-fashioned shrub rose producing myriads of small golden flowers.

Father Hugo's Rose (*R. hugonis*)

First discovered growing wild in northern China by Father Hugo, a missionary, and named in his honor. This is one of the loveliest plants known to cultivation and no rose garden is complete without it. It is the first rose to come into flower, and in late spring the slender, graceful branches are covered with myriad blooms. The flowers are single and exquisite in form, and they are of the softest shade of primrose-yellow. It blooms more profusely if not fertilized.

Frueling's Gold (*R. spinosissima* hybrid)

Bears lovely, sweetly scented, golden, cup-shaped flowers. Blooms are produced in great abundance. Vigorous growth, 3 ft. to 5 ft. high, spreading clumps. Very hardy, thrives on soil of moderate fertility.

Sweetbrier

The Sweetbrier or Eglantine rose (*Rosa rubiginosa*) is a native of England and is famed in song and story. The Eglantine rose, with its hybrids, is the only rose that possesses sweet-scented foliage. Tiny glands on the undersurface of the leaves emit a most delightful perfume, and when the plants are wet with dew, or after a warm summer shower, the fragrance is most alluring. The small, single flowers are a bright pink in color.

The Penzance Sweetbriers are hybrids of the Eglantine rose and were originated by Lord Penzance. The exquisite beauty of the small, single flowers and the scent of the foliage have endeared them to many gardeners, and they are worthy of wider recognition.

Rugosa and Rugosa Hybrids

The name *Rosa rugosa* was given to this group because of the very wrinkled appearance of the foliage. The rugosa roses are natives of Japan, China and Korea, and they are noted for their hardiness and their ability to withstand very adverse conditions. They will thrive in almost any type of soil, will endure extreme cold and will withstand neglect better than almost any other rose known. They are of particular value for planting in exposed situations and at the seashore, where they are able to withstand the effects of salt spray. They range in height from 6 ft. to 7 ft. and produce numerous erect, very spiny stems. The foliage is a deep green in color, thick and wrinkled in texture, and is practically disease- and insect-proof.

PENZANCE SWEETBRIER CULTIVARS OF MERIT

Brenda: Fragrant, single flowers of a light peach-pink
Lady Penzance: With its bright, copper-colored flowers and the sweetly-scented foliage, this is one of the most desirable of the group
Lord Penzance: Bears exquisite single flowers of a delicate fawn tint shading to ecru, and the foliage is sweetly scented
Meg Merrilies: Very vigorous in habit of growth; single, fragrant flowers of a rosy crimson
Minna: White flowers opening with the palest tinge of pink
Rose Bradwardine: Clear, rose-pink flowers with heavily scented foliage

RUGOSA CULTIVARS AND HYBRIDS OF MERIT

Agnes: Coppery-yellow buds, double flowers, pale amber-gold and very fragrant; no hips
Belle Poitevine: Grows to 6 in. high and 6 in. wide; semidouble, lavender-pink, crinkled blooms are borne intermittently throughout the season; clove fragrance and large hips
Doctor Eckener: Flowers are large, very fragrant, semidouble and of a beautiful coppery-rose shade, blended with yellow
Flamingo: The flowers are borne in clusters; buds are pointed. The single, five-petaled blooms are a flamingo pink, the color deepening as the season advances. Flowers throughout the summer and autumn; hardy and vigorous; reaches a height of 4 ft. to 5 ft.
Frau Dagmar Hartopp: A low-growing rugosa hybrid. Flowers silvery pink, single with ruffled petals; abundant bloom from June until frost; rugged and hardy, it thrives on poor, sandy soil. Good under seashore conditions.

TRAILING ROSES

There are a few roses that are of such low, trailing habit that they are particularly well suited for use as a ground cover on hillsides and embankments. A number of varieties have been introduced that are admirably adapted for this purpose.

TRAILING CULTIVARS OF MERIT

Coral Creeper: Buds deep red, flowers apricot-orange
fading to pink, semidouble in form and of good size
Little Compton Creeper: Flowers single, deep rose-pink,
borne in large, open clusters; foliage dark green and
glossy
Max Graf: Sprays of large, single, clear pink flowers
R. wichuraiana: A species rose of exceedingly rapid growth,
often producing canes from 12 ft. to 15 ft. long in a
single season. The foliage is a glossy, pale green and the
small white flowers are rather inconspicuous. The
Wichuraiana rose is extremely hardy and will grow in
almost any type of soil. It is well adapted to washed clay
banks and other unfavorable situations.

OLD-FASHIONED ROSES

Beloved by countless generations of gardeners, these old-fashioned roses are seldom seen in gardens today. There are, however, a few rosarians who have made a study of them and have brought together collections that are greatly cherished.

The Provence Rose

The Provence or cabbage rose derives its name from the Provence section of France where it was grown so abundantly. Legends tell us that it was originally cultivated by the Romans and was later introduced into other sections of Europe. The foliage is deeply wrinkled, broad and heavy, the blooms are large and globular in shape and sweetly scented. Because of the great number of petals, folded upon each other like the leaves of a cabbage, it has been called the "cabbage rose." It blooms but once during the season. Although the Provence rose will grow in almost any soil and will withstand considerable neglect, it responds remarkably to good care and cultivation, and for best growth it should be heavily pruned.

The Moss Rose

These roses are characterized by the distinctly mossy growth on the outerside of the calyx of

PROVENCE CULTIVARS OF MERIT

Anaïs Segalas: Flowers a deep tone of almost Tyrian-pink
Konigin von Danemark: Flowers a delicate flesh-pink
Unique Blanche: Deeply cupped, pure white flowers

MOSS CULTIVARS OF MERIT

Blanche Moreau: Buds heavily mossed, the double flowers
being borne in clusters; color, white tinged with pink;
vigorous and fine-flowering
Crested Moss: The Crested Moss rose is an offshoot of the
Provence rose and was first discovered in 1827 growing
in the crevice of a wall in Fribourg, Switzerland; the
large, full flowers are a bright, rose-pink in color
Gloire De Mousseux: One of the finest of the moss
roses—the flowers are of a carmine-salmon-pink shade
and are produced in great abundance
Old Pink Moss: One of the oldest roses of this type; buds
heavily mossed, flowers pale rose-pink

the opening buds. As a group they are quite hardy, but require severe pruning if good bloom is desired. In order to secure a succession of bloom, half the canes may be pruned in October and half the following May, each shoot being cut back to four or five buds.

The Damask Rose

This rose is a native of Damascus and Syria and was brought to Europe by the early Crusaders upon their return from the Holy Land. It is known to have been in cultivation in England in 1573. Damask roses are very hardy and vigorous and thrive in almost any type of soil. The foliage is large and rough, light green in color. The flowers are usually produced in trusses of three or more.

The Bourbon Rose

These roses were introduced into France in 1820 from the Isle of Bourbon and are closely related to the China or Bengal roses. They are moderately hardy and vigorous and bloom

DAMASK CULTIVARS OF MERIT

R. damascena officinalis: The original Rose of Damascus, intensely fragrant, and bearing double, rose-pink flowers

Marie Louise: Double flowers of a rich, deep pink; an old variety found growing in the gardens of Empress Josephine's Malmaison in 1813

Mme Hardy: Flowers pure white, occasionally tinged with pink; one of the most beautiful and most fragrant of the Damask roses.

BOURBON CULTIVARS OF MERIT

Adam Messerich: Fragrant flowers of a clear, rose-red; bushy in habit of growth

Louise Odier: Flesh-pink flowers of good form, produced freely throughout the season

Martha: Flowers a lovely shade of salmon-orange, produced freely on thornless canes

Souvenir De La Malmaison: Very fragrant flesh-colored flowers; of dwarf habit—hardly more than 2 ft. tall

NOISETTE HYBRID CULTIVARS OF MERIT

Bouquet D'Or: Flowers large and full, pale yellow shaded with coppery salmon

Crépuscule: A beautiful variety with flowers of an orange-pink shade, fading to apricot-yellow

Maréchal Niel: Double, fragrant flowers of a deep, golden-yellow; not hardy in the North, but one of the most beautiful of all roses for Southern gardens

Réve D'Or: Fragrant, double flowers of a soft buff-yellow shade; very vigorous in growth habit

CHINA CULTIVARS OF MERIT

Comtesse Du Cayla: Semi-single flowers, buds coppery-orange, flowers reddish-orange and yellow

Laurette Messimy: Flowers rose-pink, tinted with yellow

Old Blush: The original China rose, introduced in 1796; flowers bright pink, darkening with age

---

freely throughout the early summer, with some varieties blooming also in the autumn. The foliage is dark and lustrous.

The Noisette Rose

This rose was originated by Mr. Philip Noisette of Charleston, South Carolina, in 1817, as a result of crossing the China Blush rose with the Musk rose. Mr. Noisette sent the rose to his father in France, who produced from it the beautiful Maréchal Niel rose, so beloved throughout the South.

China or Bengal Rose

These are noted for their fine, almost evergreen foliage, which is extremely resistant to disease, and for their profuse, ever-blooming habit.

3

SPECIAL HABITATS

21.1 Prairie flowers and grasses are not only rich and varied but represent a very specific ecological system. Photo Arthur Ode

21

Prairie and Meadow

PRAIRIE

From Indiana to the Rockies, from Saskatchewan to Texas, there once existed the great American prairies. These grasslands differed from one region to another according to climatic and soil variations, but the presence of grass and the absence of trees throughout these vast areas definitely distinguished them from adjacent forested regions. In addition to these naturally occurring grasslands of America's Midwest, there are myriad similar sites, some of natural origin and some man-made, which cannot technically be called prairies. Such areas are called meadows, and these exhibit the same characteristic absence of trees and presence of grass and other herbaceous vegetation as do prairies. From a landscape standpoint, and ecologically as well, prairie and natural meadow are intrinsically valuable because they are prime habitats in which have evolved many sun-loving wildflowers. Both vegetational types also offer landscape opportunities for the creation of vistas, "open space," woodland borders and dramatic foregrounds and backdrops for architectural structures.

Early explorers and settlers frequently described the American prairie as an awesome vastness, which reminded them of almost endless oceans. "A swell and swale reminiscent of the seas," or "an ocean of grass," were common analogies. Indeed, the wagons of the pioneers were even called "prairie schooners," intimat-ing that they sailed the prairies as though upon oceans. The tall grasses of these prairies waved in rhythm with the wind, whose unbroken currents were not buffered by trees as they are in the forested regions.

Prairies are separated into several rather distinct geographic types across the continent, according to the availability of moisture. The continental distribution of rainfall determines the existence of short-grass prairie in the rain shadow of the Rocky Mountains, mid-grass prairie in the Great Plains and tall-grass prairie in the eastern reaches of the Midwest. Where rainfall exceeds 30 in. annually, deciduous forest becomes the dominant vegetational type. Throughout this vast prairie region prairie ecotypes are also determined by local soil moisture regimes, and these can be characterized as wet (lowland), mesic (upland) and dry (steep hillside). Each of these vegetational types has its characteristic flora and its unique beauty. In addition to these distinct prairie types, there are various associations with other vegetational types, such as oak-openings (prairie interspersed with oaks), pine barrens (pine and prairie) and savanna (prairie interspersed with occasional trees).

The vast, seemingly endless prairie of yesteryear, with its buffalo and Indian, has largely disappeared; it exists today only in the form of occasional relics, preserved by chance from the ubiquitous "cow and plow" of the pioneer. Areas unsuitable for farming, such as steep hillsides or undrainable wetlands, have here and there remained inviolate; likewise old settlers' cemeteries and some railroad rights-of-way also still harbor the indigenous prairie grasses and wildflowers.

Although the prairie as a continental ecosystem has largely been replaced by corn, wheat and European pasture grasses, the concepts of prairie as a landscape architectural form and of prairie grass species as range forage have made astonishing progress in recent years. The use of the major prairie grass species in restoring midwestern and western range lands emerged from the catastrophic era of the Dust Bowl in the 1930s, which was precipitated by appalling ignorance and by the wanton misuse of land, through improvident farming practices and overgrazing of the Great Plains. The U.S. Soil Conservation Service and various midwestern universities carried out pioneering research on the little-known native grasses, many of which are now available commercially and are in wide use. This commercially available stock of native grasses (and wildflowers) is also finding increasing use along roadsides, on reclaimed strip-mines, for industrial and commercial sites and in suburban home landscapes.

Prairie preservation has become an important aspect of national, state and local agency land management, and the recreation of prairies—upon suitable sites, and with appropriate kinds and numbers of grasses, wildflowers and legumes—has now achieved a popularity virtually inconceivable as recently as a decade ago. Today, nearly every major midwestern land grant university has undertaken a prairie restoration project, and prairie has been accepted as a popular design feature in landscape architecture. But recreating a prairie is a complicated undertaking at best, and a reconstruction can never be more than an approximation of the original entity. The approximation will vary in complexity according to the expertise and goals of those planning such reconstruction. The universities of Wisconsin and Iowa, among others; the Morton Arboretum, Lisle, Illinois; and the Boerner Botanical Garden, Milwaukee, Wisconsin, have done yeoman work in creating intricate prairie restorations.

Even as the original prairies of the pioneer conjured up a sense of vastness, of "oceans" of grass, so too the larger restorations can recreate this same mood. On the other hand, the smaller restorations and relics owe their popularity to another aspect of the prairie—its incredible diversity. The prairie is a climax community (a stable, self-perpetuating community of plants) of ancient lineage, developed to its fullest extent, with every possible ecological niche occupied by one or more organisms duly adapted to it through millennia of natural selection. Many of these plants are traditional garden perennials, which were originally collected from the prairie. Among these are the purple coneflower, *Echinacea purpurea;* sunflowers; goldenrods; black-eyed Susans; the lead plant, *Amorpha canescens;* and wild false indigos. The gardener who knows these prairie wildflowers as familiar perennial border plants will readily perceive that these old friends are transcendent species between prairie and what are popularly termed meadow (or "field" or "roadside") flowers in the eastern United States.

MEADOW

Meadow is a specialized habitat also dependent upon full sun and the absence of woody vegetation, and contains many of the same species as prairie. It does not represent, however, a climax community, and in the absence of intervention by man it would soon proceed through natural plant succession to woodland. Not being a recreation or relict of a specific natural community, as the prairie is, the meadow's components may contain herbaceous plants from any ecosystem that will adapt to it, as well as horticultural plants and even alien weeds. These components can be utilized architecturally in much the same way as prairie: as open space, providing and maintaining vistas; as a foil for woodland background; or to blend with formal lawns. An important ecological aspect of both meadow and prairie is their creation of habitat for ground-nesting birds and small mammals, which in turn fosters the return of hawks, owls, foxes and other predator species. This increase in diversity of animal and bird populations is aesthetically as important as the visual aspect of such landscapes.

Meadow and prairie also share similarities in

the maintenance methods necessary to perpetuate them. In order to maintain a meadow, woody vegetation such as trees and shrubs must be repelled. Mowing the area once a year will accomplish this task, without damage to the herbaceous species. In fact, meadows mowed once a year will actually increase in the diversity of sun-loving herbaceous perennials, given a nearby natural seed source or their introduction. Herbicides have also been used to reduce woody plant competition, but this is usually self-defeating from an aesthetic viewpoint, since most herbicides eradicate wild flowers while favoring grasses.

Prairie, although a natural climax vegetational community, is in a constant state of flux with the forest border, particularly in its eastern reaches or elsewhere where rainfall over extended periods is sufficient to encourage forestation. During historical drought cycles the prairie has encroached upon forest, and during periods of plentiful moisture the forest has advanced. Prairie wildfires have had a significant effect upon the history of the prairie, as a factor selecting against woody vegetation and perpetuating prairie. Fires were often deliberately set by the Plains Indians as a means of hunting game, and perhaps for other reasons as well. In addition, lightning or accidents frequently ignited such fires. With the advance of settlement, however, fires were controlled, and many prairies then developed into brush and ultimately forest. In light of these historical facts, fire has become a common and even necessary modern prairie management tool. In addition to woody vegetation, the prairie has another nemesis: Kentucky bluegrass. Bluegrass forms a dense sod in response to continual mowing or heavy grazing, and is highly competitive with the bunch grasses native to prairie. Bluegrass sod precludes the establishment of wildflowers, and once it invades an area, it is extremely persistent. Bluegrass is a cool-season grass, growing vigorously in early spring while native prairie vegetation is still dormant. Burning a prairie at this juncture not only destroys woody vegetation but seriously weakens the bluegrass sod. If burning is not feasible, prairies, like meadows, must be mowed once a year; but fire is the best tool for managing the prairie, and is equally beneficial to the meadow.

MAINTENANCE OF MEADOWS AND PRAIRIES

The management of existing meadows and relict prairies is relatively straightforward, once the basic principles are understood. Establishing a new meadow or prairie is a more complex venture. A lawn mowed several times a year is still a lawn; a lawn unmowed will undergo secondary succession, leading eventually to woodland in the forested regions of America. Lawn mowed once in the fall, or burned periodically where possible, will be maintained in meadow. Mowing or burning, thereby repelling woody vegetation, encourages the establishment of sun-loving wildflowers such as sunflowers, goldenrods, asters, milkweeds, and so on. Meadow grasses will have an entirely different aspect than mowed lawn. Even bluegrass will attain heights of 1 ft. or more, and seasonal color changes and wind motion will be evident. Meadow can be enriched by adding suitable horticultural species, or by collecting and introducing wildlings, either by transplanting or direct seeding.

Prairie restoration is a more intellectual endeavor, which requires site analysis and proper species selection. It must always be understood that the objective is to recreate an ecosystem, insofar as possible, and that the beauty is dependent not only upon architectural expression and horticultural selection but also upon the diversity of the components and the functioning of the biotic community. An existing relict can be carefully enriched by adding members to the community, either by direct seeding or with transplants. Areas with no prairie species can be seeded directly after preparation of the seedbed in much the same way as for standard lawn grasses. Seed can be obtained from several commercial sources, often from midwestern universities, botanical gardens and nature centers. Perhaps the most rewarding method of prairie restoration is to search out local prairie remnants and obtain permission to collect seed. Seed mixtures sown and raked lightly into almost any reasonably fertile topsoil will produce seedlings during the first growing season, providing they have either been stratified naturally by seeding in the fall or artificially stratified and sown in the spring. During the first year or two prairie plants are minuscule and characteristi-

21.2 *Butterfly weed* (Asclepias tuberosa), *a favorite plant of many gardens, is at home in many meadows. Photo Grant Heilman*

cally produce more roots than top growth. This is a critical period, and the new prairie should be either hand-weeded (which takes considerable expertise at identifying seedlings), or mowed at a height of 6 in. with a rotary mower, which will discourage the weeds but not harm the tiny prairie seedlings. The novice will not see the "prairie" until the third or fourth year, when the plants will indicate their presence by their beautiful blooms. Prairie plants can also be successfully sown in seed flats, stratified, and grown under greenhouse or coldframe culture until transplantable. This method produces excellent results, but it does presuppose proper equipment and ample hand labor.

The above account of prairie establishment procedures is necessarily abbreviated, but there is ample recent literature on techniques for particular prairie ecotypes and locations, and the serious amateur will want to consult them before undertaking any such project.

Only a few decades ago, as scientists and naturalists across the nation decried the devastation of the Dust Bowl and mourned the passing of the prairie ecosystem, it was impossible to foresee the rebirth of interest in this indispensable aspect of the American biota that has taken place today. This phenomenon, coupled with the understanding of meadows and their usefulness, has opened up new vistas, in a literal sense, upon the North American landscape.

MEADOW OR PRAIRIE DEMONSTRATION PROJECTS AND INFORMATION SOURCES

Cornell College
Department of Biology
Mount Vernon, Iowa 52314

Iowa State University
Department of Botany
Ames, Iowa 50010

Knox College
Galesburg, Illinois 61401

Longwood Gardens
Kennett Square, Pennsylvania 19348

Missouri Department of Conservation
Columbia, Missouri 65201

The Morton Arboretum
Lisle, Illinois 60532

Natural Vegetation Committee
5717 Baldwin
Lincoln, Nebraska 68507

New York Botanical Garden
Bronx, New York 10458

The University of Wisconsin Arboretum
Madison, Wisconsin 53700

The Wehr Nature Center
5879 South 92nd Street
Hales Corners, Wisconsin 53131

REPRESENTATIVE PRAIRIE AND MEADOW PLANTS

SCIENTIFIC NAME	COMMON NAME	HEIGHT	COLOR	BLOOM	HABITAT
Allium cernuum	nodding wild onion	1–2 ft.	pink-white	July–August	moist-mesic prairies
Amorpha canescens	lead plant	1½–3 ft.	violet	June–July	dry-mesic prairies, sandy open woods
Andropogon gerardi	big bluestem grass, turkeyfoot grass	4–6 ft.	auburn after frost	August–Sept.	moist-dry prairies
Andropogon scoparius	little bluestem grass, poverty grass	2–4 ft.	auburn-orange in autumn	August–Sept.	mesic-dry prairies, roadsides, abandoned farm fields
Anemone canadensis	windflower	1–2 ft.	white	May–July	mesic prairie, open woods
Anemone cylindrica	thimbleweed	12–20 in.	white	June–July	dry to mesic prairies
Anemone patens	pasqueflower	4–10 in.	blue	April	dry-mesic prairies
Antennaria sp.	pussytoes	4–12 in.	white	May	dry prairies, open woodlands, rock garden plant
Apocynum androsaemifolium	dogbane	1–4 ft.	pink	June–July	open woods, edges, prairies, meadows; prefers sandy, acid soil
Apocynum cannabinum	Indian hemp	1–3 ft.	white	June–August	mesic-dry prairies
Artemesia caudata	beach wormwood	1–3 ft.	green to bronze	Oct.	sandy and gravelly prairies and open woods
Asclepias amplexicaulis	sand milkweed	1–2½ ft.	greenish-purple	June–July	sandy prairies and woods
Asclepias incarnata	swamp milkweed	2–4 ft.	pink	June–August	wet meadows, prairies
Asclepias syriaca	common milkweed	1–2 ft.	pink	June–August	dry-mesic prairies, meadows
Asclepias tuberosa	butterfly weed	1–2½ ft.	orange	June–August	dry-mesic prairies, meadows, fields; common garden perennial
Asclepias verticillata	whorled milkweed	8–20 in.	white	June–August	dry-mesic prairies, open woods
Aster azureus	azure aster	1–4 ft.	blue-violet	Sept.–Oct.	dry-mesic or sandy prairies
Aster ericoides	heath aster	1–3 ft.	white	Sept.	dry-mesic prairies, sterile meadows
Aster laevis	smooth aster	1–3 ft.	blue-violet	Sept.–Oct.	dry-moist prairies, meadows
Aster novae-angliae	New England aster	1–4 ft.	violet-purple	August–Oct.	moist-mesic meadows, prairies
Aster ptarmicoides	stiff aster	1–2 ft.	white	August–Sept.	dry, gravelly dunes and hills
Aster sericeus	western silvery aster	1–2 ft.	purple-violet	Oct.	dry prairies, meadows
Baptisia leucantha	white wild indigo	2–4 ft.	white	June	moist-dry prairies, meadows, thickets
Baptisia leucophaea	cream wild indigo	1–2½ ft.	cream	June	mesic-dry prairies, meadows, dunes
Bouteloua curtipendula	side-oats, gramma grass	1–3 ft.	attractive florets and seeds	July–Sept.	dry prairies
Calamagrostis canadensis	bluejoint reed grass	2–4 ft.	purple, lead-colored florets	July–August	wet meadows, prairies
Ceanothus americanus	New Jersey tea	1½–3 ft.	white	July	dry woods, meadows, sands
Circium discolor	old field thistle	3–5 ft.	purple	August–Sept.	biennial of meadows, old fields
Coreopsis palmata	tickseed	1½–3 ft.	yellow	June–July	mesic prairies and meadows
Desmodium canadense	tick trefoil	2–4 ft.	rose-purple	July–August	mesic-wet prairies, meadows, open woods
Dodecatheon meadia	shootingstar	1 ft.	white-pink	May–June	prairie and meadow; garden and rock garden plant

(Continued)

REPRESENTATIVE PRAIRIE AND MEADOW PLANTS (Continued)

SCIENTIFIC NAME	COMMON NAME	HEIGHT	COLOR	BLOOM	HABITAT
Echinacea purpurea	purple coneflower	2–4 ft.	purple	June–Sept.	dry prairies, meadows, open woods; garden perennial
Elymus canadensis	Canada wild rye	2–3 ft.	showy tan seedheads	July–August	prairies, meadows
Erigeron strigosus	daisy fleabane	1–2 ft.	white-pink	May–Sept.	prairies, meadows
Eryngium yuccifolium	rattlesnake master	3–4 ft.	white	July–August	moist-dry prairie
Eupatorium perfoliatum	boneset	2–3 ft.	white	Sept.–Oct.	meadows, prairies
Euphorbia corollata	flowering spurge	2–3 ft.	white	June–Sept.	prairies, meadows, open woods
Fragaria virginiana	wild strawberry	5–8 in.	white	May–July	meadows, prairies, open woods, many variable sites
Gentiana andrewsii	bottle gentian	1–2 ft.	blue	Sept.–Oct.	wet-mesic prairies; requires acid soil; garden perennial
Gentiana crinata	fringed gentian	1 ft.	blue	Sept.–Nov.	wet-mesic prairies, meadows, woods; garden perennial
Geranium maculatum	wild geranium	1–2 ft.	rose-purple	May–June	moist meadows, prairies, woods
Helianthus grosseserratus	sawtooth sunflower	6–10 ft.	yellow	August–Oct.	wet-mesic prairies, meadows
Helianthus laetiflorus var. rigidus	stiff or showy sunflower	2–6 ft.	yellow	August–Oct.	dry prairies
Helianthus occidentalis	western sunflower	1–3 ft.	yellow	August–Oct.	dry-mesic prairies
Helianthus strumosus	rough sunflower	3–6 ft.	yellow	July–Sept.	wood's edges, meadows
Heliopsis helianthoides	oxeye	2–5 ft.	orange-yellow	June–Oct.	prairies, meadows, open woods
Heuchera richardsonii	alumroot	2–3 ft.	chartreuse	May–June	prairies, rocky areas
Iris virginica	blueflag	2–3 ft.	blue-violet	May–July	wet meadows, marshes
Kuhnia eupatorioides	false boneset	1–4 ft.	white	August–Sept.	dry, sandy soils, open areas
Lathyrus venosus	wild pea, vetchling	2–3 ft.	purple	June–July	prairies, meadows, stream banks
Lespedeza capitata	bush clover	2–4 ft.	cream	August–Sept.	prairies, barrens, dry meadows
Liatris aspera	blazing-star, gay-feather, Kansas gay-feather	1½–4 ft.	rose-purple	August–Sept.	prairies, garden perennial
Lilium michiganense	Michigan lily	2–6 ft.	red-orange	June–August	wet-mesic prairie, meadow, open woods
Lilium philadelphicum	wood lily	1½–2½ ft.	red-orange	June–August	dry meadows, prairies, open woods; requires acid soil; garden perennial
Lithospermum canescens	hoary puccoon	8–12 in.	golden-yellow	May–June	dry-moist prairies; several similar species in East; garden and rock garden plant
Lobelia spicata	pale lobelia	1–3 ft.	blue-white	June–August	prairies and sandy areas
Lupinus perinnis	wild lupine	1–2 ft.	blue-pink	May–June	dry meadows, prairies
Monarda fistulosa	wild bergamot	2–3 ft.	pink	July–August	meadows and prairies, tolerant
Oenothera biennis	evening primrose	2–5 ft.	yellow	July–Oct.	meadows and prairies; tolerant of site
Panicum virgatum	switch-grass	3–5 ft.	auburn autumn foliage	July–Sept.	meadows, prairies, shores
Penstemon digitalis	beard tongue	3–5 ft.	white	July–August	meadows, prairies; tolerant of site; garden perennial
Petalostemum purpureum	purple prairie clover	1–3 ft.	purple	July–August	prairies and dry meadows

REPRESENTATIVE PRAIRIE AND MEADOW PLANTS (Continued)

SCIENTIFIC NAME	COMMON NAME	HEIGHT	COLOR	BLOOM	HABITAT
Phlox pilosa	prairie phlox	1–2 ft.	red-purple	May–July	meadows, prairies, open
Polygala senega	Seneca snakeroot	16–20 in.	greenish-white	May–June	rocky barrens, dry prairies
Potentilla fruticosa	shrubby cinquefoil	3 ft.	yellow	June–Sept.	meadows, prairies; tolerant; on calcareous soils
Pycnanthemum virginianum	mountain mint	1½–2½ ft.	white	July–Sept.	woods, marshes, meadows, prairies
Ratibida pinnata	yellow coneflower	1–3 ft.	yellow	July–August	dry prairies and meadows
Rosa blanda	prairie rose	to 6 ft.	pink-white	June–August	calcareous or neutral meadows, prairies
Rosa carolina	prairie rose	to 3 ft.	pink	May–July	dry meadows and prairies
Rudbeckia hirta	black-eyed Susan	1–3 ft.	yellow	July–August	meadows, prairies, disturbed areas; acidic soils
Silphium laciniatum	compassplant	4–8 ft.	yellow	June–August	mesic prairies
Silphium terebinthinaceum	rosinweed	5–7 ft.	yellow	July–Sept.	prairies and openings
Sisyrinchium campestre	blue-eyed grass	6–10 in.	blue	May–June	prairies and sands
Solidago canadensis	Canada goldenrod	1–4 ft.	yellow	August–Sept.	meadows and prairies
Solidago gramnifolia	grassleaf goldenrod	2–5 ft.	yellow	August–Oct.	meadows, shores, prairies
Solidago nemoralis	old field goldenrod	1–3 ft.	yellow	August–Oct.	dry woods, prairies, meadows, disturbed areas
Solidago rigida	stiff goldenrod	2–4 ft.	yellow	August–Oct.	dry-mesic prairies, meadows
Solidago speciosa	showy goldenrod	2–6 ft.	yellow	August–Oct.	dry-mesic prairies, meadows; garden perennial
Sorghastrum nutans	Indian grass	3–5 ft.	purple flowers, bronze autumn foliage	August–Sept.	prairies, meadows, dry slopes
Spartina pectinata	cordgrass, sloughgrass	3–6 ft.	brown autumn foliage	July–August	marshes, shores, wet meadows and prairies
Spiraea alba	meadowsweet	3–5 ft.	white	July–August	wet prairies, meadows, shores
Spiranthes cernua	nodding ladies' tresses	1–2 ft.	cream		wet meadows, prairies, bogs, shores
Sporobolus heterolepis	prairie dropseed grass	2–3 ft.	seeds very ornamental	August	dry-moist prairies, and dry rock (limestone and serpentine) in Northeast
Stipa spartea	needlegrass	2–4 ft.	decorative seeds	June	dry prairies, open woods
Thalictrum dasycarpum	purple meadow rue	3–4 ft.	'white-purple	June–July	wet prairies, stream banks
Tradescantia ohiensis	spiderwort	2–3 ft.	blue-rose	June–August	meadows, prairies, sandy open woods; garden perennial, often escaped
Verbena stricta	blue vervain	2–3 ft.	blue-purple	June–Sept.	meadows, prairies, swamps
Veronia noveboracensis	ironweed	3–7 ft.	violet	August–Oct.	meadows, stream banks
Veronicastrum virginicum	culversroot	3–5 ft.	white	July–August	rich soil, meadows and prairies
Vicea americana	American vetch	2–3 ft.	blue-purple	May–August	dry-moist prairies and shores
Viola pedata	bird's-foot violet	3–6 in.	violet-purple, white	May–June	dry prairies, meadows, dunes; infertile acid soils, rock gardens
Viola sagittata	arrowleaf violet	2–5 in.	violet-purple	May–June	dry meadows and prairies
Zizea aurea	golden alexander	1–2 ft.	yellow	May–June	meadows, moist prairies, damp woods

22.1. Daffodils (**Narcissus**) *are so well suited to planting in woodlands that this scene is a very familiar one. Photo Grant Heilman*

22

The Woodland Garden

One of the most beautiful expressions of landscape art is to be found in the woodland garden. Here the ideals are not those of the flower garden, where perfection of bloom or variety in horticultural forms is the desideratum, but rather a representation of unaltered natural forms. Only wild flowers as they grow in nature should be included, and they should be given a setting closely resembling in appearance and physical condition that of their natural habitat. Since such a woodland is fundamentally a garden, it is not a copy or reproduction of nature, but rather a place for growing wild flowers in their accustomed way. It is, in fact, a garden of flowers either in their native habitat, or so recently brought from the wild that they have changed not at all in appearance or in their cultural requirements.

Purists may wish to cultivate in their woodland garden only plants that are native to the local area or certain geographic regions. Those with more eclectic tastes or different interests may bring plants into the woodland garden which come from farther away, but are nonetheless near relatives, or have cultural requirements that are very similar to those of the natives.

THE SITE

The owner of property containing a mature woodland has the ideal situation for a garden of woodland flowers. Indeed, the development of such a tract into a woodland garden is just as logical and natural as is the development of the open sunny spaces into gardens of herbaceous flowers.

For many centuries gardeners have been devoting their effort and skill to developing sun-loving plants, but it is only within the last half century in this country that serious effort has been made with the flora of the forest. We now recognize this as a whole new phase of gardening, with its own techniques.

THE DESIGN

The limitations of a woodland area should be recognized in the very beginning and every effort should be made to turn into assets those features of the place that might otherwise be regarded as liabilities. A woodland garden must necessarily be developed along naturalistic lines. The informal grouping of the trees themselves determines, to a very large extent, the nature of the design.

There is a general impression that an informal design in planning any type of garden is a much more simple and less intricate thing than a formal scheme. On the contrary, the opposite is usually true. There is usually something very straightforward and quite obvious about the design of a formal garden, whereas the design of an informal area, if studied, possesses a

423

22.2. The coming together of woodland plantings and more formalized portions of the garden provides the contrast of smooth lawn and clean line. Photo Carlton Lees

subtle quality and charm that is difficult to define.

Planning the woodland garden does not necessarily require exact plotting of ground areas or the spacing out of plants on a predetermined planting plan. But there should be forethought in the planning of major masses of foliage and flowers for the sake of good composition and balance, and for the separation of the plants into groups that are congenial and require similar soil conditions. If the site includes areas of dissimilar soil conditions, the plants must be assigned to the spaces where they naturally belong and in which they will develop to their fullest potential. Thus a certain tract might have dry soil on the upper levels, neutral soil in a large area, acid soil where oak trees stand and wet soil along a stream valley. Whether the plan is actually committed to paper or not, it should be sufficiently definite to keep the plants in the situations where they thrive best and to allot the more difficult conditions to those plants that are best able to withstand them.

The person who is a novice in the art of gardening with wildflowers will find that it is possible to develop very attractive groups of plantings by using some of the more easily grown bulbs and perennials that adapt themselves readily to woodland conditions. Masses of pale lavender-blue phlox under a group of white birches in early spring; English primroses and wood anemones blooming along a woodland path; foxgloves lifting their stately spires against a background of deep forest green — such delightful pictures may be obtained with a moderate expenditure of time and money.

However, the experienced gardener may not be content to limit his or her attention to the more easily grown woodland plants. This person will want to be challenged a bit more, and will attempt to naturalize some of the more fastidious woodland flowers. An adventure of this sort is full of interest and delight.

Woodland Paths

The paths in a woodland area should be as natural in appearance as possible. The surface should be kept free of encroaching growth, sharp stones, small stumps and snags of all kinds. A natural surface of fallen leaves is pleasant, but if the paths are frequently used a more permanent surface may be desirable.

The materials best suited for such a purpose are tanbark, pine needles and wood chips. Tanbark is readily procurable in many areas of the country and it makes an extremely satisfactory surface. It is a reddish, woodsy brown, and provides a soft, springy surface upon which to walk. Tanbark also has the advantage of drying out very quickly after a rain and never becoming soggy. Since tanbark will, in time, disintegrate and have to be renewed, it is a wise practice to add a small amount each season. Pine needs are always attractive but soon disintegrate and will give comparatively short service unless a very thick layer is used. And unless one is within easy range of a pine grove, they may be difficult to procure. Wood chips may usually be obtained at small cost. They are easily spread and form a very fine surface. In appearance they are somewhat less attractive than other materials, but this objection to their use may be overcome by applying a light covering of either tanbark or pine needles over the chips. Wood chips disintegrate very slowly and will give good service for a number of years.

Developing Small Areas

One need not necessarily have a piece of natural woodland on one's property in order to have the enjoyment of wildflowers in early spring. Often, even in a small suburban property, there is a semishaded spot under a group of trees where some of the woodland plants can be made to feel at home. In such an area the dainty little wood anemone, the spring beauty, hepatica, dog-tooth violet, jack-in-the-pulpit, Solomon's-seal, mertensia, bloodroot, *Phlox divaricata, Trillium grandiflorum* and many other woodland plants can be naturalized quite easily. And small though the area may be, one can have the joy of watching for the first flowers of spring—the lovely, glistening white flowers of the bloodroot, which turn always to catch the rays of sunlight, and the exquisite, dainty flowers of the hepaticas nestling among the leaves. Later in the spring the delicate lavender-blue of wild phlox and the gleaming white of trilliums will make a lovely harmony.

A natural woodland area has a soil rich in humus that provides ideal conditions for native plants. However, when one undertakes to develop a small wild garden under trees that have but recently been planted, one may find that the soil lacks the qualities of a natural woodland soil. It may be heavy in texture and lacking in humus, for example. In such a case it should be carefully prepared before any planting is done. Generous quantities of rotted leaf mold and compost should be worked into the soil so that it will provide congenial conditions for the woodland plants that are to make it their home.

SOIL REQUIREMENTS

Woodland plants vary greatly in their soil requirements; in their native habitats they are found growing where the soil, and other conditions, best meet their needs.

Some woodland plants prefer soils that are alkaline or nearly neutral in reaction, others thrive best in moderately acid soils, a few grow only in soils that are intensely acid, and some are indifferent to soil conditions. The moisture conditions of the soil are also a matter for consideration, as some plants prefer a moist or moderately moist woodsy soil, while others prefer a somewhat dry soil.

It is therefore important to become familiar with the soil requirements of the plants one wishes to grow, and to provide conditions for them that are congenial and will be favorable for their best development.

All natural woodland soils, especially those of the deciduous hardwood forests, are rich in humus, due to the decomposition of leaves and branches that is contantly taking place on the forest floor. It is in woodlands of this type—where the shade is not too dense and the soil is well supplied with humus and is only mildly acid—that most of our woodland flowers are happily at home. These are the flowers that may be grown in a home woodland area and that, once well established, will often spread, as they require only their natural conditions.

However, a few of our most beautiful woodland plants, such as the pink lady's slipper *(Cypripedium acaule)*, the trailing arbutus *(Epigaea repens)*, and some of the lovely native azaleas and rhododendrons, will thrive only in areas where the soil is quite acid. It is useless to attempt to grow plants in this group unless one is willing to make the effort necessary to provide conditions that will meet their specific needs. This may be done by providing soil that is rich in humus and strongly acid and by maintaining the correct degree of acidity from year to year. (For the various methods, see under Acidity of Soil in the index.)

Increasing the acidity of the soil is important, but it is not always the only conditioning process necessary. For rhododendrons, azaleas, mountain laurel, some of the cypripediums and many of the ferns, the soil should be moist but porous and well drained.

SHRUBS AND SMALL TREES FOR THE WOODLAND

In almost every natural woodland an undergrowth of native shrubs will be found. Some of these shrubs are of great beauty and should be carefully preserved, while others are weedy in character and should be kept under control or completely eradicated.

If some of the more desirable shrubs are not available in a piece of woodland, they may be purchased from any nursery that makes a specialty of native plant materials. Such shrubs will add greatly to the beauty and interest of the planting.

Among the native shrubs most worthy of a place in a woodland planting, because of the beauty of their foliage, fruit or flowers, are the red chokeberry *(Aronia arbutifolia);* the native azaleas, such as the flame azalea *(Rhododendron calendulacuem),* the pinxter flower *(R. periclymenoides)* and the beautiful pink-shell azalea *(R. vaseyi);* the spice bush *(Lindera benzoin)* with its fragrant yellow flowers in very early spring; mountain laurel *(Kalmia latifolia),* the glory of many a hillside woodland in late spring; the beautiful dwarf-growing Carolina rhododendron *(R. carolinianum)* and the larger *R. catawbiense* and *R. maximum,* if space permits. The witch hazels, including *Hamamelis mollis, H. vernalis, H. virginiana* and the handsome cultivars of *Hamamelis* x *intermedia,* are other large shrubs that are all at home in the woodland garden too.

There are also a number of small trees that

should be included, if they are not already growing in the woodland, such as the eastern dogwood *(Cornus florida),* which is one of our most beautiful small native trees; the redbud or Judas tree *(Cercis canadensis),* bearing deep pink flowers in early spring; the lovely silverbell tree *(Halesia carolina)* with its dainty bell-like flowers; and the shadbush or service berry *(Amelanchier canadensis),* bridelike when in bloom.

CAUTION: Many of our beautiful woodland wildflowers are becoming increasingly rare as their habitats continue to be destroyed by the onward march of civilization. Each year more forest is lost to housing developments, industrial and shopping complexes, and highway projects. Efforts to establish wildflower sanctuaries in densely populated urban areas often fail to preserve populations of rare plants in sufficient numbers to ensure their continued existence over large portions of their natural range. Digging plants from the woods to bring into the garden can only serve to complicate this serious problem. Besides, many plants that are dug in the wild fail to survive transplanting into the garden unless done by an expert. Such transplanting should be attempted only as a rescue effort when native plants are being threatened with eradication, and even then it should be done only with extreme care.

Most wildflowers can be propagated by means of seeds, cuttings or divisions. Many of the better wildflower nurseries have considerable expertise in these methods. Those wildflower nurseries that clearly state it is their policy not to dig plants in the wild (except as a rescue effort, which many nurseries actually do) are by far the most responsible and usually the best sources of wildflowers for the garden.

NATIVE WOODLAND FLOWERS OF SPECIAL MERIT

Anemone quinquefolia (wood anemone, wind flower)

The dainty white blossoms of the wood anemone are among the most exquisite of all woodland flowers, blooming from early April

22.3 In most woodlands, violets (Viola papilionacea) make unbroken ground carpets; although this spring flower is fragrant and lovely, the plants can invade areas where they are not wanted. Photo Grant Heilman

to late May. The slender, delicate stems are hardly more than 6 in. in height, and the deeply lobed leaves are borne in whorls below the flowers.

Distribution: From Canada south to Georgia and west to Kentucky and Ohio.

Preferred habitat: Open woodlands, hillsides; particularly along the borders of moist, open woods.

Soil requirements: Moist, moderately acid soil.

Culture: The wood anemone is somewhat difficult to establish. Plants should be purchased in containers from a nursery.

Period of bloom: April to June.

Aquilegia canadensis (American columbine)

Unfortunately *Aquilegia canadensis* is disappearing from many of its native habitats. The small flowers are scarlet and yellow and are borne on slender stems that vary in height from 1 ft. to 2 ft.

Distribution: From Nova Scotia to Florida, and west to Minnesota and Tennessee.

Preferred habitat: Rather dry, rocky ledges; partial shade.

Soil requirements: Thrives best in a soil that is very nearly neutral. It can tolerate neither extreme acidity nor pronounced alkalinity.

Culture: Plants should be purchased from a nursery. Despite its long tap roots *Aquilegia canadensis* may be transplanted readily and it is not difficult to establish, provided that soil conditions are favorable.

Period of bloom: April to May.

Arisaema triphyllum (Jack-in-the-pulpit)

This wilding is one of the most beloved denizens of our woods and it is particularly lovely when planted among ferns. Its floral hood is yellow-green in color, often with brown-purple stripes, and is quite pale when growing in the sun. Later the berries turn a bright scarlet.

Distribution: From Nova Scotia westward to Minnesota and southward to the Gulf States.

Preferred habitat: Moist woodlands among underbrush.

Soil requirements: Thrives best in neutral soil,

being able to tolerate neither extreme acidity nor pronounced alkalinity.

Culture: Plants may be purchased from many nurseries. If soil conditions are congenial, the plants are easy to establish, and they spread rapidly. They may be grown readily from seed.

Period of bloom: April–July.

Cimicifuga racemosa (black cohosh, snakeroot)

So many of our woodland flowers come during the spring months that one rejoices to find something for midsummer bloom, and it is during July and August that the tall, stately white spires of cohosh or snakeroot add their share of beauty to a woodland planting. The plants vary in height from 3 ft. to 8 ft.

Distribution: From Maine to Georgia and westward from Ontario to Missouri.

Preferred habitat: Deep, moist woods, wooded hillsides, woodland borders.

Soil requirements: Prefers a rich woodland soil but is indifferent to soil acidity, thriving in either neutral or acid soil.

Culture: May be transplanted very easily and becomes readily established.

Period of bloom: July–August.

Claytonia virginica (spring beauty)

Blooming soon after hepatica, the spring beauties are among the earliest of our woodland flowers. The dainty fragile blooms are borne in loose terminal racemes and the slender stems seldom reach a height of more than 8 in.

or 10 in. The flowers vary from white to pale pink.

Distribution: From Nova Scotia to Georgia and westward.

Preferred habitat: Moist, open woods, low meadows.

Soil requirements: Thrives best in soil that is very nearly neutral.

Culture: Most effective when planted in drifts or masses. The plants should be spaced from 4 in. to 6 in. apart.

Period of bloom: March and April.

Cypripedium acaule (moccasin flower, pink lady's slipper)

The clear pink blooms of the moccasin flower are startling in their beauty when come upon in some deep forest glade, and one feels a sense of triumph when one achieves this beauty in a woodland planting. The flowers are borne on stems hardly more than 10 in. in height.

Distribution: From Canada southward to North Carolina, and westward to Minnesota and Kentucky.

Preferred habitat: Deep, rocky or sandy woods. It is found in both dry and moist situations and has been known to thrive well in full sun, although it definitely prefers partial shade.

Soil requirements: Intensely acid woodland soil.

Culture: Plants should be purchased from a nursery. No attempt should be made to transplant them from the wild. During the first season after planting they should be kept constantly moist and mulched with pine needles. *Cypripedium acaule* is not difficult to establish provided that the soil conditions are congenial, as the acidity of the soil is the secret of success. In planting cypripediums, the crown should never be entirely buried, the tip being approximately ¼ in. above the surface. It is best to plant cypripediums in very early spring while entirely dormant, or in late August and early September, the latter month being preferred.

Period of bloom: May and June.

Cypripedium calceolus var. pubescens (yellow lady's slipper)

The yellow lady's slipper is of such rare beauty and easy culture that it should be included in every woodland planting. The flowers are of a soft luminous yellow hue, borne on slender stems varying in height from 12 in. to 18 in.

Distribution: From Nova Scotia to Alabama, westward to Minnesota, Louisiana, Arizona and Oregon.

Preferred habitat: Rich, moist, stony soil in deciduous woods.

Soil requirements: Rather indifferent to soil acidity, thriving equally well in neutral or somewhat acid soil.

Culture: The plants should be purchased from a nursery. They are easy to establish and thrive exceedingly well if the surroundings are congenial. Planting directions as for *C. acaule.*

Period of bloom: May and June.

Dodecatheon meadia (shooting-star)

The dainty, cyclamenlike flowers are borne on tall, slender, leafless stems, which often reach a height of 20 in. or more. The blossoms vary in color from flesh-white to pink and are as exquisite as tiny butterflies. The leaves form a rosettelike growth close to the ground.

Distribution: Pennsylvania southward to Georgia and westward from Texas to Manitoba.

Preferred habitat: Moist hillsides, open woods, tops of cliffs. Thrives in full sun or partial shade.

Soil requirements: Best in soil that is very nearly neutral. It can tolerate neither extreme acidity nor pronounced alkalinity.

Culture: The plants are listed in many catalogues. They are of easy culture and grow well if supplied with ample moisture, provided soil conditions are congenial.

Period of bloom: April and May.

Epigaea repens (trailing arbutus, mayflower)

Few woodland flowers are more universally beloved than the trailing arbutus, and it is tragic, indeed, that where once it flourished so abundantly it is now fairly rare because of thoughtless vandalism. The fragile beauty of its blossoms and their exquisite fragrance have endeared it to many generations, and fortunately it is not difficult to cultivate if one has proper soil conditions.

Distribution: From Newfoundland to Florida, and west to Kentucky.

Preferred habitat: Wooded hillsides and rocky woods, particularly under or near cone-bearing evergreens.

Soil requirements: Intensely acid, woodland soil.

Culture: Trailing arbutus is very difficult to transplant so it is advisable to purchase well-established pot-grown plants from a nursery that specializes in the propagation of woodland flowers. It is useless to attempt to grow trailing arbutus unless the soil is intensely acid, with a pH of 4.5 or below. During the first season, the plants should be mulched with a light covering of pine needles, and the soil about the plants should never be allowed to dry out.

Period of bloom: April and May.

Erythronium americanum (dog-tooth violet, trout lily)

The narrow, lancelike leaves of the dog-tooth violet are a grayish-green, often mottled or streaked with brown, and they are almost as decorative in the woodland garden as are the flowers themselves. The nodding, slightly fragrant blooms are borne on slender stems, varying in height from 4 in. to 12 in. The flowers of *E. americanum* are a pale russet-yellow, occasionally tinted with purple. Some of the species native to the West Coast (such as *E. oregonum, E. revolutum, E. tuolumnense* and others) can be grown in eastern gardens also, and are very beautiful, being obtainable in shades of yellow, mauve and rose.

Distribution: From Nova Scotia to Florida and Alabama.

Preferred habitat: Moist, open woods, along brooksides and stony banks.

Soil requirements: Prefers a neutral, or very nearly neutral, soil.

Culture: The bulbs should be purchased from nurseries and not dug from the wild. They

are smooth and egg-shaped, and produce small round offsets from the base. The foliage disappears entirely soon after the flowering season is over.

Period of bloom: April and May.

Hepatica americana (liverleaf)

The hepaticas are among the first of the spring flowers to appear, sometimes even blooming under the snow. Hardly more than 3 in. in height, the dainty, cup-shaped flowers, in delicate tints of lilac, deep lavender, and white, are borne above the leathery, bronze-tinted leaves. The foliage is evergreen and the new leaves appear after the flowers.

Distribution: From Canada to northern Florida and westward to Missouri, although more common in the East.

Preferred habitat: Open woodlands and wooded hillsides.

Soil requirements: Hepatica prefers a woodland soil rich in humus and of a neutral or slightly acid reaction.

Culture: Plants should be purchased from a nursery, and they should be planted in clumps, being spaced from 4 in. to 6 in. apart. Although they usually succeed well under cultivation in widely varying situations, a partially shaded location is best.

Period of bloom: March and April.

Mertensia virginica (Virginia bluebells)

One of the most delightful of all our wild-flowers, it may be used in happy combination with woodland ferns and with some of the spring bulbs. The buds are a lavender-pink in color and the open flowers are a clear and lovely blue. The nodding blooms are borne on stems varying in height from 12 in. to 15 in. The foliage disappears entirely after the blooming season is over. *Mertensia* comes into flower at the same time that the silverbell tree *(Halesia carolina)* is in bloom, and it is enchantingly lovely when planted beneath the spreading branches.

Distribution: Southern New York, southward to Tennessee and Alabama, and westward to Kansas.

Preferred habitat: Low meadows, banks of streams, moist hillsides, thriving in both full sun and partial shade.

Soil requirements: Thrives most luxuriantly in soil that is very nearly neutral. Does not tolerate pronounced acidity or alkalinity.

Culture: Plants should be purchased from a nursery; when they are once well established, they increase rapidly from self-sown seed. As soon as the seed has ripened, the foliage begins to wither and shortly disappears entirely. *Mertensia* should be planted in an upright position at a depth of approximately 2½ in. to 3½ in.

Period of bloom: May and June.

Phlox divaricata (wild blue phlox)

One of the most easily grown of our woodland plants, wild blue phlox has found its way into many cultivated gardens. The dainty flowers are of a soft lavender-blue and are borne in great profusion. While the plants do well in an open, sunny border, they are most happily at home in a woodland setting and one sometimes sees a wooded hillside carpeted with them. Although the plants are somewhat creeping in habit, the flower stalks reach a

height of about 12 in. *Phlox divaricata* blooms at about the same time as do many of the spring bulbs, and it combines most delightfully with the large-flowered trilliums and *Scilla campanulata*. There are few woodland flowers more completely accommodating than the wild blue phlox. It asks only a chance to establish itself, and will give generously of its bloom and beauty in the spring.

Distribution: Quebec to Michigan, south to Georgia and Alabama.

Preferred habitat: Open, rocky woods, wooded hillsides. Thrives equally well in either full sun or partial shade.

Soil requirements: More or less indifferent to soil conditions, but thrives best in a soil that is very nearly neutral in its reaction.

Culture: *Phlox divaricata* is of exceedingly easy culture, and when it has become well established in a woodland garden it will increase rapidly and become more luxuriant and beautiful each year. The plants may be increased by cuttings and also by the division of old clumps.

Period of bloom: May and June.

Sanguinaria canadensis (bloodroot)

Fleeting though the blooms may be, bloodroot contributes its full share of beauty to the spring. The pure white of the petals and the gold of the stamens are lovely in great masses in the filtered sunlight of open woods, though hardly more than a few inches in height. *S. canadensis* 'Multiplex' is a handsome double-flowered form. Its blossoms last longer than those of the species.

Distribution: Nova Scotia to Florida, and westward to Nebraska.

Preferred habitat: Low hillsides, rich, stony ground along the borders of woods and along shady roadsides.

Soil requirements: Relatively indifferent to soil acidity, thriving equally well in neutral or somewhat acid soil.

Culture: Bloodroot may be transplanted successfully at almost any season, and when it has once become well established, it may spread considerably. It is most effective when used in large clumps. Plants may be purchased from a nursery or they may be transplanted with care from the wild.

Period of bloom: April and May.

Trillium grandiflorum (white wake-robin)

There are few woodland flowers more exquisite in form than the large-flowering trilliums. The beautiful, pure white blossoms of *T. grandiflorum* are borne on strong, upright stems that often reach a height of 15 in. or more. As with all the trilliums, the parts are in threes: three sepals, three petals, twice three stamens, and a whorl of three leaves—hence the name, *Trillium.*

SOIL REQUIREMENTS OF HERBACEOUS WOODLAND PLANTS

GROUP 1—INDIFFERENT TO SOIL ACIDITY (pH 4–9)

Actaea pachypoda	white baneberry
Actaea rubra	red baneberry
Anemone canadensis	Canada anemone
Anemonella thalictroides	rue anemone
Cimicifuga racemosa	black cohosh, snakeroot
Convallaria majalis	lily-of-the-valley
Cypripedium calceolus var. pubescens	yellow lady's slipper
Habenaria psycodes var. grandiflora	purple fringed orchid

Heuchera americana	alumroot
Iris cristata	crested iris
Lupinus perennis	blue lupine
Myosotis laxa	forget-me-not
Myosotis scorpioides	forget-me-not
Podophyllum peltatum	mayapple
Polygonatum biflorum	Solomon's-seal
Polygonatum commutatum	great Solomon's-seal
Sanguinaria canadensis	bloodroot
Tiarella cordifolia	foamflower
Trillium erectum	wake-robin
Viola conspersa	dog violet
viola palmata	common blue violet

GROUP 2—CIRCUMNEUTRAL OR VERY NEARLY NEUTRAL (pH 6–8)

Aquilegia canadensis	American columbine
Arisaema triphyllum	jack-in-the-pulpit
Campanula rotundifolia	bluebell
Claytonia virginica	spring beauty
Cypripedium reginae	showy lady's slipper
Dicentra cucullaria	Dutchman's-breeches
Dodecatheon meadia	shooting-star, American cowslip
Epimedium grandiflorum	barrenwort
Erythronium americanum	dog-tooth violet, trout lily
Gentiana andrewsii	bottle or closed gentian
Gentiana crinita	fringed gentian
Hepatica acutiloba	liverleaf
Hepatica americana	liverleaf
Mertensia virginica	Virginia bluebells
Mitella diphylla	bishop's cap, coolwort
Orchis spectabilis	showy orchis
Phlox divaricata	wild blue phlox
Polemonium reptans	greek valerian
Smilacina racemosa	false Solomon's-seal
Trillium catesbaei	rosy wake-robin
Trillium grandiflorum	white wake-robin
Uvularia grandiflora	merrybells
Viola blanda	sweet white violet
Viola canadensis	canada violet

GROUP 3—MODERATELY ACID (pH 4–6)

Anemone quinquefolia	wood anemone
Aquilegia caerulea	Rocky Mt. columbine
Cornus canadensis	bunchberry
Galax urceolata	galax
Gaultheria procumbens	wintergreen or checkerberry
Habenaria ciliaris	yellow fringed orchid
Houstonia caerulea	bluets or quaker ladies
Mitchella repens	partridgeberry
Viola pedata	bird's-foot violet

GROUP 4—VERY ACID (pH 3.5–5)

Clintonia borealis	clintonia
Cypripedium acaule	moccasin flower, pink lady's slipper
Epigaea repens	trailing arbutus, mayflower
Iris verna	dwarf iris

Distribution: Minnesota to Quebec, southward to Missouri, Georgia and South Carolina.

Preferred habitat: Rich, rocky woodlands, and moist but well-drained woodland glades.

Soil requirements: Prefers a woodland soil that is very nearly neutral in its reaction. Does not tolerate pronounced acidity or alkalinity.

Culture: Trillium grandiflorum is one of the most easily grown members of this group, and when the clumps have become well established, they will bloom happily on year after year. The tubers should be planted in the autumn, placed at a depth of about 3 in. to 4 in. with the bud pointing upward.

Period of bloom: May and June.

Other excellent species to grow include *T. catesbaei* (rosy wake-robin) with pink or rose flowers; *T. erectum* (purple trillium) with brownish-purple flowers; *T. sessile* (toadshade) with maroon or yellow-green flowers; and *T. undulatum* (painted trillium) with white flowers veined with rose at the base.

22.4 *The unfurling crosiers of cinnamon fern* (Osmunda cinnamomea) *fascinate children and adults too. Photo Anita Sabarese*

PLANTS FOR THE WOODLAND GARDEN

SCIENTIFIC NAME	COMMON NAME	HEIGHT	COLOR	SEASON OF BLOOM	SOIL	HABITAT
Actaea rubra	red baneberry	1–2 ft.	white	April–June	well-drained, indifferent to acidity	open woods
Anemone canadensis	Canada anemone	1–2 ft.	white	May–August	indifferent to acidity	low, moist ground
Anemone quinquefolia	wood anemone	4–8 in.	white	April–June	moderately acid	moist, open woods
Anemonella thalictroides	rue anemone	5–9 in.	white, tinged with pink	March–May	indifferent to acidity	thin, moist woodlands
Aquilegia canadensis	American columbine	1–2 ft.	scarlet and yellow	April–May	circumneutral	dry, rocky ledges
Aquilegia caerulea	Rocky Mt. columbine	2–3 ft.	blue and white	May–June	moderately acid	open woods
Arisaema triphyllum	jack-in-the-pulpit	12–30 in.	yellowish green	April–July	circumneutral	moist woodlands
Campanula rotundifolia	bluebell	6–18 in.	light purple	June–Sept.	circumneutral	rocky cliffs, sandy fields Sun or shade
Cimicifuga racemosa	black cohosh, snakeroot	3–8 ft.	white	June–July	indifferent	deep, moist woods
Claytonia virginica	spring beauty	6–12 in.	pale pink	March–May	circumneutral	open, moist woods
Clintonia borealis	clintonia	8–10 in.	buff, sometimes greenish tinge		very acid	cool, moist woods
Convallaria majalis	lily-of-the-valley	6–8 in.	white	May–June	indifferent	sun or shade; rich, moist
Cypripedium acaule	moccasin flower	8–12 in.	crimson-pink	April–May	very acid	wooded hillsides
Cypripedium calceolus var. *pubescens*	yellow lady's slipper	12–18 in.	yellow	May–June	indifferent	moist, rich, stony soil
Cypripedium reginae	showy lady's slipper	18–24 in.	white, stained crimson	June–July	circumneutral	swamps, wet woodlands
Dicentra canadensis	squirrel corn	8–12 in.	greenish white		indifferent	fertile, light soil
Dicentra cucullaria	Dutchman's-breeches	5–9 in.	white, yellow tipped	April–May	circumneutral	thin woods, dry rocky slopes
Dicentra eximia	wild bleeding-heart	12–18 in.	pink	May	indifferent	rocky ledges in open woods
Digitalis (*see* Biennials)						
Dodecatheon meadia	shooting-star, American cowslip	8–20 in.	fleshwhite to pink	April–May	circumneutral	moist hillsides, open woods
Epigaea repens	trailing arbutus, mayflower	trailing	pink	April–May	very acid	rocky woods, wooded hillsides under cone-bearing trees
Erythronium americanum	dog-tooth violet, trout lily	4–8 in.	yellow	April–May	Circumneutral	moist woods, along brooks
Galax urceolata	galax	1–2 ft.	yellow	April–Oct.	moderately acid	open woods and pastures
Gaultheria procumbens	wintergreen or checkerberry	2–5 in.	white	July–August	moderately acid	dry, evergreen woods
Gentiana andrewsii	bottle or closed gentian	1–2 ft.	violet-blue	August–Oct.	circumneutral	borders of woods, banks of streams
Gentiana crinita	fringed gentian	1–3 ft.	sky blue	Sept.–Oct.	circumneutral	low, moist meadows and bogs
Habenaria ciliaris	yellow fringed orchis	18–24 in.	orange-yellow	July–August	moderately acid	meadows, moist, sandy places
Habenaria psycodes var. *grandiflora*	large purple fringed orchis	to 5 ft.	lilac pink	July–August	indifferent to acidity	wet woods, swampy places
Hepatica acutiloba	liverleaf	3 in.	brighter than triloba	March–May	circumneutral	open, rich woodlands

PLANTS FOR THE WOODLAND GARDEN (Continued)

SCIENTIFIC NAME	COMMON NAME	HEIGHT	COLOR	SEASON OF BLOOM	SOIL	HABITAT
Hepatica americana	liverleaf	3 in.	lilac, white, pale lavender	March–May	circumneutral	open, rich woodlands
Heuchera americana	alumroot	18–24 in.	whitish-green	May–July	indifferent to acidity	moist, open
Houstonia caerulca	bluets or Quaker ladies	3–6 in.	white, tinted with blue-violet	April–Oct.	moderately acid	moist, grassy places and sandy fields
Iris cristata	crested iris	3–6 in.	violet with orange crest	April–May	indifferent to acidity	hillsides and along streams; needs protected spot in North
Iris verna	dwarf iris	4–8 in.	violet-blue, yellow centers	April–May	very acid	wooded hillsides
Lupinus perennis	blue lupine	1–2 ft.	violet-blue	May–June	indifferent	barren fields
Mertensia virginica	Virginia bluebells	1–2 ft.	sky blue, buds pink	March–May	circumneutral	low meadows, banks of streams; sun or shade
Mitchella repens	partridgeberry	Trailing	white and pink	June	moderately acid	woods and shaded borders of fields
Mitella diphylla	bishop's cap	8–12 in.	white	April–May	circumneutral	damp rocks, deep wooded slopes
Myosotis laxa	forget-me-not	6–12 in.	bright blue, but inconspicuous	May–July	indifferent	moist, banks of brooks
Myosotis scorpioides	forget-me-not	6–12 in.	bright blue, larger	May–July	indifferent	moist, banks of brooks
Orchis spectabilis	showy orchid	5–10 in.	rosy-lavender and white	May–June	circumneutral	moist stony soil
Phlox divaricata	wild blue phlox	9–18 in.	lavender-blue	April–June	circumneutral	rocky woods
Podophyllum peltatum	mayapple	12–18 in.	white	April–May	indifferent to acidity	moist, shaded
Polemonium reptans	Jacob's ladder	8–12 in.	blue-violet	April–May	circumneutral	thin, dryish woods
Polygonatum biflorum	Solomon's-seal	18–30 in.	greenish-white	April–June	indifferent to acidity	thickets, dry wooded slopes
Polygonatum commutatum	great Solomon's-seal	8 ft.	yellowish-green	April–June	indifferent to acidity	thickets, dry wooded slopes
Sanguinaria canadensis	bloodroot	10 in.	white	April–May	indifferent to acidity	borders of woods, along shaded roadsides
Tiarella cordifolia	foamflower	6–10 in.	white	May–June	indifferent to acidity	rich, moist woods
Trillium catesbaei	rosy wake-robin	12–18 in.	rose, pink	May–June	circumneutral	rich, rocky woods
Trillium erectum	wake-robin	7–12 in.	maroon	April–May	indifferent to acidity	rich, moist woodlands
Trillium grandiflorum	large flowering trillium	10–18 in.	white, then pink	May–June	circumneutral	rich, rocky woods
Viola blanda	sweet white violet	3–5 in.	white, purple veins	April–May	circumneutral	moist or dry situations
Viola canadensis	Canada violet	5–15 in.	white, tinged purple	May–June	circumneutral	well-drained, upland woods
Viola conspersa	dog violet	3–5 in.	light blue-purple	April–June	indifferent to acidity	moist woods, shady borders of roads and fields
Viola palmata	common blue violet	3–7 in.	violet-purple	April–June	indifferent to acidity	low moist ground
Viola pedata	bird's-foot violet	4–8 in.	lilac or blue-violet	April–June	moderately acid, dry sandy	open banks, thin woods

SHRUBS FOR THE WOODLAND GARDEN

SCIENTIFIC NAME	COMMON NAME	DECIDUOUS (D) OR EVERGREEN (E): HEIGHT IN FEET	COLOR OF BLOOM AND SEASON	FRUIT AND AUTUMN EFFECT	SOIL AND HABITAT
Aronia arbutifolia	red chokeberry	D; 9	pinkish; May	red fruit and leaves	moist
Aronia melanocarpa	black chokeberry	D; 1½–3	white; May	black, red leaves	well drained
Clethra alnifolia	white alder, sweet pepperbush	D; 4–9	white; July–August	inconspicuous, yellow leaves	wet, peaty or acid sandy; edges of woods and field
Cornus alba	dogwood	D; 5–10	cream; May–June	bluish-white, red twigs	moist to dry
Cornus amomum	silky dogwood	D; 5–10	white; June	blue	moist to dry
Cornus racemosa	gray dogwood	D; 3–15	cream; June	white or pale blue	moist to dry
Cornus stolonifera	golden-twig dogwood	D; 8	dull white; May	white	moist to dry
Hamamelis virginiana	witch hazel	D; 8–12	yellow; Oct. or Nov.	black seeds, yellow leaves	indifferent; thickets, edges of woodlands
Ilex glabra	inkberry	E; 4–8	white; July	black berries through winter; evergreen	wet
Ilex verticillata	winterberry, black alder	D; 6–15	inconspicuous; July	red fruit and leaves	wet; swamps, wet thicket
Kalmia latifolia	mountain laurel	E; 8	pink; June	inconspicuous, evergreen	slightly acid and moist; rocky hillsides, woodland
Leiophyllum buxifolium	sand myrtle	E; 1	white; May–June	inconspicuous, evergreen	acid
Leucothoë fontanesiana	drooping leucothoë	E; 3–5	white; April	inconspicuous, evergreen	acid; mountains
Lindera benzoin	spice bush	D; 6–12	pale yellow; March–April	gold leaves, scarlet berries	fertile; wet woods, swamp
Paxistima canbyi	cliff-green	E; 1	reddish; April–May	inconspicuous	well drained
Pieris floribunda	fetter bush	E; 3–5	white-pink; April–May	flower buds about to burst all winter, evergreen	acid
Rhododendron arborescens	sweet azalea	D; 9–12	white; June–July	red leaves	acid
Rhododendron calendulaceum	flame azalea	D; 12	yellow-scarlet; June	inconspicuous	acid
Rhododendron canadense	rhodora	D; 3	rosy-purple; April–May	inconspicuous	acid
Rhododendron carolinianum	Carolina rhododendron	E; 9	pink; May–June	inconspicuous, evergreen	moderately acid
Rhododendron catawbiense	Catawba rhododendron	E; 6–18	rosy-lilac; May–June	inconspicuous, evergreen	moderately acid
Rhododendron maximum	rosebay rhododendron	E; 30	pink or white; May	inconspicuous, evergreen	moderately acid
Rhododendron minus	Piedmont rhododendron	E; 10	rosy-pink; June–July	inconspicuous, evergreen	moderately acid
Rhododendron periclymenoides (nudiflorum)	pinxter flower	D; 6–8	pink; April–May	inconspicuous	acid or lime
Rhododendron prinophyllum (roseum)		D; 9	pink; April–May	inconspicuous	acid or lime
Rhododendron vaseyi	pinkshell azalea	D; 15	various; April–May	inconspicuous	acid
Rhododendron viscosum	swamp azalea	D; 4–7	pink, white; June–July	inconspicuous	moist
Sambucus canadensis	elder	D; 5–8	white; June–July	purple fruit	moist
Vaccinium angustifolium	low-bush blueberry	D; 1½	white; May–June	scarlet leaves, blue berries, July–Aug.	acid; dry, rocky, sandy hills
Vaccinium corymbosum	high-bush blueberry	D; 4–10	white; May–June	scarlet leaves, blue berries, Aug.–Sept.	acid; deep swamps, moist woods
Vaccinium vacillans	dwarf late blueberry	D; 1–3	purple; May	crimson leaves, berries	acid; dry, open woods, shaded thickets
Viburnum acerifolium	dockmackie	D; 5	white; June	black	dry
Viburnum cassinoides	withe-rod	D; 6	white; May	black	wet
Viburnum dentatum	arrow-wood	D; 5–15	white; June	blue	moist
Viburnum lentago	nannyberry	D; 30	white; May	black	moist
Viburnum prunifolium	plum-leaved haw	D; 30	white; April	black	moist

FERNS FOR THE WOODLAND GARDEN

SCIENTIFIC NAME	COMMON NAME	TYPE (DECIDUOUS OR EVERGREEN)	HEIGHT	HABITAT
Adiantum pedatum	American maidenhair fern	D	2 ft.	shade
Asplenium platyneuron	ebony spleenwort	E	½–1 ft.	rocky woods
Asplenium trichomanes	maidenhair spleenwort	E	½ ft.	clefts in rocks
Athyrium filix-femina	lady fern	D	2–3 ft.	partial shade or full sun
Botrychium virginianum	rattlesnake fern	D	1–2 ft.	open woods
Camptosorus rhizophyllus	walking fern	E	4–10 in.	limestone cliffs in shade
Cystopteris bulbifera	berry bladderfern	D	1–2 ft.	moist bank or brookside in shade
Dennstaedtia punctilobula	hayscented fern	D	2 ft.	sun or shade
Diplazium pycnocarpon	narrowleaf spleenwort	D	2–3 ft.	rich woods
Dryopteris cristata	crested wood fern	E	1–2 ft.	on hummocks in grassy bogs
Dryopteris cristata var. *clintoniana*	clinton wood fern	E	2–3 ft.	moist woods
Dryopteris dilatata	mountain wood fern	E	2 ft.	mountain peaks in shade
Dryopteris marginalis	leather wood fern	E	2–3 ft.	rocky woods
Dryopteris spinulosa	toothed wood fern	E	2–3 ft.	shade
Gymnocarpium dryopteris	oak fern	D	½ ft.	shade
Lygodium palmatum	Hartford or climbing fern	D	4 ft.	partial shade
Matteuccia pensylvanica	ostrich fern	D	4–6 ft.	banks of streams; sun or shade
Onoclea sensibilis	sensitive fern	D	1–2 ft.	Bogs
Osmunda cinnamomea	cinnamon fern	D	3–4 ft.	roadsides and damp woods
Osmunda claytoniana	interrupted fern	D	3–4 ft.	sun or shade
Osmunda regalis	royal fern	D	3 ft.	sun or shade
Polypodium vulgare	common polypody	E	½ ft.	rocky woods
Polystichum acrostichoides	Christmas fern	E	1–2 ft.	rich woods
Pteretis nodulosa	ostrich fern	D	4–6 ft.	banks of streams; sun or shade
Thelypteris hexagonoptera	beech fern	D	1 ft.	shade
Thelypteris phegopteris	narrow beech fern	D	½–1 ft.	brookside banks

23.1 Running water and shade are cooling elements in any garden, but waterlilies are special. Photo Grant Heilman

23

Water and Bog Gardens

WATER GARDENS

The natural pond or the garden pool may be readily converted into a water garden by the use of water plants. It is often assumed that so exquisite a flower as a water lily is difficult to grow and that it requires special care. Actually, however, once they are established, the hardy species of *Nymphaea* thrive without much attention. Some of the species are native to this country and are common in the quiet waters of inland ponds. The tender kinds, including *Nymphaea caerulea,* the Egyptian lotus, need more care and are most satisfactorily grown in the greenhouse or removed to the greenhouse for the winter. A practical alternative may be the heated pool, which can substantially extend the outdoor season for tender species.

It is supposed that water lilies require abundant space and that one must have a pond of considerable size in which to raise them. While the larger species spread to a circle about 6 ft. across, the dwarf species, with small leaves and exquisitely small flowers, are suitable for garden pools hardly more than 3 ft. or 4 ft. in diameter. Such pools can be created from the same kind of heavy polyethelene sheathing that is used in backyard swimming pools, or variously shaped pools can be purchased.

HARDY WATER LILIES OF MERIT

***Nymphaea odorata* (fragrant water lily)**
The white pond lily of the northern states is hardy and dependable. The leaves are dark green and numerous. The flowers are about 4 in. across, the upcurving white petals encircling yellow stamens.

Many hybrid varieties of *Nymphaea odorata* are readily available.

N. odorata rosea is the pink Cape Cod water lily.

N. odorata minor is a small plant with tiny flowers. It requires a depth of only 12 in. and spreads to a circle only 3 ft. in diameter.

N. odorata caroliniana bears rose or flesh-colored flowers with yellow stamens. The leaves are large, sometimes 12 in. across.

N. odorata 'Yellow Pygmy' has clear yellow flowers. The variety 'Helen Fowler' is a good pink. Flowers of *aurora* change color on successive days, yellow the first day, then red-orange and finally red.

439

23.2 Tropical waterlily (Nymphaea) flowers are large and brilliant and generally rise above the water's surface, whereas hardy waterlily flowers tend to float on the surface and are less extravagant in their color range. Photo Anita Sabarese

N. marliacea albida and *N. gladstoniana* are among the best white water lilies. They are free-growing plants, blooming continuously all season, and they produce large fragrant flowers. Those of *N. marliacea albida* have pink sepals while *N. gladstoniana* has enormous blooms.

N. Marliacea rosea, similar to *N. marliacea albida* in habit, has deep pink blossoms. Other good pinks are 'Formosa' and 'Pink Opal'.

N. marliacea chromatella is still one of the best yellows, bearing blossoms 6 in. across with canary-yellow petals and bright yellow stamens in generous numbers. As it is a vigorous grower, it should be divided every few years to avoid crowding of the leaves in the center of the plant.

Considered among the best modern hardy water lilies are Attraction, large, garnet-red; 'Paul Harriet', changing as it matures from yellow through orange to red; 'Comanche', changing from rose to apricot; Gonnere, a very showy white; 'Pink Sensation', a rich fragrant pink; 'Rose Arey', a brilliant, very fragrant pink; and the pygmy 'Helvolla', which is sulphur yellow. All these water lilies are hardy in Zones 5 and 6.

Among the best of the night-blooming tropicals are 'Mrs. G. S. Hitchcock', a large, rose pink; 'H. C. Harrstick', with large, vivid red blooms; 'Missouri', giant, creamy-white; 'Emily Grant Hutchins', a giant red-pink; and the bright red 'Red Flare'.

Propagation by Seed

Sow the seeds in pans of sand. Cover the seeds lightly with screened sand and place the pan in water at a temperature of 70° to 80° F. in such a way that the surface of the sand is above the water but in contact with it. After soaking them all day, submerge the pans to a depth of 18 in. or more. After the plants have formed the first floating leaf, they may be transplanted to flats with 2 in. of soil containing well-rotted cow manure. Thereafter the young plants should be potted as they develop and require more space.

Cultural Requirements

The requirements for culture are quiet water with a trickling inlet and outlet, a depth of 18 in. for the smaller sorts and 2 ft. or 3 ft. for the larger species, full sunshine, and 2 cu. ft. or 3 cu. ft. of prepared soil for each plant.

The soil may be a mixture of 2 parts good garden soil and 1 part well-rotted cow manure, or, if natural sources are available, a mixture of equal parts garden soil and pond muck. If neither manure nor muck is obtainable, a ½ qt. of bone meal to each plant may be mixed with the soil.

For convenience in keeping the pool neat, the soil is placed in tubs, half barrels or boxes. Cypress is the best wood for tubs and boxes but the barrels are usually made of oak. The soil bed should be almost 12 in. deep and so placed that its surface is 12 in. to 18 in. below the surface of the water. In planting, the tub is half-filled with soil, and the tuber placed on the soil so that the growing end is upward and about level with the rim of the tub, being held in this position while more soil is filled in around it. The upper 1 in. or 2 in. should consist of sand. In planting water lilies in a natural pond, the tubers may be squeezed down into the muck of the bottom. If the muck does not hold them and they float instead, the tubers should be pinned down with a curved wire. A suitably sized wire basket is an ideal planting container for natural ponds. Such baskets hold the plants in place, yet at the same time give the roots an opportunity to grow outward into the soil. The best time for planting is April.

Winter Care

Once established, hardy water lilies will require no special care. To carry hardy water lilies through the winter, the only protection necessary is the muck and water above them. If the ice does not freeze to the bottom where the tubers are, no harm will be done to them.

The pool itself may be protected against ice pressure in several ways. If it is small, it may be covered with boards, a mound of leaves and litter heaped above it. This will conserve ground heat and delay and mitigate freezing. The larger pool may be protected by a number of floating logs As the ice freezes, the logs, being somewhat soft, will absorb the pressure and thus relieve the concrete from a strain that might otherwise crack it.

OTHER WATER GARDEN PLANTS

Other aquatic plants attractive in pools or on pond margins are floating heart, which has roots in the muck; forget-me-not; parrot-feather; primrose willow; primrose creeper; water hyacinth; water snowflake; umbrella palm. Water snowflake has charming, small white and pale yellow blossoms, which rest on the water like little butterflies.

Plants that keep the water clear and refreshed by their natural process of charging it with oxygen are known as oxygenating plants. *Cabomba* and *Anacharis* are both plants with small light green leaves — much smaller than those of watercress — floating on the surface, and they grow in shallow water about 4 in. to 12 in. deep. *Sagittaria* (arrowhead) is another oxygenating plant. It grows above shallow water to a height of 3 ft., and bears arrowhead leaves.

The shores of a natural pond may be made much more attractive by groups of pickerel rush, bull rush, papyrus, yellow flag *(Iris pseudacorus)*, purple flag *(Iris versicolor)* and arrowhead *(Sagittaria* spp.), most of which grow up from water a few inches deep and stand erect. Such shrubs as button bush *(Cephalanthus occidentalis)*, Spice bush *(Benzoin aestivale)* and sweet pepper bush *(Clethra alnifolia)* are also suitable for the larger masses of foliage on the pond side.

INSECT PESTS

Water plants seem to be troubled by only a few enemies.

Aphids sometimes are found on the leaves. The easiest way to be rid of them is to wash them off into the water with the spray of a hose. The goldfish will then dispose of them.

A leaf miner occasionally destroys leaves, making tunnels that are easily seen. The only certain method of coping with it is to cut off and destroy all affected leaves as soon as the trouble is detected. If the plant is healthy, it should be able to replace the lost leaves with new ones.

A remarkable insect is the leaf-eating *Hydrocampa propiralis,* which constructs boats from bits of leaves and cruises about the pond. Picking them off the leaves by hand and catching them in a net while navigating is recommended as the most effective means of control.

Algae are not damaging but confer upon the pool a disagreeable greenish discoloration. The water can be cleared by putting copper sulphate in it at the rate of 1 lb. per 500,000 gallons. A pool 3 ft. deep and with 13 ft. by 30 ft. of surface will need only $1/8$ oz. of copper sulphate. The crystals of copper sulphate should be crushed, put into a cloth bag or the foot of an old stocking, and drawn through the water until dissolved.

BOG GARDENS

A true bog, as it occurs in nature, is the end result of thousands of years of plant succession, and is a very specific habitat. Normally, it represents the last vestiges of a glacial lake, filled in by eons of accumulations of decaying sphagnum moss, which floated upon the ancient lake. As such, it is cold, wet and acid, and is inhabited by plant species that will withstand its severe conditions. A gardener fortunate enough to own such a habitat must realize such good fortune and preserve it.

The gardener encountering a degraded bog, or merely a poorly drained location, can certainly aspire to create a bog garden in an approximation of that created by nature. The two essentials are a continuous supply of water and a soil that is capable of retaining it. The first may be provided by water pipes in which tiny holes have been bored at intervals of 2 ft. or 3 ft., the pipes being buried at a depth of approximately 2 in. The second requisite may be provided by mixing equal portions of sand and peat moss with generous quantities of humus. The mixture should be deep, 18 in. if at all possible, and a 1-in. layer of peat moss should be spread over the surface. Particular attention must be paid to maintaining a highly acid condition, in the range of pH 4.5 to 5.5.

A small bog garden may contain only a few herbaceous plants; a large area might have trees and shrubs as well, with the herbaceous plants representing the center of an ancient lake, the shrubs its margins and the trees the shoreline. The only subsequent care of the bog after the plants have become established is the maintenance of acidity and the occasional removal of interlopers—undesirable plants that may have crept in.

PLANTS FOR THE BOG GARDEN

TREES

Betula pumila	swamp birch
Larix laricina	tamarack
Picea mariana	black spruce
Thuja occidentalis	white cedar

SHRUBS

Andromeda glaucophylla	bog rosemary
Cephalanthus occidentalis	buttonbush
Chamaedaphne calyculata	leatherleaf
Cornus stolonifera	red-osier dogwood
Gaultheria procumbens	wintergreen
Ilex verticillata	winterberry
Ledum groenlandicum	Labrador tea
Taxus canadensis	Canada yew
Vaccinium spp.	blueberry

HERBACEOUS PERENNIALS

Caltha palustris	marsh marigold
Clintonia borealis	bluebead lily
Cypripedium acaule	moccasin flower, pink lady's slipper
Cypripedium reginae	showy lady's slipper
Drosera rotundifolia	sundew (insectivorous)
Habenaria hyperborea	leafy green orchid
Habenaria psycodes	purple fringed orchid
Lobelia siphilitica	great lobelia
Mimulus ringens	monkeyflower
Sarracenia purpurea	pitcher plant (insectivorous)
Sphagnum species	sphagnum moss
Symplocarpus foetidus	skunk cabbage

AQUATIC PERENNIALS

Pontederia palustris	pickerel weed
Sagittaria latifolia	arrowhead
Utricularia vulgaris	bladderwort (insectivorous)

24.1 The integration of rock outcroppings and plantings with lawns and trees is not often as successful as in this example from The New York Botanical Garden. Photo Carlton Lees

24

Rock and Wall Gardens

Of all the specialized interests in gardening, none encompass as varied or absorbing a choice of plant materials as those available to the rock gardener. This type of gardening depends primarily upon the wild or native species of plants that are available by the thousands from among dozens of plant families. These may be annuals, biennials, herbaceous perennials, shrubs or bulbs that emanate from the mountains, bogs, woodlands, heaths or arid plains of virtually every continent.

The American Rock Garden Society defines the rock garden as one that provides suitable cultural conditions for alpine, saxatile and other low-growing plants, usually simulating as artfully as possible the terrain and general appearance of the natural habitat of the plants themselves. In 1864 the Austrian botanist Kerner von Merilaun decided to try a pioneering experiment. He collected thriving alpines from his native Alps and attempted to grow them in the lowlands. To accomplish this, Von Merilaun constructed a garden on a slope covered with rubble stones, boulders and stone chippings. This scree, which he built at the Royal Botanical Gardens in Innsbruck, was designed to represent in miniature the "Steingeroellhalde" of the valleys in the Tyrolese Alps. This unique "garden" was then—and is still today, more than a century later—the most successful demonstration of what a rock garden should be and how alpine plants could be grown successfully in an artificially created habitat.

Since the rock garden does not have the same tradition-bound history as the Japanese or Chinese garden, public opinion in this country is still divided about its popularity. As a result this type of gardening has passed through many ups and downs in its 100-year history, probably reaching a low during the early 1900s. Directors of botanical gardens throughout Europe originally started the construction of rock gardens because of the increasing scientific interest in the plants themselves, rather than to produce rock garden showcases. These alpine plant collections, or "alpinums," as they were called, were the forerunners of our present rock gardens. The imaginative alpinums were usually constructed in the shape of miniature mountains and stone hills, or even in the form of volcanoes. The plant material was collected from the wild: in alpine meadows, on screes, and among rocks above timberline. Since these plants were moved from high to low altitudes, they had a short lifetime and were replaced quite frequently. Propagating from seed or cutting was not perfected until the early 1920s.

However, this new garden style soon became very popular, with the result that the rocks and plants lost their original significance and the alpinum its intent. Unfortunately, all that remained was a conglomerate of miniature mountains, planted with trees that soon grew completely out of scale. The rock gardens, during these early years, did not have the privacy that is so much desired, as they were built quite often on street corners or between sidewalks and frequently were even badly ornamented with miniature mountain huts, mountain goats and dwarfs. This debasement of the original rock garden standards and concepts continued into the early 1930s.

ROCK GARDENS

The first and most fundamental consideration in constructing a rock garden is the relationship of individual plants and plant groups to the overall composition. Without an awareness of this relationship, the amateur may become bewildered by the very abundance of species from which to choose. As a result of such abundance he may not always make careful choices and the mistakes may not appear until several years have passed.

The designer, in attempting to visualize the ultimate appearance of the rock garden, should be greatly influenced by both the site and the locality. The interrelation of mass, texture, form, color and detail is the product of the exercise of the rock gardener's adherence to this principle of composition.

Scale

A basic principle to bear in mind is that the garden must relate to the human scale. (No miniature Matterhorns!) We have to reduce the overpowering size of the universe and bring it down to more comfortable proportions in a small, private world. Since most rock gardens are man-made, they also must have a definite unity of design with certain aesthetic and utilitarian functions. After all, a garden is not nature, but rather a work of art. It is something created artificially that merely makes use of natural means to form a different, though harmonious picture. More variations of plant material can be shown on a smaller scale than can be found in nature. In one sense, a rock garden is a synthesis or condensation of the rocky alpine landscapes of great mountains. When well done, it is believable.

24.2 In all rock gardens, rocks should be in second place to plants. Photo Anita Sabarese

Fig. 24.1
Perspective view of patio area landscaped with rock garden plants

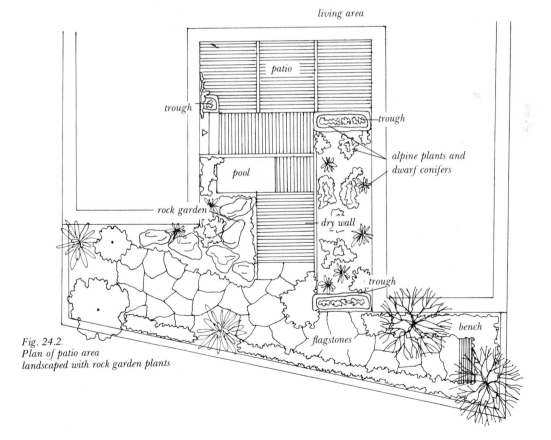

Fig. 24.2
*Plan of patio area
landscaped with rock garden plants*

By choosing highly cultivated and hardy plants for difficult locations, and by grouping them together aesthetically, we often can create new plant communities that may be superior in effect to the communities of natural plants themselves.

Choice of Site

The particular effect to be developed in any rock garden depends largely upon the condition of the site to be used. Quite often, the first choice for a rock garden is a site that is not needed for any other purpose or one that proves to be difficult to tie in with the general design of the garden as a whole. Though all these reasons may seem valid, they are expedient, and such a site may not necessarily be the best one for our purpose.

Generally speaking, most rock gardens can be classified as either formal or informal (naturalistic). Within this framework, we can more readily visualize which kind of rock garden will best fit into the existing landscape with which we have to work.

Before deciding on a site, one should observe the sunrise, sunset and sun exposure at high noon, and also the main wind direction. Although a southern exposure ensures the maximum amount of sunlight for sun-loving plants, it also exposes them to prolonged summer heat and to the injurious effect of the alternate freezing and thawing action in winter. An eastern or even a northern exposure is generally preferable for a diversity of plants.

Avoid a site that cannot be drained properly. Bear in mind that although alpines grow under widely different aspects and factors, they generally do not tolerate sour, badly drained soil. In addition, alpines will not grow when exposed to drought or to cutting winds. Do not build a rock garden under the overhanging branches of trees or between buildings where drafts and shade will discomfort or inhibit most any plants selected to grow there.

A factor that may indirectly affect the choice for a rock garden location is the provision of water for pools and streams. Water is found in its natural bodies only in a few gardens, and if desired in others, it usually must be brought in artificially. A watercourse is not necessarily essential in a rock garden, but its presence surely enhances such an area.

In selecting a spot for a rock garden, there is one point to be remembered which, at first glance, may seem of secondary importance: ease of access for the bulky and often heavy material and equipment that will be required in the course of construction. Difficult access can add considerably to the cost of the rock garden, not only in terms of the time and labor involved but also because of the damage done to already established lawns or other parts of the garden.

No work should be started before a suitable site has been selected and the decision made from which direction the garden most likely will be seen to its best advantage. Foreground and background as part of the composition must be considered in choosing the site. On most small properties a suitable background planting will be needed, so that the informal rock garden will block out, in a natural way, any extraneous or distracting objects. Such a backdrop will also serve as a frame to keep the eye from straying away from the garden itself.

The immediate foreground, also important in the overall design, is the perfect place for an alpine lawn, with stepping stones set among the plants for easy access to rock outcrops behind. In a hot, sunny location, ground covers such as *Antennaria dioica*, *A. parviflora*, *Mazus reptans*, *Cerastium tomentosum*, *Sagina* spp., *Phlox subulata*, and so on, can be used. A small pond or a stretch of closely trimmed turf also can serve as foreground for a rock garden. Turf brought up to the planting areas, and occasionally even to and around the rocks, can provide a neat and pleasing appearance.

Construction

A natural rock garden is usually better placed some distance from the more formal part of the garden which, as a rule, surrounds the house. A prime consideration in building a rock garden should be the rocks themselves which, after all, determine the garden's character. No garden builder can ignore this basic fact. The aim, of course, should be to select and arrange the rocks in such a manner that each appears as a

Fig. 24.3
Rock garden construction

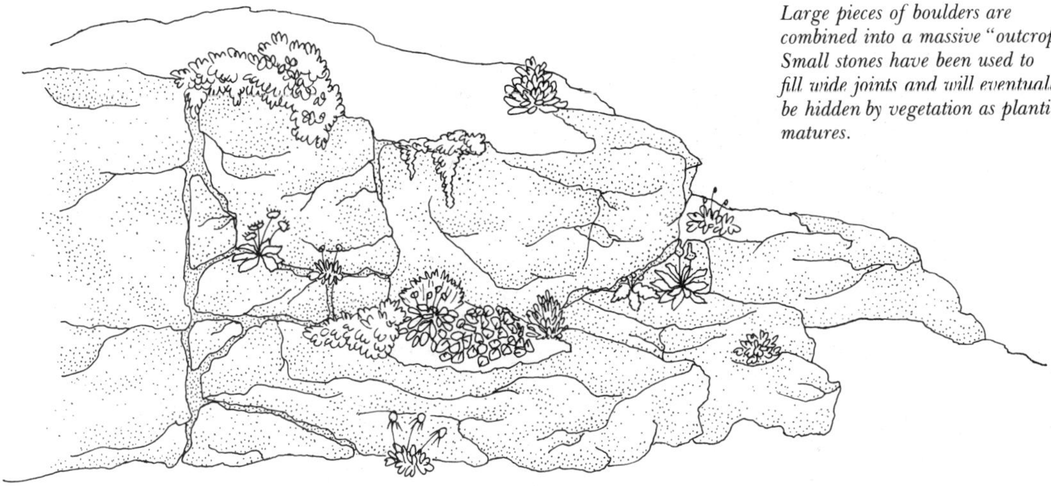

Large pieces of boulders are
combined into a massive "outcrop."
Small stones have been used to
fill wide joints and will eventually
be hidden by vegetation as planting
matures.

Cliff face consists of a number of
separate stones skillfully combined.

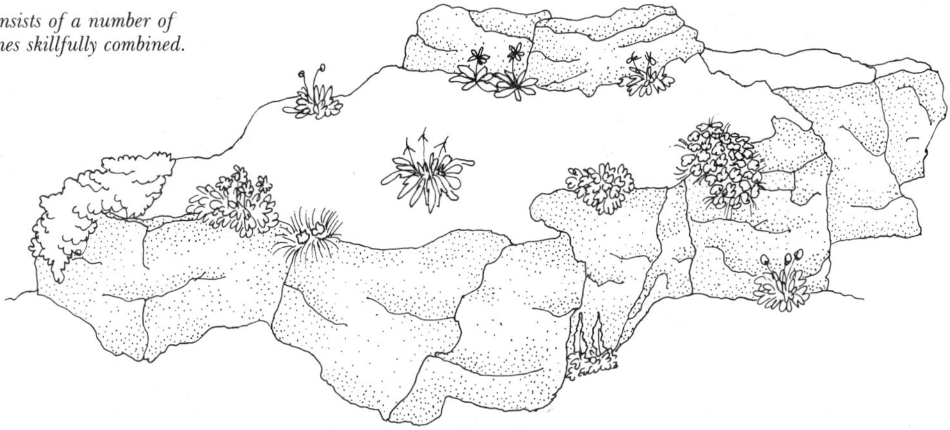

natural deposit that was there originally and
has not been disturbed. A rock garden is not a
meaningless jumble of rocks, mixed as to geographical type, showing drill marks and glaring
newly exposed surfaces. Nor should the rocks
be set up in an unnatural, shaky or unaesthetic
position.

The best stone for the rock garden is one of
local origin. Porosity is a factor of considerable
importance because the stone stores moisture
and is always cool underground. Alpine plants
thrive in association with stone and will press
their roots as closely as possible to its sides. In
this respect, the sandstones and limestones are
the best material for rock gardens. Though
granite is also good, it is hard and yields an acid

reaction to the soil. Quartz is too hard and too conspicuous.

Unstratified and Stratified (Sedimentary) Rock

Boulders and hardheads (igneous rocks such as basalt, trap and granite, which weather to round boulders) can never be used to make a stratified outcropping. Instead, their place is on a rugged, boulder-strewn slope. Some may be scattered, while others are arranged in dense steep clusters. On a rather steep slope the dominance of the rock should give the effect of a stream-cut bank, with the softer material laying bare the outcropping boulders. Stream valleys and pond areas are excellent locations for rock gardens. The size of the rocks used should be determined by the scale of the garden. Large stones give the effect of strength; however, a big boulder in a small garden makes the area seem smaller, while too many small stones create an artificial and weak effect. Only weathered boulders should be selected, and these should be embedded in the soil to their weathered line or to the level of their widest circumference.

It is necessary to understand the jointing of stratified or sedimentary rock in order to obtain a natural effect. The lines of stratification are traceable throughout the entire formation. In the garden it does not matter at what angle the strata are inclined, so long as this angle is consistently maintained throughout the placed stonework. A backward tilt to each elevation has the advantage of holding some of the rainfall and conducting it into the soil. This stone material offers the ingenious gardener ample opportunity to create a variety of crevices and planting spots, some in full sun and others where it is cool and shaded behind a bend or rock.

A limestone formation is especially suitable for most informal garden effects. Where this type of stone occurs naturally, it would be difficult to find a better or simpler rock for the garden. And if the limestone is porous, irregular in form and already weathered to a rather neutral color, the rock gardener is fortunate indeed.

Sandstone is another stratified rock that is widely used. It, too, has a large water-holding capacity and is easy to move around.

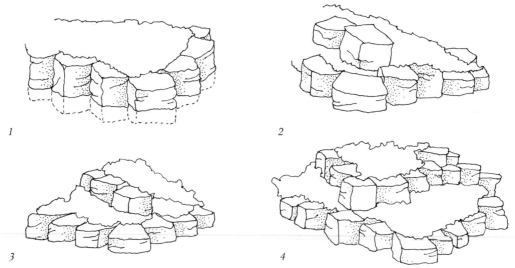

Fig. 24.4

Construction of a small rock garden with quarried stratified rocks. 1. First planting pocket is completed. The stones are buried to one-third or one-fourth of their total height and each one slightly overlaps the stone behind it. 2. Begin the next elevation with the corner stone touching the stone below it. 3. The baseline of the next elevation shapes the planting pocket of the lower bed into a roughly triangular form. 4. The finished product is stepped planting.

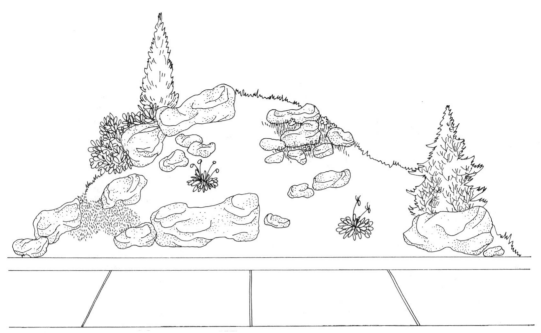

Fig. 24.5
Moraine. This garden emulates the debris left after a glacier recedes.

Moraine and Erratic Rock

Glaciers and water transported the erratic blocks of rock millennia ago southward from distant places. Frost, rain and wind then combined to change granite, feldspar and porphyry into round, smoothed-off and dome-shaped rocks. No one stone ever matches another in size or shape.

This individual expression of the solitary stone must be worked out in the construction of the moraine. Erratic blocks in a rock garden cannot be used the same way as stratified or sedimentary rocks; they have to rest on the ground. They have to be embedded as if they had been resting there forever. To do this is not an easy task, either aesthetically or physically. The individual stones all must face a common main direction. If the moraine lies against a stone wall, then the main direction is parallel to the wall. In that case the joints of a paving would be diagonal to the main direction.

The mound rises from one side of the field evenly to the opposite side. Here the largest stone will dominate. The surface of the stones must have all the same inclined plane to the lowest point. This order in direction to the side and top is the architectonic element that avoids confusion.

Drainage and Staking

An important consideration in planning a rock garden is drainage. Alpine plants prefer a cool, moist stand. However, the water should flow by the roots and not become stagnant. Clayey soil is the main enemy of rock plants. Where soil of this type predominates, it is wise to build the rockery entirely of imported soil made up to specification. An ideal mixture is equal proportions of rough sand with gravel, sphagnum peat and friable loam. The subsoil should be loosened deeply before it is covered with the new soil mix.

After the contours of the surface have been

roughly shaped according to the plan, the site should be staked out to reveal the various natural features the gardener wishes to emphasize. These stakes will indicate such points as the major rocks, a waterfall or possibly a bend in the walk. In this early process a newspaper pattern suggesting stones is often easier than stakes to help visualize the final result. To indicate the walkway, sawdust or lime may be used. Some particularly large rock may show promise of becoming the dominant part of the ridge or cliff. In certain situations such a rock can be the main attraction of the entire composition, yet still remain in harmony with its surroundings. When placing the stones, it is best to start from a central group and work outward.

Pathways

Once the stones are in place, the approach to the garden is the next consideration. A rock garden should be arranged so that the visitor is forced to view the grounds slowly and deliberately, just as he or she would do while climbing a mountain. As in the mountains, one can see the modest beauty of the little cliff and scree dwellers best only if one climbs slowly, step by step.

A trail through the interior parts of a rock garden should be so designed that it links the most interesting views. The path should be lower than the surrounding planting beds, since it also has to serve as a drainage canal for heavy rains, besides helping to regulate the flow of water.

Bold groupings of stones should be placed on curves, suggesting a natural reason for the bend. A dwarf tree or shrub will provide the same effect. Follow the more gradual contours and interrupt them by steps only when some higher elevation must be crossed. It is important that these steps blend into the natural strata line. Although the approach to the garden should be convenient, it must never monopolize the entire scene.

Selection of Shrubs

Together with the rocks, the small shrubs and slow-growing conifers form a setting or skeletal framework in which the more colorful variable herbaceous material creates its pattern. Such woody plants will be at their best in winter when the rest of the garden lies dormant.

Among the conifers are many universally liked dwarfs that exist in a range of forms. Hardiness and lack of boldness make these ideal plant material when they are used either singly or in groups. They are almost free of insect and fungi pests. (Some of the very compact varieties might have to be treated against red spider, which can be done in early spring with a systemic insecticide—see index.) Once they are rooted, these plants will rarely need any maintenance. Since the goal of a rock garden is to reproduce an "alpine" atmosphere, anything formal should be avoided. For this reason, the globose forms and others of a neat and formal outline are the least useful for our purposes.

Prostrate forms of *Juniperus* should be used sparingly because they eventually spread over a large area that could be better occupied by alpines. The greatest care in the choice of suitable species is important on the higher parts or tops of the outcrops. Anything with an upright or pyramidal habit would be out of place in such locations. In nature, there might be a tree either gnarled or dwarfed by wind; a windswept veteran with substantially exposed stem and branches is therefore most desirable in the higher parts of the rock garden.

Before actual planting begins, stakes are used again, as they were for the placement of the rocks. It is a good idea to write the name of the article on the stake, such as: "pine," "spruce," "faucet," "stone," and so on. More important features are sometimes indicated by heavier stakes, or by ends of stakes colored or keyed to indicate various things. From a distance the stakes can be studied in their positions, and if there is any dissatisfaction with the plan, the design can be changed before actual planting starts.

DWARF CONIFERS OF SPECIAL MERIT

The following list contains examples of the most common groups of slow-growing conifers, all of which are suitable for the rock garden.

Their rates of growth are slower but vary from one kind to another. The foliage of a dwarf variety or cultivar is essentially the same as that of the typical full-sized variety, but the trunk is either abbreviate or fails to form. A tree thus compacted becomes a shrub, with drooping, twisting or creeping branches or twigs. With few exceptions, dwarf forms have been the discoveries of nursery staff, who set them aside and cared for them either as cuttings from sports or abnormal growths such as witches' broom, or from juvenile forms, or as seedlings.

Abies balsamea var. hudsonia

A truly dwarf form of our native balsam fir, forming a flat-topped, deep green bush, reaching about 2½ ft. high and 4 ft. wide in about thirty years.

Cedrus libani 'Sargentii'

An attractive miniature weeping tree, producing a 12-in. to 14-in. stem before the branches start to weep; growth more restrained.

Chamaecyparis lawsoniana 'Elwoodii'

A slender, spirelike pyramid. Leaves semijuvenile, very blue. In fifteen years it reaches a height of about 3 ft. to 4 ft. and about 10 in. in width.

Chamaecyparis obtusa 'Nana'

A must in the rock garden, this is a low, flat shrub with horizontal branches. The dark green leaves resemble thick, twisted moss. At thirty years, the plant is only 10 in. to 15 in. high, and 15 in. to 20 in. wide at its base. The stronger-growing plant found under this name is 'Nana Gracilis'.

Chamaecyparis pisifera 'Filifera Aurea'

A broadly conical shrub. The branches are horizontal, with pendulous, bright yellow branchlets, except where shaded. In about thirty years it reaches a height of about 8 ft. to 15 ft.

Cryptomeria japonica 'Vilmoriana'

A truly dwarf plant, forming a dense, dark green globe that becomes deep reddish-bronze in winter. At thirty years it will be 20 in. to 30 in. high.

Juniperus communis 'Compressa'

A gem among dwarf conifers, this is a columnar shrub, rarely growing over 3 ft. high. The small needlelike leaves spread to reveal their glaucous inner surface.

Juniperus communis 'Echiniformis'

The hedge-hog juniper makes a tiny, prickly hummock 1 ft. to 2 ft. high and wide.

Juniperus procumbens 'Nana'

A compact plant with short branches which form a prostrate mat. Leaves are a deep blue-green and spiny. At twenty years this plant is 12 in. to 15 in. high and 3 ft. to 3½ ft. wide.

Picea abies 'Inversa'

A slow-growing weeping spruce with completely pendulous branches. With age it becomes a striking specimen.

Picea abies 'Nidiformis'

A dense spreading bush with branches that form a series of tight layers. The needles are rather thin and narrow. At twenty years it is about 20 in. high and 40 in. wide.

Picea glauca var. albertiana 'Conica'

One of the really perfect, slow-growing dwarf conifers, making a symmetrical cone. At twenty years it is about 4 ft. high and 2 ft. wide.

Pinus strobus 'Nana'

A dwarf, low-spreading variant of the eastern white pine, with crowded branchlets and bluish-green needles. At twenty years this tree will be about 24 in. tall and 30 in. wide.

Thuja plicata 'Rogersi'

A very attractive, compact pyramid or cone with foliage exposed to the sun and a lovely old gold color during the growing season. At twenty years it is about 3 ft. high and 2 ft. wide.

Thujopsis dolabrata 'Nana'

A low, spreading plant with slender branches and lustrous green scale-leaves. Usually less than 2 ft. high.

Tsuga canadensis 'Bennett'

A flat-topped plant with branches spreading horizontally. Terminal shoots are fanlike with weeping tips. At twenty years it is about 20 in. high and 3 ft. wide.

OTHER SHRUBS SUITABLE FOR THE ROCK GARDEN

Berberis wilsonae

Of very spreading habit, almost prostrate. The very small leaves are a dull, pale green in color, becoming a brilliant scarlet in autumn. The branches are very spiny and the abundant fruit is salmon-red. A native of western China.

Calluna vulgaris (heather)

One of the most familiar shrublets in Europe. A great number of forms are cultivated in gardens, varying in color of flower and foliage, time of flowering and growth habit. All are easily grown in lime-free soils.

Cotoneaster adpressus

A gem for the rock garden, being a compact, wide-spreading shrub with bright red fruit and small leaves that turn scarlet in autumn. Native to western China.

Cytisus decumbens

A prostrate rock garden shrublet with evergreen twigs resembling a small broom. The flowers are bright yellow in May and June. Native to southern Europe.

Daboecia cantabrica (St. Daboec's heath)

One of the most charming and useful of dwarf shrubs, producing long racemes of very showy, rose-purple, cup-shaped flowers from June to November. It will need some winter protection. Native to western Europe.

Daphne cneorum (garland flower)

This is a great favorite because of its lovely fragrance. The fine, rather needlelike leaves are evergreen, and the rose-pink flowers are borne in small clusters at the end of the branches in April and May. A difficult plant to establish. Native to central and southern Europe.

Erica carnea (spring heath)

Forms dense hummocks and mats of fine evergreen foliage hardly more than 12 in. in height. The small rosy red flowers last throughout the winter until April. Today there are innumerable cultivars available in a very wide range of colors from white to purple. All are lime-tolerant. Native to the Alps.

Jasminum parkeri

A dwarf or prostrate shrub normally forming a low mound of densely crowded greenish stems bearing small, pinnate leaves and tiny yellow flowers in summer. Native to northwestern India.

Leiophyllum buxifolium (box-leaved sand myrtle)

An evergreen shrub with very small, glossy foliage. It prefers an open sunny position and a moist, sandy soil of high acidity. The clusters of white flowers, which open in May and June, are borne at the very ends of the branches. Native to the pine barrens of southern New Jersey.

Potentilla fruticosa (shrubby cinquefoil)

A low shrub of dense, somewhat irregular growth, averaging 1½ ft. to 2 ft. in height. It blooms from June until the fall. The flowers range from pale lemon-yellow to dark golden-yellow. It is native to Europe, Asia and North America.

Rhododendron spp.

There are many dwarf forms of dense, compact habit that are suitable for the rock garden. Although a number of these are difficult to maintain in cultivation, the following are meritorious:

R. ferrugineum (alpine rose): A small, spreading shrub with reddish leaves that are scaly underneath. The June-blooming flowers are rose-crimson.

R. impeditum: A dwarf alpine shrub only a few centimeters high, with tiny leaves. Flowers are purplish-blue and bloom in April and May. From Yunan, China.

R. imperator: A dwarf shrub, often creeping, with small narrow leaves. The May-blooming flowers are pink, borne even on very young plants. Native to Burma.

R. intricatum: A small, densely twiggy shrub, with small, olive-green aromatic leaves. Flowers are funnel-shaped and lavender-blue, blooming in April and May. Native to Szechwan, China.

Rubus calycinoides

A creeping alpine evergreen, forming dense mats of short-jointed, tip-rooting stems. The small leaves are glossy green and gray-felted beneath. The white flowers are usually concealed beneath the leaves. A most useful ground cover for the rock garden. Native to Taiwan.

Selection of Herbaceous Perennials

A rock garden is a very distinctive type of flower garden, which should be characterized not only by rocks and plants but more particularly by such kinds of plants as are generally associated with rocky conditions. There are no fixed rules defining an alpine plant; however, it is best described as one that flourishes within the alpine zone. Strictly speaking, true alpines live above the treeline and are mostly of dwarf stature. Saxatile plants are those that do best and look most natural growing among rocks, though they may be found in either sun or shade at lower elevations also.

Place individual plants where they will show to their best advantage. For a correct arrangement and effect, one must become familiar with the plants—their color, their size and time of bloom. The other fundamental problems to consider are their growth habits and rates of growth.

There are two major groups of perennials for rock gardens: (1) those whose chief effect is derived from massing; and (2) those that are seen to best advantage when planted not too far off the path. To Group 1 belong:

Alyssum saxatile	*Campanula portenschlagiana*
Arabis alpina	*Iberis sempervirens*
Aubretia	*Phlox subulata*

These quite rapid-growing dwarf spreaders will provide the immediate foundation. To avoid rather too flat an appearance, their drifts of color can be interspersed with plants of slightly taller habit.

Some plants are grown for their overall beauty but are unable to provide bold dashes of color. In this group are the delights of the experts; such plants as:

Achillea tomentosa	*Draba polytricha*
Cyclamen europaeum	*Gentiana acaulis*
Douglasia vitaliana	

These plants should be close to eye level and near the paths.

Plant Arrangement

Form, color, height and texture are but a few of the characteristics to be taken into consideration when selecting suitable plant partners. The unbelievable number of types and species of plants should be placed neither in rank-and-file order nor casually or frivolously scattered. Every opportunity should be utilized to plant them according to their known ecological demands, so that they can establish themselves permanently. For example, in early spring when the grass paths are still partly moist, we find in the bright sun the warmth-loving *Muscari*, *Crocus* and *Puschkinia*. Thriving in the cool and moist places, mostly in the shade of shrubs, are the cool-loving bulbs such as snowdrop, *Scilla*, *Chionodoxa* and winter aconite. These bulbs do best when not crowded by grasses and other herbs.

Heathers tie in easily with dwarf pines, and with such undemanding perennials as *Antennaria*, *Hieracium* and the creeping thyme. A complete ground cover showing the full beauty of these plants may only be developed in sandy soil that is poor in nutrients. Wildflowers brought into the rock garden are happiest where they are in association with plants of the same habitat, and where they can grow undisturbed together and form a plant carpet.

In selecting plant material and choice of position, one should also make sure that each plant is in harmony with the rest of the planting, and that the individual beauty of a plant will not be lost or overwhelmed in the larger group. The loveliest and most precious perennial may seem a weed if not planted in the right location and community.

The distance between plants in a group depends mainly upon their rate of growth during the growing season. As a rule, plants used as ground cover grow quickly, and the choice is generally a question of how the plants are able to compete with each other. For groupings, we have to determine how many individuals to plant together or whether it would be best perhaps to plant only one individual. Not all perennials are sociable in large groups.

Decision making in this area is determined by the way plants are found in nature. A plant usually found growing in a solitary state, such as *Carlina acaulis,* should not be set out in groups in the garden. A similar approach may be taken in deciding intermediate groupings of three to five plants with *Adonis vernalis* or *Anemone alpina. Arenaria,* heathers and *Dryas octopetala* are generally massed.

Care and Maintenance

The maintenance of a rock garden is primarily a matter of weeding only. Weeds, of course, should be destroyed as soon as they appear. Do not allow them to become established, as they are then more difficult to remove and are likely seriously to weaken delicate plants and injure them when pulled. A mulch of stone chips around the plants helps to control the weeds. Stone chips also have the added advantages of keeping the soil from washing off slopes and preventing the soil surface from baking and forming a crust. Furthermore the soil below the chips stays cooler and water will not evaporate as readily. No mud will splash onto the plant and the foliage, resting on stone chips, will dry faster.

Winter protection of the rock garden is rarely necessary, though it helps to cover some of the more tender plants with evergreen branches. This should be done only after the ground is frozen 1 in. to 2 in. deep. Otherwise the plants may not harden sufficiently, with the result that they will go into the winter with soft growth and will be winter-killed. In areas where regular snowfall can be expected, snow fencing may be erected around the rockery. The fence will not only act as a windbreak but will help to retain more snow on the planted area. Snow is the best and most natural winter protection for alpines.

In the spring the established rock garden will require some attention. An early inspection will reveal where plants have been heaved out of the soil by frost action, or where soil has been washed away. Plants that have been heaved out should be promptly reset, firmed in and mulched with soil and stone chips, and the lost soil should also be replaced. Some alpines appear to grow their way out of the soil naturally, and these require mulching every year with fresh soil and stone chips.

TROUGH GARDENS

Many of us are bewitched by the charm of miniature alpine landscapes, mostly unspoiled by man's handiwork. But we may well ask, Will they grow in our garden? The answer is not easily answered unless conditions of soil, aspect and position are known. Yet, although no straightforward answer can be given, there is a solution. It lies in trough- and miniature gardening. In small compass, conditions can be artificially produced to suit the requirements of these delightful miniature gardens. At the same time trough-gardening can provide a new means of gardening even for city dwellers, whose sole available space usually consists of a few yards of paving or concrete slabs. Troughs and miniature gardens also look delightful flanking a lawn or arranged on a terrace. This type of gardening is primarily for the hobby gardener, the elderly or the admirer of the smallest and rarest plants.

Unfortunately, a number of alpines are not easy to grow in the rock garden because of our varied climate and temperature extremes. However, in a trough, where growing conditions are more under the control of the cultivator, the majority of alpine minatures can be grown successfully over a number of years.

Unless used with the greatest care, the dwarf and slow-growing conifers are not easy to place in the rock garden. In the trough, however, they add that touch of character that is so necessary and desirable in this type of gardening, and the root restriction which the trough imposes helps the plants retain their dwarf stature. All the dwarf trees must be on their own roots.

Another aspect of this method of gardening is that each miniature trough or sink is in itself an artistic creation; but, unlike a painting, it is a living thing, providing a series of enchanting pictures that change with each passing season.

There are more practical sides to trough gardening. Many elderly people who are unable to cope with the physical aspects of gardening still have an active "green thumb." These people frequently find trough-gardening very satisfactory because troughs, arranged on stilts of stone or wood to suit the gardener's height, eliminate the necessity of strenuous bending. And last but not least, this type of gardening will also keep off that arch enemy of all rock plants, the slug.

One of the most charming plant containers is the old antique stone trough, though the prices for these today are rising rapidly because each is unique. However, very attractive inexpensive troughs can be made of concrete or bricks. A more portable but equally satisfactory container can even be made of a mixture of equal parts of fine peat, fine perlite, vermiculite and cement. The inside of the 1-in.-thick walls of these man-made containers is reinforced with chicken wire. For drainage, wooden dowels can be pressed into the wet cement and pulled or drilled out later.

But the most important aspect of trough and table gardens is neither the material nor the form of the container. Far more important is good drainage. Alpines are utterly intolerant of badly drained soil. Wherever they are grown, it is essential to make certain that water does not stagnate around their roots. Alpines like plenty of water and are accustomed to growing in places where, especially during spring and early summer, vast amounts of water from melting snow and ice flow past their roots. Yet they will not endure having their roots surrounded by perpetually soggy soil.

Soil

Since we are not dependent on the existing ground, decisions on what soil to use are not difficult. Choice or preparation of a light, permeable mix should be paramount, and peat or rotted pine needles make an ideal starting material. The loose substance in the soil should

24.3 If you don't have a rock garden but enjoy alpine plants, you can grow them in a container. Photo Carlton Lees

remain, since we have a permanent planting in the trough that should not be renewed every year.

Alpines can generally be grouped in two categories: (1) the lime-loving type, to which, with a few exceptions, all *Dianthus, Aubrieta, Arabis* and *Alyssum* belong, as do the vast majority of saxifrages; and (2) those that do better without lime, most of whose members belong in the family Ericaceae. Most of the alpines will thrive in a mixture of peat, pine needle mold and sand in equal parts. The addition of small quantities of bone meal and charcoal chippings is all that is needed. For lime-loving plants, some granulated limestone should also be added. During the growing season an occasional feeding with an organic liquid fertilizer will help invigorate the plants.

Fig. 24.6
Natural stone trough. Old horse and pig troughs are excellent planters for rock garden plants

Provision for the essential good drainage must be made before the container is filled. A layer of coarse ash, gravel, or stone chips at the bottom of the container is sufficient. Over this, spread a layer of some rough organic material such as semidecayed leaves or coarse peat. This will prevent the finer compost that is used on top from filtering into and obstructing the drainage. With the drainage arranged for, fill the container to the brim with whatever compost has been chosen and prepared. It should be moist but not wet when used.

Fig. 24.8
A light, portable, frost-proof container This container can be easily made out of equal parts of cement, sphagnum, peat, and perlite. For reinforcement it is wise to sandwich a 1-in.-mesh chicken wire within the concrete.

Alpines on Tufa

A block of tufa can be used as a garden ornament and will certainly command the attention of passers-by. These chunks of porous rock can be purchased through any major garden center. Rooted cuttings or seedlings of alpines can be planted in existing holes in the tufa, or extra holes can be drilled in with a screwdriver. The stone is so porous that it will retain water for quite a long time, and the roots of the plants will penetrate into the material. This, in reality, is a miniature alpine garden. The tufa rock—a hermit from the mountains placed in an urban environment—emphasizes the contrast between tender plant and heavy structure. This is

Fig. 24.7
Round table garden. This garden is made of a large concrete drainpipe, 3 ft. to 4 ft. in diameter, buried up to 30 in. above ground level.

an ideal situation for such cliff-dwelling plants as the saxifrages and *Sempervivum*.

Plants Suitable for Troughs

In selecting plants for troughs, leaf and flower forms should be carefully studied from the aesthetic point of view, because the trough should be pleasing to look at throughout the year. Plants that are fast-growing should be avoided, and tender plants that are not winter-hardy should be omitted. Bear in mind that, contrary to a normal planting in a garden, the influence of frost comes not only from above the container but from all sides also. Of course, the type of plant material is determined by the location of the trough. Ideally, a sunny place should be selected. However, saxifrages and some ericaceous plants prefer to be on the shady side of a building but not under overhanging branches of trees.

Plants that dwell in higher mountain regions and cliffs have very precise requirements. Often the place in the garden is limited for a special alpinum. A trough or table garden, however, is an alpinum in miniature. With this form of gardening, there is the possibility of growing the rarest and daintiest alpine plants, with a good prospect of success.

Miniature dwarf conifers will improve the appearance of the sink or trough garden enormously. However, it is essential that all dwarf conifers be on their own roots, because grafted plants will lose their natural dwarf characteristics within a few years and will have to be replaced. Since a number of these conifers are surface rooters, they will require some shade during the hottest part of the day. Placing rocks

CONIFERS SUITABLE FOR TROUGH GARDENS

	ANNUAL GROWTH IN INCHES
Abies balsamea 'Nana'	1/2
Cedrus libani 'Nana'	1
Chamaecyparis obtusa 'Compacta'	1/4
Chamaecyparis obtusa 'Minima'	1/4
Chamaecyparis obtusa 'Nana'	1
Chamaecyparis pisifera 'Nana'	1/2
Cryptomeria japonica 'Bandai-sugi'	3/4
Cryptomeria japonica 'Vilmoriniana'	3/4
Juniperus communis 'Compressa'	1/2
Juniperus communis 'Echiniformis'	1/2
Picea abies 'Humilis'	1/4
Picea abies 'Pygmaea'	1
Pinus parviflora 'Brevifolia'	1/2
Pinus nigra pygmaea	1/8
Pinus sylvestris 'Beauvronensis'	1
Taxus baccata 'Pygmaea'	1/2
Thuja orientalis 'Minima Glauca'	1/2

over the roots on the surface of the compost will also be helpful. A drafty position should be avoided, and protection from the main wind direction in winter is advisable.

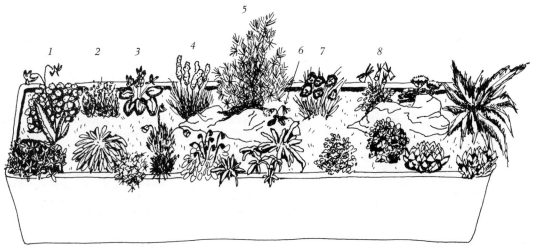

1. Helichrysum milfordiae
2. Hypericum coris
3. Cyclamen europaeum
4. Petrophytum hendersonii
5. Picea abies *'Pygmaea'*
6. Soldanella alpina
7. Dianthus simulans
8. Aquilegia jonesii

Fig. 24.9
Plants of the high mountains on the window sill

WALL GARDENS

Wall gardens, among the most practical and useful forms of rock gardens, can be created in "dry walls"—that is, walls that usually are built without mortar or cement. The wall is constructed in such a way that it holds plants which, in the wild, grow in crevices of cliffs. This type of gardening is very low in maintenance and plants more often thrive in such situations than they do in the soil of the rock garden. At the same time, they can be admired more readily since they can easily be seen at eye level.

Construction

"Dry walls" are built without any of the frost-proof foundation usually required for masonry walls. A low wall up to about 2 ft. in height can be built directly on the ground. For taller walls, however, it is better to place a layer of fairly large rocks 18 in. to 20 in. beneath the surface of the ground, or a trench can be dug as wide as one-third of the height of the wall, and about

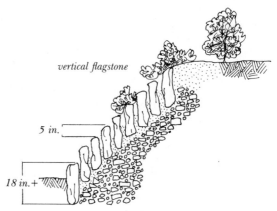

Fig. 24.11
Cyclopean wall (cross-section)

12 in. deep. This trench is filled to ground level with 2 in. to 3 in. of crushed stone.

As in the rock garden, large rocks are to be preferred, and the soil mix, which takes the place of mortar, is the same as in the rock garden: i.e., equal proportions of rough sand and gravel, sphagnum peat and a good, friable loam. Every device for holding the stones together should be used: joints should be overlapped, larger openings should be filled with smaller stone chips, tie stones should be used to hold wall to the existing bank (see sketch), and so on. Stones with round surfaces should be discarded. The individual pieces of rock must slope slightly downward toward the back of the wall. This is to prevent the rocks from slipping out of the wall as a result of frost action, and also to direct the flow of rainwater into the wall. The face of the wall must never be vertical but should slope at an angle of 2 in. for every vertical foot. The base of the wall should be equal to one-third of the height of the wall. Experience has shown that wall gardens should never be higher than 4 ft. or 5 ft. It is better to make several walled terraces rather than one tall dry wall. For higher walls, the size of the rocks should be increased to ensure greater stability and permanence.

In laying the rocks, each layer should be more or less horizontal. The prepared soil is

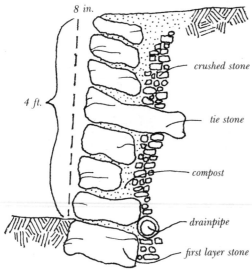

Fig. 24.10
Dry wall (cross-section)

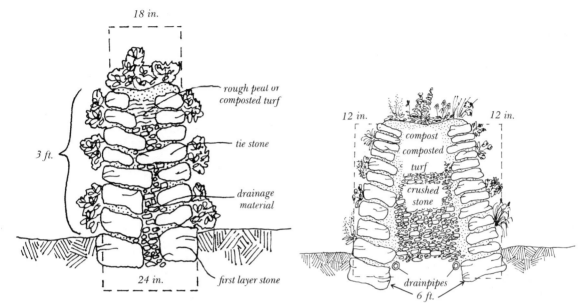

Fig. 24.12
Double dividing wall (cross-section)

Fig. 24.13
Wall mound (cross-section)

placed over the top of this first layer of rocks, and crushed stone or stone chips from the trimmed stones are packed behind each layer of stones. This will give the wall greater stability and ensure better drainage behind it. The stones in the second layer are then laid so that their joints do not coincide with those of the layer below. This process is repeated until the desired height is reached. Every so often a large rock should reach from the face of the wall back to the solid bank. This "tie stone" will give extra strength to the wall.

Planting Techniques

The most practical method of planting the wall is to set the plants in place as the wall goes up. The rootballs of the potted plants are loosened, and the roots disentangled and stretched as far back as possible on top of the stones and between the joints. Before the next rock is placed on top, some fine soil or peat should be sifted over the roots and then watered well. In walls that have already been established, the planting procedure is somewhat more complicated. In this situation, plants must be taken out of small pots and tucked securely into the crevices. To hold them in place and keep them moist for a longer period, sphagnum moss should be wedged around the plants, and the wall should then be syringed down frequently until the plants have become firmly established in their new home. On a sunny south side it would be practical to hang sheets of cheese cloth over the wall, which then is easily kept wet until the first rainy season.

The types of plants that can be used in a wall garden vary tremendously. One should take advantage of the many possibilities and grow some of those plants that are difficult to cultivate in an ordinary rock garden. Because of the better drainage, plants will have a longer life span and are less likely to rot.

ROCK PLANTS SUITABLE FOR TROUGH GARDENS

SCIENTIFIC NAME	HEIGHT AND SPREAD IN INCHES	COLOR
Androsace carnea	3 × 4	pink
Androsace chamaejasme	2 × 3	white
Androsace sempervivoides	2 × 6	pink
Androsace villosa	2 × 4	white
Anemone baldensis	3 × 6	white
Aquilegia jonesii	3 × 4	blue
Aquilegia saximontana	4 × 6	blue
Arabis androsacea	1 × 4	white
Arenaria tetraquetra	2 × 6	white
Armeria caespitosa 'Bevans variety'	2 × 6	pink
Artimesia glacialis	1 × 6	silver
Astilbe x *crispa*	6 × 8	rose
Campanula allionii	2 × 8	purple
Campanula elatines	3 × 8	violet
Campanula pilosa	4 × 6	pale blue
Campanula piperi	6 × 6	lilac-blue
Campanula rainieri	3 × 6	china blue
Campanula zoysii	2 × 4	pale blue
Cassiope lycopocioides	1 × 4	white
Cassiope mertensiana	9 × 6	white
Cassiope selaginoides	3 × 6	white
Corydalis cashmiriana	4 × 4	blue
Cyclamen europaeum	4 × 6	crimson
Cyclamen repandum	6 × 6	deep pink
Cytisus ardonii	4 × 8	yellow
Daphne petraea	4 × 6	rose-pink
Dianthus glacialis	2 × 6	deep pink
Dianthus neglectus	4 × 6	rose
Dianthus simulans	3 × 6	deep pink
Douglasia laevigata	2 × 6	rose-red
Douglasia vitaliana	1 × 6	yellow
Draba bryoides imbricata	2 × 4	yellow
Draba dedeana	1 × 4	white
Draba mollissima	2 × 6	yellow
Draba polytricha	2 × 4	yellow
Dryas octopetala minor	2 × 6	white
Edraianthus pumilio	2 × 6	lavender
Erigeron compositus	2 × 6	lavender
Erinus alpinus	3 × 6	lilac
Gentiana farreri	6 × 6	light blue
Gentiana verna	3 × 4	blue
Gentiana dalmaticum	6 × 6	pink
Globularia cordifolia	2 × 6	lavender
Gypsophila aretioides	1 × 6	white
Helichrysum milfordiae	1 × 6	white
Hypericum rhodopeum	4 × 8	yellow
Iberis saxatilis	3 × 6	white
Ilex mariesii	8 × 4	shrub
Iris pumila cretica	2 × 8	lavender blue
Kalmiopsis leachiana	9 × 6	rose pink
Leiophyllum buxifolium 'Nanum'	9 × 12	white
Lewisia brachycalyx	1 × 3	white
Lewisia rediviva	2 × 4	pale pink
Oxalis adenophylla	3 × 6	rose
Papaver alpinum	6 × 6	White, yellow, red
Penstemon davidsonii	3 × 8	lilac
Penstemon rupicola	4 × 8	crimson red

ROCK PLANTS SUITABLE FOR TROUGH GARDENS (Continued)

SCIENTIFIC NAME	HEIGHT AND SPREAD IN INCHES	COLOR
Petrocallis pyrenaica	2 × 5	lavender
Petrophytum caespitosum	1 × 6	white
Phlox bryoides	1 × 6	white
Phlox douglasii	2 × 6	lilac
Phyteuma comosum	3 × 6	lilac
Phyteuma pauciflorum	2 × 6	blue
Polygonum tenuicaule	2 × 5	white
Potentilla verna nana	1 × 6	gold
Primula allionii	2 × 4	rose red
Primula farinosa	2 × 3	pink
Primula marginata	4 × 6	lavender-blue
Primula minima	2 × 4	rose
Primula rosea	4 × 6	reddish-blue
Pulsatilla vernalis	4 × 6	white with violet back
Rhododendron impeditum	6 × 9	lavender
Rhododendron imperator	6 × 6	pale purple
Rhodothamnus chamaecistus	9 × 6	bright rose
Saponaria caespitosa	2 × 6	pale pink
Saponaria ocymoides 'Rubra Compacta'	1 × 6	carmine
Saxifraga (all small and compact varieties)	—	—
Sempervivum (all are ideal)	—	—
Silene acaulis	2 × 6	rose-pink
Silene pusilla	2 × 4	white
Soldanella montana	4 × 6	lavender
Talinum okanoganense	1 × 3	white
Townsendia wilcoxiana	2 × 4	lavender-blue
Viscaria alpina	4 × 4	rose

ROCK AND WALL PLANTS THAT ARE COMPARATIVELY EASY TO GROW

*A — acid   L — lime   N — neutral   **FL — filtered light

SCIENTIFIC NAME	COMMON NAME	SEASON OF BLOOM	HEIGHT IN INCHES	COLOR	SOIL*	EXPOSURE**
Achillea clavennae	silver alpine yarrow	May – June	4 – 12	white	L	sun, dry
Achillea tomentosa	wooly yarrow	June – Sept.	4 – 8	yellow	L	sun, dry
Adonis amurensis	Amur adonis	March – April	4 – 12	yellow	L or N	sun
Adonis vernalis	spring adonis	March – April	4 – 12	yellow	L or N	sun
Aethionema warleyense	Warley rose candytuft	June – July	4 – 6	pink	L	sun, dry
Ajuga reptans	bugle	May – June	6	blue	N	sun or FL
Alyssum saxatile (Aurinia saxatilis)	basket-of-gold, goldentuft	April – June	12	yellow	N	sun
Androsace sarmentosa	rock jasmine	May – June	4 – 6	pink	L or N	sun
Aquilegia canadensis	columbine	May	10	red	N	sun or FL
Arabis albida	wallcress	March – April	6	white	L or N	sun
Arenaria grandiflora	showy sandwort	June – Sept.	4	white	N	sun
Arenaria montana	mountain sandwort	June – Sept.	4 – 6	white	N	sun
Armeria caespitosa	thrift	June – July	3 – 4	pink	N	sun
Armeria maritima	thrift	June – July	4 – 6	pink-red range	N	sun
Aster alpinus	rock aster	May – July	10	violet-blue range	N	sun
Aubrieta deltoidea	aubretia	May – June	6 – 8	purple	L	sun
Bruckenthalia spiculifolia	spike heath	July – August	6	pink	A or N	sun
Calluna vulgaris	heather	July – Oct.	10	white, shades of purple	A	sun
Campanula carpatica	Carpathian harebell	June – Oct.	8	purple	L or N	sun
Campanula portenschlagiana		June – August	4 – 6	blue	L or N	sun
Ceratostigma plumbaginoides	leadwort	July – August	6 – 12	blue	N	sun or FL
Chrysogonum virginianum	golden star	June – August	9	yellow	N	sun or FL
Corydalis lutea		April – August	10	yellow	N	sun or FL
Dianthus gratianopolitanus	cheddar pink	July	3 – 6	rose	L	sun
Dianthus deltoides	maiden pink	May – Oct.	8	rose	L	sun
Draba sibirica	whitlow-grass	April – May	3	yellow	L or N	sun
Gentiana acaulis	spring gentian	May	2 – 5	blue	L	sun
Geranium dalmaticum	crane's bill	June	4 – 6	rose	L or N	sun
Globularia cordifolia	shrubby globularia	May – July	3	gray-blue range	L	sun
Gypsophila repens	creeping baby's breath	May – Oct.	4	pink-white range	N	sun
Haberlea rhodopensis		May	3 – 4	lavender	N	FL
Helianthemum nummularium	sun rose	June	6 – 8	yellow	L	sun
Heuchera sanguinea	coralbells	June – Sept.	12	rose red	N	sun
Hypericum calycinum	St. John's wort	June – Sept.	12 – 18	yellow	N	sun or FL
Hypericum olympicum	St. John's wort	July	6 – 8	yellow	N	sun
Iberis saxatilis	candytuft	May	4 – 6	white	L	sun
Iberis sempervirens	candytuft	April – June	8	white	L or N	sun or FL
Iris cristata	crested iris	May – June	4 – 6	lilac-blue range	N	sun or FL
Iris pumila	dwarf Crimean iris	May – June	6 – 10	lilac, blue, yellow	N	sun
Iris verna	vernal iris	May	4	blue-lilac range	N	sun or FL
Lavendula officinalis nana	lavender	July – August	8 – 10	blue	N	sun
Leontopodium alpinum	edelweiss	May – July	6	gray-yellow range	L	sun
Lewisia cotyledon	bitter root	May	8 – 10	pink	N or A	FL
Lewisia rediviva	bitter root	May – June	2 – 3	pink	N or A	sun
Linum alpinum	Alpine flax	May – Sept.	6 – 8	blue	N	sun
Linum flavum	yellow flax	June – August	10 – 12	yellow	N	sun
Lychnis alpina	Alpine campion	May	6	pink	L or N	sun
Lychnis x haggeana		June – July	10	red	N	sun
Nepeta mussiniu	catmint	July	12 – 15	blue	N	sun
Oenothera caespitosa	evening primrose	July	8	white, pink	N	sun
Penstemon menziesii	beard tongue	July	6 – 8	purple	N or A	sun or FL
Penstemon newberryi	mountain pride	July	15	rose	N or A	sun or FL

ROCK AND WALL PLANTS THAT ARE COMPARATIVELY EASY TO GROW (Continued)

*A—acid   L—lime   N—neutral   **FL—filtered light

SCIENTIFIC NAME	COMMON NAME	SEASON OF BLOOM	HEIGHT IN INCHES	COLOR	SOIL*	EXPOSURE**
Phlox bifida	prairie phlox	May	4–6	lilac, blue	N	sun
Phlox divaricata	blue phlox	April	8	lilac, blue	N	sun or FL
Phlox stolonifera	creeping phlox	May	6	carmine	N	sun or FL
Phlox subulata	moss phlox	April	4	blue-pink range, white	N	sun
Potentilla alba	cinquefoil	April	4	white	N	sun
Potentilla tridentata	three-toothed cinquefoil	June–July	6–10	white	A	sun or FL
Potentilla villosa		April–May	2	yellow	L or N	sun
Primula auricula	auricula	April–May	6–8	yellow	L	sun or FL
Primula denticulata		April–May	10–12	white, pink	N	sun or FL
Primula marginata		April–May	3–6	lavender, blue	L or N	sun or FL
Primula sieboldii	Siebold primrose	May–June	12	rose, white	N	sun
Pulsatilla vulgaris	pasque flower	March–May	10–12	violet, lilac	L	sun or FL
Saponaria ocymoides	rock soapwort	April–July	10	pink	N	sun
Sedum acre	gold moss	June–Sept.	2	yellow	N	sun
Schivereckia podolica		May–June	4	white	L or N	sun
Sempervivum (many species)	houseleek, hen-and-chickens	May–June	4	yellow, red	L or N	sun
Silene caroliniana	wild pink	June–July	3–4	pink	A	sun or FL
Silene schafta		June–July	4–6	purple, pink	N	sun or FL
Thymus serpyllum	mother of thyme	June	3–4	rose, purple	N	sun
Tunica saxifraga	tunicflower	June–Sept.	6	pink	N	sun
Veronica repestris	cliff speedwell	June–August	6–8	blue, white	N	sun
Veronica spicata nana	dwarf speedwell	June–August	6	blue	N	sun

25.1 Gently cascading water and many shallow pools invite birds. Photo Anita Sabarese

25

Inviting the Birds

We live in a world blessed with an abundance of life. The seasons come and go. Growth, fruition and decay follow in unending sequence. The birds remind us with their amazing migrations and their songs that nature's laws are slow to change, and that they, too, are subject to the protection as well as the stern necessities of these laws.

Almost all species of songbirds and game birds are our friends and allies in the never-ending process of controlling insects. The warblers, flycatchers, thrushes, creepers, thrashers, mockingbirds, woodpeckers and grackles are busy most of the time, eating the eggs, larvae and mature insects. A pair of yellow-billed cuckoos will consume thousands of tent caterpillars in a season.

If we provide suitable habitat, we will have quantities of resident birds and many of the migrants as well. The most important considerations are water, an open area of lawn or meadow, a thicket of shrubs, some trees and *no* cats. Water is essential, even if it is only a small pool with an inlet that can be opened periodically to keep the water fresh. A meadow or lawn and a nearby copse of bushes for cover, for berries and for nesting places will satisfy the ground birds. A few tall trees in a grove will delight the twig-inspecting birds who feed on insects, borers and young buds. Such birds as vireos, warblers, thrushes, woodpeckers and titmice seek

tall trees in a grove. The meadowlark, quail, field sparrow, goldfinch and bobolink need pastures and hay fields. Bluebirds, nuthatches, downy woodpeckers and flickers prefer old orchards with broken or hollow branches for nesting places. Many of the songbirds are content to live close to our homes, especially if there are mature trees and shrubs and gardens nearby. The house wren, phoebe, robin, catbird, cardinal, song sparrow and chipping sparrow all nest in confidence as our close neighbors. For winter shelter, large evergreens are particularly important and should be an integral part of the plan to invite the birds.

When complete habitat is provided for as many different species of birds as possible, the beautiful and exciting predatory species of hawks and owls may occasionally visit the sanctuary, enhancing immeasurably the birdwatcher's pleasure. In providing bird habitat, the homeowner is also providing suitable habitat for interesting mammals and insects as well. Chipmunks, squirrels, fireflies, butterflies and moths—all should be welcome visitors in the natural landscape created to attract birds.

A constant and varied food supply is as important as good locations for nests. If we will plant the trees and shrubs and garden flowers that provide the birds with the food they like, we will have many birds. In the year-round life of birds, many species of trees and shrubs seem attractive in one way or another. But those listed at the end of the chapter have associations that are noteworthy.

WINTER FEEDING

Winter feeding, if it is kept up regularly, is a great benefit to the winter residents and migratory birds. A feeding tray, or a tray with a hopper from which the seeds pour out as they are needed, set well off the ground and protected by a collar of fine mesh wire to keep off the cats and squirrels, will provide a safe and happy spot for the birds to gather. Casting crumbs and seed upon the snow is inadequate, temporary and wasteful.

The junco, nuthatch, chickadee, titmouse, fox sparrow, song sparrow, cardinal, downy woodpecker, hairy woodpecker, flicker and blue jay are the most frequent feeders at a winter station in eastern states. But in some winters, bluebirds, white-throated sparrows and robins will stay all winter in the latitude of Philadelphia. If a feeding station is established, the birds must have the assurance that the food will be supplied all winter, for winter is no time to migrate.

Fully as important as the grain and seed supply is the fruit of bushes that will stay fresh in the cold weather. The best of these are *Crataegus cordata* (Washington thorn), *Ilex verticillata* (winterberry) and the cotoneasters. If we would have the birds through the winter, we should provide for them. (See lists at end of chapter.) Balls of suet hung in loose mesh bags or secured within hardware cloth are especially attractive to downy and hairy woodpeckers and chickadees.

NESTING SITES

Nesting houses are also a means of attracting birds, especially the species whose habitual home sites have been destroyed or curtailed by modern developments.

The purple martins prefer colony houses on very tall poles.

The barn swallows will settle for a porch roof if there is no barn available.

The phoebe, which loves a running stream and likes to build its nest under a stone bridge, will accept a ledge under an accessible roof.

The house wren prefers a box with a hole just its size. But if it cannot have perfection, it will drive out the English sparrows and occupy a box with a larger hole.

The bluebird loves a low hollow branch in a low tree. But it will accept a deep nesting box on a post if it is placed from 4 ft. to 6 ft. above the ground. The box should be provided with a perch, and the entrance should face south or southeast.

Birds are very suspicious of cats. If you give them every inducement but do not keep the cats away, you are not really inviting the birds to make their home with you. Every post that supports a bird box should be provided with a flaring collar of tin or wire mesh several feet above the ground. A well-established climbing rose on the post will do almost as well as the wire.

One final precaution: leave natural places natural. Woodpeckers carve out nesting holes in dead branches of trees. Leave a few dead branches for them. Red-winged blackbirds and marsh wrens love to build in swamps. Do not drain all of the swamps. Chimney swifts like abandoned chimney flues. Do not use your fireplaces until the young birds have left the nest. Great blue herons, little green herons and mallard ducks need secluded ponds. Do not cut down the trees beside the pond. Preserve the woodland for the hermit thrush, the vireo, the wood thrush, the ovenbird, the ruffed grouse and woodcock. Keep all these natural areas as sanctuaries for the birds.

FLOWERS ATTRACTIVE TO BIRDS

Few garden flowers are attractive to birds, but those that are bring the rare and colorful hummingbird. This remarkable little creature poises beside a blossom and reaches its bill down to the base of the tube for the nectar. Its favorite flowers are columbine, flowering tobacco, coralbells, petunia, phlox and vesper iris.

The goldfinches come to the seed trays of the sunflowers and to the goldenrod, thistle bloom and orange cosmos. Hummingbirds and butterflies hover over the blooms of the butterfly weed.

TREES ATTRACTIVE TO BIRDS

Apple	Nesting sites for bluebirds. Feeding for nuthatches, flickers and chickadees
Arborvitae	Nesting sites for catbirds and waxwings
Black cherry	
Cherry (orchard var.)	Fruits for most of the small birds
Chokecherry	Jays, robins, catbirds, cardinals (70 species of birds have been counted)
Elm	Nesting sites for orioles. Seed for many songbirds, bark insects for woodpeckers and creepers
Flowering crabs	Fruits for songbirds
Flowering dogwood	Fruits for many birds
Hemlock	Shelter in storms. Nesting sites for hummingbirds
Hackberry	Fruits for many birds
Hawthorns	Fruits in quantity in autumn and early winter
Holly	Fruits for the winter residents and migrants
Larch	Feeding for creepers, chickadees
Mountain ash	Fruits in quantity in August and early autumn
Mulberry	Fruits in quantity in summer
Pines	Cones for crossbills, robins, white-throated sparrows, warblers, kinglets and many other birds
Red cedar	Berries for waxwings, catbirds and sparrows
Shadbush	Fruits for many species
Spruces	Shelter in storms and nesting places
White birch	
Yellow birch	Feeding for warblers, finches, chickadees

SHRUBS ATTRACTIVE TO BIRDS

Blueberry	Berries	Junipers	Berries and shelter
Boxwood	Shelter and nesting	Rosa multiflora	Fruit
Bush dogwoods	Berries	Sumac	Fruit
Butterfly weed	Flowers for hummingbirds	Sweetleaf	Berries
Chokeberry	Berries	Trumpet creeper	Flowers for hummingbirds
Cotoneasters (all var.)	Berries	Viburnum (most var.)	Berries
Elderberry	Berries	Virginia creeper	Berries
Firethorn	Berries and shelter	Winterberry	Berries

26

Flower Boxes

In many towns and villages throughout Europe flower boxes contribute almost as much to the charm and beauty of the community as does the picturesque architecture. One sees them everywhere — at windows, on balconies, on lamp posts, between gas pumps at filling stations. Flower boxes are used not only at the windows of private homes but also on public buildings, hotels, hospitals, banks, government and private office buildings and shops. Even in the poorer districts, material poverty is often so clothed with flowering beauty and living greenery that one feels there is no poverty of the spirit among those who dwell there.

In our own country, there recently has been a tremendous upsurge of interest not only in flower boxes but also in the whole technique of growing plants in containers outdoors. One sees window boxes more and more frequently on city homes and at apartment windows, as well as on homes in the suburbs and country. And many a porch, terrace and patio is made bright with flower boxes. Indeed, these portable planting boxes may be used to create a veritable garden in miniature. If a wise selection of plant materials is made, the boxes can be kept bright with color and bloom from early spring until mid-autumn and will be a source of joy throughout the season.

In order to provide the most favorable growing conditions for the plants, there are a number of points that must be considered: the size and type of box; the material of which the box is made and provision for drainage; the soil mixture; the program of general maintenance and the selection of plants best suited to the exposure.

SIZE AND TYPE OF BOX

Determining the size of the flower box is of major importance. Small boxes have several disadvantages. They tend to dry out very quickly and in extremely hot weather the soil may become overheated. When this occurs the plants suffer seriously, as it is difficult for them to obtain the nutrients from the soil that they need. Overheated soil is the cause of frequent failures in maintaining flower boxes in good condition. On the other hand, large boxes become extremely heavy when filled with soil, and hanging them properly from a window or balcony may become a problem. The advantage of commercial planting mixes — those that have been lightened with perlite — is obvious here as compared to the weight of garden soil.

For window and porch boxes the most satisfactory dimensions are: a length of from 32 in. to 48 in., depending upon the length of the window; a minimum width of 10 in.; a minimum depth of 8 in. (inside measurements). Root development in flower boxes is necessarily very restricted and there is considerable competition between the plants for available nutrients. In boxes that are too narrow or too shallow, plants fail to make good growth.

For terraces, patios and in penthouse gardens, planting boxes may be built according to dimensions that are suited to the location and best meet the specific needs of the plants to be grown.

MATERIALS

The materials of which flower boxes are made has an important bearing upon the growth and vigor of the plants they will contain.

Metal boxes have decided limitations. The cheaper types rust out after a year or two and must be replaced. And since metal is a conductor of heat, the soil in such boxes tends to become seriously overheated in hot weather, with the result that the normal development of the plants is greatly retarded. Metal boxes are also often too shallow to permit good root development and frequently they lack adequate provision for drainage.

Within recent years fiberglass and various "soft" polyurethane plastics have come into use for flower boxes. Such boxes offer many advantages. They are lightweight, do not rust or crack, are extremely durable, provide good insulation against heat and cold, are resistant to acids and chemicals and the color does not fade. In addition to their use at windows, these plastic flower boxes can also be used as easily movable, decorative features on terraces and patios. Indoors they may be used on deep window sills, on plant stands and on room dividers.

Wood also is an excellent material for plant boxes. If a suitable wood is selected and the box is well made, it should give service for many years. One type of wood that possesses remarkable ability to resist decay is cypress. Initially, it is more expensive than other woods but will outlast them by many years. Redwood should be avoided for conservation reasons, in favor of faster-growing, nonendangered species such as white pine. Cedar is also excellent. Cheap grades of lumber or kinds that are subject to decay should not be used. In the long run it is more economical to use the best wood available, preferably cypress or cedar, with white pine as

third choice. Exterior grade plywood is also extremely useful for building window boxes. Its advantages are strength and freedom from warping. A disadvantage is the appearance of cut ends, but this can be overcome by design.

CONSTRUCTION

There is a great difference between a really well-built flower box and one that has been carelessly constructed. As the sides of a flower box will be subject to considerable pressure, it is essential that it be constructed with care. Boards from $7/8$ in. to $1\frac{1}{4}$ in. in thickness should be used, depending upon the size of the box. Brass screws should be used throughout instead of nails, as nails are likely to pull out if the boards begin to warp. The corners should be reinforced with angle irons screwed onto the inside near the top. This will strengthen the box and prevent the boards along the front and rear from pulling away from the end pieces. Holes to permit the drainage of surplus water should be bored in the bottom. The holes should be about $1/2$ in. in diameter and should be spaced from 6 in. to 8 in. apart.

In hot climates or wherever boxes will be exposed to long hours of hot sun, an insulated type of box can be constructed that will prevent the soil from becoming seriously overheated. A $3/4$-in. board may be used along the front, faced with a light $3/16$-in. board, a dead air space of about $1/2$ in. being left between the two boards. This space will provide excellent insulation if it is filled with dry sphagnum moss; alternatively, a Styrofoam lining may be fabricated. Styrofoam is impervious to water and has excellent insulating value.

After the box has been completed, the inside should be brushed over with cuprinol or some equally good wood preservative that is nontoxic to plants. (Creosote should not be used as it is toxic to plants.) The outside of the box should be painted with a good-quality paint.

Wooden boxes can be made in a variety of styles. A molding around the front or a little scalloped apron at the base adds greatly to the attractiveness of the box.

A self-feeding, self-watering window box may be built if desired. Such a box has a double bottom. The lower portion, which should be approximately 3 in. in depth, provides a place for the removable metal tray that contains the nutrient solution. Wicks made of glass wool carry the nutrients to the plants. Perlite, vermiculite or a mixture of either or both with peat moss should be used in the box instead of soil. The plants should be taken from their pots and planted, with the ball of earth surrounding their roots, directly in the mixture.

There should be a row of holes in the bottom of the box spaced approximately 9 in. apart and the wicks should be about 9 in. long. Five inches of the wick should be poked down through the hole in the box into the metal tray. The remaining portion of the wick should be slit down into four sections, each section being spread out over a 1-inch bed of vermiculite in the bottom of the box. Both the vermiculite and the wicks should be thoroughly wet with the solution. The remaining vermiculite should be moistened with the solution and placed in the box, which is then ready for planting.

The tray should be kept filled with the nutrient solution. Beyond this, no further feeding or watering is required.

It is important that adequate provision be made for drainage in all types of flower boxes. Unless this is done, the soil in the boxes becomes completely saturated with water during periods of heavy rain; under such conditions plants become starved for oxygen and fail to thrive. Before the soil is put into the box, a 1-in. layer of small pieces of broken flower pot, small stones, sifted hard-coal cinders or smashed bricks should be spread over the bottom. Above this is a piece of wet burlap, a piece of fine mesh plastic or nylon screening, or a thin layer of thoroughly moistened sphagnum moss should be spread in order to prevent the soil from sifting down into the drainage area.

SOIL MIXTURE

A good commercial potting mix, such as Cornell Mix or a similar type, is ideal for window boxes because it is lightweight and free of the diseases and insect pests found in ordinary garden soil. A combination of such a mix and well-rotted compost or leaf mold also can be used. It is important to incorporate in the soil mix adequate humus for retention of moisture and to ensure excellent drainage. A soil with a pH range between 6.3 and 7.0 will be satisfactory for nearly all plants that are commonly grown in window boxes. The box should be filled to within about ¾ in. of the top.

If desired, the flower boxes may be filled with moist peat moss, vermiculite or perlite in which the pots containing the plants may be sunk. This procedure has several advantages. It makes it easy to change the plants from season to season or to replace a plant which is not doing well, and it obviates the necessity of obtaining soil which, in city areas especially, is often a great problem. The filler should be kept moist at all times and the potted plants should be watered whenever the soil appears dry on the surface. The disadvantage is the expense involved. Plants in pots cost considerably more than plants in plant bands, flats or other commercial containers, and it is sometimes difficult to obtain certain plants such as lobelia, alyssum and marigolds in pots.

MAINTENANCE

In caring for flower boxes the three essentials of good maintenance are watering, feeding and the removal of faded blooms.

Since the soil in flower boxes dries out much more rapidly than the soil in garden beds, the plants need more frequent watering. A mulch of peat moss on the surface of the soil will help conserve the moisture and will be of great benefit. The peat moss should be moistened well before it is used. A mulch ½ in. to 1 in. in depth usually is sufficient for such purposes. Watering the boxes is best done in the late afternoon or early evening, but do not water or syringe so late that the plants go into night with water on the foliage and flowers. In extremely dry, hot weather it may be necessary to water boxes that have a southern or southwestern exposure early in the morning and again during the middle of the day. Syringing the foliage with a fine spray several times a week also will help keep the plants in good condition. This is particularly necessary in the case of city window boxes in order to remove the coating of soot that forms on the leaves and is a serious hindrance to the normal transpiration of the plants. As in other types of gardening, to overwater a flower box is almost as serious as to underwater it. Since few plants can thrive in saturated, water-logged soil, watering must be carefully regulated, and in cool, cloudy weather it should be suspended altogether until the soil appears dry once more.

In order to encourage vigorous growth and abundant flowering, supplemental feeding is recommended. Beginning about a month after planting, a weekly application of a high-analysis, water-soluble fertilizer that also contains the various trace elements should be made, being mixed at the rate of 1 teaspoonful to 1 gallon of water. A small portion may be sprayed over the foliage if desired (see foliar feeding in the index), or it may all be applied directly to the soil.

If such plants as petunia, pansy, lantana, verbena, marigold and a number of others are to be kept in continuous bloom throughout the season, it is necessary to remove the faded flowers to prevent the formation of seed. The removal of dead flowers also greatly improves the appearance of the flower box. Some plants, such as pansies, will give a second period of bloom if they are cut back severely and allowed to develop a new growth of vigorous young shoots.

PLANNING FOR SUCCESSION OF BLOOM

If expense does not have to be considered, it is possible to have bloom in window boxes from very early spring until late autumn.

In the early spring boxes containing pansies, English daisies, violas, forget-me-nots, wallflowers and a few pots of scillas, poet's narcissus or some of the other spring bulbs are particularly appealing.

Later in this season geraniums, potted petunias, verbenas, lobelia, lantanas and many other plants will be in flower and, with good care, will continue in bloom until early autumn.

In August some of the colchicums and autumn crocus may be planted near the front of the box. These will provide a bit of color when the annuals are removed to make way for the chrysanthemums, which will carry the season

of bloom well along into the fall season.

During the winter small evergreens, such as very small box bushes, may be planted in the boxes. These will then be removed and planted elsewhere in the early spring, at which time the pansies and their companions will again be ready to hold the center of the stage for a brief time.

PLANTS SUITABLE FOR FLOWER BOXES

FULL SUN

ageratum	pansy
candytuft	*Phacelia campanularia*
English daisy	*Phlox drummondii*
forget-me-not	portulaca
geranium	snapdragon
lantana	sweet alyssum
lobelia	verbena
nasturtium	viscaria
Nierembergia caerulea	wallflower

LIMITED SUN	PARTIAL SUN	FULL SHADE
Browallia major	achimenes	English ivy
coleus	coleus	ferns
heliotrope	fuchsia	syngonium
impatiens	impatiens	
lobelia	tuberous begonia	
nemesia	wax begonia	
torenia		
wax begonia		

LOW-GROWING (for front of box)	MEDIUM HEIGHT	TALL
achimemes	browallia	coleus
ageratum	candytuft	fuchsia
English daisies	heliotrope	geranium
forget-me-not	nemesia	impatiens
lobelia	nasturtium	lantana
Nierembergia caerulea	petunia	tuberous begonia
pansy	verbena	
Phacelia campanularia	viscaria	
Phlox drummondii 'Nana'	wax begonia	
portulaca		
sweet alyssum		
torenia		
viola		

FLOWERING PLANTS OF TRAILING HABIT	VINES
achimenes	Canary Island ivy
fuchsia (trailing form)	English ivy
lantana (trailing form)	grape ivy
lobelia (trailing form)	ground ivy
nasturtium (trailing form)	*Lotus bertheloti*
sand verbena	strawberry geranium
sweet verbena	*Vinca major variegata*
Thunbergia alata	*Vinca minor*

GOOD PLANT COMBINATIONS

SUNNY EXPOSURE   PARTIAL SHADE

geranium: pink   lantana: yellow   achimenes: purple   *Browallia major:* blue
petunia: white   nasturtium: orange-yellow   fuchsia: purple to mauve   impatiens: coral
lobelia: light blue   verbena: white   impatien: soft pink   nemesia: blue
vinca: variegated   torenia: white

petunia: purple   geranium: red   wax begonia: pink   tuberous begonia: pink
verbena: pink   petunia: white   coleus: pink tones   achimenes: trailing; purple
ageratum: lavender   lobelia: deep blue   torenia: deep blue
sweet alyssum: white   grape ivy

4

FLAVOR
AND FRAGRANCE

27

The Home Vegetable Garden

The home garden, when properly planned and planted, will supply a variety of vegetables for family use throughout the entire growing season. Moreover, a carefully planned vegetable garden will provide enough additional produce for canning and freezing. Such a garden is also one of the greatest sources of pleasure and recreation for the homeowner. As fresh vegetables are an important item in one's diet, the necessity of having them fresh and in sufficient amounts is apparent.

The following points should be helpful:

1. Plan and plant the garden so that it will be a pleasure. Figure out how much of each vegetable you will need for canning, for eating fresh, or for freezing, and grow only those vegetables that will give high yields.

2. Figure out how much ground you can properly care for. It is better to have a small garden properly maintained than to plant so much that you will be discouraged with it by midsummer. A plot 40 ft. wide and 60 ft. long will furnish an adequate supply of fresh vegetables for a family of six grown people and enough extra to can and freeze.

3. If the ground has not been previously planted, dig it up in the fall. Freezing and thawing weather will improve its physical condition. Fork in a good application of manure or compost if it is available: 1 ton will not be too much for a plot 40 ft. by 60 ft.

If lime has not been applied for several years, have the soil tested. Lime is best applied after the manure has been dug in. It should be raked in to a depth of 2 in. if possible. If it is not possible to prepare the land in the fall, the same suggestions hold true for spring preparation.

4. During the early or late winter months before it is possible to plant outside, plan your garden on a piece of paper so that no time will be lost or mistakes made at planting time.

Order your seed from a reputable seed merchant at an early date so as to be sure of getting the best varieties. Remember that several varieties of the same vegetable may be planted at the same time, which will mature several weeks apart.

5. When planning a garden, the following points should be observed:

(a) The earliest and latest planting date for each vegetable. Beets, for example, may be planted as soon as the ground is workable in the spring and planted until midsummer. Most varieties mature in sixty days.

(b) The time of year at which each vegetable grows best. The small, quick-maturing varieties of radishes do best when planted in the spring and fall and should not be planted during the hot summer months. They mature in twenty-five to thirty days.

(c) The period over which each vegetable may be harvested. Sweet corn may be

476

harvested over a period of ten to fourteen days, while radishes may last for only several days if the weather is hot and the soil quite dry. Tomatoes are harvested over a period of two months.

(d) Those vegetables that mature at the same time or have similar growth habit should be planted together. Asparagus and rhubarb are two examples and are perennials. They should be planted at one end of the plot, where they will not interfere with soil preparation each year.

(e) The planting distances of vegetables in the home garden may be somewhat modified where hand cultivation is to be practiced entirely. Cabbage, broccoli, cauliflower are usually set 2½ ft. to 3 ft. apart for machine cultivation, or 2 ft. apart for hand tilling.

(f) Plant tall-growing crops at one end of the garden and not next to the smaller ones that would be shaded too much for them. For example, beets should not be planted next to overshadowing sweet corn.

(g) Plant those vegetables next to each other that are susceptible to the same insects and diseases so that they may be controlled more easily. Cabbage, broccoli, brussels sprout and cauliflower belong to the same group, while eggplant, peppers, potatoes and tomatoes belong to another. Vine crops, which include squashes, pumpkins, melons and cucumbers, are also in one group.

(h) Plan to have the soil producing all the time. As soon as one crop is removed, plant another in its place. Early peas will mature in seventy to eighty days or about July 15. They may be followed by late beets, turnips, lettuce, snap beans or spinach. This is known as successive cropping.

(i) Practice intercropping by planting a quick-maturing crop between those that take a longer time to mature. Radishes or lettuce may be intercropped with peas, for example.

(j) Rotation. Some vegetables give better results if not planted in the same place the same year. It is poor practice to plant cabbage or any of its close relatives after the early crop has been removed, as the following crop may be very inferior in both quality and size.

Other points that might be helpful:

(1) If parsley is planted, have it on the outside edge next to the house so you won't have to walk through the entire garden to get to it.

(2) A path 4 ft. wide and 60 ft. long through the garden may be bordered with ageratum, zinnia, marigold, calendula or other easy-to-grow flowers. This will allow for rows 18 ft. long each side of the path, which can be easily cared for.

(3) With only a limited amount of time — perhaps during evening hours — many homeowners find a garden 50 ft. by 50 ft. is more practical.

SOWING SEEDS IN FLATS

A successful vegetable garden requires one to become knowledgeable in the sowing of seed and the growing of seedlings both indoors and out. While corn and beets, for example, are sown directly in the garden, some of the most important crops—tomato, pepper, eggplant and cabbage—must be started indoors and set out as small plants after danger of frost has passed.

Growing Media Used in Soil Mixtures

1. Soil.
2. Sand: small rock grains from 0.05mm to 2.0mm in diameter.
3. Peat: remains of aquatic, marsh or swamp vegetation; high water-holding capacity; contains some nitrogen.
4. Sphagnum moss: remains of acid-bog plants. Relatively sterile; light in weight; holds ten to twenty times its weight in water.
5. Vermiculite: micaceous mineral heated to 2,000° F., forming small, porous, spongelike kernels; sterile; light in weight; absorbs large amounts of water.
6. Perlite: gray-white material of volcanic origin; processed like vermiculite and has similar properties.

7. Leaf mold or compost.
8. Well-rotted manure.
9. Sawdust: absorbs nitrogen; well-rotted.

Soil Mixtures

1. A standard soil mixture 2–1–1 (2 parts soil, 1 part peat moss, 1 part sand).
2. Any of the growing media listed above can be used in various combinations with soil.
3. Some media such as sand or sphagnum moss can be used alone.

Steps in Preparing Seed Flats

1. Cover bottom of flat with coarse material or newspaper.
2. Heap soil mixture into seed flat.
3. Pack mixture around sides with edge of hand or fingers.
4. Add mixture so that it is level with the top of the flat and firm slightly.
5. Make furrows with planting board.
6. Sow seed from envelope. Uniform seed distribution is desirable. Thickness of sowing depends on type of vegetable and percentage of germination. A stand of ten to twelve seedlings per inch is desirable for many vegetables.
7. Cover seed with fine sand, vermiculite or sphagnum moss.
8. Firm surface.
9. Cover with soaked burlap.
10. Water with *mist* nozzle.
11. Label with name of vegetable, variety, source of seed and date planted.

Desirable Characteristics of Vegetable Garden Soil

1. Warms early in spring.
2. Retains moisture.
3. Easy to work.
4. Drains quickly.
5. Does not bake or pack.
6. Remains fertile.

Importance of Organic Matter in the Garden

1. Improves physical structure.
2. Eases water penetration.
3. Improves aeration.
4. Reduces crusting.
5. Provides source of energy for soil microorganisms.
6. Helps make soil nutrients available.
7. Yields CO_2, which with the organic matter may increase photosynthesis.

GARDEN EQUIPMENT

Many garden operations can be accomplished with little effort if proper equipment is at hand:

A spade and fork are necessary for preparing the soil as well as for harvesting some of the crops.

A rake is used for smoothing or fining the soil just after it is spaded, and also to rake in fertilizers that have been applied.

A hoe is necessary to make rows, to cover the seed, to move the soil toward some plants, to cut off weeds, and to make holes for setting plants.

A stout line and stakes are necessary for making rows straight.

Other implements that increase efficiency are hand weeders, trowels and hand cultivators, which have several attachments for marking rows, cutting weeds and making furrows.

COMMERCIAL FERTILIZERS

Commercial fertilizers cannot take the place of organic matter in the soil, but they do much to supplement it and are especially desirable where land is intensively cropped.

The three elements most essential for garden crops are nitrogen, phosphorus and potash. Generally speaking, nitrogen is used to promote leaf and vegetative growth; phosphorus promotes root growth and hastens maturity; and potash increases general sturdiness and resistance to disease.

A complete fertilizer is one that contains nitrogen, phosphorus and potash. It is usually described by figures giving the percentages of each element, i.e., a fertilizer that contains 4 percent of nitrogen, 8 percent of phosphorus and 4 percent of potash is called a 4–8–4.

As plants need a well-regulated diet, an understanding of the use of fertilizers and of the reasons for their application will greatly help the gardener.

Every plant has three stages of growth: the germinating and sprouting; the vegetative; and the fruiting. In the germinating stage, the seed absorbs moisture which, when given heat, changes the concentrated food contained in each seed to a simple form and is sufficient to make a sprout appear through a surface of soil.

From the time the first true leaves begin to turn green until the fruit begins to form, the plant is in the vegetative state. From the time the flowering first begins to form, the plant is in the fruiting stage.

Since plants such as lettuce and spinach are eaten in the vegetative stage, and tomatoes, peppers and eggplant in the fruiting stage, it is easy to understand that fertilizer requirements vary greatly. When placed in the soil, both phosphorus and potash are available to plants over a long period. On the other hand, nitrogen has various forms that differ widely in the rates at which they become available. Nitrogen may be classified into three types: (1) Inorganic, available as soon as dissolved in water: example, nitrate of soda, which is available in all soil conditions; (2) organic, which must undergo complete decomposition before nitrogen is available: examples, tankage and dried blood, available in about a month if the soil is warm, as the bacteria that promote decay are not otherwise active; and (3) those that are halfway between (1) and (2). These last must be changed to the nitrate form: example, ammonium sulphate, which becomes available in a week or two after being applied. No. 1 is used early in the spring when the soil is cold and can be used at other times also for quick results. The effect of an application lasts only two or three weeks and for continuous quick growth over a long period, Nos. 1, 2 and 3 should be mixed together and applied.

Many complete fertilizers are on the market, some having fancy trade names, others using the firm name and having the contents described by figures.

As already noted, a 100-lb. bag of a good complete fertilizer each season is a great aid in the production of a 50 ft. by 50 ft. garden.

Where fertilizers have been applied to the first crop, the succeeding crop's requirements are usually satisfied without applying additional fertilizer.

Methods of Applying Fertilizer:

1. Broadcasting over the surface and raking in just previous to planting.

2. Scattering in the drill or furrow and raking into the soil just previous to planting.

3. Broadcasting between rows during the growing season.

4. Drilling in with an attachment on the seed planter.

5. Applying in narrow bands, 3 in. to 4 in. away from the plants and covering with soil (the most approved method).

Note: Fertilizer will prevent germination if it comes in contact with the seed. It will also burn the foliage if it is spread on it.

CONTROL OF VEGETABLE DISEASES

In many cases when vegetables have been started early in coldframes or hotbeds, instead of in the garden, diseases will appear after transplanting them into the open. The cause can often be traced to insufficient care in preparing the seedbed. A number of diseases are able to winter over in old seedbeds and gardens, while many of the more damaging diseases are also carried over by the seed, such as early and late blights of celery; leaf blights and fruit rots of cucumbers, eggplant, melons and squashes; black rot and black leg of cabbage, turnips and cauliflower; early blight, leaf spot and bacterial canker of tomatoes; and others. Therefore, it is highly important to use clean seed and also to clean the seedbed soil when starting the crop.

Investment in good seed justifies safeguarding the crop in the seedbed. While the use of disease-free seed and clean seedbed soil are important steps in producing strong healthy plants, so too is good seedbed management. Healthy plants in seedbeds usually mean a disease-free crop in the garden.

Since many important garden vegetable diseases get their start in the seedbed or coldframe, even in spite of the precautions already mentioned, we must guard against infection from outside sources. Such sanitary and protective steps consist of the following:

1. Avoid overfrequent and excessive watering of beds; instead, water more heavily at longer intervals; water only in the forenoon and ventilate well to hasten drying as soon as possible. Proper watering, heating and ventilating of beds not only ensures sturdy, vigorous-growing plants, but also provides conditions that are not favorable for damping-off and other diseases.

2. Discard spotted, wilted and otherwise diseased plants, for they are starters of infection.

3. Avoid introducing old plant debris and contaminated soil into seedbeds and coldframes.

Remember that thorough protection of the vegetable crop against diseases may be accomplished easily while it occupies so limited a space.

CULTURAL DIRECTIONS

Artichoke – Globe

The globe artichoke is a tender perennial, which must be protected to withstand freezing temperatures.

Botanical Name: *Cynara scolymus*

Soil Preparation

The globe artichoke requires large amounts of plant food. The soil should be manured at the rate of ¼ ton to 500 sq. ft., and should also receive an application of a 4 – 8 – 4 or 5 – 10 – 5 fertilizer at the rate of 1 lb. to 35 sq. ft. Heavy clay soils should be avoided for best results.

Propagation

Seed is sown in flats during February or the early part of March in a greenhouse or hotbed. When the seedlings are 3 in. high, transplant to 3 in. pots and plant outside after all danger of freezing temperatures has passed. The plants are set 3 ft. apart in rows that are 4 ft. apart.

During the following year many suckers will develop at the base of the plant. Remove all but

APPROXIMATE SEED QUANTITIES OF VEGETABLES

Asparagus	1 oz. – 800 – 1,000 plants
Beans	1 lb. – 100 ft.
Beet	1 oz. – 50 – 75 ft.
Broccoli	
Brussels sprout	
Cabbage	¼ oz. will give 700 plants
Cauliflower	
Kale	
Chard	1 oz. – 100 ft.
Carrots	1 oz. – 100 ft.
Celery	¼ oz. – 500 – 800 plants
Corn, Sweet	1 lb. for 125 hills
Cucumber	½ oz. – 25 hills
Endive	¼ oz. – 50 ft.
Eggplant	¼ oz. – 750 plants
Kohlrabi	¼ oz. – 75 – 100 ft.
Leek	1 oz. – 100 ft.
Lettuce	¼ oz. – 750 plants
Muskmelon	1 oz. – 35 – 50 hills
Watermelon	1 oz. – 35 – 50 hills
Parsley	½ oz. – 100 ft.
Onion seed	1 oz. – 100 ft.
Onion sets	1 qt. – 50 ft.
Parsnip	¼ oz. – 100 ft.
Peas	1 lb. – 40 – 50 ft.
Pepper	¼ oz. – 600 plants
Pumpkin	1 oz. – 20 hills
Rhubarb	1 oz. – 75 – 100 ft.
Radish	1 oz. – 75 – 100 ft.
Spinach	1 oz. – 75 ft.

VEGETABLES THAT CAN BE GROWN IN POTS AND PLANTED OUTSIDE

Beans, Lima	Cucumber	Melon
Corn, Sweet	Gourd	Watermelon

six to eight of them when about 8 in. high. If removed with a knife so as to obtain a root system with them, they may be transplanted to a new location.

As the parent plants are unproductive after the fourth year, constant renewing is necessary to keep up production.

Fertilization and Cultivation

A complete fertilizer may be applied during the growing season if needed. The plants should receive clean cultivation to suppress weed growth and thereby conserve moisture.

VEGETABLES THAT CAN BE TRANSPLANTED

Asparagus	Cabbage	Leek
Beet	Cauliflower	Lettuce
Broccoli	Endive	Onion
Brussels sprout	Eggplant	Parsley
Celery	Kale	Pepper
Chard, Swiss	Kohlrabi	Rhubarb
		Tomato

Harvesting

Plants grown from seed do not produce buds the same year. Suckers will in many cases produce a few buds the same year.

Artichoke—Jerusalem

Botanical Name: *Helianthus tuberosus*

Origin

A tall perennial plant, known to be cultivated by the Indians. The edible portion is the tuber, which develops in the ground. The part above ground closely resembles the sunflower when in bloom.

Soil

Practically any type of soil will give good results if it is in a fair state of productivity. An application of manure plus the use of a 4–8–4 or 5–10–5 commercial fertilizer broadcast at the rate of 1 lb. to 50 sq. ft. just before planting will be beneficial.

Planting

The tubers may be planted whole or cut like potatoes just before planting, which takes place in early spring or fall. The planting distance is 18 in. to 24 in. in the row and 3½ ft. to 4 ft. between the rows; they should be covered with 2 in. of soil.

Harvesting

The tubers may be dug in the fall after top growth ceases, or left in the ground until spring. It is important that all of the tubers be removed; otherwise those left will become a nuisance if other crops are grown in the same place.

Storage

The tubers may be stored by putting them in any type of container with sufficient soil to prevent drying out. They may be left outdoors in this container all winter and even if the temperature falls to 20° below zero they will not be affected; in fact, a little frost may improve the flavor.

Asparagus

Botanical Name: *Asparagus officinalis*

(Derived from the Greek word meaning to swell or be ripe)

Origin

Known as food in Europe more than 2,000 years ago; grown here since colonial days.

Soil

Asparagus will grow on almost any soil, but its growth and development are retarded by too much moisture. A sandy, well-drained soil is best. Also, as a sandy soil warms up quickly in the spring, maturity is hastened. Soil should be plowed or spaded deeply; 10 in. is not too much. Before plowing, well-rotted manure should be spread over the whole area about 2 in. deep; fork or disk the soil until it is very fine.

Planting

Asparagus roots will produce a crop one or two years earlier than if they are grown from seed. One-year-old roots are preferable, because they can stand transplanting much better than the larger ones at two years of age. Plant in trenches 6 in. to 8 in. deep, 18 in. apart in the rows, with rows 4 ft. apart. Cover with 3 in. of soil and as the plants grow, pull more soil around them.

Sowing

Sow the seed as soon as frost is out of the ground in rows 18 in. apart, two seeds to the inch. Germination is slow, but may be hastened by soaking seed in water for two to three days before planting. Germination takes about thirty days, and it is advisable to mix radish seed, $\frac{1}{4}$ radish to $\frac{3}{4}$ asparagus, to keep rows marked and the soil from packing. Sow 1 oz. of asparagus seed to each 40 ft., and cover seed $\frac{1}{2}$ in.

Transplanting

When the plants are 3 in. high, thin out 4 in. apart. In the latter part of August or in the following spring move to permanent position, setting plants 18 in. apart in trenches 8 in. to 10 in. deep and 4 ft. to 5 ft. apart. Cover plants with 2 in. of soil and as they begin to grow, add more soil. Plants must be set in trenches as they have a tendency to rise as they grow old. No crop can be expected for the first two years, as it takes that length of time for the roots to become well established. With good care an asparagus bed should last ten to fifteen years.

Intercropping

When first set out, asparagus plants are so small that there is sufficient space between the rows to plant lettuce, radishes, spinach, beets, turnips, carrots, etc.

Cultivation

Keep ground well loosened at all times to a depth of 1 in. to suppress weed growth and to conserve moisture.

Fertilizers

An application of well-rotted manure applied in the late fall or early spring will promote quick, succulent growth. Nitrate of soda, $\frac{1}{2}$ oz. to each plant applied just before growth starts in the spring, will promote good growth and high quality. Stop harvesting as soon as hot weather begins and broadcast a complete fertilizer, formula 4-8-4, at the rate of 1 lb. to 75 ft. between the rows. This application promotes vigorous growth, resulting in a large amount of food being stored in the roots, which will really furnish the next season's crop. The fertilizers that are applied one season as well as the care given that season are materially responsible for next season's crop.

Harvesting

Cut the shoots 1 in. to 2 in. below the ground, either early in the morning or late in the after-noon; the best length is 6 in. to 8 in. In hot weather, cut twice a day to prevent the shoots from becoming spindly. If not cut immediately before cooking, keep in a cool moist place. An asparagus bed can be cut over a period of six to eight weeks.

Remarks

If white tips are desired, set the plants in rows 7 ft. to 8 ft. apart and ridge plants up in early spring before growth starts. Forty plants are sufficient for a family of six.

Varieties

Choose a variety that resists rust, produces good shoots and is not sensitive to hot weather. Also be aware of its canning and freezing capacities.

Bean

Botanical Name: *Phaseolus*

Origin

The American cultivated beans were first known to cultivation only about 400 years ago in North and South America. The string bean is the oldest, having been introduced about the end of the fifteenth century. This also applies to the lima bean, which came into cultivation soon afterwards. There are two general types of beans: those grown for their edible pod, as the string or snap bean, and those grown for the seed, as the shell, kidney and lima bean.

Soil Type and Preparation

Bush snap beans: For the first and second crops the soil should be fairly light, but for the summer and fall crops, the soil may be much heavier. The soil does not have to be as fertile as for most of the other crops as too much plant growth, encouraged by a rich soil, lessens the productivity. Add a little well-rotted manure or a commercial fertilizer such as a formula 4-8-4 and fork it in to a depth of 6 in. to 8 in., but if the soil is good or even average, such an application of manure or fertilizer is not advisable.

Bush limas: These require a much more fertile soil and one that is retentive of moisture during the hot summer months.

Pole snap beans and pole lima beans: Require much more fertile soil than either of the bush beans.

When and How to Plant

Bush snap beans (string beans): May be planted after all danger of frost is over until the middle of August, 2 in. apart in the row and 2 ft. apart between the rows. Cover with 1 in. of soil. Seed should germinate in a week, and the plants should be mature in forty-five to sixty days. One lb. of seed per 100 ft. of row.

Bush limas: Seed may be sown after all danger of frost is over until the first week in June — 4 in. apart in the row and 2 ft. apart between the rows. Recent experiments have proven that a much higher percentage of germination results when care is taken to plant lima beans eye-downward. Cover with $1\frac{1}{2}$ in. of soil and they should germinate in ten days. Beans should mature in 85 to 100 days. One lb. of seed plants 100 ft. of row.

Pole snap beans: Plant after all danger of frost is over and keep until July 1 in hills 3 ft. apart. To make hills, remove one or two shovelfuls of soil, put in a shovelful of manure, cover with 4 in. of soil. Use poles about 7 ft. long, inserting 1 ft. into the ground and set before planting the seed. Plant six to eight seeds, cover with 1 in. of soil, and when 4 in. high thin out, leaving the four best plants. One-half oz. per pole.

Pole lima beans: Seed may be planted eye-downward after all danger of frost is over until the third week in May. Prepare hills and plant in the same way as for pole snap beans. One-half oz. of seed per pole.

Succession and Intercropping

Bush snap beans: For a succession, plant every ten days to two weeks.

Pole snap beans: An early and late planting.

Bush lima beans: Two plantings are best.

Pole lima beans: Only one planting is necessary, as they bear all season.

Moisture Requirements

When too much moisture is present, excessive vegetative growth reduces the yield. The soil should be kept only slightly moist for the best results. Limas require more moisture than string beans.

Cultivation

Shallow and frequent to remove weeds.

Fertilizers

Pole snap beans and pole lima beans: A small handful of formula 4 – 8 – 4 applied in a ring around each hill when the blossoms first appear will give good results. When the first crop has been picked, a second application will invigorate the plants to produce a second crop.

Bush lima beans: These may also have a complete fertilizer broadcast between the rows, when they are beginning to bloom, at the rate of 1 lb. to 75 ft.

Harvesting

Bush snap beans and pole snap beans: These beans should be harvested any time before the pods begin to toughen and before the bean itself begins to mature. Both the quality and flavor are superior when the beans are harvested while still young. Do not allow the beans to become overripe as this condition has a tendency to stop plant growth and affects future development. Pick every two or three days, and only when the vines are dry, to prevent bean rust. This disease does not harm the vines but impairs the appearance of the pods. Keep the beans in a cool place after harvesting to prevent deterioration by loss of moisture.

Bush lima beans and pole lima beans: These should not be harvested until the pods are well filled. This may be determined by holding them up to the light. Harvest while the pods still have their attractive green color; do not leave them until they begin to turn yellow. Keep them in a cool, moist place after harvesting. The quality is best if they are eaten as soon after picking as possible.

Remarks

A 100 ft. row yields 50 lb. snap, or 20 pecks pole snap, or 75 lb. bush lima, or 20 pecks pole lima.

Beet

Botanical Name: *Beta vulgaris*
(Derived from vague resemblance of the seed to the second letter of the Greek alphabet, beta)

Origin

Originating in the Canary Islands and countries around the Mediterranean Sea, beets have been under cultivation for over 2,000 years.

Soil Preparation and Fertilizer

Beets may be grown in practically all types of soil, but one that is friable and well drained gives best results. Plow or fork over soil to a depth of 6 in. to 8 in. and then fork or disk in a liberal application of well-rotted manure to a depth of 4 in. to 6 in. Pulverize soil thoroughly, rake it over very evenly, broadcast and rake in a complete fertilizer, at the rate of 1 lb. to every 50 or 75 sq. ft.

Sowing

As soon as the frost is out of the ground, sow seed in rows 15 in. apart, three seeds to 1 in.; cover with ½ in. of soil, firmly pressed. These seeds germinate in ten to fourteen days.

Thinning

When the plants are 2 in. high, they should be thinned to 1½ in. apart. These thinnings may be eaten as greens. When the beets are 1¼ in. in diameter, pull up every other one; these will be large enough to eat and those that are left in the ground will have room to develop full.

Succession

For a continuous supply, plant seed every two weeks. One oz. of seed plants 75 ft.

Starting Under Glass

Seed may be started indoors, three weeks before outdoor planting date, in finely pulverized ordinary garden soil. Avoid excessive watering. Plants may, if desired, be transplanted while still indoors, 1½ in. apart each way. These plants set out of doors the same time as seed is planted will mature two to three weeks earlier. Growth may be further hastened by broadcasting a complete fertilizer formula 4–8–4, at the time of transplanting, at the rate of 1 lb. to 50 sq. ft. to 75 sq. ft.

Cultivation

Beets need shallow cultivation until plants are half grown; after this it is not necessary, as their leaves will shade the ground, control weed growth and hold moisture in the soil.

Harvesting

Beets are ready for pulling when they are 1½ in. to 3 in. in diameter; size depends on the variety. Keep in a cool moist place until they are used. After beets mature, they can be left in the ground one or two weeks before they begin to deteriorate.

Broccoli

Botanical Name: *Brassica oleracea* var. *italica*

Origin

Known in western Asia for over 2,000 years.

Soil

Any soil is satisfactory, if it is well provided with organic matter and a moderate supply of moisture. As the root system is very shallow and fibrous, proper preparation cannot be over emphasized. Soil should be well worked to a depth of 6 in. to 8 in.

Fertilizer

A good application of well-rotted manure or 4–8–4 fertilizer forked in and then pulverized well.

Sowing

As broccoli prefers a cool season, it is best to make two plantings, one in the spring (as soon as frost is out of the ground) and the other two months later, both sown at the rate of ⅛ oz.

seed to 50 ft. of row. Sow seed indoors in flats ¼ in. deep, in rows 2 in. apart. Several hundred seeds should germinate in seven days. When 4 in. high, transplant 18 in. apart in rows 2½ ft. to 3 ft. apart; transplant only the best plants. Seed may be started in coldframe or hotbed eight weeks before it can be sown in the open.

Moisture

A continuous supply of moisture is necessary for good growth and production; otherwise the plants will bear prematurely and the quality will be inferior.

Cultivation

Shallow, clean cultivation should be practiced frequently to conserve moisture whenever the soil has a tendency to pack.

Harvesting

The first crop looks like heads of green cauliflower and should be about 3 in. in diameter. It should be cut with 4 in. to 6 in. of skin just before the heads begin to separate. The second and succeeding crops come as small individual heads from shoots that appear after the first head has been cut. It has the best flavor when cut early in the morning. To prevent wilting and to conserve the flavor, keep in a shallow pan of water in a cool place until used.

Fertilizer

Just before the first crop is mature, a good commercial fertilizer (4–8–4) may be applied at the rate of 1 tbs. to each plant. Make a ring of fertilizer 6 in. from the stem of the plant and cover with 1 in. of soil.

Brussels Sprout

Botanical Name: *Brassica oleracea* var *gemmifera*

This vegetable is grown for its small lateral buds, which swell and mature in the axils of leaves along the main stem.

Soil and Fertilizer

The same as for broccoli.

Planting

Two crops, the spring and fall ones, are the most satisfactory as the buds are not firm when grown in hot weather. Seed may be sown inside as with cabbage, and the plants set out when the ground thaws out; or it may be sown inside at the same time the plants are set. Seed for the late crop is sown outside between May 20 and June 15. Cultural requirements are the same as for cabbage.

Harvesting

The buds are mature when they are hard and from 1 in. to 1½ in. in diameter. They may be broken off, trimmed and stored in a cool, moist place. A well-developed plant will produce from ⅔ qt. to 1 qt. of the best grade of buds. The plants may be left outside during freezing weather as they are very hardy.

Cabbage

Botanical Name: *Brassica oleracea* var. *capitata*

Origin

Cabbage was known as food more than 4,000 years ago in western Asia.

Soil Type and Preparation

May be grown on any fairly fertile soil, but a sandy loam is best for both the early crop and the late crop, if the ground is well supplied with manure.

Fertilizer

The same as for broccoli.

When and How to Plant

For a continuous supply, three crops should be planted. Seed for the first crop should be sown indoors or in a hotbed between the first two weeks of February, six to eight weeks before the date for setting out. Sow the seed in fairly light soil in rows 3 in. apart and cover with ¼ in. of soil. Seed should germinate in a week. When plants are 2 in. high, prick out 2 in. by 2 in. They should be grown in a temperature of 70° F. Plants may be transplanted 3 in. by 3 in., or in individual 3 in. pots, three weeks later, but this is not necessary. Plants may be transplanted to the garden as soon as the ground is workable, but the plants must be hardened off beforehand in order to withstand the unfavorable weather conditions. Set out in the garden 18 in. apart in the rows and 2 ft. to 2½ ft. apart between the rows. Set the plants out a little deeper than they were inside.

Succession and Intercropping

Early crop should mature the first week in July. The second crop, planted from the middle of March to April 1, should be ready to harvest from the last of July till the middle of August. Seed for the late crop may be sown outdoors in the open ground from the middle of June until July 1. This should mature by October, and it may be stored. Intercropping is not practical.

Moisture Requirements

Cabbage requires a liberal supply of moisture for maximum development. Lack of moisture causes the heads to form prematurely. Too much moisture causes improper soil conditions.

Cultivation

The root system of the cabbage is very fibrous and extremely close to the surface of the ground. For this reason cultivation should be light, but frequent enough to control weeds.

Manures and Fertilizers

Cabbage requires large amounts of nitrogen, phosphorus and potash. Manures when applied in liberal amounts keep the soil in good physical condition and furnish a part of the nutrients, but unless the soil is very rich, commercial fertilizers high in nitrogen, phosphorus and potash, such as formulas 4–8–4 or 5–8–7, should be used. This should be broadcast at the rate of 1 lb. to 25 sq. ft. and raked in just before planting. It may be applied broadcast between the rows when, or just after, the plants are set out.

Harvesting

Do not harvest until the heads are solid, for soft heads are inferior and undeveloped. Cut several of the outer leaves with the head, for these will protect the head and keep it from deteriorating until used. If it is not harvested as soon as the heads are hard, the heads will burst. If the heads become hard, but the cabbage is not to be used for a week or so, simply give the plant a good jerk to break some of the roots, and leave it in the field until the head is wanted.

Cabbage, Chinese

Botanical Name: *Brassica pekinensis*

Origin

Probably a native of China, where it has been under cultivation for 1,500 years.

When and How to Plant

Does best on a rich soil, which will retain moisture. Sandy loam or loam soil well enriched with decayed manure before plants are set out is excellent. Seed may be sown outside as soon as the soil is slightly warm, or about May 1, and any time up until July 1. Distances should be 2 ft. to 2½ ft. between the rows and 8 in. to 12 in. between plants. For fall crop, seed is sown about July 1; thin out when plants are 3 in. high. For general care and cultivation, see Cauliflower. This vegetable cannot be transplanted.

Moisture

Plenty of moisture is required. Should the supply fail, a seed stalk will form before the head has fully developed. For this reason a muck soil, which is also rich in organic matter, will give good results.

Fertilizer

A good commercial fertilizer, such as 4–8–4, is very beneficial if applied ten days to two weeks after thinning. Apply at the rate of 1 lb. to 100 ft. between the rows.

Harvesting

Heads should be harvested when fully matured and developed. They should be firm, but the size depends on the variety. Cut from the roots as with celery. Remove the loose outer leaves until the bleached interior shows. Keep in a cool moist place; consume as soon as possible. It may, however, be kept several weeks under proper conditions.

Carrot

Botanical Name: *Daucus carota* var. *sativa*

Origin

Carrots were known as food in temperate sections of Asia over 2,000 years ago.

Soil

The best soil for this vegetable is a deep, mellow loam that will not become too compact. Since carrots have a deep root system and cannot penetrate a hard soil, the soil should by all means be fairly light. A hard, compact soil tends to force the carrots to put forth fibrous roots, which are very disfiguring. Never plant this crop on a sod land, but on land that has been prepared well beforehand by thorough plowing or forking. Apply a liberal amount of well-rotted manure, disk or fork this in, and then rake over the soil, making sure all the lumps are out and the soil is finely pulverized. If sod land must be used, plant two or three deep-rooted crops over the area first, such as corn or potatoes.

When and How to Plant

The seed should be planted in early spring, as soon as the ground is workable. There are usually two crops: the spring one, for summer consumption, and the fall one, sown in June or July, depending on the locality, and harvested in November. Those harvested late are usually stored or frozen for winter use. Since both crops are treated alike, they can be discussed together, except for dates. Sow the seed at the rate of 1 oz. per 100 ft. Allow 1 ft. between the rows, and since the seed is usually a long time in germinating, lettuce seed may be mixed with it. The lettuce seed will quickly germinate and mark the rows, so that cultivation will be easier until the carrots appear. Plant the seed immediately before or after a rainfall if at all possible, for they require a good deal of moisture in order to germinate. In a month's time the carrots should be from 3 in. to 4 in. in height. At that time they should be thinned and the lettuce

should be removed. Thin the carrots ¾ in. to 1½ in. apart. The lettuce may be transplanted if desired. These thinnings are very young and tender and are delicious when served whole.

Succession

The early crop is followed by a fall crop, which should be planted about June 1. This receives the same treatment as the first one.

Moisture Requirements

Carrots need plenty of moisture particularly when the seeds are germinating. However, they should receive only a moderate supply when they really begin to grow, for too much moisture will make the roots crack, especially when they are reaching full size.

Cultivation

Cultivate to keep all the weeds out. However, the cultivation should be fairly shallow to prevent the formation of adventitious side roots that disfigure the main root so much. After the plants are 8 in. high, the tops will begin to fall over a bit, thereby making a natural mulch or ground cover that will prevent the weeds from coming up, and will conserve all the moisture necessary for the proper maturity of the crop.

Fertilizers

Three to four days after thinning it is advisable to apply a good commercial fertilizer such as 5–10–5, scattered over the area on a dry day. See Beet for rate of application.

Harvesting

The early crop is harvested about July 1, depending on the date planted and the nature of the weather of the locality. The roots should be pulled only as they are needed, for the fresher they are when cooked, the better they will be. The late crop is harvested about November and is usually stored.

Cauliflower

Botanical Name: *Brassica oleracea* var. *botrytis*

Origin

Known as food in western Asia 2,000 years ago.

Soil

Same as for cabbage, Brussels sprout, and broccoli.

When and How to Plant

Being a cool season crop, seed should be sown indoors about February 15. Sow in a sandy loam soil, 3 in. between rows; cover with ¼ in. of soil. When the plants are 1½ in. high, transplant to 2 in. apart each way. Keep at a temperature of 55° to 60° F. to develop a good root system and stocky tops. One more transplanting is advisable, but not usually practiced. Harden off plants a week before setting out, about April 15, 18 in. apart in rows 2½ ft. to 3 ft. apart.

Seed for the second or fall crop may be sown in the open ground between the middle of June and July 1. One-eighth oz. of seed should produce at least 100 plants. Germination takes one week.

Moisture

Soil should be well supplied with moisture, especially when heads are beginning to form.

Cultivation

Keep weed growth suppressed at all times, but cultivation should be shallow to avoid root injury. For best results, cauliflower should be grown as quickly as possible.

Manures and Fertilizers

Manure is most effective if applied when the ground is being prepared. A complete fertilizer, 4–8–4, will hasten growth and may be applied at the rate of 1 tbs. to each plant, two weeks after the plants have been set out. A second application at the same rate may be applied just as the tiny heads appear.

Shading

As the heads begin to form, the outside leaves should be brought together and tied at the top to keep heads completely shaded.

Harvesting

In two weeks to a month after the head has been tied up, depending on the variety and weather, it should be ready to harvest. Properly matured heads should be firm and show no signs of discoloration or breaking. Cut the head off at its junction with the leaves; trim off any discolored leaves, leaving a few trimmed to within 1 in. of the top of the head. These will give protection until the head is ready for use. Store in a cool, moist place.

Celeriac

Botanical Name: *Apium graveolens* **var.** *rapaceum*

Origin

Probably first grown in Europe although the date is not known. Closely related to celery and similar to it in many ways. The thick tuberous root is the edible portion; the leaves resemble those of celery, but they are a darker green and smaller. Celeriac has a hollow stem and is a much slower growing plant.

Soil

The soil requirements are the same as for celery.

Planting

The seeds may be started in the open ground, but two crops may be grown, the first one started indoors and the second one in the open ground. The first crop should be sown indoors not later than March 1, since it is slow to germinate and to grow, and it should be transplanted once about April 1. Plants should be ready to set out in the open ground the middle of April, but this depends mainly on the locality and the seasons. This crop is set out in the open ground as celery is, but the distance between the rows may be lessened, for this vegetable is not hilled up more than 2 in. to be blanched. The leaves and stems are never used, only the enlarged root stem.

Harvesting

This first crop should be harvested on or before September 1; the second or late crop will provide the succession. Pull up, clean off side roots and top, and use as soon as convenient.

Succession

The second crop should be started in the open ground from the middle to the last of

May, with the same distance between the rows. When the plants are 2 in. high, they should be thinned to 6 in. apart.

After thinning or transplanting, from a week to ten days later, an application of a good commercial fertilizer should be put on at the rate of 1 lb. to 35 sq. ft. Put it down the rows as close to the plants as possible and then cultivate it in. If the soil was not very rich with manure to begin with, another application equal to the first may be made a month later.

Cultivation

Shallow cultivation is necessary. The leaves should eventually spread so that no weed growth will be possible. Then cultivate only occasionally.

Celery

Botanical Name: *Apium graveolens*
(Possibly derived from the Greek word for parsley: *selinon*.)

Origin

In its wild state, celery has a wide geographical range in the Old World. It was not used for food until the sixteenth century.

Soil

Celery does best on soils that are well supplied with organic matter and that do not contain an overabundance of clay. Land that has not previously been planted for several years should be manured and dug or plowed the fall before planting, and these operations should be repeated in the spring. If manure is not available, any organic matter such as leaf mold may be used with good results. A complete fertilizer, such as a 4–8–4, 5–10–5 or 4–12–4, should be broadcast at the rate of 1 lb. to 50 sq. ft. and raked in just before setting out the plants.

When and How to Plant

Celery does best in the cooler parts of the year, and the spring and fall crops are therefore most practical. All varieties do not mature at the same time, so it is possible to plant several simultaneously and have a continuous supply for home use.

(1) Early crop: For the first crop, sow seed in a hotbed or coldframe about ten weeks before planting in the open ground, which may be done as soon as danger from heavy frost is past. Broadcast the seed after watering the soil and cover very lightly with fine sand. The temperature should be between 60° and 75° F. Four to five weeks after planting the seed the plants will be large enough to transplant, though this is not necessary, as a little thinning in the seedbed will prove to be more satisfactory and faster growth will be made if transplanting is not practiced. Ten days before the plants are set in the field, withhold all water to harden them off. The plants are set 6 in. in the row and 2 ft. to 3 ft. between the rows.

Cultivation

Shallow cultivation will control weeds and thereby conserve moisture. The root system is very fibrous and shallow, so cultivation should not be more than 1 in. deep.

Blanching

Celery must be blanched in order to prevent development of the green coloring that gives it a bitter taste, and to cause the rapid growth of the undeveloped stalks in the crown. Boards 8 in. wide may be placed on both sides of the plants as close as is possible without injury, and kept in place by stakes 18 in. long, driven 6 in. to 10 in. into the ground at sufficient intervals to hold the boards upright. The distance between the boards at the top should be 3 in. to 4 in. Be sure to have all leaves in a vertical position to protect the center leaves during blanching. These small undeveloped leaves receive a stimulus when light is withheld, and in two weeks they should be the same height as the outside leaves. Then the celery is ready to be harvested. By blanching only a few plants at a time, the early crop will last at least six weeks. There are numerous other methods of excluding light, but the principle is to keep it from the leaf stalks, make the plant compact and force the heart of the plant to respond to the stimulus of limited overhead light. Waterproof blanching paper and cardboard collars are two other materials used for this purpose. Soil should not be used for the early crop—it has too many injurious organisms when it is warm.

Harvesting

The early crop is harvested by cutting off the stalk 2 in. below the ground. Trim off outside leaves, which are usually tough in warm weather. Store in a cool place.

(2) Late crop: Seed is planted in a prepared seedbed, in a coldframe or in the garden from April 10 to May 10. Plants should be set in the garden between June 20 and July 20. Transplant 6 in. apart in the row and leave 4 ft. between the rows. Intercropping with radishes, beets, lettuce or any other quick-maturing crop is practical.

Blanching

The late crop is of the highest quality when blanched with soil. It can remain in the ground and survive a heavy freeze if the tops are adequately protected. About two months after the plants have been set in the field, begin to hill them up by pulling the soil toward them. Keep it even with the center of the plant but do not allow the soil to reach the center, or growth will be inhibited. Hill up ten days later and repeat if necessary until the plants are 12 in. to 18 in. in height.

Fertilizers

One lb. of a high-grade complete fertilizer containing nitrogen, phosphorus and potash is applied to every 25 sq. ft. to 50 sq. ft. at planting time. A quick-acting nitrogenous fertilizer such as nitrate of soda, applied just before the bleaching process, will hasten the development of tender succulent stalks. One lb. to 100 ft. of row is sufficient.

Chard, Swiss

Botanical Name: *Beta vulgaris,* var. *cicla*

Origin
Unknown.

Soil

Fairly rich soil is good, and an application of well-decayed manure turned under before planting is beneficial.

Sowing

Sow seed as early in spring as the ground can be worked, in rows 18 in. to 30 in. apart, and when plants are 3 in. high, thin 3 in. apart. Thinnings may be used as greens. When plants are 7 in. to 9 in. high, thin to 9 in. apart. A crop matures in sixty days, but careful cutting before that time does no harm. One sowing will last until the crop is killed by autumn frost.

Cultivation
Cultivate shallowly and sufficiently often to keep down weeds.

Fertilizers

Two weeks after the last thinning, an application of 4–8–4 at the rate of ¾ lb. to 75 ft. will be beneficial, but it is not absolutely necessary. Spread in rows between plants and cultivate in shallowly. A second application, same method and amount, about the middle of August, will help ensure the crop for the rest of the season, but it is not necessary unless poor growth is being made.

Harvesting

Harvest by removing the outer leaves with a sharp twist, taking care not to injure the small, undeveloped leaves in the center. Keep in a cool moist place, and use as soon as possible.

Chicory

Botanical Name: *Cichorium intybus*

Origin

Also known as French endive and Witloof chicory; the origin and date of introduction are doubtful, but it is definitely known not to have been cultivated by the ancients.

Soil

Will give good results on any soil that will grow root crops, such as carrots, etc.

Planting

Start outside June 1, for the crop will mature and go to seed if started earlier. Top of plant is of no value. The roots, sometimes used as a substitute for coffee, may be forced to produce fresh shoots that are eaten as a salad vegetable at any time during the winter. Seed is sown in rows, 1½ ft, to 2 ft. apart, covered with ½ in. of soil. When plants are 2 in. to 3 in. high, thin apart.

Moisture

A constant, well-regulated supply of moisture is necessary to make good plants and to prevent the plants from sending up a seed stalk.

Cultivation

Cultivation is the same as for any root crop.

Fertilizers

Thorough preparation before putting in the crop is best for good results. No additional feeding should be necessary.

Harvesting

Roots should be harvested late in the fall before the ground freezes; they should be removed with a fork or a spade completely and carefully so as not to injure them in any way.

Forcing

The main use of chicory is for forcing during the winter months, using the tender blanched shoots for salad. To force the roots properly, they may be taken out of storage at any time, using only a few for each forcing, so that the supply will last all winter. They should be started at intervals of every two weeks, for one crop will last about a month, and the next crop may be coming on to take its place when it is exhausted. The roots should be placed upright in sand; if there is no sand, ashes may be used; all light should be excluded, and they should be kept moist at a temperature of 50° to 55° F. As they sprout, they should be covered with the sand until the shoots are 3 in. long. They should be cut and used as soon as possible. Each crop may be cut on the average of three times during the month they are forced, and much better shoots are obtained from the good strong roots.

Corn, Sweet

Botanical Name: *Zea mays*, var. *saccharata*

Origin

Grown by the Indians in Mexico and eastern North America before this continent was discovered.

Soil

Corn requires a well-drained soil, high in organic matter. A good application of a well-decayed manure is the best source of organic material. Early crops do best on a sandy loam soil, which warms quickly in the spring, but later crops prefer a heavier soil that will retain moisture.

When and How to Plant

Seed may be sown as soon as the soil has warmed up, or about May 1 to 10. Plant three to four seeds in hills 2 ft. to 3 ft. apart each way. Mix a small handful of commercial fertilizer with the soil in the bottom of each hill and cover the seeds with 1 in. to 1½ in. of soil. Seed germinates in one week to ten days. Thin to three plants to each hill, when plants are from 3 in. to 6 in. high.

Intercropping

May be practiced with squash, melons or pumpkins, string beans, lettuce and other quick-maturing crops. Plant every ten to fourteen days for a continuous supply.

Cultivation

Should be frequent, beginning when plants first appear. Practice shallow cultivation, pulling the soil toward the hills each time. Three to four cultivations are all that are necessary. Cultivation must cease as soon as the tassel appears.

Manures and Fertilizers

When plants are 4 in. to 8 in. high, broadcast 4–8–4 between the rows at the rate of 1 lb. to 50 ft. to 75 ft., and cultivate in carefully and shallowly. Another application is sometimes made just before the tassels appear, but is not necessary in every case, being advisable only if growth is not satisfactory.

Harvesting

Harvest when the silk has begun to turn brown. Corn should be used just as soon as picked, as the sugar content is highest at that time. The flavor of corn cooked just minutes after it has been picked is so far superior to that purchased in markets that this can hardly be overemphasized.

Cress

Botanical Names: *Lepidium sativum* — Garden cress; *Nasturtium officinale* — Watercress

Origin

Probably of Persian origin; its cultivation dates from a very early period.

When and How to Sow

Garden cress is a cool season crop, the leaves being used for salad or for garnishing and goes quickly to seed in hot weather. Sow seed in any garden soil as weather conditions permit. Sow in rows 12 in. apart and thin as needed for use.

If leaves are cut without injuring the crown, the plant will keep bearing for several weeks. It should be ready for use four to six weeks after planting.

Watercress may be grown in any stream where the water is pure and fresh. Once established in a good stream, it will last indefinitely. It is a perennial, which will throw out roots from the joints and which may also be propagated from seed or pieces of stem. It may also be grown in the garden in well-prepared, very moist soil, by starting the seed indoors and transplanting to the garden. If given plenty of moisture, plants should last some time. If grown like ordinary vegetables it will be a failure.

Cucumber

Botanical Name: *Cucumis sativus*

Origin

Native of southern Asia, in cultivation for over 4,000 years.

Soil

Heavy soil is best because it tends to be more fertile and retentive of moisture. If well-decayed manure is available, it should be used in liberal quantities and should be well forked in before planting.

Sowing

When ground has become thoroughly warm (May 1 to 15), plant in hills 4 ft. apart each way. If available, a forkful of well-rotted manure placed at the bottom of each hill and covered with 4 in. of soil gives excellent results. In each hill plant twelve seeds, $\frac{1}{2}$ in. deep. Seeds germinate in ten days and plants should be thinned out gradually, so that when they are 4 in. high there should be four plants to each hill. A less satisfactory method is to sow seeds in rows 4 ft. to 6 ft. apart, six or eight seeds to 1 ft., and thin plants to 1 ft. apart after they are 2 in. to 4 in. high. Cucumber plants cannot be satisfactorily transplanted. Four to six hills is enough for a family planting.

Succession

For a continuous supply, there must be at least two plantings between May 1 and July 10. If a few radish seeds are sown in each hill, they will germinate quickly and attract all the insects. As soon as the cucumbers appear, pull up the radishes and destroy them, insects and all.

Moisture

Without a continuous supply of moisture, vines will not develop properly and fruit will be small. Heavy land, well prepared, is an excellent retainer of moisture.

Cultivation

Should be shallow and constant until vines cover the ground. Do not step on the vines — the tissues are easily crushed and killed and the stems often cannot put out new shoots below the injury.

Fertilizer

Cucumbers must have a maximum amount of nitrogen; if the soil is rich, a complete fertilizer, applied when plants are 4 in. high, will promote satisfactory growth. If it was impossible to put manure in the hills before planting, complete fertilizer should be applied, a small handful to each hill, when the plants are about 3 in. high. Applied to plants grown in rows, 1 lb. is sufficient for 50 ft.

Harvesting

Do not pick cucumbers until leaves are dry in the morning, as disease is easily spread by disturbance of damp foliage. Harvest fruit before it begins to turn yellow; in a cool moist place, it will keep a week.

Remarks

The small gherkin, used for pickling, is planted July 1 and given the same treatment as the cucumber. As gherkin plants are somewhat smaller, they need only be thinned to from six to seven plants per hill.

Eggplant

Botanical Name: *Solanum melongena*

Origin

Used as food in India several thousand years ago. The varieties cultivated in America are long and ovate in shape, while those cultivated in India are even longer, slender and slightly curved.

Soil

A sandy loam soil yields the best crop. It should have plenty of well-decayed manure forked in to a depth of 6 in., and it should be finely pulverized, at any time before the plants are set.

Sowing

Eggplant requires warm soil conditions and a long period in which to mature, and north of Virginia it must be started indoors. Seed may be sown in flats from February 15 to March 15, in soil with a high percentage of sand. Seed germinates in ten days to two weeks. When plants are 1½ in. high, transplant 2 in. each way. The temperature should be 75° F. at all times; when plants begin to crowd, transplant to individual 3-in. pots, and then to larger pots as the plants grow. They should be in 6-in. pots one month after they are in 3-in. pots. If plants

show any tendency to turn yellow, water with nitrate of soda (1 oz. dissolved in 1 gallon of water). Plants should not be set out before June 1, and even later if the ground is not thoroughly warm; if set out earlier they are checked by cool nights and cool soil conditions. When set out, plants should be 4 in. to 6 in. high. Planting distance should be 3 ft. between rows, 2 ft. between plants.

Moisture

Eggplant is distinctly fussy about moisture; if it has too little, the leaves turn yellow, become spotted and drop; if too much, the flowers will not set fruit.

Cultivation

Should be exceedingly shallow as roots are very near the surface. Cultivate just enough to keep down weeds.

Fertilizer

A small handful of a complete fertilizer, 4-8-4, should be placed in a ring around each plant when it is set out. This should be cultivated in lightly. At any time satisfactory growth is not being made, a second application of fertilizer is advisable.

Harvesting

Always cut the fruit from the plant. It is best when about 4 in. in diameter. Keep in a cool place until ready to use; do not keep more than four days.

Endive

Botanical Name: *Cichorium endivia*

Origin

In very early times endive was cultivated in Egypt.

Soil

Should be rich and heavy. Prepared with plenty of organic matter (compost or well-decayed manure) to a depth of 6 in. before planting. Ground at the base of a slope is best because of the greater supply of moisture available.

Sowing

Sow seed from June 1 to August 1 in rows 18 in. apart. When plants are 2 in. high, thin to 1 ft. apart. Thinned plants may be transplanted. One-fourth oz. of seed will plant 50 ft. of row. An early sowing may be made as soon as the ground can be worked in spring, but is not as satisfactory as the later one, for the ground warms up too quickly.

Moisture

A continuous supply is essential for good endive.

Cultivation

Three weeks before crop is harvested, plants must be blanched to make them more tender and less bitter. Draw outside leaves over the heart and center leaves until they come together at the top. Put a piece of waterproof paper around them to hold them in place and tie with string or an elastic band. This must be done on a dry day as the inside leaves rot quickly if tied when wet. When the endive is blanched, the plants should be cut as close to the ground as possible and stored in a cool, moist place.

Kale

Botanical Name: *Brassica oleracea* var. *acephala*

Origin

First known in Europe, and cultivated for several thousand years.

Soil

A well-drained, sandy loam, well prepared with plenty of decayed manure or other organic matter, is ideal for kale. Prepare to a depth of 6 in. to 8 in., and dig in manure any time before planting. Kale will, however, grow on any soil that is fairly rich.

Sowing

Sow in place, 1/8 oz. seed to 50 ft. in rows 18 in. to 2 ft. apart, as soon as the soil can be worked in the spring. Seed germinates in seven to ten days, and when plants are 3 in. high, they should be thinned to one plant to every 8 in. to

10 in. Sow again in midsummer for fall and winter crop. Plan on sixty to eighty days to maturity.

Cultivation

Should be frequent and shallow. All weed growth must be suppressed.

Fertilizer

A complete fertilizer, 4–8–4, applied to plants a month after thinning, will prove beneficial. Apply at the rate of 1/2 lb. to 25 ft. of row.

Harvesting

When leaves are sufficiently mature, they should be bright green and of an attractive appearance. When old, they become dark green and tough. Cut and keep in a cool, damp place and use as soon as possible. If allowed to remain on the plant too long, they become tough. The fall or winter crop may be left in the field, covered lightly with salt hay or straw, and the leaves cut when desired. They will keep until late into the winter.

Kohlrabi

Botanical Name: *Brassica caulorapa*

Origin

Date of introduction uncertain, for there are no wild types. An extreme varietal form of wild cabbage.

Soil

Any well-prepared soil is satisfactory. After first working, an application of manure should be well turned under and the soil should be pulverized. Soil should be prepared to a depth of 6 in.

Sowing

No advantage is gained by early or by indoor sowing. First crop should be sown as soon as the frost is out of the ground; then sow every two weeks until August 1. Sow in rows 18 in. apart at the rate of 1/4 oz. seed to 75 ft. Cover lightly with soil, and when plants are 3 in. to 4 in. high, thin to 6 in. to 8 in. apart. The thinnings may be transplanted to another row and will take about an extra week to develop. Leave and transplant only the strongest seedlings. Days to maturity, fifty to sixty.

Cultivation

Keep soil loose at all times, but do not cultivate deeply near plants.

Fertilizer

About five days after thinning, plants will be in condition to benefit by additional fertilizer, and a small amount (¾ lb. to row of 50 ft.) of nitrate of soda or ammonium sulphate may be broadcast between rows and lightly raked in. If fertilizer remains on the leaves, they will burn.

Harvesting

Kohlrabi is a member of the cabbage family and is peculiar because the edible portion is a swollen stem, which develops just at the level of the ground; it should be used when this is the size of a silver dollar. It becomes tough and flavorless as it grows larger. Pull up the entire plant to avoid disease from the rotting of roots and leaves.

Leek

Botanical Name: *Allium porrum*

Origin

First known in Mediterranean countries, leeks have been grown since prehistoric times.

Soil

Leeks prefer a soil that is very rich, supplied with plenty of decayed vegetable and animal matter. Prepare as early as weather will permit by plowing or digging and then pulverizing.

Sowing

About February 15, seed should be sown indoors in any good garden soil in a temperature of 60° to 70° F. Germination takes about ten days. When plants are 2 in. to 4 in. high, transplant 2 in. apart each way. First week in May, set plants out 6 in. apart in rows 2 ft. to 3 ft. apart.

Seed sown in open ground does not produce leeks of large size and highest quality, but does give satisfactory results. Seed should be sown ¼ in. deep at the rate of 1 oz. to 100 ft., in rows 2 ft. to 3 ft. apart, as soon as ground is in workable condition. As the root system is meager, leek plants take at least two weeks to become established before noticeable growth takes place. Since the plants do not all mature at the same time, only one planting is necessary. Leeks may be left in the ground until the soil freezes.

Cultivation

Keep the soil friable at all times; as the plants begin to grow, hoe the soil toward them.

Fertilization

When the plants are from 4 in. to 6 in. high, apply a complete fertilizer, about 1 tsp. to each plant; put over each plant a paper collar made of waterproof paper. The collar should be 3 in. high and 2 in. in diameter. This hastens upward growth; they should grow 3 in. to 4 in., hilling the soil about the plants; continue to do so until plant grows, always keep soil hilled up to the collar. Some of the plants will be mature about August 15, but will not deteriorate if left in the ground until late fall.

Another method of planting: set the plants in trenches 6 in. deep, 4 ft. apart, and, as they grow, fill in soil to blanch them.

Moisture

Plants must have a continuous and liberal supply of moisture in order to make maximum growth.

Harvesting

Plants may be dug before freezing weather.

Lettuce

Botanical Name: *Lactuca sativa*

Remarks

Lettuce is best if grown during the cooler times of the year. Only the cos, or romaine type is adapted to warmer conditions.

Soil Preparation

Lettuce responds to an abundance of decayed organic matter and just as good results may be obtained with it as with commercial fertilizers, on soils of a fine structure. The soil should be spaded to a depth of 6 in. or more and plenty of well-rotted manure worked in. A complete fertilizer may be added at this time if deemed necessary.

Planting

April to May 15, then again in August. Seed may be sown in flats in a greenhouse or hotbed for transplanting outside. Seed should be sown six to seven weeks before transplanting outside. The young plants grow most satisfactorily at a temperature between 50° and 60° F. Too high a temperature makes the plants spindly and nonheading. At high temperatures the sugar changes rapidly to starch, which results in a disagreeable and bitter flavor. When the plants are about 2 in. high they are pricked into other flats, 2 in. apart each way. They are kept in these flats until set in the garden, which should be preceded by a hardening-off period. The plants are set 8 in. apart in rows 15 in. apart.

Lettuce seed may be planted in the open ground as soon as the frost has disappeared, the plants being thinned out to 8 in. apart when crowding begins to occur. These plants may be set out and will mature a week or so later than those that have not been moved. One oz. of seed is sufficient for 3,000 plants.

Cultivation

Shallow, and frequent enough to control weeds.

Succession

For a continuous supply sow seed every two weeks or plant varieties that mature at different dates.

Fertilizers

Lettuce quickly responds to nitrogen which, with plenty of moisture available, will promote a rapid, succulent, crisp growth.

Harvesting

Loose-leaf varieties may be harvested in any stage of development before they become tough. Heading varieties should be allowed to mature. As only a few heads mature at a time, it will not be a case of a feast or a famine if seed is sown every two weeks. The root may be cut close to the ground, removing all leaves with it. If the heads are pulled up some of the leaves may be injured.

Muskmelon, cantaloupe

Botanical Name: *Cucumis melo*

Origin

Origin doubtful; presumably they were first known either in Africa or Asia. Not cultivated before the Christian era.

Soil Type and Preparation

Melons grow well in many soils that are either sandy or slightly sandy in character. Heavy clay soils should be avoided. The more sand the soil contains, the earlier a crop may be planted. An application of well-rotted manure is advisable before planting, or it may be somewhat supplemented by a complete fertilizer broadcast at the rate of 1 lb. to 35 sq. ft. and raked in before planting.

When and How to Plant

Melons are very tender, and must not be planted until the soil is thoroughly warm, from May 10 until the middle of June. For best results, sow seeds in hills 4 ft. apart each way, and for large varieties, 4 ft. to 6 ft. apart. To make a hill, remove two shovelfuls of soil, insert one shovelful of well-rotted manure, and cover with 6 in. of well-firmed soil. Plant six to eight seeds per hill and cover with ½ in. of soil. Hills should be at least 12 in. in diameter, and the seeds placed 2 in. apart in the hill. One oz. of seed is enough for twenty hills. Seed should germinate and appear above the ground in about two weeks; when plants are 3 in. to 4 in. high, thin out to the three best plants. Seed may also be sown indoors in pots a month before setting out of doors. Two plants may be grown in each pot and two pots set out in each hill.

Succession

By one planting of two or more varieties, early and late, a continuous supply may be obtained without successive plantings.

Moisture

The plants should be kept continuously moist. This is very necessary to ensure proper vine development and maximum fruit production. Plants require much more moisture when fruit begins to mature than they do during the growing stage.

Cultivation

Keep soil lightly cultivated between rows at all times, but do not cultivate too close to the plants; weeds near the plants should be carefully pulled out to avoid disturbing roots of vines. As the vines shade the ground, they conserve the moisture near the plants, and cultivation is most needed where ground is exposed to sun.

Fertilizers

A commercial fertilizer is needed for good growth and production. Apply 4-8-4, at the rate of ½ oz. per hill in a ring around each hill, 4 in. to 6 in. away from the plants, and cover with 1 in. of soil taken from between the rows. Apply after thinning.

Harvesting

Yield: ten to fifteen melons per hill. Melons are ready for harvesting when the stems part easily from the fruit with a very slight pull. They are not mature until the stems begin to separate and should never be cut if highest quality is desired. If not picked at this stage, they will become overripe and too soft for use. In four or five days after reaching this state, they will completely detach themselves. If picked when stems part easily, the flesh is firm. Vines will continue producing fruits from three weeks to a month.

Okra

Botanical Name: *Hibiscus esculentus*

Origin

Asiatic in origin, but not cultivated during ancient times. Grown in the warmer parts of the United States since the eighteenth century.

Soil Type and Preparation

Any good garden soil will give good results if enriched before planting with manure or commercial fertilizer.

When and How to Plant

Okra is a tender plant, giving good results only in hot weather. Sow seeds from the middle of May to the middle of June, in rows 2½ ft. to 3 ft. apart. When plants are 3 in. to 4 in. high, thin the dwarf varieties 12 in. to 18 in. apart, and the larger varieties 18 in. to 30 in. apart. Not easily transplanted unless enough soil is moved to prevent root disturbance.

Cultivation

Keep soil well stirred and weeds suppressed.

Fertilizers

A liberal application of manure or complete fertilizer should be well worked in when the soil is prepared. If plants do not grow steadily, apply 1 tsp. of fertilizer to each plant as a side dressing.

Harvesting

Pods should be gathered while young — 1 in. to 2 in. long. For continuous growth, do not allow pods to mature. Two plantings are often made in the South, but only one is possible in the North.

Onion

Botanical Name: *Allium cepa*

Origin

Probably first known in parts of Asia. Grown by the ancient Egyptians, it is one of the oldest of cultivated vegetables.

It also is one of the hardiest of vegetables and may be sown as soon as the frost is out of the ground in the spring. Onion sets may also be planted at the same time.

Onion Sets

These are immature onions that have been produced by close seeding during the preceding season. Seed may also be sown in flats in a hotbed or greenhouse and the plants transplanted to the garden at any time soil and weather conditions permit.

Soil Preparation

Thorough preparation cannot be overemphasized. The organic and nutrient and water content should be high. The onion plants feed within a limited range, due to their sparse root system. Heavy applications of commercial fertilizers are often necessary, at the rate of 1 lb. to 20 sq. ft. or 25 sq. ft., being worked into the soil before planting.

Planting

Seed may be sown in flats in a greenhouse two months before the earliest planting date in the field. Four to five seeds are sown per inch. Before setting in the field, the tops are cut back to a height of 3 in. or 4 in. They are set 4 in. to 6 in. in rows 15 in. to 18 in. apart. Seed may be sown in rows, planting three or four seeds per inch. The plants are thinned to between 4 in. and 6 in. apart when well established but before the onion begins to swell.

Onion sets are planted the same distance apart, in and between the rows, as transplanted plants. One lb. of small onion sets will plant 100 ft.

Succession

If sets are planted early and followed by plants from seed, either indoors or out, there should be a steady supply, as sets mature in 90 to 100 days, and seed onions in 150 to 180 days. Plants started from seed should be put in the open ground when sets are put out.

Moisture

A continuous, well-regulated supply of moisture is absolutely necessary.

Cultivation

Should be shallow and frequent, and should begin as soon as the plants appear. Wait until tops straighten out, about one week, before weeding between the seedlings, to avoid disturbing plants. Keep rows free from weeds.

Harvesting

Tops are practically dead before plants are mature. Pull or dig and leave in sun for a few days to dry out and to toughen the skins. This will improve the keeping quality.

Storing

Onions should be thoroughly cured by being exposed to sun for several days. Do not try to remove the soil until the onions are entirely cured; then it will come off easily without washing. Only the onions grown from seed will keep for any length of time. Store in a cool, dry place spread out on a flat, dry surface. They do not need moisture and should keep five to six months.

Parsley

Botanical Name: *Petroselinum hortense*

Origin

Indigenous to southern Europe. Known to the Greeks only as a wild plant. Mentioned in a list of plants for Charlemagne's garden, and introduced into England in 1548.

Soil

Varieties used for leaves may be grown in any soil, but require ample food material; those that are grown for their root system need a deep 6-in. to 8-in., well-drained soil.

Sowing

Seed requires about three weeks to germinate and may be sown in the open ground at any time after soil can be easily worked until August 1. Sow in rows 18 in. apart; barely cover with soil. One packet of seed is sufficient for a family. Seed may also be started in hotbeds two months before it can be sown outside. Transplant when 1 in. high, 2 in. each way, and later move into the garden when the ground is workable. Transplant 8 in. apart in rows 18 in. apart.

Parsley may also be sown in coldframes about August 1. Keep plants covered with hay in the frames all winter and transplant to garden in early spring.

Cultivation

Keep soil lightly cultivated and free from weeds.

Moisture

In dry weather parsley is greatly benefited by thorough watering two or three times a week.

Fertilizer

Plants will thrive without fertilizing, but will be much larger if commercial fertilizer, 4–8–4, or well-rotted manure is applied just before planting.

Harvesting

First leaves may be picked about seventy-five days after seed is sown. Kept in water, they will remain fresh for several days. Never pick plant clean; some leaves should be left around the center of the crown to ensure continuous growth.

Parsnip

Botanical Name: *Pastinaca sativa*

Origin

Grown since the beginning of the Christian era. Native of Europe and Asia.

Soil

Parsnips need a very fertile, but fairly heavy soil, deep and well drained. If too heavy, roots become distorted; if too sandy, superfluous fibrous roots form.

Fertilizers

To get long, straight roots, apply all manures and fertilizers. such as a 4–8–4, before the land is plowed, and turn under to a depth of at least 8 in. The long tap root forms before the parsnip begins to develop, and if fertilizer is too close to the surface, roots will not be encouraged to grow down.

Sowing

Sow seed as early as possible in spring, 1 in. deep, at the rate of ⅛ oz. to 50 ft. They should be in rows 18 in. to 2½ ft. apart. They germinate in twelve to eighteen days and rows may be marked by radish seed mixed with parsnip seed. When plants are 2 in. to 4 in. high, thin 4 in. to 6 in. apart.

Intercropping

Parsnips, being a long-season crop, may be intercropped with any quick-maturing crop such as beets, lettuce, radishes or spinach.

Cultivation

Should be constant, but not deep.

Moisture

A constant supply of moisture is essential for smooth, long, well-developed roots.

Harvesting

Parsnips may be harvested before the ground freezes, or may remain in the ground, protected by coarse hay or straw, until spring. Freezing tends to reduce the bitter flavor present in the fall. Dig parsnips out; never try to pull them.

Pea

Botanical Name: *Pisum sativum*

Origin

This vegetable is a native of Europe and has been cultivated since antiquity.

Soil

Peas should be grown in a sandy loam that is rich in organic matter. The soil should be well prepared during the fall previous to planting, for the crop is planted early in the spring, often before the frost is all out of the ground. If the soil is carefully prepared in the fall, very little work is necessary in the spring. Plenty of well-rotted manure mixed into the soil will give the best results.

Planting

Peas are divided into two groups, smooth-seeded and wrinkled. The smooth varieties may be planted two weeks before the wrinkled type, because they can stand moister and cooler soil conditions—as soon as enough of the frost is out of the ground to make it easily workable. The wrinkled sorts should be put in two weeks later, for by that time the soil is drier and warmer, conditions essential for this type. The seed for both types should be sown in rows 2½ ft. apart and 1½ in. to 2 in. in the row. Thin them if it seems necessary. Make a trench 4 in. deep, and cover the seed to the depth of 1 in., filling in the trench as the plants grow. One lb. of seed is sufficient for 50 ft. of garden row. The plants cannot be transplanted successfully.

Succession

For a continuous supply, seed should be sown every ten days. They should not be planted after hot weather sets in, for they will neither mature nor thrive properly. A fall crop may be sown about August 1, but it is not nearly as productive as the spring crop. They should be mature in from sixty to eighty days, depending on the variety.

Moisture

Peas do not require an abundance of moisture but they do need a continuous supply of it. Practice clean, shallow cultivation for the best results.

Training

Peas do not need a definite system of training unless they grow to a height of more than 2 ft. Training is then necessary to keep them off the ground and to facilitate harvesting.

Twiggy brush such as that from birch trees is the best for training the taller growing varieties. The brush should be put from 6 in. to 10 in. apart in the row any time before the vines begin to spread.

Fertilizer

If the land is not very fertile, an additional application of a complete fertilizer may be given during the blooming period. Use the fertilizer at the rate of 1 lb. for every 75 ft., broadcast between the rows and lightly cultivated in.

Harvesting

The wrinkled varieties should be harvested when the pods are well filled out, while the smooth-seeded sorts are best when the pods are only about half full, for the peas lose their flavor as they grow larger and more mature. Both varieties are best when harvested either early in the morning or late in the evening, never during the hot part of the day. The quality becomes inferior in a very short time if, after picking, they are not kept in a very cool place.

Pepper

Botanical Name: *Capsicum annuum (frutescens)*

Origin

Native of South America and cultivated for centuries.

Soil Type and Preparation

Sandy loam is best, though any type will give fair results. For preparation, see eggplant.

When and How to Plant

Should be started indoors from February 1 to March 1. Sow in soil composed of 2 parts garden loam to 1 part sand. Put in rows 3 in. apart, and cover seed with $1/4$ in. of soil. Seed will sprout in ten days to two weeks, and when plants are $1^1/2$ in. high, transplant to 2 in. by 2 in. The temperature should not be lower than 70° F. A month to six weeks later, transplant again to 3 in. by 3 in. or 4 in. by 4 in. Set out of doors as soon as the ground has warmed up and all danger of frost is over. Set 18 in. in the row and $2^1/2$ ft. between the rows.

Moisture Requirements

Continuous moisture supply is necessary, but too much will promote excessive leaf growth with less fruit.

Cultivation

Practice shallow cultivation. The plants may be slightly hilled up, as they grow. When the first peppers are ready to harvest, cultivation should cease. Keep all weeds out even when the time for cultivation has ended.

Fertilizers

A complete fertilizer such as 4–8–4 or 5–8–7 should be used, as the average soil is usually deficient in nitrogen, phosphorus and potash. If the soil is not very fertile, fertilizer should be applied just before or when the plants are set out. If applied when setting out, mix about 2 tbs. with the soil at the bottom of the hole into which the plants are to be set. Another application may be made when the fruits are just beginning to form, to hasten growth and maturity. This is applied in the form of a circle around each plant 3 in. to 4 in. away from the stem and covered with soil. Two tbs. of fertilizer per plant is enough.

Harvesting

All sweet peppers are green until they reach a stage beyond which they no longer increase in size, and at that time they turn red. They are usually harvested in the green stage. Red sweet peppers are usually used only for their color. They may be picked at any time after they have reached the desired size.

Storing

If the entire plant is pulled up and hung upside down in a cellar, the peppers will remain in good condition for as long as three weeks.

Potato

Botanical Name: *Solanum tuberosum*

Origin

Native to the Peruvian Andes of South America; discovered there in the latter part of the sixteenth century.

Soil Type and Preparation

A light, well-drained, loamy soil is best. As potatoes are very heavy feeders, the soil should be plowed or forked as deeply as possible and a liberal amount of well decayed manure incorporated. Fresh manure should never be used unless it is applied in the fall previous to planting. If fresh manure is applied in the spring it will make too much nitrogen available to the plants right away, which will cause them to make an excessive amount of top growth and little root growth. Lime should never be applied to the soil as it activates organisms that cause potato diseases. All manure applied should be turned under as deeply as possible.

When and How to Plant

Early crop may be planted as soon as the frost is out of the ground, and succeeding crops may be planted until the first week in July. Make the trenches from 4 in. to 6 in. deep and 2½ ft. to 3 ft. apart. Plant the potatoes 15 in. to 18 in. apart in the trench and cover with 2 in. of soil. Use only disease-free or certified seed. Potatoes should be prepared for planting ten days beforehand, being cut so that there are at least two eyes for each section, with a small piece of

the potato attached. Spread the pieces in a box not more than two layers deep, and sprinkle them with sulphur. The sulphur should come in contact with all the cut surfaces, causing them to dry out and to toughen up. This is known as "suberization," and it prevents the potato from rotting before the plant gets a good start. Potatoes are sometimes planted without this treatment and potato skins are also planted, but the results in both cases are variable. Seed potatoes should be planted at the rate of 3 lb. to 4 lb. every 50 ft. Sprouts should appear above the ground in two weeks. The later crops are all treated in the same way.

Cultivation

Keep the soil loose and friable at all times. When the plants are 4 in. to 6 in. high, begin to hoe the soil toward them. Kill all weeds before they have a chance to develop enough to compete with the potatoes. Hoe the soil around the plants gradually at intervals of ten days to two weeks, taking the soil from between the rows, Continue until the plants have grown so long that working between the rows is impossible.

Manures and Fertilizers

An application of a complete commercial fertilizer, 4−8−4, at the rate of 1 lb. to 50 ft., may be broadcast between the rows one month after the plants have sprouted, if the soil was not very fertile to begin with.

Harvesting

The early crop may be dug from the time vines begin to die until they are actually dead. Leaving the potatoes outside on the ground in the sun for a day to toughen up the skin makes them easier to handle, and prevents them from bruising so easily. The late crop should not be dug until the vines are dead. Leave outside for a day in the sun, as with the early crop.

Storing

Requirements for storing potatoes are a temperature of 50° F., a medium amount of humidity and uniform conditions. They may be stored in bags, boxes or in piles, provided there is an allowance for proper air circulation. They will keep for five months or more.

Yield

One to 2 bushels per 100 ft. for early crop. Larger yield for late crop.

Pumpkin

Botanical Name: *Cucurbita pepo*

Origin

Found in the western hemisphere and grown for its large edible fruits.

Soil, Sowing, Cultivation, etc.

See Squash.

Remarks

The chief difference between squash and pumpkin is in the stems. Squash stems are round and tender, pumpkin stems are hard, square and woody. Pumpkins cannot stand freezing, so they should be picked before a heavy frost.

Radish

Botanical Name: *Raphanus sativus*

(Derived from the Latin, *radix,* meaning root)

Origin

The radish is probably native to western Asia, but it has been under cultivation for so long that its origin is unknown. The turnip, the onion and the radish are the oldest vegetables known.

Sowing

Sow as early as possible. The seeds need a cool moist period in which to germinate. Sow four seeds to the inch at the rate of 1 oz. to 100 ft. rows 12 in. apart. Thin when plants are 2 in. high to ¾ in. apart, or twelve to fourteen plants to a ft. Sow seed every two weeks to provide a continuous supply. Seed of the early spring varieties may be sown April 15 to June 1. Seed of summer types may be sown from June 1 until July 15. Seed for the early spring varieties may be sown from August 1 until September 1, as they will not mature in hot weather. A sowing may also be made in the hotbed, where they will come to maturity and be enjoyed as an early delicacy.

Cultivation

Cultivate at least once a week; or four times before harvesting.

Moisture

Plenty of moisture is needed for germination and for growing. If too moist when they mature, they will crack; if too dry, they will become pithy and pungent much sooner than they otherwise would do.

Harvesting

If roots remain in the ground too long, they become woody and crack. Pull out as soon as they mature.

Rhubarb

Botanical Name: *Rheum rhaponticum*

Origin

Discovered after the Christian era in the desert and subalpine regions of southern Siberia and the Volga River.

Soil

Any soil is satisfactory; if it is well prepared before plants are set out, they should last for eight or nine years. Work in a liberal application of well-decayed manure as deeply as possible and cultivate until it is finely pulverized.

Planting

As seed does not always come true to type, it is best to buy good one- or two-year-old plants. Set them out as early as possible in the spring, 18 in. apart in rows 30 in. to 36 in. apart for hand cultivation. The advantage of spring planting is that the soil is in the best condition, but rhubarb can easily be transplanted whenever the tops are dead.

Rutabaga: See Turnip

Salsify

Botanical Name: *Tragopogon porrifolius*

Origin

Salsify is also known as the oyster-plant, for its flavor is said to slightly resemble that of the oyster.

Soil and Fertilizers

See Parsnip.

Punch holes in the ground 1 ft. in depth. Put manure in the bottom, then add garden soil with 1 tsp. of commercial fertilizer. Leave the level about 2 in. below that of the ground. Put in four to five seeds per hole, and when they are up, thin to one seedling per hole. The rows should be 15 in. to 18 in. apart, and the holes 6 in. apart.

Planting

Sow seed as early in the spring as possible, or as soon as the ground can be worked. One-eighth oz. of seed to 50 ft. of row is sufficient.

Intercropping and Harvesting

See Parsnip.

Spinach

Botanical Name: *Spinacia oleracea*

Origin

Probably Persian in origin, and introduced into Europe in the fifteenth century. The New Zealand type, totally unrelated, was introduced from that country.

Soil Preparation and Type

For both the cool season or broad-leaved type and the warm-season or trailing type (New Zealand), the soil should be rich and well prepared by spading to a depth of 6 in., with well-rotted manure disked or forked in. Soil should be finely pulverized. Both types react very favorably to lime, which should not be applied in direct contact with the manure, but after the manure has been spaded in, at the rate of 1 lb. to 35 sq. ft. Lime should be used if the soil has not been limed for several years.

When and How to Plant

(1) *Cool-season type:* Plant in the open ground as early in the spring as possible. Spinach can be planted during a February or March thaw; sow seed at the rate of 1 oz. to 50 ft. in rows 12 in. apart. The plants are not usually thinned, and mature in from forty to fifty days. May also be sown in late September or October, and protected by a covering of salt marsh hay before the ground freezes. This crop is ready to use very early the following spring.

(2) *Warm-season type:* New Zealand spinach seed germinates slowly, and should be soaked in water twenty four to forty eight hours before planting. It may be sown in the open ground from May 1 to June 1. Plant in rows 3 ft. apart. six to eight seeds to each 1 ft., and thin 12 in. apart when plants are 3 in. to 4 in. high. Seed may also be started indoors about April 1 in flats or in pots. If started in flats, plants when 2 in. high should be transplanted to pots, one plant to a pot containing good garden soil. About May 15 they may be transplanted into the open ground, same distance as above.

Cultivation

(1) *Cool-season type:* Keep soil well loosened, keep weeds down.

(2) *Warm-season type:* Cultivate carefully and shallowly until plants begin to run; after that pull weeds but do not cultivate.

System of Training

For New Zealand spinach, or warm-season type, plants grow quickly when well established. Rapid growth usually takes place three to four weeks after the seeds have germinated. As crop is dependent on well-established plants, nothing should be picked until about June 15. All yellow leaves should be removed.

Manures and Fertilizers

(1) *Cool-season crop:* When plants are half-grown, top dress with nitrate of soda or am-

monium sulphate at the rate of 1 lb. to 100 sq. ft. applied as for beets, and cultivated in.

(2) *Warm-season crop:* Plants are benefited by a complete fertilizer if applied just as cultivation is stopped.

Harvesting

(1) *Cool-season type:* Can be picked only once. Best method is to cut individual plants by the roots, and wash.

(2) *Warm-season type:* Harvested by breaking off the tips, 3 in. to 4 in. long. Plant continues to send out new shoots until killed by frost.

Squash

Botanical Name: *Cucurbita*, various species

Origin

Tropical America, about 1490.

Types

Squash is of three types, summer, fall and winter. The summer or bush type will mature in sixty to seventy days and should be used before it reaches maturity and while the skin is still soft. The fall type matures more quickly and does not store as well as the winter type, which it otherwise resembles. The winter type will take 90 to 130 days and should be well matured before harvesting.

Soil

Squash likes a fairly light soil, containing plenty of organic matter. Work the soil to a depth of 6 in. to 8 in. and spade in a liberal quantity of well-rotted manure, as the squash plant is a heavy feeder. Summer squash should be planted in hills 4 ft. apart each way; fall and winter squash in hills 6 ft. to 8 ft. apart each way.

Sowing

For summer types, it is advisable to make at least two plantings for a continuous supply. For the fall and winter types, one planting is sufficient. Except in regard to distance of hills, planting, cultivating and fertilizing are the same for all types. Sow seed as soon as the frost

is out of the ground in hills prepared by removing one or two shovelfuls of soil and putting in a shovelful of manure; this should be packed firmly and covered with 4 in. of soil. A good squash hill should be about 1½ ft. in diameter and about 3 in. above ground level. If commercial fertilizer such as 4−8−4 is substituted for manure, mix one handful with at least one shovelful of soil before planting the seed. Plant six seeds to the hill, 2 in. apart; cover with 1 in. of soil and pack down firmly. Seed should germinate in about ten days. When the plants are about 3 in. high, thin out to the three best plants. If more are left, the size and the quality of the fruit will be inferior.

Plants may also be started indoors in small containers about three weeks before seed is sown in the open ground. Use any good garden soil, and sow several seeds in each container.

Thin out to two and set out when all danger of frost is past, being careful not to disturb the soil about the roots.

Moisture

Squash requires a continuous but not a heavy supply of moisture to ensure steady growth and maximum production

Cultivation

Practice shallow cultivation from the time the plants begin to grow until they have extended into the rows so far that cultivation would injure them. Do not cultivate within 6 in. of the plant, as the easily injured fibrous roots are very close to the surface. Once cultivation is impracticable, plants should be weeded to prevent the weeds from taking water and nourishment needed by the plants. To avoid disturbing the roots of the squash plants, weeds growing close to the plants should be cut rather than pulled out.

Fertilizer

If soil had not been thoroughly enriched before seeds were planted, a good commercial fertilizer may be added, just after thinning the plants. Another application is made just before the vines begin to run, at the rate of $1/2$ oz. to 1 oz. per hill, applied in a ring 6 in. away from the plants and covered with 1 in. of soil, taken from between the rows.

Harvesting

Summer squash may be harvested any time before the skin hardens. Pick all fruits before the skin hardens. If fruit is allowed to ripen, the vines will stop growing.

Fall or winter types are mature when the stems turn to a light greenish yellow. They may

27.1, 27.2. Summer squash (Cucurbita pepo) *(page 504)* and zucchini (Cucurbita pepo *var.* melopepo 'Zucchini'), *above, are prolific and popular, but more gardeners should learn to pick these vegetables when they are only 4 in. to 6 in. long. Photos Bill Swan*

then be cut and exposed to the sun for two weeks until the stem turns grayish and shrivels, or they may be left on the vines until the same condition is reached. Do not pull the fruit; cut the stalk. Winter squash should remain in the sun two weeks after reaching maturity, as evaporation reduces the high water content, making the fruit more edible and in better condition for storing.

Remarks

Squash and pumpkins may be interplanted in corn when the corn is about 3 in. high. Plant two to three seeds in every fourth row to every four to five corn hills.

Tomato

Botanical Name: *Lycopersicon esculentum*

Origin

First known as food in Peru. Until comparatively recently tomatoes were cultivated for ornamental purposes only. Even in colonial days the fruit was considered deadly poisonous to eat, and was known as the ornamental love apple.

Soil

The soil should not be very acid in reaction, nor should it react as alkaline. It should be well drained; a sandy loam is the best. Early tomatoes particularly require a light soil and do best with a southeastern exposure. Land that has grown corn or potatoes the previous year is good for tomatoes, especially if it is plowed or forked over in the autumn. Just before setting out the plants, fork in a very liberal supply of well-decayed manure and work the soil well to a 6 in. depth, being certain that the texture is very fine.

When and How to Plant

North of the latitude of Philadelphia the season is too short to ensure fruit from seed planted in the open ground for the first crop; therefore people buy their tomato plants, which should be set out when all danger from frost is past. Plants 6 in. to 10 in. in height, set 2 in. deeper than they were growing in the seedbed, are the best size to set out.

Seed may, however, be sown indoors in March in a light loam soil. Sow in rows 3 in. apart, four seeds to the inch, and cover with ½ in. of soil. In a temperature of 75° F., they should germinate in about ten days. The best plants for transplanting come from the seeds that germinate first. When plants are a week old, about 2 in. high, with true leaves showing, transplant 2 in. apart each way into flats of the same soil as that in which they were sown; two to three weeks later transplant 4 in. apart each way into the same soil and at the same temperature. Should the seedlings turn yellow, let them dry out slightly and then water with 1 oz. of nitrate of soda to 1 gallon of water. As with the purchased plants, the best plants should be 6 in. to 10 in. high. Set out deeper than they were in the flats indoors. and when all danger of frost is past. If the plants are not to be staked, set out 4 ft. apart each way. When the fruit begins to ripen, dry hay beneath the plants will prevent rotting due to moisture.

Staking is, however, a much more satisfactory method for the early crop, although it does not give as large a crop. Set out 3 ft. between rows and 1½ ft. between plants. Put stakes 3 in. away from the plants a week after they have been set out, or put them in before planting. Stakes should be 6 ft. high, and driven 18 in. into the ground. Plants should be tied to stakes in three or four places; use raffia or soft rope and a figure-8 knot to prevent the plants coming too close to the stake or being cut. A second method is to fasten three wire hoops 2 ft. in diameter to three stakes and to slip these over the plants, so that the plant can spread inside the hoops but cannot touch the ground. Hoops (or cylinders) can be made from welded-wire farm fencing, but the wire openings are large enough so that you can harvest the ripe fruit.

Pruning

All side branches should be pruned off until the fruiting period is well advanced, as they sap the strength of the good fruit and will set fruit of poor quality and size. The branches grow in the joints of the stems, between the leaf and the main stalk. True fruiting spurs come directly from the stem. Unstaked plants are practically impossible to prune.

Cultivation

Cultivate carefully and shallowly until plants are established and really begin to grow. In any case, cultivate sufficiently often to keep soil stirred and to suppress weed growth. When they are well started, begin to hill them very slightly. Cultivate until plants have so grown together that it is impossible to get through the rows without disturbing the plants. By this time they should be covering the ground enough to prevent weed growth and to conserve moisture.

Fertilizing

When plants are set out, put a small handful of good fertilizer, preferably 4–8–4, in each hole and thoroughly mix with the soil. Or scatter a handful in a ring, 6 in. in diameter, around each plant one week after they are set out. This should be covered with soil. At the last cultivation, apply a 4–8–4 or a 5–8–7, 2 lb. to 100 ft., broadcast lightly down the row and hoed in.

Harvesting

Allow tomatoes to ripen on the vines and do not pick them when the foliage is wet. They may also be picked when the first tinge of red shows and stored in a warm, dark place, where they will take about a week to ripen. Well-grown plants should each yield 12 lb. of tomatoes.

Turnip

Botanical Name: *Brassica rapa*

Origin

Native of southern Europe, and under cultivation for more than 4,000 years.

Soil

Any good garden soil is satisfactory. Should be prepared to a depth of 6 in. to 8 in.

Sowing

Sow in open ground as soon as soil can be worked, at the rate of ¼ oz. to 50 ft., in rows 18 in. apart. Cover seed with ¼ in. of soil, and when plants begin to crowd, thin to 3 in. apart. For fall crop, maturing in sixty days, sow July 15 to August 10.

Cultivation

Should be shallow and sufficiently frequent to prevent soil packing.

Fertilizer

Complete fertilizer, applied before the spring crop is planted. Late crop does not need any, as fertilizers are not all used up by preceding crop.

Harvesting

Spring crop should be harvested when 1½ in. to 2½ in. in diameter. Fall crop any time before ground freezes.

Watermelon

Midget type is excellent for the home garden. (For culture, see Muskmelon, page 496.)

VEGETABLE INSECTS AND DISEASES

Asparagus

The most common pests are two kinds of beetles. These can be controlled by spraying with either carbaryl (Sevin) or malathion, from one to three times at three-day intervals when the beetles first appear. Do not harvest until at least three days after treatment.

Bean

Beans are subject to virus diseases. Use of virus-resistant varieties such as Topcrop, Tendercrop and Resistant Cherokee will avoid such problems.

Among the insects that infest beans are the Mexican bean beetle, the flea beetle and the bean weevil. Spraying with carbaryl (Sevin) when the beetles first appear will provide control.

Beet

The one serious pest on this plant is the leaf miner, which results in unsightly blotches on the leaves. Spray with malathion when the miners appear, and at seven-day intervals thereafter as needed. Allow seven days after treatment before harvesting the crop.

Broccoli, Brussels sprout, cabbage and cauliflower

Members of the Cole family are subject to the clubroot disease caused by the organism *Plasmodiophora brassicae*. To control this disease, pour a cupful of a solution made by dissolving 6 tbs. of terraclor (PCNB) per gallon of water into each hole at transplanting time.

Cabbage aphids, cabbage worms and cabbage root maggots are three pests that frequently attack cabbage and related plants. Spraying with diasinon will control the worms and aphids. The material should be applied when the insects first appear and applied weekly thereafter as needed. Allow seven days after the last application before harvesting.

To control the root maggot, pour 1/2 cup of a solution (made with 2 tsp. of 25 percent Diazinon emulsifiable concentrate per quart of water) when setting out plants and again on soil around each plant seven days later.

Corn

The corn borer and the corn earworm are the two most destructive pests of sweet corn. Carbaryl (Sevin) or diazinon sprays applied to the foliage and silk when tassels begin to emerge, and every four to five days through silking, will provide control. To kill overwintering corn borer larvae, gather and destroy all cornstalks in late fall.

The bacterial disease known as wilt is the most destructive disease of corn. Several wilt-resistant varieties are available. Consult seed catalogues or contact your County Agricultural Agent for the names of resistant strains.

Cucumber

A fungus disease known as scab and a virus disease, mosaic, frequently affect cucumbers. Scab can be prevented by using resistant varieties such as Marketmore and Tablegreen 65. Mosaic can be avoided by using the varieties Challenger and Early Set, as well as the two above-mentioned varieties, which are resistant to scab.

Insects infesting cucumbers include cucumber beetles, squash vine borers and aphids. Methoxychlor sprays will control the beetles and borers; malathion sprays will control the aphids. Both types of spray should be applied when the vines are dry.

Eggplant

The most destructive fungus disease of eggplant is verticillium wilt. Unfortunately, there is as yet no effective control.

Rotting of the fruits caused by several other fungi can be avoided by spraying with zineb as the first fruits ripen and repeating in ten days.

Lettuce

Aphids and leafhoppers are the two most common pests of lettuce. Malathion sprays applied when aphids first appear will provide control. A carbaryl (Sevin) spray applied when leafhoppers appear, and at weekly intervals as needed, is effective. Where malathion is used, allow fourteen days on leaf lettuce, or seven days on head lettuce, before harvest. Where a carbaryl spray is used, wait fourteen days on leaf lettuce and three days on head lettuce before harvest.

Muskmelon

A fungus disease known as fusarium wilt is very prevalent and destructive. Varieties known to be resistant to this disease include Burpee Hybrid, Gold Star, Iroquois and Delicious 51.

Cucumber beetles and squash vine borers may attack muskmelons. For control, see under Cucumber above.

Onion

The fungus disease known as blotch is occasionally serious on onions. Spraying with Maneb in mid-June and repeating several times at weekly intervals will control this disease.

Two common pests of onions are thrips and maggots. The former can be controlled by spraying with malathion when the insects first appear and at five-day intervals as needed; five days must elapse before harvest. The latter can be controlled by spraying with 1 tbs. of 25 percent Diazinon emulsified concentrate in 1 qt. of water per 25 ft. of row at planting time.

Pea

Several fungus diseases affect peas. including powdery mildew, wilt and root rot. Mildew can be controlled with sulphur-containing sprays. There is no effective control for wilt and root rot except to sow the seed in a new area and as early as possible in spring.

The only serious pests are aphids, which can be controlled by spraying with malathion several times at weekly intervals starting when the insects first appear. Three days must elapse after the last treatment before harvest.

Pepper

The virus disease known as mosaic is perhaps the most prevalent. Several mosaic-resistant strains are available, including Keystone, Midway, Staddon's Select and Yolo Wonder.

Borers and flea beetles are two of the pests that attack peppers. The former can be controlled by spraying with carbaryl (Sevin) as needed, and the latter by spraying with Diazinon early in the growing season.

Potato

Few home gardeners have the desire and sufficient space to grow potatoes. For those who do, the following diseases must be combated or avoided for successful culture: scab, early and late blight and viruses. Adjusting the soil reaction with sulphur to reach an acidity of pH 5.2, and the use of resistant varieties such as Cherokee, Norland or Russet Rural, will control or prevent scab. Spraying with Maneb every seven to ten days, starting when the plants are 6 in. in height, until the vines are dead, will control the blight diseases.

Among the insects that attack potatoes are the Colorado potato beetle, aphids, flea beetles and leafhoppers. Spraying with carbaryl (Sevin) when any of these pests appear and repeating as needed will provide control.

Pumpkin

See Cucumber, page 508.

Radish

Maggots. See root maggots under Broccoli, Brussels Sprout, Cabbage and Cauliflower.

Rhubarb

The only serious fungus disease of rhubarb is a leaf spot. Spraying early in the growing season with Maneb and reappearing at ten-day intervals, as necessary, will provide control. Removal and discarding of above-ground parts in the fall will reduce the possibility of infections the following spring.

Spinach

Leaf miner is the most common pest. See Beet for control.

Squash

See Cucumber, page 506, for pest control.

Tomato

The tomato is probably the most popular and most successfully grown vegetable (or fruit) in the home garden. Nevertheless, it is subject to a number of fungus diseases and insect pests that must be controlled to assure success and bountiful yields.

The most destructive fungus diseases are fusarium wilt and verticillium wilt, which enter the plants via the roots. Complete failure of a crop can result when susceptible varieties are used. Fortunately, resistant varieties have been developed. Among those resistant to both types of wilt are Campbell 1327, Heinz 1350, Jet Star, Springset and Supersonic. Other resistant varieties are also available; check with your local garden center.

During very rainy seasons the fungus disease known as early blight will cause leaves to turn yellow and die prematurely, starting when the first fruits appear. Spraying weekly with Maneb will control this blight.

Blossom-end rot is one of the most common diseases of tomato fruits, particularly of the first-formed ones, which begin to blacken and decay at the lower blossom end. No fungus parasite is involved: the rot results from lack of moisture when the plants are making rapid growth, and a lack of calcium in the soil. Applying lime to the soil in spring, and providing adequate moisture when needed, will help to prevent blossom-end rot.

Among the insects that attack tomatoes are cutworms, flea beetles, hornworms, aphids and whiteflies. Cutworms appear early in the growing season, just after the plants are set out. Pouring ½ cup of a solution containing 1 tbs. of Diazinon per gallon of water around each plant when transplanting will provide control. For gardeners who do not want to use a chemical, a paper collar placed around each plant at transplanting time also provides control.

Hornworms—those large, green, ugly larvae of one of the sphinx moths—are among the most voracious pests, capable of completely defoliating a tomato plant within a few days. Where only a few plants are grown, the simplest procedure is to hand-pick the larvae as soon as leaves are being chewed. Where many plants are involved, spraying with either carbaryl (Sevin) or dipel will provide control.

Aphids can be controlled by an occasional application of malathion.

Whiteflies are probably one of the most common pests to tomatoes, but the damage they cause is minimal. However, because they develop in such great numbers, many home gardeners feel they cause a great amount of damage. Spraying with Diazinon or with resmethrin will control this pest.

28

The Fruit Garden

A carefully planned and well-maintained fruit garden can be a constant source of satisfaction to the homeowner. Besides yielding a bountiful and varied supply of fruit throughout the growing season, it may also occasionally even be a source of profit—which surely is a factor that cannot be denied. In addition, fruit trees can play an important part in the overall home landscape, and a healthy and thriving fruit garden around one's home can add immeasurably to one's gardening pleasure.

Many choice varieties of fruit—often far superior in quality to those grown commercially—may be produced in the home garden. When fruit is to be shipped a great distance, as it so often is in our country, it is usually necessary to pick it long before it is fully ripe and much of its potential sweetness and flavor never develops in consequence. Fruit grown in the home garden may be harvested at its finest stage of ripeness and will possess a quality unobtainable in the commercial market.

In addition to their purely utilitarian uses, most fruit trees have a decidedly decorative value. There are few things more beautiful than an apple tree in full bloom, and both pear and apple trees are often very picturesque in outline. They may be used as shade trees upon the terrace or the lawn, they may be planted along the driveway, or they may be espaliered, i.e., trained against some supporting structure such as a fence or wall. Espaliered fruit trees are often seen in English gardens and in France, and they are becoming increasingly popular in this country. An "espalier" is a trellis or open support upon which a vine or a woody plant may be trained. Apple trees, pears, peaches, plums, nectarines and quinces may be very readily used in this way. Such trees are usually trained to a given number of branches (see illustration), and they should preferably be grown on a wall facing southeast. Espaliered fruit trees are especially useful in limited space—as well as in a small urban garden or on a rooftop.

It is necessary first to decide and plan what fruits are needed for the home garden. When this decision has been made, the order for stock should be placed well in advance of planting time. There are many excellent catalogue companies that provide the home gardener with good quality and wide choice of varieties. If ordering is delayed nurseries will be in their rush season and certain varieties may be exhausted. Therefore, by ordering early and stating the desired shipping date, the stock will arrive in ample time for best planting. One should plan to set the stock as soon as the frost is out of the ground.

CHOOSING VARIETIES AND DWARFED TREES

The home gardener should specify the varieties wanted, but should avoid new highly ad-

511

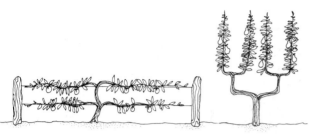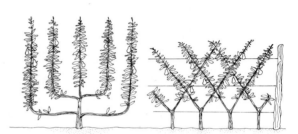

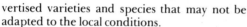

Fig. 28.1
Four examples of espaliered fruit trees

vertised varieties and species that may not be adapted to the local conditions.

A dwarf fruit tree is a standard variety grafted to a dwarfing rootstock. This root stock causes the tree to make less annual growth and remain a smaller tree throughout its life. These dwarf trees are better suited to the home garden because they come into bearing at an earlier age, require less space, and are easier to spray and prune.

They are available in two basic sizes: the very dwarf, which are generally trained as espalier (but need not be), and "no-ladder" trees, which grow only 10 ft. to 12 ft. tall. The very dwarf trees are grafted onto Malling IV rootstock, the mid-sized onto Malling VII. (Malling is the agricultural research station in England that developed this system of controlling apple tree size.) Since the Malling XI rootstock has a shallow root system, these trees should be staked, but trees grown on Malling VII need not be. They are particularly useful in small gardens.

The point of the graft should be left above ground in planting; if it is covered, roots will form above the union and the tree will become standard in size.

SELECTING THE PROPER GRADE

Trees

Trees are graded according to their height and thickness of trunk, and are priced accordingly. Fruit trees are offered in two or three sizes of one- and two-year-old stock. The A, or

best, grade costs only a few cents more than a smaller tree. It seems to be a matter of preference as to whether one- or two-year-old stock is planted. However, there is no doubt that the best should be purchased, regardless of age.

The five main advantages in purchasing one-year trees are:

1. Not as many roots broken off in transplanting.
2. Easily pruned to desired height.
3. No branches broken in shipping.
4. Better selection of main branches the following year.
5. More quickly handled and planted.

Bush Fruits

Bushes are more easily handled and set out than trees. A well-grown two-year-old bush will give excellent results and possibly produce fruit sooner and in large quantities than a one-year-old bush. The only reason for buying a one-year-old bush is to be sure that it is of the best grade, as sometimes a two-year-old bush is inferior in size and appearance at the end of its first year's growth.

CARE OF STOCK BEFORE PLANTING

Often the stock is received before planting conditions are satisfactory. The land may not yet be prepared, or it may be too wet. Other growing materials arriving at the same time of year may also necessitate a delay in planting for a short time.

As soon as the stock is received, it should be removed from the package to prevent sweating and possible deterioration. It may be planted temporarily in a trench or kept in a cool damp cellar for several days. In any case, the roots should not be permitted to dry out. Plant the stock before the buds begin to open; otherwise, if dry soil conditions exist, watering may be necessary. The roots also should have a chance to establish themselves before the warm weather begins. For this reason the earlier the stock is planted in the spring, the greater the chance it will have to establish its root system before the buds begin to swell. This should result in a greater shoot growth the first season when planted.

Nursery stock may be planted either in the spring or in the fall. In some cases fall planting is advisable, especially if the stock is to be planted on heavy land that is apt to be too wet at the proper planting time in the spring, so that the period of adjustment after transplanting is long past when conditions are favorable for growth in the spring. Weather conditions are more stable in the fall and the soil may be in better condition for planting.

The advantages of spring planting are that the stock makes considerable top and root growth before winter and is better able to survive its first winter, particularly if it is a severe one.

LAYING OUT AND PLANTING THE ORCHARD

Definite planting distances are recommended for each fruit. These should be meticulously observed. The distances in most cases may seem enormous, especially after the trees are planted, but it should be borne in mind that these distances are based on recommendations obtained from many experiments. In many cases, one is puzzled about placing trees next to each other that have different planting distances. This is easily solved: If apples and sour cherries are to be planted in adjacent rows, how far should the sour cherries be planted from the apples? Take the sum of the two planting distances as 35 ft. for apples and 20 ft. for sour cherries, which equals 55 ft., and divide by 2.

Twenty-seven feet would be the correct distance to plant the sour cherries from the apples.

Be sure to plant the trees in a straight line, as once they are set they will remain a picture of your accuracy. Establish a baseline along which the first row of trees is to be planted and take all your measurements from it. Wire or mason's twine is very practicable for this purpose. Then measure off the required distance for each tree on this line and insert a small stake at that point. To lay out the second row, measure the required distance from the baseline at each end and set up another line.

The only piece of equipment for planting that one really needs is a round, pointed shovel. Dig the hole and lay aside the topsoil. When the subsoil, often yellowish in color, appears, place it in a separate pile. Make the hole just wide enough to receive the roots without crowding. Dig deep enough to allow the tree to be set 2 in. or 3 in. deeper than in the nursery. Make the two sides of the hole parallel and thus have the bottom as wide as the top. This will allow the soil to be packed uniformly around the roots and will avoid any danger of leaving air spaces. Fill the hole, using good soil first. When the roots are covered, the soil should be firmed if it is not too wet. Then the subsoil should be put on top and firmed again. Manure or fertilizer should not be put into the hole at planting time, but can be used as a topdressing or mulch after planting is completed.

POLLINATION

"Pollination" may be defined as the transfer of pollen from the stamen to the stigma or female part of the blossom. Pollen of many varieties of fruits is not borne in large quantities and is not carried far by the wind. The pollen merely falls on the stigmas or is carried on the bodies of insects that visit the flowers.

In some varieties of fruits this pollen is capable of fertilizing the ovules of the same variety, while others must receive pollen from another variety to be successfully cross-fertilized. The causes of "self-unfruitfulness" are as follows:

1. Lack of viable pollen.
2. Discharge of pollen at a time when pistil is not receptive.

3. Production of insufficient viable pollen by some varieties.

4. In some fruits and varieties the male flowers and female flowers are borne on separate plants.

These causes of self-unfruitfulness show that some plants are somewhat modified in order to avoid self-fertilization and to secure cross-fertilization.

Many years ago, fruit trees were grown from seed. This resulted in the development of numerous worthless variants. Little was known or done about pollination. However, this was not very important at the time as so many different variants were interplanted that cross-pollination took place naturally.

As new varieties were developed, fruit growers began to select fewer but better varieties. These varieties were propagated by cuttings or grafting, the individual trees arranged in rows, planted apart at a definite distance and given proper cultural methods.

But many trees of a single variety planted on a large acreage were too far away from trees of any other variety for cross-pollination to be successful.

In a test at an eastern state agricultural experimental station, apple trees of the applied variety 'Wealthy' formed 7 fruits from each 100 blossoms pollinated with its own pollen. When the pollen of the 'Delicious' variety was applied to the stigmas of the 'Wealthy,' a 31 percent set was the result.

If a fruit tree fails to set fruit because of lack of proper pollination, this condition may be corrected in one of two principal ways:

1. The quickest method is to place bouquets of blossoms of another variety in the tree at blooming time. These bouquets should be placed in a pail of water so that the flower will last as long as possible, and should be hung in the uppermost part of the tree. The method, to be successful, depends entirely on the presence of bees or other insects.

2. The second method is to top-graft a different variety into the tree. It usually requires three or four years to get results by this method. Meanwhile bouquets of blossoms may be used in order to keep up production as described above.

Before planting varieties of fruit trees, it is well worth the time to write to your County Cooperative Extension Agent for further advice.

GROWING AND FRUITING HABITS

There is considerable variation in the time it takes a tree to come into bearing, but with other conditions being favorable, it may be only a varietal difference. In some varieties of apples, individual trees take as long as eight years to begin bearing, while most varieties of peaches and sour cherries fruit within three years.

Until a tree begins to produce blossom buds, it usually makes a rapid vigorous growth if it is in a healthy condition. Young trees may make as much as 4 ft. or 5 ft. of growth in a single season. The buds formed are vegetative and contain only leaves. As the tree gets ready to bear fruit, a marked change is noticeable. Fruit buds are larger and more plump, as they have flower parts in them. Short spurlike growths occur on the pear and apple, while modifications of this appear on cherries and plums. Peach buds become larger, with two large buds surrounding a center one. A change has obviously taken place in the vigor of the tree. Terminal growth has slowed down to 18 in. or 20 in. The tree is leaving its vegetative period to enter its productive period.

Apple

Apples are borne terminally on spurs, and laterally and terminally on shoots. The fruit bud is a mixed bud and contains three to eight blossoms (normally five) and a whorl of leaves.

The spurs are rough-looking and irregular in their method of growth. When a spur fruits, a small bud forms at one side of it. This bud cannot fruit the next year because it has no flowers in it. This is due to the fruit on that spur, which has prevented it from further development. It must have one season's time in which to develop into a fruit bud other than the year when fruit is borne. Therefore, it is conclusive that a spur will not produce fruit every year but may do so every other year. When a tree bears a heavy crop one year and none the next, its fruit spurs have all borne at the same time and it is called a biennial bearer. An annual-bearing tree has some spurs that bear each year, but no spur bears in successive years.

Fruit spurs are productive until ten or twelve years old, and may not be more than 6 in. to 10 in. long at that time.

Cherry

The fruiting habits are very similar to those of the plum. The sour cherry often produces fruit buds on the previous season's growth, the fruits being formed near the lower part of it. Each bud usually contains from two to four flowers.

Grape

Grape buds are produced on the current season's growth. The bud, which is within a single covering, is divided into three parts. The primary or main fruit-producing bud is the largest. The secondary bud is somewhat smaller and not as productive, while the smallest or tertiary bud expands as a shoot but produces no fruits. Usually, when the primary bud is not damaged by a late spring frost, the other buds fail to develop. This bud grows as a shoot and with favorable conditions may make between 10 ft. and 20 ft. of growth. The three to five clusters of blossoms are borne very near the lower end.

Peach

Peaches are borne from lateral buds formed on the previous season's growth. The buds are borne one, two or three at a node. If three, the two outside buds are fruit buds and contain only one blossom each and no leaves, while the center bud is a vegetative (leaf) bud.

Pear

This fruit is very similar to the apple in growth habit.

Plum

Fruit buds are borne axially on spurs. Each fruit bud contains from one to three blossoms. Leaf buds are also on the same spur but are smaller in size. The terminal bud, as in the peach, is always a vegetative bud.

Quince

Fruit buds are lateral on the previous season's growth. The bud expands as a shoot in the spring, and after making several inches of growth, a single flower blossoms on the end of it. This habit of growth makes the quince a very twiggy small tree.

Miscellaneous

The flowers of red and black raspberries and blackberries are borne in clusters that contain leaves and that come from axillary buds on the cane of the previous season's growth. Old canes are removed after fruiting.

TREE FRUITS

Apple

Botanical Name: *Pyrus malus*

Soil
A deep, well-drained, loamy soil, well supplied with organic matter, gives excellent results. Heavy clay soils, with a hard and impervious subsoil, should be avoided.

Planting Age of Trees
One- and two-year-old trees are the best as they recover very quickly from the effects of transplanting and are lowest in price and easily handled. Older trees may be planted if sufficient soil is moved with the roots, but this operation is expensive and the tree's recovery is not very rapid.

Time of Planting

Apple trees may be planted during the late fall or early spring months when they are in a dormant condition. In areas north of Philadelphia early spring planting is preferable to fall planting as a precaution against winter injury. Bear in mind that the root system of a tree is active long before noticeable top growth has begun to take place. Therefore, late fall or early spring planting is most desirable in order that the root system will become established before the growing season begins. A tree that is well established on its root system before top growth actually begins will make more vigorous growth the first season.

Planting Distance

Standard apple trees should be planted 40 ft. apart in the row and between the rows. They may, however, be set as close as 30 ft. apart each way if space is extremely limited and the varieties are not of the most vigorous types.

Method of planting

Dig a hole just large enough to receive the roots without crowding and deep enough to set the tree 2 in. deeper (except grafted dwarf trees) than it was formerly growing in the nursery. When removing the soil keep both the topsoil and subsoil separate. Be sure to make the sides of the hole parallel and the bottom as wide as the top.

Trim off any broken, injured or excessively long roots to within bounds and place the tree in the hole. Put the topsoil in first and firm it around the roots. Then put the subsoil in and firm it again.

The purpose of pruning and training young trees is to establish a strong framework of branches, which will satisfactorily carry the future load of fruit.

Pruning a One-year Tree

The top of a one-year-old apple tree should be cut back to a height of 36 in. from the ground after it has been set out.

Pruning a Two-year Tree

Two-year-old trees may contain many branches. In this case it is essential to choose the branches for the framework and remove the others when the tree is planted. Choose three or four branches making at least a 45° angle with the trunk, and about 6 in. apart. Of course, they are not on the same plane but are spaced uniformly around the tree for balance. The lowest branch should be at least 18 in. from the ground. Trees that are less vigorous should be pruned back more severely, but the principle is the same in every case. Crossing, closely parallel, weak, broken and low branches should be removed. However, it is best to leave branches that are not too thick or that do not directly compete with each other, as they materially aid in increasing the total growth.

Time of Pruning Young Apple Trees

Pruning may be done at any time that the trees are in dormant condition. However, as winter-killing begins at the tip of a branch, pruning should not be practiced until the coldest part of the winter is past, and not later than the time at which the buds begin to swell.

Pruning Nonbearing Young Apple Trees

Pruning should be as light as possible until the tree reaches its bearing age. This age varies greatly according to the variety. Remove one of two closely parallel branches; one of two crossing branches, as well as branches that are weak, cause crowding or appear diseased. Do not remove any branch that may not be interfering at present just to get rid of it. Such branches are a great help to the tree for several years. Do not allow any of the so-called scaffold branches to grow beyond the leader. This will necessitate some cutting back each year as the leader should be several inches longer than the others. Always cut back to buds on one-year-old wood or to lateral branches on older wood. Permit some branches to fill in the center of the tree without overcrowding.

Pruning Young Bearing Trees

For several years after a tree begins to bear its crops are not very heavy. Pruning should be light so as not to cause an overvegetative condition, which will throw it out of bearing.

Pruning Bearing Trees

Pruning is beneficial to a fruit-bearing tree, but it may be overdone if not thoroughly understood. Before you prune or permit others to prune your trees, you should be thoroughly informed on the subject and should understand its principles. Less damage is caused by lack of pruning than by pruning the wrong way. When a fruit tree reaches the bearing stage, it can be kept in a high state of production for many years.

When a tree begins to bear and form fruit-producing points, it becomes less vegetative and vigorous than it was previously. The amount of terminal growth is less, and is made within a period of three to four weeks. Fruit spurs have formed, which are to bear the fruit. Severe pruning may throw it out of bearing. The procedure for pruning is as follows:

1. Study the tree from a distance of 15 ft. to 20 ft. Try to visualize how it should look when properly pruned.
2. First remove all dead and diseased wood, water sprouts and suckers.
3. If any large branches must be removed, make your decision on the ground and not up in the tree. Branches look entirely different from the two points of view. One is justified in removing a large branch if it is:

   (a) Rubbing against another.
   (b) Running parallel to another only a few inches away.
   (c) Heavily shaded by a branch above it.
   (d) Growing up through the center of the tree through many other branches.
   (e) Too close to the ground.
   (f) Growing back toward the center, and interfering with other branches.
   (g) Broken or diseased.
   (h) Long and spindly (weak).

4. Thin out the remaining branches by removing:

   (a) Crossing, crowding, parallel, broken or diseased branches.
   (b) Weak and spindly branches.
   (c) Those growing in the wrong direction.

5. If the branches are extra long and growing out of bounds, cut them back to within the same area as the others. Always cut back to lateral branch on wood more than one year old. One-year growth may be cut back to an outside bud. Cut back to promote bushy, lateral growth.
6. Scrape the loose bark off with the back of the saw, a hoe or tree scraper. This will remove hibernating places for the codling moth, scale and other insects.

Duration of Bearing

Many varieties of apple trees bear fruit four or five years after planting and reach their full bearing from the twelfth to fifteenth year, while some varieties do not begin to bear until they are at least eight years old. Some varieties live much longer than others, while factors such as soil, fertilization, insects and diseases, etc., should not be overlooked. However, with good cultural methods, a tree should bear over a period of forty years.

Overcoming Failure to Bear

The principal causes of failure to bear fruit are:

1. Insufficient nitrogen.
2. Severe or improper pruning.
3. Lack of pollinating insects.
4. Wrong varieties.
5. Lack of pollen supply at time needed.

Cultivation

Weeds compete with trees for food and water. This competition is most harmful when the trees are newly set or are just about to bear. By keeping weed growth suppressed, the tree is able to make a better and faster start. Cultivation should consist of removing weeds from around the young trees and mowing the weeds between the rows, or by frequent disking. Cultivation should cease from four to six weeks before fall begins, so the trees will be hardened off and in good condition to withstand the cold winter months. By allowing the weeds to grow at the above late date they actually compete with the tree for favorable results.

If cultivation is not possible, as is the case in some backyards, on lawns or on stony ground, the next best treatment is to keep the weed or grass growth cut. Two cuttings per season is usually sufficient. If possible, these cuttings should be used as a mulch under the tree.

Fertilizing Nonbearing Trees

Nonbearing trees are those that have not reached the bearing age. The importance of feeding them to produce a large bearing framework for future years is apparent. If a tree is making from 12 in. to 18 in. or more of terminal growth each year, an application of fertilizer will not be beneficial. If, however, such a tree is making only 1 in. to 4 in. of growth, fertilization would prove to be extremely valuable and justifiable.

A nonbearing tree should be fertilized with particular reference to its age. A two-year-old tree should receive from 4 oz. to 8 oz., and this amount may be gradually increased as the tree gets older. However, the maximum amount that seems to give best results on a bearing tree is between 5 lb. and 7 lb.

A high-grade complete fertilizer or some form of nitrogen may be used. For best results the nitrogen should be available to the tree as soon as spring growth begins.

All fertilizers should be spread under the outer branches around the tree. It is not necessary to spade or rake them into the soil.

When trees are growing on a lawn, the best method is to make holes with a stick or bar under the outer branches from 12 in. to 18 in. apart, 1½ in. in diameter, and about 6 in. deep. Fill them almost to the top with fertilizer. It is not necessary to cover these holes with soil or other material. This method puts the fertilizer down where the roots will get it, and also prevents the unsightly and uneven lawn that would otherwise be the result.

Fertilizing Bearing Trees

Bearing trees should be fertilized regularly in most cases. Besides producing a crop of fruit, a bearing tree should make from 8 in. to 14 in. of terminal growth each year. Many bearing trees are biennial bearers, which means that they bear a heavy crop one year and few if any fruits the following year. However, fertilization should be just as regular as with an annual bearer, since a fruit spur will not bear two years in succession and each type of tree requires about the same amount of food. Fertilizers help to form fruit buds for the succeeding year's crop and also materially aid in the setting of blossoms that form fruits. Five lb. to 7 lb. of a complete fertilizer is sufficient for a full-grown tree.

Thinning

When a tree contains an overabundance of fruits, some should be removed to prevent

APPLE VARIETIES OF MERIT

'Cortland': A cross between Ben Davis and McIntosh to extend the McIntosh season. A good keeper and very high in quality.

'Delicious': A popular, well-known variety. Bears young and biennially.

'McCoun': A variety similar to Cortland but ripening later.

'McIntosh': Ripens in September. One of the finest varieties for general purposes. Tree is very hardy and vigorous. Plant 'Wealthy' with it for pollination purposes.

'Milton': A cross between 'Yellow Transparent' and 'McIntosh.' Very high quality, tree very vigorous and hardy.

'Paragon': One of the longest-keeping varieties—similar to 'Winesap.'

'Rome Beauty': All-purpose fall and winter cooking apple.

'Stayman Winesap': Ripens October 5–10. A very profitable apple for the Middle Atlantic and central states. Good keeper. Usually bears biennially. Should be planted with 'Delicious,' 'McIntosh' or 'Grimes Golden' for pollination purposes.

'Wealthy': One of the best varieties, ripening the last two weeks in August. Fine for culinary and dessert purposes. Starts bearing when young and bears heavy crops. Usually bears every other year.

'Yellow Transparent': An early yellow variety ripening in July. Bears early, heavy annual crops. When the fruits are half mature, they may be thinned and used for cooking.

CRAB APPLE VARIETIES OF MERIT

'Dolgo': Ripens in mid-August. Brilliant crimson.

'Hyslop': Pale yellow, covered with dark crimson.

'Transcendent': Ripens in September, a very good variety. Large size.

branches from breaking as well as to increase the size of the remaining fruit. Thinning should be practiced from four to five weeks after the fruits have begun to form. Only one apple should be left in a cluster, and individual apples should be from 6 in. to 8 in. apart on a limb or branch. If one side of a tree has practically no fruits and the other side is heavily laden, good-sized fruits will develop with little thinning. When removing fruits, leave the stem on the spur and use a pair of shears.

With early ripening varieties such as the 'Early Harvest,' 'Yellow Transparent' and 'Red Astrachan,' thinning may be delayed until six

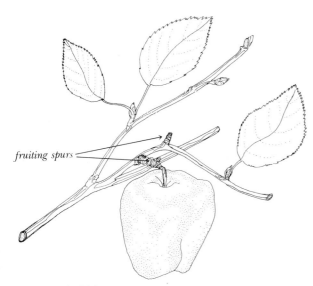

fruiting spurs

Fig. 28.2
Fruiting spur of an apple tree

weeks after the blossoms have set. Then the fruits to be removed are large enough and soft enough to use for pies, applesauce and the like, and come at a time of year when apples are particularly high in price.

Cherry

Botanical Name: *Prunus avium*—sweet cherry.
Prunus cerasus—sour cherry.
Prunus avium x *P. cerasus*—hybrids of the sweet and sour varieties, also known as the Dukes

Soil
A well-drained, loamy soil is suitable for all species.

Planting Age of Trees
Grade A one- or two-year-old trees are preferable as they are, figuratively speaking, the "cream of the crop."

Time of Planting
Same as for apple.

Planting Distance
Sweet cherry trees, 30 ft. by 30 ft.; sour or pie, 20 ft. by 20 ft.; Dukes or hybrids, 25 ft. by 25 ft.

Method of Planting and Overcoming Failure to Bear
See Apple.

Duration of Bearing
Twenty-five years for the sour, and up to forty years for the Dukes and sweet cherries.

Pruning One-year Tree
A one-year-old cherry tree usually contains a few lateral branches. Cut the top back to within 24 in. to 36 in. from the ground and prune all strong laterals back to 6 in. to 8 in. Weak growth should be removed.

Two-year Tree
Select from three to five branches within 15 in. from the ground, which are uniformly spaced 3 in. to 5 in. apart, and which are not on the same plane, but which nevertheless balance the tree. This procedure is very simple to follow if the tree was planted when one year old. If a two-year tree is being pruned at planting time, it is best to leave the three to five best branches for the framework and cut back the center branch to the uppermost one that remains. Those branches selected are then cut back to at least 15 in. to 20 in. if the tree has made a vigorous growth during the first year it was planted. The laterals on a newly set two-year tree should be cut back to 6 in. or 8 in. in length.

Time of Pruning
Same as pear or peach.

Pruning Young Nonbearing Trees
Most varieties of cherry trees bear in two to five years after setting out. Pruning should be very light and consists of removing only weak, competing and diseased branches. Slight heading back of the one-year wood is usually necessary in order to promote a bushy habit of growth.

Pruning Bearing Trees
The bearing cherry tree requires only light pruning until it reaches an age of fifteen to

twenty years, at which time it responds to the heavier pruning that is necessary in order to invigorate it and prolong its bearing life.

Cultivation
See Apple.

Fertilization
Pie or sour cherries and the hybrids, or Dukes, may be fertilized with the same materials and in the same manner as apple trees, except that the amount should be from one-half to two-thirds as much. Sweet cherry trees, or excessively large pie cherry trees, should receive the same amount as a full-sized bearing apple tree.

Thinning
This is unnecessary with all cherry trees in the home garden.

Harvesting
Sour or pie cherries may be harvested as soon as they begin to turn red. They may be used for cooking at this stage, or left on the tree over a period of approximately three weeks.

Sweet and Duke varieties should not be harvested until they are sweet but firm and ready to eat. Do not allow these varieties to remain on the tree after they once become ripe, as a rainfall will cause great loss from cracking and possibly brown rot.

All varieties of cherries will keep much longer if picked with the fruit stalks or "stems" attached to the fruit.

SWEET CHERRY VARIETIES OF MERIT

(All varieties described bear in four years)
'Bing': One of the largest, black oxheart varieties. Tree is quite small and a slow grower.
'Black Tartarian': A very large, vigorous-growing oxheart. Fine in quality and black in color.
'Lambert': Very large, purplish-red color. Very vigorous.
'Napoleon': A yellow-fleshed variety with a red cheek. Known also as 'Royal Ann.'
Note: The 'Bing', 'Lambert' and 'Napoleon' will not bear cherries if planted alone or even together. If any one or all of these varieties are planted, a 'Black Tartarian' should also be planted for cross-pollination purposes.

SOUR CHERRY VARIETIES OF MERIT

(All varieties are self-fertile and may be planted alone).
'Early Richmond,' 'Montmorency': Both are hardy, vigorous varieties, ripening a week apart. The 'Montmorency' is more highly colored.

Peach and Nectarine

Botanical Name: *Prunus persica*

Soil
A sandy loam soil is best. Silt will, however, give fair results.

Planting Age of Trees
One year old.

Planting Distance
18 ft. to 20 ft. apart each way is the standard distance, although 16 ft. apart each way is not too close for the home orchard.

Method of Planting
See Apple.

Pruning a One-year Tree
The purpose of pruning and training young peach trees is to develop a framework of bowl-shaped branches that will produce the greatest load of fruit close to the ground.

Low-headed peach trees are preferred, which branch between 18 in. and 22 in. from the ground. Oftentimes one-year peach trees contain several small branches. After cutting the main stem back to the height described, the remaining lateral branches should be cut back to 4 in. to 6 in. in length. This should be done as soon as the tree is planted.

Pruning after First Season
When the tree is in its second season, remove all side branches that form at an angle of less than 45° with the trunk. Remove any branches that are but a few inches above ground level. Prune out suckers or strong branches that fill in

Fig. 28.3
Young peach tree

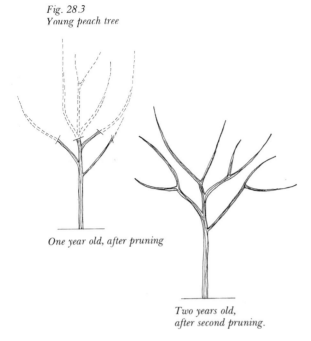

One year old, after pruning

Two years old,
after second pruning.

and shade the center of the tree. Remove one of two limbs of equal size that tend to divide the tree and form a Y. Cut back slightly the stronger framework branches.

Time of Pruning

Pruning should not be done until all danger of near or below freezing temperatures is past, as many varieties are susceptible to these low temperatures.

Pruning Young Nonbearing Peach Trees

Peach trees come into bearing during their third or fourth year so that their nonbearing period is very short. During this period a vigorous, spreading, bushy framework should be developed. Eighteen in. to 24 in. of terminal growth is most satisfactory. Pruning should consist of thinning out weak and inferior wood; cutting back several inches on the one-year wood to produce a bushy and stocky framework and to remove competing or crossing and too closely parallel branches. The center should be allowed to become filled in but not clogged.

Pruning Bearing Peach Trees

Peaches are borne on growth formed the previous season. The principle involved is to have a good supply of fruiting wood each year, which makes cutting back a necessary practice instead of an injury, as would be the result with apple trees. If peach trees were not pruned, the fruit would be borne on the terminal ends of the branches at such a height as to cause the limbs to break. Fourteen ft. is a good height for a peach tree.

The procedure in pruning a peach tree is as follows:

1. Cut out all dead, diseased and broken branches.
2. Thin out weak, crossing and parallel branches.
3. Keep the center open and allow water sprouts to grow, but thin them out if too many are present.

(A water sprout is a type of vigorous, succulent growth that develops on the trunk or limbs of a tree. Severe pruning encourages water sprouts to develop.)

4. Cut back to strong lateral branches to promote vegetative growth.
5. Do not allow the center to become clogged with nonfruiting wood.
6. Cut back one-year growth to 15 in. in length. Lateral growth will then be encouraged.
7. Keep the tree within bounds.

If a healthy tree fails to grow vigorously after several years of bearing, the branches should be cut back severely, but always to a lateral branch. This will invigorate new growth much better than fertilizers.

Duration of Bearing

A peach tree is an annual bearer of heavy crops over a period of twenty to twenty-five years, although some trees may be productive for as long as forty years.

Overcoming Failure to Bear

Early spring frosts, killing winter temperatures and lack of food are the main causes of failure to bear. The first two mentioned may be avoided by planting cold-resistant varieties, and the food supply may be given them in the form of commercial fertilizer and organic matter. Very few varieties are self-unfruitful when grown alone, but it is well to look into this matter before planting some of the newer varieties. The 'J. H. Hale' should be planted with another variety.

PEACH VARIETIES OF MERIT

1. Early Yellow: 'Jerseyland,' 'Golden Jubilee,' 'Triogem'
2. Early White: 'Raritan Rose,' 'Carman'
3. Midseason Yellow: 'Sunhigh,' 'Halehaven,' 'Elberta'
4. Midseason White: 'Red Rose,' 'Champion'
5. Late Yellow: 'Afterglow'
6. Late White: 'Belle of Georgia,' 'Late Rose'

'Bonanza': a very dwarf peach suited to small backyards. May also be grown in tubs.

NECTARINE

'Garden State': yellow
'Surecrop': Recommended for the home fruit garden

Cultivation

Peach trees respond well to cultivation, although results may also be adequate if otherwise grown. The soil should be disked or cultivated at frequent intervals during the growing season and cultivation should cease when the varieties begin to ripen. Cultivate at intervals sufficient to prevent weed growth from competing with the trees and to keep a 2 in. soil mulch at all times.

Fertilization

A general rule is to apply from one-half to two-thirds as much fertilizer to a peach tree as to an apple tree, and the application should be made at approximately the same time. See Apple.

Thinning

When about the size of a 25-cent piece, peaches should be thinned to about 4 in. apart. This practice will result in larger and higher quality fruits. When a tree is overcrowded with fruits the stone will be as large in a small fruit as in a larger fruit. Therefore, thinning tends to increase the proportion of flesh to the size of the stone or peach pit.

Harvesting

Peaches should be harvested when they are mature but firm. If they are left on the tree until fully ripe too many will drop and become inferior in appearance and salability. At the time of maturity the undercolor, which changes from green to yellow or white, is very apparent. Two or three days after picking, the peaches are in prime condition for eating or preserving. Some varieties first become soft on one side, usually the most highly colored side. If packed in this stage, the other side will soften up within a short time.

Pear

Botanical Name: *Pyrus*

Soil

A deep, loamy soil with good drainage.

Planting Age of Trees

See Apple.

Time of Planting

See Apple.

Distance Between Trees

30 ft. by 30 ft.

Method of Planting

See Apple.

Duration of Bearing

Thirty to forty years or more.

Pruning a One-year Tree

A one-year-old pear tree should be pruned back to a height of 30 in. to 36 in. Usually it is a straight whip without any lateral branches. If lateral branches are present, prune them back to 4 in. to 6 in. in length if they are vigorous. If lateral growth is weak, it is best to cut them out entirely.

Pruning a Two-year Tree

Four or five branches are selected as scaffold branches for the future framework of the tree. The same principles are practiced as with apples. The reason for leaving more scaffold branches than with apples is that the pear is quite susceptible to fire blight. If it developed on a limb from which all the main laterals developed, the entire tree would be killed within a short time. By training several branches as described, the removal of one will not seriously injure the tree.

Time of Pruning

The pear is hardier than the peach but not as hardy as the apple. Therefore, do not prune until freezing weather has passed in order to avoid winter-killing.

Pruning Nonbearing Trees

Light pruning is the answer here, for reasons discussed in the case of the apple. There are many varietal habits of growth, so allow the tree to grow naturally with a little thinning and heading back when necessary.

Pruning Bearing Trees

See Apple.

Overcoming Failure to Bear

See Apple.

Cultivation

Not entirely necessary, as with the peach, although it is helpful to give young trees a good start when possible. Keep weed growth suppressed as with the apple.

Fertilization

This may vary somewhat according to the variety and its ultimate size. Medium-sized trees may be fertilized like the peach. Large-sized trees should receive the equivalent amounts that are supplied to bearing apple trees.

Harvesting

Pears contain their best flavor if not allowed to mature fully on the tree. Pick them when they begin to turn yellow, or, with green or russet varieties, when they part easily from the spur. They should be juicy and sweet several days later.

PEAR VARIETIES OF MERIT

(All varieties listed bear within four years, except 'Beurre Bosc')

'Anjou': Very good quality, green late variety, best for eating and salads.

'Bartlett': This variety needs no introduction, being as well known as the 'Elberta' peach. It should be planted with another variety as in most cases it is self-sterile.

'Beurre Bosc': A very large russet yellow color and one of the longest keepers. Does not bear until eight or nine years old.

'Clapps Favorite': Resembles the 'Bartlett,' ripening about a week earlier. Has a tendency to become soft when fully ripe more quickly than the 'Bartlett.'

'Gorham': A similar variety to 'Bartlett,' bears about ten days later.

'Seckel': One of the highest quality small russet pears. A vigorous grower. Not as subject to fire blight as the 'Bartlett.'

'Tyson': Small to medium, pale, yellow, very good quality for an early dessert pear.

Plum

Botanical Names: *Prunus domestica* — European plum
Prunus salicina — Japanese plum
Prunus insititia — French or damson plum

Soil

A heavy silt or clay loam is most desirable, although some varieties give good results in the lighter soils.

Planting Age of Tree

See Apple.

Time of Planting

See Apple.

Planting Distance

30 ft. by 30 ft. for *P. domestica* and *P. salicina* species. Twenty to 25 ft. apart each way for *P. insititia* species.

Method of Planting

See Apple.

Overcoming Failure to Bear

See Apple.

Duration of Bearing

Usually 20 to 30 years.

Pruning, Cultivation, Fertilization and Thinning
See Cherry.

PLUM VARIETIES OF MERIT

'Burbank': A yellow-fleshed variety with a dark red skin. Good for culinary and dessert purposes. Hardy.
'Damson': Not used for eating but an excellent variety for canning in various ways. Very vigorous and prolific.
'Green Gage': A yellowish green variety, which is very high in quality.
'Italian Prune': A dark, purplish skin with greenish-yellow flesh. Very solid and fine for canning or eating.

Harvesting
The European types may be harvested when mature but firm. They include the prune plums, which will keep for as long as two weeks under ordinary conditions. However, they have the best flavor when allowed to fully mature on the tree. This is indicated by the stem easily parting from the twig.

The Japanese types are much softer, and once they begin to ripen, deteriorate rather rapidly. They may, however, be picked when firm to prolong their keeping period.

The *P. insititia* types keep as well, if not better, than many of the *P. domestica* types. They usually ripen several weeks later.

Quince

Botanical Name: *Cydonia oblonga*

Soil
A well-drained, rich loamy soil.

Planting Age of Trees
Two-year-old trees are most desirable as the quince is a comparatively slow grower.

Time of Planting
Early spring planting gives excellent results but fall planting is permissible in regions where the temperature does not go below zero.

Distance Between Trees
Quince bushes are set from 15 ft. to 20 ft. apart each way.

Method of Planting
See Apple.

Pruning a First-year Tree
The quince is pruned back slightly to stimulate new shoot growth. No definite system is followed.

Pruning a Second-year Tree
Thin out the weaker, inferior branches and cut back the remaining shoots from one-third to one-half their length, especially if the tree has been set out that season. Two-year-old trees that have been growing in their permanent position for a year do not require as severe pruning as those recently planted.

Pruning the Bearing Quince Bush
Remove a small amount of the twiggy growth each year and cut back any branches that have the tendency to grow out of bounds.

Duration of Bearing
A quince bush will bear for 25 years or more.

Overcoming Failure to Bear
There should be no trouble in this respect. See Apple.

Cultivation
See Apple.

Fertilization
See Peach.

Thinning
Fruits will be larger if thinned out from 6 in. to 8 in. apart. In most cases, however, there is little need of it.

Harvesting
The quince may be harvested when it has attained its fullest development, which is around 3 in. in diameter. It is such a hard fruit that it will keep from four to six months without any special care except in handling.

SMALL BUSH FRUITS

Blackberries

Botanical Name: *Rubus* (various)

Soil

The blackberry will grow on any fertile soil where the moisture conditions are satisfactory. As it bears its crop in midsummer, lack of moisture is often the cause of low yields. Once it is established, it will spread rapidly if not kept within bounds.

Planting

The plants are usually set out in the early spring months. Early planting is most favorable for the best results. The tops are cut back to 12 in. to 18 in. and the plants set 3 ft. apart in the row; 6 ft. to 8 ft. between the rows is not too far apart. Suckers may be set out any time after August 1, but the results are apt to be questionable because of dry weather conditions at that time of year. Set the plants slightly deeper than they grew in the nursery.

Culture

Vigorous, vegetative suckers grow up one year, fruit the following summer, and die. It is therefore necessary to permit suckers to grow but they must be kept within bounds. Plants may be trained to wires, or several canes may be tied to a stake. The plants must be kept in rows or hills, which makes it necessary to remove all suckers appearing in the middle of the row. This should be done by pulling up the roots and not by cutting, as new suckers will readily sprout from the old stumps. Enough space should be left to allow for cultivation and care in picking.

Cultivation or Mulching

If cultivation is the method chosen, it should be done frequently enough to keep weed growth suppressed. Blackberry roots are close to the surface, so cultivation should be shallow.

A mulch will suppress weed growth and conserve moisture, and if this method is chosen, enough mulch should be applied between the

BLACKBERRY VARIETIES OF MERIT

'Blowers': Mid-season, good quality, productive.
'Brewer': Mid-season, productive, glossy attractive berry.
'Eldorado': The largest and sweetest variety. Very hardy, vigorous and productive.
'Iceberg': A novelty, white-fruited.

plants and in the row to keep weeds from growing up through it. Grass clippings, hay, leaves, etc., will give satisfactory results.

Fertilizers

Fertilizers should be applied early in the spring when growth begins, to encourage good strong sucker development that is to fruit the following year. A complete fertilizer containing nitrogen, phosphorus and potash is strongly recommended. The rate of application will depend on the fertility of the soil. Some cases have been known in which blackberries did better without any fertilizer than others did with a heavy application, due to soil and moisture differences. An application of 1 lb. to 50 ft. of row early in the spring when the plants begin to fruit heavily is a medium application. Manure may also be applied with good results.

Pruning

Fruiting canes may be removed at any time after the crop is harvested until growth begins the following spring. Weak and broken canes should be removed. Thin the others out so that they are at least 6 in. apart. This is not necessary if plants are grown in hills, but never allow more than five or six canes per hill. Cut the tops back to a height between 4 ft. and 5 ft. This varies with the variety and the vigor of growth. Three or four strong laterals may be left per cane if cut back to three or four buds. Cut out the weak ones entirely.

Cutting back should be practiced only in the spring, as winter-killing always starts at the tip. If the canes are cut back in the fall, winter-killing will begin at the point of detachment.

If some of the weak suckers are removed during the growing season, the remaining ones will have more room in which to develop.

Blueberries

Botanical Name: *Vaccinium corymbosum*

Blueberry culture is a comparatively recent development, due in part to the increased market demand for a greater supply of large, high-quality berries. The problem is to adapt these berries to many soils that have been growing other crops with different soil requirements.

Soil

Blueberries produce best results on an acid soil that is well drained, but retentive of moisture. Soil that has previously grown garden crops is usually not suitable because it is not acid enough. However, the addition of decomposed leaves, peat, woodland turf or sawdust will materially help to make the soil acid. Aluminum sulphate may be applied at the rate of 1 lb. to 75 sq. ft. or 100 sq. ft., but its effect is only temporary. Aluminum sulphate should not supplant the addition of the above suggested materials, but it may be used satisfactorily in conjunction with them if applied each year and worked into the soil.

Land that has not previously been planted to garden or other crops is suitable for growing blueberries, especially if acid-loving plants such as sweet ferns, wild blueberries, white cedar, oak or pines are growing on it.

The land should be plowed after all superfluous growth is removed and allowed to lie fallow for one season. Frequent cultivation or disking during the year will prevent growth and also improve the land's physical condition. If water has the tendency to stand on the surface for a period of several days during the growing season, the plant roots will suffer from lack of oxygen. Such places should be drained.

Setting the Plants

Blueberry plants are set during early spring or late fall months. Early spring planting usually gives best results. Do not allow the roots of the plants to dry out before setting in the ground. The plants are set 4 ft. apart in the row and from 6 ft. to 8 ft. apart between the rows. Dig the holes wide enough to avoid crowding the roots and deep enough to set the plants 2 in. deeper than they were growing before. Firm the soil around the plants and water if the soil is dry. Several varieties should be planted, as cross-pollination is necessary to produce good yields.

Soil Management

Blueberry plantations may be managed by two methods: clean cultivation and mulching.

If clean cultivation is practiced, it should be shallow, at intervals of two or three weeks from early spring to midsummer to control weeds and thus conserve moisture. Deep cultivation or hoeing to a depth of more than 2 in. will destroy part of the plant's fibrous root system. Do not cultivate within several inches of the base of the plant for this reason.

Plants may be mulched with satisfactory results but cultivation should precede this treatment for at least a year after the plants are set. Shavings, peat moss, pine needles, oak leaves or lawn clippings are suitable mulching materials. The important point is to apply enough of the mulching between the rows and around the plants to prevent weed growth and to conserve moisture. Three in. or 4 in. of mulch are usually necessary.

Fertilization

Fertilizers are applied just as growth begins in the spring and again four to six weeks after the first application. A 4–12–4 fertilizer applied at the rate of 1 lb. to 100 sq. ft. will give good results. Cultivate the fertilizer into the soil soon after applying it if the mulch system is not used.

Pruning

Pruning should be done early in the spring before growth begins. During the first three years pruning consists of removing a few of the smaller lateral shoots and thinning out the bushy growth. The plants should not be permitted to bear fruit for the first year after setting. To prevent bearing, remove the flower clusters when they appear. Pruning after the third year consists in removing from one-fourth to one-third of the old wood, besides removing weak twigs and branches lying on the ground.

Blueberry Varieties

As many new varieties are being developed, it is strongly recommended that you write to your local Cooperative Extension Service for their advice on this subject. The 'Cabot,' 'Pioneer,' 'Rancocas,' 'Jersey,' 'Dixie' and 'Rubel' are excellent varieties.

Gooseberries and Currants

Botanical Names:
$\begin{cases} \text{Gooseberry} - \textit{(American) R.} \\ \quad \textit{hirtellum} \\ \quad \textit{(European) R.} \\ \quad \textit{grossularia} \\ \text{Currant} - \textit{Ribes,} \text{ various} \end{cases}$

The growing, fruiting and cultural methods are so similar that gooseberries and currants may be discussed together.

Both are very hardy and winter injury is an uncommon occurrence.

Soil and Location

A moist, fertile, well-drained loam soil, supplied with organic matter, is ideal. They should not be planted in low places where late frosts occur, as they bloom early.

Planting

Both fruits may be planted in the fall or spring with equally good results, although in some cases fall planting is preferable.

Good strong one- or two-year-old plants may be set. The planting distance is from 4 ft. to 6 ft. apart in the row with 6 ft. between the rows.

Broken and extra long roots should be cut back. The tops are cut back to a height of 6 in. to 8 in. Cutting back depends to a great extent on the size of the root system and the size of top.

Set the plants slightly deeper than originally growing in the nursery and firm the soil around them.

General Care

Practice shallow cultivation to suppress weed growth. Plants may be mulched with leaves, straw or other material during the growing season, but the mulch should be removed in the early fall to discourage rodents.

GOOSEBERRY VARIETIES OF MERIT

(American varieties produce twice as many berries as other varieties but they are very small; European varieties are more susceptible to mildew than American ones and the berries are larger.)

'Chautauqua': European. Large. Comparatively free from mildew. Seeds large. Plant is hard to propagate.

'Downing': Adapted to all conditions in this country. Very productive, high in quality. American.

'Houghton': Small. Old, well-known variety. Adapted to a good many soils.

'Poorman': One of the largest American kinds. Pinkish, sweet, excellent. Produces about 2 qt. when five years old. Berries hang on a long time.

Fertilizers

Stable manure may be broadcast around the plants early in the spring. Complete fertilizers give most satisfactory results as they contain more readily available plant food. Four oz. per plant as growth begins in the spring is usually sufficient. This is applied in a narrow band 6 in. to 8 in. away from the main stalk, and raked or hoed in.

Pruning

Both bear fruit at the base of the one-year-old wood and on spurs of older wood. The principle of pruning is to maintain a steady supply of new wood and to prevent old, partially fruiting canes from accumulating in any great number so as to interfere with the younger growth. All wood four years or older should be removed at the base of the plant. At the same time remove spindly and short shoots. Eight or ten strong shoots are sufficient, ranging in age from one to four years. By removing the old canes, we keep the new canes coming.

A little "heading back" of the new canes is necessary. In some sections where borers are a pest it is not recommended to any great extent.

Gooseberries are more difficult to propagate than currants. By heaping soil around the plant and covering 3 in. or 4 in. of the base of the one-year canes, roots will form. This should be done in late June or July. By the middle of September the soil may be removed and those canes that have rooted may be severed from the plant and set in another location. Another method is to cut back the one-year growth 6 in., remove the tips and plant in the open ground. They will root quite readily. This is best done in the early spring before the growth process is perceptible.

RED CURRANT VARIETIES OF MERIT

'London Market' (London Red): Berries medium to large, deep red, rather acid, mid-season to late; clusters compact, with short stems. Bush upright, somewhat resistant to borers and diseases: most resistant of any variety to the white pine blister rust.

'Perfection': Berries large, bright crimson, slightly subacid, mid-season, clusters compact, very long, easy to pick. A heavy yielder. Berries sometimes scald in hot weather if not picked as soon as ripe. Bush more or less spreading, throwing up canes from below the ground; canes break easily.

'Red Cross': Berries large, firm, light red, subacid, hang on to bushes well: mid-season; clusters of medium length, well filled, easy to pick. Cracks easily. Plant is not long-lived. Fruit ripens unevenly.

'Wilder': Berries large, dark red, mild subacid, hang on bushes well. Mid-season; clusters large, compact, easy to pick. Bush upright and large.

WHITE CURRANT VARIETIES OF MERIT

'White Dutch': Earliest and sweetest of white ones. Small berries and not uniform. Good in quality. Sweeter than the red ones.

White Grape: The best. Medium in size, berries fairly large, but not uniform. Rick flavor. Bush very productive.

White Imperial: Berries large, pale yellow, almost sweet; clusters medium length and loose. Bush spreading, very productive. A desirable variety; considered to have the best dessert quality of all currants.

BLACK CURRANT VARIETIES OF MERIT

'Champion': Wild flavor. Ripens after the red currants. Mildest of the black varieties. Larger than 'Perfection' (Red). Most susceptible to white pine blister rust.

Red Raspberries

Botanical Name: (European) *Rubus idaeus*
(American) *Rubus ideaus strigosus*

Soil

A deep loamy soil is most desirable for red raspberries because it is best for the plants and easier to cultivate. Heavy silts and clay soils should be avoided because low aeration results in poor growth and lower yields. Thorough drainage and an adequate supply of moisture are essential.

The soil should be thoroughly pulverized previous to planting. Sod land should be prepared by growing some vegetable on it at least two years in advance.

Planting

New stock or suckers that developed the previous year should be planted in the following spring, before growth begins. Suckers may also be dug up and planted during the month of August but the first suggestion gives best results under average conditions.

Plants are set 3 ft. to 4 ft. apart in the rows, allowing 6 ft. to 8 ft. between the rows. Before planting, the tops of the plants, if set in the spring, should be cut back to 12 in. Set the plants 3 in. deeper than they were formerly growing to protect them from drought.

Cultivation

Tillage should be thorough and more regular than for most other crops. The root system is quite shallow and cultivation should not be deeper than 3 in.

Fertilizer

The application of commercial fertilizers should be planned with caution since too much nitrogen will cause excessive growth and weak canes that may bend over and touch the ground. A fertile soil is necessary to begin with. Given sufficient cultivation· to suppress weed growth, it should be adequate.

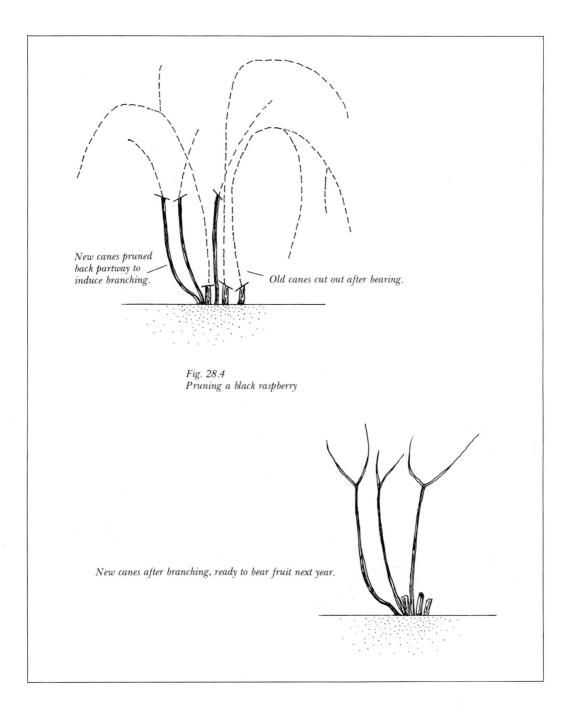

New canes pruned back partway to induce branching.

Old canes cut out after bearing.

Fig. 28.4
Pruning a black raspberry

New canes after branching, ready to bear fruit next year.

RED RASPBERRY VARIETIES OF MERIT

'Indian Summer': Ever-bearing variety. The first crop ripens early in July, the second from early September to severe frost.

'Latham': Fruit very large, plants hardy and resistant to mosaic. Flavor is only fair.

'New Milton': A late variety. Excellent for market and home use. Vigorous, productive and hardy.

'September': An outstanding ever-bearing variety. Hardy, vigorous and productive. Berries of fine quality.

'Sunrise': Earliest, long season, good quality.

'Taylor': An outstanding variety. Vigorous, hardy, very productive. Berries of superior quality.

Training and Pruning

Red raspberries fruit on the same principle as blackberries. Suckers grow one year, fruit the next and die. The principle of pruning is also the same. Varieties vary greatly in their habit of growth and should be treated accordingly when thinned out. The tops are cut back before growth begins in the spring. Cut the canes back from 6 in. to 18 in. Severe cutting will reduce the crop. With some very vigorous varieties more cutting back is practical than with others. The canes should be cut back to a height of 3½ ft. to 4½ ft.

Disease and Pest Control

See instructions at the end of this chapter.

Purple and Black Raspberries

Botanical Name: (purple raspberries) *R. occidentali* x *R. idaeus* (black raspberries) *Rubus occidentalis*

Soil

Soil requirements are practically the same as for the red raspberry. Although their water requirements are greater, these may do well on the heavier soils because the root systems are much more vigorous.

PURPLE AND BLACK RASPBERRY VARIETIES OF MERIT

'Allen'	'Clyde'	'Huron'
'Black Hawk'	'Cumberland'	'Pearl'
'Bristol'	'Dundee'	'Sodus'

Planting

Early spring planting is most satisfactory. The plants should be spaced 4 ft. apart in the rows and with 6 ft. between the rows. They should be cut back to 6 in. when setting out and the spot marked with a stick.

Propagation

Purple and black raspberries do not produce suckers as do red raspberries. All new growth comes from a definite place in the crown of the plant, and propagation is done by covering the ends of the new growth with soil during the months of July and August. This is called "tip-layering."

Pruning

Three fruiting canes are sufficient for each plant. These are summer pinched during the summer to a height of 3½ ft. to 4 ft. The following spring laterals are pruned so they are 8 in. to 10 in. long.

Strawberries

Botanical Name: *Fragaria* species

Remarks

A large patch of strawberries may be planted at small cost and will bring quicker returns and high yields sooner than any other fruit crop. They are the first fresh fruit to appear on the markets in early spring.

Soil

Soil is more important than location. A soil for strawberries should contain plenty of organic material, be well drained and fertile. The time of ripening may be extended or delayed several days. A sandy soil warms up most quickly in the spring months. Plant growth will therefore be stimulated sooner than on silt or heavy loam soils which do not warm up as quickly. Too much nitrogen will cause excessive plant development, which will result in crowding and lower yields. The soil should be well firmed before planting.

Getting the Plants

Strawberry plants are botanically described as perfect or imperfect. A perfect blossom has both stamens and pistils, while an imperfect blossom has only one or the other. Imperfect varieties should be interplanted with perfect ones so that cross-pollination will ensure a good yield of berries. The perfect and imperfect varieties should bloom at the same time. While this was a problem in the past, today over 99 percent of the varieties sold are perfect ones.

Time to Plant

Early spring is the best time to plant strawberries, and the earlier the better. They may be set in the fall but this practice is not recommended as the yield is reduced the following year and heaving is very apt to occur during the winter.

The planting distance depends on the variety, method of training and fertility of the soil. The usual distance is 15 in. to 20 in. in the row and 3½ ft. to 4 ft. between the rows.

Strawberries are prepared for planting by removing old and decayed leaves and trimming the roots to about 3 in. Soak the roots in a pail of water and keep the plants in the shade until ready to set in the ground.

Setting the Plants

The ideal time to set plants in the garden is on a cloudy day or late in the afternoon. Be sure to keep the roots moist at all times by keeping them in a container that is covered with paper or wet burlap. Do not allow the roots to be exposed to the sun for over two minutes before planting.

Mark out the rows with a tight line. If planting is difficult because of the line, a furrow 1½ in. deep may be made with a hoe or other garden implement, using the line as a guide before removing it. The crown center of the plant where the tiny leaves are developing should be just flush or level with the surface of the soil. If set too deeply, it will be covered with soil and will rot; if set too high, the roots will dry out, as they will not be in contact with a sufficient supply of moisture. The plants should be well firmed in the soil to prevent drying out, and to keep the moisture in contact with the roots.

Care of Newly Set Plants

Blossoms that will appear after the plants are set out should be removed to allow all the strength to go into the formation of plants and roots instead of fruit the first year.

Keep weed growth suppressed by practicing shallow cultivation.

About a month to six weeks after planting, runners will appear. The first two plants on each one will develop first and will, therefore, produce more fruit the following year than those rooting late in the season. Four runners per plant is sufficient. Others may be cut off. If these runners are spaced around the plant and a small stone set next to where the leaves are appearing, they will take root very easily. On a commercial basis, very little training and pruning is practiced, and so by the end of the growing season the row has a matted appearance and is called the matted row system. As the new plants form, the row gradually closes in and more hand weeding is necessary as it is impossible to hoe or cultivate between the plants.

However, if plants are not going to be dug up from the middle of the row for planting the following spring, they might just as well be kept hoed out during the first year. Leave a path 12 in. wide that will facilitate harvesting the next summer.

When new runners appear, the soil should be slightly mounded 12 in. each side of the parent plant and 2 in. to 3 in. higher than the level of the field. This will supply soft soil in which the runners will root, besides facilitating better drainage.

The bed should be weeded late in the fall and

all weeds especially clover and chickweed, which overwinter, removed.

Manures and Fertilizers

An application of well-rotted manure is a decided advantage. Cow manure, however, should be avoided because of its high weed content. The amount of 500 lb. to a plot 50 ft. by 50 ft. will bring good results. It should be plowed in at any time previous to planting. A cover crop should be plowed under a year in advance of setting the plants to allow time for decomposition to take place if it is used as a substitute for manure.

Lime is not essential and should not be applied in any great quantity as the strawberry prefers an acid soil.

A complete fertilizer should be used for best results. It may be applied at the time of setting the plants at the rate of 1 lb. to 50 sq. ft., and raked in or applied after the plants are established. In the latter case, it is applied on a dry day by broadcasting it over the plants at the mentioned rate. An old broom or fine brush should be used to remove any of it from the leaves, which will be burned if moisture is present. This application should be raked or cultivated into the soil.

Winter Protection

In sections where winter weather is variable and accompanied by alternate freezing and thawing, the plants should be protected to prevent them from heaving. Coarse material such as straw or hay is best applied after the ground freezes. Cover to a depth of ½ in. to 1 in. This material prevents the soil from thawing out very rapidly and thus prevents heaving. Fine material in any quantity, such as pine needles, should be avoided as it may pack too tightly and kill the plants.

Spring Treatment

Winter covering should be removed after all danger is past of a heavy frost that would kill the blossoms. About two-thirds of the straw is removed and placed in the space left between the rows. It serves as a mulch and makes kneeling a pleasure instead of a pain to the average gardener. The plants will grow up through the remaining covering, which will settle down around the base of them and keep the berries clean and off the ground.

There has been much discussion as to the feasibility of spring fertilization. It is well to remember at this point that the fruit buds are formed the season before. Nitrogenous fertilizers promote vigorous succulent growth, which may result in overcrowding and in soft berries. The main requirement until the fruit is harvested is water. It is the care the plants receive the first season that is so important for the production of the next year's crop.

Harvesting

The picking season for a particular variety ranges from seven to fourteen days. Beds fruiting the second or third time are earlier than those bearing their first crop.

Pick the berries in the coolest part of the day and do not pick when the vines are moist, unless absolutely necessary. Gather the fruit at least every other day, as it becomes soft very quickly after reaching maturity. Put the fruit in a cool place in the shade immediately after picking. Do not hold more than two berries in the hand at a time.

Renewing or Renovation

After the crop has been harvested, a vigorous treatment is necessary to instigate new life in the patch.

1. Remove all material used for a mulch and destroy or compost it.
2. Rake the patch very vigorously. Many plants will be removed but this is unimportant for future yields.
3. Cultivate the rows to a width of 2 ft. This will narrow them considerably but it must be done.
4. Apply a complete fertilizer—1 lb. to every 50 ft. of row.
5. Keep weed growth suppressed.

It is not advisable to keep a patch for more than three years, and two years is more generally recommended.

Potted Plants

Some nurseries sell potted strawberry plants, which can be set out in August and will bear

STRAWBERRY VARIETIES OF MERIT

'Fresno'	'Northwest'	'Tioga'
'Jersey Belle'	'Shasta'	
'Midway'	'Sparkle'	

fruit the following spring. One hundred such plants cost as much as 1,000 dug from the patch in the spring. Also the yield is a comparatively small one.

Pots filled with soil are plunged into the earth next to spring-set plants when the runners are somewhat developed. The first joint on each runner is placed on the soil in the pot. The roots that develop grow into the soil in the pot. Plants from later joints that develop are firmly rooted in the ground by August and need no help from the parent plant. The runner on both sides of the plant growing in the pot is cut and the pot removed with its plant.

Home-grown plants will give excellent results if the bed has received reasonable care and if they are free from disease. Nurseries sell excellent plants, which are satisfactory provided they are properly packed and shipped.

Plants may be dug from the patch with a trowel and moved to their new location with soil on the roots. Old and decayed leaves should be removed before planting. Two or three leaves per plant are sufficient to begin with.

If plants are received by mail or express, the package should be opened as soon as received to avoid sweating and deterioration. Set the plants in a trench temporarily, to prevent the roots from drying out.

Disease and Pest Control
See instructions at the end of this chapter.

VINE FRUITS

Grape

Botanical Name: *Vitis labruscana*

Soil
The grape does well on any fertile soil, but it shows a preference for the medium to silt-loam types.

Planting Age of Vines
One- or two-year-old vines.

Time of Planting
Early spring, as soon as the frost is out of the ground.

Distance Between Vines
6 ft. by 6 ft., or 6 ft. by 8 ft.

Method of Planting
Set 2 in. deeper than they were originally growing in the nursery.

Pruning and Training
The best time for pruning is late winter or very early spring before the sap starts to run. There are several systems of training and pruning the grape. They will not be discussed in detail here, but the important facts about pruning and training are as follows:

1. The best fruits are borne on pencil-sized canes and between the second and twelfth bud from the base.
2. A vine can supply forty to sixty buds.
3. Therefore, the best system is one that contains four pencil-sized canes, each cane having from ten to fifteen buds.

Grade A, one- or two-year vines should be planted early in the spring before the buds begin to swell. Cut the vine back to two or three buds at planting time. As the new shoots develop, train them off the ground to a stake or two wires that have been fastened to posts.

Set posts 3 ft. into the ground and 4½ ft. out of the ground, 15 in. to 18 in. apart. Attach the first lengthwise wire 18 in. from the ground, the second 18 in. from the first and the third 18 in. from the second.

The vine should be trained up to the top wire and tied and cut. This will form the trunk. The following year, growth will appear from all the lateral buds and the system of training will

Fig. 28.5. Growth and pruning of a grapevine.

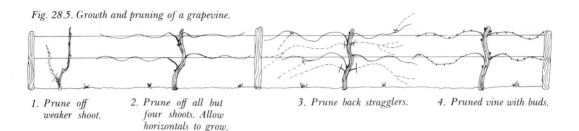

1. *Prune off weaker shoot.* 2. *Prune off all but four shoots. Allow horizontals to grow.* 3. *Prune back stragglers.* 4. *Pruned vine with buds.*

be established when the vine is pruned early the next spring. Select two pencil-sized canes near the middle wire. Train one on each side of the main stem and cut back to ten to twelve buds. Repeat this process on the top wire, and tie the canes in place with soft string or binder twine. Tight tying is not necessary as the string serves only as a support for the canes. The other canes should be removed, but be sure to leave two buds on four canes, so that they will be fully developed to produce the crop near each cane the following year.

Often only two wires are used, as the bottom wire serves mainly for support.

Lateral growths on one-year-old canes are cut back to four buds if pencil-sized.

The new wood should be kept as close to the head as possible. This is to keep the fruiting wood from growing out of bounds. As a vine gets eight to ten years old, its vigor diminishes, which is well attested to by the shortening of the annual growth. When the vigor decreases, it is time to renew the vine. One will notice in most instances that canes are persistent in growing at the base of the trunk. Cut the trunk off so as not to injure these canes and train one up to take the place of the old one that was removed. The results obtained will be remarkable, with an increase of vigor to a productive result for several years to come.

Training and Pruning a Grape Arbor

A grape arbor, besides furnishing shade, should also be productive. As much more space is allowed each vine than when trained to wires, the system of training is somewhat different. Vines may be planted 4 ft. apart on the sides. The general tendency is to permit the vines to grow year after year without pruning. Then, when someone begins to prune them proper-

ly, the owner thinks that they are being ruined.

The vigor of a vine is considerably increased by pruning. Cutting back the previous season's growth will give better results than the application of additional fertilizer will. Cut back the previous season's growth approximately one-fourth of its length each year until the arbor is covered. Thin out canes that are less than pencil-sized thick, and leave several of those larger cut back to two or three buds. Practice thinning out and cutting back each year thereafter and do not allow a vine to go without any pruning.

When a vine becomes unproductive and there is an excess of nonfruiting wood present, severe pruning is essential. It may be necessary to cut it back almost to the ground in order to stimulate vigorous growth, which, in turn, is trained up as previously described.

Duration of Bearing

Fifty years or more.

Cultivation

Weed growth should be suppressed by using a mulch or by cultivation and hoeing.

Fertilization

Apply approximately one-half lb. of a complete fertilizer to a bearing vine in a ring about 2 ft. away from the trunk, or broadcast over the surface just as growth begins in the spring. Young nonbearing vines should receive from one-half to one-third of the above amount and at the same time.

Thinning

Thinning is not necessary if a bearing vine is pruned and trained as suggested, as it can comfortably care for the entire crop.

GRAPE VARIETIES OF MERIT

'Agawam': Large, red. About 2½ times as large as the 'Concord. Not highly colored. Good flavor, but hard to swallow. Very vigorous grower.

'Brighton': Never plant alone. This is the only variety that must be cross-pollinated. Recommended for cooler parts of the country. On heavy soil, plant 8 ft. by 8 ft. It is usually planted 6 ft. by 6 ft.

'Caco': Red in color. Yield and quality good. One of the best all-purpose grapes.

'Cardinal'

'Concord': An old variety. Widely grown except in the warmer sections. Can be depended upon. Will grow without any cultivation. Likes moisture.

'Delaware': About ³/₁₆ in. in diameter. Leaves are tiny and many. Must spray thoroughly to control mildew. Small, red, compact. Late and excellent flavor. Red, small bunches.

'Emperor'

'Green Mountain': Medium late, white, dark green, sprightly flavored.

'Malaga'

'Moore's Early': Black in color, ripens two weeks earlier than the Concord. Not so high in quality. Berries crack easily. Bunch not compact. Shoulders (upper part of grapes) not very good.

'Portland': Early white, vigorous and excellent flavor.

'Seedless'

'Thompson'

'Worden': Ripens ten days before the 'Concord.' Berries larger than the 'Concord.' In wet, rainy weather the berries will crack. When ripening on the bunch, those that ripen first will not wait until the others ripen (tend to shell). Highly recommended, more so than the 'Concord.'

Harvesting

Grapes should not be harvested until they are fully ripe, at which time they have reached their highest sugar content and flavor. Each bunch should be handled carefully and preferably removed with a pair of scissors to prevent shattering or other injury.

SPRAYING OF FRUIT TREES AND BUSH AND VINE FRUITS

Equipment

Any type of hand- or machine-driven sprayer, if used properly, will distribute sprays to control diseases and insects satisfactorily so long as all parts of the leaves and fruit are covered with the proper pesticide.

Compressed air sprayers of 1½ gallon to 5 gallon capacity are suitable for spraying low-growing fruit trees. A stepladder will increase efficiency and thoroughness in covering taller fruit trees. Pressures ranging from 30 lb. to 50 lb. are built up by pumping a rod inside the sprayer up and down by hand.

Knapsack sprayers ranging from 2 gallons to 6 gallons in capacity are strapped onto the operator's back. Pressure is maintained by pumping a lever with one hand while spraying with the other.

"Trombone" or slide sprayers discharge a continuous spray at pressures up to 180 lb. These sprayers have a smooth, double action pump, which works both on the in and out strokes. They are relatively inexpensive and are among the most reliable kinds.

Bucket-pump sprayers are small, powerful brass pumps of the plunger type, capable of developing pressures up to 250 lb. Most of these produce a continuous high-pressure spray.

Wheelbarrow, cart and barrel sprayers have capacities ranging from 7 gallons to 50 gallons, and pressures ranging up to 250 lb. These are most useful for larger gardens and for greenhouses.

Garden hose jar-sprayer attachments are fixed to the garden hose, and the water pressure does the work. Dilute the insecticide concentrate in the jar according to the manufacturer's instructions, then turn on the water and spray as directed. If properly used with the right pesticide, these jar-sprayer attachments save much time and energy.

Spray Schedules

The spray schedules listed below are for home gardeners with only a few trees to maintain, not for commercial growers.

Trees and fruits are attacked by insects and disease at various stages in their development. As in many other cases, prevention is better than cure, for once an insect or disease attacks a fruit, it decreases in value. Therefore, sprays should be applied to prevent them from gaining a foothold. Certain insects and diseases must be controlled at a definite time or over a definite period. Some materials, especially those that keep fungus diseases under control, may be used in place of others. Instructions for using these substitutes should be closely observed.

Apple

Apple trees are subject to attack by so many insects, mites, fungi and bacteria that an intensive spray program must be carried out to produce top-quality fruit. Aphids, maggots plum curculio, codling moths, leaf rollers and sawflies are among the most common pests. Scab, powdery mildew and rust are three of the most prevalent fungus diseases, and fire blight is the most destructive bacterial disease.

Most of these pests and fungus parasites can be controlled by spraying with a so-called multipurpose spray, which is readily obtainable in garden supply stores. At least eight applications of a multipurpose spray at ten-day intervals are required, starting with the green-tip stage. Gardeners desiring to prepare their own multipurpose mixture may do so by mixing the following wettable powders (WP) dry, per gallon of water:

3 tbs. kelthane 35% WP
2 tbs. malathion 25% WP
3 tbs. methoxychlor 50% WP
2 tbs. captan 50% WP

This mixture will control most of the insects, mites and fungus diseases to which apples are subject.

The blossom blight stage of the fire blight disease cannot be controlled with any of the above-mentioned sprays. Bordeaux mixture or an antibiotic such as agrimycin must be used at the full-bloom stage to control the bacterial disease.

Among the practices that will help to reduce certain pests are: collecting and disposing of all fallen leaves in the fall to reduce scab infections the following year (the apple scab fungus *Venturia insequalis* lives through the winter on the fallen leaves); pruning back twigs infected by the

BEARING YIELDS OF FRUITS AND BERRIES

(Yields vary according to size, age, vigor of plant and growing conditions)

TREE FRUITS	ANNUAL YIELD PER PLANT
Apple – dwarf	1¼ to 1½ bushel
standard	5 to 10 bushel
Pear – dwarf	1¼ to 1½ bushel
standard	1 to 4 bushel
Plum	1 to 2 bushel
Peach	2 to 4 bushel
Sour cherry	1 to 2 bushel
Sweet cherry	1 to 2 bushel
Quince	½ to 1 bushel

SMALL FRUITS	ANNUAL YIELD PER PLANT
Blackberries	1 to 1½ quarts
Blueberries	4 quarts
Currants	3 quarts
Grapes	1¼ to ½ bushel
Gooseberries	3 to 4 quarts
Raspberries	1½ quarts
Strawberries	¾ to 1 quart

fire blight organism to sound wood, and placing them in the trash can or otherwise properly disposing of them; and picking up and disposing at a distance of all fruits that drop prematurely in early June to reduce plum circulio infestations (fruits that drop in late August and September should be picked up and disposed of to reduce apple maggot infestations).

Grape

The grape vine is susceptible to several fungus diseases, including black rot, downy mildew and powdery mildew, as well as to the depredations of insects, including grapeberry moth, flea beetle, leaf roller, cane girdler and leafhopper. To control most of these pests, apply a multipurpose spray just before bloom, repeat immediately after bloom, then ten days later and again two weeks after that.

Peaches, Apricots, Nectarines, Plums, Prunes and Cherries

All these should be sprayed with a mixture of benomyl, malathion and methoxychlor just before the blossoms open in spring, followed by a benomyl spray at full bloom. Five multipurpose sprays, as described under apple, should be applied at ten-day intervals after the full-bloom spray.

A benomyl spray should be applied to all stone fruits a week or so before harvest to control brown rot.

Other practices that help to reduce diseases of stone fruits include the removal of dried, mummified fruits from the trees in winter; cutting out and discarding black knot-infested twigs; and the collection and distant disposal of all fallen leaves.

Stone fruits, particularly peaches, are susceptible to the peach tree borer, which feeds on the inner bark and sapwood at the trunk base. The appearance of an amberlike gummy substance at or above the soil line is one indication of the presence of borers. Digging out the borers with a knife or wire near the exudation will provide control. Another method is to apply paradichlorobenzene (PDB—available in drug and garden supply stores) in September, in a circular, $1/2$-in.-deep trench about 2 in. from the trunk. Then cover the PDB with 3 in. of soil in the form of an Indian tepee. The soil covering should be removed in five or six weeks. Still another method is to spray or paint the trunk base with methoxychlor in late May and again about three weeks later.

Pear

Pear trees are subject to many of the diseases and pests that affect apple trees. Hence the spray schedules are much the same. One pest peculiar to pear, the psylla, requires an additional spray of Bordeaux mixture and oil at the green-tip stage.

Strawberry

Strawberry plants are susceptible to fungus leafspot, fruit rot, tarnished plant bug and several species of mites.

Apply a multipurpose spray soon after removing the mulch, as spring growth starts. Repeat the spraying at seven-day intervals up to fourteen days before the fruit is to be picked.

After harvest, apply the multipurpose spray twice at a monthly interval.

29.1 *A great many kinds of herbs—for flavor and fragrance—are organized here in an easy-to-manage fashion. Photo Ruth Clausen*

29

The Herb Garden

The herb garden was one of the earliest expressions of garden art during the period of the Renaissance. Throughout Europe physic gardens were found within the cloistered walls of the monasteries and from these gardens were dispensed a variety of medicinal herbs, in an effort on the part of the monks to alleviate the suffering and distress of their people. It was an era when the enjoyment of plants for their beauty alone, while not entirely forgotten, was at least secondary in importance to their more practical uses. People were interested primarily in growing plants for medicinal purposes, for flavorings in cookery, for the dyeing of materials and in some cases for fragrance alone. An intimate knowledge of such plants was general throughout the countryside, as is evidenced by the wealth of plant names in most European languages. The superstition and folklore regarding these plants were passed on from generation to generation.

The herb garden of the Middle Ages was laid out on formal lines with quaintly patterned beds, narrow paths and prim edgings. During the Elizabethan era in England the herb garden was an important feature, and the patterned beds upon the broad terraces surrounding the manor houses became more and more intricate in design. The early colonists brought with them to this country knowledge and understanding of the use of herbs, and it was not long before many of the old, familiar plants were flourishing in the dooryard gardens of New England.

During the nineteenth century the interest in herbs declined steadily, and the herb garden became an almost forgotten thing of the past. Within the last few decades, however, there has been a great reawakening of interest in the culture and uses of herbs, and we have again come to appreciate them.

THE SMALL HERB GARDEN

Although one occasionally sees a new herb garden with intricate, primly patterned beds reminiscent of earlier days, most herb gardens today are simple affairs. Sometimes the herbs are relegated to the vegetable garden, or are used as a foreground planting in a shrub border where many of them adapt very readily. Some gardeners who have no other available space tuck them in at random among the perennial garden beds and borders.

One of the most ideal locations for a small herb garden is a sunny space near the kitchen door. Such a space may be made very attractive and can have a definite charm if a simple design is evolved and if materials are selected with care. Where space permits, a few mellow old bricks could be used to make a small terrace bordered with herbs. Two small bay trees in tubs and a few pots of rosemary and a bench would lend added interest. If there is no available space for even a small terrace, perhaps a walk could be bordered with narrow herb beds, or space found for a little herb patch beside the door, bordered with marigold and parsley, with tarragon and basil, pineapple sage and lavender planted close against the house wall. Just a few feet of sunny space—that is all that is needed for an effective and pleasing herb garden.

While working in the kitchen one can derive a great deal of pleasure from slipping out for a moment to pluck a few fresh sprigs from the herb bed and so add flavor or embellishment to whatever food is being prepared. And few plants will give so generously in return for the time and labor expended upon them as will the herbs.

The selection of herbs to be grown in a small herb garden will depend to a considerable extent upon personal preference. The variety of different herbs need not be large—a half dozen or so will suffice to give a subtle tang to many a dish. And no matter how small the garden, a

29.3 Chives (Allium schoenoprasum) *for garnish*

few herbs, such as lavender and lemon verbena, should be included for fragrance.

Among the herbs most generally grown for culinary use are the following:

chives	marjoram	summer savory
dill	mint	sweet basil
basil	rosemary	tarragon

Herbs are usually divided into several groups, although there is more or less overlapping. The aromatic herbs are those grown for fragrance; the culinary herbs are those grown to be used as flavorings in cookery; the medicinal herbs continue to play an important part in modern medicine; and those grown for coloring give us some of our most beautiful dyes.

CULTURAL REQUIREMENTS

Most herbs may be grown very easily from seed; small plants may be purchased or they may be obtained through a friendly exchange of cuttings and divisions among gardeners.

29.2 Lavender (Lavandula officinalis) *for scent*

Some of the plants commonly grown in the herb garden will need frequent division and pruning in order to keep them within bounds and to prevent them from crowding out some of the less aggressive plants. The various mints are in this class, and chives will benefit from being lifted and divided each year.

The majority of herbs prefer a position in full sun and thrive in a not-too-fertile, sandy loam soil that is well drained. When grown in rich garden beds, they make more luxuriant vegetative growth but seem to lose some of their fragrance and flavor.

There are a few herbs that prefer light shade rather than full sun, and a few that prefer a moist location.

If the foliage is to be used for fragrance or flavoring, the herbs should be cut just as the flowers are about to open, for with most herbs it is at this stage that the essential oils are most abundant. The most favorable time for cutting is early in the morning, after the dew has dried but before the plants have been touched with

29.5 Lemon balm (Melissa officinalis) *for cool refreshment. Photos (29.2, 29.3, 29.4, 29.5) Grant Heilman*

hot midday sun. When herbs are to be cut for flowers, as in the case of lavender and chamomile, they should be cut when in full bloom. If the seeds are to be used, the seed heads should be cut when they are no longer green. Those herbs that are harvested for their roots should be dug in the autumn after growth has ceased.

Some herbs can be grown on a sunny window sill during the winter months, where they offer a welcome bit of green as well as flavorings. Basil, mint, rosemary and parsley are among those that will thrive if favorable conditions are provided. They may be grown either in pots or in small window boxes.

For indoor culture the soil should be fairly fertile. A good sandy loam to which some compost has been added will give good results. Herbs will thrive best if they are grown in a south or southeast window in a very cool room, although they will adapt themselves to varied conditions. It is a wise practice to syringe the foliage once a week.

29.4 Basil (Ocimum basilicum) *for pungency*

HERBS FOR FLAVORING

angelica	*Angelica archangelica*
anise	*Pimpinella anisum*
balm	*Melissa officinalis*
basil	*Ocimum minimum, O. basilicum*
borage	*Borago officinalis*
burnet	*Sanguisorba officinalis, S. minor*
caraway	*Carum carvi*
catnip	*Nepeta cataria*
chamomile	*Anthemis nobilis*
chervil	*Anthriscus cerefolium*
chives	*Allium schoenoprasum*
coriander	*Coriandrum sativum*
costmary	*Chrysanthemum balsamita*
cress	*Barbarea verna*
dill	*Anethum graveolens*
fennel	*Foeniculum vulgare*
fennel flower	*Nigella sativa*
horehound	*Marrubium vulgare*
lovage	*Levisticum officinale*
marjoram, sweet	*Origanum majorana*
marjoram, pot	*Origanum onites*
mint, apple	*Mentha rotundifolia variegata*
mint, curled	*Mentha crispa*
peppermint	*Mentha piperita*
rue	*Ruta graveolens*
saffron	*Crocus sativus*
sage	*Salvia officinalis*
savory, summer	*Satureja hortensis*
savory, winter	*Satureja montana*
sorrel	*Rumex acetosa*
spearmint	*Mentha spicata*
sweet flag	*Acorus calamus*
tarragon	*Astemisia dracunculus*
thyme, common English	*Thymus vulgaris*
thyme, lemon	*Thymus serpyllum citriodorus*
watercress	*Nasturtium aquaticum*

HERBS FOR FRAGRANCE

ambrosia	*Chenopodium botrys*
balm	*Melissa officinalis*
basil	*Ocimum*
bee balm	*Monarda didyma*
bergamot	*Monarda fistulosa*
bergamot, white	*Monarda fistulosa alba*
geranium, apple	*Pelargonium odoratissimum*
geranium, balm	*Pelargonium melissinum*
geranium, citronella	*Pelargonium crispum*
geranium, lemon	*Pelargonium limoneum*
geranium, rose	*Pelargonium graveolens*
geranium, skeleton	*Pelargonium denticulatum*
lavender, English	*Lavandula angustifolia (L. spica, L. vera)*
lavender, French	*Lavandula dentata*
lavender-cotton	*Santolina chamaecyparissus*
marjoram, pot	*Origanum onites*
marjoram, sweet	*Origanum majorana*
mint, apple	*Mentha rotundifolia*
mint, creeping	*Mentha requieni*
mint, curled	*Mentha crispa*
mint, orange	*Mentha citrata*
pennyroyal	*Mentha pulegium*
peppermint	*Mentha piperita*
rosemary	*Rosmarinus officinalis*
rue	*Ruta graveolens*
savory, summer	*Satureja hortensis*
savory, winter	*Satureja montana*
southernwood	*Artemisia abrotanum*
spearmint	*Mentha spicata*
thyme	*Thymus*
verbena, lemon	*Lippia citriodora*
woodruff, sweet	*Asperula odorata*
wormwood, beach	*Artemisia stelleriana*
wormwood, common	*Artemisia absinthium*
wormwood, Roman	*Artemisia pontica*

HERBS
(*not hardy in North)

COMMON AND BOTANICAL NAMES	ANNUAL, BIENNIAL OR PERENNIAL; HEIGHT	PROPAGATION; USES	EXPOSURE; SOIL REQUIREMENTS
Ambrosia *Chenopodium botrys*	A; 2 ft.	seed; fragrance	sunny; any soil
Angelica *Angelica archangelica*	B; 2–3 ft.	sow seed as soon as ripe; food, perfume	cool climate; prefers a rather moist soil
Anise *Pimpinella anisum*	A; 2–3 ft.	seed; food, perfume, medicine	warm, sunny; moderately rich, well-drained loam
Balm (Lemon Balm) *Melissa officinalis*	P; 2½–3 ft.	seed; medicine, food, perfume	warm, sheltered position; poor, light soil
Basil *Ocimum minimum*	A; 1 ft.	seed; seasoning, fragrance	sunny; well drained
Bee Balm *Monarda didyma*	P; 2–3 ft.	seed, division; medicine, perfume, food	sun or partial shade; dry, well-drained soil
Bergamot *Monarda fistulosa, M. f. alba*	P; 3 ft.	division; fragrance	sun or partial shade; any soil

HERBS (Continued)

COMMON AND BOTANICAL NAMES	ANNUAL, BIENNIAL OR PERENNIAL; HEIGHT	PROPAGATION; USES	EXPOSURE; SOIL REQUIREMENTS
Borage			
Borago officinalis	A; 1½–2 ft.	seed; food	sunny; dry, well-drained soil
Burnet	P; 1–1¼ ft.	seed, division; medicine, food	full sun; any garden soil, prefers lime
Sanguisorba minor			
Sanguisorba officinalis	P; 5 ft.	division, seed; flavoring	sunny; any garden soil
Caraway	B; 2 ft.	seed; medicine, perfume, food	sunny; dry, well-drained soil
Carum carvi			
Chamomile	P; 1 ft.	seed, rooting stems; medicine	sunny; dry, well-drained soil
Anthemis nobilis			
Sweet			
Matricaria chamomilla	A; 2 ft.	seed; flavoring	full sun; ordinary soil
Chervil	A; ½–1 ft.	seed; food, medicine	sun or partial shade; any good garden soil
Anthriscus cerefolium			
Chives	P; 10 in.	bulbs, seed, division of clumps; flavorings for salads, omelets, sauces	sunny; any good garden soil
Allium schoenoprasum			
Clary			
Salvia sclarea	B; 3 ft.	seed; perfumes, food	full sun; rocky, dry soil
Coriander	A; 1½ ft.	seed; medicine, perfume, food	sunny; prefers a warm light soil
Coriandrum sativum			
Costmary	P; 3 ft.	root cuttings; medicine, food	sunny; dry, well-drained soil
Chrysanthemum balsamita			
Cress			
Barbarea verna	B; 2 ft.	seed; flavoring for salad	sun; any meadow soil
Cumin	A; 4–8 in.	seed; medicine, perfume, food	sunny; any good garden soil
Cuminum cyminum			
Dill	A; 2½–3 ft.	seed (do not transplant); food, for pickling, for vinegars	sunny; any ordinary garden soil
Anethum graveolens			
Fennel Flower			
Nigella sativa	A; 1 ft.	seed; condiment, perfume	full sun; any garden soil
Florence Fennel			
Foeniculum vulgare, var. *dulce*	A; 6–10 in.	seed; food	full sun; light, well-drained soil
Geranium, scented, in variety			
Pelargonium spp.	P*; 1–3 ft.	cuttings; fragrance	sunny; any garden soil
Horehound			
Marrubium vulgare	P; 3 ft.	seed; medicine, as a drink	full sun; poor, light, dry soil
Horseradish	P; 18–30 in.	root cuttings; food, medicine	sun; any soil
Armoracia rusticana			
Hyssop	P; 18–24 in.	seed; medicine, perfume, food	sunny; ordinary garden soil, not too rich. Prefers lime
Hyssopus officinalis			
Lavender	P; 2–3 ft.	cuttings, seed; fragrance, food	full sun; light, well-drained soil high in lime content
Lavandula vera (*L. officinalis, L. spica*)			
Lavandula dentata	P; 2–3 ft.	cuttings, seed; fragrance	full sun; any garden soil
Lavender-Cotton	P; 2 ft.	cuttings; fragrance	sunny; garden soil, not hardy. Winter over in coldframes
Santolina chamaecyparissus			
Lemon Verbena	P; 4–5 ft.	cuttings of half-ripe wood; flavor, perfume	very sensitive to frost. Best grown in pots; good garden loam
Lippia citriodora			
Lovage	P; 6 ft.	seed; medicine, perfume, food	sunny; rich, moist soil
Levisticum officinale			
Mint, Apple	P; 30 in.	cuttings, divisions; flavoring, fragrance	sunny; good garden soil
Mentha rotundifolia			
Mint, Curled	P; 3 ft.	cuttings, divisions; flavoring, fragrance	sunny; good, deep soil
Mentha crispa			
Parsley			
Petroselinum hortense	B; 6–10 in.	seed; medicine, food	full sun; prefers a rather moist soil

(Continued)

HERBS (Continued)

Peppermint	P; 2–3 ft.	cuttings, runners; medicine, perfume, food	sunny; deep, moist soil
Mentha piperita			
Perennial Marjoram			
Origanum majorana (O. onites)	P; 2 ft.	seed; flavoring, fragrance	sunny; any garden soil
Pot Marigold			
Calendula officinalis	A; 12–15 in.	seed; medicine, food	sunny; any rich garden soil
Pot Marjoram	P; 2 ft.	seed, cuttings; medicine, perfume, food	sunny; any garden soil
Origanum vulgare			
Rosemary	P; 3–6 ft.	seed, cuttings; medicine, perfume	sunny, sheltered position; dry, well-drained soil
Rosmarinus officinalis			
Rue	P; 2 ft.	seed, cuttings; perfume, food	sunny; prefers a well-drained yet moist soil
Ruta graveolens			
Saffron	P; 4 in.	seed, corms; perfume, flavoring, coloring	sunny; garden soil
Crocus sativus			
Sage	P; 2–3 ft.	seed, cuttings; medicine, perfume, food	sunny; any well-drained garden soil
Salvia officinalis			
Savory,			
Summer			
Satureja hortensis	A; 1–1½ ft.	seed; medicine, food	sunny; any good garden soil
Winter			
Satureja montana	P; 15 in.	seed; seasoning, fragrance	sunny; any garden soil
Sesame			
Sesamum orientale	A; 2 ft.	seed; medicine, food	full sun; any well-drained garden soil
Sorrel	P; 3 ft.	seed; salad flavoring	sunny; any garden soil not too alkaline
Rumex acetosa			
Southernwood	P; 2–3 ft.	division; fragrance, medicine	sunny; any garden soil
Artemisia abrotanum			
Spearmint	P; 2–3 ft.	cuttings, runners; perfume, food	sunny; deep, moist soil
Mentha spicata			
Sweet Basil	A; 1½–2 ft.	seed; flavoring, medicine, perfume	sunny; well-drained soil
Ocimum basilicum			
Sweet Cicely	P; 2–3 ft.	seed, division; food	sun or partial shade; any ordinary garden soil
Myrrhis odorata			
Sweet Fennel			
Foeniculum officinale	A; 3 ft.	seed; food	full sun; well-drained soil
Sweet Flag			
Acorus calamus	P; 5 ft.	division; perfume	sunny; moist
Sweet Marjoram	A; 8–12 in.	seed; medicine, perfume, food	sunny; dry, well-drained
Origanum majorana hortensis			
Sweet Woodruff	P; 8 in.	division; fragrance, flavoring	partial shade; thrives well in either moist or dry soil
Asperula odorata			
Tansy	P; 3 ft.	seed, division; medicine, perfume	full sun; any garden soil
Tanacetum vulgare			
Tarragon	P; 3 ft.	root cuttings; perfume, flavoring	prefers light shade; any good soil
Artemisia dracunculus			
Thyme	P; 6–8 in.	seed, cuttings; medicine, perfume	sunny; rocky banks, any well-drained sunny position
Thymus spp.			
Watercress	P; 5 in.	seed or stem cuttings; salad seasoning	sunny; pool or stream margins
Nasturtium aquaticum			
Wormwood	P; 2½–4 ft.	seed, division; medicine, food	sunny; any garden soil
Artemisia absinthium			
Roman Wormwood			
Artemisia pontica	P; B; 4 ft.	seed, division; fragrance	sunny; thrives even in poor soil
Beach Wormwood			
Artemisia stelleriana	P; 2½ ft.	seed, division; fragrance	sunny; any soil

5

CULTURAL METHODS
AND PRACTICES

30

Soils and Soil Improvement

No subject is of more fundamental importance to the gardener than that of soil management. In order to handle garden soils intelligently, and to maintain or increase the fertility of the soil, it is necessary to have a thorough knowledge not only of the soil itself but also of the manner in which plants receive their nutrients from the soil.

Comparatively few soils provide ideal conditions for plant growth, but if a wise program of soil management is put into effect, much may be accomplished in improving the structure, the fertility and the water-holding capacity of soils of widely varying types.

There are certain factors affecting plant growth over which a gardener has very little control, such as climate, rainfall, sunshine and humidity; but over the various factors of soil management he has very definite control. The soil is a heritage from the past. Not only for our own immediate benefit should we conserve, maintain and increase its fertility; it is our obligation to do so for the generations who are to follow us.

The formation of the soil is a process that has continued since earliest geologic times when the surface of the earth was composed entirely of rock. The action of sun and frost, air and water, upon these rock surfaces has resulted in a gradual process of disintegration and the consequent slow formation of soils. Eons ago the first land plants grew in the hollows and crevices of the rocks where this newly formed mineral soil had found lodgement. As these primitive plants died, they decayed and formed food for other plants, and gradually, as the millennia passed, this decaying organic matter became mixed with the mineral soil, thus enriching it and increasing the earth's vegetation. The same process continues today as algae, mosses and lichens, nature's pioneer plants, gain footholds in the bare rock of glacial and volcanic areas, and gradually break down rock into primitive soils.

In areas of the world where primeval forest growth abounds, we often find deep, porous soils, rich in humus, which are classed as peaty soils. Such soils are also found in peat bogs and are composed almost entirely of partly decayed organic matter. The world's grasslands produce soils equally rich in organic matter. In other areas we find soils that are classed as mineral soils, composed largely of mineral matter, And in between these two extreme types, the peaty soils and the mineral soils, we find many soils of widely varying character.

Most soils, as we find them in our gardens today, are composed of five intermingled components: the mineral substances obtained from the slow disintegration of rock surfaces; humus or decaying organic matter; minute living organisms such as the bacteria, protozoa and fungi that are present in large quantities in most soils; water, which holds in solution the dissolved mineral salts; and air. In sections where the soil has been under cultivation for many years or where the program of soil management has been poor, we find soils that have lost much of their humus content and that, in many cases, have become depleted of their mineral elements. It is these soils that present the greatest problems.

TYPES OF SOIL

Soils are generally grouped into three classes according to structure: sand, silt or clay. These classes are determined by the size of the soil particles. Sand contains 20 particles or less to a millimeter, silt 20 to 200 particles to a millimeter and clay 200 or more. A soil of ideal texture is a mixture of sand, silt and clay, being classed as a good garden loam. The structure of the soil has a very direct bearing upon its water-holding capacity, upon its warmth in early spring, upon the ease with which it can be worked or handled, and upon the penetration of plant roots and the consequent nutrition of the plant.

Clay Soils

A clay soil has a water-holding capacity many times higher than that of a sandy soil because each soil particle is capable of holding a film of water upon its surface. Therefore a clay soil possessing 200 particles per millimeter is capable of holding many times as much water as sand that possesses only 20 particles to the same area. The water-holding capacity of clay soils may be an asset in seasons of extreme drought, but it is, on the whole, almost as much of a liability. A heavy clay soil is very slow in drying out in the spring, and all planting operations and general cultural practices must therefore be delayed. It does not absorb the sun's rays as readily as does a soil of lighter texture and, therefore, does not warm up as quickly in the spring, thus delaying the normally eager spring growth of plants. If left uncultivated too long after a rain, a clay soil will form a hard, baked crust that makes it impossible for either air or moisture to reach the roots of the plants, and in some cases it will form deep cracks. On the other hand, if it is plowed or cultivated or otherwise handled when it is too wet, it will form hard lumps that are exceedingly difficult to break down. A clay soil is one of the most difficult of all soil types to handle wisely, and every effort should be made to improve its structure. Much may be accomplished by the addition of sand, humus and compost, and even sifted coal ashes will be of some benefit. It is also an advantage to spade or plow clay soils in the autumn, leaving them in a very rough condition throughout the winter. The action of the frost will have a beneficial effect on the close texture of the soil, making it somewhat more mellow and friable.

Sandy Soils

These possess many of the advantages that are lacking in soils of a decidedly heavy texture. They warm up quickly in the spring, they are easy to work; on the other hand, sandy soils are not retentive of moisture and many of the soluble plants foods may be lost through leaching. It is quite as important, therefore, to improve the structure of sandy soils as it is to improve the structure of heavy clay soils. This may be accomplished most successfully by the addition of liberal quantities of organic matter.

Loam Soils

The ideal soil for most garden operations is a fertile loam, which is a mixture of sand, clay and humus. It should be porous enough in texture to provide good drainage and adequate aeration; it should be spongy enough to retain an ample supply of moisture; it should contain sufficient humus to provide favorable conditions for the growth of the soil bacteria, which play such an important part in plant nutrition; and it should contain all the mineral elements necessary for the healthy, normal growth of plant life. A soil of this type is the desideratum of every gardener, and with a good program of soil management and an intelligent understanding of the needs of growing plants, much may be accomplished in building a soil that will very nearly approximate the ideal.

HUMUS

An adequate supply of humus in the soil is one of the most important factors in a program of good soil management.

Humus serves many functions in improving the structure and character of any soil. It increases the water-holding capacity of soils; it modifies the soil structure; it readily absorbs the sun's rays and consequently increases and stimulates plant growth in early spring; it prevents the leaching of soluble plant foods; it liberates compounds which, in turn, act upon the chemical elements in the soil, thus making available to the plants mineral nutrients that would otherwise remain in insoluble form; and it promotes the bacterial action in the soil to a very marked degree.

The value of humus in increasing the water-holding capacities of soils can hardly be over-emphasized. It is unlike the particles of mineral soils in that it does not merely hold the water on its surface; it soaks it in like a sponge. In a series of recent experiments to test the water-holding capacities of soils of varying types, it was found that 100 lb. of sand will hold 25 lb. of water; 100 lb. of clay will hold 50 lb. of water; and 100 lb. of humus will hold 190 lb. of water. From 20 to 40 percent of the water-holding capacity of soils is due to their humus content; in seasons of prolonged drought soils high in humus content will remain moist in both the upper and lower soil horizons far longer than soils that are deficient in humus, and plant growth is correspondingly greater.

Humus is also of great value in improving the texture of soils, as it has the ability to modify the soils structure to a very marked degree. A soil that is of mellow, friable texture, the kind we class as an ideal garden loam, is made up of crumbs of soil held together in a granule, and it is the humus that furnishes the binding material for these soil particles. A soil of this texture permits the rapid renewal of moisture and food nutrients. It also permits easy root penetration, which is an important factor, as the roots travel to the water and nutrients in the soil, not vice versa. When a clay soil is deficient in humus, it becomes tight and compact in structure. The penetration of the roots is therefore restricted and the nutrition of the plant is often seriously limited in consequence. Such a soil has a ten-

dency to become hard and baked when it is dry, and is far less permeable to water than soil of a more open structure. Not only does the water penetrate the soil less readily but it is also more quickly evaporated. Soils of this type may be greatly improved in texture by the application of liberal amounts of humus. When sandy soils are deficient in humus, many valuable plant nutrients are lost through leaching and plant growth also suffers seriously from lack of moisture in times of drought. It is, therefore, quite as important to see that sandy soils are well supplied with humus as it is to maintain an adequate humus supply in clay soils.

Mineral fertilizers supplement, but in no way replace, humus. Experiments have proved that mineral fertilizers are much more effective if they are applied either with, or immediately following, an application of humus, than if they are applied alone. At the Maryland Experimental Station, crop yields have shown an increase varying from one-fifth to one-third more when manure and mineral fertilizers were applied together than when double the amount of either was applied alone. This same principle would apply to the building up of soil fertility in the garden.

Sources of Humus

Peat

The various forms of peat provide an excellent source of humus. Technically, peat may be defined as the partially carbonized organic residue of plants, the decomposition of which has taken place under standing water. The peats may be classed into several groups: those of deep water, marsh, swamp and bog origin. When the process of decay of such substances as tree trunks, mosses, sedges and grasses takes place under water, the decomposition is greatly retarded because of the exclusion of air, and the resulting product, known as peat, differs considerably from the humus that is found in upland forests.

Peat is rich in organic matter, is highly absorbent and retentive of moisture, and has the added advantage of being comparatively free from weed seeds and harmful fungi. Peat is usually somewhat acid in its reaction and it must, therefore, be used with discrimination. It is of particular value for use in connection with the planting of broad-leaved evergreens, such as rhododendrons, laurel, and many of the acid-loving woodland plants, but it should not be used too liberally in connection with plants that are not acid-tolerant. The actual fertilizing value of peat is comparatively low. It contains some nitrogen, the amount varying from 1 to 3.5 percent, depending upon the source of the peat, and it is extremely low in phosphorus and potash.

The two kinds of peat most readily obtainable are imported peat and domestic peat. The imported peat comes in tightly packed bales, weighing about 200 lb. It is largely of bog origin, being a sphagnum type of peat, and it is very low in nitrogen content. When it is to be incorporated in the soil, or used as a mulch, the handling will be greatly facilitated if the bale is thoroughly soaked before it is opened. When dry, imported peat's light, fluffy texture makes it hard to manage.

Domestic peat has a higher moisture content, is darker in color and finer in texture. In general it is considered a better source of humus than the imported peat, as it may be more evenly worked into the soil and its effect is more lasting.

Leaf Mold

An excellent and usually readily available source of humus. It is highly retentive of moisture, is rich in organic matter, and has the ability to change into a more readily available form various nitrogenous materials in the soil. Leaf mold varies considerably in its reaction upon the soil. Oak leaves and pine needles, when decayed, form a leaf mold that is definitely acid in its reaction. However, the majority of our deciduous trees form a leaf mold that is very mildly acid or entirely neutral in reaction. The best and most abundant source of leaf mold is the natural forest floor. A small but readily available supply may be kept at hand by making a compost of leaves each autumn. Many municipalities provide leaf mold to residents, and it is also commercially available in many areas.

The Compost Pile

A good compost pile is a valuable adjunct to any garden, and no matter how small one's place may be there will always be some organic materials that can be converted into compost. The end product of a compost pile is a soil that is exceedingly high in humus content and rich in plant nutrients. Such soils are of particular value as potting soils for house plants and for use in the preparation of seed flats. Compost is also valuable as a topdressing for lawns and in the preparation of the soil in hotbeds and cold-frames, and it is used extensively to enrich and improve the texture of the soil in flower gardens and on vegetable plots. Indeed, there are so many uses for a good compost that the supply never seems to be quite sufficient to meet one's needs.

The building of a compost pile is a simple matter. A partially shaded location is preferable to one in full sun, as it will be possible to maintain a more even degree of moisture. A pile of convenient, workable size is one from 4 ft. to 6 ft. in width, 3 ft. to 4 ft. in height, and of any desired length. The foundation of the pile should consist of some coarse material, such as inverted sods or weed stalks, and upon this foundation alternating layers of organic refuse and soil should be built up, animal manures being included whenever they are obtainable as they greatly increase the fertility of the compost. Almost any type of organic material may be used with the exception of very woody materials and plants that are diseased. Grass clippings, sod, weeds, refuse from the vegetable garden, and all types of animal manures are excellent materials, as are vegetable peelings and fruit rinds. Through the process of composting, all may be converted into potential wealth for the gardener.

The decomposition of organic matter is due to the activity of certain organisms, and the rate of decomposition in a compost pile will be greatly accelerated if these microorganisms are present in sufficient numbers. This may be accomplished through the addition of soil to the pile (a healthy soil is teeming with biologic life); through the use of some well-rotted compost from another pile; or through the use of one of the numerous commercial activators on the market.

Since these organisms, which play such an important part in the decomposition of organic materials, are less tolerant of acid conditions, it is wise to add an occasional sprinkling of ground limestone to the pile during the process of construction. The moisture content of the pile is also important. The top of the pile should be concave, in order to catch as much rain as possible, and if dry materials such as hay or straw are used the pile should be thoroughly soaked during the process of building. It should have a moist, spongy consistency at all times. An occasional turning is advisable, rebuilding the pile so that the outer portion is placed in the center of the new pile.

The time required to convert raw organic materials into a good humus suitable for garden use will depend upon a number of factors, such as climatic conditions, the moisture content of the pile, the types of materials used and whether or not an activator is used. Bacterial action is more rapid in warm climates than in colder regions; green materials will decompose more rapidly than more woody materials, and some of the new commercial activators will speed the process of decomposition to such an extent that it is possible to obtain an excellent humus in three or four mild or warm months.

Making Compost Weed-free

When using compost as a topdressing on lawns, or for a seedbed in a coldframe, or for flats in which seeds are to be started, it is a great advantage to have material that is weed-free.

There are various methods of producing compost that will be entirely free of viable weed seeds. One of the methods best adapted to the facilities available to the home gardener is a process developed by the University of Rhode Island in which granular calcium cyanamide is used. Not only does this method kill all the weed seeds, but it also increases the nutritive value of the compost, as calcium cyanamide, commonly known as Cyanamid, contains 20 percent nitrogen and the equivalent of 70 percent hydrated lime.

The process is simple. The compost, which should be well decomposed and moderately moist, should be sifted through a 1/4-in.-mesh wire screen. It should then be mixed thoroughly with the Cyanamid at the rate of 13 lb. of Cyanamid to each cubic yard of compost. The easiest way to measure a cubic yard is to have a bottomless box that holds 1 cu. yd. or an exact fraction thereof. The box may be filled and lifted away and refilled again as many times as necessary. One of the best ways of adding the Cyanamid in the correct proportion, and ensuring that it is well distributed through the compost, is to place the compost in the measuring box layer by layer, adding a proportionate amount of Cyanamid as the layers are built up. If four layers are used, slightly more than 3 lb. of Cyanamid should be sprinkled over each layer. The Cyanamid should never be applied in excess of 13 lb. per cubic yard, as it might result in the burning of turf or plants when the compost is used.

The mixing may be done by shoveling the material back and forth on a cement floor or some other level surface. After it has been thoroughly mixed, it should be screened again and then stored under a shelter in a wooden bin or in some place where the pile will not be disturbed.

It usually takes from four to six weeks to obtain a complete kill of all weed seeds, provided the weather is mild. It takes considerably longer in cold weather, so the work should preferably be done during the warm months.

Although the above method is more thorough, it should be noted that a properly functioning compost pile, which will heat to 160° F., can be almost as efficient in eliminating most weed seeds. This can be accomplished with ease by piling compost in a sunny place and covering it with black plastic. If the compost consists mainly of leaves, it will be ready in a couple weeks; more fibrous material (such as corn husks) will take longer.

Cover Crops

Cover crops are often spoken of as "green manures." The term is applied to crops that are grown for the sole purpose of being plowed or spaded under, in order to improve the physical texture of the soil, to increase its organic content and its fertility. Such a procedure is one of the best and also least expensive methods of improving poor, worn-out soils. It is, on the whole, more suitable for large-scale operations than for use on small areas. It may play a very important part, however, in the initial preparation of the soil for a vegetable garden or a fruit orchard, or for a lawn area.

The most valuable cover crops, from the standpoint of increasing the fertility of the soil, are the legumes, such as soybeans, alfalfa, the clovers and the vetches. The legumes actually increase the nitrogen content of the soil through the aid of the nitrogen-fixing bacteria. These highly specialized bacteria, which have the ability to take nitrogen from the air, are minute, rod-shaped bodies that are found in the soil under certain favorable conditions. When these bacteria come into contact with the roots of certain legume plants, they enter the root hairs, causing a slight irritation that results in the growth of a tiny, round ball called a nodule. These bacteria take nitrogen from the air and supply it to the plant. The plant, in return, furnishes other food matter to the bacteria, which enables them to multiply rapidly. This relationship is called "symbiosis." There is a slight difference in the forms of bacteria found on different types of legumes — one form living on one group of legumes, another living only on certain other types. Some legumes, such as alfalfa, are very dependent upon the nitrogen-fixing bacteria and the plants are unable to make vigorous, normal growth, or to survive at all, unless these bacteria are present in the soil. Other legumes, such as soybeans, are considerably less dependent and will make reasonably good growth on soil where no bacteria are present. When grown under such conditions, however, these crops are no more valuable than a nonleguminous crop, as they do not increase the nitrogen content of the soil unless the bacteria are present. In order to ensure the presence of these nitrogen-fixing bacteria in the soil, all legume crops should be inoculated, before planting, with a specially prepared inoculant carrying the exact type of bacteria needed for the particular legume to be grown. Such inoculants are obtainable from any commercial seed house.

The value of legumes as cover crops can hardly be overemphasized. A well-grown leguminous crop that is plowed under at the proper stage of growth will frequently add from 100 lb. to 150 lb. of actual nitrogen to the soil per acre. This would practically equal 100 tons to 15 tons of good animal manure.

The stage of growth at which cover crops are plowed under has a very direct influence upon the value of the crop. The nitrogen and mineral content are highest shortly before maturity. Therefore, the crop should be plowed under when it is in a slightly immature stage.

If cover crops are to be grown on soils of very low fertility, the eventual value of the crop as a soil improver will be greatly increased if the cover crop receives the benefit of an application of commercial fertilizer, and if conditions are made generally favorable for good growth. There is little to be gained from growing a cover crop on land that is so poor it can support little in the way of plant growth. Under such conditions, the benefits will hardly justify the cost of seed and labor.

It is a generally accepted fact that the crops planted immediately after the plowing under of a cover crop (particularly a nonleguminous crop) will thrive infinitely better if a fairly liberal application of a commercial fertilizer is made at the time that the crop is turned under. The same principle applies to the plowing under of a heavy growth of sod. This is because the process of decomposition is carried on by certain of the bacteria in the soil. These bacteria need to use the nitrogen in the soil in order to carry on their activities, and unless a surplus of nitrogen is present the plants suffer in consequence. By applying a highly nitrogenous fertilizer, such a surplus may be assured.

DESIRABLE COVER CROPS*

Leguminous Crops

Alfalfa

A perennial crop, which consequently requires a longer time to become established than the annual and biennial crops, but there are instances when its use as a cover crop is justified. In a case where a country property is purchased and there are open fields that will eventually be put into lawns, no better use can be made of the land than to put it into alfalfa.

*Dates recommended for plowing under are applicable to the latitude of Pennsylvania and Ohio. In any locality, cover crops should be turned under when slightly immature.

Time and rate of seeding: The seed may be sown in early spring or late summer at the rate of 10 lb. to 12 lb. per acre and it should be inoculated. If the field is weedy, late summer sowing is preferable.

Soil requirements: A well-drained soil of reasonably good fertility with a pH of 6.5 or above.

Time of plowing under: Hay may be harvested for a number of years and the crop plowed under in the fall or in the spring when the ground is desired for some other purpose, such as a lawn area, garden or orchard. When plowed under, the tops and roots contain approximately 2.65 percent nitrogen, and as much as 150 lb. per acre of actual nitrogen may be added to the soil.

Hairy Vetch
A winter annual and one of the most valuable of all soil builders.

Time and rate of seeding: May be sown early in September at the rate of 3 pecks to 4 pecks per acre. The seed should be inoculated.

Soil requirements: It thrives best on a sandy, well-drained soil with a pH of 6.5 or slightly above.

Time of plowing under: Should be plowed under about the middle of May. If turned under at this season, the top growth and roots will contain approximately 3.75 percent nitrogen.

Mammoth Red Clover
Being a biennial, red clover must occupy the ground for a considerable length of time and is therefore not as well suited for a cover crop as are some of the other legumes, although it is considered by many as a splendid soil builder.

Time and rate of seeding: Should be sown very early in the spring, preferably with a small grain crop such as oats, or on a wheat crop

sown the previous fall. Rate of seeding: 8 lb. to 12 lb. per acre. Inoculate seed.

Soil requirements: A soil of at least moderate fertility, with a pH above 5.5.

Time of plowing under: Should be plowed under just before full bloom the year after sowing.

Soybeans
One of the most valuable of all cover crops, as they are a summer annual and make rapid growth.

Time and rate of seeding: Soybeans should be sown in May or early June at the rate of 2 bushels per acre.

Soil requirements: If grown on very poor soil, a complete fertilizer should be added. Soil should have a pH above 5.

Time of plowing under: It is very important that soybeans be plowed under before the vines have become too mature. The most generally accepted practice is to turn them under when the beans in the pods are about half grown. At this stage, the tops and roots will contain approximately 2.65 percent nitrogen.

Sweet Clover
A biennial, which possesses tremendous soil-building potentialities.

Time and rate of seeding: Sweet clover should be sown early in the spring either on, or with, a small grain crop. The usual rate of seeding is 10 lb. to 12 lb. per acre.

Soil requirements: Sweet clover is one of the few legumes that will grow well on very poor soil. It does reasonably well on washed clay land. Its one definite requirement is a soil high in lime content with a pH of 6.5 or above.

Time of plowing under: The crop may be plowed under the spring following seeding. In order to secure good results, it is essential that it be turned under before it reaches maturity. If plowed under between April 15 and May 1, the maximum percentage of nitrogen will be secured, often running as high as 3.75 percent.

Nonleguminous Crops

Rye

Rye is considered the most valuable of all the nonlegumes as a cover crop. Although it does not increase the actual nitrogen content of the soil appreciably, it adds a considerable amount of organic matter.

Time and rate of seeding: Rye should be sown during early September, being seeded at the rate of 1½ bushels to 2 bushels per acre.

Soil requirements: Rye succeeds reasonably well on a soil of average fertility and is almost entirely indifferent to soil pH, thriving on decidedly acid soil.

Time of plowing under: Rye should be plowed under in the spring when it has reached a height of approximately 10 in. At this time the plant contains a greater percentage of nitrogen than at any other stage of its development, sometimes running as high as 1.75 percent.

Rye and Hairy Vetch

These two may be sown in combination, and make an excellent cover crop.

Time and rate of seeding: They should be seeded early in September at the rate of 5 pecks per acre, the mixture containing 60 lb. of rye to 20 lb. of hairy vetch.

Soil requirements: Soil pH above 6.5 because of the vetch.

Time of plowing under: About the middle of May.

ANIMAL MANURES

Long before commercial fertilizers were developed, the good qualities of animal manures in improving and maintaining soil fertility were known and appreciated. Not only does animal manure increase the fertility of the soil but it also serves other important functions as well. It increases the organic content of the soil; it improves the physical structure of the soil; it increases the bacterial activity to a very appreciable degree; and it has, in general, a very beneficial effect upon the soil.

Contrary to popular belief, the actual elements of fertility contained in animal manures are very meager when compared with those contained in most inorganic commercial fertilizers. The following table indicates the usual percentages found in various types of manure.

	NITROGEN	PHOSPHORUS	POTASSIUM
Poultry Manure	1.0	0.8	0.4
Sheep Manure	0.95	0.35	1.0
Horse Manure	0.7	0.25	0.55
Cow Manure	0.6	0.15	0.45
Pig Manure	0.5	0.35	0.4

It is even more startling to realize that, low as the above percentages may seem, only one-half of the nitrogen, one-half of the potassium and one-sixth of the phosphorus are readily available for use by the plants. It can be seen, therefore, that the actual fertility added to the soil by an application of animal manure is very slight, and that the benefits derived from such an application are those more directly concerned with the physical character of the soil.

The value of animal manure, from a standpoint of fertility, depends to a considerable extent upon the method of handling. If a high percentage of the nutrients it contains as fresh manure are to be conserved, it must be handled with care. The most generally accepted practice is to store manure under cover, to keep it piled in watertight pits and to keep the stack constantly moist, never allowing it to dry out or to become fire-fanged through overheating. If manure is not properly handled, it may lose a very large percentage of its nutrients and become practically valueless from the standpoint of increasing the actual fertility of the soil.

The rate of application of stable manure varies from what is considered a moderate application of 15 tons per acre to an extremely heavy application of 40 tons per acre; or from 700 lb. per 1,000 sq. ft. to 2,000 lb. per 1,000 sq. ft.

Fresh manure should never be used where it will come into direct contact with the root formation of the plants as it is liable to cause severe burning. Most gardeners prefer to use manure after it has become partially rotted. In this form the nutrients are more readily available and the danger of any harmful effects is largely mitigated. On large-scale operations, manure is usually spread upon the surface of the soil and is then plowed in. On smaller areas, it is forked or spaded into the soil.

Dehydrated Manures

There are various forms of dry, shredded and pulverized manures on the market. From the standpoint of economy, such manures are a poor investment. During the process of dehydrating, some of the nitrogen is lost, and comparatively little actual fertility is added to the soil. For the same expenditure, far better results may be obtained from the use of domestic humans and commercial fertilizers.

Liquid Manures

The type of liquid manure formerly used to a considerable extent by gardeners was made by immersing a bushel of manure in a barrel of water. The modern method—which consists of dissolving a highly concentrated nitrogenous fertilizer, such as nitrate of soda, urea or ammonium sulphate, or a well-balanced complete fertilizer, in water and thus applying it to the plant—is far superior for its economy, ease of application and the reliability of the results.

ARTIFICIAL MANURE

In these days when manure is often difficult to obtain, it is a source of satisfaction to the gardener to be able to make an artificial manure that is very similar in every way to the natural product. This may be done by mixing commercial fertilizers and lime with straw, hay, weeds, grass clippings, leaves or any other garden refuse. It is essential that this work be undertaken in the late spring or early summer as the decomposition of the material is dependent upon bacterial action, and correct temperature and abundant moisture are factors of vital importance. To each ton of straw or other litter, the following ingredients should be added:

60 lb. sulphate of ammonia
30 lb. superphosphate
25 lb. potassium chloride
50 lb. ground limestone

The method of making artificial manure resembles that for making compost, previously outlined, but for convenience it is repeated here. The pile should be approximately 4 ft. to 6 ft. wide, 4 ft. high and any desired length. A 4-in. layer of composting material should be placed upon the surface of the ground. This should be liberally sprinkled with the fertilizing ingredients and should then be thoroughly soaked with water. This process should be repeated until the pile has reached the desired height. The top of the pile should be slightly hollow, or concave, so that it will retain as much water as possible. Unless the rainfall is unusually heavy, the pile should be soaked daily for the period of a week or more in order that the bacterial action may be promoted as rapidly as possible. After the process of decomposition has started, a thorough weekly soaking will usually be sufficient. The sides as well as the top of the pile should be soaked, and the pile should be kept moist at all times. Within three or four months the material should have become sufficiently decomposed, and it will have a composition very similar to a good quality barnyard manure. One ton of straw will produce approximately 3 tons of organic material.

PLANT NUTRITION

In order to provide for an adequate supply of nutrients in the soil it is essential to understand something of the method by which plants manufacture their food from the elements obtained from the soil and the air.

Fifteen elements are known to be essential for the nutrition of plants. Three of these elements, carbon, hydrogen and oxygen, are obtained from water or from the atmosphere. The remaining twelve, nitrogen, phosphorus, potassium, calcium, magnesium, boron, copper, manganese, molybdenum, iron, sulphur and zinc, are normally obtained from the soil. These mineral nutrients in the soil can be utilized by the plant only when they are in solution and can be absorbed through the root hairs. When foliar feeding is practiced there is absorption of the minerals through the leaves.

From these fifteen essential elements a plant is able, in the presence of light, to manufacture sugars, proteins and other complex organic substances that are used for the maintenance of existing tissues and for the production of new tissue. As long as these essential elements are present in sufficient amounts, the plant is able to continue this process of food manufacture. However, if one or more of these elements is not available to the plant in sufficient quantity, the production of food becomes limited and the growth and vigor of the plant are affected.

The twelve mineral elements that are essential for normal growth are divided into two general groups: the major elements; and the minor, or trace, elements. In the first group we find nitrogen, phosphorus, potassium, calcium and magnesium. Since the days of early scientific investigation it has been recognized that these elements are essential for plant growth and that each of them fulfills an important function.

The three elements most likely to be deficient in soils that have been brought under cultivation are nitrogen, phosphorus and potassium.

Nitrogen

Nitrogen is an essential element for plant growth. Its most important function is to stimulate vegetative development, and it is therefore particularly necessary in the production of leaves and stems. If an excess of nitrogen is applied, the effects are decidedly harmful, as it will result in an overluxuriant growth of foliage at the expense of flowers and fruit, and maturity will consequently be delayed. The cell walls of the stems will also become weakened and the plant's resistance to disease will be appreciably lowered.

Nitrogen is seldom found in the soil in a free state, being almost invariably found in combination with other elements. Soils are usually lowest in available nitrogen during the early spring months and it is at this season that quickly available nitrogenous fertilizers are of particular value. It also sometimes happens that in prolonged periods of heavy rain during the summer much of the available nitrogen is leached out of the soil, and when such a condition occurs an immediate application of nitrogen should be made.

When applying nitrogen in any of the inorganic forms, the material should not come into direct contact with the foliage of the plant as it may cause severe burning. If it is accidentally dropped onto the foliage, it should be washed off immediately with a strong spray of water.

Nitrate of Soda

The most quickly available form of nitrogen is nitrate of soda, which contains approximately 15 percent nitrogen. Upon application it is almost immediately available to the plant. It is more quickly available in acid soils than in alkaline soils. It should be used only on well-established plants that are making active growth, and the soil should be moist when an application is made. Nitrate of soda may be applied in the dry form, the substance being scattered upon the surface of the soil at the rate of 1 lb. to 100 sq. ft., or it may be applied in the form of a solution, being dissolved in water at the rate of 1 oz. to 2 gallons of water. In soils where lime is not present, the long-continued use of nitrate of soda may cause a toxic condition because of an undue accumulation of sodium carbonate.

Calcium Nitrate

Contains 15 percent nitrogen. It is readily available, but leaves a decidedly alkaline residue in the soil and is therefore not as generally used as nitrate of soda. The rate of application is approximately the same.

Ammonium Sulphate

A by-product obtained in the manufacture of coal gas, ammonium sulphate contains approximately 20 percent or more of nitrogen in a readily available form. In warm soils it is often as quickly available as is nitrate of soda, and it has been proven that in alkaline soils its availability is even quicker and greater than nitrate of soda. When it is used over a period of many years it has a tendency to develop an acid reaction in the soil, but any difficulty of this nature may be readily overcome by the use of lime. When ammonium sulphate is applied to acid soils, the results will be more satisfactory if it is used in combination with superphosphate than if it is used alone. The usual rate of application varies from 1 lb. to 2 lb. per 100 sq. ft., or, in the form of a solution, 1 oz. to 2 gallons of water.

Urea

This is a synthetic form of nitrogen, a combination of ammonia and carbon dioxide. It contains 46 percent nitrogen in a form that is quickly soluble, but it is not as quick in its action as nitrate of soda. As it is a highly concentrated form of nitrogen, urea must be used with care and discretion. When applied dry it should be mixed with sand, in order that an even distribution may be secured. It is usually applied at the rate of ½ lb. per 100 sq. ft. In the liquid form it is used at the rate of 1 oz. to 7 gallons of water.

Ammonium Phosphate

Obtainable in two forms—as mono-ammonium phosphate, which contains 10 percent nitrogen and 48 percent phosphoric acid; and as di-ammonium phosphate, which is more highly concentrated and contains 21 percent nitrogen and 53 percent phosphoric acid. The usual rate of application for ammonium phosphate varies from 1 lb. to 2 lb. per 100 sq. ft.

Cyanamid

Another synthetic product of fairly high concentration, being composed of calcium cyanamide and calcium hydroxide. Cyanamid contains from 20 to 25 percent of nitrogen and is highly alkaline in its reaction. The usual rate of application for cyanamid is approximately 1 lb. per 100 sq. ft.

Urea-form Fertilizers

A recent advance in the field of chemical fertilizers, and one that is a great boon to gardeners, is the development of a fertilizer that releases the nitrogen which it contains slowly, over a period of many months, and thereby entirely eliminates the danger of "burning." One of the greatest objections to the commercial chemical fertilizers used so widely in the past has been the danger of burning plant tissues. Many a lawn and many young plants in both the vegetable and flower garden have been injured in this way. Organic fertilizers have been preferred by many gardeners because there is considerably less danger of burning, although in the case of organic fertilizer a delayed nitrogen burn sometimes occurs a month or more after application.

The principal source of nitrogen in the urea-form fertilizers is a urea-formaldehyde compound that releases nitrogen slowly and will not cause burning, even under the most adverse conditions.

One of the great advantages of fertilizers of this type is that the nitrogen needs of a plant for the entire season may be supplied in a single application. This is a factor of considerable importance in the management of large areas of turf, and in fertilizing shrub plantings, flowerbeds and long-season vegetables. It is of less importance in the case of quickly maturing flower and vegetable crops.

In general, the organic forms of nitrogen are less highly concentrated than the inorganic forms and are more slowly available to the plants.

Cottonseed Meal

Contains approximately 7 percent of nitrogen, which becomes slowly available over a long period of time. It is more readily available in warm soils than in cold soils. The usual rate of application varies from 2 lb. to 5 lb. per 100 sq. ft. There is practically no danger of overstimulation of the plants or of burning when cottonseed meal is used, and in addition to nitrogen it supplies other elements of fertility in small amounts. The usual analysis is 7 percent nitrogen, 2 to 3 percent phosphorus, and 2 percent potash.

Castor Pomace

Very similar to cottonseed meal in general composition, castor pomace contains slightly less nitrogen. The nitrogen content usually averages about 5 percent and a somewhat heavier application is therefore made.

Dried Blood

An excellent organic source of nitrogen, containing from 9 to 14 percent. The nitrogen is in a form that is readily soluble and therefore quickly available to the plant. The usual rate of application varies from 2 lb. to 3 lb. per 100 sq. ft.

Phosphorus

Phosphorus is an essential element in all functions of plant growth and it is particularly associated with the production of fruits and seeds. It also induces good root development, contributes toward the formation of strong cell walls and, in general, hastens maturity. In addition, phosphorus helps to balance an overabundance of nitrogen in the soil. Phosphorus is fixed in the soil soon after it is applied and it does not leach out. As it does not travel in the soil, it must be absorbed by the plant at the point where it falls. There is practically no danger from excessive applications. The acidity of the soil determines to some extent the availability of phosphorus, it being more available in slightly acid soils than in definitely alkaline soils. The presence of ammonium sulphate increases its availability, while the presence of calcium carbonate, sodium nitrate and iron salts decreases it.

Superphosphate

The most commonly used source of phosphorus, superphosphate is obtainable in various grades — 16, 20, or 45 percent. It is the product that results from treating raw phosphate rock with sulphuric acid. The rate of application varies from 3 lb. to 10 lb. per 100 sq. ft., according to the needs of the soil.

When superphosphate is applied as a top-dressing, its penetration is very slow. It is wise, therefore, to work it thoroughly into the soil whenever possible, either by lightly forking it in or by cultivating it in with a hand weeder.

Basic Slag

A by-product in the manufacture of steel, basic slag is sometimes used as a source of phosphorus. It usually contains from 10 to 25 percent phosphoric acid and from 40 to 50 percent lime. The phosphorus in basic slag is practically all available, as it becomes water-soluble as soon as it is acted upon by carbon dioxide. The rate of application is approximately the same as for superphosphate.

Bone Meal

Raw bone meal is made from finely ground bone and contains from 3 to 4 percent nitrogen and from 20 to 25 percent phosphoric acid. Although the phosphorus content may seem high, it is held in a tricalcium form, and is very slowly available. The small percentage of nitrogen is quickly available but the phosphorus becomes available so slowly that, in many instances, the use of bone meal is of doubtful value. It is true that it is one of the safest and most foolproof fertilizers one can use — but unless it is applied many months before it is needed, the plants will derive practically no benefit from it. Steamed bone meal is even less valuable than raw bone meal as during the process of steaming some of the nitrogen is lost. The fineness of bone meal has a very direct effect upon its availability, and weather conditions also have some influence as, regardless of the time of year when it is applied, it seldom becomes available until warm weather. On the whole, when plants are in need of phosphorus, it is wiser to apply it in the form of superphosphate than in the form of bone meal.

Rock Phosphate

The material that is used in the manufacture of superphosphate. It usually contains from 66 to 80 percent calcium phosphate, but its availability is very low and its use is not recommended.

Potassium

Potassium is particularly valuable in promoting the general vigor of the plant, and it increases the resistance of the plant to certain diseases. Potassium also plays an important part in sturdy root formation. In general, it has a balancing influence upon other plant nutrients.

Potassium Chloride

One of the most commonly used sources of potash. Potassium chloride contains from 48 to 50 percent in a readily available form, as it is immediately soluble. The usual rate of application is 1 lb. to 100 sq. ft.

Muriate of Potash

Contains approximately 45 percent potash and is applied at the same rate.

Potassium Sulphate

Another inorganic source of potash, containing approximately 48 percent potash. It is readily soluble and therefore quickly available to the plant.

Wood Ashes

These are also a valuable source of potash although much less highly concentrated than the inorganic forms. Wood ashes vary tremendously in composition. Ash produced from hardwood trees, and that has not been leached by exposure to rain, often runs as high as 10 percent available potash, while wood ashes produced from softwood trees, or wood ashes that have been exposed to rain, may contain less than 2 percent potash. Wood ashes also run high in lime content, sometimes containing as much as 40 percent. The type of wood ashes most readily available on the market is a high-grade, unleached hardwood ash. Wood ashes are usually applied at the rate of 50 lb. to 75 lb. per 1,000 sq. ft.

The Trace Elements

The minor or trace elements of essential minerals are boron, copper, iron, manganese, molybdenum, sulphur and zinc.

The term "trace" refers not to the amount of the element in the soil but to the amount needed by the plant. Although these elements are needed only in infinitesimal amounts, they are of great importance, and may mean the difference between healthy and sickly, stunted growth. A number of plant diseases are caused by a lack of one or more of the trace elements. In certain crops spectacular increases in yield resulted where the required minerals were supplied to meet the needs of the plants.

Trace elements are usually present in most soils. However, some soils lack one or more of these important minerals, or if present they may be in a form unavailable to the plants. Some soils in Florida and in the Southwest were found to be deficient in certain elements. Remarkable improvement in the growth of oranges, pecans and other fruits and vegetables occurred when the needed trace element was supplied.

Many of the complete commercial fertilizers contain the trace elements that are most likely to be deficient in the soil. The manufacturers of high-analysis, quickly soluble fertilizers usually include them in their formulas.

Some organic fertilizers are a poor source of trace elements, while others are a very rich source. Only when the raw materials that are the components of an organic fertilizer contain the trace elements will they be present in the finished product. Thus a good organic fertilizer should contain a variety of organic materials. The best organic sources of trace elements are dried blood and fish emulsion, which contain the major and minor elements in highly soluble form.

The development of the chelating agents has made it possible to make certain trace elements, such as iron and zinc, more readily available to plants than has been possible heretofore. The word "chelate" (pronounced "key-late") is derived from the Greek word for claw, as the chelates may be likened to two claws that catch and hold metal ions.

The best program for the gardener to follow is to use either organic or inorganic fertilizers that contain the trace elements.

Complete Fertilizers

For general garden use, for lawns, for the vegetable and fruit garden, for the flower border and for trees and shrubs, an application of a well-balanced complete fertilizer is the most satisfactory method of supplying the needed plant nutrients. Such fertilizers are usually based on a ratio of 1 percent nitrogen, 2 percent phosphorus and 1 percent potash, or 1 percent nitrogen, 3 percent phosphorus and 1 percent potash, or any desired multiple of these ratios—such as 2-6-2, 4-12-4; 5-10-5, 15-30-15. Whenever the analysis of a complete commercial fertilizer is stated in this way, the first numeral denotes the percentage of *nitrogen,* the second numeral the percentage of *phosphorus* and the third numeral the percentage of *potash.* In addition to these three essential elements of fertility, which are always present in any "complete" fertilizer, there are also usually present some of the minor, or trace, elements that are needed in very small amounts, such as manganese, iron and sulphur. In preparing commercial fertilizers, most reliable firms make it a practicce to supply the required amount of nitrogen in two, sometimes three, forms: in a quickly available inorganic form; in a somewhat more slowly available form; and in a very slowly available organic form. Such a practice greatly increases the value of any fertilizer from the standpoint of the gardener, as it means that the nitrogen becomes available for the plant's use over a long period of time.

The time and rate of application of complete commercial fertilizers vary considerably with the individual requirements of the plant and the purpose of the application. The most approved fertilizer practices are discussed in detail in the various chapters on Lawns, Roses, Perennials, Greenhouse Gardening, and so on.

Soluble Fertilizers

The development of high-analysis, quickly soluble, complete fertilizers has solved many problems for the gardener, as they can be applied both to the soil and to the foliage without danger of harming plant tissues, provided they are used in proper concentration.

The quickly soluble fertilizers are water-soluble salts, to be dissolved in water before use. The concentrated solutions are uneconomical, because of the costs of packing and shipping large amounts of liquid. It is wiser to use the salts. Directions given on the package should be followed carefully.

Soluble fertilizers contain the same nutrient elements as do the standard complete fertilizers—nitrogen, phosphate and potash—and often in the same proportions, but usually in higher analysis. Some brands contain most of the trace elements and some also vitamins and hormones. This is an advantage if they are to be used for foliage feeding.

These high-analysis, soluble fertilizers can be used to advantage in many ways. They can be applied directly to the soil to promote the growth and vigor of house plants, flowering plants of all types, vegetables, ornamental trees and shrubs. Being in solution, the nutrients become almost immediately available to the plant. They can be applied as a spray to the foliage of the plant (see Foliar Feeding, page 561). They can be used as a pre-planting dip for seeds to quicken germination and promote a more vigorous growth of the young seedlings. They may be used as a dip for leafy, softwood cuttings to develop more vigorous plants. They may be used as a solution in which to soak bulbs and tubers, such as tulips and tuberous begonias, in order to increase their vigor and size of bloom. And they may be used very satisfactorily on small lawn areas. They are not practical on extensive areas of lawn unless application can be made by a commercial outfit that has the necessary equipment.

It has been found that when young seedlings or rooted cuttings are to be transplanted, or when older plants are to be moved from one location to another, they will suffer less of a setback if given an application of a high-analysis soluble fertilizer. In the case of young plants, best results will be obtained if the fertilizer is applied to the propagating bed, seedbed or flat in which the plants are growing, about three days before the time of transplanting. The benefits will be greater than if the application is made at the actual time of transplanting. In the case of purchased plants it is, of course, not possible to follow this procedure. When the application is made at the time of transplanting, one cup of the solution should be allowed for a small plant, two cups for a large plant. The solution should be poured around the plant before the hole has been completely filled.

These starter or booster solutions may be used to great advantage in the vegetable garden when setting out tomatoes, cabbage, cauliflower, broccoli, pepper and celery plants, and they are also very valuable when transplanting annuals, biennials and perennials in the flower garden.

High-analysis, soluble fertilizers are more expensive per unit of plant food than the standard complete fertilizers, but they more than justify the additional expense. They are easy to mix and apply; the danger of "burning" plant tissue is eliminated; they are procurable in small quantities; and there is no waste.

In handling these soluble fertilizers, a number of precautions should be taken. Soluble salts should not be stored in lightweight paper containers because the container will deteriorate. Glass mason jars with screw tops are excellent for long periods of storage. If a solution is to be kept over from one application to another, it should be stored in a glass or earthenware jug, *not* in a metal container.

After years of research the University of Wisconsin developed a method of feeding plants that was so revolutionary it was granted a patent by the U.S. Patent Office.

Highly concentrated fertilizer is packed in a very small plastic bag, which resists deterioration in the soil. The plastic is punctured with microscopic holes that allow water to seep in and dissolve some of the fertilizer. The dissolved fertilizer can only be forced out when enough water accumulates inside to create internal pressure.

By controlling the make-up of the fertilizer and the size of the holes in the plastic, a package will continue to supply plant food over a period of from three to five years, as the dissolved fertilizer is released at a rate equal to absorption by the plant. The packet acts as a reservoir, slowly releasing the nitrogen, phosphate and potash in correctly controlled proportions. When this method is used there is no danger of injury to tender roots, and it also means a great saving of time and labor.

This method is recommended for the feeding of established trees and for trees at time of planting, for roses at time of planting and for established beds, for potted plants and for perennials when feasible.

More recently, pelletized fertilizers that have the same basic effect have been developed, and are proving equally useful in the same applications.

When chelates are applied to the soil, the metal does not combine with other elements to form insoluble compounds but remains free to be taken up and used by the plants. On the other hand, when simple iron compounds are used, they often combine to make insoluble compounds and thus become unavailable to the plants. This explains why plants sometimes suffer from iron chlorosis or iron starvation when the soil actually contains sufficient iron for normal plant growth, and it also explains why additional applications of simple iron compounds on soils definitely deficient in iron often fail to correct the chlorotic condition. It is their ability to hold the iron in the form in which plants can readily use it that gives the chelates their great importance.

The symptoms of iron deficiency in plants are not difficult to detect. In mild cases the veins of the leaf appear to be a darker green than the areas between the veins. If the deficiency is pronounced, the areas between the veins gradually become a lighter green, then yellowish in appearance, and, finally, in a severe case of iron chlorosis, the foliage becomes a very pale ivory color. Unless the condition is corrected it will eventually cause the death of the plant.

Iron chelates are used extensively in citrus groves and in the great commercial flower- and vegetable-growing sections of California and Florida and many other areas. In some instances the effects of an application have been little short of miraculous. In one citrus grove the foliage on orange trees that were suffering from acute iron chlorosis became green again within six weeks and the vigor of the trees was entirely restored.

Iron chelates are also of great value to the home gardener for the treatment of ornamental plants that are suffering from iron starvation, and for use on orchard trees and vegetable crops.

Among ornamental plants suffering from iron chlorosis that have responded well to applications of the iron chelates are azalea, camellia, chrysanthemum, gardenia, gladiolus, hydrangea, magnolia, oak, the rhododendrons and the roses.

Iron chelates may be applied directly to the soil in either powder or liquid form, or may be dissolved in water and applied as a foliar spray. When applied to the soil in powder form, the powder should be spread evenly over the surdace of the soil beneath the plant at the recommended rate, and it should then be watered in thoroughly until the soil is moist to a depth of at least 6 in. It will be easier to obtain an even coverage if the powder is mixed with dry sand or fertilizer. The powder may, if desired, be dissolved in water and either sprayed onto the soil or applied with a watering can.

When a foliar spray is applied, it is important to make sure that all leaf surfaces are thoroughly covered. When foliar sprays are being applied to outdoor plants, there will be less danger of injury if the application is made during the middle third of the growing season. It is not advisable to apply foliage sprays to plants when they are in blossom or in fruit.

Products are also available consisting of small vials of trace elements that can be inserted directly into the xylem of large trees, by tapping them in with a hammer. The ease of application is a major consideration in choosing this method.

Foliar Feeding

Trees, shrubs, roses, many flowering plants and vegetables respond well to foliar feeding, and it is becoming a common practice among amateur gardeners as well as among professional gardeners.

Foliar feeding is of particular value in supplying trace elements where a deficiency exists, and often on cold, wet soils nitrogen and phosphorus can be made more readily available to the plant through foliar feeding than through application to the soil.

Through scientific research with radioisotopes it has been proved that at least one-half of the nitrogen in a good all-soluble, high-analysis fertilizer enters the leaf directly within a few hours after application, and that a reasonable percentage of the phosphorus and potassium is also absorbed in this way. In addition to these major elements (nitrogen, phosphorus and potash), many of the minor or trace elements such as iron, zinc, boron and manganese may also be applied in the form of foliage sprays.

In purchasing soluble fertilizers to be used for foliar feeding, it is wise to make sure that they contain these trace elements. In certain

soils there may be definite deficiency of some of the trace elements, whereas in other soils they may be present but unavailable to the plant, and one of the most satisfactory ways of supplying them is through foliar feeding.

Experiments have shown that "chelated" (organic) forms of some of these minor elements are very effective in overcoming deficiencies when applied as foliar sprays. Iron in the "chelate" form has proved very effective in controlling chlorosis of lawns, deciduous fruits and vegetables, and zinc in the "chelate" form is effective in controlling a number of conditions attributable to a deficiency of this element.

Some plants can absorb nutrients through their leaves more readily than others. Absorption normally takes place more readily through the lower surface to the leaves than through the upper surface. Where the leaves possess a heavily waxed surface, it has been found that the absorption of nutrients is usually very restricted or entirely inhibited.

There are many satisfactory types of applicators on the market suitable for applying liquid fertilizers as foliar sprays. It is important not to use too concentrated a solution, and the manufacturer's directions should be followed carefully.

Excellent results have been obtained from the foliar feeding of many types of plants. Greenhouse and indoor plants seem to respond particularly well. Orchids, anthuriums, philodendron, African violets, gloxinias, achimenes, streptocarpus, crotons, ferns and certain forms of cactus, such as the Christmas cactus, have shown excellent results. In some cases the increase in the health and vigor of the plants has been spectacular. At the Montreal Botanical Garden where young African violet plants that were yellowish and sickly in appearance were given a foliar feeding, the response was almost immediate. Within a few days the leaves had turned a dark green and the plants had a totally different appearance. The accepted practice in many greenhouses is to give two or three weekly feedings at first, followed by monthly feedings. Sometimes one or two feedings applied at a critical time in the life of a plant are all that is necessary.

Certain insecticides may be applied at the same time that foliar feedings are given, which means a considerable saving of labor.

It must be borne in mind that foliar feedings do not take the place of root feedings; they are definitely a supplementary feeding, but not a substitute.

SOIL TESTS

Since it is sometimes difficult to determine deficiencies that are not very obvious yet may be of considerable importance, it is well to have an occasional soil analysis made. Soil samples may be sent to any of the state Agriculture Experimental Stations for analysis.

Obtaining Soil Samples

The season when the sample is taken, the method of obtaining the sample and the preparation of the sample are all factors of importance in soil analysis.

Time of Sampling

The most reliable information concerning the need for fertilization and for the application of lime may be obtained from samples taken either in the early spring or in late fall. During the active growing season the nutrient level of the soil is affected to some extent by the growth of the plants that occupy the area. Heavy rainfalls also very definitely affect the nutrient level and low tests are frequently secured after periods of prolonged leaching. Nitrates and ammonia nitrogen are the most variable, as they are the elements most easily lost by leaching.

Method of Sampling

A trowel or spade may be used to make a V-shaped hole, 6 in. or 7 in. deep. Remove the loose dirt from the hole, then cut a thin, uniform slice off the straight side of the hole from top to bottom. If the sample is being taken from a lawn area, it should represent the zone of the feeding roots, which will vary from 3 in. to 6 in. If the area to be tested is of considerable size, or if it varies in texture to any marked degree, it will be necessary to obtain several samples. If there is a decided variance in the general character of the soil, one section being of a sandy texture and another having a more dense structure, the samples should be kept separate. If the soil is uniform in character, the samples may be mixed together, forming a composite sample.

Preparing the Sample

After the sample has been obtained, the soil should be spread out to dry on a clean sheet of paper. Care should be taken to prevent the soil from becoming contaminated with dust, fumes or chemicals of any kind.

After the soil has dried out thoroughly, it should be packed for shipment.

SOIL ACIDITY

The relative acidity or alkalinity of the soil is commonly expressed in terms of the symbol pH. The neutral point in the scale is 7. Soil testing below a pH 7 is acid; soil testing above pH 7 is alkaline.

The pH values are based on logarithms, 10 being the base. Therefore, a soil testing pH 5 is 10 times as acid as soil testing pH 6; while a soil testing pH 4 is 100 times as acid as soil testing pH 6. (In going either up or down the pH scale from the neutral point of pH 7, the value of the unit is 10 times greater than the next one approaching 7.)

Most herbaceous plants and the majority of our commonly grown trees and shrubs prefer a soil that is very nearly neutral in its reaction. A few plants seem to be entirely indifferent to soil conditions and will thrive equally well in soil with either a neutral, acid or alkaline reaction, while some plants definitely prefer a strongly acid soil and others a soil of pronounced alkalinity. In general garden practice, it is well to maintain a soil reaction as nearly neutral as possible, ranging between a pH 6 and a pH 7.

The reaction of the soil is not a stable factor, as there is a tendency for soils, except in very arid regions, to become slowly more and more acid. This is due to the fact that, with the gradual seepage of rainwater through the soil, elements such as calcium and sodium are dissolved more rapidly than the more strongly acid elements such as carbon and silicon.

Every gardener should know how to make

SOIL-TESTING SCALE

pH 9.5	intensely alkaline
pH 9.	strongly alkaline
pH 8.5	definitely alkaline
pH 8.	moderately alkaline
pH 7.7	slightly alkaline
pH 7.	neutral
pH 6.5	very slightly acid
pH 6.	slightly acid
pH 5.5	moderately acid
pH 5.	moderately acid
pH 4.5	definitely acid
pH 4.	strongly acid
pH 3.5	intensely acid

simple, rapid tests to determine the pH of the soil. There are now many excellent yet inexpensive soil-testing outfits on the market, and such a kit should be considered an essential part of one's equipment. Complete directions accompany each outfit and these should be followed precisely.

Increasing the Acidity of the Soil

It is a comparatively simple procedure either to increase the degree of acidity in the soil or to bring an acid soil to a more nearly neutral level.

Many woodland plants such as the azaleas, mountain laurel, the rhododendrons, trailing arbutus and the pink lady's slipper prefer a definitely acid soil. For such plants a pH ranging between 4.5 and 5.5 is desirable.

When such plants are to be grown, the soil should be tested; and if it does not fall within this range, measures should be taken to increase the acidity. This may be accomplished in a number of ways.

Method No. 1. The ideal method, and the one strongly recommended if the existing soil is fertile and of good texture, is to incorporate into the soil certain organic materials that will increase its acidity. The following materials may be used for this purpose:

Acid muck from swamps and stream banks
Oak leaf mold
Peat moss, of the coarse, *acid* type
Rotting bark and wood from old logs and stumps of hemlock or oak
Sawdust (partly rotted) from hemlock or oak trees
Sphagnum moss, finely ground.

After the organic materials have been worked thoroughly into the soil, another soil test should be made to determine whether the acidity has been brought to the desired level.

Method No. 2. Where the existing soil is of poor quality or where raised beds are to be used, it is advisable to prepare a special soil mixture that will provide the desired amount of humus and the correct degree of acidity. Such a mixture should contain at least 50 percent decayed organic matter. The following mixture is recommended: 50 percent coarse, acid peat, 25 percent rotted oak leaf mold, 25 percent sandy loam. If, after testing, this does not provide the desired degree of acidity, a small quantity of a chemical may be added according to the directions given in Method No. 3.

Method No. 3. There are a number of chemicals that may be applied to the soil to increase the acidity. Among the most satisfactory for this purpose are aluminum sulphate and sulphur. These may be used as a surface application, being spread evenly over the area and watered in thoroughly, or they may be mixed with the soil as the bed is being prepared.

The rate of application is given in the table on the next page.

A number of fertilizers such as ammonium sulphate, ammonium phosphate, cottonseed meal and urea, have an acid reaction and when applied to the soil over a period of years tend to increase its acidity. Therefore fertilizers of this type should be selected for use on plants that are known to thrive best in acid soils. Some fertilizer companies offer special mixtures suitable for such plants. Fertilizers that are known to be definitely alkaline in their reaction, such as nitrate of soda, calcium nitrate, Cyanamid, bone meal and wood ashes, should not be used on acid-loving plants.

TABLE FOR INCREASING SOIL ACIDITY

CHANGE FROM pH	SULPHUR, LB. PER 100 SQ. FT.	ALUMINUM SULPHATE; LB. PER 100 SQ. FT.
8.0 – 7.0	2.0	4.5
8.0 – 6.5	3.0	7.0
8.0 – 6.0	4.0	10.0
8.0 – 5.5	5.5	13.5
8.0 – 5.0	7.0	17.5
7.5 – 7.0	1.75	3.5
7.5 – 6.5	2.0	5.0
7.5 – 6.0	3.5	7.5
7.5 – 5.5	5.0	11.5
7.5 – 5.0	6.5	15.5
7.0 – 6.5	1.5	2.5
7.0 – 6.0	2.0	5.5
7.0 – 5.5	3.5	9.0
7.0 – 5.0	5.0	13.0
6.5 – 6.0	1.5	3.0
6.5 – 5.5	2.5	6.5
6.5 – 5.0	4.0	10.5
6.0 – 5.5	1.5	3.5
6.0 – 5.0	3.0	7.5
5.5 – 5.0	1.5	4.0

Source: A. Laurie and V. H. Reis, *Floriculture,* p. 374, 1942.

Lime

Lime serves several important functions. It is of particular value in correcting the acidity of the soil; in addition, it also changes the structure of the soil, hastens bacterial action in the soil, aids in the liberation of plant foods that would otherwise remain in the soil in unavailable form, hastens the decomposition of organic matter, and supplies a small amount of calcium, which is one of the essential plant foods.

Lime is usually applied either in the form of ground limestone or as hydrated lime. Hydrated lime is quicker in its action but not as lasting in its effect.

Lime should never be used in combination with animal manures or with nitrogenous fertilizers, as this causes the rapid release of ammonia.

When lime is applied, it should be spread over the surface of the ground and should then be thoroughly mixed with the upper few inches of soil. It should not be plowed or spaded deeply into the soil.

The rate of application depends entirely upon the forms in which the lime is applied, and the texture of the soil. The table opposite will serve as a general guide.

An excessive application of lime has a very injurious effect upon some plants, causing a condition known as lime-induced chlorosis. This is regarded as a physiological disease, and it is due directly to a deficiency of iron in the plant tissues. The symptoms are very marked in most plants, and are apt to appear on young growth in the early spring, although they may be noticed at almost any time during the growing season. The leaves present a characteristically mottled appearance, being either yellow or whitish in color. The mid-rib of the leaf and the veins remain a very dark green, and the mottling takes place in the areas between the veins.

Iron is absolutely essential for the production of chlorophyll, which is the green coloring matter of the leaf, and when iron is not present in sufficient quantities, the chlorophyll fails to develop. This deficiency of iron in the plant is very closely associated with the lime content of the soil, as the solubility of iron in the soil is dependent, to a large extent, upon the degree of soil acidity. Iron is readily soluble in a definitely acid soil, but as the pH of the soil approaches the neutral point, the iron becomes less and less soluble. In soils that are decidedly alkaline comparatively little iron, or, in extreme cases, no iron at all is available for the plant. Therefore the long-continued use, or excessive application of lime, bone meal, wood ashes and certain inorganic fertilizers tends to increase the alkalinity of the soil to a point where it is not favorable for certain forms of plant growth due to this precipitation of iron, which consequently becomes unavailable to the plant.

In general garden practice, it is well to maintain the soil at a pH slightly below the neutral point, and not to increase its alkalinity beyond a pH of 7.5, which seems to be the limit of safety for many plants. There are, of course, special plant groups that are definitely more acid- or alkaline-tolerant, and some that prefer a decidedly acid soil; but for the majority of garden plants a pH slightly below neutral is the safest.

If a condition of lime-induced chlorosis occurs, it may be corrected by the use of the iron chelates.

RATE OF APPLICATION OF LIME

(As it is not advisable to apply more than 50 lb. of hydrated lime or 75 lb. of ground limestone per 1,000 sq. ft. at any one time, it will be necessary to make several successive applications on strongly acid soils and raise the pH gradually. It is often detrimental to a plant's growth to make an excessively heavy application of lime at one time.)

	LIGHT SANDY SOIL				MEDIUM SANDY SOIL			
	HYDRATED LIME		GROUND LIMESTONE		HYDRATED LIME		GROUND LIMESTONE	
SOIL ACIDITY	*per 1,000 sq. ft.*	*per acre*	*per 1,000 sq. ft.*	*per acre*	*per 1,000 sq. ft.*	*per acre*	*per 1,000 sq. ft.*	*per acre*
pH 4.0	60 lb.	2610 lb.	90 lb.	3915 lb.	80 lb.	3480 lb.	120 lb.	5220 lb.
pH 4.5	55 lb.	2392 lb.	82 lb.	3567 lb.	75 lb.	3263 lb.	112 lb.	4872 lb.
pH 5.0	45 lb.	1957 lb.	67 lb.	2914 lb.	60 lb.	2610 lb.	90 lb.	3915 lb.
pH 5.5	35 lb.	1522 lb.	52 lb.	2262 lb.	45 lb.	1957 lb.	67 lb.	2914 lb.
pH 6.0	None	None	None	None	None	None	None	None

	LOAM AND SILT LOAM				CLAY LOAM			
	HYDRATED LIME		GROUND LIMESTONE		HYDRATED LIME		GROUND LIMESTONE	
SOIL ACIDITY	*per 1,000 sq. ft.*	*per acre*	*per 1,000 sq. ft.*	*per acre*	*per 1,000 sq. ft.*	*per acre*	*per 1,000 sq. ft.*	*per acre*
pH 4.0	115 lb.	5002 lb.	172 lb.	7482 lb.	145 lb.	6307 lb.	217 lb.	9439 lb.
pH 4.5	105 lb.	4567 lb.	157 lb.	6827 lb.	135 lb.	5872 lb.	202 lb.	8787 lb.
pH 5.0	85 lb.	3697 lb.	127 lb.	5524 lb.	100 lb.	4356 lb.	150 lb.	6525 lb.
pH 5.5	65 lb.	2827 lb.	97 lb.	4219 lb.	80 lb.	3480 lb.	120 lb.	5220 lb.
pH 6.0	None	None	None	None	None	None	None	None

NOTE: A light application of lime at the rate of 25 lb. per 1,000 sq. ft. has proved beneficial on certain soils, even though the soil has a pH value of 6.0.

SOIL CONDITIONERS

Soil conditioners are effective in improving the structure and physical condition of certain types of soil. They should not be used indiscriminately, as it is a waste of time and money to apply them to soils that will receive little or no benefit.

Calcium sulphate (gypsum) is a soil conditioner that displaces those elements, especially sodium, that make a soil sticky and hard to work. Applied at a rate of 9 oz. to 28 oz. per square yard, according to the clay in the soil, it results in better workability within several weeks.

The gardener must bear in mind that soil conditioners are not fertilizers and do not increase the nutrient content of the soil. Soil conditioners have been developed for the purpose of maintaining in porous and loose condition clay soils that are normally heavy and tight in structure. On such soils, which are difficult to handle and which present many problems, soil conditioners have proved of great value. Soils of a light, sandy nature and soils high in organic content show little benefit, and rarely justify the use of such conditioners.

Under tillage conditions, heavy clay soils have a tendency to become more and more compact and to provide poor conditions for plant growth. They contain little pore space and consequently have low air capacity, they lack the ability to absorb water readily, thus making the application of soluble fertilizers difficult, and they are extremely difficult to handle when the moisture content is high. They are thus problem soils.

If a soil conditioner put out by a reliable firm is used, and if the directions on the package are followed, such soils may be maintained in a crumbly and friable condition throughout the season. Water will percolate freely, there will be sufficient pore space for an adequate supply of oxygen for plant needs, and good response can be obtained from soluble fertilizers. A soil so conditioned can grow thrifty, vigorous plants.

Decaying organic matter is nature's soil conditioner, but such material is not always available to the gardener in sufficient quantity to be effective, and in such cases the chemical soil conditioners fill a long-felt need. One lb. of a synthetic soil conditioner is equivalent to several bushels of a natural soil conditioner in improving the structure of fine-particled clay soils. Chemical soil conditioners have several advantages over natural soil conditioners. Results will be obtained more quickly, as within a few days after the application of a synthetic conditioner the soil particles will be crumbly and mellow. Also, this improvement in the soil structure will last over a longer period than will be the case in the necessarily limited use of organic materials.

Soil conditioners can be incorporated into the soil most satisfactorily when the soil is nei-

ther too wet nor too dry. The surface of the soil should preferably be slightly dry, with moist soil just below the surface. The soil conditioner should be worked into the soil to a depth of 6 in., the soil being well pulverized during the process. The more thoroughly the chemical is mixed with the soil, the better the results. After the conditioner has been thoroughly incorporated into the soil, a moderate watering will speed up the chemical reaction. Best results will be obtained if seed sowing and transplanting are delayed for several days after application.

It is a simple matter to determine whether or not a certain soil will benefit from an application of a soil conditioner. The following test will give a reliable indication: Take a *small* handful of the soil; add four or five drops of water to the soil, using a medicine dropper; mix the soil and water together thoroughly until every tiny granule of soil crumbles; then roll the soil between the palms of your hands into the form of a cigarette. If the cigarette holds its shape, it is an indication that the structure of the soil will be greatly improved by an application of a soil conditioner. If the soil remains granular and cannot be formed into the shape of a cigarette, it is evident that a soil conditioner is not needed and that the soil will derive no benefit from its use. If a "weak cigarette" is formed, which flops over at the end when lifted, this indicates that the application of a soil conditioner will be of enough benefit to warrant its use.

When used on a large scale, soil conditioners are very expensive; but in preparing soil for house plants, seedbeds and coldframes, and in special limited areas in the garden and on small areas to be seeded to lawn grasses, great benefit will be derived from their use if the soil is a heavy clay one.

In the vegetable and cutting garden treatment may be limited to the actual rows or hills where the plants are to be grown.

31

The Control of Weeds and
Undesirable Plants

In the larger sense every tree, vine, shrub and herb is a weed if it grows in the wrong place or if its growth habits are such that more desirable plants are crowded out. One of the fundamental characteristics of most plants, whether they be weeds or not, is to extend their dominion, often at the expense of their neighbors.

In forest country the encroachment of seedling trees very quickly pushes the margins of the woodlands out into the fields, and a time-honored annual chore of the farmer in such regions is to cut back the young seedlings in order to maintain the meadows. In a well-balanced agriculture, however, many native weeds are held in check by the very completeness of the use of the land. The annual cutting of a hayfield will usually destroy seedling trees and weeds in their first season of growth, while the cultivation of crop fields eliminates many weeds in an early stage of growth and prevents them from maturing. Thus it is only along the fencerows and stone walls that separate the fields that seedling trees, shrubs and weeds survive and are a source of infestation of the farmer's fields. One of the few virtues of these weeds is that they serve a useful purpose by providing food and shelter for birds and wildlife.

But on land that has been left idle in that zone that seems to surround so many of our cities, where it is no longer profitable to farm yet where the time for real estate development is not yet ripe, the weeds and weedtrees often have a twenty-year head start on the ultimate

homeowner. By the time there is a demand for home sites in such areas, they have all too frequently already become jungles of honeysuckle, sumac, poison ivy, ailanthus and *Rosa multiflora,* and the new owner of the property is faced with serious problems. Even on well-established and carefully maintained home properties it is necessary to exert constant vigilance in order to prevent the introduction and encroachment of undesirable plants. Many gardeners and property owners alike have lived to regret the day they failed to realize the danger of permitting a few trailing runners of Japanese honeysuckle to form a pleasant mat of green beneath some trees, or to take immediate action against the small patch of poison ivy that had established itself along the fencerow at the far end of their property, or when they failed to dig out the lovely tawny daylilies that appeared in their flower border.

There are some trees and shrubs, such as the ailanthus and the sumacs, which, if left to their own devices, tend to form such rank jungles of growth that their eradication involves a costly program. Certain vines also can become devastatingly rampant if neglected, though if kept within bounds they are of great ornamental value. In this group we find akebia, wisteria and trumpet creeper.

There are also the ubiquitous, rank-growing perennials, such as the above-mentioned tawny daylily, the plume poppy and bouncing bet, which form vigorous colonies on the perimeter

567

of many cultivated areas and threaten to invade our gardens at the slightest opportunity. And there are still other plants which, quite frankly, are weeds — some of them comparatively harmless, others with dangerous potentialities. It is therefore important for every homeowner and gardener to know which trees and shrubs, which vines and herbaceous plants have a tendency to dominate and crowd out the more desirable plants, and which weeds are likely to become a serious menace. It is important, also, that everyone become familiar with the latest and most approved means of eradication or, at least, of a reasonable degree of control if an orderly economy of plants is to be maintained.

As people have become more aware of what constitutes natural plant communities, the concept of "weeds" has expanded to include plants that are alien to any given ecosystem. Thus Norway maples are considered weeds in a sugar maple grove in New England, and the black locust is a weed among the native oaks of Europe. That this concept is valid in a practical as well as a scientific sense is borne out by the fact that, once introduced, it is the alien organism that usually becomes rampant; in its new setting it frequently has no natural controls, and has not been restricted to a narrow niche through long evolutionary pressures. Indeed, the most common of our pernicious perennial weeds — Japanese honeysuckle, ailanthus, Kudzu vine and Japanese knotweed — are invasive aliens.

Even as the subject of weeds has become more controversial, so have the methods used for their control. Recent legislation has outlawed the casual use of the most widely used brushkillers, 2,4,5-T and silvex, for environmental reasons. Many other commonly used compounds may eventually meet the same fate. Thus, knowledge and timely awareness have become even more necessary tools in mankind's unrelenting and age-old battle with "weeds."

TREES THAT MAY BECOME WEEDS

Ailanthus (*Ailanthus altissima*)

The ailanthus, also known as the tree-of-heaven, was imported into this country from China, where it is greatly revered. No other tree is able to thrive under such adverse conditions and it is found growing in city yards and in alley where scarcely any other green thing could. Under favorable conditions it grows very rapidly, often, when young, making as much as 6 ft. of growth in a single season, and it attains an ultimate height of about 75 ft. Although ailanthus has definite value as a tree for city planting, it deserves no place in more open areas. It reseeds prolifically and the young seedlings soon grow into dense, junglelike thickets, often crowding out desirable native trees and other plant materials of superior quality. This already has happened in parts of New England, New York, Pennsylvania, California and in some other states where the ailanthus has thus "gone wild."

Measures of Control

Young seedling trees should either be cut down as soon as they appear, or they should be destroyed by spraying. Fortunately the wood of the ailanthus is soft and light and the task of cutting is therefore comparatively easy, but it is a task that should not be postponed. Ailanthus may also be controlled effectively by spraying with a brushkiller containing dicamba plus 2,4-D (see pages 579 – 80). The spray may be applied as a dormant spray during the winter months or during the summer. If sprouts from unkilled sections develop, they should be sprayed as soon as they are 1 ft. or 2 ft. high. The top of the stumps also should be sprayed immediately as soon as the trees have been cut down.

Sumac *Rhus* spp.

Both the staghorn sumac (*Rhus typhina*) and the smooth sumac (*Rhus glabra*) are weedtrees common in the eastern part of the United States. They are softwooded, quick-growing, shrublike trees, which form continuous thickets and rapidly convert open fields into veritable jungles. They spread both by adventitious sprouts from their shallow roots and by seeds, and often take over abandoned land by the acre. The sumacs are decorative in form, the foliage has brilliant autumn coloring, and the red-berried seed heads are strikingly handsome, but their weediness far outweighs their beauty and they should never be allowed to spread out of bounds.

Measures of Control

Merely cutting the plants down is not a satisfactory measure of control, as they spring up again the following year with a growth more dense than before. They can be eradicated by grubbing out the roots—a long, slow task. But the most effective means of control is a brushkiller containing dicamba plus 2,4-D. This may be applied either as a dormant spray during the winter or as a summer spray. One thorough application will usually result in the complete eradication of sumac. If subsequent growth occurs, a second application should be made.

Miscellaneous Weed Trees

In this group we have such trees as the wild cherry, the poplars, the hackberry and the mulberry, and some of the maples, birches and pines.

The wild cherries harbor tent caterpillars, which spread to orchard trees and to the flowering crabs; they should be eliminated from the home grounds, from roadsides and from hedgerows. A watchful eye with the axe constitutes one method of eradication. They may also be controlled by either summer or dormant spraying with dicamba plus 2,4-D.

In spite of their many fine qualities, some of the birches, poplars and pines occasionally may become weedtrees, as they reseed prolifically and have a tendency to spread into open land, thus reestablishing the forest. Therefore, if open fields are to be maintained, or if a cherished view or vista is to be kept clear of encroachment, it is imperative that these young seedling trees be systematically destroyed through the annual use of the axe, brushhook, chopping knife, mower or sprayer. All of these trees also may be successfully controlled by either summer or dormant spraying with one of the brushkillers containing dicamba plus 2,4-D.

The hackberry *(Celtis occidentalis)* and the mulberry, both *Morus alba* and *Morus rubra* may be considered weedtrees in almost any situation, and under most circumstances both should be completely eliminated. Small seedling trees may be readily cut down, or eradicated by spraying with a brushkiller as directed.

VINES WITH DANGEROUS POTENTIALITIES

Akebia *(Akebia quinata)*

Akebia is a stemmed, ornamental vine with attractive foliage that is often planted on fences, porches and pergolas. Unless care is taken to keep its growth within bounds, however, it is capable of spreading over the ground as a dense mat and of obtaining a stranglehold on all shrubs and trees in its path, eventually killing everything within its reach.

Measures of Control

Keep the vine strictly within bounds by judicious pruning. If it has been permitted to grow unchecked, it may be eradicated by spraying with one of the brushkillers containing dicamba plus 2,4-D.

Bittersweet *(Celastris scandens* and *Celastris chinensis)*

Although bittersweet is a perennial favorite because of its brilliant coloring and decorative fruit, it must be kept within bounds as it has a propensity to clamber over surrounding trees and shrubs and in time cause considerable damage. The native bittersweet, *C. scandens,* only bears flowers on the terminal branches, and therefore is not as invasive as the oriental species, although individual plants may need to be controlled on certain trees.

Measures of Control

Careful pruning will keep bittersweet under control, and where eradication is desired, it may either be cut down or sprayed with one of the brushkillers containing dicamba plus 2,4-D.

Dodder *(Cuscuta)*

Known also as love-vine, strangleweed and hellbind, euphemisms that speak for themselves, dodder is one of the few parasitic plants that invade the garden, and it can become a very insidious and destructive pest. It is a leafless, annual vine. After the seed has germinated, the slender orange tendrils reach out until they come into contact with some neighboring plant, and they then entwine themselves about the stem. Being a true parasite, tiny suckers arising along the stems pierce the stalk of the plant it contacts, and thenceforth the dodder draws its nourishment entirely from the host plant, completely losing its contact with the ground. The dodder plant has the appearance of a tangled mass of tiny, orange, threadlike suckers and tendrils. It produces no green foliage, but bears clusters of small white flowers. The seeds mature in August, at which time they drop to the ground and lie dormant during the winter, germinating the following spring. When allowed to go unchecked, dodder can become a very serious problem in the garden. It attacks annuals, perennials and vines indiscriminately, and once it has become established, is very difficult to eradicate completely.

Measures of Control

It is useless to attempt to disentangle the dodder plant from the plant it has attacked, as new growth will start again if the tiniest piece is left attached to the host plant. The only sure measure of control is ruthlessly to root up or cut down the entire host plant or such portion of the plant as has been attacked, and to discard it immediately. A preemergence herbicide, such as dacthal, applied to the soil before dodder seeds germinate, can give reasonable control in an area known to be infested and where no injury to ornamentals will result.

Japanese honeysuckle *(Lonicera japonica)*

About seventy-five years ago a new decorative climber was imported into this country that unfortunately was destined to become one of our most troublesome and devastatingly destructive weed-vines—the Japanese honeysuckle. Because of its attractive appearance and its fragrant blossom, it is still frequently planted by property owners who are completely unaware of the liability they are incurring. When this vine once gets out of bounds, it spreads rapidly under trees and in open, sunny areas as well, and it obtains a stranglehold on anything that comes within its reach. In some areas of the country it has destroyed many acres of young forest growth. It has smothered out large areas of cropland, and entire farms have even been abandoned because of its devastations.

Measures of Control

In the past Japanese honeysuckle has been one of the most difficult of all plants to control, once it gained headway; but the new brushkillers have proved very effective, and it can now be eradicated completely by spraying with dicamba plus 2, 4-D. The spray should be applied when the plants are in full leaf and are making active growth, June to September being the most favorable period. If the growth is dense, more than one application will be necessary. A vigorous and thorough program of spraying, followed by a careful checkup the following season, will be necessary if effective control is to be secured. Better than eradication, however, is prevention. Don't plant it—don't tolerate it on your property under any circumstances!

Kudzu vine *(Pueraria lobata)*

Introduced as an ornamental from China in 1885, this rapacious plant has become a vicious pest throughout the Southeast. It is extremely difficult to control. Brushkillers or even soil sterilants may be necessary.

Poison ivy *(Rhus toxicodendron)*

The tremendous increase in the spread of poison ivy during the past fifty years should be sufficient proof that we have been playing a losing contest with some of our weed enemies. Poison ivy is a vine native to the United States that is now found growing rampantly in disturbed woodland from New Hampshire southward to Virginia, and it is extending its habitat annually. In some woodlands which, twenty years ago, were a joy to explore for the wealth of wildflowers they contained, poison ivy has gradually established itself as a permanent ground cover and has completely overwhelmed the lovely native azaleas and viburnums, the ferns and the wild flowers. It has become a serious economic pest in many an orchard and its rampant growth along roadsides and hedgerows spoils the enjoyment of the countryside for those who are susceptible to it—and very few people are immune.

In areas where poison ivy is only starting its invasion, prompt action on the part of the property owners may avert disaster. Here the rule should be: Don't let it become established! In sections where it has already become rampant, a united effort should be made on the part of the entire community to eradicate it.

Although this plant has a deservedly bad reputation and cannot be tolerated in areas frequented by people, it nevertheless has beautiful fall coloration and is valued as a wildlife plant. Human responses toward it should take these factors into consideration.

Measures of Control

If poison ivy spread only by extending its runners over the surface of the ground, its control would be relatively simple, as these ground trailers seldom bear fruit. But once it has attained height by attaching itself to a fence post, a tree or the wall of a building, it blooms and sets seed. Birds carry the seeds to new locations and its spread thus becomes much more rapid. So, wherever poison ivy has started to ascend trees or posts or walls, its stems should be cut with an axe or pruning saw if it is inadvisable to spray it because of the possibility of injury to the host plant or to nearby plants. Needless to say, this should be done by someone who is not susceptible. Otherwise a curved pruning saw blade may be attached to a long pole, thus enabling the worker to stand at a considerable distance while cutting the stems.

In the past, the eradication of large areas of poison ivy was an almost impossible task, but some of the chemical and hormone sprays now available have proved remarkably effective, and

today it is a relatively easy matter to eliminate it completely.

The following sprays have proved effective controls:

Amitrole (see page 578): Available as amitrole, Amitrole T, Aminotriazole or Cytrol. This is one of the most effective controls for poison ivy. One application will usually result in complete eradication. Application may be made at any time after the leaves have become fully expanded until they begin to change color in the autumn. Early spring and dormant applications are not advisable. A fairly coarse spray is preferable to a fine, mistlike spray, and the application should be made on a day when there is little wind in order to avoid the danger of having the spray drift onto other plants that might prove sensitive to it.

It is not necessary to contact all the leaves on the poison ivy vine in order for the spray to be effective. Those leaves that are easily accessible should be painted or sprayed with amitrole, and this is usually sufficient. Be sure that no spray touches the leaves of desirable plants, however.

Although some trees may be somewhat resistant to amitrole (see list on page 578), it should be kept off the foliage of all desirable plants. It is not absorbed through corky bark. It is illegal to use amitrole on land that will be planted to food crops.

AMS, ammonium sulfamate (see page 577): Available as Ammate X or Ammate X-Nl.

Now that poison ivy may be so effectively eradicated by use of sprays, entire communities are undertaking to rid themselves of this scourge. Roadside spraying is being done on an extensive scale in many parts of the country, and in some areas spraying is being done for individual property owners on a custom basis.

Wisteria

Although one of the most beautiful of all vines, wisteria can become a rampant weed-vine if allowed to get out of bounds. Its capacity to reach ever higher and to wrestle with anything with which it comes into contact and to pull it from its fastenings makes it a bad neighbor for shutters, downspouts, gutters and shingles. Another unfortunate characteristic of wisteria is its habit of spreading by long, trailing runners on the surface of the ground, from which it sends down roots at intervals and forms new plants. Thus, if left unchecked, wisteria can take possession of a large area very rapidly and can completely crowd out all existing growth. There is a tragic example of exactly this situation near an old, deserted house in the South where a single wisteria vine has spread out in every direction until its rampant, unrestrained growth now covers an area of more than an acre, forming an almost impenetrable jungle.

Measures of Control

The pruning saw and pruning shears are the most important tools for keeping wisteria in check, and a vine should never be allowed to get out of control.

When young plants spring up from runners, they may be controlled by spraying with a brushkiller containing dicamba plus 2,4-D. Wisteria is fairly resistant to sprays of this type, however, so that several applications may be necessary.

SHRUBS WITH UNDESIRABLE CHARACTERISTICS

There are some shrubs that seem to possess an unquenchable spirit for conquest and that will quickly encroach upon more desirable plantings if given the least opportunity. And there are other shrubs that are so weedy in character they do not deserve a place in any well-designed planting scheme. In these two groups we find, among others, matrimony vine, the ubiquitous knotweed, coralberry and St. John's wort.

Matrimony vine (Lycium halimifolium)

Matrimony vine is a shrub with slender, drooping branches, useful as a ground cover on eroded banks, but it should never be used in a shrubbery border or in plantings about the house. It spreads rapidly from underground suckers and in a comparatively short time will completely take over quite an extensive area. It is difficult to eradicate by cutting down or grubbing out, as young suckers will almost invariably appear and it will soon reestablish itself. It is, however, extremely sensitive to sprays containing dicamba plus 2,4-D and may be completely killed by one application.

Elaeagnus (Elaeagnus umbellata)

This shrub, closely related to Russian olive (E. angustifolia), has been planted as a highway divider screen in some areas of the United States and serves its purpose very well. It is dense and tolerant of air pollution, highway salt and other factors. Unfortunately, it flowers and fruits profusely, and while this is a happy situation for birds, the result is that the seeds are carried long distances and germinate readily wherever dropped. The plant, therefore, has the potential of becoming a widespread nuisance.

To get rid of elaeagnus, cut the trunks to the ground and paint the remaining stubs with 2,4-D.

Multiflora rose (Rosa multiflora)

This shrubby rose was introduced into the United States for use on farms for hedgerows to provide dense barriers, reduce wind erosion of tilled fields and provide wind protection for crops while at the same time creating shelter for birds and small animals. It was loudly touted as "living fence" and much sold by mail-order retailers.

As long as farm fields were tilled, grazed, or mowed, there was no problem with this rose; it stayed in its place. But since so much farmland has been abandoned, multiflora rose has self-sown to the extent of forming impenetrable thickets in once open fields. This is an excellent example of a plant being useful, but of not understanding the restrictions necessary to keep it so. This rose, escaped from the hedgerow, has now become a serious weed pest in some areas of the United States.

Remove established plants by cutting to the ground, and paint the remaining stubs with 2,4-D.

St. John's wort *(Hypericum aureum)*

A shrub that grows up to 3 ft. tall, St. John's wort is not only of a weedy nature but also possesses the unfortunate characteristics of reseeding so prolifically that young plants spring up all over the place, making it a doubly undesirable resident on one's property. The coralberry *(Symphoricarpus vulgaris)* spreads rapidly also, and homeowners should be alert to the first sign of either of these shrubs, so that they can be kept within bounds.

PERENNIALS WITH AGGRESSIVE TENDENCIES

There are a number of perennial plants that tend to spread rapidly and have the potential to become serious pests in lawns. This occurs when they escape from the confines of the garden itself, or from nearby woodlands and less well-cultivated areas. And there are other undesirable perennial plants that are sometimes unwittingly brought into the garden, the owner being entirely unaware of their aggressive characteristics. In some instances, such plants appear suddenly as voluntary invaders in the garden, and unless immediate steps are taken to eliminate them they will soon gain such headway that the more *desirable plantings* will be overwhelmed and crowded out. Some of these perennials such as the plume poppy *(Macleaya cordata)*, reseed so prolifically that they very soon become unwanted on one's property unless all the flower stalks are cut off before the seed has matured. The piquant and dainty little English daisy can also become a source of annoyance in lawns unless the flower heads are cut off before the seeds have formed and ripened. It is particularly important to do this because they hold a very strategic position, since these daisies are always used as edging plants along the front of beds or borders, and are thus in close proximity to areas of turf in the garden. The only practical control for such aggressive

and unwelcome perennials is spraying when in active growth with a low rate of dicamba (Banvel D) (see page 580).

Other plants, such as false dragonhead *(Physostegia virginiana)*, send their long, underground shoots out in every direction and in an incredibly short time will completely take over large areas in the garden at the expense of less aggressive plants. When a plant such as the tawny daylily *(Hemerocallis fulva)* has once gained a roothold in the flower garden, it seems ruthless in its determination to take command. To eradicate it, every particle of the root must be dug out, as the plant will grow again if even a small portion is left in the ground.

Japanese bamboo *(Polygonum cuspidatum)*

This is an extremely invasive weed, which grows into dense, nearly impenetrable masses 7 ft. to 8 ft. tall, and so completely dominates areas where it grows that few other plants, with the exception of established trees, can compete with it. Its stoloniferous growth habit (spreading by underground stems) makes it very difficult to keep in place.

The common name, Japanese bamboo, is misleading because this plant is in the same family as knotweed, buckwheat and rhubarb. The true bamboos *(Bambusa* spp.) belong to the grass family. The stems of *Polygonum* have conspicuous nodes in the manner of bamboo, but it is a herbaceous perennial, whereas bamboo is a woody perennial.

Polygonum resists weedkillers (herbicides). One called Roundup (trade name) will kill the plant only if it is applied when the plants are in bloom. Roundup is not available to homeowners and can be used only by a licensed individual, so professional service is needed. If there is a small colony of the plants, persistent and continual hand digging may be an alternative. Be aware, however, that the roots penetrate downward several feet and even small pieces left remaining in the soil will resprout.

Japanese knotweed *(Polygonum seiboldii)*

This is a rank perennial, also known as Japanese bamboo, that spreads rapidly from deep roots, throwing up stems 5 ft. to 7 ft. tall. It is very persistent and difficult to eradicate. Because of the extremely rank character of its growth, it will quickly crowd out everything in its path and eventually form an expensive thicket. It is the better part of wisdom never to permit it to become established on one's property.

Japanese knotweed is an extremely difficult weed to control. Where there are no desirable trees, repeated applications of dicamba (Banvel D) will bring it under control. A very effective treatment and one that is safe for tree roots but not for grass is the use in noncrop areas of glyphosate (Roundup) by professional applicators.

Since the eradication of these undesirable perennials is such a laborious undertaking, the wise gardener takes the trouble to find out in the first place which plants possess dangerous or unpleasant potentialities; then, should they inadvertently appear, undertakes immediate measures of control. It cannot be overemphasized that an informed mind, eternal vigilance and prompt action will bring their rewards.

Listed below are some of the worst offenders among herbaceous plants:

SCIENTIFIC NAME	COMMON NAME
Ajuga genevensis	bugle
Apios americana	wild bean
Bellis perennis	English daisy
Bocconia cordata	plum poppy
Campanula rapunculoides	grandmother's bluebells
Coronilla varia	
Hemerocallis fulva	tawny daylily
Physalis alkekengi	Chinese lantern
Physostegia virginiana	false dragonhead
Plumbago larpentae	leadwort
Saponaria officinalis	bouncing bet
Sedum sarmentosum	stringy stonecrop

WEEDS THAT REALLY ARE WEEDS

There are many plants that really are weeds and do not masquerade as decorative vines or handsome shrubs, or ingratiate themselves by producing such attractive flowers that they thus gain admittance to one's garden. Among these weeds some are comparatively innocuous and easy to control. In this group we find such weeds as common lamb's quarters, Pennsylvania smartweed, Indian mallow, common chickweed, rough pigweed, common purslane, common ragweed and many other annual weeds that may be readily controlled by ordinary cultivation. There are other weeds, however, that present a very different problem—weeds that are capable of becoming a persistent menace in the flower bed, vegetable garden or orchard. It is important to know which weeds are in this class and to be able to recognize these perennials and biennials when they first appear so that immediate control measures can be taken. It is often a comparatively simple matter to eradicate such weeds in the very beginning, but this becomes increasingly difficult to do after they are once established and have begun to spread. The worst offenders in this group are bindweed, Canada thistle, Johnson grass, the palmetto, prickly pear cactus and quack grass.

Field bindweed *(Convolvulus arvensis)* and hedge bindweed *(Convolvulus sepium)*

Both these bindweeds are unbelievably prolific and insidious weeds and have been among the most difficult of all to control. In some parts of the country these two types of weeds have become so rampant that vast areas of agricultural land have had to be abandoned because of them. Their habit of obtaining a stranglehold on all plants with which they come into contact makes them a most serious menace in garden and crop field, and immediate measures of control should be undertaken as soon as they appear, as they spread very rapidly from slender tuberous roots.

Measures of Control

Spray with 2,4-D amine. As bindweed is somewhat tolerant of sprays of this type, more than one application may be necessary. The most favorable time to make the first application is when the plants are just coming into bloom, although reasonably good results may be obtained at other times if the plants are making vigorous growth. Poor results are usually obtained from spraying during the hot, dry summer months when plants are making but little growth.

Canada Thistle *(Circium arvuse)*

The Canada thistle is one of the most pernicious of all weeds, and legal measures have been taken in many states to prevent its spread. The roots are tough and deep, and as they spread out in every direction from the parent plant, new shoots are formed at frequent intervals. Within the space of a single season a few plants will develop into an extensive patch. When once firmly entrenched, Canada thistles are capable of crowding out most other plants. Many a gardener and farmer has lived to rue the day when he failed to take prompt action against this invader, which can become such a very serious menace in the garden, in the orchard and on farm fields.

Measures of Control

1. Small patches may be smothered out (see page 576).
2. Spray with amitrole. This herbicide is an excellent control for Canada thistle. For best results it should be applied to young growth in the spring when the plants are between 6 in. and 15 in. high. Results are not good if spraying is done after the plants have reached the bud or bloom stage. Good coverage with the spray is essential. Plants should not be mown or otherwise cut down after treatment. About three weeks after application of the spray the plants should be plowed or deeply spaded under. Amitrole cannot be used on land to be planted with food crops.
3. Spray with 2,4-D (see page 579). As Canada thistles are somewhat resistant to sprays of this type, more than one application is usually necessary. The first application should be made when the plants are in the bud stage. Following this initial application a careful watch should be kept, as new shoots appear they should be sprayed while still in the rosette stage, being at this time between 4 in. and 6 in. in height.

Johnson grass

In some sections of the country Johnson grass is a serious pest, in fact, the most troublesome of any of the perennial grasses. It is a deeply rooted grass and spreads very rapidly.

Prior to the introduction of some of the new chemicals, it had been extremely difficult to control.

Measures of Control

1. Small patches may be smothered out.
2. Spray with dalapon (see page 579). Application should be made in the spring when the grass is well developed and making active, fast growth. Good coverage is essential. A second application may be necessary.
3. For turf renovation, professional applicators can expect very good control with glyphosate (Roundup).

Quack grass

This is one of the perennial grasses that has become a serious weed in many parts of the country. It spreads very rapidly, as the long, underground stems trail along for great distances just below the surface of the ground and root at every joint.

Measures of Control

1. Small patches may be smothered out.
2. Spray with amitrole. Application should be made in the spring when the grass is 4 in. to 6 in. high. When the grass shows a whitish color, usually about two weeks after treatment, it should be plowed or spaded deeply under so that all the treated grass is completely covered. (Amitrole cannot be used on land to be planted with food crops.)
3. Spray with dalapon. Application should be made in the spring when the grass is in full leaf and is making fast, active growth. Good coverage is essential. A second treatment may be necessary if a complete kill is not secured with the first application.
4. In noncrop areas or for turf renovation, professional applicators can spray with glyphosate (Roundup), and plow or spade over three days later.

EFFECTIVE MEASURES OF WEED CONTROL

In general, the most effective measures of control for weeds and other undesirable plants include cultivation, smothering by means of an effective mulch, and control or possibly even complete eradication by use of chemical spray or granular treatments.

Cultivation

Many annual weeds in the flower garden, the vegetable garden and the orchard, as well as some perennial weeds, may be controlled very satisfactorily by good cultivation. It is, of course, the age-old method of weed control and will probably continue to be used by gardeners throughout the world for centuries to come. It is the method most frequently used for the control of weeds in the flower garden, where other methods, such as the use of chemical sprays and granulars, are not feasible. In this connection it should be pointed out that the use of deep mulches is rapidly replacing cultivation in vegetable gardens, and to some extent this is becoming an accepted form of weed control in flower gardens also.

Cultivation should be timely and thorough. In normal seasons a good cultivation every ten days or two weeks will keep most weeds under control, although in very rainy seasons more frequent cultivations may be necessary. The soil should never be stirred with a cultivator when it is too wet, as this will tend to injure the structure of the soil, making it lumpy and cloddy. This is particularly true when one is working with heavy loam or clay soils. A good test to determine whether the soil is dry enough for cultivation is to pick up a handful of earth and squeeze it tightly in the palm of the hand. If, when it is dropped, it breaks up into a crumbly mass it is a sign that it is sufficiently dry for cultivation. But if the soil remains in a solid lump, it is evident that it is too moist to work with.

Mulches

There are various materials that may be used very satisfactorily for mulches (see Chapter 8).

The application of a mulch has become an increasingly popular practice among gardeners within recent years, and mulches have proved

their value in the flower garden, the vegetable garden and the orchard. In addition to being a very effective method of controlling weeds, a mulch also helps not only to conserve the soil's moisture but also to maintain a more even soil temperature. These cooler summer soil temperatures create generally more favorable growing conditions for the plants.

On small areas where weedy grasses spring up so readily from bits of trailing roots and stems, one of the most effective methods of eradication is to smother all growth with a very heavy, impervious mulch. Boards, building paper or even heavy layers of newspapers may be used. At the end of several weeks, both the roots and tops of the weeds will be dead, provided that all light and air have been excluded. Small patches of Canada thistle, bindweed and other weeds of this type may also be eradicated in this way.

Herbicides

Chemicals that can be used to kill weeds are called herbicides. Diesel oil and AMS work by direct contact, killing only that part of the plant that is treated with the herbicide; repeat treatments are usually necessary to control perennial weeds. There is very limited residual action. Systemic herbicides are usually absorbed by the foliage, and sometimes by the stems and roots. These herbicides move through the plant by a method called translocation, and they adversely affect the plant internally, frequently causing its death.

Some chemicals applied to the soil prevent seed germination: these are known as pre-emergence herbicides. Most herbicides are absorbed through the foliage, but some can be picked up by the roots or even through green bark. Also of great importance is the persistence of the preemergence herbicide in the soil, which determines how long it will be effective. A crop cannot be safely planted until after the herbicide residue has degraded and become neutral or inert.

Herbicides can be applied either as sprays or as granules. Formulations vary in degrees of concentration. Always read the label very carefully for exact amounts to use and methods of application.

CHEMICAL SPRAYS

The United States Department of Agriculture, the State Experimental Stations and many large commercial concerns have carried out extensive experiments in an effort to discover and develop effective measures of weed control through the use of chemical and hormone sprays, and remarkable advances have been made. In fact, so great has been the progress in these fields that large-scale agricultural operations have practically been revolutionized in many areas of the country. It is now possible to eradicate, or least bring under reasonable control, weeds occurring along roadsides, in crop fields, in gardens and in orchards, while heretofore it had seemed useless even to make an attempt to do so, because measures of control were so limited.

AMS (ammonium sulfamate, Ammate X)

This chemical weedkiller is nonpoisonous to people and to animals, and has no lasting ill effects upon the soil. It is effective against certain types of weeds and against many woody plants, such as blackberry and other brambles, green brier, hickory, poison ivy, poison oak, the sumacs and the willows. As there is less danger of drifting than with certain other types of sprays, it is particularly useful as a control for underbrush and for weeds in orchards. One disadvantage of ammonium sulfamate, however, is that it will injure grasses, and care must therefore be taken when it is used. The directions on the container concerning rate and method of application should be followed with the utmost care.

Borates

Borates are effective weedkillers in areas where complete soil sterilization is not a detriment. They render the soil toxic to all plant growth for a number of years, and are therefore of particular value for use on such areas as tennis courts and driveways. Borates should be applied in powder form at the rate of 3 lb. to 4 lb. per square yard (16 ft. by 16 ft.).

SYSTEMIC SPRAYS

One of the most revolutionary advances in the field of weed control has been the development of organic compounds that act as systemic, hormone-type weedkillers. These chemicals are absorbed by the foliage, and sometimes by stems and roots. Very small amounts of systemic sprays moved through the plant cause internal changes that can kill the plant. Examples are 2,4-D, 2,4,5-T, silvex, dicamba, amitrole and glyphosate. Of these, 2,4,5-T and silvex have been withdrawn from commerce for environmental reasons. 2,4-D when combined with picloramis is illegal in certain states.

Some of these systemic sprays act as growth-regulating substances, which kill a plant either by upsetting its balance of growth so completely that it is no longer adapted to its environment, or by exciting it into such activity that it literally grows itself to death. In some cases the leaves become distorted in shape; in other cases development is arrested and flowers do not open. The parts of the plant below ground become enlarged and then split open, causing the plant to die soon afterwards. Other hormone-type sprays affect the formation of chlorophyll within the plant.

These systemic sprays can be selective by affecting some plants and not others. In general, most broad-leaved weeds are sensitive to the phenoxy type, such as 2,4-D, while many narrow-leaved plants, especially grasses, are markedly resistant to such sprays. Because small amounts of these systemic herbicides can kill plants, they should be applied with low pressure and a coarse spray to avoid the danger of droplets drifting onto nearby desirable plants. Spray on calm days only to minimize such drift.[1]

Although 2,4-D is not very long-lasting in the soil, dicamba is both persistent and soluble. Because it can wash down to the roots of trees and readily be absorbed by the tree, it can cause serious damage. A combination of dicamba plus 2,4-D has been more effective than any systemic spray when used alone.

Precautions

When using any of the still-legal phenoxy-type sprays, certain precautions should be observed. It must be borne in mind that most broad-leaved plants are susceptible and the spray should not be allowed to drift onto nearby vegetation lest severe damage be done. A sprayer once used for the application of a hormone spray should never be used for any other purpose. It is extremely difficult to eliminate all traces of the mixture, no matter how carefully the sprayer is cleaned. There have been instances where serious damage has resulted. Be sure to consult your state extension service about current regulations governing herbicide use in your area.

Amitrole

This systemic spray is manufactured under such trade names as Amitrole T, Aminotriazole, Cytrol, Amizol and Weedazol. It has proved particularly effective against many stubborn plants by affecting the formation of chlorophyll, thus interfering with the normal growth of the plant. Since chlorophyll is basic to the manufacture of food within the plant, amitrole possesses outstanding qualities of translocation and has proved superior to some of the phenoxy-type sprays in controlling certain plants. It is most effective if applied when the plants are in active growth and after they are well leafed out, and it may be used effectively up to within a few weeks of frost. Early spring and dormant applications are not advisable. One application is usually sufficient for complete eradication, but under some conditions a follow-up treatment may be necessary.

Aminotriazole has many advantages as a herbicide. It does not volatilize and form vapors that might prove harmful to sensitive plants. It dissolves readily in water and is easy to apply; it

WEEDY PLANTS THAT ARE SENSITIVE TO AMITROLE

Bermuda grass	quack grass
buck brush	Russian knapweed
Canada and sow thistles	poison ivy
cattails and tules	poison oak
horsetail rush	prickly ash
leafy spurge	white ash
nut grass (sedges)	white, scrub and red oak

PLANTS THAT MAY SHOW SOME RESISTANCE TO AMITROLE

(At rates required for ordinary control)

apple	rhododendron
creeping myrtle	sassafras
dogwood	smooth sumac
English ivy	spice bush
Japanese honeysuckle	viburnum
lilacs	Virginia creeper
pachysandra	walnut
red maple	wild grape

is nontoxic to humans and animals; it is not a fire hazard; and it is not corrosive to spray equipment. It is readily inactivated in heavy soils and does not build up a toxic residue if it is used at the prescribed rates. Nevertheless, because of possible harmful effects it is illegal to use Aminotriazole on land that will be later used for food crops. Therefore, it is obvious that this (and any herbicide) is a last resort, not a preferred control measure.

As Aminotriazole is a comparatively nonselective weedkiller, precautions must be taken in its use. However, unless plants that are sensitive to it come into direct contact with the spray there is no danger of permanent damage. If a small amount of spray drifts onto evergreens or deciduous trees or shrubs, the leaves may turn white. The new growth of grass may also turn white but will resume its normal color within a few weeks unless too much was sprayed on the foliage, in which case the plant could be killed.

Dalapon

Dalapon is a systemic herbicide that is very effective in the control of weedy grasses such as Bermuda grass, Johnson grass and quack grass. It is readily translocated within the plant and causes a gradual yellowing of the leaves. It induces a dormancy of the crown and rhizome buds; if used at prescribed rates, the dormant buds fail to develop and a high percentage of kill results.

It should be applied when the grasses are in full leaf and are making active, fast growth. Good coverage is essential in order to provide for sufficient absorption by the plant.

In using dalapon, certain precautions should be taken. Direct contact with the skin should be avoided as it may cause irritation. All spraying equipment should be flushed out after use and before storage.

2,4-D

The scientific name of this hormone spray is 2,4 dichlorophenoxyacetic acid, which, for common usage, has been shortened to 2,4-D. It was one of the first organic sprays to be developed and it is widely used as a weedkiller. 2,4-D is an effective control for most of the broad-leaved lawn weeds, such as buckhorn plantain, broad-leaved plantain, dandelion and lawn pennywort. It is also used extensively to control such weeds as mustard and yellow rocket when they become troublesome in grain fields. It is a selective weedkiller, as it has the ability to kill many weeds that are troublesome on lawns and in grain fields without injuring the lawn grasses or the grain crop itself. It is not very effective as a control for the common chickweed clover and prostrate knotweed.

Among the other advantages of 2,4-D are the facts that it is nontoxic to people and to animals, it is noninflammable, and it has only a very temporary effect upon the soil, which is soon dissipated after a few good rains. However, seeds should not be planted immediately in soil that has been sprayed with 2,4-D. It has been found that 2,4-D is less effective when used during periods of excessive rainfall or prolonged drought than it is when used under more normal conditions. Additional applications may be necessary when used under these less favorable weather conditions.

Extensive experiments have shown that the ester form of hormone spray is the most effective. This has been found to be particularly true when stubborn plants are to be eradicated. However, it has one serious drawback: it is a volatile substance, which can be picked up by wind drift and carried to surrounding vegetation.

Though the weedkillers 2,4,5-T and silvex (2,4,5-TP) seemed to represent a distinct advance in weed control measures, and for a number of years were widely used on home properties, in park areas and for roadside spraying, neither is any longer considered desirable for use around dwellings, and dicamba is suggested as a suitable replacement. It is effective against a wide range of woody plants, and is among the best means of eradicating poison ivy and Japanese honeysuckle. It is also effective in killing tree stumps and preventing resprouting. In addition, dicamba: (1) will kill weeds and woody plants without harming grasses; (2) is nonpoisonous to human beings and to animals; (3) does not cause a fire hazard and is noncorrosive to spray equipment; and (4) may be mixed with water for high-volume spraying, or with oil for low-pressure spraying.

Best results will be obtained if the plants are in full leaf at the time that the application is made. In most cases the results have been obtained when the spraying was done between midsummer and early autumn. Complete coverage of the foliage is necessary. When areas of brush are being sprayed, the size of the bushes or saplings is very important. Spraying should not be attempted on brush that is over 6 ft. in height. If the brush exceeds this height, it is advisable to cut it back and then to spray the stubble with silvex plus 2,4-D mixed with oil. This may be done at any time of the year, either during the growing season or during the winter when the plants are dormant. The tops and sides of the stumps should be sprayed thoroughly. This same treatment may be accorded the stumps of trees that have been cut down. A single application will usually reduce resprouting as much as 75 percent, although a few stumps may require a second application. Stumps also can be treated at any time throughout the year.

Usually 2,4-D is applied as a spray using low-volatile ester forms for easy leaf penetration and to reduce the likelihood of damage to nearby sensitive plants. The amine forms are not volatile but they penetrate foliage more slowly and are more easily washed from the leaves by rain before sufficient 2,4-D has penetrated the leaf. 2,4-D can also be applied to turf in the granular form.

Silvex or 2,4,5-TP (Kuron)

Similar to 2,4,5-T in action, but at one time more readily available to homeowners as a common clover and chickweed killer. When mixed with 2,4-D, it also is a very effective killer of trees and shrubs. However, for environmental reasons silvex has been withdrawn from commerce.

Dicamba (Banvel D)

This is not a phenoxy but a benzoic, similar in its action. It will control many broad-leaved weeds that are not controlled by 2,4-D, especially prostrate knotweed in lawns. It is commonly used with 2,4-D to control weedy trees and shrubs. Since it is long-lasting and soluble, it can be leached down to tree roots and absorbed, thereby effectively damaging or killing the trees. For this reason, great care should be exercised in using dicamba.

Glyphosate (Roundup)

A systemic that is long-lasting in plants but leaves no soil residue that can hurt the trees or crops that follow. This is a newer chemical available to professional applicators; at present it is only labeled for use before planting certain grain crops, or for turf renovation or non-crop use.

Preemergence Herbicides

Some chemicals applied as a spray or as granules to the soil surface will prevent weed seeds from germinating. Usually such chemicals must be applied before weeds emerge from the soil. They are not effective against established weeds. Chemicals of this type are widely used in the preparation of land for the production of farm crops and for certain commercial vegetable and flower crops. In addition, they are being used to an increasing extent by the home gardener. Such herbicides may be applied to bare soil or to areas where nonsensitive, established plants are growing, and will prevent all growth of weeds for a period varying from three to six weeks. Preemergence treatments are also being used to a considerable extent on lawn areas to prevent the germination of crabgrass seeds. The following preemergence treatments will give good control under favorable conditions:

DCPA (Dacthal)

Available as a 75 percent wettable powder for spraying, or as a 2.3 percent granular that can be applied with a drop-type lawn spreader or a "Cyclone"-type spreader. DCPA is used to control many seedling weeds on established transplants in vegetable and flower gardens, landscape plantings and especially for crabgrass control in lawns. In gardens, it must be applied to a newly raked or cultivated, weed-free soil surface. For crabgrass control on lawns, it is applied about the time forsythia is in flower. Follow the directions on the package for amounts to use, for the crops on which it can be used, and for the names of weeds that are controlled by the use of Dacthal.

Trifluralin (Treflan)

This is most useful to the homeowner in 5 percent granular form, but it also is used as an emulsifiable concentrate by farmers. It is applied to the soil before planting some crops, or on established plantings of some vegetable crops, as well as on flower beds and landscape plantings. Trifluralin must be incorporated (mixed) into the soil immediately after application. It does not control such weeds as galinsoga and common ragweed. Consult the label for a list of crops that respond to its use.

SUSCEPTIBILITY OF SOME COMMON WEEDS
TO 2,4-D AND DICAMBA

I — intermediate   R — resistant   S — susceptible   I — intermediate   R — resistant   S — susceptible

COMMON NAME	2,4 – D	DICAMBA	COMMON NAME	2,4 – D	DICAMBA
ash	R		mugwort	I – R	
bindweed, field	I	I	mustards	S	S
black medic	I		oak, white	I – R	
burdock, common	S	S	onion, wild	I – S	I
buttercup, creeping	S		pepperweed, field	S	
Canada thistle	I	I – S	pigweed, redroot	S	S
carpetweed	I	S	pineapple weed	I – R	
carrot, wild	I	I	plantain	S	I
chickweed, common	I	S	poison ivy	I	I
chicory	S	S	pokeweed	S	
cinquefoil	I – S		purslane, common	I	S
clover, white	R	S	ragweed, common	S	S
cocklebur, common	S	S	rose, multiflora	I – R	
dock, curly	I	S	shepherd's purse	S	S
English daisy		S	smartweed, Pennsylvania	S – I	S
fleabane, rough	I	S	sorrel, red	I	S
grass	R	R	speedwell, common	I	
ground ivy	I – R	S	speedwell, thyme leaf	I	
grounsel, common	I – R	R	spurge, prostrate	I – R	S
hawkweed	I – R		stinging nettle	I – S	I
healall	I		stitchwort		S
henbit	R	S	tree-of-heaven	I	
hyacinth, water			trumpet creeper	I	
knotweed, prostrate	I – R	S	violet	R	
lamb's quarters	S	S	walnut, black	S	
lettuce, prickly	S		willow	S	I
mallow, common	I – R	I	wood sorrel, yellow	I – R	S – I
morning-glory	S	S	yarrow	I – R	I

32

Plant Diseases and Insect Pests

Pest control, in gardens, is a controversial and often emotional subject. The word "chemical" became suspect because of the widespread and often overuse of pest control materials in the 1940s, 1950s and 1960s. While achieving the immediate beneficial results, many of these materials came to be recognized as having impact on the environment far beyond the specific crops or plants to which they were applied. Rachel Carson's *Silent Spring* probably did more than any other single work to alert the world to these problems and introduced the general public to the very concept of "ecology." While biologists and naturalists understood the complex interrelationships of the natural world, "environment" and "ecology" were not the common household words they are today.

The use of chemical pest control materials, DDT, for example, was made possible by the enormous surge forward in knowledge in chemical science; the flaw was lack of information or insight. No one really took into account the aftereffects of these seemingly marvelous materials at the time, nor was there any knowledge of how very quickly insect pests in particular could adapt to these materials and in effect outwit the chemists. Now we know better.

Great strides have been made in developing new pesticides ("chemicals," if you will) with concern for their environmental inpact, both immediate and long-term. The very fact that DDT, Chlordane and a host of other materials are banned from use, and that certain other products may be used only by a trained and licensed pesticide applicator, is evidence of progress.

It behooves every gardener to give serious thought as to how best to use pest control materials, and to investigate alternate methods and techniques such as comparison planting.

PLANT DISEASES

Plant diseases may be grouped into three general classes: those brought about by unfavorable environment or by some physiological disturbance; those caused by fungi and by bacteria; and those caused by a virus, a mycoplasmalike organism or a viroid.

In the first group we find plants suffering from malnutrition, from an improper balance of food elements in the soil, from an excess of one or more food nutrients, from extreme soil acidity, or from extreme alkalinity, as, for example, might be caused by limestone. The symptoms are very much the same in most cases. Growth is retarded, the foliage becomes a sickly yellowish-green, and the root systems are poorly developed. For the control of such physiological diseases, refer to Chapter 30 on Soils and Soil Improvement.

In the second group we find the majority of our common plant diseases, those caused by fungi and bacteria. Fungi are minute forms of plant life, which are too small, for the most part, to be seen with the naked eye. They differ primarily from other plants in that they possess none of the green coloring matter known as chlorophyll. All fungi are classed as parasites as they cannot live except on some other plant or animal. Some forms, such as the rust fungi, can exist only on living plants; other forms live only on dead plants; and a few forms can live on either living or dead plant tissue. Some fungi attack many different plants, while other forms can live on one kind. Some forms are very short-lived while others live on in the soil for many years. Most fungi produce small seedlike bodies that are called spores. These tiny spores are very easily carried from one plant to another by the wind and other means, and the spread of fungus diseases is therefore often very rapid. When supplied with sufficient moisture these spores germinate and produce new fungus plants. Since they require a certain amount of moisture in order to germinate, it may be readily understood why fungus diseases are apt to be much more prevalent in wet seasons than in dry seasons.

Bacteria are also a form of plant life, even more minute in size than the fungi. There are many different kinds of bacteria, but those that attack plants do not usually produce spores. They differ from fungi in this respect, since they cannot be blown about by the wind. To be spread from plant to plant, bacteria generally must depend upon some mechanical means such as human hands, insects and garden tools, for example, or upon the splashing of raindrops from leaf to leaf, or the spattering caused by heavy rains upon the surface of the soil. It is in just this way that the dreaded leaf spot of delphiniums is spread. The bacteria causing this disease winter over in the soil, and with the spring rains they are spattered up onto the lower leaves.

The infections due to viruses are a large group of plant diseases. Viruses are ultramicroscopic and are chemically composed of protein and nucleic acid; they can be purified and crystallized like many chemical compounds. Yet viruses are subject to mutation and other variations usually associated only with living things. Viruses are spread by contaminated pruning instruments and by insects, while in some cases, they seem to be transmitted in the seed itself.

Some of the commonest symptoms of a virus infection are curling of leaf tissue, yellowing of leaves, a mottled effect due to the alternating of green and yellow patches, and a bushy type of growth.

Mycoplasmalike organisms are midway between bacteria and viruses both in size and other properties. Aster yellows and several of the witch's broom diseases, previously thought to be caused by viruses, are now believed to be caused by these organisms.

Viroids have only recently been recognized as still another group of plant parasites. They are small molecules of infectious ribonucleic acid, about fifty times smaller than typical plant viruses and lacking a protein coat. Chrysanthemum stunt and chrysanthemum chlorotic mottle, formerly thought to be caused by viruses, are now known to be caused by viroids.

INSECT PESTS

Many scientists have devoted their lives to the study of insects and, as a result of their patient investigations, information is now available regarding the habits and life histories of practically all of our common insect pests. Nearly 1 million species of insects have already been classified, nor is this figure astonishing when we realize that insects constitute the largest group in the animal kingdom. It has been estimated that 75 percent of all known kinds of living animals belong to the insect world, and there are certainly many species in remote sections of the earth that have not, as yet, been discovered.

Continual warfare has been waged between mankind and insects since the dawn of history, and it is sobering to learn that in spite of all that modern science has achieved, no insect pest has ever been known to be completely exterminated. So probably the best that we can hope for in our gardens is to keep insects under control, and this can be done only by prompt and concerted effort. In order to give our gardens intelligent care, there are certain things we should know about the common insect pests. We should know something of their life histories, their feeding habits and the various measures of control.

Insects, in common with all other animals, begin life from a single cell known as the egg. In most cases the eggs are fertilized by the male and are then deposited in some suitable place by the adult female. Sometimes, however, fertilization does not seem to be necessary and the females produce living young without mating. This remarkable phenomenon is known as parthenogenesis, and the most common example is the aphid. Throughout the summer months generation after generation of aphids is produced, consisting entirely of females that have developed from unfertilized eggs. As many as ninety-eight generations have been produced in this manner during this period. In the autumn males suddenly appear, and the eggs that are to carry the species over the winter are fertilized.

Insect eggs vary greatly in size, shape and coloring, most of them being very small. The number laid by one female varies from a single egg, which is exceptional, to as many as 1 million. The average number is probably about 100. Some species lay eggs all at one time, while in the case of other species they are laid in successive batches. Instinct almost invariably guides the female to lay her eggs where the newly hatched young will be able to find suitable food. After the eggs are laid, the mother's responsibility usually comes to an end and she gives her young no further heed. From the moment of hatching the young insects are thrown entirely upon their own resources. There are a few cases where the adult insects prepare elaborate nests and provision them with food for the young, but this is the exception rather than the rule. The time each insect spends within the egg varies considerably. In the majority of cases it is about two weeks. In the case of the house fly it is only eight hours, and in other cases the period is decidedly prolonged, the winter frequently being passed in the egg stage. The life cycle of most insects is completed within a year. A few species such as the ants, the honeybees and wireworms live longer than a year. The shortest life as yet known among insects is ten days.

In studying the life histories of insects, we find that they are grouped into three classes: those without a metamorphosis; those with a simple, or gradual metamorphosis; and those with a complete or complex metamorphosis. A "metamorphosis" may be defined as a noticeable change in the form of an animal between the time of hatching, or birth, and the time of maturity.

Those insects that do not undergo a metamorphosis constitute a relatively small group, and include such species as spring tails and fish moths that are of little or no importance to the gardener. When the young of these species are hatched, they are perfectly formed and resemble the adults in every respect except size.

In the second group, those having a simple or gradual metamorphosis, we find many of our old acquaintances such as the grasshoppers, squash bugs, the scale insects and the aphids. In the case of many species in this group, the newly hatched young are very similar to the adults except for the absence of wings. In some species, however, the difference is more noticeable. The young insects in this group are described as nymphs. In general they have the same feeding habits as their parents and are often found together with their parents. As they grow, their wings develop and they become more and more like the adults.

We find the largest number of insect species in the last group, those that pass through a complete metamorphosis, having four distinct life stages: the egg stage, the larva stage, the pupa stage and the adult stage. In most cases the newly hatched young in no way resemble the adults and have totally different habits. The young are known as larvae (singular: larva). When the larvae become full grown, they pass into the pupa stage and later the adult form emerges. All growth is made in the larva stage. No growth ever occurs in the adult stage. Little beetles never grow into big beetles, nor do little butterflies grow into big butterflies.

The way in which insects grow is very interesting. They do not grow gradually, almost imperceptibly, as do the young of most other animals. The body wall is incapable of expanding, and increase in size can take place only through a series of molts. An entirely new skin is created within the old skin. When this is ready, a fluid known as the molting fluid is poured forth by certain specialized cells in the body. This loosens the outer skin, enabling the insect to crawl forth. Ordinarily four or five molts occur before the nymphs or larvae become full grown. In some species an insect passes through as many as twenty molts. In the case of a nymph the final molt results in a fully developed adult, whereas in the case of a larva the final molt carries the insect into the pupa stage.

The pupa stage is one of the most important in the life of an insect, for it is during this period that it undergoes the wonderful transformation from an often sluggish larva into an alert, highly developed adult—a bee, a moth, a beetle, a fly—according to the species. Most larvae make very careful provision for the safeguarding of the pupa, protecting it under bark or rubbish of some kind, hiding it in the long grass, enfolding it within a leaf or burying it in the soil. In a few species, such as the lady beetles, the pupa is found exposed, with the tip of the body merely fastened to a leaf. The protection about the pupa varies considerably with the different species. In the case of many of the flies the larva retains its own mottled skin and pupates within it. The skin undergoes something of a change, however, becoming hard and forming a waterproof and in most cases a completely airtight case. In some species the larva spins a cocoon for the protection of the pupa and in other species it constructs intricate little chambers within the soil. The period of pupation varies greatly. Many species pass the winter in the pupa stage, while others spend only a few days within the pupa case.

The Control of Insect Pests

Various natural factors enter into the control of insect pests. Weather conditions have a considerable influence upon the prevalence of some species. For example, most of the eggs of the gypsy moth are killed during a cold, open winter, whereas they will survive a snowy winter. If heavy rains occur during the time that the eggs are hatching, certain species suffer severe losses. This may help to explain the reason why certain insects are much more numerous in some seasons than in others.

On farms we use crop rotations to control certain insects and resort to deep plowing in order to expose the larvae of other species at a critical time in their development. But here the farmer has a decided advantage over the gardener, for it would be neither practicable nor possible to use these methods in the flower garden.

Probably few people realize what staunch allies we have in the birds, when it comes to the control of insects. Among the more common species that feed on insects are the purple grackle, European starling, English sparrow, cardinal, meadow lark, catbird, crow, robin, flicker and the common Herring gull. These birds consume large numbers of insects, which they extract from turf by scratching or pecking holes in infested lawns, and also from weeds, flowers, trees, shrubs and farm crops. Birds also carry insects to their nests to feed their young.

Many of the smaller mammals also are useful in controlling insects. Moles, skunks, toads and some species of snakes depend almost entirely upon insects for their food. Predatory parasites play an important part in insect control, too. These are insects that are harmless in themselves from the viewpoint of the gardener but that prey upon other insects. In most parts of the country natural parasites exist and are a constant source of help. When alien insects are brought into the country—and most U.S. garden pests are of foreign origin—one of the most effective means of control is the introduction of these predatory parasites. For example, when the gypsy moths were creating such havoc in New England a decade or so ago, insect parasites were imported from Europe and Asia and were of inestimable value. The Australian lady beetle was imported into California to help control the cottony cushion scale on citrus fruits, and one of the most interesting examples of insect control is found in the case of the Japanese beetles. The beetle has existed for many years in Japan but it never was considered a serious pest because it had been kept more or less under control by its natural enemies. Some years ago, however, a few beetles were brought into this country on a shipment of plants from Japan. For a year or so they escaped notice and then, too late, we woke up to the fact that they were increasing in such alarming numbers that they threatened to become a very serious pest.

It is doubtful whether, in the history of this country, any pest has increased so rapidly or proved so destructive. The government appropriated millions of dollars to aid the fight against the Japanese beetles and to prevent their spread into uninfested territory. And one of the most important measures of control has been the importation of some of the natural parasites that have so successfully kept the beetle in check in its native home. The two that have proved most valuable are a parasitic fly that lays its eggs upon the adult beetle, the larvae boring their way into the body of the beetle, and a parasitic wasp that attacks the beetle in the larva stage.

In spite of the fact, however, that these natural factors are constantly at work to prevent the increase and spread of insect pests, the gardener will find that it is impossible to depend upon them for complete control, except in rare instances. It is necessary, therefore, to resort to other means, such as chemical control through the use of poison sprays, dusts and fumigants; or to mechanical control through the use of traps, tree bands and hand picking. In controlling insect pests by these means, it is necessary to determine the type of pest one is fighting, to decide upon the remedy to be used and to apply it promptly and thoroughly.

Insects are grouped into two distinct classes: those with chewing mouth parts and those with sucking mouth parts. In the first group we have caterpillars and beetles of every kind and description, and other less important insects such as grubs and grasshoppers. These feed largely upon the foliage of growing plants while grubs and borers feed upon the roots. Among this group of insects we find some of our gardens' worst enemies, such as the aster beetles, the iris borer, the rose beetle, the Japanese beetle, the yellow wooly-bear caterpillar, the cabbage looper and many others. The insects in this group chew and swallow solid plant tissues and they may, with very few exceptions, be controlled by the use of stomach poisons.

In the second group, those insects having sucking mouth parts, we find such familiar enemies as the aphids, the various scale insects and the leafhoppers. Instead of being equipped with jaws with which they can cut and chew their food, these insects have delicate tubelike mouth parts with which they are able to pierce through the outer layer of plant tissue and suck the juices from within. These long, needlelike beaks are usually jointed and they may point forward, upward or downward. When not in use they are generally laid back on the breast between the front legs. It is not possible to control the insects in this group by coating the outer surface of the plant with poison dusts or sprays, as they are able to pierce through the poisoned layer and can then draw their nourishment from the plant, quite unharmed. It has been found, however, that these sucking insects can be controlled by contact poisons — poisons that come into direct contact with the body.

THE GARDEN MEDICINE SHELF

It is wise for every gardener to become familiar with some of the standard reliable remedies that are used in controlling insect pests and diseases and to keep a sufficient quantity on hand for ordinary use. An orderly, well-stocked medicine shelf for the garden is not only a great source of satisfaction in itself but also means that in an emergency you will find yourself prepared.

For the average flower garden, comparatively little is needed in the way of equipment. A quart measure, a measuring spoon (the kind that comes in little sets is very useful), a sprayer and a dust gun are really all that are necessary. The size of the sprayer and dusting outfit will depend largely upon the extent of one's gardening operations. In a small garden a hand sprayer such as may be purchased from any hardware store will probably be entirely adequate. For a large garden a sprayer of the knapsack or bucket type would be more satisfactory.

Insecticides and Miticides

In order to be effective in combatting insect pests in the garden, an insecticide must measure up to certain definite requirements. It must not repel the insects against which it is to be used; it must give reasonably quick results; it must not burn the foliage of tender plants; it must spread uniformly when applied and adhere well to the foliage of the plant; it must keep its strength during storage; it must be reasonable in price; and it should have as low toxicity as possible for humans and animals, as well as untargeted insects.

Within recent years, as the result of extensive scientific research, a number of new insecticides have been discovered and developed which make it possible for the gardener to obtain complete control of many insect pests that heretofore were difficult to combat.

Stomach poisons are used as a control for insects with chewing mouth parts, such as beetles of various types, cabbage worms, etc., that actually eat foliage, fruit or flowers. Contact insecticides are used to control insects with sucking mouth parts that suck the juices from the plant tissues, such as the aphid, red spider, etc. In order to be effective, most contact insecticides must come into direct contact with the body of the insect, as they kill the insect either by clogging up the breathing tubes or by entering the body and causing a chemical reaction upon the body tissues. As some contact sprays are effective against certain sucking insects and not effective against others, it is important that the proper spray or dust is selected for use. Some of the newer chemicals are effective both as contact and stomach poisons.

Aramite

An excellent miticide, also sold under the names Aracide and Niagaramite, for use on ornamental and nonfood plants. It is compatible with sulphur and with most of the commonly used insecticides and fungicides. It should not be used with lime sulphur and other highly alkaline materials, or with Bordeaux mixture.

Bacillus thuringiensis

As an insecticide, this microbe is effective in the control of many kinds of caterpillars. It is harmless to humans and animal pets. The insecticide is sold under the trade names Agritol, Bakthane L69, Biogard, Biotrol, Dipel, Larvatrol and Thuricide.

Cedo-O-Flora

This pesticide—made with petroleum distillates, soap and cedar and hemlock oils—is effective in controlling scale, mealy bugs and mites on most house plants.

Cygon

Also known as dimethoate and Rogor, this is effective in controlling mealy bugs and other insects on yews and other plants. It should not be used on Chinese holly, chrysanthemums and Easter lilies because it is toxic to these. Some varieties of azaleas, fern, gloxinia, hydrangea, Schefflera and African violets may also be injured by its use.

Cythion

A premium grade of malathion, this is recommended for controlling sucking insects on plants grown indoors. Its odor is less offensive than that of ordinary malathion.

Diazinon

Also sold under the name Spectracide. It controls soil insects such as wireworms and root worms, as well as turf pests such as chinch bugs and many insects infesting ornamental plants. It may injure gardenia, hibiscus, pilea and stephanotis.

Dormant Oil Sprays

Petroleum oils, properly prepared, are used to control many pests that live through the winter on the buds, twigs and trunks of trees and other woody plants.

Dursban

This pesticide can control chinch bugs, sod webworms and Japanese beetle grubs in lawns, in addition to such other pests as ants, centipedes and millipedes.

Imidan

Also known as Prolate, this preparation controls many chewing insects, including gypsy moth caterpillars, elm spanworms and a wide variety of sucking insects.

Kelthane

This is perhaps the most widely used mitekiller. It also is sold under the name of Dicofol and is effective against most species of mites on trees, shrubs and food plants.

Malathion

This, the most widely used organic phosphate insecticide, controls a great number of pests including aphids, the crawler stage of scales, mealy bugs and many chewing insects. The premium-grade Cythion, mentioned earlier, has a less offensive odor. Malathion injures some crassulas, some cacti, ferns, petunias, sweet peas, violets, gloxinias, some red carnations and some rose varieties.

Methoxychlor

An effective insecticide with long residual action, this is used to control the elm bark beetles that spread the Dutch elm disease fungus. It is also effective in combatting Mexican bean beetles, many fruit and vegetable pests and borers on numerous fruit, ornamental and shade trees.

Nicotine Sulphate

Sold under the name Black Leaf 40, this insecticide has long been used to control sucking insects on both indoor and outdoor plants. It is highly toxic if swallowed, inhaled or spilled on the skin. However, it is less toxic to cacti, succulents and ferns in controlling scales, aphids and mites. It breaks down rapidly so that food plants, herbs, etc., can be consumed within a few days of its use.

Ovotran

Also known as Ovex, Difensen and Chlorfenson, this pesticide kills all stages of mites, including the eggs. It is toxic to the leaves of some ornamental plants early in the growing season, so read the directions carefully before using it.

Pyrethrum

This insecticide is extracted from the flowers of a species of *Chrysanthemum* grown in central Africa and Ecuador. It is effective against many chewing and sucking insects.

Resmethrin

This synthetically manufactured pyrethroid, also known as SBP 1382 and Synthrin, is effective against many household and greenhouse insects, particularly whiteflies.

Rotenone

A botanical insecticide extracted from derris and cube roots grown in Peru, this is sold in various commercial forms as a dust or spray. It is moderately toxic to animals and highly toxic to fish.

Sevin

Also known by the common name carbaryl, this has been one of the most widely used insecticides for control of many kinds of chewing and some sucking insects. Repeated use will result in an increase in mite populations, however. Sevin is also toxic to bees and will defoliate Boston ivy and Virginia creeper vines. For these reasons it should be used only as a last resort and then with great care to limit the spray to infected plants.

Zectran

Also known as Mexacarbate, this pesticide is effective against a wide range of insects infesting shade trees, flowers and shrubs, as well as snails and slugs, which attack nonfood plants.

Systemic Insecticides

Systemics are substances that can be absorbed through either the roots or leaves of plants and translocated in the sapstream in sufficient amounts to kill insects and related pests feeding or breeding in the plants. In other words, what systemics actually do is to kill insects, nematodes and other pests from the inside of the plant rather than from the outside, as do conventional sprays. Systemics are more efficient than chemicals sprayed onto the leaves because they spread throughout the plant as it grows, and they do not wash off in rainy weather. Another advantage is that they present little or no danger to nearby wildlife, unless the plants are eaten by them. Systemic insecticides are currently being used primarily by commercial arborists, nursery staff and professional flower growers on nonfood crops. A few can also be used on nonbearing fruit trees. The following are the most frequently used systemics:

Cygon (previously described under Insecticides)

This chemical is sprayed on azaleas, camellias and gardenias, and when enough of it enters the leaves, it becomes toxic to lace bugs, leaf miners, mites, scales and whiteflies. Sucking insects and mites on narrow-leaved evergreens and on birch, boxwood and holly can also be controlled with Cygon. However, it should be used only on those plants listed on the container.

Di-Syston (also known as Disulfoton)

Will control sucking insects, mites and some chewing insects on birch, holly, mimosa (*Albizia*) and roses. It is available in both granular and liquid forms, or impregnated on fertilizer.

Meta-Systox R

When applied to the soil around certain plants, this pesticide becomes toxic to sucking pests such as aphids, leafhoppers, scales and whiteflies, as well as to mites. It is also very toxic to insects when applied as a foliage spray.

Fungicides

Benlate (also sold under the name benomyl)

Widely used to control fungus diseases of roses and other ornamental plants as well as fruit and shade trees and lawn grasses.

Bordeaux Mixture

This is one of the oldest and still one of the most useful fungicides. The following procedure is suggested for preparing small quantities of Bordeaux: dissolve 4 oz. of copper sulphate crystals in 1 gallon of water. Then dissolve 2 oz. of hydrated lime in 2 gallons of water. Finally, add the copper sulphate solution to the limewater. This makes 3 gallons of approximately 4–2–50 Bordeaux mixture.

Wherever Bordeaux mixture is mentioned in this book as a disease-preventing material, one of the so-called fixed coppers may safely be substituted. Among the fixed coppers on the market are basic copper sulphate, tribasic copper sulphate, Basi-Cop, Microcop, Copper 53 Fungicide and T-B-C-S 53. Other copper fungicides are sold under such trade names as Bordo, Bordo-Mix, C-O-C-S, Kocide 101, Miller 658, Ortho Copper Fungicide and Coprantol.

Captan (Orthocide)

An organic fungicide for use on fruits, vegetables and ornamentals. Controls various turf diseases such as brown patch and copper spot, and early and late blight on potatoes. It also has proved effective as a control for black spot and leaf rust on roses, and when used for treating rose cuttings, it acts as a preventive against crown gall. It should not be used in combination with oil sprays or with lime, but it is compatible with most insecticides. Available both as a wettable powder and a dust. It is not effective against mildew.

Dithane M-45

Effective in preventing many fungus diseases of ornamental plants.

Dithane Z 78

This has proved an excellent control for azalea petal blight, and is also used as a control for black spot on roses and for downy mildew on cucurbits. It may be used either as a dust or as a spray.

Ferbam

Also sold under the names Fermate, Karbam Black, Carbamate, Coromate and Vancide FE. Among the first so-called carbamates to be marketed, Ferbam is an excellent control for certain plant diseases such as septoria leaf diseases of chrysanthemums, rusts on antirrhinums and carnations, some botrytis blights and anthracnoses, downy mildew, black spot on roses, black rot on grapes, apple scab, apple rust and brown rot of stone fruits.

Karathane (Also known as Dinocap and Mildex)

Used to control powdery mildew on many ornamental plants, including roses, phlox and tuberous begonias. Karathane should not be applied when the temperature is above 85°F. or during periods of very humid weather, as it is apt to cause damage under such conditions. It is important to follow instructions concerning rate of application carefully. Karathane also has some value as a miticide.

Lime sulphur

Used as a standard dormant spray for fruit trees and also sometimes for roses. As a summer spray it is used for volutella blight of boxwood. As a dormant spray it is used at a dilution of 1 to 9; as a summer spray at a dilution of 1 to 50. It should not be used when the temperature is over 85°F.

Manzate

A good control for black spot on roses and for cercospora leaf spot and downy mildew. It is a protectant and should be applied *before* infections appear. Manzate controls all common tomato and potato diseases, including early and late blight.

Phaltan

Also sold under the common name folget, this is used to control certain fungus diseases of fruit trees, black spot and mildew of roses and many others.

Sulphur

This has long been used to control powdery mildews and many other plant diseases; it also controls spider mites. However, it is not wise to apply sulphur when the air temperature is above 85°F., as it may cause severe burning.

Systemic Fungicides

The systemic fungicides control plant diseases in an entirely different way from sprays and dusting powders. These systemic compounds are absorbed by plants through their roots and leaves, and they are very helpful in the control of some of the most baffling plant diseases.

Arbotect 20-S

The effective ingredient is thiabendazole; used to protect elms against the Dutch elm disease and to cure mildly affected ones.

Lignasan BLP

This is a soluble form of Benlate, which is injected into elm trees both as a preventive and as a therapeutic treatment for the fatal Dutch elm disease.

Thiabendazole (also sold as Merfect and Tobaz)

An effective systemic fungicide for controlling certain turf diseases, as well as the decay of bulbs and corms of ornamental plants.

Antibiotics

Antibiotics are substances produced by fungi that have the power to destroy other fungi or the toxins produced by them. Since the chemical structure of many antibiotics has been determined, it is now possible for them to be produced synthetically in laboratories.

Some of the results from the use of antibiotics on plants have been almost as dramatic as have the cures effected through their use in human diseases. For example, as the result of a single application of the antibiotic, Actidione, to the galls on red cedars that spread cedar-apple rust, spore production was completely arrested. And through the use of a streptomycin spray, fire blight—one of the most dreaded diseases among orchardists, and heretofore extremely difficult to combat—has been brought under almost complete control. Such bacterial diseases as tobacco wildfire, bacterial spot of peppers and tomatoes, bacterial soft rot of potato seed pieces, angular leaf spot of cucumber and bacterial blight of celery have all been controlled experimentally with the new antibiotics.

Aureomycin is effective in treating seed infected with bacterial black rot. Another antibiotic, cyclohexamide, sold under the name Actidione Ferrated, is an excellent control for a number of turf diseases such as brownpatch, dollar spot, melting out and snow mold.

The production of antibiotics is costly. They are therefore so expensive that their use is frequently not justified for large-scale operations, but for certain hard-to-control diseases that have not yielded to other measures, they offer great possibilities.

General Purpose Dusts and Sprays

There are many excellent all-purpose dusts and sprays on the market. In order to be of greatest value to the home gardener, an all-purpose dust or spray should offer good control for the following: *Insect pests*—aphids, red spider mites, caterpillars and beetles of most types. *Diseases*—the various leaf spots, mildews and rusts. This is by no means an all-inclusive list but covers the pests and diseases most likely to be a problem in the average home garden.

In purchasing an all-purpose dust or spray, it is wise to know what ingredients it contains and what pests and diseases it may be expected to control.

It is possible to prepare an all-purpose spray

mixture that will be as effective as a commercial product, yet much less expensive. Such a mixture should contain a good general fungicide, a miticide and a control for both sucking and chewing insects. It is very important that the ingredients used be compatible, as otherwise serious complications may result.

The following mixtures are recommended. The tablespoons and teaspoons should be slightly rounded.

3 tsp.	= 1 tbs.	4 cups	= 1 qt.
4 tbs.	= 1/4 cup	2 pt.	= 1 qt.
16 tbs.	= 1 cup	4 qt.	= 1 gal.
2 cups	= 1 pt.	8 fl. oz.	= 1 cup

1. 2 tbsp. malathion, 25% wettable powder
   3 tbsp. Methoxychlor, 50% wettable powder
   2 tbsp. Manzate or Orthocide 406
   1 gallon water
   plus a sticker-spreader used according to the manufacturer's directions.
2. 4 tbsp. malathion, 25% wettable powder
   2 tbsp. Sevin, 50% wettable powder
   1 tbsp. Zineb, 65% wettable powder
   1/2 tsp. Karathane or Mildex, 25% wettable powder
   1 gallon water
   plus a sticker-spreader used according to the manufacturer's directions.
   Because of the broad-scale effect of Sevin, it is recommended that this preparation be adopted as a last resort, and then targeted to specific plants.
3. 4 tbsp. malathion, 25% wettable powder
   2 tbsp. Methoxychlor, 50% wettable powder
   2 tbsp. Captan, 50% wettable powder
   1/2 tsp. Karathane or Mildex, 25% wettable powder
   1 gallon water
   plus a sticker-spreader used according to the manufacturer's directions.

The several ingredients should be mixed dry, then enough water added to make a very thin paste. The mixture should then be poured into the sprayer, preferably through a fine screen or cheesecloth. More water should be added and the mixture stirred.

TABLE OF DILUTIONS
(Number of tablespoonfuls to 1 gallon of water)

TABLESPOONFULS		DILUTION
1/4	..	1 to 1,000
1/2	..	1 to 500
1	..	1 to 250
1 1/4	..	1 to 200
2 1/2	..	1 to 100
5	..	1 to 50
10	..	1 to 25

PRECAUTIONS

As many insecticides and some fungicides are deadly poisons, they must be handled with care.

Every possible precaution should be taken to protect children, birds, dogs and other animals from inhaling or ingesting these mixtures.

Such materials should always be kept in a locked cupboard, never on open shelves.

Soil Fumigants

Chloropicrin (sold under the trade name Larvacide)

An excellent soil fumigant. Destroys nematodes, weed seeds and some fungi. It causes injury to living plants and should only be used on fallow ground or on bare soil in benches or in containers being prepared for planting. Directions should be followed with great care as it is somewhat dangerous to use.

D-D Mixture

A soil fumigant that is an effective control against root knot nematodes, wireworms and other insects and some weeds. It is most effective on sandy soils. It is available in liquid form. On large-scale operations it should be applied with a special applicator. On small areas application can be made by hand.

Ethylene Dibromide

An effective soil fumigant that is available in liquid form for large-scale operations and also in capsule form, which is very convenient for home gardeners as the capsules can be easily pressed into the soil. Available in garden supply stores under names such as Bromofume, Dowfume W-85, Pestmaster EDB85 and Soil Brom-86, Ethylene Dibromide is toxic to both plants and animals. It is most effective when the soil is moist and the temperature 60° F. or above. No planting should be done for at least two weeks after application.

Mobilawn
Used to control noncyst-forming nematodes infesting boxwood, Japanese holly and many other woody plants without harming the plants. It also controls lawn chinch bugs on St. Augustine grass and nematodes on African violets.

Nicotine
One of the most generally used fumigants in greenhouses. Commercial preparations such as Nicofume contain free nicotine. This material comes in cans under pressure and is vaporized by opening the can and setting fire to its contents.

Vapam
Also sold as SMDC, VPM and Metam, this is used as an all-purpose fumigant to control soil fungi, nematodes and weed seeds.

DISEASE AND INSECT PESTS OF TREES AND SHRUBS

Betula (birch)

Insect Pests – Leaf Miner
Attacks gray, paper and European white birch.

Identification: Mature larvae are about ½ in. long, whitish with black spots on thorax. The adult sawfly is black and about ¹⁄₁₆ in. long.

Injury: The larvae feed upon the tissues between the upper and lower leaf surfaces, causing a browning of the foliage. If the infestation is severe, the tree appears blighted.

Life history: The adult sawfly emerges in spring when the leaves are about half open and the eggs are laid in the new leaves. Upon hatching, the young larvae begin feeding within the leaf. There are several generations. The eggs are always laid in the new leaves. Infestation is therefore heaviest when the first brood hatches, later broods being confined more to the tips of the branches. The mature larva passes the winter in an earthen cell in the soil at the base of the tree.

Control: Diazinon, Meta-Systox or Sevin sprays will control the birch leaf miner. The first spray should be applied about May 1; if the spring is a cold one, the first application can be delayed a week or so. For best control, two additional applications should be made at ten-day intervals. To control the second brood of leaf miners, spray again about July 1 and July 10.

Tent Caterpillar
Attacks chiefly blackcherry, chokecherry and apple. Also sometimes found on birch, elm, hawthorn, maple, oak, pear, plum and roses.

Identification: Hairy caterpillars that are black, with a white stripe down the back and brown and yellow stripes along the sides. At maturity the caterpillars measure 2 in. to 2½ in. in length. The moths are a light reddish-brown, with two diagonal stripes across each of the forewings.

Injury: The tent caterpillars are a serious and a very unsightly pest of orchard and roadside trees in many sections throughout the country. They are voracious feeders and can completely defoliate a tree in a remarkably short time.

Life history: The female moth lays from 150 to 350 eggs, depositing them in a circle about a

PLANTS THAT ARE SELDOM ATTACKED BY PESTS AND DISEASES

ANNUALS

Arctotis stoechadifolia var. *grandis*	African daisy
Brachycome	Swan River daisy
Browallia	bush violet
Cynoglossum	hound's tongue
Delphinium	larkspur
Euphorbia marginata	snow-on-the-mountain
Gilia	thimble flower
Gomphrena	
Helichrysum	everlasting
Hunnemannia	Mexican tulip poppy, golden-cup
Incarvillea	
Mirabilis	four o'clock
Molucella	bells of Ireland
Nemesia	
Nemophila	
Nierembergia	cupflower
Nigella	love-in-the-mist
Portulaca	purslane, moss rose
Scabiosa	pincushion flower
Schizanthus	butterfly flower
Papaver rhoeas	Shirley poppy
Trachymene	blue lace flower

PERENNIALS

Adonis	pheasant's-eye
Ajuga	bugle
Anagallis	pimpernel
Anaphalis	everlasting
Anchusa	bugloss, alkanet
Artemisia	mugwort
Aubrietia	
Baptisia australis	blue false indigo
Boltonia	
Cerastium tomentosum	snow-in-summer
Cimicifuga	black cohosh, snakeroot
Crucianella	crosswort
Dicentra eximia	fringed bleeding-heart
Dicentra spectabilis	bleeding-heart
Echinacea	purple coneflower

Echium	viper's bugloss
Eupatorium	thoroughwort
Geum	
Helianthemum	sun rose
Helianthus	hardy sunflower
Hemerocallis	daylily
Hesperis	sweet rocket
Hypericum	St. John's wort
Iberis sempervirens	hardy candytuft
Kniphofia	torch lily
Liatris	blazing star
Limonium	sea lavender
Linum perenne	perennial flax
Lychnis	campion
Mertensia	Virginia bluebells
Nepeta mussinii	catmint
Papaver nudicaule	Iceland poppy
Papaver pilosum	Olympic poppy
Penstemon	beard-tongue
Physostegia	false dragonhead
Platycodon	balloon flower
Plumbago larpentiae (*Ceratostigma plumbaginoides*)	leadwort
Potentilla	cinquefoil
Salvia azurea	azure sage
Saponaria ocymoides	rock soapwort
Scabiosa	pincushion flower
Serpervivum	houseleek
Silene	campion, catchfly
Spiraea filipendula	spirea, bridal-wreath
Stokesia cyanea	Stokes' aster
Thalictrum	meadow rue
Thermopsis	false lupine
Trollius	globeflower
Verbascum	mullein

BIENNIALS

Bellis perennis	English daisy
Cheiranthus cheiri	English wallflower
Dianthus barbatus	sweet William
Viola	violet

twig or branch on the host tree. The egg mass is covered with a sticky substance that is dark brown in color and becomes very hard and shiny. The young larvae hatch out in early spring and gather in the fork of the tree, where they spin their weblike nest. They remain in the nest during the night and on dark, rainy days, but leave it on clear days to feed nearby. The caterpillars become full grown in about a month. The pupa stage is passed in a yellowish-white cocoon usually found on tree trunks or on buildings. The adult moths emerge in about three weeks. The winter is passed in the egg stage.

Control: Prune twigs that have egg masses in winter or spray the trees with Sevin as soon as the caterpillars appear in spring.

Buxus (box)

**Disease — Nectria Canker *or* Volutella Blight
(Leaf Cast or Twig Blight)**

Symptoms: In midsummer, particularly during a long spell of damp weather, some branches turn straw color. Salmon-pink spore pustules will be found on the backs of the leaves and along the stems. In the canker form the disease often follows severe winter injury.

Control: This is a fungus disease, so it is important to remove and destroy all affected twigs. Cut out all branches where winter injury is evident. The annual removal and destruction of all leaves that have lodged in the crotches is recommended. Four applications of a copper fungicide or lime sulphur have proven very effective in preventing canker. The first application should be made after the dead leaves and dying branches have been removed and before growth starts in the spring; the second, when the new growth is half completed; the third, after spring growth has been completed; and the fourth, after fall growth has been completed.

Insect Pests — Box Leaf Miner
Identification: The adult form of the box leaf miner is a yellowish fly, slightly smaller than a mosquito. These flies may readily be distinguished by their very definite yellow coloring. The larvae are only about 1/10 in. long when full grown, and they are a muddy white in color.

Injury: The lower, more protected branches are usually the first to become infested. Leaves in which the miners are at work gradually turn yellow and drop prematurely. Bushes that are badly infested present a scraggly, unhealthy appearance.

Life history: The adult flies emerge from the pupa stage in late April or early May. The emerging period for the entire brood extends over several weeks. The average life of the adult fly is about two days, and soon after emerging the females deposit their eggs within the leaf tissues, piercing through the epidermis on the undersurface. The eggs hatch during the next two or three weeks, and the tiny larvae feed within the tissues of the leaves throughout the summer and autumn and the early spring of the following year. In late March or early April the larvae pass into the pupa stage; three or four weeks later the adult flies emerge and the life cycle begins again.

Control: When the adult flies are seen in late May, spray the box leaves with Cygon, Diazinon, malathion or Sevin.

Box Psylla
Identification: Small, greenish insects about 1/8 in. long, the body covered with a white, waxy secretion. They are usually found at the tips of the young shoots.

Injury: The young nymphs feed upon the young, growing shoots, sucking the juices from the plant and causing a very characteristic curling of the leaves at the tips of the branches. The damage done by the box psylla is usually not very serious unless the bushes are heavily infested.

Life history: The adults emerge in late April or early May and the females lay their eggs upon the tips of the young shoots. Several weeks later the nymphs hatch out and begin feeding.

Control: Spray in mid-May and again two weeks later with Diazinon, malathion or Sevin.

Mites (boxwood)
Identification: Minute animals hardly visible to the naked eye, their presence may usually be detected by their characteristic injury.

Injury: The mites suck the juices from the young, tender leaves of the new growth causing the foliage to lose its fresh, bright green color. The infested leaves at first become mottled, later taking on a dull, grayish-brown appearance and dropping prematurely.

Life history: The winter is passed in the egg stage, the eggs being infinitesimal, round, pinkish dots. The first brood hatches in April and as they breed rapidly four or five generations are produced during a single season.

Control: The dormant oil spray recommended for scales destroys many overwintering mites. Cygon, Diazinon, Kelthane or Tedion applied during May and June will also control mites.

Nematodes
Symptoms: Foliage becomes yellow, growth appears stunted and unhealthy for no apparent reason. Shallow root mat observed upon examination.

Control: Some species of nematodes can be controlled by drenching the soil with Nemagon as directed by the manufacturer. Other species can be controlled with Dasanit or Mocap. A nematologist can determine which species is involved and what the recommended treatment should be. Such an expert can readily be located through your local county agent or a nearby state college.

Oyster Shell Scale
Identification: Small, grayish-white scales resembling an oyster shell in shape. They are usually found clustered in masses along the lower branches and the innermost twigs.

Injury: The scales suck the juices from the bush, greatly lowering its vigor and vitality. If the infestation is not checked, it will eventually cause death.

Life history: During the winter the eggs are protected by the hard, shell-like covering of the old scales. The young hatch out about the end of May or early in June. At this stage they are soft-bodied and look like small yellowish-white specks crawling about on the branches. Soon after hatching they select a place to feed and pierce through the outer bark. As the season advances, the hard, shell-like covering is formed.

Control: Spray with a dormant oil to control overwintering scales. Where infestations are heavy, follow with a Meta-Systox R or malathion spray when the young are crawling about in May and June.

Camellia

Disease—Camellia Flower Blight
The blight first appeared in California in 1938 and has now spread throughout the Pacific Coast states and Gulf states, including other southern states from Texas to Virginia. As it is a fungus disease, areas where it has been found have been placed under rigid quarantine and every precaution has been taken to prevent its further spread.

Symptoms: Small brown specks appear on the petals, a darkening of the veins is evident and the flower becomes brown in the center. The entire bloom gradually turns brown, but not slimy, a symptom characteristic of azalea flower blight. When infected flowers drop, the moist soil and mulch in turn become infected. From January to March, the large, black sclerotia that have formed about the plant develop mushroomlike apothecia from which the spores are catapulted, alighting on the opening petals.

Control: To control flower blight, pick off and discard all old camellia blossoms before they fall. Benlate, ferbam, sulphur or Fore sprays all help to prevent infections, which also can be prevented by placing a 3-in. mulch of wood chips or other suitable material around the base of each plant. Such a barrier will prevent the fungus bodies in the surrounding soil from ejecting their spores into the atmosphere and onto the leaves.

Insect Pests—Nematodes
Identification: Foliage becomes yellow, growth appears stunted and unhealthy for no apparent reason.

Control: See page 595.

Mites (Southern Red Mite)
Identification: Leaves become unhealthy in appearance, with a yellow or grayish cast. See page 594 for *Injury* and *Life history.*

Control: Spray with Diazinon or Kelthane.

Tea Scale
Identification: The scales are found on the undersurface of the leaves. When young, the female is light yellow and thin, later becoming brown, elongated and hard. The male is soft, white and narrow. White cottony threads seem to entangle the scales.

Injury: The upper surface of the leaves has a yellowish, blotched appearance. Bush appears unhealthy; foliage drops prematurely.

Life history: The eggs hatch in from one to three weeks, depending upon the weather. The newly hatched crawlers, which are flat and yellow in color, attach themselves to the new growth within a few days. The first molt occurs in eighteen to thirty-six days, the second seven days later. Eggs are laid forty-one to sixty-five days after birth and there are many overlapping generations during the spring, summer and early fall months.

Control: Spray with malathion to control the young crawler stage. Repeat the treatment at two-week intervals for heavily infested plants. In the southern states, oil emulsions such as Volck are quite effective on outdoor plants.

Clematis

Insect Pest—Root-knot Nematode
Identification: Plant appears stunted for no apparent reason. Wilting sometimes occurs, resulting in death.

Control: See pages 595 and 665.

Cornus (dogwood)

Insect Pests—Borer (dogwood borer, *Thamnosphecia scitula*)
Identification: Small adult moths with blue-black margins on their clear wings. Caterpillar, whitish with brown head, approximately $\frac{1}{2}$ in. long.

Injury: The young borers penetrate the bark and feed in the cambium layer. A badly infested tree may have as many as fifty borers. The trunk may become completely girdled, causing the death of the tree, or branches may be girdled at the base and die. Tree greatly weakened.

Life history: Moths emerge from the pupa stage during late spring to midsummer. The eggs are laid by the female moths in roughened places on the bark. Young larvae hatch and begin their feeding.

Control: In the latitude of New York, paint or spray the trunk with Methoxychlor three times at twenty-day intervals starting in mid-May. Endosulfan (Thiodan) spray applied in early June and repeated two weeks later also provides control. In some states this material can be used only by arborists and nursery staff under official permit from the state Department of Agriculture.

Precautions: As young, newly transplanted dogwood trees are particularly susceptible to attacks from borers because of their reduced vitality, it is a wise precaution to wrap the trunk with burlap. It is also wise at all times to prevent dogwood trees from being damaged by rabbits, or by the lawn mower or any other mechanical equipment, as it is in such roughened areas that the eggs of the adult moths are laid.

Crataegus (hawthorn)

Disease – Cedar-apple Rust
Symptoms: In midsummer orange-yellow spots appear on the leaves. One type of spore is borne on the upper surface of the leaf and another type on the lower surface.

Control: See under *Juniperus,* page 598.

Insect Pest – Lace Bug
Identification: Small, sluggish insects with lace-like wings, which feed on the undersides of leaves depositing small, brown, sticky spots of excreta.

Control: Spray with Diazinon, malathion or Sevin.

Euonymus

Insect Pest – Euonymus Scale
Attacks euonymus and bittersweet, and is sometimes found on pachysandra and ivy growing near euonymus.

Identification: Female scale resembles a tiny, dark brown oyster shell, males are white and very slender. In a severe infestation the leaves and stems may appear almost completely covered with the white males, with a smaller proportion of brown females.

Injury: Foliage turns yellow, leaves drop prematurely, branches begin to die back. Euony-

mus trained to a vine form is most apt to be seriously affected.

Life history: The eggs are laid under the shell of the female and hatch in late spring. The pale yellowish crawlers are usually seen in late May or June. A second brood appears in late August or early September.

Control: Heavy infestations can be eliminated only by applying both dormant and summer sprays. In late March or early April spray with "superior"-type dormant oil plus Ethion. The summer spray should be applied from June 5 to June 15, depending on the locality and season. The dosage is 2 tsp. of 50 percent malathion liquid or 4 tbs. of 25 percent malathion wettable powder per gallon of water. Cygon or Meta-Systox R may be substituted for the malathion.

Hedera helix (English ivy)

Insect Pests – Aphids
Identification: Small black plant lice clustered along the tips of the shoots.

Control: See page 610.

Spider Mites
Identification: Foliage appears unhealthy, dusty, grayish brown in appearance.

Control: See page 629.

Juniperus virginiana (red cedar)

Disease – Cedar-apple Rust
Attacks apples, hawthorns and ornamental crab apples. Bechtel's and many native crabs are very susceptible. Asiatic varieties show more resistance.

Nature of the disease: The fungus that causes the disease, *Gymnosporangium juniperi-virginianae,* winters over in the galls on cedars. In the spring gelatinous rays that bear many spores are produced (when the disease is sometimes called a cedar flower). These spores infect the apple. Several stages of the life cycle are completed on the apple. In June reinfection of the cedar may occur.

Symptoms: This fungus, like many rusts, must have two different plants as hosts in order to complete its life cycle. In this case the two hosts are the ordinary cedar, *Juniperus virginiana,* and the crab or ordinary domestic apple. On the leaves of apples, the infection first appears as small yellow spots that enlarge, deepen in color and frequently have reddish borders. On the undersurface of the leaf the tissue develops a cushion or blister on which small tubular projections appear. On the twigs, small swollen areas develop, which also bear many tubular projections. In the case of the cedar, galls, commonly called apples, are produced with small round indentations.

Control: On apple, hawthorn and other rosaceous hosts, as many as six applications may be needed for good control. These applications should be made every ten days, and should consist of a wettable sulphur or a mixture of wettable sulphur and Ferbam. The initial application should be made just before an expected rainy spell and as soon as the leaves emerge in spring. On junipers, when the gelatinous protrusions develop in spring, spray the galls thoroughly with 1 oz. (3 tbs.) of Actidione TGF in 3 gallons of water.

Kalmia latifolia (mountain laurel)

Disease—Leaf Spot

A fungus disease that is most apt to be troublesome on mountain laurel when it is growing in a very shady or damp location.

Symptoms: Brown or grayish spots appear on the leaves and the foliage may become badly disfigured.

Control: Hand-pick infected leaves, collect fallen ones and destroy them. Where the disease has been severe the previous year, spray with Benlate plus a spreader-sticker when the buds open, and repeat twice, ten and twenty days later. An additional application may be necessary in September or October if wet weather prevails.

Liriodendron tulipifera (only one species encountered in United States) (tulip tree)

Insect Pests—Tulip Tree Scale

Usually found on tulip trees; occasionally attacks magnolia and linden.

Identification: Large, dark brown, soft scales are found along the twigs and branches.

Injury: Reduces the vigor of the tree and in the case of very heavy infestations may cause its death.

Life history: The winter is spent in the nymph stage, the small, partly grown nymphs clinging tightly to the twigs of the host tree. The nymphs grow rapidly during the spring and begin producing young by midsummer.

Control: Malathion, applied in early fall.

Magnolia

Insect Pest—Magnolia Scale

Identification: The magnolia scale is the largest of any of the scale insects. The female is $1/2$ in. across and is covered with a whitish wax. If the infestation is severe, the branches appear to be covered with a white, cottony substance.

Injury: Trees become weakened and leaves are small.

Life history: The young nymphs hibernate in young wood. They molt early in the spring and again in June, starting the secretion of wax. By August they produce living young.

Control: A dormant oil (Scalecide) spray in early spring just before new growth emerges will control the adult, overwintering scales. The crawler stage appears in late summer. Hence the use of a malathion or Sevin spray should be delayed until late August or early September.

Malus spp. (crab apple)

Disease—Cedar-apple Rust
Symptoms: Orange-yellow spots appear on the leaves in midsummer.

Control: See page 597.

Picea (spruce)

Insect Pest—Spruce Spider Mite
Indication: Foliage becomes grayish and unhealthy in appearance. Tiny webs are sometimes evident.

Life history: See page 605.

Control: See page 605.

Pinus (pines)

Disease—Blister-rust
Nature of the disease: There are many forms of blister-rust that attack various species of pine, the most common being the fungus *Cronartium ribicola*, which causes the stem blister-rust of the white pine and of other five-needle pines. Young trees are most susceptible, and on older trees it is the young branches that are first attacked.

Part of the life cycle of the fungus must be passed on an alternate host plant, the currant and the gooseberry being the hosts. When the covering of the blisterlike fruiting bodies on the pines has broken, the fine, powdery spores are liberated and blown in every direction. However, these spores cannot infect other pine trees because they must find lodgment on the leaves of the currant or·gooseberry in order to complete their cycle.

Symptoms: The injury is very characteristic and the young shoots are the first portion of the tree to become affected. When infection sets in, the bark becomes somewhat swollen, but it is not until the spring of the second or third year that the orange-colored fruiting bodies appear. At the point where these fruiting pustules appear on the tree a cankerous scar is left, and in many cases the branch becomes completely girdled and dies. If the infection extends into the trunk of the tree, the growth becomes characteristically stunted and compact, and there is a decidedly yellowish cast to the foliage.

Control: In forest plantings, eradicate the alternate hosts such as the European black currant *(Ribes nigrum)* within a 1-mile radius, and all wild currants within 900 feet. To eliminate cankers on pine, prune off cankered lateral branches or excise stem cankers by removing bark at least 4 in. above and below, and 2 in. on either side of discolored bark. Paint wounds with orange shellac followed by tree paint.

Insect Pests—Pine Spittlebug
Most injurious on Scots pine but also attacks white, pitch, red and Virginia pines and Norway spruce.

Identification: The young nymphs live in a frothy substance resembling the lightly beaten white of an egg.

Injury: The young feed on the twigs, ejecting undigested sap that causes the branches to become covered with a black, sooty mold. If infestation is not checked, it may cause the death of the tree within a few years.

Life history: The eggs are laid during the summer months at the base of the terminal buds, hatch the following May and the young begin feeding.

Control: Spray with malathion or Methoxychlor in mid-May and again in mid-July, directing the spray forcefully so as to hit the little masses of spittle that cover the insect.

Pine False Webworm
Identification: Larvae about 1 in. long, greenish-gray striped with purplish-red.

Injury: Larvae feed within a loose webbing, chewing off the needles and pulling them into the web. Trees can become completely defoliated if infestation is severe.

Life history: The adults emerge from their earthen cells between mid-April and early May, and the eggs, which are laid on the needles, hatch within a few weeks and the larvae begin feeding. In late June the mature larvae make silken tubes along the twigs and drop to the ground.

Control: Spray with Dylox or Methoxychlor when the larvae begin to feed in June.

Pine Webworm
Identification: Larvae are a yellowish-brown with two dark stripes along each side.

Injury: The larvae feed in silken webs near the ends of the terminal shoots.

Life history: The winter is passed in the pupa stage in the ground near the tree. Adults emerge from June to August.

Control: Same as for pine false webworm.

Redheaded Pine Sawfly
Identification: The larvae are whitish with brown heads when young, later becoming yellow with six rows of black spots.

Injury: The larvae live in groups and feed voraciously upon the needles of the pine, often completely defoliating young trees. They begin feeding about May and continue until late in the autumn.

Life history: The larvae winter over in the pupa stage, encased in tough, papery cocoons in the ground beneath the trees. The adult fly lays her eggs in slits in the needles. Young larvae begin feeding as soon as hatched. There are often two overlapping broods.

Control: As soon as an infestation is observed, spray the trees with Methoxychlor. Additional applications may be necessary in June, July and August because of the overlapping broods.

White Pine Sawfly
Identification: Larvae yellowish with four rows of black dots.

Control: Spray with Methoxychlor as soon as the larvae begin to feed in late spring.

White Pine Weevil
One of the most serious pests on white pines in the East. Sometimes attacks Scots and pitch pines and Norway spruce.

Identification: Adults are about ¼ in. long, reddish-brown, with a long, curved snout. Grubs are yellow, footless, ⅓ in. in length.

Injury: The grubs kill the terminal leader, girdling it as they mine into the bark, and causing it to turn brown and then die. Wilting and drooping of terminal shoots in the spring is the first sign of infestation.

Life history: Adults hibernate under trashy cover on the ground; begin feeding in May and the female lays two to three eggs in cavities which she cuts in the bark of the leader shoot. Grubs hatch in six to ten days and begin feeding on the inner bark. They pupate in the wood and emerge as beetles during the summer.

Control: Cut out and destroy all infested branches in order to kill the insects before they emerge as beetles. Spray valuable trees with Meta-Systox R in early May and repeat two weeks later. Where the tree's central leader is destroyed, a new leader may be encouraged to develop by tying the strongest of the next-lowest lateral shoots in an erect position with a small stick and a soft rope. Pruning the dead leader branch at a 45° angle, rather than straight across, will encourage the development of a new leader.

Platanus (sycamore)

Disease — Anthracnose (Leaf and Twig Blight)
Most common on sycamores; sometimes attacks oaks.

Symptoms: Foliage appears to be scorched. Leaves drop after they are dead and the tree may become defoliated.

Control: See page 602.

Pyracantha (firethorn)

Disease — Fire Blight
Attacks apples, pears, quinces, crab apples, hawthorns and pyracantha.

Nature of the disease: A bacterial disease that is spread from one plant to another by insects and by contaminated pruning shears.

Symptoms: The branches begin to die back, and look as if they had been burned by fire.

Control: Prune out infected branches, cutting well below the blighted region. Spraying with the antibiotic Agri-strep, as directed on the container. will control the blossom blight phase of this disease. The spray should be applied during the blossoming period at four- to five-day intervals. The initial application should be made when the first blossom opens and the last when the period of full bloom has been reached.

Insect Pests — Lace Bug
Identification: Small whitish and lacelike insects about ⅛ in. long are found on the undersurface of the leaves.

Life history: See page 603.

Control: See page 603.

Webworm
Identification: Small caterpillars feeding near the tips of the branches within a web.

Life history: See page 600.

Control: See page 602.

Quercus (oak)

Disease — Anthracnose (Leaf and Twig Blight)
Most common on sycamores but sometimes attacks oaks. The disease is caused by the fungus *Gnomonia quercina*. The asexual stage of this fungus, *Gloeosporium quercinum*, is rather common in the northern states on white and red oaks, American elm and black walnut.

Symptoms: The usual type of lesion appears as elongated brown spots along the main veins of the leaf. The infected tissue causes the death of the surrounding leaf tissue, and two or more lesions may involve an entire leaf. An infected tree may appear from a distance to be scorched. The leaves soon drop after they are dead, and the tree may become completely defoliated by early summer. Sometimes the young twigs become infected and turn brown as they start to grow. This symptom is often confused with frost injury. Cankers may also appear on the twigs. The center of the canker is usually sunken with a slightly raised margin. The repeated killing of the young branches often produces a gnarled type of growth.

Control: Three applications of Maneb or Zineb sprays will control this disease; the first application should be made when the leaves expand, the second when the leaves reach full size and the third, two weeks later. Difolatan sprays also provide control.

Rhododendron

Insect Pests — Rhododendron Borer

Sometimes attacks azaleas and mountain laurel.

Identification: Larvae are yellowish-white and about $\frac{1}{2}$ in. long. Adult moths black with three yellow bands.

Injury: The larvae bore into the sapwood under the bark and usually cause the branches to wilt or break off. The general vigor of the bush is affected and leaves turn brown.

Life history: The eggs are laid by the female moth on the twigs in May and June. The young larvae begin tunneling into the branches soon after hatching.

Control: Spray or paint the trunk and larger branches with Methoxychlor three times at twenty-day intervals, starting when the adults begin to emerge.

Lace Bug

Symptoms: Leaves begin to show yellowish stippling on upper surface, with rusty flecks on the underside; small, whitish, lacelike insects are found on the undersurface.

Life history: See page 603.

Control: See page 603.

Rhododendron spp. (azalea)

Disease — Azalea Flower Blight (also called Flower Spot and Petal Blight)

A most devastating disease, prevalent from Maryland southward to Florida, westward along the Gulf to Texas, and also in California.

Nature of disease: A fungus disease. The summer spores are formed inside the petals during periods of moist weather and are spread from flower to flower and bush to bush by wind, rain and insects. The spots on the petals — white spots on colored petals, brownish spots on white petals — indicate where each spore has landed. Within twenty-four hours in rainy or humid weather tiny black sclerotia form in the limp, slimy petals. Many of these drop to the ground or remain in the shriveled flowers. In very early spring the sclerotia on the ground send up little stalks. From the tiny sacs that develop on the top of the stalks the spores are catapulted into the air to find lodgement on the lower petals, and the cycle begins again.

Symptoms: Infection is first evidenced by a white, slimy spot on the petals. Flowers on the lower branches are the first to become affected. The disease spreads with incredible speed, particularly in warm, humid weather, and all the flowers become limp and slimy, the beauty of the blooms being completely ruined.

Control: The most important factor in control of azalea flower blight is prompt and persistent picking of infected flowers. In some plantings it has been found advisable to remove all the blossoms, including the uninfected ones. In larger plantings where it is impossible to do this, spraying the soil surface with Ferbam before flowering kills the ascospores which are formed in the fruiting structures. Protection of the flowers during their blooming period can be provided with Benlate sprays applied at five-day intervals. The first application should be made when the flowers begin to show color. This treatment should protect the plant for more than one year.

Insect Pests—Lace Bug
Identification: Small insects about ⅛ in. long, whitish and lacelike in appearance, are found on the undersurface of the leaves. Brown droplets of liquid are sometimes evident.

Injury: Lace bugs, both in the adult and nymph stage, suck the juices from the plant, causing a whitish speckling of the foliage and a gradual blanching and dying.

Life history: During the winter the eggs are embedded in the undersides of the leaves. The young nymphs hatch out in the spring and begin feeding. Several generations are produced during the year, damage being continued quite late into the autumn.

Control: As soon as the eggs hatch in spring, spray the undersides of the leaves with Meta-Systox R as directed on the container. Repeat in summer and fall if additional lace bugs appear.

Mites
Identification: The mites, almost infinitesimal in size, are found on the lower surface of the leaves, and tiny webs are sometimes observed. Foliage appears grayish, dusty and unhealthy.

Injury: Mites feed on both upper and lower surfaces of leaves, and if numerous will cause complete defoliation.

Life history: Eggs are laid on leaf surfaces, hatch in a few days and populations build up rapidly.

Control: Spray with a miticide such as Kelthane or Ovotran.

Whitefly
Identification: Tiny whiteflies on under surface of leaves.

Injury: Grayish speckling on the leaves. Bush appears unhealthy if infestation is heavy.

Life history: See page 611.

Control: Malathion sprays will control the nymphal stage of whitefly. The adult stage can be controlled with the synthetic pyrethroid, Resmethrin.

Syringa (lilac)

Disease—Powdery Mildew
Symptoms: Late in the summer a white coating appears on the foliage, giving it a dusty appearance.

Control: Benlate or Karathane sprays will control this disease.

Insect Pests—Lilac Borer
Attacks lilac, ash, mountain ash and privet.

Identification: Larvae from ¾ in. to 1½ in. in length, white with brown head. Adult a clear-winged moth.

Injury: The larvae tunnel under the bark and into the wood. Sawdust from new borings is sometimes noted. Old branches may become riddled with holes and die slowly. If the infestation is heavy and no control measures are undertaken, the health and vigor of the entire bush may be seriously affected.

Life history: The borer passes the winter in its tunnel within the branch, usually near the ground. It feeds for a short time in the spring and then pupates in its tunnel near the outer bark. Adults emerge during the spring and summer, according to the locality, and the females lay their eggs at the base of the branches or in roughened places on the bark. After hatching, the young larvae start tunneling into the stems. There is only one generation a year.

Control: Since the partly grown insects pass the winter in the stems of lilacs, the infested branches should be cut out and destroyed. Spray or paint the trunks and limbs at the end of April and repeat three times at ten-day intervals (in the latitude of New York City) with Methoxychlor. In more southerly areas, spray two to three weeks earlier. In more northerly areas, spray one to two weeks later.

Scale (Oyster Shell Scale)
Identification: Grayish scales, resembling miniature oysters, are found on twigs and branches.

Injury: The health and vigor of the bush is affected by scale and heavily infested twigs and branches die.

Life history: The winter is passed in the egg stage under the female shells. The young crawlers hatch in late May or June. After moving about for a few hours they penetrate the bark with their beaks.

Control: Spray the plants early in spring with lime sulphur while they are still in a dormant condition. If the dormant spray is not applied, or if the scale infestations are particularly heavy, spray with Diazinon in early June and repeat twice at two-week intervals.

Taxus (yew)

Insect Pest—*Taxus* Mealy Bug
Identification: The female is small, about ³/₈ in. long, and is covered with a white, waxy substance.

Injury: The mealy bugs suck the juices from the plant and cause a decline in vigor and appearance.

Life history: The nymphs winter over in crevices in the bark. They become mature about June and give birth to living young. There are two or three broods during the season. The adults disappear in the autumn.

Control: Good control is available by spraying with malathion or Cygon when the young stage is crawling about. In the area of Long Island and Connecticut, the latter part of May is the proper time to spray; in cooler regions, the application should be made a week or two later.

Thuja (arborvitae)

Insect Pests—Arborvitae Leaf Miner
Identification: Larvae very small, ¹/₅ in. long, color green with reddish tinge, head black.

Injury: Larvae make tunnels in the terminal leaves as they feed. Tip growth appears whitish and finally turns brown. In severe infestations the entire tree may be affected.

Life history: The small, gray moths emerge from the infested leaves in late spring or early summer. Eggs are laid, hatch within a few weeks, and the larvae begin to feed.

Control: If infestation is very slight, cut off and destroy the affected tips. Spray with malathion in mid-June and early July, when eggs are hatching.

Bagworm
Attacks arborvitae, hemlock, red cedar, larch, juniper, pine and spruce. Sometimes found on locust, soft maples, linden and sycamore.

Identification: The characteristic, grayish, spindle-shaped bags, an inch or two long, make identification of the bagworm easy. The bags are usually seen hanging near the tips of the branches, and they vary somewhat in appearance, as the outer covering is made from the needles, leaves and twigs of the host tree. The larvae are dark, brownish-black in color with white to yellowish, black-spotted head and thorax. When full grown they are about 1 in. long.

Injury: The larvae feed on the needles or leaves of the host tree. If present in great numbers they can do considerable damage, sometimes completely defoliating a tree and after several years, if left unchecked, causing its death.

Life history: The eggs winter over in the bag and the larvae hatch out in late spring. As it feeds, each larva constructs its own case, weaving a band of silk around itself and attaching it to a leaf or petiole whenever it stops to eat. Four molts take place and pupation occurs in late summer. The male moth mates with the female through an opening in the base of her bag. The maggotlike female lays from 500 to 1,000 eggs in the pupal case in her bag and then dies.

Control: If the infestation is light, the bags may be picked off during the winter and discarded in the trash can. Spray with Diazinon, malathion or Sevin when the young worms first appear. The time of this appearance varies from May 1 to June 1, depending on the locality. Spray seven to ten days later if live bagworms are still present.

Spruce Spider Mite

Attacks arborvitae, hemlock, juniper and spruce.

Identification: Minute, dark green to nearly black mites with pinkish legs. Webbing between the needles may often be detected.

Injury: The mites cause the foliage of the arborvitae to turn brown, the hemlock needles appear nearly white, the junipers appear yellowish and the spruce needles gray. If the infestation is severe, young trees die quickly. The lower branches of older trees are usually

the first to show injury and die. Injury is most pronounced in hot, dry seasons.

Life history: The winter eggs are laid in October at the base of the needles. The eggs hatch in April or May. As a new generation occurs every four to five weeks, the mite population builds up very rapidly.

Control: Spray with lime sulphur or with a "superior"-type dormant oil in early spring just before new growth emerges. Or spray in mid-May with chlorobenzilate, Kelthane, Meta-Systox R or Tedion to kill the young mites of the new generation. Repeat in September if necessary.

Tsuga (hemlock)

Insect Pest — Spruce Spider Mite
Identification: Needles appear whitish, giving the tree an unhealthy appearance.

Control: See above.

Ulmus (elm)

Disease — Dutch Elm Disease
Nature of the disease: The disease is caused by the fungus *Ceratostomella ulmi.* The European elm bark beetle has proved to be the principal carrier of the disease. The beetles winter over in dead or diseased wood, emerging in the spring. They migrate to healthy trees where, during the process of feeding in newly formed twig crotches, they place fungus spores of the disease into the wounded tissues of the tree, whence it soon spreads through the entire vascular system.

Symptoms: In the case of acute attacks the foliage of the entire tree may wilt rather quickly. The leaves may or may not turn yellow before wilting. Soon afterwards the tree may drop its leaves. However, the disease usually presents a more chronic condition, and only a few branches at a time are attacked. For this reason it is often difficult to distinguish from other diseases. The presence of branches bearing wilted or yellow leaves should be investigated at once. If the disease is present, a diagonal section through the twig will show a whole or partial brown ring. Sometimes the ring consists of a series of brown spots.

Control: Spraying elms with Methoxychlor in March or early April will control the bark beetles that spread the causal fungus. Two chemical compounds, Lignasan BLP and Arbotect 20–S, have recently been developed as aids in the control of Dutch elm disease. These compounds are injected under pressure into the trunks of elms as preventives or as therapeutic treatment for mildly affected trees.

Strict sanitation practices, including prompt removal and destruction of diseased trees, are perhaps the most important control practice.

Two recently developed hybrid elms, Urban and Sapporo Autumn Gold, are said to have natural immunity to the disease.

Insect Pests – Cankerworm

Both the fall and the spring cankerworm usually appear in cycles. For several successive years they will be present in vast numbers, and they will then almost disappear for a few years, only to return for another upswing of the cycle.

Fall Cankerworm

Attacks elms, oaks and apples. Sometimes attacks birch, linden and maple trees and cherry, plum and other fruit trees. During the end of their feeding period they occasionally attack roses, rhododendron and other shrubs growing nearby.

Identification: Male moths brownish-gray with a 1¼-in. wing spread. Female moths are gray, and completely wingless, ½ in. in length. Larvae are about 1 in. long, brownish on the upper surface, green below, with three narrow white stripes along the body above the spiracles, and a yellow stripe below. They have a charac-

teristic of dropping from a branch or leaf on a silken thread and then climbing back again.

Injury: Larvae feed on the foliage, causing great damage if the infestation is heavy.

Life history: The moths emerge in the late autumn, usually after there have been freezing temperatures. The wingless females crawl up the trunk of the host tree to deposit their grayish eggs in a compact, single-layered mass. The eggs hatch in early spring about the time the leaves begin to unfold, and the larvae feed on the foliage until early summer. When fully mature they drop to the ground and spin a silken cocoon in which they pass the pupa stage, at a depth of 1 in. to 4 in. Only one generation is produced in a year.

Control: Spray the leaves with Dipel or Thuricide *(Bacillus thuringiensis),* or with Imidan while the worms are small.

As a precautionary measure a 4-in. to 6-in. band of heavy paper, cotton batting or Balsam wool may be bound about the trunk of a tree and smeared with Tree Tanglefoot in late September. This will entangle many of the female moths as they ascend the trunk to lay their eggs. Great care must be taken not to let the Tree Tanglefoot come into direct contact with the bark of the tree as it may cause serious injury. This measure of control is, at best, only partially effective, but many moths will be destroyed. It is best suited to use on individual trees on a lawn rather than on trees grouped closely in a grove or woodland. Tree Tanglefoot can be purchased at most garden centers, and is also useful to trap house flies.

Spring Cankerworm

Attacks elms and apples; less often injures oaks, hickory, cherry and maple.

Identification: Female moths are gray, wingless, and may be distinguished from the fall cankerworm moth by the dark stripe down the back and the rows of stiff, reddish spines on the first seven joints of the abdomen. The larvae are about 1 in. long and vary in color from green to brownish-black, usually having a yellow stripe under the spiracles.

Injury: The caterpillars are voracious feeders, often completely skeletonizing the leaves and causing defoliation of a tree. They are one of the most annoying of tree pests. When they are present in great numbers, one can actually hear the crunching of the leaves as they feed, and their droppings fall in the form of a rain of tiny black pellets on terraces, furniture and unwary guests. Where infestations are very severe for a number of years, the ravages of cankerworms may cause the death of trees through defoliation. At best, the trees are so weakened that they become extremely vulnerable to other pests and diseases.

Life history: Moths hatch in early spring, and the wingless females crawl up the trunk to lay their eggs. The brownish-purple oval eggs are laid in loose clusters under the bark scales on the main trunk of the tree and on some of the larger branches. The eggs hatch in about thirty days, and the caterpillars begin their feeding period. When mature, they drop to the ground and pass the period of pupation in the soil at the foot of the host tree.

Control: See control for fall cankerworm. If the practice of tree banding is followed, the material should be freshly applied before the female moths begin to ascend the tree trunks in the spring.

Elm Leaf Beetle

Attacks American, English and Scotch elms and *Zelkova serrata.* The slippery, rock and winged elms are usually not attacked by the elm leaf beetle.

Identification: The adult beetle is slender, about ¼ in. in length, yellow to olive green in color, with a dark line near the outer edge of each wing, which becomes less distinguishable prior to hibernation. Larvae are yellow but so spotted and striped that they appear almost black, about ½ in. in length.

Injury: The adult beetles feed on the young foliage of the tree in the spring as it unfolds, making many small holes, but most of the damage is done in the larval stage. The larvae are voracious feeders and when infestation is heavy they practically skeletonize the leaves. Foliage takes on the appearance of brown lace, and the tree may become completely defoliated. The vigor of the tree is greatly weakened so that it becomes an easy victim of other pests and diseases. Three years of defoliation will usually cause the death of the tree.

Life history: The adult beetles emerge from their winter hiding places in early spring and begin feeding. They lay their yellow, lemon-shaped eggs in clusters of five to twenty-five on the underside of the leaves in late spring and early summer. The egg-laying period continues for several weeks, a single female laying about 500 eggs. The eggs hatch in five to six days and the larvae begin their feeding period, which lasts from fifteen to twenty days. The larvae then drop or crawl to the ground and pass into the pupa stage at the base of the tree. The period of pupation is very brief; in six to ten days the adult beetles emerge and the life cycle of the second generation begins. The number of generations in a season varies from one to four, depending upon the climate. During the latter part of the summer the beetles usually crawl into houses to hibernate until spring, often being found in cellars or attics.

Control: Spray carefully with Sevin after the leaves are partly expanded, taking care that spray reaches only the affected tree. Repeat about three weeks later. The masses of grubs or pupae around the base of the tree can be destroyed by wetting the soil with a dilute solution of malathion prepared from the emulsifiable concentrate.

DISEASES AND INSECT PESTS OF FLOWERING PLANTS

Althea (hollyhock)

Diseases — Anthracnose

A fungus disease, *Colletotrichum malvarum*, that causes severe losses in some parts of the country.

Symptoms: The foliage becomes covered with irregular, dark brown spots and the leaves wither and fall. Sunken spots varying in color from pale yellow to black appear on the stems and petioles of the leaves. When young plants in the seedbed are attacked, the leaf stalks usually collapse.

Control: Spray the plants with Benlate after periods of wet weather.

Cercosporose

A rather uncommon fungus disease caused by *Cercospora althaeina*.

Symptoms: Large, dark, angular spots appear on the leaves. The spots are surrounded by darker margins, and as the disease progresses the center becomes a light ashen-gray. Upon this light center small black dots may be distinguished. When the infection is severe, the plants lose nearly all of their foliage.

Control: Gather and destroy all above-ground parts of the plant in the fall. Spraying the plants with Bordeaux mixture or Fore several times during the growing season will control this disease.

Rust

Nature of the disease: A fungus disease caused by *Puccinia malvacearum*. It was first discovered in Chile, and from there was introduced into France. It was brought into this country in 1886 on some infected seed and has spread with alarming rapidity to almost every section of the United States where hollyhocks are grown. It renders the plants most unsightly and is very insidious.

Symptoms: Leaves and stems become covered with raised pustules, a light rusty-brown in color. If the infection is severe, the whole plant may wither and die. In mild cases, however, the lower leaves are killed but the plant continues to grow and flower.

Control: Remove and destroy the first leaves on which the rust is evident. Frequent spraying with wettable sulphur, Zineb or Fore is effective. Two or three applications a week may be necessary, since new leaves develop rapidly and it is essential to have a fungicide present on the new leaves as early as possible.

Insect Pests — Japanese Beetle *(Popillia japonica)*
Identification: Large, handsome beetles, a metallic greenish-bronze in color, with two conspicuous and several small white spots near the tip of the abdomen. During the middle of the day they are very active, making rapid flight when disturbed. In the evening they are more sluggish.

Injury: The beetles feed upon both the foliage and the flowers and can completely demolish a plant in a very short time.

Life history: See page 652.

Control: See page 652.

Leaf Roller
Identification: Small, active caterpillars about 1/4 in. long, olive green in color.

Injury: The caterpillars feed upon the foliage, their work being very characteristic as they roll and tie the leaves together with fine silken threads.

Life history: See page 615.

Control: See page 615.

Stalk Borer (Common)
Identification: Slender caterpillars about 1 in. or 2 in. in length. The young caterpillars are brown with white stripes. When full grown they lose their stripes and become a solid dirty gray in color.

Injury: The stalk borer makes a small, round hole in the stem and tunnels up through the stalk, causing the injured shoot to suddenly wilt and die.

Life history: See page 615.

Control: See page 616.

Yellow Wooly-bear Caterpillar
Identification: A caterpillar about 2 in. in length when full grown. The body is completely covered with long hairs, which vary in color from pale yellow to reddish-brown.

Injury: The caterpillars feed upon the leaves.

Life history: See page 623.

Control: See page 623.

Antirrhinum (snapdragon)

Diseases — Anthracnose
A fungus disease caused by *Colletotrichum antirrhini* that is rather common on greenhouse plants and frequently found on outdoor plants started under glass.

Symptoms: Small brownish spots with a dark, narrow margin appear on the leaves. Canker-ous formations develop on the stems, frequently girdling them. Growth is seriously affected and badly diseased plants may succumb entirely to the fungus.

Control: Spray with Captan, Maneb or Zineb. Take cuttings only from healthy plants. When watering plants, avoid wetting the leaves.

Blight
A fungus disease caused by *Phyllostictia antirrhini,* very prevalent in some parts of the country.

Symptoms: Yellowish, somewhat circular spots appear on the foliage. Stems brownish. Occasionally dark shrunken areas resembling cankers are found on the stems. In the center of each leaf spot there is a minute black pimple, which readily distinguishes blight from other diseases attacking antirrhinums. Young seedlings die off rapidly when affected with blight, apparently rotting off at the ground line. Older plants are more resistant but will eventually succumb unless the disease is checked.

Control: Same as for anthracnose above.

Rust
Nature of the disease: A fungus disease caused by *Puccinia antirrhini.* The spores of the fungus are readily blown about by the wind and the disease spreads rapidly from plant to plant. As the spores require a certain amount of moisture for germination, rust is more prevalent during a rainy season than during a dry season.

Symptoms: Stems and leaves become covered with rusty-brown pustules. If rust is allowed to gain headway, the plants will be killed in a comparatively short time.

Control: In the greenhouse, spray the plants several times at weekly intervals with Maneb or Zineb. Rust-resistant varieties should be used when snapdragons are grown outdoors.

Wilt

Nature of the disease: A fungus disease that attacks the plant through the roots. It is usually first introduced on infected seed and the fungus lives over in the soil for many years. Extremely moist conditions favor its spread.

Symptoms: Plants suddenly wilt and die as if from lack of water. When the stem is split open, the sap tubes will be found to be dark and discolored.

Control: Pasteurizing the soil with steam will control several species of fungi that cause the wilt disease.

Aquilegia (columbine)

Diseases — Root Rot or Crown Rot

Nature of the disease: A fungus disease caused by certain fungi known as *Sclerotinia sclerotiorum*. It is becoming more and more prevalent and causes serious losses in some areas of the country. The long-spurred types seem to be more susceptible than the old-fashioned short-spurred varieties.

Symptoms: Plants show general lack of vigor and rot off at the crown. They may be attacked at any time during the growing season or they may fail to winter over.

Control: No effective control other than steam-pasteurization of soil, available from professional nurserymen.

Insect Pests — Aphids

Identification: Soft-bodied, licelike insects that are usually found clustered near the tips of the young, growing shoots. They are light green in color and vary in size, the newly hatched young being considerably smaller than the adults.

Injury: Aphids suck the juices from the plant and cause a general lack of vigor and stunted growth.

Life history: In the North aphids pass the winter in the egg stage, while in the South where the winters are mild they continue to breed throughout the year. The eggs, which are small, black and glossy in appearance, hatch early in the spring and the young aphids begin feeding immediately. This first brood matures in about two weeks and from then on, until autumn, living young are produced from unfertilized eggs. These are all females and reproduction takes place with startling rapidity as each mature female gives birth daily to several young and nearly 100 generations are sometimes produced in a single season. In the autumn males appear, and the eggs that carry the aphids over the winter are fertilized. The life history of the aphids is one of the most remarkable in the entire animal kingdom.

Control: Sprays containing malathion or Meta-Systox R are very effective in controlling aphids.

Leaf Miner *(Phytomyza miniscula)*

Identification: Small worms that feed within the tissues of the leaf, making a white serpentine trail. The trail usually crosses itself several times and ends in a small spot about 1/8 in. in diameter. Eight to ten larvae sometimes develop within a single leaf.

Injury: The foliage becomes badly disfigured and the vitality of the plant is lowered.

Life history: The adult flies, which are small and dark brown in color, appear early in May. They feed for a short time, doing no noticeable damage, and then deposit their eggs on the underside of the leaves. The eggs hatch within a few weeks and the larvae immediately tunnel their way into the leaves, where they feed for about ten days. They then pass into the pupa state, the tiny pupa being attached to the leaf. A short time later the adult flies emerge and the life cycle begins again. There are several generations each summer, the last appearing about the middle of September. The winter is passed in the pupa state, the pupa case being buried in the soil close to the plants.

Control: Pick off infested leaves as soon as they are visible. In the fall all plant remains should be removed and discarded. Spray with malathion or Meta-Systox R in late May or early June.

Whitefly

Though whiteflies are generally regarded as greenhouse pests, they also occasionally attack plants in the open. This is particularly apt to happen if the garden is located near a greenhouse or conservatory.

Identification: Very small, whitish flies about 1/16 in. long with four wings. They are usually found on the undersurface of the leaves.

Injury: Whiteflies suck the juices from the plant causing a general reduction of vigor. The leaves turn yellow, and if the infestation is severe the plant eventually dies.

Life history: The females deposit their minute yellow eggs on the underside of the leaves upon which they are feeding. The young nymphs that hatch from the eggs are very small and almost flat, being a pale green, somewhat transparent color. The nymphs feed for about four weeks and pass through four molts before they become full grown. The average life of an adult fly is between thirty and forty days, and many generations are produced during the year.

Control: Malathion sprays will control the nymphal stage. The synthetic pyrethroid, Resmethrin, will control both the nymphal and adult stages.

Begonia, tuberous

Tuberous begonias grown outdoors are comparatively free from pests and diseases. Plants grown in greenhouses or indoors are more subject to trouble, and difficulties are sometimes encountered.

**Diseases – Bacterial Leaf Spot
(*Xanthomonas begoniae*)**

Seldom causes trouble if tubers are obtained from a reliable source.

Symptoms: Spots appear on the leaves, disfiguring the foliage of the plant.

Control: Remove and discard all affected leaves. Spray with a 2–2–50 solution of Bordeaux mixture. Repeat every week or ten days. Three to four applications recommended. The new Reiger *elatior* begonias are particularly susceptible.

Mildews

Two species of fungi, *Oidium geginiae* and *Erysiphe cichoracearum*, frequently attack begonias.

Symptoms: Leaves become affected with a powdery, grayish-white mildew that spreads rapidly over the entire surface of the leaf unless checked. Plants become sickly and fail to flower well.

Control: Spray thoroughly at the first sign of trouble with Benlate, Karathane or wettable sulphur.

Insect Pests – Mealy Bug

Identification: Scales covered with a white, waxy secretion appear on the stems and sometimes on the undersurface of the leaves.

Life history: The entire life cycle is completed on the plant. The female deposits eggs in a wax-covered sac at rear of body, then dies. Sacs are usually found in the axils of stems or leaf petioles. Hatching occurs in ten days and the young nymphs begin feeding.

Control: Spray with malathion.

Mites
Identification: The young shoots are attacked and the underside of the leaves turn a rusty-brown, having a glazed appearance. The leaves have a tendency to curl. Infinitesimal mites may be seen under a hand lens. The plants gradually become sickly and unhealthy in appearance and fail to bloom well. Infestation is most likely to occur when tuberous begonias are grown near gloxinias, cyclamen and other susceptible plants.

Life history: See page 594.

Control: See page 595.

Thrips
Identification: Dark streaks appear on the stems, leaves and flowers. Plants appear stunted and malformed.

Life history: See page 657.

Control: See page 657.

Slugs and Snails
Identification: Slugs and snails can cause severe damage if present in great numbers. They feed at night, chiefly upon the petals of the flowers and the tender foliage of young shoots.

Control: Use a good commercial bait. Such mixtures usually contain metaldehyde, which is the most effective control.

Calendula (pot marigold)

Diseases – Mosaic
Nature of the disease: Aphids and leafhoppers are probable carriers of the disease in very much the same way that mosquitoes carry malaria to human beings. In sucking the juices of a diseased plant these insects pick up the infectious virus, later transmitting it to healthy plants.

Symptoms: The foliage has a curiously mottled appearance, blotched and streaked with yellow and in some cases the leaves become distorted in shape.

Control: When once injected, the virus penetrates to every part of the plant and there is no known cure for the disease.

All diseased plants should be pulled up and destroyed in order to lessen sources of infection. Spray with Meta-Systox R to control the insect vectors.

Soft Rot
A fungus disease that is apt to be prevalent during damp seasons. The resting bodies of the fungus, known as sclerotia, resemble little hard, black balls.

Symptoms: Plants rot away. The rotted tissues are frequently covered with a white mold.

Control: Remove and destroy all infected plants. Set new plants in steam-pasteurized soil.

Insect Pests – Aphids
Identification: Soft-bodied, louselike insects, which are usually found clustered near the tips of the young shoots. They are light green in color and vary in size, the newly hatched young being considerably smaller than the adults.

Injury: Aphids suck the juices of the plant and cause stunted growth and a general lack of vigor.

Life history: See page 610.

Control: See page 610.

Black Blister Beetle (also known as *Aster Beetle*)
Identification: A slender jet-black beetle about 1/2 in. in length, with prominent head and neck.

Injury: The beetles feed upon the flowers, completely destroying them in a short time.

Life history: See page 614.

Control: See page 614.

Cabbage Worm
Identification: Small velvety, green caterpillars, somewhat more than 1 in. in length when full grown.

Injury: Large, irregular holes eaten in the foliage.

Life history: The winter is passed in the pupa stage and the adult butterflies, which are white with three or four black spots on the wings, emerge early in the spring. The females lay their small yellow eggs one at a time upon the undersurface of the leaves of the various host plants. Several hundred eggs are laid by each female. The very small green caterpillars hatch out in about a week and begin feeding immediately. They develop rapidly, becoming full grown within a few weeks, and then pass into the pupa stage. Several weeks later the adult butterflies emerge. One generation swiftly succeeds another throughout the summer until sometimes as many as five or six broods are produced.

Control: Spray with *Bacillus thuringiensis* or, less preferably, with Sevin.

Stalk Borer (common)
Identification: Slender caterpillars about 1 in. to 2 in. in length when full grown. The young caterpillars are brown with white stripes. When full grown they lose their stripes and become a solid dirty gray.

Injury: The stalk borer makes a small round hole in the stem and tunnels up through the stalk, causing the injured shoot suddenly to wilt and break over.

Life history: See page 615.

Control: See page 616. Clean cultivation about the garden in order to destroy breeding places is important.
   Cut off and destroy infested shoots or insert a small wire with a hook on the end of it into the tunnel and drag the borer out.

Whitefly
Identification: Very small, whitish flies about $1/16$ in. in length. They have four wings and are found usually on the undersurface of the leaves on plants near greenhouses.

Injury: Whiteflies suck the juices from the plant, causing a general lack of vigor.

Life history: See page 611.

Control: See page 611.

Callistephus (aster, annual)

Diseases – Leaf Spot
   A fungus disease prevalent in some part of the country, caused by *Septoria callistephi*, *Ascochyta asteris* and *Botrytis* sp.

Symptoms: Small dark spots appear on the leaves, gradually becoming larger.

Control: Spray thoroughly at monthly intervals, or more often if necessary, with Captan or Maneb.

Rust
   A fungus disease caused by *Coleosporium solidaginis*, one stage of which is passed on asters and closely related plants, the other stage being passed on pine trees.

Symptoms: Orange-colored patches of rust appear on the leaves, and unless the disease is checked the leaves turn yellow and die.

Control: Spray with Maneb or Zineb several times early in the growing season.

Wilt

A fungus disease caused by *Fusarium oxysporium* var. *callistephi,* which attacks the plants through the roots.

Symptoms: Young plants in the seedbed are frequently attacked and rot off at the ground line. The time of transplanting and of blossoming seem to be susceptible periods for older plants. The lower leaves are usually affected first, turning a yellowish-green in the early stages, later becoming withered and black. Occasionally only one side of the plant is affected. Dark streaks develop in the cortex of the stem and in severe cases the stems and roots rot away entirely. Plants sometimes die quickly when attacked, although others occasionally linger on for months producing a few small blooms.

Control: Benomyl soil drench gives excellent control of *Fusarium* when used at the rates given on the label. Wilt-resistant seed is also available from the major seed companies.

Yellows

Nature of the disease: Yellows is caused by a mycoplasmalike organism in the sap of the plant. The aster leafhopper *(Macrosteles fascifrons)* is the principal vector of the disease, which apparently cannot be spread by any other organism. One can handle diseased plants without any fear of spreading the infection. Many other closely related plants are attacked by the yellows and the disease is carried over the winter by various perennial hosts.

Symptoms: Plants become dwarfed if attacked when young. Older plants have a curiously bushy and erect habit of growth, the young branches that arise from the axils of the leaves being thin and yellowish in color. Leaves that are not mature at the time infection takes place turn bright yellow; this is first evidenced by a slight yellowing along the veins. Occasionally only one side of a plant is affected. The injury to the flowers is very characteristic of the disease, the blossoms becoming dwarfed and distorted and frequently developing only on one side. Plants are practically never killed outright, usually living on until cut down by frost.

Control: The aster leafhopper that spreads the disease can be controlled by spraying with Diazinon or Meta-Systox R. When grown commercially, asters are frequently covered with cheesecloth to exclude the leafhopper.

Insect Pests — Black Blister Beetle
(also known as *Aster Beetle*)

Identification: A slender jet-black beetle about $\frac{1}{2}$ in. in length, with prominent head and neck.

Injury: The beetles feed voraciously upon the flowers, completely destroying them in a short time.

Life history: The winter is passed in the larva stage, the grubs pupating early in the spring. The adult beetles appear about the middle of June.

Control: Sprays containing Methoxychlor are effective in controlling this pest.

Buffalo Tree Hopper

Identification: A small green insect about $\frac{3}{8}$ in. long, triangular in shape with a two-horned enlargement at the front.

Injury: The nymphs and adult insects feed upon the plants and do considerable damage if they become numerous.

Life history: The eggs are deposited in slits in the bark of trees and occasionally in the bark of rose bushes. The winter is passed in the egg stage. Late in the spring the small green nymphs hatch out and begin feeding on the sap of various plants. They become full grown by August and the adult females die as soon as they have deposited their eggs.

Control: Clean cultivation in and about the garden will help to control this pest. Spraying with malathion or Cygon in June is also usually effective.

Leaf Miner *(Phytomyza miniscula)*
Identification: Small worms that feed within the tissues of the leaf, making a white serpentine trail. The trail usually crosses itself several times and ends in a small spot about ⅛ in. in diameter. Eight to ten larvae sometimes develop within a single leaf.

Injury: The foliage becomes badly disfigured and the vitality of the plant is lowered.

Life history: See page 610.

Control: Cultivate the ground about the plants as early as possible in the spring in order to destroy the pupa cases before the flies emerge.

Leaf Roller *(Choristeunera roseacana)*
Identification: Small caterpillars about ½ in. in length when full grown. They vary in color from yellow to light green.

Injury: The caterpillars feed upon the flower buds and the foliage, rolling and tying the leaves in a very characteristic manner with fine silken threads.

Life history: The female moths deposit their eggs in tiny masses upon the foliage of the host plants. The young caterpillars hatch out a few weeks later and begin feeding. They become full grown in about a month and pupate within the rolled leaves. The pupa stage extends over a period of about two weeks. The adult moths then emerge and the life cycle begins again. Two broods are generally produced during the season.

Control: Sprays containing Cygon applied before the leaves are rolled will provide control.

Root Aphids
Identification: Soft-bodied, whitish-gray insects found clustered along the roots or near the crown of the plant.

Injury: Root aphids suck the juices from the plant, causing it to become dwarfed and stunted. The foliage frequently turns yellow, indicating general lack of vigor. The presence of aphids can only be determined by lifting some of the infested plants and examining the roots.

Control: Wetting the soil near the base of the plant with a dilute solution of Diazinon or one made from the emulsifiable concentrate of malathion will control root aphids.

Stalk Borer (Common)
Identification: Slender caterpillars about 1 in. or 2 in. in length. The young caterpillars are brown with white stripes. When full grown they lose their stripes and become a solid, dirty gray in color.

Injury: The stalk borer makes a small, round hole in the stem and tunnels up through the stalk, causing the injured shoot to wilt suddenly and break over.

Life history: The common stalk borer passes the winter in the egg stage, the eggs being laid on grasses and weeds in the autumn. The larvae hatch very early in the spring. When small they attack the stems of grasses, but as they grow they become more ambitious and move on to larger plants. They change frequently from the stem of one plant to that of another, seldom remaining long in one place. The caterpillars become full grown about August 1 and pass into the pupa stage within the stem of the plant upon which they happen to be feeding at the time. Late in September the adult moths emerge and the females deposit their eggs.

Control: Clean cultivation about the garden in order to destroy breeding places is one of the most important measures of control. Spray with a methoxychlor-Kelthane mixture in early summer to control the borers before they enter the stems. If this has not been done, the borers can be killed with a flexible wire, or by sticking straight pins through the stalk in several places (this will not harm the stem).

Tarnished Plant Bug

Identification: A small, very active bug about ¼ in. in length. The oval body is somewhat triangular in front. Coppery-brown in color, with dark brown and yellow flecks on the back.

Injury: The bugs puncture the shoots just below the flower heads, causing the buds to droop and die. The injury completely destroys any chance of bloom. It is believed that, while feeding, the tarnished plant bug injects some substance into the sap that is highly injurious to the plant and has the effect of a poison.

Life history: The adults live over the winter in the shelter of long grasses; with the first warm days of spring they become very active and begin feeding. The eggs are usually laid in the stems of herbaceous plants, and occasionally in growing fruit such as peaches. Two generations are produced during the season.

Control: Apply a Methoxychlor spray each week during the period when adults are to be seen. Clean cultivation both in and about the garden will destroy breeding places and help also to keep the tarnished plant bug under control.

Whitefly

Identification: Very small whitish flies, about ¹⁄₁₆ in. in length, with four wings. They occur usually on the undersurface of the leaves.

Injury: Whiteflies suck the juices from the plant, causing a general lack of vigor. Leaves turn yellow, and if the infestation is severe the plant will eventually die.

Life history: See page 611.

Control: See page 611.

White Grubs

The grubs of the Asiatic garden beetle, the June beetle and various other species cause damage to garden plants.

Identification: Large, fleshy grub worms, grayish-white in color, with a brown head and six prominent legs. They are usually found in a curled position buried in the soil.

Injury: The grubs feed upon the roots, causing the plant to become stunted and weakened. If the infestation is severe, the plants may die.

Life history: The larvae winter over in the soil. In late spring the adults emerge from the soil at night, feeding while it is dark and returning to the soil at daybreak. The females deposit their eggs several inches below the surface of the soil, generally selecting grassy fields or weedy areas. The eggs hatch in two or three weeks and the young grubs begin feeding on the roots of nearby plants. Some species complete their growth in one year while others require from two to four years. The most common species requires three years, and the grubs cause the greatest damage during the second feeding season. During the winter they burrow down below the frost line. Grub worms are particularly troublesome on grassy or weedy ground.

Control: Diazinon, Dursban or Dylox will control grubs. An annual treatment during August is necessary. Water the area well immediately after applying the insecticide.

Campanula (Canterbury-bells)

Disease—Root Rot

Nature of the disease: The root rot of *Campanula* is caused by the fungus *Pellicularia rolfsii*. It is particularly troublesome during hot, wet weather. The fungus produces small brown, resting bodies resembling mustard seed.

Symptoms: Plants show signs of wilting; tips of the branches dry up, foliage turns a pale yellowish-green, roots become rotted. Occasionally only a single branch is affected.

Control: Soil-infesting fungi can only be controlled by pasteurizing the soil with steam.

Insect Pest—Rose Chafer (*Macrodactylus subspinosus,* also known as Rose Beetle or Rose Bug)

Identification: Grayish-fawn long-legged beetles, about ½ in. in length.

Injury: The beetles feed upon the flowers.

Life history: See page 653.

Control: See page 654.

Canna

Disease—Bud Rot

A bacterial disease caused by *Xanthomonas* spp. Some varieties seem to be much more susceptible than others.

Symptoms: The young buds become a mass of rotted tissue and the foliage becomes spotted. The disease is seldom fatal and vigorous plants will often entirely outgrow it. When plants are severely attacked, however, there is considerable loss of bloom.

Control: Use only healthy root stocks for propagation. Suspicious ones should be dipped into a streptomycin solution before planting; Streptomycin bud and leaf sprays might also help. Avoid overwatering, overcrowding and poor ventilation.

Insect Pests—Corn Ear Worm

Identification: Large striped worms about 2 in. in length when full grown. They vary in color from light green to brown and the stripes, which run lengthwise on the body, are alternating light and dark. The head is yellow, the legs almost black.

Injury: The caterpillars feed upon both the foliage and the flower buds, soon causing considerable damage.

Life history: The adult female moths deposit their eggs upon the host plants, flying only in the evening or on dark, cloudy days. The eggs are laid singly and an individual moth will deposit anywhere from 500 to 2,000 during her lifetime. The eggs hatch in from three to five days and the larvae feed ravenously for about three weeks. At this time they have reached their full growth and drop to the ground, where they burrow into the soil to form a small cell-like structure in which the pupa stage is passed. Two to three weeks later the adult moths emerge and the life cycle begins again. Two to three generations are produced each year, and the winter is passed in the pupa stage 4 in. to 5 in. below the surface of the soil. Before entering the pupa stage, the larvae carefully prepare small exit tunnels through which the moths may crawl when they are ready to emerge. The moths vary in color from light gray to brown.

Control: Spray with Sevin, being careful to limit spray to infected plants.

Greenhouse Leaf Tier

Although primarily a greenhouse insect, the leaf tier is often troublesome on garden flowers.

Identification: Slender, yellowish-green caterpillars, with a broad white stripe running lengthwise down the back and a dark green band in the center of the stripe. When full grown they are about ¾ in. in length.

Injury: The caterpillars feed upon the leaves, often completely skeletonizing them. They also form a light web, which draws the edges of the leaves together in a very characteristic way.

Life history: The brownish adult moths usually fly at night and the females lay their eggs upon the underside of the leaves of the host plants. The eggs hatch in about two weeks and the larvae begin feeding. When the caterpillars are full grown and ready to pupate, they roll the edge of the leaf over and fasten it with a delicate web. Within this shelter they spin their silken cocoons. Ten days later the adult moths emerge. The life cycle takes forty days and several generations are produced each season.

Control: Spray with Methoxychlor when the caterpillars begin to feed.

Leaf Roller

Cannas are attacked by two distinct species of leaf rollers. The Lesser Canna Leaf Roller and the Larger Canna Leaf Roller. These are both very prevalent in some sections of the South but are seldom seen in the North.

Injury: The caterpillars feed upon both the foliage and the blossoms, rolling and tying the leaves together with fine silken threads.

Control: See page 615.

Rose Weevil

Identification: Dull and brownish-gray beetles slightly over ¼ in. in length with a white line running diagonally across each wing.

Injury: The beetles feed upon the foliage,

unopened buds and flowers. Most of their feeding is done at night.

Control: Spray with Methoxychlor.

Saddle-back Caterpillar

Identification: A caterpillar about 1 in. in length and of very striking appearance. It is brown at each end, the main part of the body light green with a little purple saddle over the back. It also possesses stinging, poisonous hairs.

Injury: The caterpillars feed upon the foliage and the flowers.

Control: Spray with Methoxychlor.

Caution: Do not touch the caterpillars with bare hands as certain hairs on the body inject a poison into the skin that causes a very unpleasant stinging sensation.

Spotted Cucumber Beetle

Identification: A yellowish-green beetle about ¼ in. in length with 12 very conspicuous black spots on its back. The head and antennae, which are almost two-thirds as long as the body, are black.

Injury: The beetles feed upon the leaves, buds and flowers.

Life history: The adult beetles hibernate during the winter in long grass and near the base of woody plants. They become active very early in the spring, when they begin feeding. The females deposit their eggs in the ground and, upon hatching, the young larvae bore into the roots of nearby plants where they feed until they become full grown. Early in July they pass into the pupa stage, which lasts for about a week, at which time the adult beetles emerge. Two generations are produced each season in the South and one or two in the North.

Control: Spray with Diazinon.

Centaurea (bachelor's-button)

Disease—Root Rot
Symptoms: Plants become sickly and rot off near the crown and white mold is often found on the lower portion of the stem.

Control: Destroy infected plants. Replace infested soil with clean soil or steam-pasteurize old soil.

Rust
Symptoms: Rusty spots appear on the leaves and stems.

Control: Wettable sulphur or Ferbam sprays will control the rust diseases.

Insect Pest—Root Aphids
Identification: Soft-bodied white or grayish-green insects found clustered along the roots or near the crown of the plant.

Injury: Root aphids suck the juices from the plant causing it to become dwarfed and stunted. Foliage turns yellow.

Control: See page 615.

Cheiranthus (wallflower)

Insect Pests—Diamond-back Moth Caterpillar
Identification: Small, slender caterpillars about 2/5 in. long, light green in color. The caterpillars are very active and when disturbed they usually drop from the plant, suspending themselves by a fine silken thread.

Injury: The caterpillars feed upon the foliage, often completely skeletonizing it.

Control: Spray with Imidan.

Potato Flea Beetle
Identification: Small, very active beetles about 1/16 in. long, of a dark, somewhat metallic color. The hind legs are longer than the front legs and enable the beetle to jump like a flea when disturbed.

Injury: The beetles feed upon the foliage, making many small round or irregular holes. The leaves have the appearance of being peppered with fine shot. The foliage becomes badly disfigured and the vitality of the plant is greatly weakened.

Life history: See page 646.

Control: See page 646.

Chrysanthemum

Diseases—Blight
Caused by the fungus *Cylindrosporium chrysanthemi.*

Symptoms: Dark blotches about 1/2 in. in diameter appear on the foliage. The disease spreads rapidly. The leaves turn yellow, become somewhat shriveled and drop. Severely infected plants die in a comparatively short time.

Control: Destroy all badly infected plants. Spray thoroughly with Bordeaux mixture.

Leaf Spot
A fungus disease caused by *Septoria chrysanthemi* that is very prevalent in some parts of the country and causes severe losses.

Symptoms: Dark brownish-black spots of circular or somewhat irregular outline appear on the leaves. The spots enlarge until they merge together and the entire leaf becomes involved. The lower leaves are usually the first to be affected. The vitality of diseased plants is seriously affected and growth is stunted. The diseased leaves become black and shriveled and drop prematurely. In severe cases the plant may become entirely defoliated.

Control: Handpick and discard leaves showing spotting. Spray weekly with Captan, Maneb or Zineb.

Mildew

A fungus disease caused by *Erysiphe cichoracearum* that is particularly prevalent in damp, rainy weather.

Symptoms: Leaves become covered with a white, powdery growth. In the most advanced stages the affected areas turn black.

Control: Spray with Benlate or wettable sulphur. Sulphur sprays, however, should not be applied when the temperatures are high, that is, 80°F. or over.

Root Rot

A fungus disease caused by *Sclerotium rolfsii* that is particularly troublesome during hot, wet weather. The resting bodies of the fungus resemble small brown mustard seeds.

Symptoms: Plants show signs of wilting—the tips of the branches dry up, the foliage turns a pale yellowish-green and roots become rotted. Occasionally only a single branch is affected.

Control: Use clean soil or steam-pasteurize infested soil.

Rust

Nature of the disease: Rust is a fungus disease caused by *Puccinia chrysanthemi*. It is thought to be a native of Japan and was introduced into this country in 1896 by way of Europe. It spread very rapidly until it is now prevalent throughout most of the country where chrysanthemums are grown. It attacks only the chrysanthemum, as yet having been found on no other host plant. The fungus is comparatively short-lived and soon dies out, unless it is continually transmitted from one living plant to another. Some varieties seem to be more susceptible than others.

Symptoms: In the early stages small, rusty blisters about the size of a pinhead are found on the lower surface of the leaves. Very occasionally they occur on the upper surface. At this stage the blister is covered by the epidermis of the leaf. As the disease progresses, the epidermis breaks away, exposing a mass of dark, brownish spores. When plants are badly affected, the undersurface of the leaves may be almost entirely covered with these rust spores. The leaves gradually shrivel and die, and the plants become stunted and fail to produce good bloom.

Control: Remove infected leaves as soon as possible. Set new plants further apart and provide better ventilation. Spray with Ferbam or Zineb when severe infections are likely to occur.

Stunt

A disease first found in 1945 on greenhouse chrysanthemums, it is caused by a viroid.

Symptoms: Plants are stunted in growth and the leaves pale green.

Control: Use only healthy, disease-free plants for propagation.

Wilt

Nature of the disease: A fungus disease caused by *Verticillium albo-atrum*. The fungus lives for some time in the soil. The disease is more prevalent on greenhouse plants than on plants grown in the open, although it sometimes causes considerable trouble in the garden.

Control: If the soil in which plants have become diseased is to be used again, it must be pasteurized or treated with some effective chemical such as chloropicrin.

Yellows

Symptoms: Leaves turn yellow. Plants become stunted and fail to produce normal bloom, the blossoms being distorted and frequently developing only on one side. The plants are only infrequently killed.

Control: See Yellows in Asters, page 614.

Insects—Aphids
Identification: Soft-bodies, louselike insects that are usually found clustered near the tips of the young shoots or on the underside of the leaves. Chrysanthemums are attacked by several different species, some being pale green in color while others are brown and black.

Injury: Aphids suck the juices from the plant, causing a general lack of vigor and stunted growth.

Life history: See page 610.

Control: See page 610.

Gall Midge
Identification: Small cone-shaped galls about $1/2$ in. long are found on the leaves, stems and flower buds. When on the leaves they are almost always found on the upper surface. Within the galls small maggotlike larvae are found.

Injury: The foliage becomes disfigured and the flowers are badly distorted. If the infestation is very severe, the tips of the stems become dwarfed and curiously gnarled, and no flower buds develop.

Life history: The adult midge is a tiny, two-winged fly and the females deposit their bright, orange-colored eggs on the tips of the young tender shoots. The larvae hatch within one to two weeks, depending upon temperature, and for several days after hatching they move about upon the surface of the plant. They then bore into the tissues and as a result of the irritation the little galls are formed. The larvae feed until they reach full development, then pupate within the gall. When the pupa is fully developed

and while it is still enclosed in the pupal skin, it pushes itself out of the gall and the adult flies emerge. It is a peculiar fact that the flies always emerge shortly after midnight and the females lay their eggs very early in the morning—about dawn. Frequently the discarded pupal skin may be seen protruding from the opening of the empty gall. The period from the time the larvae penetrate the tissues of the plant until the adults emerge from the pupa stage varies from twenty-one to forty-six days.

Control: Diazinon or Methoxychlor sprays are effective against the gall midge.

Greenhouse Leaf Tier
Although primarily a greenhouse insect, the leaf tier is often troublesome on outdoor chrysanthemums.

Identification: Slender, yellowish-green caterpillars, having a broad white stripe running lengthwise with the body with a dark green band in the center of the stripe. When full grown they are about $3/4$ in. in length.

Injury: The caterpillars feed upon the leaves, often completely skeletonizing them. They also form a light web that draws the edges of the leaves together in a very characteristic way.

Life history: See page 618.

Control: See page 618.

Nematodes
Identification: The chrysanthemum leaf nematode is a dreaded pest in both garden and greenhouse. Too small to be seen except under a microscope, it is best identified by the characteristic injury to the plant.

Injury: The first indication of trouble is the appearance of dark spots on the undersurface of the foliage. The leaves begin to turn brown or black between the veins and gradually wither and hang down along the stem, giving the plant an unsightly appearance.

Life history: The nematodes enter the plant through the stomata on the undersurface of the leaves, and they move about on the plant by swimming up the stems in a film of water when moisture is present.

Control: Propagate by taking cuttings only from the tops of long, vigorous shoots. Avoid replanting chrysanthemums in the same area year after year. As soon as the soil has warmed, mulch the surface with peat moss or some other material. This helps to prevent infection of the lower leaves by nematodes that may have survived in old infested leaves. Diazinon sprays applied three times at two- to three-week intervals, from July to early September, will also help to control this pest.

Tarnished Plant Bug
Identification: A small, very active bug about ¼ in. long. The oval body is somewhat triangular in front, and coppery-brown in color with dark brown and yellow flecks on the back.

Injury: The bugs puncture the shoots just below the flower heads, causing the buds to droop and die. The injury completely destroys any chance of bloom. It is thought that, while feeding, the tarnished plant bug injects some substance into the sap that is highly injurious to the plant and has the effect of a poison.

Life history: See page 616.

Control: See page 616.

Chrysanthemum coccineum (Pyrethrum atrosanguineum, painted daisy)

Disease—Yellows
Symptoms: Plants become dwarfed if attacked when young. Leaves that are not mature at the time infection takes place turn bright yellow. Blossoms become dwarfed and distorted, frequently developing only on one side. Plants are seldom killed outright, usually living on until cut down by frost.

Control: See page 614.

Cleome (spider plant)

Insect Pest—Harlequin Bug (Harlequin Cabbage Beetle)
Identification: The body is flat, shield-shaped and about ½ in. in length, and the back is gaily decorated with red and black markings.

Injury: Both the young nymphs and the adults suck the sap from the plant tissues. If the infestation is severe, it will cause the death of the plant.

Life history: The harlequin bug is a distinctly southern insect, incapable of surviving the cold of northern winters. In the extreme South it feeds and breeds during the entire year. In the more northerly part of its range the adults find shelter in long grass or under piles of rubbish in the winter, emerging with the first warm days of spring. The eggs are usually laid on the underside of the leaves of host plants, and they are very amusing in appearance as they resemble tiny white kegs. They are set on end, about a dozen being glued together, and each one is bound with two black bands that look like miniature barrel hoops. There is even a black dot set in the very place for a bung hole. The time of hatching varies from four to twenty-five days according to weather conditions. The young nymphs begin feeding as soon as they have hatched. At the end of eight weeks, after passing through five molts, they become full grown. Three and sometimes four generations are produced during the season.

Control: Handpick bugs in small areas. Spray with Naled or Rotenone on larger areas.

Coleus

Insect Pests—Orthezia

Identification: The young nymphs are very tiny, dark green and wingless, with a row of waxy plates extending back over the body. The adult females have a very conspicuous white, fluted egg sac, which extends back from the body for a distance two or more times the diameter of the body.

Injury: Although primarily a greenhouse insect, orthezias frequently infest bedding plants when grown in the open and cause considerable trouble. They are closely related to the scales and mealy bugs and suck the juices from the plant tissues.

Control: Spray with malathion or nicotine sulphate.

Whitefly

Identification: Small whitish flies about $1/16$ in. long with four wings, usually found on the undersurface of the leaves.

Injury: Whiteflies suck the juices from the plants, causing a general lack of vigor. If the infestation is severe, the plant eventually dies.

Life history: See page 611.

Control: See page 611.

Yellow Wooly-bear Caterpillar

Identification: A caterpillar about 2 in. in length when full grown. The body is completely covered with long hairs, which vary in color from pale yellow to reddish-brown.

Injury: The caterpillars feed upon the foliage.

Life history: The winter is passed in a cocoon made from the wooly coat of the caterpillar and silk which it spins. These pupa cases are usually found under piles of dead leaves or loose brush. The adult moths, which emerge early in the spring, are pure white with a few black spots on each wing. The females deposit the eggs in small patches on the leaves of the host plants. The larvae hatch out within a few days and begin feeding, attaining full size in about two months. There are usually two generations during the season.

Control: Spray with Sevin when the caterpillars begin to feed, being careful to limit spray to infected plants.

Cosmos

Diseases—Botrytis Rot

A fungus disease seldom prevalent except in very wet seasons.

Symptoms: Attacks foliage, stems and flower buds. The affected parts appear to be covered with a greenish mold.

Control: Pull up and destroy badly infected plants. Spray with Benlate or Botran.

Wilt

A bacterial disease caused by *Pseudomonas solanacearum,* which also causes the wilt of potatoes and tomatoes.

Symptoms: Leaves turn a sickly yellow. Plants wilt and die.

Control: Destroy all wilted plants. Heavily infested soil must be pasteurized with steam.

Insect Pests—Aphids

Identification: Soft-bodied, louselike insects, which are usually found clustered near the tips of the young shoots. They are light green and vary in size, the newly hatched young being considerably smaller than the adults.

Injury: Aphids suck the juices from the plant and cause a general lack of vigor and stunted growth.

Life history: See page 610.

Control: See page 610.

Spotted Cucumber Beetle
Identification: A yellowish-green beetle about ¼ in. in length with 12 very conspicuous black spots on its back. The head and antennae, which are about two-thirds as long as the body, are black.

Injury: The beetles feed upon the leaves, buds and flowers.

Life history: See page 618.

Control: See page 619.

Stalk Borer (Common)
Identification: Slender caterpillars about 1 in. or 2 in. in length. The young caterpillars are brown with white stripes. When full grown they lose their stripes and become a solid dirty gray in color.

Injury: The stalk borer makes a small round hole in the stem and tunnels up through the stalk, causing the injured shoot to wilt suddenly and break over.

Life history: See page 615.

Control: See page 616.

Dahlia

Diseases – Mildew
A fungus disease caused by *Erysiphe polygoni*, which is apt to be prevalent in damp, rainy weather.

Symptoms: Leaves become covered with a powdery white growth. In the most advanced stages the affected areas turn black.

Control: See page 620.

Root Rot
A fungus disease caused by a species of *Botrytis*, which always gains entrance through bruised areas on the surface of the tubers.

Symptoms: Affected tubers rot during storage, becoming soft in the center and having a spongy, water-soaked appearance.

Control: Handle tubers with care in order to avoid bruising. Store in a cool and dry place. Dust any scarred places with finely powdered sulphur.

Stunt
Closely resembling mosaic, it is transmitted through the roots.

Symptoms: Plants become yellowish-green in color, leaves are small, flowers poor and malformed. The growth of the plant is curiously bushy and stunted, and the flower buds do not appear until very late in the season.

Control: Pull up and discard all diseased plants. Use tubers from healthy plants for propagating.

Dahlias are subject to various physiological disorders caused by lack of water at time of blossoming, hot weather and intense sunshine, too much shade, excessively rich soil, etc. Such conditions are apt to cause stunted growth, distorted blossoms, and burning along the tips of the leaves. All of these can usually be overcome by good cultural methods.

Insect Pests – Corn Ear Worm
Identification: Large, striped worms about 2 in. long when full grown. They vary in color from light green to brown, and the stripes, which run

lengthwise on the body, are alternating light and dark. The head is yellow, the legs almost black.

Injury: The caterpillars feed upon the foliage and the flower buds, causing considerable damage.

Life history: See page 617.

Control: Spray with Sevin when the worms begin to feed, being careful to limit spray to infected plants.

Cutworms
Identification: Smooth, plump little caterpillars, about 1 in. long when full grown and varying in color from greenish-gray to muddy brown.

Injury: Cutworms are exceedingly destructive as they sever the stem at or near the ground line, causing the immediate death of the plant. Young plants are most susceptible to attack, but older plants also are frequently injured.

Life history: There are numerous species of cutworms that are injurious to flowering plants. In most species, the adult moths deposit their eggs on the stems of weeds and grasses. The larvae conceal themselves in the ground during the day, emerging to feed only at night. They start feeding early in the spring and continue until midsummer, when they pass into the pupa stage. Most species produce only one generation a year, the winter being passed in the larval stage in little cell-like structures in the soil.

Control: Sprays containing Diazinon or Dursban will protect plants susceptible to cutworms.

European Hornet
Identification: A small hornet with a dark body and two gauzy wings.

Injury: European hornets cause serious trouble in some areas of the country by gnawing or peeling off the tender bark on the stems of dahlia plants. Sometimes the stem becomes completely girdled and the portion above dies.

Control: Locate the nests and blow Diazinon powder into the openings. Apply a Diazinon spray to the main stems in mid-July.

Greenhouse Leaf Tier
Although primarily a greenhouse insect, the leaf tier is often troublesome on dahlias.

Identification: Slender, yellowish-green caterpillars, having a broad white stripe running down the back with a dark green band in the center of the stripe. When full grown they are about ¾ in. in length.

Injury: The caterpillars feed upon the leaves, often completely skeletonizing them. They also form a light web, which draws the edges of the leaves together in a very characteristic way.

Life history: See page 618.

Control: See page 618.

Leaf-cutter Bee
Injury: The bees first make a tunnel in the stem and then construct their nest within it. In most cases they cause the death of the shoot.

Life history: The bees cut a neat circular piece of a growing leaf, usually preferring roses; with this they build a nest composed of thimble-shaped cells within the tunnel that has already been prepared in the stem of some half-woody plant. The cells are arranged one above another. When they are completed, each contains a single egg, some nectar and some pollen. The young bees develop within the nest until ready for flight, a period of about a month or so.

Control: There is no control except to cut out and discard wilted or dying shoots containing the nests.

Spotted Cucumber Beetle
Identification: A yellowish-green beetle about 1/4 in. long with twelve very conspicuous black spots on its back. The head and antennae, which are almost two-thirds as long as the body, are black.

Injury: The beetles feed upon the leaves, buds and flowers and do considerable damage if they become numerous.

Life history: See page 618.

Control: See page 619.

Stalk Borer (Common)
Identification: Slender caterpillars about 1 in. to 2 in. long. The young caterpillars are brown with white stripes. When full grown they lose their stripes and become a solid dirty-gray.

Injury: The stalk borer makes a small round hole in the stem and tunnels up through the stalk, causing the injured shoot suddenly to wilt and break over.

Life history: See page 615.

Control: See page 616.

Tarnished Plant Bug
Identification: A small, very active bug about 1/4 in. in length. The oval body is somewhat triangular in front, coppery-brown in color, with dark brown and yellow flecks on the back.

Injury: The bugs puncture the shoots just below the flower heads, causing the buds to droop and die. The injury completely destroys any chance of bloom. It is thought that while feeding, this bug injects some substance into the sap that is highly injurious to the plant and has the effect of a poison.

Life history: See page 616.

Control: See page 616.

Delphinium (larkspur)

Diseases — Bacterial Leaf Spot
Nature of the disease: A bacterial disease of an insidious nature caused by *Pseudomonas delphinii.* The bacteria remain alive in the soil during the winter and are spattered up onto the leaves with the early spring rains. The disease spreads rapidly so that the entire plant is soon affected. The original source of infection may usually be traced to the purchase of diseased plants. In rare instances it has been found that infection was carried on the seed.

Symptoms: Dark spots of irregular outline appear upon the leaves. The lower leaves are usually the first to be affected. The spots occasionally appear on the stems and on the flower buds and in some cases the leaves become distorted.

Control: Remove and destroy affected leaves as soon as noticed. Cut and discard old stems in autumn. Streptomycin sprays may be helpful.

Black Rot (also known as Root Rot and Crown Rot)
A fungus disease caused by *Sclerotium delphinii.* The fungus spreads rapidly through the soil and is particularly prevalent on low, poorly drained land; it is also favored by damp, rainy weather.

Symptoms: Plants wilt and die suddenly, rotting off at the crown, or fail to come through the winter. The crown and roots sometimes become covered with a yellowish, moldy growth, which has a characteristically strong odor of decay.

Control: This fungus attacks a large number of garden plants and may therefore by widely distributed in the soil. Delphiniums should not be planted where the disease is known to have been present, unless the soil is first replaced with clean soil that has been either steam-pasteurized or drenched with Terraclor (4 oz. in 25 gallons of water).

Burning of the Leaves

Although this condition may appear alarming it is not in the true sense a disease. It is a physiological condition caused by intense summer sunshine, and seldom results in any permanent injury to the plant.

Symptoms: Leaves have a curious metallic sheen on the undersurface and in some cases the edges begin to dry and curl up.

Mildew

A fungus disease caused by *Erysiphe polygoni* that is particularly prevalent in damp, rainy weather. It is very disfiguring to the appearance of a plant but seldom causes death.

Symptoms: Foliage becomes covered with a white powdery growth. In the most advanced stages the affected areas turn black.

Control: See page 620.

Insect Pests — Aphids

Identification: Soft-bodied, louselike insects that are usually found clustered near the tips of the young shoots. The species that infest delphiniums are usually black in color and they vary considerably in size, the newly hatched young being smaller than the adults.

Injury: Aphids suck the juices from the plant,

causing a general lack of vigor and stunted growth.

Life history: See page 610.

Control: See page 610.

Cyclamen Mite (Pallid Mite)

Identification: A minute creature, hardly visible to the naked eye. The adult mites are pale brown in color, somewhat glossy, and have four pairs of legs. The presence of cyclamen mites is usually detected by their very characteristic injury.

Injury: Both the leaves and flower spikes become blackened and very much distorted. Stems become twisted and flower buds fail to open. Injury usually is evident on young, succulent growth.

Life history: The eggs, which are infinitesimal in size, are laid either about the base of the plant or on the leaves. The young begin feeding as soon as they have hatched.

Control: Spray with Kelthane when the plants are young, and repeat several times at weekly or ten-day intervals.

Stalk Borer (Common)

Identification: Slender caterpillars about 1 in. to 2 in. long when full grown. The young caterpillars are brown with white stripes. When full grown they lose their stripes and become a solid dirty-gray in color.

Injury: The stalk borer makes a small round hole in the stem and tunnels up through the stalk, causing the injured shoot suddenly to wilt and break over.

Life history: See page 615.

Control: See page 616.

Dianthus (carnation)

Diseases — Alternaria Leaf Spot
Nature of the disease: The disease is caused by the fungus *Alternaria dianthi.* The lower leaves are usually more seriously infected than those at the top of the plant. When the stem becomes infected, that part of the plant above the infection dies.

Symptoms: The disease appears as spots on the leaves, which become infected near the tip and die back, and sometimes on the stems, especially at the nodes. The spots are white, with the center occupied by a black fungus growth.

Control: Spray before and after benching at two- to three-week intervals with Captan or Zineb. Avoid wetting the leaves when watering the plants.

Bud Rot
Nature of the disease: The disease is caused by the fungus *Fusarium poae.* Mites are usually found associated with the disease and are believed to carry the spores. The fungus can sometimes be seen with the naked eye.

Symptoms: This disease affects only the flowers of the plant. In some cases the buds either do not open or fail to expand perfectly, while others are only slightly abnormal. The petals are first infected, then the sepals. The entire flower may rot and turn brown.

Control: Destroy all rotting buds. Control weeds in and around the greenhouse. Spray with a good miticide. Diazinon sprays may also be helpful.

Leaf Spot
Nature of the disease: The disease is caused by the fungus *Septoria dianthi* and is most abundant on the lower part of the leaves. The diseased part often becomes contracted, causing the leaves to be bent and curled.

Symptoms: Circular or oblong spots, which are blanched or pinkish with purple borders, develop on the leaves. In the center of the spot are small black dots. The stem may also become infected.

Control: Leaf spot is best controlled in the greenhouse by keeping the foliage as dry as possible and, when necessary, by spraying occasionally with Ferbam or Bordeaux mixture.

Rust
Caused by the fungus *Uromyces dianthi,* the infection usually extends throughout the entire plant.

Symptoms: The rust is first characterized by swollen yellow areas on the leaves and stem. These soon break open and expose the brown spores. The whitish ruptured edges of the epidermis give a ragged appearance to the pustules.

Control: Cuttings should be taken only from healthy plants. Cultural practices are important in controlling rust. Good ventilation is essential and the foliage should be kept as dry as possible. Syringing should be avoided and only surface watering should be done. Where wetting the foliage is unavoidable, spray weekly with Zineb or Captan.

Stem Rot
Caused by the fungus *Pellicularia filamentosa.*

Symptoms: This is a very common disease of carnations. It may attack cuttings or older plants. In the case of cuttings and plants that have recently been potted, the plants may appear to damp-off. On older plants the rot usually starts at an injury in the cortex of the stem. As the infection spreads, it girdles the stem and the plant then wilts and dies. In this type of infection, the rot is more or less dry and corky.

Control: In commercial greenhouses Terraclor can be used as a soil drench on living carnation plants.

Dianthus (garden pink)

Diseases — Root Rot
Caused by *Sclerotium rolfsii,* the same fungus that attacks many other plants.

Symptoms: Leaves wither and die. Plants rot off at the crown.

Control: See page 617.

Digitalis (foxglove)

Disease — Leaf Spot
A fungus disease caused by *Phyllosticta digitalis,* which is very prevalent in some sections of the country.

Symptoms: Leaves have an unhealthy, rusty-brown appearance. Young seedlings are especially subject to attack, though older plants also are susceptible.

Control: Leaf spot may be readily controlled by spraying with Bordeaux mixture or Ferbam as soon as trouble is detected.

Insect Pests — Mite *(Red Spider)*
Identification: Minute mites, some red in color, others greenish-yellow and black.

Injury: Red spider usually feeds on the undersurface of the leaves, puncturing the outer tissues and sucking on the juices of the plant. The foliage has an unhealthy, curiously glazed appearance and frequently drops prematurely. Fine silken threads will be found spun across the undersurface of the leaves.

Life history: The minute eggs are laid on the undersurface of the leaves, and usually are attached to the web. Each female lays from two to six eggs per day, depositing about seventy in all. The eggs hatch in four to five days and the young mites begin feeding. The females pass through three molts, the males through only two. The life cycle covers a period of thirty-five to forty days.

Control: Spray with Kelthane.

Thrips
Identification: Young thrips are lemon-yellow, adults amber, about $1/20$ in. in length. Usually found within infested flower buds.

Injury: Flowers are affected, not the foliage. Flower buds turn brown and either fail to open or are distorted.

Life history: See page 657.

Control: Spray with Cygon or Diazinon.

Fritillaria imperialis (crown imperial)

Disease — Gray Bulb Rot
Caused by *Pellicularia (Rhizoctonia) tuliparum,* the same fungus that attacks tulips and other bulbs.

Symptoms: Dry rot begins at the nose of the bulb. The flesh of the bulb becomes a reddish-gray in color. In the advanced stages of the disease the bulbs rot away entirely.

Control: Remove and destroy all infected plants, using a "bulb sticker," a special apparatus used to aid in planting bulbs. Select clean bulbs and plant in soil that has been steam-pasteurized or treated with Benlate. Avoid poorly drained planting sites.

Gaillardia (blanket flower)

Disease — Yellows
Symptoms: Plants become dwarfed if attacked when young. Older plants have a curiously bushy habit of growth. Leaves that are not mature at the time that infection takes place turn a bright yellow. Occasionally only one side of the plant is affected. The blossoms become dwarfed and distorted. Plants are rarely killed outright, living on until frost.

Control: See page 614.

Galtonia

Insect Pest — Bulb Fly *(Merodon equestris)*
Identification: Small brown scars are sometimes found upon the outer scales. Bulbs are suspiciously soft and light in weight. Upon cutting the bulb open, large, fat, grayish- to yellowish-white maggots are found, 1/2 in. to 3/4 in. in length.

Injury: The maggots feed upon the tissues and render the bulbs practically worthless.

Life history: See page 634.

Control: Apply 2 oz. (10 level tbs.) of Proxol 80 SP in 10 gallons of water as a drench per 100 ft. of row. Direct stream to base of plants at the beginning of adult fly activity (early May to June). Repeat treatment annually.

Gladiolus

Diseases — Bacterial Blight
A bacterial disease caused by *Xanthomonas gummisudans;* some varieties seem very susceptible, while others are quite resistant.

Symptoms: In the early stages dark, water-soaked spots appear on the leaves. The diseased areas spread gradually until the entire leaf is affected. There is usually a very characteristic, somewhat sticky, exudation of the infected areas, which gradually dries until it becomes a thin film. The corms are seldom affected.

Control: Cut off and destroy all infected leaves. Spray three times at ten-day intervals, starting when the leaves are 3 in. tall.

Dry Rot
Nature of the disease: Dry rot is a fungus disease caused by *Stromotinia gladioli.* It is becoming increasingly prevalent and causes severe losses. The *Primulinus* varieties seem to be particularly susceptible. The fungus lives over the winter in the soil in the form of minute resting bodies known as sclerotia, which are found on the base of decayed leaves.

Symptoms: Dark, reddish-brown blotches are found on the corms. These spots are sunken with raised margins, and are usually most numerous on the lower part of the corm near the old bulb scar. When corms that are badly diseased are planted, the growing plants may become affected later in the season, the leaves turning yellow and rotting off at the ground level. In advanced stages the roots and the corm itself rot away. When diseased corms are lifted and stored in the autumn, the dry rot continues, and frequently the corms become entirely mummified before spring.

Control: Use a new planting area each year, or steam-pasteurize the soil. In Florida, Botran-treated soil provides control.

Hard Rot
Nature of the disease: Hard rot is a fungus disease caused by *Septoria gladioli.* It is particularly prevalent on young plants grown from seed or from small cormels. It may spread directly from the old corm to the new corm and cormels, or it may first attack the leaves. In an apparent endeavor to resist the disease and to check its spread on the corm, a layer of corklike tissue is frequently built up around the infected area.

Symptoms: Reddish-brown spots appear on the leaves, producing a rusty caste. As the disease advances, minute black specks appear in the center of the leaf spots. These are the fruiting bodies of the fungus, and later this center frequently drops out, giving the leaves a shothole appearance. The corms are also affected, dark brown spots with a water-soaked margin being found on both the upper surface and the base. In severe cases the corm becomes a hard, shriveled mummy. When badly diseased corms are planted, spindly, unhealthy growth results and the plants eventually die.

Control: Discard all badly infected corms and, if possible, plant clean corms in clean fields. It may be possible to kill the fungus in corms that are not badly infected by dipping them in a suspension made by mixing 2 oz. of Tersan 75 per gallon of water. Corms should be dried before storing. For leaf spot of seedlings or first-year plants, spray with a copper fungicide.

Neck Rot or Scab

A bacterial disease caused by *Pseudomonas marginata;* the bacteria are carried on infected corms.

Symptoms: This disease usually manifests itself by the appearance of light brown streaks on the lower leaves near the ground line. Upon close observation minute brown spots are apparent, which enlarge as they become black and merge into one another. The blackened leaves rot off at the base and frequently the entire plant is killed.

The corms are also affected. Dark, burnt-looking streaks are found on the bulb scales and the corms are covered with brownish or blackened sunken spots having a slightly raised margin. In the advanced stages of the disease the entire corm has a rough, scabby appearance and is covered with a varnishlike secretion. The outer husk is frequently stuck to the corm with this sticky exudation. In some cases the husk is entirely destroyed.

Control: Discard corms that show disease symptoms. Plant healthy corms in a new area. The bulb mite *Rhizoglyphus echinopus* is associated with the severity of scab.

Penicillium Rot
Nature of the disease: A fungus disease caused by *Penicillium gladioli.* It always gains entrance through wounded tissues. Small, light brown sclerotia or resting bodies are found in the infected corms.

Symptoms: The entire corm becomes a mass of dark, porous, rotted tissue.

Control: In handling the corms, care should be taken to avoid wounding them. To prevent initial infection, corms should be stored in a cool, dry cellar with the temperature ranging from 35° to 45°F. Prompt curing and drying of corms is imperative. Freshly harvested corms should be cured at 85°F. for ten or fifteen days. Dipping the corms in Benlate (2 tbs. per gallon of warm water, 80° to 85°F.) for fifteen to thirty minutes will also provide some control.

Insect Pests—Black Blister Beetle
Identification: A slender, jet-black beetle about $1/2$ in. long, with prominent head and neck. Its best means of identification is a yellow exudate.

Injury: The beetles feed upon the flowers.

Life history: See page 614.

Control: See page 614.

Corn Ear Worm
Identification: Large striped worms about 2 in. in length. They vary in color from light green to brown, and the stripes that run lengthwise with the body are alternating light and dark. The head is yellow, the legs almost black.

Injury: The caterpillars feed upon the foliage and the flowers.

Life history: See page 617.

Control: Spray with Sevin, being careful to limit spray to infected plants.

Gladiolus Thrips
Identification: The adult thrips are black-winged insects about 1/16 in. in length. In the immature stage they are wingless, pale yellow and very active.

Injury: The thrips feed upon the leaves, buds and flowers of the gladioli, causing a very characteristic injury. Affected flowers open imperfectly, the flower spike is apt to nod, and small, silvery-white streaks may be found on both the flowers and the leaves.

Life history: The adults appear early in the spring and feed within the tissues of the leaf, where the eggs are laid. The eggs hatch into small, wingless insects that continue feeding until they are full grown, at which time they pass into a quiescent stage and emerge as adults.

Control: Spray with Diazinon, Cygon or Methoxychlor during the early part of the growing season. These materials should be used before flowers are formed because they may damage the delicate petals. Soaking corms for three hours just before planting in a solution of 1½ tbs. of Lysol mixed in 1 gallon of water will also help to control thrips. Storing the corms at a temperature of 40° to 45°F. is effective.

Stalk Borer (Common)
Identification: Slender caterpillars about 1 in. to 2 in. long. The young caterpillars are brown with white stripes. When full grown they lose their stripes and become a solid, dirty gray.

Injury: The stalk borer makes a small, round hole in the stem and tunnels up through the stalk, causing the injured shoot suddenly to wilt and break over.

Life history: See page 615.

Control: See page 616.

Wooly Aphids
Gladiolus corms are occasionally attacked by wooly aphids during storage. This is particularly true if they are stored in or near a conservatory or greenhouse.

Identification: Small, soft-bodied insects with a whitish, wooly covering are found clustered on the corms.

Injury: The insects suck the juices from the tissues of the corms and weaken their vitality.

Control: Dust corms with Sevin powder before storage. Spray plants during the growing season with Diazinon or malathion.

Heliotrope

Insect Pests—Greenhouse Leaf Tier
Identification: Slender, yellowish-green caterpillars, having a broad white stripe running lengthwise down the back, with a dark green band in the center of the stripe. When full grown they are about ¾ in. in length.

Injury: The caterpillars feed upon the leaves, often completely skeletonizing them. They also form a light web, which draws the edges of the leaves together in a very characteristic way.

Life history: See page 618.

Control: See page 618.

Orthezia
Identification: The young nymphs are very tiny, dark green, and wingless, with a row of waxy plates extending back over the body. The adult females have a very conspicuous white, fluted egg sac, which extends back for a distance two or more times the diameter of the body.

Injury: The orthezias are closely related to the scales and suck the juices from the plant tissues.

Control: See page 623.

Hemerocallis (daylily)

Insect Pests—Tarnished Plant Bug
Identification: Small, coppery-brown, very active bug about ¼ in. long.

Injury: The bugs puncture the stems just below the flower bud, causing the buds to droop and die.

Control: See page 616.

Thrips
Identification: Young thrips are lemon-yellow, adults amber, about 1/20 in. long.

Injury: Petals are streaked; foliage often has a silvery sheen.

Control: See page 657.

Hyacinth

Diseases—Black Rot

The fungus *Sclerotinia bulborum* causes black rot. It lives over winter as flat-bodied sclerotia, about ½ in. broad; these are white at first, but later turn black.

Symptoms: The leaves become yellowish and the plants are retarded in growth; later they wither and are easily detached from the bulbs, which then become a mass of black, rotted tissue.

Control: Special care should be taken to pasteurize the soil where the disease has been pres-

ent. Bulbs that are badly infected should be destroyed. Dusting PCNB (Terraclor) over bulbs in furrows before covering may provide some control.

Gray Bulb Rot
Symptoms: Dry rot begins at the nose of the bulb, and the flesh of the bulb becomes a reddish-gray in color. In the advanced stages of the disease the bulbs rot away entirely.

Control: See page 659.

Soft Rot
A bacterial disease caused by *Erwinia carotovora.*

Symptoms: Flower stalks rot off at the base. Bulbs either come "blind" and fail to form flower buds, or the flower head becomes distorted.

Control: Store the bulbs in a dry, well-ventilated room. Separate them so that they are not in contact with each other. Avoid excessive watering, especially about the bulbs. Avoid excessively high temperatures in forcing bulbs.

Yellow Rot
Caused by the bacterium *Xanthomonas hyacinthi;* some varieties seem much more susceptible to yellow rot than others.

Symptoms: The tip of the leaf is usually affected first, a characteristically yellow or brownish stripe appearing down the midrib that causes the leaf to die. The sap tubes of the bulb become filled with a yellowish slimy substance, and in time the entire bulb is destroyed.

Control: Destroy all plants affected by this rot. No other control measure is available.

Insect Pests—Bulb Mite (*Rhizoglyphus echinopus*)
Identification: Minute whitish mites, beadlike in form. These are found in large numbers

within the bulb scales. Reddish-brown spots appear at the point of injury.

Injury: The mites suck the juices from the plant tissues and the bulbs become soft and mushy. The vitality of the bulb is weakened and as a result growth is generally stunted—the leaves turn a sickly yellow, and the flower buds either fail to develop or they produce distorted flowers.

Life history: The eggs are laid inside the bulb scales and hatch out into six-legged nymphs. After passing through a molt, these change to an eight-legged form. It is in this stage that they are the most destructive. They molt again before becoming adults, and several generations are produced each year. The mites frequently migrate through the soil from decaying bulbs to healthy ones.

Control: Discard all bulbs in which heavy infestation is evident. Avoid planting clean bulbs in previously infested ground, unless the soil has been steam-pasteurized. Bulbs also may be freed of mites by dipping them in hot water at 122°F (50°C.) for a few minutes, but this treatment cannot be used safely if roots have started to develop.

Bulb Fly *(Merodon equestris)*
Identification: Bulbs are suspiciously soft and light in weight and small brown scars are sometimes found on the outer scales. Upon cutting the bulb open, large fat maggots, grayish- to yellowish-white in color, are found.

Injury: The maggots feed upon the tissues and render the bulbs practically worthless.

Life history: The adult fly is yellow and black in color and very hairy, resembling a bumblebee in appearance although it is considerably smaller. The female lays her eggs either in the neck of the bulb or at the base of the leaves. Upon hatching, the young maggots bore their way into the bulb and begin feeding. They are

equipped with strong, slightly hooked mouth parts, which are admirably adapted for this purpose. The pupa stage is passed sometimes within the bulb, sometimes in the soil.

Control: Apply 2 oz. (10 level tbs.) of Proxol SP in 10 gallons of water as a drench per 100 ft. of row. Direct stream to base of plants at beginning of adult fly activity (early May to June). Repeat treatment annually.

Lesser Bulb Fly *(Eumerus tuberculatus)*
Identification: Bulbs become soft and light in weight, and upon examination maggots will be found feeding within the tissues. The maggots are grayish- to yellowish-white in color, about 1/2 in. in length when full grown, and the body is decidedly wrinkled in appearance. They may be distinguished from the larvae of the bulb fly *(Merodon equestris)* by this characteristic.

Injury: The maggots feed upon the tissues and ruin the bulbs.

Life history: The adult fly is blackish-green, with white markings on the sides of the abdomen. It is about 1/3 in. long, with an almost hairless body, and in general appearance it resembles a small wasp. The eggs are laid at the base of the leaves or in the neck of the bulb, and the larvae tunnel down into the bulb as soon as they have hatched. Two generations are usually produced during the season.

Control: Same as for bulb fly *(Merodon equestris).*

White Grubs
Identification:

Injury:

Life history: See page 616.

Control:

Ipomoea (morning-glory)

Insect Pest—Golden Tortoise Beetle or Gold Bug
Identification: A small, golden-colored beetle about ¼ in. long. Occasionally black stripes or dots are found on the body. The beetle is turtle-shaped, being flat on the underside with the head and legs partially hidden.

Injury: The beetles feed upon the foliage.

Life history: The adult beetles hibernate during the winter in dry, sheltered places, and they usually do not come out of hiding until late spring. The eggs, which are laid on the leaves of the host plants, hatch in about a week or ten days and the larvae begin feeding. Their feeding is confined largely to the underside of the leaves. After feeding for a short time, they pass into the pupa stage. A few weeks later the adults emerge.

Control: Spray with Diazinon when the beetles begin to feed.

Iris

Diseases—Leaf Spot
Nature of the disease: A fungus disease caused by *Didymellinia macrospora*. It is becoming more and more prevalent in many sections of the country and causes severe losses. The fungus lives over the winter on the dead leaves, and infection on the new growth usually becomes apparent about the middle of June. Some varieties seem to be much more susceptible than others.

Symptoms: In the early stages small brown spots appear on the leaves. The spots enlarge as the disease progresses, the center becoming lighter and the margin decidedly darker. The foliage gradually turns brown and is killed entirely.

Control: Spray plants three times at ten-day intervals with Fore, Maneb or Zineb, starting when the leaves are 4 in. tall. Raking and destroying old iris leaves in the fall or early spring will also help materially to avert this prevalent disease.

Sclerotial Rot
Nature of the disease: Sclerotial rot of iris is caused by the fungus *Sclerotium delphinii,* the same fungus that attacks many other plants. It is particularly prevalent during damp weather and where irises are planted on low, poorly drained land.

Symptoms: Leaves turn a yellowish-brown; leaf stalks and flower stalks rot off at the base.

Control: Discard all diseased rhizomes. Treat infested soil with PCNB (Terraclor) as directed by the manufacturer.

Soft Rot
A bacterial disease caused by *Erwinia carotovara* that is very prevalent and destructive in some parts of the country. It is frequently spread by the iris borer.

Symptoms: The affected leaves and stems have a yellowish, unhealthy appearance, and at the base they become a mass of ill-smelling, rotting pulp. This disagreeable odor is very characteristic of the disease and distinguishes it from the less serious sclerotial rot.

Control: Elimination of the iris borer (see below) is one of the first essentials in controlling soft rot. Discard all heavily infected rhizomes. Remove diseased portions of mildly infected rhizomes and soak the rhizomes in a streptomycin solution. Plant rhizomes shallowly so that deleterious bacteria on or near the surface are killed by the sun's rays.

Insect Pest—Iris Borer
Identification: The borers are pinkish-white with a row of dark spots on each side of the body. When full grown they measure about 2 in. In spring the presence of the borers may be detected by the characteristic "bleeding" of the leaves at the point where they enter.

Injury: The borers tunnel down through the leaf into the rhizome, feeding upon the plant tissues as they continue their peregrinations. They weaken the vitality of the plant to a very serious extent and cause sickly, stunted growth.

Life history: The winter is passed in the egg stage and the young larvae hatch out late in March or early in April. The tiny caterpillars crawl up the leaves, make a small hole in the outer surface, and as soon as they are safely within the tissues of the leaf begin tunnelling their way down into the rhizome, feeding as they go. They become full grown about August 1, at which time they pass into the pupa stage. At the end of three weeks the adult moths emerge, and early in the autumn they lay their eggs near the base of the leaves or on the rhizomes that appear above the surface of the ground. The moths fly only at night.

Control: Collect and destroy all old iris leaves in autumn, leaving only the short fans of young leaf growth. This practice removes all eggs deposited on them. In the spring, spray the leaves when they are 6 in. to 8 in. tall with Cygon or malathion, and repeat the treatment three times at two-week intervals.

Lantana (shrub verbena)

Insect Pests—Orange Tortrix
Identification: Whitish, brown-headed caterpillar. Adult moths are grayish-fawn with dark mottlings.

Injury: The caterpillars roll and tie the leaves upon which they feed. They are a distinctly southern pest and sometimes cause considerable injury.

Control: Spray with Sevin when the caterpillars are young, being careful to limit spray to infected plants.

Orthezia
Identification: The young nymphs are very tiny, dark green and wingless, with a row of waxy plates extending back over the body. The adult females have a very conspicuous white, fluted egg sac, which extends back for a distance two or more times the diameter of the body.

Injury: The orthezias are closely related to the scales and suck the juices from the plant.

Control: See page 623.

Whitefly
Identification: Very small, whitish flies about $1/16$ in. long. They are usually found on the undersurface of the leaves.

Injury: Whiteflies suck the juices from the plant, causing a general lack of vigor. Leaves turn yellow and if the infestation is severe, the plant will eventually die.

Life history: See page 611.

Control: See page 611.

Lathyrus odoratus (sweet pea)

Diseases—Anthracnose
Nature of the disease: The anthracnose of the sweet pea is caused by *Glomerella cingulata*, the same fungus that produces the bitter rot of the apple and the ripe rot of the grape. It is confined almost entirely to sweet peas grown in the open; only in rare instances has it been found on greenhouse plants. The spores of the fungus are carried on the seed and the disease is usually transmitted in this way.

Symptoms: The growing tips of the plant wilt and die, becoming white and brittle. As the disease progresses, the entire plant becomes affected and the flower buds dry up and fail to open. When an infected leaf is examined under a hand lens, it is found to be covered with very small pustules of a peculiar salmon-pink color. These pustules are also prominent on the seed pods. Small cankers are sometimes produced on the stems and leaf petioles.

Control: Gather and destroy all infected plant parts after the flowering season. Choose only seed from pods that are plump and sound in appearance for planting. An occasional application of Zineb spray during the growing season also helps to control this disease.

Collar Rot (also known as Stem Rot)
Nature of the disease: Collar Rot is caused by *Sclerotinia sclerotiorum,* a fungus that attacks a number of different plants. The fungus penetrates the stem at the ground level, clogging up the vessels and preventing the flow of sap from the roots to the upper portion of the plant. After a plant has succumbed, it soon becomes covered with a moldy white growth, which is the mycelium of the fungus. The small, black sclerotia or resting bodies of the fungus are later found both on and within the affected parts of the plant. The fungus lives over in the soil from year to year.

Symptoms: Young seedlings are particularly susceptible to this disease although older plants are occasionally also attacked. The plants wilt at the tip, the leaves show a peculiar flagging, and the stem rots off at the ground line. The roots are practically never affected. The disease spreads quickly from plant to plant and is always fatal.

Control: If collar rot has proved troublesome, fresh soil that is known to be free from the disease should be used or, alternatively, the soil may be sterilized with formaldehyde. Use 1 pint of 40 percent formaldehyde to 12½ gallons of water at the rate of 1 gallon to every square foot. Let the soil stand for twenty-four hours. Fork over and aerate well, and do not plant seed for several weeks.

Mildew
Caused by the fungus *Microsphaera alni.*

Symptoms: Leaves turn yellow and drop prematurely. The white, powdery growth so typi-

cal of mildew is more apt to be found on the dead and fallen leaves than on the growing plant.

Control: See page 620.

Mosaic
Symptoms: Leaves become a mottled yellow and green in color and have a tendency to curl. Flower stalks become twisted and fail to make normal growth. If the plants are affected when young, they frequently remain dwarfed and stunted.

Control: See page 612.

Root Rot
Sweet peas are attacked by several forms of root rot. The control is practically the same in all cases.

Black Root Rot *(Thielaviopsis basicola)*
Symptoms: Plants affected with black thielavia root rot have practically no root system except a dark, charred-looking stub. The new roots are destroyed as soon as they are formed. The disease occasionally spreads up the stem for 2 in. or 3 in. above the ground. The affected plants seldom die but remain dwarfed and stunted, being a sickly color and producing no bloom.

Pellicularia Root Rot *(Pellicularia filamentosa)*
Symptoms: Roots become rotted, plants wilt and finally collapse entirely. Stems frequently also become affected, being covered with reddish, sunken spots. Young seedlings seem to be more susceptible to attack than older plants.

Shredded Root Rot *(Aphanomyces euteiches)*
Symptoms: The underground portion of the stem becomes rotted and the tissues have the appearance of being shredded. The roots usually rot away entirely.

Control: Destroy all diseased plants. Disinfect the soil thoroughly with formaldehyde. Use 1 pt. 40 percent formaldehyde to 12½ gallons of water at the rate of 1 gallon to every square foot. Let the soil stand for twenty-four hours, then fork it over and aerate it well. Do not plant the seed for several days.

Streak

Nature of the disease: Streak is a bacterial disease caused by the bacterium *Erwinia herbicola*. The bacteria are carried on the seed and are spattered up onto the plant by heavy rains. They gradually destroy the tissues of the plant.

Symptoms: The disease usually makes its appearance just as the plants are coming into bloom. Peculiar spots or streaks, varying in color from light reddish-brown to dark brown, appear on the stems. This condition is usually first apparent near the ground line but spreads gradually to other portions of the plant. In some cases the streaks merge and the stem becomes entirely girdled, killing the plant. In the advanced stages of the disease, water-soaked spots are found on the leaves, petioles and flowers.

Control: Dip seeds in a streptomycin solution before planting them.

Insects — Aphids

Identification: Soft-bodied, louselike insects usually found clustered along the tips of the young growing shoots. The species that most commonly infests sweet peas is pale green in color.

Life history: See page 610.

Control: See page 610.

Nematodes (*Meloidogyne incognita*) causing
Root Knot

Identification: Swellings are found on the roots; singly, in pairs or in strings, often giving the root a beaded appearance. The swellings range from being very small to almost as large as the root nodules, with which they must not be confused. The root nodules, which are peculiar to sweet peas and all other members of the legume family, are lobed outgrowths that are attached

to the root at one end, whereas the galls or swellings caused by nematodes produce a swelling of the entire affected portion of the root. Upon cutting open a swelling, the minute worms may frequently be seen with a hand lens.

Injury: Infested plants become sickly and fail to make normal growth. Leaves turn yellow and flower production is seriously affected. The plants usually linger on for a long time before dying.

Life history: See page 665.

Control: See page 665.

Root Aphids

Identification: Soft-bodied, grayish-white insects found clustered along the roots or near the crown of the plant.

Injury: Root aphids suck the juices from the plants, causing them to become dwarfed and stunted. The foliage frequently turns yellow, indicating a general lack of vigor.

Control: See page 615.

Lilium (lily)

Diseases — Botrytis Rot

Nature of the disease: A fungus disease, *Botrytis illiptica*, which is very prevalent in some sections of the country. Its spread is particularly favored by cool, wet weather. The spores are carried from one plant to another by wind and other agencies. The fungus lives over the winter on dead and decaying leaves and other garden refuse.

Symptoms: Spots that range in color from orange to brown appear on the leaves, stems and flower buds. A small dark area will be found in the center of each lesion. The spots gradually enlarge and in the latter stages of the disease, when the spores of the fungus begin to develop, the affected areas appear to be covered with a grayish mold. In severe cases the stem of the plant rots off, the flower buds fail to develop and the disease spreads down into the bulb.

Control: Gather and destroy all leaves of infected plants as soon as they are seen. Spray with Bordeaux mixture or Benlate three or four times at ten-day intervals, starting in late spring.

Bulb Rot
A fungus disease caused by *Rhizopus necans.*

Symptoms: In the early stages a slightly darkened appearance is noted in the flesh of the bulb about the roots. As the disease progresses, the bulb softens at the base and the entire heart may become rotten. The rotted portion is brown and cheesy. When bulbs are seriously affected, the flower stalks are usually dwarfed and frequently break over, and if any blooms are borne they are distorted and malformed.

Control: Avoid wounding bulbs at digging time. There is no effective control once the fungus has penetrated the bulbs.

Leaf Spot
A fungus disease that is caused by *Cercospora richardiaecola.*

Symptoms: Brown spots appear on the foliage of the calla lily, and as the disease progresses the spores of the fungus form a powdery, mildewlike substance on the surface of the leaves.

Control: Avoid wetting the leaves on greenhouse-grown plants. Keep plants well spaced and ventilate the greenhouse.

Mosaic
Nature of the disease: Mosaic is a vicious disease that is becoming more and more serious and in some parts of the country is entirely wiping out

large colonies of lilies. The disease is carried from one plant to another by aphids in much the same way that mosquitos carry malaria to human beings. In sucking the juices of a diseased plant, the aphids pick up the infectious virus, later transmitting it to healthy plants. The virus penetrates to every portion of the plant. If infection occurs late in the summer the disease may not become active until the following season. Therefore, apparently healthy bulbs may be carriers of the disease.

Symptoms: In the early stages the leaves have a curiously mottled appearance, being blotched and streaked with yellow. The disease usually progresses slowly. The second year the leaves and stems become twisted and distorted and no flowers are formed. Eventually the plant succumbs entirely but it will usually linger on for a number of years.

Control: Bulbs from diseased plants should not be used for propagation, since the virus is carried in them from year to year. The melon aphid, which carries the virus, can be controlled to a certain extent by spraying the plants frequently with malathion.

Rust
Nature of the disease: The fungus *Uromyces holwayi* causes rust. Some varieties are much more susceptible than others. Regal and Bermuda lilies are seldom attacked. Candidum lilies are very susceptible, particularly when planted in shady places.

Symptoms: Small, brown, rusty patches appear both on the upper and undersurface of the leaves.

Control: Pick and destroy infected leaves. Ferbam-sulphur sprays will provide control in areas where rust is prevalent.

Insect Pests — Aphids
Identification: Soft-bodied, louselike insects that are usually found clustered near the tips of the young, growing shoots. They vary in size,

the newly hatched young being considerably smaller than the adults.

Injury: Aphids suck the juices from the plant, causing a general lack of vigor and stunted growth. They are also carriers of the mosaic disease on lilies. Every effort should therefore be made to keep them under control.

Life history: See page 610.

Control: See page 610.

Stalk Borer (Common)
Identification: Slender caterpillars 1 in. to 2 in. long and brown with white stripes. When full grown they lose their stripes and become a solid, dirty gray.

Injury: The stalk borer makes a small, round hole in the stem and tunnels up through the stalk, causing the injured shoot suddenly to wilt and break over.

Life history: See page 615.

Control: See page 615.

Lobelia

Insect Pest—Red-banded Leaf Roller
Identification: Small active caterpillars, about ³/₄ in. in length. They are greenish, with a distinctive red band from which they derive their name.

Injury: The caterpillars feed upon the leaves, rolling them together in a very characteristic fashion.

Life history: See page 615.

Control: Spray with Diazinon early before the leaves are rolled.

Lobularia maritima (sweet alyssum)

Insect Pests—Cabbage Worm
Identification: Small velvety-green caterpillars, somewhat more than 1 in. long when full grown.

Injury: The caterpillars feed upon the foliage.

Life history: See page 613.

Control: See page 613.

Potato Flea Beetle
Identification: Small black beetles ¹/₁₆ in. long, which jump like a flea when disturbed.

Injury: The beetles feed on foliage, making many small holes.

Life history: See page 646.

Control: See page 646.

Lunaria (honesty)

Insect Pest—Harlequin Bug (Harlequin Cabbage Beetle)
Identification: The body is flat, shield-shaped and about ³/₈ in. long, the back being gaily decorated with red and black markings.

Injury: Both the young nymphs and the adults suck the sap from the plant tissues, and if the infestation is severe it may cause the death of the plant.

Life history: See page 622.

Control: See page 622.

Muscari (grape hyacinth)

Diseases — Rot
Symptoms: A white, moldy growth appears on the surface of the ground near the plants. Bulbs become rotten.

Control: No effective control is available. Discard diseased bulbs and plant disease-free bulbs in a new location.

Smut
Symptoms: The flowers are imperfect and become covered with a greenish-brown smut. The smut spores replace the ovaries and anthers of the flowers, utterly ruining their beauty.

Control: Pick off and discard all infected flowers as soon as the disease is detected in order to prevent the spread of the smut spores.

Narcissus

Diseases — Botrytis Bulb Rot
A fungus disease similar to the rot that affects tulips.

Symptoms: Leaves and stems become covered with unsightly spots. Small black, resting bodies known as sclerotia are frequently found in the rotting tissues of the bulbs.

Control: Dip bulbs in Benlate and dry them rapidly after treatment.

Gray Bulb Rot
Symptoms: Dry rot begins at the tip of the bulb. The flesh of the bulb becomes reddish-gray and the diseased portions are often covered with dark brown sclerotia or resting bodies. The bulbs finally rot away entirely.

Control: Dig up and destroy all diseased bulbs. Disinfect soil with formaldehyde or some other appropriate chemical before replanting bulbs in the same area.

Insect Pests — Bulb Fly (*Merodon equestris*)
Identification: Small brown scars are sometimes found upon the outer scales. Bulbs are soft and light in weight. Upon cutting the bulb open, large, fat maggots are found. The color varies from grayish- to yellowish-white, and when full grown they are about $1/4$ in. long.

Injury: The maggots feed upon the tissues and render the bulbs practically worthless.

Life history: See page 634.

Control: See page 634.

Lesser Bulb Fly (*Eumerus tuberculatus*)
Identification: Bulbs become soft and light in weight and upon examination maggots will be found feeding upon the tissues. The maggots are grayish- to yellowish-white, about $1/2$ in. long when full grown, and the body is very wrinkled. They may be readily distinguished from the larvae of *Merodon equestris* by this characteristic wrinkled appearance.

Injury: Same as that of the bulb fly.

Life history: See page 634.

Control: See page 634.

Bulb Mite (*Rhizoglyphus echinopus*)
Identification: Minute whitish mites, beadlike in form, found in large numbers within the bulb scales. Reddish-brown spots appear at the point of injury.

Injury: The mites suck the juices from the plant tissues and the bulbs become soft and mushy. The vitality of the bulb is weakened and as a result growth is stunted. The leaves turn a sickly yellow and the flower buds either fail to develop or produce distorted blooms.

Life history: See page 634.

Control: See page 634.

Nematodes

Identification: Upon cutting open an infested bulb a brown ring will be found. With a hand lens, one may detect the nematodes, which are minute worms of a transparent color hardly more than $1/25$ in. long.

Injury: Plants make stunted growth. The leaves become curiously twisted and distorted and lie prostrate on the ground, turning yellow and dying prematurely. Thickened specks or speckles are produced upon the leaves and are very characteristic of this infestation.

Life history: The eggs — 400 to 500 — are laid by a single female and deposited within the tissues of the plant. Upon hatching, the larvae usually remain within the plant, but occasionally they migrate through the soil to other hosts. It is during this stage that they so often find their way into the greenhouse or into the garden when fresh soil is brought in. Located in the mouth of each worm is a sharply pointed, spearlike apparatus, which is used to bore through the root tissues when a new host plant is attacked, and also while feeding. During the first two to three weeks after hatching the male and female larvae are identical in size and shape. During the molting period, however, when the old skin is shed, the female undergoes a distinct change, becoming pear-shaped and pearly-white in color. The male remains spindle-shaped.

In the South the worms winter over in the open. In the North they are usually killed by the cold unless harbored in frames or in greenhouses.

Control: Destroy all badly infested bulbs. Bulbs that are only lightly infested or of which

one may be suspicious may be given the following treatment:

Submerge bulbs for three hours in water kept at a temperature of 110°F. Then plunge immediately into cold water.

Oenothera (evening primrose)

Insect Pest — Primrose Flea Beetle (*Altica torquata*)

Identification: A small, very active beetle that is metallic blue in color.

Injury: Both the larvae and the adult beetles feed upon the foliage. If the infestation is severe, the leaves of the primrose may become completely skeletonized.

Life history: The adult beetles usually appear early in June and the females deposit their eggs upon the leaves of the host plant. Upon hatching, the larvae feed for a short time and then pass into the pupa stage, the second generation emerging late in July. The winter is passed either in the pupa or adult stage.

Control: Spray plants with Sevin when the larvae begin to feed, being careful to limit spray to infected plants.

Paeonia (peony)

Diseases — Anthracnose

A fungus disease that occasionally attacks peonies.

Symptoms: Spots appear on the stems and leaves. In the early stages the center is almost white, with a dark, reddish border. Later in the season the spots become sunken, with a small black pimple in the center.

Control: Remove and discard diseased portions of the plant. Frequent sprayings with a copper fungicide will provide control.

Botrytis

Nature of the disease: A fungus disease caused by *Botrytis paeoniae* that is very destructive in many parts of the country. It is particularly prevalent in damp, rainy seasons. Small, black resting bodies, known as sclerotia, are formed in the diseased stems and the fungus is carried over the winter in this manner.

Symptoms: Young shoots rot off at the ground line when 5 in. to 8 in. tall, the stems having a water-soaked, cankerous appearance. The rotted portion later becomes covered with a soft brown mass of spores. The flower buds turn brown and fail to open, and the flower stalk is usually affected for several inches below the bud. During a severe outbreak of the disease 90 percent of the flower buds may fail to develop. Open flowers also occasionally are affected, turning dark brown and becoming a mass of rotting petals. The leaves are usually the last part of the plant to show any trace of infection, being attacked first at the tips. Large, irregular spots appear, dark in the early stages, later fading to light brown. Dark concentric rings within the lesions on both the leaves and the stems are very characteristic of the disease.

Control: In early fall cut all above-ground parts to ground level and discard them. In spring spray the plants with Benlate when the young tips break through the ground. Follow in two weeks with another application. If leaf blight and bud blast develop later, a third application may be necessary.

Leaf Blotch

A fungus disease caused by *Cladosporium paeoniae.*

Symptoms: Large spots, 2 in. to 3 in. in diameter, appear on the leaves late in the season. The spots are very characteristic, being purple on the upper surface and dull brown on the lower surface. In damp weather the spots on the lower surface appear to be covered with a feltlike substance, olive green in color.

Control: As the fungus lives over the winter on the old leaves, the disease may be kept almost entirely under control by cutting off and destroying all top growth after the plants have become dormant in the autumn.

Mosaic

Symptoms: Leaves become blotched with alternating rings of light and dark green. The spots vary considerably in size, some being small with narrow margins and others being large with much wider margins. Frequently only one or two stalks in the clump are affected.

Control: See page 612.

Phytophthora Blight

Caused by the fungus *Phytophthora paeoniae.*

Symptoms: Large, dark brown spots appear on the leaves, resembling those of botrytis but lacking the concentric markings. The buds are usually blighted and fail to open, and the crown of the plant may become rotted.

Control: Because infections occur in the roots and lower portions of the stems, fungicidal sprays are of no value. Confirmed cases should be lifted out together with adjacent soil and thrown into the trash can. Planting healthy clumps in a new location where the soil is well-drained usually prevents further trouble.

Stem Rot

A fungus disease caused by *Sclerotinia sclerotiorum;* damp, rainy weather is particularly favorable to its spread.

Symptoms: Stalks suddenly wilt, due to rotting at the base. Large, black, resting bodies or sclerotia are found in the pith at the base of the plant and readily distinguish this disease from any other.

Control: Same as for phytophthora blight.

Wilt

Caused by the fungus *Verticillium albo-atrum*.

Symptoms: Plants show signs of wilt and gradually die. The sap tubes become clogged, and when the stem is split open they appear as greenish streaks.

Control: See page 610.

Insect Pests — Ants

Ants are frequently found on peonies, being attracted by the sweetish, sticky substance that is exuded from the buds. While they do no direct harm themselves, it is very probable that they carry the spores of fungus diseases from one plant to another, provided such spores are present. It is recommended that the soil about the plants be treated with Diazinon or Dursban.

Nematodes causing Root Gall

Identification: Swollen places are found on the roots, which are caused by microscopic worms. The roots are often short and stubby, the fine rootlets being covered with galls. The crown of the plant is also occasionally swollen.

Injury: The growth of the plant is very seriously affected if the infestation is severe.

Life history: See page 665.

Control: See page 665.

Oyster Shell Scale

Identification: Small, grayish-white scales, resembling an oyster shell in shape, are found clustered in masses along the stems.

Injury: The scales suck the juices from the plant, causing general lack of vigor and the eventual death of the infested shoots.

Life history: During the winter the eggs are protected by the hard, shell-like covering of the old scales. The young hatch out at the end of May or early in June. At this stage they are soft-bodied and look like small, yellowish-white specks on the stems. Later in the season the hard, shell-like covering is formed.

Control: Remove all above-ground parts at ground level in the late fall. Spray the plants with malathion in late May and again in mid-June.

Rose Chafer (*Maciodactylus subspinosus*, also known as Rose Beetle or Rose Bug)

Identification: Grayish-fawn, long-legged beetles, about ½ in. in length.

Injury: The beetles feed upon the flowers, completely destroying them in a very short time.

Life history: See page 653.

Control: See page 654.

Rose Curculio (*Rhynchites bicolor*)

Identification: Bright red beetles with black legs and snout, about ¼ in. long.

Injury: The beetles eat holes in the unopened buds and also feed to some extent upon the leaves. Buds either fail to open or produce flowers riddled with holes.

Life history: See page 654.

Control: See page 654.

Stalk Borer (Common)

Identification: Slender caterpillars about 1 in. to 2 in. long. The young caterpillars are brown with white stripes. When full grown they lose their stripes and become a solid, dirty gray.

Injury: The stalk borer makes a small round hole in the stem and tunnels up through the stalk, causing the injured shoot suddenly to wilt and break over.

Life history: See page 615.

Control: See page 615.

Pelargonium (geranium)

Diseases — Bacterial Leaf Spot
Caused by *Xanthomonas pelargoni*, this may be present on young as well as on old leaves.

Symptoms: The affected area first shows as a water-soaked dot that can be seen only in transmitted light. As the spots become older, they turn brown in color and are usually irregular though sometimes circular in shape. Several spots may appear on a single leaf. The tissue between the spots may also turn brown and die, but the original spots show up clearly in the dead area.

Control: Out of doors the plants should be planted where they will get plenty of sunlight and air. In the greenhouse plants should be kept in a well-ventilated house and care should be taken to see that the tops are not splashed when watering. If necessary, spray with a copper fungicide.

Bacterial Spot
Caused by the *Pseudomonas erodii*. It may start at the margin of the leaf and give rise to the angular areas, or it may start by a small translucent spot.

Symptoms: The soft leaf tissue is invaded between the veins, which give rise to a rather large elongated area that converges toward the base of the leaf. Occasionally the infected areas are more or less round and may retain the original color or become brownish or pinkish in color.

Control: See Bacterial Leaf Spot, column one.

Cercospora Leaf Spot
Caused by the fungus *Cercospora brunkii.*

Symptoms: The spots are small, light brown or pale brick-red in color, more or less circular in shape, and have a narrow, slightly raised and darker border. It can be differentiated from bacterial spot in that the borders of the spots are raised and darker in color than in the center of the spot, while in bacterial spot the borders are colorless.

Control: See Bacterial Leaf Spot, column one.

Dropsy
Nature of the disease: Dropsy is believed to be caused by a warm, damp soil that stimulates root growth and a moist, cool air that inhibits transpiration. The disease is more common in late winter.

Symptoms: The leaves develop water-soaked areas, which become brown and corky. The leaf yellows first around the spot, and later becomes entirely yellow and drops off. The stems and petioles develop corky ridges.

Control: Give the plant plenty of light and good ventilation. Avoid overwatering.

Petunia

Disease — Mosaic
Symptoms: The foliage becomes mottled yellow and green. The leaves are frequently distorted and the growth of the plant is stunted.

Control: See page 612.

Insect Pests — Orthezia
Identification: The young nymphs are very tiny, dark green and wingless, with a row of waxy plates extending back over the body. The adult

females have a very conspicuous white, fluted egg sac, which extends back from the body for a distance two or more times the diameter of the body.

Injury: The orthezias are closely related to the scales and suck the juices from the plant tissues.

Control: See page 623.

Potato Flea Beetle
Identification: Small, very active black beetle about 1/16 in. long. The hind legs are longer than the front legs, enabling the beetle to jump like a flea when disturbed.

Injury: The beetles feed upon the foliage, making many small round or irregular holes. The leaves have the appearance of being peppered with fine shot. The foliage becomes badly disfigured, and if the infestation is very serious it may cause the death of the plant.

Life history: The adults hibernate during the winter under leaves or trash and emerge early in the spring. The minute eggs are laid in the soil about the plants. The larvae are small, slender, whitish worms. They feed to some extent upon the roots and underground stems of weeds and cultivated plants but do comparatively little damage. After feeding for a few weeks, they pass into the pupa stage in the soil. A short time later the adult flea beetles emerge. There are usually two generations a year.

Control: Spray with Sevin when the beetles first appear, being careful to limit spray to infected plants.

Yellow Wooly-bear Caterpillar
Identification: A caterpillar about 2 in. long when full grown. The body is completely covered with long hairs, which vary from pale yellow to reddish-brown.

Injury: The caterpillars feed upon the foliage.

Life history: See page 623.

Control: See page 623.

Phlox

Diseases — Leaf Spot
A fungus disease caused by *Septoria divaricata.* The fungus lives over the winter on the fallen leaves and is ready to reinfect the new growth in the spring.

Symptoms: Dark spots, ranging from brown to black, appear on the leaves and eventually the plant may become almost completely defoliated.

Control: Remove and destroy infected plant parts in the fall. Spray several times at two-week intervals in late spring with a copper fungicide.

Mildew
Caused by the fungi *Erysiphe cichoracearum* and *Sphaerotheca humuli.*

Symptoms: The foliage becomes covered with a white, powdery substance. In the most advanced stages the affected areas turn black. Mildew is very disfiguring to the plant and is injurious to its growth. It is especially prevalent in damp seasons.

Control: See page 620. In the autumn remove the tops and rake up and destroy fallen leaves. It is well to divide the clumps and give the plants plenty of space.

Phlox Blight
Nature of the disease: In the past it was thought that phlox blight was caused either by a fungus or by injury from some insect or mite, but investigations carried on at Cornell and at the New Jersey Agricultural Experimental Station tend to prove that the trouble is attributable to the peculiar growth habits of certain types of phlox. In the *P. paniculata* types the new shoots

in the spring are borne on the stem of the previous season's growth, and these new shoots obtain their water and nutrients through the old stems. As growth advances, the old stems begin to decay and there is an apparent disturbance in the flow of nutrients into the young and vigorously growing shoots, causing the characteristic symptoms of phlox blight (the theory being that the growing tips draw the moisture from the lower leaves). Some varieties appear to be much more susceptible than others, and when phlox plants are grown in a very moist climate the trouble is less severe. The *P. suffruticosa* types of phlox seldom suffer from blight, as the new shoots start from a much lower point on the old stems or directly from the crown, and they soon become established on their own roots.

Symptoms: The lower leaves of the plant become spotted and gradually turn brown and die. In the majority of cases only the lower portion of the plant is affected. The upper portion continues to make good growth, appears healthy and vigorous, and produces normal bloom. In occasional instances the disease progresses slowly upward, eventually killing the entire stem.

Control: Various measures of control are recommended. The removal of the first shoots in early spring will induce the formation of new bud growth, either directly from the crown of the plant or at a point lower down on the old stem, and it has been found that such growth is comparatively free from blight. Another measure that is proving very satisfactory is to prune back the old stalks to sound wood and to paint them with Bordeaux mixture.

Insect Pests — Black Blister Beetle
Identification: A slender jet-black beetle about ½ in. long, with very prominent head and neck. It exudes a yellow, oily fluid from the joints of its legs when disturbed.

Injury: The beetles feed upon the flowers, completely destroying them in a very short time.

Life history: See page 614.

Control: See page 614.

Corn Ear Worm
Identification: Large striped worms about 2 in. long when full grown. They vary from light green to brown, and the stripes, which run lengthwise on the body, are alternating light and dark. The head is yellow, the legs almost black.

Injury: The caterpillars feed upon the plants.

Life history: See page 617.

Control: See page 617.

Nematodes
Identification: The nematodes are microscopic worms. Their presence is usually detected by their characteristic injury to the plant.

Injury: Plants are dwarfed and stunted and few flowers develop. Foliage frequently becomes spotted and distorted. Small, swollen, knotty growths are found upon the roots.

Life history: See page 665.

Control: See page 665.

Physalis alkekengi (Chinese-lantern plant)

Insect Pest — Tortoise Beetle (Gold Bug)
Identification: A small golden beetle about ¼ in. long. Occasionally black spots or stripes are found on the body. The beetle is turtle-shaped, flat on the underside, with the head and legs partially hidden.

Injury: The beetles feed upon the foliage.

Life history: See page 635.

Control: See page 635.

Primula (primrose)

Diseases — Chlorosis
A physiological disease thought to be due to intense soil acidity.

Symptoms: Leaves become somewhat mottled yellow and white. Plants fail to make vigorous growth.

Control: An application of an iron chelate (sequestrene of iron) to the soil or to the leaves will help restore their normal green color.

Rot
The disease is caused by *Botrytis cinerea*, which is very prevalent under conditions of extreme dampness.

Symptoms: Plants rot off at the crown, becoming covered with a gray mold.

Control: Avoid excessive watering of plants growing in greenhouses. Spraying with Botran several times at two-week intervals might provide control.

Insect Pest — Potato Flea Beetle
Identification: A small, very active, metallic blue beetle. The hind legs are longer than the front legs, enabling the beetle to jump like a flea.

Injury: The beetles feed upon the foliage, making many small round or irregular holes. The leaves have the appearance of being peppered with fine shot.

Life history: See page 646.

Control: See page 646.

Reseda (mignonette)

Diseases — Leaf Spot or Blight
A fungus disease caused by *Cercospora resedae.*

Symptoms: Small, slightly sunken spots with pale yellowish-brown margins appear on the leaves. As the disease progresses, dark specks that are the fruiting bodies of the fungus develop in the center of the spots and the leaves gradually wither and die.

Control: Spray with a copper fungicide several times at ten-day intervals during the growing season.

Insect Pests — Cabbage Looper
Identification: Greenish caterpillars with a white line along each side of the body and two lines near the middle of the back. The middle half of the body is without legs, and when resting or moving the caterpillar is usually in a very characteristic humped position.

Injury: The caterpillars feed upon the leaves.

Life history: The winter is passed in the pupa stage, the delicate, white pupa cases being attached to a leaf of some host plant. The small, grayish-brown moths emerge in spring, and the females lay their eggs singly upon the upper surface of the leaves of the host plants. The moths fly only at night. After hatching, the larvae feed for three to four weeks and then pass into the pupa stage. During the summer the pupa stage lasts only two weeks, and there are usually three or four generations during the season.

Control: See page 613.

Cabbage Worm
Identification: Small, velvety-green caterpillars

somewhat more than 1 in. in length when full grown.

Injury: Large irregular holes eaten in the foliage.

Life history: See page 613.

Control: See page 613.

Rose

Diseases — Black Spot
Nature of the disease: Black spot is caused by the fungus *Diplocarpon rosea.* The winter spores, which are protected during the cold months by minute sacs, mature at about the time that roses begin their growth in the spring. These spores are carried to the leaves by wind, splashing rain, and other agencies, and when conditions of temperature and moisture are favorable they germinate, sending out tiny germ-tubes that penetrate the outer covering or cuticle of the leaf. When safely within the leaf these germ-tubes develop a vegetative, threadlike structure known as mycelium.

About two weeks after infection has taken place, these mycelia produce millions of secondary or summer spores. These are readily blown about by the wind, eventually settling on nearby plants. If conditions happen to be extremely favorable, they germinate within a few hours. Thus successive crops of these summer spores are produced throughout the season at intervals of from two to three weeks and the disease gains tremendous headway as the season advances unless proper measures of control are taken. The fungus lives over the winter on dead and decaying leaves in the form of special winter spores.

Symptoms: Black spots appear on the foliage. Leaves turn yellow and drop prematurely. The spots are somewhat circular in shape, having irregular margins, and they occasionally reach a diameter of $1/2$ in. or more. They are confined entirely to the upper surface of the leaf. The disease first makes its appearance early in the summer and becomes particularly virulent later in the season. It saps the vitality of the plant to a great extent and in severe cases causes complete defoliation.

Control: Black spot cannot be cured but it *can* be kept under control. After a leaf is once attacked and the minute germ-tubes have penetrated through the outer tissues, there is no chemical known that will kill the fungus and not be injurious to the growing plant at the same time. The problem, therefore, is to prevent infection; fortunately, with a reasonable amount of care, this is possible. The importance of prompt and systematic attention cannot be overemphasized. If the foliage is coated with an effective fungicide the spores will fail to germinate, and will be unable to start new centers of infection. As a matter of further precaution all leaves that drop to the ground should be immediately raked up and placed in the trash can. As the spores require a certain amount of moisture in order to germinate, it is essential that the foliage be protected particularly well during rainy weather.

There are a number of excellent commercial products on the market that are combination sprays or dusts for the control of black spot and other rose diseases, as well as many insect pests. A preparation of this sort is very convenient and it is the practical solution to the problem of disease and insect control for the average gardener.

For rosarians and commercial growers who may wish to prepare their own combination spray, the following formula is recommended:

Phaltan, 50% wettable powder	4 tsp.
Sevin, 50% WP	2 tbs.
malathion, 25% WP	4 tbs.
water	1 gal.

Mix the four dry ingredients together, then add enough water to make a very thin paste. Pour this mixture into the spray tank, preferably through a fine screen or cheesecloth, add water and stir. Because of the broad-scale effect of Sevin on beneficial insects, the spray should be carefully limited to infected plants.

Regardless of the type of spray used, frequent applications must be made if good control is to be obtained. During periods of rainy weather applications should be made at five- or six-day intervals; during dry weather at eight- to nine-day intervals. A two-week interval between applications is too long and will not give satisfactory control. Both the upper and the undersurface of the leaves must be reached. There are few accomplishments that bring greater satisfaction to the gardener than rose beds filled with vigorous, healthy bushes that have luxuriant, disease-free foliage. If spraying is done thoroughly and frequently, this achievement is well within the realm of possibility, and one in which a rose grower may take justifiable pride.

Bronzing of Leaves

Nature of the disease: A physiological disease due to some functional disturbance in the growth of the plant. It may sometimes be due to very rapid growth caused by the drastic pruning of some particular shoot.

Symptoms: A single leaf or several leaves on the same shoot become a mottled bronze in color, turn yellow and drop prematurely.

Control: No effective control.

Canker, Brown

Nature of the disease: Brown canker is a disease caused by *Cryptosporella umbrina,* a fungus that has gained much headway during the past decade and causes severe losses in many areas of the country.

Symptoms: In the early stages small, purplish-red areas appear on the stems and the petioles of the leaves. As the disease progresses, the spots develop a lighter center with a definite purple margin. When the leaves and flowers are affected the same characteristic cinnamon-buff spots appear. Usually only the outer, more exposed petals of the flowers are affected. When the flower buds are attacked they either fail to open or produce distorted, malformed blooms. In some cases a branch becomes completely girdled by brown canker and occasionally an entire plant will succumb to the disease if it is not checked.

Control: The sprays recommended for black spot will keep brown canker fairly well under control. Spraying should begin early in the spring and continue throughout the growing season.

All diseased canes should be removed at time of pruning. Do not use any type of winter mulch such as peat moss or leaves that will keep the canes moist for long periods.

Canker, Stem

Stem canker is caused by *Leptosphaeria conio-thyrium,* the same fungus that causes cane blight of raspberries.

Symptoms: In the early stages stem canker appears as a slender, purple stripe on the branches. As the disease progresses, the affected area becomes dry and brown and somewhat sunken and the stem may become partially or entirely girdled. It reduces the vigor of the plant, causing sickly, weakened growth above the point of attack.

Control: The fungus of stem canker usually enters through wounds or scars on the stems. The best measure of control is to prune stems back to a point below infection, and when cutting blooms always to cut close to a bud or leaf axil. It is a wise precaution to dip the shears in a 7 percent denatured alcohol solution.

Leaf Rust

Nature of the disease: Leaf rust is a fungus disease caused by *Phragmidium mucronolatum.* It causes the foliage to become unhealthy in appearance and if the infection is severe the vitality of the plant is seriously affected.

Symptoms: In the early stages bright orange-colored pustules are found on the undersurface of the leaves. As the disease progresses, the pustules become brick-red in color.

Control: Occasional applications of Zineb or a mixture of Ferbam and sulphur provide control.

Affected leaves should be picked off and destroyed. All fallen leaves should be raked up and discarded in the autumn.

Mildew

Nature of the disease: Mildew is a fungus disease caused by *Sphaerotheca pannosa* var. *rosae*. It is a moldlike growth, the greater portion being confined to the outer surface of the leaves. The minute white threads form a network with their numerous strands and at frequent intervals chains of egg-shaped spores are borne on upright branches. When mature, these spores are blown about by the wind and eventually settle on nearby plants. As soon as temperature and moisture conditions are favorable, they germinate and establish new centers of infection. The individual spores are comparatively short-lived but new ones are constantly being produced. Special spores are produced to carry the fungus over the winter months and these are ready to start growth as soon as spring comes.

The original source of infection may usually be traced to spores brought into the garden when new plants were purchased. Mildew is often very troublesome on roses grown under glass, and as the spores are blown about by the slightest wind, it is probable that roses growing in a garden some distance away might become infected in this way.

Mildew is especially prevalent during damp, rainy seasons as the spores are then provided with ideal conditions for germination. Some varieties are much more susceptible to mildew than others. The crimson ramblers and closely related forms are highly susceptible.

Symptoms: In the early stages grayish or whitish spots are found on the young leaves and shoots. These spots gradually enlarge and the stems, foliage and unopened buds become almost completely covered with a white, powdery substance. In the most advanced stages the affected areas turn black. Not only is mildew very disfiguring but it also seriously affects the vigor and growth of the plants. If it is not checked, the foliage and flower buds become dwarfed and malformed and many of the leaves drop prematurely.

Control: As soon as hybrid teas and hybrid perpetuals have been pruned in early spring, the dormant plants should be sprayed with commercial lime sulphur. During the growing season mildew may be curbed by using any one of the following materials: Acticione PM, Benlate, Karathane or Phaltan. (The last also controls black spot.) Some of these materials cannot be used when the air temperature is over 85°F. Observe the precautions on the container.

Stem Rust

A fungus disease caused by *Phragmidium speciosum*.

Symptoms: Bright orange cankerlike spots appear on the petioles of the leaves and the stems of the young shoots. The affected shoots frequently become distorted.

Control: All infected shoots should be cut off and placed in the trash can.

Insect Pests — Aphids

Two species of aphids attack roses: the rose aphid *(Macrosiphum rosae)* and the small green rose aphid *(Myzaphis rosarum)*. The latter is usually the most troublesome in greenhouses but it is also frequently found on outdoor roses in the South and in California. The identification, injury and control of the two species are practically the same.

Identification: Green, soft-bodied, louselike insects with globular or pear-shaped bodies. They are usually found clustered along the tips of the young growing shoots.

Injury: Aphids suck the juices from the plant, reducing its vigor and vitality and in many cases causing the leaves and flowers to become unsightly and distorted.

Life history: In the North the rose aphids pass the winter in the egg stage. The eggs are small, glossy-black in color and are attached to the bark near the buds. The eggs hatch early in the spring, as soon as plant growth begins, and the young aphids begin feeding. The first brood that hatches out from the eggs matures in about two weeks, and from then on, through the balance of the season, living young are produced. As each female gives birth daily to several young, they multiply with startling rapidity. These living young are produced from unfertilized eggs and are all females. In the autumn males appear and fertilize the eggs, which carry the species over the winter. In the South they do not pass through an egg stage, as the winters are mild and they breed throughout the year.

Control: See page 610.

Japanese Beetle *(Popillia japonica)*
Identification: Large, handsome beetles, a metallic greenish-bronze in color, with two conspicuous and several small white spots near the tip of the abdomen. During the middle of the day they are very active, making rapid flight when disturbed. In the evening they are more sluggish.

Injury: The Japanese beetles have been among the most destructive of our garden pests. They feed voraciously upon the foliage, buds and open flowers, and may completely skeletonize a bush in a very short time. They are gregarious in habit and sometimes as many as twenty or thirty beetles will be found clustered on a single flower bud.

Life history: Japanese beetles were first seen in Riverton, New Jersey, in 1916. The adult beetles appear early in July and for about six weeks they feed upon fruit and shade trees, field crops and vegetables and many ornamentals. The female beetles deposit their eggs in the soil, usually selecting an open, sunny area where the grass is short. The larvae hatch in several weeks and begin feeding on decaying vegetable matter in the soil and also to a considerable extent upon the roots of grasses and other plants. At this stage they do considerable damage to lawns and golf courses. At the approach of cold weather the grubs burrow down into the soil to a depth of 6 in. to 12 in. and construct a little earthen cell in which they pass the winter. In the spring the grubs work their way toward the surface again and feed for several weeks before passing into the pupa stage. The pupa stage extends over a period of about six weeks. The adult beetles then emerge.

Control: When the foliage is attacked, the adult beetles may be sprayed with Methoxychlor or individual plants carefully with Sevin. In home gardens it is advisable to hand-pick the beetles by knocking them in a can containing kerosene and water. The use of beetle traps is not advised because the Geraniol bait attracts more beetles into the rose garden than the traps themselves can catch. If traps are to be used, they should be placed outside the garden and baited with a mixture of Geraniol and Eugenol. Apply Diazinon to grass plots or borders in the rose garden to control the larval stage of the Japanese beetle. "Milky disease" spore dust, sold under the trade name Doom, can also be distributed over large areas of grass bordering a rose planting. This material, though acting more slowly than chemical substances, eventually reduces the beetle population. It should not be used in areas that have been treated with insecticides.

Leaf Roller
There are a number of caterpillars of this type that attack roses. The life history, injury and control are practically the same in all cases.

Rose Leaf Tier *(Choristoneura rosaceana):* Small caterpillar varying from yellow to light green and distinguished by an oblique band running across the body.

Red-banded Leaf Roller (Argyrotaenia velutinana)
Small caterpillar, similar to the above but readily distinguished by the red band on the body.

Injury: The caterpillars feed upon the foliage and the blossoms, their work being very characteristic, as they roll the leaves together and web them with fine, silken threads.

Life history: The moths vary somewhat in appearance according to the species. They deposit their eggs in tiny masses on the foliage and within a few weeks the caterpillars hatch and begin feeding. They become full grown in about a month and pupate within the rolled leaves. Several weeks later the moths emerge and the life cycle begins again. Two broods are usually produced during the summer.

Control: See page 615.

Mites (Red Spider)

The species of mite most commonly found on roses and on many other garden plants, such as phlox and hollyhocks, is the two-spotted spider mite *(Tetranychus urticae)*, commonly called red spider.

Identification: Almost infinitesimal in size, they are less than $1/50$ in. long. The body is oval with two dark spots on the back.

Injury: The mites feed on the undersurface of the foliage. Leaves take on an unhealthy appearance, becoming gray, reddish- or yellowish-brown. Tiny webs are made on the undersurface of the leaves, and sometimes on the tips of new shoots and on flower buds. If the infestation is severe and remains unchecked, the plant may become completely defoliated.

Life history: The female lays her eggs on the undersurface of the foliage. Upon hatching, the young mites feed for a few days, then pass into a resting stage. They then molt, begin active feeding again, and pass into a resting stage again before developing into adults. The time required from egg to adult depends upon the temperature. When temperatures are low, ranging around 55°F., it requires forty days. When temperatures reach 75°F., it requires only five days. In midsummer, particularly when the humidity is high, mite populations build up very rapidly.

Control: Frequent applications of sulphur, either alone or in combination sprays, help to control this mite. When sulphur sprays fail to provide adequate control, the gardener can use any one of several excellent mite killers. Among these are Chlorobenzilate, Kelthanc or Tedion. Most of these materials are compatible with fungicides. Follow the manufacturer's directions on compatibility and dilutions.

Rose Chafer (*Macrodactylus subspinosus,* also known as Rose Beetle or Rose Bug)

Identification: Grayish-fawn, long-legged beetles about $1/4$ in. in length.

Injury: The beetles feed chiefly upon the flowers. Sometimes a dozen or more will be found clustered upon a single bloom, which soon is completely demolished. Beyond any doubt, rose chafers are the most destructive of our rose pests. They appear in hordes just as the first roses are coming into bloom and their depredations continue throughout the height of the rose season.

In closely built suburban areas rose bugs are seldom seen and cause little damage, due probably to the fact that conditions are not so favorable for them, as the land is too intensively cultivated. In country districts, however, where open fields abound, and particularly where the soil is of a sandy texture, conditions are ideal and they make the most of their opportunities by increasing in alarming numbers. They are not apt to be so numerous where the soil is of a heavy clay texture, as it is more difficult for the females to deposit their eggs, and consequently they never gain much headway where such soil conditions exist.

Life history: The adult rose beetles appear early in June and feed for about six weeks. Toward the end of this period the females deposit their eggs. Under normal conditions each female deposits three sets of eggs, about twelve being laid at one time. The beetle selects a rough, grassy place where the soil is somewhat sandy, burrows into the ground for a depth of 3 in. to 6 in. and lays her eggs singly in tiny soil pockets. The eggs, which are oval, white and smooth in appearance, hatch in about two weeks. The larvae feed both on decaying vegetable matter and the roots of weeds and grasses, reaching maturity about the latter part of October. They then burrow down into the soil to a depth of about 12 in. and curl up in little earthen cells for the winter. In the spring the grubs work their way up toward the surface again and usually feed for a short time before they pupate. The pupa stage varies from three to four weeks. The adult beetles then emerge just as the first roses are coming into bloom.

Control: Spray with Methoxychlor when the insects first appear, and repeat as often as required.

Rose Curculio (*Rhynchites bicolor*)
Identification: Bright red beetles with black legs and snout. Small in size, measuring only about ¼ in.

Injury: The beetles eat holes in the unopened buds and in the fruits, and also feed upon the leaves and flower stems to some extent. Many of the injured buds fail to open; the petals of those that do expand are usually riddled with holes.

Life history: The beetles appear early in June. The eggs, which are oval in shape, are deposited in the holes that the beetles bore in the buds and young fruits. Within a week or ten days the eggs hatch and the small, white, legless larvae feed upon the seeds and flower petals until they are full grown. In late summer the grubs migrate down to the ground near the base of the plant, where they enter the pupa stage and pass the winter.

Control: Daily hand-picking of infested buds is helpful, and collecting and destroying the fruits or hips will lessen the infestation for the coming year because this practice destroys the larvae. Since the weevils are still likely to be abundant after the blooming season, the plants may be sprayed with Sevin mixed with Kelthane, with care to limit this spray to infected plants. Although this pest is usually not troublesome on hybrid teas, it has been known to cause serious damage to cultivated roses that grow near wild roses.

Rose Leafhopper (*Edwardsiana rosae*)
Identification: Small, narrow, yellowish-white insects. They are very active and hop quickly from one leaf to another when disturbed.

Injury: The nymphs and adults usually feed from the undersurface of the leaves, sucking the juices from the plant. The leaves at first appear yellow and somewhat faded; if the infestation is severe, they later turn brown and die.

Life history: The adult females deposit their eggs in late summer under the bark of the rose bushes. The winter is passed in the egg stage and the young nymphs hatch out early in May. They begin feeding immediately, then pass through several molts before reaching the adult stage.

Control: Diazinon sprays provide good control.

Rose Midge (*Dasineura rhodophaga*)
Identification: Adult is a very minute, yellowish-brown fly; larva small, whitish to orange.

Injury: The maggots feed on the flower buds, which as a result become blackened and distorted.

Life history: The adult female lays her eggs within the flower and leaf buds. Larvae feed on the buds, and when grown, they drop to the ground and pupate. The life cycle covers only two to three weeks in midsummer and successive generations are produced.

Control: On outdoor roses, Diazinon sprays are effective. In greenhouses, control of this pest is obtained with standard Malathion sprays or aerosols.

Rose Scale (*Aulacaspis rosae*)
Identification: Small, snow-white scale insects, usually found clustered thickly along the branches and twigs. The female scales are circu-

lar in shape, about $\frac{1}{10}$ in. in diameter. The male scales are considerably smaller, and are long and narrow in shape.

Injury: The scales feed upon the plant juices, causing weakened growth and general lack of vigor. If sufficiently numerous, they can cause the death of the plant.

Life history: The young scales emerge from beneath the scale of the female parent and for the first few days crawl about actively upon the plant. They find a favorable location, then insert their threadlike mouth parts into the bark and begin feeding. After a short time they pass through the first molt; at this stage they lose their legs, and the scalelike covering forms over the body. The scale is composed of fine threads of wax that have exuded from the wall of the body and have become practically welded together. The female scales molt twice, remaining under the scale for the period of their entire life. The males pass through four molts; at the end of this period they become minute, two-winged, yellowish insects with three pairs of legs, and with eyes and antennae. They do not feed in this stage but move about actively, mating with the female scales. The female scales continue to feed for a short time after mating.

Control: Prune out badly infested canes. In early spring while plants are still dormant, spray with commercial lime sulphur, 1 part to 9 parts of water. The temperature should be above 45°F. when the application is made.

A miscible oil, applied as a dormant spray, will also give fairly satisfactory control.

Malathion, applied as a spray during the summer, will eliminate some of the scales in the crawler stage.

Rose Slugs

Three distinct species of slugs are apt to be troublesome on roses:

Rose Slug (Endelomyia aethiops):

Identification: Greenish when young, becoming more yellow as they grow older, $\frac{1}{2}$ in. to $\frac{3}{4}$ in.

Injury: The slugs do most of their feeding at night, skeletonizing the upper surface of the leaves. The foliage becomes unsightly and eventually dries up and drops off.

Life history: The adult flies are black, about $\frac{1}{5}$ in. long, and possess four wings. They appear at about the time that the rose bushes start growth in the spring, and the females deposit their eggs between the tissues of the leaves. The eggs hatch about ten days later and the slugs begin feeding, attaining full growth in two or three weeks. When mature they burrow into the soil to a depth of 1 in. or 2 in. and construct a cocoon in which they pupate during the winter. The following spring the flies emerge and the life cycle begins again.

Control: Prevent infestation by cleaning up and destroying all rubbish. Spray infested plants with Diazinon or carefully with Sevin in June.

Bristly Rose Slug (Cladius isomerus):

Identification: Yellowish-green, about $\frac{3}{8}$ in. long, the body covered with little bristly hairs.

Injury: When young the slugs merely skeletonize the leaves, feeding upon the undersurface, but as they grow older they eat large irregular holes along the edge of the leaves.

Life history: The adult is a black, four-winged fly, slightly larger than that of the rose slug. The female deposits her eggs just under the surface of the leaf petiole. The eggs, which are small, white and round, hatch in seven to ten days and the young slugs make rapid growth. Six or more generations are produced during the season. The winter is passed in the pupa stage, the cocoons, which are very thin and transparent, being protected by rubbish and old leaves.

Control: Same as for rose slug.

Coiled Rose Slug (Allantus cinctus):

Identification: The upper surface of the body is green, with a metallic sheen. There are numerous white spots on the body and a wide band runs across the middle of the abdomen. The slug is about ¾ in. long.

Injury: The slugs feed along the edge of the leaves, with the tip of the body usually coiled beneath the leaf. The entire leaf surface is, in time, destroyed by them.

Life history: The adult flies appear in early spring and the females deposit their eggs, singly, upon the undersurface of the leaves. The larvae hatch out within a few days and begin feeding. When full grown they bore into the pith of a dead or decaying branch and pass into the pupa stage. Two broods are produced each season, the winter being passed in the pupa stage.

Control: Same as for rose slug.

Rose Stem Borer (*Oberea maculata*)
Identification: The larvae, which are seldom seen unless an infested shoot is slit open, are small, whitish caterpillars.

Injury: The larvae feed within the shoots, making small tunnels that weaken the branches and eventually cause their death.

Life history: The adult of the rose stem borer is a wasplike insect, which appears early in the summer. The females puncture the shoots and deposit their eggs within the tissues. A short time later the larvae hatch out and begin feeding within the stem.

Control: Infested shoots should be cut off and discarded.

Rose Stem Girdler (*Agrilus aurichalceus*)
Identification: Small, whitish caterpillars. Their presence may be detected by the characteristic swelling of the shoot.

Injury: The larvae tunnel their way into the stem, making short, spiral mines. The shoots swell over the affected area.

Life history: The adult beetles appear in June and July and the females deposit their eggs on the bark of the branches. Upon hatching, the larvae tunnel their way into the shoots and begin feeding. When full grown they construct little cells in the pith of the plant and pass into the pupa stage.

Control: Cut off and discard all infested shoots.

Rose Weevil (*Pantomotus cervinus*, also known as Fuller Rose Beetle)
Identification: Dull, brownish-gray beetle, slightly over ¼ in. long, with a white line running diagonally across each wing.

Injury: The larvae feed upon the roots to some extent and the adult beetles feed upon the foliage, buds and open blooms. They are most commonly found on greenhouse roses but occasionally become a serious menace to roses grown in the open. Most of their feeding is done at night.

Life history: The female beetle lays her eggs in late summer in crevices of bark or at the base of the host plant. The larvae feed on the roots and the pupae stage is passed in the soil.

Control: Dusting the soil surface with Diazinon will control the larval stage of this pest.

Thrips (*Frankliniella tritici*)
   The Flower Thrip is the species most commonly found on roses.

Identification: Adults are very small, about ¹/₂₀ in. long, brownish-yellow to amber with an orange thorax. The young are lemon-yellow.

Injury: The thrips feed only upon the flowers, causing the buds to turn brown. Blooms are distorted and buds frequently fail to open. The thrips may often be observed inside the petals, usually near the base. They have a preference for light colors.

Life history: The thrips breed in grasses and weeds and migrate to the garden. The entire life cycle covers only two weeks, and generations build up very rapidly.

Control: Sprays containing malathion or Cygon are effective provided they are applied frequently. Infested buds and open flowers should be picked off and discarded.

Rudbeckia laciniata cv. 'Hortensia' (golden-glow)

Diseases — Mildew
Caused by the fungus *Erysiphe cichoracearum.*

Symptoms: Foliage becomes covered with a white, powdery growth. In most advanced stages the affected areas turn black.

Control: Spray with Karathane or Benlate as soon as the mildew appears. Repeat a few times at two-week intervals.

Root Rot
Symptoms: Plants show signs of wilting, the tips of the branches dry up, the foliage turns a pale yellowish green, and the roots become rotted.

Control: See page 617.

Insect Pests — Aphids
Identification: Soft-bodied, louselike insects, usually found clustered along the tips of the growing shoots. The species that attacks golden-glow is a dark reddish-brown in color.

Injury: Aphids suck the juices of the plant,

causing general lack of vigor and stunted growth.

Life history: See page 610.

Control: See page 610.

Stalk Borer (Common)
Identification: Slender caterpillars about 1 in. to 2 in. in length. The young caterpillars are brown with white stripes. When full grown they lose their stripes and become a solid dirty gray in color.

Injury: The stalk borer makes a small, round hole in the stem and tunnels up through the stalk, causing the injured shoot suddenly to wilt and die.

Life history: See page 615.

Control: See page 616.

Salvia farinacea (mealycup sage)

Insect Pests — Aphids
Identification: Soft-bodied, louselike insects, usually found clustered near the tips of the young, growing shoots and along the flower stems. The species that attacks mealycup sage is black.

Injury: Aphids suck the juices from the plant, causing a general lack of vigor and stunted growth. The leaves at the tips of the growing shoots become curled and distorted and the flower heads are stunted and malformed.

Life history: See page 610.

Control: See page 610.

Tagetes (marigold)

Diseases — Wilt

The wilt of marigolds is caused by the same bacterium that causes wilt in tomatoes and various other vegetables.

Symptoms: The lower leaves turn yellow in the early stages, and this condition gradually spreads over the entire plant. The sap tubes become brown, and the plants eventually wilt and die.

Control: At present no remedy is known. Diseased plants should be pulled up and destroyed.

Yellows

Symptoms: Leaves turn yellow. Plants become stunted and fail to produce normal bloom. The plants are seldom killed outright, usually lingering on until frost.

Control: See page 614.

Insect Pest — Tarnished Plant Bug

Identification: A small, very active bug about ¼ in. long. The body is oval in shape, being somewhat triangular in front. Coppery-brown in color with dark brown and yellow flecks on the back.

Injury: The bugs puncture the shoots just below the flower buds, causing the buds to droop and die. The injury completely destroys any chance of bloom. It is thought that while feeding, the tarnished plant bug injects some substance into the plant that is highly injurious and has the effect of a poison.

Life history: See page 616.

Control: See page 616.

Tropaeolum (nasturtium)

Disease — Wilt

The wilt of nasturtiums is caused by *Pseudomonas solanacearum*, the same bacterium that causes wilt of potatoes.

Symptoms: The lower leaves turn yellow in the early stages and this condition gradually spreads over the entire plant. The sap tubes become brown and the plants eventually wilt and die.

Control: Avoid planting nasturtiums near potatoes, tomatoes, eggplants and other plants subject to the same disease. Do not plant nasturtiums in soil that harbors the bacteria unless it has been steam-pasteurized.

Insect Pests — Aphids

Identification: Black, soft-bodied, louselike insects usually found clustered on the tips of the young, growing shoots.

Injury: Aphids suck the juices from the plant, causing the leaves and stems to become curled and distorted.

Life history: See page 610.

Control: See page 610.

Cabbage Looper

Identification: Greenish caterpillars with a white line along each side of the body and two lines near the middle of the back. The middle half of the body is without legs, and when either resting or moving, the caterpillar is in a very characteristic humped position.

Injury: The caterpillars feed upon the leaves.

Life history: See page 648.

Control: See page 613.

Cabbage Worm
Identification: Small, velvety-green caterpillars somewhat more than 1 in. long when full grown.

Injury: The caterpillars feed upon the foliage.

Life history: See page 613.

Control: See page 613.

Tulipa (Tulip)

Diseases — Blossom Blight
   A fungus disease caused by *Phytophthora cactorum* that seems to be particularly prevalent when tulips are planted in wet locations.

Symptoms: The flower stalks turn white and gradually shrivel just below the flower buds. Buds droop over and fail to develop.

Control: Pick off and discard all diseased flower stems. Very little is as yet known about blossom blight and no satisfactory measure of control has been found.

Botrytis Blight (also known as Fire Disease)
   A fungus disease caused by *Botrytis tulipae* that is currently occasioning severe losses in many areas of the country. Every effort should by made to keep it under control.

Symptoms: The leaves, stems and flowers become covered with unsightly spots. In the early stages the spots appear as small, yellowish areas with a dark, water-soaked margin. As the lesions enlarge, they become covered with a moldy growth and appear a light gray in color. The bulbs are also frequently affected, with deep, yellowish-brown lesions found in the fleshy scales. Black sclerotia or resting bodies develop on the dead stalks and are also found within the outer scales of the bulbs. When plants are severely affected, the stalks rot and break over; the leaves become twisted and distorted and the flower buds are blighted.

Control: A careful inspection of the bulbs should be made before they are planted, and all that show infection should be discarded. The outer husks should be removed to disclose any diseased spots on the scales beneath. As soon as the disease appears in a tulip bed, individual plants should be removed in such a way as to avoid scattering the spores or leaving parts of infected bulb scales in the soil. Destroy all blossoms and leaves that show infection.
   Good protection of outdoor plants can be achieved by frequent applications of Botran. During a rainy spring season the applications must be thorough and frequent, as often as every three days. The applications should be discontinued as soon as the blooms begin to open, so that the flower petals will not be spotted with spray residue.

Gray Bulb Rot
   A fungus disease caused by *Pellicularia (Rhizoctonia) tuliparum.*

Symptoms: Dry rot begins at the tip of the bulb. The flesh of the bulb becomes a reddish-gray in color and the diseased portions are often covered with dark brown sclerotia or resting bodies. The bulbs finally rot away entirely.

Control: Remove and destroy all infected plants. Select clean bulbs and plant in soil that has been treated with Benlate.

Insects — Bulb Mite (*Rhizoglyphus echinopus*)
Identification: Minute, whitish mites, beadlike in form, are found in large numbers within the bulb scales. Small, reddish-brown spots appear at the point of injury.

Injury: The mites suck the juices from the plant tissues and the bulbs become soft and mushy. The vitality of the bulb is weakened and as a result growth is stunted. The leaves turn a sickly yellow and the flower buds either fail to develop or produce distorted blooms.

Life history: See page 634.

Control: See page 634.

Verbena

Insect Pests — Leaf Roller (*Choristoneura rosaceana*)
Identification: Small caterpillar about 1/2 in. in length when full grown. They vary from yellow to light green and are distinguished by an oblique band running across the body.

Injury: The caterpillars feed upon the foliage and the flowers, their work being very characteristic as they roll the leaves together and web them with fine silken threads.

Life history: The female moths deposit their eggs in tiny masses on the foliage and within a few weeks the caterpillars hatch out and begin feeding. They become full grown in about a month and pupate within the rolled leaves. Several weeks later the moths emerge and the life cycle begins again. Two broods are usually produced during the season.

Control: See page 615.

Red Spider Mites
Identification: Tiny mites, some red, others greenish, yellow or black.

Injury: Red spiders usually feed on the undersurface of the leaves, puncturing the outer tissues and sucking the juices of the plant. The foliage has an unhealthy, whitish and curiously glazed appearance. Fine silken threads are sometimes found, spun across the undersurface of the leaves.

Life history: See page 629.

Control: See page 629.

Yellow Wooly-bear Caterpillar
Identification: A caterpillar about 2 in. long when full grown. The body is completely covered with long hairs that vary from pale yellow to reddish-brown.

Injury: The caterpillars feed upon the foliage.

Life history: See page 623.

Control: See page 623.

Viola (pansy)

Diseases — Anthracnose
A fungus disease caused by *Colletotrichum violae-tricoloris*. The spores of the fungus are carried on the seed and infection may usually be traced to this source.

Symptoms: Small brown spots with a narrow, dark border appear on the foliage and the petals. The flowers are usually malformed and fail to produce seed. If the disease is not checked, the plants eventually die.

Control: Spray twice at five-day intervals with Maneb, Zineb or Fore as soon as the first browning occurs.

Leaf Spot
A fungus disease caused by *Cercospora violae*.

Symptoms: Dead-looking spots appear on the leaves. In the very early stages the spots are

small with dark margins, but they rapidly become larger until the whole leaf is involved. The petals of the flowers also become blotched and spotted; flower buds fail to open or produce distorted bloom.

Control: Occasional applications of Maneb or Zineb sprays will provide control.

Rust
A fungus disease caused by *Puccinia violae.*

Symptoms: Rust is small, reddish-brown pustules found upon the leaves and stems.

Control: Pull up and discard all infected plants. Spray others with Maneb or Zineb.

Yellows
Symptoms: Plants become dwarfed and stunted. Foliage turns a greenish-yellow.

Control: See under *Aquilegia,* page 614.

Insect Pests—Aphids
Identification: Pale green, soft-bodied, louselike insects usually found clustered along the tips of the young growing shoots.

Injury: Aphids suck the juices from the plant, causing it to have a sickly, unhealthy appearance.

Life history: See page 610.

Control: See page 610.

Violet Sawfly
Identification: Small, sluglike larvae, bluishblack with conspicuous white spots on the back and sides. When full grown they are about ½ in. long.

Injury: The larvae are usually found close to the ground, feeding upon the lower leaves, but if the infestation is severe the entire plant may be eaten.

Life history: Eggs are laid on lower surface of the leaves; pupation takes place in stalks of pithy plants and adults emerge in about two weeks.

Control: Spray with Sevin, being careful to limit spray to infected plants.

Zantedeschia (calla lily)

Diseases—Root Rot
Nature of the disease: The disease is caused by the fungus *Phytophthora richardia.* If the roots are examined, they are found to be infected. The feeder roots start rotting at the tips, and the infection sometimes spreads through the root to the corm. The rot in the corm is more or less dry and spongy.

Symptoms: The plants appear normal for a time, then the older outer leaves begin to yellow along the margins, and gradually the whole leaf yellows and droops. Other leaves are affected progressively inward. However, new leaves continue to develop. If flowers are developed, the spathe usually does not open properly and its tip may turn brown.

Control: Clean dormant rhizomes, then dip dip them in hot water at a temperature of 122°F. for one hour. Cool and dry. Dormant rhizomes can also be soaked for one hour in a formaldehyde solution, 4 oz. in 1½ gallons of water.

Soft Rot
Nature of the disease: The disease is caused by the bacterium *Bacillus carotovorus.* The top of the corm at or just below the top of the soil is usually attacked first. The plant may rot off at this point. Sometimes it spreads downward through the corm, producing a soft, mushy rot with a foul odor.

Symptoms: The leaf stalks are often attacked near the base. Water-soaked areas develop, which later become dark and slimy. The leaf blade yellows at the tip and along the margins, and as the infection spreads, becomes entirely yellow, shrivels and dies. If the flower is attacked, it turns yellow and the stalk eventually falls over.

Control: See Calla Root Rot.

Zinnia

Diseases—Leaf Spot
A fungus disease caused by *Cercospora zinniae.*

Symptoms: Large, dark spots appear on the leaves. Usually not troublesome except in very wet weather.

Control: Spray with Bordeaux mixture or any other copper fungicide.

Mildew
A fungus disease caused by *Erysiphe cichoracearum.*

Symptoms: Foliage becomes covered with a white, powdery growth. In the most advanced stages the affected areas turn black.

Control: Spray with Benlate or Karathane as soon as the mildew appears.

Sclerotium Disease of Zinnia
Nature of the disease: The disease is caused by the fungus *Sclerotinia sclerotiorum,* which attacks the plant at ground level. The vegetative growth of the fungus completely fills the vessels of the plant and deprives the leaves of water.

Symptoms: The disease attacks the plant at ground level and works upward. The stems become blackened and the leaves turn yellow and wilt. The stem finally collapses. The reproductive bodies resemble small bumps on the surface of the stem. Sometimes they become quite large.

Control: In flower beds where the disease has occurred, replace the top 4 in. of soil with clean soil.

Insect Pests—Black Blister Beetle
Identification: A slender, jet-black beetle about $\frac{1}{2}$ in. long with prominent head and neck. The best identification is the yellow, oily, blistering fluid exuded when handled.

Injury: The beetles feed upon the flowers.

Life history: See page 614.

Control: See page 614.

Japanese Beetles (*Popillia japonica*)
Identification: Large, handsome beetles of a metallic greenish-bronze color. There are two conspicuous and several small white spots near the tip of the abdomen. During the middle of the day they are very active, making rapid flight when disturbed. In the evening they are more sluggish.

Injury: The beetles feed upon both the foliage and the flowers, completely demolishing a plant in a very short time.

Life history: See page 652.

Control: See page 652.

Leaf Roller (Red-banded)
Identification: Small caterpillars varying in color from yellow to light green, readily distinguished by the red band on the body.

Injury: The caterpillars feed upon the foliage, their work being very characteristic as they roll and tie the leaves together with fine silken threads.

Life history: See page 615.

Control: See page 615.

Stalk Borer (Common)

Identification: Slender caterpillars about 1 in. to 2 in. long when full grown. The young caterpillars are brown with white stripes. When full grown they lose their stripes and become a solid dirty gray.

Injury: The stalk borer makes a small, round hole in the stem and tunnels up through the stalk, causing the injured shoot suddenly to wilt and break over.

Life history: See page 615.

Control: See page 616.

Tarnished Plant Bug

Identification: A small, very active bug about ¼ in. long. The body is oval, being somewhat triangular in front; coppery-brown in color, with dark brown and yellow flecks on the back.

Injury: The bugs puncture the shoots just below the flower heads, causing the buds to droop and die. The injury completely destroys any chance of bloom. It is thought that while feeding, the tarnished plant bug injects some substance into the sap that is highly injurious to the plant and has the effects of a poison.

Life history: See page 616.

Control: See page 616.

MISCELLANEOUS INSECT PESTS, RODENTS AND ANIMALS

Mice

Meadow Mouse

Identification: Small, dark brown mouse with coarse fur. The ears are almost entirely concealed and the tail is much shorter than that of the common house mouse. The meadow mice make little runs readily visible just under the surface of the soil.

Injury: The meadow mouse does most of its feeding at the surface of the ground, nibbling at the roots and crowns of many herbaceous plants and gnawing the bark of trees, shrubs and vines at or just above the ground level, in many cases completely girdling them and causing their death.

Pine Mouse

Identification: The pine mouse is smaller than the meadow mouse. It is reddish-brown and has an exceedingly short tail, which is about the same length as the hind foot. The burrows of the pine mouse are well below the ground level, with occasional small openings upon the surface.

Injury: The pine mouse does all of its feeding below the surface of the ground. It has a particular fondness for tulip and lily bulbs, and it feeds also upon the roots of herbaceous plants, trees and vines. In areas that are severely infested with pine mice, the destruction is often alarming. Literally thousands of bulbs may be destroyed in a single season by them and fruit trees forty or fifty years of age have been known to be killed outright by the work of these little creatures. One of the greatest tragedies is that one is seldom aware of their presence until considerable damage has been done.

Control: Mice can be controlled by using ready-prepared mouse bait, available in hardware and garden supply stores. Warfarin and Fumarin are anticoagulants also used to control rats and mice. They cause death by producing internal hemorrhages.

Moles

In parts of the country where moles are prevalent, they are classed among the most troublesome of our garden pests. The natural food of moles consists of beetle grubs, cutworms and various other insects found in the soil. Moles do not normally feed upon the roots of plants or upon bulbs. Their annoyance to the gardener is caused by the upheaval of the soil when they are tunneling close to the surface. Not only are these tunnels unsightly but they are often most damaging to lawn areas and to garden plants because they break the contact between the upper inch or so of soil with the soil beneath, thus depriving the grasses or plants of water and food. Unless the damage is quickly repaired, the plants suffer seriously and eventually die. Where mole infestations are heavy the damage may be very great, as a lawn or a garden bed may become a network of underground tunnels.

Moles live in colonies and they maintain certain tunnels as regular routes used by all members of the colony. From these main runways side tunnels diverge that are made by individual moles in their search for food. These minor tunnels are used only once and are usually fairly short and end abruptly. When attempting to eradicate moles, it is necessary to determine which tunnels are the main runways. This may be done by pressing down all the tunnels evident in a given area. The main tunnel will soon be heaved up again, whereas the side tunnels will not. Traps should always be set and poisons placed in the main runs only.

Mole runs are often used by mice, rats, shrews and pocket gophers. These are usually old runs abandoned by the moles in search of new feeding grounds. They may be distinguished by the presence of openings through which the other creatures using them enter and emerge.

Control: One of the most effective measures of control is to reduce to a minimum the grub population in lawns and garden beds. Limited areas can be kept free of moles by burying an 18-in.-high strip of ½-in. hardware cloth in an upright position.

Traps: There are several types of strong, steel mole traps on the market and some of them are very satisfactory if properly handled. It is wise to handle the traps with rubber gloves, and the results will be better if several traps are set at the same time. One trap should be set at the point where the main tunnel divides, and one or two other traps should also be set along the branch tunnels. The soil should be pressed down very firmly at the spots where each trap is set.

Rabbits

During the winter rabbits often seriously damage trees and shrubs by gnawing the bark just above the ground level. If the plant is completely girdled, it will die; many valuable specimens have been lost as a result of damage done by rabbits. Young trees are more susceptible to damage than older trees.

Protecting trees and shrubs: A 3-ft.-tall cylinder of fine-meshed chicken wire, or "hardware cloth" with a ¼-in. mesh or ordinary screen wire may be used to protect the trunks of trees and to encircle shrubs, but this method involves considerable labor and expense if done on a large scale. Susceptible, dormant deciduous trees and shrubs can also be protected by painting or spraying the trunks up to a height the rabbits can no longer reach. The following are some of the more effective deterrents: Arasan 42-S, made by the DuPont Company; M-S Ringwood Repellent, made by Medical Service Corporation, Chicago, Illinois; and REPEL, made by Leffingwell Company, Brea, California.

Ants

Injury: Although ants seldom cause any direct injury to plants, they can be a source of great annoyance in the flower garden. They are often found on peony buds, where they feed on the sweet secretions exuded by the opening flowers, and they are very frequently found on plants that are infested with plant lice, as they are fond of the honey dew given off by the aphids. In some parts of the South ants are very troublesome, as they carry off newly sown seed before it has had time to germinate.

Control: The most effective means of control is to destroy ants in their nest. Sprays or baits containing Diazinon or Baygon are best.

Nematodes

Description: Nematodes are microscopic, threadlike creatures that have become one of our most devastating plant pests in many areas. Some nematodes are harmless and live only on dead organic matter, but many species feed on living plants, causing varying degrees of damage. Nematodes are equipped with a minute, spearlike feeding mechanism, which enables them to pierce the plant cells and suck out the juices.

Injury: The root-knot nematodes puncture the roots of the host plant just behind the root tip, where they drain the plant's food supply. Small, characteristic root knots are found in the area surrounding the female nematode.

Some species damage the stems, leaves and flowers, and it is often difficult to trace such injury to nematodes. The plants become yellow and stunted and wilt badly on hot days. Among the plants thus attacked by nematodes of this type are camellias, lilies, sweet peas and boxwood.

The stem nematodes attack narcissus, iris, crocus and freesias. They live in the bulb scales, flower stalks and leaves of bulbous plants, causing short, stubby flower stalks, deformed flowers, and twisted, thick, crescent-shaped, yellowish leaves. Small, scaly, raised lumps on the leaves and flower stalks indicate the presence of nematodes.

The chrysanthemum nematode is one of the more common types. It lives within the leaves and buds of the chrysanthemum and other closely related plants, causing triangular-shaped, dark brown spots. Eventually the entire leaf becomes brown and limp, and if the infestation is severe the plant may become completely defoliated.

How nematodes are spread: Nematodes can move only very short distances under their own power and are usually introduced into a garden when infected plants are unknowingly brought in. Once they have gained entrance to a garden, they are spread by cultivators, on the hands and shoes of those working in the garden, by animals, by the splashing of raindrops or water from a hose and in countless other ways.

Every possible precaution should be taken to prevent the introduction of nematode-infested plants. New plants obtained either through gift or purchase should be carefully inspected for any evidence of infestation.

Control: Where nematodes are known to exist, control measures consist of strict sanitation and soil sterilization. In greenhouses, and where small plants are grown, all pots, flats, benches and tools should either be scrubbed with or dipped in a formalin solution (1 part commercial formalin to 50 parts of water). Such equipment should not be used until all of the formaldehyde odor has disappeared. All soil used for potting or in benches, and all sand used in propagating beds, should be sterilized.

When areas of garden soil have become infested with nematodes, all plants must be removed preparatory to thorough soil fumigation. The materials that are recommended are D-D, ethylene dibromide, vapam and chloropicrin. When any of these fumigants are injected into warm, moist soil, they vaporize and kill all nematodes with which they come in contact. If soil is to be fumigated, all debris must be raked off and the soil should then be turned with a spade or spading fork. It should be raked again and watered lightly.

There are several methods of application. Holes 8 in. to 10 in. deep may be made 10 in. apart in a square pattern over the area to be treated. The amount of fumigant to be used should comply with the directions on the container, the usual quantity being approximately 2 qt. per 1,000 sq. ft. or 15 gallons per acre. Injectors are available that can be hand-operated and greatly facilitate the work. These are regulated to release the desired amount in each hole. Capsules containing the fumigant are also available, which can be inserted into the soil by hand. Whatever the method used, the hole should be closed and tramped down, then watered to seal in the gas.

The treated area can be planted in about three weeks, provided all odor of the fumigant has gone. It is wise, however, to turn the soil before planting.

The most favorable time to apply the fumigant is in the spring after the soil is warm. The soil temperature should preferably be between 55° and 60°F. Treatment can, however, be done at any time during the summer or early autumn.

Certain flowering plants require specific treatment.

For bulbs such as *Narcissus*, see page 642.

For chrysanthemums, see page 621.

For boxwood, see page 595.

Deer

One of the most effective controls for deer is bone tar oil, which is an odor-producing chemical. It is available under the trade name of Magic Circle Deer Repellent, manufactured by the J. C. Ehrlich Chemical Company, Reading, Pennsylvania. This chemical should be mixed with water as directed. It is either sprayed on the ground in a circle about the plants or sprayed directly onto the plants that are to be protected. It should not be used on young seedlings.

The first application should, if possible, be made before the deer develop the habit of feeding on an area, and subsequent applications should be made at monthly intervals. If deer have already formed a feeding habit, a solution stronger than normal should be used. Evergreens, fruit trees, shrubs, flowers and vegetables may all be effectively protected.

Another effective deer repellent is REPEL, mentioned earlier under rabbit control.

Recently, the Cary Arboretum has tested the use of human hair as a deer-repellent. Tennis-ball-sized parcels of hair tightly packed in plastic-mesh bags, which are suspended 3 to 5 feet apart in the branches of susceptible shrubs and small trees, have conferred protection for at least one winter.

Woodchucks

Woodchucks may be controlled by the use of poisonous gas, by trapping and by repellents such as Magic Circle Deer Repellent (see above).

In some states "bombs" are available through the Fish and Wild Life Service or through the local game warden. These may be placed in the mouth of the den, but the instructions should be followed with great care. There are usually two openings to a woodchuck den and it is necessary to locate both in order to plug up the exit with soil before the bomb or poisonous gas is used. Carbon monoxide gas may be piped through a hose from the exhaust pipe of a car into the mouth of a den, closed except for the small opening made for the hose. This must be done carefully; there must be no leakage. Control measures of this type should preferably be taken in early spring before the adult woodchucks become active and the young leave the den.

There are also a number of very effective traps on the market and special woodchuck lures may be obtained as bait. These may be used at any time during the growing season.

33

Coldframes and Hotbeds

COLDFRAMES

A coldframe is an indispensable adjunct, even to the smallest garden. It is, as the name implies, an unheated glass-covered structure, in which the plants receive heat from the penetration of the sun's rays through the sash.

There seems to be a very common belief that coldframes are useful only for the protection of plants during the winter months and that at other seasons of the year they lie idle. Winter protection, however, is but one of the many uses to which coldframes may be put. Indeed, a really enterprising gardener will find that the frames are in use during every month of the year—that there is never a time from one season's end to another when they lie fallow.

Uses of Coldframes in Early Spring

Hardening-off Plants

During the early spring months, coldframes may be used to harden off seedlings that have been started in the greenhouse or in the house. This hardening-off process is a factor of considerable importance, as young seedlings often suffer a serious setback if moved directly from indoors to the garden. The coldframe provides an ideal transition, as the plants may be protected from sudden drops in temperature and will have an opportunity to become gradually hardened-off. When pots or flats are moved to the frames, they should be placed on a bed of gravel in order that drainage may be facilitated. There is also less danger of trouble from slugs and pill bugs if cinders are used.

Uses of Coldframes in Spring and Summer

Seed Sowing

A coldframe also offers very satisfactory facilities for the starting of young seedling plants throughout the spring and summer months. (See directions for seed sowing, Chapter 34. The hardy and half-hardy annuals may be sown in the frames early in the spring, many weeks before seed could be sown in the open ground; perennials also may be sown in the spring, and the young transplanted seedlings may be carried on in the frames until they are ready to be moved to the nursery rows or to their permanent place in the garden; biennials may be sown during the summer months, and as many of them, such as the foxgloves, Canterbury-bells and wallflowers, need winter protection in cold climates, they may be carried on in the frames until spring.

Propagation by Cuttings

During the late spring and summer months a coldframe may be converted into a propagating case, the soil being temporarily replaced with sand or peat moss or some other medium satisfactory for the rooting of cuttings. (See plant propagation, Chapter 34.)

667

Uses of Coldframes in Autumn

Seed Sowing

Most perennials and some annuals may be sown very successfully in the autumn, and there are many benefits to be gained if such a practice is followed. The object is not to secure germination during the autumn, but to have the seeds remain dormant during the winter months. They will then germinate very early in the spring and the young seedlings will have a vigor and lustiness which usually surpasses that of spring-sown seedlings. Better germination is also frequently secured. A coldframe offers ideal conditions for autumn sowing. The seeds may be sown either in a well-prepared seed bed or in flats. It is essential that good drainage be provided, and if flats are used they should be placed on a layer of gravel. The seeds should not be sown until just before the onset of winter, when the ground begins to freeze. There will then be no danger of having the seed germinate before spring. At the time of sowing the soil should be watered so that it is moderately damp, but not excessively wet. If the soil becomes dry during the winter a light watering should be given, preferably during a spell of warm weather. It is a wise practice to inspect the frame every few weeks to check up on the condition of the soil. After the seeds have been sown, the sash should be placed over the frames, being raised slightly to provide adequate ventilation. In order to exclude the winter sunshine and to maintain a more even soil temperature, it is well to place a lath sash over the glass. This slat shade should be removed very early in the spring so that the soil may warm up as rapidly as possible. As soon as the soil in the frame has begun to thaw, the seeds should be given the usual care. The soil should not be allowed to dry out, adequate ventilation should be provided, and the sash should be removed on warm, sunny days.

Uses of Coldframes in Winter

Protection of Less Hardy Plants and Tender Bulbs

Not only are coldframes useful during the winter months for the protection of the less hardy plants and newly started perennials but they also make it possible to grow some of the tender bulbs, which cannot be grown in the open ground in areas where the winters are of extreme severity. In this group we find the lovely bulbous iris, the dwarf gladioli of the nanus and colvillei types, which are so decorative as cut flowers, and the St. Brigid anemones. If planted in the autumn in frames, these bulbs will give abundant bloom in the spring.

Storage of Bulbs and Plants for Forcing

Coldframes may also be used for the storage of bulbs and plants that are later to be forced indoors. Such plants as bleeding-heart, *Astilbe japonica* and *Mertensia* may be handled very successfully in this way. Chrysanthemum plants that are of the less hardy type may be lifted in the autumn and carried over the winter in the frames, and cuttings may be made from these stock plants in the spring.

Location

Coldframes should preferably be located on ground that is very gently sloping in order that good drainage may be assured, a south or southeastern exposure being considered ideal. The frames should be placed with the high end toward the north, the sash sloping toward the south so that full benefit may be obtained from the rays of the sun. Whenever possible a sheltered spot should be chosen with a wall or hedge on the north to afford protection against winter winds. If a sheltered spot is not available, however, a temporary winter windbreak may be constructed of corn stalks, or boughs braced against a snow fence. If a gravel walk is laid immediately in front of the frames, it will greatly facilitate easy access in wet weather and will prove a significant convenience. Sufficient space should be left at the rear of the frames for the comfortable removal of the sash. The frames should be easily accessible and water should be piped to them.

It is occasionally possible to make use of a steep bank in constructing coldframes, so that much of the backbreaking work usually associated with managing coldframes may be eliminated. A concrete or cinderblock wall should be built up along the upper side of the path to a level of approximately 3 ft. The frames may be placed on the top of the bank if the height of the bank corresponds with the desired height of the frames, or a section of the bank may be dug back to provide a level area for the frames. Thus, the frame is raised to a position where it can be reached as easily as a greenhouse bench. Small-sized sashes should be used, since they can be reached only from the front.

Construction

Of the many materials that are available, wood and concrete block are the most satisfactory for the construction of coldframes. Stone, brick and solid concrete also may be used, but while they are extremely durable materials, the additional expense is hardly justifiable. Sometimes in old colonial gardens one will come upon ancient frames of brick built a century or more ago and still providing shelter for young seedlings.

Wood is the least expensive material and if a good grade of cypress or cedar is selected, wooden frames will last for many years. Though difficult to obtain, cypress will resist decay better than almost any other wood and it is, therefore, particularly well adapted for locations where it will be exposed to dampness and to the weather. It is folly to construct frames of cheap lumber that does not possess the ability to resist decay, as the boards will have to be replaced after a few years. Wooden frames are very easily constructed, and as they do not require highly skilled workmanship, they may readily be made at home. It is also possible to purchase frames from some of the large seed firms and greenhouse construction companies. These are shipped "knocked down" and are easily assembled. Such commercial frames are very satisfactory, and they may readily be moved from one section of the garden to another if a change in the general arrangement of the working area should be desired, or if one is moving to a new property. These ready-made frames may be obtained both in the standard size and in a small size that is admirably adapted for use in suburban gardens.

Frames constructed of concrete blocks are more permanent than wooden frames, but they cannot be moved from one location to another.

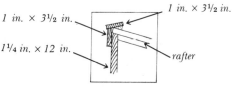

Fig. 33.1
Coldframe construction

1 in. × 3½ in.

1 in. × 3½ in.

1¼ in. × 12 in.

rafter

Enlarged section of back rail

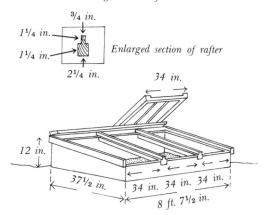

¾ in.

1¼ in.

1¼ in.

2¼ in.

Enlarged section of rafter

34 in.

12 in.

37½ in.

34 in. 34 in. 34 in.

8 ft. 7½ in.

Dimensions are based on standard coldframe sash.

The initial cost may be considerably higher than for wooden frames, but it is the only cost, as no replacement will be necessary. The concrete blocks should extend into the ground a few inches below the frost line for the locality and should be laid with mortar joints. The appearance of the frames will be greatly improved if a cement-sand mortar finish is applied as a surface coat over the concrete blocks.

Regardless of the material used, coldframes should be so constructed that the back is approximately 6 in. higher than the front. This slope will permit the water to drain easily from the sash and will also offer the maximum amount of surface for the penetration of sunlight.

The front of the frame may vary in height from 6 in. to 12 in. If the frames are to be used as a seedbed and to winter small plants such as pansies and English daisies, a height of 6 in. will be sufficient. If large plants such as foxgloves and Canterbury-bells are to be wintered over in the frames, a height of 12 in. will be needed. Cross-ties usually extend from the back of the frame to the front at intervals of every 3 ft. in order to provide additional support for the sash. These ties should be dovetailed into the walls of the frame; a projection in the center of each cross-tie will keep the sash from slipping out of position.

The standard size for coldframe sash used by practically all commercial growers and by most private gardeners is 3 ft. by 6 ft. For the home garden, where operations are on a limited scale and where convenience is a matter of considerable importance, a smaller size is often more satisfactory. Small sash, measuring 2 ft. by 4 ft., or 3 ft. by 3 ft., may be obtained from various firms, and they have many advantages. They are much lighter and therefore easier to handle than the standard-size sash. In addition, the entire area within the frame can be reached from the front with comparative ease, which greatly facilitates such operations as seed sowing and transplanting.

Most coldframe sashes are made of wood and they may be purchased either glazed or unglazed. The process of glazing is a rather simple one and considerable expense may be saved if this is done at home.

Coldframe sash may also be made of fiberglass, which has the advantage of allowing the penetration of ultra-violet rays. Sash made of fiberglass is lighter in weight than glass sash and, because it is unbreakable, is easier to handle. It is, however, less transparent, and does not provide as much protection against extreme cold as does sash made of glass.

When not in use during the summer months, the sashes should be neatly stacked, preferably under cover where they will not be exposed to the weather. It is a matter of sound economy to keep the coldframe sash in good condition. All cracked or broken panes of glass should be replaced and the sashes should be kept well painted. If attention is given to these details, coldframe sash should last for many years.

Management

There are a few general rules that should be followed in the management of coldframes. The most important factors to be considered are ventilation, watering, protection against extreme cold and protection against extreme heat.

Ventilation

During the late winter and early spring the sash should be partially raised for a brief period on clear, sunny days, when the temperature ranges above 45°F., the object being to keep an even temperature. As the season advances, the sash may be raised for a longer period each day, and on warm days it may be removed entirely during the middle of the day. The sash should be lowered or replaced before the temperature begins to drop in the afternoon, in order to conserve as much heat as possible. On windy days the sash should be raised on the opposite side from the direction of the wind, in order to protect the plants from a direct draft. With the approach of warm weather, the sash may be removed entirely. When sashes are to be raised slightly, small blocks of wood may be placed between the edge of the frame and the sash. A block measuring approximately 1 in. by 4 in. by 6 in. is excellent for this purpose, as it enables one to regulate the size of the opening.

Watering

It is an accepted rule among gardeners that plants grown under glass, either in greenhouses or in frames, should be watered when the temperature is rising rather than when it is falling. It is, therefore, advisable, and particularly so early in the season, to water the frames in the morning, in order that the foliage of the plants may be dry at night. In cold, cloudy weather water should be withheld as much as possible to avoid trouble from various fungus diseases.

Protection Against Extreme Cold

During periods of extreme cold additional protection should be given. Straw mats, light frames filled with straw, heavy sisal-craft paper and similar materials may be used for this purpose. In mild climates no protection other than that of the sash is necessary.

Summer Shade

In the summer months some provision must be made for protecting the seedbeds and the young seedling plants in the frames from intense sunshine. Lath sashes are very satisfactory for this purpose. They are light and easy to handle, permit a free circulation of air, and a filtered sunshine reaches the plants. Burlap tacked onto lath frames also makes a very satisfactory shade.

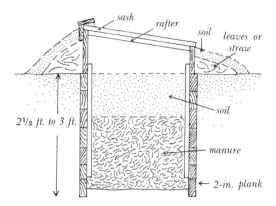

Fig. 33.2
Cross-section of a hotbed

HOTBEDS

Hotbeds differ from coldframes in that they are supplied with some form of artificial heat. They may be heated by the old method of fermenting manure, or by the more modern method of specially devised, shallowly buried electric cables. In occasional instances where hotbeds are located in close proximity to a greenhouse, they may be heated as a part of the greenhouse unit, which is a very satisfactory arrangement. The construction and management of the hotbed will usually be determined by the type of heating to be used.

Uses of Hotbeds

Since the soil in a hotbed is maintained at a warm and fairly constant temperature, it provides excellent facilities for the germination of most seeds and for the growing of a wide variety of young seedling plants. Some plants with a short season of growth, such as lettuce, may be carried through to maturity in the hotbed, although the majority of plants started in the hotbed are later transplanted to the garden or field. Seeds may be sown in the hotbed several weeks before it is advisable to make use of the coldframes, and the young seedlings will make much more rapid growth. Later in the season when there is no longer any need for artificial heat, the hotbed may serve as a coldframe and be used to fulfill the same functions.

Types of Organic Hotbeds

Manure Hotbeds

A pit approximately 2½ ft. deep is necessary if manure is to be used, the dimensions for width and length being determined by the size of the frames and the number of frames de-

sired. If the earth walls of the pit are firm, no inside wall need be constructed. If, however, there is any danger that the earth walls may crumble, it will be necessary to construct supporting walls. Walls made of wood will be of only temporary value as they will lack durability in such a location, but materials such as cement block, stone and brick are excellent. The upper part of the frame is similar in construction to a coldframe.

Manure-heated hotbeds should be started in early March, and it is necessary to use fresh horse manure obtained from stables where straw has been used for bedding. Approximately 4 cu. yd. of manure will be required for a single-sash hotbed. The manure should be piled near the hotbed, and every three or four days the heap should be turned, throwing the outside toward the center. When the entire pile has begun to heat evenly, which is evidenced by steam arising from the pile, the manure may be placed in the pit. It should be spread evenly in 6-in. layers, each layer being firmly tramped and packed. After the manure has been placed in the pit to a depth of 2 ft., a thin layer of straw should be spread over it and the soil should then be added. The depth of soil may vary from 4 in. to 6 in., and it should be of a mixture suitable for a seedbed. A soil thermometer should be placed so that the mercury extends well down into the soil and the sash should remain tightly closed. For the first few days the thermometer will register a high degree of heat, ranging well above 90°F. When the soil temperature has cooled down to 75°F., the bed is ready for use and the seeds may be sown.

In extremely cold climates it is well to bank manure about that portion of the bed which extends above the surface of the ground, as this will increase the warmth within the frame to a very appreciable extent.

Hotbeds Filled with Raked Leaves

Raked leaves can be used in place of fresh horse manure, and the procedure is the same. The leaves should be spread evenly, in successive 6-in. layers, then each layer firmly tramped and packed, and immediately covered with topsoil. The temperature within the frame will not rise as high as with horse manure, but raked leaves are a good substitute where manure is either unobtainable or too expensive.

Hotbeds with Wood Chips

This material, often used as a mulch or in walkways, can be used successfully in any of the above-described deep frames. A generous sprinkling of unslaked lime (quicklime) should be on top of each 6 in.- to 8-in. layer of firmly packed wood chips. This should be repeated until a depth of 27 in. to 30 in. is reached. A thin layer of leaves or pine needles should then be placed on top, to prevent the topsoil from being washed into the chips.

When cleaning out these organic hotbeds each year, the half-rotted medium can be mixed with topsoil and sand for use as an excellent compost in the garden and for potting.

Electric Hotbeds

Various types of electric units have been especially designed to heat hotbeds. One of the most satisfactory is the insulated electric cable, which may be buried in the soil and will provide uniform heat. The procedure for the construction of such a bed is as follows: A pit approximately 12 in. deep should be excavated. It should be of sufficient size to extend 1 ft. or more beyond the sides and ends of the proposed frame. The pit should be filled with 6 in. of slag or gravel. The frame may be placed di-

rectly on this bed. The outside of the frame should be banked with soil to provide insulation against the penetration of cold air. A layer of burlap or of sphagnum moss should be placed over the gravel and 1 in. of sand spread over the surface of the bed. The electric cable is then laid upon the sand in uniform loops in order that the heat may be evenly distributed. Approximately sixty ft. of flexible, lead-covered cable will be required for a two-sash hotbed, if the voltage is 110–120. This will provide for ten coils spaced approximately 7 in. apart, the ends of the cable being connected with a thermostat. The thermostat should be installed on the inside of the frame with the switch box on the north side of the bed. The thermostat should be regulated so that a uniform temperature is maintained. Tender plants will require a temperature ranging from 60° to 75°F.; half-hardy plants will prefer a temperature of 50° to 60° F.; and those that are truly hardy will thrive well in a temperature ranging from 45° to 60°F.

Approximately 400 watts will be required to provide heat for a two-sash hotbed (6 ft. × 6 ft.) in a moderately cold climate. Electricity required will usually average 1 kilowatt hour per square yard of hotbed per day.

The soil that is to be used for the seedbed may be placed over the cable to a depth of 6 in. If flats are to be used, 3 in. of sand may be spread over the cable and the flats may be placed upon the sand.

The one great disadvantage of an electric hotbed is that the current may go off because of a severe storm or some other emergency. In such a case the plants are apt to suffer serious injury, and every effort should be made to protect them, through the use of straw mats, old blankets or other materials that will provide temporary insulation.

Hot Water or Steam Pipes

One of the most satisfactory and also most economical ways to provide heat for the hotbeds is to install a system of pipes that may be connected with the heating system in the dwelling house or greenhouse. The pipes may be placed around the top of the frame on the inside or they may be placed beneath the soil. As a second option, such a system provides for a uniform heat, which may be maintained at a minimum of expense and labor.

Management

The management of a hotbed is similar in most respects to the management of a cold-frame. There is, however, more danger from damping-off, as the plants are somewhat more susceptible to attack because of the greater degree of heat and humidity. Every precautionary measure should be taken to control an outbreak of this disease. (See index for the control of damping-off.)

Since artificial heat is provided, the plants grown in a hotbed are more tender than those grown in a coldframe and more sensitive to sudden fluctuations in temperature. So ventilation and watering must be done with care.

Hotbeds are usually started upon the approach of spring weather. In the latitude of New York and Philadelphia, early March is usually the most favorable time.

34

Propagation

There are few subjects of more vital interest to the avid gardener than propagation. Although the art of propagation dates to the very origin of plant cultivation, more progress has been made by scientists within the past few decades than had occurred over many previous centuries. As a result, though many of the old and established practices may still be followed with good results, recent scientific discoveries have revolutionized some of the techniques of propagation.

Plant propagation falls into two main categories: (1) sexual propagation, or the use of seeds to produce new plants; and (2) asexual or vegetative propagation, which includes producing new plants by one of several means — (a) by cuttings, (b) by division of plant parts, (c) by bulbs or offsets, (d) by layering, (e) by grafting and budding, or (f) by spores. (Although fern spores are produced asexually, they may be sown in much the same manner as seeds.)

The success of a large proportion of the plant propagation methods to be discussed is attributable to the creation of special environments in which temperature, humidity, light and ventilation are controlled. While high initial and operating costs may not deter some people from installing a home greenhouse, it is far more likely that most will be satisfied with more ordinary and less expensive alternatives.

674

PROPAGATING UNITS

Propagating Cases

Flowerpots, small shallow planter boxes, greenhouse flats and aquariums may all be converted into very satisfactory propagating cases for seeds or cuttings.

Seeds

When only a few seeds are sown, a small flowerpot or a plastic shoebox that is narrow enough to fit on a window sill or even an aquarium will give excellent results and can be easily cared for, even in small homes or cramped quarters.

Cuttings

When only a few cuttings are to be rooted, the double flowerpot is one of the most satisfactory devices. A small 3-in. or 4-in. pot is placed within a larger pot, the hole in the bottom of the small pot being tightly closed with a cork. The rim of the small pot should be level with the area of sand in the large pot. The intervening space below and about the sides should be filled with sand or with a sand and peat moss mixture. The small pot should be kept filled with water, and the gradual seepage through the

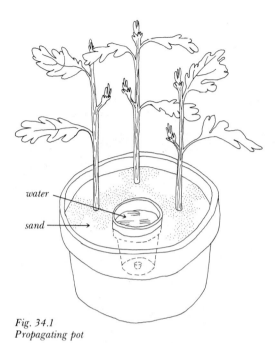

Fig. 34.1
Propagating pot

porous clay of the pot will keep the rooting medium uniformly moist. If a large glass jar, such as a bell jar, is inverted over the pot, it will prevent an excessive evaporation of moisture and will provide very favorable conditions for the rooting of the cuttings.

If many seeds are to be sown or cuttings rooted, and if space permits, a plastic greenhouse flat will accommodate both seeds and cuttings. When cuttings are to be rooted, it is important to conserve moisture and maintain high humidity. A simple system for covering cuttings in a flat entails slipping two wire hangers over either end of the flat and draping a small sheet of plastic across the top or, more simply, slipping the whole unit inside a plastic bag and tying the end of the bag to close it.

Fluorescent Lighting

Fluorescent light gardening offers the individual whose living quarters have low natural light sources an excellent opportunity to participate in home gardening. An inexpensive unit may be constructed, using paired fluorescent lighting tubes designed especially for this purpose. In order to provide a full spectrum of light, one tube should be rated "daylight" and the other "natural." An industrial reflective light fixture can house the tubes, with the plants any distance from 3 in. to 15 in. below the lights, depending upon the stage of growth. Home temperatures are usually adequate for this purpose, and humidity may be easily controlled by setting the pots in trays of moist gravel.

Coldframes and Hotbeds

The standard coldframe is simply a box of varying dimensions with a transparent cover. It usually is 6 ft. wide and its length is a multiple of 3-ft. increments, designed to accommodate standard 6 ft. by 3 ft. hinged sashes that fit snugly across the top of the box. Ideally, the frame faces south and is 9 in. to 12 in. lower in the front so that the sash slopes downward. The bottom or floor of the frame should be prepared in accordance with what is to be grown in it; that is, pot plants can be hardened-off by placing them in a 3-in. bed of gravel, whereas plants or cuttings grown *in situ* require addi-

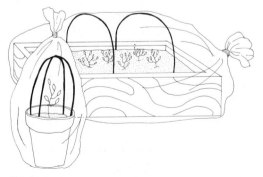

Fig. 34.2
Wire coat hangers are bent to provide framework over which plastic is wrapped and sealed.

tional soil preparation. A lath or green shade cloth placed across the top of the sashes is an excellent method of shading tender cuttings and plants.

Since the coldframe will probably become a permanent structure, it would be wise to use high-grade, durable materials such as concrete block or brick for the foundation and high-grade wood for the frame. Another type of coldframe that can be constructed easily is one with double exterior walls. The space between the walls can be filled with manure in late winter or early spring and subsequent decomposition will generate heat, giving a head start on the growing season. In the fall the wall should be filled with leaves or straw for additional winter protection.

The addition of electrical heating units to a coldframe, while usually not requiring excessive modifications, expands a frame's usefulness immeasurably. Installation of any of these electrical units is best done by a qualified electrician, since there is a risk of receiving an electrical shock when improperly installed.

Home Greenhouses

Glass Greenhouses

Perhaps the most versatile and certainly the most attractive propagating unit is the glass greenhouse. Among the most popular home greenhouses are the relatively inexpensive window sill units and the attached "lean-to" types. Normally, these are both constructed against an east-facing window or door, and since they are both attractive and practical, they soon become an integral part of the home.

Plastic Greenhouses

With the introduction and improvement of plastics, it is possible to construct an inexpensive and very satisfactory home propagating unit. The use of plastic materials for this purpose enables the home gardener to obtain the desired degree of temperature, humidity and adequate ventilation without incurring the high expense involved in building and maintaining the traditional glasshouse. However, there is one major drawback to such greenhouses—since the plastic materials used for them deteriorate and have only a brief life span, they must

be replaced at least every other year, sometimes even annually.

There are so many types of greenhouses to fill such diverse needs that it is important to analyze fully the eventual use for which your greenhouse is intended. Local extension services will yield information about minimum structural requirements for each locality, taking into account snow load, winds and temperatures. Helpful booklets outlining current costs and recent advances in the entire field are also available.

Greenhouses that are primarily devoted to plant propagation may contain a special bench area reserved specifically for starting plants. The propagating bench, which has an enclosed base, is filled with sand and/or perlite and may feature bottom heat and an overhead mist system. Cuttings generally are started directly in the bench medium, while seeds are started in separate trays or pots. The sophistication of the system depends upon the frequency with which it will be used and the types of materials to be propagated.

Work Areas

The greenhouse should contain an area that is reserved for such activities as potting up plants and making cuttings. Ideally, this area should be adjacent to but should not interfere with the propagating unit. It should contain ample room to store the many tools, pots, soil mixes and frequently used chemicals, and it should also provide a bench or space at which to work. Nothing is more frustrating for a conscientious gardener than to begin a project, only to realize halfway through that a major search must be made for a particular item.

PROPAGATING MEDIA AND SOIL MIXTURES

A variety of materials may be used to germinate seeds and to root cuttings. In addition to being sterile, all the media must meet certain other criteria. They must be:

1. Firm and dense enough to hold cuttings or seeds in place during rooting or germination;

2. Of a consistency that will not alter drastically dry or wet, since excessive shrinkage while drying causes root damage; and

3. Porous enough to drain properly yet retain enough moisture so that frequent watering will not be necessary.

Media Components

Perlite
Used to increase aeration in a mixture. It is derived from a type of volcanic rock and is processed into light, porous, sterile particles that hold many times their own weight in water.

Vermiculite
Used to increase the water-holding capacity of a soil medium. It is made from a micalike ore that is composed of thousands of separate layers with a very small amount of water between each layer. When subjected to very intense heat, expansion of the moisture takes place and each layer is separated into many tiny cells.

Sphagnum Moss
Also used to increase the water-holding capacity of a medium. It is derived from the bog plant *Sphagnum* and is usually shredded before incorporation. It may be used either as the entire medium in flats, pots and seedpans, or 1 in. of sphagnum moss may be used on top of a light, sandy, sterile soil. Alternatively, a mixture of sterile sand and peat or sphagnum moss also may be used.

Sand
Used to add body and drainage to a soil medium; also excellent when used alone for rooting cuttings.

Peat Moss
Used in heavy mixtures to lighten and increase porosity; it is derived from partly decomposed aquatic plants.

Germinating Media

The following media combinations are the most frequently and successfully used to germinate seeds or root cuttings. The combination that best suits your purposes will be discovered through experimentation.

1. 1 part sterilized garden loam
   1 part coarse sand or perlite
   1 part moist peat moss

2. 1 part vermiculite
   1 part sphagnum moss

3. Sphagnum moss

4. Sand

Container Sterilization

One of the most satisfactory ways for the home gardener to disinfect seedpans and pots is to place them in a large kettle, such as a canning kettle, and boil them for half an hour.

Soil and Tool Sterilization

Baking
This method is suitable for sterilizing small quantities of soil for use in seedpans. The seedpan, pot or container should be sterile. Fill the container with soil. Cover and place in an oven heated to 180°F.—the temperature should not be allowed to exceed 200°F. Bake for fifteen minutes (no longer). Be advised that this process creates a very unpleasant odor, and while some people are willing to tolerate it, others are not.

Chemicals

Chemicals such as formaldahyde or methyl bromide, which are used in commercial greenhouses, really should not be used by homeowners; they are extremely dangerous.

Prepackaged Sterilized Soils

Sterilized soils can readily be purchased in a wide variety of mixes and quantities, and this is probably the easiest way to be assured of a sterile medium. Separate ingredients may be purchased and combined to create a customized medium. Local nursery staff generally mix their own soils and some are equipped to sell small amounts of this to the home propagator.

SOWING SEEDS INDOORS

First refer to the various germinating media and select the most suitable and convenient mixture.

In Soil Mixture

Bear in mind when sowing seeds indoors that the texture of the soil is of far greater importance than its fertility.

In order to provide a good medium for seed germination, the soil must be loose and mellow.

Fill the pots, seedpans, flats or whatever container will best serve the purpose. Level the mixture and press firmly with a flat block of wood or similar object that serves as a tamper. This should bring the surface of the soil about ⅜ in. below the rim. When pots or seedpans are used, the seeds are usually sown broadcast over the surface of the soil. The seed should be sown as evenly as possible. Heavy seeding should be avoided, as it will result in spindly, weak plants due to overcrowding. When very fine seeds are sown no covering is necessary, as they may be pressed gently into the soil with a float or small tamper. Larger seeds should be covered with a finely sifted layer of the soil mixture or with sand. When flats are used, the seeds may be sown either broadcast or in drills, the rows being spaced from 1½ in. to 2 in. apart. The soil should be firmed lightly after the seeds have been sown.

As soon as sowing has been completed, the flats or seedpans should be watered. The most satisfactory method, particularly in the case of very fine seed, is the subirrigation method. The seedpan or flat should be placed in a pan of water and allowed to remain until the surface of the soil has become dark and moist in appearance. It should then be removed and any surplus water allowed to drain off. This method is far superior to the overhead method. If, however, the overhead method is employed, a very fine spray should be used, such as a fog nozzle. A rubber bulb sprinkler is very satis-

factory for the purpose if only a small number of pots are being handled. At no time should the seed boxes be allowed to dry out, and they should be kept carefully shaded until the seeds have germinated. Shading will greatly facilitate the conservation of moisture and will hasten germination. A pane of glass covered with newspaper or a small burlap frame may be used very satisfactorily. It is essential, however, that some provision be made for the circulation of air, and the covering should be raised very slightly, being laid on small sticks placed across the pot or flat. A covering of light, plastic material is excellent for this purpose, as it not only retains the moisture but also provides for a movement of air.

Germination will be hastened if the pots or flats are placed in a warm, dark place, the ideal temperature ranging from 60° to 70°F. In a greenhouse the seed boxes are sometimes placed along the heat pipes underneath the benches, and in the home a radiator may be used to serve the same purpose. As soon as the seeds have germinated, the covering should be removed and the seedlings should be placed in full light. If the seedpans or flats are placed in a sunny window, they should be turned every two or three days, as the seedlings have a tendency to lean toward the light. Watering should be done both regularly and carefully. The seed boxes must never be allowed to dry out, but an excess of moisture must also be avoided.

In Vermiculite and Sphagnum Moss

When used alone, vermiculite frequently becomes a sticky, poorly aerated, almost greasy medium. However, mixing vermiculite with spagnum moss easily remedies this condition and results in an excellent soil-less, sterile medium for seed germination. A dilute nutrient solution is preferable when watering young seedlings.

In Sphagnum Moss

Shredded or milled sphagnum moss is one of the best of media for the germination of seeds. It is inexpensive, readily obtainable from any horticultural supply house, easy to use, a high percentage of germination is usually secured, there is no danger of overwatering, and, as it is a completely sterile medium, it entirely eliminates all danger of damping-off. Germination takes place in an incredibly short time, the young seedlings make rapid growth, and if mineral nutrient solutions are supplied, many plants may be carried on in the sphagnum well beyond the seedling stage.

Sphagnum moss grows in bogs in certain areas of the country, most of it being obtained from bogs in New Jersey and Wisconsin. As it comes from the bog, it is long and stringy and must be shredded before it is suitable for use as a medium for seed germination. Horticulturally milled sphagnum is available commercially. Shredding may also be done at home by rubbing the long, dry sphagnum through a wire screen such as hardware cloth. Sphagnum moss may be used to start seedlings in flats, in seedpans, in pots, in hotbeds and in coldframes. In flats, pots and seedpans it may be used either as the entire medium, or 1 in. of fine sphagnum moss may be used on top of a light, sandy, sterile soil or a mixture of sterile sand and peat moss.

When sowing seeds on sphagnum moss, the procedure is very simple. The moss should be moistened slightly to increase the ease of handling and the flat or seedpan should be filled until it is level. The surface should then be firmed until the moss is about 1/2 in. below the rim and it should be watered thoroughly. As this firm, smooth surface is favorable to the growth of green algae, it has been found advisable, after the flat or pot has been allowed to drain for a few minutes, to add an additional layer of finely shredded moss about 1/8 in. in depth. This should be given a light sprinkling and the seeds should then be sown either broadcast or in drills. When sowing fine seeds no covering is necessary, but with larger seeds, such as zinnias and marigolds, it is advisable either to poke them down into the sphagnum or to add a light covering of the shredded moss. After the seed has been sown a light sprinkling should be given, a fine, mistlike spray from an atomizer being ideal. The flat or seedpan should then be covered with a pane of glass or with a sheet of translucent glass substitute that has been tacked on a frame. The seed boxes should not be exposed to direct sunlight until after the seeds have germinated. Little watering is necessary, merely enough to keep the sphagnum moist. As soon as germination has taken place, the covering should be removed, and from this time on, considerable care must be taken to see that the sphagnum does not dry out. Fortunately there is no danger of overwatering.

Seedling plants that are to be transplanted while still quite small may be grown very satisfactorily in sphagnum without the use of nutrient solutions. If, however, the seedlings are to be held for any length of time beyond the cotyledon stage, it will be found advisable to apply a well-balanced solution in order to obtain vigorous growth. The solution should be applied at intervals of every few days in a quantity sufficient to saturate the moss. A commercially prepared mixture may be used, or a very satisfactory mixture may be made at home by using either of the following formulas:

1. 2 tsp. of a 12–12–6 fertilizer added to 1 gallon of water
2. 6 tsp. of a 4–12–4 fertilizer added to 1 gallon of water

By withholding the nutrient solution, seedlings growing in sphagnum moss may be held for some time in an arrested state of development without suffering any permanent setback. When transplanted from the flat or seedpan they will continue normal growth. Under certain conditions this offers definite advantages. Where the viability of seeds is affected by even a brief period of storage, they can be germinated immediately on sphagnum and held in a retarded state until normal growth is desired. In other cases a succession of plants ready for transplanting may be obtained from one sowing by holding some of the seedlings in a retarded state.

One of the greatest advantages of growing plants in sphagnum is the ease with which they may be transplanted. If removed carefully, there is usually much less disturbance to the root system than when seedlings are grown in soil. Seedling plants may also be shipped with ease when grown in pots or bands filled with sphagnum, as it is so light in weight. If they are knocked out of the pots for shipment, the sphagnum ball will hold its shape well.

The most important advantage of all, however, in starting seedlings in sphagnum is the fact that absolutely no losses are encountered from damping-off, which frequently takes such a toll when seedlings are started in nonsterile media.

In Sand

Seeds may also be germinated very successfully in pure sand. If the sand is sterile, all danger of damping-off will be eliminated. Sand of a somewhat coarse grade is preferable to very fine sand. If seedlings are to be held for any length of time, a nutrient solution should be applied. Many growers using this method feel that it is advisable to apply a nutrient solution before the seeds are sown. This may be done by placing the pot or seedpan in a pan of the solution and leaving it until the surface has become moist. The solution is commonly used at the rate of 1 cupful of the solution to each quart of sand. The usual procedures in sowing seeds in other media are followed when seeds are being germinated in sand.

GERMINATION FACTORS

Successful sexual propagation is represented by the production of seed. Essentially, a seed is a neat and compact package which contains an embryo that carries a genetic code and is accompanied by a food supply. Should the seed's basic production have been faulty or inadequate, then no matter what technique is implemented germination will never occur and the seed may be considered inviable.

Viable seeds that are unable to germinate because of their own physiological makeup are referred to as dormant, or as being recalcitrant. Seeds capable of germinating immediately if provided the proper environment are considered nondormant, or in a state of quiescence. The distinction between the two is that the first is controlled by internal factors while the latter is controlled by external factors.

For germination to occur, the following conditions must exist: (1) the seed must be viable or capable of germination; (2) internal or physiological controls must signal that it is time for

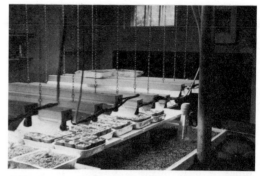

A place to grow spring seedlings was created with available single-unit fixtures, even though two-, three- or four-tube fixtures are recommended. Fixtures are wired in groups of three. Polyethylene over a 5 ft. by 8 ft. table, with 1 in. by 3 in. strips at the edges, provides a waterproof base. Moist vermiculite contributes humidity (34.1).

Height of light fixtures is changed by adjusting chain (34.2).

Bottom heat for germination is provided simply by placing newly sown flats on top of fixtures (34.3).

Aluminum foil cake pans and plastic bags—just right for germinating seeds. Holes are punched in the pan bottoms (34.4).

Seedlings are pricked off as soon as possible and grown close to the lights. Above tomatoes, the lights have to be moved up a link or two nearly every day (34.5). Photos Carlton Lees

germination to occur; and (3) the appropriate external environmental conditions must exist.

There are several forms of dormancy. These include:

1. Dormancy regulated by the external seed coat even though the internal seed is non-dormant.

2. Dormancy caused by an immature seed embryo.

3. Dormancy caused by the internal physiology of the seed.

4. A combination of internal and external dormancies.

Obviously, the home propagator must know how to treat the many different types of seeds in order to produce a wide variety of plants. Many seeds will germinate under widely varying conditions of temperature and light. However, there are some seeds that have special requirements and maximum germination cannot be obtained unless these requirements are met.

Methods of Removing Seed Coat Dormancy

Several methods of removing dormancy caused by an impervious, hard seed coat are available.

Method 1: Soaking

Seeds are soaked in water in order to modify hard seed coats, remove inhibitors, soften seeds and/or reduce germination time. The length of time will vary considerably, some seeds requiring only twenty-four hours, other seeds requiring several weeks. As a general rule, the seeds should be soaked until they begin to swell. After the seeds have been soaked, they should not be allowed to dry out before sowing, and the soil should be moist but not excessively wet at the time that they are sown. If the process is continued for more than a few days, the mass of seed should be stirred and aerated occasionally. Natural growth inhibitors can be removed by soaking the seeds for a short period, rinsing them repeatedly and then blotting them dry. Frequently, seed soaking can reduce the time required for germination. However, if such

SEEDS AFFECTED BY SEED COAT DORMANCY

(All are members of the legume or bean family)

Albizia	*Gymnocladus*
Caragana	*Laburnum*
Cladrastis	*Robinia*
Cytissus	*Sophora*
Genista	*Wisteria*
Gleditsia	

soaking is practiced indiscriminately, it can damage some seeds.

Method 2: Scalding

In the case of some very dry, hard-shelled seeds, such as seeds of the Kentucky coffee tree, scalding water may be used with considerable success. Boiling water is poured over the seeds and allowed to cool gradually. Once again, this process should be used only when absolutely necessary, since exposure to the high temperature of boiling water may destroy the seeds' viability.

Method 3: Mechanical Aids

There are also a number of mechanical aids that may be employed very successfully, such as filing and clipping. In the cases of some extremely large seeds a very minute hole may be bored.

The germination of some seeds is greatly increased if they are scarified prior to sowing. Scarification—a process that scratches the surface of a hard seed coat, making it more permeable to water—is commercially performed by specially designed machines. However, mechanical sophistication is not necessary to scarify seeds; successful results may be had simply by scratching or nicking the surface of the seed coat with a file. Care should be taken not to damage the inner parts of the seed during this process.

Method 4: Acid Scarification

Using sulphuric acid to scarify hard seed coats can yield most successful results but this procedure must be performed with extreme caution. Dry seeds should be covered with sulphuric acid in a proportion of 1 part seed to 2 parts acid. From time to time, stir the seeds gently. Drain off the sulphuric acid as soon as the seed coat has been reduced to paper thinness. Follow this by washing the seeds thoroughly for ten minutes, then either plant the seeds immediately or dry them and place in storage.

Moist-chilling Stratification for Simple Dormancy

Simple dormancy of the embryo (internal seed) may be handled by the procedure known as moist-chilling stratification. This treatment, which is used on many trees and shrubs, exposes seeds for a prescribed period of time to low temperature and prescribed humidity. For seeds with a very hard seed coat, stratification should be preceded by a moist, warm treatment period to break down the seed coat. After soaking the seeds in warm water for twenty-four hours (if necessary), drain off the water and mix the seeds in a moist but not wet medium of 1 part sand and 1 part milled sphagnum moss then wrap the mixture in a plastic bag. The medium to seed ratio should be about 3 to 1. Store the seeds at 40°F. To maintain a consistent temperature, store the seed in your refrigerator and check the package periodically to make sure the medium is still moist. This process is known as "after-ripening" and usually requires about three months' time. At the end of this period, the seed should be planted immediately and germination allowed to proceed at a relatively cool temperature.

Warm Stratification for Double Dormancy

Seeds characterized by double dormancy would normally require two years to germinate. This time span can be significantly reduced by the following procedure: In the fall, clean, dry seed is set in a mixture of equal parts of sand and moist peat moss. This should then be placed in a plastic bag and set in an area with a constant temperature range of 65° to 75°F. After a period of three months the seeds and moist medium are transferred to the refrigerator for an additional three months. At the conclusion of the cool period the seeds should be

SIMPLE DORMANCY WOODY PLANTS REQUIRING MOIST-CHILLING STRATIFICATION

SCIENTIFIC NAME	COMMON NAME	STRATIFICATION TIME REQUIRED (IN MONTHS)
Abies spp.	fir	2 – 3
Acer spp.	maple	3
Berberis spp.	barberry	3
Betula spp.	birch	3
Carya spp.	hickory	4
Cedrus spp.	cedar	2
Chamaecyparis spp.	false cypress	3
Clematis spp.	clematis	3
Cornus spp.	dogwood	3
Fagus spp.	beech	3
Fraxinus spp.	ash	2 – 3
Liquidambar spp.	sweet gum	3
Magnolia spp.	magnolia	3 – 4
Malus spp.	apple, crab apple	3
Nyssa spp.	tupelo	3
Picea spp.	spruce	2 – 3
Pinus spp.	pine	2 – 3
Prunus spp.	cherry, plum, peach	3
Pyrus spp.	pear	3
Sorbus spp.	mountain ash	3
Thuja spp.	arborvitae	2
Tsuga spp.	hemlock	3

WOODY PLANTS REQUIRING NO DORMANCY PERIOD

Some woody plants will germinate as soon as they are sown after ripening. Alternatively, these seeds may be collected when ripe, stored in a cool dry location and sown in the spring. Among the plants included in this group are:

Alnus spp.	alder
Catalpa spp.	catalpa, Indian bean
Cercidiphyllum spp.	Katsura tree
Clethra spp.	sweet pepperbush
Deutzia spp.	deutzia
Enkianthus spp.	enkianthus
Erica spp.	heath and heather
Euodia spp.	euodia
Hydrangea spp.	hydrangea
Kalmia spp.	mountain laurel
Kolkwitzia spp.	beautybush
Leucothoë spp.	leucothoë
Philadelphus spp.	mock-orange
Pieris spp.	andromeda
Potentilla spp.	cinquefoil
Rhododendron spp.	rhododendron, azalea
Spiraea spp.	spirea
Weigela spp.	weigela

sown, as described in the moist-chilling procedure. The initial warm, moist treatment is essential to break down hard seed coats. Although this process may be carried on outdoors, it may prove difficult because weather conditions are so variable, and rodents are inevitably attracted to the seed mixture.

DOUBLE DORMANCY WOODY PLANTS REQUIRING WARM STRATIFICATION

Cotoneaster spp.	cotoneaster
Crataegus spp.	hawthorn
Hamamelis spp.	witch hazel
Halesia spp.	silverbell
Helleborus spp.	hellebore
Ilex spp.	holly
Juniperus spp.	juniper
Paeonia spp.	peony
Stewartia spp.	stewartia
Taxus spp.	yew
Viburnum spp.	viburnum

Dry Storage

Most native and some cultivated annual, biennial and perennial herbaceous plants fail to germinate until after a period of dry cool storage at 45° to 50° F.

Growing Annuals from Seed

Annual flowers and vegetables can be grown very readily from seed. They may be grouped into three general classifications: those that are extremely hardy and may be sown in the open ground early in the spring as soon as the soil is in condition for planting; those that are half-hardy and may be sown in the open ground after all danger of frost is over; and those that are either extremely tender and delicate or make such slow growth that it is advisable to sow them in either the greenhouse or hotbed, where they may be kept under carefully controlled conditions until they are well started and the weather settled.

If early bloom is desired, many of the hardy and half-hardy annuals may also be started under glass. The rapidly growing kinds such as zinnia and marigold should not be sown more than six weeks before time for transplanting to

the garden, as they will become spindly and leggy if held too long indoors. Slow-growing annuals such as lobelia, petunia, snapdragon, salpiglossis and verbena may be sown from eight to ten weeks before the time for transplanting to the open.

Raising Biennials from Seed

Practically all biennial flowers may be grown very easily from seed. The seeds are usually sown in coldframes during the summer months. When the seedlings have reached sufficient size, they are transplanted and are usually carried on in the frames until autumn. Those that are tender are wintered in the frames, while those that are hardy may be transplanted to the open ground. For details regarding time of sowing and method of handling, see Chapter 19 on Biennials.

Raising Perennials from Seed

Many perennials can be raised very successfully from seed. However, this method of propagation is not suitable for all perennials, especially those cultivars and hybrids such as phlox that do not come true from seed. There are others that develop so slowly when grown from seed that it is far more practical to resort to the division of old clumps or to some other means of vegetative reproduction.

Seed Viability

Some seeds retain their vitality for many years, whereas others must be planted as soon as they are ripe if good germination is to take place. The seeds of most of our commonly grown annual and perennial flowers retain their vitality for at least a year and some of them for two years or even longer.

With the majority of garden flowers we can expect a percentage of germination ranging from 75 to 85%, and in some cases an even higher percentage may be obtained if conditions are favorable.

If seed has been carried over from one season to the next, or if there is any reason to

PERENNIALS PROPAGATED BY SEED

Achillea spp.	yarrow	*Eupatorium* spp.	mist flower
Aconitum spp.	monkshood	*Gaillardia* spp.	blanket flower
Althaea spp.	hollyhock	*Geum* spp.	geum
Alyssum spp.	alyssum, madwort	*Gypsophila* spp.	baby's-breath
Amsonia spp.	bluestar	*Helenium* spp.	sneezeweed
Anchusa spp.	bugloss, alkanet	*Helleborus* spp.	Christmas rose
Aquilegia spp.	columbine	*Hesperis* spp.	sweet rocket
Arabis spp.	rock cress	*Heuchera* spp.	coralbells
Arenaria spp.	sandwort	*Iberis* spp.	candytuft
Artemisia spp.	mugwort	*Linum* spp.	flax
Asclepias tuberosa	butterfly weed	*Lobelia* spp.	cardinal flower
Aubrieta spp.	aubrieta, purple rock cress	*Lupinus* spp.	lupine
Baptisia spp.	false indigo	*Macleaya* spp.	plume poppy
Boltonia spp.	boltonia	*Monarda* spp.	horsemint, bee balm
Campanula spp.	bellflower	*Myosotis* spp.	forget-me-not
Centaurea spp.	knapweed	*Oenothera* spp.	evening primrose
Centranthus spp.	valerian	*Penstemon* spp.	beard-tongue
Cerastium tomentosum	snow-in-summer	*Physostegia* spp.	false dragonhead
Chelone spp.	turtlehead	*Platycodon* spp.	balloon flower
Chrysanthemum coccineum	pyrethrum, painted daisy	*Primula* spp.	primrose
Cimicifuga spp.	black cohosh, snake root	*Salvia* spp.	sage
Coreopsis spp.	tickseed, coreopsis	*Scabiosa* spp.	pincushion flower
Delphinium spp.	larkspur	*Sedum* spp.	stonecrop
Dianthus spp. (single types)	sweet William, dianthus	*Thalictrum* spp.	meadow rue
Dicentra spp.	bleeding-heart	*Veronica* spp.	speedwell
Dictamnus spp.	gas plant	*Viola* spp.	violet
Digitalis spp.	foxglove		

doubt its viability, it is wise to run a test for germination before the seed is sown. A number of methods can be used in testing seed, one of the simplest being the blotting paper method. The seeds are placed between two sheets of blotting paper, which are kept constantly moist and at a temperature ranging between 65° and 70°F. If several varieties of seed are to be tested, the paper may be marked off into small squares. The percentage of germination may be determined by dividing the number of seeds that have sprouted by the total number tested.

When seeds are to be held for any length of time, they should be stored in a dry place with a range of temperature varying from 45° to 50°F. Viability depends upon seed variety, but storage conditions are a major determinant in preserving quality seeds successfully.

Meeting Special Requirements

Though most seeds germinate under a wide variety of conditions, some require special treatment and attention to ensure maximum germination. For example, the seeds of certain flowers will not germinate well if the temperatures at the time of sowing are too high; other seeds will not germinate well if the temperatures are too low. For most garden plants, the optimum temperature range within which seeds will give the best germination is known, other conditions being favorable. Seeds with definite temperature requirements for maximum germination will, with a few exceptions, sprout under less favorable temperature conditions, but the percentage of germination will become increasingly lower as the temperature varies from the optimum.

In the case of seeds in the low temperature range (see the following list), every effort should be made to provide conditions that are as nearly ideal as possible in order to secure the best germination. Such seeds should be sown during cool weather whenever possible, or the seed flats should be placed in as suitably cool a location as is available. For seeds in the very low temperature group, the following procedure is recommended for best results: The seeds should be mixed with damp, sterile sand and moist peat moss and placed in the crisper compartment of the home refrigerator. As soon as the seed has germinated, the sand, peat moss and sprouted seed may be sown in drills in a flat, coldframe or seedbed, and from this point on they may be handled in the usual manner.

Seeds in the high temperature range should not be sown outdoors until the soil is thoroughly warm. If started early indoors, the seedpans or flats should, if possible, be placed in a location where a temperature above 68°F. can be maintained.

Pansy seed has rather unique requirements, as it fails to germinate well unless there are wide fluctuations in temperature. When sown where a constant temperature is maintained, with no fluctuations whatsoever, pansy seed will not germinate at all. It will sprout with moderate variations in temperature, but the wider the fluctuations the better the germination. This explains why pansy seed usually germinates best in the early autumn when hot days alternate with cool nights.

Some seeds pass through alternating periods of dormancy. They will germinate well when fresh, then, a few months later, will become completely dormant and will appear to have lost their vitality. Six months later they will again show a high percentage of germination. Primrose seed is in this class. Perennial seed that does not sprout yet remains firm and shows no signs of rotting may be passing through such a period of dormancy and should be left in the seedbed.

It has been found that some seeds will germinate best in the dark, while other seeds will give the highest percentage of germination in the light, other conditions being favorable. There are also some species whose seeds are so indifferent that they will germinate well either in the dark or in the light.

Preventing Damping-off

One of the greatest handicaps in sowing seeds in soil is the prevalence of the fungi that cause the damping-off of young seedlings. Therefore, when seeds are to be sown in cold-

FRESH SEED REQUIRING CHILLING TO GERMINATE

Alyssum spp.	alyssum, madwort
Antirrhinum spp.	snapdragon
Dianthus spp.	pink
Iberis spp.	candytuft
Lathyrus spp.	sweet pea
Lupinus spp.	lupine
Matthiola spp.	stock
Phlox spp.	phlox

OPTIMUM TEMPERATURE RANGE FOR BEST GERMINATION

HIGH 68° to 86°F.)

Ageratum spp.	floss flower, ageratum
Aquilegia spp.	columbine
Cleome spp.	spider plant
Dahlia spp.	dahlia
Ipomoea spp.	morning-glory
Lobelia spp.	lobelia
Nicotiana spp.	flowering tobacco
Salvia spp.	salvia, sage
Tagetes spp.	marigold
Verbena spp.	verbena, vervain
Zinnia spp.	zinnia

LOW (55° to 68°F.)

Alyssum spp.	alyssum, madwort
Antirrhinum spp.	snapdragon
Calendula spp.	calendula, pot marigold
Chrysanthemum spp.	chrysanthemum
Torenia spp.	wishbone flower
Viola spp.	violet

VERY LOW 42° to 55°F.)

Delphinium spp.	larkspur
Lactuca spp.	lettuce

INDIFFERENT

Aster spp.	aster
Phlox spp.	phlox

VARIABLE

Petunia spp.	petunia
Viola tricolor var. *hortensis*	pansy

frames, hotbeds or in soil indoors, every possible precaution should be taken to prevent the growth and spread of these fungi, which attack the young seedlings either before they emerge or at a later stage, causing the stem to rot away at the ground level. The loss of one or two plants may not seem serious, but it is a danger signal that should be carefully heeded, as the fungus spreads rapidly and hundreds of plants may become affected in a very short time. Un-

LIGHT REQUIREMENTS FOR BEST GERMINATION

SCIENTIFIC NAME	COMMON NAME
LIGHT REQUIRED	
Ageratum spp.	floss flower, ageratum
Alyssum spp.	alyssum, madwort
Antirrhinum spp.	snapdragon
Begonia spp.	begonia
Clarkia spp.	clarkia, godetia
Lobelia spp.	lobelia
Nicotiana spp.	flowering tobacco
Petunia spp.	petunia
Viola spp.	violet
DARK REQUIRED	
Impatiens spp.	impatiens, balsam
Dahlia spp.	dahlia
Delphinium spp.	larkspur
Scabiosa spp.	pincushion flower
Verbena spp.	verbena, vervain
Zinnia spp.	zinnia
INDIFFERENT	
Aster spp.	aster
Calendula spp.	pot marigold
Phlox spp.	phlox
Salvia spp.	sage
Tagetes spp.	marigold
Torenia spp.	wishbone flower

fortunately, the very conditions that are most favorable for the germination and growth of young seedlings are also the conditions most favorable for the growth and spread of the fungi that cause the destructive damping-off. These fungi cannot grow in absolutely dry soil, but under conditions of warmth and moisture they develop rapidly. Consequently, the disease is apt to be more serious in damp, cloudy weather than it is in bright, sunny weather; and it is more serious where there is inadequate ventilation than where there is good circulation of air. Weak plants are invariably more susceptible to attack than strong ones, and the overcrowding of young seedlings tends to aggravate the spread of the disease.

In order to ensure complete control of damping-off, the seed, the soil and the containers (if old pots or flats are used) should be sterilized.

Seed Treatment

The treatment of the seed is very simple and will ensure the preemergence control of damp-ing-off. This protection of the seeds has become an accepted practice in many commercial greenhouses, and it should be quite as generally adopted by home gardeners, as it is a very important factor in the successful control of the disease. The most effective means of protecting seeds is to dust them at the time of sowing with a good seed protectant such as Ferbam, benomyl or Captan. These protectants are fungicides that will give good control against seed decay, damping-off and various seedling blights. Some seed firms now offer seeds that have already been treated with a protectant.

Transplanting

When the first or second pair of true leaves has developed, young seedlings should be transplanted in order to prevent overcrowding and to induce better root development. They may either be transplanted into other flats, or transplanted singly into small, 2½-in. pots. If the young seedlings are strong and vigorous and if weather conditions are favorable, they may also be transplanted into the coldframes; and in some exceptional cases, they may even be transplanted directly into the open ground.

A mixture of 1 part sand (or perlite), 1 part loam and 1 part peat moss is a good blend for transplanting. The soil should be neither too wet nor too dry at the time of transplanting. If it is moist enough to form a fairly firm ball when pressed together in one's hand, yet dry enough to crumble when the ball falls to the ground, it is of excellent consistency for transplanting. After the soil has been made level, it should be firmed and marked off into rows from 2 in. to 3 in. apart. The young plants should be spaced from 2 in. to 3 in. apart in the row, depending upon their size and vigor.

In order that the roots may receive as little injury as possible, the seedlings should be very carefully removed from the seedbed. The pointed end of a small label is excellent for this purpose. If the small seedling plants are massed together in a clump, as so often happens when seeds have been sown thickly, the soil should be shaken gently from the roots and the individual plants carefully separated from the group. Only a small number of seedlings should be removed at a time, because no more

PERIOD OF GERMINATION AND LONGEVITY FOR FLOWER SEEDS

SCIENTIFIC NAME	COMMON NAME	PERIOD OF GERMINATION (IN DAYS)	APPROXIMATE LONGEVITY (IN YEARS)
Achillea spp.	yarrow	14	4
Ageratum spp.	floss flower	14	4
Agrostemma spp.	corn cockle	14–21	4
Althaea spp.	hibiscus, marsh mallow	14–21	2–3
Alyssum spp.	alyssum, madwort	21–28	4
Amaranthus spp.	annual poinsettia	14–21	4–5
Ammobium spp.	everlasting	14	1–2
Anagallis spp.	pimpernel	21	4–5
Anchusa spp.	bugloss	14–21	3
Anemone spp.	windflower	28–40	2
Anthemis spp.	chamomile	14	2
Antirrhinum spp.	snapdragon	10–14	3–4
Aquilegia spp.	columbine	30–50	2
Arabis spp.	rock cress	21	2–3
Armeria spp.	thrift	21	2
Aster spp.	aster	14	1–2
Aubrieta spp.	aubrieta	25	2
Bellis sp.	daisy	10–14	2–3
Boltonia spp.	boltonia	20	5
Brachycome spp.	brachycome	10	3–4
Browallia spp.	bush violet	28–40	2–5
Calendula spp.	pot marigold	14	5–6
Campanula spp.	bellflower	14	3
Celosia spp.	woolflower	6–10	4
Centaurea spp.	knapweed	20	1–2
Cheiranthus spp.	wallflower	14	2–3
Chelone spp.	turtlehead	20–30	1–2
Chrysanthemum spp.	chrysanthemum (annual)	11–18	4–5
Clarkia spp.	clarkia, godetia	14	2–3
Cobaea spp.		21	2
Coleus spp.	coleus	14	2
Coreopsis spp.	tickseed	21	2
Cosmos spp.	cosmos	10–14	3–4
Cyclamen spp.	cyclamen	50	4–6
Cynoglossum spp.	hound's tongue	14	2–3
Dahlia spp.	dahlia	10	2–3
Datura spp.	thorn apple	15–21	3–4
Delphinium spp.	larkspur	15–21	1
Dianthus spp.	pink	6–10	4–5
Digitalis spp.	foxglove	15	2
Dimorpotheca spp.	Cape marigold	15–21	1
Erigeron spp.	fleabane	14	2
Eschscholzia spp.	California poppy	10	2
Euphorbia spp.	spurge	21–28	3
Gaillardia spp.	blanket flower	15–20	4
Gerbera spp.	gerbera	14	1
Geum spp.	geum	21	2
Gypsophila spp.	baby's breath	10–14	4
Helianthus spp.	sunflower	10–14	2–3
Helichrysum spp.	everlasting	7	1–2
Heliotropium spp.	heliotrope	21	1–2
Hesperis spp.	rocket	18	3–4
Hibiscus spp.	rose mallow	15–30	3–4
Hunnemannia spp.	Mexican tulip poppy, golden-cup	14	2–3

PERIOD OF GERMINATION AND LONGEVITY FOR FLOWER SEEDS (Continued)

SCIENTIFIC NAME	COMMON NAME	PERIOD OF GERMINATION (IN DAYS)	APPROXIMATE LONGEVITY (IN YEARS)
Iberis spp.	candytuft	14	2–3
Impatiens spp.	impatiens, balsam	15	2
Ipomoea spp.	morning-glory	10	5
Kniphofia spp.	torch flower	21	2
Lathyrus spp.	sweet pea	21	3–4
Lavatera spp.	tree mallow	14–35	4–5
Lilium spp.	lily	21	1
Limonium spp.	sea lavender	14–21	2–3
Linaria spp.	toadflax	15	2–3
Linum spp.	flax	21–30	1–2
Lobelia spp.	lobelia	10–15	3–4
Lunaria spp.	money plant	14–21	1–2
Lupinus spp.	lupine	10	2
Lychnis spp.	catchfly, campion	21–30	2–3
Matricaria spp.	matricary	11–14	2–3
Matthiola spp.	stock	14	5
Mesembryanthemum spp.	ice plant	14	3–4
Myosotis spp.	forget-me-not	14	2
Nemesia spp.	nemesia	18–21	2–3
Nepeta spp.	catmint	17	2–3
Nicotiana spp.	flowering tobacco	10	3–4
Nigella spp.	fennel flower	14	1–2
Oenothera spp.	evening primrose	31	2
Papaver spp.	poppy	12	3–5
Pelargonium spp.	geranium	30–40	1
Penstemon spp.	beard-tongue	17	2
Petunia spp.	petunia	10	2–3
Phlox spp.	phlox	10–15	1–2
Physostegia spp.	false dragonhead	25	2–3
Platycodon spp.	balloon flower	12–15	2–3
Polemonium spp.	Jacob's ladder	20	2
Portulaca spp.	moss rose	14	3
Pyrethrum spp.	painted daisy	21	1
Ranunculus spp.	buttercup	30–40	6–7
Reseda spp.	mignonette	11–14	2–4
Rudbeckia spp.	coneflower	21	2–3
Salpiglossis spp.	salpiglossis	14	6–7
Salvia spp.	sage	14	1
Saponaria spp.	soapwort	10	2
Scabiosa spp.	pincushion flower	14–21	2–3
Schizanthus spp.	butterfly flower	21	4–5
Senecio spp.	groundsel	10	2–3
Stokesia spp.	Stokes' aster	28	2
Tagetes spp.	marigold	7	2–3
Thalictrum spp.	meadow rue	30	1
Thunbergia spp.	black-eyed Susan vine	14	2
Tithonia spp.	Mexican sunflower	25	2
Torenia spp.	wishbone flower	14	1–2
Tropaeolum spp.	nasturtium	10	6–7
Verbena spp.	verbena, vervain	14	1
Vinca spp.	periwinkle	14	1–2
Viola spp.	violet	14	1
Zinnia spp.	zinnia	5–10	6–7

than a few moments should elapse between the time when the young plants are lifted from the seedbed and when the operation of transplanting is completed. If the roots are exposed for any length of time they may dry out, causing the plant to suffer a serious setback. The roots should be kept covered with soil as much as possible during the operation, and under no condition should the young plants be exposed to direct sunlight.

Long, straggly roots should be pinched back in order to induce a vigorous, well-branched, fibrous root system. A hole large enough to receive the roots without crowding them should be made with the pointed end of a label, small stick or pencil point. The roots of the plant should be placed in the hole, and the soil should then be pressed firmly about the roots and stem so that they cannot be easily dislodged. In transplanting delphinium or similar seedlings, care must be taken not to cover the crown with soil as these plants are very subject to rot unless the crown is slightly above the surface of the soil. Transplanting ability may be tested by pulling sharply on the tip of a leaf. If you are left holding a tiny portion of the leaf between the fingertips while the plant itself appears undisturbed, then the transplanting is being done properly.

Most seedlings are easily handled, being picked up by the leaves with the thumb and forefinger. In the case of very tiny seedlings, such as begonias and primroses, it is sometimes more convenient to use a small pair of forceps.

Never move seedlings about by their stems. A small crimp in the delicate stem of a young seedling will usually result in the weakening or destruction of its internal anatomy, preventing the translocation of water and nutrients throughout the plant. When handling a small number of plants, it may be more convenient to use small pots rather than flats for the transplanting of seedlings. Fill the pots with the prepared soil mixture and tamp it down lightly so that the soil surface is about ¾ in. below the rim of the pot. Make a hole in the center of the pot deep and wide enough so that the roots will spread comfortably and the plant will sit at the proper level, then firm the soil. Once again, test the first few plants by pulling on the tip of a leaf to make sure that they are being planted properly.

Do not let the newly transplanted seedlings sit too long without watering them in. Transplanting is at best a severe shock to young seedling plants, as many of the tiny root hairs that supply moisture and nutrients to the plant are inevitably injured or destroyed, and can recover only with prompt watering. Furthermore, to prevent rotting of the seedlings' tender stems it is a good idea to add a very weak solution of Benlate or a similar fungicide to the water at this time. Use a fine spray or fog nozzle when watering, and then shade the new transplants for a few days until they have reestablished themselves. The ideal weather for transplanting is a cloudy or rainy day when moist air is at its peak and direct sunlight is absent.

Seed Sowing in the Open

The seed of many annual flowers may be sown directly in the garden where they are to bloom. Some of the perennials and biennials, as well as many annuals, may be sown in outdoor seedbeds, being transplanted to their permanent position in the garden after they have made some growth in the nursery plots. The disadvantages of sowing seeds in the open ground are that one is unable to control conditions of temperature and moisture, and it is more difficult to provide an ideal seedbed. Heavy rains often cause the soil to become too firmly compacted before the seeds germinate and may also seriously injure the delicate young seedlings. Long hours of hot sunshine may cause the soil to dry out too rapidly and to form a hard crust unless frequent attention is given to watering; but in spite of all these handicaps, seed sowing in the open can be done successfully in the majority of cases if careful attention is given to a few essential details. A well-prepared seedbed will do much to offset the vagaries of nature.

The time of sowing will depend, to a large extent, upon the kind of seed. South of the New York area, a few of the very hardy annuals such as snapdragon, poppy, cornflower, larkspur, balsam, cosmos and calliopsis may be sown in the autumn where they are to flower. The secret of success in autumn sowing lies in the fact that the seeds should not be sown until late in the season. They will then lie dormant in the soil throughout the winter and will germinate with the first warm days of spring, many weeks before the soil is in condition for the sowing of seeds. These autumn-sown seedlings are unusually sturdy and vigorous and will give an abundance of early bloom. For the more tender annuals spring sowing is preferable, and it is wise to wait until the soil is mellow and warm and workable. It is unwise to attempt the sowing of seed when the soil is wet and heavy and sticky. Seed of most annuals will not germinate well and plants tend to do poorly in heavy, unaerated soil. Unless the soil will crumble readily after it has been pressed firmly in the hand, it is best to wait for more suitable planting conditions.

If the garden soil is a mellow loam, one need not be greatly concerned about the preparation of a special seedbed, particularly in the case of the more sturdy plants such as lupines, zinnias and marigolds. If, however, one is dealing with a heavy soil that will have a tendency to form a hard, baked crust, it is necessary to prepare a special seedbed. This may easily be done by working compost, sand and finely pulverized moist peat moss into the upper 6 in. of soil. This will make the soil more retentive of moisture and, most important of all, will prevent it from forming a hard crust through which the young seedlings cannot penetrate. In the case of very fine seeds, such as petunias and ageratum, it is advisable to sift the top 1 in. of soil and the final light covering. With larger seeds this precaution is not necessary. The depth of sowing will depend upon the size of the seed. In general, seeds should be sown at a depth corresponding to twice the diameter of the seed. Large seeds such as those of lupines and sweet peas should be planted about ¾ in. deep; zinnias and marigolds about ¼ to ½ in.; while petunia, nicotiana and ageratum seeds are so fine that they need only be barely covered with a light sprinkling of sand or fine mellow soil.

After the seeds have been sown, the soil should be watered with a very fine spray and should not be allowed to dry out until the seeds have germinated and the young plants have become well established. Providing some light shade during germination will help retain moisture. If the seeds have been sown in the garden where they are to flower, shading is usually not feasible, but in an outdoor seedbed in the nursery it is possible. A lath frame forms a very satisfactory shade as it permits free circulation of air and admits a small amount of direct sunshine. Inexpensive shades may be easily made by tacking pieces of burlap on 2-in. by 3-in. wood strips or other small-scale lumber.

In preparing a seedbed in the nursery, it is essential to select a well-drained location; and the natural drainage will be improved if the bed is raised a few inches above the surrounding ground.

VEGETATIVE REPRODUCTION

Rooting Media and Propagating Units

Experimentation will reveal which of several rooting media should be used when propagating with cuttings. The medium used usually depends upon the type of plants to be propagated and the sophistication of the propagating facilities. Regardless of whether the propagating unit is a modest 3-in. flowerpot or an elaborate greenhouse mist bed, one must remember that the aim is to conserve moisture and maintain high humidity. Several media are suggested below. Do not be tempted to include water as one of the media; while roots may very well be formed, water induces a distinct type of root tissue to develop and gardeners frequently have difficulty successfully transplanting to soil cuttings with this type of root formation.

The following rooting media are suggested:

1. Moderately coarse, sterile sand

2. 1 part coarse sand, 1 part peat moss

3. 1 part coarse sand, 1 part perlite

4. 1 part coarse perlite, 1 part medium perlite.

As conditions that favor the rooting of cuttings also provide excellent conditions for the growth of fungi, it is advisable initially to water in the cuttings with a dilute preparation of a fungicide such as Benlate or Ban-rot; and this should be followed with a fungicide spray every ten days to two weeks. Captan 50 W, used at a concentration of 2 tsp. per gallon of water, is a good fungicide spray.

Substances That Promote Root Formation

Root-forming compounds known as plant hormones have a very direct influence upon plant growth and hasten the root development of both succulent and hardwood cuttings.

There are a number of excellent commercial preparations on the market. Detailed instructions are given for their use on the container. The directions should be followed with care since some hormones are too strong for certain plants, not only causing damage but also actually stunting the rooting process. These plant hormone substances may be used with a wide variety of cuttings. They mark a distinct advance in the technique of propagation, as root formation can be stimulated on many plants, such as magnolias and certain dogwood species, which are difficult to propagate.

In general, rooting hormones are available in three concentrations: No. 1 for soft tissue (house plants); No. 2 for semiripened wood (as in many shrubs); and No. 3 for hardwoods (most trees).

Mist Sprays for Cuttings

The development of mist spraying has been a great boon to propagators. It is a practice now widely used by commercial growers and can also be adapted for use by the home gardener who wishes to propagate plants by softwood cuttings on a fairly large scale.

Mist spraying of softwood cuttings has many advantages. At no point in their development do the cuttings dry out, as the foliage is kept constantly moist. Since shade is not necessary when mist spraying is used, the plants receive ample sunlight and the danger of having the cuttings suffer from lack of sufficient air circulation is greatly lessened. As a consequence there is less opportunity for disease to gain headway. A high percentage of rooting is usually obtained with mist spraying, and resultant growth is healthy and vigorous. By this method it is possible to root cuttings of larger size. This, of course, is a decided advantage when propagating trees and shrubs, as it is often possible to save from one to three years of growing time. Mist spraying has also made it possible to propagate plants that were hitherto extremely diffi-

cult to grow from cuttings but in many instances can now be easily rooted.

The procedure is simple and can be adapted for use in greenhouses, in coldframes and in outdoor propagating beds. However, it is essential that there be good draingage where mist spraying is to be used. Pipes containing a series of nozzles that give off a very fine mist are installed above the propagating area. The mist spray may be regulated by hand or it may be controlled automatically by a time-clock, or by an "electronic leaf." The number of applications required will depend to a considerable extent upon the weather, and good judgment must be exercised on the part of the operator if it is controlled manually. Constant mist will supply far more water than is needed and is definitely detrimental to most cuttings. A time-clock may be set so that it will go on and off—so many seconds on, so many seconds off; but here again, the intervals must be regulated to some extent according to the weather. The most satisfactory control is through the use of a device known as an "electronic leaf." This consists of two carbon contact points, embedded in a small block of plastic that is on a short stand. This is inserted in the rooting medium with the cuttings. The surface of the plastic dries off a little more rapidly than do the leaves of the cuttings. When there is no longer a film of moisture covering the plastic, the contact is broken and the mist spray is automatically turned on, going off again as soon as the leaves are thoroughly moist.

When cuttings are first inserted in the medium, the "leaf" is placed at its farthest point from the jets. As the cuttings begin to root it is gradually moved closer to the jets, which reduces both the frequency and quantity of mistings. After the cuttings are rooted, the application of mist should gradually cease and lath shade should be provided. The cuttings should then go through a hardening-off process before being removed from the bed.

Stem Cuttings

Stem cuttings may be grouped into three separate classes: softwood cuttings; cuttings made from half-ripened wood; and hardwood cuttings, which are those made from hard or dormant wood. Practically all greenhouse plants and all herbaceous perennials as well as some shrubs may be propagated by softwood cuttings. Many shrubs and vines, and some trees, are propagated by cuttings made from half-ripened wood, while others are most successfully propagated by hardwood cuttings.

Softwood Stem Cuttings of Herbaceous Plants

Stem cuttings are sometimes referred to as "slips," the term being frequently applied to small shoots that are pulled or "slipped" from a plant for the purpose of propagation.

Time of Making Cuttings

Softwood stem cuttings of herbaceous perennials such as delphiniums, phlox and chrysanthemums should preferably be taken in the spring just as the plants are starting into growth, although they may be taken at any time during the growing season when young, nonflowering shoots are obtainable. Cuttings of *Viola* and of the majority of rock plants such as *Phlox divaricata, Phlox subulata, Arabis* and *Iberis* are most successful when taken during June and July after the flowering season is over.

Making the Cutting

The parent plants from which the cuttings are taken should be vigorous, healthy and preferably well branched. The cuttings should usually be taken from the terminal growth, preferably from nonflowering shoots. Growth that is too soft and succulent should be avoided, as cuttings taken from such shoots are apt to rot before root formation has taken place. Shoots that are somewhat older and are brittle enough to snap when bent double should be selected. Old fibrous stems are unsatisfactory as they root very slowly and have a tendency to produce inferior plants. In some cases old plants can be headed back in order to induce a growth of new lateral shoots suitable for cuttings.

Softwood cuttings vary in length from 2 in. to 4 in. A sharp, clean, slightly diagonal cut should be made a short distance below a node or joint, a node being the point at which the leaf is attached to the stem. There are occasional exceptions to this generally accepted rule of cutting

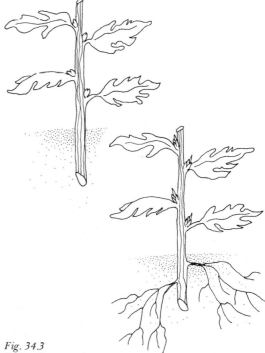

Fig. 34.3
Softwood stem cutting

slightly below a joint, as a few plants have been found to root more readily if the cut is made midway between the nodes or slightly above a node. After the cuttings have been taken, it is advisable to plunge them in cold water or to wrap them in damp newspaper for about a half hour or more to prevent them from wilting. This practice does not apply to geraniums or to other plants that exude a milky juice such as *Euphorbia mili:* (crown-of-thorns). Cuttings from such plants should be sprinkled lightly with water and spread out on a surface where they will be exposed to the air for several hours. This will give the bleeding cells an opportunity to become sealed and there will be less danger of rot after the cutting is placed in the propagating case.

In preparing the cutting, all flower buds should be removed and the leaf surface should be slightly reduced. The leaves should be removed from one or two nodes at the base of the cutting with a sharp knife, not pulled or stripped off. The leaf area at the top should not be reduced unless there is an excessive amount. In the case of coleus and a few other plants with large, succulent foliage a portion of the leaves may be removed, but as a general practice it is well to leave as much leaf area at the top of the cutting as possible. The leaves of a softwood cutting aid in the manufacture of food for the plant and they consequently have an important part to play in the development of the new root system.

Planting the Cutting

After the cuttings have been prepared, they should be inserted in the propagating case. The depth will vary somewhat with the type of cutting but, in general, it should be such that one or two nodes are buried. The rooting medium should be pressed firmly about the cuttings and a thorough watering should be given after the cuttings are in place. Shade should be provided for the first few days at least, and in some cases for a much longer period. One may be guided by the condition of the foliage. The leaves should be firm and should never be allowed to show any appearance of wilting. Plants differ greatly in this respect. As the roots begin to form, it is important that full sunlight be provided.

Temperature

Temperature is of considerable importance. For the majority of plants a temperature ranging between 65° and 75°F. is ideal, although some plants require somewhat lower or a much higher degree of heat. Root formation is usually greatly stimulated if bottom heat is provided. If possible, the temperature of the rooting medium should be 5° to 10° warmer than the surrounding air. In greenhouses the bottom heat is supplied by the pipes that comprise the regular heating system or by an automatically controlled electric heating cable. In a hotbed it may be supplied by manure or by an electric cable, while in the house it may be supplied by radiator pipes, if they are accessible.

Moisture

An adequate supply of moisture and sufficient circulation of air are also important factors. For the majority of plants a moderate degree of moisture is desirable. The sand of a rooting medium should never be allowed to dry

PERENNIALS PROPAGATED BY STEM CUTTINGS

Achillea spp.	yarrow
Alyssum spp.	alyssum
Arabis spp.	rock cress
Artemisia spp.	mugwort
Aster spp.	aster
Aubrieta spp.	aubrieta
Campanula spp.	bellflower
Centaurea spp.	cornflower
Chrysanthemum spp.	chrysanthemum
Coreopsis spp.	coreopsis, tickseed
Delphinium spp.	larkspur
Dianthus spp.	pink
Dicentra spp.	bleeding-heart
Dictamnus spp.	gas plant
Eupatorium spp.	mist flower
Gaillardia spp.	blanket flower
Geum spp.	geum
Gypsophila spp.	baby's-breath
Helenium spp.	sneezewort
Helianthus spp.	sunflower
Heliopsis spp.	orange sunflower
Hesperis spp.	sweet rocket
Heuchera spp.	coralbells
Iberis spp.	candytuft
Linum spp.	flax
Lobelia spp.	lobelia
Lychnis spp.	campion
Lupinus spp.	lupine
Lythrum spp.	loosestrife
Monarda spp.	horsemint
Myosotis spp.	forget me-not
Nepeta spp.	mint (many)
Oenothera spp.	evening primrose
Penstemon spp.	beard-tongue
Phlox spp.	phlox
Physostegia spp.	false dragonhead
Platycodon spp.	balloon flower
Potentilla spp.	cinquefoil
Rudbeckia spp.	coneflower
Salvia spp.	sage
Saponaria spp.	soapwort, bouncing bet
Sedum spp.	stonecrop
Silene spp.	catchfly, campion
Teucrium spp.	germander
Verbascum spp.	mullein
Veronica spp.	speedwell
Viola spp.	violet

out completely, nor should it be allowed to become wet to the point of sogginess. Cacti and other succulents require a rather dry environment, while a few of the large-foliaged greenhouse plants prefer a very high degree of humidity. Success with cuttings will depend upon selecting the rooting medium that will best maintain appropriate moisture levels.

Air Conditions

There should be sufficient circulation of air so that moisture does not remain on the leaves constantly or for too long a time. However, direct drafts should always be avoided, as they are usually very harmful to young cuttings.

Potting Up

Depending upon the time of year, about two to four weeks will be required for the rooting of most softwood cuttings. Evidence of root formation will usually be indicated by the beginning of new top growth. When the roots are well developed and have reached a length of ½ in. or more, the cuttings should be removed from the sand. They may then be potted up in small pots or planted in flats or frames. A sandy loam with a small proportion of leaf mold is ideal for this first potting. After the young plants have become well established, they may be allowed a richer diet.

Softwood and Half-ripened Stem Cuttings of Shrubs and Trees

Many shrubs and trees may be propagated by softwood and half-ripened stem cuttings. Softwood cuttings are generally taken during the late spring or early summer, while half-ripened stem cuttings should be taken during the late summer months, the exact time depending upon the growth and variety of the plant.

The cuttings should be taken from the tip end of the shoots and the wood should be just brittle enough to snap off when bent double. Avoid soft, fast-growing suckers as well as old brittle growth.

When making these tender cuttings, take special care in order to limit transpiration or water loss. Try to take the cuttings in cloudy weather or in the early morning of a day when you will have time to insert them in the rooting medium. During the interim the cuttings should be kept wrapped in damp burlap or placed in a plastic bag and kept out of the sun. The cuttings should vary in length from 4 in. to 6 in. and a clean cut should be made below a node. The leaves should be removed from the lower portion of the stems and the base dipped in the appropriate rooting hormone before inserting the cuttings in the propagating unit.

Selecting the right time to take these cuttings is most critical and can dramatically affect the percentage of successful rooting, as well as the length of time it takes for the cuttings to produce roots. In general, softwood and half-ripened stem cuttings are taken from deciduous trees and shrubs as well as from broad-leaved evergreens.

Hardwood or Dormant Stem Cuttings

Many deciduous trees and shrubs may be propagated very readily by means of dormant or hardwood cuttings. These cuttings should be taken in the autumn after the leaves have fallen, in the winter or the very early spring. In the case of a few shrubs, such as *Hibiscus* and *Diervilla,* only the tips of the branches should be used. With the majority of shrubs and trees, however, the branches may be cut into sections varying from 6 in. to 10 in. in length. The cuttings should be made from healthy wood of the current season's growth.

Since these cuttings are made when temperatures are very low, be careful not to cause tissue damage by bringing frozen cuttings into a warm work area. If you must work in a heated area, allow the cuttings to warm slowly in the

Fig. 34.4
Hardwood stem cuttings

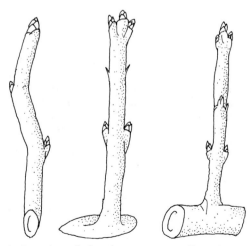

simple cutting   *heel cutting*   *mallet cutting*

TREES AND SHRUBS PROPAGATED
BY STEM CUTTINGS

Berberis spp.	barberry
Buddleia spp.	butterfly bush
Buxus spp.	boxwood
Cercis spp.	redbud
Chaenomeles spp.	quince
Chamaecyparis spp.	false cypress
Clethra spp.	sweet pepperbush
Cotoneaster spp.	cotoneaster
Deutzia spp.	deutzia
Elaeagnus spp.	Russian olive
Euonymus spp.	burning bush
Forsythia spp.	forsythia
Hamamelis spp.	witch hazel
Ilex spp.	holly
Kerria spp.	kerria
Kolkwitzia spp.	beautybush
Ligustrum spp.	privet
Lonicera spp.	honeysuckle
Philadelphus spp.	mock-orange
Pieris spp.	andromeda
Syringa spp.	lilac
Taxus spp.	yew
Viburnum spp.	viburnum
Weigela spp.	weigela

sun first. In most cases there should be at least three or four buds on each section of stem used as a cutting. A clean, slightly diagonal cut should be made just below a bud at the bottom of each cutting. Be sure to use a sharp knife when taking these cuttings; dull tools will almost certainly mash the bases of the cutting, creating an ideal site for disease to set in and consequently destroying or limiting your success. After the cuttings have been made, they should be tied in bundles of convenient size with the lower or butt ends even and the cuttings facing in the same direction. A label should be attached to each group and the bundles should then be buried in slightly moist sand, soil, peat moss or sawdust. A cool cellar with a temperature ranging between 40° and 45°F. provides an ideal storage place for hardwood cuttings during the winter months. If such a place is not available, however, the bundles of cuttings may be buried below the frost line in a well-drained spot outdoors in sand or in light, sandy soil. During this period of storage a callus will form over the butt ends of the cuttings. In the spring when the ground is workable, the cuttings may be removed from storage and planted out in nursery rows. By

autumn the cuttings should be well rooted and the young plants may be then shifted to more ample quarters in the nursery.

Two other types of specialized hardwood cuttings are the "heel" and "mallet" forms. The "heel" cutting simply includes a tiny portion of the previous year's growth. The "mallet" type is a lateral shoot that includes a 1/4-in. section from the previous year's vertical growth. Both types give the same results as a simple tip cutting and are usually reserved for use with coniferous, or narrow-leaved, evergreen cuttings.

Hardwood cuttings are usually used in propagating deciduous woody plants and coniferous evergreens. Certain evergreens, such as spruces (*Picea* spp.), hemlocks (*Tsuga* spp.), firs (*Abies* spp.), pines (*Pinus* spp.) and some junipers (*Juniperus* spp.), are more easily propagated by air layering methods, however (see index).

Leaf Cuttings

Among the more commonly grown house plants there are several that may be very easily propagated by leaf cuttings, various methods being used to meet the requirements of the individual plant. In general, plants with thick, fleshy leaves may be most readily propagated this way as the leaves contain a sufficient supply of reserve food.

The *Saintpaulia, Gloxinia, Peperomia* and Rex *Begonia* may be propagated by removing an entire leaf from the plant and inserting the petiole, or leaf stem, in the rooting medium. *Sansevieria* may be increased by cutting the leaves into lengths varying from 3 in. to 5 in. and inserting them in the propagating case. In the case of *Kalanchoë*, the leaf should be removed from the plant and laid flat upon the surface of the sand, being weighted down with pebbles. The new plants are produced from latent buds in the indentations along the margins of the leaves. Occasionally these young plantlets begin to grow while the leaf is still attached to the parent plant. In the propagation of Rex *Begonia* and *Streptocarpus,* the usual practice is to make a slight cut through the main veins of the leaf just below the point where they fork. The leaf is then placed flat on the sand or other rooting medium, being pinned in place with small wire hairpins or weighted down with pebbles. An-

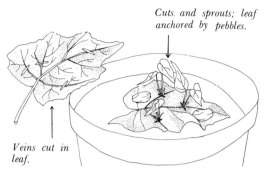

Cuts. and sprouts; leaf anchored by pebbles.

Veins cut in leaf.

Fig. 34.5.
Begonia: *whole-leaf cutting*

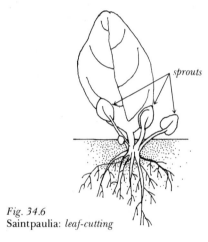

sprouts

Fig. 34.6
Saintpaulia: *leaf-cutting*

other method of propagating begonias is to cut the leaf into the shape of a V, each piece containing a large vein. The point of the V is then inserted in the sand and the new plant will develop at this point.

Root Cuttings

After the plants have been lifted, the roots may be cut into lengths varying from 2 in. to 3 in. These small pieces of root should then be planted in greenhouse flats or frames, being placed in a horizontal position at a depth of approximately 1 in. Pure sand, sand and peatmoss in mixture, or a light sandy soil will

PERENNIALS PROPAGATED BY ROOT CUTTINGS

Anchusa	bugloss
Anemone japonica	Japanese anemone
Asclepias	butterfly weed
Ceratostigma	
plumbaginoides	blue leadwort
Dicentra spectabilis	bleeding-heart
Dictamnus	gas plant
Echinops	globe thistle
Gypsophila paniculata	baby's-breath
Macleaya cordata	plume poppy
Oenothera	evening primrose
Papaver orientale	Oriental poppy
Phlox	
Polygonatum	Solomon's-seal
Romneya	canyon poppy
Stokesia	Stokes' aster
Thermopsis	false lupine
Trollius	globeflower
Yucca	Adam's-needle

give equally satisfactory results as a rooting medium.

If the cuttings are taken in the autumn, they may be carried over the winter in the coldframe, and by spring the new plants will be ready to set out in the nursery. If the cuttings are given mild bottom heat in the greenhouse propagating bench, the development of new root and top growth will be very rapid. Root cuttings may be taken at almost any season of the year, but the most favorable time will usually be indicated by the plant's natural habit of growth. *Anemone japonica,* which flowers in the autumn, may be propagated most successfully if lifted late in the season after the blooming period is over. Phlox may be successfully propagated by this method at almost any season and the root cuttings develop new plants so readily that they may even be planted in small shallow drills in the open ground.

Propagation by Division

Clumps

The division of old clumps is one of the simplest of all methods of propagation. A few shrubs and many of the herbaceous perennials may be propagated very successfully in this way.

The plants should be lifted from the soil and

PERENNIALS PROPAGATED BY DIVISION OF CLUMPS

Achillea spp.	yarrow	*Eupatorium* spp.	mist flower
Aconitum spp.	monkshood	*Euphorbia* spp.	spurge
Ajuga spp.	bugle	*Filipendula* spp.	meadowsweet
Alyssum saxatile	goldentuft	*Gaillardia* spp.	blanket flower
Amsonia spp.	amsonia	*Helianthus* spp.	sunflower
Anchusa spp.	bugloss	*Hemerocallis* spp.	daylily
Aquilegia spp.	columbine	*Heuchera* spp.	coralbells
Arabis spp.	rock cress	*Hosta* spp.	plantain lily
Artemisia spp.	mugwort	*Iris* spp.	iris
Aster spp.	aster	*Linum perenne*	perennial flax
Astilbe spp.	spirea	*Lupinus* spp.	lupine
Aubrieta spp.	aubrieta, purple rock cress	*Macleaya cordata*	plume poppy
Baptisia spp.	false indigo	*Mertensia* spp.	Virginia bluebells
Boltonia spp.	boltonia	*Monarda* spp.	horsemint
Campanula spp.	bellflower	*Oenothera* spp.	evening primrose
Centranthus spp.	valerian	*Paeonia* spp.	peony
Cerastium tomentosum	snow-in-summer	*Penstemon* spp.	beard-tongue
Ceratostigma plumbaginoides	blue leadwort	*Phlox* spp.	phlox
Chelone spp.	turtlehead	*Physostegia* spp.	false dragonhead
Chrysanthemum spp.	chrysanthemum	*Primula* spp.	primrose
Cimicifuga spp.	black cohosh, snakeroot	*Pyrethrum* spp.	painted daisy
Clematis spp.	clematis	*Rudbeckia* spp.	coneflower
Coreopsis spp.	coreopsis	*Scabiosa* spp.	pincushion flower
Delphinium spp.	larkspur	*Sedum* spp.	stonecrop
Dianthus spp.	pink	*Thalictrum* spp.	meadow rue
Dicentra spp.	bleeding-heart	*Trollius* spp.	globeflower
Doronicum spp.	leopard's bane	*Veronica* spp.	speedwell
Echinops spp.	globe thistle		

pulled apart with care to prevent the roots and crown from being injured. In cases where the crowns have become tough and hard, two spading forks or hand forks may be used to loosen them. In occasional instances where no alternative seems possible, a clean cut can be made with a strong butcher's knife or with a sharp spade.

For certain herbaceous perennials the frequent division of the clumps is desirable from the standpoint of good cultural methods; in other cases it is employed only when there is a need to increase the stock. Hardy asters and chrysanthemums deteriorate rapidly if left undisturbed over a period of many years, for example, and they should therefore be systematically lifted and divided every two or three years, whether new plants are desired or not. On the other hand, peonies should not be divided more frequently than once in seven or eight years and they may often be left undisturbed for many years with no apparent injury to the plant. Bleeding-heart should never be disturbed unless an increase of stock is desired,

as the plants will increase in beauty as the years pass.

The season of the year most favorable for the division of old clumps will vary with the plant's natural habit of growth. Hardy asters and chrysanthemums should be divided during the early spring just as growth starts. Phlox is best divided in the early autumn after the period of bloom has passed, although it may be divided at almost any season of the year with reasonable success. Bleeding-heart should always be divided in the autumn, never in the spring if one wishes to have bloom the same season. Peonies should be lifted and divided in September.

Rhizomes

A rhizome is a horizontal underground, or partially underground, stem which, in most cases, produces roots, shoots and leaves. A rhizome may be distinguished from a root by the presence of nodes. A true root has no nodes. The rhizomes of some plants penetrate quite deeply into the soil, while in the case of certain irises, the rhizomes rest upon the surface of the ground, being only partially subterranean. Plants of this type may be readily propagated by a division of the rhizomes. In the case of the bearded iris, the plant may be lifted from the soil and the rhizomes gently separated, each rhizome having two or three sprouts for new growth (see page 284 for illustration). The rhizomes of some plants bear no prominent shoots and in such cases the rhizome should be cut into short pieces. These sections should then be planted in sand until they have rooted. The majority of rhizomatous plants should be propagated when dormant. In the case of the bearded iris, however, the most favorable time is the season immediately following the blooming period.

Tubers

Tubers are thickened underground stems bearing conspicuous buds or eyes. Among flowering plants, the dahlia is the most prominent member of this group, while the Irish potato and the Jerusalem artichoke are well known among the vegetables. The tubers may be cut into sections, as in the case of the potato, or they may be planted whole, as in the case of the dahlia. It is essential that each tuber have at least one healthy bud. When dahlias are propagated by tubers, a small portion of stem should be attached to each tuber.

"Bulbous" Propagation

Bulbs and Bulbils

There are numerous bulblike structures, commonly called bulbs, but which in reality may be tubers or rhizomes (as described above) or corms. Bulbs are, botanically, modified leaves, buds and stems that usually occur underground. They are composed largely of fleshy, scalelike leaves and they contain large quantities of stored plant food. There are two general types of bulbs: the tunicated type, which is composed of close-fitting layers of leaf tissue covered with a dry husk, such as the hyacinth and tulip; and the scaly type, which is composed of thick, loose, overlapping scales, such as the lily.

Many bulbs are readily increased by natural separation. A fully matured bulb, known as a "mother bulb," will, under favorable conditions, produce one or more bulbs of flowering size and a number of small bulbils. These small bulbils should be removed when the mother bulb is dug and should be planted in flats or in nursery plots, as they will usually require several years to reach blooming size.

Corms and Cormels

A corm is a round, fleshy, underground base of a stem. It is solid, being composed almost entirely of undifferentiated stem tissue, and is unlike a bulb in this respect. Among the most familiar examples of plants grown from corms are the crocus, cyclamen, gladiolus, ixia and tritonia. Each year one, and in some cases several new corms of flowering size are formed on top of the mother corm, which deteriorates at the end of the growing season. Many small cormels are also usually formed at the base of the new corm. When the plants are dug in the autumn, the new, flowering-size corms may be separated and stored for spring planting. In general practice these corms are planted the following season to produce bloom. If, however, a very rapid increase of stock is desired, as in the case of a new or very expensive variety, these large corms may be cut into sections so that more plants may be produced. The tiny cormels should be stored until planting time in the spring. They may then be planted in rows, being treated very much like seed, and they will reach blooming size in from one to three years.

Propagation by Specialized Shoots

Layering

Layering is one of the simplest and most dependable methods of propagation, although it is adapted only to those plants that possess a characteristic habit of growth and that root readily when their branches come into contact with the soil. It is of especial value in the propagation of some of the broad-leaved eve   eens, such as certain varieties of rhododendron and magnolia. *Daphne cneorum* and *Forsythia* may also be propagated by layering.

There are several different types of layering: tip-layering, simple layering, serpentine layering, mound layering and air layering.

Fig. 34.7
Layering

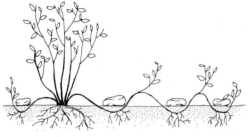

simple layering   serpentine layering

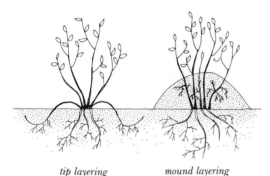

tip layering   mound layering

Tip layering: The method commonly used in the propagation of black raspberries and plants with arching stems. In late summer the supple canes are bent over, the tip being anchored in the soil. A new plant will soon form, which may be severed from the parent plant and transplanted to any desired position.

Simple layering: Usually done during the spring and summer months. If the branch is woody in character, a notch should be cut in it about 18 in. from the tip. The notch should be propped open with a match or some very small piece of wood. The branch should then be bent over to the ground, the portion where the notch occurs being covered with soil. The leaves should be removed from that portion of the stem that is to be buried. The tip end of the branch should be left exposed. If necessary the branch may be pegged down with a forked stick, or it may be held in place by the weight of a small stone. After the layer has rooted, it may be severed from the parent plant, and when the new plant is well established, it may be transplanted the following spring.

Serpentine layering: A method frequently used in the propagation of vines with long flexible stems, as it enables one to obtain a large number of new plants (see sketch, left). In continuous layering the entire shoot except the tip is covered with soil. Continuous layering can be used only with a rather limited group of plants, as many types will not send up shoots from buds that are buried in the soil. This method is of particular value in the propagation of *Hedera* spp. (ivy) and *Salix* spp. (willow).

Mound layering: Plants of a characteristically bushy habit of growth may frequently be propagated successfully by mound layering. This method is of particular value in the propagation of *Hydrangea, Cotoneaster, Chaenomeles, Calycanthus* and *Ribes.* The plants should be pruned back severely, preferably a year before the layering is to be done, in order to encourage the production of new shoots at the base. The soil should be mounded up about the entire base of the plant in the spring and these new basal shoots will strike root at the nodes. This method of propagation is somewhat slow, as it will frequently require from one to two years for the new plants to become well established.

Air layering: Used more than 2,000 years ago by the Chinese, for a long time the use of air layering in this country was largely limited to the propagation of a few greenhouse plants, such as the rubber plant and certain species of the *Dracaena.* But today, due to the development of new techniques and to the use of plastic materials that have the ability to hold moisture in without hindering the movement of air, air layering has come into much wider use. Both professional and amateur gardeners are finding it an excellent method of propagating such plants as *Ilex* and *Rhododendron.*

The most favorable time for air layering is just as the buds start into growth in the spring. A stem or branch of the previous season's

Fig. 34.8
Air layering

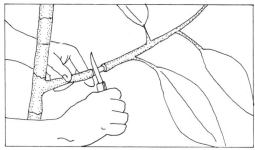

One-in. length of stem is trimmed to induce new growth.

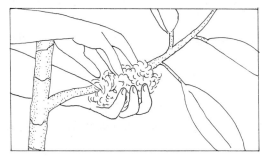

Damp sphagnum moss is clustered around open area.

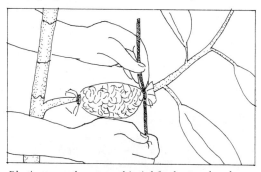

Plastic secures the moss and is tied firmly at each end.

PLANTS THAT CAN BE ROOTED BY AIR LAYERING

Acer spp.	maple
Betula spp.	birch
Carya spp.	hickory
Catalpa spp.	catalpa
Cercis spp.	redbud
Cornus spp.	dogwood
Crataegus spp.	hawthorn
Enkianthus spp.	enkianthus
Ilex spp.	holly
Magnolia spp.	magnolia
Malus spp.	apple, crab apple
Populus spp.	poplar
Prunus spp.	cherry, plum, peach, almond (ornamental and fruiting)
Rhododendron spp.	rhododendron, azalea
Salix spp.	willow
Syringa spp.	lilac
Taxus spp.	yew
Tsuga spp.	hemlock
Viburnum spp.	viburnum

growth should be selected. A cut should be made from 1½ in. to 2 in. long, extending approximately one-third of the way through the stem. The cut should be made with a sharp knife and may be made either toward or away from the tip. The flap of bark made by the cut should be entirely removed. The cut should then be dusted with a dusting powder such as Hormodin No. 3. A small paintbrush is excellent for this purpose. Fine sphagnum moss, which has either been horticulturally milled or rubbed through a ½-in. screen, should be used to bind the wound. The moss should be thoroughly moistened and then squeezed until no water drips from it. Moss that is soggy when it is applied may cause fermentation and discourage rooting. After the moss has been moistened and the excess water squeezed out, it should be rolled into a ball and then cut in half. These two pieces should be bound around the wounded area on the stem. A 6 in. by 6 in. piece of polyethylene or vinyl plastic should then be wrapped tightly around the ball of moss. The plastic should be sealed at both the top and bottom with strips of waterproof tape. The strip of tape should completely seal the plastic and be bound several times around the stem of the plant, as it is important that a complete seal be made that will prevent rainwater from seeping through or interior moisture from escaping.

When roots have formed at the point where the cut was made, the branch should be severed from the parent plant, the plastic covering should be removed, and the newly rooted plant should be planted either in a pot of ample size or in a nursery bed.

Suckers

Some plants may be propagated by means of suckers, which are leafy shoots produced from adventitious buds on the underground parts of a plant. Certain varieties of *Malus* and *Prunus* produce suckers very rapidly, and *Syringa* may be propagated by this method. If the tree or shrub that is to be propagated has been grafted, it is important to make certain that the sucker has been produced from a bud above the graft. If it happens to have come from a bud below the graft, it will be similar to the stock upon which the tree or shrub was grafted and will not possess the desirable characteristics of the grafted plant. Certain species of *Salix* and *Populus* may be very readily propagated by means of suckers.

Runners

Some plants, such as *Fragaria* spp. (strawberries), *Nephrolepis exaltata* 'Bostoniensis' (Boston fern) and *Saxifraga stolonifera* (strawberry saxifrage), may be readily propagated by means of runners. In plants of this type the stems creep along the surface of the ground and strike root at the widely spaced nodes, producing new plants that continue to receive nourishment from the parent plant until they are well established. The connecting stem may be severed at any point between the old plant and the new plant, and the new plant may then be moved to its new location.

Stolons

A stolon is a slender branch which, under favorable conditions, will take root. Stolons may be produced either above ground or below ground, the new plant being produced from the bud at the end of the stolon. Some of the bent grasses may be very readily increased by the planting of stolons. The sod is broken into small pieces and the stolons are strewn upon the surface of the well-prepared seedbed, being covered with approximately ½ in. of soil. The soil should be kept moist until growth has started, and at no time should the stolons be allowed to dry out.

Some shrubby plants also take root very naturally by means of stolons and may be readily propagated in this way. In this group we find *Cornus stolonifera* and *Salix* spp. and some species (old-fashioned) roses such as 'Harrison's Yellow.'

Grafting

Fruit trees do not come true from seed, as most of our orchard varieties are hybrids. In order to perpetuate a variety, vegetative propagation or a vegetative union is necessary.

Grafting and budding are the two common methods of propagating fruit trees. An undesirable variety may be replaced by a more desirable one by grafting. Pollination troubles can be solved by grafting the proper variety on one branch of an unproductive tree, because the presence of another or pollinating variety will result in cross-fertilization, causing fruits to form on the heretofore nonproductive variety. When the trunk of a tree has been girdled by mice, bridge grafting will save the tree.

Bridge Grafting

This is the only way to save trees girdled by mice.

1. Remove soil from around the trunk of the tree until the live bark on the roots is exposed.

2. Trim off rough edges of the bark with a sharp knife at the base of the tree and also on the root.

3. Take a piece of dormant one-year-old wood (previous season's growth) and measure the distance to be bridged over. Allow 1¼ in. on the bark and also on the root, and cut with a sharp knife.

4. Cut out a piece of bark above and below the girdled area, into which the ends of the scion should fit snugly. (A scion is a young shoot used for grafting.)

5. Make a slanting cut, 1¼ in. long, on each end of the scion and place each end in the part where the bark was removed.

6. Place the scions 2 in. apart around the trunk.

7. Two small brads without heads should be used to hold the scion firmly in place at each end. They should be nailed through the middle two-thirds of each scion, each end of which is properly fitted above and below the girdled area.

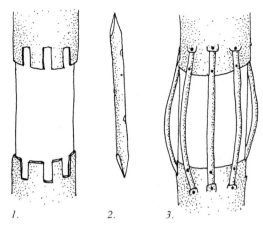

Fig. 34.9
Bridge graft. (1) stock (with dead or damaged bark removed); (2) scion (buds may be removed); (3) scions wedged into stock to facilitate new growth over wound. All unions should be carefully covered with grafting wax.

8. Apply grafting wax over the united areas to keep them airtight.

Whip Grafting

Used to propagate nursery stock and may be done in midwinter when most orchard operations are at a standstill.

One-year-old root stocks should be used: (The stock is that part which is to receive the scion.) They may be grown from seed or purchased from firms in midwestern and far western states that make a specialty of this. The procedure is as follows:

1. Cut the root from the one-year whip and below any green tissue.

2. Cut the root into 3 in. lengths.

3. Make a clean slanting cut about 1½ in. to 2 in. in length. The next cut on the root is made parallel to the edge of the root and should be 1¼ in. to 1½ in. long.

4. Select a piece of scion wood from the middle of one-year terminal growth with three buds on it. Cut it 1¼ in. below the third bud and proceed as in No. 3.

5. Join the two tongues together and be sure that the cambium layer of one side of the root is in contact with one side of the scion. (Cambium is the layer of cells that lies between the bark and the wood; these cells grow and multiply rapidly.)

6. Wrap tightly with waxed string and store in moist sand or leaves in a damp, cool place with a temperature of approximately 45°F. until they have united. As soon as the soil can be prepared in the spring, set the plants 6 in. apart in rows 3 ft. apart. Set deep enough to cover all but the top bud. Remove the string before planting.

This method may also be practiced on young trees in the nursery row that are not over one year old. If older, the smaller branches may be successfully grafted in this way.

Cleft Grafting

A method used to top-work trees, especially when the limb to be grafted is somewhat larger than the one-year scion to be grafted. A limb may vary from ½ in. to 2 in. diameter. This type of grafting is most successful if done early in the spring when the bark is loose, before growth has made much progress. It may be

Fig. 34.10
Whip grafting

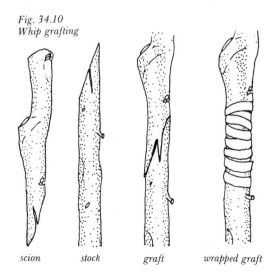

scion   stock   graft   wrapped graft

Fig. 34.11
Cleft graft

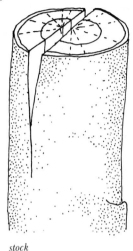

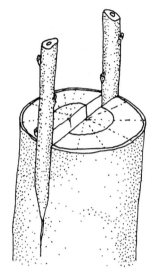

stock   scion   *Scion inserted in stock. All cut surfaces*
                                                              require thorough waxing.

done after that, however, if the scions are dormant. The procedure is as follows:

1. Saw the limb off at the desired point where the limb is to be grafted.

2. With a sharp knife smooth the edges so the cambium layer may be easily seen.

3. A grafting chisel is placed on the center of the stump and driven into the stock to a depth of 3 in. to 4 in. with a wooden mallet or club.

4. The scion of the desired variety should have been taken from the terminal growth of a bearing tree, which should be the previous season's growth.

5. The tip of the scion should be cut off, and the second cut is made 1½ in. below the third bud.

6. That part of the scion below the third bud is cut to make a wedge. The side with the bud should be slightly thicker than the side that will be in toward the center of the stump. This wedge should be 1¼ in. in length.

7. The cleft is opened with the end of a wedge-shaped chisel and the scion inserted so

that its cambium layer is in direct contact with that of the stock. One scion is inserted on each side of the stock if it is more than 1 in. in diameter, and the chisel is removed. The pressure from the sides of the split stock holds the scions firmly in place. Keep in mind that the scions should be uniform in size so that they fit well and have equal pressure from both sides of the stock.

8. Cover the exposed area immediately with grafting wax to prevent drying out and to inhibit the entrance of disease organisms and the accumulation of excess moisture.

An extra large branch may be cleft grafted by making two clefts at right angles to each other. In this case four scions are necessary. A small piece of wood, or a wedge, must be put in the center to prevent the scion from being crushed, since there is greater pressure on a larger limb.

When the grafting of an individual limb is finished, the entire exposed area should be waxed over to prevent drying out, to inhibit the entrance of moisture and to inhibit disease organisms. The grafts should be checked occasionally to make sure that the wax is properly protecting it. When grafting is done after considerable growth has been made, it is best to cover the entire scion with wax, which keeps it in a dormant state a little longer while the scion is uniting with the stock.

Cleft grafting is very satisfactory on apples and pears but more difficult on plums and cherries and almost impossible with peaches.

Bark Grafting

This must be done in the spring after the sap starts to flow, or the bark will not easily separate from the cambium layer. This graft is most practical on limbs that are too large to be cleft grafted. The limb is removed at the desired place and a smooth area is selected where the graft is to be placed.

Preparing the Scion

1. The scion should contain three buds and be cut from the terminal growth 1½ in. below the third bud for all three types of bark grafting.

2. *(a)* Directly opposite the lower bud make an abrupt cut to the center and then straight down to the end; or

(b) Make a sloping cut on the side opposite the lowest bud to the end of the scion, or 1½ in.

There are two ways of bark grafting.

1. *(a)* Make a cut 1¼ in. long on the stock and at right angles to the stub that is to receive the graft.

(b) Pry the two corners up with a sharp knife and insert the scion prepared as in either *(a)* or *(b)*. Force it under the bark until the outer bud is directly at the point of the stock and the scion.

(c) Fasten it securely by driving two small brads into it through the bark.

(d) Put the grafts 2 in. apart around the stub, and cover exposed, newly cut tissues with grafting wax. Best results are obtained if, in addition, raffia is wound tightly around the stub two to three times and tied securely to hold the bark tightly against the scion.

2. Bark grafts may also be made in the same way as a bridge graft. Preparation for the scion has been discussed. A piece of bark is removed as described in bridge grafting. One side of the scion is cut as described in *(a)* or *(b)*, inserted, fastened with brads and waxed over. This is the easiest method for the amateur to follow.

Budding

This type of grafting is done during August or in the early part of September when the bark slips easily. Its main use is to propagate young trees of the desired variety.

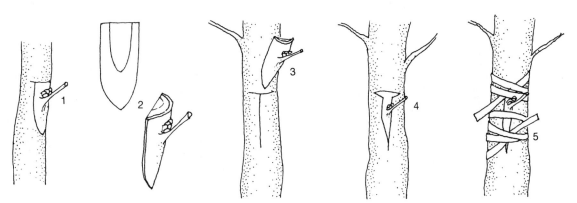

Fig. 34.12

Budding   1. Cut off bud.   2. Back and side views of bud. Note that sliver of wood must be removed before insertion in stock.   3. Cut and insertion in stock.   4. Bud inserted.   5. Protective raffia wrapping holds bud in place.

1. At the point where the budding is to be done, that is, as close to the ground as possible, make a cut in the shape of a T: its vertical distance ¾ in. long and the horizontal distance ½ in.

2. The bud to be used is selected from the terminal growth on the current season's growth. Be sure that the bud is well developed. Remove the leaf next to the bud, but leave on part of its stem.

3. Using a sharp knife, remove the bud with some of the wood and bark attached to it. When properly removed it looks like a shield.

4. Loosen carefully the corners of the T-shaped cut in the stock and slip the bud in under the corners.

5. Use raffia, rubber bands or waxed string to wind above and below the bud.

6. Two weeks later the bud should be united. The bud remains dormant until the following spring, at which time stock is cut back to the bud, which develops into the desired limb.

Pruning and Training of Grafts

Grafts, especially those on large limbs that have been cleft or bark grafted, must be properly understood. If two or more grafts are made on a stub, only one should be allowed to fully develop. The best one should be selected before next season's growth starts. It is cut back to promote lateral branches. The other is cut back to two or three buds, the purpose being to keep it alive so that it will help to heal over the stump but not compete with the one selected. The principle used to train grafts until maturity or bearing is the same as with young trees planted in the ground.

It is best to graft one side of a tree at a time if it is more than eight years old. The side not grafted can be grafted the following year.

35

Garden Practices

A good garden program includes such general practices as soil preparation, cultivation, watering, feeding, pruning, winter protection, protection against frost, preventing transplanting losses, and control of pests and diseases.

The application of these practices to various types of gardens and to special plant groups has been discussed in preceding chapters, but it is well to understand some of the underlying principles involved.

DIGGING

Double-digging

Dig an initial trench across the end of the bed 2 ft. wide and 1 ft. deep. This soil is then moved to the farther end of the bed to be used in filling the final trench. Spread manure in the trench and fork it into the ground as deeply as possible. Dig the next trench 2 ft. wide and 1 ft. deep, turning the soil into the first trench and enriching it with a layer of manure when half the soil has been moved in. Break up and enrich the bottom of the second trench and continue across the bed in this way.

Trenching

This operation is the same as double-digging except that 2 ft. of soil are removed in each trench. The topsoil of the second trench is placed in the bottom of the first, and the lower foot of soil then becomes the topsoil of the first trench. This is only practical to do, however, when the garden soil is a very deep loam. Where the topsoil is only 1 ft. in depth, fresh soil can be hauled in for the fill and the lower foot of subsoil discarded.

CULTIVATION

Soil cultivation serves several important functions. It destroys weeds; breaks the crust that forms on heavy soils after a rain; aerates the soil, thus permitting air to reach the roots of the plants; and establishes a dust mulch on the surface that helps to conserve the moisture in the soil.

Under normal conditions the ground should be cultivated as soon as possible after a rainfall. If the soil is extremely sandy it may be cultivated almost immediately. Heavy clay soils should be dried out sufficiently, as it is imperative that such soils not be worked when they are too wet, because this will seriously injure the physical condition of the soil. There are occasional instances when it is unwise to cultivate the soil after a rain. Such a situation occurs during a period of drought when only a light rain has fallen. Under such circumstances it is wiser to allow the plants to derive what they can from

707

the meager supply of surface moisture, which would be almost entirely dissipated and lost if the surface were stirred.

One of the most important functions of cultivation in the garden is the destruction of weeds. It is essential that cultivations be given so frequently that weeds never have an opportunity to gain headway. If the weeds are less than 1 in. in height at the time that the cultivation is done, it will not be necessary to remove them because they will wilt as soon as they have been uprooted and will disappear entirely within a very short time.

Various types of small hand weeders are available for the cultivation of flower beds, borders and nursery plots. A small inexpensive hand weeder with three flexible wire prongs is one of the most efficient. For more extensive areas, such as shrubbery borders and the vegetable garden, there are the long-handled prong cultivators, hoes of many varied types (the small half-moon type being one of the most satisfactory) and the wheel hoes, which are exceedingly useful in the cultivation of long rows.

WATERING

Soil nutrients are available to plants only when dissolved in water. Therefore, thorough watering is a necessity. Frequent light waterings tend to do infinitely more harm than good. If only the few surface inches of soil are moist, and if there is not enough water to allow for a sufficient depth of penetration, the plant roots will be drawn upward toward the surface in their search for moisture. If this process continues, the plants will become more and more shallow-rooted. And it is a well-established fact that shallow-rooted plants are less vigorous than those that are deeply rooted, as such plants can derive their nutrients from only a very limited soil area and suffer seriously during periods of drought. It is therefore a wise practice to water thoroughly, even if less frequently.

The most favorable times for watering are late afternoon and evening, or very early in the morning, though evening watering is preferable, provided that the water is applied only to the soil and is not sprinkled on the plants. The

evaporation of moisture is considerably less at such times, and the plants are consequently able to derive more lasting benefit from the application. Young seedling plants must never be allowed to suffer from lack of moisture, however.

The method of watering, or of supplying constant moisture, will vary considerably, being dependent upon the type of plant being handled and, to some degree, upon the extent of one's gardening operations. One of the most satisfactory ways of maintaining a constant and uniform supply of moisture in the soil is to sink pieces of 4-in. drain tile in the ground, one open end being level with the surface of the soil. If these pieces of tile are kept filled with water, there will be a gentle and very gradual seepage of moisture throughout the soil. This method is of particular value in providing moisture for trees and shrubs. It may also be used in large flower beds and borders, as the tile openings are inconspicuous and are seldom noticed. English primroses, which are extremely dependent upon moisture, will usually thrive when water is supplied this way.

The usual method of supplying water to plants is through the use of a sprinkling can or a garden hose. There are various attachments available for the hose. An adjustable nozzle, which is capable of throwing both a fine, mist-like spray and a comparatively heavy stream of water, is one of the most useful. Rose attachments similar to those used on a watering can may also be obtained and are very useful where a gentle, steady spray is desired. There are also various types of satisfactory automatic sprinklers that will relieve the tedium of hand watering. Sprinklers should be left in place until an area is thoroughly soaked, and should then be moved on to another section of the garden or lawn. A special device particularly useful for watering trees and shrubs is a water sword, which may be attached to a hose and plunged deeply into the ground.

There is comparatively little danger of too liberal applications of water when watering is done artificially, but during prolonged periods of excessively heavy rains the soil may become so saturated with moisture that plant growth suffers seriously in consequence. Under such conditions much of the available nitrogen in the soil is leached away and plants are unable to make normal growth. The ground also becomes so densely saturated with water that the aeration of the soil is seriously checked and plants fail to thrive because their roots are unable to obtain sufficient air. Large trees sometimes die as a result of such a condition. Under these circumstances it is well to apply additional nitrogen to the soil to stimulate plant growth and to make up for the deficiency in nitrogen due to leaching. In areas where trees are beginning to show ill effects from such a condition, — evidenced by a browning of the leaves and a generally unthrifty appearance — holes should be bored in the soil beneath the spread of the branches to increase the supply of oxygen and to permit air to reach the roots.

FEEDING

All plants are dependent upon mineral nutrients for their growth and development, and it is essential that an adequate supply of those necessary elements be maintained in the soil. A detailed discussion of the value of soil tests, the mineral nutrients needed for plant growth, and the form in which these nutrients may be applied, will be found in Chapter 30 on Soils and in various other chapters dealing with special plant groups.

There are, however, a few fundamental principles that should be observed in the application of all fertilizers.

Under no condition should water-soluble commercial fertilizers be allowed to come into contact with seeds at the time that they are sown, or into direct contact with the roots of trees, shrubs or herbaceous plants at the time of planting. The germination of most seeds will be seriously affected if commercial fertilizers are used in the drill at the time of sowing. The most approved method of supplying nutrients to young plants is to place the fertilizer in drills 3 in. or 4 in. away on each side of the row. The drills should be from 2 in. to 3 in. deep and the fertilizer should be covered with a small quantity of soil. This method is especially recommended for vegetables and for flowers in the cutting garden that are grown in rows.

The most satisfactory way to apply fertilizer to garden beds and borders is to broadcast it over the surface of the soil at the prescribed rate and to cultivate it in very lightly. The soil should then be thoroughly watered so that the fertilizer may become more readily available to the plants. If individual plants within the border are to be fertilized, a shallow furrow in the form of a ring may be made several inches from the crown of the plant and the fertilizer placed in the furrow. Care must be taken to keep the fertilizer from coming into contact with the foliage, as it may cause severe burning. Pelletized, slow-release fertilizers may be safely used, if the directions are followed carefully.

When fertilizers are to be applied in the form of a solution, they may be dissolved in the desired quantity of water and applied with a watering can from which the rose or sprinkler has been removed.

PRUNING

It is important that every gardener acquires a knowledge of the fundamental principles of pruning. One should understand why pruning is necessary, and at what season of the year it should be done. And one should also be familiar with the most approved pruning practices.

The primary purposes of pruning are: to restore a proper balance between root and top growth at the time of transplanting; to remove injured, diseased or dead wood; to increase both the quantity and quality of flowers and fruit; to control the structure of a tree or shrub and to guide its growth; to improve the appearance and symmetry of a plant; and to aid in the rejuvenation of old trees, shrubs or vines.

In order to prune a tree or shrub intelligently, it is necessary to understand that there is always a definite relationship in all plants between root growth and top growth. If there is a reduction in normal root growth, there must be a compensating reduction in top growth. This is why the judicious pruning of trees and shrubs at the time of transplanting is a matter of such paramount importance. In bare root transplanting it is almost inevitable that some of the roots will be severed entirely or severely injured. Therefore, in order to compensate for this reduction in root growth, the top must be pruned; moreover, because the plant has suffered some degree of shock and will require time to reestablish itself, it is not able to sustain its usual amount of top growth; consequently, severe pruning is recommended.

Although each tree and shrub has a natural form, its symmetry and appearance may be controlled to a considerable degree by judicious pruning. No attempt should be made, however, radically to change the shape or form of a plant, except for such specific applications as topiary, bonsai and hedge trimming. Pruning should serve as an aid in building a strong framework and in guiding the natural growth. After ornamental trees have attained their full development and have been trained to the desired form, comparatively little pruning is necessary. Systematic yearly care includes the removal of broken branches and of any dead or diseased wood, and the cutting away of any branch that may be interfering with the development of other branches. In the case of shrubs the same general principles hold true: in many cases some of the old wood should be cut away entirely in order to stimulate the production of vigorous new growth. The pruning requirements of the various groups of shrubs are discussed fully in Chapter 14.

Just as the removal of roots necessitates the reduction in top growth, so does the severe pruning of top growth disturb the equilibrium of the normal function of the roots, and nature tends to restore the balance by the production of new shoots and branches. In many cases this is the goal with fruit trees and with flowering shrubs, where the production of vigorous, young, flowering and fruiting wood is the desideratum. Some plants bear flowers and fruit on new growth, and such growth may be encouraged by the annual pruning out of old wood. Many of our flowering shrubs, most roses, the small bush fruits, and the grapevines may be found in this group.

Such pruning is also associated with the rejuvenation of old trees and shrubs that have become weak and unthrifty through age or neglect. Invariably, vigorous pruning is followed by an increase in top growth, but moderation must be practiced. This is particularly true in the rejuvenation of old trees. If very severe pruning of large trees seems necessary or advisable, the process should be extended over a period of several years. If excessively heavy pruning of top growth is attempted at one time, it will usually cause the formation of much undesirable growth in the nature of water sprouts and suckers. These rampant, upright shoots are entirely unproductive, injure the form and appearance of the tree and rob the more desirable growth of nourishment. Not only should they be removed if they occur, but their production should be controlled by judicious pruning.

Pruning Equipment

Elaborate pruning equipment is not usually necessary. Most pruning may be accomplished efficiently with three or four tools—a pair of good pruning shears, a pair of lopping shears with extended handles, one or two pruning saws and a pair of pole pruners usually are the only tools necessary. It is essential that the shears be sharp, as much damage can be done with dull tools. Pruning shears should always be kept well sharpened and properly tightened, and they should be oiled at frequent intervals.

Pruning Practices

To make a close, clean cut, and to avoid injury to the bark, the shears should be held with the blade next to the portion of the twig or branch that is to remain upon the plant. A ragged cut, with torn and mutilated bark, reflects only discredit upon the person responsible for the pruning. In cutting back small branches, the cut should be made at a slight angle, just above a bud (see page 185). If the cut is made above an outside bud the growth will be directed outward, and the form will be open and spreading. If a more compact, upright growth is desired, the cut should be made above an inside bud. When branches have opposite rather than alternate buds, one of the buds may be removed, and the growth may thus be guided in any desired direction.

If large branches are to be removed, the final cut should be made as close to the main trunk as possible so that the wound may heal rapidly and there may be no disfiguring stump. If the limb is comparatively large, more than one cut may be advisable. The first cut should be made from below, about 1 ft. from the main trunk, and it should extend only halfway through the branch. The second cut should be made from above, at a distance 3 in. or 4 in. farther out on the branch, and it should sever the limb entirely. The final cut should consist of the removal of the stub as close to the trunk as possible.

WINTER PROTECTION

Providing adequate winter protection for trees, shrubs and flowers is a problem all gardeners in northern climes must face. The amount of protection necessary depends upon the natural hardiness of the plants, upon the severity of the climate and upon the exposure.

Winter injury to plants is usually attributable to two factors: severe cold, or loss of moisture from shoots and branches. Extreme cold will cause the twigs, stems and roots to freeze, with a consequent breaking down of the cell tissues. Excessive loss of moisture, which is quite as frequently a cause of winter-killing as is severe cold, is due largely to the effect of strong, drying winds during periods of brilliant winter sunshine. It is a well-known fact that the evaporation of moisture from the twigs, branches, canes, and, in the case of evergreens, from the leaves, continues at a slow rate throughout the winter, and that in order to supply this moisture the roots of the plant must continue to absorb water. When the evaporation is unduly accelerated by prolonged periods of winter wind and sunshine, the roots are unable to supply moisture rapidly enough, and the branches and canes become dehydrated. If this condition becomes sufficiently aggravated, it frequently results in the dying back of a large portion of the plant, or in its death.

Therefore, one of the most important preparations for winter in the case of all woody plants, and particularly in the case of broad-leaved evergreens, is to see that the soil is adequately supplied with moisture. If rainfall has been light during the autumn months, it will be necessary to soak the ground thoroughly before it freezes. Numerous trees and shrubs may be saved from winter injury if this precaution is taken. For many plants a winter protection against wind and sun also is quite as important as a protection against extreme cold.

The most approved practices for providing winter protection for herbaceous perennials, rock plants, roses, trees and shrubs have been discussed in detail in the various chapters.

PROTECTION AGAINST FROST

When sudden cold spells occur, plants may be protected from frost in numerous ways. If only a small number of plants need protection, they may be covered with baskets, boxes or lath frames over which burlap, muslin or sheets of plastic have been spread.

Smudge pots may also be used on cold nights.

One of the most effective ways of lessening frost damage is through the use of water. If plants can be subjected to a fine, gentle, continuous spray of water during a sudden drop in temperature, satisfactory protection can be obtained in many cases, even where the thermometer drops as low as 20°F. When the air temperature drops below freezing, the water sprayed onto the plants begin to form into ice. During the process of freezing the water gives off heat and enough of this heat is absorbed by the plants to prevent them from freezing, with a resultant breakdown of cell structure. As long as water is applied continuously, the plant remains above its freezing point. The application of water should begin when the temperature at plant level drops to 34°F. It must be constant throughout the period when the air temperature is below freezing, and must also be continued until all the ice has melted off the plants.

This method is used by many commercial growers, particularly where sprinkler irrigation systems are available, and often means the saving of an entire crop. Much less water is required than the amount normally used for irrigation purposes, however, as a fine, light spray is essential. In the home garden a stationary or rotary sprinkler on the end of a hose will give very satisfactory results, although it is possible to cover only a comparatively small area in this way unless a number of hoses and water connections are available. When a light frost is forecast, sufficient protection may often be obtained by watering the plants with a fine, mist-like spray several times during the evening and again early in the morning, keeping them wet until the temperature has risen above freezing.

Tall, slender plants, such as dahlias and gladioli, are not as well adapted to this method of frost protection as are lower, more bushy types, due to the weight of the ice load that builds up on the plant and is apt to cause breakage of the stalks. This does not usually happen, however, unless the temperature drops below 27°F.

If a sudden, light frost has caught one unawares and no precautions have been taken, plants can sometimes be salvaged by protecting them immediately from direct sunshine so that they will have a chance to thaw out gradually. Potted plants can be moved to a completely shaded area for this purpose.

PREVENTING TRANSPLANTING LOSSES

At the time of transplanting many feeder roots are often injured or destroyed, and the water-absorbing capacity of the root system itself is consequently greatly reduced. Unless the top growth is also appreciably reduced, or measures are taken to reduce the transpiration of water from the leaves, wilting usually occurs because the plant is unable to maintain a balance between water intake and outgo. Some plants tend to wilt more rapidly than others and are slower in making a recovery. In cases of very severe wilting there is a complete destruction of the cells and the plant dies.

The usual precaution taken by the gardener is to do the transplanting on a cloudy day when there is an abundance of moisture in the air; but this is not always possible. Artificial shade may be provided temporarily for newly transplanted stock, but this involves considerable labor and expense.

An alternative method is to spray the plants with a special material that reduces water loss before they are transplanted. In order to be effective, such a spray must have the ability to control the amount of water transpired by the leaves without stopping it completely, and it must not interfere with the proper gas exchange. A number of such sprays have been developed that meet these requirements, and these are sold under various trade names. Such sprays can be useful to the gardener, as they help to cut transplanting losses and setbacks to a minimum. Used according to the manufacturers' directions, and applied prior to transplanting, these sprays facilitate moving deciduous trees and shrubs that are in leaf, as well as evergreens that must be dug under less than optimum conditions.

CONTROL OF INSECT PESTS AND DISEASES

It requires constant vigilance on the part of the gardener to keep insect pests and diseases under control, and it is necessary to be able to recognize the first symptoms of disease, or the first manifestation of the presence of injurious insects. The effectiveness of any treatment depends upon the promptness, frequency and knowledge with which it is applied and the thoroughness of the application.

The identification and full description of the more common insect pests and diseases, as well as the most approved measures of control and application, are given in Chapter 32.

6

THE INDOOR
GARDEN

36.1 Job's tears (Coix lacryma-jobi) *in a hanging pot. Photo Grant Heilman*

36

Gardening Indoors

Contemporary houses present the gardener with many stimulating new opportunities and challenges for the dramatic and aesthetic use of plants. Great expanses of glass reaching from ceiling to floor; intricate room dividers with specially designed built-in boxes for plants; walls of brick or stone — all are adaptable to using plants with imagination and skill. Many houses have "sunken" floor wells into which large potted plants may be set, and overhead "bubble" skylights make it possible to grow large plants where least expected. When well used, plants add distinction and a very special vitality to indoor living spaces.

Houses built with less extravagant use of glass, and even the typical modest apartment or suburban dwelling, can also accommodate a wide selection of plants. Almost every American home, be it large or small, understated or opulent, can provide adequate growing conditions for some kind of living plants. By carefully choosing plants and containers to suit particular needs — and perhaps even after some trial and error to gain experience — the average indoor gardener usually can achieve the type of overall effect desired.

Never before has such a wealth of plant material been available for these purposes. For example, in recent years, plant explorers have discovered, growing in the dim light of tropical jungles, new plants that are admirably adapted to the subdued light of interiors in the modern suburban home and city apartment. Some of these plants, with their huge, glossy, deeply lobed leaves, are exotic and exciting in appearance, while others are valued for their gentler qualities of delicate leaf pattern and iridescent hues on the undersurface of the foliage.

Recently, horticulturists also have developed many new cultivated varieties with interesting leaf forms, or with variegated foliage, or splashed with white and dusted with gold — a kaleidoscope of color and form bringing life and animation to any indoor planting composition. Especially suited to the more traditional type of home are the new varieties of ivy and begonia and African violets, all of which add color, warmth and bloom to the window garden. Few foliage plants are more decorative than some of the new hybrid begonias, for example, and a pebble-filled tray containing pots of a number of varieties with contrasting leaf forms and subtle colorings possesses great beauty and distinction.

Though each person's lifestyle is different, anyone with even only a latent "green thumb" can find some time in an actively scheduled life to grow superb house plants. An important part of such success lies in the careful selection of plants, and part lies in analyzing the potential of each home to support such plants. Then, by assiduously modifying the indoor environment to suit the final choices, the indoor gardener can easily accommodate many kinds of plants.

Another important aspect of gardening in-

715

doors is the proper care and feeding of the plants. For those willing to give plants what they need and when they need it—before they begin to languish—the reward is the beauty of well-grown and thriving house plants.

INDOOR ENVIRONMENTS

Houses and lifestyles determine the success of indoor gardening. Beautiful plants, as living things, demand care and attention. Their requirements for life are few, but these needs must be supplied or the plants will not thrive. Success begins in having a knowledge of plant needs and then matching the proper plant to the appropriate indoor environment. To do this, one must first analyze the physical conditions of a house. The natural light entering windows with different exposures varies, hence different plants will thrive in different windows. Sometimes modifications can adjust the environment, making it more suitable for plants. For instance, palms, begonias and geraniums may grow well all winter in an east window with no protection from the sun's rays. However, from April to the end of September a sheer curtain should be used to soften the strong spring and summer sunlight for the palm and begonia. But since the geranium grows better in full summer sunlight, it should be moved to an uncurtained east window, where it will thrive with a group of succulents that also enjoy sunlight with no special shading. Likewise, humidity can readily be increased in an interior garden if necessary, and extra light for plant growth also can be easily added by the gardener.

In order to attain success with indoor plants, however, it is essential to learn something about each plant's cultural requirements. Then, with modifications of the environment—at times this can be something as simple as installing a curtain in an east window—it is possible to enjoy a wide variety of plants. Selections, of course, should be made with care, and the specific requirements of each plant must be met as completely as possible. In any case, it is essential that such considerations as light, temperature, ventilation and humidity are carefully studied so that the most favorable environmental conditions are established for the plants one se-

lects. Each of these factors may be modified, often with very simple procedures, to create a balanced, healthy environment for plant life. A good rule of thumb is that if a newly acquired plant lives without declining for three to six months, then it can probably thrive in that situation indefinitely. Exceptions to this general rule are *Araucaria, Aspidistra* and some palms, for example, which are able to stay green for months in low light but eventually will slowly decline because they lack proper growing conditions.

Light

Light is essential to the growth of all plants, which contain chlorophyll. The leaves serve as a manufacturing center for plant food, and this process is carried on under the direct influence of light. If the leaves are entirely deprived of light, they are unable to perform the function of food manufacture, and they gradually turn yellow and die.

Though light is the most important growth requirement for healthy plants, many people often overlook this fact in their eagerness to enjoy plants in interior situations away from windows. Supplemental electric lighting can be very effective in keeping house plants healthy (see Chapter 37). For example, a simple reading lamp, set 3 ft. or closer to a plant on an end table, can give the plant that extra bit of light it needs to maintain itself. However, it is essential that the homeowner consistently use the same light each evening for it to be effective. If this light becomes part of the usual evening illumination, then it will function both to light the room and to stimulate the nearby plant to manufacture a little extra food.

Sufficient light for plants in interior spaces away from windows may also be provided by mercury-vapor spotlights designed specifically to stimulate plant growth. Such lights are comparatively new on the commercial market, but their use in private homes is becoming as important as their present function in public buildings, where plants frequently are subjected to low light levels. These new mercury-vapor spotlights are revolutionizing the range and scope of indoor gardening, though admittedly

36.2 *A shelf full of* Begonia *at window level; the floor space below also becomes a plant place by the addition of fluorescent lights on the bottom of the shelf. Photo George Elbert*

they are still rarely used in the home. While the initial outlay may seem excessive, self-ballasted mercury-vapor lights are really no more expensive than two fluorescent tubes and the fixture they require. The mercury light is stronger over greater distance than are the fluorescent tubes, and it also needs no special fixture but can fit into any standard incandescent socket. The spotlights will not function on a rheostat, so cannot be dimmed, and they are not recommended as reading lamps because of their intensity. Their development is, however, a great step forward in modifying the general environment to satisfy the needs of plants.

Plants vary tremendously in the intensity of light required for their best development. Many of the ferns, which in their native habitat grow in dense woodland shade, require comparatively dim light, though they do demand high humidity. Most foliage plants, particularly those that are native to the tropical jungles and rain forests of Central and South America, thrive best in diffused natural light. In the home, a north window will best meet the needs of such plants, and some may even be grown

successfully in the interior of the room, away from a window. There are comparatively few foliage house plants that can tolerate direct sunlight, particularly the afternoon summer sun. Plants with variegated foliage require more light, due to the fact that the cells in the white portion of the leaves contain little or no chlorophyll, and therefore they are unable to carry on the manufacture of food.

Most flowering plants require full sunlight, or sun for at least the major portion of the day. Such plants thrive best in a window with a southern or southeastern exposure. A few flowering plants, however, such as *Achimenes, Steptocarpus* and the African violet, prefer limited sun and should be grown in a window with an eastern exposure.

When house plants are left in one position for any length of time, the leaves and stems will inevitably turn toward the light and the growth of the plant will become very unsymmetrical. In order to avoid this tendency, the pots should be turned at frequent intervals so that all portions of the plant may receive an equal amount of light. The growth will then remain symmetrical and well balanced.

Temperature

Every plant has an optimum temperature range that provides the most favorable conditions for maximum growth. Some plants suffer seriously when there are fluctuations of temperature much above or below this range, while others are able to withstand great fluctuations without suffering serious damage.

The majority of house plants thrive well in a moderate temperature, ranging between 62° and 70°F., with a somewhat cooler temperature at night. Some plants require a very warm temperature, between 75° and 80°F., and will not make satisfactory growth unless this requirement is met, while still others will thrive only in a very cool temperature, 50° to 60°F. Plants in this group are best suited to growing on a cool porch, or in a closed-off room that is not occupied.

When plants are grown on window sills or ledges, it is a wise precaution to place a heavy layer of newspaper between the plants and the window on severely cold nights. This simple preventive measure will provide excellent insulation for the plant when it needs it most.

Ventilation

Though house plants require an ample supply of fresh air, they must be protected from direct drafts and from being suddenly chilled. Ventilating should, therefore, be done in such a way that the plants are protected from direct currents of cold air. It is wise to provide a change of air at least twice a day in a room where plants are grown. In mild weather the doors or windows of the room may be opened; in severe weather it may be advisable to open the windows in an adjoining room, so that the plants are not subjected to direct drafts. Ventilation has a direct influence in mitigating the effects of coal gas and heating and cooking gas. Some plants, such as the Jerusalem cherry, are extremely sensitive and even a minute quantity of gas in the atmosphere will have a most damaging effect, causing a blackening of the buds and a discoloration of the leaves. In the fruiting stage, the fruit will drop prematurely.

Humidity

Closely associated with the problems of ventilation and watering is that of humidity. A moist atmosphere is essential to the health and vigor of most house plants. Comparatively few plants can thrive, or even survive, in a dry, almost desertlike atmosphere. It is impossible, therefore, to expect satisfactory growth unless every effort is made to increase the humidity of the atmosphere, and this may be accomplished in several very simple ways. Some heating systems are equipped with humidifying devices, and special water-holding compartments are attached to some types of radiators. If such devices are not already part of the heating system, water pans may be purchased and attached to the radiators. Another excellent method of increasing the humidity is to set the plants on metal or plastic trays that have been filled with pebbles and water. The bottom of the pots should rest on dry pebbles above the level of the water. This method may also be used with flowerpot saucers, while making sure that the water around the pebbles does not reach the bottom of the pot, since this would cause the soil to be constantly saturated.

Because of the wide interest in growing plants under fluorescent lights (see Chapter 37), many practical horticultural items are available in garden centers and specialty plant shops that cater to indoor plant growers. It is now easy to obtain rectangular plastic plant trays to hold the pebbles and the water that will increase humidity. These trays usually measure 11 in. by 22 in., and two of them fit perfectly under a standard 4-ft. fluorescent fixture. Perlite, vermiculite and long-fiber sphagnum moss is sometimes used in place of pebbles. And the molded, plastic panels used to cover fluorescent ceiling fixtures—sometimes referred to as "egg crate"—can be cut and used instead of pebbles or other material in humidity trays. Water is added almost to the top of the holes in the "egg crate," and the pots will then remain high and dry, while the humidification effect is the same as if using pebbles. This system is easier to keep clean and is lighter in weight than pebbles. The new, nonwoven capillary mat material that is used to water plants automatically from below (see index) also functions as a good source of humidity, and many people are using this material in plant trays in place of either pebbles or "egg crates." Any of these methods will increase the general level of humidity around house plants. You must choose your own system, based upon the availability of material and your personal preferences.

A daily syringing of house plants is often suggested as an ideal method of increasing humidity and cleaning leaf surfaces. This practice is the common way to increase humidity in greenhouses where a large amount of water can usually be splashed around with abandon. Though some avid indoor gardeners can afford to have wall and floor areas made of stone, concrete or other water-tolerant materials in the gardening sites of their homes, most of us, unfortunately, must avoid wetting wall and floor surfaces. Admittedly, syringing has an immediate effect upon the local environment of plants; but its long-range effect, in most homes or apartments, is questionable. Many indoor gardeners, in recent years, have purchased humidifiers for either individual rooms or even the entire house, to the total benefit of their plants and their own health as well. If you are unable to operate and maintain a humidifier, however, the alternative is simply to concentrate on plants that have proven their ability to survive low humidity.

Many house plants benefit greatly from a summer spent outdoors in dappled shade, or with only morning sunlight, or other ideal situations. Although not everyone can move house plants out for the summer, those who can usually do so willingly because of the wonderful growth a plant accomplishes in several months of ideal conditions. Often, plants that are summered outdoors live easily in houses during the moderate spring and fall months when the harsh, dry heating system of the house or apartment does not operate continually. The growth achieved in the summer outdoors on either a modest apartment terrace or at ground level may be sufficient to carry a plant through the harder winter months when it is standing in front of a coolish window.

CULTURAL PRACTICES

Most indoor plants are grown in pots or tubs of soil, and many of these containers serve their purposes well, provided they have drainage holes in the bottom. These holes should be covered with a layer of pebbles or pieces of broken clay pot to keep the soil inside and yet allow excess water to drain away. It is extremely difficult to use an undrained container for an extended period without harming the plant. For most gardeners, success is easily achieved by using containers with adequate drainage holes. The container in which the plant is growing can be hidden inside a decorative cachepot or a second container that is undrained. In effect, this is the same as placing the potted plant in a saucer. In both instances, the excess water that drains out of the soil must be emptied so that the plant will not constantly be standing in water; otherwise its roots will die from lack of oxygen in the soil saturated by stagnant water.

From a decorative point of view, many people like to standardize the color and material of the flowerpots they use. A collection of plants all in white plastic pots has a pleasing unity, even though the plants themselves have varying cultural demands.

Soil Mixtures

Different plants demand different types of soil; deciding what mix to use comes with experience and horticultural common sense.

An excellent general purpose potting mixture consists of 1 part sand, 2 parts fibrous loam, 1 part humus in the form of compost, leaf mold or peat and ½ part well-rotted cow manure. This mixture should be combined with a 5-in. potful of ground limestone or bone meal and thoroughly stirred into each bushel of the mix. The mix should then be screened before using. However, since few of us have ready access to the rural components called for above, we have modified the recipe to the following proportions:

BASIC SOIL MIX

---

1 qt. soil (from garden or yard; do not use pure clay)
1 qt. builder's sharp sand
2 qts. peat moss (sphagnum or Canadian peat)
1 tbs. dolomitic limestone or 1 tbs. bone meal

Soil

Soil taken from the garden or yard is variable, yet the mineral content and weight is useful. When minerals are available in the mix, one does not have to rely completely upon fertilizer for the trace minerals necessary for plant growth. Soil weight, combined with the sand used for drainage, is important when potting large plants that need a heavy soil for stability. When we mix soil for pot culture, anchoring the plant is important, but aeration and drainage are equally important.

Sand

Sand, which is readily obtained from a builder's yard, should be as sharp and as coarse as possible. In fact, aquarium gravel could even be substituted; it is almost impossible to find sand that is too coarse. Avoid very fine beach sand, or the sand that is used for children's sandboxes, as such fine sand will pack together with other components in the soil mix and will not provide the necessary drainage and aeration. For cacti and succulents, increase the sand to one-half the total mix, then combine it with small pebbles and finely broken brick or flowerpot shards.

Peat Moss (sometimes called Canadian peat)

Derived from sphagnum moss, peat moss is usually dark brown to reddish in color, depending on the source and moisture content. This material is acid (pH 4.5 to 4.6) and for most plants limestone is necessary to bring the pH up to about 6 to 6.5. You may need to add more or less limestone, depending upon the pH of your water supply. In the northwest and northeast parts of the country the water is generally acid, so more limestone will not be detrimental. In Florida or southern California the water is alkaline and therefore less limestone should be added.

The peat moss derived from sedges and reeds is black. It is usually sold in plastic bags in a slightly moist condition and is sometimes called humus or Michigan peat. It is generally more finely divided than the sphagnum (Canadian) peat. This type of peat moss is very useful in mixes for ferns, begonias, African violets and other plants that have delicate fibrous roots. Use it to replace half of the Canadian peat.

Lime

Lime is granular, dolomitic or ground, and is used to bring the pH level of the soil mix nearer to neutral (pH 7.0 is neutral; lower values are acid, and higher values are alkaline). One tbs. of agricultural ground limestone per quart of peat moss is usually sufficient.

Bone Meal

Made from waste animal bones, bone meal contains calcium just as limestone does and acts in the same way to make soil mix more alkaline. However, bone meal has a slow fertilizing effect that limestone lacks. It is often used as a spring-

time topdressing when it is worked into the upper few inches of soil in pots of plants that are not repotted each year, such as mature fig trees.

Perlite

A white volcanic rock that is light in weight, porous and sterile. It may be used as a replacement for sand but actually aerates soil better than sand. Perlite does not deteriorate, nor does it contain nutrients.

Vermiculite

Made by heating mica until it expands. A horticultural grade (small particles) and an insulating grade (larger particles) are available, and both types are useful as soil conditioners to aerate soil and to take the place of sand. The horticultural grade is most frequently used and is practical for the smaller flowerpots. Nutrients and water are held in the platelike structure, which contains small amounts of potassium, calcium and magnesium useful to plant growth. It is sterile when new, but after several years the particles in vermiculite break down and collapse so that it loses its aerating ability.

Mixes Made without Soil

In recent years various mixes have been developed that do not depend upon either soil or loam. These, of course, are ideal for apartment dwellers who cannot readily obtain the usual soil, and are also used extensively by people who garden under artificial light.

SOIL-LESS MIX 1

1 qt. sphagnum peat moss
1 qt. horticultural vermiculite
1 qt. perlite (coarse or medium preferred)
1 tbs. dolomitic limestone

This mix is ideal for tropical plants that require good drainage, aeration, and that have the ability to withstand drying out between watering. Use it for bromeliads, hoyas, peperomias, philodendrons, dracaenas, sansevarias, ficus, rhizomatous begonias and geraniums.

SOIL-LESS MIX 2

A	B
2 qts. sphagnum peat	3 qts. sphagnum peat
1 qt. vermiculite	2 qts. perlite
1 qt. perlite	1 qt. vermiculite
2 tbs. limestone	3 tbs. limestone

This mix is heavier and, therefore, will hold and retain moisture longer. The second choice, (B), is drained even better, and is intended for those indoor gardeners who have a tendency to water their plants too heavily. This mix should be used with plants that have fine root systems, like most gesneriads, ferns, begonias, caladiums, coleus and marantas.

SOIL-LESS MIX 3

1 qt. sphagnum peat
2 qts. perlite
2 qts. vermiculite
1 tbs. limestone

Use this for succulents, cacti and some dry-growing bromeliads.

Since the above three soil-less mixes contain no fertilizer, it is necessary to apply some that are soluble. Again, there are several methods to choose from. Some growers apply one-half strength (as directed by the manufacturer) fertilizer every other watering. Other growers fertilize with 1/8 or 1/10 strength fertilizer at every watering. Both types of applications should be omitted every fifth watering, to allow some of the extra fertilizer to leach out of the soil.

Potting

House plants should be repotted only when they will derive very definite benefit, and it has been found that plants vary greatly in their needs for frequent potting. Most flowering plants will, like the geraniums, give better bloom if they are allowed to become somewhat pot-bound. Such plants as amaryllis, the various palms, podocarpus and schefflera will also thrive well in very small pots, and these seem to suffer no ill effects from becoming extremely pot-bound. Many house plants may be grown in comparatively small pots if sufficient nutrients are provided in the form of occasional applications of a complete fertilizer (see page 722 on Feeding).

However, young plants, grown either from seed or from cuttings, must be put into larger pots at frequent intervals to accommodate their more rapid growth. The general practice is to repot such plants as soon as the pots they occupy become well filled with roots. Unless this is done, the plants may become stunted, and will be unable to make normal and vigorous growth. A pot from 1/2 in. to 1 in. larger in size is usually sufficient for the next stage of growth.

When plants are grown in pots, it is essential that ample drainage be provided. In small pots a piece of broken pot (crock) placed over the hole in the bottom of the pot will usually be sufficient. When large pots are used, and particularly if the plant is to remain in the pot for some time, it is wise to place a layer of crock in the bottom. This layer should be 3/4 in. deep in 6-in. to 8-in. pots, and up to 3 in. to 4 in. deep in pots that are 18 in. to 24 in. in diameter.

In potting your seedlings or rooted cuttings, the pot may be partially filled with soil. The plant should be held in place, with the roots spread out in a natural position. The remaining soil should then be added and pressed firmly into place with the fingers. In small pots a space of approximately 1/2 in. should be left between the surface of the soil and the rim of the pot. In potting rooted cuttings, a soil mixture consisting of 2 parts sharp sand, 1 part loam and 1 part leaf mold or peat is recommended. For young seedlings in the early transplanting stages, a mixture of 1 part sand, 1 part loam and 1 part leaf mold or peat moss will give excellent results. The pots should be watered thoroughly and shaded from direct sunlight for several days, in order that the plants may have an opportunity to become reestablished.

In repotting an established plant, the plant may easily be removed by inverting the pot and gently tapping the rim on the edge of a firm surface, such as the edge of a potting bench or a work table. The soil in the pot should be fairly moist so that it does not crumble, and while the pot is held in an inverted position, one hand should be held firmly over the ball of earth. A small quantity of soil should be placed over the drainage material and the plant then placed in the center of the new pot. If the pot is only slightly larger than the one in which the plant had previously grown, it will be necessary to remove some soil from the bottom and sides of the ball of earth surrounding the roots. This should be done with care so that the root system is kept as nearly intact as possible. The space between the old ball of earth and the side of the new pot should then be filled with the new potting soil, which should be firmed into place with the fingers or with a small potting stick.

Watering

The watering of house plants is a task that requires good judgment and common sense. It is quite as important not to overwater as it is to avoid underwatering. Not only do different species of plants vary tremendously in their moisture requirements, but individual plants also vary considerably according to the stage of growth. When plants are making active growth, forming new shoots and flower buds, they obviously require much more water than they do when they are in the resting, nonflowering stage. Although daily watering is not necessary for all house plants, it is wise to make a daily survey in order to ascertain their needs. When the surface of the soil in the pot is dry to the point of being crumbly to the touch, or if the (clay) pot gives a hollow, ringing sound when it is tapped lightly with the knuckle, the plant needs water. If water is applied to the surface of the soil by means of a watering can, the surplus water will drain out through the opening in the bottom of the pot. If watering is done by placing the pot in a pan of water, it should be allowed to remain in the receptacle until the surface of the soil becomes dark and moist in appearance. The pot should then be removed and the surplus water allowed to drain away. This method of watering is excellent for those plants that have dense, fuzzy leaves, such as the African violet and gloxinia. In any case, pots should never be allowed to stand in saucers that are filled with water, as the soil in the bottom will soon become soggy and sour, and the growth and vigor of the plant will be seriously affected. Note that the temperature of the water used should always be approximately the same as that of the room.

Feeding

Many house plants benefit by regular feedings. Applications of fertilizer should be made when the plants are making active, vigorous growth, such as during the spring and summer or after the flower buds have formed but before the flowers have begun to show color. At this period of growth a light application of fertilizer may be made at two-week intervals. No application should be made when the plants are in a resting stage during the fall and winter.

There are many excellent, rapidly soluble fertilizers on the market today that are suitable for house plants. A preparation should be chosen that contains trace elements as well as the major elements. The instructions on the container concerning the rate of application should always be followed with care. Many people use two different brands of soluble fertilizer and alternate the application of each.

GENERAL CARE OF HOUSE PLANTS

Keeping Foliage in Good Condition

Plants transpire through their leaves. When the foliage becomes coated with a film of fine dust particles, or with soot from heaters, it seriously interferes with this natural process, and the plants suffer in consequence. In order to keep the foliage of house plants with glossy leaves clean and healthy, the leaves should be syringed or cleansed at periodic intervals, at least once or twice a month. Plants with thick, hairy leaves, such as the African violets and gloxinias, should not be treated in this manner.

If one has only a few plants that require attention and they are not too large, they may be placed in the kitchen sink or in a laundry or bathtub, and syringed with a fine but fairly strong spray of lukewarm water from the faucet. Both the upper and undersurfaces of the leaves should be treated this way. The foliage should then be allowed to dry before the plants are placed again in full sunlight, in order to avoid the possibility of burning tender leaves.

In the case of large plants that cannot be moved easily, the leaves may be wiped with a damp cloth or sponge.

If plants are kept on pebbles in a metal tray, a small hand syringe may be used very effectively. The syringing should be done on a dry day and the foliage should be protected from direct sunlight while it is wet.

Dividing House Plants

Many foliage plants benefit greatly from occasional division and replanting. Not all plants can be handled in this way, however, because of their habit of growth. In general, plants that grow in clumps, with several stems rising from below the soil, each with a separate root system, may be divided successfully.

The procedure is simple. The plant should be removed from the pot. The soil should then be shaken away from the roots, and the sections should be gently pulled apart. It is important that each section have good roots. In some cases it may be necessary to cut the sections off the main stock plant with a sharp knife.

Long, straggly roots should be cut back, and in some cases it may be advisable to remove one or two of the old leaves, retaining the younger, more vigorous growth only.

Each section should be planted in a pot of sufficient size, using a good potting mixture. The soil should be worked well about the roots in order to prevent air pockets, and it then should be well firmed. After the plant has been watered, it should be placed in subdued light for several days.

PEST AND DISEASE CONTROL

House plants are subject to attacks by insects and related pests. Many pests can be present when the plants are purchased, despite the best efforts on the part of the commercial growers who raise them. So check plants carefully.

Some plants are rarely infested and require no special treatment. Others, however, are so susceptible to one or more pests that special treatments are required from time to time to keep them healthy and reasonably free of the pests.

Though syringing with a fine stream of water every few weeks will help considerably in reducing insect populations, this practice alone cannot be depended upon for good control, particularly on the plants that are most often infested with insects and mites.

Plants that are summered outdoors are more apt to be infested by insects and related pests than those kept indoors the year round.

Indoor plants with a vinelike habit (ivy, kangaroo vine, small-leaved philodendrons, wandering Jew) and those with leaves close to the soil, like African violet, are difficult to spray. Some gardeners find it more convenient to dip such plants into an insecticide-water mixture. A 1- or 2-gallon can is filled with the diluted insecticide, the flowerpot is inverted and the leaves and stems dipped into the solution. To prevent the soil from dropping into the insecticide, cover the soil surface with newspaper, cardboard or aluminum foil.

Large plants, obviously, cannot be handled in this way. These must be sprayed with the proper insecticide *in situ*, or moved to the bathroom or outdoors on a mild day and sprayed, whichever is more convenient. The very lightweight and inexpensive plastic "drop cloths" sold in hardware stores are useful for protecting rugs and walls if a plant needs to be sprayed in place.

Ready-to-use insecticides in push-button cans are available in hardware, department and garden supply stores. These usually contain rotenone, pyrethrum, malathion and other active ingredients. One of the most recently introduced insecticides in such cans for controlling certain pests on house plants, particularly whiteflies, is a synthetic pyrethroid containing Resmethrin (SBP-1382). Sold under the name Pratt Whitefly Spray, it also controls aphids and exposed thrips on African violets, begonias, coleus, philodendron and many other house plants.

When using insecticides in push-button cans, be sure to hold the nozzle at least 18 in. from the leaves and give them just a light, quick misting, not a drenching. Prolonged wetting may cause injury to the leaves or even death of the plant.

Insecticide applications should be repeated every ten days to two weeks for as long as the pests are present. The spray chart on page 726 gives details on controlling the most common pests on many kinds of house plants.

Generally speaking, fungus and bacterial diseases of the leaves are not common on house plants because the atmosphere is much too dry to favor their development. One exception, however, is the fungus disease known as powdery mildew that causes brown dead areas on the leaves. It is especially common on begonias, particularly the new Reiger *elatior* types, and on miniature roses. Spraying the leaves with benomyl (trade name Benlate) diluted as directed by the manufacturer will provide control.

More common than leaf diseases are certain diseases of the roots and lower stems. The fungi responsible for such diseases develop most frequently in waterlogged soils. When the soil surface is kept too wet, the crown of the plant will rot. This is especially prevalent in African violets, caladiums and geraniums.

Providing the proper conditions and a little "tender loving care" will assure long and continuous enjoyment of green gardens indoors.

HOUSE PLANTS

Foliage plants are an endless source of pleasure. Their variation is tremendous, ranging all the way from hanging baskets of tradescantia, to accent plants like palms, to miniatures like peperomias in a window. Some foliage plants may produce the extra bonus of flowers, like well-grown fancy-leaved geraniums. But most foliage plants do not overpower us with bloom; they respond, rather, to cultural attention by growing larger and more beautiful. While large, old specimens may be exceptionally beautiful, they can really outgrow their usefulness by becoming too large for a particular place. Before this happens, however, one can usually propagate a new plant and have it already established to replace the first, when the time comes. But there is much to be said for such venerable old house plants as twenty-year-old jade plants and Christmas cacti.

36.3 A terrarium (this one temporarily without its glass cover for the sake of better viewing) not only provides a controlled environment for small plants but also offers the opportunity to create interesting compositions. Photo George Elbert

The list of indoor plants that follows includes those that are moderately easy to maintain; attention is given only to any special requirements of each plant under discussion. If no mention of a special requirement is made, then the plant needs only the basic soil mix (page 719) and the normal amount of watering when dry (page 722), along with the usual fertilization schedule (page 722).

Aglaonema commutatum and Varieties (Chinese evergreen)

A low-light plant, it grows in jungle shade and can tolerate abusive care. Whether grown in regular potting soil or kept alive a long time in plain water, this plant will stay green and healthy in dim light, though it will not increase in size very quickly. When grown in better light, however, it responds well by making new leaves and may occasionally even produce a curious flower resembling a calla lily. A temperature range of 60° to 80°F. and moist soil is appropriate.

Araucaria heterophylla (*A. excelsa,* **Norfolk Island pine**)

This plant is a forest giant in its native home and is striking for the radial, tiered symmetry of its spikelike branches in whorls along the trunk. It will tolerate low light levels, but in such illumination will grow only very slowly. Under these conditions, plants have been known to stay green for several years but they will not produce new branches or growth. In such situations the plant is receiving only enough light to maintain itself, not enough to produce new growth. In order to flourish, this plant needs good light, so it definitely benefits from a summer spent out of doors. Afterwards it easily tolerates the winter's stay indoors. Norfolk Island pines are difficult for the average homeowner to propagate, so once it outgrows its home it should be replaced by a new seedling tree. Ideal temperatures are 50° to 55°F. at night and 68° to 72°F. during the day, though plants will tolerate just a touch of frost if grown outdoors. Only normal soil and watering are required.

Asparagus sprengeri **and Other Species and Cultivars (asparagus fern)**

Grow in bright light (curtain-filtered in summer) with a cool night temperature of 50° to 55°F. Keep soil uniformly moist when in active growth — that is, when actually making new branches — but during the winter the plant will tolerate going quite dry, because its roots are underground water-storage organs. If set outside for the summer, expect some "leaf" drop when the plant is brought back in at the end of the season. The plant will recover, though it resents the transition to a harsher environment.

Aspidistra elatior (*A. lurida,* **cast-iron plant**)

Another low-light house plant that will stay green and attractive in poor light for a long time. To make the most of this plant, summer it outdoors in medium shade. This is the ideal plant for apartments where light is insufficient for anything else — put it in a dim window, and if any plant can survive this one should. A low-light house plant is *not* a no-light house plant, however, and the more indirect light that *Aspidistra* receives, the better. The plant will tolerate temperatures from 45° to 85°F. but prefers 60° to 72°F. and a barely moist soil.

Aucuba japonica (**Japanese laurel**)

This vigorous shrub (to 3 ft.) with variegated, oval foliage is hardy outdoors in most southern states, but is adaptable to becoming a large house plant if it is kept cool and well lighted (four hours' sun daily) during its stay in the house. It needs only regular potting soil and normal care, but profits greatly from a summer spent outdoors. It prefers 40° to 50°F. at night, and normal daytime temperatures.

Begonia

Since there are many species of begonias with diverse growth habits, they have been given the following horticultural classification system by devoted begonia growers:

CATEGORY	NOTES
Canelike	strong upright grower, sometimes called angel-wing begonia
Shrublike	even stronger upright grower, main stems develop many lateral branches
Thick stem	thickened base, not quite a tuber
Semperflorens	wax begonia, ever-blooming, easiest culture
Rex cultorum	rex and rexlike hybrids; low light but high humidity
Rhizomatous	foliage-type begonia; good house plant; flowers in spring if given sufficient light
Tuberous	bulblike root stock, high humidity important; growth and flowers in summer, rests in winter
Trailing	vinelike, may be grown in hanging baskets

HOUSE PLANT SPRAY CHART

Plant	Pest	What to Look For	Treatment
African violet	Cyclamen mites. Young, glassy white to pale green, 1/100 in. Adults, pale brown, difficult to detect.	Center growth is hard, stunted, very hairy, and curls upward.	Kelthane (25% liquid) 1 tsp. per gallon water, or Kelthane in push-button cans.
	Mealy bugs. White cottony fluffs in leaf axils or along veins. Adults pink, oval, with white, powdery wax covering.	Weak plants due to sucking out of leaf juices. Bugs secrete honeydew on which sooty mold fungus grows.	Spray with nicotine sulphate (Black Leaf 40), 3/4 tsp. per quart soapy water.
Begonia	Aphids. Small, gray, green, red or black, soft-bodied insects.	Same as above	Malathion or cythion (50% liquid). 1/2 tsp. per quart water, or nicotine sulphate as for African violet.
	Mealy bugs	See African violet	Same as above
	Cyclamen mites	Stunted, distorted leaves and flowers.	Kelthane as for African violet
Cacti	Mealy bugs	See African violet	Nicotine sulphate as for African violet
	Scales. Adults have various shapes, are motionless. Young crawler stage too small to be seen with the naked eye.	Suck out juices, resulting in poor growth, weak plants. Secrete honeydew like aphids.	Same as above, nicotine sulphate
Coleus	Mealy bugs	See African violet	Same as for African violet
Ferns	Fern scale. Adult females brown and oyster-shaped. Males, thin, white, conspicuous.	Suck out juices, weaken and kill plants.	Nicotine sulphate as for mealy bugs on African violet, or Cedo-Flora as recommended by manufacturer.
	Mealy bugs	See African violet	Same as above
	Whitefly. Young, oval, thin, flat semitransparent on undersides of leaves. Adults have white, wedge-shaped wings, fly readily when disturbed.	Suck out juices, resulting in weak plants	Use synthetic pyrethroid (SBP-1382) sold as Pratt Whitefly Spray in aerosol cans.
Fuchsia	Cyclamen mites	See Begonia	Kelthane as for African violet
	Mealy bugs	See African violet	Malathion or cythion as for aphids on begonia
	Scales	Same as for scale on ferns	Same as for scale on ferns
	Whitefly	Same as for whitefly on ferns	Same as for whitefly on ferns
Gardenia	Mealy bugs	Same as for mealy bugs on African violet	Same as for scale on ferns
	Scales	Same as for scale on ferns	Same as for scale on ferns

HOUSE PLANT SPRAY CHART (Continued)

Plant	Pest	What to Look For	Treatment
Geranium	Cyclamen mites	See Begonia	Kelthane as for African violet
	Red spider mites. Tiny, yellow, orange or greenish pests on undersides of leaves. Make fine webs.	Leaves speckled gray-green or yellow	Kelthane as for cyclamen mites on African violet
	Whitefly	See Ferns	See Ferns
Ivy	Aphids	See Begonia	Same as for aphids on begonia
	Mealy bugs	See African violet	Same as for African violet
	Scales	See Ferns	See Ferns
	Spider mites	See Geranium	Kelthane as for African violet
Palms	Mealy bugs	See African violet	Malathion as for African violet
	Scales	Same as for scale on ferns	Same as for scale on ferns
Poinsettia	Mealy bugs	See African violet	Nicotine sulphate as for mealy bugs on African violet
	Spider mites	See Geranium	Kelthane as for cyclamen mite on African violet
Rubber plant	Mealy bugs	See African violet	Malathion, or cython, or nicotine sulphate as for begonia
	Scales	See scales on cacti	Same as for scales on ferns

Begonias want bright to filtered sunlight throughout the year south of Washington, D.C., St. Louis, Mo., or Sacramento, California. North of these cities a few hours of direct winter sunlight are beneficial, as in an east or west window. A night temperature of 60° to 65°F. is ideal. Although the soil should be kept moist, it is better to practice restraint in this connection because these plants can easily be overwatered. Some species need extra humidity, as noted above. A soil mix that contains an extra amount of humus, peat or leaf mold is important. See Chapter 37 for a discussion of special begonias grown under artificial light.

Brassaia actinophylla (schefflera)

These accommodating house plants are attractive either as small seedlings or as large specimen plants. Given moderate care, a small seedling can grow into a handsome large plant in several years. Young plants have small leaves with three to five radially arranged leaflets. As the plant matures more leaflets are added, eventually developing up to sixteen leaflets each 2 in. to 3 in. wide and up to 15 in. long. Scheffleras do best if they get a few hours of direct sunlight each day, although they can also adjust to less light and are slower-growing.

Keep the soil moderately dry between thorough watering.

Bromeliads

A number of new species have become available on the commercial market during the last few years because people are becoming increasingly successful in growing bromeliads, those curious plants that are closely related to pineapples. Bromeliads require bright light and some sun. They also need a very open potting mix — like an orchid's — and the cup, formed by their funneling leaves, should be filled with water. The roots need just enough water to keep the potting media barely moist, *but the water in the cup is most important.* Occasionally, it is beneficial to exchange the water in the cup with dilute fertilizer, and a 1/10 solution is recommended for this purpose. The main plant blooms only once, then produces new plants at the base.

Cacti

Another large group of varied plants, some of which make excellent house plants. In general, cacti thrive best in bright light to full sun, and they also need extra-sandy, well-drained soil and the usual temperatures. Most cacti profit from a cool winter period with only occasional watering; don't let them shrivel.

Christmas cacti and orchid cacti not only need more humus in their well-drained sandy mix but also an autumnal dry period. These types profit from a summer spent outdoors, as do the cacti described above. In return they may even reward you with a bonus of blooms, if they can manufacture the necessary food supplies.

Caladium

These colorful, foliage plants are purchased as bulblike tubers that demand a winter rest period. When grown in a bright, curtain-filtered window, they make excellent spring and summer plants. But don't rely on them for color from September to December; simply store the dry tubers in a plastic bag filled with vermiculite. Replant them from January to March in soil with extra peat, and keep them moist.

Ceropegia woodii (rosary vine, hearts-entangled)

Since this succulent vine forms a bulblike storage organ, the tuber, which stores water, you can occasionally allow the soil to become quite dry. These tubers form along the vining stem and they may be cut off, with a piece of this stem included, and planted in new pots to propagate the plants. Hang or suspend the vine in a sunny window — it is almost foolproof if given enough light, though it will also tolerate some shade.

Cissus rhombifolia and Other Species (grape ivy)

Given bright light and moderately good care, grape ivy will reward the indoor gardener with an overflowing pot full of vinelike foliage. This foliage may either be pruned into a shrublike plant, or allowed to climb with some support. Normal soil and watering is all that is required.

Coffea arabica (coffee tree)

In its natural environment, the coffee tree is a shrub that grows under other trees where it is protected from the strong tropical sun. Thus, it will flourish as a house plant if given bright light or curtain-filtered sun. Humidity of over 40 percent is very important to the health of this plant; otherwise the leaves will brown at the tips and edges. New plants may be grown from a fresh, unroasted coffee bean or older plants may be air-layered (see index). When doing this, use the main stem or upright side growth because the lateral, horizontal branches will not convert themselves into upright shoots even when they do root.

Dieffenbachia spp. and Cultivars (dumb cane)

Even in the wild, there is much variation in leaf color among *Dieffenbachia* plants. It is, therefore, easy to understand the variability of marking and color in plants that are grown horticulturally. The dieffenbachias are particularly valued for their decorative foliage. Since this foliage is large and the plants reach considerable size, they are best adapted for flanking north or west windows, or for use in low planting boxes or beds at floor level. In time, the plants will usually reach a height of 3 ft. to 4 ft. They require a warm temperature and good light, but no direct sunlight. A moderately acid loam best meets their needs and the plants should be kept moist. They are also sensitive to drafts and will not thrive if the temperature is too low.

There are many species and varieties. Among the most valuable for use as house plants are the following:

D. fournieri

A species from Colombia with broad elongate leaves that are dark green blotched with small ivory spots parallel with the lateral veins.

D. maculata

The commonest species in cultivation, with several named cultivars. 'Jenmonnii' is slender with narrow leaves 2½ in. wide and 10 in. long; the leaves are medium green with irregular ivory marking. 'Rudolph Roehrs' is a mutant with leaves that are almost completely creamy-white or chartreuse, with fine, white splotches.

D. oerstedii

This species has ovate to elongate-ovate leaves and ivory and light green markings.

Dionaea muscipula (Venus's-flytrap)

Because tubers of these plants can be purchased in the most unexpected places—even in drugstores—this should tell you that Venus's-flytrap is considered an intriguing novelty to most people. But, like the chameleons, it does not survive long in home culture. Since most of these plants are collected from the wild, they now unfortunately face almost certain extinction, victims of their own uniqueness. At best, the Venus's-flytrap is a fairly difficult greenhouse plant, and it does not make a good house plant at all. Not recommended.

Dizygotheca elegantissima (false aralia)

A warmish location (75° to 85°F. by day; 65° to 70°F. at night), combined with good bright light (curtain-filtered in summer), should reward the indoor gardener with substantial growth in this elegant house plant. If the new growth is stunted and the old leaves fall off, starting at the bottom, then the plant probably needs increased general humidity. It should never be allowed to dry out completely.

Dracaena spp. (corn plant)

Some of the dwarf types of dracaena adapt very well to the modern home. Being native to West Equatorial Africa, they are able to withstand the dry, overheated conditions so often encountered in apartments better than most other plants.

D. fragrans

Rugged, and therefore the type best adapted to unfavorable growing conditions.

D. godseffiana

Also described as the "gold-dust" dracaena. A compact, bushy plant seldom exceeding 18 in. in height, although under exceptionally favorable conditions it may attain 2½ ft. The glossy, oval-shaped green leaves are dusted with yellow and cream. This variety is more exacting in its cultural demands than many other types and prefers a moist but well-drained soil, rich in humus.

D. sanderana

Of dwarf habit, with the gray-green leaves banded with white. It is easily cultivated and will withstand dry conditions exceptionally well.

Episcia (carpet plant)

See Chapter 37.

Fatshedera pizei (shrub ivy)

Fatshedera is easier to grow than *Fatsia* (see below) because it is more tolerant of dry conditions and low light. *Fatsia japonica* was hybridized with English ivy *(Hedera helix)* to produce the hybrid, hence the name: *Fatshedera.* It combines the parental characteristics; the English ivy makes it a semierect shrub that will eventually need some support. It should be kept cool and moist with good light.

Fatsia japonica

This is a broad-leaved plant that is usually grown as a single specimen in a pot. It needs moist soil and cool conditions, with temperatures of 55° to 60°F. at night and 65° to 70° by day. A light-demanding plant that needs winter sun in the north.

Ferns

Ferns demand stable conditions and generally high humidity, a combination few homes can offer without the help of a humidifier. A few of the most tolerant ferns can stand some draft and require more light than the rest, which demand at least 60 percent humidity and up to 80 percent when making new growth.

Ferns should be grown in a soil mix that is rich in humus and kept constantly moist, but not wet. Complete drying out can kill a fern specimen, and partial drying out can cause browned edges and deformed new growth. Rooms kept cool (below 70°F.) support ferns better than warmer ones do, probably because the extra heat means extra-dry air. Many small ferns are adaptable to terrarium culture (see chapter 37). The following list includes the easiest ferns for growing indoors, but a large specimen plant of any of them is still an accomplishment! If summered outdoors, slugs are a major problem to new fern growth. To control these pests, a commercial slug bait should be used on a wet or humid evening.

Adiantum spp. (maidenhair fern)

Beautiful yet challenging as a house plant, *Adiantum* makes a wonderful greenhouse plant but is difficult to grow under lights because of the heat usually generated, especially in the summer. Some people succeed in producing fine plants with humidifiers, while others fail. Not one of the easy ferns in this list.

Cyrtomium spp. (holly fern)

A cool winter location, and a summer spent outdoors in shade with the pot plunged into cool earth, is the foolproof way to ensure a beautiful holly fern.

Davallia spp.

Since this is also known as a bear's foot fern or a squirrel's foot fern, it might be wise to abandon common names and learn, instead, the name of the botanical genus to which forty species of *Davallia* ferns are known in Asia. Those that are used as house plants are the evergreen species and should thrive if given the care summarized above.

Lygodium japonicum (Japanese climbing fern)

Needs support to twine, but is hardy and tolerant of 50 percent humidity. This is a "sun" fern that can enjoy a full four hours of winter sun in Washington D.C. and northward. In summer, curtain-filtered sun should be provided.

Nephrolepis spp. and Cultivars (Boston fern)

These ferns are old Victorian favorites that grow well for some people and turn brown for others—or, as in one case, grew in one house but died when the gardener moved to another house! Generally, however, these plants thrive in cool homes with good light.

Platycerium spp. (staghorn fern)

These bizarre plants can readily adjust to home conditions if they are provided with good light—full winter sunlight and curtain-filtered sunlight during the summer. Allow the potting medium to dry out between waterings, and then water thoroughly in a sink or tub so that the plant can be saturated (see below). Staghorn ferns thrive best in long-fiber sphagnum moss or in fern fiber medium, or a 50/50 mixture of these two ingredients. The plants produce two kinds of leaves: (1) shield leaves, which clasp the pot wall or vertical slab surface the plant is mounted upon, and which, though they turn brown with age, should nonetheless not be trimmed away because they continue to help the plant by keeping the medium from drying out too rapidly. These fronds hold water and should be watered whenever the plant is. (2) The second type of frond is the true staghorn-shaped frond, two or three of which will be produced twice a year—in the spring and fall.

Polypodium (Phlebodium) aureum (rabbit's-foot fern)

This is one of the toughest ferns. If given good light and the usual careful attention, it will reward you with sculptural blue-green new leaves and fuzzy rhizomes that become more interesting as the plant grows older and larger. But by the same token, "growing older and larger" is one of the plant's chief faults, because it can get too large for many rooms and must therefore be divided. This is best done in the early spring, just as the new leaves are beginning to grow after the winter's rest.

Pteris spp.

Again, common names are confusing and the Latin genus name is now used as a common name. Like the Boston fern and the holly fern, these are among the easiest to grow, if good light, proper humidity and a cool temperature are all consistently maintained.

Ficus elastica, F. benjamina and Other Species (ornamental fig tree)

Tropical fig trees are popular as indoor plants because they are large and dramatic, and they survive well if they receive enough light. Remember, however, that they are true *trees,* not subshrubs that can tolerate low light levels. These fig trees need a month's adjustment to new environments when moved, and the new growth must be healthy and strong if the plant is to survive. Healthy fig trees need occasional pruning to remove excess growth and to shape the tree.

Grevillea robusta (silk oak)

This Australian tree can tolerate both dry soil (between waterings) and dry air very well. It demands good light, however, and thrives in a comfortable 55° to 60°F. at night and 65° to 75°F. by day. A summer spent outdoors can add a full 12 in. of growth, but the plant may also be trimmed and kept pot-bound once it achieves the space allotted to it.

Hedera helix (English ivy)

The new varieties of English ivy introduced within recent years have become tremendously popular, and are highly valued for their decorative effect. They may be allowed to trail over the edge of a plant tray or planting box, or they may be trained upward to frame a window. They also can be trained along lattice strips against the wall in a sunroom or on a ceiling; or, if desired, some varieties may be kept to a compact, bushy form. Many lend themselves to training on architectural or animal-shaped frames in the manner of topiary. Among the numerous excellent types and varieties are:

GREEN VARIETIES

'Albany': Trailing, medium-leaved, branching
'Conglomerata erecta': Erect, slow-growing, leaves curled
'Lady Kay': Bushy, trailing, small, lance-shaped leaves
'Manda's Crested': Trailing, ruffled, star-shaped leaf

VARIEGATED VARIETIES

'Jubilee': Slow-growing, branches freely, becoming a shapely plant
'Glacier': Small-leaved, attractive
'Hahn's Variegated': Free-growing, leaves have thin white edge
'Williamsiana': Leaves have crisp white edge

The ivies are very adaptable as house plants. They will grow well in windows with any exposure, and will also thrive in indirect light in the interior of a room. They prosper in a cool temperature, and will grow in any type of soil. These ivies may be grown in water over long periods, if soluble fertilizers are occasionally added. They require a moderate amount of moisture and the leaves should be syringed at frequent intervals or sponged with soapy water.

Hoya spp. (wax plant)

These wonderful vines will literally cover a sunny east or west window if given enough time and support. While they are comparatively slow-growing, within a few years they can amass quite a quantity of vining stems with waxy green or variegated leaves. If hoyas receive sufficient light, they will flower indoors. Grow in a cactus soil mix, and keep on the dry side; allow the pot to dry out completely between waterings.

Mimosa pudica (sensitive plant)

This interesting plant reacts to the touch and to darkness by collapsing its leaflets, which are borne along the midrib of small, fernlike, compound leaves. Best grown from seed in a sunny window, these are easy and satisfying plants for children to raise. Use normal potting soil and keep moist.

Monstera deliciosa (Swiss cheese plant)

This is often sold under the name of *Philodendron pertusum* and erroneously called split-leaf philodendron. The leaves of this tall-growing, tropical climber are very decorative, being large and rounded, cut at the margins and having conspicuous holes. The plant is usually given a moss stick or piece of bark for support. A moderately warm temperature and an ordinary soil that is kept fairly moist but not saturated will help this large plant to thrive. It will make satisfactory growth in poor light, but the leaves will lose their holes as a result. In the wild, monsteras climb tree trunks and the leaves with holes are the adult foliage type. Juvenile plants, found in the wild in dense forest shade, seek tree trunks to climb upon; their leaves, which lack the conspicuous holes, maximize the leaf area exposed to the low light for manufacture of food. Thus, monsteras are good house plants because they will tolerate low light and dry air.

Palms

These decorative plants are old favorites for both pot and tub culture. Most palms need good light to make satisfactory growth. The lush, voluptuous palms so often seen in photographs of decorators' living rooms are misleading because they are used with the furniture only for advertising purposes, and were probably not "homegrown."

Palms should be given as much winter sun as possible north of Washington, D.C., and curtain-filtered sun during the summer. Normal potting soil that is topdressed every two years will allow you to keep a palm specimen in the same size pot for many years. Topdressing is best done in early spring, before new growth starts. Carefully dig out 2 in. to 4 in. of soil from around the roots at the top of the pot and refill with new soil. The minerals from the new soil will permeate downward into the old soil to enrich the entire plant.

Cayota mitis (fishtail palm)

This plant produces suckers at the base that may be chipped off and potted singly—but wait until the sucker plant has a root system of its own before doing so! Keep moist and never allow to dry out completely.

Chamaedorea elegans (parlor palm)

This dwarf species often arrives in a florist's dish garden and outlives the other components. It is a good plant for a north window or for an apartment with no direct light but good reflected light from other buildings. A reliable, beautiful little palm that is easy to care for.

Chrysalidocarpus lutescens (butterfly palm)

These are now readily available since they are grown by southern wholesalers for shipment to northern apartments. Butterfly palms need bright light and moist soil. They are clump-forming plants, and an old colony can be easily split, or the tallest canes simply removed if the plant grows too large.

Howea forsterana (sentry palm)

Also known as kentia palms, these grow best in bright light. They will withstand adverse conditions longer than the butterfly palms.

Livistona chinensis (Chinese fan palm)

This fan palm needs more light than the feather-leafed palms described above. It will thrive in an enclosed sun porch or next to a very sunny east or west window—or even in a corner with windows yielding two sunny exposures, an arrangement occasionally found in some apartments.

Phoenix roebelenii (**miniature date palm**)

Though these palms are very adaptable, they need good light to thrive. A summer spent outdoors will revitalize a poor plant so long as it is eased gradually and gently into the summer sun.

Rhapis excelsa (**lady palm**)

These graceful palms are slow-growing, hence they are comparatively expensive. They will thrive if given sufficient light. They are semitolerant of dry air, however, and the tips of the leaves will brown if humidity is too low. The canelike stems can reach 6 ft. to 8 ft. in height, while new stems are produced at the base. A clump of *Rhapis* is most decorative and not demanding, if the light requirement is met.

Peperomia spp. (radiator plant)

Among the low-growing plants of easy culture are the peperomias, which seldom exceed a height of more than 10 in. They are interesting little plants, and many varieties have highly decorative foliage. Among the species most commonly grown as house plants are these:

P. obtusifolia

Has leaves that are very popular and widely grown. They are round and waxy, borne on erect or sometimes partially procumbent stems.

P. obtusifolia 'variegata'

Attractively marked with cream and white.

P. sandersii (**P. argyreia**)

Known as the watermelon begonia, this is one of the most decorative of the group. The leaf stalks develop from a central crown and make a very symmetrical small plant. The dark green, heart-shaped leaves are interestingly marked with silver stripes.

Many other interesting types and varieties are readily available from good garden centers and nurseries. The peperomias thrive best in a moderately warm temperature and prefer good light but no direct sunlight. They are excellent for growing in a north window. For good growth they require plenty of water and high humidity. They do particularly well when placed on pebble-filled trays that are kept partially filled with water. A woodsy soil, rich in humus, best meets their needs.

Philodendron

These showy plants have two growth forms. One is nonclimbing and self-heading, and a single plant is often grown as a dramatic specimen in a pot. The other form is a tropical vine that needs some support to grow upon, and several plants or cuttings are usually grown in one pot to create a substantial effect.

The nonclimbing, self-heading types of philodendron have considerable decorative value, and they are frequently used very effectively in interiors with a modern decor. Among the most desirable varieties are:

Self-Heading

P. bipinnatifidum

An attractive species, attaining considerable size. The foliage is feathery and finely cut.

P. selloum

Has attractive, deeply cut leaves.

P. undulatum

Has erect, waxy, heart-shaped leaves.

P. wendlandii

Has oblong, glossy leaves that emerge from the crown of the plant. This species is more dwarf in habit than others, and it is often called the "bird's-nest" type because its leaves are arranged in a rosette.

The self-heading philodendrons need more light than the vining type. Thus, curtain-filtered sun or good indirect light is appropriate. They are best suited to a north window, and will do well in the interior of a room only if they receive sufficient light.

The vining philodendrons can thrive in less light than the self-heading types. There are a number of species and varieties available, including the following:

Vining Varieties

P. erubescens

The heart-shaped leaves are medium in size, deep green on the upper surface, coppery on the undersurface. This is one of the best types for growing on moss sticks or tree bark supports.

P. hastatum

Has dark green leaves that are long, narrow and arrow- or heart-shaped.

P. imbe

Has broad, lance-shaped leaves, red on the undersurface.

P. oxycardium (often listed by nurseries as P. cordatum)

The deep green, heart-shaped leaves are smaller than most other types, and the stems are slender. This philodendron is the most commonly seen. It makes an excellent trailer but may also be trained on a moss stick.

P. panduriforme

The deep green leaves are fiddle-shaped.

P. sodiroi (P. ornatum)

The large, heart-shaped leaves have a silvery hue with reddish stems. Neat and trim in habit of growth.

The philodendrons thrive in ordinary room temperatures, and since the vining types (especially *P. oxycardium*) have the ability to grow well in poor light, they are especially desirable for room interiors. Basic potting soil, fortified with ¼ part extra peat, is ideal. They require moderate watering but the soil should never be allowed to become soggy. Philodendrons thrive best in a moderately humid atmosphere; as mentioned earlier, the vining types are more tolerant in this respect than the self-heading types.

Pittosporum tobira (Japanese pittosporum)

Although this plant needs good sunlight, it is very tolerant of chilly drafts and cool nights. So, if you have a well-lighted hall or breezeway, then pittosporum will serve you admirably. Night temperatures as low as 40°F. will not harm this plant, for it is used outside both in southern gardens and in California. By judicious pruning, it may be kept to a reasonably

small size for many years. 'Variegata' has leaves variegated with creamy-white markings.

Podocarpus macrophyllus (Japanese yew)

Another shrub grown in the South and often effectively used as a house plant. It may be grown into a slender column up to 5 ft. tall and thus can fit into any narrow, upright space. The 3-in., dark green, slender leaves are distinctive. This plant is a good candidate for an entry hall because it will tolerate cold drafts. A summer outdoors is necessary if it receives poor light throughout the winter when it is semidormant and not in active growth. Good, bright, indirect light, or curtain-filtered sun, is important to its health during the spring and summer when it is actively growing.

Sansevieria spp. (snake plant)

One of the sturdiest of all house plants, the snake plant will survive poor growing conditions and amazing abuse. It is often used in combination with other plants as room dividers. The following list includes some of the more popular species and varieties:

S. hahnii

A dwarf form not more than 6 in. in height. The dark green, pointed leaves are banded with gray-green.

S. hahnii 'Variegata'

Has leaves marked with narrow, yellow stripes.

S. trifasciata

The species most commonly grown today. The gray-green leaves are erect and pointed, with dark green bands. It reaches a height of 2 ft. to 3 ft..

S. trifasciata 'Craigii'

Has leaves that are dark green in the center, with broad, yellow bands.

Sansevierias are of the easiest possible culture. They will endure dry air, poor soil and a minimum of light, but thrive best in a moderately fertile soil that is allowed to become dry between waterings.

Scindapsus aureus (Pothos)

A vining house plant similar to the vining philodendron species. It has the same cultural requirements and will adapt well to low light conditions. The variety most commonly seen in cultivation has variegated yellow and green leaves, and is attractive as a table plant or in a hanging container with the stems cascading over the edges. These plants also grow amazingly well in plain water, although better growth is achieved in soil. If grown in very low light, the yellow variegation disappears from the leaves.

Spathiphyllum Species and Varieties (spathe flower)

Good growth in low light conditions make *Spathiphyllum* plants ideal, if the humidity is sufficient. Since some species grow in tropical bogs their moisture requirement is high, so the soil should never be allowed to dry out completely. When given sufficient light, these plants will reward the grower with white, flattish, calla-like flowers on stems above the foliage; however, even without flowers the foliage is attractive. These are ideal plants for sunless windows with good reflected light, or for interiors that are several feet away from a sunny window.

Succulent Plants

Succulents will prosper where the humidity is low but the light intensity is high. Many plants in this group are as adaptable as the jade plant (*Crassula argentea*), though some experimentation may be necessary to determine which will successfully live in your home. The recent interest in house plants generally has made many more varieties of succulents available to the public, and quite a few of the new varieties are wonderful house plants.

Since succulents store water in their tissues, they can be allowed to become quite dry be-

tween waterings, and some can even safely be abandoned for several weeks as long as they receive sufficient sunlight during that time. Direct east- or west-facing windows receive the most light, and it is in these locations that succulent plants will do their best. Some extra sand in the soil mix will ensure good drainage and aeration.

Aloe vera (A. barbadensis) and Other Species

Ease of culture makes *Aloe* a particularly dependable house plant that has been cultivated for centuries for decorative and medicinal purposes. Most species have a rosette form but some can grow into treelike forms. These plants do best with four or more hours of sunlight each day.

Crassula argentea (jade plant)

The jade plant will reward the grower with masses of thick leaves and stems if given a lot of light. This is an easy succulent to grow and does well when summered outdoors in a sunny location, as long as the move is done gradually in the spring to prevent sunburning its leaves.

Euphorbia spp.

The succulent members of this group of plants from Africa and Asia resemble the cacti of the American continents and have the same cultural requirements. These plants vary tremendously in shape, from branched, treelike forms to small, rotund, cactuslike plants.

Gasteria spp.

Interesting markings on the fleshy leaves, which usually face each other in two rows, are typical of most *Gasteria*; but some have leaves in perfect rosettes. These plants are easy to grow, can tolerate less than full sun and may be left in the same pot for years.

Haworthia spp.

Resembling *Gasteria*, *Haworthia* are rosette plants which easily form basal suckers that turn an individual into a colony in a short time. These young plantlets may be pulled from the parent and potted on their own. Originating from South Africa, they will, if old enough and healthy, flower during the winter. The inconspicuous white or greenish flowers grow on long spikes, and though not spectacular, are welcome.

Kalanchoe spp.

Variety is the key word for this group of plants, which can be fuzzy-leaved or completely smooth and are grown both for foliage and flowers. *K. blossfeldiana* is sold in full bloom at Christmas time. In order for it to bloom again the following year it must have poinsettia treatment, that is, fourteen hours of complete darkness and ten hours of sunshine or bright light from September to early December.

Schlumbergera

Christmas and Thanksgiving cacti are ephiphytic plants from Brazil that are true members of the cactus family. These plants require more humus in the planting mix than other succulents and slightly more water during the spring and summer growing periods. Refrain from watering during September and October and give them fourteen hours of uninterrupted darkness during these months to ensure flowers for the holidays. When the flower buds have set, feed the soil once with a half-strength, water-soluble fertilizer, and keep it on the dry side until blooming is complete.

Sedum morganianum (burro's-tail)

A trailing succulent that grows in isolated canyon walls in Mexico, where it is partially shaded each day. It makes an ideal house plant, and will trail over the edge of its pot, so several plants should be planted together for maximum effect.

Stapelia spp. (carrion flower)

These members of the milkweed family make good trailing indoor house plants. If they are summered outdoors and make sufficient growth, they will provide the grower with the dubious reward of interesting but evil-smelling flowers. The natural pollinator of this group of plants is a fly attracted by the foul smell; this mechanism works as well in South Bend as it does in South Africa, the *Stapelia's* native region.

Syngonium (often sold as Nephthytis, arrowhead vine)

These vinelike tropical plants are very satisfactory for use in room dividers as they thrive in direct light. They may be allowed to trail, or may be trained on a piece of tree bark or a moss-covered stick. The stems cling by means of fleshy aerial roots. There are many excellent varieties of *Syngonium podophyllum* with variegated leaves, most of which will keep their variegated color even in low light. These plants are of easy culture, even growing for several months in plain water.

FLOWERING HOUSE PLANTS

Bulbs

Most bulbous plants that are grown indoors need a rest period prior to blooming. Also, after flowering, most of them need ideal conditions if they are to manufacture sufficient food to ensure new bloom the following year. It is at this point that most window gardeners fail, because bulbous plants do not usually receive sufficient light indoors. Thus, bulbs often produce their best flowers in the year they are purchased and then decline thereafter. By putting the bulbs out in the garden for the summer, however, one can sometimes keep them healthy and productive for many years.

Achimenes, tuberous begonias and the gloriosa lily are all best suited for late spring and summer bloom. Start the bulbs in late winter or early spring (January to March), using the basic soil mix enriched with additional rotted leaf mold, if available. Be careful not to overwater the pots when the bulbs are newly planted or they may rot. Keep them barely moist and warm (70°F.) and perhaps in the dark until growth appears above the soil, then move to bright light. Use common sense in covering the bulbs and in selecting pot sizes: achimenes are small bulbs, so six to eight bulbs in a 6-in. pot buried 1 in. deep is adequate. Tuberous begonias and gloriosa lily plants need at least 6-in. pots, and should be buried 1½ in. to 2½ in.

deep, depending upon the size of the bulb. The tuberous begonias need good light but no direct sun; they also need higher humidity than the achimenes and the gloriosa lily. The latter are good in an east or west window protected by a sheer curtain.

Amaryllis and callas (wrongly called calla lilies) will produce early spring flowers if started in late November or December. Purchase the largest bulbs possible and plant in 8-in. to 12-in. pots. The amaryllis should produce its flowers before the foliage appears, but the calla will produce several leaves before flowering. Both will profit from a summer spent outdoors in partial sun. Dig the bulbs in the fall before the first frost, spread them out and store for a week in a dry place, then clean off the leaves and cut back the roots. Thereafter, they should be stored completely dry in polyethelene bags of vermiculite in a frost-free location.

Tulip, hyacinth, narcissus and bulbous iris can be forced into early bloom in a window just as in a greenhouse. The iris are especially easy because they are small and the first stage of their growth can be accomplished in the refrigerator. Pot several bulbs, grouping each type in separate pots, in the fall before the ground freezes. Water them thoroughly, then bury the pots in a coldframe or a protected location, and cover with 6 in. to 12 in. of leaves, straw or some other mulch that can be easily removed when the ground is still frozen. Another method of wintering the pots is to store them in plastic bags in the refrigerator for two months. This cold-storage period is essential to the bulbs if the roots are to grow, in order to supply the leaves and flowers with water. Once the pots are removed from cold storage, they should be kept cool (60°F.) and well illuminated until they bloom.

Capsicum spp. (ornamental pepper)

These novel, small-fruited peppers are easily grown from seed. They produce an attractive, peppery-hot colored fruit that lasts for months. They are good subjects for children to grow from seed, and are not demanding in their requirements, though a few hours of sunlight each day are beneficial.

Clerodendrum (glory-bower)

These vining, shrublike plants must be trimmed regularly to be kept within bounds. They are usually considered greenhouse plants, but they make good house plants also, if given sufficient light. Variegated varieties are available that brighten these plants when they are not in flower.

Clivia miniata (Kaffir lily)

Clivias belong to the amaryllis family, are evergreen, and thus do not require as much care as do the amaryllis, which need a rest period of several months during the fall. Clivias can be grown for many years in the same large pot, but they do benefit from a topdressing of new soil every two years. They will tolerate low light during the winter if they are summered outdoors in partial sun. If they make enough food during the summer, they will reward you with orange-yellow flowers in March or April.

Gardenia jasminoides (gardenia)

Gardenias all too frequently fail to do well as house plants. This is particularly true if they have been originally grown in a greenhouse. Due to the high temperature, the low humidity and the low light intensity usually found in the average home, gardenia buds tend to drop before opening. Some plants will continue to make foliage growth under these conditions, but will produce little or no bloom. A cool sun porch offers reasonably favorable conditions. Provide good bright light and four hours of winter sun each day. Summer outdoors in partial sun.

Gesneriads

This is the common name for members of the plant family Gesneriaceae (named for the Swiss naturalist Konrad Gesner), which includes some of the newest plants to attain popularity in the United States. They are popular because they flower, and the foliage of most varieties is interesting and varied. If gesneriads are given at least 40 percent humidity, a temperature of 65° to 75°F. and good light, they make very successful house plants. The following species are the most useful in window gardens, but see also Chapter 37 for varieties that may be grown under lights.

Aeschynanthus and Columnea

Genera from different parts of the world. *Aeschynanthus* comes from the Asian tropics and *Columnea* from the American tropics. Both are vining or shrubby in habit and produce bright orange, red and yellow flowers (depending on species or variety) in the spring. Both also make good hanging plants and the soil-less Mix 2 (page 721) is ideal. Provide bright light and four hours of winter sunlight north of Washington, D.C.

Sinningia spp. (also called Gloxinia)

These plants grow from tubers (bulblike underground stems) and have been developed into large-flowered cultivars by hybridizers. Many species and varieties are miniature, however, and are ideal for light culture (see Chapter 37). Gloxinias are usually grown for summer flowers in exactly the same way as tuberous begonias—in fact, they both make good companion plants in the same well-lit but sunless window.

Streptocarpus (Cape primrose)

Like African violets, the Cape primrose has been hybridized and improved until it is much more showy and reliable in bloom than its wild ancestors. Unlike the African violet, however, Cape primroses thrive in a cool atmosphere; it is the summer heat that makes these plants decline. The soil requirements are the same as for African violets: extra humus and constant moisture. However, these plants are easier to care for, because their leaves do not spot when touched by cold water so it is not necessary to water them from below. The plants are also larger than African violets, and a good multiple-crown specimen may be as much as 18 in. across and have twelve or more open flowers on it every day from January to June. Keep as cool as possible during the summer, and repot in September. Each leaf produces flower buds at

its base, so select only two or three new leaves per stem, and cut off the old leaves that have already flowered. These can be used for propagation. The good growth you get throughout the fall will amply reward you with a profusion of spring flowers.

Impatiens spp. (balsam, patience plant)

Impatiens is one of the few house plants that will give almost continuous bloom throughout the year if conditions are favorable. The two species most commonly grown are *I. sultanii*, the old-fashioned type, and *I. holstii*. Many lovely hybrids of these two species have recently been introduced and plants are now available in a wide variety of colors: white, soft pink, salmon, coral, pale lavender, purple, cerise and brick-red. The dainty, five-petaled flowers are borne in such profusion that the plants are sometimes literally covered with bloom.

The recently imported New Guinea impatiens, and the varieties developed from them, have begun to appear on the commercial market. These wonderful plants have variegated foliage and amazingly large flowers. They thrive in full sun during winter months and in partial sun during the summer. Impatiens are heavy feeders and should be fertilized frequently to keep them in bloom. Avoid fluctuations in temperature, and never allow them to dry out completely.

Ipomoea spp. (morning-glory)

These may be grown from seed and make short-lived but pleasing house-plants. Give these delicate vines some support to climb upon, moderate moisture and a few hours of sun each day to obtain flowers. Morning-glory seeds have a very hard seed coat, so they should be nicked with a file to allow water to enter the seed and speed germination.

Orchids

In recent years many indoor gardeners have had great success in growing orchids on their window sills and under lights (see Chapter 37). Most of these people belong to a local orchid society and obtain from other equally avid members information as to varieties that will succeed in a home situation. Growing orchids without a greenhouse is challenging but not impossible, though the grower usually must modify the environment of the average home to accommodate orchid plants and make them bloom. Often it is not difficult to get the plants to grow, but it is much more of a challenge to produce the orchid flowers.

Cymbidium spp.

These orchids, particularly the miniatures, are especially suited to culture in the home. In the summer, grow them outdoors in bright shade or partial sun. They are burned by very hot sun, though they do need as much light as possible to make food for next year's blooms. In the fall bring them indoors and keep them cool—60°F.—and well lighted—four hours of morning sun in an east window is fine. If the plants are well grown, they should flower in the early spring from January to March.

Paphiopedilum spp. and Hybrids

These are semiterrestrial and exotic, with their curious, pouched flowers. They will grow in sunless north windows if the light is not obstructed by trees or other buildings. In other exposures a curtain to filter summer sun is necessary. Normal house temperatures of 70°F. in the day and 60°F. at night are suitable for these orchids. *Paphiopedilum* also likes extra limestone added to the potting mix.

Both *Cymbidium* and *Paphiopedilum* orchids thrive in a semiepiphytic mixture that drains well yet holds some moisture. A mix containing orchid fir bark in ½-in. and smaller chunks, shredded fir bark and perlite in equal proportions is satisfactory. Soak the medium in water for a day before using, because the fir bark is initially difficult to wet. Orchids should be watered when the medium is just about ready to dry out, but be wary of overwatering.

Phalaenopsis spp. and Hybrids

These also respond well to house culture, but they are more epiphytic in nature and need only the chunklike fir bark as a potting medium. Water thoroughly, then allow the medium to dry out completely between waterings. The roots should be white and plump, not shriv-

eled or darkened and soggy. *Phalaenopsis* prefers warmer temperatures, too—70°F. to 80°F. in the day and down to 65°F. at night is good.

The difficulty and skill required to grow orchids should be amply compensated for by the end result—those long-lasting and exotic blooms that are a joy to behold.

Passiflora (**passionflower**)

Another flowering vine that will reward you with exotic flowers if the plants receive enough light. The flowers, which are about 4 in. across, are intricate in detail and beautiful in coloring, with the white outer edge of the petals shading to soft mauve and blue near the crown.

Passionflowers prefer full sun but will do well with only four hours of winter sun each day. They are best suited to moderately cool temperatures and need no special soil or watering. They should be grown in large pots, and need support for the vigorous climbing stems.

Pelargonium spp. (**geranium**)

Many varieties and species of geranium *(Pelargonium)* are available and most will bloom if given sufficient sunlight. The scented-leaved types are best for windows without direct sun. All geraniums can be easily propagated by cuttings, and will grow wonderfully well outdoors in the summer. Start some cuttings in late June or early July in order to have small plants to bring indoors in September. It is almost impossible to try to overwinter the large, outdoor-grown plants indoors, because if they are severely cut back they never achieve the grace of a freshly grown plant.

Geraniums will grow in a basic potting mix, which should be allowed to dry out between watering. The small-leaved cultivars and the scented-leaf varieties are especially successful as house plants.

Saintpaulia ionantha (**African violet**)

Few plants have achieved such wide popularity as the African violet, largely because it is a house plant that readily blooms indoors. It prefers an exposure where it is protected from midday sun, and thrives well in an east or west window if given curtain-filtered sunlight throughout the summer months. The African violet is particularly well adapted to growing under lights (see Chapter 37). A warm temperature is necessary for its proper growth, and winter cold will stop the plant's growth if it is placed near a cool window. A range of temperature between 65° and 75°F. best meets its needs. African violets require a soil mix rich in humus, so modify the basic soil mix by using one-half rotted leaf mold or sedge peat in addition to the Canadian peat of the basic soil mix. You can also purchase commercially blended African violet soil, or use one of the suggested soil-less mixes (see pages 720–21).

Cold water will cause yellow spotting of African violet leaves, so the plants should be watered from below, using warm water. Allow the pots to sit in a saucer of water until the soil surface is dark, then remove the water in the saucer beneath the pot. Since humidity must be high for African violets to thrive, a pebble tray below the plants will be necessary in most homes.

Solanum pseudocapsicum (**Jerusalem cherry**)

These small, treelike shrubs are available as Christmas plants and may either be kept for several years or grown each year from seed. Christmas plants are best cut back somewhat, summered outdoors, then brought back into a well-lighted but cool window sill in the fall. Since they are not really long-lived woody plants, they can be counted on for several years only, at which time they can be restarted from seed in the early spring—just like their relative, the tomato.

37

Gardening under Artificial Light

Many homes and apartments do not provide sufficient window space to accommodate the gardening ambitions of their enthusiastic owners. But since light is the single most important limiting factor to successful indoor gardening, the vast majority of such gardeners have tried growing plants under electric lights. Their success has been great because with artificial lights the grower has complete control over all the cultural conditions needed for potted plants. Moreover, new fluorescent tubes have been developed that deliver nearly perfect light for plant growth. With just a little extra effort and expense, anyone can create an enjoyable indoor garden that will provide excellent conditions for a wide spectrum of plants. People who live in small apartments can enlarge their growing space because light gardens can be installed almost anywhere. They may fit into a shelf in a bookcase, in an unused fireplace or even in a roomy closet. Light gardens have taken over whole rooms and basements after their owners have become enthusiastically involved in their hobby. Many people have gardens that occupy several different locations throughout the house. Light gardening is also ideal for older people, because it does not involve strenuous activity, yet the rewards are great. Flowers can literally adorn one's home every day of the year, and a wonderful array of plant material is completely successful using modern light fixtures. Indeed, some plants are horticulturally superior when grown under such lights to those produced in a greenhouse.

Indoor light gardening is also a practical way of starting vegetable and flower seeds for transplanting to the outdoor garden. All the tomatoes, peppers and marigolds you will need for the entire season can be started in just a few feet of space. And you even can plant the special varieties usually available only from seed merchants, rather than taking "pot luck" at the local nursery.

LIGHT AND SOURCES OF LIGHT

All green plants must have light to flourish and grow. It does not matter where the light comes from, so long as it is of the proper wavelength and intensity for a sufficiently long period each day. In view of the fact that all artificial light creates some degree of heat, which can be damaging to plants, fluorescent lights produce the least amount of heat while at the same time delivering the most light for the least expense. They are, therefore, the lights most often used by indoor growers. While the fluorescent tubes designed for general household or industrial illumination can be used to grow plants, the newer tubes, specifically designed for gardening, are noticeably superior. These horticultural tubes, as they are called, provide the proper spectrum and balance of blue and red light rays that are of maximum value to the food-making processes of plants. Green plants must have this balance of light to make food for themselves in order to grow. Before the development of the new horticultural lamps, the older standard fluorescent tubes had to be supplemented with ordinary incandescent light bulbs so that sufficient red light rays would reach plants grown under these conditions. This is no longer necessary with the new tubes.

All fluorescent tubes produce a small amount of heat because the ballast, which is contained inside the fixture, is necessary for the efficient operation of the tubes. This small heat source is far from a limiting factor, but placement and ventilation of the fixtures are important considerations when a light garden is being planned, especially if the garden is to contain more than just a few fixtures.

The most frequently used fixture to hold the fluorescent tubes is the standard (and least expensive) 4-ft. long, double-tube fixture with a white enamel reflector. Light gardens in large areas often employ standard 8-ft. tubes. These gardens are usually built by experienced growers who started with shorter tubes, then expanded their gardening area. Short tubes (20 in.) also are available for smaller spaces such as inside bookcases or other pieces of furniture, or in confined spaces such as closets. The cost of the shorter tubes, in relation to the amount of light they produce, is somewhat higher. A single tube is not sufficient, but groups of two, four or six are ideal. In building your own light garden, put the lamps on 6-in. centers. In this way, standard double-tube fixtures will light an area of 4 ft. by 12 in. To light a greater space, use more fixtures with tubes on 6-in. centers.

Light fixtures can be built into stationary plant stands (see illustration, page 746) or a semimovable cartlike plant stand (see illustration, page 749). Efficient and attractive ready-made stands can be purchased at most garden stores or from mail-order catalogues. Fixtures can be hung very simply from the ceiling, especially in basements where such installations may be more informal. Hanging the fixtures with a chain will allow the lights to be easily raised as the plants grow upward. Lightweight but strong plastic link chain is available in garden stores for this purpose, or standard metal chain can be used. A basement installation of several

lights over a temporary table is basically all that is necessary to grow one's own seedlings for the outdoor vegetable and flower garden.

Engineering a light garden often demands a handyman's touch, but nothing really complicated is involved. Many light gardens are built like bookcases (see illustration, page 743), so that several shelves can accommodate the maximum garden with the minimum sacrifice to living space. In such gardens, of course, the upper shelves will be slightly warmer than the lower ones, as the heat generated by the fixtures will rise to the shelves above. This extra warmth is ideal for plant propagation. Some tropical plants actually grow better beneath this extra heat on the upper shelves than on the lower ones.

Types of Fluorescent Tubes

The tubes for general illumination will produce very adequate plant growth. These are common household lamps, such as "cool white," "daylight" and "warm white" tubes, and can readily be purchased from hardware stores. In recent years, lamp manufacturers have designed tubes specifically for horticultural use, and these new tubes, of course, are superior to the older ones. The original horticultural tube, the Gro-Lux tube, is well known and quite satisfactory.

However, newer tubes recently have been introduced that deliver superior light without the rosy tint of the Gro-Lux. These are called broad-spectrum tubes, and they are manufactured by various companies:

BROAD-SPECTRUM FLUORESCENT TUBES

NAME	MANUFACTURER
Ago-Lite	Westinghouse
Natur-Escent	Duro-Lite, Inc.
Verilux TruBloom	Veriluc Co.
Vita-Lite	Duro-Lite, Inc.
Wide Spectrum Glo-Lux	Sylvania

Each of these lamps is efficient and provides complete light for plant growth, yet they differ slightly because of the light-producing chemi-

37.1 This is a practical, easy-to-assemble, free-standing structure for growing a large number of plants under lights. Photo George Elbert

cals used by the manufacturer. The tubes are designed to provide the light energy most useful to plant growth—blue and red light rays—although the light itself looks white to the human eye. To our vision, all the broad-spectrum tubes deliver light of the quality of sunlight at noon. But the Vita-Lite listed above gives more ultra-violet light than does the Natur-Escent, though both are from the same manufacturer. This is important for growing and flowering succulents and orchids, as well as for developing foliage color in plants like bromeliads and begonias. Since these provide more usable light for plant growth, the small difference in price over the common fluorescent tube is amply justified.

Amount of Light

Plants grown under lights thrive in twelve to sixteen hours of light a day. An inexpensive timer for this purpose is handy but not abso-

lutely necessary. Some people habitually turn their garden lights on each morning and off each night. During occasional weekends away from home, twenty-four hours of light a day is not disastrous to the potted plants—but twenty-four hours of darkness might be! However, a prolonged period of constant light (twenty-four hours a day) is harmful to most plants, the only exception being the African violet, which will tolerate and even thrive on such a light diet.

Fluorescent tubes are brightest when they are new; after about 100 hours of use they begin to fall off, but level out to produce nearly constant (though very slowly declining) high-intensity light for about a year. It is a good idea to stagger the replacement of the tubes because new, bright tubes will burn or yellow the leaves of plants if the tubes are replaced all at once. The newer, broad-spectrum tubes last longer than the standard illuminating tubes; most growers replace their tubes after eighteen to twenty-four months of use.

Various species of plants differ in the amount of light they can utilize, and brightness or amount of light is easily controlled by the distance between the tube and the leaf surface. Some succulents demand bright, intense light. These plants will thrive only when placed 2 in. to 4 in. from the tubes, under the center of each tube's length. Most plants want less intense light, however, so for them, 8 in. to 14 in. below the lamps is the optimum distance at the center of the tube. Only ferns and some begonias will thrive further away from the tubes: 24 in. is about the maximum distance even for these low-light plants.

Since the light intensity decreases from the center to the ends of the tube, bear in mind that some orchids, most succulents, herbs and geraniums benefit from a central position under the tubes. On the other hand, gesneriads, low light orchids and terrestrial bromeliads thrive at the ends of tubes in multiple-tube systems. But you must be the judge in determining proper distances. Your plants will tell you, by their growth and appearance, whether they are obtaining sufficient light. A plant that produces large leaves with long lengths of stem between individual leaves is not getting enough light. *Lack* of light is usually what ails plants under lights, if all other cultural conditions are met. You should either put such light-deficient plants in a central position under the tube or raise them nearer to the tubes.

A plant that seems to be trying to avoid the light, with leaves curled or flattened against the pot or its stem, or a plant that develops an over-abundance of red pigment, is telling you that the light is too bright. It should either be moved to the ends of the tubes, or be lowered. Seedlings should be placed only a few inches below the tubes so they will be sturdy. As the plants grow, however, either the lights or the seedlings will have to be moved; hence easily adjustable fixtures are needed for seedling culture.

To maximize the light you are paying for, a reflector should be installed above the tubes. In this way more light will bounce down upon the leaves of the plants you are growing. Standard fixtures come with built-in reflectors. White or mirrored surfaces on the sides or back walls of light gardens will also increase the amount of light on the plant. By keeping the tubes clean and replacing them at eighteen-month intervals, you can achieve the maximum output of light for your indoor garden.

HUMIDITY AND VENTILATION

Many of the most successful plants grown under lights are those that enjoy the constant environment so easily achieved in this type of gardening. Ventilation and humidity control are factors that are closely linked. Ventilation provides fresh air but usually leads to the drying out of an indoor environment. As humidity must be conserved and constantly replenished in any garden, a balance must be achieved between ventilation and enclosure in order to conserve humidity. Small electric fans are useful in indoor gardens to move air around the plants. If these fans are used, it will be necessary to put water-filled pebble trays under the plants to increase the humidity in the immediate vicinity. This is readily achieved under linear fluorescent tubes by using the 11-in. by 22-in. by 2-in. plastic trays that fit perfectly under standard fixtures. These may be filled with small pebbles or gravel, or even with perlite if weight is a consideration.

A new product to improve humidity is the nonwoven capillary mat material that was first used on benches in commercial greenhouses to grow plants in small containers, where it provided continuous and constant watering of the pots placed upon it. This same mat material also provides excellent humidity control in indoor light gardens — plus the additional bonus of automatically watering the plants from below. Small lengths of mat material are sometimes difficult to obtain, but it will undoubtedly become more available as the demand increases. Occasionally, a local plant society or a specialty plant shop will offer shorter lengths for the average indoor grower. It has been found that many plants that once needed a contained (closed) atmosphere can now be grown in the open, if grown on mats placed in plastic trays and constantly kept moist. Undoubtedly, this new material will become more readily available as people become more familiar with it and learn to use it successfully.

TERRARIUMS AND CONTAINED ENVIRONMENTS

One of the most rewarding aspects of indoor light gardening is terrarium culture. This is due to the constancy of artificial light and to the low heating effect of artificial light, as opposed to natural sunlight filtered through a window. Many miniature tropical plants and ferns enjoy the high humidity that a terrarium provides. The miniature landscape or composition created in a small space can be a constant source of pleasure as plants flower and develop into perfect specimens in their enclosed environment. Such enclosed conditions are in fact essential for certain temperamental or rare plants grown by the fanciers of such plant groups as begonias or gesneriads.

Humidity

For terrariums to provide constant high humidity, they must be kept almost constantly closed. Sometimes, when they are in just the right spot in a house and the plants within them seem to be thriving, they may stay completely closed indefinitely. Such terrariums are ideal because they are worry-free. Though such success is rare, it does happen more than occasionally, after several attempts in different locations in a home.

Most terrariums need some attention, however, especially in hot weather, when the cover is opened slightly to allow limited air circulation and to enable heat to escape. The hottest summer days are those that can destroy a well-grown terrarium: high temperature and humidity combine to kill plant tissue, and leaves will turn brown. It is during such periods that growers must be particularly alert and observant.

Types of Containers

Various containers of clear glass or plastic make ideal terrariums, but the covers and lids that close these containers vary in convenience. The challenge of a lovely miniature garden inside a bottle with a narrow neck obviously will not appeal to everyone. These gardens are becoming almost an art form similiar to flower arranging in some metropolitan garden clubs. Most familiar "working" terrariums are built in unused fish tanks, in wide-mouthed bowls or in specially constructed glass chambers with convenient doors or access through the top of the container, which is usually fitted with a piece of glass. (Photo, page 724). Once planted, the terrarium needs little care after it has become established. The first few weeks are critical, however, because the plants are adjusting to their new environment and the grower is learning the particular idiosyncrasies of the new terrarium. During this period, if water condensation on the inside of the glass is excessive, the covering will have to be opened to allow the extra water vapor to escape. Usually, a small amount of condensed water on the glass is a healthy situation and need not be a worry. Most terrariums need to be carefully watered every few months due to very slow water loss.

Assembling the Terrarium

A terrarium is simple to assemble. All that is needed is a suitable, clean container, pebbles or gravel for drainage, potting soil and compatible plants. Try to determine the growth rates of the plants to be grown as a community, so that one will not grow so fast as to crowd out the slower

growers. Put at least 2 in. to 3 in. of gravel on the floor of the container, add barely moist soil, then use your imagination and creativity to design your own little landscape with the plants. Rocks, pieces of wood and small mounds are natural possibilities in the overall plan. A one-sided terrarium will naturally be assembled differently from one that is to be viewed from all sides. The latter type might contain a single plant set in the center of the container, there to grow into a perfect specimen in its ideal environment. Once completed, add less water than you think the terrarium needs. Then wait a day before determining whether or not more water is needed. In any case, avoid overwatering. It is *very* difficult to get extra water out, once it has been added to a terrarium.

STARTING VEGETABLE SEEDS IN A LIGHT GARDEN

By using readily available materials, anyone can start vegetable and flower plants indoors for their own home garden. Begin with a fluorescent light installation in a cool location in the house, basement—or even in the garage, if it's warm enough there. Temperature and amount of light are the critical factors for the production of sturdy seedlings. Ideally, the seedlings should receive bright fluorescent light in an area with a daytime temperature of 70° to 75°F., and a drop of at least 10°F. at night, down to 60°F. or even 55°F. A constant, warm temperature (70° to 75°F.) is ideal for germinating seeds. This can be achieved just *above* the fluorescent fixture because of the heat made by the ballast. Once the seedlings have germinated and are just beginning to emerge from the soil, they should be moved to a position 3 in. to 4 in. below the tubes, with the upper leaves kept at that distance as the plants grow.

Choosing the Seeds

When sowing seeds indoors in a light garden, select varieties of plants that actually will benefit from such an early start indoors. It is foolish to transplant bean or lettuce plants, for example, which can be so readily grown right in the garden. Tomato, pepper, eggplant, okra, melon,

37.2 *Built into a wall, this indoor light garden becomes a part of the room's architecture. Photo George Elbert*

cabbage and its many relatives, herbs and flowers—all can profit from the early indoor start. Concentrate your efforts on these plants. All members of the cabbage family enjoy a cooler daytime temperature (60°F.) than do the tomato and its relatives (70°F.). Each, however, needs a 10°F. drop at night. Only fresh seed should be used; then follow the instructions outlined below for foolproof seedling production.

Preparing Seed Flats

Plan to start ten to twelve weeks before the plants are to be set outdoors. Use standard plastic seed flats or even wooden ones. These can be the same plastic trays that are used to increase humidity in light gardens—but be sure that ample drainage holes are punched in the bottom of the pans. New flats are sterile, but before using those saved from previous years, they should be soaked for several hours in a 5 percent household bleach solution, then washed and rinsed in clear water. Fill the flats with fresh, sterile soil purchased for this purpose, or use one of the soil-less mixes (see pages 720–21). Since you are going to the trouble to set up fluorescent fixtures, do not use ordinary garden soil or old, used, possibly contaminated soil from last year. A freshly prepared, sterile soil will save you work, and will be a great time-saver.

Direct Sowing

Fill the flats with pre-moistened soil and tamp it in place. Thinly sow the seed in rows that are 2 in. to 3 in. apart. Sowing in definite rows allows you to judge easily how well the seeds are germinating. Cover the seed to a depth of twice the largest diameter of the seed, and gently tamp in place. Very tiny plant seeds like petunia should not be covered, but simply gently watered in. Label the flat, or each section, if you have planted more than one type in a flat. Water the planted seeds with warm water thoroughly and carefully, until the water runs out of the drainage holes. Allow the flat to drip dry for several hours; cover with a plastic bag, then put the flat in a warm position for germination. A good spot is over the ballast of a fluorescent light fixture.

Most vegetable and flower seeds take six to ten days to germinate, at which time the seedlings should be placed 2 in. from the tubes. Gradually remove the plastic bag. After the seeds germinate, you must judge if they are planted too thickly to thrive. If they seem too crowded for good growth, they should be thinned. If the plants are not too badly crowded, however, wait until the seedlings have two sets of true leaves, then transplant the extra plants to fresh flats of soil. Newly transplanted seedlings will wilt after they are moved, but they should recover in a day to two.

The "Jiffy 7"

An alternative to direct sowing in flats is to sow into "Jiffy 7s," which are pressed peat moss pellets. These can be purchased at most garden centers and nurseries. Sow two seeds per moistened peat pellet, and proceed as above. Once the seed germinates and the plants are 4 in. to 6 in. tall, thin the seedlings to one per pellet, selecting the strongest. At this stage the individual plants in their pellets should be transplanted to a flat of soil or into individual pots. Plants should be spaced 2 in. to 4 in. apart, herbs closer, and filled in around the "Jiffy 7" with soil. Melon, especially, responds to the "Jiffy 7" because it resents complete transplanting. The transplanting step described above allows you to care more easily for your group of seedlings, yet since most of the seedling roots will be inside the "Jiffy 7," the final shock of transplanting is less great than if the plants were directly sown into soil in a flat.

Damping-off

Once the seedlings come up, watering the flats is critical. The flat must be checked daily but care must be taken lest you overwater. The fungus infection known as "damping-off" often claims seedlings in overwet soil. Allow the surface of the soil to become dry; the plant can actually wilt ever so slightly without undue harm. Then water thoroughly until the water runs out of the drainage holes. Pay particular attention to watering the edges or the sides of the flat. It is here that flats dry out first because

of increased air circulation at the edge of the flat. Apply a weak fertilizer (¼ strength) to every second watering.

If you observe seedlings with rotten root systems and ones that fall over, or that have a constriction around the stem at ground level before they fall over, then you probably have been overwatering and your seedlings are suffering from damping-off. You can try to overcome this by scooping out the affected soil and seedlings in an attempt to isolate the seedlings that are still healthy. Water the flat with a fungicide such as Captan, using the dosage recommended on the package. The prevention of damping-off is obviously easier than the cure.

Hardening-off

Prior to being planted in their final location, these light-grown seedlings must be acclimated to the outside conditions or, to put it more technically, "hardened-off." In other words, plants grown under lights must be gradually toughened in order to survive outdoors. First, on warm spring days the flats should be moved to a shady outdoor location for just a few hours each day, all the while protecting the seedlings from drying winds. They should be returned to their indoor home at night. After several days' exposure, the plants should be moved into more sunshine, until you have them in full sun all day prior to placing them in a crude coldframe or similar structure. This can be nothing more than a shallow excavation that will hold the flats and is covered with a slightly opened storm window. The plants can remain in this coldframe for several weeks, until all danger of frost is past. They then are properly "hardened-off" and can safely be transplanted into the garden.

PLANTS THAT WILL GROW WELL UNDER LIGHTS

Annual plants that are grown under lights from seed to flowering are wonderfully rewarding. These may be started by the far-sighted gardener in early fall to help dispel the inevitable winter doldrums. Although short-lived — usually six months is average for handsome, healthy plants—seeds are easily obtained and are an excellent way to have a varied collection at little cost. To achieve constant bloom, replanting must be done at monthly intervals; but since commercial packets are generous, you should be able to make many sowings of a few seeds for pot culture. Store extra seeds in a screwtop jar in the refrigerator. When buying seed, only dwarf and miniature varieties should be selected since space is so limited in light gardening. The following plants are outstanding performers under lights.

Antirrhinum (snapdragon)

'Little Darling' and 'Little Sweetheart' are husky, dwarf plants that branch readily from the base.

Celosia

'Golden Triumph,' 'Golden Gem,' 'Crusader,' 'Fiery Feather.' These dwarf, plume types make excellent pot plants; 'Golden Triumph' is only 7 in. tall, 'Golden Gem' is 10 in. and 'Crusader' and 'Fiery Feather' (both crimson) are 10 in.

Coleus

'Carefree,' 'Magic Lace,' 'Salicifolius.' Any coleus is easy to grow under lights, but the varieties above are deeply serrated, lacelike and notched-leaf types that are the most interesting. While colorful, coleus may grow too fast and too tall unless light is bright enough. Most must be propagated by rooting cuttings several times a year.

Cyclamen

'Puck' is small and starts blooming six months after sowing. Keep cool, at a temperature of 65°F.

Impatiens

'A Go Go' is a 10 in. bicolor, red and white flower; ever-blooming. 'Tangerine' matures at 15 in., with large 1½-in. flowers.

Kalanchoe

'Scarlet Gnome' matures at 7 in. with bright red flowers; 'Yellow Tom Thumb' is 8 in. at maturity, with bright yellow flowers.

Lantana nana compacta

A dwarf plant that has bright yellow flowers and is very rewarding to grow.

Pentas

Dwarf strains are available in pink, lavender or white.

Petunia

Choose dwarf strains; very easy to grow under lights if kept pruned and if old flowers are removed promptly.

Salvia

New pastel shades, 12 in. to 15 in. tall in soft colors. 'Salmon Pygmy' is a very dwarf 6 in., and a lovely clear salmon color.

Tagetes (marigold)

Choose any of the dwarf French varieties. They are easy and effective in a light garden.

Zinnia

The 'Buttons' strain is highly recommended for cultivation under lights. Compact plants 10 in. to 12 in. high, with double yellow-orange, pink and red flowers.

FLOWERING PLANTS THAT WILL GROW WELL UNDER LIGHTS

Anthurium scherzeranum (flamingo flower)

Twelve in. tall and a relative of the well-known florist variety but more dwarf and hence

37.3 These benches on wheels are a practical solution to the production of plants under lights in a basement, heated garage or unused room. Individual plants can be moved for display when in bloom and returned afterwards. Photo George Elbert

better under lights. It will flower constantly, with bright red bracts. Pot in a porous mix — preferably an orchid mix with extra leaf mold, or sphagnum moss with charcoal added — and keep moist at all times. Keep the aerial roots covered with long-fibered sphagnum moss, and fertilize this open mix every two weeks.

Begonia

Begonias may outgrow the light garden, but the following are selected for their small size:
Cane stem begonia: *B.* 'Medora' blooms shyly, but the foliage is beautifully spotted. Everblooming varieties are *B.* 'Orange Rubra,' *B.* 'Lenore Oliver,' *B.* 'Preussen' and *B.* 'Sachen.'

Rhizomatous Begonia

These offer the most miniatures; a few are *B.*

bowerae, B. bowerae nigramarga, B. 'China Doll,' *B.* 'Chumash' and *B.* 'Many Colors.'

Reiger Begonia

These are difficult to keep growing all year. They like cool temperatures — 65° to 70°F. is best. Keep the foliage dry at all times to prevent mildew; for this malady use Benlate (benomyl systemic fungicide).

Semituberous Begonia

B. 'Weltonensis' has maplelike foliage and is a constant bloomer.

Terrarium Begonia

B. prismatocarpa and *B.* 'Buttercup' are two bright yellow ever-blooming miniatures that will quickly fill a container. They require high humidity and must be grown in an enclosed atmosphere.

Wax Begonia (*B. semperflorens*)

These may be grown either from cuttings or from seed. Keep well fertilized and pruned. *B.* 'Ballet,' *B.* 'Firefly' and *B.* 'Pink Camellia' are excellent. The calla lily types (with variegated leaves) are a bit more difficult to grow. Both *B.* 'Charm' and *B.* 'Phaline' are feasible but want a cool temperature, and must dry out slightly between waterings.

Bromeliads

Bromeliads are interesting plants, related to pineapples. They do well under lights, but the smaller species and varieties are preferred.

Perfect drainage and air circulation around the root system are keys to success with bromeliads. Terrestrial bromeliads require a porous, acid mix—one of the soil-less mixes (pages 720–21) is recommended. The ephiphytic types may be mounted (glued or tied) on pieces of cork, bark, driftwood or tree fern, with roots wrapped in sphagnum moss for the wetter-growing types. The dry-growing *Tillandsia* should not have its roots covered.

Be sure to keep water in the vase-shaped varieties that have a "cup" in the center of their rosette. Mounted plants should be misted daily. Each bromeliad plant will bloom only once, but several offshoots or "pups" will appear at the base of the original plant, and these may be used for propagation. When offshoots are one-fourth to one-third the size of the mother plant, cut them off and mount or root them in a new soil mix.

Ephiphytic Bromeliads

Aechmea x 'Royal Wine,' *A. miniata discolor* and *A.* x 'Foster's Favorite' are best grown under medium light. *Tillandsia* species, like the miniatures *T. cyanea* and *T. ionanthe*, are best grown mounted on a piece of bark or driftwood.

Terrestrial Bromeliads

Cryptanthus species and hybrids are called earth stars and range from 2 in. to 12 in. across. *C.* 'It,' *C. zonatus, C. bromelioides tricolor, C. bivittatus* and *C. fosterionus* are all good. Grow at the ends of the light tubes. *Billbergia nutans* and *B. zebrina* should be grown close to the center of the lights. *Guzmania lingulata* and *G.* 'Major' have especially large, long-lasting colorful spikes. Grow in medium light.

Cactus and Succulents

The most successful plants of this large group are those that are flat, spreading or compact, so that sufficient surface is exposed to bright light. Keep them cool at night and use an extra well-drained soil. *Schlumbergera* (Christmas cactus) and the Easter cactus are popular, especially the new cultivars with their lovely pastel flowers.

Crossandra (firecracker flower)

An ever-blooming plant that reaches 12 in. high, with bright salmon flowers. It can be grown either from seed or from basal stem cuttings. Constant feeding, using 1/8 dilution of soluble fertilizer, and keeping the soil moist at all times will give good (possibly constant) bloom. *C. undulifolia* is recommended for light garden culture.

Episcia (carpet plant)

These species and hybrids enjoy warm temperatures (above 70°F) and high humidity, though the white-flowered *Episcia* is more tolerant of cool temperatures and lower humidity. They are stoloniferous plants and can be grown as a trailer or kept to a single rosette by trimming the stolons. *E. dianthiflora* has fringed white flowers, while its hybrid *E.* 'Cygnet' has larger flowers, larger leaves and is more floriferous. *E.* 'Cleopatra' or 'Pink Brocade' has variegated pink, white and green foliage with red flowers. It is usually grown in a terrarium because it is sensitive to drafts and needs *high* humidity.

Exacum

The Persian violet produces masses of 1/2-in. blue flowers (there is a rare white form) with bright yellow stamens almost constantly. It is grown readily from seed; keep some seedlings coming, because plants tend to die back after a long period of heavy bloom.

Gesneriads

The gesneriad plant group (a botanical family) is especially successful under lights. Best known are the *Saintpaulia* (African violet) hybrids, *Sinningia speciosa* (the florist's gloxinia) and *Episcia* (listed separately). Other plants in this same group that are highly successful under lights are listed below:

Achimenes
Can be bloomed at all seasons under light. *A.* 'Blue Waltz' (purple), *A.* 'Charm,' *A.* 'Tarentella' (pink) are erect but compact plants with large flowers. Plant the small tubers ½ in. deep in porous, open soil, and do not allow to dry out.

Aeschynanthus
These are trailing vines that bloom irregularly throughout the year under lights. *A. micranthus* has small red flowers produced in profusion. *A. ellipticus* has orange-pink flowers and *A. obconicus* has a maroon calyx and red flower.

Codonanthe carnosa
This is a smaller trailer, with succulent leaves and ever-blooming habit.

Columnea
Species and cultivars of this genus are rewarding under lights. Choose the ever-blooming types, such as *C. jamaicensis*, with orange flowers and arching stems. *C.* 'Early Bird' or *C.* 'Joy' are ever-bloomers, with yellow and red flowers. *C.* 'Fanfare' is a compact grower and *C.* 'Pixie' with orange flowers is the smallest hybrid.

Gesneria
This needs warmth, high humidity and extra lime in the soil for best results. *G. cuneifolia* has red, orange or yellow flowers, depending upon the clone you obtain. *G. christii, G. citrina* and *G. saxatilis* are all excellent for terrariums. *G.* 'Lemon Drop' is a hybird that is more tolerant and adaptable to growing conditions than the species.

Koellikeria erinoides
This grows as a miniature rosette, with small pink and white flowers in a terminal spike. It is excellent in terrariums.

Kohleria
These are rhizomatous plants that may grow quite tall, but tip cuttings allow you to shorten its stature periodically. *K.* 'Connecticut Belle' is smaller than most floriferous plants, with large pink flowers and interesting mottled foliage.

Sinningia
This is the proper genus name for the florist's gloxinia, which may be too large for some light gardens. But try the new dwarf hybrids and miniatures. Some of the best are *S. concinna, S. pusilla, S.* 'Dollbaby,' *S.* 'Cindy,' *S.* 'Cindy-Ella,' *S.* 'Coral Baby' is new and a good performer, as is the white-flowering *S.* 'Snowflake.'

Smithiantha
These may be large plants, so select such dwarf varieties as *S.* 'Littleone' or the Zebrina hybrids. The flowers, in large spikes, range from yellow to orange to red.

Hoya

These tropical vines are too large for most light gardens, but the species *H. bella* is small with delicate leaves. Flowers appear on short leafless spurs year after year, so do not remove these. They flower best when allowed to become pot-bound in a well-drained mix with some extra lime or bone meal added to the original mix.

Orchids

Many orchids can be successfully grown under lights, *Paphiopedilum* and *Phalaenopsis* being the easiest to raise. However, the range of orchids is great if you can supply sufficiently high light intensity and also devote enough time to learning about them and experimenting in their culture.

Paphiopedilum
The easiest of the orchids to cultivate under light, when well grown, it will bloom year after year. Some dwarfs are *P. niveum* 'Ang Thong,'

P. concolor and *P. bellatulum. P. fairrieanum* matures at 8 in., and *P. glaucophyllum* produces a succession of flowers on the same scape.

Phalaenopsis

Known as moth orchids, these have long-lasting flowers. When they fade, cut the inflorescence back only three-quarters of the way, leaving several nodes. Within a month or two a new spike will form and the plant will bloom a second time. By that time a new spike will be coming up from a younger leaf. The modern hybrids are large but some of the species are smaller and easier to grow. *P. amboinensis* has yellow flowers and brown stripes; *P. equestris* has violet tones and small flowers on a plant that should almost always have flowers; *P. parishii* is a dwarf species with small white flowers. Other orchids to try growing under light are *Ascocentrum ampullaceum, A. curvifolum, Brassovola nodosa, Goodyeara* spp., *Lockhartia* spp., *Masdevallia* spp. and *Pleurothallis* spp.

Oxalis (wood sorrel)

These are cormous plants that will go dormant if allowed to dry out. Most growers dry the plants off once a year, place the pots in the refrigerator for several weeks, then repot to start them over. *O. regnellii* has triangular leaves and white flowers; *O. aureo-reticulata* has green leaves with gold veins and rosy-red flowers.

Pelargonium (geranium)

Dwarf and miniature geraniums are good subjects under lights, provided they are kept as cool as possible. *P.* 'Alpha' has brilliant red-orange flowers and small apple-green leaves. *P.* 'Black Vesuvius' has orange-scarlet flowers and tiny black-green leaves with a red band. Zonal geraniums have pleasing-colored leaves of such variety that it doesn't matter whether they bloom or not. The leaves are banded with green, red and cream, and are spectacular under lights. The tricolored varieties are the most desirable, such as *P.* 'Mrs. Henry Cox,' *P.* 'Mrs. Strong' and P. '*Skies of Italy.*'

Punica Granatum 'Nana'

This dwarf pomegranate is an excellent subject for bonsai under lights. Try it from seed or cuttings and you will be pleased with the lovely pendulous red or pink blossoms. The plant will even set fruit. Keep it pruned and the soil moist.

Roses

These are dwarfs that reflect the hybrid tea roses. Most grow 12 in. to 15 in. tall, but some grow only to between 5 in. and 8 in. They require the same care that outdoor roses do. They must be grown in the garden in the summer, then pruned slightly and sprayed before bringing indoors in the autumn. Keep them from becoming straggly, but do not prune them back as drastically as you would hybrid teas.

Saintpaulia spp. (African violet)

These are part of the gesneriad family, but because of their popularity and variety they are listed separately. The extensive range in plant and leaf form, color and blossoms has earned the African violet worldwide recognition. Of easy culture, it is a good plant for the beginner. If you master the African violet, you should be able to grow most plants. There are good new hybrids being developed constantly. The miniatures and trailing types (not grown as a single rosette) are popular with the more selective indoor gardeners, as are the species (about seventeen) of *Saintpaulia*.

Scilla violacea

This is a succulent bulb with 2-in. to 4-in. spotted leaves. It is dwarf and evergreen, blooms in the spring and produces sprays of blue flowers. But its real asset is the attractive foliage. Keep pot-bound and use a succulent mix. Allow to dry out between waterings, and do not overfertilize. Propagate by dividing the bulbs.

38

Greenhouse Gardening

For many people, gardening is a joyous adventure from the opening of the first winter aconite in the early spring until the frosts of autumn have robbed the garden of its beauty and driven us indoors to await the arrival of the seed catalogues. Fortunate, indeed, are those favored few among gardeners who possess a small greenhouse and can carry on their gardening activities throughout the year.

Small, private greenhouses have always been considered such a luxury that many gardeners have assumed they were something quite beyond their means and therefore gave the matter little thought. However, new types have been designed along such simple and efficient lines that construction and operating costs have been greatly reduced, and the small greenhouse is now well within the range of many a gardener. It need not be elaborate or expensive; a small lean-to, built against the house, may be constructed for only a few hundred dollars and will offer delightful possibilities for winter gardening. The money thus invested will pay big dividends in beauty and in joyous activity. Even the unheated greenhouse offers many opportunities and is a challenge to the skill and ingenuity of the gardener.

If the greenhouse can be attached directly to the house it may usually be operated on the same heating unit, which substantially reduces the cost of operation. Such a location also has the advantage of providing shelter from strong winds. If a greenhouse is to be attached to the house, it should preferably have a south or southeastern exposure. If it is not attached to the house, it should be located so that it receives a maximum amount of sunshine and is protected, if at all possible, from the prevailing winds.

Where the topography of the ground presents no problem, the greenhouse should preferably be oriented so that the length of the house runs from north to south, as this will provide for a maximum amount of sunlight during the winter months.

CONSTRUCTION

The average hobby or home greenhouse is basically a simple structure. If one is handy with tools, pre-cut and pre-fitted greenhouse kits are available today ready for assembling. These kits come complete with detailed instructions, and are, of course, the most economical to erect. Plans for greenhouses also are available from most local cooperative extension services. In any case, there are many details that must be considered in the course of constructing a greenhouse, whether it is to be heated or unheated. It is essential that the house be built of sturdy, durable materials; that satisfactory provisions be made for ventilation; that the benches be designed to meet any specially designated needs; and that the heating unit be entirely adequate.

Aluminum is considered very durable and

753

will not be affected by rust or rot. Although the initial cost may be somewhat higher than that of wood, the maintenance costs will be reduced to a minimum as the aluminum will require no painting and almost nothing in the way of repairs and replacements. A combination of wood and aluminum is also very satisfactory.

The least expensive types of greenhouses are those made of plastic instead of glass. Polyethylene film, polyvinyl chloride (PVC), clear vinyl, polyester (Mylar) or fiberglass panels are the plastics most frequently used. Such plastic greenhouses are very popular among commercial nurseries, and are used today on a very large scale. The cost of a plastic structure is a fraction of the cost of a glass greenhouse, particularly since many homeowners are adept at "do-it-yourself" techniques. Plastic-clad greenhouses obviously offer great possibilities for the average home gardener on a limited budget.

Among the other advantages of plastic greenhouses is that they have greater moisture retention and less heat loss than a glass structure. The light transmission varies from approximately 81 percent to 90 percent through a single thickness. Actually, some plants even thrive better in this lower light intensity than they do in a glass greenhouse. The chief disadvantage of plastic greenhouses is that they deteriorate under strong sunlight, and usually must be renewed in two to five years, depending upon the type of plastic that was used.

The material for the construction of the benches is usually a matter of personal preference. Wood is the most economical, if the initial cost alone is considered, but it is the least satisfactory, for it is not durable and will have to be replaced after a few years. If wood is used, however, the best grade of cypress should be selected, as cypress is more resistant to decay than any other wood available today. Regardless of what wood is selected, it should be treated with a salt-type preservative to prevent rot. Copper naphthemate is a good treatment. Beware of creosote and pentachlorophenol preservatives that are toxic to plants; these should never be used in the greenhouse. Solid concrete benches are sometimes used, but they are very expensive. One of the most satisfactory types of bench is a combination of metal and tile, which is pleasing in appearance, durable and yet not prohibitive in cost. An open, wire bench that provides good ventilation and heat distribution at a low cost also is suitable.

Benches constructed with pipe legs and an angle-iron frame are the most satisfactory. Those benches in which crops for cut flowers are to be grown should be from 6 in. to 8 in. deep. Adequate provision for drainage must be provided in the form of narrow openings between the boards or tiles that form the bottom of the bench. Benches on which potted plants are to be placed should be 2 in. or 3 in. deep. Such benches, which resemble shallow trays, should be filled with pebbles or cinders upon which the pots may rest. This will not only facilitate drainage but will aid in maintaining the desired degree of humidity as well. Don't make the benches too wide. They should be only as wide as you can comfortably reach. For side benches, build them 2 ft. to 3 ft. wide; center benches are reached from both sides and may be as wide as 6 ft. The heights of the benches will vary to fit your needs; most benches are from 30 in. to 32 in. tall.

The greenhouse should be supplied with piped water, and a sufficient number of faucets provided at convenient points. The faucets should be threaded so that a hose may be easily attached. In general, it is much more convenient to use short hoses with several faucets than one long, heavy, cumbersome hose. One faucet for every 12 ft. of greenhouse space is recommended.

Concrete makes the most satisfactory walkways for greenhouses, although cinders and gravel are sometimes used where it is necessary to maintain a very high degree of humidity, as in orchid houses. Concrete walks are easy to keep clean, will withstand wear, are impervious to dampness and are, in general, entirely satisfactory.

It is very convenient to have a small workroom or potting shed attached to the greenhouse. But if space is not available, or if the various items of expense must be kept to a minimum, the north end of the house may be utilized for this purpose. A bench of convenient height and length should be provided for use in the preparation of soil mixtures, and for such operations as seed sowing, transplanting and potting, which are an almost daily part of the greenhouse routine. Bins may be constructed underneath the bench as a storage place for surplus

38.1 Nearly every plant lover, at one time or another, dreams of a greenhouse full of flowering plants when snows are deep and temperatures cold outdoors. Photo courtesy Lord and Burnham

flats and pots and to hold the loam, peat moss, perlite, sand, leaf mold and compost used in the various soil mixtures. Adequate shelf space should also be provided for insecticides, fumigants, labels and other small items.

In managing a modest greenhouse, the most important considerations are heating, temperature control, ventilation, watering and syringing.

HEATING

Hot water is the most satisfactory form of heat for the small greenhouse. The heat is more evenly distributed than steam heat and there is less danger of a sudden drop in temperature. It is an accepted fact that in a small greenhouse practically all plants thrive better with hot water heat than with steam heat.

Thermostatically controlled oil heat is still the most satisfactory type of heating unit for greenhouses today, especially if it is an extension of the existing home heating system with a separate heating zone. However, for a very small greenhouse in a protected location, there are

some other fairly efficient heating systems. Among these are: electric, forced warm air and direct radiation. For a greenhouse of considerable size, the cost of operating any of these methods would be prohibitive, of course, but for a small hobby greenhouse, such costs need not be excessive. In any case, regardless of the choice, any heating system should be thermostatically operated, since environmental control is vital in greenhouse gardening.

Overall fuel costs for greenhouse heating can be kept to a minimum if the solar heat that accumulates within the structure is retained as long as possible. This can easily be achieved by closing the ventilators earlier each day than one would normally do, and also by carefully covering the glass during the night with straw mats or boards. In this way, the stored heat from the sun will not escape so rapidly.

TEMPERATURE

If the greenhouse is of sufficient size, it is wise to have it divided into at least two sections, and to have the heating system so planned that it is possible to maintain a moderately high temperature in one section and a much lower temperature in the other section. This will make it possible to grow a wider variety of plants, as some plants have a preference for a cool temperature, while others prefer a comparatively high temperature. If, however, the greenhouse is small, and it is not feasible to provide for more than one temperature, this need not be too great a handicap. The choice of plant materials will, of necessity, be somewhat more limited, but even the smallest greenhouse, maintained at a rather low temperature, will offer delightful opportunities for winter gardening.

In general commercial practice, greenhouse temperatures range from 40° to 45°F. in extremely cool houses to 65° to 70°F. in houses where semitropical plants are grown. These figures refer to night temperatures. During the day the temperatures will naturally rise from 10° to 15° higher. The thermometer in a greenhouse should not be placed where the direct heat of the sun will fall upon it. For a small greenhouse where but one temperature is to be maintained, a range between 50° and 55°F. at night, with a temperature varying from 10° to 15° higher during the day, will usually prove most satisfactory. Some plants are able to endure severe fluctuations in temperature, while others are extremely sensitive to such changes, and it is wise for the amateur to choose the less temperamental plants. If one is an experienced gardener and can provide conditions that very nearly approximate the ideal, it is possible to grow some of the more exotic greenhouse plants; but if one is a novice it is well to devote one's efforts to the more sturdy types, which are less exacting in their demands.

VENTILATION

An abundance of fresh air is essential for the normal, healthy growth of all plants, and at the time of construction adequate provision must be made for ventilation. Some greenhouses are equipped with ventilators on the sides as well as on the roof, and this is the most desirable type of construction. It requires care, skill and good judgment to control a ventilating system efficiently. As a general practice, the ventilators should be opened in the morning when the temperature is rising. On warm days when there is brilliant sunshine and little wind, the ventilators should be opened to the fullest extent. On very cold days a mere crack may be sufficient. The ventilators should be closed early enough in the afternoon to conserve as much heat as possible. When a strong wind is blowing, it is wise to open the ventilators on the opposite side of the house from the direction of the prevailing wind in order to prevent a direct draft of air on the plants. Sudden changes in temperature and sudden shifting from brilliant sunlight to dark clouds mean more or less constant attention to the regulation of the ventilators in a greenhouse if the heating unit is to function at its maximum degree of efficiency.

So important is fresh air to the welfare of the plants that even on days in early autumn and in the spring when it would be possible to maintain the desired temperature within the house, provided that the ventilators were kept closed, it is preferable to admit fresh air even if it necessitates maintaining a low fire.

Excellent electronically controlled devices for regulating the ventilators in greenhouses are available and such devices are well worth the extra cost, as they relieve the owner of much care and anxiety. When fluctuations in temperature occur, the ventilators are automatically opened and closed by these thermostatically activated devices.

WATERING AND SYRINGING

Greenhouse plants vary tremendously in their moisture requirements, and individual plants also vary considerably at different stages of growth. In a program of successful greenhouse management it is, therefore, essential to understand fully the moisture requirements of the plants one is handling. The requirements of all the important greenhouse plants and plant groups are discussed in detail at the end of this chapter.

There are, however, certain general principles that should be observed. Greenhouse plants should be arranged according to their watering requirements. For example, cacti and succulents do not need the amount of water that moisture-loving plants do. Watering should be done preferably when the temperature is rising, and it is, therefore, part of the usual morning routine in the greenhouse. To secure the best results, the temperature of the soil in the beds and benches should be approximately that of the surrounding air in the greenhouse. Water absorption by the plant takes place very slowly in cold soils. Greenhouse plants in ground beds frequently fail to do well because of this factor. Such a condition may be remedied, however, by running heating pipes along the sides of the beds, or by placing pipes in tiles underneath the beds. Some plants are so sensitive to temperature that it is advisable, whenever possible, to supply them with water that has been warmed to a room temperature of approximately 70° F. In this group we find such plants as poinsettia, gardenia, gerbera, lily and rose. Tanks or barrels may be kept in the greenhouse for the storage of sufficient water to supply the needs of such plants.

Most plants will make their best growth, other conditions being favorable, in soils that are uniformly supplied with a sufficient amount of moisture. In the case of greenhouse plants grown in beds and benches, the optimum moisture conditions may best be maintained by heavy watering at rather infrequent intervals. Both the amount of water and the frequency of application will be determined, to a considerable extent, by the age of the plants, the type of root system they possess and the physical structure of the soil. Large plants that are making active growth will require relatively large amounts of water. Plants with fibrous root systems will require larger amounts than those with tap roots. Heavy soils will require less frequent applications than light, sandy soils. If greenhouse beds and benches are given a fairly heavy watering at rather infrequent intervals, the plants will make a vigorous root growth that will extend deeply into the soil. If frequent, light waterings are given, the plants will have a tendency to become shallow-rooted, and will be less vigorous in consequence.

The force with which the water is applied is also a factor to be taken into consideration. A heavy stream of water should be avoided, as it causes the soil to become more and more compact and thus reduces aeration. An adjustable hose nozzle, or a rose nozzle of a size to permit a moderately fine spray, may be attached to the hose. For watering small seedlings and young

38.2 Lean-to greenhouses can be adapted to fit a house of almost any architectural style or size. Photo courtesy Lord and Burnham

growing plants, a fog nozzle or a watering can is to be preferred. The regulation greenhouse watering can with a long spout is ideal for this purpose, and a series of rose nozzles of various sizes may be obtained.

Careful attention must always be given to the watering of young seedlings. Fresh-sown seed and young seedlings are most efficiently watered by placing the seedpan or pot in a tray filled about one-third with water. By capillary action the water will soon rise to the surface in the seedpan or pot, at which time it should be removed from the tray. On bright sunny days it is often necessary to water more than once. Seed flats and young transplanted seedlings should never be allowed to dry out and they always should be kept shaded. This can be done with a sheet of newspaper.

The watering of potted plants also requires skill and good judgment as the plants vary tremendously in their moisture requirements. Some plants, such as the azalea, maidenhair fern and certain types of begonia, should never be allowed to dry out. Many other plants, including poinsettia, fuchsia, calla and clivia, require a definite rest period, during which time the amount of water should be appreciably decreased or, in some cases, entirely withheld. The requirements of the individual plants are discussed at the end of the chapter. In general, potted plants should be watered only when necessary. Plants that are making active growth and those that are in full flower will usually require liberal quantities of water. In some cases it may be necessary to water more than once a day. An excellent way to determine a potted plant's need for water is the method used by many old English gardeners—that of tapping the pot with the knuckle. If the tap resounds in a dull thud, it is an indication that the plant does not need water. If, however, the tap resounds with a hollow, ringing sound, additional moisture should be supplied to the plant. Another method is to lift the pot and test it by weight. A clay pot is always heavier than a plastic pot, and as a rule, the clay pot will dry out faster also. Plunging the pot into some sand or gravel will keep the roots cooler and the pot will not dry out as quickly. It is important that there be sufficient drainage space below the pot.

The majority of plants with smooth leaves may be watered by the overhead method without any danger of injury to the foliage. Plants with hairy or very fleshy leaves, such as African violet, should preferably be watered in such a way that no moisture comes into contact with the foliage. A watering can may be used very successfully for this purpose if the rose nozzle is removed. In some cases it is advisable to place the plants in a pan of water and to allow them to remain thus until the surface of the soil in the pot has become moist.

There are excellent automatic subirrigation systems for greenhouse benches. Such a system, which should preferably be installed at the time the house is built, has many advantages but involves considerable expense.

There are several very direct advantages to be gained from syringing. It increases the humidity and reduces the evaporation power of the air very appreciably. Thus, the transpiration of water from the leaves is reduced to a point lower than the actual absorption of water by the roots.

Syringing also has a very direct influence on the control of red spider.

During the winter syringing should be done on bright, sunny days when the temperature is rising. It is not advisable to syringe plants late in the afternoon when the temperature is dropping, as the result will be a condensation of moisture on the foliage, which may prove injurious to the plant. During the summer, however, plants may safely be syringed in the late afternoon.

In general, all plants that have smooth foliage will benefit from syringing. But plants with fleshy or hairy foliage should not be syringed, as the protracted retention of water on their surfaces is more harmful than beneficial.

HUMIDITY

The maintenance of a proper degree of humidity in the greenhouse is a matter of vital importance. Plants vary greatly in their optimum humidity requirements, just as they vary greatly in their moisture requirements. The fact that roses require a humidity of 75 percent or more, while members of the cactus family thrive best where the humidity is less than 50 percent, means that these two plant groups must be accorded very different treatment. Every gardener should be familiar with the general humidity requirements of the various plant groups. In some cases, the optimum humidity requirements of specific plants have been very definitely determined, and these are in the section on culture.

Humidity is closely associated with the respiration of plants and with the manufacture of food within the plant. It is a generally accepted fact that high humidity makes it possible for the leaf stomata to open wider and to remain open longer than is possible under conditions of low humidity. If plants are grown in an atmosphere in which the degree of humidity is far below the optimum, the transpiration from the leaves will be greater than the intake of moisture by the roots, and the growth and vigor of the plants will suffer seriously in consequence.

There is a very direct relationship between humidity and the factors of light and temperature. During dull, winter days an overabundance of humidity is not to be desired, as it may have a definitely detrimental effect upon the plants, whereas on bright, sunny days when the temperature is comparatively high, the effect will be decidedly beneficial. It is particularly needed on cold, bright days in winter when the heater is being forced to maintain the desired temperature.

There are various ways in which the humidity in a greenhouse may be increased: by syringing the plants; by wetting down the walks; and by spraying beneath the benches, particularly on the heating pipes. It is possible to maintain a higher degree of humidity in a house where the walks are made of gravel than it is in a house where the walks are of concrete. However, most growers prefer concrete because the degree of humidity can be more definitely controlled and the house can be kept dry, except when moisture is artificially applied at times when it may seem desirable to increase the humidity. In orchid houses, where a very high degree of humidity is necessary, a sprinkling or misting system is sometimes installed under the benches.

It is advisable to record the degree of humidity in a greenhouse definitively. This may be done by means of a hygrometer, or some similar device designed especially for the purpose. For the control of diseases and pests of greenhouse plants, see Chapter 32.

38.3 A home greenhouse can be used for special plant collections, such as orchids, camellias and cactus, or simply for a great mixture of winter-flowering plants. Photo courtesy Lord and Burnham

THE EFFECT OF SUMMER ON THE GREENHOUSE

With the approach of summer, the intensity of the heat in a greenhouse would become unbearable both for the plants and for the gardener if some form of shade were not provided. The ideal device for such a purpose is a roll of small strips of metal, green plastic, cheesecloth, wood or thin pieces of bamboo wired together. These may be regulated by means of pulleys and rolled up and down at will. It is a decided advantage to be able to roll them up on cool, cloudy days and to lower them on bright, sunny days when the temperature within the house is soaring. If it is not possible to obtain any of the above roller-type shades, the most satisfactory substitute is a coating of some suitable preparation applied to the outside of the glass. Such shading compounds can be purchased from any reputable garden or greenhouse supplier. They are usually obtained in either powdered or liquid form; they mix in-

stantly with water, and are available in white or green.

During the summer months when most of the plants have been removed, the greenhouse may be given a thorough cleaning. Any necessary repairs or repainting may be done at this time. The soil from the benches may be removed and fresh soil brought in, and the greenhouse may be made ready for the next winter season.

THE AMOUNT OF LIGHT AND ITS EFFECT

In recent decades a number of interesting experiments have been carried on at several of the State Agricultural Experimental Stations to determine the effect of varying light intensities on plant growth. It has been found that plants vary tremendously in their responses to light. In the case of some plants it is possible to hasten the blooming period and to increase the quantity and quality of the bloom by prolonging the day. This is accomplished by means of electric lights placed above the plants. In the case of other plants the reverse procedure, the shortening of the day, has resulted in the production of early bloom, and this, in turn, is accomplished by shading the plants with black cloth in order to exclude all light for a portion of the day. Extensive experiments have shown that some plants are not affected by either of these treatments, and in other cases the effect has been so slight that the additional labor and expense involved have not been justified.

Increasing the Length of the Day

Additional light may be supplied for a period varying from four to eight hours either at the beginning or the end of the day. The method most commonly employed by commercial growers is to provide additional light for a period of five hours, beginning at 5:00 p.m. and continuing until 10:00 p.m. The method employed in supplying the light is of considerable importance. The lights should be placed approximately 18 in. to 24 in. above the plants. For the majority of plants a 40-watt bulb may be used with excellent results; for some plants that are unusually responsive to light a 15- or 25-watt bulb will be sufficient. Either clear or frosted incandescent bulbs may be used. Ordinary nitrogen-filled bulbs have, in the majority of cases, proved to be more satisfactory than mercury, neon or sun lamps. It is essential that reflectors be used. The most desirable type of reflector is one about 8 in. in diameter and deep enough so that only the tip of the bulb extends beyond the rim. The plants should be given an opportunity to become well established in the benches before using extra light.

Reducing the Length of the Day

The usual procedure in shortening the length of the day in order to induce early flowering is to drape black cloth or some other dark, opaque material over the plants. Closely woven black sateen has proved to be one of the most satisfactory materials for this purpose, and if proper care is taken it will give good service for several seasons. In most cases a reduction of four or five hours in the length of the day is sufficient. The practice most generally followed is to place the cloth over the plants at 5 in the afternoon, allowing it to remain until 7 the following morning. The time when the short-day treatment should be initiated will depend entirely upon the normal bud-forming period of the plants.

THE UNHEATED GREENHOUSE

Although an unheated greenhouse has decided limitations, it also offers many satisfying opportunities. However, before discussing the pros and cons of such a structure, it should be pointed out that people have become increasingly aware—and justifiably so—of the need to conserve energy, and that the ordinary sources of such energy are no longer limitless, as most of us once thought they were. In other words, before deciding whether or not one should build a greenhouse, obviously the cost of heating the structure must be carefully explored. Regardless of the ultimate decision—to heat or not to heat—the avid gardener need not be discouraged. There are many delightful opportunities to indulge one's gardening interest to the fullest in an unheated greenhouse; two of the most popular methods are discussed below.

Alpine House

For a collection of rare alpine plants, or for plants difficult to grow outdoors, the unheated greenhouse is the ideal location. With plenty of ventilation near the benches, or with air conditioning during the summer months, this type of greenhouse can be used throughout the year for growing alpine plants. The glass or plastic skin will protect the plants from harsh or dry winds, while the amount of water needed also can be more carefully controlled. On sunny winter days the ventilators must be opened to prevent the temperature from rising too much and also to keep the plants in their dormant stage. In the summer the lath shading is rolled over the glass or plastic, but this shading must be at least 6 in. above in order to maintain a cooling air current between the glass or plastic and the shading.

38.4 A collection of dwarf geraniums (Pelargonium *spp.*) *in a window greenhouse that has been modified to fit the floor-to-ceiling opening. Photo courtesy Lord and Burnham*

Pit-house

This type of structure also can be described as a combination of sunken greenhouse and walk-in coldframe. In effect, it is really a greenhouse that is partially below ground. Only 12 in. to 24 in. of the sides and the roof, which is made of coldframe sash, is above ground. To ventilate the pit-house, the sash can either be partially raised or removed completely. The advantage of the pit-house over a regulation greenhouse for alpine plants is that the plants are closer to the glass, the temperature can more readily be controlled and the roof can be removed to expose the plants to the weather. The pit-house is also easier and cheaper to install.

In parts of the country where the climate is severe, it is difficult, if not impossible, to obtain any actual bloom in an unheated greenhouse during the midwinter months. But with the first warm days of spring such a greenhouse may become a veritable garden, and it will offer a wealth of material for flower arrangements in the house. Bulbs of all kinds may be forced into early bloom, and *Astilbe japonica,* bleeding-heart, *Mertensia, Aquilegia,* pansy and primrose may all be brought into flower. *Antirrhinum, Calendula,* annual larkspur and wallflower may be sown in the early autumn and the young plants carried over the winter in the benches. Although such flowers will make comparatively little growth during the winter, they will develop into sturdy plants with strong, vigorous root systems and will come into flower months ahead of spring-sown seedlings.

During the spring months the unheated greenhouse also serves the purposes of a somewhat glorified coldframe, as it affords ideal conditions for the starting of young seedlings. It is a decided advantage to have the unheated greenhouse in as protected a location as possible. Straw mats or burlap frames packed with straw may be used to provide added protection during extremely cold weather.

SELECTION OF PLANT MATERIALS

If the potentialities of a small greenhouse are to be realized to the fullest extent, the plant materials to be grown must be selected with great care. The usual desideratum is to have as much bloom as possible in the greenhouse from early autumn until late spring, and to have a wide variety of flowers that are of particular value for cutting and for decorative purposes in the house.

Annuals, perennials, bulbs and potted plants all have an important part to play, and with careful thought and planning an abundance of bloom may be had throughout the winter months.

Many of the annuals that grow so luxuriantly outdoors during the summer months and are so valuable for cutting will give an equally good account of themselves in the greenhouse. To this list we are able to add some of the more temperamental annuals, which cannot always be grown so successfully under the trying conditions of summer temperatures and humidity.

In order to obtain a succession of bloom from autumn until spring, it is necessary to plan one's program of work well in advance and to follow the schedule with exactitude and care.

Agathaea coelestris (blue daisy)

Lovely both as a potted plant and for cutting, *Agathaea coelestris* is admirably adapted to the small greenhouse. The daisylike flowers, of a soft powder blue, with golden centers, are borne in profusion throughout the winter and early spring months. The plants remain in flower over a long period of time, which makes them particularly desirable as potted plants for house decoration.

Propagation

Agathaea may be raised either from seed or from cuttings. In plants grown from seed there is a slight variation in color, and after a stock has been established it is wise to make cuttings from the most desirable plants. Cuttings made during the early spring root readily, and the young plants may be carried on in pots throughout the summer.

Culture

In early autumn the plants may be transferred to the greenhouse bench if the flowers are to be used only for cutting. If they are to be grown as potted plants, they may be shifted into 6-in. or 8-in. pots or bulb pans. The plants thrive well in a moderately cool house.

Soil Requirements

Agathaea is not particular in regard to soil. A good potting compost is all that is necessary.

Antirrhinum (snapdragon)

The snapdragon is among the most satisfactory of all greenhouse plants and will give a wealth of colorful bloom throughout the winter months.

Propagation

If autumn or early winter bloom is desired, the seeds should be sown early in June. The young seedlings should be pricked out before they become crowded, and they may be carried on in flats or in pots until they are ready to be benched in late August or early September.

Soil Requirements

A rather heavy, coarse soil, well supplied with organic matter and of good fertility, is considered ideal, although snapdragons will do well on widely varying types of soil. A soil with a slightly acid reaction is preferred, because one that is too alkaline in its reaction will cause a yellowing of the leaf margins and veins. An application of superphosphate, 5 lb. per 100 sq. ft., made at the time of planting will give excellent results, and additional feeding is usually not necessary.

Culture

When the young seedlings have developed five or six sets of leaves, they should be pinched back. The plants should be spaced 10 in. apart each way in the bench. Snapdragons prefer a cool temperature and will succeed extremely well if given a night temperature of approximately 45° to 48°F. with a rise of 10° to 15° during the day. They are one of the few plants that can be grown successfully in an unheated greenhouse, and will give an abundance of bloom during the late winter and early spring months if grown under such conditions. In a heated greenhouse they often bloom immediately after chrysanthemums and in this way excellent use is made of all available bench space. For a late planting such as this, the seeds should be sown in late August and the young seedlings carried on in flats or pots until the chrysanthemums have been removed and bench space is available. Snapdragons will usually not come into flower until late winter, but will give luxuriant bloom throughout the early spring months. It is a common practice among commercial growers not to water the foliage of snapdragons, merely watering the roots as a precautionary measure against the spread of rust, even though many strains are reputed to be rust-resistant. Throughout the flowering season the plants should be disbudded, and any small shoots that appear at the base of the leaves and in the axils of the flower stalks should be removed. Snapdragons prefer a relatively low humidity of approximately 60 percent.

Snapdragons of the forcing type, suitable for growing in the greenhouse, are available in a veritable rainbow of colors: white, yellow, apple-blossom pink, rose, apricot, scarlet, deep Indian red and wine, among others.

Aquilegia (columbine)

It is, perhaps, difficult to think of *Aquilegia* as a greenhouse plant, yet it can be forced so easily and the flowers are so exquisite for cutting that a few clumps should certainly be included. Plants that have flowered the previous season in the garden or in the nursery are ideal for greenhouse cultivation. It is well to mark the clumps at the time that they are in bloom, as it is then possible to choose plants that are unusually beautiful in form or in coloring and will therefore be of particular value as cut flowers later on in the season.

Culture

Clumps of columbine should be lifted in the autumn and placed in a coldframe where they can be given some slight protection. Late in January or early in February the dormant plants may be brought into the greenhouse and planted in a bench, or potted in 10-in. to 12-in. pots. Growth will start within a few days and by March or early April the plants will be in full flower. A cool temperature, ranging between 45° and 55°F., is preferred, as *Aquilegia* will not do well if subjected to excessive heat. After the plants have been forced, they may be replanted in the nursery.

Soil Requirements

Good potting compost.

Begonia

This plant may be grouped into four general classes: the semituberous-rooted; the tuberous-rooted; the foliage group; and the fibrous-rooted.

Semituberous Group

Propagation

These plants are propagated by petiole leaf cuttings taken from medium-sized, well-ripened leaves in November and December. The petioles should be inserted in the propagating case in such a way that the leaf blades do not come into contact with the sand. The formation of roots requires from four or five weeks, but the cuttings should not be potted up until new shoots have begun to develop from the base. A potting mixture of 1 part loam, 1 part sand and 1 part peat moss should be used, and the crown of the cutting should be placed as near the surface as possible.

Soil Requirements

A soil with a pH between 6.8 and 7.2 is preferred. For the final potting soil a mixture of 3 parts loam, 2 parts rotted manure, 1 part peat moss and 1 part sand is recommended. To each 2½ bushels of soil may be added a 4-in. pot of a 4–12–4 complete fertilizer.

Culture

The young plants may be grown on with a bottom heat of about 70°F., and as they develop they may be shifted into larger pots. The final potting in a 6-in. or 7-in. pot should be done in September. A humid atmosphere and partial shade during the summer are desirable, and pinching should be practiced in order to produce stocky, well-developed plants. Staking is advisable, as the stems are very brittle. During the growing period a night temperature of 58° to 60°F. is desirable, with a slightly higher temperature during the day.

Tuberous-rooted Group

See Summer-flowering Bulbs and Tubers, page 351.

Foliage Group

Propagation

Members of this group are propagated by means of leaf cuttings. Only well-matured leaves should be selected for propagation. One in. of the leaf margin should be cut away and the remaining portion of the leaf should be cut into triangular sections, with a small section of the petiole at the base and a vein running through the middle. The cutting should then be inserted in the propagating case, the section of petiole being completely covered.

Soil Requirements⎤
Culture   ⎦   See Semituberous Group.

Fibrous-rooted Group *(Begonia semperflorens)*

Propagation

The fibrous-rooted begonias may be propagated by seed, by stem cuttings and in the case of a few varieties, such as 'Gloire de Chatelaine,' by division. Seeds may be sown at any time from November to January. The seeds are exceedingly fine and should be handled with care. (See Chapter 34 on Propagation.) The seedlings should be pricked out as soon as they have developed their second leaf. Cuttings may be taken at any time of the year but will root most readily during March and April.

Soil Requirements⎤
Culture   ⎦   See Semituberous Group.

Bouvardia

The waxy, orange-blossom-scented flowers of the bouvardia are a source of constant joy during the brief months that they are in bloom. The flowers are so lovely for cutting and the fragrance is so delightful that a few clumps should be grown in every small greenhouse.

Propagation

New plants may be started very readily from cuttings made in late winter or early spring, and the young plants may be grown in pots. Bouvardia may also be propagated by means of root cuttings. The roots may be cut into pieces 1 in. to 2 in. long, and these may be planted horizontally in flats containing a mixture of equal parts of sand and peat moss.

Soil Requirements

Bouvardia prefers a very fibrous, mellow soil, abundantly supplied with leaf mold or some other form of organic matter. The soil should have a neutral or slightly alkaline reaction, preferably testing between pH 7.0 and pH 7.5.

If the soil is too acid in its reaction, it will cause a browning of the foliage, and in some cases a complete defoliation.

Culture

During the summer months the young rooted cuttings may be planted in the open, being benched late in August; alternatively, they may be planted directly in the greenhouse bed or bench in May and carried over the summer in their permanent location. The plants should be kept pinched back until the end of August so that they may become well branched. When the plants are moved from the open ground into the greenhouse, they must be lifted with an ample quantity of earth and the roots should be disturbed as little as possible. It is also wise to shade the plants for a few days after transplanting until they have become well established. Bouvardia prefers a moderately cool temperature, a temperature of 55°F. at night being considered ideal, with a rise of about 10° or so during the day. The plants will usually begin to flower late in September and will continue to give generous bloom throughout November and December. When the plants have finished blooming, they should be cut back, lifted and placed under the bench, water being withheld gradually. Late in January the soil may be shaken from the roots of the old plants, and they may be potted up in 5 in. or 6 in. pots. Cuttings may be made from these plants as growth starts, or the old plants may be carried over for another season of bloom. They will often bloom even more profusely during this second season.

Calendula (pot marigold)

These are among the most satisfactory of all plants for the cool greenhouse, and their gay, jaunty blossoms, in shades of orange, yellow and gold, are borne in profusion throughout the winter months. The plants are of easy culture, and will repay one generously for the small amount of labor expended upon them.

Soil Requirements

Calendula may be grown with a reasonable degree of success in almost any soil, but it does best in a rather heavy loam of high fertility. A cool, deep, rich soil is ideal, and in the preparation of the beds 1 part rotted manure should be used to every 3 parts of soil, and an application of 5 lb. of superphosphate per 100 sq. ft. should be made. The plants are more or less indifferent to soil reaction but, in general, a neutral reaction is considered best. A mulch of peat moss is beneficial because it helps to maintain a cool soil temperature.

Propagation

The seeds may be sown at any time from mid-July to late October. Seeds sown during the last week in July will come into flower about the middle of October. Seeds sown about October 10 will flower early in February. The young seedlings make rapid growth, and after being transplanted into pots or flats the plants will be ready for benching about the middle of September.

Culture

The new, improved varieties should be spaced from 12 in. to 15 in. apart each way. The size of the flower, the length and stiffness of the stem and the quality of the foliage will depend to a large extent upon the temperature under which the plants are grown. In order to produce flowers of maximum size with strong, stiff stems, the night temperature should be about 45°F. A slightly higher temperature ranging between 50° and 55°F. will produce earlier and more abundant bloom but the flowers will be somewhat smaller.

Cheiranthus cheiri (wallflower)

The English wallflowers are prized for their delightful fragrance and for their quaintly decorative quality, with colors ranging through yellow, apricot, orange, red, rust and brown. They are of easy culture and are admirably adapted to the cool greenhouse.

Propagation

Wallflowers are propagated by seed. For bloom during the winter months the seeds should be sown the previous March. The young seedlings may be pricked out into small pots or into flats as soon as they have made sufficient growth.

Soil Requirements

A good, rich compost will give excellent results.

Culture

During the summer months the young plants may be carried on in pots or they may be planted in nursery beds in the open ground. Wallflowers require a very cool growing temperature. The night temperature should range between 45° and 50°F. and the day temperature but a few degrees higher. Throughout their growing period the plants require a liberal amount of water. Wallflowers may be grown in pots, in raised benches or in solid beds, the plants being spaced approximately 12 in. apart.

Chrysanthemum

There is no other flower that can take the place of the chrysanthemums during the autumn months. They are so generous with their bloom, so lovely in form and coloring, so entirely satisfactory both for cutting and as potted plants, that they should be included in every greenhouse, no matter how limited the space may be. Many varieties that are not hardy out of doors may be grown successfully in the greenhouse, and with careful planning the period of bloom may be extended over several months. .

Propagation

Rooted cuttings of many desirable varieties may be initially purchased from commercial growers, but after the first season cuttings may be made from the stock thus obtained. These rooted cuttings should be potted up in March or early April; they may be carried on in pots, and shifted to larger pots as the plants develop, or they may be transferred to the benches. During the summer the plants should be syringed at least twice a day.

Soil Requirements

The soil in the benches should be carefully prepared. A 1-in. layer of rotted sod or coarse, strawy manure should be placed in the bottom of the bench and a soil mixture consisting of 1 part well-decomposed manure and 3 parts good sandy loam is recommended. An application of 20 percent superphosphate at the rate of 8 lb. per 100 sq. ft. may be made at the time of planting. The soil should be very slightly acid in its reaction.

Culture

If the plants are to be trained to single stems, they should be spaced from 8 in. to 10 in. apart. For the more branching types, 12 in. should be allowed. If large flowers borne on tall single stems are desired, all side shoots and all growth from the base of the plants should be removed. The pompon types of chrysanthemum should be kept pinched back until the middle of August in order to obtain sturdy, well-branched plants, six or eight flowering branches being allowed to develop. Commercial growers consider it a good practice to bench their chrysanthemums during May, June and July as this enables the young plants to become well established during the summer.

A few weeks after the plants have been benched, a 1-in. mulch of domestic peat moss should be applied. Such a mulch has a dramatic effect upon the growth and vigor of the plants, sometimes causing as much as a 50 to 100 percent increase in growth.

When the buds begin to show, weekly applications of ammonium sulphate may be made, 1 oz. dissolved in 2 gallons of water usually being sufficient.

Chrysanthemums prefer a night temperature that does not exceed 50°F.

After the flowering season is over, the plants may be lifted from the bench and placed in a coldframe, cuttings being taken from these stock plants in the early spring.

Clarkia (clarkia, godetia)

The copper-colored stems of clarkia, studded with crisp little whorls of bloom, are very lovely for cutting, and a few plants will add welcome variety for flower arrangements. If the flowers are cut just as the buds begin to open, they will last extremely well.

Propagation

For early bloom the seeds should be sown before mid-September; for later bloom, sowing should be in October or early November.

Soil Requirements

Clarkia is rather indifferent to soil conditions and will thrive in any good greenhouse compost.

Culture

The young plants make rapid growth, and they may be grown either in pots or in raised benches, the plants being spaced from 10 in. to 12 in. apart. Clarkia prefers a decidedly cool temperature of 50°F. at night.

Cyclamen

The blooms of cyclamen are like miniature butterflies poised on slender stems. If the plants are well grown, they will flower abundantly during the winter and will add their full share of jewel-like beauty to the indoor garden.

Exposure and Temperature

When used for decorative purposes in the house, a window with an eastern exposure is ideal. If maximum growth and development are desired, the temperature throughout the growing period should range between 50° and 60°F.

Propagation

Cyclamen may be propagated either by seed, or by cutting the corm into sections with one or two leaves attached to each section. The seed should be sown in the early autumn in order to produce flowering plants for the following winter. A mixture of equal parts loam and peat may be used for the seedbed and the seeds may be planted about 1 in. apart. If kept in a temperature ranging between 55° and 60°F., they will germinate in from four to five weeks. After several leaves have developed, the plants should be transplanted into 2½-in. pots. At the time of this first transplanting, the tiny corm that is forming should be placed so that its top is level with the surface of the soil. At each subsequent repotting the corm should be placed slightly higher until at the time of the last shift it is entirely above the surface of the soil.

Soil Requirements

A slightly acid soil with a pH between 6.0 and 7.0 is considered ideal. A soil decidedly light in texture should be used for cyclamen plants in the early stages of growth. For plants reaching maturity, the following soil mixture is recommended: 3 parts good loam, 1 part manure, $\frac{1}{2}$ part peat, $\frac{1}{2}$ part sand. At the time of the final potting, a 4-in. potful of a 4 – 12 – 4 complete fertilizer and a 4-in. potful of horn shavings should be added to each $2\frac{1}{2}$ bushels of soil.

Culture

During the summer months the young plants should be kept in a cool, semishaded spot, a well-ventilated, partially shaded greenhouse being satisfactory. Frequent syringing of the foliage and the maintenance of high humidity is desirable. The shade should be removed in the autumn. If, at this time, the pots are set on a staging or are elevated on overturned flower-pots, the development of the plant will be hastened. Cyclamen plants should be grown in clay pots, rather than in glazed or plastic containers. Watering must be done with care. The plants should usually be watered twice a day, the pots being set in a saucer or pan until the surface of the soil has become moist. Faded blooms and any yellowing leaves should be removed by giving the stem a quick jerk in order to snap it off at the base. The plants may be carried over for a second year by resting them after the period of bloom is over.

Delphinium (larkspur, annual)

Some of the new and greatly improved varieties of annual larkspur are exceedingly lovely and are well adapted for greenhouse culture. The plants will come into flower several months after sowing; it is also possible to plan either for an early winter crop or for a later crop to follow after the chrysanthemums have been removed from the benches.

Propagation

The annual larkspur is propagated by seed, and the young seedlings may be carried on in pots or in flats until bench space is available.

Soil Requirements

A light, fertile soil, neutral or slightly alkaline, is preferred.

Culture

A decidedly cool temperature, ranging around 50°F. at night, is most favorable for the development of the annual larkspurs. The plants are in no way exacting in regard to their soil requirements, though they should be given ample room in which to develop, being spaced 8 in. to 10 in. apart. The annual larkspurs offer a wealth of bloom, and are available in shades of violet, lavender-blue, rose, pink and white. The tall, stately flower spikes are also exceedingly fine for cutting – all in all, a most satisfactory greenhouse plant.

Dianthus (carnation)

Carnations are among the ever-dependable and ever-popular greenhouse flowers.

Propagation

Carnations are propagated by means of cuttings. The most accepted practice is to take the cuttings from established plants in November or December. Though cuttings may be taken later in the winter season, plants grown from earlier cuttings will make more vigorous growth and will produce more abundant bloom the following year. The cuttings should be taken from disease-free plants that are in vigorous growing condition. Cuttings are taken from the axillary shoots, preferably from the lower portion of the flowering stem. They should range from 3 in. to 5 in. in length and should be inserted in the propagating case with clean, sharp sand as the best rooting medium. Although it was formerly a common practice to remove a portion of the foliage, recent experiments have proved that a higher percentage of rootage is obtained if the foliage is not reduced. Under favorable conditions the cuttings should root in about four weeks, although some varieties will root more readily than others.

Soil Requirements

Carnations prefer a medium sandy loam, high in organic matter. The plants are indifferent to soil reaction, thriving equally well in neutral, mildly acid or slightly alkaline soil, within a range of pH 5.5 to 8.0. At the time of planting, an application of superphosphate, 10 lb. per

100 sq. ft., may be made. Beginning eight weeks after benching, monthly applications of a 4–12–4 commercial fertilizer may be made at the rate of 4 lb. to every 100 sq. ft. Planting distances vary from 6 in. to 12 in. apart according to the variety and, to some extent, to the fertility of the soil in the benches.

Culture

When the cuttings are well rooted, with roots from 1/2 in. to 1 in. long, the cuttings should be removed from the propagating bench and potted up in 2½-in. pots, a mixture of equal parts compost, sand and peat moss being used. Before the plants begin to be pot-bound, they should be shifted to larger pots, as carnations suffer seriously from any check of this sort, the plants becoming hard, yellow and stunted in appearance. Carnations are one of the few plants that should not be potted very firmly, and care should therefore be taken not to set the plants too deeply. Watering must also be done with care, as overwatering is often fatal to these plants.

Soon after the plants have been potted for the first time, they should be pinched back to within about 3 in. The lateral shoots should be pinched back as they develop, in order to produce symmetrical, well-branched plants. Pinching should continue until you want the flower buds to mature. If early bloom is desired, pinching should cease early in July. If late bloom is desired, pinching may be continued until after the plants are benched. It requires from ten to twenty weeks for a newly pinched shoot to produce a flower. The plants may be carried on in pots until they are ready to be benched or, as soon as danger of frost is past, they may be set in the open ground. If field culture is practiced, a more vigorous growth and greater disease resistance are obtained, though the pot-grown plants will give earlier bloom. The plants should be benched in late summer, though early summer benching is also practiced occasionally.

Disbudding

The flowering stems of carnations should be kept disbudded, all the axillary buds and shoots being removed from the upper portion.

Watering

Watering must be done with care. Carnation plants thrive best in a soil that is uniformly moist but not saturated.

Dicentra spectabilis (bleeding-heart)

There are very few perennials that can be forced as successfully as bleeding-heart, and few flowers are more beautiful or more appealing. After you have once grown them in the greenhouse, you will not want a season to pass without using at least a few plants for decorative purposes in the house or in the greenhouse itself.

Soil Requirements

Good potting compost.

Culture

Two-year-old clumps should be lifted in the autumn and heeled in a frame. Late in January the plants should be brought into the greenhouse and potted up in ample 10-in. to 12-in. bulb pans. They should then be placed in the coolest temperature available and forced slowly. During this period of growth the plants will require abundant moisture. By late March or early April the lovely, pendent, heart-shaped flowers will begin to open and the plants will then remain in bloom for many weeks if they are kept in a moderately cool temperature. After the flowering period is over, the plants may be replanted out of doors, and will show no ill effects from this gentle process of forcing.

Eschscholzia (California poppy)

Although California poppies are seldom thought of as greenhouse flowers, a few plants may well be included if one's aim is to provide a pleasant variety of flowers for cutting. Some of the large-flowering types of poppy that have been introduced recently are very decorative and lovely.

Soil Requirements

A good greenhouse compost.

Propagation

Poppy seeds should be sown in the greenhouse bench where they are to flower, as the young seedlings do not take kindly to transplanting.

Culture

The plants should be thinned out to a distance of 8 in. to 10 in. A cool greenhouse will provide nearly ideal growing conditions. The plants will come into flower in about eight to ten weeks from sowing.

Euphorbia fulgens (euphorbia)

The brilliant orange-red flowers of euphorbia are very decorative and lovely and a few plants are a welcome addition to the stock of a small greenhouse.

Propagation

Euphorbia may be propagated by softwood cuttings taken from the stock plants about May 1, or by hardwood cuttings taken in January after the parent plants have flowered. The cuttings should consist of two or three nodes, and should be rooted in a medium of equal parts of peat and sand.

Soil Requirements

A rather heavy, slightly acid soil is preferred for euphorbia.

Culture

The rooted cuttings may be benched or potted up early in July. The plants should be pinched back so that three or four stems develop from the lower portion of the plant. The plants should be spaced from 10 in. to 12 in. apart in the bench. A growing temperature of 60°F. is preferred. Sudden changes in temperature should be avoided, as they have a very harmful effect upon the plant.

Freesia

Freesia may be obtained in a wide range of colors—mauve, lavender, blue, yellow, orange, pink and carmine-rose. The delicately formed, sweetly scented flowers are lovely for cutting and freesias are exceedingly well adapted for greenhouse culture.

Propagation

If bloom is desired throughout the winter months, the bulbs may be planted in succession from August until the middle of December. They may be grown either in pots or in flats. For early bloom only large-sized corms should be used; for later bloom the smaller sizes will be entirely satisfactory. The corms should be spaced approximately 2 in. apart each way.

Soil Requirements

A potting soil consisting of 2 parts loam, 1 part leaf mold and 1 part sand is recommended.

Culture

After planting, the corms should be placed in a cool, dark place until the leaves appear. In the summer the pots or flats may be placed in a coldframe and shaded with lath sash. The pots should be kept moist but not too wet. As soon as leaf growth has started, the shade should be removed. The pots should be brought into the greenhouse before there is danger of frost. A night temperature ranging between 55° and 60°F. is satisfactory. As the flower stems are very delicate, some support is necessary and very slender bamboo stakes may be used with a number of strings crisscrossed between them. When the plants have finished flowering, water should be gradually withheld and the corms should be allowed to ripen. After the foliage has ripened sufficiently, the corms may be removed from the soil, and the largest ones may be saved for bloom the following year, being stored during the summer in a cool, dry place.

Gardenia jasminoides

The gardenia adapts well to greenhouse culture and is widely grown commercially. The blooms are in great demand for corsages and there is also a demand for pot-grown plants. The flowering period varies according to the climate. On the West Coast a long flowering period is attained, while in other parts of the country it may be comparatively short, depending upon the interval of night temperature that remains below 65°F. Plants thrive best in raised benches. Soil should be sterilized as a protection against nematodes and canker. Gardenias thrive best with a night temperature between 62° and 65°F. and a day temperature above 70°F. Humidity should be kept very high and the soil moist.

Gerbera jamesonii (Transvaal daisy)

Coming to us from the fields of the Transvaal in South Africa, the *Gerbera* has gained rapidly in popularity as a greenhouse plant. The flowers are unusually fine for cutting and are obtainable in many exquisite shades of salmon, apricot, orange-pink and cerise. Transvaal daisies are true perennials in their native habitat, but they are too tender to withstand the rigors of our winters north of Virginia and in many areas they are, therefore, best adapted to greenhouse culture.

Propagation
These daisies may be readily propagated both by seed and by the division of old established clumps. As *Gerbera* seed loses its vitality rapidly, only fresh seed should be used for propagation. The seed should be sown in March and as soon as four or five small leaves have developed, the seedlings should be transplanted directly into the beds where they are to flower. Established plants may be divided in June.

Culture
*Gerbera*s should preferably be grown in solid beds. During the summer the plants should be given a light mulch and kept carefully watered. The plants should be spaced 12 in. to 15 in. apart. A moderately cool night temperature of 55° to 60°F. is best. If given good care, the plants will produce abundant bloom throughout the winter and early spring months.

Soil Requirements
Gerbera prefers an open, well-drained oil of good fertility, with a pH value of approximately

7.0 to 7.5. In the fall and spring a weekly application of urea, 1 oz. to 7 gallons, is recommended.

Gladiolus

Both the large-flowered types of gladiolus and the primulinus hybrids, as well as many of the very exquisite dwarf varieties, may be forced in the greenhouse for early spring bloom. The culture of the latter group is, however, quite distinct from the culture of the large-flowered types; consequently the two groups will be treated separately as to culture and soil requirements.

Large-flowered and Primulinus Types of Gladiolus

Soil Requirements
Any good loam is satisfactory.

Culture
If the large-flowered and primulinus types are to be grown, corms that have been especially prepared for forcing should be obtained. These may be planted directly in a bench, the rows being spaced 12 in. apart and the corms 4 in. apart in the row, or they may be planted in flats or in pots. The method of planting will usually be determined by the amount of greenhouse space available at the time. When pot culture is followed, three corms may be planted in a 6-in. pot. In flats, the corms may be spaced 4 in. apart each way. The corms should be planted at a depth of approximately 1 in., and the soil should be at least 1 in. below the rim of the pot or flat in order to allow for watering. Greenhouse culture is practically identical with outdoor culture. The plants should be given full sun, they should be watered adequately and a moderate temperature is preferred. If bench space is not available at the time of planting, the pots or flats may be placed beneath the benches for a brief period, until the corms have started into growth, and the shoots have obtained a height of about 4 in. They should then be brought into full light. The primulinus hybrids are particularly well adapted to forcing, and as

cut flowers they are far lovelier than the large-flowered types.

Dwarf Types of Gladiolus

Soil Requirements

A light, sandy loam soil is preferred.

Culture

There are few flowers more exquisite in form and coloring than some of the dwarf gladioli and no greenhouse should be without them. Although many of these dwarf types are not hardy enough to be grown out of doors in the North, they may be grown to perfection in the small greenhouse. Most of these dwarf species, and their hybrids, have come to us from the Transvaal in South Africa, and it is to be regretted that they are not hardy enough for general culture outdoors throughout the United States, for they are utterly charming.

The corms should be planted in November, either in pots or in flats. The pots should be stored in a coldframe until mid-January, when they may be brought into the greenhouse and forced in a moderately cool temperature. The graceful flower spikes will begin to open in late March, and if a succession of bloom is desired during the spring months, the pots should be brought in from storage at intervals of every ten days.

Gloxinia

The gloxinia is a colorful, lovely plant, bountiful with its bloom, that well deserves the popularity it has attained in recent years.

The large-flowered hybrids have a wide color range and the handsome, showy blooms sometimes measure as much as 6 in. to 7 in. across. However, many gardeners prefer the more modest slipper type, with its smaller, more delicate flowers.

The colors of gloxinia range from white, delicate pink and rose to sparkling red and purple, with many lovely intermediate hues.

In many sections of the country gloxinia are not adapted to outdoor culture and should be grown either in the greenhouse or as house plants.

Propagation

Gloxinia may be grown from tubers, from leaf cuttings and from seed. Tubers may be planted at any time from November to February if favorable growing conditions can be provided. If tubers have been shipped, it is wise to plant them as soon as possible after they arrive. They may be started either in small pots or in trays, with vermiculite or milled sphagnum moss being used as the starting medium, or they may be planted directly in the pots in which they are to flower, using 5-in. pots for small tubers and 6-in. to 8-in. pots for large tubers. The top third of the tuber should be exposed above the level of the soil in the pot.

Leaf cuttings may be taken from mature, flowering plants during the spring and early summer. The leaf should be cut close to the main stem and should be placed in the shade for half an hour in order to give the end a chance to dry. The leaf may then be inserted in moist sand or vermiculite in the propagating case. Cuttings also root very readily in water or in any simple, homemade device. When new growth appears and the original leaf dies, the plant may be transplanted into a pot. Plants grown from leaf cuttings will bloom the following spring and summer.

Gloxinias may also be easily grown from seed. The seeds are very fine and require careful handling (see page 678 for details). The seeds germinate in about ten days and the young seedlings should be transplanted into flats when they have two or three pairs of leaves, then later shifted into 5-in. or 6-in. pots. When grown from seed, gloxinias will come into flower in from six to ten months. Seed sown in early January should produce flowers by midsummer.

Soil Requirements

Gloxinias require a rich, porous, well-drained soil, with a high content of organic matter. The following mixtures will give excellent results.

(1) 1 part garden loam, 1 part sand, 1 part peat moss.

(2) 1 part garden loam, 1 part leaf mold, 1 part sand. Add one 4-in. pot of bone meal per bushel of soil.

Culture

For their best development gloxinias require a moist atmosphere, a favorable temperature, a sufficient amount of light, protection from brilliant sunshine and a congenial soil.

The ideal range of temperature for gloxinias is from 68° to 72°F. during the day and 62° to 65° at night, although these plants are adapted to some fluctuation. If temperatures range much above 75°F., growth will tend to suffer.

Although gloxinias should be given as much light as possible, they should be shaded from strong sun. Insufficient light will produce leggy, spindly growth. When grown in the house, they will usually do well in a south or east window during the winter months.

Watering must be done with care. The most satisfactory method is to place the pot in a pan of water and leave it until the surface of the soil appears moist. The plant should not be watered again until the soil begins to look dry. It should never be allowed to stand in water for a long period of time. If overhead watering is practiced, the water should be poured close to the rim of the pot in order to avoid wetting the leaves or the crown of the plant. When water stands in the crown, it is conducive to crown rot and to the spread of gray mold. Ample drainage material should be placed in the bottom of the pot at the time of potting, as good drainage is essential for gloxinia.

When the period of bloom is over and the foliage begins to die down, water should be gradually withheld so the plants may become dormant. The pots should be stored in a cool place at a temperature of about 50°F., and should be watered just enough to keep the tubers from shriveling. If desired, the tubers may be removed from the pot and stored in peat moss in a cool place until their period of dormancy is over. They may then be potted up again in fresh soil in February or March.

Plants that flower in early spring can be cut back to the first pair of leaves and will usually produce excellent second bloom within eight to ten weeks. After the second period of bloom is over, prepare them for their rest period.

Heliophila

Heliophila is one of the most charming of the group of South African annuals, and as it becomes more widely known in this country, its popularity will undoubtedly increase. The long sprays of lovely clear blue flowers, similar in coloring to the flowers of the perennial flax (*Linum flavum* 'Compactum'), are borne in profusion throughout the late winter months, and they are perfectly delightful for cut flower arrangements. The fact that a few plants will produce such an abundance of bloom, and that they may be cut almost continually over a period of several months, makes them of unique value as a greenhouse flower.

Propagation

The seeds may be sown at any time during the late summer and early autumn months.

Soil Requirements

Good greenhouse compost.

Culture

Heliophila prefers a moderately cool temperature. The plants may be grown either in pots or in raised benches, the latter being preferred. A distance of from 8 in. to 10 in. between the plants will give ample space for their best development.

Iris, Bulbous

Of all the varieties and types of bulbous iris that may be grown in the greenhouse, the *Iris tingitana* hybrid, 'Wedgwood,' is the most beautiful. It is extremely well adapted to forcing and the lovely, clear blue flowers are of great value for cutting. The Spanish, English and Dutch iris may all be forced into early bloom very successfully and are available in a wide range of colors.

Soil Requirements

A soil mixture of 1 part compost, 1 part loam and 1 part sand is recommended.

Culture

Iris may be planted in September in shallow bulb pans or in flats, being spaced 1½ in. apart. A thorough watering is necessary in order to start root action. They should be stored in a coldframe until mid-November and may then be brought in and placed in a cool greenhouse with a night temperature of 45° to 50°F. If a succession of bloom is desired, a few pots or flats should be brought in from the frames at intervals of every ten days. When the buds begin to show, the temperature may be raised to 55°F., but the plants should never be subjected to a high temperature lest the quality of bloom be seriously affected. Bulbous iris requires abundant water during the growing period, but the amount should be reduced when the buds begin to develop. Only the largest-size bulbs (actually corms) should be used for forcing.

Bulbs that have been especially prepared for forcing may now be obtained and the variety 'Wedgwood' may be brought into flower by Thanksgiving. The following method of preparing bulbs for early forcing was developed by Dr. David Griffiths of the U.S. Department of Agriculture, and consists of subjecting the bulbs to a temperature of 80°F. for three weeks after they are dug in July. From the middle of August to September 25 they are held at a temperature of 50°F. They are then ready for potting.

Lathyrus odoratus (sweet pea)

So delightfully decorative are sweet peas for cut flower arrangements that they are an important crop in the small greenhouse, even though little space can be allotted to them. Some of the winter flowering types are exquisite both in form and in coloring, the flowers being borne on long, slender stems.

Propagation

Sweet peas are propagated by seed. As the seeds have a hard outer covering, germination may be hastened by soaking them for twenty-four hours before sowing. The seeds may be sown directly in the beds or in the benches where they are to flower or they may be sown in small pots or in flats, being later transplanted to their permanent position in the greenhouse. A light soil mixture should be used, consisting of equal parts of sand and loam. The time of flowering will depend to a considerable extent upon the date when the seed is sown. Seeds of the early or winter-flowering type, sown about the middle of July, will flower from October through January. This is the type best suited for greenhouse culture. If sown September 1, the flowering period will extend from February to the middle of March, and if sown late in September the plants will flower in March, April and May. For early bloom it is therefore necessary to start the seeds in midsummer.

Soil Requirements

Sweet peas thrive best in a soil that is very nearly neutral in its reaction and that is of an open and porous texture. Good drainage is essential, as the plants are seriously injured by excessive amounts of water in the soil. A good, rich, fibrous compost is considered ideal. To this may be added a 0–10–10 commercial fertilizer, applied at the rate of 4 lb. to 5 lb. per 100 sq. ft. of soil area. An excess of nitrogen in the soil is detrimental to the best development of the plants.

Culture

Sweet peas prefer a cool growing temperature, and from the time the young seedlings have begun growth they should be kept as cool as possible so that they may develop good root systems. During the summer the greenhouse should be well ventilated, and adequate shade should be provided for the seedlings. Throughout the entire growing period low temperatures should be maintained. In the winter the night temperature of the greenhouse should not go above 50°F. and day temperatures should not range over 55° to 60°F., with 65°F. as a maximum. Solid beds are preferred, rather than raised benches. The rows may be spaced from 3 ft. to 4 ft. apart, double drills being approximately 6 in. apart. The plants should remain thickly in the rows, being spaced hardly more than a few inches apart. As soon as they have become well established, they should be provided with adequate support. Wire or stout twine on wire supports may be used. When the plants come into bloom, all flowers should be picked immediately after blooming. If seed pods are allowed to form, subsequent flowering will be seriously checked and the flowers will have a tendency to become short-stemmed.

Lily, Easter

There are several species of lilies that are used for forcing, the most popular being *Lilium longiflorum giganteum* and *Lilium longiflorum* 'Erabu.'

Propagation

Bulbs are obtainable in three sizes, 5-in. to 7-in. bulbs, 7-in. to 9-in. and 9-in. to 11-in. Most commercial growers purchase the 7-in. to 9-in. size. The larger size will give more flowers per stem, but this is, of course, considerably more expensive. Its northern-grown bulbs will produce shorter plants with more blooms on a plant than southern-grown bulbs, and they are usually preferred.

Soil Requirements

Easter lilies prefer a somewhat heavy, yet porous, soil with a pH ranging between 6.0 and 7.0. A soil mixture of 4 parts silt loam, 1 part sand and 1 part well-rotted, composted manure is recommended.

Culture

Approximately thirteen weeks are required from the time of planting to the time of bloom. The bulbs should be planted in 6-in. pots, being set at a depth of 1 in. or more, and they should be placed on a bench in a greenhouse where the temperature can be maintained between 54° and 56°F. The potting soil should be fairly dry and very little water should be given until root growth has started, at which time the temperature of the greenhouse should be increased to 60°F. It is desirable that the plants be watered with warm water at approximately 70°F. After active growth has started, and the plants have attained a height of 6 in., biweekly applications of a liquid fertilizer may be given, 1 oz. of ammonium sulphate being dissolved in 2 gallons of water. The time of bloom may be slightly hastened or retarded by raising or lowering the temperature a few degrees.

Lupinus (lupine)

The annual lupines are well adapted to greenhouse culture.

The most satisfactory varieties for cutting are 'Hartwegii,' 'Azure Blue,' with flowers of a delicate mistlike hue, and 'Sutton's Tall Pink,' with flowers a lovely soft shade of pink.

Propagation

Lupine seeds may be sown either in the bench where the plants are to flower or in flats, and then transplanted into small pots.

Soil Requirements

A moderately rich soil, well supplied with organic matter, will produce fine bloom. The soil should be neutral or slightly alkaline in its reaction.

Culture

The plants may be shifted into the benches as soon as space is available, being spaced 12 in. apart. A cool greenhouse with a night temperature of 50° to 55°F. is preferred.

Matthiola (stock)

The delicate fragrance of stock adds greatly to its appeal as a cut flower, and it does extremely well under greenhouse conditions.

Propagation

The seeds should be sown in flats in early August, the young seedlings being transplanted either directly into the benches where they are to flower, or carried on in pots or flats until bench space is available.

Soil Requirements

A light, porous and well-drained soil of good fertility is considered ideal.

Culture

When the young plants are shifted to the benches, they should be spaced from 8 in. to 10 in. apart each way. The plants, which should be pinched back once in order to induce branching, will begin to flower late in the winter. The coolest possible temperature is to be desired, a night temperature of 48° to 50°F. being considered ideal. Stocks are often used to follow on after the chrysanthemums have been removed from the benches.

Narcissus (daffodil)

All the members of this group may be easily forced into early spring bloom in the greenhouse.

Soil Requirements
The bulbs should be planted in a good general purpose soil mixture of 21 parts loam, 1 part leaf mold and 1 part sand.

Culture
Narcissus planting should take place in the autumn, either in pots or in flats, and the bulbs should be placed in storage for a minimum period of twelve weeks. A coldframe or outdoor pit will provide satisfactory conditions for storage, and the pots or flats should be covered with several inches of sand or coal ashes. If the pots are brought in from storage in succession, a variance in the time of bloom and a succession of bloom will automatically be obtained. When the bulbs are first brought in from storage, they should not be placed in full light for several days. If forced at a cool temperature, 50° to 55°F. at night, the blooms will be of a superior quality and will last as long as cut flowers will.

Pelargonium (geranium)

The popularity of the geranium as a house plant has endured over many, many years. Beloved and cherished by our grandmothers, geraniums were among the few flowering plants that could be grown in the window garden a generation or more ago; and they are still beloved today, their popularity being quite undiminished in spite of the wealth of other plants that have become available in recent years.

Exposure and Temperature
Full sunlight is essential at all times. A temperature ranging between 65° and 70°F. during the day and between 60° and 65°F. at night is considered ideal.

Propagation
Geraniums are propagated by means of softwood stem cuttings. When winter bloom is desired, cuttings should be made in May.

Soil Requirements
Geraniums require a soil low in nitrogen and relatively high in phosphorus and potash. An excess of nitrogen in the soil induces a rank, vegetative growth and prevents flowering. Geraniums will thrive reasonably well in almost any ordinary garden soil. If, however, maximum growth and abundant bloom are desired, the following soil mixture will give the best results when used in the final potting: 8 parts good garden loam to 1 part well-rotted manure. To 2½ bushels of soil, add one 5-in. flowerpotful of superphosphate and one 4-in. potful of a 2-10-10 commercial fertilizer. This should be thoroughly mixed with the soil before potting. The same mixture may be used in repotting old plants. If a good potting mixture is used, no subsequent application of fertilizer will be needed. A soil with a pH between 6.5 and 7.6 is preferred.

Culture
After the cuttings have rooted, they should be potted up into 3-in. pots, and as the plants develop they may be shifted into 4-in. and 5-in. pots. Geraniums require very firm potting; they flower more abundantly when they are allowed to become slightly pot-bound, so they should be carried through the winter in 4-in. or 5-in. pots. Old plants should be grown in 6-in. and 8-in. pots. During the first summer of growth the young plants should be pinched back frequently, so that they may become symmetrical and well branched, and no flower buds should be allowed to develop until early September. The plants should then give ample bloom from October until April. In May those plants that have bloomed throughout the winter months should be severely pruned back, leaving about three strong shoots, 3 in. or 4 in. long to each plant. During the summer the plants should be placed in a partially shaded place and kept fairly dry. It is important not to encourage new growth during this rest period. In the early autumn the plants may be repotted in fresh soil and should give abundant bloom during the winter months.

Watering
Geraniums should not be watered too liberally. The plants will give better bloom if they are kept somewhat on the dry side. Overwatering

and poor ventilation are frequently the cause of a physiological leaf spot that is very disfiguring to the foliage.

Poinsettia pulcherrima

Poinsettia is the most decorative of all plants for the Christmas season, and if conditions are favorable it is possible to have well-grown, specimen plants even in the small greenhouse.

Propagation

Poinsettias are propagated by cuttings taken from mature stock plants. After the flowering season is over, the stock plants are usually lifted and placed under a bench for a period of ten or twelve weeks. The temperature of the greenhouse should range between 50° and 60°F. and the plants should be kept very dry—not dry enough, however, to allow the wood to shrivel. About April 1 the plants should be pruned back heavily and potted up or replanted in the bench. They should be watered thoroughly and the stems syringed occasionally. A rich soil should be used for the stock plants, consisting of 3 parts loam and 1 part rotted manure with a light application of superphosphate. The first cuttings may be taken early in July. They may be cut at a node or with a slight heel of old wood from the parent stem. As the plants bleed readily, the cuttings should be dropped into cold water for a few moments (not over five minutes). The cuttings should be trimmed so that only the two top leaves remain, and they should be rooted in a medium of moderately fine, sterilized sand, being shaded during the day. The cuttings should be well rooted and ready for potting in about three weeks. A mixture of 2 parts loam, 1 part sand and 1 part well-rotted manure is recommended.

Soil Requirements

Poinsettias thrive best in a soil of medium fertility with a slightly acid reaction, the pH ranging between 6.0 and 7.0. For the final potting or benching soil, the following mixture is recommended: 2 parts silt loam, 1 part manure, 1 part sand. To each 2½ bushels of soil add a 4-in. flowerpotful of superphosphate.

Culture

Poinsettia plants may either be shifted into larger pots as they develop or they may be benched. If well-branched, symmetrical plants are desired, they may be pinched back until early September. The ideal temperature for poinsettias ranges between 60° and 65°F. The temperature should never be allowed to drop below 60°F. at night, however. The plants are also extremely sensitive to drafts and are very easily injured by chilling or by overwatering. Under such conditions the leaves will turn yellow and drop.

Primula (primrose)

There are many species of *Primula* that are excellent when grown as potted plants in the greenhouse. They are very decorative when in flower and bloom over a long season.

Propagation

Primroses are propagated by seed, which should be sown in February or early March. Germination will be hastened if the seeds are soaked for a few hours before sowing. When the young seedlings have attained sufficient size, they may be transplanted into flats or small pots, a soil mixture of 3 parts good loam and 1 part well-rotted manure being used. As the plants develop, they may be shifted into larger pots. Since they have a tendency to wilt badly, primroses should be shaded after each transplanting.

Soil Requirements

These plants prefer a slightly acid soil with a pH ranging between 6.0 and 7.0. The final potting mixture should consist of 3 parts good loam, 2 parts well-rotted manure and 1 part sand. To each 2½ bushels of soil a 4-in. pot of a 4-12-4 complete fertilizer should be added. No peat should be used in the potting mixture.

Culture

Primroses require an abundance of moisture, and the pots should never be allowed to dry out. During the summer the pots may either be kept in a lightly shaded greenhouse or placed on a bed of ashes in a coldframe under a lath shade. The plants prefer a moderately cool temperature during the winter, and a range between 50° and 60°F. is considered ideal.

Reseda odorata (mignonette)

Although mignonette is prized more for its fragrance than for its bloom, some of the new and greatly improved forms are valuable for cutting and they are admirably adapted to greenhouse culture.

Propagation

Mignonette is readily propagated by seed. If bloom is desired throughout the winter months, three successive sowings should be made, one early in July, another early in August and the last early in September. The seeds should always be sown where they are to flower, as the plants suffer such a check from transplanting that they never fully recover. The procedure for growing this plant in most commercial greenhouses is to mark the bench area off into rows 6 in. by 8 in. apart. From six to eight seeds are planted at the intersection of the rows, being covered very lightly. Watering should be done with a very fine spray. After the seeds have germinated and the small seedling plants have developed the third leaf, the three strongest plants should be left and the remaining plants thinned out. The young seedling plants should be shaded from intense sunlight during the hottest part of the day until they have become well established.

Soil Requirements

A medium, light, rather turfy loam is preferred. The usual practice is to place 1 in. of well-rotted stable manure on the bottom of the bench. The remaining portion of the bench is then filled with compost.

Culture

Mignonette prefers a very cool temperature. A night temperature ranging between 45° and 48°F. and a day temperature between 55° and 65°F. is considered ideal. Watering should be done on bright mornings, and it must be done with care, as the plants may be seriously injured

by an overabundance of moisture. If water is allowed to remain on the foliage for any length of time, the leaves become spotted. When the flower spikes begin to form, all side shoots should be removed from around the top of the stem, but three or four vigorous shoots should be left at the base of the plant for later bloom. A topdressing of well-rotted compost may be applied when the plants are ready to come into flower.

Rhododendron (azalea)

There are few plants more decorative or rewarding than azaleas when they are in full bloom, and many species and varieties may be grown very successfully under greenhouse conditions, forced into bloom either for Christmas or for Easter.

Propagation

Some varieties of azalea may be propagated most successfully from cuttings, while other varieties are usually grafted. As the propagation of azaleas is a highly specialized field, it is advisable for the owner of the small greenhouse to purchase a few plants that have been specifically prepared for forcing. These can readily be obtained from a good garden center or nursery.

Soil Requirements

Azaleas require a highly acid soil with a pH between 4.5 and 5.5. The potting soil should consist of a mixture of 2 parts loam and 1 part peat moss. Yellowing of the foliage and poor root development are indicative of a lack of available iron and of a soil that is too highly alkaline. In order to correct an iron deficiency, an application of 1 oz. of a 12 percent chelated iron per 100 sq. ft. of bench area, or 4 oz. in 100 gallons of water for potted plants, will give excellent results.

Culture

Azalea plants are shipped with a small ball of earth. As soon as they have been unpacked, the ball should be immersed in a bucket of water until it has become thoroughly saturated. It should then be allowed to drain before it is potted. For the first two or three weeks the plants should be placed in a cool greenhouse where the night temperature ranges around 45°F. Azaleas require an abundance of water and a moist atmosphere. Frequent syringing of the foliage with warm water is beneficial. If the plants are to be brought into flower by Christmas, they should be kept at a temperature of 45° to 48°F. until November 5. They should then have a night temperature of 60°F., with a somewhat higher temperature of 65°F. during the day. If the plants are desired for Easter bloom, they should be kept in a very cool house (45° to 50°F.) until six weeks before Easter. All new growth that appears at the base of the flower buds should be pinched out. If this is not done, the flowers will be small and there will be many blind buds.

After the flowering period is over, the plants should be trimmed back lightly and placed in a warm, moist greenhouse in order that vigorous new growth may be encouraged. In June the pots may be sunk in the open ground or the plants may be shifted to the nursery rows. A soil mixture similar to that of the potting mixture should be used. The symmetry of the plants should be maintained by the occasional pinching back of any awkward shoots. No pinching should be done after July 1. In early autumn the plants may be lifted and brought into the greenhouse.

Rose

There are many varieties of roses that are admirably adapted to greenhouse culture and that will give abundant bloom throughout the winter months.

Propagation

Greenhouse roses may be propagated by budding, by cuttings or by grafting. Grafting is the most approved method and the one most commonly employed by commercial growers. As the propagation of roses is a highly specialized business, it is advisable for the owner of a small greenhouse to purchase only strong, healthy pot-grown plants that are suitable for forcing.

Soil Requirements

Roses prefer a slightly acid soil with a pH ranging between 6.0 and 7.0. A rich compost,

consisting of 3 parts good loam and 1 part rotted manure will give excellent results.

Culture

A temperature ranging between 58° and 62°F. at night and between 70° and 75°F. in the daytime is considered ideal for roses. These plants may be grown either in raised benches or in solid beds. Good drainage is essential and beds or benches should be narrow, preferably not over 4 ft. wide, as the best blooms are invariably produced on the outside plants. Roses may be set in their permanent position in the greenhouse between the middle of May and July 1, being spaced from 12 in. to 14 in. apart. The plants should be set a little deeper than they were when growing in the pots. During this period when the plants are becoming established, they should be watered thoroughly but at no time should the soil be allowed to become too saturated with moisture; the walks of the greenhouse should be kept damp and the foliage should be sprayed several times a day during sunny weather. The temperature also should be kept as low as possible and the greenhouse should be well ventilated. No flower buds should be allowed to form until early in September.

As the plants develop, wire may be stretched along the side of the benches and wire stakes placed beside the plants to provide support. During the growing season very shallow cultivation should be given, and at the time of flowering, applications of a complete fertilizer, 4–12–4, may be given every three or four weeks, being applied at the rate of 1 lb. to every 100 sq. ft. of bench area. Greenhouse roses will usually continue to give good results over a period of three or four years, and sometimes even longer. Plants that are to be carried over in the benches should be given a period of rest during the summer. Beginning about the middle of June water should be withheld gradually, though the plants should not be allowed to become too dry. During this period the plants should be pruned vigorously, the weak stems being pruned even more severely than strong ones. The plants should be cut back to within approximately 18 in. or 20 in. A few inches of topsoil may be removed, and the bed or bench may be refilled with rich compost.

Saintpaulia (African violet)

For cultural details, see page 740.

Schizanthus pinnatus (butterfly flower)

Seldom at its best in the garden under the heat of the summer sun, the lovely butterfly flower is one of those annuals admirably adapted to greenhouse culture. Only indoors does it reach full perfection, and a well-grown pot of *Schizanthus* is a thing of beauty. The small, orchid-shaped flowers in luminous tones of pink, lavender and white are borne in great profusion and are lovely both for cutting and as potted plants.

Propagation
Seed may be sown in early September and the plants grown on in pots for early spring bloom.

Soil Requirements
A soil composed of 2 parts good, fibrous loam and 1 part well-rotted cow manure will give excellent results.

Culture
The plants may either be grown on in pots, or they may be benched when they have reached sufficient size, being spaced not less than 12 in. apart. They thrive best in a moderately cool temperature of 45° to 50°F. If the plants are allowed to become somewhat potbound, the blooming period will be hastened.

Stevia

The chief value of stevia is as a filler-in for mixed bouquets. The small, white flowers are produced in abundance on long stems that are heavily clothed with deep green foliage.

Propagation
Stevia is propagated by stem cuttings taken from the stock plants in January. As soon as the cuttings have rooted, they may be potted up in 2½ in. pots.

Soil Requirements
A good rich greenhouse compost will give excellent results. If a light application of superphosphate is made at the time that the plants are brought into the greenhouse, the danger of oversucculent, soft-stemmed growth will be reduced.

Culture
As the plants develop, they may be shifted on into 4-in. pots and later into 7-in. pots, being grown in a cool temperature of 40° to 45°F. As soon as all danger of frost is over, the pots may either be set on a bed of gravel in a coldframe or transferred to nursery rows. During the summer the plants should be kept pinched back in order to become bushy and symmetrical. In the autumn, before the first frost, the plants should be brought into the greenhouse. They may be grown on in pots or planted in beds or benches, being spaced 12 in. apart. Stevia prefers a cool greenhouse, with a night temperature of approximately 50°F. The plants will normally come into flower shortly before the Christmas season. The flowering period may be hastened by shading the plants with black cloth for four hours a day for a period of thirty days, beginning September 1.

Tulips

For use both as potted plants and as cut flowers, tulips add their share to the galaxy of bloom in the greenhouse during the spring months, and a succession of bloom may be had over a period of many weeks.

Soil Requirements
A soil mixture consisting of 2 parts good loam, 1 part leaf mold and 1 part sand is recommended.

Culture
The bulbs should be planted in November, either in pots or in flats. Ample drainage should be provided and the tip of the bulb should be from 1 in. to 2 in. below the surface of the soil. Unless bulbs that have been especially prepared for forcing are used, tulips require

a long period of storage in order to make good root growth. They should be kept in storage in either a coldframe or an outdoor pit for approximately twelve to fourteen weeks. It is a wise plan to place a light layer of straw or excelsior over the pots or flats to afford protection for any shoots that may push through, and a 6-in. layer of ashes or sand may then be added. Early varieties may be brought in after twelve weeks of storage, late varieties at the end of fourteen weeks. If a succession of bloom is desired, the pots may be brought in at ten-day intervals. When first brought in from storage, the pots should preferably be placed in a cool, semi-dark place, as it is wise not to expose the young shoots to direct sunlight for several days. Tulips should be forced at a comparatively low temperature, 55° to 60°F. approximating the ideal. Though a high temperature is conducive to more rapid development, the quality of the flowers is seriously affected by it. After the pots have been placed in full sunlight, they should be turned every few days so that the flowers and leaves may develop evenly.

Viola (violet)

Violets are admirably suited to the cool greenhouse, and if the plants are grown under favorable conditions they will give an abundance of bloom during the winter months.

Propagation

The method of propagation usually preferred by commercial growers is that of cuttings taken from healthy terminal shoots between the middle of January and the middle of March. Violets may also be propagated by the division of the parent plant after the flowering season is over, or by root cuttings taken during February and March. After the young plants are well established, they may be planted in flats. During the summer the plants may be kept in cold-frames or they may be planted in the open ground. Some growers prefer to transplant the young plants into their permanent position in May. If this practice is followed, adequate ventilation must be provided and the greenhouse must be heavily shaded during the summer.

Soil Requirements

Violets prefer a rather heavy, sandy loam soil, well drained yet retentive of moisture. A good, moderately rich compost is considered ideal.

Culture

Violets may be grown either in solid beds or in raised benches. Most growers prefer solid beds, as it is easier to maintain a cool, moist soil. Cool growing conditions are one of the essentials for success. Single-flowering varieties prefer a night temperature of 45° to 50°F. and a day temperature ranging between 60° and 65°F. Double-flowering varieties prefer a temperature about 5° lower. High temperatures are conducive to an excessive amount of vegetative growth, which is produced at the expense of flowers. The plants require an abundance of moisture and an adequate supply of fresh air.

Zantedeschia (Arum or Calla lily)

Callas are grown for the decorative quality of their blooms when used in cut flower arrangements. There are two types: white calla and yellow calla.

Propagation

The small offsets that form around the parent rhizome may be removed. Several years of growth are required before these young plants will come into bloom.

Soil Requirements

Callas require a very rich soil. A mixture of 2 parts heavy, rich loam and 1 part well-rotted cow manure will give excellent results.

Culture

Callas may be grown either in solid beds, in raised benches or in pots. A night temperature of 55° and a day temperature ranging between 60° and 65°F. are preferred. The plants require an abundant supply of moisture throughout their growing period. After the flowering period is over, the plants should be gradually dried off and given a rest period. They may be watered occasionally but all active growth is allowed to cease. In August the topsoil from the beds may be removed. After the plants have been given a thorough soaking, a heavy mulch of well-rotted manure should be applied. Active growth will soon be resumed and the plants will begin to flower late in the autumn.

PLANTS THAT MAY BE GROWN IN POTS FOR DECORATION IN THE HOUSE

Abutilon hybridum	Chinese lantern
Acacia armata	kangaroo thorn
Acacia drummondii	Drummond's acacia
Astilbe japonica	blue daisy
Begonia spp.	spirea
Bougainvillea glabra	begonia
Browallia speciosa 'Major'	paper flower
Camellia japonica	sapphire flower
Chorizema ilicifolium	camellia
Chrysanthemum spp.	flame pea
Cineraria cruenta (Senecio cruentus)	chrysanthemum
Cyclamen persicum	Canary cineraria
Cytisus canariensis	cyclamen
Cytisus racemosus	genista
Dicentra spectabilis	florist's broom
Euphorbia fulgens (jacquiniiflora)	bleeding-heart
Felicia amelloides	scarlet plume
Fuchsia x *hybrida*	lady's-eardrops
Gardenia jasminoides	Cape jasmine
Kalanchoe spp.	beach bells
Lantana camara	yellow sage
Pelargonium x *hortorum*	geranium
Poinsettia	poinsettia
Primula spp.	primrose
Rhododendron spp.	azalea
Saintpaulia ionantha	African violet
Schlumbergera truncata	Thanksgiving cactus
Sinningia speciosa	gloxinia
Solanum pseudocapsicum	Jerusalem cherry
Strelitzia reginae	bird-of-paradise flower
Streptosolen jamesonii	firebush

CUT BRANCHES OF SHRUBS THAT MAY BE FORCED

Chaenomeles japonica	Japanese quince
Cornus florida	eastern dogwood
Forsythia spp.	forsythia
Magnolia stellata	star magnolia
Malus spp.	flowering crab apple
Prunus spp.	flowering cherry
Spiraea thunbergii	Thunberg spirea
Viburnum spp.	viburnum

VINES FOR THE GREENHOUSE

Allamanda cathartica	golden trumpet
Antigonon leptopus	coral vine
Asparagus densiflorus	Sprenger's asparagus fern
Asparagus setaceus	plumose asparagus fern
Clerodendrum thomsoniae	bleeding-heart vine
Ficus pumila	creeping fig
Hedera helix	English ivy
Jasminum grandiflorum	royal jasmine
Monstera deliciosa	split-leaf philodendron
Passiflora spp.	passionflower
Philodendron scandens spp. *oxycardium*	common philodendron
Senecio mikanioides	German ivy
Stigmaphyllon ciliatum	butterfly vine
Tradescantia fluminensis	wandering Jew
Vinca major	blue buttons

PALMS FOR DECORATIVE PURPOSES

Chrysalidocarpus lutescens	cane palm
Howea belmoreana	Belmore sentry palm
Howea forsterana	Forster sentry palm
Latania lontaroides	red latan
Livistona rotundifolia	fan palm
Microcoelum weddellianum	Weddel palm
Phœnix rupicola	Indian date palm

BULBS, CORMS AND TUBERS SUITABLE FOR FORCING

Anemone coronaria	windflower
Convallaria majalis	lily-of-the-valley
Freesia spp.	freesia
Gladiolus spp.	gladiolus
Hippeastrum vittatum hybrids	amaryllis
Hyacinthus orientalis	hyacinth
Iris spp.	bulbous iris
Lilium auratum	gold-banded lily
L. candidum	madonna lily
L. formosanum	Formosa lily
L. japonicum	Japanese lily
L. lacifolium	tiger lily
L. longiflorum	trumpet lily
L. x *maculatum* vars.	spotted lily
L. pumilum	coral lily
L. regale	royal lily
L. speciosum 'Album'	white Japanese lily
L. speciosum 'Rubrum'	red Japanese lily
Narcissus	narcissus daffodil
Rannunculus acris	buttercup
Tulipa spp.	tulip
Zantedeschia spp.	calla

PLANTS FOR THE COOL GREENHOUSE

FOR CUT FLOWERS

Antirrhinum majus	snapdragon
Bouvardia longiflora	bouvardia
Calendula officinalis	calendula
Centaurea cyanus	bachelor's-button
Cheiranthus cheiri	English wallflower
Chrysanthemum x morifolium	florist's chrysanthemum
Chrysanthemum parthenium	feverfew
Clarkia spp.	clarkia, godetia
Cynoglossum spp.	hound's tongue
Delphinium spp.	larkspur
Dianthus caryophyllus	carnation
Dimorpotheca spp.	Cape marigold
Erlangea tomentosa	erlangia
Eupatorium spp.	thoroughwort
Euphorbia spp.	spurge
Gerbera jamesonii	Transvaal daisy
Gypsophila spp.	baby's-breath
Lathyrus odoratus	sweet pea
Limonium spp.	statice
Lupinus spp.	lupine
Matthiola incana	stock
Myosotis spp.	forget-me-not
Nemesia spp.	nemesia
Piqueria trinervia	stevia
Reseda spp.	mignonette
Salpiglossis sinuata	painted-tongue
Scabiosa atropurpurea	pincushion flower
Schizanthus pinnatus	butterfly flower
Streptosolen jamesonii	firebush
Trachymene coerulea	blue lace flower
Viola spp.	violet

FOR POTTED PLANTS

Acacia spp.	acacia
Arsidia spp.	marlberry
Astilbe japonica	spirea
Begonia spp.	begonia
Browallia speciosa	sapphire flower
Calceolaria herbeohybrida	pouch flower
Camellia japonica	camellia
Chorizema ilicifolium	flame pea
Cyclamen spp.	cyclamen
Cytisus spp.	broom

Felicia amelloides	agathaea
Hydrangea macrophylla	hydrangea
Kalanchoe spp.	beach bells
Primula spp.	primrose
Schlumbergera bridgesii	Christmas cactus
Schlumbergera truncata	Thanksgiving cactus
Senecio cruentus	cineraria
Solanum spp.	nightshade
Strelitzia reginae	bird-of-paradise flower
Rhododendron spp.	azalea

FOR FOLIAGE PLANTS AND VINES

Araucaria heterophylla	Norfolk Island pine
Arecaceae	palm, numerous spp.
Asparagus densiflorus	Sprenger's asparagus fern
Asparagus setaceus	plumose asparagus fern
Aspidistra elatior	bar-room plant
Cissus rhombifolia	grape ivy
Dracaena spp.	dracaena
Ficus spp.	foliage fig
Ficus pumila	creeping fig
Grevillea robusta	silk oak
Hedera helix	English ivy
Pandanus spp.	screw pine
Peperomia spp.	radiator plant
Philodendron spp.	philodendron
Senecio mikanioides	German ivy
Vinca major	blue buttons

BULBS

Anemone coronaria	windflower
Calochortus spp.	mariposa lily
Freesia spp.	freesia
Gladiolus spp.	gladiolus
Hyacinthus orientalis	hyacinth
Iris spp.	bulbous iris
Ixia spp.	corn lily
Lilium candidum	madonna lily
L. longiflorum	trumpet lily
L. speciosum	Japanese lily
Narcissus spp.	narcissus
Ranunculus acris	buttercup
Tulipa spp.	tulip
Zantedeschia spp.	calla

FERNS FOR DECORATIVE PURPOSES

Adiantum raddianum	maidenhair fern
Adiantum tenerum 'Farleyense'	glory fern
Asplenium nidus	bird's-nest fern
Cyrtomium falcatum	holly fern
Lilium longiflorum var. croftii	Easter lily
Nephrolepis exaltata	sword fern

Paphiopedilum spp.	lady's-slipper
Phragmipedium spp.	lady's-slipper
Poinsettia (Euphorbia pulcherrima)	poinsettia
Pteris cretica	cretan brake
Rosa spp.	rose
Sinningia speciosa	gloxinia

PLANTS TO BE GROWN FOR
CUT FLOWERS

Antirrhinum majus	snapdragon	*Lupinus* spp.	lupine
Bouvardia longiflora	bouvardia	*Matthiola incana*	stock
Buddleia spp.	butterfly bush	*Myosotis* spp.	forget-me-not
Calendula officinalis	calendula	*Nemesia* spp.	nemesia
Cheiranthus cheiri	English wallflower	Orchidaceae	orchid family
Chrysanthemum spp.	chrysanthemum	*Piqueria trinervia*	stevia
Chrysanthemum frutescens 'Chrysaster'	Boston yellow daisy	*Reseda* spp.	mignonette
Clarkia spp.	clarkia, godetia	*Rosa* spp.	rose
Cynoglossum amabile	Chinese forget-me-not	*Salpiglossis sinuata*	painted-tongue
Delphinium spp.	larkspur	*Scabiosa atropurpurea*	pincushion flower
Dianthus caryophyllus	carnation	*Schizanthus pinnatus*	butterfly flower
Gerbera jamesonii	Transvaal daisy	*Ursinia* spp.	ursinia
Heliophila spp.	heliophila	*Viola* spp.	violet

SHRUBS THAT MAY BE
FORCED IN POTS OR TUBS

Astilbe japonica	spirea	*Pieris floribunda*	lily-of-the-valley shrub
Chaenomeles japonica	Japanese quince	*Prunus tomentosa*	Nanking cherry
Clethra alnifolia	sweet pepperbush	*Rhododendron* spp.	rhododendron and azalea
Daphne cneorum	garland flower	*Spiraea prunifolia*	bridal-wreath spirea
Deutzia spp.	deutzia	*Spiraea thunbergii*	Thunberg spirea
Philadelphus x *lemoinei*	Lemoine's mock-orange		

FOLIAGE PLANTS AND VINES

Arecaceae	palm, numerous spp.
Asparagus densiflorus	Sprenger's asparagus fern
Asparagus setaceus	plumose asparagus fern
Aspidistra elatior	bar-room plant
Ficus spp.	foliage fig
Ficus pumila	creeping fig
Pandanus spp.	screw pine
Philodendron spp.	philodendron
Polypodiaceae	fern, numerous spp.

BULBS

Hyacinthus orientalis	hyacinth
Tulipa spp.	tulip

POTTED PLANTS

Bougainvillea glabra	paper flower
Clerodendrum thomsoniae	bleeding-heart vine
Fuchsia spp.	fuchsia
Hydrangea macrophylla	hydrangea
Kalanchoe spp.	beach bells
Lantana camara	yellow sage
Lantana montevidensis	trailing lantana
Poinsettia (Euphorbia pulcherrima)	poinsettia
Rhododendron spp.	azalea

7

GARDENER'S MISCELLANY

39

Plant Societies

AFRICAN VIOLET

African Violet Society
Box 1326
Knoxville, TN 37901
Dues $6.00

(Saintpaulia International: *see* Gesneriad Society International)

AROID

International Aroid Society
P.O. Box 43-1853
South Miami, FL 33143
Dues $10.00

BEGONIA

American Begonia Society
8302 Kittyhawk Ave.
Los Angeles, CA 90045
Dues $5.00

BONSAI

American Bonsai Society
228 Rosemont Ave.
Erie, PA 16505
Dues $10.00

Bonsai Clubs International
445 Blake St.
Menlo Park, CA 94025
Dues $7.50

BOXWOOD

American Boxwood Society
Box 85
Boyce, VA 22620
Dues $5.00

CACTI AND SUCCULENTS

Cactus and Succulent Society
of America, Inc.
Abbey Garden Press
1675 Las Canoas Rd.
Santa Barbara, CA 93105
Dues $12.50

CAMELLIA

American Camellia Society
Milton Brown, Executive Secretary
Box 1217
Fort Valley, GA 31030
Dues $10.00

CARNIVOROUS PLANTS

Carnivorous Plants Digest
P.O. Box 72
Kelly Corners, NY 12445
Dues $10.00

Carnivorous Plant Newsletter
Pat Hansen, c/o Fullerton Arboretum
California State University
Fullerton, CA 92634

CHRYSANTHEMUM

National Chrysanthemum Society
B. L. Markham
2612 Beverly Blvd.
S.W. Roanoke, VA 24015
Dues $7.50 ($2.50 sixteen years and under)

CYCAD

International Cycad Society
Dr. Walter Harman
5988 South Pollard Parkway
Baton Rouge, LA 70808
Dues $10.00

CYMBIDIUM

Cymbidium Society of America, Inc.
Mrs. W. Eilau, Membership Secretary
469 West Norman Ave.
Arcadia, CA 91006
Dues $10.00

DAFFODIL

American Daffodil Society
William O. Ticknor, President
Daffodil Corner, Route 1, Box 93A
Tyner, NC 27980
Dues $7.50

DAHLIA

American Dahlia Society, Inc.
Charles E. Knauf, Treasurer
1649 Beech Avenue
Melrose Park, PA 19126
Dues $7.00

DELPHINIUM

American Delphinium Society
7540 Ridgeway Rd.
Minneapolis, MN 55426

EPIPHYLLUM

Epiphyllum Society of America
Box 1395
Monrovia, CA 91016
Dues $4.00

FERN

American Fern Society
Dr. J. E. Skag
Department of Biology
George Mason University
Fairfax, VA 22030
Dues $5.00

International Tropical Fern Society
8720 Southwest 34th St.
Miami, FL 33165
Dues $5.00

Los Angeles International Fern Society
4369 Tujunga Ave.
North Hollywood, CA 91604
Dues $8.00

FRUIT

North American Fruit Explorers
Robert Kurle
10 S. 55 Madison St.
Hinsdale, IL 60521
Dues $5.00

FUCHSIA

American Fuchsia Society
Mr. Fred Clark, Membership Secretary
1600 Prospect St.
Belmont, CA 94002
Dues $5.00

GARDENING AND HORTICULTURE

American Horticultural Society
Mount Vernon, VA 22121
Dues $15.00

American Rock Garden Society
3 Salisbury Lane
Malvern, PA 19355
Dues $7.00

Garden Club of America
598 Madison Ave.
New York, NY 10022
Dues $3.00

Hobby Greenhouse Association
Mr. Bernard York, President
P.O. Box 695H
Wallingford, CT 06492
Dues $5.00

Indoor Light Gardening Society of America
c/o Horticultural Society of New York, Inc.
128 West 58th St.
New York, NY 10019
Dues

Men's Gardening Club of America
5360 Merle Hay Rd.
Des Moines, IA 50323
Dues $10.00

GERANIUM

International Geranium Society
Arthur Theide
22551 Thrush
Colton, CA 92324
Dues $5.00

GESNERIAD

Gesneriad Society International
P.O. Box 549
Knoxville, TN 37901
Dues $6.00

GLADIOLUS

North American Gladiolus Council
Robert Dorsam, Membership Secretary
30 Highland Place
Peru, IN 46970
Dues $6.00

GLOXINIA

American Gloxinia/Gesneriad Society, Inc.
Mrs. J. William Rowe, Membership
Secretary, Dept. C
P.O. Box 174
New Milford, CT 06776
Dues $7.00

GOURDS

Gourd Society of America
P.O. Box 274
Mt. Gilead, OH 43338
Dues $2.50

HEMEROCALLIS

American Hemerocallis Society
Signal Mountain, TN 37377
Dues $7.50

HERBS

Herb Society of America
300 Massachusetts Ave.
Boston, MA 02115
Dues $14.00

HIBISCUS

American Hibiscus
Box 98
Eagle Lake, FL 33139
Dues $5.00

HOLLY

Holly Society of America
407 Fountain Green Rd.
Bel Air, MD 21014
Dues $10.00

HOSTA

American Hosta Society
c/o Paul Aden
980 Stanton Ave.
Baldwin, NY 11510
Dues $5.00

IKEBANA

Ikebana International
C.P.O. Box 1262
Tokyo, Japan

IRIS

American Iris Society
6518 Beachy Ave.
Wichita, KS 67206
Dues $7.50

IVY

American Ivy Society
National Center for American Horticulture
Mount Vernon, VA 22121
Dues $7.50

LILAC

International Lilac Society
Walter W. Oakes
Box 315C
Rumford, ME 04276
Dues $5.00

LILY

Lily Society, Inc.
Mrs. E. A. Holl, Executive Secretary
Box 40134
Indianapolis, IN 46240
Dues $10.00

MAGNOLIA

American Magnolia Society
Rockard B. Figlar
14876 Pheasant Hill Court
Chesterfield, MO 63017
Dues $7.00

NUTS

Northern Nut Growers' Association
4518 Holston Hills Rd.
Knoxville, TN 37914
Dues $8.00

OLEANDER

National Oleander Society
P.O. Box 3431
Galveston Island, TX 77550
Dues $3.00

ORCHID

American Orchid Society, Inc.
Botanical Museum of Harvard University
Cambridge, MA 02138
Dues $15.00

PALMS

The Palm Society
1320 South Venetian Way
Miami, FL 33139
Dues $12.50

PENSTEMON

American Penstemon Society
Mr. Orville M. Steward
c/o Mrs. Vincent Astor
P.O. Box 136
Briarcliff Manor, NY 10501
Dues $3.00

PEONY

American Peony Society
Greta M. Kessenich, Secretary
250 Interlachen Rd.
Hopkins, MN 55343
Dues $7.50

RHODODENDRON

American Rhododendron Society
Esther Berry, Executive Secretary
617 Fairway Dr.
Aberdeen, WV 98520
Dues $12.00

ROSE

American Rose Society
P.O. Box 30,000
Shreveport, LA 71130
Dues $15.50

SEMPERVIVUM

Sempervivum Society
2017 South Athol Rd.
Athol, MA 01331

WILDFLOWERS

New England Wildflower Society
Ann Spence Dinsmore, Executive Director
Framingham, MA 01701
Dues $7.50

40

Glossary

Anther

The terminal part of the reproductive organ or pollen-disseminating part of the "male" flowering plant.

Broadcast

To scatter seed, rather than to sow it in rows or drills.

Cambium

The layer of growing cells just under the bark.

Casein

A substance contained in milk which, when added to sprays and dusts, adds to their adhesive and spreading qualities.

Coniferous

Pertaining to a tree that bears woody cones containing naked seeds.

Crop Rotation

The practice of alternating crops in a garden or field to avoid (1) the plant's taking the same food elements out of the soil year after year, which are necessary to the plant's growth, and (2) the increase of the insects and diseases characteristic of one plant.

Cultivar

A term denoting a cultivated variety such as *Cornus florida* 'Cloud 9.' It may be written with single quotes or: *Cornus florida* cv. Cloud 9. Cultivars are generally reproduced by asexual (vegetative) methods so that all individuals are genetically alike.

Cultivation

The practice of stirring the surface of the soil (1) to aerate the deeper layers, (2) to break the crust that sometimes forms after the wet soil has dried in the sun, (3) to discourage weed growth, (4) to form a dust mulch.

Deciduous

A term applied to trees that drop their leaves annually, in contrast to *evergreen*.

Decomposition

Decay, usually of strawy manure, compost or other organic substances.

Dioecius

A term applied to plants that bear staminate (male) or pistillate (female) flowers, such as holly *(Ilex),* in which "female" plants bear fruit but "male" plants do not.

Dormant

The period during which a plant makes no active growth. Most plants are completely dormant during the winter season. The rest period of a plant is not identical but is controlled by internal factors characteristic of the plant itself.

Drying Off

A method of preparing bulbs for ripening or plants for resting between periods of forcing. It may be done by gradually reducing the amount

791

of water or by laying the pots on their sides in a spot protected from the sun.

Emulsion

A liquid mixture in which a fatty substance is suspended in minute globules, usually appearing like milk.

Erosion

The (usually destructive) washing away of soil or rock, as when rainfall starts gullies in a field that grow to the proportions of a deep ditch, washing away the valuable topsoil and sometimes even subsoil.

Everlastings

Flowers that are grown for their winter effects, as they hold their shape and color well when dried.

Fertilization

(1) The application of fertilizer, (2) the union of the "male" reproductive body (pollen) with the "female" reproductive body (egg) to produce offspring (seeds).

Flats

Shallow boxes, usually 16 in. by 22½ in. and varying in depth from 2 in. to 4 in. The young stages of plant growth may be carried on in flats, thus eliminating the backbreaking work of planting and transplanting tiny seedlings in nursery rows indoors or outdoors.

Forcing

A process (1) of making plants or bulbs bloom at a time that is not natural for them to do so, or (2) of making them bloom in a shorter length of time than is normal. In the first case, only duplication of their normal growing conditions may be necessary, while in the second, excess heat and moisture are necessary.

Fumigation (plant)

The control of injurious infestation by the use of toxic fumes given off by chemical substances.

Grafting

A process whereby a part of one plant, usually a shoot or bud of a tree or shrub (scion), is made to unite with a part of another plant (stock). There are many ways of performing this process.

Habitat

The region in which a plant is found growing wild.

Hardening-off

The process of gradually reducing the amount of water and lowering the temperature for plants grown indoors or under glass, in order to toughen their tissues, making it possible for them to withstand colder conditions.

Heaving

The thrusting of plants out of the ground, caused by alternate freezing and thawing during the winter. In some cases, roots may be left exposed, which may prove injurious or even fatal if they are not pressed back into the soil. A light, porous texture of the soil, or a mulch, will help to prevent this injury.

Heel

A small piece of two-year-old wood with a cutting of one-year-old wood, for a certain method of propagation.

Heeling In

A method of storing plants in the ground until conditions are favorable for planting. They are usually laid on their sides in trenches and covered with soil until only a small part of their top growth is left exposed.

Hilling Up

A practice of mounding the earth about a plant, performed for various purposes: (1) to protect half-hardy plants during the winter; (2) to bleach celery; (3) to strengthen the stand of aerial-rooted plants, such as corn; (4) to protect shallow roots or tubers from sun scorch.

Hybrid

A variety or individual resulting from the crossing of two species. An individual plant resulting from fertilization between two species, cultivars or (rarely) genera; a cross.

Insecticide

A substance that kills insects by poisoning, suffocation or paralysis. There are stomach poisons, contact poisons and fumigants. A repellent is not really an insecticide as it does not kill, but repels insects by its disagreeable properties.

Leaching
The diminishing or complete loss of soluble fertilizers from the soil caused by the percolation of water downward.

Mat (hotbed)
A straw or fabric covering used to protect plants in coldframes and hotbeds against excessive cold.

Monaecious
A term applied to plants that bear flowers of different "sexes," that is, staminate and pistillate, on the same plant.

Naturalizing
The planting of trees, shrubs, flowering plants, bulbs, mosses, etc., in such a way as to bring about the effect of natural wild growth. The establishment and reproduction of plants outside their native geographic range.

Nitrification
The change of crude forms of nitrogen, first into ammonia, then into nitrites and finally into nitrates in which form the nitrogen is available to the plant.

pH
A term that represents the hydrogen ion concentration by which scientists measure soil acidity. The pH acidity scale measures from 1 (acid) to 14 (alkaline), with 7 as neutral.

Pinching Back
The shortening of young shoots either to achieve bushy plant form, to encourage the development of a greater quantity of buds, or to enhance flower or fruit development.

Pistil
The central organ or reproductive part of a pistillate or perfect flower.

Pistillate
Often referred to as "female" flowers because they contain cells which, when fertilized, become seeds.

Pollen
The dusty substance found on the anther or terminal part of the male reproductive organ.

Pollination
The transfer of pollen from the anther of the stamen, the "male" organ, to the stigma of the pistil, the "female" organ, accomplished by wind, insects or human beings.

Pot-bound
A stage of potted plant growth when the roots become a dense mass of fibers and no longer can reach out freely to make growth. Normally potted plants should be transplanted before they become pot-bound, but some prefer to be slightly so.

Potting On
A term applied to the repeated transplantings of a plant from seedling stage to maturity in graduating sizes of flowerpots, each transplanting taking place as soon as the roots have filled the pot.

Potting Up
The transplanting of seedling plants from flats or seedpans into flowerpots; the transplanting of mature plants from outdoor positions into pots, usually for the purpose of winter or ornamental effects.

Pricking Out (pricking off)
The process of transplanting tiny seedlings from the seedpans, pots or other containers into flats.

Propagation
The increase or multiplication of plants. For different methods, see Chapter 34 on Propagation.

Repellents
Substances which, when used alone or in combination with other substances, protect plants by warding off, without killing, insects or animals.

Respiration
The process by which a plant takes in oxygen, oxidizes matter and gives off the gas.

Scabrous

Rough or gritty to the touch, as leaves.

Scarification

(1) A process of loosening the soil without turning it over, (2) a method of scratching hard-coated seeds to hasten germination.

Scion

A term given to a bud or cutting of an improved variety that is to be inserted into the rooted "stock" in the process of grafting.

Seedlings

A term usually applied to very young plants. It is also sometimes applied to mature plants that have been produced from seed, in order to distinguish them from similar plants grown from cuttings, grafts, budding, etc.

Species

A group of individuals with similar characteristics forming a subdivision of a genus. Several species may be grouped in a single genus. In *Anchusa italica, Anchusa* is the genus name, and *italica* the species name.

Stamen

The "male" pollen-bearing reproductive organ of the flower, the top part of which is the anther.

Staminate

A term used to describe a flower containing only stamens, or male reproductive organs.

Sterilization (soil)

A term commonly given to the process of making a soil, or similar material, free from all harmful organisms before it is used for sowing seed, or for transplanting purposes.

Stigma

The terminal part of the female reproductive organ, or pollen-receiving part, of the flower.

Stock

In grafting, the plant into which the scion is to be inserted, and which will assume the rooting function of the new plant. Any leaf or stem growth from the stock should be cut back close

to the root or branch, as only new growth from the scion is desired.

Stomata

Minute openings on the undersurface of a leaf through which transpiration of moisture takes place.

Stratification

An artificial method of preparing seeds for germination. Some seeds require a longer period of storage then others before germination takes place, and this is usually done by placing them between layers of peat moss, soil or similar materials that are kept moist to prevent them from drying out. Stratification is usually done in the winter so that frost action will help split hard-shelled seeds.

Subsoil

A stratum of soil lying beneath that commonly referred to as topsoil. It is less fertile. Since it contains little nutrient and few microorganisms essential to plant growth, roots do not penetrate it, except those of very large vigorous plants.

Sucker

Vegetative growth coming from the roots of a tree near the base or at a short distance.

Tamping

The process of lightly firming down freshly loosened soil, either in the open or in containers, with a flat surface such as a block of wood or a board.

Topdressing

Any material such as manure, compost, fertilizer, etc., that is placed on the surface of the ground, and that may in some cases be cultivated in. It differs from a mulch in that its primary function is to feed the plant, while the primary purpose of a mulch is to hinder weed growth and to protect from heat or cold, although a mulch may have some food value.

Transpiration

The process by which excess water is given off by the leaves of a plant, through stomata, or minute openings, primarily on the undersurface of the leaf. The greatest amount of moisture is given off when the heat rays of the sun reach the plant.

Transplanting

The process of moving seedlings or mature plants from one location to another. The first transplanting process out of the seedpan or pot is referred to as "pricking out."

Variety

A group of individuals forming a subdivision of a species with similar characteristics, but differing too slightly to form another species. *Viburnum plicatum tomentosum,* for example, is not different enough from *V. plicatum* to constitute another species but *is* different enough to need segregation.

Water Sprout

A quick, succulent shoot growth that may appear on the trunk or limbs of a tree.

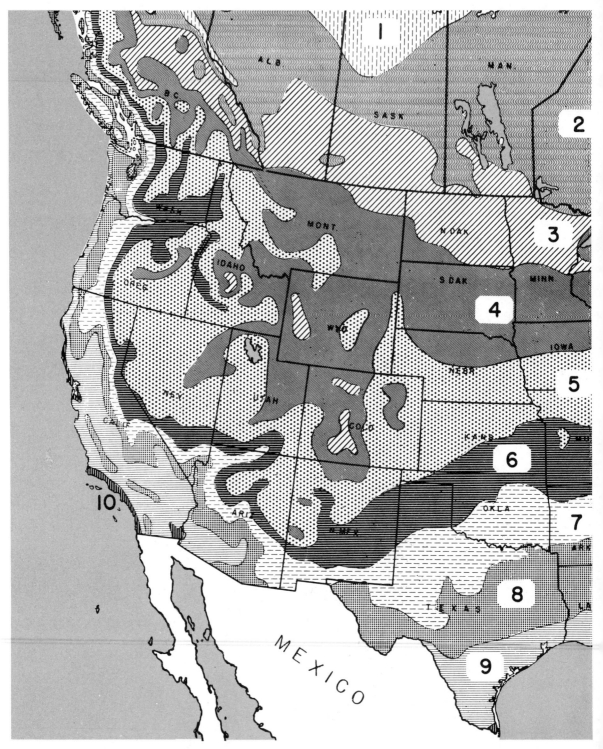

Hardiness Zone Map

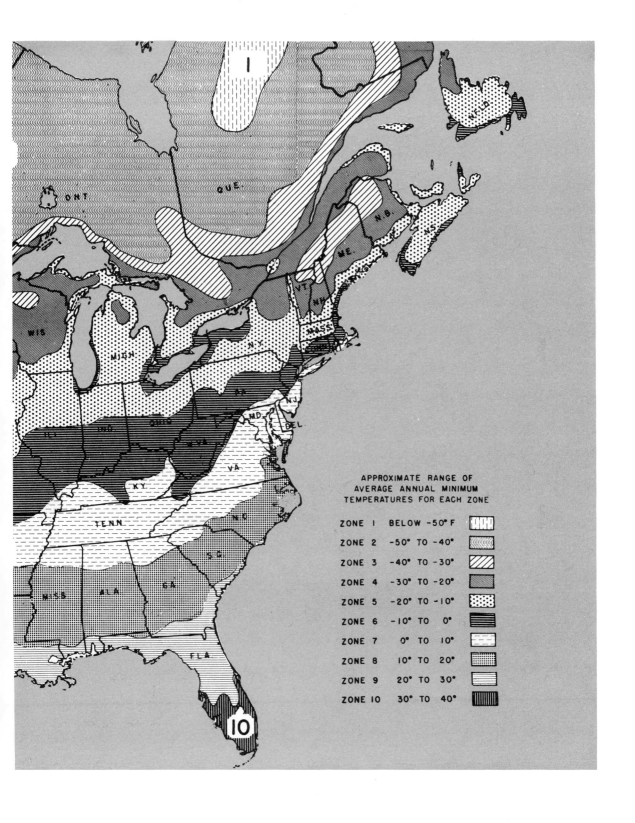

APPROXIMATE RANGE OF
AVERAGE ANNUAL MINIMUM
TEMPERATURES FOR EACH ZONE

ZONE 1   BELOW -50° F
ZONE 2   -50° TO -40°
ZONE 3   -40° TO -30°
ZONE 4   -30° TO -20°
ZONE 5   -20° TO -10°
ZONE 6   -10° TO 0°
ZONE 7   0° TO 10°
ZONE 8   10° TO 20°
ZONE 9   20° TO 30°
ZONE 10 30° TO 40°

Index